Programming ASP.NET 3.5

Other Microsoft .NET resources from O'Reilly

Related titles
ADO.NET 3.5 Cookbook™
Building a Web 2.0 Portal
  with ASP.NET 3.5
Learning ASP.NET 3.5
Learning WCF

Programming .NET 3.5
Programming ASP.NET AJAX
Programming WCF Services
RESTful.NET

.NET Books Resource Center
dotnet.oreilly.com is a complete catalog of O'Reilly's books on .NET and related technologies, including sample chapters and code examples.

ONDotnet.com provides independent coverage of fundamental, interoperable, and emerging Microsoft .NET programming and web services technologies.

Conferences
O'Reilly brings diverse innovators together to nurture the ideas that spark revolutionary industries. We specialize in documenting the latest tools and systems, translating the innovator's knowledge into useful skills for those in the trenches. Visit *conferences.oreilly.com* for our upcoming events.

Safari Bookshelf (*safari.oreilly.com*) is the premier online reference library for programmers and IT professionals. Conduct searches across more than 1,000 books. Subscribers can zero in on answers to time-critical questions in a matter of seconds. Read the books on your Bookshelf from cover to cover or simply flip to the page you need. Try it today for free.

FOURTH EDITION

Programming ASP.NET 3.5

Jesse Liberty, Dan Hurwitz, and Dan Maharry

O'REILLY®

Beijing · Cambridge · Farnham · Köln · Sebastopol · Taipei · Tokyo

Programming ASP.NET 3.5, Fourth Edition

by Jesse Liberty, Dan Hurwitz, and Dan Maharry

Published by O'Reilly Media, Inc., 1005 Gravenstein Highway North, Sebastopol, CA 95472.

O'Reilly books may be purchased for educational, business, or sales promotional use. Online editions are also available for most titles (*safari.oreilly.com*). For more information, contact our corporate/institutional sales department: (800) 998-9938 or *corporate@oreilly.com*.

Editor: John Osborn
Production Editor: Rachel Monaghan
Copyeditor: Audrey Doyle
Indexer: Julie Hawks

Production Services: Octal Publishing, Inc.
Cover Designer: Karen Montgomery
Interior Designer: David Futato
Illustrator: Jessamyn Read

Printing History:

February 2002:	First Edition.
September 2003:	Second Edition.
October 2005:	Third Edition.
October 2008:	Fourth Edition.

ISBN: 978-0-596-52956-7

[M]

Table of Contents

Preface

New ideas in web development are created all the time, and the speed with which they evolve into mature technologies is astounding. To its credit, Microsoft is one of the companies that continue to push the boundaries in web development. ASP.NET 3.5 is arguably the fastest, most efficient, most reliable, and best-supported way to create interactive web applications today. Combined with the development tools available from Microsoft (both free and commercial), it is incredibly easy to create websites that look great and perform well. The amount of code you need to write to implement quite complex things continues to reduce with each new version of ASP.NET. The ever-improving support that Visual Studio and ASP.NET have for Cascading Style Sheets (CSS), themes, and consistent layouts using master pages means it's even easier to make your sites look their best. Best of all, most of the "plumbing" (security, data access, layout, etc.) is taken care of for you by the .NET Framework and the controls that are built into ASP.NET. Want to switch from using an Access database to using SQL server? That'll take about five minutes. Want to let users log on to the site using their logon identities? That's built into ASP.NET along with four other methods of authentication. Want to make sure users don't accidentally enter the wrong type of data into a web page? You can do that without writing any code at all thanks to the built-in validation controls.

The list of possibilities is long, and with the release of ASP.NET 3.5, there are yet more new pieces in the Microsoft web development puzzle that weren't there before—and, promisingly, a number of pieces that will continue to appear in the future which we've previewed in Chapter 21 and will cover more fully in the next edition of this book.

Until such time as the fifth edition arrives, here's a list of the new features you'll find in this edition:

New ASP.NET 3.5 server controls

ASP.NET 3.5 introduces a trio of new controls. The ListView is a new data-bound control, which for those already using ASP.NET, works much like a cross between a Repeater and a DataList without the pain of using either. Combine it with the second new control, the DataPager, and you've got the best template-based data-bound control in ASP.NET today. We cover both in Chapter 8.

The third new control is another data source control which uses LINQ statements rather than SQL or XPath commands to select, alter, or create data. It is called the LinqDataSource control and we cover it in Chapter 10.

ASP.NET AJAX Extensions and the Control Toolkit

AJAX has been around awhile now, but this is the first version of this book to cover it. In Chapters 3 through 5, we look at the various controls in the ASP.NET AJAX Extensions library that now form part of ASP.NET 3.5 and those in the Microsoft-sponsored AJAX Control Toolkit available from *http://codeplex.com*.

WCF Web Services

Those of you who are already using web services in your websites will be aware that .NET 3.0 introduced the Windows Communication Framework and within it a new type of slim-line (RESTful) web service. This makes a lot more sense to use in some scenarios than those introduced originally in .NET 1.0. Chapter 16 looks at both types, the difference between them, and how to create and use them within a website.

LINQ

Probably the most compelling reason to look at .NET 3.5, the Language Integrated Query API presents a brand-new way to query for data across multiple sources in a consistent way. As Chapter 10 will demonstrate, LINQ is in no way just another data API.

New features in Visual Studio 2008

A new version of Visual Studio always includes a few new features and this edition is no different. In Chapter 2 we provide coverage of these new features, and in Chapter 20 we look at the new Web Deployment Project add-on for VS2008.

Vista and IIS 7.0

January 2007 saw the release of Windows Vista and with it a completely new version of Internet Information Services (IIS). Rewritten from scratch, IIS 7.0 is a completely different beast from its forebears, and this has a direct effect on forms-based security, site configuration, and deployment. Chapters 12, 18, and 20 will cover all these changes, respectively.

Even Vista itself has a certain impact on the development process. Its tighter grip on account permissions means that certain VS2008 functions can be performed only by an administrator. Notes throughout the book will highlight where this is the case.

Examples and sample database
> The majority of the examples in this book have been completely reworked and the database-dependent ones now also use the lightweight AdventureWorksLT sample database.

It's quite amazing just how deep and rich a feature set ASP.NET has on its own before you even start to consider the additional features of VS2008, IIS 7.0, C# 3.0, SQL Server, and the rest. Although we can't cover everything in minute detail, we hope this book does give you a good guide to working with ASP.NET 3.5 and its associated technologies.

Learning or Programming?

We have written two ASP.NET books: the one you are currently reading and another named *Learning ASP.NET 3.5* (O'Reilly). Whereas that book is aimed at complete beginners wanting to ramp up their ASP.NET skills, this book is aimed at those with at least a basic knowledge of development with ASP.NET who want to explore it in more depth. It is a way marker, mapping out and describing the various aspects of development with ASP.NET to a point where the reader has enough knowledge of it to understand what he can do and how to strike out on his own to deeper, more involved areas of the topic.

With this in mind, *Programming ASP.NET 3.5* is not aimed specifically at the total newcomer to ASP.NET development, though arguably newcomers may gain the most from it over a period of time. Nor is it targeted at the ASP.NET guru who wants in-depth knowledge of operations at the protocol level, although we hope there are a few nuggets in here that such readers didn't already know, and that they may choose to use this book as a handy fallback if their memory fails them.

Visual Basic Versus C#

A quick note on Visual Basic versus C#: some people choose a .NET book based on the language in which the examples are given. That's a natural reaction, but it's really not necessary, and here's why: there is very little actual Visual Basic or C# code in any given ASP.NET application, and what there is, you can easily translate from one to the other "on inspection." Besides, the two languages are strikingly similar, and both produce the same output. If you know one, it's quite simple to learn the other. In fact, software tools are available that can convert one language to the other with amazing accuracy. Finally, ASP.NET programmers benefit terrifically by being "bilingual"—that is, having the ability to read C# and write Visual Basic (or vice versa).

In the end, we had to choose one language over the other, and we elected to do the examples and exercises for this book in C#. However, if you prefer Visual Basic, you'll find every single example and exercise solution reproduced in Visual Basic free for download from this book's website, at *http://www.oreilly.com/catalog/ 9780596529567.*

How This Book Is Organized

Here is a summary of the chapters in this book and what you can expect from each:

Chapter 1, *Web Development in 2008*
> Provides a short introduction to how .NET has grown between v2.0 and v3.5, and in which areas it will continue to grow.

Chapter 2, *Visual Studio 2008*
> Explores Visual Studio 2008 and its new features since the previous version, and shows how you can use them to create ASP.NET applications.

Chapter 3, *Controls: Fundamental Concepts*
> Introduces the five types of control you'll use to create an ASP.NET website, and how they differ from each other. This chapter also introduces the concept of events and postbacks on a page.

Chapter 4, *Basic Controls*
> Looks at all the text-, image-, and list-related ASP.NET Server controls and AJAX server controls installed by default into Visual Studio 2008. The chapter also looks at some of the controls in the AJAX Control Toolkit that extend the functionality of the basic controls.

Chapter 5, *More Controls*
> Looks at more advanced ASP.NET Server controls and AJAX server controls installed by default into Visual Studio 2008, including the `Panel`, `UpdatePanel`, `Wizard`, `FileUpload`, and `Calendar` controls.

Chapter 6, *Website Fundamentals*
> Shows you how to use the code behind a page effectively, and how to manage state in the otherwise stateless Web. This chapter also describes the life cycle of a web page in detail and shows you how to take advantage of advanced directives.

Chapter 7, *Data Source Controls and Connections*
> Looks at the ASP.NET data source controls, how to use them, and which sources of data can be used with which control.

Chapter 8, *Using Data-Aware Controls*
> Explores the various data-bound controls supplied with ASP.NET 3.5, including the new `ListView` control. This chapter also demonstrates how they use the `DataSource` controls shown in Chapter 7 to both retrieve and save data.

Chapter 9, *ADO.NET*

Shows you the technology underlying the controls described in Chapters 7 and 8, so you understand how it all works and can take precise control when necessary.

Chapter 10, *Presenting LINQ*

Looks at the brand-new LINQ API, how it can be used to query and join diverse sources of data, and how to make use of it within ASP.NET pages.

Chapter 11, *Validation*

Demonstrates the various ASP.NET server controls dedicated to validating the contents of a form to ensure data consistency and protect against spoofing.

Chapter 12, *Forms-Based Security*

Describes in detail how to implement forms-based security to constrain user access to your website over the Internet. In addition, this chapter demonstrates how to use either the default (SQL Express) database for this or how to create your SQL Server database and use that instead to create users and roles (groups) and to facilitate authentication and authorization.

Chapter 13, *Master Pages and Navigation*

Describes some of the features that help you build professional-quality web applications. Master pages allow you to create a uniform look and feel throughout your application, and the navigation controls allow you to build site maps, menus, and breadcrumbs quickly and easily to facilitate navigation of large applications.

Chapter 14, *Personalization*

Shows you how to allow your users to tailor the look and feel of your site to their own requirements, and how to store that information so that when users return, the site remembers their preferences and state.

Chapter 15, *Custom and User Controls*

Covers the powerful yet easy-to-use technology that allows you to extend ASP.NET to create controls customized for your specific problem domain.

Chapter 16, *Web Services*

Looks at how to create and consume both ASP.NET and WCF web services, how to enable them in an AJAX environment and the various standard protocols used for services and their clients to talk to one another.

Chapter 17, *Caching and Performance*

Lays out the various ways that some or all of an ASP.NET page can be cached on the server and the different toggles that will require it to be deleted from the cache and regenerated.

Chapter 18, *Application Logic and Configuration*

Looks at how information can be stored at the application level and how the *web.config* file can be used to alter the operating parameters of your website. In particular, you'll see how to use IIS 7.0 and the Web Site Administration Tool (WAT) to alter *web.config* and then how to create custom sections of *web.config* for your own specific use.

Chapter 19, *Tracing, Debugging, and Error Handling*
> Examines the various ways to detect errors during development in ASP.NET, and how to handle errors that occur in your production code.

Chapter 20, *Deployment*
> Looks at three different ways to deploy your website: by copying the site's file directly with XCOPY, by wrapping it up into an installer with a Web Setup Project, and finally by deploying it as a part of the build process with a Web Deployment Project.

Chapter 21, *Epilogue: From Now to vNext*
> Last but not least, this chapter takes a brief look at the various .NET 3.5 web development-related beta projects currently available for download.

Appendix A, *Installing the AJAX Control Toolkit*
> Demonstrates how to install the AJAX Control Toolkit used throughout the book.

Appendix B, *Relational Database Technology: A Crash Course*
> Introduces the key concepts needed to use relational databases, such as SQL Server, used in this book.

Appendix C, *Keyboard Shortcuts*
> Describes all the keyboard shortcuts enabled in Visual Studio 2008 under its Web Development default settings.

What You Need to Use This Book

We wrote this book using Visual Studio 2008 and SQL Server 2005 on a laptop running Windows Vista. You may want to copy this setup to follow the book, but any of the following will do:

Operating systems
> Windows XP or later will do, except to follow Chapter 18's look at IIS 7.0, which is available only for Windows Vista and Windows Server 2008.

Visual Studio
> The 2008 edition of Visual Web Developer (free to download) will be more than sufficient to follow this book. If you have a paid-for copy of Visual Studio 2008, so much the better.

SQL Server
> Any edition of SQL Server 2005 or 2008 will do. If you decide to follow this text using SQL Server 2008, please note that you will need to download a slightly different version of the sample database to follow the material in Chapters 7 through 10.

Conventions Used in This Book

The following typographical conventions are used in this book:

Italic

> Indicates new terms, URLs, email addresses, filenames, file extensions, pathnames, directories, and Unix utilities

`Constant width`

> Indicates commands, options, switches, variables, attributes, keys, functions, types, classes, namespaces, methods, modules, properties, parameters, values, objects, events, event handlers, XML tags, HTML tags, macros, the contents of files, and the output from commands

`Constant width bold`

> Shows commands or other text that should be typed literally by the user

`Constant width italic`

> Shows text that should be replaced with user-supplied values

> This icon signifies a tip, suggestion, or general note.

> This icon indicates a warning or caution.

Using Code Examples

This book is here to help you get your job done. In general, you may use the code in this book in your programs and documentation. You do not need to contact us for permission unless you're reproducing a significant portion of the code. For example, writing a program that uses several chunks of code from this book does not require permission. Selling or distributing a CD-ROM of examples from O'Reilly books *does* require permission. Answering a question by citing this book and quoting example code does not require permission. Incorporating a significant amount of example code from this book into your product's documentation *does* require permission.

We appreciate, but do not require, attribution. An attribution usually includes the title, author, publisher, and ISBN. For example: "*Programming ASP.NET 3.5*, Fourth Edition, by Jesse Liberty, Dan Hurwitz, and Dan Maharry. Copyright 2009 Jesse Liberty, Dan Hurwitz, and Dan Maharry, 978-0-596-52956-7."

If you feel your use of code examples falls outside fair use or the permission given here, feel free to contact us at *permissions@oreilly.com*.

We'd Like to Hear from You

Please address comments and questions concerning this book to the publisher:

O'Reilly Media, Inc.
1005 Gravenstein Highway North
Sebastopol, CA 95472
800-998-9938 (in the United States or Canada)
707-829-0515 (international or local)
707-829-0104 (fax)

We have a web page for this book, where we list errata, examples, and any additional information. You can access this page at:

http://www.oreilly.com/catalog/9780596529567

To comment or ask technical questions about this book, send email to:

bookquestions@oreilly.com

For more information about our books, conferences, Resource Centers, and the O'Reilly Network, see our website at:

http://www.oreilly.com

Safari® Books Online

When you see a Safari® Books Online icon on the cover of your favorite technology book, that means the book is available online through the O'Reilly Network Safari Bookshelf.

Safari offers a solution that's better than e-books. It's a virtual library that lets you easily search thousands of top tech books, cut and paste code samples, download chapters, and find quick answers when you need the most accurate, current information. Try it for free at *http://safari.oreilly.com*.

Acknowledgments

From Jesse Liberty

This book is the result of the extraordinary work of three teams: the ASP.NET developers at Microsoft, my coauthors who shouldered the responsibility to turn a good book on ASP.NET into a world-class tutorial on a tremendously expanded framework, and the editorial and production team at O'Reilly who contribute more than can ever be expressed. I am deeply grateful to you all.

From Dan Hurwitz

I would like to once again thank Jesse for being an excellent colleague and good friend, and the fine folks at O'Reilly who made this book possible, especially John Osborn and Brian MacDonald. I also wish to acknowledge the outstanding contribution of our new coauthor, the other Dan. And as always, I especially want to thank my wife and family for being so supportive.

From Dan Maharry

There are a number of people connected to this project that I need to thank. Jesse and Dan H. were brave enough to let me work with them, and John Osborn was kind enough to suggest me in the first place. Lou Franco and Mike Pope also provided some additional text. Thanks to them. Having worked in publishing in a former life, I know how many others will also have touched this book before reaching you, the reader, so I thank them, too.

Thirteen months is a long time to dedicate weekends and nights to a single project, so thanks to my family and friends for necessarily distracting me every so often.

Last but not least (first and foremost even), thanks to *my wife Janey*, who endured my absence during the writing process with the patience of a saint. I love her lots and am amazed daily at how lucky I am to be married to her.

CHAPTER 1

Web Development in 2008

ASP.NET is at the heart of Microsoft's web development strategy. Version 2.0 was released in 2005 as part of .NET 2.0, and it delivered everything Microsoft had promised to drooling developers: less code to write, enhanced security and personalization features, new and overhauled controls across the board, web services, mobile support, and more. Visual Studio 2005 (VS2005) was released at the same time with a built-in web server for use locally and has proved to be an excellent, robust tool for ASP.NET development.

In the three years since that initial release, ASP.NET 2.0 hasn't changed much. On the other hand, what surrounds ASP.NET to give both web developer and web user a richer experience has changed a lot.

AJAX

It may come as somewhat of a surprise that in a world where the emphasis seemed to have been squarely on writing neat and good server-side code to improve the interaction between website and user, the current revolution starts on the client side. The proliferation of the group of technologies most commonly known as *Asynchronous JavaScript and XML*, or AJAX for short, has been rapid and its reliance on only open standards has meant that competition for the best use of AJAX has been seen across all web platforms. Its cross-browser, cross-platform nature continues to ensure that.

Whether you use it to implement the more blatantly apparent UI features, such as the instant lookups of Google Suggest, or the subtler features, such as text box watermarking and the invisible updating of selection lists based on the contents selected in others, AJAX is here to stay despite the security risks that it exposes. After the initial commotion in 2005, and the development of several free server-side AJAX libraries such as Anthem.NET and MagicAjax.NET, many asked when Microsoft would come up with its own AJAX implementation.

If you're interested in reading about some of the security risks of AJAX, have a look at *http://www.cgisecurity.com/ajax/*.

In January 2007, Microsoft answered with three distinct downloads for ASP.NET 2.0 and VS2005:

ASP.NET 2.0 AJAX Extensions 1.0
A library of client-side scripts and a half dozen core controls to place onto an ASP.NET page that render into an appropriate client-side script to enable AJAX functionality.

ASP.NET AJAX Control Toolkit
A library of almost three dozen server-side controls which demonstrate how to use and extend ASP.NET AJAX 1.0. This toolkit is under constant development at *http://www.codeplex.com/AjaxControlToolkit*.

ASP.NET AJAX Futures/ASP.NET 3.5 Extensions
Early developer releases of ASP.NET AJAX 2.0 for those who want to see how it is likely to develop. This product changes often and rapidly and is a good indicator of how other technologies Microsoft is working on will affect web developers. In late 2007, this package was wrapped into and is now part of the ASP.NET 3.5 Extensions preview package. It is likely, though, that another Futures package will appear once the 3.5 Extensions download comes out of beta.

As part of the OpenAjax Alliance, Microsoft has made the source code for the controls in the core Extensions download and the script library they render freely available under its shared source license to ensure interoperability across browsers, operating systems, and other AJAX libraries.

Visual Studio 2008 (VS2008) incorporates support for ASP.NET AJAX-enabled websites out of the box thanks to the inclusion of the .NET Framework 3.5.

.NET Framework 3.0 and 3.5

It may seem counterintuitive to say that ASP.NET is still at version 2.0 when VS2008 comes with version 3.5 of the .NET Framework, but it is true: the version number for the System.Web assembly in which ASP.NET sits has changed only in its minor version, from v2.0.50727.42 in .NET 2.0 to v2.0.50727.1434 in .NET 3.5. Rather confusingly, Microsoft decided to use the release of .NET 3.0 and .NET 3.5 to indicate the addition of new libraries to the framework rather than any specific updates to what was already there. Figure 1-1 shows the basic makeup of the .NET Framework 2.0 for ASP.NET developers.

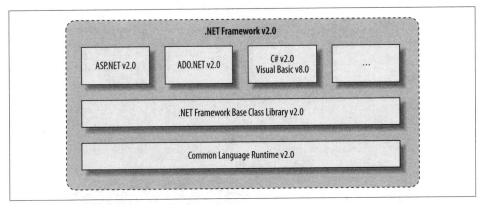

Figure 1-1. The .NET Framework 2.0 stack

November 2006 saw the release of .NET 3.0, a superset of .NET 2.0 in which the only change apart from the inclusion of interim bug fixes was the inclusion of the four WinFX libraries being developed in parallel for the launch of Windows Vista:

Windows Presentation Foundation (WPF)

Targeting mainly Windows Forms developers, WPF hasn't directly affected ASP.NET development. However, Microsoft has released a cross-platform browser plug-in hosting its own subset of the .NET runtime and WPF, origi-nally known as WPF/Everywhere. Rechristened Silverlight, the 1.0 plug-in uses JavaScript as its main language. Silverlight 2.0, however, incorporates support for C# and VB.NET and will be a central focus for the next release of .NET after 3.5 as a cross-browser, cross-platform .NET runtime.

Windows Workflow Foundation (WF)

WF allows developers to write workflow-enabled applications. Or rather, hav-ing designed the workflows of an application, WF allows the developer to create the application directly, as a series of steps creating those workflows rather than as a set of objects that incidentally go through those steps.

Windows Communication Foundation (WCF)

A reworking of the web service and interoperability stack, WCF impacts ASP.NET developers through the way it implements SOAP, WSDL, and the WS-* set of stan-dards previously implemented as Microsoft's Web Service Extensions download.

Windows CardSpace (WCS)

WCS provides a new way for Windows users to provide their digital identity online in a simple, secure way. If you use Passport to verify your users online, you might consider replacing it with WCS at some point. However, the uptake on this so far has been slow.

Figure 1-2 demonstrates how the WinFX libraries are bolted onto .NET 2.0 to pro-duce .NET 3.0. When Windows Vista was released two months later in January 2007, it included .NET 3.0 by default.

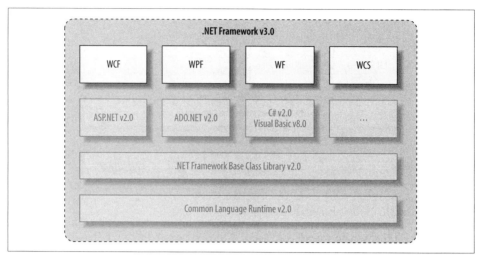

Figure 1-2. The .NET Framework 3.0 stack

.NET 3.5 is again a superset of .NET 3.0 but with a bit more meat for web developers to chew on. Once again, at its core there is just a bug-fixed version of the .NET 2.0 runtime and core libraries, as shown in Figure 1-3, but on top of that are the following items of interest for web developers.

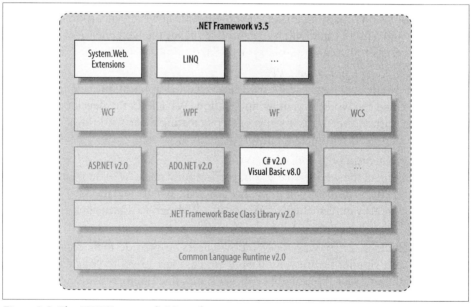

Figure 1-3. The .NET Framework 3.5 stack

C# 3.0 and Visual Basic (VB) 9.0

.NET 3.5 includes new versions of C# and Visual Basic .NET, with the majority of the new language features—anonymous types, lambda functions, anonymous methods, and more—being combined to support LINQ.

Language Integrated Query (LINQ)

LINQ is a set of .NET extensions that allow the user to query, set, and transform data from any type of data source natively in C# or VB. For example, you could join the contents of a SQL Server table with data from an in-memory data table and put the results into an XML document in one line of code. It is very powerful, and is limited only by the types of data sources for which there is a corresponding LINQ library. Indeed, several third-party libraries are already in the works for less obvious data sources, such as NHibernate and SharePoint.

System.Web.Extensions

A companion to the core ASP.NET 2.0 library, System.Web.Extensions includes an updated version of the ASP.NET 2.0 AJAX Extensions download so that AJAX is supported out of the box with .NET 3.5, three new controls for ASP development—the `ListView`, `DataPager`, and `LinqDataSource`—and a new security feature called Client Application Services that allows your smart client applications to use a centralized user database on the Web using the same personalization methods as ASP.NET.

 Remember that at any time, you can find out what version of a .NET assembly you are using by looking in *%windir%\assembly*.

Visual Studio 2008

Even if VS2008 offered no new features over VS2005 it would still be a great environment with which to build websites. As you would expect from Microsoft, though, VS2008 has been significantly improved, especially for web developers. And here's why:

The use of AJAX cannot be ignored

VS2008 now includes AJAX-enabled website projects by default, IntelliSense for JavaScript, and a debugger for it, too.

Expression Web

Microsoft released a new suite of applications for designers rather than developers in 2007 under the Expression umbrella name. Microsoft designed and fitted the Expression Web product, which also replaces FrontPage, with a brand-new and much-improved HTML and Cascading Style Sheet (CSS) editor. It is now a shared component between Expression Web and VS2008.

Scott Guthrie

The man who invented ASP.NET now also has a significant influence over the development of Visual Studio. In fact, he's now corporate vice president for the .NET Developer Division.

Chapter 2 includes a complete rundown of the new features in VS2008.

Internet Information Services 7.0

In the same way that Windows 95 represented a quantum leap from Windows 3.1, so too does IIS 7.0 from its predecessors. Totally rewritten, IIS 7.0 includes a new, secure by default, pluggable request processing stack which presents several breaking changes from IIS 6.0, as discussed at *http://mvolo.com/blogs/serverside/archive/2007/12/08/IIS-7.0-Breaking-Changes-ASP.NET-2.0-applications-Integrated-mode.aspx*. Most notably, passport authentication is no longer supported, and as Chapter 12 demonstrates, the new integrated authentication mode in IIS alters the way users are authenticated as well.

If you are migrating existing ASP.NET sites onto Vista or Windows Server 2008 from IIS 6.0 or earlier, beware.

Beyond 2008

One of the nice side effects of a new release for Visual Studio is the flattening of the stack of additional installs you need in order to work with the latest technologies. For example, by installing VS2008, you remove the need to install the following immediately:

- VS2005 Service Pack 1
- VS2005 Service Pack 1 Update for Vista Compatibility Pack
- ASP.NET 2.0 AJAX Extensions 1.0
- .NET Framework v3.0 Controls for Visual Studio
- .NET Framework v3.5

What VS2008 doesn't provide, of course, are the technology stacks that are still in development, some of which are very relevant to web development.

The Silverlight Stack

Initially touted as Microsoft's rival to Adobe's Flash Player, Silverlight's cross-platform .NET runtime looks set to be much, much more than that. Its early-adopter demonstration applications from the BBC and Major League Baseball hint at the idea of full applications streamed through this browser plug-in from data centers, as well as enabling media streaming and XBAP applications. Silverlight also includes support for the dynamic stack.

For more about Silverlight, see *Programming Silverlight 2* by Jesse Liberty and Tim Heuer (O'Reilly), available in 2009.

The Dynamic Languages Stack

At MIX07 in Las Vegas, Microsoft announced a new Dynamic Language Runtime (DLR) which is to bolt onto the core .NET runtime and provide support for dynamic languages such as Ruby and Python. The .NET runtime has always been targeted at "static" languages where types and methods are defined at compile time rather than at runtime. The DLR will include a shared dynamic type system, standard hosting model, and support to make it easy to generate fast dynamic code.

The Data Futures Stack

One of the poster children for dynamic languages is Ruby on Rails (RoR). This dynamically generates classes against a database and web pages that use those classes to enable the creation, use, alteration, and deletion of the data the database contains. It's a fantastic tool for prototyping a data-driven web application very rapidly, and the ActiveRecord wrapping pattern at the heart of RoR has been adapted into C# by several open source projects (Castle and SubSonic, to name but two).

It's also a good example of the object-relational mapping (ORM) layer, in which the properties and methods of an object map to the fields in and queries over a database table. The LINQ and ADO.NET teams are currently working on two ORM layers. LINQ to SQL (discussed in Chapter 10) is part of the .NET Framework 3.5 and is aimed at the situation in which there is a 1:1 relationship between classes and database tables. An "enterprise-level" ORM layer known as the ADO.NET Entity Framework which is aimed at situations with a 1:*n* relationship between classes and database tables is included with Service Pack 1 of .NET 3.5 and VS2008.

Also in the data-based future are two other Microsoft projects, codenamed Astoria and Jasper. Astoria, now officially christened ADO.NET Data Services, offers a new approach to accessing data over the Web through web services. It is also included with Service Pack 1 of .NET 3.5 and VS2008. Jasper, still known only as Jasper, is Microsoft's interpretation of RoR using the ADO.NET Entity Framework as the ORM glue to produce rapid web application prototypes based on a database.

These three stacks aren't mutually exclusive. The Data Futures stack, for instance, uses the dynamic stack as the basis for Jasper, whereas Silverlight and Dynamic Data controls feature in the ASP.NET 3.5 Extensions download. The point is that you may well end up with all three on your machine rather than just one.

On to VS2008

One of the tenets to being a better developer is to base what you build on solid foundations. In web development, that means knowing your HTML, CSS, and JavaScript for static web development, and knowing your tools. VS2008 (whether in one of its paid-for versions or as the freely downloadable Visual Web Developer 2008) is our choice of tool for this book, and it would be criminal if we didn't first look at all of its features, both old and new, before looking at ASP.NET itself. Investing your time in learning to use VS2008 well now will pay you back many times over in the future. The next chapter delves into VS2008 in depth.

Visual Studio 2008

Visual Studio 2008 (VS2008) is the development environment of choice for .NET developers, allowing you to create applications for desktop, web, or mobile platforms, as simple or as complex as required. It comes in several different flavors, from the free-to-download Express editions (including Visual Web Developer) to the rather expensive enterprise-level Team System editions, but at their heart they all contain the same core features:

- A convenient, easy way to access many different code files at the same time
- Dockable toolbars and information windows you can customize as and how you require
- WYSIWYG editing views for the rapid development of Windows and web forms
- A unified code editor for all .NET languages and project types offering code completion; and IntelliSense to help you write syntax-error-free code; immediate flagging of syntax errors if you do write some; support for inline, code-behind, and mixed coding models; incremental search; code outlining; collapsing text; line numbering; color-coded keywords; simple code refactorings; and code snippets
- Dynamic, context-sensitive help, which allows you to view topics and samples relevant to the code you are writing at the moment
- A built-in web server for use in testing the websites you develop, and the ability to access them for development through the filesystem, File Transfer Protocol (FTP), or Internet Information Services (IIS)
- An integrated debugger, which allows you to step through code, observe program runtime behavior, and set breakpoints, even across multiple languages and multiple processes
- Integrated support for source control software, such as Visual SourceSafe
- Support for third-party add-ins and controls to further enhance your development experience (this support is disabled in the Express editions, however)

In addition to the new classes and namespaces in version 3.5 of the .NET Framework, VS2008 also gives you:

Much tighter integration with Windows Vista

A standard user can run VS2008 without any problems in Vista, and VS2008 knows when that user will encounter permission problems, asking the user to restart it using administrative privileges as required. It also uses a number of the standard dialogs that Vista uses to provide a common user experience while developing.

AJAX, .NET 3.0, and ASP.NET 3.5 controls built in as standard

VS2005 users will recall that AJAX and .NET 3.0 controls had to be installed on top of VS2005 for them to be available. They are now part of the VS2008 install along with entries in the Visual Studio toolbox window for the three new ASP.NET 3.5 controls.

Multitargeting

VS2008 allows you to specify which version of the .NET Framework—2.0, 3.0, or 3.5—your projects should be compiled against. Once a project is targeted for a specific version, it makes available to your project only the features of the chosen .NET Framework.

Improved and enhanced IntelliSense

.NET 3.5 includes new versions of C# and Visual Basic .NET (VB.NET), and so VS2008 IntelliSense supports the new constructs within those languages. It also offers several improvements in the way VB.NET IntelliSense works. In addition, VS2008 now offers IntelliSense for JavaScript for the first time and a much-improved version for Cascading Style Sheets (CSS) as well.

Brand-new web form designer

VS2008 ships with a new web page editor. Among its new features are much-improved CSS editing facilities, the aforementioned IntelliSense for JavaScript and CSS, split-view editing where you can see code and browser views simultaneously, and full support for editing nested master pages in Design view.

Visual support for Language Integrated Query (LINQ)

This major new feature of .NET 3.5 is well supported in VS2008 with a number of new dialogs, file types, and samples that are included to help you in the development of LINQ-based applications. There is also an add-on visual debugger for LINQ, which you can install as required.

Restart Manager

It was always a bit frustrating to lose your work if VS2005 crashed, even though your documents were recovered successfully if Word failed. VS2008 now fixes that and will recover your solutions if it fails.

Unit-testing support in VS2008 Professional Edition

Unit-testing facilities were previously available only in the Team Suite editions of VS2005. They are now part of the Professional edition of VS2008 as well.

VS2008 is a program that will save you a huge amount of time in your development efforts. However, we cannot cover it adequately in a single chapter. Instead, this chapter will lay the foundation for understanding and using VS2008, and we'll point out some of the nastier traps you might run into along the way.

First Sight: The Start Page

When you open VS2008 for the first time, you'll find yourself looking at the VS2008 Start Page, as shown in Figure 2-1. This contains links for creating new projects and websites and opening existing ones. It also contains several windows with links to helpful topics for getting started, as well as up-to-date news items.

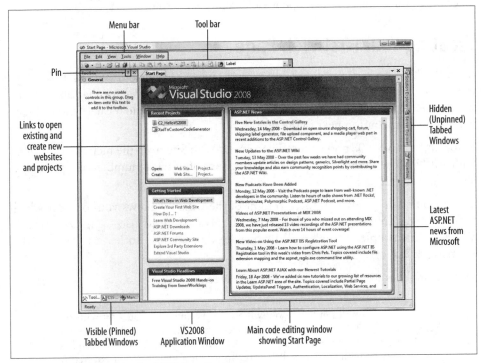

Figure 2-1. The Visual Studio 2008 Start Page

The Start Page opens in the main code-editing window inside VS2008. You can close it by clicking the X icon in the top-righthand corner or by pressing Alt-F, C. You can also disable it in the main Options dialog (Tools → Options) if you prefer not to see it at all.

The VS2008 application window surrounds the main window and is a typical collection of Windows menu items and buttons, plus several that are specific to the VS2008 integrated development environment (IDE). The left and right sides of the application window hold specialized tabs that provide access to tools and controls, and to other servers and databases in the development environment, labeled Toolbox and Server Explorer, respectively. The Solution Explorer, for exploring the files and classes associated with a particular project, appears on the right side. More windows are available through the VS2008 menu bar (see "The Integrated Development Environment," later in this chapter).

Note that you can lock open, or "pin," these tabs, as the Toolbox is in Figure 2-1, using the Pin button shown in the screenshot. Alternatively, you can hide them on one side of the VS2008 window when you're not using them, just like the Solution Explorer tab shown on the far right in Figure 2-1. You can also choose which edge of the window these tabs are attached or "docked" to by dragging them to the desired place once you've pinned them open—left, right, or bottom.

Creating Your First Web Page

It wouldn't be polite if we didn't bid a fond farewell to our old ASP.NET development tools, so your first coding effort in VS2008 will be a web page that displays the words "Goodbye Visual Studio 2005," which change to "Hello Visual Studio 2008" when you click a button next to the text.

To begin, start VS2008 and choose File → New Web Site from the menu bar (or press Shift-Alt-N). The New Web Site dialog opens, offering a number of options, as shown in Figure 2-2.

The unnamed drop down at the top right of the window allows you to select which version of the .NET Framework you want the website to use—a new feature in VS2008. This simple example will work with any version, so leave it set to .NET Framework 3.5.

In the Templates window, choose ASP.NET Web Site.

 The examples in this book will always assume that you start with the ASP.NET Web Site template, except for Chapter 16, which uses the two web service templates. The ASP.NET Reports Web Site template is used with the Crystal Reports application, which is not covered in this book.

Below the list of templates is a set of controls for setting the location and language for your website.

The first drop down, Location, allows you to work on web apps in three different manners, from three different locations: File System, HTTP, and FTP. The choice here controls much more than just a physical location, as you can read in the upcoming "Website Locations" sidebar. Leave it as File System and then use the Browse button to choose where the files for your website will be created.

Website Locations

VS2008 gives you the option of accessing the files in your web-related projects (websites, web services, and Web Application Projects) in three different ways.

File System is the default; it causes the new website folder to be created somewhere on the physical filesystem accessible to this PC and this user, either on the local machine or on the network. When you then run the website, VS2008 uses its own internal test web server to present it to the browser, instead of using IIS, the web server Microsoft provides to run websites available to the public once they are presentable.

The downside to using File System as the location is that web pages created in this way cannot be run from a browser unless VS2008 has started its test web server, created a temporary virtual directory for your site, and made it available to the browser on a URL such as *http://localhost:<portNumber>/default.aspx*.

The advantage, however, is that sharing file-based solutions is easy: you just copy the entire directory to the new machine and open it in Visual Studio.

The second option is HTTP, which indicates that IIS will be serving the pages. As such, it requires that the web application be located in an IIS virtual directory. VS2008 will automatically create this virtual directory. This is evident when you open a browser on the local machine and enter a URL such as *http://localhost/<virtual directory name>/default.aspx*.

You can also see any virtual directories created by VS2008 by opening Computer Management and looking under Default Web Site.

To access websites running under IIS on your local Windows Vista machine, you must run Visual Studio with administrator privileges; otherwise, the option to browse IIS sites will not be available.

FTP allows you to develop your website on a remote location accessible via FTP.

Note that the name of the website (as VS2008 will know it) is determined by the last folder name in this file path. By default, this will be *Website1*. Change this to *C2_HelloVS2008*, as shown in Figure 2-2.

This book uses C# as its language of choice, so leave it selected in the Language drop-down list and click OK. VS2008 will create a new website in the file location you've designated, and the markup for your first web page, named *Default.aspx*, will be shown in the main VS2008 window, as shown in Figure 2-3.

Before we go into the details of the myriad capabilities of VS2008, let's get this simple example up and running. You'll add some text to the page and a button which changes the text when pressed.

Click and drag a `Literal` control from the toolbox (it's highlighted in Figure 2-3) right into the source code between the opening and closing `<div>` tags.

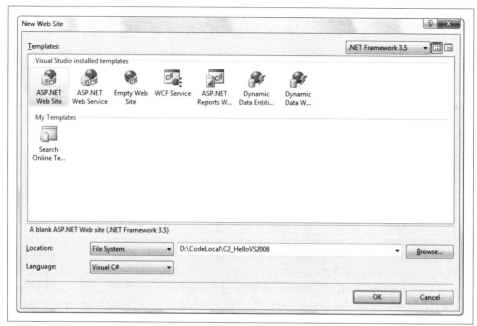

Figure 2-2. The New Web Site dialog

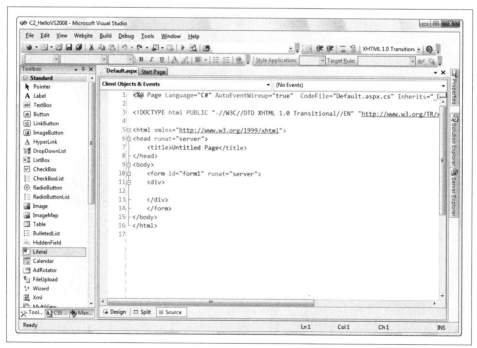

Figure 2-3. C2_HelloVS2008 created

A Literal is an ASP.NET server control that represents some literal text on the page. The actual text shown is saved in its Text property which will be altered when the button is clicked. We will look at server controls in much more detail in Chapters 4 and 5.

VS2008 will add some markup to the page to represent this control as follows:

```
<form id="form1" runat="server">
    <div>
        <asp:Literal ID="Literal1" runat="server"></asp:Literal>
    </div>
</form>
```

Add the text "Goodbye Visual Studio 2005" between the two `<asp:Literal>` tags:

```
<form id="form1" runat="server">
    <div>
        <asp:Literal ID="Literal1" runat="server">
            Goodbye Visual Studio 2005
        </asp:Literal>
    </div>
</form>
```

This is one way of setting a Literal control's Text property. Alternatively, you can set it explicitly like so:

```
<form id="form1" runat="server">
    <div>
        <asp:Literal ID="Literal1" runat="server"
            Text="Goodbye Visual Studio 2005">
        </asp:Literal>
    </div>
</form>
```

Now click the word Design at the bottom of the screen to switch from Source view to Design view. Whereas Source view lets you work directly with the markup for the page, Design view allows you to create a page visually by dragging controls from the toolbox onto the page, arranging them as needed, and then using the controls' context menus and the VS2008 Properties window to start defining how they work. At the moment, the only content on the page is the Literal control, so Design view shows only its text content.

In ASP.NET development, web pages are often referred to as *web forms* or just *forms*.

If you click the word Split at the bottom of the screen, you'll see that the main window divides into two halves, as shown in Figure 2-4. This arrangement is known as Split view. Note that while in Split view, if you select the Literal control in the design half of the window, the code for that control is also highlighted in Source view, as shown in Figure 2-4. This is true in reverse as well; selecting code in Source view will cause the visual page content it relates to (if any) to be highlighted in Design view.

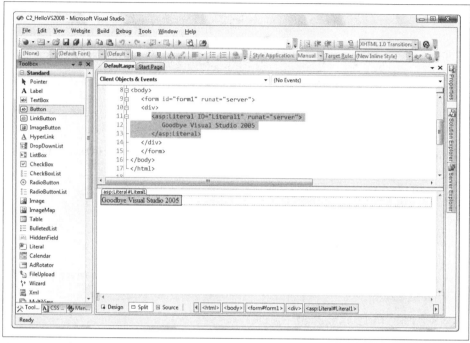

Figure 2-4. Split view in VS2008

Staying in Design view, click and drag a `Button` control from the toolbox onto the page beneath the `Literal` control. Click the `Button` control to select it and then press F4 to display the Properties window, as shown in Figure 2-5. It should be showing the `Button` control's properties and have its `Text` property highlighted.

If you press the Tab key now, the value of the `Button` control's `Text` property will be highlighted. Change it to `"Install .NET 3.5"` and press Enter to confirm this change. The text on the button in Design view changes immediately. If you switch back to Source view, you'll see that the button has been added after the label and the new value for its `Text` property has also been added:

```
<form id="form1" runat="server">
    <div>
        <asp:Literal ID="Literal1" runat="server">
            Goodbye Visual Studio 2005
        </asp:Literal>
        <br />
        <asp:Button ID="Button1" runat="server" Text="Install .NET 3.5" />
    </div>
</form>
```

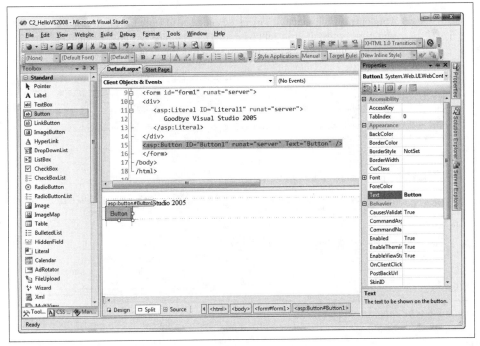

Figure 2-5. Using the Properties window

Still in Design view, double-click the Button control. All sorts of things now happen in the background. VS2008 takes your double-click as an instruction to create an event handler for the "default" event of the button. (If you don't understand what an event is, don't worry; we will explain it in detail shortly and in later chapters.) The code-behind file (the file containing the programming logic, explained in detail in Chapter 6) for *Default.aspx* is opened in the main window, and the cursor is placed in the event handler for you to start writing code there. Type in the one line of code needed to change the Literal control's Text property to "Hello Visual Studio 2008":

```
protected void Button1_Click(object sender, EventArgs e)
{
    Literal1.Text = "Hello Visual Studio 2008";
}
```

As you type, IntelliSense will try to help you locate the control you want (Literal1). It will then provide all the properties and methods of that control for you to set or invoke. Just keep typing; we'll get to IntelliSense later on.

Run the application by choosing Debug → Start Debugging from the menu (or pressing F5). VS2008 will notice that you do not have debugging enabled and will offer to create a new *web.config* file with debugging enabled, as shown in Figure 2-6. Click OK.

This prompt will *always* appear whenever you start a website for the first time without first telling it to run the site without debugging (Ctrl-F5) or changing *web.config* to switch debugging on.

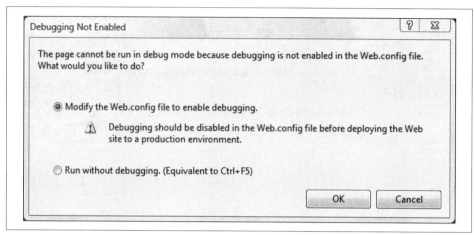

Figure 2-6. The enable debugging prompt

If script debugging is turned off in Internet Explorer, VS2008 will now ask whether you want to enable it, as shown in Figure 2-7. No script is used in this simple page, so click Yes to continue debugging. Script debugging comes in handy when you're using client-side scripts in your pages; with it enabled, Internet Explorer will alert you when any errors in the script occur and will offer to debug it in VS2008 if Java-Script is being used.

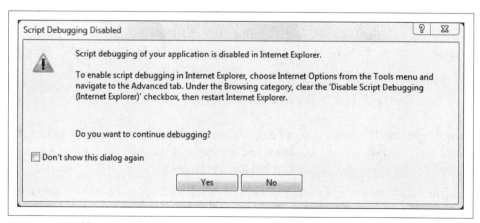

Figure 2-7. Enabling script debugging in Internet Explorer

The page now appears in Internet Explorer. Click the button and your event handler runs, changing the text as expected, as shown in Figure 2-8.

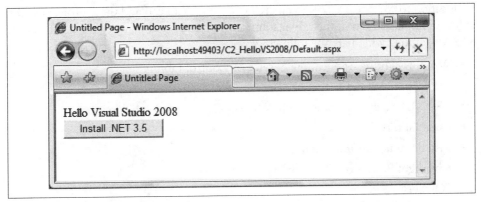

Figure 2-8. Running Hello Visual Studio 2008

You have just created a fully functional website, with controls and an event handler that responds to user action by changing the text of one of the controls. Though this is admittedly a very simple website, it is still notable how little typing you had to do because you could add controls to the page visually in Design view. VS2008 does its best to make your job easier.

 You can change which browser VS2008 uses to open web pages. Select File → Browse With, and use the resultant dialog to add details of the browser you want to use instead.

Projects and Solutions

A typical .NET web application consists of many items: content files (e.g., *.aspx* files), source files (e.g., *.cs* files), assemblies (e.g., *.exe* and *.dll* files) and assembly information files, data sources (e.g., *.mdb* files), references, icons, and miscellaneous other files and folders. VS2008 organizes these items into a folder that represents the website. All the files that make up the website are contained in a *solution*. When you create a new website, VS2008 automatically creates the solution and displays it in the Solution Explorer, shown in Figure 2-9. You can also add projects (described shortly) to the website.

Figure 2-9. The Hello Visual Studio 2008 solution and its files

In addition to websites, VS2008 can create *projects*. You can add these projects to the solution or place them in their own solution. You can build many types of projects in VS2008, among which are the following:

- Windows Forms Application, Service or Control Library
- WPF Application, Custom or User Control
- ASP.NET Web Application, AJAX Server Control, or Web Service
- Class Library
- Visual Studio or Office Add-ins
- Silverlight Project or Class Library
- SQL Server Project
- Setup, Merge Module or CAB File
- Empty Project

 You'll be able to create only Web Site Projects in Visual Web Developer 2008. If you install Service Pack 1, you'll also be able to create Web Application Projects.

Solutions

Solutions typically contain one or more projects or websites. They may contain other, independent items as well. These independent *solution items*, such as business case presentations, specification documents, or timelines, are not specific to any particular project, but apply to the entire solution. The solution items are not an integral part of the application because they can be removed without changing the compiled output. They display in the Solution Explorer (described later in this chapter) in a *Solution Items* folder and can be managed with source control.

Miscellaneous files are independent of the solution or project, but you may want to have them handy. They are not included in any build or compile but will display in the Solution Explorer and may be edited from there. Typical miscellaneous files include project notes, database schemas, and sample code files. To display the *Miscellaneous Files* folder as part of the solution, go to Tools → Options → Show All Settings → Environment → Documents, and check the checkbox for Show Miscellaneous Files in the Solution Explorer. You can even create a blank solution that does not contain any projects, but contains only solution items or miscellaneous files for editing with VS2008.

Solutions are defined by a *solution file*, created by VS2008 and named for the solution with an *.sln* extension. The *.sln* file contains a list of the projects that comprise the solution, the location of any solution-scoped items, and any solution-scoped build configurations. VS2008 also creates an *.suo* file with the same name as the *.sln* file (e.g., *mySolution.sln* and *mySolution.suo*). The *.suo* file contains data used to customize the IDE on a per-user and per-solution basis.

The solution file is placed in the Visual Studio projects location. On Windows XP or Windows Server 2003, this is typically:

> *C:\Documents and Settings\<your username>\My Documents\Visual Studio 2008\ Projects*

On Windows Vista or Windows Server 2008, this is:

> *C:\Users\<your username>\Documents\Visual Studio 2008\Projects*

You can change it to something a little easier to navigate, such as this:

> *C:\vsProjects*

Go to Tools → Options → Show All Settings → Projects and Solutions → General and change the default Visual Studio projects location.

You can open a solution in VS2008 by double-clicking the *.sln* file in Windows Explorer. Even if the *.sln* file is missing, you can still open a Web Site Project in VS2008 by clicking File → Open Web Site and selecting the folder that contains the site. A new *.sln* file will be created when you save the solution later on.

Projects and Files

A project contains content files, source files, and other files such as data sources and graphics. Typically, the contents of a project are compiled into an assembly, such as an executable file (*.exe*) or a dynamic link library (DLL) file, which can be identified by its *.dll* extension.

Most of the content of a web page or user control (we describe user controls in Chapter 15) consists of server control declarations and HTML. This content, along with any necessary directives (we describe directives in Chapter 6) and scripts comprise the *content file* for the page or user control. Content files for web pages have an extension of *.aspx*, and those for user controls have an extension of *.ascx*. There are other types of content files in ASP.NET, listed in Table 2-1.

Table 2-1. Content file types

File type	Extension
Page	*.aspx*
User Control	*.ascx*
Web Service	*.asmx*
Master Page	*.master*
Site Map	*.sitemap*
Website configuration file	*.config*

By the time the web server has sent a requested page to a browser, ASP.NET has already processed all the server controls to produce the HTML and client-side script. HTML is static content, whereas the client-side script—typically written in Java-Script or VBScript—is code executed by the browser which reacts to the user's actions on the page without any further help from ASP.NET. The client-side script can be placed within content files either in script blocks delimited by <script> tags or inline with HTML delimited by <% %> tags.

In contrast, the server-side script is compiled and run only on the web server in addition to its processing of any ASP.NET controls that have been added to the page. The server-side script can also be placed in script blocks delimited by <script> tags or inline with HTML delimited by <% %> tags, but it will be written in the .NET language specified in the Language attribute of the Page directive rather than JavaScript or VBScript. A <script> tag will also have a runat="server" attribute, to distinguish its contents from the client-side script.

ASP.NET supports *code separation*, where the server-side source code is contained in a *code-behind file* separate from the content file. The code-behind file typically has an extension indicating the programming language, such as *.cs* or *.vb*, for C# or Visual Basic (VB) .NET, respectively.

The server-side script and code contained in code-behind files are compiled into a single class. We discuss code separation and code-behind files in detail in Chapter 6.

Code-behind is the default coding model used by VS2008. When a new website is created, VS2008 automatically creates two files for the site: the content file with a default name, such as *Default.aspx*, and a code-behind file with a matching name, such as *Default.aspx.cs* (assuming you are using C#). If you change the name of the content file (highly recommended), the code-behind file will automatically assume the new name.

To see a code-behind page, right-click *Default.aspx* in the Solution Explorer and choose View Code. Alternatively, press F7 with *Default.aspx* open in the main editing window. The file *Default.aspx.cs* will open, showing the partial class definition that inherits from the System.Web.UI.Page class used to build your page (_Default). To get you started, a skeleton Page_Load event handler is provided. (We explain this event handler in Chapter 6.)

 For more on partial classes, see *Programming C# 3.0* or *Programming .NET 3.5*, both by Jesse Liberty (O'Reilly).

Templates

When you create a new project by clicking the New Project link on the Start Page (shown earlier in Figure 2-1) or by selecting File → New Project, you will get the New Project dialog box, as shown in Figure 2-10.

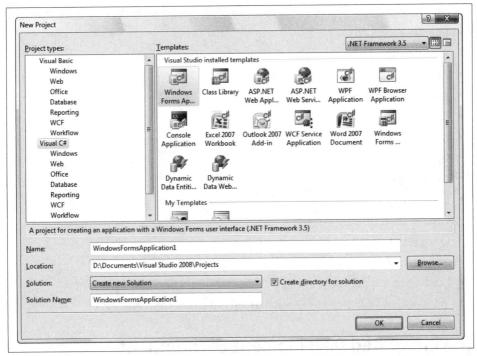

Figure 2-10. The New Project dialog box (not available in Visual Web Developer)

To create a new project, you select a project type and a template. You'll find various templates for each project type. For example, the templates for Visual C# Windows projects, shown in Figure 2-10, are different from the templates available in the Visual Basic, Visual C++, and Other Project Types sections.

 You can also create an empty solution, ready to receive whatever projects you want to add.

The template controls what items will be created automatically and included in the project, as well as default project settings. For example, if your project is a Web Site written in C#, code-behind files ending with .cs will be created as part of the project.

If the project is a website written in Visual Basic, code-behind files ending in *.vb* will be created instead. If a different template were selected, an entirely different set of files would be created.

Project names

Project names may consist of any standard ASCII characters except for the following:

- Pound or hash (#)
- Percent (%)
- Ampersand (&)
- Asterisk (*)
- Vertical bar (|)
- Backslash (\)
- Colon (:)
- Double quotation mark (")
- Less than (<)
- Greater than (>)
- Question mark (?)
- Forward slash (/)
- Leading or trailing spaces
- Windows or DOS keywords, such as `nul`, `aux`, `con`, `com1`, and `lpt1`

The Integrated Development Environment

The VS2008 IDE consists of windows for the visual design of forms, code-editing windows, menus, and toolbars providing access to commands and features. It also consists of toolboxes containing controls for use on the forms and windows providing properties and information about forms, controls, projects, and the solution.

But more important than the physical layout of the IDE is the productivity boost it provides to you, the developer. You can visually drag controls from the toolbox onto a design window or a code window. In code-editing windows, IntelliSense automatically pops up a list of all the available members for any given situation. Syntax errors are highlighted in code windows, signaling a problem even before you try to compile the project. The list goes on: a little time invested getting familiar with the IDE will reap tremendous payback.

Layout

VS2008 consists of a single parent window, which contains multiple child windows. All the menus, toolbars, design and editing windows, and miscellaneous other windows are associated with the single parent window.

A typical layout of the IDE is shown in Figure 2-11. Basically, it consists of a menu and toolbar arrangement across the top and a work surface below, flanked by other toolbars and windows.

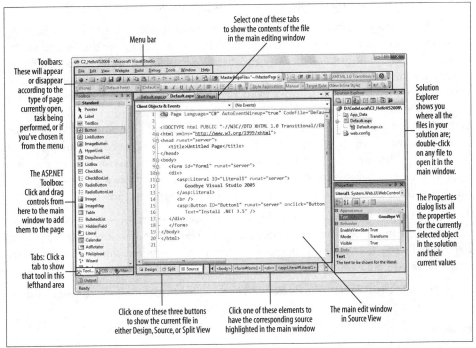

Figure 2-11. The typical IDE layout (in Source view)

When you're working on content files, such as page, user control, or master page files—all of which have visual content—you have your choice of three different views, selectable by tabs at the bottom of the screen. *Design view* shows the content in a WYSIWYG mode. *Source view* shows the source code for the content, that is, the server control declarations, any HTML and static content, and any script blocks on the page. *Split view* shows Source and Design views simultaneously, as shown in earlier in Figures 2-4 and 2-5.

VS2008 has a title bar across the top with menus below. Under the menus are toolbars with buttons that duplicate many of the common menu commands. Nearly everything you can do through menus you also can do with context-sensitive pop-up menus, as described shortly. You can easily customize the menu and toolbars by clicking Tools → Customize.

The toolbars are docked along the top of the window by default. As with many Windows applications, you can undock and move them to other locations, either free-floating or docked along other window edges. You move the toolbars by grabbing them with the mouse and dragging them where you want.

Figure 2-11 shows a Source view of a web form, with the Source window occupying the work surface in the center of the screen. When you click either the Design or the Split button at the bottom of the window, the work surface will display a visual representation of the page. In Split, Design, or Source view, you can drag and drop controls, components, or data sources from the Toolbox or Server Explorer onto the page. In Design view, this puts an accurate visual representation on the page. In Source view, it puts the control or component declaration in the source code. In Split view, the control will first appear on the pane where you placed it, and the other view will synchronize after a few seconds. You can work in any of the three views, switching to whichever is most convenient at the time, safe in the knowledge that the other two will also show your changes when you use them instead.

Along the right side of the screen in Figure 2-11 are two windows, both of which we will cover in more detail later in this chapter. The upper window is the Solution Explorer. Below that is the Properties window. Many other similar windows are available to you, and we will describe them shortly.

Right-clicking the title bar of a dockable window pops up a menu with five mutually exclusive check items:

Floating
> The window will not dock when you drag it against the edge of the VS2008 window. You can place the floating window anywhere on the desktop, even outside the VS2008 window. (This is handy for multiple-monitor setups.)

Dockable
> You can drag the window and dock it along any side of the VS2008 window.
>
> While you're dragging a window to be docked, two sets of blue docking icons will appear in the window. One icon will be located at each edge of the application window and a set of five icons will be located in the center of the current window. Dragging and releasing the window to be docked over one of these docking icons will cause it to dock against the indicated edge. The center docking icon of the set of five will cause the window to be one of the tabbed windows on the central work surface.

You can double-click the title bar or the tab to dock and undock the window. Double-clicking the title bar when a window is docked undocks the entire group. Double-clicking the tab undocks only the one window, leaving the rest of the group docked.

Tabbed Document

The window occupies the work surface, with a tab for navigation, the same as the code and design windows.

Auto Hide

The window will disappear, indicated only by a tab, when the cursor is not over the window. It will reappear when the cursor is over the tab. A pushpin in the upper-right corner of the window will be pointing down when Auto Hide is turned off and pointing sideways when it is turned on.

Hide

The window disappears. To see the window again (unhide it), use the View menu or the keyboard shortcuts listed in the View menu.

In the upper-right corner of the window are two buttons: one marked with a pushpin and the other with an X. The pushpin toggles the AutoHide property of the window. The X is the standard close window button. The work surface uses a tabbed metaphor, meaning the tabs along the top edge of that window indicate there are other windows below it. You can change to a Multiple Document Interface (MDI) style, if you prefer, by selecting Tools → Options → Environment → General and choosing Multiple Documents from the Window layout section.

You will find navigational aids along the bottom of the work surface. Depending on the context, there may be one or more buttons. When you're looking at a web page, for example, as shown in Figures 2-4, 2-11, and 2-12, three buttons labeled Design, Source, and Split allow switching between Design view, the underlying source code, and simultaneous views of both. Next to those buttons is a set of breadcrumb links representing the HTML hierarchy of the page, seen as <body> and <div> buttons in Figure 2-12. The cursor in the code window or the focus in Design view dictates which objects will be represented as buttons: one button for the current level and one more for each parent level. Clicking any of the buttons highlights that level of code in the code window.

When you switch from a design window to a code window, the menu items, toolbars, and toolbox change in a context-sensitive manner.

The code window has context-sensitive drop-down lists at the top of the screen for navigating around the application. In the HTML Editor, the left drop-down list presents Client Objects & Events and Client Script, and the right drop-down list presents event handlers. In the C# code editor, the left drop down contains a list of all the classes in the code, and the right drop down has a list of all the objects in the current class.

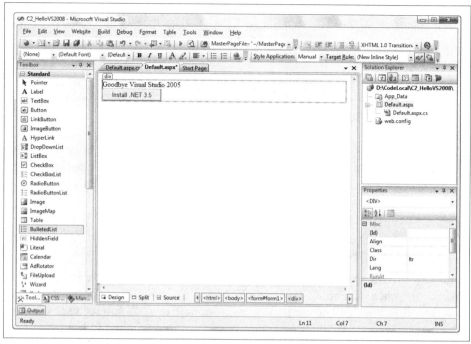

Figure 2-12. The typical IDE layout (in Design view)

The left margin of a code window shows a yellow bar next to lines that have been changed and a green bar next to lines that have been saved. This color coding is per session; it resets when the project is first loaded.

Along the bottom edge of the IDE window is a status bar, which shows such information as the current cursor position (when a code window is visible), the status of the Insert key, and any pending shortcut key combinations.

Building and Running

You can run your application at any time by selecting either Start or Start Without Debugging from the Debug menu, or you can accomplish the same results by pressing F5 or Ctrl-F5, respectively. In addition, you can start the program by clicking the Start icon ( ) on the Standard toolbar.

You can build the program (i.e., generate the *.exe* and *.dll* files for the program) by selecting a command under the Build menu. You have the option of building the entire solution or only the currently selected project.

Menus and Toolbars

The menus provide access to many of the commands and capabilities of VS2008. The more commonly used menu commands are duplicated with toolbar buttons for ease of use.

The menus and toolbars are context-sensitive (i.e., the available selection is dependent on what part of the IDE is currently selected and what activities are expected or allowed). For example, if the current active window is a code-editing window, the top-level menu commands will be the following:

- File
- Edit
- View
- Website
- Build
- Debug
- Format
- Tools
- Window
- Help

If the current window is a design window, the Table menu will also become available. Or, if the current window shows C# source code, the Refactor menu appears.

Many of the menu items have keyboard shortcuts, listed adjacent to the menu item itself. Look over the list of shortcut keys in Appendix A; many of them will become indispensable to your daily development efforts.

The following sections describe some of the menu items and their submenus, focusing on those aspects that are interesting and different from common Windows commands.

File Menu

The File menu provides access to a number of file-related, project-related, and solution-related commands. Many of these commands are context-sensitive. The following subsections describe the commands that are not self-explanatory.

Many different editions of VS2008 are available. Each may have a slightly different menu structure. Visual Web Developer in particular has a much-reduced menu selection.

New

As in most Windows applications, the New menu item creates new items that you can work on in the application. In VS2008, the New menu item has four submenu items, to handle the different possibilities:

Project (Ctrl-Shift-N)
> The New Project command brings up the New Project dialog shown in Figure 2-10.

Web Site (Shift-Alt-N)
> The New Web Site command brings up the New Web Site dialog box shown in Figure 2-2.

File (Ctrl-N)
> The File command brings up the Add New Item dialog box, as shown in Figure 2-13. It offers a range of template files, including a web form template, for adding web pages to a preexisting project. Files created in this way are located in the project directory.

Project From Existing Code
> This command brings up a wizard that walks you through the steps necessary to copy existing files to a new project.

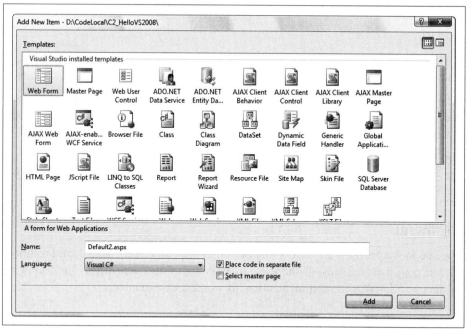

Figure 2-13. Add New Item dialog box

The New command has an equivalent button in the Standard toolbar, shown in Figure 2-14, which exposes the New Project and New Web Site commands.

Figure 2-14. The New Item icon and menu

Open

The Open menu item is used to open preexisting items. It has four submenu items:

Project/Solution (Ctrl-Shift-O)
> This opens an existing project. Radio buttons give you a choice of adding this project to the current solution or closing the current solution before opening the project.

Web Site (Shift-Alt-N)
> An Open Web Site dialog box is presented. Buttons down the left side of the dialog box give you the choice of opening a website from the filesystem, local IIS, an FTP site, or a remote website. As described in "Projects and Files," earlier in this chapter, these buttons dictate the type of access to the website—for instance, through the filesystem versus a virtual directory.

File (Ctrl-O)
> This presents a standard Open File dialog box, allowing you to browse to and open any file accessible on your network. Files that are opened are visible and editable in VS2008, but are not part of the project. To make a file part of the project, use one of the Add menu commands described later in this chapter. The Open File command has an equivalent button on the Standard toolbar.

Convert
> The Convert dialog box displays a list of converters to convert from one type of project to another—for example, from VB 6.0 to VS2008—and radio buttons to add the converted project to the current solution or to create a new solution.

Add

The Add menu item gives you options for adding a new or existing project or a new or existing website to a preexisting solution.

Advanced Save Options

Advanced Save Options is a context-sensitive submenu that is visible only when you are editing in a code window. It presents a dialog box, shown in Figure 2-15, which allows you to set the encoding option and line-ending character(s) for the file.

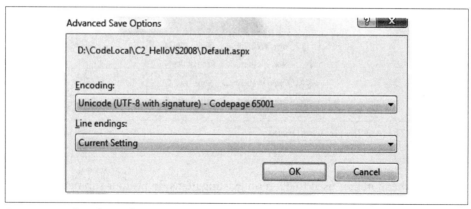

Figure 2-15. The Advanced Save Options dialog box

Export Template

The Export Template Wizard allows you to create a Visual Studio project or item template for use in the New Project (Figure 2-10) and New Item (Figure 2-13) dialogs, respectively.

Source Control

The Source Control submenu item allows you to interact with your source control program if it is installed, such as Visual SourceSafe.

Edit Menu

The Edit menu contains the text-editing and searching commands that one would expect, but also includes commands that are useful in editing code. We will discuss the most useful in the following subsections.

Cycle Clipboard Ring (Ctrl-Shift-V)

The Clipboard Ring is like copy and paste on steroids. You can copy a number of different selections to the Windows clipboard, using the Edit → Cut (Ctrl-X) and Edit → Copy (Ctrl-C) commands. Then you can use Ctrl-Shift-V to cycle through all the selections, allowing you to paste the correct one when it comes around.

This submenu item is context-sensitive and is visible only when you're editing a code window.

Finding and replacing

VS2008 offers a number of useful options for finding and replacing text, both in the current file and in a range of files.

Quick Find (Ctrl-F) and Quick Replace (Ctrl-H). Quick Find and Quick Replace are slightly jazzed names for slightly jazzed versions of the typical Find and Replace. Both commands call essentially the same dialog box and are switchable via a tab at the top of the dialog box, as shown in Figures 2-16 and 2-17.

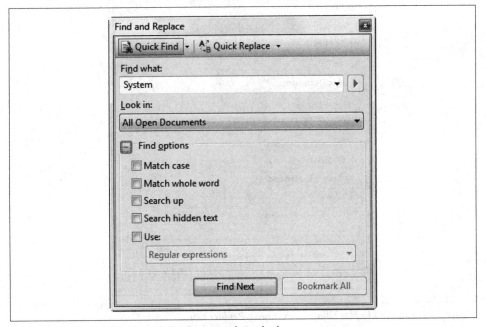

Figure 2-16. Find and Replace dialog box: Quick Find tab

The search string defaults to the text that is currently selected in the code window or, if nothing is selected, to the text immediately after the current cursor location.

The "Look in" drop-down box offers a choice of Current Document, All Open Documents, Current Project, or the current method.

You can expand or collapse the search options by clicking the plus/minus button next to Find Options. By default, "Search hidden text" is checked, which allows the search to include code sections currently collapsed in the code window. The Use checkbox allows the use of regular expressions (see the upcoming "Regular Expressions" sidebar) or wildcards. If the Use checkbox is checked, the Expression Builder button to the right of the "Find what" text box will become enabled, providing a handy way to insert valid regular expression or wildcard characters.

Once a search string has been entered in the "Find what" text box, the Find Next button becomes enabled. In Quick Find mode is a Bookmark All button, which finds all occurrences of the search string and places a bookmark (described in "Bookmarks," later in this chapter) next to the code.

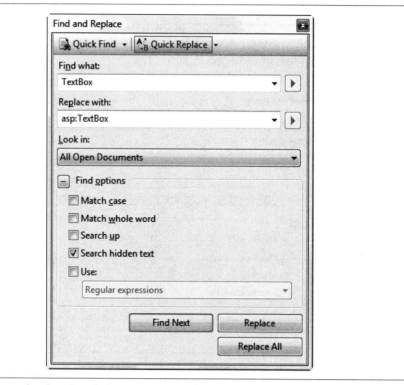

Figure 2-17. Find and Replace dialog box: Quick Replace tab

In Quick Replace mode, there is also a "Replace with" text box, and buttons for replacing either a single or all occurrences of the search string.

Regular Expressions

Regular expressions are a language unto themselves, expressly designed for incredibly powerful and sophisticated searches. A full explanation of regular expressions is beyond the scope of this book. For a complete discussion of regular expressions, see the SDK documentation or *Mastering Regular Expressions*, Third Edition, by Jeffrey E.F. Friedl (O'Reilly).

Find In Files (Ctrl-Shift-F). Find In Files is a powerful search utility that finds text strings anywhere in a directory or in subdirectories (subfolders). It presents the dialog box shown in Figure 2-18. It is similar to the Quick Find dialog in Figure 2-16, but with additional options to restrict the files being searched to those with a given file extension, and to indicate where to list the search results once available.

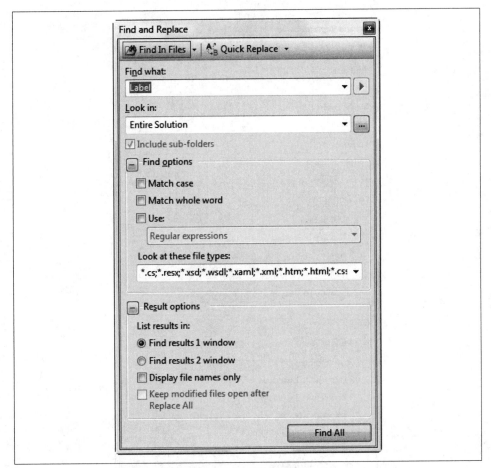

Figure 2-18. Find and Replace dialog box: Find In Files tab

Replace In Files (Ctrl-Shift-H). Replace In Files is identical to the Find In Files command, described in the preceding section, except that it allows you to replace the target text string with a replacement text string. The Replace In Files dialog box is shown in Figure 2-19.

This command is useful for renaming forms, classes, namespaces, projects, and so on. Renaming objects is a common requirement because you don't want to be saddled with the default names assigned by VS2008.

Renaming should not be difficult, but it can be. Object names are spread throughout a project, often hidden in obscure locations such as solution files, and throughout source code files. Though all of these files are text files and can be searched and edited, it can be a tedious and error-prone task. The Replace In Files command makes it simple, thorough, and reasonably safe. Of course, you can always undo a Find and Replace operation if you make a mistake.

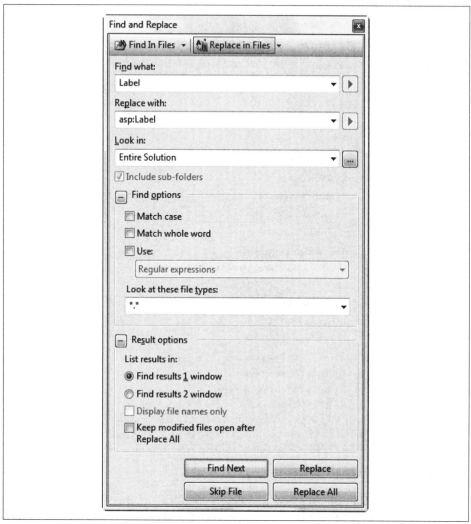

Figure 2-19. Find and Replace dialog box: Replace In Files tab

Find Symbol (Alt-F12). Clicking the Find Symbol command will bring up the Find Symbol dialog box shown in Figure 2-20. This allows you to search for symbols (such as namespaces, classes, and interfaces) and their members (such as properties, methods, events, and variables). It also allows you to search in external components for which the source code is unavailable.

The search results will be displayed in a window labeled Find Symbol Results. From there, you can move to each location in the code by double-clicking each result.

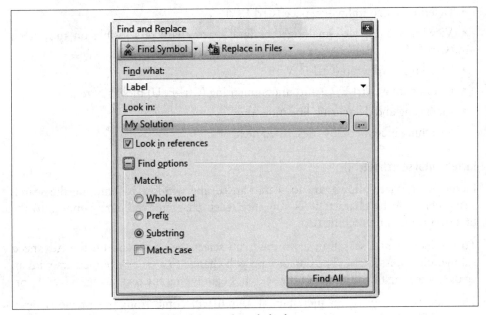

Figure 2-20. Find and Replace dialog box: Find Symbol tab

Go To (Ctrl-G)

The Go To command brings up the Go To Line dialog box, which allows you to enter a line number and immediately go to that line. It is context-sensitive and is visible only when you are editing a text window.

Insert File As Text

The Insert File As Text command allows you to insert the contents of any file into your source code, as though you had typed it in. It is context-sensitive and is visible only when you are editing a text window.

A standard file browsing dialog box is presented for searching for the file to be inserted. The default file extension will correspond to the project language, but you can search for any file with any extension.

Advanced

The context-sensitive Advanced command is visible only when you are editing code. It has many submenu items. These include commands for the following:

- Creating or removing tabs in a selection (converting spaces to tabs and vice versa)
- Forcing selected text to uppercase or lowercase

- Deleting horizontal whitespace (Ctrl-E, \)
- Viewing whitespace—making tabs and space characters visible on the screen (Ctrl-E, S)
- Toggling word wrap (Ctrl-E, W)
- Commenting (Ctrl-E, C) and uncommenting (Ctrl-E, U) blocks of text
- Increasing and decreasing line indenting
- Searching incrementally (described next)

Incremental search (Ctrl-I)

Incremental search allows you to search an editing window by entering the search string character by character. As you enter each character the cursor moves to the first occurrence of matching text.

To use incremental search in a window you select the command on the Advanced submenu or press Ctrl-I. The cursor icon will change to a pair of binoculars with an arrow indicating the direction of the search. Begin typing the text string to search for.

The case sensitivity of an incremental search will come from the previous Find, Replace, Find In Files, or Replace In Files search (described earlier).

The search will proceed downward and from left to right from the current location. To search backward you use Ctrl-Shift-I.

The key combinations listed in Table 2-2 apply to incremental searching.

Table 2-2. Incremental searching

Key combination	Description
Esc	Stop the search.
Backspace	Remove a character from the search text.
Ctrl-Shift-I	Change the direction of the search.
Ctrl-I	Move to the next occurrence in the file for the current search text.

Bookmarks

Bookmarks are useful for marking spots in your code and easily navigating to them later. Several context-sensitive commands are on the Bookmarks submenu (listed in Table 2-3, along with their shortcut key combinations). Unless you add the item to the task list, bookmarks are lost when you close the file, though they are saved when you close the solution (as long as the file was still open).

Table 2-3. Bookmark commands

Command	Key combination	Description
Toggle Bookmark	Ctrl-K, Ctrl-K	Place or remove a bookmark at the current line. When a bookmark is set, a blue rectangular icon will appear in the column along the left edge of the code window, as shown in Figure 2-20.
Previous Bookmark	Ctrl-B, P	Move to the previous bookmark.
Next Bookmark	Ctrl-B, N	Move to the next bookmark.
Previous Bookmark in Folder	Ctrl-Shift-K, Ctrl-Shift-P	Move to the previous bookmark in the folder.
Next Bookmark in Folder	Ctrl-Shift-K, Ctrl-Shift-N	Move to the next bookmark in the folder.
Clear Bookmarks	Ctrl-B, Ctrl-C	Clear all the bookmarks.
Previous Bookmark in Document	None	Move to the previous bookmark in the current document.
Next Bookmark in Document	None	Move to the next bookmark in the current document.
Add Task List Shortcut	Ctrl-K, Ctrl-H	Add an entry to the Task List (described in "View Menu," later in this chapter) for the current line. When a task list entry is set, a curved arrow icon appears in the column along the left edge of the code window, as shown in Figure 2-21.

The Bookmarks menu item appears only when a code window is the current window.

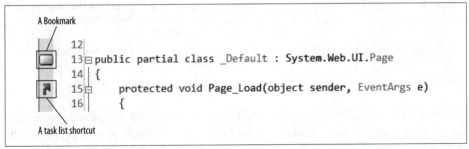

Figure 2-21. Icons in the code window representing a bookmark and a task list shortcut

Outlining

VS2008 allows you to *outline*, or collapse and expand, sections of your code to make it easier to view the overall structure. When a section is collapsed, it appears with a plus sign in a box along the left edge of the code window. Clicking the plus sign expands the region. For example, in Figure 2-22, the Page_Load event handler has been collapsed whereas the Button1_Click handler has not.

You can nest the outlined regions so that one section can contain one or more other collapsed sections. Several commands facilitate outlining, as shown in Table 2-4.

```
      protected void Page_Load(object sender, EventArgs e)|...|

      protected void Button1_Click(object sender, EventArgs e)
      {
          Literal1.Text = "Hello Visual Studio 2008";
      }
```

Figure 2-22. Code outlining at work

Table 2-4. Outlining commands

Command	Key combination	Description
Hide Selection	Ctrl-M, H	Collapses currently selected text. In C# only, this command is visible only when automatic outlining is turned off or the Stop Outlining command is selected.
Toggle Outlining Expansion	Ctrl-M, M	Reverses the current outlining state of the innermost section in which the cursor lies.
Toggle All Outlining	Ctrl-M, L	Sets all sections to the same outlining state. If some sections are expanded and some are collapsed, all will become collapsed.
Stop Outlining	Ctrl-M, P	Expands all sections. Removes the outlining symbols from view.
Stop Hiding Current	Ctrl-M, U	Removes outlining information for the currently selected section. In C#, this command is visible when automatic outlining is turned off or the Stop Outlining command is selected.
Collapse to Definitions	Ctrl-M, O	Automatically creates sections for each procedure in the code window and collapses them all.
Start Automatic Outlining	None	Restarts automatic outlining after it has been stopped.

You can set the default behavior for outlining with the Tools → Options menu item. Select Text Editor and then the specific language for which you want to set the options. You can set the outlining options for VB.NET under Basic → VB Specific, and for C# under C# → Advanced.

IntelliSense

Microsoft IntelliSense technology makes the lives of programmers much easier. It has real-time, context-sensitive help available, which appears under your cursor. Code completion automatically completes words for you, reducing your typing. Drop-down lists provide all methods and properties possible in the current context, available at a keystroke or mouse click.

Unlike previous versions of Visual Studio, IntelliSense works in all code windows, including the C# code-behind files, but also within server-side (script) and client-side (HTML) code in content files, that is, in *.aspx* and *.ascx* files.

You can configure the default IntelliSense features by selecting Tools → Options and then the language-specific pages under Text Editor.

Most of the IntelliSense features appear as you type inside a code window, or allow the mouse to hover over a portion of the code. In addition, the Edit → IntelliSense menu item offers the commands shown in Table 2-5.

Table 2-5. IntelliSense commands

Command	Key combination	Description
List Members	Ctrl-K, L	Displays a list of all possible members available for the current context. As you enter keystrokes, the list is incrementally searched. Press any key to insert the highlighted selection into your code; that key becomes the next character after the inserted name. Use the Tab key to select without entering any additional characters.
		You can access this by right-clicking and selecting List Member from the context-sensitive menu.
Parameter Info	Ctrl-K, P	Displays a list of the number, name, and type of parameter required for a method, sub, function, or attribute.
Quick Info	Ctrl-K, I	Displays the complete declaration for any identifier (such as a variable name or class name) in your code. You can also enable this by hovering the mouse cursor over any identifier.
Complete Word	Ctrl-K, W	Automatically completes the typing of any identifier once you type in enough characters to uniquely identify it. This works only if you are entering the identifier in a valid location in the code.
Insert Snippet	Ctrl-K, X	Displays a selection of code snippets to insert, such as the complete syntax for a `switch case` block or an `if` block.
Surround With	Ctrl-K, S	Displays a selection of code snippets to surround a block of code, such as a class declaration.
Generate Method Stub	Ctrl-K, M	With the cursor over a method call, will automatically generate a code skeleton for that method.
Implement Interface Implicitly	None	With the cursor over an inherited interface, will automatically generate implicit interface member declarations, meaning that member calls will not include the interface name in their declarations.
Implement Interface Explicitly	None	With the cursor over an inherited interface, will automatically generate explicit interface member declarations, meaning that member calls will include the interface name in their declarations.
Implement Abstract Class	None	With the cursor over an inherited abstract class, will automatically generate class member declarations.
Remove Unused Usings	None	Automatically removes any `using` statements that refer to namespaces not used in the code.
Sort Usings	None	Sorts the `using` statements in a code file alphabetically by namespace.
Remove and Sort	None	A combination of both Remove Unused Usings and Sort Usings.

The member list presents itself when you type a dot following any class or member name.

Every member of the class is listed, and each member's type is indicated by an icon. There are icons for methods, fields, properties, events, and so forth. In addition, each icon may have a second icon overlaid to indicate the accessibility of the member: public, private, protected, and so on. If there is no accessibility icon, the member is public.

 If the member list does not appear, ensure that you have added all the necessary using statements. You should also remember that IntelliSense is case-sensitive in C#. Occasionally, C# needs a rebuild before it will reflect the most recent changes.

Table 2-6 lists all the different icons used in the member lists and other windows throughout the IDE. The accessibility icons are listed in Table 2-7.

Table 2-6. Object icons

Icon	Member type
	Class
	Constant
	Delegate
	Enum
	Enum item
	Event
	Exception
	Global
	Interface
	Intrinsic
	Macro
	Map
	Map item
	Method or function
	Module
	Namespace
	Operator
	Property
	Structure
	Template
	Typedef

Table 2-6. Object icons (continued)

Icon	Member type
◆◆	Union
❶	Unknown or error
◆	Variable or field

Table 2-7. Object accessibility icons

Icon	Accessibility type
⊡	Shortcut
✉	Internal
🔒	Private
♘	Protected

Two of the subcommands under the IntelliSense menu item, Insert Snippet and Surround With, tap into a great feature to reduce typing and minimize errors: *code snippets*. A code snippet is a chunk of code that replaces an alias. For example, the alias switch would be replaced with the following:

```
switch (switch_on)
{
    default:
}
```

After the replacement, the switch expression switch_on is highlighted in yellow and the cursor is in place, ready for you to type in your own expression. In fact, all the editable fields will be highlighted, and you can use the Tab key to navigate through them or Shift-Tab to go backward. Any changes made to the editable field are immediately propagated to all the instances of that field in the code snippet. You press Enter or Esc to end the field editing and return to normal editing.

To add a snippet to your code, you can either select Insert Snippet from the menu; press Ctrl-K, X; or start typing the name of the snippet in the code, select it from the IntelliSense dialog, and press the Tab key.

A code snippet can also surround highlighted lines of code—for instance, with a for construct. To surround lines of code with a code snippet construct, highlight the code and then select Surround With from the menu or press Ctrl-K, S.

View Menu

The View menu provides access to the myriad windows available in the VS2008 IDE. You will probably keep many of these windows open all the time; others you will use rarely, if at all.

When the application is running, a number of other windows, primarily used for debugging, become visible or available. You can access these windows via the Debug → Windows menu item, not from the View menu item.

VS2008 can store several different window layouts. In particular, it remembers a completely different set of open windows during debug sessions than it does during normal editing. These layouts are stored per user, not per project or per solution.

The following subsections discuss the areas that may not be self-explanatory.

Solution Explorer (Ctrl-Alt-L)

You use the Solution Explorer to manage projects and solutions. The Solution Explorer presents the solution and projects and all the files, folders, and items contained within them in a hierarchical, visual manner. The Solution Explorer is typically visible in a window along the upper-right side of the VS2008 screen, although you can close or undock it and move it to other locations, as you can with all the windows accessible from the View menu. A typical Solution Explorer is shown in Figure 2-9.

You will find several menu buttons along the top of the Solution Explorer window. These buttons are context-sensitive, meaning they may or may not appear, depending on the currently selected item in the Solution Explorer.

Table 2-8 details the purpose of each button.

Table 2-8. Solution Explorer buttons

Button	Name	Shortcut key	Description
	Properties	F4	If the currently highlighted item is a solution or a project, this button displays the Properties page for that item. Otherwise, it moves the cursor to the Properties window for that item.
	Refresh	None	Refreshes the Solution Explorer display.
	Nest Related Files	None	Toggles between nested and non-nested views of related files, such as *Default.aspx* and *Default.aspx.cs*.
	View Code	None	Displays source code on the work surface. It is visible only for page and user control files.
	View Designer	None	Displays the visual designer on the work surface. It is visible only for items with visual components.
	Copy Web Site	None	Puts the Copy Web Site dialog, described fully under the Website menu item, on the work surface.
	ASP.NET Configuration	None	Opens the ASP.NET Configuration utility, described in Chapters 12 and 18.

You can display miscellaneous files in the Solution Explorer: go to Tools → Options, and then go to Environment → Documents. Check the checkbox labeled Show Miscellaneous Files in the Solution Explorer.

Most of the functionality of the Solution Explorer is also available through the VS2008 menu items, though performing a given chore in the Solution Explorer rather than in the menus is often easier and more intuitive. Right-clicking any item in the Solution Explorer will pop up a context-sensitive menu. Three different pop-up menus from the Solution Explorer are shown in Figure 2-23. From left to right, they are for a solution, a web page, and a source code file.

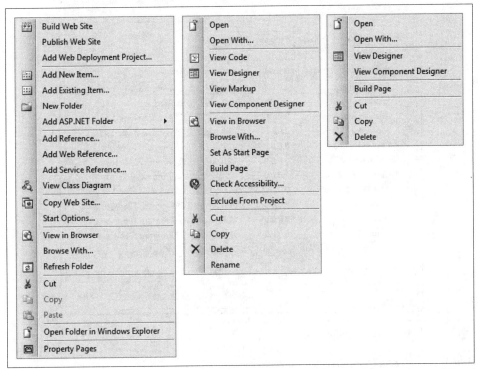

Figure 2-23. Solution Explorer context-sensitive menus for solutions, web pages, and source files

A few commands are available only through the Solution Explorer context menus:

View Code/View Designer/View Markup

The Code and Markup menu items are available only when you are looking at a content file, that is, files with an extension of *.aspx* or *.ascx*. The Code menu item displays the C# code-behind file on the work surface (i.e., a file with an extension of *.cs*). The Markup menu item has the same effect as clicking the Source button at the bottom of the work surface, displaying the underlying HTML and script of the content file.

The Designer menu item is available whenever Design view is available. It has the same effect as clicking the Design button at the bottom of the work surface, switching to a WYSIWYG Design view.

Add Reference

The Add Reference command brings up the Add Reference dialog box shown in Figure 2-24. This allows you to reference assemblies or DLLs external to your application, making the public classes, methods, and members contained in the referenced resource available to your application.

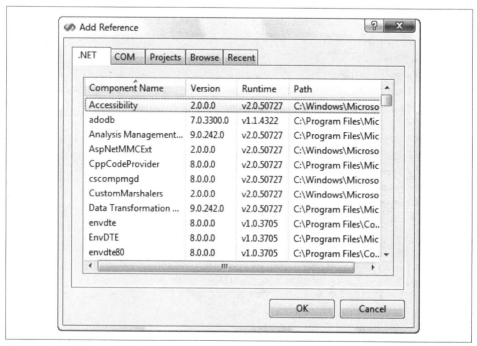

Figure 2-24. Add Reference dialog box

Add Web Reference/Add Service Reference

The Add Web Reference and Add Service Reference commands, available in the Solution Explorer by right-clicking a project, allow you to add a reference to a web service to your project, thereby making it a consuming application of a web service.

We cover web services, web references, and service references in Chapter 16.

Server Explorer (Ctrl-Alt-S)

The Server Explorer allows you to access any server to which you have network access. If you have sufficient permissions, you can log on, access system services, open data connections, access and edit database information, access message queues and performance counters, and more.

> Visual Web Developer uses a pared-down version of the Server Explorer, referred to as the Database Explorer. As you might imagine, it is limited to working only with databases.

A typical Server Explorer is shown in Figure 2-25. It is a hierarchical view of the available servers. In this figure, just one server (the local machine named *Precision*) is available. As you can see, you can drill down into a data connection allowing you to view the tables, views, stored procedures, and more in the AdventureWorksLT database. These objects, and all other objects in this tree view, are directly accessible and editable from the window.

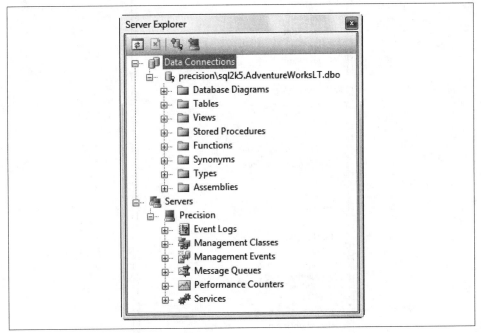

Figure 2-25. The Server Explorer

Properties window (F4)

The Properties window displays all the properties for the currently selected item. Some of the properties may be grouped under a common heading (such as Font), indicated by a plus sign next to their entries in the window. The property values on the right side of the window are editable.

One thing that can be confusing is that certain items have more than one set of properties. For example, a Form content file can show two different sets of properties, depending on whether you select the source file in the Solution Explorer or the form, as shown in Design view.

A typical Properties window while in Design view is shown in Figure 2-26.

The name and type of the current object are displayed in the field at the top of the window. In Figure 2-26, the current object is an object named Button1 of type Button, contained in the System.Web.UI.WebControls namespace.

Figure 2-26. Properties window

You can edit most properties in either the Properties window or declaratively (i.e., manually) in Source view. You can set the properties in the Font group directly in the Properties window by clicking the plus sign to expand the group and editing them in place.

The Properties window has several buttons below the name and type of the object. The first two buttons on the left toggle the list by category or alphabetically (as shown in Figure 2-26). The next two buttons from the left (visible only in Design view) toggle between displaying properties for the selected item and displaying events for the selected item. The rightmost button displays property pages for the object, if there are any.

Some objects have both a Properties window and Property Pages. The Property Pages display additional properties other than those shown in the Properties window.

The box below the list of properties displays a brief description of the selected property.

Visible Aids

The Visible Aids menu item is available only in Design view and toggles the display of various visual aids on the page or user control. For example, you can toggle visible borders around block-level elements, the highlighting of margins and padding for an element, and the display of icons representing nonvisual ASP.NET controls placed on the page.

Formatting Marks

The Formatting Marks menu item is available only in Design view and toggles the display of items such as HTML breaks, spans, and divs.

Object Browser (Ctrl-W, J)

The Object Browser is a tool for examining objects (such as namespaces, classes, and interfaces) and their members (such as methods, properties, variables, and events). A typical Object Browser window is shown in Figure 2-27.

The objects are listed in the pane on the left side of the window, and members of the object, if any, are listed in the right pane. The objects are listed hierarchically, with the ability to drill down through the tree structure. The icons used in this window were listed earlier in Tables 2-6 and 2-7.

Right-clicking an object or a member brings up a context-sensitive pop-up menu with various menu options.

Error List (Ctrl-W, E)

Available in all editor views, the Error List window displays errors, warnings, and messages generated as you edit and compile your project. Syntax errors flagged by IntelliSense are displayed here, as well as deployment errors. Double-clicking an error in this list will open the offending file and move the cursor to the error location.

Task List (Ctrl-W, T)

In large applications, keeping a to-do list can help. VS2008 provides this functionality with the Task List window. You can provide shortcuts to comments in the Task List along with token strings, such as TODO, HACK, and UNDONE. Also, the compiler populates the Task List with any compile errors. Clicking a line in the Task List will take you to the relevant line of code in the code editor.

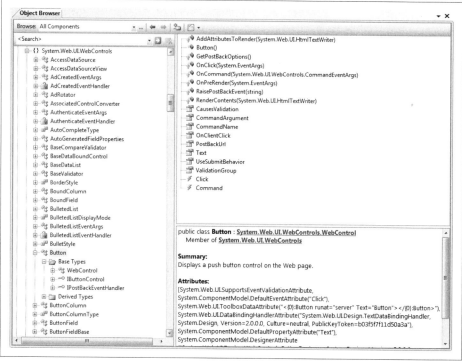

Figure 2-27. Object Browser

Toolbox (Ctrl-W, X)

The Toolbox window displays the toolbox if it is not currently displayed. The toolbox is where you'll find the various ASP.NET server controls to use in your projects. You can drag controls from the toolbox directly onto Source or Design view. If it is currently displayed, nothing happens, and it does not toggle the display.

Class View (Ctrl-W, C)

The Class View window shows all the classes in the solution in a hierarchical manner. A typical Class View window, somewhat expanded, is shown in Figure 2-28. The icons used in this window were listed earlier in Tables 2-6 and 2-7.

As with the Solution Explorer, you can right-click any item in the Class View window to expose a pop-up menu with a number of context-sensitive menu items. This can provide a convenient way to sort the display of classes in a project or solution or to add a method, property, or field to a class.

The button on the left above the class list allows you to create virtual folders for organizing the classes listed. These folders are saved as part of the solution in the *.suo* file.

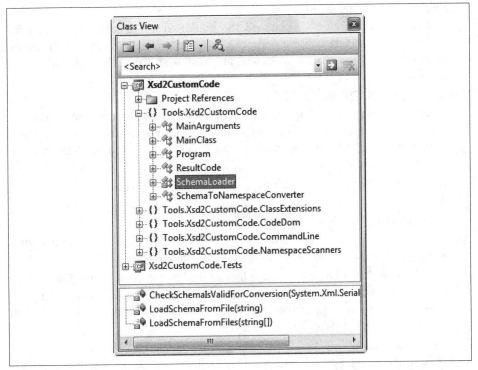

Figure 2-28. Class View window

These folders are virtual; they are used only for viewing the list. As such, they have no effect on the actual items. Items copied to the folder are not physically moved, and if the folders are deleted, the items in them will not be lost. If you rename or delete an object from the code that is in a folder, you may need to drag the item manually into the folder again to clear the error node.

The button on the right allows you to choose which class members to show or not to show in the Class View window.

Output (Ctrl-W, O)

The Output window displays status messages from the IDE, such as build progress. You can set the Output window to display by default when a build starts by going to Tools → Options → Projects and Solutions → General and checking "Show Output window when build starts."

This window is available in all editor views.

Other windows

Several other windows have been relegated to a submenu called Other Windows:

Bookmark window (Ctrl-W, B)

The Bookmark window displays all the bookmarks you have created in your code. Each bookmark is listed with its location and with its name (if you choose to give it one). You can create, delete, and temporarily disable bookmarks from this window.

Command window (Ctrl-W, A)

The Command window is used to enter commands directly, bypassing the menu system or executing commands that are not contained in the menu system. (You can add any command to the menu or to a toolbar button using Tools → Customize.)

For a comprehensive discussion of Command window usage, consult the SDK documentation.

Document Outline (Ctrl-W, U)

The Document Outline menu item is available in either Design or Source view when a page or user control is visible on the work surface.

The Document Outline displays the hierarchical structure of a web page or user control, including directives, script blocks, HTML elements, and server controls. Clicking any item in the Document Outline will immediately select that item on the work surface, but not vice versa.

Resource View (Ctrl-W, R)

This window displays the resource files included in the project. *Resources* are nonexecutable data deployed with an application, such as icons and graphics, culture-specific text messages, and persisted data objects.

Macro Explorer (Alt-F8)

VS2008 offers the ability to automate repetitive chores with macros. A macro is a set of instructions written in VS2008, either created manually or recorded by the IDE, and saved in a file. The Macro Explorer is one of the main tools for viewing, managing, and executing macros. It provides access into the Macro IDE.

We describe macros further in "Tools Menu," later in this chapter.

Refactor Menu

Refactoring, to quote the Microsoft MSDN Library, is "the process of improving your code after it has been written, by changing the internal structure of the code without changing the external behavior of the code."

In English, this means after you write your code, you may change the code to enhance readability and maintainability. VS2008 makes this easy.

 For details on refactoring, we recommend the book *Refactoring: Improving the Design of Existing Code* by Martin Fowler et al. (Addison-Wesley).

The Refactor menu item is available when you're looking at a code window for a web page, user control, or language source code file. It is also available from context menus when you right-click an identifier in a Class View, Object Browser, or Solution Explorer window.

The refactoring menu items will modify your code, for example, extracting common code to a method and then calling that method in the place from which it was extracted. You also can use refactoring to rename methods, and all references to the renamed method will automatically be updated as well across all files in the project and across all projects of the same language. Before any changes are committed, an optional Preview Changes dialog box will appear, giving you the opportunity to accept or cancel the changes. A project that is unable to build successfully can still be refactored, though ambiguous references might not update properly.

The following functions are available under the Refactor menu item:

Rename (F2)

To rename a code symbol such as a method, class, namespace, field, local variable, property, or type, click the symbol in your code and select the Rename menu item, press F2, or right-click the symbol and select Refactor → Rename from the pop-up menu.

The Rename dialog box will appear which contains a text box for the new name to be entered. A read-only text box will show the current cursor location. Several context-sensitive checkboxes will present options. "Preview reference changes" will be checked by default. Other options might include "Search in comments," "Search in strings," and "Rename overloads."

After you click OK, the program will process for a bit before displaying the Preview Changes dialog box, if that option was left checked. The top pane will list all the files and lines of code where the symbol is to be renamed. Clicking any of the lines will show the source code in context in the bottom pane of the dialog box.

Click Apply to apply the changes or Cancel to cancel the operation.

Alternatively, type a new name and then click the smart tag that appears at the end of the name and choose the Rename option.

Extract Method (Ctrl-R, Ctrl-M)

As described earlier, the Extract Method option extracts duplicate code and turns it into a method, leaving a call to that new method in place of the old (duplicate) code.

The new method is inserted into the source file in the same class immediately following the current method. If no instance data is referenced by the new method, the method will be declared a static method.

The Extract Method dialog box will preview the new method signature. You can click OK to create the new method or click Cancel to cancel. If you wish to revert after creating the new method, use Edit → Undo (Ctrl-Z).

Encapsulate Field (Ctrl-R, Ctrl-F)

A public member variable can be accessed externally and its value altered without the knowledge or consent of its class, breaking encapsulation. A better practice is to declare private fields and use properties with get and set accessors to control external access to the field.

The Encapsulate Field function creates a property from an existing public field and updates the code to refer to the new property rather than the field. The previously public field is converted to private, and the get and set accessors are created. If the original field had been declared as read-only, the set accessor will not be created.

Extract Interface

If multiple classes, structs, or interfaces use a common set of members, it can be beneficial to extract those common members into an interface, which is then implemented by the original classes, structs, or interfaces.

This menu item is available only when the cursor is in the class, struct, or interface containing the members to extract into an interface. The new interface is created in a new file. The Extract Interface dialog lets you enter the name of the new interface, the new filename, and which public members to include in the new interface.

Promote Local Variable to Parameter (Ctrl-R, Ctrl-P)

This function converts a local variable to a parameter of a method, indexer, constructor, or delegate. It also updates all the calls to that local variable.

Remove Parameters (Ctrl-R, Ctrl-V)

This function removes parameters from methods, indexers, constructors, or delegates. It updates all the calls to the now defunct parameter. The easiest way to invoke this function is to right-click anywhere within the declaration of the object (e.g., method, struct, property) where you want to remove the parameter(s), and then select Refactor → Remove Parameters from the context menu.

Reorder Parameters (Ctrl-R, Ctrl-O)

Similar to the Remove Parameters function, this menu item allows you to change the order of parameters in methods, indexers, constructors, or delegates. It updates all the calls to the modified objects to reflect the new order of parameters.

Website Menu

The Website menu item mostly provides an alternative to, and works in conjunction with, the Solution Explorer. It allows you to add new or existing items, references, or web references, all affecting the current selection in the Solution Explorer. We described these menu items earlier in this chapter.

In addition, the Website menu item provides other menu items, some of which are redundant with the Solution Explorer and others which are not.

Start Options

The Start Options menu item opens the Property Pages dialog box with the Start Options for the current website, as shown in Figure 2-29. This allows you to specify settings such as the start page or URL, the server to use, and the debugger to use. This menu item is unavailable on the Solution Explorer.

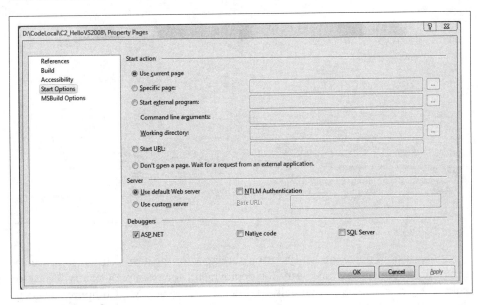

Figure 2-29. Start Options

Copy Web Site

The Copy Web Site menu item, which is also available as an icon at the top of the Solution Explorer, allows you to easily copy all or part of one website to a new website. If the new website does not exist, Copy Web Site will create it. Figure 2-30 shows the Copy Web Site window.

To copy a website, click the Connections drop-down menu at the top of the window then navigate to the target location. If the target location does not exist, you will be prompted to create it. Highlight the files and folders on the left that you wish to copy and then click the right-facing arrow in the middle to copy those selected items.

A number of other self-explanatory controls exist, such as buttons for refreshing the list, deleting items, synchronizing directories, and viewing the log.

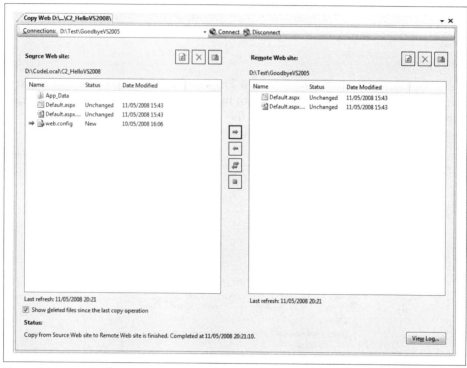

Figure 2-30. Copy Web Site

This process does not create an IIS virtual directory for the new website, so if you are using virtual directories (necessary for deployment, for example), you will have to make the virtual directory manually. To do so, right-click My Computer or go to Control Panel → Administrative Tools → Computer Management and drill down through Services and Applications → Internet Information Services → Web Sites to Default Web Site. Then right-click and select New → Virtual Directory and follow the wizard.

ASP.NET Configuration

The ASP.NET Configuration menu item is also available as an icon at the top of the Solution Explorer. It brings up the ASP.NET Web Site Administration Tool (WAT), which we will cover in detail in Chapter 18.

Project Menu

The Project menu provides functionality related to project management. It is visible only when the solution is selected in the Solution Explorer. All of the functionality exposed by the Project menu is available in the Solution Explorer by right-clicking the solution. Accomplishing your goals in the Solution Explorer is often easier and more intuitive, but the menus lend themselves to keyboard use.

Each command under this menu pertains to the object currently highlighted in the Solution Explorer.

Add New Item (Ctrl-Shift-A)

The Add New Item command brings up the Add New Solution dialog box, which lets you add new items based on templates, such as a text file, stylesheet, class file, and so forth. This command is not for adding a new project to the solution; you do that using the File → New → New Project command.

Add Existing Item (Shift-Alt-A)

The Add Existing Item command brings up the Add Existing Item – Solution Items dialog box, which allows you to browse your filesystem for existing items to add to the solution.

Add New Solution Folder

Solution folders are used to organize solution items within a solution. The Add New Solution Folder command lets you add a folder to the solution. These solution folders are virtual, which means no corresponding physical folder is on your filesystem. Instead, the solution folders are remembered within the solution file (*.sln*). Any solution items added to the solution folder are physically stored in the project file along with the *.sln* file and other solution items.

Set StartUp Projects

Visual Studio must know which project, or projects, in a solution will be the startup project(s). The Set StartUp Projects command brings up the Solution Properties Pages dialog box, with the Startup Project page displayed. You can select either the current project as the startup project, any specified project from the solution, or multiple projects. By default, the first project created in a solution becomes the startup project.

If multiple projects are selected, the startup page for each project will execute sequentially, so multiple browser windows will be opened.

Project Dependencies and Project Build Order

The Project Dependencies and Project Build Order commands, visible only when a solution contains multiple projects, present the Project Dependencies dialog box that allows you to control the dependencies and build order of the projects in a solution. You can also access this dialog from the Solution Explorer by right-clicking a solution. The dialog box has two tabs: one for dependencies and one for build order.

For each project in a solution, the Project Dependencies tab allows you to specify which projects it depends upon. The dependent projects will be built first.

The Project Build Order tab presents a list of all the projects in the order in which they will be built. You can't change the build order from this tab. It is inferred from the dependencies.

Build Menu

The Build menu offers menu items for building the current project (highlighted in the Solution Explorer) or the solution. It also exposes the Configuration Manager for configuring the build process. We will cover the Build menu in Chapter 20.

Debug Menu

The Debug menu allows you to start an application with or without debugging, set breakpoints in the code, and control the debugging session. We will cover the Debug menu along with the topic of debugging in Chapter 19.

Data Menu

The context-sensitive Data menu is visible only when in Design view. It is not available when editing code pages. The commands under it are available when appropriate data controls are on the form. We will cover data controls and data binding in Chapters 7 through 10.

Format Menu

The Format menu is visible only in Design view, and the commands under it are context-sensitive to the control(s) currently selected. This menu offers the ability to control the size and layout of controls, though many of the menu options are grayed out for certain web form controls. The Fomat Menu allows you to:

- Align controls with a grid or with other controls in six different ways.
- Change the size of one or more controls to be bigger, smaller, or identical in size.
- Control the spacing horizontally and vertically.
- Move controls forward or backward in the vertical plane (Z order) of the form.

To operate on more than one control, you can select the controls in one of several ways:

- Hold down the Shift or Ctrl key while clicking controls to be selected.
- Use the mouse to click and drag a selection box around all the controls to be selected. If any part of a control falls within the selection box, that control will be included.
- To unselect one control, hold down the Shift or Ctrl key while clicking that control.
- To unselect all the controls, select a different control or press the Esc key.

When you operate on more than one control, the last control selected will be the baseline. In other words, if you are making all the controls the same size, they will all become the same size as the last control selected. Likewise, if you're aligning a group of controls, they will all align with the last control selected.

As controls are selected, they will display eight resizing handles. These resizing handles will be black for all the selected controls except the baseline, or last control, which will have white handles.

With that in mind, all of the commands under the Format menu are fairly self-explanatory.

Tools Menu

The Tools menu presents commands accessing a wide range of functionality, ranging from connecting to databases to accessing external tools to setting IDE options. We describe some of the more useful commands in the following subsections.

Connect to Device

The Connect to Device command brings up a dialog box that allows you to connect to either a physical mobile device or an emulator.

Connect to Database

The Connect to Database command brings up the dialog box that allows you to select a server, log in to that server, and connect to the database on the server. Microsoft SQL Server is the default database (surprise!), but the Change button allows you to connect to any number of other databases, including any for which there are Oracle or ODBC providers.

Code Snippets Manager (Ctrl-K, B)

The Code Snippets Manager command brings up the Code Snippets Manager dialog box, which allows you to maintain the code snippets, described in "IntelliSense," earlier in this chapter. This dialog box allows you to add or remove code snippets for any of the supported languages. You can import code snippets and search online for code snippets.

Choose Toolbox Items

The Choose Toolbox Items command brings up the Choose Toolbox dialog box shown in Figure 2-31. This dialog box has four tabs: one for adding (legacy) COM components, one for adding .NET CLR-compliant components, one for Windows Presentation Foundation (WPF) components, and one for Windows Workflow Foundation (WF) activities. All of the components available on your machine (including registered COM components and .NET components in specific directories—you can browse for .NET components if they are not listed) are listed in one or the other of these tabs. In either case, check or uncheck the box in front of the component to include or not include the desired component.

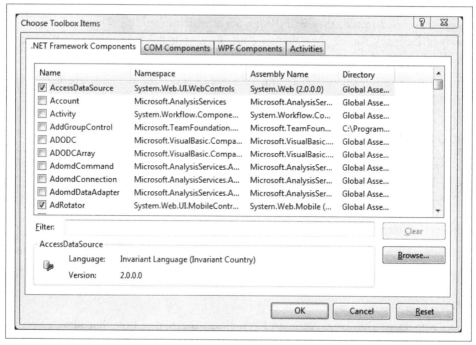

Figure 2-31. Choose Toolbox Items dialog box

 When you want to add a .NET component to the toolbox, it is generally easier to just drag it from Windows Explorer onto the toolbox.

You can sort the components listed in the dialog box by clicking the column head by which you wish to sort.

Macros

Macros are a wonderful feature, allowing you to automate tasks in the IDE. Macros can either be coded by hand using VS2008 or be recorded as you perform the desired task. If you allow the IDE to record the macro for you, you can subsequently examine and edit the macro code it creates. This is similar to the macro functionality provided as part of Microsoft Word or Microsoft Excel.

Macro recording doesn't work for anything inside a dialog box. For example, if you record the changing of some property in a project's Property Pages, the recorded macro will open the Property Pages but won't do anything in there.

You can easily record a temporary macro by using the Macros → Record Temporary-Macro command or by pressing Ctrl-Shift-R. Then you can play back this temporary macro using the Macros → Run TemporaryMacro command or by pressing Ctrl-Shift-P. You can save the macro with the Macros → Save TemporaryMacro command, which will automatically bring up the Macro Explorer, described next.

You manage macros with the Macro Explorer window, accessed via a submenu of the Macros command or by pressing Alt-F8, shown in Figure 2-32.

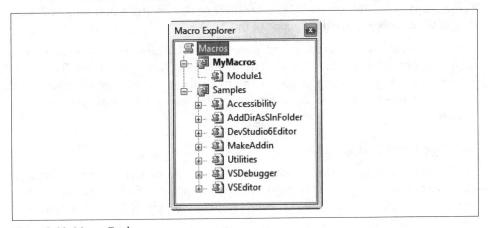

Figure 2-32. Macro Explorer

Right-clicking a macro in the Macro Explorer pops up a menu with four items:

Run
> Runs the highlighted macro. You also can run the macro by double-clicking the macro name.

Edit
> Brings up the macro-editing IDE, in which all the macros for the user can be edited. The macro language is VB.NET, regardless of the language used for the project. You can also invoke the macro-editing IDE using the Macros → Macro IDE command, or by pressing Alt-F11.

Rename
> Allows you to rename the macro.

Delete
> Deletes the macro from the macro file.

All the macros are contained in a *macro project* called, by default, MyMacros. This project is composed of a binary file called *MyMacros.vsmacros* (unless you have elected to convert it to the multiple-files format), which is physically located in a folder called *VSMacros80* in the current projects directory for each user. You can create a new macro project by using the Macros → New Macro Project command or by right-clicking the root object in the Macro Explorer and then selecting New Macro Project. In either case, you will get the New Macro Project dialog box, which will allow you to specify the name and location of the new macro project file.

External Tools

Depending on the options selected at the time VS2008 was installed on your machine, you may have one or more external tools available on the Tools menu. These might include tools such as Create GUID or Dotfuscator Community Edition. (Use of these tools is beyond the scope of this book.)

The Tools → External Tools command allows you to add additional external tools to the Tools menu. When you select it, you are presented with the External Tools dialog box. This dialog box has fields for the tool title, the command to execute the tool, any arguments and the initial directory, and several checkboxes for different behaviors.

Import and Export Settings

The Import and Export Settings command brings up the Import and Export Settings dialog box, which is a wizard for importing and exporting IDE environment settings. With this wizard, you can transfer your carefully wrought IDE settings from one machine to the next.

Customize

The Customize command allows you to customize many aspects of the IDE user interface. (The Options command, described in the following section, allows you to set other program options.) It brings up the Customize dialog box, which has two tabs and a button, allowing customization in three different areas:

Toolbars

    This tab presents a checkbox list of all the available toolbars, with checkmarks indicating toolbars that are currently visible. You can control the visibility of specific toolbars by checking or unchecking them in this list or you can use the View → Toolbars command.

    You can also create new toolbars, rename or delete existing toolbars, or reset all the toolbars back to the original installation version on this tab. Checkboxes allow you to control tool tips and icons.

Commands

The Commands tab allows you to add or remove commands from a toolbar or modify buttons on the toolbar.

To add a command to a toolbar, select the category and command from the lists in the dialog box and then use the mouse to drag the command to the desired toolbar.

To remove a command from a toolbar, drag it from the toolbar to anywhere in the IDE while the Customize Commands dialog is showing.

The Modify Selection button is active only when a button on an existing toolbar is selected. It allows you to perform such chores as renaming or deleting the button, changing the image displayed on the button, changing the display style of the button (e.g., image only, text only), and organizing buttons into groups.

Keyboard

The Keyboard button brings up the Environment → Keyboard page, which is also accessible under the Tools → Options command described next. This page allows you to define and change keyboard shortcuts for commands.

Options

The Options command brings up the Options dialog box. This dialog box allows you to set a wide array of options, ranging from the number of items to display in lists of recently used items to HTML Designer options.

The dialog box displays a hierarchical list of categories on the left side. Selecting any category allows you to drill down through the tree structure. Clicking a detail item brings up the available properties on the right side of the dialog box.

Most of the available options are fairly self-explanatory. If you have any questions about specific settings, clicking the Help button at the bottom of the Options dialog box will bring up context-sensitive help about all the properties relevant to the current detail item.

Window Menu

The Window menu is a standard Windows application Window command. It displays a list of all the currently open windows, allowing you to bring any window to the foreground by clicking it. All the file windows currently displayed in the IDE have tabs along the top edge of the work surface, below the toolbars (unless you have selected MDI mode in Tools → Options → Environment → General), and you can select a window by clicking a tab. The following options are available when any window is active:

Auto Hide All

Hides all dockable windows. Clicking a window's pushpin icon turns Auto Hide off for that window.

New Horizontal/Vertical Tab Group

Creates another set of windows with its own set of tabs.

Close All Documents

Closes all the documents that are open in VS2008.

New Window

Creates a new window containing the same file as the current window (use this to open two windows to the same source file).

Split

Creates a second window in the current window for two different views of the same file.

Remove Split

Removes a split window.

If a dockable window, such as the Solution Explorer or Class View, is currently selected, five more menu items become available: Floating, Dockable, Tabbed Document, Auto Hide, and Hide. We described these in "Layout," earlier in this chapter.

Help Menu

The Help menu provides access to a number of submenus. We describe the ones that are not self-explanatory in the following subsections.

Dynamic Help (Ctrl-F1, D)

If you are developing on a fast enough machine, Dynamic Help is a wonderful thing. Otherwise, it is quite a performance hog. (You can disable it by unchecking all the checkboxes under Tools → Options → Environment → Dynamic Help.) Alternatively, closing the window is sufficient to prevent the performance hit, and that way it is available when you need it.

With that said, using Dynamic Help is simple. Open a Dynamic Help window by clicking this menu item or pressing Ctrl-F1 followed by the D key. Then, wherever the focus is, whether in a design, code, or dockable window, the context-sensitive hyperlinks will appear in the Dynamic Help window. Click any of these links to bring up the relevant help topic in a separate window.

Contents (Ctrl-F1, I), Index (Ctrl-F1, I), and Search (Ctrl-F1, S)

The Contents, Index, and Search commands provide different views into the SDK help system, allowing you to search by a (pseudo) table of contents, an incremental index, or a search phrase, respectively. The first type of search is an indexed search, and the latter two are full text searches, so you may get different results using the different search types using the same phrase.

 The Help system exposed by these commands is the same Help system exposed in two other places by the Start button:

- Programs → Microsoft Visual Studio 2008 → Microsoft Visual Studio 2008 Documentation
- Programs → Microsoft Visual Studio 2008 SDK → Microsoft Visual Studio 2008 SDK Documentation

This Help tool uses a browser-type interface, with Forward and Back navigation and Favorites. The list of topics is displayed in the lefthand pane, and the help topic itself, including hyperlinks, is displayed on the right.

Index Results (Ctrl-F1, T)

When you're searching for Help topics by Index, many topics are often available for a given index entry. In these cases, the multiple topics are listed in an Index Results window. This window will display automatically if this is the case. The Index Results command allows you to view the Index Results window if it has been closed.

Check for Updates

The Check for Updates command will check for service releases for your currently installed version of VS2008. For this command to work, your machine must be connected to the Internet. If an update is available, you will be prompted to close the IDE before the service release is installed.

CHAPTER 3
Controls: Fundamental Concepts

Controls are the building blocks of a graphical user interface (GUI). Some controls you're probably familiar with include buttons, checkboxes, and listboxes. Controls provide a means for a user to indicate a preference, enter data, or make selections. They can also provide infrastructure support in areas, such as validation, data manipulation, master pages, and security.

There are five types of web controls. We will cover in detail each of the following, except for HTML controls, in this and subsequent chapters:

HTML controls

These are the original controls available to any HTML page. They work in ASP.NET in the same way they work in other web pages. We will use HTML controls where appropriate in this book, but we will not discuss them in detail. For a good resource on HTML controls, see *HTML and XHTML: The Definitive Guide*, Sixth Edition, by Chuck Musciano and Bill Kennedy (O'Reilly).

HTML server controls

These are based on the original HTML controls but are enhanced to enable server-side processing.

ASP.NET server controls

These rich and flexible server-side controls are integrated into the ASP.NET programming model. They are rendered to the client as HTML and provide the same functionality as HTML server controls, and more.

ASP.NET AJAX server controls

These additional controls use the AJAX set of technologies to enhance pages using ASP.NET server controls. They are rendered to the client as HTML and JavaScript.

User controls and custom controls

These controls are created by the developer. We will discuss user and custom controls in more detail in Chapter 15.

ASP.NET server controls (sometimes called ASP controls because the way they can be coded in content files resembles classic ASP) are at the heart of ASP.NET, replacing classic client-side HTML controls with a server-side implementation that integrates with and follows the object-oriented programming model of the .NET Framework. Most important, ASP.NET server controls remove all the inconsistencies of how attributes are set in HTML controls: ASP.NET server controls are predictable.

ASP.NET server controls can be either declared in a content file (a page file, user control file, or master page file) similar to classic HTML elements, or programmatically instantiated and manipulated in C# (or other .NET language) assemblies.

In addition to straightforward form elements such as text boxes, labels, buttons, and checkboxes, ASP.NET server controls include several broad categories that provide rich functionality with little developer coding. These include the following:

Validation controls
> These controls provide a full range of built-in form validation capability. Chapter 11 discusses validation controls.

Data source controls
> These controls provide data binding to various data stores, including Microsoft SQL Server and Access and other relational databases, XML files, and classes implemented in code. We cover data source controls in Chapter 7.

Data view controls
> These controls are various lists and tables that can bind to a data source for display and editing. We cover data view controls in Chapter 8.

Personalization controls
> These controls allow users to personalize their view of a site, including rearrangement of the page itself. User information can be saved automatically and transparently and can be persisted from one session to the next. We cover personalization controls in Chapter 14.

Login and security controls
> These controls handle the common chores of logging in to a site and maintaining user passwords. We cover login and security controls in Chapter 12.

Master pages
> These help create websites with a consistent layout and user interface. We cover master pages in Chapter 13.

Rich controls
> These are controls for implementing features such as menus, tree views, and wizards, among others.

Version 1 of ASP.NET introduced server-side controls, both the HTML and the ASP.NET server variety. The latter gave a taste of the rich potential with the Validation, AdRotator, and Calendar controls. Version 2 expanded this with new classes of controls to handle data binding, security, login, and so forth.

Version 2 still ships with .NET v3.5, but it includes three new controls. The ListView and DataPager are data view controls, which we'll cover in Chapter 8. The LinqDataSource object is a data source control and will be covered in Chapter 10.

ASP.NET server controls offer significant improvements over the old-style HTML controls. These include the following:

- The ability to have the page automatically maintain the state of the control, discussed in detail in Chapter 6.

- The ability to detect the level of the target browser. "Up-level" DHTML-enabled browsers are sent scripts for client-side processing. On "down-level" old-fashioned browsers, all processing is done on the server. The appropriate HTML is generated for each browser.

- The use of a compiled language instead of an interpreted script, resulting in better performance.

- The ability to bind to a data source (as discussed in Chapters 7 and 8).

- The ability to raise events via controls on the browser, and to easily handle events via code on the server.

ASP.NET AJAX controls (which we will refer to as AJAX controls for simplicity) complement core ASP controls offering the option for a great deal of the processing to happen on the user's browser. The net effect is a tremendous increase in both the real and the perceived performance of ASP.NET applications.

Several sets of ASP.NET AJAX controls are available for use with ASP.NET pages at the moment. This book will concentrate on two in particular:

Core controls

These controls are installed with Visual Studio 2008 (VS2008) and provide the basic functionality for any control using Microsoft's implementation of AJAX. Originally, they were offered as the ASP.NET AJAX 1.0 Extensions for VS2005 users.

AJAX Control Toolkit controls

A joint effort from the open source community and Microsoft, the toolkit contains two types of controls. Extenders enhance the functionality of an ASP control in some way, but have no function of their own without a control to extend. Standalone controls, as their name suggests, work by themselves.

Each web page and server control is represented by a class derived from the System.Web.UI.Control class. For example, the ASP.NET Button control is represented by the Button class, the HTML Button control is represented by the HtmlButton class, and the AJAX ConfirmButton control is represented by the ConfirmButtonExtender class. In addition, the Page class is derived from the Control class. As such, all pages and controls share all of the properties, methods, and events which are members of the Control class. We will cover these later in this chapter, in "ASP.NET Server Control Class Hierarchy" and "AJAX Server Control Class Hierarchy."

Events

The two models of program execution (which are not necessarily mutually exclusive) are *linear* and *event-driven*. The key to understanding ASP.NET is that it is event-driven.

Linear programs move from step 1, to step 2, and so on, to the end of all the steps, as shown in Figure 3-1. Flow control structures within the code (such as loops, if statements, and method calls) may redirect the flow of the program, but essentially, once the program execution begins, it runs its course, unaffected by anything the user or system may do. Before GUI environments, most computer programs were linear.

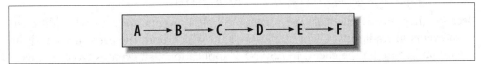

Figure 3-1. Linear program execution

In contrast, event-driven programming responds to something happening, such as a button being pressed, as shown in Figure 3-2. A website or web form waits until some user action occurs and then an event dispatcher triggers the code that deals with the particular event.

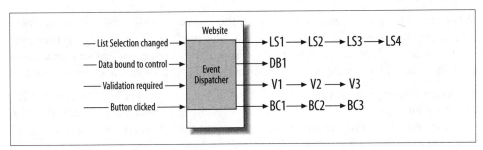

Figure 3-2. Event-driven program execution

Most often, events are generated by user actions, but events can be raised by the web server as well. For example, the system will raise an event when the user's session expires, or when an unhandled error has occurred.

In ASP.NET, some objects may raise events while other objects may have assigned event handlers. For example, a button may raise the Click event, and the page may have a method to handle the button's Click event (such as Button1_Click). Your code in the event handler then responds to the button being clicked in whatever way is appropriate for your application.

The main point to remember here is that server controls are objects that can raise events. Any action a user takes with a server control on the browser raises an event. Your server-side code responds to that event, running the code you have placed in the event handler method.

ASP.NET Events

ASP.NET has thousands of events. The application has events (such as Start and End), each session has events (again, such as Start and End), and the page and most of the server controls can raise events. All ASP.NET events are handled on the server. Some events cause an immediate posting to the server, while other events are stored until the next time the page is posted back to the server.

Because they are handled on the server, ASP.NET events are somewhat different from events in traditional client applications, in which both the event itself and the event handler are on the client. In ASP.NET applications, an event is typically raised on the client (such as by the user clicking a button displayed in the browser) but is handled on the server.

Consider an ASP.NET web page with a button control. A Click event is raised when the button is clicked. Unlike an HTML button control, the ASP.NET button has an attribute, runat, which adds server-side processing to all the normal functionality of an HTML button when set to "server".

When the Click event is raised once again, the browser handles the client-side event by posting the page to the server. This time, however, an event message is transmitted to the server. The server determines whether the Click event has an event handler associated with it, and if it does, the event handler will be executed on the server.

An event message is transmitted to the server via an HTTP POST. ASP.NET *automagically* (that's a technical term) handles all the mechanics of capturing the event, transmitting it to the server, and processing the event. As the programmer, all you have to do is create your event handlers.

Many events, such as MouseOver (which is raised when you move your cursor over an item on the page using the mouse), are ineligible for server-side processing because they kill performance. All server-side processing requires a postback (a round trip to the server and back), and you do not want to post the page every time the mouse hovers over the control. If these events are handled at all, it is on the client side (using script) and is outside the scope of ASP.NET.

 As all AJAX controls are also ASP.NET controls, the same can be said about events for the former as for the latter. The difference between the two is that AJAX controls may use JavaScript to elicit a response to an event on the client side as well as a response from the server. They may define their own additional events for a server-side response as well.

Event Arguments

Events are implemented with *delegates*. A delegate is an object that encapsulates the description of a method to which you may assign responsibility for handling the event.

 For a complete discussion of delegates, see *Programming C# 3.0*, Fifth Edition, by Jesse Liberty and Donald Xie (O'Reilly).

By convention, all ASP.NET event handlers take two parameters and return void. The first parameter represents the object raising the event. By convention, it is called sender, though that is not a requirement. We will demonstrate how to use the sending object later in this chapter, in the section, "Multiple Controls to One Event Handler."

The second parameter, called the *event argument*, contains information specific to the event, if there is any. For most events, the event argument is of type EventArgs, which does not expose any properties. So, the general prototype for an event is the following:

```
private void EventName (object sender, EventArgs e)
```

For some controls, the event argument may be of a type derived from EventArgs and may expose properties specific to that event type. For example, the AdRotator control's AdCreated event handler receives an argument of type AdCreatedEventArgs, which has the properties AdProperties, AlternateText, ImageUrl, and NavigateUrl.

Application and Session Events

ASP.NET supports the application and session events familiar to classic ASP programmers. If you're not familiar with these terms, *application* refers to the website itself. Thus, the Application_Start event is raised when the website is started and begins to receive requests through the web server that is hosting it. This is a good time to initialize resources that will be used throughout the application, such as database connection strings (but not the database connection itself). Similarly, the

Application_End event is raised when the website is stopped, for whatever reason. This might happen because you have chosen to reboot the machine hosting the web server, or to stop the web server from accepting further requests for the website, or yet a number of other things. This is the time to close resources and do any other housekeeping that may be necessary. Garbage collection will automatically take care of freeing up memory, but if you allocated unmanaged resources, such as components created with languages that are noncompliant with the .NET Framework, you must clean them up yourself.

Likewise, there are session events. A *session* starts when a user first requests a page from your application, and ends when the application closes the session or the session times out. A Session_Start event is raised when the session starts, at which time you can initialize resources that will be session-specific, such as opening a database connection, though it is probably better to open a database connection when it is needed and to close it immediately when finished with it. When the session ends, there will be a Session_End event.

Page and Control Events

An ASP.NET page and the controls it contains all have events that are inherited from the Control class (or the TemplateControl class in the case of the Error event). All of these events pass an event argument of type EventArgs that exposes no properties. The most common of these events are listed in Table 3-1. (You can find a complete list of all properties, methods, and events for every class in the online documentation at *http://msdn2.microsoft.com/library*.)

Table 3-1. Some common page and control events

Event name	Description
DataBinding	Occurs when the control binds to a data source
Disposed	Occurs when the control is released from memory
Error	For the page only; occurs when an unhandled exception is thrown
Init	Occurs when the control is initialized
Load	Occurs when the control is loaded to the Page object
PreRender	Occurs when the control is about to be rendered
Unload	Occurs when the control is unloaded from memory

Binding a control to a data source means that the control and the data source are tied together so the control knows to use that data source to populate itself. Chapters 8 and 9 provide a complete description of data controls and data binding.

Postback Versus Nonpostback Events

Postback events cause the form to be posted back to the server immediately. These include click-type events, such as Button.Click. In contrast, many events (typically change events such as TextBox.TextChanged, or selection events such as CheckBox. CheckedChanged) are considered nonpostback because the event is not posted back to the server immediately. Instead, the control caches these events until the next time a post occurs. You can force controls with nonpostback events to behave in a postback manner by setting their AutoPostBack property to true.

Table 3-2 summarizes the ASP.NET controls with postback and nonpostback events. Core ASP.NET AJAX controls are marked with an asterisk.

Table 3-2. Postback and nonpostback controls

Postback	Nonpostback
Button	BulletedList
Calendar	CheckBox
DataGrid	CheckBoxList
DataList	DataPager
FileUpload	DropDownList
GridView	ListBox
ImageButton	Panel
ImageMap	RadioButtonList
LinkButton	RadioButton
ListView	ScriptManager*
Menu	ScriptManagerProxy*
Repeater	TextBox
	Timer*
	UpdatePanel*
	UpdateProgress*

Types of Postback

With the arrival of AJAX, there are two types of postback to understand. A *normal (synchronous) postback* occurs when all the nonpostback events that have occurred on the page are collected together with the page's view state and form values, everything is sent to the server, and a new HTML page is generated to send back to the browser. Nothing else will happen on your site until that page has been regenerated and sent back. This is the only type of postback ASP.NET developers have known before AJAX, and web users know it by the blanking and redrawing of the page after a button press or some other action which causes a postback.

In an AJAX world, there is now a *partial-page*, or *asynchronous*, postback as well, where the server updates on an ad hoc basis only the controls that need to be updated. This targeted updating is a very slick feature of AJAX and prevents the blanking and redrawing of a page that would otherwise occur during a postback. However, it's worth noting here that despite its name, when a partial-page update occurs, a full postback to the server *does* occur—that is, all the contents of the page are sent back to the server—but only the content of the control being updated is returned.

You enable partial-page postbacks on a page using the UpdatePanel control, which we cover in Chapter 5. We also provide a brief demo of this later in this chapter.

IsPostBack

The Page object exposes the IsPostBack property. This is a read-only Boolean property that indicates whether the page is being loaded for the first time or whether it is being loaded in response to a client postback. There are many expensive operations (such as getting data from a database, populating lists, and reading binary files) that you will want to perform only the first time the page is loaded. If the page is posted to the server and then reloaded, there will be no need to repeat the operation, because any data entered or populated is retained (using view state, described in Chapter 6) on subsequent posts. By testing the value of IsPostBack, you can skip the expensive operations, as in the following code snippet:

```
protected void Page_Load(Object sender, EventArgs e)
{
    if (!IsPostBack)
    {
        //  Do the expensive operations only the
        //  first time the page is loaded.
    }
}
```

Events in Visual Studio 2008

The VS2008 integrated development environment (IDE) can automatically handle much of the work required to implement events in ASP.NET. Indeed, you can always access a list of the events you might want to handle.

When you're working on a content page in Design view or Source view, you can always find an event list for the content currently selected in the Properties window by selecting Design view and then clicking the events button (the lightning bolt) in the Properties window. For example, the events for a Button control placed on the page are shown in Figure 3-3, with the events button indicated. Double-clicking in the whitespace to the right of the event name will create an empty handler for the event with a default name, as shown in Figure 3-5, and will wire up the associated delegate. If you'd prefer to give it another name, type the name into the space next to the event name in the Properties window then press Enter.

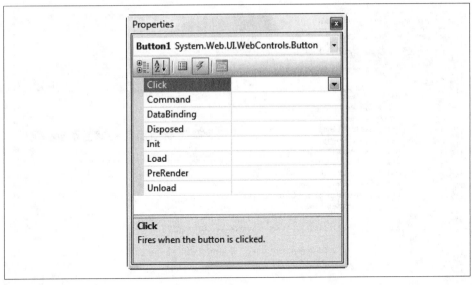

Figure 3-3. Button events

When you're working on a code page (*.cs* or *.vb*), there are always two context-sensitive drop-down controls at the top of the Edit window, as shown in Figure 3-4. The one on the left displays the classes and controls in your page, and the one on the right displays all the methods and events for the class or control selected on the left. Selecting an event that doesn't have a handler will generate an empty handler for the event with a default name, as shown in Figure 3-5, and will wire up the associated delegate.

In Design view, double-clicking any control will also generate an empty handler for the control's default event with a default name, as shown in Figure 3-5, and will wire up the associated delegate.

> Unless you tell it otherwise, VS2008 concatenates the ID of the control with an underscore and the name of the event being handled to generate the default name for an event handler. For example, Button1_Click is the default name for the method that handles the Click event of the Button control with ID Button1.

Every control has a default event, typically the one most commonly implemented for that control. Predictably, the default event for the Button class is the Click event. You can create the default event handler just by double-clicking the control in Design view. Thus, had you not created the Button1_Click event handler, as shown earlier, you could open Design view and double-click the button. The effect would be identical: an event handler named Button1_Click would be created, and you'd be placed in the event handler ready to type your code to implement the method.

The default events for some of the most common web controls are listed in Table 3-3.

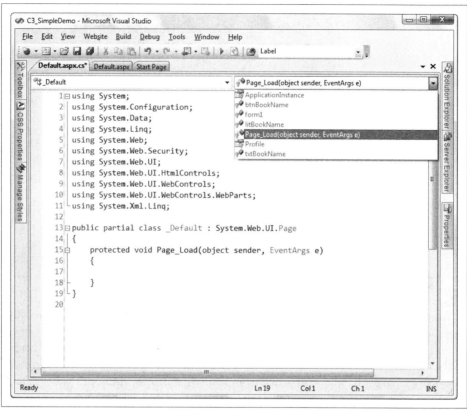

Figure 3-4. The code-behind editing window, showing the Classes & Controls and Methods & Events drop downs

Table 3-3. Default events for some ASP.NET controls

Control	Default event
AdRotator	AdCreated
BulletedList	Click
Button	Click
Calendar	SelectionChanged
CheckBox	CheckedChanged
CheckBoxList	SelectedIndexChanged
DataGrid	SelectedIndexChanged
DataList	SelectedIndexChanged
DropDownList	SelectedIndexChanged
HyperLink	Click
ImageButton	Click
ImageMap	Click
Label	Has no default event

Table 3-3. Default events for some ASP.NET controls (continued)

Control	Default event
LinkButton	Click
ListBox	SelectedIndexChanged
Menu	MenuItemClick
RadioButton	CheckedChanged
RadioButtonList	SelectedIndexChanged
Repeater	ItemCommand

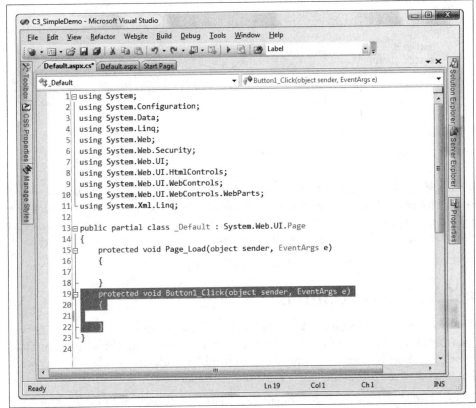

Figure 3-5. VS2008 generating the default handler for the Button control's Click event

The default event for the Page object is the Load event. VS2008 automatically includes the following code snippet to handle the Page_Load event in every new page you add to your website:

```
protected void Page_Load(object sender, EventArgs e)
{

}
```

Multiple Controls to One Event Handler

A single event handler can handle events from several different controls. For example, you may have a generic button click event handler that handles all the buttons on your form. You can determine which button raised the event by testing the value of the sender parameter. This can eliminate a great deal of duplicate code and can make your program easier to read and maintain.

In the following code snippet, a button click event handler casts the sender object (i.e., the control that raised the event) to the Button type and then assigns the ID property of that button to a string variable:

```
private void BtnClick(object sender, System.EventArgs e)
{
    Button b = sender as Button;
    switch (b.ID)
    {
        case "btnDoThis":
            //  code to do this
        case "btnDoThat":
            //  code to do that
    }
    //  code to do stuff common to all the buttons
}
```

To hook up the BtnClick handler once it has been created, go to Design view and select the control whose event it will handle. In the Properties window, click the lightning bolt icon to show the control's events, type in the name of the handler in the space next to the event you want it to handle, as shown in Figure 3-3, and press Enter.

ASP.NET Server Controls

The primary control type used in ASP.NET is the ASP.NET server control. Server controls may have methods and event handlers associated with them, and this code is processed on the server. (Some server controls provide client-side script as well, but even then the processing is done, again, on the server.)

If the control has a visual component (e.g., labels, buttons, and tables), ASP.NET renders classic HTML to the browser, taking the target browser capabilities into account. If the ASP.NET server control requires client-side script to implement its functionality, for example, with the validation controls described in Chapter 11, browser-appropriate script is generated and sent to the browser. However, server-side validation will be performed as well.

This is a key point and bears repeating: what is sent to the client is plain vanilla HTML, so ASP.NET programs can be run on any browser by any manufacturer. All processing is done on the server, and all ASP.NET server controls are presented to the browser as standard HTML. Sending script is an optimization and is never required.

ASP.NET server controls offer a consistent programming model. For example, in HTML, the input tag (<input>) is used for buttons, single-line text fields, checkboxes, hidden fields, and passwords. For multiline text fields, you must use the <textarea> tag. With ASP.NET server controls, each different type of functionality corresponds to a specific control. For example, all text is entered using the TextBox control; the number of lines is specified using a property. In fact, for ASP.NET server controls in general, all the declared attributes correspond to properties of the class which represents the control.

The ASP.NET server controls include all the functionality provided by HTML controls, and much more. This includes basic controls (such as buttons, labels, checkboxes, and tables), advanced data controls (such as data sources, lists, and grids), validation controls, security and login controls, and rich controls (such as the Calendar, AdRotator, Menu, and DynamicImage controls).

In the content file, the syntax used to implement ASP.NET server controls is of this form:

```
<asp:controlType ID="ControlID" runat="server"
    thisProperty="this value"
    thatProperty="that value"/>
```

Here, the control tag always begins with asp:, which is known as the *tag prefix*. The controlType is the type, or class, of the control, such as Button, CheckBoxList, or GridView. An ID attribute allows you to refer to this instance of the control programmatically. The runat attribute tells the server this control is to be processed on the server.

You might think that the runat attribute would be set to "server" by default rather than having to set it for every control, since the most common scenario is for server controls to be processed on the server. However, that is not the case: you must include this attribute with every declaration of every server control. If you omit it, there will be no errors if you choose to view the page in a browser, but the control will be ignored and will not be rendered. VS2008 will, however, highlight the control in Source view saying that the attribute is missing.

The control will render properly if you omit the ID attribute, but it cannot be referenced and manipulated elsewhere in code.

You can declare additional attributes within the angle brackets. For example, you can declare Text and Width attributes for a TextBox like this:

```
<asp:TextBox ID="txtBookName" runat="server"
    Width="250px"
    Text="Enter a book name."/>
```

ASP.NET server controls use well-formed XHTML syntax, though ASP.NET is tolerant of missing quotation marks around attribute values. (See the upcoming "Well-Formed XHTML" sidebar for a description of well-formed XHTML.) Specifically, the angle brackets must be self-closing, as shown earlier, or have closing elements. So, the TextBox shown earlier could equivalently be written this way:

```
<asp:TextBox ID="txtBookName" runat="server"
    Width="250px"
    Text="Enter a book name."></asp:TextBox>
```

In addition, many ASP.NET server controls can make use of inner HTML, which is content between the opening tag and the closing tag. In the case of a TextBox control, for example, the Text property can be specified as inner HTML rather than as an attribute of the opening element. So, the control shown earlier could again be equivalently written in this way:

```
<asp:TextBox ID="txtBookName" runat="server"
    Width="250px">Enter a book name.</asp:TextBox>
```

You implement ASP.NET server control attributes as properties of the server control class, and you can access them programmatically. Once a control has been declared or otherwise instantiated in code, you can retrieve or set its properties programmatically. Using this example, your code could set or change the Text property with the following line of code:

```
txtBookName.Text = "Programming ASP.NET 3.5";
```

As explained earlier in this chapter, most ASP.NET server controls expose events which can be hooked into and handled in your page's code. Later chapters will look at specific control events, why it's useful to handle them, and how to do it.

A Simple Demonstration

The following example will demonstrate many of the features provided by VS2008 to minimize typing and errors when using controls, including:

- Dragging and dropping controls onto either the Design or Source view of the web page
- IntelliSense to display and auto-complete properties declaratively in the Source view of the web page
- Using a Properties window for entering properties in either the Design or Source view of the web page

Well-Formed XHTML

XHTML is a World Wide Web Consortium (W3C) standard, of which the current version is 1.1. It defines HTML as a well-formed XML document. Many web browsers are very forgiving, and ill-formed HTML will work fine, but the world is moving toward a stricter syntax to increase the robustness of the Web. Well-formed code has a huge benefit for authoring tools and is worthwhile when handcoding since it decreases confusion and ambiguity.

Here are some of the rules of well-formed HTML:

Close all tags

Several HTML tags, such as <p>, <tr>, and <td>, are routinely left unclosed. In well-formed HTML, there will always be a closing tag, such as </td>. Many tags, such as <br>, <hr>, <input>, and <img>, can be made self-closing by putting the closing forward slash within the tag itself. This makes it well formed, as in this example:

```
<input type="submit"
id="btnBookName"
value="Book Name"
onServerClick="btnBookName_Click"
runat="server" />
```

No overlapping tags

Some browsers are tolerant of overlapping tags, but well-formed HTML requires that tags do not overlap. For example, consider the overlapping tags in the following line of HTML:

```
<b>This is <i>the year</b>for the Giants.</i>
You can express this instead in this way:
<b>This is</b> <i><b>the year</b>for the Giants.</i>
```

Case sensitivity

Like all HTML and ASP pages, ASP.NET is generally not case-sensitive. The one glaring exception is that C# is always case-sensitive. With that said, it should be noted that script components, that is, code intended to be rendered to the browser as executable script, are XML files, and as such should follow XML conventions. According to these conventions, element types and attributes are case-sensitive. This will usually matter only if you use an XML editing tool to work with the script components or if you are creating an XML file (such as an advertisement file for use with the AdRotator control, described in Chapter 5). However, it is a good practice to follow the XML guidelines. Element types and attributes are usually lowercase, except for multipart names (such as onServerClick), which use camel notation with initial lowercase. For other HTML tags, being well formed requires that start and end tags have matching case. This book will generally use lowercase for all HTML tags.

—continued—

Quotation marks

In well-formed HTML, all attributes are enclosed in quotation marks.

Single root

The top-level element in a page must be <html>. Remember to close it at the end with </html>.

Reserved characters

There are only five built-in character entities in XML:

```
&lt;    <
&gt;    >
&amp;   &
&quot;  "
&apos;  '
```

If any of these characters are used in script, they must be "escaped" by using the corresponding character entity or by enclosing the entire script block in a CDATA section. (CDATA is an XML type.)

HTML controls are divided into two categories: *input* and *container*. HTML input controls do not require a closing tag (though to be well formed, they should be made self-closing with a trailing /) and have Name, Value, and Type attributes, which may be accessed and controlled programmatically.

HTML container controls, on the other hand, must have a trailing / or a closing tag. They do not have Name, Value, or Type attributes. Instead, the content found between opening and closing tags may be accessed programmatically using the InnerHtml or InnerText property. The difference between these two properties is that InnerText provides automatic HTML encoding and decoding of special characters, such as < or >. If you use the InnerHtml property, these characters will be interpreted as being part of the HTML and will not display in the final output.

All ASP.NET server controls are declared on the page using well-formed XHTML syntax and are rendered on a page also using well-formed XHTML.

Open VS2008 and click New Web Site. Select ASP.NET Web Site, ensuring that the language is set to C# and the target framework is set to .NET Framework 3.5. Call the new website "C3_SimpleDemo", as shown in Figure 3-6, and click OK.

This will create a new website with a page called *Default.aspx*. The IDE will show the Source view of *Default.aspx* on the work surface, with the Toolbox on the left side of the screen and the Solution Explorer and Properties windows on the right. The code shown in Example 3-1 (reformatted slightly for better readability on this page) will be inserted by default.

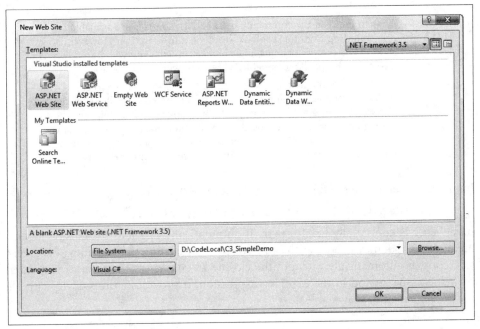

Figure 3-6. The VS2008 New Web Site dialog

Example 3-1. Default boilerplate code

```
<%@ Page Language="C#" AutoEventWireup="true"
        CodeFile="Default.aspx.cs" Inherits="_Default" %>

<!DOCTYPE html PUBLIC "-//W3C//DTD XHTML 1.0 Transitional//EN"
   "http://www.w3.org/TR/xhtml1/DTD/xhtml1-transitional.dtd">

<html xmlns="http://www.w3.org/1999/xhtml">
<head runat="server">
   <title>Untitled Page</title>
</head>

<body>
   <form id="form1" runat="server">
   <div>

   </div>
   </form>
</body>
</html>
```

Replace the default title text with something more meaningful, such as "A Simple Demo Of ASP.NET Server Controls". Inside the <div> element, type in a header element:

```
<h1>A Simple Demo Of ASP.NET Server Controls</h1>
```

Though many of the commonly used HTML controls are available for drag and drop from the Toolbox, header controls are not. However, as soon as you type an opening angle bracket, IntelliSense will drop down a complete list of all the possible HTML and web server controls.

You can enter the first few characters of the control's name to get to it or use the mouse to slide down and select the control. Pressing the Tab key will insert the currently selected control. When you type the closing angle bracket the closing tag will automatically pop into place with the cursor positioned between the opening and closing tags, ready for typing. You can also press Ctrl-Space bar to wake up IntelliSense.

Immediately following the first header, enter a second header control, as follows:

```
<h2>The date and time is <% =DateTime.Now.ToString( ) %>.</h2>
```

IntelliSense is continually helpful here. It automatically provides the closing h2 element, and as soon as you enter the <% characters, indicating the beginning of server-side code, it automatically provides the closing %> characters. As soon as you enter each successive period in the DateTime expression, it provides a drop down with all the possible members available next.

Remember that C# is case-sensitive. If you are not using the correct case, the code will not work, and IntelliSense will not display anything.

You can place server-side code inline (without being wrapped within a <script> block) in a content file by enclosing the code within the <% %> characters, as we did in the preceding code snippet. This works because the browser ignores anything between the script block characters, not rendering it to the page. The ASP.NET runtime, however, recognizes that content as it processes the page. When the runtime sees valid framework code, it processes it. In this case, that code returns a text string containing the current date and time, which is then incorporated directly into the rendered output.

Switch to the page's Design view by clicking the Design button at the bottom of the work surface. That header will display the following:

```
The date and time is .
```

It does this because the script that provides the date and time will not run until the page is run.

While still in Design view, put your cursor at the end of the <h2> sentence. The <h2> block will be highlighted so you know which block-level element you're working in. Press Enter a couple of times to see a new paragraph created and to see VS2008 highlight these on the page in the same way it highlighted the <h2> block.

Commenting Your Code

Commenting in ASP.NET is particularly difficult. As an ASP.NET developer, you may be working with HTML, C#, VS2008, JavaScript, VBScript, and Transact-SQL, among others. Each language has its own unique syntax for comments, and one language can overlap another.

Here is a summary of the different ways to comment:

HTML

```
<!-- text to be commented goes in here -->
```

JavaScript

```
// commented text follows //
/* multiline
   comment */
```

C#

```
// commented text follows //
/* multiline
   comment */
```

Visual Basic.NET and VBScript

```
' commented text follows a single quotation mark
REM  comments can also follow the REM keyword
```

Transact-SQL

```
-- commented text follows two dashes
/* multiline
   comment */
```

XML commenting

VS2008 can automatically convert XML comments placed in the code-behind file into well-formatted documentation:

```
/// In C#, the XML comments follow three slashes.
''' In Visual Basic.NET, comments follow 3 single quotes.
```

Page (.aspx) or user control (.ascx) file

These characters actually indicate server-side code, but they behave as comments because they do not render unless there is valid code:

```
<% The comments go here. %>
```

ASP.NET controls

There is no comment within an ASP.NET control. Because any unrecognized attributes are ignored, some developers prepend any attributes they wish to comment out with XX.

Now drag a TextBox control from the Toolbox (under the Standard category) into the second paragraph block on the form. A TextBox control will appear on the work surface and will be selected. In the Properties window on the right side of the window, change the ID property from the default value, TextBox1, to txtBookName. At the same time, change the Text property from the blank default to "Enter a book name.", and change the Width property to 250. The Width property will display 250px, for pixels.

It is always a good practice to assign a meaningful name to any controls that will be referenced in code—for example, txtBookName or txtPassword, rather than txtA or txtB. This makes it much easier to read and write any code in the page and understand what that TextBox is meant to contain.

Before proceeding any further, click the Source button at the bottom of the work surface to see the code generated by VS2008. Between the <div> tags, you should see something similar to the following (reformatted to fit on this page):

```
<h1>A Simple Demo Of ASP.NET Server Controls</h1>
<h2>The date and time is <% =DateTime.Now.ToString() %>.</h2>
<p> </p>
<p>
    <asp:TextBox ID="txtBookName" runat="server"
        Width="250px">Enter a book name.
    </asp:TextBox>
</p>
```

VS2008 inserted paragraph elements with enclosed nonbreaking spaces where you pressed the Enter key. More significantly, it inserted a TextBox ASP.NET server control with the Width property set and the Text property contained in the inner HTML.

You can edit the generated HTML and ASP.NET server control declarations directly in the Source window, edit the design in the Design window, or change the properties in the Properties window. In any case, all other views of the page will immediately reflect those changes. Try it in Split view. As soon as the page is changed in one view, a warning pops up asking to synchronize views.

Moving on, drag a Button control from the Toolbox (again under the Standard category) onto the work surface after the TextBox, either in Design or Source view. Change its ID to btnBookName and its Text property to Book Name.

If you're working in Design view, press Enter after the button to insert a new line. If you're in Source view, enter a <p> HTML element after the closing </p> tag of the paragraph containing the Button. Then drag a Literal control onto the page in either case. Change its ID to litBookName and leave its Text property blank.

The goal here is to enable the user to type a book name into the text box, click the button, and have that book name display as the Text property of the Literal control.

To accomplish this, you need to hook up the click event of the button to an event handler as described previously in this chapter. Switch to Design view if you're not in it already, and then double-click the button. Double-clicking a control tells VS2008 you want to implement the default event for that control; for buttons, the default event is Click.

The code-behind file, *Default.aspx.cs*, will open with a code snippet for the click event handler method in place and the cursor inside the method, ready to accept your typing. Enter the following highlighted line of code:

```
protected void btnBookName_Click(object sender, EventArgs e)
{
    litBookName.Text = txtBookName.Text;
}
```

Switch back to the content file, *Default.aspx*, by clicking the tab at the top of the work surface, or by pressing F7. Go to Source view by clicking the Source button at the bottom of the work surface. The onclick attribute has been added to the button control, with its value set to the name of the event handler method to which you added the line of text.

Run your web page by pressing F5 or clicking the Debug → Start menu item. If this is the first time you have run the page, you will be prompted to create a configuration file to enable debugging. Click OK in that dialog box and then Yes if you are prompted about script debugging.

The page will appear in a browser with the current date and time displayed in the second header you entered. Change the text in the text box and click the button. The text you entered will display in the label below the button. The page will look something like that shown in Figure 3-7.

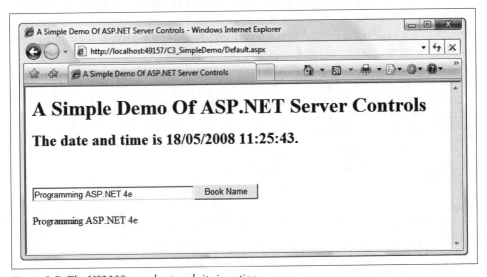

Figure 3-7. The VS2008 new demo website in action

ASP.NET and Browsers

We'll say it just one more time: *the browser never sees the ASP.NET server control.* The *server* processes the server control and sends standard HTML (and JavaScript in the case of AJAX controls) to the browser.

ASP.NET considers browsers to be either *up-level* or *down-level*. Up-level browsers support script versions 1.2 (ECMAScript, JavaScript, and JScript), Cascading Style

Sheets (CSS), and HTML 4.0; typical up-level browsers would include Internet Explorer 4.0 and later releases. Down-level browsers, on the other hand, support only HTML 3.2.

ASP.NET can tell you which browser is being used to display the page. This information is made available via the HttpRequest.Browser property. HttpRequest.Browser returns an HttpBrowserCapabilities object whose many properties include a number of Booleans, such as whether the browser supports cookies, frames, and so forth.

You will find that you don't often need to check the HttpBrowserCapabilities object because the server will automatically convert your HTML to reflect the capabilities of the client browser. For example, validation controls (considered in Chapter 11) can be used to validate customer data entry. If the user's browser supports client-side JavaScript, the validation will happen on the client (and then again on the server to prevent spoofing). However, if the browser does not support client-side scripting, the validation will be done server side only.

From within your browser, view the source for the web page displayed in Figure 3-7. This source is shown in Example 3-2. No server controls exist; all the controls have been converted to traditional HTML tags, and a hidden field with the name VIEWSTATE has been inserted into the output. This is how ASP.NET maintains the state of the controls. When a page is submitted to the server and then is redisplayed, the controls are not reset to their default values. Chapter 6 discusses *state*.

Example 3-2. The HTML for the simple demo page

```
<!DOCTYPE html PUBLIC "-//W3C//DTD XHTML 1.0 Transitional//EN"
    "http://www.w3.org/TR/xhtml1/DTD/xhtml1-transitional.dtd">
<html xmlns="http://www.w3.org/1999/xhtml">
<head>
    <title>
        A Simple Demo Of ASP.NET Server Controls
    </title>
</head>
<body>
    <form name="form1" method="post" action="Default.aspx" id="form1">
    <div>
        <input type="hidden" name="__VIEWSTATE" id="__VIEWSTATE"
            value="/wEPDwULLTE0OTM4MjIxMjEPZBYCAgMPZBYCAgIPFgIeBFR1eHQFF
                lByb2dyYW1taW5nIEFTUC5ORVQgNGVkZPgvK6z45xjHejh5FHcCrmwdqpYS"
        />
    </div>

    <div>
        <h1>A Simple Demo Of ASP.NET Server Controls</h1>
        <h2>The date and time is 18/05/2008 11:25:43.</h2>
        <p> </p>
```

Example 3-2. The HTML for the simple demo page (continued)

```
    <p>
        <input name="txtBookName" type="text"
          value="Programming ASP.NET 4e" id="txtBookName"
          style="width:250px;" />
        <input type="submit" name="btnBookName"
          value="Book Name" id="btnBookName" />
    </p>
    <p>Programming ASP.NET 4e</p>
  </div>
  <div>
      <input type="hidden" name="__EVENTVALIDATION"
        id="__EVENTVALIDATION"
        value="/wEWAwLUl+qLCwKe8vzpDAKG1LbDDVAZsm/3kxuzyjo8qIo3/hRaOWO2" />
  </div>
  </form>
</body>
</html>
```

CSS-Friendly Adapters for ASP.NET

Although both ASP.NET server controls produce valid XHTML, the point is often made that some do not actually produce the correct XHTML for the content they are displaying. A common case in point is the Menu control which you'll meet in Chapter 13. When this control renders on a page, it produces a menu using a <table> element to precisely control the positioning of its contents on the page as specified in its properties.

Many people will argue this is wrong for two reasons. First, a menu is a list of options, so using a <ul> list makes more sense semantically than seeing it as tabular data. The second reason, <table> versus <ul> aside, is that the XHTML generated by ASP.NET server controls isn't very useful for styling with CSS.

For this reason, and because they want to encourage the use of core web standards such as CSS, the ASP.NET team released the ASP.NET CSS Friendly Adapters in November 2006. This package is not officially supported by Microsoft, but it allows the developer to specify exactly what XHTML is rendered by a server control given the level of browser asking for a page.

The adapters are not incorporated into VS2008 as, for example, the ASP.NET AJAX Extensions were. However, you can still download them from *http://www.asp.net/cssadapters* and use them if you want. The ability to control exactly what XHTML a control renders on a page is something Microsoft is looking to enable for existing controls in the future (ASP.NET 3.0, perhaps?). In the meantime, the new ListView server control gives you a flavor of where this effort might take developers as it actually does offer this level of control. You'll find more on ListView in Chapter 8.

ASP.NET Server Control Class Hierarchy

All the ASP.NET server controls that have a visual aspect when rendered to the browser are derived from the WebControl class. This class provides the properties, methods, and events common to all of these controls. Among these are common properties, such as BorderColor, BorderStyle, and BorderWidth, as well as the RenderBeginTag and RenderEndTag methods.

The WebControl class and several other ASP.NET server controls (e.g., Literal, PlaceHolder, Repeater, and XML) derive from System.Web.UI.Control, which derives from System.Object. The Control class provides base properties such as ID, EnableViewState, Parent, and Visible; base methods such as Dispose, Focus, and RenderControl; and life cycle events such as Init, Load, PreRender, and Unload.

The WebControl class and the controls derived from Control are in the System.Web.UI. WebControls namespace. These relationships are shown in Figure 3-8.

All of the properties, events, and methods of WebControl and System.Web.UI.Control are inherited by the ASP.NET server controls. Table 3-4 lists many of the commonly used properties inherited by all the ASP.NET server controls from either the Control or the WebControl class. All of them are read/write unless stated otherwise.

Table 3-4. Commonly used properties inherited by all ASP.NET server controls

Name	Type	Values	Description
AccessKey	String	Single-character string	Pressing the Alt key in combination with this value moves focus to the control.
BackColor	Color	Azure, Green, Blue, etc.	Background color.
BorderColor	Color	Fuchsia, Aqua, Coral, etc.	Border color.
BorderStyle	BorderStyle	Dashed, Dotted, Double, NotSet, etc.	Border style. Default is NotSet.
BorderWidth	Unit	*nn*, *nn*pt	Width of the border. If of the form *nn*, where *nn* is an integer, then in units of pixels. If of the form *nn*pt, where *nn* is an integer, then in units of points.
CausesValidation	Boolean	true, false	Indicates whether entering control causes validation for controls that require validation. Default is true.
Controls	ControlCollection		A collection of all the control objects contained by this control. *Read-only*.

Name	Type	Values	Description
CssClass	String		CSS class. See the "CSS Styles" section that follows.
Enabled	Boolean	true, false	If disabled, control is visible but grayed out and not operative. Contents are still selectable for copy and paste. Default is true.
EnableTheming	Boolean	true, false	Indicates whether theming applies to this control.
EnableViewState	Boolean	true, false	Indicates whether this control persists its view state. Default is true.
Font	FontInfo		See Table 4-1 in Chapter 4.
ForeColor	Color	Lavender, LightBlue, Blue, etc.	Foreground color.
Height	Unit	nn, nn%	If of the form nn, where nn is an integer, then in units of pixels. If of the form nn%, then a percentage of the height of the container. For down-level browsers, will not render for Label, HyperLink, LinkButton, or any validator controls, or for CheckBoxList, RadioButtonList, or DataList when their RepeatLayout property is Flow.
ID	String		Programmatic identifier for the control.
Parent	Control	Control on the page	Returns a reference to this control's parent control in the page control hierarchy. Read-only.
SkinID	String	Skin filename	Specifies which skin file from a theme directory to apply to this control. See Chapter 14 for more on this.
ToolTip	String		Text string displayed when the mouse hovers over the control; not rendered in down-level browsers.
Visible	Boolean	true, false	If false, control is not rendered; default is true.
Width	Unit	nn, nn%	Works like the Height property, but determines the width of a control.

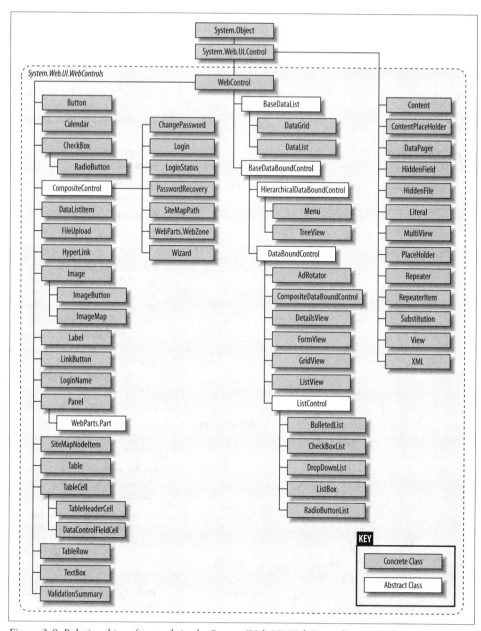

Figure 3-8. Relationships of controls in the System.Web.UI.WebControls namespace

CSS Styles

CSS provides a means to apply uniform and consistent styles across an entire website. It is a W3C standard, first supported in Internet Explorer 4.0 and Netscape 4.0.

For a complete discussion of CSS, see the following O'Reilly books: *HTML and XHTML: The Definitive Guide*, Sixth Edition, by Chuck Musciano and Bill Kennedy, and *CSS: The Definitive Guide*, Third Edition, by Eric Meyer.

To see how ASP.NET and VS2008 support CSS, open the *C3_SimpleDemo* website you created earlier. Right-click the website root in the Solution Explorer and click Add New Item. Select Style Sheet from the list of templates and leave the default name. (You can change the name if you want.)

This will add the new stylesheet file to the website and display the contents on the work surface, including two lines of boilerplate code:

```
body {
}
```

Replace that code with the contents of Example 3-3. No period precedes the body class name, but a period does precede the other two class names, indicating they are generic classes.

Example 3-3. Stylesheet.css

```
body
{
    font-size: 12px;
    color: blue;
    font-family: arial, helvetica, verdana, sans-serif;
    text-decoration: underline;
}
.button
{
    font-weight: bold;
    font-size: 14px;
    color: red;
    background-color: Yellow;
    font-family: arial, helvetica, verdana, sans-serif;
}
.label
{
    font-weight: bold;
    font-size: 18px;
    color: green;
    font-family: arial, helvetica, verdana, sans-serif;
}
```

Now add a new web form to the site and call it *CssDemo.aspx*. The form will be opened in Source view on the work surface. Add the following <style> element inside the <head> element:

```
<style>@import url(StyleSheet.css); </style>
```

Now add two ASP.NET server controls to the page: a Button and a Label. Set the CssClass property of the Button to button and that of the Label to label. (Note how VS2008 provides some IntelliSense help to fill in the names of the styles. This is new to VS2008.) Add some text to the Label control. The declaration of the two controls within the page file should look something like that listed in Example 3-4.

Example 3-4. The controls in CssDemo.aspx

```
<asp:Button ID="Button1" runat="server"
   Text="Button" CssClass="button" />

<asp:Label ID="Label1" runat="server"
   Text="Label" CssClass="label"></asp:Label>
```

Right-click *CssDemo.aspx* and select View In Browser. Note how the two controls reflect the styles set in the stylesheet file, *StyleSheet.css*. The body style is first applied to all the content on the page, and then each subsequent style in the stylesheet is applied cumulatively to the page. This is why both the button and the label are underlined (set in body style) but neither has blue text (overridden in the .button and label styles). This is why they are called *cascading* stylesheets.

AJAX Server Controls

AJAX server controls are rapidly growing in popularity. Like the ASP.NET server controls, they also can have methods and event handlers associated with them. The code for these methods and handlers is also processed on the server side. The two key differences between AJAX server controls and ASP.NET server controls are as follows:

- AJAX server controls add script to the page which *is* run and processed within the browser. Some of the scripts may interact with the server in some way, but they are run on the client side. All ASP.NET server control processing is done on the server.

- All AJAX server controls depend on one particular control to be present on the page for them to work at all. This is the ScriptManager control, which we'll discuss in a minute. ASP.NET server controls have no such reliance.

AJAX server controls also offer the same consistent programming model as ASP.NET server controls. Those controls formerly in the ASP.NET AJAX Extensions 1.0 download are now integrated into VS2008 and are accessed with the same syntax as ASP.NET server controls.

```
<asp:controlType id="ControlID" runat="server"
    thisProperty="this value"
    thatProperty="that value"/>
```

In addition to the core AJAX server controls included with VS2008, Microsoft also leads a community project to build a set of useful AJAX server controls, called the AJAX Control Toolkit. You can find it online at *http://www.codeplex.com/ ajaxcontroltoolkit*. Appendix A covers its installation.

If you want to add controls from the AJAX Control Toolkit to a page, you again use the same syntax but with a different tag prefix to denote that this is an addition to rather than a part of ASP.NET 2.0. For example:

```
<cc1:controlType id="ControlID" runat="server"
    thisProperty="this value"
    thatProperty="that value"/>
```

VS2008 automatically uses cc1 as the tag prefix for toolkit controls, but you can change this if you like.

Extending the Simple Demonstration

In this example, you'll copy a page you created earlier and then add some AJAX controls to it so that you can see how they can enhance the standard set of controls as well as providing their own functionality. (If you haven't installed the AJAX Control Toolkit yet, follow the instructions in Appendix A to do so.)

Open the *C3_SimpleDemo* website you created earlier. Right-click the application root in the Solution Explorer and click Add New Item. Select AJAX Web Form from the list of templates, call it *AjaxDemo.aspx*, and click OK. Double-click *Default.aspx* in the Solution Explorer to open it and copy the headings as well as the TextBox, Button, and Literal controls from that page to *AjaxDemo.aspx* underneath the ScriptManager control that's already on the page.

Switch to Design view and add an UpdatePanel control from the AJAX Extensions section of the Toolbox to *AjaxDemo.aspx*. Now select and drag the TextBox, Button, and Literal controls into the UpdatePanel, as shown in Figure 3-9.

Now select the Button, and open its Common Tasks panel by clicking the small arrow button (known as a *smart tag*) that appears in the top-right corner and click Add Extender. The Extender Wizard dialog, as shown in Figure 3-10, appears with a list of AJAX extender controls from the Control Toolkit that you can apply to the Button. Select the ConfirmButtonExtender, leave its ID at the default, and click OK.

The ConfirmButtonExtender control doesn't have any UI, except for a small green icon that now appears next to the ID of the Button when selected. This is the standard way to identify whether an ASP.NET server control has an AJAX extender control applied to it. Switch to Source view to confirm that the extender has been added to the page, and add the text "Are you sure about this?" to its ConfirmText property.

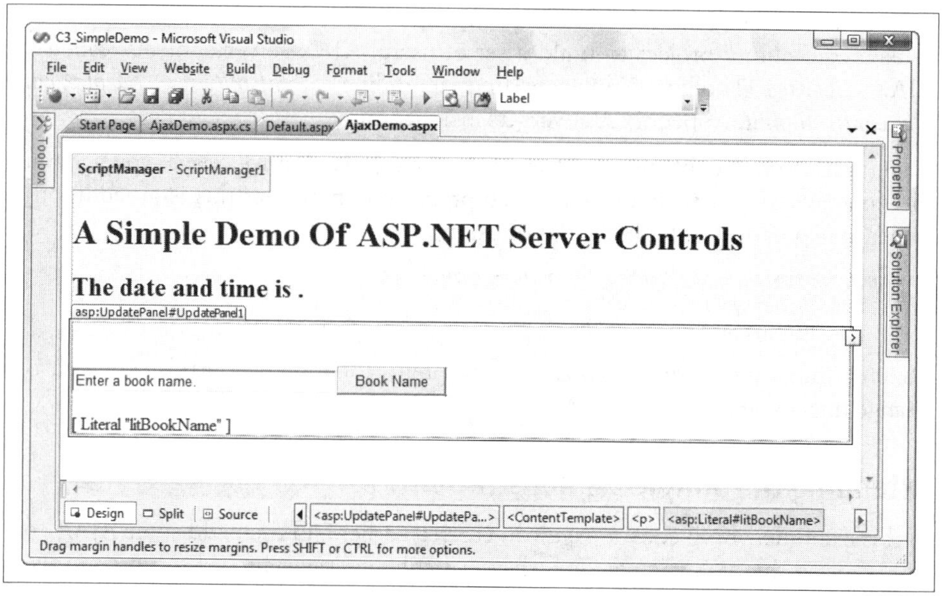

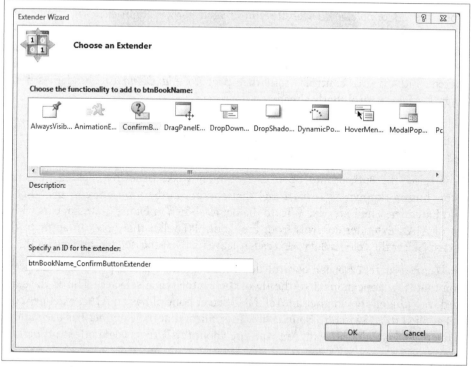

Figure 3-9. AjaxDemo.aspx in Design view

Figure 3-10. The Extender Wizard

The last task is to rehandle the Button's click event. Switch back to Design view and double-click the button. When the code-behind file opens, enter the following high-lighted line of code for the Click handler as you did before:

```
protected void btnBookName_Click(object sender, EventArgs e)
{
    litBookName.Text = txtBookName.Text;
}
```

Run your web page by pressing F5. On the surface, everything looks the same as the earlier demo page, *Default.aspx*. However, if you click the button, a dialog now appears asking you to confirm whether to proceed. This is the ConfirmButtonExtender at work. If you click OK, the page continues as normal. If you click Cancel, nothing happens.

A second, subtler thing happens here which does not happen if you click the button and then click OK. The Literal control is updated to reflect the text in the TextBox as before, but the date and time in the heading are not. Also, the page itself does not go blank and redraw itself as usually happens when a page posts back to the server. This is the UpdatePanel control at work. When a control inside an UpdatePanel raises a postback event, a partial-page postback occurs and only the contents of the UpdatePanel are updated rather than the entire page.

You can find the full source for *AjaxDemo.aspx* in Example 3-5 with the additional code highlighted for your reference.

Example 3-5. The source code for AjaxDemo.aspx

```
<%@ Page Language="C#" AutoEventWireup="true"
    CodeFile="AjaxDemo.aspx.cs" Inherits="AjaxDemo" %>
<%@ Register Assembly="AjaxControlToolkit"
    Namespace="AjaxControlToolkit" TagPrefix="cc1" %>
<!DOCTYPE html PUBLIC "-//W3C//DTD XHTML 1.0 Transitional//EN"
    "http://www.w3.org/TR/xhtml1/DTD/xhtml1-transitional.dtd">

<html xmlns="http://www.w3.org/1999/xhtml">
<head runat="server">
    <title>A Simple Demo Of ASP.NET Server Controls</title>

    <script type="text/javascript">
        function pageLoad( ) {
        }
    </script>

</head>
<body>
    <form id="form1" runat="server">
    <div>
        <asp:ScriptManager ID="ScriptManager1" runat="server" />
        <h1>
            A Simple Demo Of ASP.NET Server Controls</h1>
```

Example 3-5. The source code for AjaxDemo.aspx (continued)

```
    <h2>
        The date and time is
        <% =DateTime.Now.ToString( ) %>.</h2>
    </div>
    <asp:UpdatePanel ID="UpdatePanel1" runat="server">
        <ContentTemplate>
            <p> </p>
            <p>
            <asp:TextBox ID="txtBookName" runat="server"
                Width="250px">Enter a book name.</asp:TextBox>
            <asp:Button ID="btnBookName" runat="server"
                OnClick="btnBookName_Click" />
            <cc1:ConfirmButtonExtender
                ID="btnBookName_ConfirmButtonExtender"
                runat="server" ConfirmText="Are you sure about this?"
                Enabled="True" TargetControlID="btnBookName" />
            </p>
            <p>
                <asp:Literal ID="litBookName" runat="server"></asp:Literal>
            </p>
        </ContentTemplate>
    </asp:UpdatePanel>
    </form>
</body>
</html>
```

AJAX Server Control Class Hierarchy

Like the ASP.NET server controls, all the AJAX server controls are also derived ultimately from System.Web.UI.Control. However, although the majority of the controls are related to how a page looks and presents itself, only six are derived from the WebControl class. The remainder is derived from System.Web.UI.ExtenderControl, an abstract class that defines hooks into the standard ASP.NET server controls.

Figure 3-11 shows this hierarchy in full. Note that the controls marked with an asterisk are not directly AJAX-related, and if they aren't in a box (or System.Object and System.Web.UI.Control) they're in the AjaxControlToolkit namespace.

The ScriptManager Control

Remember that to enable ASP.NET AJAX in the page, the first thing you need to do is add a ScriptManager control. ScriptManager takes care of the client-side script for all the server-side controls. Every page that uses ASP.NET AJAX requires one and only one instance of the ScriptManager. Don't forget to add one to your page, if it isn't there already, and then leave it alone. The ScriptManager does have a number of properties for controlling how it works, but these are beyond the scope of this book.

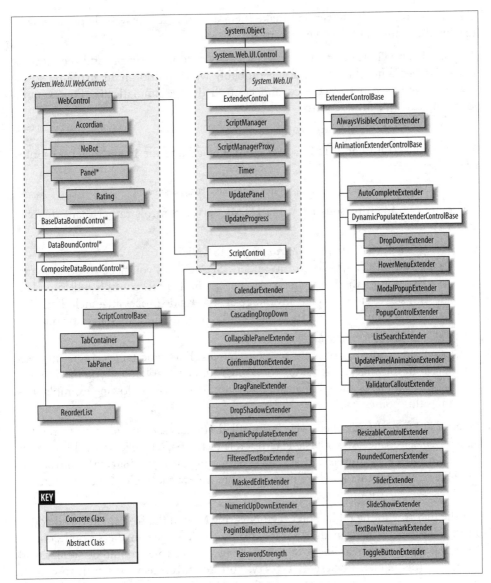

Figure 3-11. AJAX server control hierarchy

HTML Server Controls

This book focuses on using ASP.NET server controls. However, understanding and using HTML and HTML server controls can be useful in real-life applications.

Normal HTML controls such as `<h1>`, `<a>`, and `<input>` are not processed by the server, but rather are sent directly to the browser for display. You can expose standard

HTML controls to the server and make them available for server-side processing by turning them into HTML server controls.

To convert an HTML control to an HTML server control, simply add the attribute `runat="server"`. In addition, you will probably want to add an `id` attribute, so the control contents can be accessed and controlled programmatically. For example, start with a simple input control:

```
<input type="text" size="40">
```

You can convert it to an HTML server control by adding the `id` and `runat` attributes, as follows:

```
<input type="text" id="BookTitle" size="40" runat="server">
```

There are two main reasons for using HTML server controls rather than ASP.NET server controls:

Converting existing HTML pages to run under ASP.NET
>   To convert an HTML file to run under ASP.NET, all you need to do is change the extension of the file to *.aspx*. However, the HTML controls will run client side, not server side. To take advantage of server-side processing, including automatic maintenance of state (see Chapter 6), you must add the `runat` attribute.

Using HTML tables for page layout
>   Server-side controls consume server resources. For static tables commonly used to lay out the page, server-side processing is unnecessary unless you need to refer to one or more of the table elements in your code. The following example illustrates this point.

Open VS2008 and add a new web form called *HtmlServerControls.aspx* to the *C3_SimpleDemo* website. Add a basic HTML table to the page by clicking Table → Insert Table. Give it two columns and six rows. Now drag an Input (Button) control from the HTML tab on the Toolbox onto the page below the table. Give the button a `runat="server"` attribute.

For the first row in the table, enter the text string `Name` in the first column and add an Input (Text) control from the HTML area of the Toolbox in the second column. Give that input control an ID of `txtName`. The next three rows should be similar, with input controls named `txtStreet`, `txtCity`, and `txtState`. Leave the fifth row in the table empty. Leave the second column in the last row empty, but give it an ID of `tdInnerHtml`. The design should look something like that shown in Figure 3-12, where the controls are named as indicated.

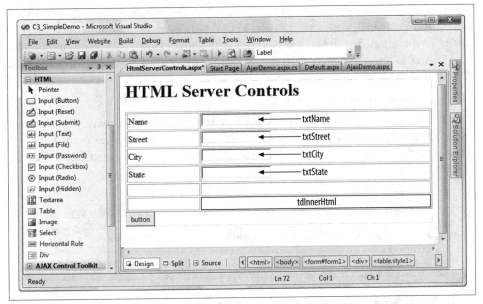

Figure 3-12. HtmlServerControls.aspx

Be certain that all the named controls have the runat="server" attribute as well. Add it if they do not. All the other table elements on the page need neither an ID nor a runat attribute because they are used for static display and will not be processed on the server.

Now add the onServerClick attribute to the button. You can add this using the Properties window, or you can add it directly to the markup for the page.

```
onServerClick="Button1_OnServerClick"
```

Press F7 to view the code-behind file for the page if VS2008 hasn't already opened it for you, and add the code for the event handler:

```
protected void Button1_OnServerClick(object sender, EventArgs e)
{
    string strHtml = "";
    strHtml += txtName.Value + "<br/>";
    strHtml += txtStreet.Value + "<br/>";
    strHtml += txtCity.Value + ", " + txtState.Value;
    tdInnerHtml.InnerHtml = strHtml;
}
```

 If you want the control to handle the event on the client side, you should use the traditional onClick attribute. In this case, you must provide client-side scripting to handle the event.

You can have an onClick and an onServerClick attribute for the same control, in which case the client-side code will be run first, followed by the server-side code. We will demonstrate this later in this chapter.

If you take a look at the server-side Click event handler, which is executed every time the button is clicked, you'll see that an HTML string is constructed containing the values of the input text fields, interspersed with some HTML to control line breaks. This string is then assigned to the InnerHtml property of the table cell with the tdInnerHtml ID attribute:

```
tdInnerHtml.InnerHtml = strHtml
```

If you use the InnerText property instead of the InnerHtml property, the resultant page will display the < and > symbols. As written, however, the resultant page will look something like Figure 3-13, after values are entered in the text fields and the button is clicked.

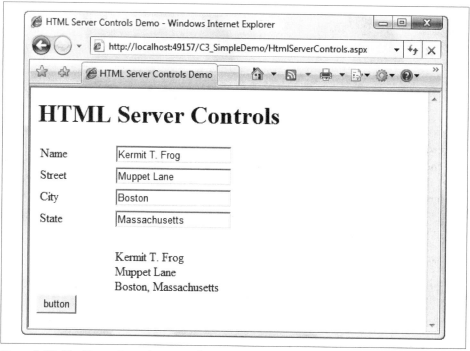

Figure 3-13. HtmlServerControls.aspx with InnerHtml populated

Table 3-5 lists HTML tags and the category to which they belong. In the example shown in Figures 3-12 and 3-13, the two types of input controls are text fields and a button. Both happen to use the <input> HTML tag, though as you can see in Table 3-5, other input controls do not use those tags.

Table 3-5. HTML tags and their categories

HTML tag	Category	HTML server control name	Description
`<head>`	Container	`HtmlHead`	`<head>` element. Other elements can be added to its `Controls` collection.
`<input>`	Input	`HtmlInputButton` `HtmlInputCheckbox` `HtmlInputFile` `HtmlInputHidden` `HtmlInputImage` `HtmlInputPassword` `HtmlInputRadioButton` `HtmlInputReset` `HtmlInputSubmit` `HtmlInputText`	`<input type=button	submit	reset>` `<input type=checkbox>` `<input type=file>` `<input type=hidden>` `<input type=image>` `<input type=password>` `<input type=radio>` `<input type=reset>` `<input type=submit>` `<input type=text	password>`
`<img>`	N/A	`HtmlImage`	Image.
`<link>`	N/A	`HtmlLink`	`Href` property gets/sets the URL target.
`<textarea>`	Input	`HtmlTextArea`	Multiline text entry.
`<a>`	Container	`HtmlAnchor`	Anchor.
`<button>`	Container	`HtmlButton`	Customizable output format, usable with Internet Explorer 4.0 and later browsers.
`<form>`	Container	`HtmlForm`	Maximum of one `HtmlForm` control per page; default method is POST.
`<table>`	Container	`HtmlTable`	Table, which can contain rows, which can contain cells.
`<td> <th>`	Container	`HtmlTableCell`	Table cell; table header cell.
`<tr>`	Container	`HtmlTableRow`	Table row.
`<title>`	Container	`HtmlTitle`	Title element.
`<select>`	Container	`HtmlSelect`	Pull-down menu of choices.
	Container	`HtmlGenericControl`	Any HTML control not listed here.

You never actually use the name of the HTML server control shown in Table 3-5 in a content file such as a page, user control, or master page. What goes in your HTML code is the HTML tag with the addition of the `runat="server"` attribute; and usually with the addition of an ID attribute.

You can convert any HTML control to server-side processing with the addition of the `runat="server"` attribute. Those not listed explicitly in Table 3-5 will be treated as an `HtmlGenericControl`. As with any other container control, this allows programmatic access to the control's inner HTML.

All the HTML server controls derive from the System.Web.UI.Control class and are contained in the System.Web.UI.HTMLControls namespace. Figure 3-14 shows the HTML server control hierarchy.

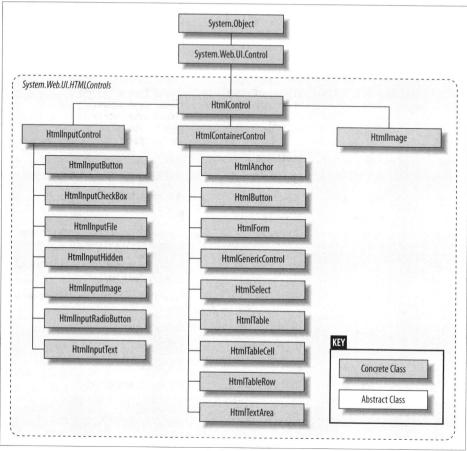

Figure 3-14. The HTML server control object hierarchy

Client-Side Processing

Server-side processing is at the heart of ASP.NET, but as AJAX controls prove, the judicious addition of script to be run on the browser can be a distinct advantage. It can speed up a page's execution by controlling how it communicates with the server and it can provide a much-improved user experience as well.

It may strike you as odd, though, that despite this hoo-ha about JavaScript, this book won't look at writing any JavaScript (or any VBScript, for that matter) directly onto the page, except in this section. That's not to say the authors of this book dismiss it, but rather that it isn't core to the topic of writing ASP.NET pages and you simply don't need to know what JavaScript is being generated by the AJAX controls used here. It just works.

There are exceptions to the rule, of course: some ASP.NET server controls use client-side scripting to provide responses to user actions without posting back to the server. For example, validation controls typically download a script to the browser so that invalid data is caught and flagged to the user without requiring a round trip to the server. In these cases, this client-side script is provided by ASP.NET and you, the developer, do not have to write or manage that script.

As you will see, you can call client-side code from any ASP.NET server control. In addition, the ASP.NET Button server control has a property, OnClientClick, which lets you specify client-side script to execute when the button is clicked.

Conventional and server HTML controls expose a number of events that can execute a script when they are raised. This script can be contained in a script block in the content file or contained inline with the attributes in the control declaration. Previously, you saw the onclick and onserverclick attributes for the HTML Button control for handling click events. Table 3-6 lists a few of the commonly used events available to HTML controls.

Table 3-6. Commonly used HTML events

Event	Description
onblur	Fires when the control loses input focus
onfocus	Fires when the control receives focus
onclick	Fires when the control is clicked
onchange	Fires when the value of the control changes
onkeydown	Fires when the user presses a key
onkeypress	Fires when the user presses an alphanumeric key
onkeyup	Fires when the user releases a key
onmouseover	Fires when the mouse pointer is moved over the control
onserverclick	Raises the ServerClick event when the control is clicked

To take an example of handcoded client-side script in action, create a new web form called *ClientSideProcessing.aspx* in your *C3_SimpleDemo* website. In the Source view of the content file, add the following script block between the closing </head> tag and the opening <body> tag:

```
<script language=javascript>
    function ButtonTest()
    {
        alert("Button clicked - client side processing");
    }
```

```
   function DoChange( )
   {
      document.getElementById("btnSave").disabled=false;
   }
</script>
```

The language is specified with the `language` attribute in the opening `<script>` tag, in this case JavaScript. In this example, two different functions are implemented. `ButtonTest` uses the `alert` method to pop up a dialog box. `DoChange` enables a Save button. This addresses the scenario where you want a Save button to be disabled until the user makes a change to some data, at which point the Save button should become enabled.

 Learning JavaScript is beyond the scope of this book. See *JavaScript: The Definitive Guide*, Fifth Edition, by David Flanagan (O'Reilly).

Add the following controls to the form: an HTML button, two ASP.NET buttons, an HTML input text box, and an ASP.NET TextBox. You can drag the controls onto the form, rename the button controls, and add the attributes shown in Example 3-6. The two HTML controls have `ID` and `runat` attributes, making them server controls. `btnServer` has the `OnClientClick` property set, and `btnSave` has its `Enabled` property set to false.

Example 3-6. Controls in Default.aspx for ClientSideProcessing
```
<h1>Client-Side Processing</h1>
<input id="btnHTML" runat=server type="button"
   value="HTML Button" onclick="javascript:ButtonTest( );"
   onserverclick="btnHTML_ServerClick"/>

<asp:Button ID="btnServer" runat="server"
   Text="ASP.NET Button" OnClientClick="javascript:ButtonTest( );" />
<br />
<input id="txtHTML" type="text" runat="server"
   onchange="javascript:DoChange( );" />
<br />
<br />
<asp:TextBox ID="TextBox1" runat="server"
   onchange="javascript:DoChange( );"></asp:TextBox>
<br />
<asp:Button ID="btnSave" runat="server" Text="Save" Enabled=false />
```

Double-click `btnHTML` in Design view to create an event handler in the code-behind file. Add the following highlighted line of code:
```
protected void btnHTML_ServerClick(object sender, EventArgs e)
{
   txtHTML.Value = "An HTML server control";
}
```

Double-click btnServer in Design view to create an event handler for that button and add the following highlighted line of code in the code-behind file:

```
protected void btnServer_Click(object sender, EventArgs e)
{
    txtHTML.Value = "An ASP.NET server control";
}
```

Now run the page. Initially, the Save button will be disabled (grayed out). Clicking the HTML button will cause the JavaScript function ButtonTest to execute, popping up a dialog box with the message "Button clicked – client side processing." Once that dialog is cleared, the server-side code will run, populating the HTML input box with the string "An HTML server control." Similarly, clicking the ASP.NET Server button will pop up the same dialog box, and then will populate the HTML input box with the string "An ASP.NET server control." Changing the contents of either of the text boxes and tabbing out of the text box will enable the Save button.

 The ability to call client-side script from an ASP.NET server control, other than using the Button.OnClientClick property, is essentially an undocumented feature. It works by taking advantage of the fact that any attributes declared with the control that are unrecognized by ASP.NET are passed unchanged to the browser.

You can see this by viewing the source for the page in the browser. The ASP.NET TextBox from the earlier code snippet is rendered to the browser in this way:

```
<input name="TextBox1" type="text" id="TextBox1"
    onchange="javascript:DoChange();" />
```

Because onchange is a valid event for an HTML input control, it correctly processes the JavaScript function.

CHAPTER 4

Basic Controls

Chapter 3 introduced controls. Though it briefly mentioned both server and classic HTML controls, most of the coverage was on ASP.NET server controls, the body of ASP.NET, and on ASP.NET AJAX server controls, the clothes to make the body more presentable.

 As noted previously, server controls are known variously as "ASP controls," "ASP.NET controls," "ASP.NET server controls," "Web controls," and "Web server controls." In this book, we will use "ASP.NET server control" or "server control." Likewise, we will use the term "AJAX server control" for clarity. When we refer to "server control," it should be clear from the context whether this means only ASP.NET server controls or whether it includes HTML and AJAX server controls as well.

Chapter 3 covered topics common to all ASP.NET and AJAX server controls, such as events, syntax, programmatic access to controls at runtime (using the ID property), and the use of Visual Studio 2008 (VS2008) to build your website using controls. However, it did not go into significant detail about any specific controls save the AJAX ScriptManager control.

This chapter provides a wealth of detail about many of the basic ASP.NET and AJAX controls, including the TextBox, Button, CheckBox, and RadioButton controls, lists, and images. It discusses the features and properties common to many controls, and the AJAX extender controls which enhance their functionality.

The next chapter will look at the more advanced server controls included as part of ASP.NET in VS2008 and the AJAX Control Toolkit, such as the UpdatePanel, MultiView, Wizard, FileUpload, AdRotator, ModalPopup, and Calendar controls. Other chapters will focus on data controls, validation controls, login and security controls, and so on.

If you haven't already downloaded and installed the AJAX Control Toolkit, now would be a good time to do so. Turn to Appendix A and follow the instructions on how to install and integrate it into VS2008.

Visual Studio Is Not Mandatory

It's fair to say that this book relies on Visual Studio to do a fair amount of the code generation for you as you work through the examples. Such features as the Toolbox, the data source wizards you'll see in Chapter 7, the Language Integrated Query (LINQ) editors in Chapter 10, and much more all speed up our development time, and the debugger is a fantastic piece of work. However, that's not to say it's the only way to do it. Before we start getting comfortable with VS2008, let's look at a little example to show that you really can write a web page with a simple text editor and how much easier it is to do the same thing in VS2008.

You will create the same simple web page in two different ways: once using a text editor (Notepad) and then again using VS2008.

 This is the only time in the entire book that you will create a website without using VS2008, and it requires you to have Microsoft Internet Information Services (IIS) installed. If you don't have it installed, you cannot run the page without opening it in VS2008.

XP users can install it via Control Panel → Add\Remove Programs → Windows Components. Vista users will find the option under Control Panel → Programs and Features → Turn Windows features on or off. In both cases, you'll need administrative privileges to install it, and you can accept the default options.

Using either technique, the resultant web page should look something like that shown in Figure 4-1. This page will demonstrate some of the properties, events, and methods common to all ASP.NET server controls.

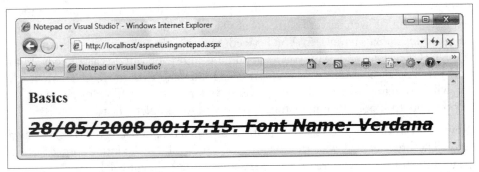

Figure 4-1. ASPNETUsingNotepad.aspx

To create this web page without the benefit of VS2008, open Notepad or your favorite editor that is capable of creating a flat text file (not Microsoft Word, for example, unless you want to jump through hoops). Enter into the file the code in Example 4-1.

Example 4-1. ASPNETUsingNotepad.aspx

```
<%@ Page Language="C#" %>
<script runat="server">
   void lblTime_Init(object sender, EventArgs e)
   {
      lblTime.Font.Name = "Verdana";
      lblTime.Font.Size = 20;
      lblTime.Font.Underline = true;
      lblTime.Font.Bold = true;
      lblTime.Font.Italic = true;
      lblTime.Font.Overline = true;
      lblTime.Font.Strikeout = true;
      lblTime.Text = DateTime.Now.ToString() +
         ". Font Name: " +
         lblTime.Font.Name;
   }
</script>

<html>
   <head runat="server">
      <title>Notepad or Visual Studio?</title>
   </head>
   <body>
      <form id="form1" runat="server">
         <h2>Basics</h2>
         <asp:Label ID="lblTime" runat="server"
                    OnInit="lblTime_Init" />
      </form>
   </body>
</html>
```

To see your page processed by ASP.NET on a web server, you need to access the page in a browser via localhost. Localhost is the domain that browsers use to make requests to an IIS web server on the local machine. The default home directory for IIS is *c:\inetpub\wwwroot*, so you'll need to save the file in this directory as *ASPNETUsingNotepad.aspx*. If you're an administrator, you can do this directly, but if not, you'll need to save it in your *Documents* folder and then move it. The text editor will just refuse to save the file directly, but moving the file will give you the opportunity to supply an administrative password to complete the move.

Now you can open a browser and point it at *http://localhost/ASPNETUsingNotepad.aspx*. The browser will wait a moment while the ASP.NET runtime processes the page and returns the rendered HTML, as shown earlier in Figure 4-1.

Using Virtual Directories

When building websites, it's a common practice to save your website's files to a directory other than *c:\inetpub\wwwroot* and then to create a virtual directory in IIS which maps to that location under localhost. For example, to access a website at *http://localhost/chapter2*, you can create a virtual directory in IIS called *chapter2* and point it at whichever directory the website is stored in. This has the advantage that you can tweak a lot more settings in IIS for a virtual directory than for a physical one directly saved under IIS's home directory. It also means the website doesn't get lost if you change the IIS home directory to something other than *c:\inetpub\wwwroot* for some reason. The virtual directory isn't connected to the location of the home directory and will always point to the same folder.

To create a virtual directory under localhost in IIS, follow these steps:

1. Select Start → Control Panel → Administrative Tools → Internet Information Services.
2. When the IIS window appears, expand the tree on the lefthand side until you find *<local computer>* → Web Sites → Default Web Site.
3. Right-click Default Web Site.
4. From the drop down, select New → Virtual Directory and follow the wizard, filling in the name of the virtual directory you want to use and the folder containing your website.

In contrast, the ASP.NET Development Server (the web server built into VS2008) may appear to use virtual directories, but it doesn't. Instead, when you ask VS2008 to run a site in your browser, it spins up a new instance of the server whose home directory is the folder that contains the website you're working on. Then it simply serves pages, images, and the like directly from that folder.

Now you'll create an equivalent web page using VS2008. Open the integrated development environment (IDE) and create a new website called *C4_BasicControls*. When *Default.aspx* opens, close it and delete it from the site in the Solution Explorer. Add to the site a new web form called *ASPNETUsingVS2008.aspx*, making sure to clear the box marked "Place code in separate file". Change the `<title>` element text to `"Notepad or Visual Studio?"`, delete the `<div>` element in the form, and switch to Design view. Drag a `Label` control onto the page and select it. In the Properties window, change the `Label`'s ID property to `lblTime` and then click the lightning bolt icon in the window to show a list of events for the `Label`. Double-click the box next to Init, and VS2008 will generate the skeleton code for that event handler and will switch back to Source view with the cursor in the right place for you to start writing code. Copy the highlighted code for the handler from Example 4-1 and note that as you type, the IntelliSense feature in VS2008 helps you write your code more quickly and with fewer mistakes. The finished code looks something like Example 4-2.

Example 4-2. ASPNETUsingVS2008.aspx

```
<%@ Page Language="C#" %>

<!DOCTYPE html PUBLIC "-//W3C//DTD XHTML 1.0 Transitional//EN"
 "http://www.w3.org/TR/xhtml1/DTD/xhtml1-transitional.dtd">

<script runat="server">

    protected void lblTime_Init(object sender, EventArgs e)
    {
        lblTime.Font.Name = "Verdana";
        lblTime.Font.Size = 20;
        lblTime.Font.Underline = true;
        lblTime.Font.Bold = true;
        lblTime.Font.Italic = true;
        lblTime.Font.Overline = true;
        lblTime.Font.Strikeout = true;
        lblTime.Text = DateTime.Now.ToString() +
            ". Font Name: " +
            lblTime.Font.Name;
    }
</script>

<html xmlns="http://www.w3.org/1999/xhtml">
<head runat="server">
    <title>Notepad or Visual Studio?</title>
</head>
<body>
    <form id="form1" runat="server">
    <h2>Basics</h2>
    <asp:Label ID="lblTime" runat="server"
      OnInit="lblTime_Init" Text="Label"></asp:Label>
    </form>
</body>
</html>
```

Run the page by either pressing F5 or selecting the Debug → Start menu item. You will see the same results as the previous page, shown earlier in Figure 4-1.

You can also repeat the exercise using a web form with its code in a separate file. Add to the site a new web form called *ASPNETUsingCodeBehind.aspx*, making sure the box marked "Place code in separate file" is checked, and follow the instructions again for *ASPNETUsingVS2008.aspx*. When you're done, select Edit → IntelliSense → Organize Usings → Remove Unused Usings, to remove references to framework libraries that aren't necessary. The results in the browser will be the same as will the HTML generated in the *.aspx* file. The code-behind page will look a bit different, as shown in Example 4-3.

Example 4-3. ASPNETUsingCodeBehind.aspx.cs

```
using System;

public partial class ASPNETUsingCodeBehind : System.Web.UI.Page
{
    protected void Page_Load(object sender, EventArgs e)
    {

    }
    protected void lblTime_Init(object sender, EventArgs e)
    {
        lblTime.Font.Name = "Verdana";
        lblTime.Font.Size = 20;
        lblTime.Font.Underline = true;
        lblTime.Font.Bold = true;
        lblTime.Font.Italic = true;
        lblTime.Font.Overline = true;
        lblTime.Font.Strikeout = true;
        lblTime.Text = DateTime.Now.ToString() +
            ". Font Name: " +
            lblTime.Font.Name;
    }
}
```

These three examples demonstrate a `Label` control, an event handler, and properties being set for a control. This simple web page has static HTML text and a `Label` web server control. The `Label` control has been assigned an ID of `lblTime`, which allows the control to be referred to in the code.

Of more interest is the `onInit` attribute, which declares a method (known as a *delegate* in this case) to be bound to the `Init` event. The `Init` event, a member of the `Control` class, is called when a control is initialized. It is the first step in each control's life cycle. All `WebControl` objects, because they are derived from `Control`, have an `Init` event.

In Examples 4-1, 4-2, and 4-3, the `Init` event is handled by a method called `lblTime_Init`, defined in the code block at the top of the *.aspx* file or in the code-behind file. The `lblTime_Init` method sets several properties of the label's font (`Name`, `Size`, etc.) and sets the value of the `Text` property. The `Text` property value is a concatenation of the current date and time, a literal string, and the name of the font used. Because `DateTime.Now` is of type `DateTime`, it must be converted to a string in the C# code.

The results, shown in Figure 4-1, are not pretty, but they are instructive. The figure shows how several text attributes—bold, italic, overline, underline, and strikeout—can be applied to a `Label`.

Fonts deserve special mention. Fonts contain the *subproperties* listed in Table 4-1.

Table 4-1. Subproperties of the Font object

Subproperty	Type	Values	Description
Bold	Boolean	true, false	Makes the text bold; default is false.
Italic	Boolean	true, false	Italicizes the text; default is false.
Name	String	Verdana, Courier New, etc.	Automatically updates the first item in the Names property. The font must be installed and available to the client browser. Note that default installed fonts vary by OS.
Names	String	Times New Roman, etc.	Ordered array of font names. Stores a list of available font names. The Name property is automatically updated with the first item in the array.
Strikeout	Boolean	true, false	Puts a line through the text; default is false.
Underline	Boolean	true, false	Puts a line under the text; default is false.
Overline	Boolean	true, false	Puts a line over the text; default is false. Will not render on down-level browsers.
Size	FontUnit or string	Small, Smaller, Large, Larger, or an integer representing point size	Sets the size of the font either as a named size preset in the browser or in points.

When used in HTML, subproperties are accessed declaratively in code in the following form:

```
Font-Size = "small"
```

When used in code blocks, subproperties are accessed programmatically in this form:

```
lblTime.Font.Size = new FontUnit("Small");
```

Or, when used in Visual Basic:

```
lblTime.Font.Size = 20
```

Web Forms: Plain or AJAX?

You may notice as you add new items to your website that the Add New Item dialog box offers two kinds of basic page—a web form and an AJAX web form—and the same option for a master page (see Figure 4-2). The AJAX web form item is simply a plain web form with references to the ASP.NET AJAX libraries included already, so you can use AJAX controls right away. The same is true of the difference between Master Page and AJAX Master Page in the figure.

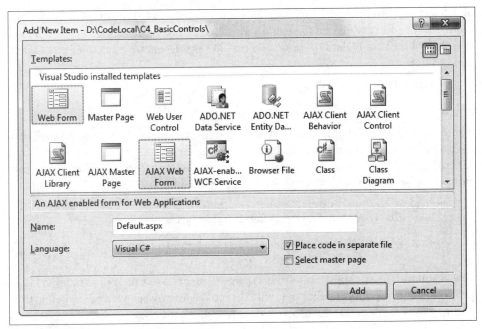

Figure 4-2. Web form or AJAX web form?

To convert a plain web form to support AJAX, add a reference to *System.Web. Extensions.dll* in the project references and a `ScriptManager` control to the form.

For the remainder of this chapter, we're going to discuss the various controls available to you. We'll explain how to use each one, give you examples to work with, and then see how the AJAX Toolkit controls can extend their functionality.

Label Controls and Literal Controls

Both `Label` and `Literal` controls are used to control the text displayed on a page at runtime. The text to be displayed is set in the controls' `Text` property, as shown in Example 4-4.

Example 4-4. Declaring labels and literals

```
<asp:Literal ID="Literal1"
    runat="server" Text="This is a literal" />

<asp:Label ID="Label1"
    runat="server" Text="This is a label" />
```

So, why have two controls for plain text? The answer is one of context. Add a new page called *LabelsAndLiterals.aspx* to the *C4_BasicControls* website, and add the code from Example 4-4 to it. Press Ctrl-F5 to run the page (or right-click the page and select View in Browser) and then have a look at the HTML generated by the two controls by right-clicking the page in the browser and selecting View Source. The key is that the Label control has wrapped its text in <span> tags whereas the Literal control has not:

```
This is a literal

<span id="Label1">This is a label</span>
```

The <span> elements enable you to control the formatting of the text in a Label control, which is why the Label control has many display-related properties whereas the Literal control has none. For example, you can add text formatting to Label controls inline or through a Cascading Style Sheet (CSS) like so:

```
<asp:Label  ID="Label2" runat="server" ForeColor="Blue"
    Font-Bold="True" Text="This is a label styled inline" />

<asp:Label  ID="Label3" runat="server" CssClass="StandardText"
    Text="This is a label styled with CSS" />
```

The resultant HTML shows how the <span> elements use the appropriate XHTML properties. Furthermore, ASP.NET will detect what browser version is being used and will use <font> tags if the browser does not support CSS.

```
<span id="Label2" style="color:Blue;font-weight:bold;">
    This is a label styled inline
</span>

<span id="Label3" class="StandardText">
    This is a label styled with CSS
</span>
```

The Label control has another trick up its sleeve as well. If you set its AssociatedControlID property to the ID of another form element, like this:

```
<asp:Label ID="Label4" runat="server" Text="This is a form label"
    AssociatedControlID="form1" />
```

the control will generate an HTML <label> element with its for attribute set to the value of AssociatedControlID. The compiler will also check that the nominated ID also exists on the form, rather than create a semantically incorrect HTML form:

```
<label for="form1" id="Label4">This is a form label</label>
```

So, why use a Literal at all? Because in some situations those <span> elements are invalid XHTML—notably in the <head> area of a page. For example, if you were generating the title of a page dynamically from a database, you would use:

```
<head>
    <title>
        <asp:Literal id="PageTitle" text="Page Title" runat="server" />
    </title>
</head>
```

rather than:

```
<head>
    <title>
        <asp:Label id="PageTitle" text="Page Title" runat="server" />
    </title>
</head>
```

because the result of using the Label would be invalid:

```
<head>
    <title>
        <span id="PageTitle">Page Title</span>
    </title>
</head>
```

The HTML elements surrounding the text are also why you can use AJAX controls to extend the functionality of a Label control but not of a Literal control. Once the server has rendered your ASP.NET page as XHTML and JavaScript, that JavaScript can target the HTML elements, <span> or <label>, generated by a Label control, but there's nothing to reference in a Literal control.

TextBox Control

You can use the TextBox control for both user input and read-only text display. You can configure it to be single-line or multiline, or to act as a password entry box, hiding the text being typed in it. If you set it to multiline, it automatically wraps the text it contains unless the Wrap property is set to false. Its Text property sets and retrieves the text content within the box. The text it contains can exceed the length of the control displayed on the page, in which case the beginning of the text is scrolled off to the left of the box.

Table 4-2 lists the frequently used properties of the TextBox control. If you omit any of these values from the control, the default value will apply. All the properties listed in the table are read/write properties.

Table 4-2. Some properties specific to the TextBox control

Name	Type	Values	Description
AutoPostBack	Boolean	true, false	Determines whether automatic postback to the server will occur if the user changes the contents of the control and then selects another control on the form. If false, the postback to the server will not occur until the page is posted, either by a button or by another control with AutoPostBack set to true. Default is false.
Columns	Int32	0, 1, 2, etc.	Width of the text box as measured in the width of the widest characters in the current font. Default is 0, which indicates that the property is not set. Use the Width property for fine-grained control instead.

Table 4-2. Some properties specific to the TextBox control (continued)

Name	Type	Values	Description
MaxLength	Int32	0, 1, 2, etc.	Maximum number of characters allowed. If MaxLength is greater than Columns, and if the current length of the value of the text box is larger than Columns, only a portion of the string will display, and users must use the Home, End, or arrow key to see all of the text.
			The default value is 0, which does not impose a limit on the number of characters entered into the text box.
ReadOnly	Boolean	true, false	If true, the contents cannot be changed by the user, although there is no visual indication to this effect. The contents of the text box can still be changed programmatically, however. Default is false.
Rows	Int32	0, 1, 2, etc.	Number of lines of text in a multiline text box. The default is 0, which imposes no limit on the number of lines. Has an effect only if TextMode is set to MultiLine.
Text	String		Content of the TextBox.
TextMode	TextBoxMode	SingleLine, MultiLine, Password	SingleLine, the default value, displays a single line of text. MultiLine allows multiple lines of text and displays a vertical scroll bar, even for Rows = 1. The text wraps automatically to fit the width of the box. The Enter key enters a carriage return/line feed. The mouse or Tab key causes focus to leave the box. Password displays any text entered as a nonalphanumeric character (which one is specific to the browser you're using) and then clears the text box on posting. The value is not case-sensitive. Note that for security reasons, this mode makes the Text property not settable from code.
ValidationGroup	String		Specifies which validation group, if any, this control is a member of. See Chapter 11 for a discussion of validation.
Wrap	Boolean	true, false	Indicates whether text within a multiline text box should wrap. If false, the text box will have a horizontal scroll bar. Default is true.

In addition to the events inherited from the WebControl class, such as Init, Load, and PreRender, the TextBox control raises the TextChanged event when the contents of the text box have changed and the control loses focus. This is not a postback event unless the AutoPostBack property is set to true.

When a TextBox control is declared in a content file (*.aspx* or *.ascx*), the TextChanged event handler method is specified with the OnTextChanged attribute. TextChanged is the default event handler created by VS2008 when you double-click a TextBox in Design view. This event handler is passed a standard EventArgs argument.

TextBox Behavior

The following example demonstrates the basic use of a TextBox, including handling the TextChanged event. This example has two text boxes: one to input text, and a second, read-only control to echo the contents of the first box. The finished web page should look something like that shown in Figure 4-3, after changing the text in the input box.

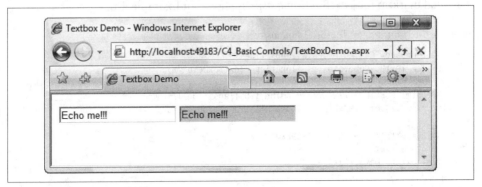

Figure 4-3. TextBoxDemo.aspx

Add to your *C4_BasicControls* site a new web form called *TextBoxDemo.aspx*. Drag two TextBox controls onto the page. Set the ID property of the first to txtInput and the second to txtEcho. Set the AutoPostBack property of txtInput to true so that the form will automatically post back whenever the contents of the control changes. Set the BackColor property of txtEcho to LightGray and the ReadOnly property to true. The former will give a visual clue that the latter has been set, and txtEcho won't accept text. Finally, add some text to txtInput.

To echo the contents of txtInput in txtEcho, you'll make use of the TextChanged event of txtInput. This event fires when the contents of a text box changes and then the text box loses focus. To bind this event with the method to copy the text to txtEcho, switch to Design view and double-click the TextBox. The OnTextChanged attribute will be added to the txtInput declaration in the content file, and the code-behind file will open with a code skeleton in place of the event handler. Enter the highlighted line of code from Example 4-5.

Example 4-5. The TextChanged event handler in TextBoxDemo.aspx.cs

```
using System;
using System.Web.UI;

public partial class TextBoxDemo : Page
{
```

```
    protected void txtInput_TextChanged(object sender, EventArgs e)
    {
        txtEcho.Text = txtInput.Text;
    }
}
```

The final markup for *TextBoxDemo.aspx* is shown in Example 4-6.

Example 4-6. Markup for TextBoxDemo.aspx

```
<%@ Page Language="C#" AutoEventWireup="true"
    CodeFile="TextBoxDemo.aspx.cs" Inherits="TextBoxDemo" %>

<!DOCTYPE html PUBLIC "-//W3C//DTD XHTML 1.0 Transitional//EN"
    "http://www.w3.org/TR/xhtml1/DTD/xhtml1-transitional.dtd">

<html xmlns="http://www.w3.org/1999/xhtml">
<head runat="server">
    <title>Textbox Demo</title>
</head>
<body>
    <form id="form1" runat="server">
    <div>
        <asp:TextBox ID="txtInput" runat="server" AutoPostBack="true"
            OnTextChanged="txtInput_TextChanged" Text="Enter some text" />
        <asp:TextBox ID="txtEcho" runat="server"
            BackColor="lightgray" ReadOnly="true" />
    </div>
    </form>
</body>
</html>
```

Run the page and you'll see that txtInput contains "Enter some text". When you change the contents of the control and tab out of the text box, the page will be posted back, the TextChanged event will be raised, and the event handler specified in the OnTextChanged attribute, txtInput_TextChanged, will execute, populating txtEcho.

TextBox Extenders

The TextBox control serves its purpose very well, but it gives users no help or hints on how to complete the information that is required of them. For example, in what format should a date be given? Is this a good password? The AJAX Control Toolkit contains several TextBox extender controls to provide this functionality and alternative ways to change the value in a TextBox without typing it in directly:

Autocomplete

> This extender control displays a list of possible values for the TextBox based on the text already added to the box. This list is generated on the fly by querying a web service in the background.

Calendar

For TextBoxes that require a date value, the CalendarExtender displays a standard Calendar control (see Chapter 5 for more on that) next to the TextBox as soon as the TextBox gets the focus. The user can then choose a date from the Calendar and that date as a string is then shown in the TextBox in the format you specify.

FilteredTextBox

This allows you to specify a list of the characters that may be added to the value in the text box. Characters that are not in the list won't be allowed into the box.

MaskedEditExtender

This specifies a format for the string to be added to the TextBox. For example, if the extender specifies a 10-digit ISBN string, the MaskedEditExtender will add hyphens between the appropriate numbers to create the correct string.

NumericUpDownExtender

This extender control adds "up" and "down" buttons to the side of the TextBox that increase and decrease a numeric value (if there is one) in the TextBox. You can also define sequences of non-numeric values for the TextBox. Clicking the buttons then calls a web service in the background that tells the extender which is the next or previous value in the sequence.

PasswordStrength

For TextBox controls where users need to add a password, PasswordStrength provides feedback to users as they type regarding how strong the password they've entered is so far and what they'll need to add to the string to make it the required strength.

PopupControlExtender

A more generic version of the CalendarExtender control, this extender allows you to associate another control or group of controls with a text box to make setting the value for the text box simpler. Indeed, this can extend almost any ASP.NET server control, as you'll see at the end of this chapter.

Slider

This defines a range of numeric values to which the TextBox can be set and then replaces the text box with a slider graphic which the user can drag to the appropriate value. We cover sliders separately at the end of this chapter.

TextBoxWatermarkExtender

This displays hint text in the TextBox that is visible when the text box contains no user-entered or programmatically set value. The watermark disappears as soon as the user clicks on the TextBox.

To demonstrate how you can use some of these extender controls with a TextBox, the next example extends *TextBoxDemo.aspx* to make it easier to enter a date into a TextBox. Add to the *C4_BasicControls* website a new AJAX web form called *TextBoxDemoWithAJAX.aspx*. Next, add the highlighted code from Example 4-6 to *TextBoxDemoWithAJAX.aspx* below the `ScriptManager` control, and then add the event handler code for `txtInput_OnTextChanged` from Example 4-5 to *TextBoxDemoWithAJAX.aspx.cs*.

The first change is to replace the "Enter some text" text in `txtInput` with a watermark saying the same thing, so the user doesn't have to delete it before she can actually write what she wants there.

With *TextBoxDemoWithAJAX.aspx* in Source view, drag a `TextBoxWatermarkExtender` from the Toolbox onto the page underneath the two TextBoxes. Set the `TargetControlId` for the extender to `txtInput` and the `WatermarkText` to "Enter a Date". Delete the `Text` property from `txtInput`, as it's no longer necessary, and then run the page. You'll see the watermark in the TextBox disappear as soon as you click it. If you delete the contents of the TextBox and click elsewhere on the page, the watermark will reappear.

To differentiate the watermark from text you've actually typed in, you can define a CSS class for watermarks and set the extender's `WatermarkCssClass` property to that. For example, the following CSS style works quite well:

```
<style type="text/css">
    .watermark
    {
        color : Gray;
        background-color : #dddddd;
        font-size: smaller;
        font-style:italic;
    }
</style>
```

You can add an AJAX Toolkit Extender control to an ASP.NET server control in Design view if you prefer. Select the target control for the extender on the page and a small arrow appears by its top-right corner. Clicking this *smart tag* will expand the control's Common Tasks dialog. You'll see an option to Add Extender. Clicking this will present another dialog box showing all the available extenders for that type of control. Select one and click OK.

Note, however, that not all of the properties of the AJAX Control Toolkit controls are visible in the Properties window in Design view, so you'll still need to use IntelliSense in Source view to see all of those.

With the hint text now a watermark, you can use a couple of other extenders to help users specify a date they want in the format you want. You could just use a `Calendar` control (see Chapter 5), it's true, but this is neater and also allows the user to just type the date straight into the box.

Drag a `CalendarExtender` onto the page under the `TextBoxWatermarkExtender`. Set its `TargetControlId` to `txtInput`. Now run the page and see that when the TextBox gets the focus, a calendar appears below it, as shown in Figure 4-4. Now you can select the date from the calendar or type it directly into the TextBox.

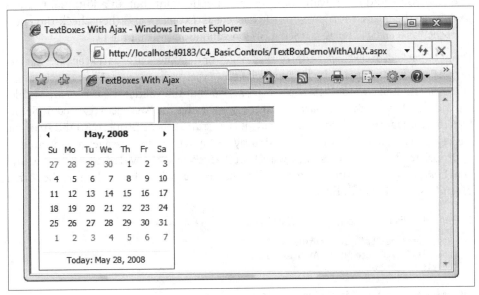

Figure 4-4. The CalendarExtender at work

Once you've selected a date from the calendar, the TextBox reflects that in its default format: MM/dd/yyyy. To change the format, use the Format property of the CalendarExtender. For example, set format="dd/MM/yy". A list of CalendarExtender's useful properties appears in Table 4-3.

Table 4-3. CalendarExtender properties

Name	Type	Value range	Description
Animated	Boolean	true, false	True if the calendar should pop up with an animation. False if it should just appear. Default is false.
CssClass	String		Specifies the CSS class that should be applied to the calendar when it is visible.
FirstDayOfWeek	String	Monday, Tuesday, Wednesday, etc.	Specifies the day to display as the first day of the week on the calendar.
Format	String	Use the same format strings as the standard .NET DateTime object.	Specifies the format of the selected date to be used in the text box after the date has been selected.
PopupButtonID	String		Specifies the ID of a button control that must be clicked before the calendar appears. If this is set, the calendar will not appear if the text box simply gets the focus. To display the calendar, users have to click the button first.

The CalendarExtender helps people write the date in the format you want, but it doesn't preclude them from writing their own version of the date directly into the TextBox. You could use a watermark to give a better hint, but an additional route is to enforce the desired format with the MaskedEditExtender and then check the entry with the MaskedEditValidator. (See more on validation in Chapter 11.)

Drag a MaskedEditExtender onto the page under the CalendarExtender. Set its TargetControlId property to txtInput, its MaskType property to date, its Mask to 99/99/9999, and its ErrorTooltipEnabled to True so that the validator's errors are visible. Now drag a MaskedEditValidator onto the page under the MaskedEditExtender. Set its ControlToValidate property to txtInput, its ControlExtender property to the ID of the MaskedEditExtender control, and its Display to "dynamic" so messages are inserted as appropriate. Then add messages with EmptyValueMessage, InvalidValueMessage, and ToolTipMessage properties. These additions, along with the code for the other extenders, are shown in Example 4-7.

Example 4-7. Full source code for TextBoxDemoWithAJAX.aspx.cs

```
<%@ Page Language="C#" AutoEventWireup="true"
   CodeFile="TextBoxDemoWithAJAX.aspx.cs"
   Inherits="TextBoxDemoWithAJAX" %>

<%@ Register Assembly="AjaxControlToolkit"
   Namespace="AjaxControlToolkit" TagPrefix="cc1" %>

<!DOCTYPE html PUBLIC "-//W3C//DTD XHTML 1.0 Transitional//EN"
   "http://www.w3.org/TR/xhtml1/DTD/xhtml1-transitional.dtd">

<html xmlns="http://www.w3.org/1999/xhtml">
<head runat="server">
   <title>TextBoxes With Ajax</title>

   <script type="text/javascript">
      function pageLoad( ) {
      }

   </script>

   <style type="text/css">
     .watermark
     {
        color: Gray;
        background-color: #dddddd;
        font-size: smaller;
        font-style: italic;
     }
   </style>
</head>

<body>
   <form id="form1" runat="server">
```

```
<div>
    <asp:ScriptManager ID="ScriptManager1" runat="server" />

    <asp:TextBox ID="txtInput" runat="server" AutoPostBack="true"
        OnTextChanged="txtInput_TextChanged" Text="Enter some text" />
    <asp:TextBox ID="txtEcho" runat="server"
        BackColor="lightgray" ReadOnly="true" />

    <cc1:TextBoxWatermarkExtender ID="TextBoxWatermarkExtender1"
        runat="server" TargetControlID="txtInput"
        WatermarkText="Enter a date" WatermarkCssClass="watermark" />
    <cc1:CalendarExtender ID="CalendarExtender1" runat="server"
        TargetControlID="txtInput" Format="MM/dd/yyyy" />
    <cc1:MaskedEditExtender ID="MaskedEditExtender1" runat="server"
        TargetControlID="txtInput" Mask="99/99/9999" MaskType="Date"
        ErrorTooltipEnabled="True" CultureInfo="en-us" />
    <cc1:MaskedEditValidator ID="MaskedEditValidator5"
        runat="server" ControlExtender="MaskedEditExtender1"
        ControlToValidate="txtInput"
        EmptyValueMessage="Date is required"
        InvalidValueMessage="Date is invalid"
        Display="Dynamic" TooltipMessage="Enter a date" />
</div>
</form>
</body>
</html>
```

Now run the page. See how the `MaskedEditExtender` applies itself to the `TextBox` when you type directly into the text box, and fits in nicely with `CalendarExtender`.

This example leaves the date format at the default, but it must be set anyway in the `CalendarExtender` to agree with the `MaskedEditExtender`. If you decide to use a different format, or if your users don't all use the same culture settings as you do, make sure the `CalendarExtender` and `MaskedEditExtender` controls agree on the format using the `CultureName` property for the `MaskedEditExtender` and the `Format` property for the `CalendarExtender`.

When the page is posted back and the selected date is reflected in `txtEcho`, `txtEcho` by default will show the date in the default format for the default culture on the server. You might need to experiment with culture and format values, before the extenders and `txtEcho` all show the same date in the same format. See *http://msdn2.microsoft.com/en-us/library/5hh873ya.aspx* for more on cultures and dates in general and *http://asp.net/learn/ajax-videos/video-131.aspx* for more on how this applies to the `MaskedEdit` controls in particular.

A list of useful properties for the `MaskedEditExtender` is given in Table 4-4. Note that it validates only numbers, times, and dates. For any other specific value you'll need one of the other `Validation` controls covered in Chapter 11.

Table 4-4. Useful MaskedEditExtender properties

Name	Type	Value range	Description
Mask	String	A sequence of the characters in Table 4-5	Defines the format of the string to be entered in the text box. For example, 99/99/9999 for a date, or LL99LLL for a current UK vehicle registration number.
Filtered	String		A string containing the characters allowed in place of "C" in the Mask property.
MaskType		None, Number, Date, Time, DateTime	Specifies what the value entered into the target TextBox will be verified as unless set to None, in which case no verification is made.
Autocomplete	Boolean	true, false	True to add in a default value to the TextBox.
AutoCompleteValue	String		Default value for AutoComplete if MaskType is set to None.
AcceptAMPM	Boolean	true, false	True to display an A.M. or P.M. sign for values with MaskType=time.
AcceptNegative		left, right, none	For MaskType=number, set to none if the minus sign is not allowed, and set to left or right if it is allowed and should be shown to the side of the number.
DisplayMoney		left, right, none	For MaskType=number, set to none if the local currency symbol is not allowed, and set to left or right if it is allowed and should be displayed to the side of the number.
ErrorTooltipEnabled	Boolean	true, false	True if a tool tip message should be shown when the user holds the mouse pointer over the targeted TextBox control.

Table 4-5. Mask characters

Character	Represents
9	Only a numeric character
L	Only a letter
$	Only a letter or a space
C	Only a custom character defined in the Filtered property
A	Only a letter or a custom character
N	Only a numeric or custom character
?	Any character
/	Date separator
:	Time separator
.	Decimal separator

Table 4-5. Mask characters (continued)

Character	Represents
,	Thousand separator
\	Any C# escape character
X{y}	Indicates the character represented by X should be repeated y times in the mask

An escape character in C# is a backslash (\) , followed by one of a small set of letters which allow you to specify a character in a string you wouldn't otherwise be able to use. For example, you use a double quote (") to specify the beginning and end of a string. If you want to use a double quote in a string, you can escape it as \":

```
string a = "Dave said, \"How much is that book?\" to the shopkeeper."
```

The full set of C# escape characters is available at *http://blogs.msdn.com/csharpfaq/ archive/2004/03/12/88415.aspx.*

HiddenField Control

Hidden fields are a common trick of the HTML web developer's trade for carrying information within a page when you do not want that information to be visible to the user—that is, the hidden field provides a way to store state information in the page. For example, you might want to keep track of whether a form on the page has been completed, has been saved as a draft, or is being edited for the first time.

Often, an easier and more elegant way to accomplish this task is to use one of the state mechanisms provided by the .NET Framework (see Chapter 6 for a complete discussion of state). However, sometimes this is impossible, perhaps for performance, bandwidth, or security reasons. (Performance and bandwidth are mostly two sides of the same coin.)

In HTML pages, you might use something such as the following code snippet to implement a hidden field:

```
<input type="hidden" id="FormStatus" value="Draft Saved">
```

Indeed, ASP.NET uses a hidden field to implement view state. You can see this by examining the source that is rendered to the browser, via the View → Source menu command in Internet Explorer. (Other browsers have analogous commands.) You will see something similar to the following, where the value attribute encodes all the information saved in view state:

```
<input type="hidden" name="__VIEWSTATE"
    value="/wEPDwUJLOCH1BR...YfL+BDX7xhMw=" />
```

To reap the benefits of server-side processing, you can use an ASP.NET HiddenField control to generate these hidden fields for use both by the browser and on the server.

In addition to accessing the hidden value through the control's Value property, ASP.NET also defines an event called ValueChanged for the HiddenField control. This fires on postback when the Value property of the control is different from the previous posting. The event does not cause a postback itself, and unlike most nonpostback controls, the HiddenField does not expose an AutoPostBack property to force an instantaneous postback. As with all nonpostback controls (explained in Chapter 3), notification of the event will be cached until the form is posted back by some other control, at which point the event will be raised in server code.

These features are demonstrated in Example 4-8, in a file called *HiddenFieldDemo.aspx*. The file contains a TextBox (txtSecretValue) for entering a new value for the HiddenField control (hdnSecretValue), an HTML button (used to execute a client-side function without causing a postback to the server), and an ASP.NET Button called btnPost (to force a postback to the server). A Label (lblSecretValue) displays the contents of the hidden field.

Example 4-8. HiddenFieldDemo.aspx

```
<%@ Page Language="C#" AutoEventWireup="true"
    CodeFile="HiddenFieldDemo.aspx.cs" Inherits="HiddenFieldDemo" %>

<!DOCTYPE html PUBLIC "-//W3C//DTD XHTML 1.0 Transitional//EN"
    "http://www.w3.org/TR/xhtml1/DTD/xhtml1-transitional.dtd">

<html xmlns="http://www.w3.org/1999/xhtml">
<head runat="server">
    <title>HiddenField Control Demo</title>
</head>
<body>
    <script type="text/javascript" language="javascript">
        function ChangeHiddenValue( )
        {
            alert("Entering ChangeHiddenValue");
            var hdnId = "<%=hdnSecretValue.ClientID%>";
            var hdn = document.getElementById(hdnId);
            var txt = document.getElementById("txtSecretValue");
            hdn.value = txt.value;
            alert("Value changed");
        }
    </script>

    <form id="form1" runat="server">
    <div>
        <asp:HiddenField ID="hdnSecretValue" runat="server"
            onvaluechanged="hdnSecretValue_ValueChanged" />
        Enter secret value:
        <asp:TextBox ID="txtSecretValue" runat="server" />
        <br />
        <br />
        <input id="Button1" type="button" value="button"
            onclick="ChangeHiddenValue( )" />
```

Example 4-8. HiddenFieldDemo.aspx (continued)

```
      <asp:Button ID="btnPost" runat="server" Text="Post" />
      <br />
      <br />
      <asp:Label ID="lblSecretValue" runat="server" />
   </div>
   </form>
</body>
</html>
```

The HTML button calls the `ChangeHiddenValue` function, highlighted in the code list-ing. This function has two alert methods that are helpful in debugging; they can be omitted or commented out.

`ChangeHiddenValue` demonstrates two equivalent ways of getting a reference to a con-trol on the page, both using the JavaScript `getElementById` method. This method returns a reference to the first object it finds on the page with the specified ID attribute.

In the first technique, a reference is obtained to the `HiddenField` control via the `ClientID` property, which returns the actual ID of the `<input type="hidden">` element as rendered on the page by ASP.NET:

```
var hdnId = "<%=hdnSecretValue.ClientID%>";
```

Enclosing the server-side code in `<% %>` tags tells ASP.NET to evaluate that code and place the results there in place of the tags and their contents.

In the second technique, the `ID` attribute of the `TextBox` control is passed directly to the `getElementById` method in the script rather than by injecting it:

```
var txt = document.getElementById("txtSecretValue");
```

The `HiddenField` `ValueChanged` event is handled by a server-side method, `hdnSecretValue_ValueChanged`, as indicated by the `HiddenField`'s `OnValueChanged` attribute in Example 4-8. The event handler from the code-behind file, *HiddenFieldDemo.aspx.cs*, is shown in Example 4-9.

Example 4-9. HiddenFieldDemo.aspx.cs

```
using System;
using System.Web.UI.WebControls;

public partial class HiddenFieldDemo : System.Web.UI.Page
{
    protected void hdnSecretValue_ValueChanged
       (object sender, EventArgs e)
    {
       HiddenField hdn = sender as HiddenField;
       lblSecretValue.Text = hdn.Value;
    }
}
```

The first line in hdnSecretValue_ValueChanged obtains a reference to the control that raised the event, carried in the sender argument. It casts sender as type HiddenField. Then the Value property of the HiddenField object is used to set the Text property of lblSecretValue.

After you enter a secret value and click the Post button, you'll see a web page much like Figure 4-5. The Post button does not have an event handler because you don't need it to perform any function other than to cause a postback to the server.

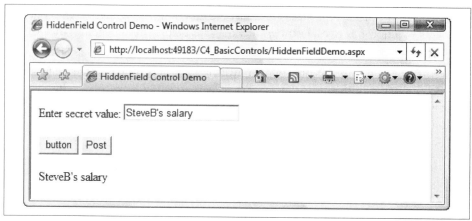

Figure 4-5. HiddenFieldDemo at work

Button Controls

Button controls are controls that post the form back to the server, enabling server-side processing to commence. There are three types of ASP.NET button controls, all members of the System.Web.UI.WebControls namespace:

Button
> This is the standard button.

LinkButton
> The LinkButton control is a cross between a standard button and a HyperLink control (described in the next section). A LinkButton appears to the user as a hyperlink (i.e., the text is colored and underlined), but it performs the standard postback behavior.

ImageButton
> The ImageButton control performs the same function as the standard button, except that an image bitmap takes the place of the button on the browser UI. For the ImageButton control, there is no Text attribute but there is an AlternateText attribute, which specifies what text to display on nongraphical browsers instead of the image.

The event handler uses an `ImageClickEventArgs` event argument rather than the `EventArgs` argument used in the event handlers for the `Button` and `LinkButton` controls. This event argument exposes two fields containing the x and y coordinates of the location where the user clicked on the image.

In addition to all the properties, methods, and events inherited from `WebControl`, all three button types have the following two events:

Click
> This event is raised when the control is clicked and no command name is associated with the `Button` (i.e., no value has been assigned to the `Button` control's `CommandName` property). The method is passed an argument of type `EventArgs`.

Command
> This event is raised when the control is clicked and a command name such as `Sort` or `Select` has been assigned to the `Button` control's `CommandName` property. The event is passed an argument of type `CommandEventArgs`, which has these two members:

> CommandName
> > The name of the command.

> CommandArgument
> > An optional argument for the command set in the `Button` control's `CommandArgument` property. You could then write a single method to handle the `Command` event for all the `Button` controls on your page and have it take its cue from the differing `CommandName` and `CommandArgument` values assigned to the different buttons.

> All three types of `Button` controls implement the `IButtonControl` interface. This interface requires the `Click` and `Command` events, plus properties such as `Text` and `CausesValidation`, among others, which we will describe shortly. The `IButtonControl` interface is what causes a control to act like a button.

Button Behavior

To demonstrate the three `Button` controls, add to the *C4_BasicControls* website a new web form called *ButtonDemo.aspx*. Now add a `Button`, a `LinkButton`, and an `ImageButton` control to the page. Each control will perform the same task: transferring control to another web page.

> For the code in the *ButtonDemo* website to work correctly, you will need an image file for the `ImageButton` control. This example uses a file called *popflyduck.png*, located in the *website* directory, but you can use any image file you want.

Now switch to Source view if you're not there already and set the controls' properties to match those highlighted in Example 4-10.

Example 4-10. ButtonDemo.aspx

```
<%@ Page Language="C#" AutoEventWireup="true"
    CodeFile="ButtonDemo.aspx.cs" Inherits="ButtonDemo" %>

<!DOCTYPE html PUBLIC "-//W3C//DTD XHTML 1.0 Transitional//EN"
    "http://www.w3.org/TR/xhtml1/DTD/xhtml1-transitional.dtd">

<html xmlns="http://www.w3.org/1999/xhtml">
<head runat="server">
    <title>Button Demo</title>
</head>

<body>
    <form id="form1" runat="server">
    <div>
        <asp:Button runat="server" ID="btnLink"
            Text="Link to target page" onclick="btnLink_Click"
            ToolTip="Click here to go to target page" />
        <asp:ImageButton runat="server" ID="imgLink"
            ImageUrl="~/popflyDuck.png" onclick="btnLink_Click"
            AlternateText="Link to target page"
            ToolTip="Click here to go to target page" />
        <asp:LinkButton runat="server" ID="lnkLink"
            ToolTip="Click here to go to target page"
            Font-Names="Impact" Font-Size="X-Large"
            onclick="btnLink_Click">
                Link to Target Page
        </asp:LinkButton>
    </div>
    </form>
</body>
</html>
```

All three controls bind the same method, btnLink_Click, to their Click event. This should be added to the code-behind file, *ButtonDemo.aspx.cs*, as Example 4-11 shows.

Example 4-11. The Click event handler code in ButtonDemo.aspx.cs

```
using System;

public partial class ButtonDemo : System.Web.UI.Page
{
    protected void btnLink_Click(object sender, EventArgs e)
    {
        Response.Redirect("http://www.ora.com");
    }
}
```

The resultant web page is shown in Figure 4-6.

The difference between a standard Button control and the other two variants is that both the LinkButton and the ImageButton controls' functionality is implemented using client-side scripting. This is readily apparent for the LinkButton at least if you

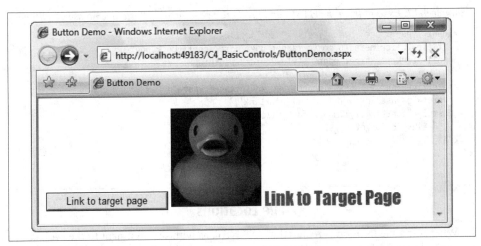

Figure 4-6. ButtonDemo.aspx in action

look at the markup rendered to your browser resulting from the *ButtonDemo.aspx* web page, an excerpt of which is shown in Example 4-12. In this listing, the Java-Script "manually" initiates a postback and is called by the `<a>` element generated by the LinkButton. In effect, this re-creates the automatic postback of the form associated with a standard HTML button because by default, the `<a>` element generated by the LinkButton will not post a form back when it is clicked.

It also means that if a user has JavaScript disabled in his browser, a LinkButton will not send the user to your intended destination because the postback will not occur.

Remember, this markup is output by ASP.NET, not written by you.

Example 4-12. Excerpt from the HTML and JavaScript generated by ButtonDemo.aspx

```
<script type="text/javascript">
//<![CDATA[
var theForm = document.forms['form1'];
if (!theForm) {
    theForm = document.form1;
}
function __doPostBack(eventTarget, eventArgument) {
    if (!theForm.onsubmit || (theForm.onsubmit() != false)) {
        theForm.__EVENTTARGET.value = eventTarget;
        theForm.__EVENTARGUMENT.value = eventArgument;
        theForm.submit();
    }
}
//]]>
</script>


<div>
    <input type="submit" name="btnLink" value="Link to target page"
        id="btnLink" title="Click here to go to target page" />
```

Example 4-12. Excerpt from the HTML and JavaScript generated by ButtonDemo.aspx (continued)

```html
<input type="image" name="imgLink" id="imgLink"
    title="Click here to go to target page" src="popflyDuck.png"
    alt="Link to target page" style="border-width:0px;" />

<a id="lnkLink" title="Click here to go to target page"
    href="javascript:__doPostBack('lnkLink','')"
    style="font-family:Impact;font-size:X-Large;">
        Link to Target Page
</a>
</div>
```

File Locations

Whenever a file location is required in ASP.NET, as with the argument to the Redirect method or properties like ImageButton.ImageUrl, there are four ways to represent a URL:

Relative

> The location is specified with respect to the application root directory. It starts with a period (.) or the name itself, but not with a slash (/).

Application relative

> The location is relative to the application root. It uses the tilde (~) operator, which resolves to the application root directory as in this example:
>
> ```
> BackImageUrl="~/images/SunflowerBkgrd.jpg"
> ```
>
> This would refer to a file in the *images* folder underneath the application root.
>
> The advantage to using relative or application relative addressing is it makes deployment easier. For a complete discussion of deployment issues, see Chapter 20.

Absolute

> In this case, a path on the local machine starts with a slash (/), indicating a folder on the current hard drive or a drive, plus a path.
>
> If the application is deployed to a machine with a different directory structure, the code may have to be changed to prevent errors.

Fully qualified

> This can be one of several types. A Universal Naming Convention (UNC) formatted name specifies a location anywhere on the network. It is of the following form:
>
> ```
> \\server-name\shared-resource-pathname
> ```
>
> It can be a URL to a page on the Internet, of the form:
>
> ```
> http://www.SomeDomainName.com
> ```
>
> It can be a location served from the local machine, as in:
>
> ```
> //localhost/websites/TargetPage.aspx
> ```

.NET provides several methods to convert between one type of location and another. For example, Server.MapPath(url) takes a relative or application relative address and returns the equivalent absolute address on the server. The Path and VirtualPathUtility classes contain several more such converter methods.

Button Control Extenders

Buttons don't offer much scope for functional extension. You click them, they post back the form to the server, and that's it. However, one button-specific extender in the AJAX Control Toolkit—the `ConfirmButtonExtender`—makes use of the period between the button being clicked and the form being posted to the server. It displays an alert box for the user to confirm that the postback, or whatever action you've attached to the `Button_Click` event, should proceed by clicking OK. If the user clicks Cancel, no postback will occur. Figure 4-7 shows this in action.

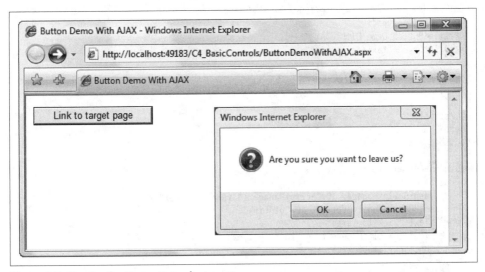

Figure 4-7. The ConfirmButtonExtender in action

The `ConfirmButtonExtender` can target all three types of ASP.NET Button controls, but in the demonstration page shown in Figure 4-7, it has been shown extending only a standard `Button` control. To build this page, add an AJAX web form called *ButtonDemoWithAJAX.aspx* to the *C4_BasicControls* website used in this chapter. Copy the markup for the `Button` control `btnLink` from *ButtonDemo.aspx* and paste it under the `ScriptManager` control. Next, copy the handler code for its `Click` event from *ButtonDemo.aspx.cs* to *ButtonDemoWithAJAX.aspx.cs*. Run the page to make sure it works as the original page does.

Now drag a `ConfirmButtonExtender` control to the page. Set its `TargetControlID` property to `btnLink` and its `ConfirmText` property to `"Are you sure you want to leave us?"` as shown in Example 4-13. Run the page again. This time, when you click the button an alert box pops up asking you to confirm that you want to navigate away. If you click Cancel, the form is not posted back.

Example 4-13. ButtonDemoWithAJAX.aspx

```
<%@ Page Language="C#" AutoEventWireup="true"
    CodeFile="ButtonDemoWithAJAX.aspx.cs"
    Inherits="ButtonDemoWithAJAX" %>

<%@ Register Assembly="AjaxControlToolkit"
    Namespace="AjaxControlToolkit" TagPrefix="cc1" %>

<!DOCTYPE html PUBLIC "-//W3C//DTD XHTML 1.0 Transitional//EN"
    "http://www.w3.org/TR/xhtml1/DTD/xhtml1-transitional.dtd">

<html xmlns="http://www.w3.org/1999/xhtml">
<head runat="server">
    <title>Button Demo With AJAX</title>
    <script type="text/javascript">

        function pageLoad() {
        }

    </script>
</head>
<body>

    <form id="form1" runat="server">
        <div>
            <asp:ScriptManager ID="ScriptManager1" runat="server" />
            <asp:Button runat="server" ID="btnLink"
                Text="Link to target page"
                ToolTip="Click here to go to target page"
                OnClick="btnLink_Click" />

            <cc1:ConfirmButtonExtender ID="ConfirmButtonExtender1"
                runat="server" TargetControlID="btnLink"
                ConfirmText="Are you sure you want to leave us?">
            </cc1:ConfirmButtonExtender>
        </div>
        </form>
</body>
</html>
```

One subtlety to the ConfirmButtonExtender is when the alert box will pop up once the button has been clicked. By default, it appears immediately, but you can delay it to the point immediately before the form is sent back to the server for processing if you set its ConfirmOnFormSubmit property to true. This can be useful for forms that contain client-side validation code that will run after the button is clicked but before the confirm dialog appears.

The ConfirmButtonExtender has one more property—OnClientCancel—the value of which is a client-side script that will run if the user clicks Cancel in the alert box.

HyperLink Control

A HyperLink control behaves very similarly to an HTML <a> element control, except that you can program it using server code. Indeed, the control is rendered on the client browser as an HTML anchor element (i.e., <a>) with the control's properties reflected in the element's attributes.

The HyperLink control has four control-specific properties:

ImageUrl
> Sets the path to an image to be displayed by the control rather than text set in the Text property.

NavigateUrl
> The target URL to navigate to once the user clicks on the hyperlink.

Text
> The text string that will be displayed on the browser as the link. If the Text and ImageUrl properties are both set, the ImageUrl takes precedence. The text will be displayed if the image is unavailable.
>
> If the browser supports tool tips and the ToolTip property (inherited from the WebControl class) has not been set, the Text value will display as a tool tip. If the ToolTip property has been set, the ToolTip text string will display as a tool tip.

Target
> Defines the window or frame that will load the linked page. The value is case-insensitive and must begin with a character in the range of a–z, except for the special values shown in Table 4-6, all of which begin with an underscore. Note that these are the standard HTML values for the target attribute of an <a> element.

Table 4-6. Special values of the Target attribute

Target value	Description
_blank	Renders the content in a new unnamed window without frames.
_new	Not documented, but behaves the same as _blank.
_parent	Renders the content in the parent window or frameset of the window or frame with the hyperlink. If the child container is a window or top-level frame, it behaves the same as _self.
_self	Renders the content in the current frame or window with focus. This is the default value.
_top	Renders the content in the current full window without frames.

To demonstrate a HyperLink control, add a new web form called *HyperLinkDemo.aspx* to the *C4_BasicControls* website. On the page are a HyperLink control and a DropDownList. The value selected in the list will determine the value of the HyperLink control's Target property, which you can then verify by clicking the link. The content file is shown in Example 4-14.

Example 4-14. HyperLinkDemo.aspx

```
<%@ Page Language="C#" AutoEventWireup="true"
    CodeFile="HyperLinkDemo.aspx.cs" Inherits="HyperLinkDemo" %>

<!DOCTYPE html PUBLIC "-//W3C//DTD XHTML 1.0 Transitional//EN"
    "http://www.w3.org/TR/xhtml1/DTD/xhtml1-transitional.dtd">

<html xmlns="http://www.w3.org/1999/xhtml">
<head runat="server">
    <title>HyperLink Demo</title>
</head>

<body>
    <form id="form1" runat="server">
    <div>
        <asp:HyperLink ID="hypLink" runat="server"
            NavigateUrl="http://www.microsoft.com"
            ToolTip="Visit Microsoft" Font-Names="Verdana">
            Show Microsoft.com
        </asp:HyperLink>  in 
        <asp:DropDownList ID="ddlTarget" runat="server" AutoPostBack="true">
            <asp:ListItem Text="A New Window" Value="_blank" Selected="True" />
            <asp:ListItem Text="This Window" Value="_self" />
        </asp:DropDownList>
    </div>
    </form>
</body>
</html>
```

To keep it simple, the HyperLink control's Target property is set when the page loads (as highlighted in Example 4-15) and the DropDownList's AutoPostBack property is set to true so that the Target property is reset whenever the value selected in the list changes.

Example 4-15. HyperLinkDemo.aspx.cs in full

```
using System;

public partial class HyperLinkDemo : System.Web.UI.Page
{
    protected void Page_Load(object sender, EventArgs e)
    {
        hypLink.Target = ddlTarget.SelectedValue;
    }
}
```

When the *HyperLinkDemo* page is run, it looks like Figure 4-8.

Switch between the two values in the DropDownList and verify that the hyperlink does or does not open a new window when clicked. You can also see how the <a> element's Target attribute changes by examining the generated markup for the web page on your browser.

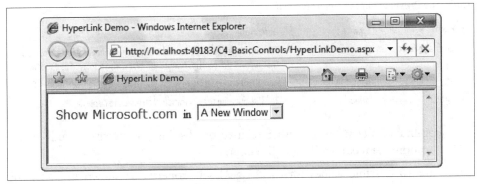

Figure 4-8. HyperLinkDemo.aspx in action

 A HyperLink control may look similar to a LinkButton control, but they are fundamentally different. Once clicked, a HyperLink control immediately navigates to the target URL without a postback. A LinkButton control, meanwhile, will post back the form to the server once clicked and will navigate to a URL only if its Click event handler is written to do that. It could just as easily display some text on the screen or refresh some data displayed on the page.

Images

Images are an important aspect of most websites. ASP.NET provides several ASP.NET server controls for displaying images. Two of them, the Image and the ImageMap controls, are covered in this section. The AdRotator control, which also displays images, will be covered in the next chapter.

Image Control

The Image control has limited functionality: it is used for displaying an image on a web page or, alternatively, displaying some text if the image is unavailable. It raises no events for user interaction, other than those inherited from Control, such as Init and Load. However, which image it displays and where it is aligned on the page can be set in code, so it is a legitimate alternative to using a static HTML <img> element.

 If you need an image to have the same functionality as a button (i.e., to capture mouse clicks), you should use either the ImageButton control, or a HyperLink control with its ImageUrl property set.

In addition to the properties inherited from the WebControl class, the Image control has the read/write properties shown in Table 4-7.

Table 4-7. Properties of the Image control

Name	Type	Description
AlternateText	String	The text displayed in the control if the image is unavailable. In browsers that support the ToolTips feature this text is also displayed as a tool tip.
ImageAlign	ImageAlign	Alignment options relative to the text of the web page. See Table 4-8.
ImageUrl	String	The URL pointing to the location of an image to display.

The ImageUrl property can be either relative or absolute, as described fully in the "File Locations" sidebar, earlier in this chapter.

There are 10 possible values for the ImageAlign property, as shown in Table 4-8. They each correspond to one of the valid values for the HTML <img> element's align attribute, with the exception of NotSet. If you need better control of image and text placement, you will probably want to position it with CSS.

Table 4-8. Members of the ImageAlign enumeration

Values	Description
NotSet	Not set. This is the default value.
AbsBottom	Aligns the lower edge of the image with the lower edge of the largest element on the same line.
AbsMiddle	Aligns the middle of the image with the middle of the largest element on the same line.
Top	Aligns the upper edge of the image with the upper edge of the highest element on the same line.
Bottom	Aligns the lower edge of the image with the lower edge of the first line of text. Same as Baseline.
Baseline	Aligns the lower edge of the image with the lower edge of the first line of text. Same as Bottom.
Middle	Aligns the middle of the image with the lower edge of the first line of text.
TextTop	Aligns the upper edge of the image with the upper edge of the highest text on the same line.
Left	Aligns the image on the left edge of the page with the text wrapping on the right.
Right	Aligns the image on the right edge of the page with the text wrapping on the left.

To see how the various ImageAlign values affect the appearance of a web page, create a new web form called *ImageDemo.aspx* in your *C4_BasicControls* website. As highlighted in Example 4-16, the form contains two Image controls and a DropDownList containing all the possible values for the Image control's ImageAlign property. There are also a few horizontal lines and some text to demonstrate the difference in the alignments.

> For the code in *ImageDemo.aspx* to work correctly, you will need an image file for the ImageUrl. These examples use *popflyduck.png*, located in the *website* directory. You can use any image file you want.

Example 4-16. ImageDemo.aspx

```
<%@ Page Language="C#" AutoEventWireup="true"
    CodeFile="ImageDemo.aspx.cs" Inherits="ImageDemo" %>

<!DOCTYPE html PUBLIC "-//W3C//DTD XHTML 1.0 Transitional//EN"
    "http://www.w3.org/TR/xhtml1/DTD/xhtml1-transitional.dtd">

<html xmlns="http://www.w3.org/1999/xhtml">
<head runat="server">
    <title>Image Control Demo</title>
</head>
<body>
    <form id="form1" runat="server">
    <div>
        <p>
            <asp:Image ID="img1" runat="server"
                AlternateText="Popfly Duck" ImageUrl="~/popflyDuck.png" />
            This is a sample paragraph which is being used to demonstrate
            the effects of various values of ImageAlign. As you will see,
            the effects are sometimes difficult to pin down, and vary
            depending on the width of the browser window.
        </p>
        <hr />
        <asp:Button ID="Button1" runat="server" Text="Sample Button" />
        <asp:Image ID="img2" runat="server"
            AlternateText="Popfly Duck" ImageUrl="~/popflyDuck.png" />
        <hr />
        <asp:DropDownList ID="ddlAlign" runat="server"
            AutoPostBack="True">
            <asp:ListItem Text="NotSet" />
            <asp:ListItem Text="AbsBottom" />
            <asp:ListItem Text="AbsMiddle" />
            <asp:ListItem Text="Top" />
            <asp:ListItem Text="Bottom" />
            <asp:ListItem Text="BaseLine" />
            <asp:ListItem Text="TextTop" />
            <asp:ListItem Text="Left" />
            <asp:ListItem Text="Right" />
        </asp:DropDownList>
    </div>
    </form>
</body>
</html>
```

Much like *HyperLinkDemo.aspx*, the ImageAlign property of the two Image controls is set when the page loads, and the DropDownList's AutoPostBack property is set to true so that when a new value is selected from the list the page posts back and the ImageAlign properties are reset. The code that sets the property in *ImageDemo.aspx. cs* appears in Example 4-17. Note that when being set programmatically, the ImageAlign property must be set to one of the predefined ImageAlign enumeration values rather than a simple string.

Example 4-17. The code-behind file in ImageDemo.aspx.cs

```
using System;
using System.Web.UI;
using System.Web.UI.WebControls;

public partial class ImageDemo : Page
{
    protected void Page_Load(object sender, EventArgs e)
    {
        switch (ddlAlign.SelectedIndex)
        {
            case 0:
                img1.ImageAlign = ImageAlign.NotSet;
                img2.ImageAlign = ImageAlign.NotSet;
                break;
            case 1:
                img1.ImageAlign = ImageAlign.AbsBottom;
                img2.ImageAlign = ImageAlign.AbsBottom;
                break;
            case 2:
                img1.ImageAlign = ImageAlign.AbsMiddle;
                img2.ImageAlign = ImageAlign.AbsMiddle;
                break;
            case 3:
                img1.ImageAlign = ImageAlign.Top;
                img2.ImageAlign = ImageAlign.Top;
                break;
            case 4:
                img1.ImageAlign = ImageAlign.Bottom;
                img2.ImageAlign = ImageAlign.Bottom;
                break;
            case 5:
                img1.ImageAlign = ImageAlign.Baseline;
                img2.ImageAlign = ImageAlign.Baseline;
                break;
            case 6:
                img1.ImageAlign = ImageAlign.Middle;
                img2.ImageAlign = ImageAlign.Middle;
                break;
            case 7:
                img1.ImageAlign = ImageAlign.TextTop;
                img2.ImageAlign = ImageAlign.TextTop;
                break;
            case 8:
                img1.ImageAlign = ImageAlign.Left;
                img2.ImageAlign = ImageAlign.Left;
                break;
            case 9:
                img1.ImageAlign = ImageAlign.Right;
                img2.ImageAlign = ImageAlign.Right;
                break;
```

Example 4-17. The code-behind file in ImageDemo.aspx.cs (continued)

```
        default:
            img1.ImageAlign = ImageAlign.NotSet;
            img2.ImageAlign = ImageAlign.NotSet;
            break;
        }
    }
}
```

Figure 4-9 shows this page in action.

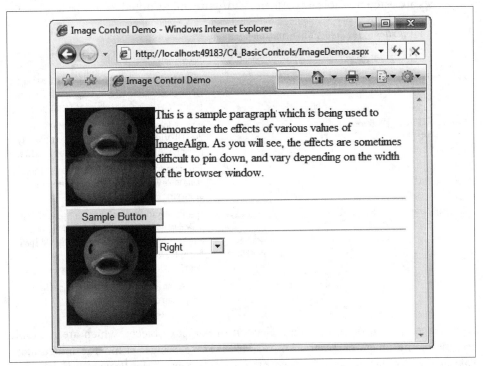

Figure 4-9. ImageDemo.aspx in action

 One of the AJAX Control Toolkit controls, the SlideShow, targets Image controls and uses a web service in the background to replace the image after a period of time with a new image, as its name would suggest.

ImageMap Control

HTML provides the <map> element to define *hotspots* on an image. Each hotspot is a defined area of the image that acts as a hyperlink to another area or website. These are known as *image maps*. The ImageMap server control provides this functionality in ASP.NET. Common uses include:

- An image of a map of the world defining a different URL to navigate to depending on which continent or country the user clicks.
- Allowing a user to change the color scheme and font of a website by clicking different areas of an image representing those choices. The hyperlinks in this case are often to a client-side function which the browser executes instead of navigating to a different URL.

The ImageMap control derives from the Image class, and adds a number of properties and a single event, Click, to that class to provide the image map functionality. These properties are listed in Table 4-9. All are read/write unless noted.

Table 4-9. Properties of the ImageMap control

Name	Type	Values	Description
AlternateText	String		The text will be displayed in the control if the image is unavailable. In browsers that support the ToolTips feature this text is also displayed as a tool tip.
GenerateEmpty-AlternateText	Boolean	true, false	If true, forces an empty alt attribute in the rendered HTML even if the AlternateText property is empty (" ") or not specified. The default is false.
			This property is provided to support the web pages compatible with assistive technology devices, such as screen readers.
HotSpotMode	HotSpotMode	Inactive, Navigate, NotSet, PostBack	Specifies the action taken when a hotspot is clicked. Individual hotspots may specify different modes. Navigate immediately navigates to the URL specified by the NavigateUrlproperty, whereas PostBack causes a postback to the server.
HotSpots	HotSpotCollection		A collection of HotSpot objects contained by the ImageMap control. Read-only.

Each ImageMap control contains a collection of HotSpot objects, which are clickable regions of the image corresponding to HTML <area> tags within the image map. HotSpots will either raise a Click event on the server, if the HotSpotMode is set to PostBack, or immediately navigate to the URL specified by the NavigateUrl property, if the HotSpotMode is set to Navigate.

There are three types of hotspots:

RectangleHotSpot
Defines a rectangular region (in pixels) of the image with Top, Bottom, Left, and Right properties, relative to the upper-left corner of the image

CircleHotSpot
Defines a circular region (in pixels) of the image with X and Y properties specifying the center of the circle, relative to the upper-left corner of the image, and the Radius property specifying the radius of the circle in pixels

PolygonHotSpot

Defines a many-sided region (in pixels) of the image with a comma-separated list of x and y coordinates of endpoints of line segments outlining the region, relative to the upper-left corner of the image

All of the `HotSpot` objects have in common the read/write properties listed in Table 4-10.

Table 4-10. Properties of a HotSpot object

Name	Type	Values	Description
AlternateText	String		The text displayed in the control if the image is unavailable. In browsers that support the ToolTips feature this text is also displayed as a tool tip.
HotSpotMode	HotSpotMode	Inactive, Navigate, NotSet, PostBack	Specifies the action taken when a hotspot is clicked. Individual hotspots may specify different modes. Navigate immediately navigates to the URL specified by the NavigateUrl property, whereas PostBack causes a postback to the server.
NavigateUrl	String		Specifies the URL to navigate to when a hotspot with a HotSpotMode set to Navigate is clicked. Allows either relative or absolute references, as described in the "File Locations" sidebar earlier in this chapter.
PostBackValue	String		The value of the clicked HotSpot object passed by the ImageMapEventArgs event argument. Relevant only if the HotSpotMode is set to PostBack.
Target	String		Specifies the browser window in which the target page will be displayed. The values of the Target property are the same as those listed in Table 4-6 for the HyperLink control. Relevant only if the HotSpotMode is set to Navigate.

To demonstrate all of these properties and the `Click` event, add a new web form called *ImageMapDemo.aspx* to your *C4_BasicControls* website. This web page is shown in Figure 4-10 after the Yes hotspot has been clicked. This example has two image maps. The one at the top of the page contains three rectangular hotspots—Yes, No, and Maybe—and a circular hotspot around a question mark in the image. The second image map has three polygonal hotspots defined: one above the band, one below, and the band itself.

The markup for *ImageMapDemo.aspx* is shown in Example 4-18 and the code-behind file in *ImageMapDemo.aspx.cs* is shown in Example 4-19. The only code of interest in the latter is the event handler method, `imgmapYesNoMaybe_Click` (highlighted), which is executed whenever a hotspot with a `HotSpotMode` set to `PostBack` is clicked.

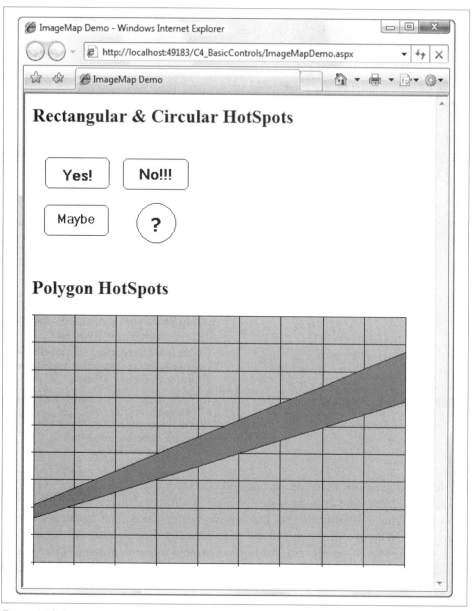

Figure 4-10. ImageMapDemo.aspx in action

 For the code in *ImageMapDemo.aspx* to work correctly, you will need the image files for the ImageMap controls. These examples use *YesNoMaybe.gif* and *plot.gif*, which you'll find in the download folder for this site on *http://www.oreilly.com*.

Example 4-18. ImageMapDemo.aspx

```
<%@ Page Language="C#" AutoEventWireup="true"
   CodeFile="ImageMapDemo.aspx.cs" Inherits="ImageMapDemo" %>

<!DOCTYPE html PUBLIC "-//W3C//DTD XHTML 1.0 Transitional//EN"
   "http://www.w3.org/TR/xhtml1/DTD/xhtml1-transitional.dtd">
<html xmlns="http://www.w3.org/1999/xhtml">
<head runat="server">
   <title>ImageMap Demo</title>
</head>

<body>
   <form id="form1" runat="server">
   <div>
      <h1>Rectangular &amp; Circular HotSpots</h1>
      <asp:ImageMap ID="imgmapYesNoMaybe" runat="server"
         ImageUrl="~/YesNoMaybe.gif" HotSpotMode="Postback"
         OnClick="imgmapYesNoMaybe_Click">
         <asp:RectangleHotSpot PostBackValue="Yes"
            Bottom="60" Top="21" Left="17" Right="103"
            AlternateText="Yes please" />
         <asp:RectangleHotSpot HotSpotMode="PostBack"
            PostBackValue="No" Bottom="60" Top="21"
            Left="122" Right="208" AlternateText="No thanks" />
         <asp:RectangleHotSpot PostBackValue="Maybe" Bottom="122"
            Top="83" Left="16" Right="101"
            AlternateText="Well maybe" />
         <asp:CircleHotSpot HotSpotMode="Navigate" X="165" Y="106"
            Radius="25" NavigateUrl="http://www.ora.com"
            Target="_blank"
            AlternateText="I'll have to think about it." />
      </asp:ImageMap>
      <asp:Label ID="lblMessage" runat="server" />

      <h1>Polygon HotSpots</h1>
      <asp:ImageMap ID="imgmapPlot" runat="server"
         ImageUrl="~/plot.gif" HotSpotMode="PostBack"
         OnClick="imgmapYesNoMaybe_Click">
         <asp:PolygonHotSpot Coordinates="4,245,4,3,495,3,495,45,"
            AlternateText="Above the band"
            PostBackValue="Above the band" />
         <asp:PolygonHotSpot Coordinates="4,245,495,45,495,112,3,264"
            AlternateText="In the band"
            PostBackValue="In the band" />
         <asp:PolygonHotSpot Coordinates="495,45,495,112,495,320,4,320"
            AlternateText="Below the band"
            PostBackValue="Below the band" />
      </asp:ImageMap>
   </div>
   </form>
</body>
</html>
```

Example 4-19. ImageMapDemo.aspx.cs

```
using System;
using System.Web.UI;
using System.Web.UI.WebControls;

public partial class ImageMapDemo : Page
{
    protected void imgmapYesNoMaybe_Click(object sender, ImageMapEventArgs e)
    {
        lblMessage.Text = "The PostBackValue is " + e.PostBackValue;
    }
}
```

In the declaration of the first image map, imgMapYesNoMaybe, an image file is specified, *YesNoMaybe.gif*, which is located in the same directory as the page itself.

The default HotSpotMode for this image map is set to PostBack. The Yes and Maybe hotspots assume this value, the No hotspot explicitly specifies the same value, and the question mark hotspot uses a different HotSpotMode of Navigate. In this last case, the NavigateUrl and Target properties provide direction as to where and how to navigate. For the postback hotspots, the OnClick attribute of the image map binds the Click event to the imgmapYesNoMaybe_Click method contained in the code-behind file, shown highlighted in Example 4-19.

The second image map, imgmapPlot, defines three irregularly shaped hotspots. Each hotspot is defined by a set of x, y coordinates. In this example, the hotspots are simple, with only four straight sides each. In a more typical usage—say, a map of the United States, with each state defined as a hotspot—you might have many dozens of nodes specified. The more nodes there are, the finer and more accurate the hotspot. However, don't go too crazy trying to make the outline perfect, because most users click near the middle of the hotspot, and if they are too close to the edge of the region and get the adjoining region by mistake, they will just click the Back button and try again a little more carefully.

The Click event argument is of type ImageMapEventArgs. It exposes a single public property, PostBackValue. This corresponds to the HotSpot property of the same name declared with each HotSpot in the example. This property is retrieved in the Click event handler in Example 4-19 and is used to populate the Text property of the Label control on the page.

Selecting Values

Several ASP.NET server controls allow the user to select a value or values:

CheckBox

    Allows selection of Boolean data

CheckBoxList
: A group of CheckBox controls that can be dynamically created and bound to a data source

RadioButton
: Allows only a single option to be selected from a group

RadioButtonList
: A group of RadioButton controls that can be dynamically created and bound to a data source

ListBox
: Allows selection of one or more items from a predefined list

DropDownList
: Similar to a ListBox, but allows only a single selection and displays the list only once the user has clicked it

BulletedList
: Formatted with bullets and can be simple text or a link

All of these controls derive from the WebControl class, as shown in Figure 3-8 in Chapter 3. The RadioButton derives further from the CheckBox class, and the list controls all derive from the abstract ListControl class. We consider each of these controls and their AJAX Control Toolkit extenders in detail in upcoming sections. Also included in this section are two standalone AJAX controls, the Slider and Rating controls, which also allow you to select a value.

CheckBox Control

A CheckBox control provides a means for a user to select Boolean data (i.e., Yes/No or True/False). If you have several checkboxes arranged together (not to be confused with a CheckBoxList, discussed next), you can select multiple options. No option is mutually exclusive of another.

The CheckBox and RadioButton controls implement the ICheckBoxControl interface. This interface provides for a single property called Checked, and a single event called CheckedChanged.

CheckBox behavior

To demonstrate the Checked property and CheckedChanged event with respect to a CheckBox control, add to the *C4_BasicControls* website a new web form called *CheckBoxDemo.aspx*. It uses one of three CheckBox controls to control the appearance of a Label control, as shown in Figure 4-11. Clicking any of the checkboxes in this example—Underline?, Overline?, or Strikeout?—imposes that font attribute on the text string in the Label control.

The markup for *CheckBoxDemo.aspx* is shown in Example 4-20.

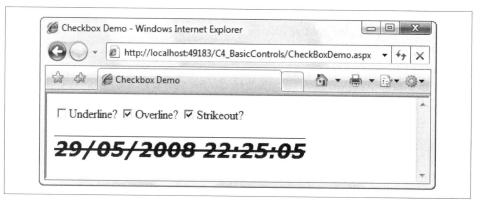

Figure 4-11. CheckBoxDemo.aspx in action

Example 4-20. CheckBoxDemo.aspx

```
<%@ Page Language="C#" AutoEventWireup="true"
    CodeFile="CheckBoxDemo.aspx.cs" Inherits="CheckBoxDemo" %>

<!DOCTYPE html PUBLIC "-//W3C//DTD XHTML 1.0 Transitional//EN"
    "http://www.w3.org/TR/xhtml1/DTD/xhtml1-transitional.dtd">

<html xmlns="http://www.w3.org/1999/xhtml">
<head runat="server">
    <title>Checkbox Demo</title>
</head>
<body>
    <form id="form1" runat="server">
    <div>
        <asp:CheckBox ID="chkUnderline" runat="server"
            Text="Underline?" AutoPostBack="true"
            oncheckedchanged="chkUnderline_CheckedChanged" />
        <asp:CheckBox ID="chkOverline" runat="server"
            Text="Overline?" AutoPostBack="true"
            oncheckedchanged="chkOverline_CheckedChanged" />
        <asp:CheckBox ID="chkStrikeout" runat="server"
            Text="Strikeout?" AutoPostBack="true"
            oncheckedchanged="chkStrikeout_CheckedChanged" />
        <br />
        <br />
        <asp:Label ID="lblTime" runat="server"
            oninit="lblTime_Init" />
    </div>
    </form>
</body>
</html>
```

Each ASP.NET server control in this example, the Label and the three CheckBox controls, has an event handler. The Init event for the Label is handled to set the common format and content (the current date and time) of the label every time the page is posted. The CheckBox controls have their default CheckedChanged event handled.

This event passes a standard `EventArgs` argument, which does not expose any properties.

All these event handler methods are contained in the code-behind file listed in Example 4-21.

Example 4-21. Event handlers in CheckBoxDemo.aspx.cs

```
using System;

public partial class CheckBoxDemo : System.Web.UI.Page
{
    protected void lblTime_Init(object sender, EventArgs e)
    {
        lblTime.Font.Name = "Verdana";
        lblTime.Font.Size = 20;
        lblTime.Font.Bold = true;
        lblTime.Font.Italic = true;
        lblTime.Text = DateTime.Now.ToString( );
    }
    protected void chkUnderline_CheckedChanged
        (object sender, EventArgs e)
    {
        lblTime.Font.Underline = chkUnderline.Checked;
    }

    protected void chkOverline_CheckedChanged
        (object sender, EventArgs e)
    {
        lblTime.Font.Overline = chkOverline.Checked;
    }

    protected void chkStrikeout_CheckedChanged
        (object sender, EventArgs e)
    {
        lblTime.Font.Strikeout = chkStrikeout.Checked;
    }
}
```

When you run *CheckBoxDemo.aspx*, you'll see that each time you check or uncheck a CheckBox, the page will post back, and the text displayed will refresh with the new time and will be underlined, overlined, or ruled through depending on the state of each CheckBox.

Like all controls derived from `WebControl`, CheckBox controls have an ID property. But as the sample code in Example 4-20 shows, several other properties are not inherited from `WebControl`. These are listed in Table 4-11. Some, such as `AutoPostBack` and Text, are common to several other controls. Checked and TextAlign, meanwhile, are specific to the CheckBox class. All are read/write. Table 4-12 lists the CheckBox events.

Table 4-11. CheckBox properties not inherited from WebControl

Name	Type	Values	Description
AutoPostBack	Boolean	true, false	Determines whether automatic postback to the server will occur if the user changes the contents of the control. If false (the default), postback to the server will not occur until the page is posted, either by a button or other postback control or by a control with AutoPostBack set to true.
Checked	Boolean	true, false	Indicates whether the CheckBox control is checked. Default is false.
Text	String		The text label associated with the CheckBox.
TextAlign	TextAlign	Left, Right	Dictates whether the text label is on the left or right of the CheckBox. Default is Right.

Table 4-12. CheckBox events

Name	Description
CheckedChanged	This event is raised when the Checked property is changed. This event will not immediately post back to the server unless AutoPostBack is set to true.

CheckBox extenders

The AJAX Control Toolkit contains two extender controls that specifically target CheckBox controls:

ToggleButtonExtender

    Allows you to replace the checkbox graphic with your own custom graphics to indicate whether it has been checked or not

MutuallyExclusiveCheckBoxExtender

    Allows you to specify a group of CheckBoxes from which only one can be selected at any time

To demonstrate how you can use these together, the next example extends *CheckBoxDemo.aspx*, replacing the Strikeout? checkbox with our own graphics and making the Underline? and Overline? checkboxes mutually exclusive. Figure 4-12 shows the net result.

Add to the *C4_BasicControls* website a new AJAX web form called *CheckBoxDemoWithAJAX.aspx*. Add the highlighted code from Example 4-20 to *CheckBoxDemoWithAJAX.aspx* under the ScriptManager control, and add all the event handler code highlighted in Example 4-21 to *CheckBoxDemoWithAJAX.aspx.cs*.

To use the ToggleButtonExtender, you'll need to add to the website one graphic to represent an unchecked CheckBox and another to represent a checked CheckBox. If you have none on hand, try using *ToggleButton_Checked.gif* and *ToggleButton_Unchecked.gif* from the AJAX Control Toolkit sample website in the *ToggleButton* directory. With that done, drag a ToggleButtonExtender onto the page beneath the three CheckBoxes. It has five mandatory properties to set, as listed in Table 4-13.

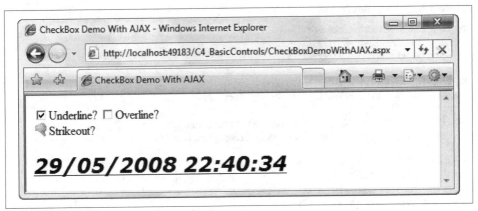

Figure 4-12. CheckBoxDemoWithAJAX.aspx in action

Table 4-13. ToggleButtonExtender mandatory properties

Name	Type	Description
CheckedImageUrl	String	The location of the image representing a checked CheckBox
ImageHeight	Integer	The height of the image
ImageWidth	Integer	The width of the image
TargetControlId	String	The ID of the CheckBox control being extended
UncheckedImageUrl	String	The location of the image representing an unchecked CheckBox

The ToggleButtonExtender has several more optional properties, listed in Table 4-14, which cover such circumstances as what happens when the CheckBox is disabled and alternative text for each image.

Table 4-14. ToggleButtonExtender optional properties

Name	Type	Description
CheckedImageAlternateText	String	Alternative text for screen readers describing the image for CheckedImageUrl
DisabledCheckedImageUrl	String	The location of the image representing a checked CheckBox that has been disabled on-screen
DisabledUncheckedImageUrl	String	The location of the image representing an unchecked CheckBox that has been disabled on-screen
UncheckedImageAlternateText	String	Alternative text for screen readers describing the image for UncheckedImageUrl

Set the ToggleControlExtender properties as highlighted in Example 4-22 and run the page to see how images now take the place of the standard checkbox.

Example 4-22. CheckBoxDemoWithAJAX.aspx

```
<%@ Page Language="C#" AutoEventWireup="true"
   CodeFile="CheckBoxDemoWithAJAX.aspx.cs"
   Inherits="CheckBoxDemoWithAJAX" %>

<%@ Register Assembly="AjaxControlToolkit"
   Namespace="AjaxControlToolkit" TagPrefix="cc1" %>

<!DOCTYPE html PUBLIC "-//W3C//DTD XHTML 1.0 Transitional//EN"
   "http://www.w3.org/TR/xhtml1/DTD/xhtml1-transitional.dtd">

<html xmlns="http://www.w3.org/1999/xhtml">
<head runat="server">
   <title>CheckBox Demo With AJAX</title>
   <script type="text/javascript">
      function pageLoad( ) {
      }
   </script>
</head>

<body>
   <form id="form1" runat="server">
   <div>
      <asp:ScriptManager ID="ScriptManager1" runat="server" />
      <asp:CheckBox ID="chkUnderline" runat="server"
         Text="Underline?" AutoPostBack="true"
         oncheckedchanged="chkUnderline_CheckedChanged" />
      <asp:CheckBox ID="chkOverline" runat="server"
         Text="Overline?" AutoPostBack="true"
         oncheckedchanged="chkOverline_CheckedChanged" />
      <asp:CheckBox ID="chkStrikeout" runat="server"
         Text="Strikeout?" AutoPostBack="true"
         oncheckedchanged="chkStrikeout_CheckedChanged" />

      <cc1:ToggleButtonExtender ID="ToggleButtonExtender1"
         runat="server" TargetControlID="chkStrikeout"
         CheckedImageUrl="ToggleButton_Checked.gif"
         CheckedImageAlternateText="Disable Strikeout"
         UncheckedImageUrl="togglebutton_unchecked.gif"
         UncheckedImageAlternateText="Enable Strikeout"
         ImageWidth="19" ImageHeight="19" />

      <cc1:MutuallyExclusiveCheckBoxExtender
         ID="MutuallyExclusiveCheckBoxExtender1" runat="server"
         targetControlId="chkUnderline" Key="Decoration" />
      <cc1:MutuallyExclusiveCheckBoxExtender
         ID="MutuallyExclusiveCheckBoxExtender2" runat="server"
         targetControlId="chkOverline" Key="Decoration" />

      <br />
      <br />
```

Example 4-22. CheckBoxDemoWithAJAX.aspx (continued)

```
        <asp:Label ID="lblTime" runat="server" OnInit="lblTime_Init" />
    </div>
    </form>
</body>
</html>
```

Next, you need to make the chkOverline and chkUnderline boxes mutually exclusive using MutuallyExclusiveCheckBoxExtender (MECBE) controls. Drag an MECBE onto the page under the ToggleButtonExtender. Set its TargetControlID to chkUnderline. Now add a second MECBE to the page under the first. Set its TargetControlId to chkOverline. Make the two checkboxes mutually exclusive by giving both MECBEs the same Key value—it doesn't actually matter what value you use as long as it isn't the same as another Key group name on the page. In Example 4-22, it's set to Decoration.

Now run the page. Note how you can't add overlines and underlines to the label at the same time. Furthermore, if you do try to do so, the Label updates correctly when one box is checked, and the other is unselected automatically.

RadioButton Control

A RadioButton control is very similar to, and in fact is derived from, a CheckBox control. The essential difference between the two classes is that RadioButton controls are typically grouped using the GroupName property, and only one RadioButton in the group can be checked (i.e., its Checked property is true) at one time. Changing the Checked property of one RadioButton control in the group to true changes the Checked property of all other controls in the group to false. In addition, radio buttons typically display as round, as opposed to the square checkboxes.

If you compare and contrast a RadioButton with a CheckBox extended with an MECBE, you might not perceive any difference between the two. But consider the case where you have two groups of RadioButtons on a page and you need to ensure that a particular choice in one group precludes a selection in the other group while others do not. MECBEs can work *across* the RadioButton groups as required.

To demonstrate, add a new web form called *RadioButtonDemo.aspx* to your *C4_BasicControls* website. This page contains three RadioButton controls to set the font size of a label. Each radio button is part of the group grpSize and all are set to post back when selected. The markup for *RadioButtonDemo.aspx* is shown in Example 4-23.

Example 4-23. RadioButtonDemo.aspx

```
<%@ Page Language="C#" AutoEventWireup="true"
    CodeFile="RadioButtonDemo.aspx.cs" Inherits="RadioButtonDemo" %>

<!DOCTYPE html PUBLIC "-//W3C//DTD XHTML 1.0 Transitional//EN"
    "http://www.w3.org/TR/xhtml1/DTD/xhtml1-transitional.dtd">

<html xmlns="http://www.w3.org/1999/xhtml">
<head runat="server">
    <title>RadioButton Demo</title>
</head>

<body>
    <form id="form1" runat="server">
    <div>
        <asp:RadioButton ID="rdoSize10" runat="server" Text="10pt"
            GroupName="grpSize" AutoPostBack="true"
            OnCheckedChanged="grpSize_CheckedChanged" />
        <asp:RadioButton ID="rdoSize14" runat="server" Text="14pt"
            GroupName="grpSize" AutoPostBack="true"
            OnCheckedChanged="grpSize_CheckedChanged" />
        <asp:RadioButton ID="rdoSize16" runat="server" Text="16pt"
            GroupName="grpSize" AutoPostBack="true"
            OnCheckedChanged="grpSize_CheckedChanged" />
        <br />
        <br />
        <asp:Label ID="lblTime" runat="server" OnInit="lblTime_Init" />
    </div>
    </form>
</body>
</html>
```

You can see in Example 4-23 that all three RadioButton controls name the same method, grpSize_CheckedChanged, to handle their CheckedChanged event. This method, plus another to set the text and initial font attributes for the Label control, is saved in the code-behind file for the page, *RadioButtonDemo.aspx.cs*, listed in Example 4-24.

Example 4-24. RadioButtonDemo.aspx.cs

```
using System;
using System.Web.UI;

public partial class RadioButtonDemo : Page
{
    protected void grpSize_CheckedChanged(object sender, EventArgs e)
    {
        if (rdoSize10.Checked)
            lblTime.Font.Size = 10;
        else if (rdoSize14.Checked)
            lblTime.Font.Size = 14;
        else
            lblTime.Font.Size = 16;
    }
```

Example 4-24. RadioButtonDemo.aspx.cs (continued)

```
protected void lblTime_Init(object sender, EventArgs e)
{
    lblTime.Font.Name = "Verdana";
    lblTime.Font.Size = 20;
    lblTime.Font.Bold = true;
    lblTime.Font.Italic = true;
    lblTime.Text = DateTime.Now.ToString( );
}
}
```

The result of running it is shown in Figure 4-13.

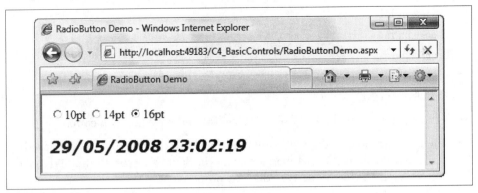

Figure 4-13. RadioButtonDemo.aspx in action

Note that the grpSize_CheckedChanged method uses an if...else block to change the text size depending on which button is selected, but there are several ways to achieve the same end here. For example, you could use a C# switch statement to make it easier to add additional radio buttons in the future:

```
protected void grpSize_CheckedChanged(object sender, EventArgs e)
{
    RadioButton rb = (RadioButton)sender;

    switch (rb.ID)
    {
        case "rdoSize10":
            lblTime.Font.Size = 10;
            break;
        case "rdoSize14":
            lblTime.Font.Size = 14;
            break;
        case "rdoSize16":
            lblTime.Font.Size = 16;
            break;
    }
}
```

You could even replace the switch statement in this example with a much shorter statement:

```
lblTime.Font.Size = new FontUnit(rb.Text);
```

However, this line works only because the Text property for the Checkbox controls has been set to values which are also valid as values for Font.Size.

Selecting from a List

ASP.NET provides five server controls for selecting single or multiple items from a list:

- BulletedList
- CheckBoxList
- DropDownList
- ListBox
- RadioButtonList

All of these controls are derived from ListControl and have much in common:

- The ListItem object (the object that encapsulates the information displayed by individual items in the list) works exactly the same way for all the ListControl objects, with a Value property and a Text property.

- The Items property of the control contains the collection of all the ListItems.

- ListItem objects can be added to the Items collection either statically, that is, declaratively in the content file, programmatically through the Add method, or from a data source.

  You can access the Data Source Configuration Wizard or the ListItem Collection Editor dialog box by clicking the control's smart tag, the little icon in the upper-right corner of the control.

- The SelectedIndex and SelectedItem properties of the control point to the selected item with the lowest index. For single-select controls, such as the DropDownList, the RadioButtonList, and the ListBox (if the SelectionMode property is set to ListSelectionMode.Single, the default value), the selected index is the lowest index by definition. For multiselect controls, such as CheckBoxList and the ListBox with the SelectionMode property set to ListSelectionMode. Multiple, these properties will refer to the selected item with the lowest index. To discover any other selected items, you'll need to iterate through the control's Items collection and test the Selected property of each ListItem therein.

- The SelectedValue property of the control retrieves or specifies the value of the selected item.

- The `AppendDataBoundItems` property of the control allows items added through data binding (described in Chapter 8) to be added to the `Items` collection, rather than replacing the `Items` collection, which is the default behavior. This is useful if you want to add a value statically—such as the text "(Select a value)"—and then add the remaining items by using data binding.
- All five controls raise and respond to the `SelectedIndexChanged` event.

The `ListBox` and `DropDownList` controls differ from the other list controls (`BulletedList`, `CheckBoxList`, and `RadioButtonList`) in that they appear to the user to be a single control (a listbox or a drop-down list) rather than a collection of links, buttons, or checkboxes. The `ListBox` and `DropDownList` controls lend themselves to longer lists because they scroll.

Table 4-15 summarizes the differences among the five list controls.

Table 4-15. Differences among the five list controls

Characteristic	BulletedList	CheckBoxList	RadioButtonList	DropDownList	ListBox
Single selection only	✗		✗	✗	
Able to select more than one item		✗			✗
Displays the entire list by default	✗	✗	✗		✗ (using a vertical scroll bar if necessary)
Displays a single item at a time, along with a button for seeing the entire list				✗	
Best for short lists	✗	✗	✗		
Best for long lists				✗	✗

The following sections describe the controls and objects related to selecting items from a list.

ListItem Object

As mentioned earlier, all five server controls are derived from the `ListControl` class. A `ListControl` control contains a collection of `ListItem` objects called `Items`. Each `ListItem` object has four read/write properties, detailed in Table 4-16.

Table 4-16. Properties of the ListItem object

Name	Type	Description
Enabled	Boolean	If set to `false`, makes an item invisible when the list is displayed, although it remains in the `Items` collection.
Selected	Boolean	A value indicating whether the item has been selected or not.

Table 4-16. Properties of the ListItem object (continued)

Name	Type	Description
Text	String	The text string displayed for a ListItem.
Value	String	A value associated with a ListItem. The value is not displayed, but it is available programmatically.

When dealing with lists, displaying one thing to the user but passing something different to your code is common. For example, if you're presenting your users with a list of states, the list might display state names, such as Massachusetts. But when your users select an item, the program will pass the selected item as MA. Massachusetts would be the ListItem object's Text property, and MA would be the Value property. This comes in handy, for example, when translating the site into another language. In this case, you need only translate the contents of the Text property and leave the Value property alone:

```
<asp:ListItem value="air">By air</asp:ListItem>
<asp:ListItem value="air">Par avion</asp:ListItem>
<asp:ListItem value="air" text="Auf dem Luftweg" />
```

If only the Text property is set for a ListItem, the same value is also used for the Value property of the ListItem:

```
<asp:ListItem>Item 7</asp:ListItem>
<asp:ListItem text="Item 7"></asp:ListItem>
<asp:ListItem text="Item 7"/>
```

If both a Text property and inner HTML content are specified, the inner HTML content will be displayed. For example, consider the following line:

```
<asp:ListItem text="Item 7">Item 8</asp:ListItem>
```

If you used that line, "Item 8" would be displayed on the web page.

CheckBoxList Control

The CheckBoxList is a parent control containing a collection of CheckBox items. It is very similar to the group of CheckBox controls shown previously in *CheckBoxDemo.aspx* in Figure 4-11, except all the child checkboxes are handled as a group. The CheckBoxList control derives from ListControl rather than directly from WebControl.

The CheckBoxList control is better suited than individual checkboxes for creating a series of checkboxes out of data from a database, although either type of control can be bound to data. Chapter 8 discusses data binding.

There are three ways to add items to the Items collection of a CheckBoxList:

- Declaratively using the <asp:ListItem> control element
- Programmatically from an array or other collection
- Dynamically from a data source such as a database

Adding items declaratively

To demonstrate how to add list items declaratively in the content file, add a new web form called *CheckBoxList-DeclarativeItems.aspx* to your *C4_BasicControls* website. You'll also use some of the CheckBoxList control's properties to set its appearance and behavior.

Drag a CheckBoxList control onto the page from the Toolbox and then, in Source view, add six list items as shown in Example 4-25.

Example 4-25. CheckBoxList-DeclarativeItems.aspx

```
<%@ Page Language="C#" AutoEventWireup="true"
    CodeFile="CheckBoxList-DeclarativeItems.aspx.cs"
    Inherits="CheckBoxList_DeclarativeItems" %>

<!DOCTYPE html PUBLIC "-//W3C//DTD XHTML 1.0 Transitional//EN"
    "http://www.w3.org/TR/xhtml1/DTD/xhtml1-transitional.dtd">

<html xmlns="http://www.w3.org/1999/xhtml">
<head runat="server">
    <title>CheckBoxList Demo - Declaring Items Individually</title>
</head>

<body>
    <form id="form1" runat="server">
    <div>
        <asp:CheckBoxList ID="cblItems" runat="server"
            RepeatDirection="Horizontal" RepeatColumns="2"
            RepeatLayout="Flow">
            <asp:ListItem>Item 1</asp:ListItem>
            <asp:ListItem>Item 2</asp:ListItem>
            <asp:ListItem>Item 3</asp:ListItem>
            <asp:ListItem>Item 4</asp:ListItem>
            <asp:ListItem>Item 5</asp:ListItem>
            <asp:ListItem>Item 6</asp:ListItem>
        </asp:CheckBoxList>
    </div>
    </form>
</body>
</html>
```

Because no events are handled in this page, and hence no event handlers, there are no additions to be made to the code-behind file, *CheckBoxList-DeclarativeItems.aspx.cs*. When you run the page, you'll see that the six list items have been split alternately into two columns, as shown in Figure 4-14. This is because the list's RepeatColumns property is set to 2 and the RepeatDirection property is set to Horizontal.

The CheckBoxList has a number of properties that determine how the items in the list are displayed on the page. These and other key read/write properties appear in Table 4-17.

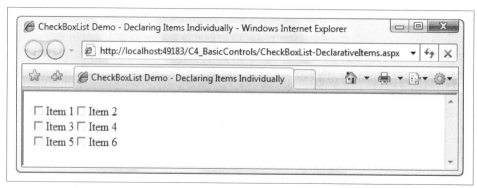

Figure 4-14. CheckBoxList-DeclarativeItems.aspx in action

Table 4-17. Properties of the CheckBoxList control

Name	Type	Values	Description
AutoPostBack	Boolean	true, false	Determines whether automatic postback to the server will occur if the user changes the contents of the control. If false, postback to the server will not occur until the page is posted, either by a button or by another control with AutoPostBack set to true. Its default value is false.
CellPadding	Integer	Integer	Distance in pixels between the border and contents of a cell. The default is -1, which indicates the property is not set.
CellSpacing	Integer	Integer	Distance in pixels between the border and contents of a cell. The default is -1, which indicates the property is not set.
DataSource	Object		Source that populates the control.
RepeatColumns	Integer	Integer	Number of columns to display.
RepeatDirection		Horizontal, Vertical	Horizontal specifies that items are loaded from left to right, and then top to bottom. Vertical specifies items are loaded top to bottom, and then left to right. Default is Vertical.
RepeatLayout		Flow, Table	Flow specifies items are displayed without a table structure. Table specifies that items are displayed in a table structure. Default is Table.
Selected	Boolean	true, false	Indicates that a list item has been selected. Default is false.
TextAlign	TextAlign	Left, Right	Dictates whether the text label is on the left or right of the checkboxes. Default is Right.

You can manually type the ListItem objects into the content file (IntelliSense will help minimize the typing), or you can use the Collection Editor. To use the Collection Editor, select the CheckBoxList in Design view, click the smart tag (the little icon in the upper-right corner of the control in Design view), and select Edit Items from the Smart Tag menu. The dialog box shown in Figure 4-15 will appear. Use this dialog box to add or remove ListItem objects and change their properties.

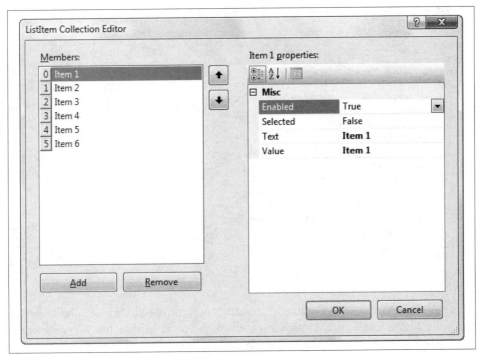

Figure 4-15. The ListItem Collection Editor

Adding items programmatically from an array or collection

Sometimes you do not know at design time what checkboxes you want to create. For example, you may want your program to populate the list depending on the value of other controls on the page. In these cases, you need to be able to add items to the Items collection programmatically.

To demonstrate, add a new web form called *CheckBoxList-ArrayItems.aspx* to your *C4_BasicControls* website. In this example, ListItem objects are added both declaratively, just like the previous example, and programmatically in the code-behind page. Indeed, the markup for *CheckBoxList-ArrayItems.aspx* is exactly the same as the previous example, with the single exception of a new line, highlighted in Example 4-26.

Example 4-26. CheckBoxList-ArrayItems.aspx

```
<%@ Page Language="C#" AutoEventWireup="true"
    CodeFile="CheckBoxList-ArrayItems.aspx.cs"
    Inherits="CheckBoxList_ArrayItems" %>

<!DOCTYPE html PUBLIC "-//W3C//DTD XHTML 1.0 Transitional//EN"
    "http://www.w3.org/TR/xhtml1/DTD/xhtml1-transitional.dtd">

<html xmlns="http://www.w3.org/1999/xhtml">
<head runat="server">
```

Example 4-26. CheckBoxList-ArrayItems.aspx (continued)

```
      <title>CheckBoxListDemo - Populating Items From An Array</title>
</head>
<body>
   <form id="form1" runat="server">
   <div>
      <asp:CheckBoxList ID="cblItems" runat="server"
         RepeatDirection="Horizontal" RepeatColumns="2"
         RepeatLayout="Flow"
         oninit="cblItems_Init">
         <asp:ListItem>Item 1</asp:ListItem>
         <asp:ListItem>Item 2</asp:ListItem>
         <asp:ListItem>Item 3</asp:ListItem>
         <asp:ListItem>Item 4</asp:ListItem>
         <asp:ListItem>Item 5</asp:ListItem>
         <asp:ListItem>Item 6</asp:ListItem>
      </asp:CheckBoxList>
   </div>
   </form>
</body>
</html>
```

This new line is the key to the page, assigning an event handler for the CheckBoxList control's Init event which is implemented in the code-behind file, *CheckBoxList-ArrayItems.aspx.cs*, the highlighted code in Example 4-26. This method creates a string array of book categories to add to the list of checkboxes and then uses a foreach loop to iterate through the array to add them to the list. In each iteration of the loop, a new ListItem object is created and added to the Items collection of the CheckBoxList control. The code in full is highlighted in Example 4-27.

Example 4-27. The code-behind file, CheckBoxList-ArrayItems.aspx.cs

```
using System;
using System.Web.UI;
using System.Web.UI.WebControls;

public partial class CheckBoxList_ArrayItems : Page
{
   protected void cblItems_Init(object sender, EventArgs e)
   {
      // create an array of items to add
      string[] Categories =
         { "SciFi", "Fiction", "Computers", "History", "Religion" };
      foreach (string category in Categories)
      {
         cblItems.Items.Add(new ListItem(category));
      }
   }
}
```

When you run the page, you'll see that the list items added programmatically come after those added declaratively, as shown in Figure 4-16.

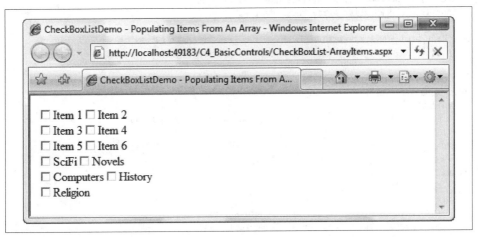

Figure 4-16. CheckBoxList-ArrayItems.aspx in action

You can modify the code in Examples 4-26 and 4-27 to add Value properties for some of the ListItems created in the CheckBoxList declaration, as well as in all the ListItem objects created in the cblItems_Init event procedure. This is demonstrated in *CheckBoxList-ArrayItemsAndValues.aspx*, copied from *CheckBoxList-ArrayItems.aspx* and modified. The resultant web page is shown in Figure 4-17.

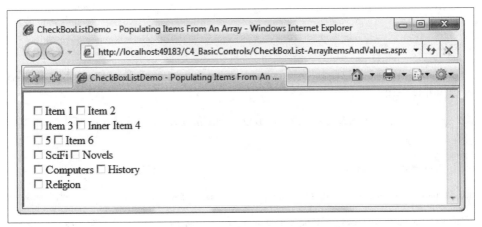

Figure 4-17. CheckBoxList-ArrayItemsAndValues.aspx in action

The markup for *CheckBoxList-ArrayItemsAndValues.aspx* is listed in Example 4-28; the highlighted lines of code are the ones that differ from Example 4-26.

Example 4-28. CheckBoxList-ArrayItemsAndValues.aspx

```
<%@ Page Language="C#" AutoEventWireup="true"
    CodeFile="CheckBoxList-ArrayItemsAndValues.aspx.cs"
    Inherits="CheckBoxList_ArrayItemsAndValues" %>

<!DOCTYPE html PUBLIC "-//W3C//DTD XHTML 1.0 Transitional//EN"
    "http://www.w3.org/TR/xhtml1/DTD/xhtml1-transitional.dtd">

<html xmlns="http://www.w3.org/1999/xhtml">
<head runat="server">
    <title>
        CheckBoxListDemo - Populating Items and Values From An Array
    </title>
</head>

<body>
    <form id="form1" runat="server">
    <div>
        <asp:CheckBoxList ID="cblItems" runat="server"
            RepeatDirection="Horizontal" RepeatColumns="2"
            RepeatLayout="Flow"
            oninit="cblItems_Init">
            <asp:ListItem Value="1">Item 1</asp:ListItem>
            <asp:ListItem Value="2" Text="Item 2" />
            <asp:ListItem Text="Item 3" />
            <asp:ListItem Text="Item 4">Inner Item 4</asp:ListItem>
            <asp:ListItem Value="5"></asp:ListItem>
            <asp:ListItem>Item 6</asp:ListItem>
        </asp:CheckBoxList>
    </div>
    </form>
</body>
</html>
```

The changes to the cblItems_Init event handler from Example 4-27 are highlighted in Example 4-29.

Example 4-29. The code-behind file, CheckBoxList-ArrayItemsAndValues.aspx.cs

```
using System;
using System.Web.UI;
using System.Web.UI.WebControls;

public partial class CheckBoxList_ArrayItemsAndValues : Page
{
    protected void cblItems_Init(object sender, EventArgs e)
    {
        // create an array of items to add
        string[] Categories =
            { "SciFi", "Fiction", "Computers", "History", "Religion" };
        string[] Code =
            { "sf", "nvl", "cmp", "his", "rel" };
```

Example 4-29. The code-behind file, CheckBoxList-ArrayItemsAndValues.aspx.cs (continued)

```
    for (int i=0; i<Categories.Length; i++)
    {
        cblItems.Items.Add(new ListItem(Categories[i], Code[i]));
    }
  }
}
```

In `cblItems_Init`, listed in Example 4-29, where you previously created a single string array to hold the `Text` properties, there are now two string arrays: one for the `Text` properties and one for the `Value` properties. You now use the overloaded `Add` method, passing in a single argument consisting of a `ListItem` object and a `for` loop rather than a `foreach` loop to iterate through both arrays in a single iteration.

> An object may overload its methods, which means it may declare two or more methods with the same name. The compiler differentiates among these methods based on the number and type of parameters provided.
>
> For example, the `ListItemCollection` class overloads the `Add` method. One version takes a string, and the other version takes a `ListItem` object.

Finally, in creating the static `ListItems`, you used several different methods of creating `Values` and `Text`, including instances of missing `Text` (Item 5), missing `Values` (Item 3, Item 4, Item 6), and a divergent `Text` property from inner HTML content (Item 4). The differences between Figures 4-16 and 4-17 can be seen in Items 4 and 5.

You can see that if the `Value` is missing, the `Text` is displayed. If the `Text` is missing, the `Value` will be displayed. If the `Text` is different from the inner HTML content, the inner HTML content will be displayed.

Adding items from a data source

The real power of adding items programmatically comes when you can use a data source to populate the items in a `CheckBoxList` control. The ultimate data source, obviously, is a database. We will cover how to bind information from a database into your controls in Chapters 7 through 10. However, you can use the array we just created to demonstrate binding to a data source.

Add to your *C4_BasicControls* website a new page called *CheckBoxList-ArrayItemsDataBind.aspx*, and copy the code for the previous example to it. Modify only the `cblItems_Init` event handler method in the code-behind file. Replacing the `for` loop and second array in `cblItems_Init` in Example 4-29 with two lines of code (which specify the data source and then bind to it), the method now appears as shown in Example 4-30.

Example 4-30. The code-behind file, CheckBoxList-ArrayItemsDataBind.aspx.cs

```
using System;
using System.Web.UI;
using System.Web.UI.WebControls;

public partial class CheckBoxList_ArrayItemsDataBind : Page
{
    protected void cblItems_Init(object sender, EventArgs e)
    {
        // create an array of items to add
        string[] Categories =
            { "SciFi", "Novels", "Computers", "History", "Religion" };
        cblItems.DataSource = Categories;
        cblItems.DataBind();
    }
}
```

You might expect the results to be unchanged from Figure 4-17, but that is not the case. Instead, you get the results shown in Figure 4-18.

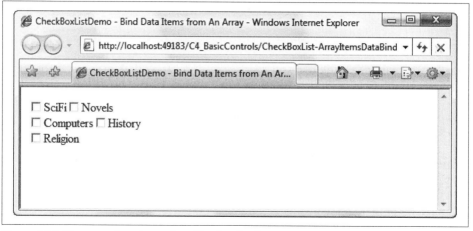

Figure 4-18. Unexpected results produced by data binding

In the previous example, using the for loop, ListItems were added by the Init method after the control was created. In this example, the preexisting ListItem objects were replaced by the new data source because the ListControl.Items collection is initialized by the data source, so any previously defined ListItem objects are lost.

That is the default behavior when data binding to a ListControl object. However, you can set the AppendDataBoundItems property of the control to true, in which case the data-bound items will be *added* to the existing Items collection, rather than *replacing* the existing Items collection.

Responding to user selections

When a user checks or unchecks one of the checkboxes in a CheckBoxList, the SelectedIndexChanged event is raised. This event passes an argument of type EventArgs, which does not expose any properties. By handling this event, you can respond to the user selection on one of the checkboxes. As with most ASP.NET server controls, if AutoPostBack is set to true the response occurs immediately. Otherwise, the response occurs the next time the form is posted to the server.

To see this, copy the previous example to a new page, *CheckBoxList-RespondingToEvents.aspx*, and then add the highlighted code from the content file in Example 4-31.

Example 4-31. CheckBoxList-RespondingToEvents.aspx

```
<%@ Page Language="C#" AutoEventWireup="true"
    CodeFile="CheckBoxList-RespondingToEvents.aspx.cs"
    Inherits="CheckBoxList_RespondingToEvents" %>

<!DOCTYPE html PUBLIC "-//W3C//DTD XHTML 1.0 Transitional//EN"
    "http://www.w3.org/TR/xhtml1/DTD/xhtml1-transitional.dtd">

<html xmlns="http://www.w3.org/1999/xhtml">
<head runat="server">
    <title>CheckBoxList - Responding To Events</title>
</head>

<body>
    <form id="form1" runat="server">
    <div>
      <asp:CheckBoxList ID="cblItems" runat="server"
          oninit="cblItems_Init" AutoPostBack="true"
          OnSelectedIndexChanged="cblItems_SelectedIndexChanged">
          <asp:ListItem>Item 1</asp:ListItem>
          <asp:ListItem>Item 2</asp:ListItem>
          <asp:ListItem>Item 3</asp:ListItem>
          <asp:ListItem>Item 4</asp:ListItem>
          <asp:ListItem>Item 5</asp:ListItem>
          <asp:ListItem>Item 6</asp:ListItem>
      </asp:CheckBoxList>
        <asp:Label ID="lblCategory" runat="server"></asp:Label>
    </div>
    </form>
</body>
</html>
```

You'll also need to add a new method to handle the event in the code-behind file, *CheckBoxList-RespondingToEvents.aspx.cs*, as highlighted in Example 4-32. This method checks to see whether any items are selected. If no items are selected, the method sets the Label control with an appropriate message. If at least one item is selected, the method iterates over all the items in the CheckBoxList and builds up a string indicating which items are checked, to be displayed by the Label.

Example 4-32. CheckBoxList-RespondingToEvents.aspx.cs

```csharp
using System;
using System.Text;
using System.Web.UI;
using System.Web.UI.WebControls;

public partial class CheckBoxList_RespondingToEvents : Page
{
   protected void cblItems_Init(object sender, EventArgs e)
   {
      // create an array of items to add
      string[] Genre =
         { "SciFi", "Fiction", "Computers", "History", "Religion" };
      cblItems.DataSource = Genre;
      cblItems.DataBind( );
   }

   protected void cblItems_SelectedIndexChanged
      (object sender, EventArgs e)
   {
      if (cblItems.SelectedItem == null)
      {
         lblCategory.Text = "<br />No genres selected.";
      }
      else
      {
         StringBuilder sb = new StringBuilder( );

         foreach (ListItem li in cblItems.Items)
         {
            if (li.Selected)
            {
               sb.Append("<br/>" + li.Value + " - " + li.Text);
            }
         }
         lblCategory.Text = sb.ToString( );
      }
   }
}
```

When you run this page you'll see how it responds to your selecting and deselecting checkboxes in the list, as shown in Figure 4-19.

Note that you used the StringBuilder class in cblGenre_SelectedIndexChanged to create the string, rather than concatenating each string value onto the previous value, as in this line of C# code:

```csharp
str += "<br/>" + li.Value + " - " + li.Text;
```

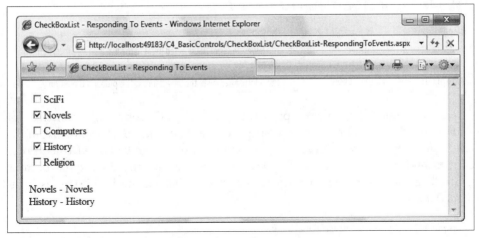

Figure 4-19. CheckBoxList_RespondingToEvents.aspx in action

This is the preferred approach to building up a string because when you write the following code, it only appears as though you are concatenating the second part of the string onto firstString:

```
String firstString = "Hello";
firstString += " world";
```

What is actually happening, however, is that a second string is being allocated and assigned to your string reference, and the first string is being destroyed. If you do this a lot (e.g., in a tight loop), it is very inefficient because creating and destroying the string objects are time-consuming operations. The StringBuilder class provides a more efficient way of constructing strings, because it does not require that a new string be created with every modification. Once the string has been constructed in the StringBuilder, you then call its ToString( ) method to retrieve it, as we demonstrated in Example 4-32:

```
lblCategory.Text = sb.ToString( );
```

RadioButtonList Control

The RadioButtonList control is very similar to the CheckBoxList control. Both are derived from the ListControl class and share all of the same properties, events, and methods. The only difference between the two (aside from the round versus square shape) is that the RadioButtonList control can have only one item selected at a time. When an item is selected, any other selected item is deselected.

The RadioButtonList and the CheckBoxList controls share two properties inherited from ListControl, shown in Table 4-18.

Table 4-18. Selection properties inherited from the ListControl class

Name	Type	Description
SelectedIndex	Integer	The lowest index of the selected items in the list. If equal to -1, nothing was selected.
SelectedItem	ListItem	The selected item with the lowest index. This property is read-only.

To demonstrate how these properties are useful, copy the contents of *RadioButtonDemo.aspx* to a new web page, called *RadioButtonListDemo.aspx*, in the *C4_BasicControls* website. Also copy the contents of the *RadioButtonDemo.aspx.cs* code-behind file to *RadioButtonListDemo.aspx.cs*. Replace the three radio buttons controlling the font size with a single RadioButtonList, calling it rblSize, as highlighted in Example 4-33.

Example 4-33. RadioButtonListDemo.aspx

```
<%@ Page Language="C#" AutoEventWireup="true"
    CodeFile="RadioButtonListDemo.aspx.cs"
    Inherits="RadioButtonListDemo" %>

<!DOCTYPE html PUBLIC "-//W3C//DTD XHTML 1.0 Transitional//EN"
    "http://www.w3.org/TR/xhtml1/DTD/xhtml1-transitional.dtd">

<html xmlns="http://www.w3.org/1999/xhtml">
<head runat="server">
    <title>RadioButtonList Demo</title>
</head>

<body>
    <form id="form1" runat="server">
    <div>
       <asp:RadioButtonList ID="rblSize" runat="server"
          AutoPostBack="true"
          onselectedindexchanged="rblSize_SelectedIndexChanged">
          <asp:ListItem Text="10pt" Value="10" />
          <asp:ListItem Text="14pt" Value="14" />
          <asp:ListItem Text="16pt" Value="16" />
       </asp:RadioButtonList>
       <br />
       <br />
       <asp:Label ID="lblTime" runat="server" OnInit="lblTime_Init" />
    </div>
    </form>
</body>
</html>
```

The code-behind file for this page also needs a few changes, as highlighted in Example 4-34. Instead of a handler for the CheckedChanged event of each individual RadioButton, you now need a handler for the SelectedIndexChanged event of the RadioButtonList. When this event is raised and the page posts back to the server, the method checks the RadioButtonList control's SelectedIndex property to see whether any of the items in the list have been selected and then uses the Value of that item to set the font size of the text in the Label. If no item has been selected, the SelectedIndex property is equal to -1. If an item has been selected, SelectedIndex will be greater than -1.

Example 4-34. RadioButtonListDemo.aspx.cs

```
using System;
using System.Web.UI;

public partial class RadioButtonListDemo : Page
{
    protected void lblTime_Init(object sender, EventArgs e)
    {
        lblTime.Font.Name = "Verdana";
        lblTime.Font.Size = 20;
        lblTime.Font.Bold = true;
        lblTime.Font.Italic = true;
        lblTime.Text = DateTime.Now.ToString();
    }

    protected void rblSize_SelectedIndexChanged
        (object sender, EventArgs e)
    {
        //  Check to verify that something has been selected.
        if (rblSize.SelectedIndex > -1)
        {
            int size = Convert.ToInt32(rblSize.SelectedItem.Value);
            lblTime.Font.Size = size;
        }
    }
}
```

Note that we could have written the last two highlighted lines of code in the preceding snippet as a single line, as follows:

```
lblTime.Font.Size = Convert.ToInt32(rblSize.SelectedItem.Value);
```

However, the more verbose version used in the example makes the code easier to read and debug, and that's always a preferable thing.

The final page is shown in Figure 4-20 after selecting a font size.

When you run the page, you'll see that a RadioButtonList looks similar to the individual radio buttons used earlier in the chapter, but it is much easier to work with programmatically as demonstrated even in this simple example. Rather than a cumbersome if or switch statement, you can use the control's SelectedItem and SelectedIndex properties; a much quicker and more readable solution.

The SelectedIndex property represents the lowest integer value index of all the selected items. The SelectedItem property returns the ListItem object in the list pointed to by SelectedIndex. From the ListItem object, you can then retrieve its text and value, select or deselect it, and change any of its HTML attributes.

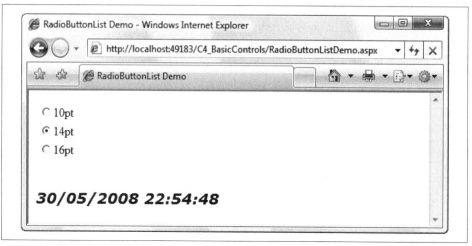

Figure 4-20. RadioButtonListDemo.aspx in action

Because a RadioButtonList, by definition, can have at most a single selected item, SelectedIndex and SelectedItem will tell you which item is selected. When you apply it to a CheckBoxList control or other multiselect ListControl control, however, you must remember that SelectedIndex and SelectedItem return only the first selected item in the list. To find out whether there are more, you must iterate through the list's Items collection, as shown in Example 4-34, and check each ListItem's Selected property to see whether it is set to true.

DropDownList Control

DropDownList controls display a single item at a time with a button for displaying the list. Only a single item can be selected.

DropDownList behavior

To demonstrate a DropDownList, add to the *C4_BasicControls* website a new web form called *DropDownListDemo.aspx*, and drag a DropDownList control and a Label onto it from the Toolbox. The aim of the page will be to have the item selected in the DropDownList reflected in the Label's text, as shown in Figure 4-21.

To ensure the DropDownList posts back to the server and updates the Label, its AutoPostBack property is set to true and its SelectedIndexChanged event is bound to a method in the code-behind file. Example 4-35 shows the markup for the page.

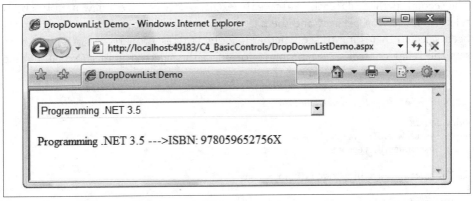

Figure 4-21. DropDownListDemo.aspx in action

Example 4-35. DropDownListDemo.aspx

```
<%@ Page Language="C#" AutoEventWireup="true"
    CodeFile="DropDownListDemo.aspx.cs" Inherits="DropDownListDemo" %>

<!DOCTYPE html PUBLIC "-//W3C//DTD XHTML 1.0 Transitional//EN"
    "http://www.w3.org/TR/xhtml1/DTD/xhtml1-transitional.dtd">

<html xmlns="http://www.w3.org/1999/xhtml">
<head runat="server">
    <title>DropDownList Demo</title>
</head>

<body>
    <form id="form1" runat="server">
    <div>
        <asp:DropDownList ID="ddlBooks" runat="server"
            AutoPostBack="true"
            OnSelectedIndexChanged="ddlBooks_SelectedIndexChanged" />
        <br />
        <br />
        <asp:Label ID="lblBookInfo" runat="server"></asp:Label>
    </div>
    </form>
</body>
</html>
```

The code-behind file, *DropDownListDemo.aspx.cs*, contains handlers for two events, as shown in Example 4-36. In the Page_Load method, items are added to the list in two steps. First, a two-dimensional string array is created to hold the Text and Value properties for the items. Then, the code loops through the items in the array adding a ListItem object to the list's Items collection.

The second method, ddlBooks_SelectedIndexChanged, fires once a new item has been selected in the DropDownList and the page has posted back. It makes sure an item has been selected by testing to see whether its SelectedItem property is not -1 and then sets the Label control's Text property to reflect the selected item's Text and Value properties.

Example 4-36. DropDownListDemo.aspx.cs

```
using System;
using System.Web.UI;
using System.Web.UI.WebControls;

public partial class DropDownListDemo : Page
{
    protected void Page_Load(object sender, EventArgs e)
    {
        if (!IsPostBack)
        {
            // Build 2 dimensional array for the lists
            // First dimension contains bookname
            // 2nd dimension contains ISBN number
            string[,] books = {
                {"Learning ASP.NET 2.0 with AJAX", "9780596513976"},
                {"Beginning ASP.NET 2.0 with C#", "9780470042583"},
                {"Programming C#","9780596527433"},
                {"Programming .NET 3.5","978059652756X"},
                {"Programming .NET Windows Applications","0596003218"},
                {"Programming ASP.NET 3e","0596001711"},
                {"WebClasses From Scratch","0789721260"},
                {"Teach Yourself C++ in 21 Days","067232072X"},
                {"Teach Yourself C++ in 10 Minutes","067231603X"},
                {"XML & Java From Scratch","0789724766"},
                {"XML Web Documents From Scratch","0789723166"},
                {"Clouds To Code","1861000952"},
                {"C++ Unleashed","0672312395"}
            };

            // Now populate the list.
            for (int i = 0; i < books.GetLength(0); i++)
            {
                // Add both Text and Value
                ddlBooks.Items.Add(new ListItem(books[i, 0], books[i, 1]));
            }
        }
    }

    protected void ddlBooks_SelectedIndexChanged
        (object sender, EventArgs e)
    {
```

Example 4-36. DropDownListDemo.aspx.cs (continued)

```
    //  Check to verify that something has been selected.
    if (ddlBooks.SelectedIndex != -1)
    {
        lblBookInfo.Text = ddlBooks.SelectedItem.Text +
            " --->ISBN: " + ddlBooks.SelectedValue;
    }
  }
}
```

The `Page_Load` method runs every time the page is reloaded, but it's often not a good idea to have all the code it contains be executed each time the method is run. For instance, in many applications, the contents of lists and other controls are filled from a database, which can be an expensive operation. Hitting the database only when necessary makes the implementation more efficient. It also means that any selections made from a list are carried over postbacks. They would otherwise be lost when a list is rebound to a database or other data source.

The approach most often taken is to have this database access occur only when the page is first loaded, and for this purpose you test to see whether the `IsPostBack` property is true. The `IsPostBack` property is `false` when the page is first loaded, but it is set to `true` whenever the form is posted back to the server as a result of user action on one of the controls.

DropDownList extenders

The AJAX Control Toolkit contains two extender controls that target the `DropDownList` control. Both aim to make the selection of items from the list a little bit easier.

`CascadingDropDown`

In a situation where you have several related `DropDownLists` on the same page, updates the items in one list based on the choices made in other lists

`ListSearchExtender`

Helps the user work through very long (and unsorted) lists more quickly by allowing the user to start typing out the choice he wants from the list and highlighting the first option from the list that matches what he has typed

The `CascadingDropDown` extender control uses a web service (see Chapter 16) in the background to do the hard work, so this section will look solely at using the `ListSearchExtender`.

To demonstrate, you'll add the `ListSearchExtender` to a copy of *DropDownList.aspx* to make it easier to search through the list to find the book you want to select. Figure 4-22 shows this in action.

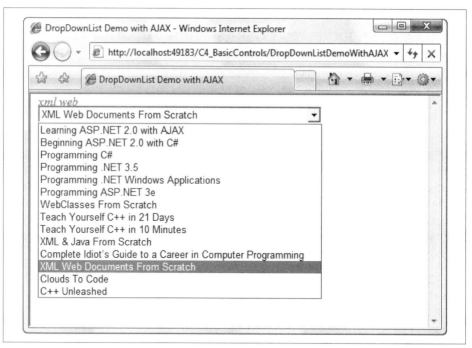

Figure 4-22. The ListSearchExtender in action

Add a new AJAX web form to the *C4_BasicControls* website and call it *DropDownListDemoWithAJAX.aspx*. Copy the DropDownList and Label controls from *DropDownListDemo.aspx* to the new page underneath the ScriptManager control. Similarly, copy Page_Load and ddlBooks_SelectedIndexChanged from *DropDownListDemo. aspx.cs* to *DropDownListDemoWithAJAX.aspx.cs*.

Now drag a ListSearchExtender onto the page under the DropDownList. Set its TargetControlID property to ddlBooks and run the page. Observe that when the DropDownList is in focus, typing the first few letters of a book in the list puts the focus straight on the book in the list. Now, this behavior is true of an unextended DropDownList too, but the ListSearchExtender allows you to see what you've typed on top of the list as well, which a DropDownList by itself would not allow you to do.

Now tidy up the UI of the ListSearchExtender a bit more with PromptText, PromptPosition, and PromptCssClass. If you use this last property, you'll also need to add the relevant CSS styles to your stylesheet. Example 4-37 shows the markup for *DropDownListWithAJAX.aspx* with the differences between it and *DropDownList.aspx* highlighted. There's no change to the code-behind file.

Example 4-37. DropDownListDemoWithAJAX.aspx

```
<%@ Page Language="C#" AutoEventWireup="true"
   CodeFile="DropDownListDemoWithAJAX.aspx.cs"
   Inherits="DropDownListDemoWithAJAX" %>

<%@ Register Assembly="AjaxControlToolkit" TagPrefix="cc1"
   Namespace="AjaxControlToolkit" %>

<!DOCTYPE html PUBLIC "-//W3C//DTD XHTML 1.0 Transitional//EN"
   "http://www.w3.org/TR/xhtml1/DTD/xhtml1-transitional.dtd">

<html xmlns="http://www.w3.org/1999/xhtml">
<head runat="server">
   <title>DropDownList Demo with AJAX</title>

   <script type="text/javascript">

      function pageLoad( ) {
      }

   </script>
   <style type="text/css">
      .PromptStyle {
      color: Red;
      font-style:italic;
      }
   </style>
</head>

<body>
   <form id="form1" runat="server">
   <div>
      <asp:ScriptManager ID="ScriptManager1" runat="server" />
      <asp:DropDownList ID="ddlBooks" runat="server"
         AutoPostBack="true"
         OnSelectedIndexChanged="ddlBooks_SelectedIndexChanged" />

      <cc1:ListSearchExtender ID="ListSearchExtender1" runat="server"
         TargetControlID="ddlBooks" PromptPosition="Top"
         PromptText="Type name of book to find it more quickly"
         PromptCssClass="PromptStyle" />
      <br />
      <br />
      <asp:Label ID="lblBookInfo" runat="server"></asp:Label>
   </div>
   </form>
</body>
</html>
```

The ListSearchExtender can also target a ListBox control.

ListBox Control

ListBox controls are very similar to DropDownList controls, except that multiple list items are visible on the screen by default (with the aid of a vertical scroll bar if necessary), and multiple items can be selected from it at once (by changing the SelectionMode property from the default value of Single to Multiple).

To demonstrate, add a new web form called *ListBoxDemo.aspx* to the *C4_BasicControls* website, and then add two ListBox controls to the form from the Toolbox. One will allow only single-item selection and the other will allow multiple-item selection, as shown in Example 4-38.

The first ListBox, with an ID of lbxSingle, is a single-selection listbox. The Rows property has been set to 6, and six items are displayed. Because the control has been populated with more than six items, a vertical scroll bar automatically appears. If a new item is selected, the first item is deselected. As with most of the examples in this chapter, AutoPostBack has been set to true so that the effects of the change are visible immediately.

The second ListBox control, with an ID of lbxMulti, is a multiple-selection listbox with its SelectionMode property set to Multiple. The Rows property has not been set, so the default four rows are visible. Because it is a multiselect listbox, the standard Windows techniques of multiselection can be used.

Example 4-38. ListBoxDemo.aspx

```
<%@ Page Language="C#" AutoEventWireup="true"
    CodeFile="ListBoxDemo.aspx.cs" Inherits="ListBoxDemo" %>

<!DOCTYPE html PUBLIC "-//W3C//DTD XHTML 1.0 Transitional//EN"
    "http://www.w3.org/TR/xhtml1/DTD/xhtml1-transitional.dtd">

<html xmlns="http://www.w3.org/1999/xhtml">
<head runat="server">
    <title>ListBox Demo</title>
</head>
<body>
    <form id="form1" runat="server">
    <div>
        <h2>Single Selection</h2>
        <asp:ListBox ID="lbxSingle" runat="server"
            AutoPostBack="true" Rows="6"
            onselectedindexchanged="lbxSingle_SelectedIndexChanged" />
        <br />
        <br />
        <asp:Label ID="lblSingle" runat="server"></asp:Label>

        <h2>Multiple Selection</h2>
        <asp:ListBox ID="lbxMulti" runat="server" AutoPostBack="true"
            SelectionMode="Multiple"
            onselectedindexchanged="lbxMulti_SelectedIndexChanged" />
```

Example 4-38. ListBoxDemo.aspx (continued)

```
      <br />
      <br />
      <asp:Label ID="lblMulti" runat="server"></asp:Label>
   </div>
   </form>
</body>
</html>
```

The code-behind file, *ListBoxDemo.aspx*, is shown in Example 4-39. Both `ListBox` controls are populated from the same array when the page is initially loaded, but the techniques used to identify the selected item(s) in each `ListBox` are different, illustrating again the different uses of the `SelectedItem` and `SelectedIndex` properties.

The event handler for the single-selection listbox is similar to the one for the `DropDownList` or any other single-select `ListControl`, such as the `RadioButtonList`.

The event handler for the multiselect listbox shows two different techniques for building up the string of selected items. The first technique is like that used for the `CheckBoxList`. It first checks to see whether any items in the list are selected, and if so, it iterates through the collection of `ListItem` objects, checking each to see whether the `Selected` property is true. If the item is selected, the `Text` and `Value` properties will be added to the `StringBuilder` for output to a label.

The second technique, commented out in Example 4-39, uses the `ListBox` control's `GetSelectedIndices` method to return an integer array of indexes of all the selected items. That array is iterated, with each selected `ListItem` being instantiated to get its `Text` and `Value` properties.

Example 4-39. ListBoxDemo.aspx.cs

```
using System;
using System.Web.UI;
using System.Web.UI.WebControls;

public partial class ListBoxDemo : Page
{
    protected void Page_Load(object sender, EventArgs e)
    {
        if (!IsPostBack)
        {
            // Build 2 dimensional array for the lists
            // First dimension contains bookname
            // 2nd dimension contains ISBN number
            string[,] books = {
                {"Learning ASP.NET 2.0 with AJAX", "9780596513976"},
                {"Beginning ASP.NET 2.0 with C#", "9780470042583"},
                {"Programming C#","9780596527433"},
                {"Programming .NET 3.5","978059652756X"},
                {"Programming .NET Windows Applications","0596003218"},
                {"Programming ASP.NET 3e","0596001711"},
```

Example 4-39. ListBoxDemo.aspx.cs (continued)

```
              {"WebClasses From Scratch","0789721260"},
              {"Teach Yourself C++ in 21 Days","067232072X"},
              {"Teach Yourself C++ in 10 Minutes","067231603X"},
              {"XML & Java From Scratch","0789724766"},
              {"XML Web Documents From Scratch","0789723166"},
              {"Clouds To Code","1861000952"},
              {"C++ Unleashed","0672312395"}
        };

        //  Now populate the list.
        for (int i = 0; i < books.GetLength(0); i++)
        {
            //  Add both Text and Value
            lbxSingle.Items.Add(new ListItem(books[i, 0], books[i, 1]));
            lbxMulti.Items.Add(new ListItem(books[i, 0], books[i, 1]));
        }
    }
}

protected void lbxSingle_SelectedIndexChanged
    (object sender, EventArgs e)
{
    //  Check to verify that something has been selected.
    if (lbxSingle.SelectedIndex > -1)
    {
        lblSingle.Text = lbxSingle.SelectedItem.Text +
            " ---> ISBN: " + lbxSingle.SelectedValue;
    }
}

protected void lbxMulti_SelectedIndexChanged(object sender, EventArgs e)
{
    if (lbxMulti.SelectedItem == null)
    {
        lblMulti.Text = "No books selected.";
    }
    else
    {
        StringBuilder sb = new StringBuilder();

        foreach (ListItem li in lbxMulti.Items)
        {
            if (li.Selected)
            {
                sb.AppendFormat("<br/>{0} ---> ISBN: {1}", li.Text, li.Value);
            }
        }
        lblMulti.Text = sb.ToString();
    }
```

Example 4-39. ListBoxDemo.aspx.cs (continued)

```
    //  Alternative technique
    //  foreach (int i in lbxMulti.GetSelectedIndices())
    //  {
    //     ListItem li = lbxMulti.Items[i];
    //     sb.AppendFormat("<br/>{0} ---> ISBN: {1}", li.Text, li.Value);
    //  }
    //  lblMulti.Text = sb.ToString();
    }
}
```

When you run the page and make a few selections, it should look like Figure 4-23.

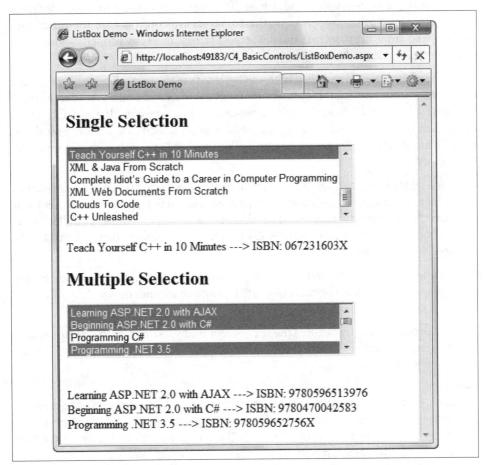

Figure 4-23. ListBoxDemo.aspx in action

ListBox controls have two read/write properties in addition to those inherited from ListControl. These properties are shown in Table 4-19.

Table 4-19. ListBox properties not inherited from ListControl

Name	Type	Values	Description
SelectionMode	ListSelectionMode	Single, Multiple	Determines whether a ListBox is in single-selection mode or multiple-selection mode. Default is Single.
Rows	Integer		Number of rows displayed. Default is four.

BulletedList Control

The BulletedList control provides an ASP.NET server control analog to the HTML ordered (<ol>) and unordered (<ul>) lists. The appearance and functionality of the list are controlled with properties of the BulletedList control. Like the other controls derived from ListControl, the BulletedList has an Items property, which is a collection of ListItem objects.

The style of the bullet is specified with the BulletStyle property. The valid values are contained within the BulletStyle enumeration, with values such as Circle, Disc, Numbered, LowerAlpha, UpperAlpha, LowerRoman, and UpperRoman. If the BulletStyle property is not set, a value of NotSet is the default, in which case the browser determines what style of bullet to use, typically the same as Disc, although this may vary by browser.

If the BulletStyle property is set to a numeric or alphabetic style, such as Numbered, LowerAlpha, UpperAlpha, LowerRoman, or UpperRoman, the starting value can be set using the FirstBulletNumber property. The default value is 1. Numeric bullet styles (Numbered, LowerRoman, UpperRoman) display numbers, and alphabetic types display the alphabetical equivalent.

The DisplayMode property determines appearance and functionality. It can be any one of the three values of the BulletedListDisplayMode enumeration:

Text
> The default value; this causes the list content to display as text. No events will be associated with the control if this value is used, that is, there is no user interaction with this control.

HyperLink
> Each ListItem is displayed as an underlined link. When an item is clicked, no server-side events are raised, and the form is not posted back to the server. Rather, like the HyperLink control itself, the user is navigated directly to the URL specified in the Value property of the ListItem that was clicked.
>
> The Target property of the BulletedList control works in conjunction with the DisplayMode set to HyperLink, dictating the browser window in which the target page will be displayed. The values of the Target property are the same as those listed in Table 4-5 for the HyperLink control.

`LinkButton`

Each `ListItem` is displayed as an underlined link, exactly like the `HyperLink`. However, when the user clicks an item, the `BulletedList.Click` event is raised and the page is immediately posted back to the server. A server-side event handler, specified by the `OnClick` attribute of the `BulletedList` control, is executed.

BulletedList behavior

The example shown in Figure 4-24, *BulletedListDemo.aspx*, demonstrates the different bullet styles, starting numbers, and display modes, as well as event handling with the `BulletedList` control. The content file for the example is shown in Example 4-40, and the event handler methods from the code-behind file are shown in Example 4-41.

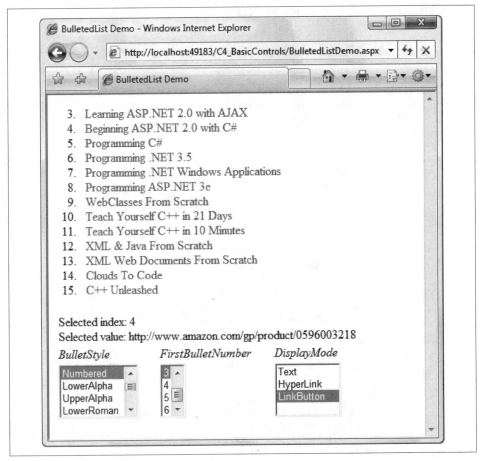

Figure 4-24. BulletedListDemo.aspx in action

Example 4-40. BulletedListDemo.aspx

```
<%@ Page Language="C#" AutoEventWireup="true"
    CodeFile="BulletedListDemo.aspx.cs" Inherits="BulletedListDemo" %>

<!DOCTYPE html PUBLIC "-//W3C//DTD XHTML 1.0 Transitional//EN"
    "http://www.w3.org/TR/xhtml1/DTD/xhtml1-transitional.dtd">

<html xmlns="http://www.w3.org/1999/xhtml">
<head runat="server">
    <title>BulletedList Demo</title>
</head>

<body>
    <form id="form1" runat="server">
    <div>
        <asp:BulletedList ID="bltBooks" runat="server"
            Target="_blank" onclick="bltBooks_Click" />
        <table>
            <tr>
                <td colspan="3" id="tdMessage" runat="server"></td>
            </tr>
            <tr>
                <td><em>BulletStyle</em></td>
                <td><em>FirstBulletNumber</em></td>
                <td><em>DisplayMode</em></td>
            </tr>
            <tr>
                <td>
                    <asp:ListBox ID="lbxBulletStyle"
                        runat="server" AutoPostBack="true"
                        onselectedindexchanged="lbxSelectedIndexChanged">
                        <asp:ListItem>NotSet</asp:ListItem>
                        <asp:ListItem>Numbered</asp:ListItem>
                        <asp:ListItem>LowerAlpha</asp:ListItem>
                        <asp:ListItem>UpperAlpha</asp:ListItem>
                        <asp:ListItem>LowerRoman</asp:ListItem>
                        <asp:ListItem>UpperRoman</asp:ListItem>
                        <asp:ListItem>Disc</asp:ListItem>
                        <asp:ListItem>Circle</asp:ListItem>
                        <asp:ListItem>Square</asp:ListItem>
                        <asp:ListItem>CustomImage</asp:ListItem>
                    </asp:ListBox>
                </td>
                <td>
                    <asp:ListBox ID="lbxBulletNumber"
                        runat="server" AutoPostBack="true"
                        onselectedindexchanged="lbxSelectedIndexChanged">
                        <asp:ListItem>1</asp:ListItem>
                        <asp:ListItem>2</asp:ListItem>
                        <asp:ListItem>3</asp:ListItem>
                        <asp:ListItem>4</asp:ListItem>
                        <asp:ListItem>5</asp:ListItem>
                        <asp:ListItem>6</asp:ListItem>
                    </asp:ListBox>
```

Example 4-40. BulletedListDemo.aspx (continued)

```
            </td>
            <td>
                <asp:ListBox ID="lbxDisplayMode"
                    runat="server" AutoPostBack="true"
                    onselectedindexchanged="lbxSelectedIndexChanged">
                    <asp:ListItem>Text</asp:ListItem>
                    <asp:ListItem>HyperLink</asp:ListItem>
                    <asp:ListItem>LinkButton</asp:ListItem>
                </asp:ListBox>
            </td>
        </tr>
    </table>
  </div>
  </form>
</body>
</html>
```

In Example 4-40, the BulletedList control has three ListItem objects in its Items collection, all added statically. It so happens that all the list items represent websites. In anticipation of the HyperLink DisplayMode being applied, each ListItem has its Value property set, which supplies the URL to navigate to. The Target property of the BulletedList control is set to _blank, which according to Table 4-5, will cause the new page to open in a new, unnamed browser window.

The OnClick attribute of the BulletedList control binds the Click event to the bltBooks_Click method in the code-behind file, shown highlighted in Example 4-41.

Example 4-41. BulletedListDemo.aspx.cs

```
using System;
using System.Web.UI;
using System.Web.UI.WebControls;

public partial class BulletedListDemo : Page
{
    protected void Page_Load(object sender, EventArgs e)
    {
        if (!IsPostBack)
        {
            // Build 2 dimensional array for the lists
            // First dimension contains bookname
            // 2nd dimension contains ISBN number
            string[,] books = {
                {"Learning ASP.NET 2.0 with AJAX", "9780596513976"},
                {"Beginning ASP.NET 2.0 with C#", "9780470042583"},
                {"Programming C#","9780596527433"},
                {"Programming .NET 3.5","978059652756X"},
                {"Programming .NET Windows Applications","0596003218"},
                {"Programming ASP.NET 3e","0596001711"},
                {"WebClasses From Scratch","0789721260"},
                {"Teach Yourself C++ in 21 Days","067232072X"},
```

Example 4-41. BulletedListDemo.aspx.cs (continued)

```
            {"Teach Yourself C++ in 10 Minutes","067231603X"},
            {"XML & Java From Scratch","0789724766"},
            {"XML Web Documents From Scratch","0789723166"},
            {"Clouds To Code","1861000952"},
            {"C++ Unleashed","0672312395"}
        };

        //  Now populate the list.
        for (int i = 0; i < books.GetLength(0); i++)
        {
            //  Add both Text and Value
            bltBooks.Items.Add(new ListItem(books[i, 0],
                "http://www.amazon.com/gp/product/" + books[i, 1]));
        }
    }
}


protected void lbxSelectedIndexChanged(object sender, EventArgs e)
{
    ListBox lb = (ListBox)sender;
    string strID = lb.ID;
    string strValue = lb.SelectedValue;

    switch (strID)
    {
        case "lbxBulletStyle":
            BulletStyle style =
                (BulletStyle)Enum.Parse(typeof(BulletStyle), strValue);
            bltBooks.BulletStyle = style;
            //  The CustomImage style is a special case.
            if (style == BulletStyle.CustomImage)
            {
                bltBooks.BulletImageUrl = "togglebutton_checked.gif";
            }
            break;

        case "lbxBulletNumber":
            bltBooks.FirstBulletNumber = Convert.ToInt32(strValue);
            break;

        case "lbxDisplayMode":
            BulletedListDisplayMode displayMode =
              (BulletedListDisplayMode)Enum.Parse
                  (typeof(BulletedListDisplayMode), strValue);
            bltBooks.DisplayMode = displayMode;
            break;

        default:
            break;
    }

}
```

Example 4-41. BulletedListDemo.aspx.cs (continued)

```
protected void bltBooks_Click
    (object sender, BulletedListEventArgs e)
{
    BulletedList b = (BulletedList)sender;
    tdMessage.InnerHtml = "Selected index: " +
        e.Index.ToString() + "<br />" + "Selected value: " +
        b.Items[e.Index].Value + "<br />";
}
}
```

The event handler for this Click event will concatenate the Index and the Value properties of the clicked ListItem, along with some HTML elements, and assign that string to the InnerHtml property of an HTML server-side control. This event handler method requires an event argument of type BulletedListEventArgs, which exposes a single property, Index. This property returns the zero-based index of the clicked ListItem in the Items collection.

However, to retrieve the actual Text or Value of the clicked ListItem, you must have a reference to the specific BulletedList control that raised the event. In this example, there is only a single BulletedList control and the ID is known to us: bltList. However, a more generic technique is used here where a single event handler will work with any number of controls. You first cast the object that raised the event, encapsulated in sender, to an object of type BulletedList, and then index into the ListItems collection represented by the Items property of that BulletedList object. This is accomplished in the following line of code from Example 4-40:

```
BulletedList b = (BulletedList)sender;
```

Though not directly related to the BulletedList control, some interesting techniques are used with the ListBox controls on the page.

All three of the ListBox controls have AutoPostBack set to true, so you will see the results of changing a value immediately. Also, all three controls use the same event handler method, lbxSelectedIndexChanged, for the SelectedIndexChanged event.

In the lbxSelectedIndexChanged method in the code-behind file in Example 4-41, the first line of code gets a reference to the control that raised the event by casting sender to a ListBox object:

```
ListBox lb = (ListBox)sender;
```

Then the ID and SelectedValue properties of the listbox can be retrieved.

A switch block is used to take action appropriate for each listbox. The ListBox that sets the FirstBulletNumber property is straightforward, converting the SelectedValue, contained in the string variable strValue, to an integer and assigning that integer to the FirstBulletNumber property:

```
bltBooks.FirstBulletNumber = Convert.ToInt32(strValue);
```

The case blocks for the other two ListBoxes are a bit more interesting. The goal is to determine the item selected, either a BulletStyle or a DisplayMode, and apply that to the BulletedList. In both cases, this is accomplished using the static Enum.Parse method. This method converts a name or value of an enumerated constant into its equivalent enumerated object. You must pass it the type of the enumerated constant and the value of the constant.

So, looking at the case for lbxBulletStyle (lbxDisplayMode is equivalent), the Type of the enumeration is obtained from the typeof operator, which returns a System.Type object. The value of the selected constant is contained in strValue. Given these two arguments, Enum.Parse returns an object, which you then cast to the desired type and assign to a variable:

```
BulletStyle style =
    (BulletStyle)Enum.Parse(typeof(BulletStyle), strValue);
```

This variable can then be used to set the appropriate property:

```
bltBooks.BulletStyle = style;
```

In the case of lbxBulletStyle, you must make a special case of the CustomImage style to assign the BulletImageUrl property. Here you can compare BulletStyle directly with the enumerated constants to see whether there is a match:

```
if (style == BulletStyle.CustomImage)
{
    bltBooks.BulletImageUrl = "togglebutton_checked.gif";
}
```

BulletedList extenders

It would be great if the ListSearchExtender demonstrated earlier could also be applied to a BulletedList control. Unfortunately, there is no scope for this, as a BulletedList doesn't offer the user a place to type in her choice. However, the AJAX Control Toolkit contains the PagingBulletedListExtender (PBLE) control, as shown in Figure 4-25.

Rather than using user input to help find the correct choice in the list, the PBLE breaks the list into groups of choices based on two properties, IndexSize and MaxItemPerPage. It then adds an index above the list which the user can click to browse through the list more easily.

To re-create this, add to the *C4_BasicControls* website a new AJAX web form called *BulletedListDemoWithAJAX.aspx*. Copy to this new form the contents of the <div> element from *BulletedListDemo.aspx* under the ScriptManager in *BulletedListDemoWithAJAX.aspx*, and the event handlers from its code-behind page. Now add a PBLE to the new page under the main BulletedList control, bltBooks. Set its TargetControlId property to bltBooks, its ClientSort property to true, and its IndexSize to 3, and then run the page. See how the BulletedList is now augmented with an index which you can use to browse the list more efficiently.

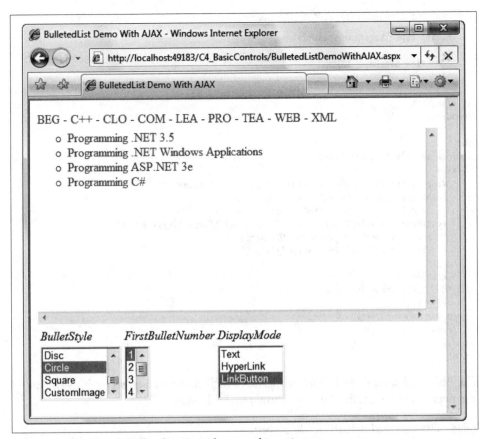

Figure 4-25. The PagingBulletedListExtender control in action

Example 4-42 highlights the additions in *BulletedListDemoWithAJAX.aspx* over the original code in Example 4-40 to enable the PBLE. There are no changes in the code-behind file.

Example 4-42. BulletedListDemoWithAJAX.aspx

```
<%@ Page Language="C#" AutoEventWireup="true"
   CodeFile="BulletedListDemoWithAJAX.aspx.cs"
   Inherits="BulletedListDemoWithAJAX" %>

<%@ Register Assembly="AjaxControlToolkit"
   Namespace="AjaxControlToolkit" TagPrefix="cc1" %>

<!DOCTYPE html PUBLIC "-//W3C//DTD XHTML 1.0 Transitional//EN"
   "http://www.w3.org/TR/xhtml1/DTD/xhtml1-transitional.dtd">

<html xmlns="http://www.w3.org/1999/xhtml">
<head runat="server">
   <title>BulletedList Demo With AJAX</title>
```

Example 4-42. BulletedListDemoWithAJAX.aspx (continued)

```
    <script type="text/javascript">

        function pageLoad( ) {
        }

    </script>
</head>

<body>
    <form id="form1" runat="server">
    <div>
        <asp:ScriptManager ID="ScriptManager1" runat="server" />
        <asp:BulletedList ID="bltBooks" runat="server"
            Target="_blank" OnClick="bltBooks_Click" />
        <cc1:PagingBulletedListExtender ID="PagingBulletedListExtender1"
            runat="server" TargetControlID="bltBooks"
            ClientSort="true" IndexSize="3" />

        <table>
            ... as shown in Example 4-40 ...
        </table>
    </div>
    </form>
</body>
</html>
```

The PBLE has several read/write properties which all have an effect on how the index it generates is presented. These are shown in Table 4-20.

Table 4-20. PagingBulletedListExtender properties

Name	Type	Description
ClientSort	Boolean	Organizes the index entries alphabetically rather than leaving them to echo the order of the list items.
Height	Integer	Specifies a fixed height for the entries in the bulleted list.
IndexSize	Integer	Specifies the number of characters in each index entry. Has no effect if MaxItemPerPage is set.
MaxItemPerPage	Integer	Overrides IndexSize. Specifies the number of list items in each page of the list. The index entries will reflect the first item on each page.
SelectIndexCssClass	String	Sets the CSS class name for the index entry currently selected by the user.
UnselectIndexCssClass	String	Sets the CSS class name for any index entries not currently selected by the user.

Sliders and Ratings

The AJAX Control Toolkit introduces two new controls to web forms that are commonly used metaphors for a user's feelings toward a purchase or service:

Slider

> Presents the user with a sliding scale of values (e.g., 0–100) and a "handle" which the user can slide from left to right (or down to up) with the mouse to increase or decrease its value.

Ratings

> Presents the user with a set of values which are often much smaller than those in a slider (e.g., 0–5) where each value is visually represented by one of two images depending on what the value is. For example, the AJAX Control Toolkit sample website uses filled and empty star images, much like you would see on Amazon.com, to reflect the current rating value.

It's much easier to show these controls than to describe them. Figure 4-26 shows both of them in action in *SlidersAndRatingsDemo.aspx*, which you'll build next.

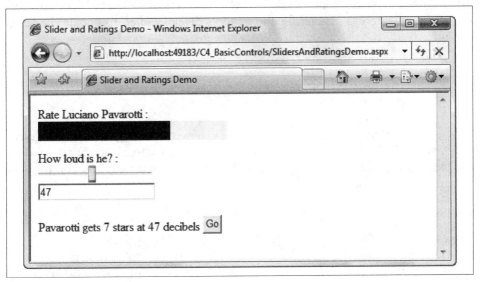

Figure 4-26. Slider and Ratings controls in action

To build the page, add to the website a new AJAX web form called *SlidersAndRatingsDemo.aspx*. Add a Ratings control to the form with some explanatory text.

Now you need to define how the current rating value will be displayed onscreen. You can tie four different CSS styles into a Ratings control, as listed in Table 4-21.

> Because it's customary for online ratings to be given in terms of "stars," the Ratings control style properties are named as such for ease of use. However, this example just uses blocks of color defined in CSS rather than any particular images. The AJAX Control Toolkit sample website, on the other hand, does demonstrate a Ratings control using star images.

Table 4-21. Style properties for the Ratings controls

Property name	Purpose of CSS style
StarCssClass	Defines the generic style for a "star"—height, width, background color, etc.
FilledStarCssClass	Defines the style for a selected "star".
EmptyStarCssClass	Defines the style for an unselected "star".
WaitingStarCssClass	When the user changes the rating value, confirms to the user that it has recorded this new value by briefly changing (flashing) the style of the selected stars. This is the "flashing confirmation" style.

Create four CSS styles for these four mandatory properties and set them accordingly. The full markup for *SlidersAndRatingsDemo.aspx* in Example 4-43 shows one possibility.

Add a Button (btnSubmit) and a Label (lblChoices) to display the results of the rating, and then an event handler for the button's Click handler, to update the Label control:

```
protected void btnSubmit_Click(object sender, EventArgs e)
{
    lblChoices.Text = String.Format("Pavarotti gets {0} stars",
        Rating1.CurrentRating.ToString( ));
}
```

Now run the form, change the rating, noting how the control uses the different styles. Click the button to see the current value of the Ratings control reflected on the page. Table 4-22 shows some optional properties for the Ratings control with which you can experiment.

Table 4-22. Optional properties for the Ratings control

Name	Type	Values	Description
CurrentRating	Integer		The initial rating for the Ratings control until the user changes it.
MaxRating	Integer		The maximum value for CurrentRating.
ReadOnly	Boolean		Set to true if CurrentRating should not be changed.
RatingAlign	Orientation	Horizontal, Vertical	Sets whether the stars should be set horizontally or stacked vertically. Default is Horizontal.
RatingDirection	RatingDirection	LeftToRightTopToBottom, RightToLeftBottomToTop	Sets which way to increase or decrease the CurrentRating value.
OnChanged	String		Client script that should run after the CurrentRating value has been changed.

The Slider control is actually an extender for a text box control, which stores the actual slider value. It also requires a second control, Label or Textbox, which is bound to it and displays the numeric value of the slider.

Add to the page two text boxes, called txtHiddenSlider and txtVisibleSlider, with empty text properties beneath the Ratings control. Now add the Slider extender to the page. Set the targetControlId and boundcontrolId properties to txtHiddenSlider and txtVisibleSlider, respectively. You can see the final markup for this page in Example 4-43. You'll also need to update the Click event handler for the Button to reflect the slider's value in the Label control, as shown in Example 4-44.

Example 4-43. SlidersAndRatingsDemo.aspx

```
<%@ Page Language="C#" AutoEventWireup="true"
    CodeFile="SlidersAndRatingsDemo.aspx.cs"
    Inherits="SlidersAndRatingsDemo" %>

<%@ Register Assembly="AjaxControlToolkit"
    Namespace="AjaxControlToolkit" TagPrefix="cc1" %>

<!DOCTYPE html PUBLIC "-//W3C//DTD XHTML 1.0 Transitional//EN"
    "http://www.w3.org/TR/xhtml1/DTD/xhtml1-transitional.dtd">

<html xmlns="http://www.w3.org/1999/xhtml">
<head runat="server">
    <title>Slider and Ratings Demo</title>
    <script type="text/javascript">
      function pageLoad( ) {
      }
    </script>

    <style type="text/css">
      .ratingStar
      {
         font-size: 0pt;
         width: 25px;
         height: 25px;
         margin: 0px;
         padding: 0px;
         cursor: pointer;
         display: block;
         background-repeat: no-repeat;
      }
      .filledRatingStar
      {
         background-color: Black;
      }
      .emptyRatingStar
      {
         background-color: Yellow;
      }
```

Example 4-43. SlidersAndRatingsDemo.aspx (continued)

```
        .savedRatingStar
        {
            background-color: Green;
        }
    </style>
</head>

<body>
    <form id="form1" runat="server">
    <div>
        <asp:ScriptManager ID="ScriptManager1" runat="server" />
        Rate Luciano Pavarotti :
        <cc1:Rating ID="Rating1" runat="server"
            StarCssClass="ratingStar"
            FilledStarCssClass="filledRatingStar"
            EmptyStarCssClass="emptyRatingStar"
            WaitingStarCssClass="savedRatingStar"
            CurrentRating="3" MaxRating="10" />
        <br />
        <br />
        How loud is he? :
        <asp:TextBox ID="txtHiddenSlider" runat="server"></asp:TextBox>
        <asp:TextBox ID="txtVisibleSlider" runat="server"></asp:TextBox>
        <cc1:SliderExtender ID="SliderExtender1" runat="server"
            TargetControlID="txtHiddenSlider"
            BoundControlID="txtVisibleSlider" />
        <br />
        <br />
        <asp:Label ID="lblChoices" runat="server" />
        <asp:Button ID="btnSubmit" runat="server" Text="Go"
            OnClick="btnSubmit_Click" />
    </div>
    </form>
</body>
</html>
```

Example 4-44. SlidersAndRatingsDemo.aspx.cs

```
using System;
using System.Web.UI;

public partial class SlidersAndRatingsDemo : Page
{
    protected void btnSubmit_Click(object sender, EventArgs e)
    {
        lblChoices.Text = String.Format
            ("Pavarotti rates {0}/{1} stars at {2} decibels",
            Rating1.CurrentRating.ToString(),
            Rating1.MaxRating.ToString(),
            txtHiddenSlider.Text);
    }
}
```

Run the page. Notice the value in the text box changes with the Slider. If you change the value in the TextBox, the Slider will update after the TextBox loses the focus. Try setting the slider's Minimum and Maximum properties to adjust the value bounds on the slider, and the Steps property to a value greater than 1 for sliding up the values faster. Table 4-23 lays out all of the Slider's optional properties.

Table 4-23. Properties for the Slider control

Name	Type	Values	Description
Decimals	Integer		Number of decimal places the slider value uses. Default is 0.
EnableHandleAnimation	Boolean		Enables or disables the animation of the slider handle after the user has manually changed the value in the bound TextBox. Default is false.
HandleCssClass	String		CSS class that defines an alternative look for the slider's handle.
HandleImageUrl	String		URL for the image to be used as the slider's handle.
Length	Integer		Width or height of the slider in pixels.
Maximum	Integer		Maximum value for the slider.
Minimum	Integer		Minimum value for the slider.
Orientation	SliderOrientation	Horizontal Vertical	The slider's orientation.
RailsCssClass	String		CSS class that defines an alternative look for the slider's rail.
RaiseChangeOnlyOn-MouseUp	Boolean		If true, a change event is raised only for the bound TextBox when the *left* mouse button dragging the slider has been raised.
Steps	Integer		Number of steps in the slider's range. The default is the number of whole integers between Maximum and Minimum.
TooltipText	String		Text to display when the mouse pointer is held over the slider.

In the next chapter, we look at more advanced controls and compound controls.

CHAPTER 5

More Controls

In the preceding chapter, we covered many of the standard ASP.NET controls and the AJAX extenders that you can use to enhance their functionality beyond the remit of the traditional HTML controls to which they correspond. In this chapter, we'll look at two more groups of controls:

Panel controls
> Those ASP.NET server controls and AJAX controls which can enclose a number of other controls and allow you to control the presentation and contents of the child controls in one

More standard controls from the toolbox
> Those ASP.NET server controls that offer a richer level of functionality than those you saw in Chapter 4, such as the MultiView, Wizard, and Calendar controls

What this chapter does not offer is coverage of all the other controls in the Visual Studio toolbox, of which there are several dozen. Many which have a specific functionality, such as validation, data access, personalization, or navigation, are covered in individual chapters later in the book.

Panel Controls

The Panel control is used as a container for other controls much as a <div> (or a <span> to a lesser extent) acts in plain HTML. It serves several functions:

- To control the visibility of the controls it contains
- To control the appearance of the controls it contains
- To make it easier to generate controls programmatically

The Panel control is derived from WebControl and has the read/write properties shown in Table 5-1. The Panel control has no methods or events not inherited from the Control or WebControl class. Specifically, there are no events raised by user interaction.

Table 5-1. Properties of the Panel control not inherited from Control or WebControl

Name	Type	Values	Description
BackImageUrl	String		The URL of an image to display as the background of the panel. If the image is smaller than the panel, it will be tiled.
Direction	ContentDirection	LeftToRight, RightToLeft, NotSet	The direction to display text in a container control. Default is NotSet.
GroupingText	String		Causes the Panel to render to the browser as a <fieldset> element rather than a <div> element. The value of this property is used for the <legend> element.
HorizontalAlign	HorizontalAlign	Center, Justify, Left, NotSet, Right	Specifies the horizontal alignment of the contents, overriding any CSS styles that are already set on it. Default is NotSet. Note there is no VerticalAlign property.
ScrollBars	ScrollBars	Auto, Both, Horizontal, None, Vertical	Specifies the visibility and location of scroll bars. Default value is None.
Wrap	Boolean	true, false	If true (the default), the contents of the panel will wrap. If false, the contents will not wrap.

 The Panel may seem like a humble control, but it is the basis for many of the excellent AJAX controls and extenders, as you'll see later in this section. In particular, the UpdatePanel is an ASP.NET AJAX control that works in the same way as a regular Panel control, but allows for the asynchronous updating (i.e., without posting back the whole page) of the controls it contains. It's probably the most important AJAX control after the ScriptManager.

To demonstrate this control, create in Visual Studio 2008 (VS2008) a new website solution called *C5_MoreControls*, and add a new web form called *PanelDemo.aspx*. On this page, you'll work with two Panel controls, as shown in Figure 5-1. The first panel demonstrates how to control the appearance and visibility of child controls and how to add controls programmatically. The second panel demonstrates the use of the GroupingText, ScrollBars, and Wrap properties to control the appearance of the control.

The first of the Panel controls in this example, with an ID of pnlDynamic, is highlighted in Example 5-1. It has some static content between the opening and closing Panel tags.

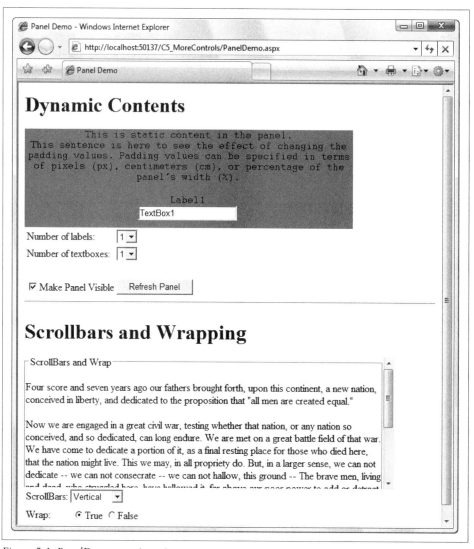

Figure 5-1. PanelDemo.aspx in action

Example 5-1. The first half of PanelDemo.aspx

```
<%@ Page Language="C#" AutoEventWireup="true"
   CodeFile="PanelDemo.aspx.cs" Inherits="PanelDemo" %>

<!DOCTYPE html PUBLIC "-//W3C//DTD XHTML 1.0 Transitional//EN"
"http://www.w3.org/TR/xhtml1/DTD/xhtml1-transitional.dtd">
<html xmlns="http://www.w3.org/1999/xhtml">
<head runat="server">
   <title>Panel Demo</title>
</head>
```

Example 5-1. The first half of PanelDemo.aspx (continued)

```
<body>
    <form id="form1" runat="server">
    <div>
        <h1>Dynamic Contents</h1>
        <asp:Panel ID="pnlDynamic" runat="server" BackColor="Fuchsia"
            Height="150px" Width="80%" HorizontalAlign="Center"
            Font-Names="Courier" ScrollBars="Auto">
            This is static content in the panel.
            <br />
            This sentence is here to see the effect of changing the
            padding values. Padding values can be specified in terms
            of pixels (px), centimeters (cm), or percentage of the
            panel's width (%).
            <p />
        </asp:Panel>

        <table>
            <tr>
                <td>
                    Number of labels:</td>
                <td>
                    <asp:DropDownList ID="ddlLabels" runat="server">
                        <asp:ListItem Text="0" Value="0" />
                        <asp:ListItem Text="1" Value="1" />
                        <asp:ListItem Text="2" Value="2" />
                        <asp:ListItem Text="3" Value="3" />
                        <asp:ListItem Text="4" Value="4" />
                    </asp:DropDownList>
                </td>
            </tr>
            <tr>
                <td>
                    Number of textboxes:</td>
                <td>
                    <asp:DropDownList ID="ddlBoxes" runat="server">
                        <asp:ListItem Text="0" Value="0" />
                        <asp:ListItem Text="1" Value="1" />
                        <asp:ListItem Text="2" Value="2" />
                        <asp:ListItem Text="3" Value="3" />
                        <asp:ListItem Text="4" Value="4" />
                    </asp:DropDownList>
                </td>
            </tr>
            <tr>
                <td colspan="2"> </td>
            </tr>
            <tr>
                <td>
                    <asp:CheckBox ID="chkVisible"
                        Text="Make Panel Visible" runat="server" />
                </td>
```

Example 5-1. The first half of PanelDemo.aspx (continued)

```
        <td>
            <asp:Button ID="btnRefresh"
                Text="Refresh Panel" runat="server" />
        </td>
    </tr>
</table>
```

pnlDynamic has several properties defined, including BackColor, Height (in pixels), Width (in percentage of the browser window), Font-Names, and HorizontalAlign. Note that this control does not have a property for vertical alignment.

The Scrollbars attribute is set to Auto, which causes a horizontal or vertical scroll bar, or both, to be present only if necessary. Because the Wrap property is true by default, the static text will wrap within the space available; hence this first Panel control will never require a horizontal scroll bar. However, as you add enough labels and/or text boxes to the panel, a vertical scroll bar will appear as necessary.

The value for the Height attribute is an integer representing the number of pixels. The px as part of the value is optional, but it does serve to self-document. For example, the following two lines are equivalent:

```
Height="250px"
Height="250"
```

Alternatively, you can express the Height as a percentage, if it is contained within a fixed-size container, such as another Panel control. If it is not within a fixed-size container and it has no content, the panel will be only a single line high, no matter what percentage value is used. If the Height attribute is missing, the Panel control automatically sizes itself vertically to contain all of its children controls.

The Width attribute can be either an integer number of pixels or a percentage of the browser window. This example shows the latter. If the Width attribute is missing, the Panel control will default to a width of 100%.

Beneath pnlDynamic, an HTML table contains two DropDownList controls, a CheckBox control, and a Button control. Further content is added dynamically to the panel, depending on the values selected in the two drop downs: ddlLabels and ddlBoxes. There's also a CheckBox to make the panel visible or invisible. None of these three controls has its AutoPostBack property set, so to see any of the changes take effect, you need to click the button, which posts the form. This triggers the Page_Load event handler for this page—shown in Example 5-2—which then makes the necessary adjustments to the panel.

Example 5-2. Page_Load for pnlDynamic

```
using System;
using System.Web.UI;
using System.Web.UI.WebControls;
```

Example 5-2. Page_Load for pnlDynamic (continued)

```csharp
public partial class PanelDemo : Page
{
    protected void Page_Load(object sender, EventArgs e)
    {
        // First take care of the panel w/ the dynamically generated controls
        // Show or hide Panel contents.
        pnlDynamic.Visible = chkVisible.Checked;

        // Generate Label controls.
        int numlabels = Int32.Parse(ddlLabels.SelectedItem.Value);
        for (int i = 1; i <= numlabels; i++)
        {
            Label lbl = new Label();
            lbl.Text = "Label" + (i).ToString();
            lbl.ID = "Label" + (i).ToString();
            pnlDynamic.Controls.Add(lbl);
            pnlDynamic.Controls.Add(new LiteralControl("<br />"));
        }

        // Generate TextBox controls.
        int numBoxes = Int32.Parse(ddlBoxes.SelectedItem.Value);
        for (int i = 1; i <= numBoxes; i++)
        {
            TextBox txt = new TextBox();
            txt.Text = "TextBox" + (i).ToString();
            txt.ID = "TextBox" + (i).ToString();
            pnlDynamic.Controls.Add(txt);
            pnlDynamic.Controls.Add(new LiteralControl("<br />"));
        }
    }
}
```

The handler starts by setting the panel's Visible property to reflect whether the checkbox is checked. When the panel is not visible, its contents are not visible either. Likewise, when the panel is visible, all of its contents are visible.

Then there are two for loops, one each for labels and text boxes, which generate the contained controls. After converting the entry in the appropriate DropDownList control to an integer, the for loop iterates through the procedure for the specified number of times.

The procedure is similar in each of the two cases. A new control is instantiated, and then the Text and ID properties are assigned. The control is added to the Controls collection of the panel, and finally a LiteralControl containing some HTML is added to the collection as well. Note that the LiteralControl class is not the same as the Literal control we saw in Chapter 4, although both are used to render basic text to the browser. LiteralControl is in fact the base class that all ASP.NET server controls use to render their static text.

Note how the font name specified inside the Panel tags affected the static text and labels in the panel but not the contents of the text boxes. This is because it applies only to the literal contents of the <div> corresponding to the Panel control and not to the <input> elements corresponding to the TextBox controls.

The second Panel control in this example, with an ID of pnlScroll, is highlighted in Example 5-3, which shows the rest of the code in *PanelDemo.aspx*.

Example 5-3. The second half of PanelDemo.aspx

```
    <h1>Scrollbars and Wrapping</h1>
    <asp:Panel Height="200px" ID="pnlScroll" runat="server"
        Width="90%" GroupingText="ScrollBars and Wrap">
        <asp:Label ID="lblPanelContent" runat="server"></asp:Label>
    </asp:Panel>
    <table>
        <tr>
            <td>
                ScrollBars:</td>
            <td>
                <asp:DropDownList ID="ddlScrollBars"
                    AutoPostBack="true" runat="server"
                    OnSelectedIndexChanged="ddlScrollBars_SelectedIndexChanged">
                    <asp:ListItem Text="None" Selected="True" />
                    <asp:ListItem Text="Auto" />
                    <asp:ListItem Text="Both" />
                    <asp:ListItem Text="Horizontal" />
                    <asp:ListItem Text="Vertical" />
                </asp:DropDownList>
            </td>
        </tr>
        <tr>
            <td>
                Wrap:</td>
            <td>
                <asp:RadioButtonList ID="rblWrap" runat="server"
                    AutoPostBack="true" RepeatDirection="Horizontal"
                    OnSelectedIndexChanged="rblWrap_SelectedIndexChanged">
                    <asp:ListItem Text="True" Value="true" Selected="True" />
                    <asp:ListItem Text="False" Value="false" />
                </asp:RadioButtonList>
            </td>
        </tr>
    </table>
  </div>
  </form>
</body>
</html>
```

As you can see, pnlScroll has only one new property declared: GroupingText. This has the effect of putting a border around the panel with the string value of the GroupingText property as a caption within the border.

The only content within pnlScroll is a Label control, lblPanelContent. To demonstrate the Panel control's scroll bar feature, Page_Load is extended to set the Label's Text property to a rather lengthy text string. This text string contains some HTML paragraph elements to force line breaks. This addition to the code-behind page, *PanelDemo.aspx.cs*, is shown in Example 5-4.

As with pnlDynamic, an HTML table is added under pnlScroll containing two controls associated with this panel. One is the DropDownList ddlScrollBars which sets the value of the panel's Scrollbars property, and the other is a RadioButtonList setting the Wrap property. AutoPostback is set to true for both of these, so no further user action is required to see them take effect. New code is required to handle their default SelectedIndexChanged events and to make changes to pnlScroll, as shown in Example 5-4.

Example 5-4. Additions to PanelDemo.aspx.cs

```
using System;
using System.Web.UI;
using System.Web.UI.WebControls;
using System.Text;

public partial class PanelDemo : Page
{
   protected void Page_Load(object sender, EventArgs e)
   {
      ... code as in Example 5-2 ...

      // Next take care of the Scrollbar panel.
      StringBuilder strText = new StringBuilder("<p>Four score and seven years ago
our fathers brought forth, upon this continent, a new nation, conceived in liberty,
and dedicated to the proposition that \"all men are created equal.\"</p>");
      strText.Append("<p>Now we are engaged in a great civil war, testing whether
that nation, or any nation so conceived, and so dedicated, can long endure. We are
met on a great battle field of that war. We have come to dedicate a portion of it,
as a final resting place for those who died here, that the nation might live. This
we may, in all propriety do. But, in a larger sense, we can not dedicate -- we can
not consecrate -- we can not hallow, this ground -- The brave men, living and dead,
who struggled here, have hallowed it, far above our poor power to add or detract.
The world will little note, nor long remember what we say here; while it can never
forget what they did here.</p>");
      strText.Append("<p>It is rather for us, the living, we here be dedicated to
the great task remaining before us -- that, from these honored dead we take
increased devotion to that cause for which they here, gave the last full measure of
devotion -- that we here highly resolve these dead shall not have died in vain;
that the nation, shall have a new birth of freedom, and that government of the
people by the people for the people, shall not perish from the earth.</p>");

      lblPanelContent.Text = strText.ToString();
   }
   protected void ddlScrollBars_SelectedIndexChanged(object sender, EventArgs e)
   {
```

Example 5-4. Additions to PanelDemo.aspx.cs (continued)

```
    DropDownList ddl = (DropDownList)sender;
    string strValue = ddl.SelectedItem.ToString( );
    ScrollBars bars = (ScrollBars)Enum.Parse(typeof(ScrollBars), strValue);
    pnlScroll.ScrollBars = bars;
}


    protected void rblWrap_SelectedIndexChanged(object sender, EventArgs e)
    {
        RadioButtonList rbl = (RadioButtonList)sender;
        pnlScroll.Wrap = Convert.ToBoolean(rbl.SelectedValue);
    }
}
```

In the event handler for the SelectedIndexChanged event of the drop-down list, ddlScrollBars_SelectedIndexChanged, the Scrollbars property of the panel is set. The technique of setting the value from the ScrollBars enumeration is exactly as described in Example 4-41 in Chapter 4 for the BulletedListDemo example.

Of course, it's not the only way to do it. The following code does the same job by pulling all the possible values for a Panel control's Scrollbars property into an array and then checks the selected value against that:

```
    ScrollBars theEnum = new ScrollBars( );
    ScrollBars[] theScrollBars =
        (ScrollBars[])Enum.GetValues(theEnum.GetType( ));

    foreach (ScrollBars scrollBar in theScrollBars)
    {
        if (scrollBar.ToString( ) == strValue)
        {
            pnlScroll.ScrollBars = scrollBar;
        }
    }
```

In the event handler method for the SelectedIndexChanged event of the radio button list, a reference to the radio button list is obtained by casting sender to a variable of type RadioButtonList. Then the Wrap property of pnlScroll is set appropriately by converting the SelectedValue of the control to a Boolean.

If the text string in strText did not have any HTML tags in it, it would display a single, very long line if Wrap were set to false. As it is, with each "line" enclosed in the paragraph tags, when Wrap is set to false it displays as three separate paragraphs.

The Panel Control and AJAX

The Panel control is the AJAX user's best friend, offering as it does a blank canvas on which to add some subtle and some not so subtle effects. In particular, the UpdatePanel is one of the core AJAX controls now available by default in .NET 3.5

---

along with the `ScriptManager`. It enables (asynchronous) partial-page rendering, or rather, it enables the controls it contains to post back and update from the web server asynchronously, without forcing the entire page to post back as well. You'll see more on this in the next section of the chapter.

Before then, you'll look at the following AJAX Control Toolkit controls which either extend the basic `Panel` or offer its functionality but in a slightly enhanced way:

DropShadowExtender
> Emphasizes the existence of the panel on the web page by adding a drop shadow behind it which you can customize as you see fit.

DragPanelExtender
> Allows the user to drag and drop the panel and its contents anywhere on the page.

CollapsiblePanelExtender
> Enables the panel to be "collapsed" (made invisible) and "expanded" based on whether a nominated control has been clicked or the user's mouse has passed over the panel.

Accordion
> Builds on the idea of the `CollapsiblePanelExtender` to offer a number of collapsible panes stuck together where only one can be expanded at any time.

Tabs
> Similar to the `Accordion`, the `Tabs` control offers the idea that a number of `Panels` are stacked on top of each other with only the topmost control being visible. Each panel has a header which is visible, and clicking it moves its corresponding contents to the top of the stack and makes them visible.

PopUpControlExtender
> Attaches an `UpdatePanel` to a nominated control and makes it invisible until such time as the nominated control comes into focus (is selected), when the `UpdatePanel` and its contents become visible ("pop up") and you can choose the value for the control from the contents of the `Panel` control.

Notice that all of these controls work on the idea of making a form or some static content available on a page in the most user-friendly way possible; an extension of the original intent of the `Panel` control.

Panel Extenders

The AJAX Control Toolkit contains two extender controls that specifically target the `Panel` control: the `DropShadowExtender` and the `DragPanelExtender`. To demonstrate, the next example extends *PanelDemo.aspx*, giving the top panel a drop shadow and allowing it to be dragged anywhere over the page. You can see the result in Figure 5-2.

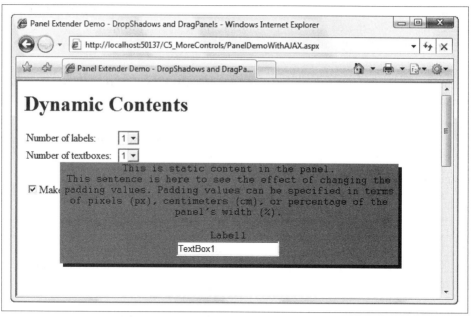

Figure 5-2. PanelDemoWithAJAX.aspx in action

Add a new AJAX web form to the *C5_MoreControls* website, call it *PanelDemoWithAJAX.aspx*, and copy the code for the pnlDynamic panel, its contents, and the associated HTML table, as given in Example 5-1, under the ScriptManager control. Copy also the code for only the Page_Load event handler in Example 5-2 to *PanelDemoWithAJAX.aspx.cs*.

Now drag a DropShadowExtender from the VS2008 Toolbox so that it is under pnlDynamic but above the HTML table. Set its targetControlId property to pnlDynamic and run the page. Once you make the panel visible, you'll see the drop shadow based around the bottom right of the panel, as in Figure 5-2. You can customize the shadow's presentation and behavior a little using the five properties shown in Table 5-2.

Table 5-2. DropShadowExtender properties

Name	Type	Default	Description
Opacity	Float	0.5	Sets the transparency level of the shadow from 0.0 (totally transparent) to 1.0 (fully opaque)
Radius	Integer	5	Sets the radius in pixels of the shadow's rounded corners if Rounded is set to true
Rounded	Boolean	False	Sets whether the shadow has rounded corners
TrackPosition	Boolean	False	Sets whether the drop shadow should follow the targeted Panel if it moves on the page
Width	Integer	5	Sets the width of the shadow

To demonstrate, change the control's Opacity to 0.2, Rounded to true, and Radius to 10 and run the page again.

Now drag a DropPanelExtender from the Toolbox so that it is under the DropShadowExtender. Again, set its targetControlId property to pnlDynamic and run the page. You should notice a few issues:

- You can drag the panel up the page but apparently not down the page. The issue here is that you can't drag the panel below the end of the content on the page. To give yourself a bit more space to experiment with the DragPanelExtender, set the style property for the main div on the page to height:800px;.

- The drop shadow stays where it was originally created even when you drag and drop the panel elsewhere. Set the DropShadowExtender's TrackPosition property to true to fix this.

Notice how, even though the Panel or its shadow may sometimes obscure the button, the two DropDownLists do still affect the Panel in the same way as before. It's simply that the Panel has acquired new functionality. Example 5-5 highlights where a change has been made in *PanelDemoWithAJAX.aspx* over the original in Example 5-1.

Example 5-5. PanelDemoWithAJAX.aspx

```
<%@ Page Language="C#" AutoEventWireup="true"
    CodeFile="PanelDemoWithAJAX.aspx.cs"
    Inherits="PanelDemoWithAJAX" %>

<%@ Register Assembly="AjaxControlToolkit" Namespace="AjaxControlToolkit"
TagPrefix="cc1" %>

<!DOCTYPE html PUBLIC "-//W3C//DTD XHTML 1.0 Transitional//EN"
"http://www.w3.org/TR/xhtml1/DTD/xhtml1-transitional.dtd">
<html xmlns="http://www.w3.org/1999/xhtml">
<head runat="server">
    <title>Panel Extender Demo - DropShadows and DragPanels</title>

    <script type="text/javascript">

        function pageLoad( ) {
        }

    </script>

</head>

<body>
    <form id="form1" runat="server">
    <div style="height:800px;">
        <asp:ScriptManager ID="ScriptManager1" runat="server" />
        <h1>Dynamic Contents</h1>
```

Example 5-5. PanelDemoWithAJAX.aspx (continued)

```
        <asp:Panel ID="pnlDynamic" runat="server" BackColor="Fuchsia"
            Height="150px" Width="80%" Font-Names="Courier"
            HorizontalAlign="Center" ScrollBars="Auto">
            This is static content in the panel.
            <br />
            This sentence is here to see the effect of changing the padding values.
            Padding values can be specified in terms of pixels (px),
            centimeters (cm), or percentage of the panel's width (%).
        </asp:Panel>
        <cc1:DropShadowExtender ID="DropShadowExtender1" runat="server"
            TargetControlID="pnlDynamic" TrackPosition="true">
        </cc1:DropShadowExtender>
        <cc1:DragPanelExtender ID="DragPanelExtender1" runat="server"
            TargetControlID="pnlDynamic">
        </cc1:DragPanelExtender>

        <table>
          ... contents of table as in Example 5-1 ...
        </table>
    </div>
    </form>
</body>
</html>
```

In this example, you drag and drop the Panel by selecting the Panel itself. It's also possible to associate another control on the page with the panel you want to move, by setting the DragPanelExtender's DragHandleID property to the other control's ID. Having done that, the only way to move the Panel, then, will be to drag and drop the "handle" control.

Collapsible Panels and Accordions

You can get a lot of mileage out of toggling a Panel's Visible property to keep a page more user-friendly, hiding controls or forms from view until required. Indeed, *PanelDemo.aspx* demonstrated this earlier in the chapter, as well as the fact that the page must be posted back to the server before the change in its visibility occurs.

Naturally, AJAX presents several options to hide or make visible a panel and its contents without posting the page back to the server. In this section, you'll look at the CollapsiblePanelExtender, which provides the most direct mapping to the "toggle panel visibility by clicking a button" action in an AJAX world, and the Accordion, which stacks several collapsible panels on top of each other and substitutes the toggle button to click with a visible part of the panel itself.

In the next example, *CollapsiblePanelDemo.aspx*, you'll use and experiment with a CollapsiblePanelExtender (CPE) control, to hide and make visible the contents of a Panel (a RadioButtonList) in several ways. Figure 5-3 shows the final page.

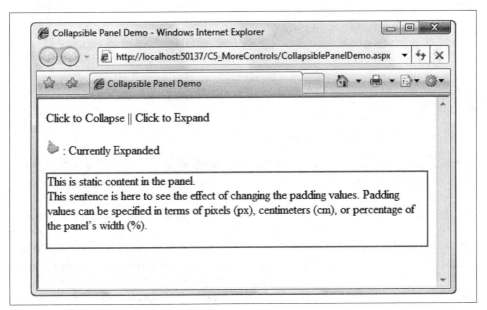

Figure 5-3. CollapsiblePanelDemo.aspx in action

To follow this example, you'll need *ToggleButton_Checked.gif* and *ToggleButton_Unchecked.gif*, which you can find either in the code download for this book or in the ToggleButton demo in the AJAX Control Toolkit sample website.

Add a new AJAX web form to the *C5_MoreControls* website and call it *CollapsiblePanelDemo.aspx*. Add two Label controls to the page under the ScriptManager control and give them the IDs of lblCollapse and lblExpand. Give them some text as shown in Figure 5-3. Now copy the code for the pnlDynamic panel and its contents, as given in Example 5-1, under the two Labels.

Now add a CPE control to the page under the panel. You want pnlDynamic to collapse, so set the extender's TargetControlID property to pnlDynamic. Running the page doesn't do much at the moment as the collapse and expand actions aren't hooked up to anything, so that's the next task. Set CollapseControlID to lblCollapse and ExpandControlID to lblExpand to wire up the labels. Also set Collapsed to true so that the panel is initially hidden when the page loads.

Run the page, and even if it doesn't look like you can, click the text to expand or collapse the panel. Label controls are deliberately in this example to emphasize that no postbacks are being used to collapse or expand the panel; they do not auto-postback a page when you click them.

A CollapsedPanelExtender will retain its state if a page is posted back to the server, so the panel it contains and the subordinate controls it targets will also retain the state they had before the postback.

So far, so not-too-thrilling, so let's look at some of the CPE's properties in Table 5-3 and put them to use.

Table 5-3. CollapsiblePanelExtender properties

Name	Type	Default	Description
AutoCollapse	Boolean	false	Sets whether the panel will collapse if the cursor moves off it.
AutoExpand	Boolean	false	Sets whether the panel will expand if the cursor moves onto it.
CollapseControlID	String		The ID of the control to click to toggle the panel collapsing.
Collapsed	Boolean	false	Sets whether the panel is collapsed when the page is initially loaded.
CollapsedImage	String		The URL of the image shown by the Image control named in ImageControlID when the panel is collapsed. Has no effect if ImageControlID is not set.
CollapsedSize	Integer	0	The width of the panel in pixels when collapsed.
CollapsedText	String		The value for the Text property of the Label control named in TextLabelID when the panel is collapsed. Has no effect if TextLabelID is not set.
ExpandControlID	String		The ID of the control to click to toggle the panel expanding.
ExpandDirection	Horizontal, Vertical	Vertical	The direction in which a panel is expanded/collapsed.
ExpandedImage	String		The URL of the image shown by the Image control named in ImageControlID when the panel is expanded. Has no effect if ImageControlID is not set.
ExpandedSize	Integer		The width of the panel in pixels when expanded. Overrides the target Panel control's Width property.
ExpandedText	String		The value for the Text property of the control specified by TextLabelID when the panel is expanded. Has no effect if TextLabelID is not set.
ImageControlID	String		The ID of the Image server control whose URL property will change when the panel is resized.
ScrollContents	Boolean	false	Sets whether scroll bars will be added around the panel if its contents are too large to be shown all at once when expanded. Note that these scroll bars are in addition to any that may be made visible through the Panel control's own Scrollbars property.
TextLabelID	String		The ID of the Label control whose Text property will change when the panel is resized.

Now you'll add a bit more interaction on the page besides the actual hiding and expanding of the panel. The CPE allows you to specify other controls whose values change depending on whether the panel is collapsed or visible. First consider a text control such as a Label. Add a Label control with an ID of lblState to the page and clear its Text property. Now set the CPE's textLabelID to lblState, and then use its ExpandedText and CollapsedText properties to set the Label's text when the panel has been expanded and collapsed, respectively.

You can also use the CPE to toggle between images to represent the expanded or collapsed state of the panel. Add an Image control with an ID of imgToggle to the page. Set the CPE's ImageControlID property to imgToggle and then set its ExpandedImage and CollapsedImage properties accordingly.

Finally, you'll make a few UI tweaks. The CPE's ExpandDirection property allows you to specify whether the resizing of the panel should be animated in a horizontal or vertical direction, and its CollapsedSize property lets you specify the width in pixels of the panel when collapsed, if you'd prefer it to be something other than zero. The final page is listed in Example 5-6. You can also set AutoExpand or AutoCollapse to true if you want to toggle the state of the panel by mousing over it.

Example 5-6. CollapsiblePanel.aspx in full

```
<%@ Page Language="C#" AutoEventWireup="true"
    CodeFile="CollapsiblePanel.aspx.cs"
    Inherits="CollapsiblePanel" %>
<%@ Register Assembly="AjaxControlToolkit"
    Namespace="AjaxControlToolkit" TagPrefix="cc1" %>

<!DOCTYPE html PUBLIC "-//W3C//DTD XHTML 1.0 Transitional//EN"
    "http://www.w3.org/TR/xhtml1/DTD/xhtml1-transitional.dtd">
<html xmlns="http://www.w3.org/1999/xhtml">
<head runat="server">
    <title>Collapsible Panel Demo</title>

    <script type="text/javascript">

        function pageLoad( ) {
        }

    </script>

</head>

<body>
    <form id="form1" runat="server">
    <div>
        <asp:ScriptManager ID="ScriptManager1" runat="server" />
        <p>
            <asp:Label ID="lblCollapse" runat="server" Text="Click to Collapse" />
            ||
            <asp:Label ID="lblExpand" runat="server" Text="Click to Expand" />
        </p>
```

Example 5-6. CollapsiblePanel.aspx in full (continued)

```
    <p>
        <asp:Image ID="imgToggle" runat="server" /> :
        <asp:Label ID="lblState" runat="server" />
    </p>
    <p>

        <asp:Panel runat="server" ID="pnlDynamic"
            BorderWidth="2px" BorderColor="red">
        This is static content in the panel.
        <br />
        This sentence is here to see the effect of changing the padding values.
        Padding values can be specified in terms of pixels (px), centimeters (cm),
        or percentage of the panel's width (%).
        <p />
        </asp:Panel>
        <cc1:CollapsiblePanelExtender ID="CollapsiblePanelExtender1"
            runat="server" TargetControlID="pnlDynamic"
            CollapseControlID="lblCollapse" ExpandControlID="lblExpand"
            Collapsed="true" ExpandedText="Currently Expanded"
            CollapsedText="Currently Collapsed" TextLabelID="lblState"
            ExpandedImage="ToggleButton_Checked.gif"
            CollapsedImage="ToggleButton_Unchecked.gif"
            ImageControlID="imgToggle"
            ExpandDirection="Horizontal" CollapsedSize="100" />
    </p>
  </div>
  </form>
</body>
</html>
```

Moving now to look at the Accordion control, you'd be forgiven for looking at the next example in Figure 5-4 and thinking that it is just a collection of CollapsiblePanelExtender controls wired up in a specific way. The Accordion control is in fact its own standalone control deriving from System.Web.UI.WebControls.WebControl rather than System.Web.UI.ExtenderControl.

Every Accordion control contains one or more AccordionPanes, which contain a Header area and a Content area. The user will click the Header area to reveal the contents of the AccordionPane to which it belongs. Only one pane can be shown at a time.

 One of the best features of the Accordion control is that you can bind data from databases or another data source to it rather than having to write it all out longhand. We cover binding data to controls in Chapters 7 through 10.

Add a new AJAX web form to the *C5_MoreControls* website and call it *AccordionDemo.aspx*. The Accordion doesn't rely on any other controls, so just drag an Accordion control onto the page under the ScriptManager and drag two AccordionPanes into the Accordion. Give both AccordionPanes a header and a content area as highlighted in Example 5-7.

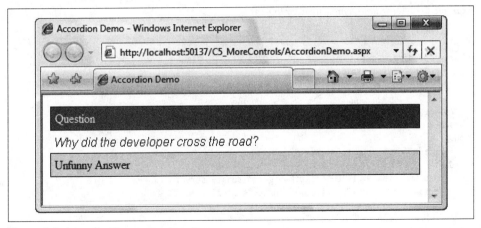

Figure 5-4. AccordionDemo.aspx in action

Example 5-7. AccordionDemo.aspx

```
<%@ Page Language="C#" AutoEventWireup="true"
    CodeFile="AccordionDemo.aspx.cs" Inherits="AccordionDemo" %>

<%@ Register Assembly="AjaxControlToolkit"
    Namespace="AjaxControlToolkit" TagPrefix="cc1" %>

<!DOCTYPE html PUBLIC "-//W3C//DTD XHTML 1.0 Transitional//EN"
    "http://www.w3.org/TR/xhtml1/DTD/xhtml1-transitional.dtd">
<html xmlns="http://www.w3.org/1999/xhtml">
<head runat="server">
    <title>Accordion Demo</title>

    <script type="text/javascript">

        function pageLoad( ) {
        }

    </script>

    <style type="text/css">
        .header
        {
            background-color: Aqua;
            padding : 5px;
            border : solid 1px black;
            color : Black;
        }
        .selectedheader
        {
            background-color: Green;
            padding : 5px;
            border : solid 1px black;
            color : Yellow;
        }
```

Example 5-7. AccordionDemo.aspx (continued)

```
      .content
      {
         padding: 5px;
         font-style: italic;
         font-family: Arial;
      }
   </style>
</head>
<body>
   <form id="form1" runat="server">
   <div>
      <asp:ScriptManager ID="ScriptManager1" runat="server" />
      <cc1:Accordion ID="Accordion1" runat="server"
         HeaderCssClass="header" ContentCssClass="content"
         HeaderSelectedCssClass="selectedheader"
         FadeTransitions="false" TransitionDuration="2000"
         FramesPerSecond="5" AutoSize="Limit">
         <Panes>
            <cc1:AccordionPane runat="server" ID="pane1">
               <Header>Question</Header>
               <Content>Why did the developer cross the road?</Content>
            </cc1:AccordionPane>
            <cc1:AccordionPane runat="server" ID="pane2">
               <Header>Unfunny Answer</Header>
               <Content>The chicken had a gun</Content>
            </cc1:AccordionPane>
         </Panes>
      </cc1:Accordion>
   </div>
   </form>
</body>
</html>
```

Save and run the page. You'll see that the Accordion expands the first pane and collapses the second by default. Clicking the header for the second pane will expand its contents and collapse those of the first. You can add as many AccordionPanes into the Panes collection as you have data, although it may be worth noting that too many will clutter the screen and will not help users find the information or the bit of the form they require.

Table 5-4 presents a list of properties controlling the display of the Accordion on the page you'll use to tweak the control in *AccordionDemo.aspx*.

Table 5-4. Accordion control properties

Name	Type	Default	Description
AutoSize	Fill, Limit, None	None	Determines how much space the Accordion will take up on the page.
ContentCssClass	String		Sets the default CSS for the content area of all its child AccordionPanes.

Table 5-4. Accordion control properties (continued)

Name	Type	Default	Description
FadeTransitions	Boolean	false	Sets whether the contents of a newly expanded AccordionPane fade into view.
FramesPerSecond	Integer	15	Sets the speed of the animation between AccordionPane objects.
HeaderCssClass	String		Sets the default CSS class for the header areas of all child AccordionPanes whose content areas are currently hidden.
HeaderSelectedCssClass	String		The default CSS class for the header area of the currently selected AccordionPane.
RequireOpenedPane	Boolean	true	Sets whether the Accordion must always have the contents of one pane visible to the user.
SelectedIndex	Integer	0	The index of the AccordionPane in the Accordion that should be open when the page is loaded initially and the index of the pane currently selected after that.
SuppressHeaderPostbacks	Boolean	false	Sets whether postback events which would have been raised by controls in an AccordionPane header area should be suppressed. So, if you have a hyperlink in the header, the browser navigates to that URL when clicked rather than resizing the Accordion.
TransitionDuration	Integer	500	Length in milliseconds of the animation between AccordionPane objects.

Now to demonstrate these properties: first, set RequireOpenedPane to false and run the page again. Note the top pane is still open by default on initial load, but you can now collapse it without having any other pane expanded. It's still true that only one AccordionPane can be expanded at any one time; you can't change that. If you want to change the pane that opens initially on-screen, set the Accordion's SelectedIndex property to a value other than 0 (zero). This value represents the (zero-based) index of the pane you want to be opened in the list of panes in your markup. Therefore if you want the fourth pane in your Accordion to be open initially, set SelectedIndex to 3.

The Accordion displays both the header and contents of its panes as plain text by default. Example 5-7 suggests some basic CSS styles that you can use to differentiate between the header of a currently expanded (selected) pane and the headers of panes that are not currently selected. Set the Accordion's HeaderSelectedCssClass and HeaderCssClass to these styles, respectively, to link them. You can also style the contents of AccordionPanes using the Accordion control's ContentCssClass property.

You can also tweak the animation that occurs when a user switches between panes. Like a CollapsiblePanelExtender, when a pane is deselected its content area collapses into its header, and when it is selected its content area extends from the header into an area big enough to show the pane's contents, or to the size specified by the Accordion control's Height property.

You can control how quickly that collapse or expansion of the content area occurs using the TransitionDuration and FramesPerSecond properties. The former defines how long (in milliseconds) the complete collapse/expansion animation will take, and the latter determines how many steps will occur in the animation per second, effectively determining how smooth the animation will appear.

You can also control how the contents of the pane appear in a new expanded area on-screen using the FadeTransitions property. If you set this property to true, you will see the contents fade into view once the pane has expanded fully. Setting it to false will have the contents simply appear.

One final property to consider for the Accordion—AutoSize—controls how much space the Accordion takes up on the page. It takes one of three values:

None

> The Accordion will take up exactly enough space to show the currently expanded pane and all the other headers. When a new pane is selected, the other contents of the page may be moved up or down depending on the new size of the Accordion.

Limit

> The Accordion will take up exactly the space on the page given by its Height CSS property. If content in the selected pane doesn't fill the space, it will add whitespace so that it does. If content overfills the selected pane, scroll bars will be added to the pane accordingly.

Fill

> The Accordion will take up exactly the space on the page as determined by its Height CSS property. If content in the selected pane doesn't fill or overfills the space, it will be shrunk or expanded accordingly.

It's also worth noting that each AccordionPane also has a HeaderCssClass and a ContentCssClass property with which you can override the choice of style made in the Accordion's properties of the same name.

From Columns to Stacks

From working on the y-axis to working on the z-axis, the next AJAX Control Toolkit server control stacks Panel controls on top of each other, much as Windows Property pages do (see Figure 5-5), rather than below each other as Accordions do. This tabbed interface is often the easiest for users to understand and the TabContainer control gives you the chance to use it on a web page.

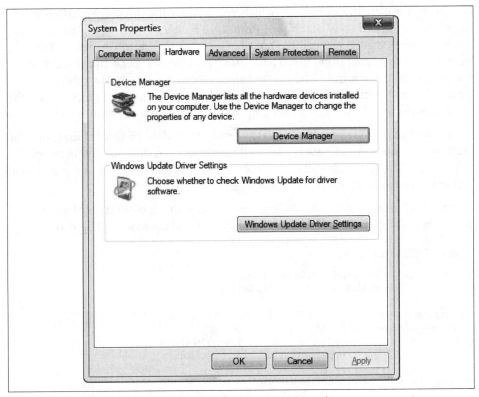

Figure 5-5. Windows Property pages, which also use a tabbed interface

As with the Accordion, there are two pieces to the puzzle here. The Accordion has its AccordionPanes and the TabContainer has its TabPanels, which also provide the idea of header text and contents, albeit in a different way:

```
<cc1:TabContainer>
    <cc1:TabPanel HeaderText=" header1 ">
        <ContentTemplate>
            content for tabpanel 1
        </ContentTemplate>
    </cc1:TabPanel>

    ...

    <cc1:TabPanel HeaderText=" header n ">
        <ContentTemplate>
            content for tabpanel n
        </ContentTemplate>
    </cc1:TabPanel>
</cc1:TabContainer>
```

As you can see, in contrast to AccordionPane, TabPanels use their HeaderText property for their tab header contents and a ContentTemplate to contain everything to be displayed in that panel.

Let's work through an example, in which you'll adapt the original *PanelDemo.aspx* page into a tabbed-style interface. Add a new AJAX web form to the *C5_ MoreControls* website, and call it *TabDemo.aspx*. Copy the top panel, pnlDynamic, along with its contents from *PanelDemo.aspx* onto the new page and place it under the ScriptManager control. The TabContainer doesn't rely on any other controls (again like the Accordion control), so just drag one onto the page under the ScriptManager and then use its Smart Tag menu to add TabPanel controls to it.

For the first TabPanel, set its HeaderText property to "Number of Labels" and copy the DropDownList control, ddlLabels, from *PanelDemo.aspx* into its ContentTemplate. Copy the ddlBoxes DropDownList control into the ContentTemplate for the second TabPanel and give it the HeaderText "Number of TextBoxes".

Finally, copy btnRefresh onto the page and under the TabContainer. Example 5-8 shows the markup code with the new TabContainer and contents highlighted.

Example 5-8. TabDemo.aspx

```
<%@ Page Language="C#" AutoEventWireup="true"
   CodeFile="TabDemo.aspx.cs" Inherits="TabDemo" %>

<%@ Register Assembly="AjaxControlToolkit"
   Namespace="AjaxControlToolkit" TagPrefix="cc1" %>
<!DOCTYPE html PUBLIC "-//W3C//DTD XHTML 1.0 Transitional//EN"
   "http://www.w3.org/TR/xhtml1/DTD/xhtml1-transitional.dtd">

<html xmlns="http://www.w3.org/1999/xhtml">
<head runat="server">
   <title>Tab Demo</title>

   <script type="text/javascript">

      function pageLoad( ) {
      }

   </script>
</head>

<body>
   <form id="form1" runat="server">
   <div>
      <asp:ScriptManager ID="ScriptManager1" runat="server" />
      <asp:Panel ID="pnlDynamic" runat="server" BackColor="Fuchsia"
         Height="150px" HorizontalAlign="Center" ScrollBars="Auto">
         This is static content in the panel.
         <br />
         This sentence is here to see the effect of changing
         the padding values. Padding values can be specified
         in terms of pixels (px), centimeters (cm), or percentage
         of the panel's width (%).
         <p />
      </asp:Panel>
```

Example 5-8. TabDemo.aspx (continued)

```
    <br />
    <hr />
    <br />
    <cc1:TabContainer ID="TabContainer1" runat="server"
        Height="200" ActiveTabIndex="1">
        <cc1:TabPanel ID="TabPanel1" runat="server"
            HeaderText="Number of labels">
            <ContentTemplate>
                <p>How many labels should be added to the panel?</p>
                <asp:DropDownList ID="ddlLabels" runat="server">
                    <asp:ListItem Text="0" Value="0" />
                    <asp:ListItem Text="1" Value="1" />
                    <asp:ListItem Text="2" Value="2" />
                    <asp:ListItem Text="3" Value="3" />
                    <asp:ListItem Text="4" Value="4" />
                </asp:DropDownList>
            </ContentTemplate>
        </cc1:TabPanel>
        <cc1:TabPanel ID="TabPanel2" runat="server"
            HeaderText="Number of textboxes">
            <ContentTemplate>
            <p>How many textboxes should be added to the panel?</p>
                <asp:DropDownList ID="ddlBoxes" runat="server">
                    <asp:ListItem Text="0" Value="0" />
                    <asp:ListItem Text="1" Value="1" />
                    <asp:ListItem Text="2" Value="2" />
                    <asp:ListItem Text="3" Value="3" />
                    <asp:ListItem Text="4" Value="4" />
                </asp:DropDownList>
            </ContentTemplate>
        </cc1:TabPanel>
    </cc1:TabContainer>
    <br />
    <br />
    <asp:Button ID="btnRefresh"
        Text="Refresh Panel" runat="server" />
    </div>
    </form>
</body>
</html>
```

You'll also need to copy the code pertaining to the two DropDownList controls from
the Page_Load handler in *PanelDemo.aspx.cs* into *TabDemo.aspx.cs*, as shown in
Example 5-9.

Example 5-9. TabDemo.aspx.cs

```
using System;
using System.Web.UI;
using System.Web.UI.WebControls;

public partial class TabDemo : Page
```

Example 5-9. TabDemo.aspx.cs (continued)

```
{
    protected void Page_Load(object sender, EventArgs e)
    {
        // Generate label controls
        int numlabels = Int32.Parse(ddlLabels.SelectedItem.Value);
        for (int i = 1; i <= numlabels; i++)
        {
            Label lbl = new Label();
            lbl.Text = "Label" + (i).ToString();
            lbl.ID = "Label" + (i).ToString();
            pnlDynamic.Controls.Add(lbl);
            pnlDynamic.Controls.Add(new LiteralControl("<br />"));
        }

        // Generate textbox controls
        int numBoxes = Int32.Parse(ddlBoxes.SelectedItem.Value);
        for (int i = 1; i <= numBoxes; i++)
        {
            TextBox txt = new TextBox();
            txt.Text = "TextBox" + (i).ToString();
            txt.ID = "TextBox" + (i).ToString();
            pnlDynamic.Controls.Add(txt);
            pnlDynamic.Controls.Add(new LiteralControl("<br />"));
        }
    }
}
```

If you run the page now, you'll see something similar to Figure 5-6.

The page works the same way as *PanelDemo.aspx*. Just choose values in the two DropDownLists and click the button. The TabContainer affects nothing in their operation or the way they can be referenced from the code-behind file—just the way in which they are displayed on-screen.

You can tweak the TabContainer presentation using the properties shown in Table 5-5.

Table 5-5. TabContainer's UI-related properties

Name	Type	Default	Description
ActiveTabIndex	Integer	−1	The (zero-based) index of the TabPanel currently visible on the page.
CssClass	String	ajax__tab_xp	The parent CSS class with which you want to style the TabContainer and its panels (more on this shortly).
Height	Integer		The height in pixels of the TabContainer.

Table 5-5. TabContainer's UI-related properties (continued)

Name	Type	Default	Description
Scrollbars	Auto, None, Both, Horizontal, or Vertical	None	Sets whether a TabPanel should contain scroll bars if its content overfills the space available.
Width	Integer		The width of the TabContainer as a percentage of the width of the page.

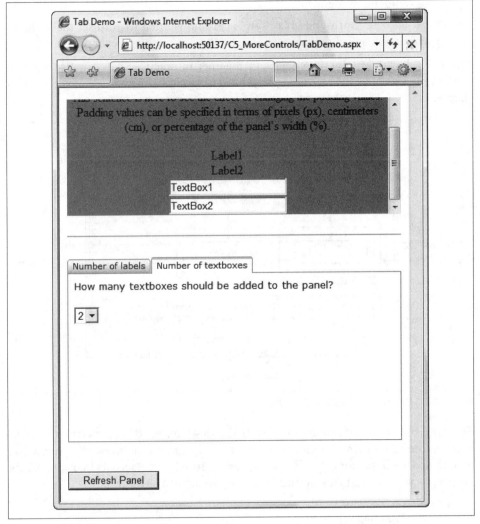

Figure 5-6. TabDemo.aspx in action

You can format all the tab headers and their contents using two CSS styles:

- ajax__tab_body formats the text contents of the tab.
- ajax__tab_header formats the area containing all the headers of the tabs.

Three additional styles allow you to change the appearance of an individual tab header:

- ajax__tab_tab formats the text in the tab header.
- ajax__tab_inner surrounds ajax__tab_tab and is often used to set the righthand background image of the tab.
- ajax__tab_outer surrounds ajax_tab_inner and is often used to set the lefthand background image of the tab.

Figure 5-7 illustrates how these styles fit together in practice. You can also see this working in *TabPanelStylesDemo.aspx*, which is available in the download for this chapter.

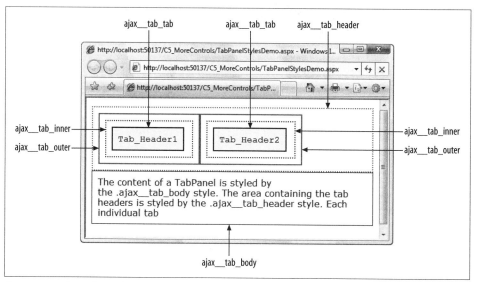

Figure 5-7. The TabPanel and its CSS styles

To apply your own definitions to these five styles, you must first specify a "parent class" in the TabContainer's CssClass property. In Figure 5-7, all five styles have a 2px border and their padding attributes are set to 10px. The TabContainer's CssClass property is set to DemoStyles, so the five styles are defined as follows:

```
<style type="text/css">
    .DemoStyles .ajax__tab_header {
        font-family:Courier New; padding: 10px; border:dotted 2px red;}

    .DemoStyles .ajax__tab_outer {
        padding:10px;border:solid 2px green;}
```

```
.DemoStyles .ajax__tab_inner {
    padding:10px;border:dotted 2px blue;}

.DemoStyles .ajax__tab_tab {
    padding:10px;border:solid 2px black;background-color:yellow;}

.DemoStyles .ajax__tab_body {
    font-family:verdana;border:1px solid black;padding:10px}
</style>
```

You can also go further and define CSS styles for a tab header when the cursor is hovering over it by using the `.ajax__tab_hover` class. For instance:

```
.DemoStyles .ajax__tab_hover .ajax__tab_outer {}
.DemoStyles .ajax__tab_hover .ajax__tab_inner {}
.DemoStyles .ajax__tab_hover .ajax__tab_tab {}
```

Similarly, you can also define specific CSS styles for the currently selected tab header by using the `.ajax__tab_active` class:

```
.DemoStyles .ajax__tab_active .ajax__tab_outer {}
.DemoStyles .ajax__tab_active .ajax__tab_inner {}
.DemoStyles .ajax__tab_active .ajax__tab_tab {}
```

Both of these sets of styles will override the defaults for tab headers when applicable.

 You can find the default styles which the AJAX Control Toolkit uses for the TabPanel in *<toolkitInstallDirectory>\AjaxControlToolkit\ Tabs\ Tabs.css*.

Finally, you can also set a TabPanel's Enabled property to `true` or `false` to make it visible or not visible in the container area.

The UpdatePanel Control

The majority of the controls you've seen thus far in this chapter and in Chapter 4 have had some sort of graphical component. The Panel control does not, nor does the UpdatePanel, which you'll look at next. Available initially in Microsoft's ASP.NET AJAX Extensions download and now included directly in .NET 3.5, the UpdatePanel has much the same purpose as the Panel control—to identify and isolate a set of controls on a page—but with a different intention once the controls have been added to the panel.

If you'll recall from Chapter 3, the UpdatePanel is a server-side control that enables the common AJAX pattern of partial-page updates. Or rather, as well as being able to make the controls it contains visible or invisible, the UpdatePanel lets you isolate content you want to update independently from the rest of the content on the page.

One of the best features of the UpdatePanel is exactly how easy it is to enable this partial-page postback. You just drag one or more UpdatePanel controls onto your page and then drag controls you want updated into the UpdatePanel. Each UpdatePanel is updated individually and asynchronously, without affecting one another or anything else on the page.

 You can disable all UpdatePanels on a page by setting the ScriptManager's EnablePartialRendering property to false on that page.

It's time to demonstrate. Add a new AJAX web form to the *C5_MoreControls* website and call it *UpdatePanelDemo.aspx*. First, you need to establish what the page does when it posts back normally. Add two labels, lblTime and lblCounter, and a button, btnStdPostBack, to the page below the ScriptManager control. Delete lblTime.Text and set lblCounter.Text to 0. Set btnStdPostback.Text to "Standard Postback".

```
<p>
    Time:
    <asp:Label ID="lblTime" runat="server" /><br />
    Number of page_loads:
    <asp:Label ID="lblCounter" runat="server" Text="0" />
</p>
<p>
    <asp:Button ID="btnStdPostback" runat="server"
    Text="Standard Postback" />
</p>
```

Switch to the code-behind page and add the following code to the Page_Load handler:

```
protected void Page_Load(object sender, EventArgs e)
{
    // Get counter1 and increment it
    int counter = Int32.Parse(lblCounter.Text);
    lblCounter.Text = (++counter).ToString();

    // Set current date and time
    lblTime.Text = DateTime.Now.ToString();
}
```

Now run the page. lblTime displays the time the page was last loaded, and lblCounter displays the number of times it has been reloaded as a result of postbacks. So far, so boring; every time you click the button, the whole page is posted back and all the values are updated on the page accompanied by a flicker of the page in the browser as it is reloaded.

Next, copy the two labels, paste them below the button, and call them lblTime2 and lblCounter2. Add a new button under them, called btnAsyncPostback, and adjust the Page_Load routine to update the new labels as well, as shown in Example 5-10. Note that all the code is in the one function. Run the page and verify that all the labels update with the same values regardless of which button is pressed.

Example 5-10. UpdatePanelDemo.aspx.cs

```
using System;
using System.Web.UI;

public partial class UpdatePanelDemo : Page
{

    protected void Page_Load(object sender, EventArgs e)
    {
        // Get counter1 and increment it
        int counter = Int32.Parse(lblCounter.Text);
        lblCounter.Text = (++counter).ToString();

        // Get counter2 and increment it
        counter = Int32.Parse(lblCounter2.Text);
        lblCounter2.Text = (++counter).ToString();

        // Set current date and time
        lblTime.Text = DateTime.Now.ToString();
        lblTime2.Text = DateTime.Now.ToString();
    }
}
```

Now drag an UpdatePanel control onto the page from the AJAX Extensions part of
the Toolbox in VS2008. Cut and paste lblTime2, lblCounter2, and btnAsyncPostback
into the UpdatePanel. If you do this in Source view, you'll need to add a
<ContentTemplate> child element to the UpdatePanel and cut and paste the controls
into it. In Design view, the content template is created automatically. Either way, the
code for the page thus far should resemble that in Example 5-11. (You'll also find it
in the download for the chapter, saved as *UpdatePanelDemoPart1.aspx*.)

Example 5-11. UpdatePanelDemo.aspx with one UpdatePanel

```
<%@ Page Language="C#" AutoEventWireup="true"
    CodeFile="UpdatePanelDemo.aspx.cs"
    Inherits="UpdatePanelDemo" %>

<!DOCTYPE html PUBLIC "-//W3C//DTD XHTML 1.0 Transitional//EN"
    "http://www.w3.org/TR/xhtml1/DTD/xhtml1-transitional.dtd">
<html xmlns="http://www.w3.org/1999/xhtml">
<head runat="server">
    <title>UpdatePanel Demo</title>
    <script type="text/javascript">

        function pageLoad( ) {
        }

    </script>

</head>
```

Example 5-11. UpdatePanelDemo.aspx with one UpdatePanel (continued)

```
<body>
    <form id="form1" runat="server">
    <div>
        <asp:ScriptManager ID="ScriptManager1" runat="server" />
        <h1>
            Update Panel Demo Part 1</h1>
        <p>
            Time:
            <asp:Label ID="lblTime" runat="server" /><br />
            Number of page_loads:
            <asp:Label ID="lblCounter" runat="server" Text="0" />
        </p>
        <p>
            <asp:Button ID="btnStdPostback"
                runat="server" Text="Standard Postback" />
        </p>
        <br />
        <hr />
        <br />
        <asp:UpdatePanel ID="UpdatePanel1" runat="server">
            <ContentTemplate>
                <p>
                    Time:
                    <asp:Label ID="lblTime2" runat="server" /><br />
                    Number of page_loads:
                    <asp:Label ID="lblCounter2" runat="server" Text="0" />
                </p>
                <p>
                    <asp:Button ID="btnAsyncPostback"
                        runat="server" Text="Async Postback" />
                </p>
            </ContentTemplate>
        </asp:UpdatePanel>
    </div>
    </form>
</body>
</html>
```

Run the page again. Note that clicking btnStdPostBack updates both sets of labels as before, but clicking btnAsyncPostback updates only the values for lblTime2 and lblCounter2, as shown in Figure 5-8. Because btnAsyncPostback is in the UpdatePanel, ASP.NET AJAX understands that when it is clicked, only the controls inside the UpdatePanel should be updated. Hence, an asynchronous or "partial-page" update occurs and there is no flicker in the browser as the whole page reloads.

Thus, one of the most useful aspects of AJAX is demonstrated. It is not without its caveats, however.

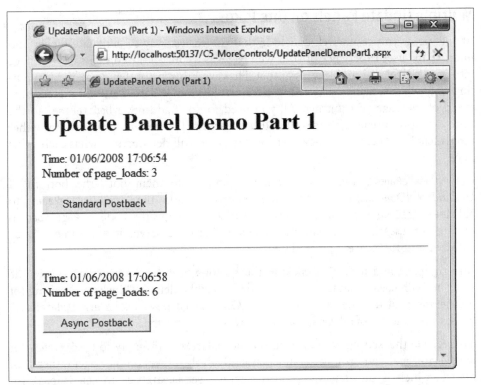

Figure 5-8. A partial-page postback

Click `btnAsyncPostback` a few times so that the partial-page update occurs several times and the counters are out of sync. Now click `btnStdPostback` again so the whole page updates. Note how the counters are back in sync again. One has been added to the number shown by `lblCounter2` for the latest `Page_Load`, but `lblCounter` is now equal to `lblCounter2` rather than just having one added to it.

This demonstrates a key point. When a partial-page update occurs through an `UpdatePanel`, the whole page, its view state, and the rest is actually posted back to the server, and the values for the new version of the page are calculated but only the values for the controls in the `UpdatePanel` are sent back.

Thus, each time a partial-page update occurred, the value in `lblCounter` did actually increase, but it wasn't updated on-screen. When the full-page postback happened, `lblCounter` was incremented and updated at last. It always matched `lblCounter2`, but it wasn't updated.

Also worth noting at this time is the button—or more generally, the control—that kicks off the partial-page postback in the `UpdatePanel` doesn't actually have to be contained within it. We will show this in a later part of this demonstration.

Multiple Update Panels on One Page

At this point you could well conclude that the easiest way to eliminate flicker and improve the user experience of your web pages is to put all the contents of your page into one UpdatePanel and leave it at that. However, this is not that great an idea: putting only what actually will need to be updated in an UpdatePanel will increase the speed of the page even further. All you need to do is add other UpdatePanel to the page as appropriate and set the UpdatePanel's UpdateMode property to either Conditional or Always. The next part of this demo will demonstrate what each value does.

Copy UpdatePanel1 and all its contents, and paste them onto the bottom of *UpdatePanelDemo.aspx*. Rename the controls inside the new UpdatePanel to lblTime3, lblCounter3, and btnAsyncPostback2, and copy the code in Page_Load to update lblTime3 and lblCounter3 on postback to the server in the same way as lblTime2 and lblCounter2 are updated.

Run the page and note that clicking the buttons in either UpdatePanel causes the labels in both UpdatePanels to be updated. This is the default (Musketeer) setting for UpdatePanel: all for one and one for all. One partial postback in any UpdatePanel causes the contents of all UpdatePanel controls to be updated.

To override this setting, you need to set the UpdateMode property to Conditional for any UpdatePanel you want to act independently of the others on the page, rather than Always, which is the default. To demonstrate, set UpdateMode to Conditional for UpdatePanel2 and run the page again.

You'll see now that clicking btnAsyncPostback (which is not inside UpdatePanel2) does not cause the labels in UpdatePanel2 to update. However, clicking btnAsyncPostback2 still causes the labels in both UpdatePanels to update, because UpdatePanel1 still has its UpdateMode set to Always. Set UpdateMode to Conditional for UpdatePanel1 for both UpdatePanels to post back to the server by themselves.

While we're covering "modes," note that UpdatePanel has a second property called RenderMode, which determines whether the server renders it as a span or a div. Run the page again and see that both UpdatePanels are rendered as <div> elements—for example, <div id="UpdatePanel2"> ... </div>.

Now set the RenderMode property for UpdatePanel2 to inline (rather than the default of block) and run the page again. View the source and you'll see that UpdatePanel2 is now rendered as <span id="UpdatePanel2"> ... </span>.

 You'll find the code for this part of the demo in the download as *UpdatePanelDemo2.aspx*.

Table 5-6 lists a full set of properties for the UpdatePanel.

Table 5-6. UpdatePanel properties

Name	Values	Default	Description
ChildrenAsTriggers	Boolean	true	If one UpdatePanel is nested in another, set the parent UpdatePanel ChildrenAsTriggers property to false if its contents should not update when a control inside its nested UpdatePanel starts a postback.
ContentTemplate			Reference to the content template for the UpdatePanel.
Controls			Read-only. Gets the collection of all the UpdatePanel child controls.
IsInPartialRendering	Boolean	false	Read-only. Returns true if the UpdatePanel is currently being updated by a partial-page postback. Returns false otherwise.
RenderMode	Block, Inline	block	Specifies whether the UpdatePanel should be treated as a block-level element on the page (like a `<div>`) or inline inside another block element (like a `<span>`).
RequiresUpdate	Boolean	true	Read-only. Returns true if the control's Update method has been called or its UpdateMode is set to Always.
Triggers			Read-only. Returns the collection of the triggers that will cause the UpdatePanel to partially post back. See the next section for more information.
UpdateMode	Always, Conditional	Always	Sets whether the contents of the UpdatePanel will be updated on all asynchronous postbacks or only when it is explicitly set for postback by a trigger.

Now you can isolate UpdatePanel controls from each other. The next common issue with UpdatePanel controls is that the control (a Button, a DropDownList, etc.) causing the updates in the UpdatePanel is trapped inside the panel as well. From a UI standpoint, this may not be a good thing. Fortunately, you can nominate a control outside an UpdatePanel to asynchronously update its contents by adding a new AsyncPostBackTrigger object to the UpdatePanel triggers collection, as we'll demonstrate next.

In *UpdatePanelDemo.aspx*, cut and paste all the buttons from the three areas to the bottom of the page. You can run the page at this point to confirm that all three buttons now initiate only full-page postbacks. The trick now is to add a `<triggers>` collection to both UpdatePanel controls with each containing an AsyncPostBackTrigger object, where the ControlID is the associated button and the EventID is Click, as highlighted in Example 5-12.

Example 5-12. Using UpdatePanels with AsyncPostBackTriggers

```
<%@ Page Language="C#" AutoEventWireup="true"
    CodeFile="UpdatePanelDemo.aspx.cs"
    Inherits="UpdatePanelDemo" %>

<!DOCTYPE html PUBLIC "-//W3C//DTD XHTML 1.0 Transitional//EN"
    "http://www.w3.org/TR/xhtml1/DTD/xhtml1-transitional.dtd">
<html xmlns="http://www.w3.org/1999/xhtml">
<head runat="server">
    <title>UpdatePanel Demo (Part 3)</title>

    <script type="text/javascript">

        function pageLoad() {
        }

    </script>
</head>

<body>
    <form id="form1" runat="server">
    <div>
        <asp:ScriptManager ID="ScriptManager1" runat="server" />
        <h1>
            Update Panel Demo Part 3</h1>
        <p>
            Time:
            <asp:Label ID="lblTime" runat="server" /><br />
            Number of page_loads:
            <asp:Label ID="lblCounter" runat="server" Text="0" />
        </p>
        <br />
        <hr />
        <br />
        <asp:UpdatePanel ID="UpdatePanel1"
            runat="server" UpdateMode="Conditional">
            <ContentTemplate>
                <p>
                    Time:
                    <asp:Label ID="lblTime2" runat="server" /><br />
                    Number of page_loads:
                    <asp:Label ID="lblCounter2" runat="server" Text="0" />
                </p>
            </ContentTemplate>
            <Triggers>
                <asp:AsyncPostBackTrigger
                    ControlID="btnAsyncPostback" EventName="Click" />
            </Triggers>
        </asp:UpdatePanel>
        <br />
        <hr />
        <br />
```

Example 5-12. Using UpdatePanels with AsyncPostBackTriggers (continued)

```
<asp:UpdatePanel ID="UpdatePanel2"
    runat="server" UpdateMode="Conditional">
    <ContentTemplate>
        <p>
            Time:
            <asp:Label ID="lblTime3" runat="server" /><br />
            Number of page_loads:
            <asp:Label ID="lblCounter3" runat="server" Text="0" />
        </p>
    </ContentTemplate>
    <Triggers>
        <asp:AsyncPostBackTrigger
            ControlID="btnAsyncPostback2" EventName="Click" />
    </Triggers>
</asp:UpdatePanel>
<br />
<hr />
<br />
<p>
    <asp:Button ID="btnStdPostback"
        runat="server" Text="Standard Postback" />
</p>
<p>
    <asp:Button ID="btnAsyncPostback"
        runat="server" Text="Async Postback" />
</p>
<p>
    <asp:Button ID="btnAsyncPostback2"
        runat="server" Text="Async Postback 2" />
</p>
</div>
</form>
</body>
</html>
```

No alterations to the code-behind page are needed. Run the page again, and you'll see that the buttons now work with their associated UpdatePanel controls as before. The AsyncPostBackTrigger objects use their ControlID and EventID properties to identify a specific event occurring on a page to trigger a partial postback. The example identifies a Button's Click event for each UpdatePanel, but it could equally identify the SelectedIndexChanged event for a DropDownList or a ListBox.

 You'll find the code for this part of the demo in the download as *UpdatePanelDemo3.aspx*.

Using the UpdateProgress Control

The demos in this chapter are necessarily short so we can cover all the relevant material on UpdatePanel without making the chapter any longer than it has to be. Thus, it may not have occurred to you to ask what happens if a partial-page update takes a long time to complete. Actually, nothing happens, which might leave your users wondering whether the page is broken or whether they've done something wrong. The best way to assure them that neither of these is the case is to add an UpdateProgress control to the page, the easiest analogy for which is the "Loading" screen you will have seen while many large Flash animations load in your browser. This demonstration isn't as fancy as one of those, but you'll get the idea.

Taking *UpdatePanelDemo.aspx*, move the buttons back to their UpdatePanel and delete the trigger collections. You know from earlier in this section that all the partial postbacks in this page occur almost instantaneously, so you'll need to create an artificial delay. In Design view, double-click btnAsyncPostback to generate an event handler for its Click handler. Now add the following line of code to "pause" the postback for five seconds:

```
protected void btnAsyncPostback_Click(object sender, EventArgs e)
{
    System.Threading.Thread.Sleep(5000);
}
```

Run the page and click btnAsyncPostback to see how long it feels. Back in VS2008, add an UpdateProgress control to the page—it doesn't need to be in or near any UpdatePanels—and set its AssociatedUpdatePanelID to UpdatePanel1.

Now add a message to the UpdatePanel. In Design view, VS2008 will automatically create the ProgressTemplate for the control which contains the message. In Source view, you'll need to add a <ProgressTemplate> child element to the UpdatePanel and cut and paste the controls into that:

```
<asp:UpdateProgress ID="UpdateProgress1" runat="server"
    AssociatedUpdatePanelID="UpdatePanel1">
    <ProgressTemplate>
        <p style="color:Red;">Please wait. This page is loading.</p>
    </ProgressTemplate>
</asp:UpdateProgress>
```

Run the page again and click btnAsyncPostback. After 0.5 seconds, the UpdateProgress control kicks in and the contents of the ProgressTemplate are added to the screen until the update is complete, as shown in Figure 5-9.

You can tweak how it works using the DisplayAfter property to set the number of milliseconds the control will display after the asynchronous update was started. This can help prevent the UpdateProgress control from flashing if the asynchronous update happens very quickly. Use the DynamicUpdate property to set whether the page should include a blank area for the UpdateProgress control's contents, or whether it

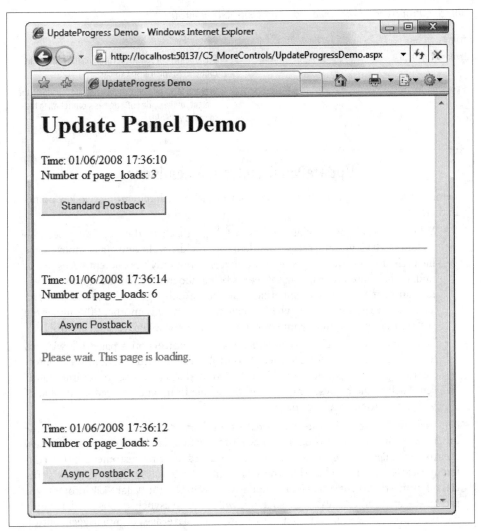

Figure 5-9. The UpdateProgress control in action

should just be added dynamically to the page (as is the case in this example). Table 5-7 provides a full list of UpdateProgress properties.

Table 5-7. Properties for the UpdateProgress control

Name	Values	Default	Description
AssociatedUpdatePanelID	String		The ID of the UpdatePanel this control is associated with.
DisplayAfter	Integer	500	The number of milliseconds after an UpdatePanel starts posting back before the UpdateProgress control is shown on the page.

Table 5-7. Properties for the UpdateProgress control (continued)

Name	Values	Default	Description
DynamicUpdate	Boolean	true	Sets whether any space is set aside on the page for the control even when it isn't visible.
ProgressTemplate			Gets and sets a reference to the template containing the contents of the UpdateProgress control when the control is visible.

UpdatePanel Controls: A Reminder

Before we leave the topic of UpdatePanel controls, it's worth reiterating two key points in their use:

- When a partial-page update occurs, a full postback to the page *does* occur—including all view state, script, (hidden) form fields, and events (a complete page life cycle does occur, albeit under the covers)—but only the content necessary to update the content in the UpdatePanel is being updated. So, in the context of performance, it's worth remembering that the partial-page update is an iceberg. You only see about 10% of what's going on, but there is another 90% under the surface that will hammer your connections if you abuse UpdatePanel controls.

- Don't add just a single UpdatePanel for all the controls on a page. It's wiser to use individual panels for each set of controls dealing with a certain set of information and an action upon it. That way, only that certain set of information is sent back to the browser, rather than the whole form, and you reduce the bandwidth used to update your page.

The trick, then, is to make sure each UpdatePanel does or does not act in sync with the other. For example, when you add a new customer to a database from a DetailsView control in one UpdatePanel, you will want the DataGrid showing customer data (in a different UpdatePanel) to update, but you won't want the Repeater showing today's special offers in a third UpdatePanel to be updated as well. Use the UpdateMode property for the UpdatePanel set to Conditional so that it will cause an asynchronous postback only when an appropriate event is raised from within the UpdatePanel or by a trigger control.

It's time to leave the world of panels for other controls whose purpose is not a million miles away from that of the Tab or Accordion control.

MultiView and View Controls

Sometimes you may want to break a web page into different pieces, displaying only a single piece at a time, with easy transitions from piece to piece. So far, this scenario isn't any different from an Accordion or TabContainer control. However, the MultiView, View, and Wizard controls add the notion of an order to visit their panels, whereas Tabs and Accordions do not.

The classic use of this addition technique is to walk a user through a number of steps within the context of a static page, such as the checkout procedure from an online store, or the procedure to transfer funds from one account to another. You can also use these controls to create wizard-like applications, although there is now a Wizard control, described shortly, for this exact purpose.

 In fact, the View and MultiView controls were originally designed for mobile devices, which explains their limited capabilities for style (which you'll see in a minute) and their high utility in pages optimized for low-res screens.

ASP.NET provides the View control to manage the chunks—that is, the content in a section of the page: one View control per chunk. All of the View objects are contained together within a MultiView object, which makes one View object, called the *active view*, visible at a time.

As shown in Figure 3-8 in Chapter 3, both the View and MultiView controls derive not from WebControl, but directly from System.Web.UI.Control.

The MultiView control has a read-only property called Views, of type ViewCollection, which is a collection of the View controls contained within the MultiView. As with all .NET collections, the elements in the collection are indexed. Hence, the MultiView control has a property called ActiveViewIndex, which gets or sets the zero-based index of the currently active view. If no view is active, ActiveViewIndex will be –1, which is the default value.

The MultiView control has four properties, listed in Table 5-8, that correspond to the four CommandName attributes which you can assign to buttons for automated navigation of the views.

Table 5-8. MultiView CommandNames

Field	Default CommandName	Description
NextViewCommandName	NextView	Navigates to the next higher ActiveViewIndex. If currently at the last view, sets ActiveViewIndex to –1, and nothing is displayed.
PreviousViewCommandName	PrevView	Navigates to the next lower ActiveViewIndex. If currently at the first view, sets ActiveViewIndex to –1, and nothing is displayed.
SwitchViewByIDCommandName	SwitchViewByID	Navigates to the View with the ID specified in the CommandArgument property.
SwitchViewByIndexCommandName	SwitchViewByIndex	Navigates to the View with the index specified. Can use the CommandArgument attribute to specify the index.

For example, a Button, ImageButton, or LinkButton with the CommandName NextView will automatically navigate the MultiView control to the next View when that button is clicked, with no additional code required. The developer (that's you) does not have to write a Click event handler for the button.

You can also set or retrieve the active view by calling the SetActiveView or GetActiveView method of the MultiView control. SetActiveView takes a reference to a View object as an argument, and GetActiveView returns a reference to a View object.

 An important point to remember is that all the controls on all the Views, even those Views not currently visible, are available to the app and server-side processing. Not only are they available to code, but also they participate in View state and are part of the Controls collection of the page.

Every time a view is changed, the page is posted back to the server and a number of events are raised by both the MultiView and View controls.

Whenever the active view changes, the ActiveViewChanged event is raised by the MultiView control. At the same time, the View control that is now active raises the Activate event, and the View control that is now inactive raises the Deactivate event.

All of these events have an event argument of type EventArgs, which you will remember is a placeholder and provides no additional information about the event. However, as with all event handlers, a reference to the sender is passed to the event handler, as we will demonstrate shortly.

The View control has a Visible property of type Boolean, which can be set to control the visibility of specific View objects or retrieved to determine programmatically which View is visible.

Neither the MultiView nor the View control has any style properties. That is not too surprising for the MultiView, because it is just a container for the Views. In the case of the View control, if you want to impose style properties, you must apply them to each control contained within the View. Another technique would be to embed a Panel control in the View and set the style properties of the Panel control.

The following example, *MultiViewDemo.aspx*, demonstrates many of the features of the MultiView and View controls. The web page, after some navigation has occurred, is shown in Figure 5-10.

MultiViewDemo, shown in Design view in Figure 5-11, consists of a single web page with a MultiView control, MultiView1. MultiView1 contains four View controls (vwFirst, vwSecond, vwThird, and vwLast), along with other controls for navigating the MultiView. The page also contains controls for displaying data from and about the MultiView and its contained Views.

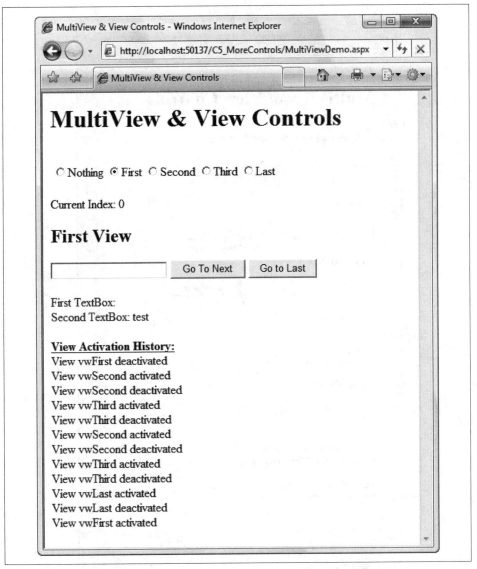

Figure 5-10. MultiViewDemo.aspx in action

Each of the four Views contains buttons for navigation. In addition, the first two Views contain a TextBox for demonstrating how controls on a View are accessible to the application even when that View is not visible.

To create this example, add to the chapter's website a new web form called *MultiViewDemo.aspx*. The complete content file for this example is listed in Example 5-13, with the MultiView and View controls highlighted. We will look first at the MultiView and View controls in this source file and then at the other controls on the page.

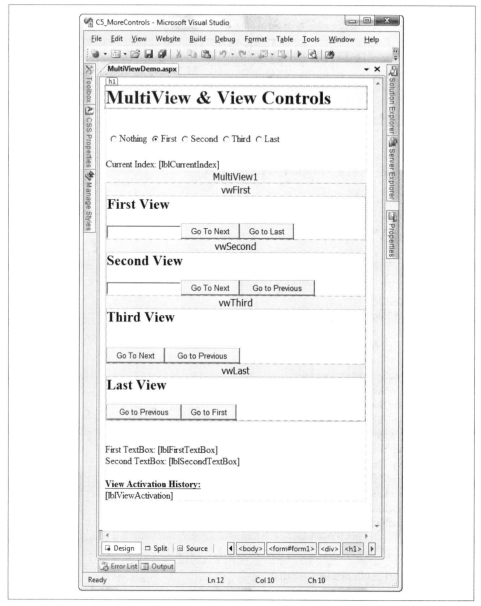

Figure 5-11. MultiViewDemo in Design view

Example 5-13. Default.aspx for MultiViewDemo

```
<%@ Page Language="C#" AutoEventWireup="true"
    CodeFile="MultiViewDemo.aspx.cs" Inherits="MultiViewDemo" %>

<!DOCTYPE html PUBLIC "-//W3C//DTD XHTML 1.0 Transitional//EN"
    "http://www.w3.org/TR/xhtml1/DTD/xhtml1-transitional.dtd">
```

Example 5-13. Default.aspx for MultiViewDemo (continued)

```
<html xmlns="http://www.w3.org/1999/xhtml">
<head runat="server">
   <title>MultiView & View Demo</title>
</head>

<body>
   <form id="form1" runat="server">
   <div>
      <h1>MultiView & View Controls</h1>
      <br />

      <asp:RadioButtonList AutoPostBack="True" ID="rblView"
         OnSelectedIndexChanged="rblView_SelectedIndexChanged"
         RepeatDirection="Horizontal" runat="server">
         <asp:ListItem Value="-1">Nothing</asp:ListItem>
         <asp:ListItem Value="0" Selected="True">First</asp:ListItem>
         <asp:ListItem Value="1">Second</asp:ListItem>
         <asp:ListItem Value="2">Third</asp:ListItem>
         <asp:ListItem Value="3">Last</asp:ListItem>
      </asp:RadioButtonList>
      <br />
      Current Index:
      <asp:Label ID="lblCurrentIndex" runat="server"></asp:Label>
      <br />

      <asp:MultiView ID="MultiView1" runat="server"
         ActiveViewIndex="0"
         OnActiveViewChanged="MultiView1_ActiveViewChanged">

         <asp:View ID="vwFirst" runat="server"
            OnActivate="ActivateView" OnDeactivate="DeactivateView">
            <h2>First View</h2>
            <asp:TextBox ID="txtFirstView" runat="server" />
            <asp:Button CommandName="NextView" ID="btnNext1"
               runat="server" Text="Go To Next" />
            <asp:Button CommandArgument="vwLast"
               CommandName="SwitchViewByID" ID="btnLast"
               runat="server" Text="Go to Last" />
         </asp:View>

         <asp:View ID="vwSecond" runat="server"
            OnActivate="ActivateView" OnDeactivate="DeactivateView">
            <h2>Second View</h2>
            <asp:TextBox ID="txtSecondView" runat="server" />
            <asp:Button CommandName="NextView" ID="btnNext2"
               runat="server" Text="Go To Next" />
            <asp:Button CommandName="PrevView" ID="btnPrevious2"
               runat="server" Text="Go to Previous" />
         </asp:View>

         <asp:View ID="vwThird" runat="server"
            OnActivate="ActivateView" OnDeactivate="DeactivateView">
```

Example 5-13. Default.aspx for MultiViewDemo (continued)

```
            <h2>Third View</h2>
            <asp:Button CommandName="NextView" ID="btnNext3"
                runat="server" Text="Go To Next" />
            <asp:Button CommandName="PrevView" ID="btnPrevious3"
                runat="server" Text="Go to Previous" />
        </asp:View>

        <asp:View ID="vwLast" runat="server"
            OnActivate="ActivateView" OnDeactivate="DeactivateView">
            <h2>Last View</h2>
            <asp:Button CommandName="PrevView" ID="btnPrevious4"
                runat="server" Text="Go to Previous" />
            <asp:Button CommandArgument="0" ID="btnFirst"
                CommandName="SwitchViewByIndex" runat="server"
                Text="Go to First" />
        </asp:View>
    </asp:MultiView>
    <br />
    <br />
    First TextBox:
    <asp:Label ID="lblFirstTextBox" runat="server" />
    <br />
    Second TextBox:
    <asp:Label ID="lblSecondTextBox" runat="server" />
    <br />
    <br />
    <strong>
        <span style="text-decoration: underline">
            View Activation History:
        </span>
    </strong>
    <br />
    <asp:Label ID="lblViewActivation" runat="server" />
  </div>
  </form>
</body>
</html>
```

The MultiView control highlighted in Example 5-13 is declared with an ID of MultiView1. The ActiveViewIndex attribute is set to 0, so the first view in the Views collection will display. If this property is not set, it will default to –1 and none of the View controls will display.

The OnActiveViewChanged attribute binds an event handler method in the code-behind file, MultiView1_ActiveViewChanged (listed in Example 5-14), which will fire every time the active index changes.

Example 5-14. ActiveViewChanged event handler in MultiViewDemo.aspx.cs

```
protected void MultiView1_ActiveViewChanged(object sender, EventArgs e)
{
    lblFirstTextBox.Text = txtFirstView.Text;
    lblSecondTextBox.Text = txtSecondView.Text;
    rblView.SelectedIndex = MultiView1.ActiveViewIndex + 1;
}
```

This event handler does two things. First, it retrieves the values of the two text boxes on the first two Views and displays them on the page in the labels that were placed there for that purpose. Second, it sets the RadioButtonList at the top of the page, rblView, to the proper value. This code is relatively straightforward because the RadioButtonList.SelectedIndex and the MultiView.ActiveViewIndex properties are of type integer. However, you must compensate for the fact that the lowest value of the ActiveViewIndex property is –1 whereas the lowest index of the RadioButtonList is 0. That is, they are offset by one.

Four View instances are declared: vwFirst, vwSecond, vwThird, and vwLast. All of them declare event handlers for both OnActivate and OnDeactivate:

```
<asp:View ID="vwThird" runat="server"
    OnActivate="ActivateView" OnDeactivate="DeactivateView">
```

The Activate event is handled by a method called ActivateView and the Deactivate event by DeactivateView, as listed in Example 5-15. They retrieve the contents of the Label control holding the activation history, append the ID and action of the current View, and assign the string back to the Label.

Example 5-15. Activate and Deactivate event handlers for MultiView.aspx.cs

```
protected void ActivateView(object sender, EventArgs e)
{
    string str = lblViewActivation.Text;
    View v = (View)sender;
    str += "View " + v.ID + " activated <br/>";
    lblViewActivation.Text = str;
}

protected void DeactivateView(object sender, EventArgs e)
{
    string str = lblViewActivation.Text;
    View v = (View)sender;
    str += "View " + v.ID + " deactivated <br/>";
    lblViewActivation.Text = str;
}
```

Because sender is of type object, it must first be cast to type View before assigning it to a reference to View and obtaining properties of the View object, such as the ID property.

Each View object contains navigation buttons. The .NET Framework makes it particularly easy to set them up. (It's harder to explain in words than to actually do it.) If a button has its CommandName attribute set to one of the default values (Sort, Select, Update, Insert, Delete), the corresponding action will automatically occur. So, the first View object, vwFirst, will have buttons labeled "Go to Next" and "Go to Last", with CommandNames of NextView and SwitchViewByID, respectively. The first is easy; it just navigates to the next View.

The SwitchViewByID action requires an ID to switch to, so the CommandArgument attribute is used to pass in that argument:

```
<asp:Button ID="btnLast" runat="server" Text="Go to Last"
    CommandArgument="vwLast" CommandName="SwitchViewByID" />
```

Each View control contains content in addition to navigation buttons. This content includes standard HTML elements and ASP.NET server controls.

Run the page now and you'll see that these server controls are accessible to the application even when their View is not displayed.

The next step is to update the RadioButtonList at the top of the page. As you have seen, the SelectedIndex property is set by the code in MultiView1_ActiveViewChanged every time the active view changes. When the SelectedIndex changes due to user action the SelectedIndexChanged event is fired, which calls rblView_SelectedIndexChanged:

```
<asp:RadioButtonList AutoPostBack="True" ID="rblView"
    OnSelectedIndexChanged="rblView_SelectedIndexChanged"
    RepeatDirection="Horizontal" runat="server">
```

This method, listed in Example 5-16, consists of a single line that sets the ActiveViewIndex property of the MultiView to the SelectedValue of the RadioButtonList.

Example 5-16. SelectedIndexChanged event handler for MultiViewDemo.aspx.cs

```
protected void rblView_SelectedIndexChanged(object sender, EventArgs e)
{
    MultiView1.ActiveViewIndex =
        Convert.ToInt32(rblView.SelectedValue);
}
```

The final bit of code is contained in the event handler for the PreRender event of the Page (listed in Example 5-17), where lblCurrentIndex is populated with the index of the currently active view. This code cannot be run in Page_Load because Page_Load is called before the label is updated.

 See Chapter 6 for complete coverage of the Page class life cycle.

Example 5-17. Page_PreRender event handler for MultiViewDemo.aspx.cs

```
protected void Page_PreRender(object sender, EventArgs e)
{
    lblCurrentIndex.Text = MultiView1.ActiveViewIndex.ToString( );
}
```

Now that you've seen how to use the `MultiView` class to create a simple paged application, you can expand it to more complex uses. Sometimes, though, you want a traditional Windows-style wizard on your page. In that case, you can use the `Wizard` control, discussed next.

The Wizard Control

Users expect modern applications to provide wizards to walk them through multistep processes. These UIs are distinguished by the use of magic. Sorry, just kidding.

`Wizard` controls provide the infrastructure to present the user with successive steps in a process, providing access to all the data collected in all the steps, with easy forward and backward navigation.

Similar to the `MultiView` control, the `Wizard` control contains a collection of `WizardStep` objects. These `WizardStep` objects derive from the `View` class, as you can see in Figure 5-12, and the relationship between `WizardSteps` and the `Wizard` control is analogous to the relationship between the `View` and `MultiView`.

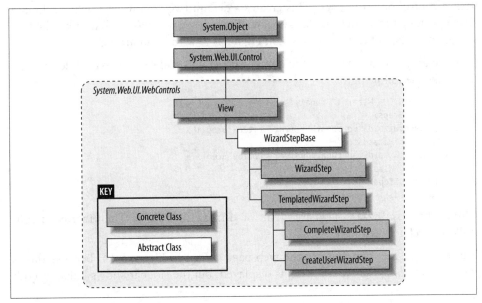

Figure 5-12. View class hierarchy

As with the MultiView control, all of the controls on all of the WizardStep controls are part of the page's control hierarchy and are accessible via code at runtime regardless of which specific WizardStep is currently visible. Every time a user clicks on a navigation button or link, the page posts back to the server. It will not, however, post onward to another page, a process known as *cross-page posting*, which we'll look at more in Chapter 6.

The Wizard control takes care of all the plumbing required to implement navigation, both linear (going from one step to the next or back) and nonlinear (going from any step to any other step). It automatically creates the appropriate buttons, such as Next, Previous, and Finish (on the very last step). The first step does not have a Previous button and the last step does not have a Next button. It also makes provisions for steps that can be navigated to only a single time. In addition, by default, the Wizard displays a toolbar with navigation links, enabling the user to go to any step from any other step.

You can customize almost every aspect of the look and feel of the Wizard with styles and templates. This includes all the various buttons and links, the header and footer, the sidebar, and the WizardStep controls.

The best way to explore the Wizard control is to look at an example. In this example, you will create a whimsical wizard to guide you through the steps you follow when waking up in the morning.

Create for the chapter's website a new web page called *WizardDemo.aspx*. Drag a Wizard control onto the page. This creates a default two-step wizard, which, though sparse, is fully functional. In Design view, you will see the two sidebar links, the first step, and the Next button, as shown in Figure 5-13 with its smart tag.

Looking at the Source view of the content page, you will see the Wizard declaration looks like the following:

```
<asp:Wizard ID="Wizard1" runat="server">
    <WizardSteps>
        <asp:WizardStep runat="server" title="Step 1">
        </asp:WizardStep>
        <asp:WizardStep runat="server" title="Step 2">
        </asp:WizardStep>
    </WizardSteps>
</asp:Wizard>
```

Within the <asp:Wizard> tags are a pair of <WizardSteps> tags. The WizardStep controls are declared within those tags.

Run this page and you will see the web page shown in Figure 5-14. Because this is the first step, only the Next button is displayed, but the sidebar shows links for both steps.

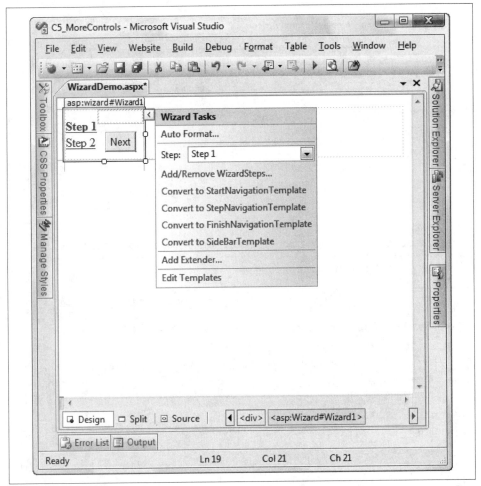

Figure 5-13. A fresh Wizard control in Design view and its smart tag

Let's put a bit more meat on this example's bones. Click the content area of the first WizardStep and type in some text—for example, an <h2> heading that says "Wake Up," as shown in Figure 5-15.

Next, switch to Design view, open the smart tag of the Wizard control, as seen in Figure 5-13, then select Add/Remove WizardSteps. This will bring up the Wizard-Step Collection Editor, as shown in Figure 5-16. Add five more steps so there are a total of seven. For each (including the first two), enter a value for the Title and the ID, as listed in Table 5-9.

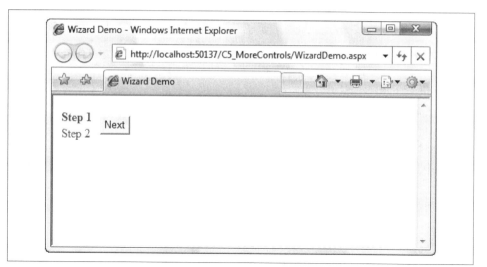

Figure 5-14. A fresh Wizard control in action

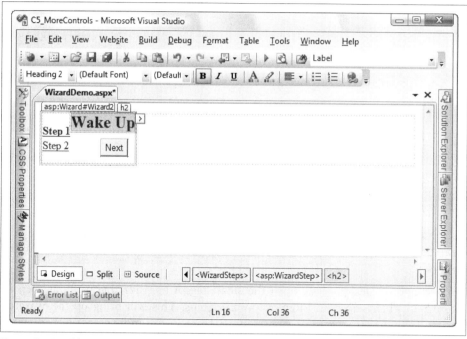

Figure 5-15. Adding content to a Wizard step

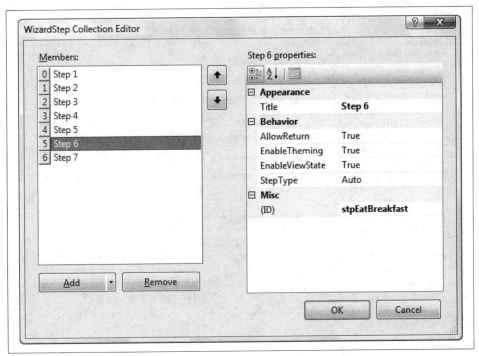

Figure 5-16. WizardStep Collection Editor

Table 5-9. WizardSteps for WizardDemo

ID	Title
stpWakeUp	Step 1
stpShower	Step 2
stpTakeMeds	Step 3
stpBrushTeeth	Step 4
stpGetDressed	Step 5
stpEatBreakfast	Step 6
stpFinish	Step 7

Select each step in turn by clicking "Step 2", "Step 3", and so on, and add content to each step as you did with Step 1. You can also use the drop-down list in the smart tag to switch between steps, but it is easier to switch to Source view and edit the WizardStep declarations directly. When you are done, the Wizard control declaration should look something like that shown in Example 5-18.

Example 5-18. Wizard declaration after adding steps

```
<asp:Wizard ID="Wizard1" runat="server" ActiveStepIndex="1">
    <WizardSteps>
        <asp:WizardStep ID="stpWakeUp" runat="server" title="Step 1">
            <h2>Wake Up</h2>
        </asp:WizardStep>
        <asp:WizardStep ID="stpShower" runat="server" title="Step 2">
            <h2>Shower</h2>
        </asp:WizardStep>
        <asp:WizardStep ID="stpTakeMeds" runat="server" Title="Step 3">
            <h2>Take Medicine</h2>
        </asp:WizardStep>
        <asp:WizardStep ID="stpBrushTeeth" runat="server" Title="Step 4">
            <h2>Brush Teeth</h2>
        </asp:WizardStep>
        <asp:WizardStep ID="stpGetDressed" runat="server" Title="Step 5">
            <h2>Get Dressed</h2>
        </asp:WizardStep>
        <asp:WizardStep ID="stpEatBreakfast" runat="server" Title="Step 6">
            <h2>Eat Breakfast</h2>
        </asp:WizardStep>
        <asp:WizardStep ID="stpFinish" runat="server" Title="Step 7">
            <h2>Out The Door</h2>
        </asp:WizardStep>
    </WizardSteps>
</asp:Wizard>
```

The Wizard control has many properties for controlling appearance and behavior. Table 5-10 lists some of the most important Wizard properties other than those relating to the appearance of the buttons. The button-related properties are listed in Table 5-11. You'll see many of these properties as you continue with *WizardDemo.aspx*.

Table 5-10. Wizard properties not related to style or button display

Name	Type	Description
ActiveStep	WizardStepBase	Read-only. The currently displayed step in the WizardSteps collection.
ActiveStepIndex	Integer	The zero-based index of the currently displayed step in the WizardSteps collection.
CancelDestinationPageUrl	String	The URL the user navigates to when clicking the Cancel button.
CellPadding	Integer	The number of pixels between the cell's contents and border. Default is 0.
CellSpacing	Integer	The number of pixels betweens cells. Default is 0.
DisplayCancelButton	Boolean	If true, a Cancel button will be displayed. Default is false.
DisplaySideBar	Boolean	If true, the default, the sidebar area will be displayed.
FinishDestinationPageUrl	String	The URL the user navigates to when clicking the Finish button.

Name	Type	Description
FinishNavigationTemplate	ITemplate	The template used to specify content and styles for the navigation area of the Finish step, either the last step or the step with StepType = Finish.
HeaderStyle	TableItemStyle	Read-only. Style properties for the header area.
HeaderTemplate	ITemplate	The template used to specify content and styles for the header area displayed at the top of every step.
HeaderText	String	Text displayed in the header area.
NavigationButtonStyle	Style	Read-only. The style properties that specify the appearance of the buttons in the navigation area.
NavigationStyle	TableItemStyle	Read-only. The style properties for the navigation area.
SideBarButtonStyle	Style	Read-only. The style properties that specify the appearance of the buttons in the sidebar area.
SideBarStyle	TableItemStyle	Read-only. The style properties for the sidebar area.
SideBarTemplate	ITemplate	The template used to specify content and styles for the sidebar area.
SkipLinkText	String	Rendered as alternative text with an invisible image to work with assistive technologies. Default is "Skip Navigation Links", localized for server locale.
StartNavigationTemplate	ITemplate	The template used to specify content and styles for the navigation area of the Start step, either the first step or the step with StepType = Start.
StepNavigationTemplate	ITemplate	The template used to specify content and styles for the navigation area of all the steps other than Start, Finish, and Complete.
StepStyle	TableItemStyle	Read-only. The style properties for the WizardStep objects.
WizardSteps	WizardStepCollection	Read-only. A collection of WizardStep objects.

Table 5-11. Wizard properties related to button displays

Property	Type	Description
CancelButtonImageUrl FinishStepButtonImageUrl FinishStepPreviousButton-ImageUrl NextStepButtonImageUrl PreviousStepButtonImageUrl StartStepNextButtonImageUrl	String	The URL of the image displayed for the button.
CancelButtonStyle FinishStepButtonStyle FinishStepPreviousButton-Style NextStepButtonStyle PreviousStepButtonStyle StartStepNextButtonStyle	Style	Read-only. The style properties that specify the appearance of the button.

Table 5-11. Wizard properties related to button displays (continued)

Property	Type	Description
CancelButtonText FinishStepButtonText FinishStepPreviousButton-Text NextStepButtonText PreviousStepButtonText StartStepNextButtonText	String	The text displayed on the button.
CancelButtonType FinishStepButtonType FinishStepPreviousButton-Type NextStepButtonType PreviousStepButtonType StartStepNextButtonType	ButtonType	The type of button rendered as the button. Possible values are Button, Image, and Link.

Many of the properties are of type TableItemStyle. This class, which derives from System.Web.UI.WebControls.Style, contains properties used to format the table rows and cells that make up the Wizard control. The TableItemStyle class has many properties, including BackColor, BorderColor, BorderStyle, BorderWidth, CssClass, Font, ForeColor, Height, HorizontalAlign, VerticalAlign, Width, and Wrap.

When you are setting the properties of a Wizard control in VS2008 in Design view, the properties that are of type TableItemStyle appear in the Properties window with a plus sign next to them. Clicking the plus sign expands the list to display the TableItemStyle properties as subproperties, as seen in Figure 5-17. Properties set in this manner will be contained in separate elements within the Wizard control declaration in the content file, as in the highlighted code in the following snippet:

```
<asp:Wizard ID="Wizard1" runat="server" ActiveStepIndex="1">
    <WizardSteps>
        ... all seven wizard steps ...
    </WizardSteps>

    <HeaderStyle BackColor="#666666" BorderColor="#E6E2D8"
        BorderStyle="Solid" BorderWidth="2px"
        Font-Size="0.9em" ForeColor="White"
        HorizontalAlign="Center" Font-Bold="True" />
/asp:Wizard>
```

When working in Source view, you can also add the TableItemStyle type properties directly to the Wizard control declaration. For example, to add those properties set in Figure 5-16, you would add the following:

```
<asp:Wizard ID="Wizard1" runat="server" ActiveStepIndex="1"
    HeaderStyle-backcolor="#666666" HeaderStyle-bordercolor="#E6E2D8"
    HeaderStyle-borderstyle="Solid" HeaderStyle-borderwidth="2px"
    HeaderStyle-font-size="0.9em" HeaderStyle-forecolor="White"
    HeaderStyle-HorizontalAlign="Center"
    HeaderStyle-font-bold="True">
```

```
<WizardSteps>
    ... all seven wizard steps ...
    </WizardSteps>
</asp:Wizard>
```

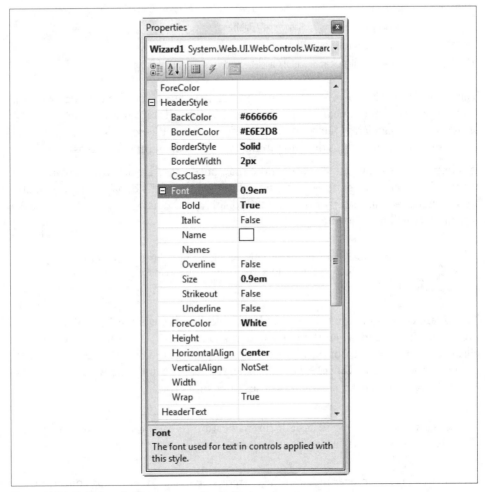

Figure 5-17. TableItemStyle type properties in Design view

The WizardStep class has a StepType property, which has one of the values of the WizardStepType enumeration listed in Table 5-13. By default, the StepType is Auto, in which the navigation UI is determined by the order of the steps in the WizardSteps collection. The first step has only a Next button, the last step has only a Previous button, and all the other steps of StepType Auto have both Previous and Next buttons.

Alternatively, you can assign a different value to the StepType property to modify the default behavior, as described in Table 5-12. For example, you can create a confirmation page, with no navigation buttons at all, by changing the StepType to Complete.

Table 5-12. WizardStepType enumeration members

Member	Description
Auto	Navigation UI determined automatically by the order in which the step is declared. The default value.
Complete	The last step to display. No navigation buttons are rendered; all sidebar links will be rendered as plain text.
Finish	The final data collection step. Renders only Finish and Previous buttons.
Start	The first step. Renders only a Next button.
Step	Any step other than Start, Finish, or Complete. Renders Previous and Next buttons.

The WizardStep class has one additional property of particular interest: AllowReturn. This property enforces linear navigation, meaning that all steps in the wizard must be visited in order, which is handy if all steps must be completed and information and options in subsequent steps depend on the choices made in previous steps.

It is impossible to navigate to a step more than once with AllowReturn set to false. If the DisplaySideBar property is true (the default) so that the sidebar is displayed, any step with AllowReturn set to false will still display in the navigation links, but clicking that link will have no effect.

 The AllowReturn property only disallows user interaction; program code can force a return to a step even if the AllowReturn property is false.

The Wizard control has six events, listed in Table 5-13. One is the ActiveStepChanged event, which is raised when the current step has changed. The other five events are all raised in response to button clicks. As noted in Table 5-13, all the button click events other than CancelButtonClick have an event argument of type WizardNavigationEventArgs, which exposes three properties:

Cancel
: Set this Boolean value to true if the navigation to the next step should be canceled. The default is false.

CurrentStepIndex
: The zero-based integer index of the current step in the WizardSteps collection.

NextStepIndex
: The zero-based integer index of the step that will display next. If the Previous button has been clicked, for example, the value of NextStepIndex will be one less than the CurrentStepIndex.

Table 5-13. Wizard control events

Event	Event argument	Description
ActiveStepChanged	EventArgs	Raised when a new step is displayed
CancelButtonClick	EventArgs	Raised when the Cancel button is clicked

Table 5-13. Wizard control events (continued)

Event	Event argument	Description
FinishButtonClick	WizardNavigationEventArgs	Raised when the Finish button is clicked
NextButtonClick	WizardNavigationEventArgs	Raised when the Next button is clicked
PreviousButtonClick	WizardNavigationEventArgs	Raised when the Previous button is clicked
SideBarButtonClick	WizardNavigationEventArgs	Raised when a sidebar button is clicked

The Wizard control has three methods of particular interest, listed in Table 5-14.

Table 5-14. Wizard methods

Method name	Return type	Description
GetHistory	ICollection	Returns a collection of WizardStepBase objects in the order they were accessed, where index 0 is the most recent step visited, index 1 is the step before that, and so on. (It is essentially like a browser history list, but for steps in a wizard.)
GetStepType	WizardStepType	The type of step, as listed in Table 5-12.
MoveTo	Void	Moves to the WizardStep object passed in as a parameter.

Now, let's return to the *WizardDemo.aspx* example, where you will apply many of the properties, methods, and events we just listed and discussed.

First, add a bit of text to each WizardStep. The content of each step can include text and HTML, other ASP.NET server controls, and user controls (covered in Chapter 15), enabling the easy reuse of UI and code.

Next, set the StepType of Step 1 to Start and of Step 7 to Finish. Set the AllowReturn property of Step 3 to False, so you can access that step only one time. Finally, add one additional WizardStep to the WizardSteps collection, with a StepType of Complete. The new <WizardSteps> section of the Wizard declaration will now look like Example 5-19, with the modified code highlighted (except for the added text content).

Example 5-19. A final set of WizardSteps for WizardDemo.aspx

```
<WizardSteps>
    <asp:WizardStep ID="stpWakeUp" runat="server" title="Step 1"
        StepType="Start">
        <h2>Wake Up</h2>
        Rise and shine sleepy head.
    </asp:WizardStep>

    <asp:WizardStep ID="stpShower" runat="server" title="Step 2">
        <h2>Shower</h2>
        Make it cold!
    </asp:WizardStep>
```

Example 5-19. A final set of WizardSteps for WizardDemo.aspx (continued)

```
    <asp:WizardStep ID="stpTakeMeds" runat="server" Title="Step 3"
        AllowReturn="false">
        <h2>Take Medicine</h2>
        Only do this once.
    </asp:WizardStep>

    <asp:WizardStep ID="stpBrushTeeth" runat="server" Title="Step 4">
        <h2>Brush Teeth</h2>
        Don't forget to floss.
    </asp:WizardStep>

    <asp:WizardStep ID="stpGetDressed" runat="server" Title="Step 5">
        <h2>Get Dressed</h2>
        Got to look good.
    </asp:WizardStep>

    <asp:WizardStep ID="stpEatBreakfast" runat="server" Title="Step 6">
        <h2>Eat Breakfast</h2>
        The most important meal of the day.
    </asp:WizardStep>

    <asp:WizardStep ID="stpFinish" runat="server" Title="Step 7"
        StepType="Finish">
        <h2>Out The Door</h2>
        Meet the world!
    </asp:WizardStep>

    <asp:WizardStep ID="stpComplete" runat="server"
        Title="Complete" StepType="Complete">
        <h2>Complete!</h2>
        Your morning routine is now complete.
    </asp:WizardStep>
</WizardSteps>
```

Next, add a drop down along with several labels to the page below the Wizard control. The labels will be used to display various types of information and the drop down will be used to demonstrate how step navigation can occur programmatically outside the Wizard control. The code snippet from the content file shown in Example 5-20 declares these additional controls.

Example 5-20. Additional controls for WizardDemo.aspx

```
<br />
Select a step: 
<asp:DropDownList ID="DropDownList1" runat="server"
    AutoPostBack="True"
    OnSelectedIndexChanged="DropDownList1_SelectedIndexChanged">
    <asp:ListItem>1</asp:ListItem>
    <asp:ListItem>2</asp:ListItem>
    <asp:ListItem>3</asp:ListItem>
```

Example 5-20. Additional controls for WizardDemo.aspx (continued)

```
    <asp:ListItem>4</asp:ListItem>
    <asp:ListItem>5</asp:ListItem>
    <asp:ListItem>6</asp:ListItem>
    <asp:ListItem>7</asp:ListItem>
</asp:DropDownList>
<p>
    Active Step: 
    <asp:Label ID="lblActiveStep" runat="server" />
</p>
<p>
    ActiveStepIndex: 
    <asp:Label ID="lblActiveStepIndex" runat="server" />
</p>
<p>
    StepType: 
    <asp:Label ID="lblStepType" runat="server" />
</p>
<p>
    Button Info: 
    <asp:Label ID="lblButtonInfo" runat="server" />
</p>
<p>
    <u>History</u>
</p>
<p>
    <asp:Label ID="lblHistory" runat="server" />
</p>
```

Go back to Design view, click the smart tag of the Wizard control, and select Auto Format. Select one of the format schemes presented; in this example, we use Simple. This will automatically apply a number of formatting properties, as you will see momentarily.

In the Properties window for the Wizard control, set the DisplayCancelButton property to true.

While in Design view with the Wizard control selected, click the Events icon (the lightning bolt) in the Properties window. Double-click the cell next to ActiveStepChanged to insert an event handler with the default name (Wizard1_ ActiveStepChanged) for that event. Do the same for the CancelButtonClick event. For the FinishButtonClick event, enter the name Button_Click, which will insert a skeleton event handler with that name in the code-behind file. You should also enter Button_Click for each of the NextButtonClick, PreviousButtonClick, and SideBarButtonClick events. Finally, double-click the DropDownList control under the Wizard control to generate an empty handler for its SelectedIndexChanged event.

Now add the highlighted code from Example 5-21 to *WizardDemo.aspx.cs.*

Example 5-21. WizardDemo.aspx.cs

```csharp
using System;
using System.Collections;
using System.Web.UI;
using System.Web.UI.WebControls;

public partial class WizardDemo : Page
{
    protected void Wizard1_ActiveStepChanged
        (object sender, EventArgs e)
    {
        lblActiveStep.Text = Wizard1.ActiveStep.Title;
        lblActiveStepIndex.Text = Wizard1.ActiveStepIndex.ToString( );
        lblStepType.Text = Wizard1.ActiveStep.StepType.ToString( );

        //  get the history
        ICollection steps = Wizard1.GetHistory( );
        string str = "";
        foreach (WizardStep step in steps)
        {
            str += step.Title + "<br/>";
        }
        lblHistory.Text = str;
    }

    protected void Wizard1_CancelButtonClick
        (object sender, EventArgs e)
    {
        lblActiveStep.Text = "";
        lblActiveStepIndex.Text = "";
        lblStepType.Text = "";
        lblButtonInfo.Text = "Canceled";
        Wizard1.Visible = false;
    }

    protected void Button_Click
        (object sender, WizardNavigationEventArgs e)
    {
        string str = "Current Index: " +
            e.CurrentStepIndex.ToString( ) +
            ".   Next Step: " + e.NextStepIndex.ToString( );
        lblButtonInfo.Text = str;
    }

    protected void DropDownList1_SelectedIndexChanged
        (object sender, EventArgs e)
    {
        int index = DropDownList1.SelectedIndex;
        WizardStepBase step = Wizard1.WizardSteps[index];
        Wizard1.MoveTo(step);
    }
}
```

The reference to the System.Collections namespace is needed so you can use the ICollection object returned by the GetHistory method of the Wizard control.

The ActiveStepChanged event handler, Wizard1_ActiveStepChanged, is fired every time the current step changes, whether through user interaction or programmatically. This method gathers three pieces of information, populates the labels, and displays a history of the steps accessed.

The first label displays the currently active step. The ActiveStep property of the Wizard control returns a WizardStep object. The Title property of that object gives you the information you want. The second label is filled with the ActiveStepIndex property value. Because it is of type Integer, it must be converted to a string. The third label displays the StepType property of the WizardStep class, which is of type WizardStepType and therefore must be converted to a string for assignment to the Text property of the TextBox.

Second, the Wizard1_ActiveStepChanged method calls the GetHistory method of the Wizard class, which returns a collection of WizardStep objects (strictly speaking, it returns a collection of WizardStepBase objects, from which WizardStep derives). The collection is iterated and the Title property of each step is appended to a text string, which is then assigned to the lblHistory label. The most recent step accessed has an index of 0; the previous step has an index of 1, and so on.

All the buttons and links, other than the Cancel button, use the same event handler method: Button_Click. This method fills lblButtonInfo with the current-step index and the next-step index, both of which are properties of the event argument.

The Cancel button's Click event handler, Wizard1_CancelButtonClick, clears all the labels and hides the Wizard control.

The DropDownList control on this page lets the user move to any of the WizardSteps. When one of its values is selected, the SelectedIndexChanged handler for the control gets the new value for its SelectedIndex property. This value is used as an index into the WizardSteps collection to get a reference to the desired WizardStep object (actually a WizardStepBase object, from which WizardStep is derived). Then the MoveTo method of the Wizard is called to move programmatically to that step. The really interesting thing here is that it is possible to move multiple times to a step, such as Step 3, even if that step's AllowReturn property is set to false.

As a result of setting the event handlers and the Auto Formatting, the Wizard declaration will now look something like that shown in Example 5-22.

Example 5-22. Wizard declaration after adding event handlers and formatting

```
<asp:Wizard ID="Wizard1" runat="server" ActiveStepIndex="1"
    BackColor="#E6E2D8" BorderColor="#999999" BorderStyle="Solid"
    BorderWidth="1px" DisplayCancelButton="True"
    Font-Names="Verdana" Font-Size="0.8em"
```

```
    onactivestepchanged="Wizard1_ActiveStepChanged"
    oncancelbuttonclick="Wizard1_CancelButtonClick"
    onfinishbuttonclick="Button_Click"
    onnextbuttonclick="Button_Click"
    onpreviousbuttonclick="Button_Click"
    onsidebarbuttonclick="Button_Click">

    <stepstyle backcolor="#F7F6F3" bordercolor="#E6E2D8"
        borderstyle="Solid" borderwidth="2px" />

    <WizardSteps>
        ... as given in Figure 5-18 ...
    </WizardSteps>

    <sidebarbuttonstyle forecolor="White" />
    <navigationbuttonstyle backcolor="White" bordercolor="#C5BBAF"
        borderstyle="Solid" borderwidth="1px" font-names="Verdana"
        font-size="0.8em" forecolor="#1C5E55" />
    <sidebarstyle backcolor="#1C5E55" font-size="0.9em"
        verticalalign="Top" />
    <HeaderStyle BackColor="#666666" BorderColor="#E6E2D8"
        BorderStyle="Solid" BorderWidth="2px"
        Font-Size="0.9em" ForeColor="White"
        HorizontalAlign="Center" Font-Bold="True" />
</asp:Wizard>
```

Running the web page and navigating through several of the steps will yield something similar to Figure 5-18.

The Wizard control is a fairly well-defined control, with obvious uses. You could walk your user through entering his preferences or setting up a stock sale. Anytime you want a clearly defined series of steps for the user to follow, the Wizard control is useful.

The FileUpload Control

Often an application needs to allow users to upload files to the web server. The FileUpload control makes it easy for the user to browse for and select the file to transfer, providing a Browse button and a text box for entering the filename. Once the user has entered a fully qualified filename in the text box, either by typing it directly or by using the Browse button, the SaveAs method of the FileUpload control can be called to save the file to disk.

In addition to the normal complement of members inherited from the WebControl class, the FileUpload control also exposes several *read-only* properties of particular interest, listed in Tables 5-15 and 5-16.

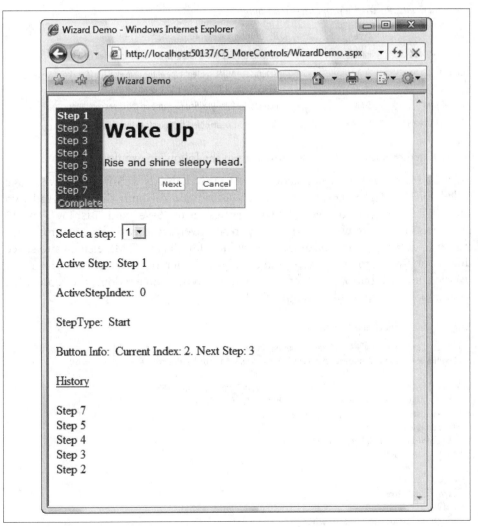

Figure 5-18. WizardDemo.aspx after some navigation

Table 5-15. FileUpload properties (read-only)

Name	Type	Description
FileContent	Stream	Returns a Stream object that points to the file to upload.
FileName	String	Returns the name of the file to be uploaded, without any qualifying path information.
HasFile	Boolean	If true, indicates the control has a file to upload.
PostedFile	HttpPostedFile	Returns a reference to the file which has been uploaded. Exposes the read-only properties listed in Table 5-16.

Table 5-16. HttpPostedFile properties (read-only)

Name	Type	Description
ContentLength	Integer	Returns the size of the file, in bytes, of an uploaded file.
ContentType	String	Returns the MIME content type of the uploaded file (e.g., text\html, text\css, or text\javascript).
FileName	String	Returns the fully qualified filename on the client computer.
InputStream	Stream	Returns a Stream object that points to the uploaded file.

We will demonstrate all of these properties in the following example.

To see a FileUpload control in action, add to the chapter's website a new web page called *FileUploadDemo.aspx*. Drag a FileUpload control onto the page. Add two ASP.NET Button controls, with Text properties set to "Save" and "Display", and ID properties set to btnSave and btnDisplay, respectively. Add two Label controls with IDs set to lblMessage and lblDisplay. Sprinkle a few
 HTML elements to space things out. Switch to Design view and double-click each button to create Click event handlers for each button in the code-behind file. When you are done, the content file should look something like Example 5-23.

Example 5-23. FileUploadDemo.aspx

```
<%@ Page Language="C#" AutoEventWireup="true"
   CodeFile="FileUploadDemo.aspx.cs" Inherits="FileUploadDemo" %>

<!DOCTYPE html PUBLIC "-//W3C//DTD XHTML 1.0 Transitional//EN"
   "http://www.w3.org/TR/xhtml1/DTD/xhtml1-transitional.dtd">
<html xmlns="http://www.w3.org/1999/xhtml">
<head runat="server">
   <title>FileUpload Control Demo</title>
</head>

<body>
   <form id="form1" runat="server">
   <div>
      <h1>FileUpload Control</h1>
      <asp:FileUpload ID="FileUpload1" runat="server" />
      <br />
      <asp:Button ID="btnSave" runat="server"
         Text="Save" OnClick="btnSave_Click" />
      <asp:Button ID="btnDisplay" runat="server"
         Text="Display" OnClick="btnDisplay_Click" />
      <br />
      <br />
      <asp:Label ID="lblMessage" runat="server" />
      <asp:Label ID="lblDisplay" runat="server" />
   </div>
   </form>
</body>
</html>
```

In the code-behind file, add the highlighted code from Example 5-24. Note that you'll need to change <c:\\SaveDirectory> to the directory to which you want your files saved.

Example 5-24. FileUploadDemo.aspx.cs

```csharp
using System;
using System.IO;        //needed for StringBuilder class
using System.Text;      //needed for Stream class
using System.Web.UI;

public partial class FileUploadDemo : Page
{
    protected void btnSave_Click(object sender, EventArgs e)
    {
        StringBuilder str = new StringBuilder();
        if (FileUpload1.HasFile)
        {
            try
            {
                str.AppendFormat("Uploading file: {0}", FileUpload1.FileName);

                // Save the file
                FileUpload1.SaveAs("<c:\\SaveDirectory>"
                    + FileUpload1.FileName);

                // show info about the file
                str.AppendFormat("<br/>Saved As: {0}",
                    FileUpload1.PostedFile.FileName);
                str.AppendFormat("<br/>File Type: {0}",
                    FileUpload1.PostedFile.ContentType);
                str.AppendFormat("<br/>File Length (bytes): {0}",
                    FileUpload1.PostedFile.ContentLength);
                str.AppendFormat("<br/>PostedFile File Name: {0}",
                    FileUpload1.PostedFile.FileName);
            }
            catch (Exception ex)
            {
                str.Append("<br/><b>Error</b><br/>");
                str.AppendFormat(
                    "Unable to save <c:\\SaveDirectory>{0}<br />{1}",
                    FileUpload1.FileName, ex.Message);
            }
        }
        else
        {
            lblMessage.Text = "No file uploaded.";
        }
        lblMessage.Text = str.ToString();
        lblDisplay.Text = "";
    }

    protected void btnDisplay_Click(object sender, EventArgs e)
    {
```

Example 5-24. FileUploadDemo.aspx.cs (continued)

```
      StringBuilder str = new StringBuilder( );
      str.AppendFormat("<u>File:  {0}</u><br/>", FileUpload1.FileName);
      if (FileUpload1.HasFile)
      {
         try
         {
            Stream stream = FileUpload1.FileContent;
            StreamReader reader = new StreamReader(stream);
            string strLine = "";
            do
            {
               strLine = reader.ReadLine( );
               str.Append(strLine);
            } while (strLine != null);
         }
         catch (Exception ex)
         {
            str.Append ("<br/><b>Error</b><br/>");
            str.AppendFormat("Unable to display {0}<br/>{1}",
               FileUpload1.FileName, ex.Message);
         }
      }
      else
      {
         lblDisplay.Text = "No file uploaded.";
      }
      lblDisplay.Text = str.ToString( );
      lblMessage.Text = "";
   }
}
```

In btnSave_Click, the event handler for the Save button, the HasFile property of the FileUpload control is used to test whether a valid, fully qualified filename is entered in the control text box. If the text box is blank or the filename entered is not a valid file, this test will fail, and lblMessage will display "No file uploaded.".

Assuming there is a valid file to upload, the code in the try block is executed. The key statement here calls the SaveAs method of the FileUpload control, using a hard-coded path along with the FileName property to pass in a fully qualified filename. This statement may fail for any number of reasons, including insufficient disk space, an invalid path, or security issues (more on that in a moment).

If the SaveAs fails, the catch block will come into play, displaying an error message in lblMessage, including ex.Message, the Exception Message property.

 It's not a security best practice to echo exception messages to the user, because they can reveal sensitive information, but it suffices for this demo. Usually you would log this exception in the event log, in a database table, or in an email to the web administrator for further review.

If the SaveAs is successful, a number of pieces of information about the uploaded file are displayed in lblMessage, retrieved from properties of the FileUpload.PostedFile property (which is of type HttpPostedFile).

After saving a file, the page will look something like that shown in Figure 5-19.

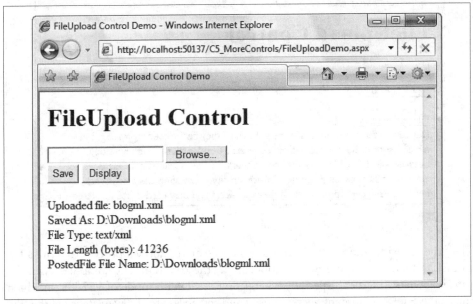

Figure 5-19. FileUploadDemo after saving a file

The event handler for the Display button's Click event is similar, except that instead of displaying information about the file, it displays the contents of the file itself. It does this by using the FileContent property to retrieve the contents of the uploaded file as a Stream object, which is then used to instantiate a StreamReader object. The ReadLine method of the StreamReader class is then used to step through the file, line by line, concatenating the lines to display in lblDisplay.

After displaying a file, in this case a text file containing a blog post, the page will look something like that shown in Figure 5-20.

Whenever you talk about uploading a file to a web server from clients, security is a big concern. There are two considerations. First, opening your web server in this way can present a huge security hole, and you should do it only with care and careful consideration. Not only can uploaded files contain viruses, Trojan horses, and other malicious software, but it would be dangerous to allow the client to browse the directory structure of the web server itself. For that reason, you will almost always want to either hardcode the target directory or at least severely circumscribe where the uploaded files can be saved.

Figure 5-20. FileUploadDemo displaying a file

The other consideration is the permissions necessary to allow a process to write a file to disk. When developing a web application, the development computer typically runs its own web server, especially when using the default mode of VS2008, in which the ASP.NET Development Server is used and the access to the website is via the file-system and in the security of the user running VS2008. In this situation, you will probably never run into any file permission problems.

However, when the website is deployed to a production web server and the website is accessed via Internet Information Services (IIS) and a virtual directory, problems will arise. This is because the account under which ASP.NET runs must have write permission for the directory in which the uploaded files are to be saved. In Windows 2000/XP, this account is named ASPNET. In Windows Server 2003, it's called NET-WORK SERVICE.

With a FileUpload control and good security precautions in place (e.g., checking the file's MIME types and file extensions), your users will be able to send their own files to your site, increasing your site's versatility.

 ASP.NET sets a default maximum size (4 MB) for files that the FileUpload control can upload. You can set this up to a maximum of 2 GB by setting the maxRequestLength attribute for the <system.web>/ <httpRuntime> in your *web.config* file. See Chapter 18 for more on configuring your website.

The AdRotator Control

The AdRotator control gets its name because it is most often used to display advertisements on web pages. It displays an image randomly selected from a list stored in either a separate XML file or a data-bound data source. In either case, the list contains image attributes, including the path to the image and a URL to link to when the image is clicked. The image changes every time the page is loaded.

In addition to the properties inherited from WebControl, the AdRotator control has the properties listed in Table 5-17, and an event you can handle called AdCreated. This occurs once per round trip to the server after creation of the control, but before the page is rendered.

Table 5-17. Properties of the AdRotator control

Name	Type	Description
AdvertisementFile	String	The path to an XML file that contains the list of advertisements and their attributes. We describe this file in detail shortly.
AlternateTextField	String	The element name from the AdvertisementFile or data field from which the alternative text is stored. Default is AlternateText.
DataMember	String	The name of the specific list of data the control will bind to if the control is not using an XML file for ads.
DataSource	Object	An object from which the control can retrieve data.
DataSourceID	String	The ID of the control from which the AdRotator can retrieve data.
ImageUrlField	String	The element name from the advertisement file or data field from which the URL for the image is stored. Default is ImageUrl.
KeywordFilter	String	Filters ads displayed to include only those with the specified keyword in the AdvertisementFile.
NavigateUrlField	String	The element name from the advertisement file or data field in which the URL to navigate to is stored. Default is NavigateUrl.
Target	String	The browser window or frame that displays the contents of the page linked to when the AdRotator is clicked.

The Target property is used to specify which browser window or frame is used to display the results of clicking the AdRotator control. It dictates whether the resultant page displaces the contents in the current browser window or frame, opens a new browser window, or does something else. The values of the Target property must begin with any letter in the range of a to z, case-insensitive, except for the special values shown in Table 4-6 in Chapter 4, which begin with an underscore. These are the same values recognized by the Target property of the HTML <a> element.

The Advertisement File

The advertisement file is an XML file that contains information about the advertisements to be displayed by the AdRotator control. Its location and filename are specified by the AdvertisementFile property of the control.

You can save the advertisement file anywhere in your website, but the recommended location is the special *App_Data* folder, because ASP.NET will never send files from that folder to the browser. VS2008 creates this folder by default for new websites.

The location of the advertisement file can be relative to the website root directory or can be absolute. If its location is something other than the web root, you will need to ensure the application has sufficient rights to access the file, especially after deployment.

The AdvertisementFile property cannot be set simultaneously with the DataSource, DataMember, or DataSourceID property. In other words, if the data is coming from an advertisement file, it cannot simultaneously come from a data source, and vice versa, or else an error occurs.

The advertisement file and the AdvertisementFile property are optional. If you want to create an advertisement programmatically, without the use of an advertisement file, place the code to display the desired elements in the AdCreated event.

As an XML file, the advertisement file is a structured text file with well-defined tags delineating the data.

Those who understand schemas can find the schema for the advertisement file in *%Program Files%\Microsoft Visual Studio 9.0\Xml\ Schemas\adrotator.xsd*.

Table 5-18 lists the standard elements, which are enclosed in angle brackets (< >) and require matching closing tags.

Table 5-18. XML elements used in the advertisement file

Tag	Description
Advertisements	Encloses the entire advertisement file.
Ad	Delineates each separate ad.
ImageUrl	The URL of the image to display. Required.
NavigateUrl	The URL of the page to navigate to when the control is clicked.
AlternateText	The text displayed in the control if the image is unavailable. In browsers that support the ToolTips feature this text is also displayed as a tool tip.
Keyword	The advertisement category. The keyword can be used to filter the advertisements displayed by the control by setting the AdRotator KeywordFilter property.

Table 5-18. XML elements used in the advertisement file (continued)

Tag	Description
Impressions	A value indicating how often the ad should be displayed relative to the other ads in the file.
Height	The height of the image being displayed.
Width	The width of the image being displayed.

Because this is XML and not HTML, it is much less forgiving of files that are not well formed. These tags are case-sensitive: ImageUrl will work; ImageURL will not.

For a complete description of well-formed XML, see the "Well-Formed XHTML" sidebar in Chapter 3.

In addition to the tags listed in Table 5-18, you can include your own custom tags to have custom attributes. The sample advertisement file in Example 5-25 contains a custom attribute called Animal, which will hold the animal pictured on the cover of each book. (No, O'Reilly authors have no say in selecting the animal that goes on their books.)

Example 5-25. ads.xml, sample advertisement file

```
<?xml version="1.0" encoding="utf-8" ?>
<Advertisements xmlns="
    http://schemas.microsoft.com/AspNet/AdRotator-Schedule-File-1.2">
    <Ad>
        <ImageUrl>ProgAspNet.gif</ImageUrl>
        <NavigateUrl>
            http://www.oreilly.com/catalog/progaspdotnet3/index.html
        </NavigateUrl>
        <AlternateText>Programming ASP.NET</AlternateText>
        <Keyword>Web</Keyword>
        <Impressions>50</Impressions>
        <Animal>stingray</Animal>
    </Ad>
    <Ad>
        <ImageUrl>LearningASP.gif</ImageUrl>
        <NavigateUrl>
            http://www.oreillynet.com/catalog/9780596513979/
        </NavigateUrl>
        <AlternateText>Learning ASP.NET 2.0 With AJAX</AlternateText>
        <Keyword>Windows</Keyword>
        <Impressions>40</Impressions>
        <Animal>stingray</Animal>
    </Ad>
    <Ad>
        <ImageUrl>ProgCSharp.gif</ImageUrl>
        <NavigateUrl>
            http://www.oreilly.com/catalog/9780596527433/
        </NavigateUrl>
        <AlternateText>Programming C# 3.0</AlternateText>
```

Example 5-25. ads.xml, sample advertisement file (continued)

```
        <Keyword>Language</Keyword>
        <Impressions>40</Impressions>
        <Animal>African Crowned Crane</Animal>
    </Ad>
    <Ad>
        <ImageUrl>ProgVB.gif</ImageUrl>
        <NavigateUrl>
            http://www.oreilly.com/catalog/progvb2005/index.html
        </NavigateUrl>
        <AlternateText>Programming VB .NET</AlternateText>
        <Keyword>Language</Keyword>
        <Impressions>30</Impressions>
        <Animal>grebe</Animal>
    </Ad>
</Advertisements>
```

All the elements in the advertisement file are parsed and placed in the adProperties dictionary. This dictionary can be used programmatically to access attributes, either standard or custom, by placing code in the AdCreated event handler.

Example 5-25 shows a sample advertisement file that contains references to books and websites for several excellent programming books. :)

> The NavigateUrl element of an Ad should be on one line, or else the AdRotator will try to interpret the whitespace as part of the URL to link to. It's split across three lines in Example 5-25 purely for clarity.

Using AdRotator

Now all you need is a web page with an AdRotator control and some graphics to use this advertisement file, as shown in the next example, *AdRotatorDemo.aspx*. After creating a new web form for the chapter website and calling it *AdRotatorDemo.aspx*, drag an AdRotator control onto the page, along with a Label control to display the animal. The content file should look something like Example 5-26.

Example 5-26. AdRotatorDemo.aspx

```
<%@ Page Language="C#" AutoEventWireup="true"
    CodeFile="AdRotatorDemo.aspx.cs" Inherits="AdRotatorDemo" %>

<!DOCTYPE html PUBLIC "-//W3C//DTD XHTML 1.0 Transitional//EN"
    "http://www.w3.org/TR/xhtml1/DTD/xhtml1-transitional.dtd">

<html xmlns="http://www.w3.org/1999/xhtml">
<head runat="server">
    <title>AdRotator</title>
</head>

<body>
    <form id="form1" runat="server">
```

Example 5-26. AdRotatorDemo.aspx (continued)

```
    <div>
        <h1>
            AdRotator Control</h1>
        <asp:AdRotator ID="ad" runat="server" Target="_blank"
            AdvertisementFile="ads.xml" OnAdCreated="ad_AdCreated" />
        <br />
        Animal:
        <asp:Label ID="lblAnimal" runat="server" />
    </div>
    </form>
</body>
</html>
```

The event handler for the AdRotator control is contained in the code-behind file, as highlighted in Example 5-27.

Example 5-27. AdRotatorDemo.aspx.cs

```
using System;
using System.Web.UI;
using System.Web.UI.WebControls;

public partial class AdRotatorDemo : Page
{
    protected void Page_Load(object sender, EventArgs e)
    {

    }
    protected void ad_AdCreated(object sender, AdCreatedEventArgs e)
    {
        if ((string)e.AdProperties["Animal"] != "")
            lblAnimal.Text = (string)e.AdProperties["Animal"];
        else
            lblAnimal.Text = "Not Applicable";
    }
}
```

Make certain that the advertisement file called *ads.xml*, listed in Example 5-25, is located in the website root directory, along with the image files specified within that file: *ProgAspNet.gif*, *ProgCSharp.gif*, *ProgVB.gif*, and *LearningASP.gif*. You'll find them in the download for this book.

The results of running *AdRotatorDemo* are shown in Figure 5-21. To see the images cycle through, refresh the view on your browser.

This control raises an AdCreated event, which occurs on every round trip to the server after the control is created but before the page is rendered. An attribute in the control declaration, called OnAdCreated, specifies the event handler to execute whenever the event fires. The event handler is passed an argument of type AdCreatedEventArgs, which has the properties listed in Table 5-19.

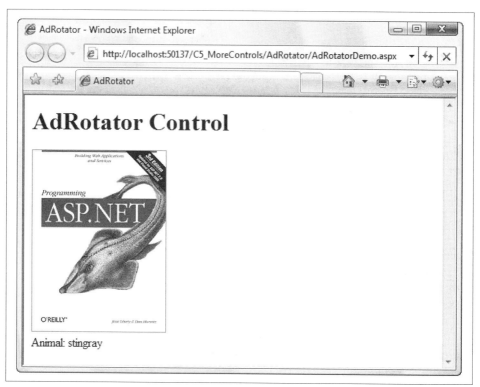

Figure 5-21. AdRotatorDemo.aspx in action

Table 5-19. Properties of the AdCreatedEventArgs class

Property	Description
AdProperties	Gets a dictionary object that contains all the advertisement properties contained in the advertisement file.
AlternateText	The alternative text displayed by the browser when the advertisement image is unavailable. If the browser supports tool tips, this text will be displayed as a tool tip.
ImageUrl	The URL of an image to display.
NavigateUrl	The URL of the web page to display when the control is clicked.

Every time the ad is changed (i.e., every time the page is reloaded), the event handler, ad_AdCreated, fires and updates lblAnimal contained on the page. ad_AdCreated first tests to be certain a value is in the Animal attribute. If not, "Not available." is displayed.

AdProperties returns a Dictionary object. When the AdProperties property is invoked, it implicitly calls the Item method of the Dictionary object, which returns the value corresponding to the dictionary entry whose key is Animal. This value is then cast, or converted, to a string. In C#, this is done with the following syntax:

```
(string)e.AdProperties["Animal"]
```

The Calendar Control

The ASP.NET Calendar control is a rich web control that provides several capabilities:

- Displays a calendar showing a single month
- Allows the user to select a day, week, or month
- Allows the user to select a range of days
- Allows the user to move to the next or previous month
- Programmatically controls the display of specific days

The Calendar control is customizable, with various properties and events. Before digging into all the detail, have a look at a bare-bones *.aspx* file showing a simple Calendar control. Add to the chapter website a new web form called *Calendar-Simple.aspx*, and drag a Calendar control onto the page.

Example 5-28 contains the code with the Calendar declaration highlighted, and Figure 5-22 shows the results. There is no code-behind file with this example other than the default boilerplate created by VS2008.

Example 5-28. Calendar-Simple.aspx

```
<%@ Page Language="C#" AutoEventWireup="true"
    CodeFile="Calendar-Simple.aspx.cs" Inherits="Calendar_Simple" %>

<!DOCTYPE html PUBLIC "-//W3C//DTD XHTML 1.0 Transitional//EN"
    "http://www.w3.org/TR/xhtml1/DTD/xhtml1-transitional.dtd">
<html xmlns="http://www.w3.org/1999/xhtml">
<head runat="server">
    <title>Simple Calendar Demo</title>
</head>

<body>
    <form id="form1" runat="server">
    <div>
        <asp:Calendar ID="Calendar1" runat="server"></asp:Calendar>
    </div>
    </form>
</body>
</html>
```

Pretty spiffy; zero manual coding yields a web page with a working calendar that displays the current month. The user can select a single day (though at this point nothing happens when a day is selected, other than it being highlighted) and move through the months by clicking the navigation symbols (< and >) on either side of the month name.

In addition to the properties inherited by all the ASP.NET server controls that derive from WebControl, the Calendar control has many properties of its own. The most important ones are listed in Table 5-20.

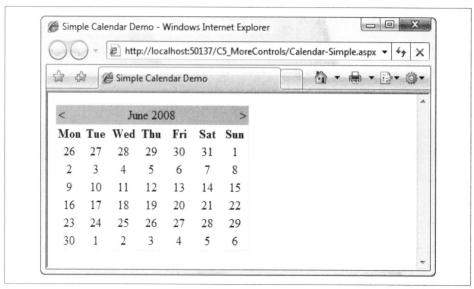

Figure 5-22. A bare-bones Calendar control in Calendar-Simple.aspx

As you can see in Table 5-20, the aforementioned navigation symbols are specified by the NextMonthText and PrevMonthText properties as > and <, respectively. These HTML character entities normally display as the greater than (>) and less than (<) symbols. However, in the Calendar control, these symbols are displayed as underlined. This is because all the selectable elements in the Calendar control are rendered to the browser like LinkButton controls, hence the underlines.

Table 5-20. Read/write properties of the Calendar control

Name	Type	Values	Description
Caption	String		Text to display on the page above the calendar.
CaptionAlign	TableCaption-Align	Bottom, Left, NotSet, Right, Top	Specifies horizontal and vertical alignment of the Caption property value.
CellPadding	Integer	0, 1, 2, etc.	Distance in pixels between the border and contents of a cell. Applies to all the cells in the calendar and to all four sides of each cell. Default is 2.
CellSpacing	Integer	0, 1, 2, etc.	Distance in pixels between cells. Applies to all the cells in the calendar. Default is 0.
DayNameFormat	DayName-Format	Full, Short, FirstLetter, FirstTwoLetters	Format of days of the week. Values are self-explanatory, except Short, which is the first three letters. Default is Short.
FirstDayOfWeek	FirstDayOfWeek	Default, Sunday, Monday, ... Saturday	Day of week to display in the first column. Default (the default) specifies system setting.

Table 5-20. Read/write properties of the Calendar control (continued)

Name	Type	Values	Description
NextMonthText	String		Text for next month navigation control. The default is >, which renders as the greater than sign (>). Applies only if the ShowNextPrevMonth property is true.
NextPrevFormat	NextPrevFormat	CustomText, FullMonth, ShortMonth	To use CustomText, set this property and specify the actual text to use in NextMonthText and PrevMonthText.
PrevMonthText	String		Text for previous month navigation control. Default is <, which renders as the less than sign (<). Applies only if the ShowNextPrevMonth property is true.
SelectedDate	DateTime		A single selected date. Only the date is stored; the time is set to 00:00:00 (12:00 A.M.).
SelectedDates	DateTime		Collection of DateTime objects when multiple dates are selected.
SelectionMode	Calendar-SelectionMode		Described later in this section.
SelectMonthText	String		Text for month selection element in the selector column. Default is >>, which renders as two greater than signs (>>). Applies only if the SelectionMode property is set to DayWeekMonth.
ShowDayHeader	Boolean	true, false	If true, the default, the days-of-week headings are shown.
ShowGridLines	Boolean	true, false	If true, grid lines between cells are displayed. Default is false.
ShowNextPrev-Month	Boolean	true, false	Indicates whether the next and previous month navigation elements are shown. Default is true.
ShowTitle	Boolean	true, false	Indicates whether the title is shown. If false, the next and previous month navigation elements will be hidden. Default is true.
TitleFormat	TitleFormat	Month, MonthYear	Indicates whether the title is month only or month and year. Default is MonthYear.
TodaysDate	DateTime		The date in the calendar that is formatted as the current date.
UseAccessible-Header	Boolean	true, false	Specifies whether a header accessible to assistive technologies is to be used.
VisibleDate	DateTime		Any date in the month that you want to display. *Initially not set.*

Selecting Dates in the Calendar

If you want to give the user the ability to select a single day, an entire week, or an entire month, you must set the SelectionMode property. Table 5-21 lists the legal values for the SelectionMode property.

Table 5-21. Members of the CalendarSelectionMode enumeration

Member	Description
Day	Allows the user to select a single day. This is the default value.
DayWeek	Allows the user to select a single day or an entire week.
DayWeekMonth	Allows the user to select a single day, an entire week, or an entire month.
None	Nothing on the Calendar can be selected.

To see the effects of setting the SelectionMode property, add another new web form to the chapter website and call it *Calendar-SelectionMode.aspx*. Once again, add a Calendar control to the empty page, but add the following highlighted attribute to the Calendar:

```
<asp:Calendar ID="Calendar1" runat="server"
    SelectionMode="DayWeekMonth">
</asp:Calendar>
```

The resultant calendar, with the entire month selected, looks like Figure 5-23. (It's saved as *Calendar-SelectionMode.aspx* in the download for the chapter.)

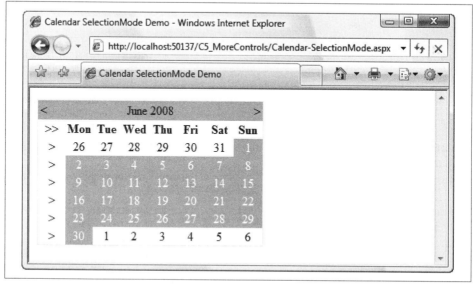

Figure 5-23. A Calendar control with a month selected

When the SelectionMode property is set to DayWeek, an extra column containing the ≥ symbol is added to the left side of the calendar. Clicking one of those symbols selects that entire week.

Similarly, when the SelectionMode property is set to DayWeekMonth, in addition to the week selection column, a ≥≥ symbol (two "greater than or equal to" symbols) is added to the left of the Day Names row. Clicking that symbol selects the entire month, as shown in Figure 5-23.

Controlling the Calendar's Appearance

A number of read/write properties, all of type TableItemStyle, control the style for each part of the calendar. These TableItemStyle type properties are listed in Table 5-22 and are demonstrated in the next example, *Calendar-Styles.aspx*, shown in finished form in Figure 5-24.

Table 5-22. Calendar control properties of type TableItemStyle

Name	Sets style for...
DayHeaderStyle	Days of the week
DayStyle	Dates
NextPrevStyle	Month navigation controls
OtherMonthDayStyle	Dates that are visible but are not in the current month
SelectedDayStyle	Selected dates
SelectorStyle	Week and month selection column
TitleStyle	Title section
TodayDayStyle	Today's date (or the date represented by the value of the TodaysDate property)
WeekendDayStyle	Weekend dates

These TableItemStyle type properties work the same way in VS2008 for the Calendar control as we described previously for the Wizard control. When you work in Design view, the properties appear as in Figure 5-17, and when you work in Source view, the properties appear in IntelliSense in their expanded form. The format of the declaration also follows the same pattern described for the Wizard control.

In addition to the TableItemStyle type properties there are four read/write Boolean properties that control various aspects of the calendar, shown in Table 5-23.

Table 5-23. Boolean properties controlling various aspects of the Calendar control's appearance

Property	Default	Controls visibility of...
ShowDayHeader	true	Names of the days of the week
ShowGridLines	false	Grid lines between the days of the month
ShowNextPrevMonth	true	Month navigation controls
ShowTitle	true	Title section

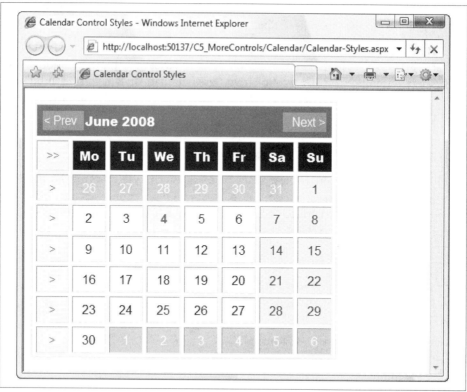

Figure 5-24. Calendar-Styles.aspx in action

You could click the Calendar control smart tag in Design view and select one of the Auto Format formats, but in this example you will choose your own styles. You can do this in the Properties window after selecting the Calendar control in either Design or Source view.

To see how these style properties are used, copy the Calendar control from *Calendar-SelectionMode.aspx* to a new web form, *Calendar-Styles.aspx*. The complete content file for this latest example is listed in Example 5-29, with the Calendar declaration highlighted, and the finished page is shown in Figure 5-24 (or at least as best as it can be in grayscale rather than color). You can see what styles to set for this example by looking at the declarations in Example 5-29.

Example 5-29. Calendar-Styles.aspx in full

```
<%@ Page Language="C#" AutoEventWireup="true" CodeFile="Calendar-Styles.aspx.cs"
   Inherits="Calendar_Styles" %>

<!DOCTYPE html PUBLIC "-//W3C//DTD XHTML 1.0 Transitional//EN"
"http://www.w3.org/TR/xhtml1/DTD/xhtml1-transitional.dtd">
<html xmlns="http://www.w3.org/1999/xhtml">
```

Example 5-29. Calendar-Styles.aspx in full (continued)

```
<head runat="server">
    <title>Calendar Control Styles</title>
</head>
<body>
    <form id="form1" runat="server">
    <div>
        <asp:Calendar ID="Calendar1"
            runat="server" SelectionMode="DayWeekMonth"
            CellPadding="7" CellSpacing="5"
            DayNameFormat="FirstTwoLetters" FirstDayOfWeek="Monday"
            NextMonthText="Next >" PrevMonthText="< Prev"
            ShowGridLines="True" DayStyle-BackColor="White"
            DayStyle-ForeColor="Black" DayStyle-Font-Names="Arial">

            <DayHeaderStyle BackColor="Black"
                Font-Names="Arial Black" ForeColor="White" />
            <SelectedDayStyle BackColor="Cornsilk" Font-Bold="True"
                Font-Italic="True" Font-Names="Arial" ForeColor="Blue" />
            <SelectorStyle BackColor="Cornsilk"
                Font-Names="Arial" ForeColor="Red" />
            <WeekendDayStyle BackColor="LavenderBlush"
                Font-Names="Arial" ForeColor="Purple" />
            <OtherMonthDayStyle BackColor="LightGray"
                Font-Names="Arial" ForeColor="White" />
            <TodayDayStyle BackColor="Cornsilk" Font-Bold="True"
                Font-Names="Arial" ForeColor="Green" />
            <NextPrevStyle BackColor="DarkGray"
                Font-Names="Arial" ForeColor="Yellow" />
            <TitleStyle BackColor="Gray" Font-Names="Arial Black"
                ForeColor="White" HorizontalAlign="Left" />
        </asp:Calendar>
    </div>
    </form>
</body>
</html>
```

Programming the Calendar Control

The Calendar control provides three events that are not inherited from other control classes and are of particular interest. By providing event handlers for the events, you can exercise considerable control over how the calendar behaves. These events are:

- SelectionChanged
- DayRender
- VisibleMonthChanged

The following sections describe each of these in detail.

SelectionChanged event

The SelectionChanged event fires when the user makes a selection—either a day, a week, or an entire month—in the Calendar control. The event is not fired if the selection is changed programmatically or if you reselect the currently selected day. The event handler is passed an argument of type EventArgs.

The next example demonstrates handling the SelectionChanged event. Whenever you select a new date, it displays text strings with today's date, the selected date, and the number of days selected.

Copy the calendar control from *Calendar-SelectionMode.aspx* (the one without all the styles) to a new web form called *Calendar-SelectionChanged.aspx*. Add the default named event handler for the SelectionChanged event by double-clicking the Calendar control in Design view. This will add the OnSelectionChanged attribute to the Calendar declaration in the content file and will open the code-behind file with the event handler skeleton in place. In the Calendar1_SelectionChanged method, type in the highlighted code from Example 5-30, as well as the highlighted helper method, lblCountUpdate.

Example 5-30. Calendar-SelectionChanged.aspx.cs

```
using System;
using System.Web.UI;

public partial class Calendar_SelectionChanged : Page
{
    protected void Calendar1_SelectionChanged(object sender, EventArgs e)
    {
        lblTodaysDate.Text = "Today's date is "
            + Calendar1.TodaysDate.ToShortDateString( );
        if (Calendar1.SelectedDate != DateTime.MinValue)
        {
            lblSelected.Text = "The date selected is "
                + Calendar1.SelectedDate.ToShortDateString( );
        }
        lblCountUpdate( );
    }

    private void lblCountUpdate( )
    {
        lblCount.Text = "Count of days selected:  "
            + Calendar1.SelectedDates.Count.ToString( );
    }
}
```

You must also add three Label controls to the bottom of the page to display the information from the calendar. *Calendar-SelectionChanged.aspx* is listed in full in Example 5-31, with the style attributes of the Calendar control omitted because they are the same as the previous example. Additions for this example are highlighted.

Example 5-31. Calendar-SelectionChanged.aspx in full

```
<%@ Page Language="C#" AutoEventWireup="true"
    CodeFile="Calendar-SelectionChanged.aspx.cs"
    Inherits="Calendar_SelectionChanged" %>

<!DOCTYPE html PUBLIC "-//W3C//DTD XHTML 1.0 Transitional//EN"
    "http://www.w3.org/TR/xhtml1/DTD/xhtml1-transitional.dtd">
<html xmlns="http://www.w3.org/1999/xhtml">
<head runat="server">
    <title>Calendar SelectionChanged Demo</title>
</head>

<body>
    <form id="form1" runat="server">
    <div>
        <asp:Calendar ID="Calendar1"
            runat="server" SelectionMode="DayWeekMonth"
            OnSelectionChanged="Calendar1_SelectionChanged">
        </asp:Calendar>
        <br />
        <asp:Label ID="lblCount" runat="server" />
        <br />
        <asp:Label ID="lblTodaysDate" runat="server" />
        <br />
        <asp:Label ID="lblSelected" runat="server" />
    </div>
    </form>
</body>
</html>
```

Running the page and selecting a date or dates will result in a screen similar to the one shown in Figure 5-25.

Looking at Example 5-31, you can see this example adds the OnSelectionChanged property to the Calendar control. This property binds the SelectionChanged event to the Calendar1_SelectionChanged method in the code-behind file, shown in Example 5-30. Three Label controls have been added after the Calendar control. The first of these, lblCount, is used to display the number of days selected. The other two labels, named lblTodaysDate and lblSelected, are used to display today's date and the currently selected date, respectively.

All three of these labels have their Text property set in the SelectionChanged event handler method. Looking at that method in Example 5-30, you can see that lblTodaysDate is filled by getting the Calendar control's TodaysDate property, with the following line of code:

```
lblTodaysDate.Text = "Today's date is "
    + Calendar1.TodaysDate.ToShortDateString();
```

The ID of the Calendar control is Calendar1. TodaysDate is a property of the Calendar control that returns an object of type System.DateTime. To assign this to a Text property (which is an object of type String), you must convert the DateTime to a String.

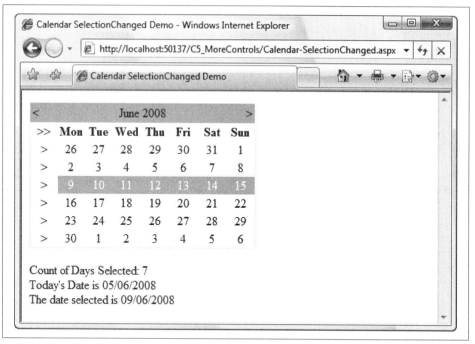

Figure 5-25. Calendar-SelectionChanged.aspx in action

You do this with the ToShortDateString method, which returns a shorter (mm/dd/yy) version of the date.

> The DateTime structure has many methods for converting a DateTime object to other formats based on the current culture for the website. For the lowdown on DateTime format strings, go to *http://blogs.msdn. com/kathykam/archive/2006/09/29/.NET-Format-String-102_3A00_- DateTime-Format-String.aspx*.

lblSelected is filled by the following line of code:

```
if (Calendar1.SelectedDate != DateTime.MinValue)
{
   lblSelected.Text = "The date selected is "
      + Calendar1.SelectedDate.ToShortDateString( );
}
```

To detect whether any date has been selected, you test to see whether the currently selected date, Calendar1.SelectedDate, is equal to DateTime.MinValue. DateTime. MinValue is a constant representing the smallest possible value of DateTime, and is the default value for the SelectedDate property if nothing has been selected yet. MinValue has the literal value of 12:00:00 A.M., 1/1/0001 CE. There is also a MaxValue that has the literal value of 11:59:59 P.M., 12/31/9999 CE.

CE (Common Era) is the scientific notation for the span of years referred to as AD (*Anno Domini*) on the Gregorian calendar. BCE (Before Common Era) is the scientific equivalent of BC (Before Christ).

If the user has selected a date, the Text property of lblSelected will be set to the string value of the SelectedDate property.

The Label control, lblCount, displays the number of days selected. The SelectionChanged event handler calls the lblCountUpdate method, which sets the Text property of lblCount. To set that control, you must determine how many dates were selected. The Calendar control has a SelectedDates property that returns a SelectedDates collection. SelectedDates is a collection of DateTime objects representing all the dates selected in the Calendar control. Count is a property of the SelectedDatesCollection object that returns an integer containing the number of dates in the collection. Because the Count property is an integer, you must use the ToString method to convert it to a string so it can be assigned to the Text property:

```
Calendar1.SelectedDates.Count.ToString( );
```

Though SelectedDates (the collection of selected dates) and SelectedDate (the single selected date) both contain DateTime objects, only the date value is stored. The time value for these objects is set to 0 (equivalent to 12:00 A.M.) in C#.

The range of dates in the SelectedDates collection is sorted in ascending order by date. When the SelectedDates collection is updated, the SelectedDate property is automatically updated to contain the first object in the SelectedDates collection.

The user can navigate from month to month by clicking the month navigation controls located on either side of the month title. The user can also select a single day by clicking that day, an entire week by clicking the week selector control, or the entire month by clicking the month selector control.

However, you can give the user much more flexibility than this. To demonstrate, you must add several controls and methods. Create in the chapter's website a new web form called *Calendar-MoreSelections.aspx* and copy across the Calendar, Labels, and event handler code from *Calendar-SelectionChanged.aspx*.

To enable the user to navigate directly to any month in the current year, add a DropDownList containing all the months of the year and a button, labeled TGIF, which selects all the Fridays in the currently viewed month.

The Calendar control also allows the user to select a range of dates. You might expect to be able to use the standard Windows techniques of holding down the Ctrl or Shift key while clicking on dates, but this does not work. However, you can put controls on the page to select a starting day and ending day. In *Calendar-MoreSelections*, you will add a pair of TextBox controls to accept a starting day and an ending day for a range of dates. A Button control can force the selection of the range of dates.

The markup for this is shown in Example 5-32, with the new additions highlighted.

Example 5-32. Calendar-MoreSelections.aspx in full

```
<%@ Page Language="C#" AutoEventWireup="true"
    CodeFile="Calendar-MoreSelections.aspx.cs"
    Inherits="Calendar_MoreSelections" %>

<!DOCTYPE html PUBLIC "-//W3C//DTD XHTML 1.0 Transitional//EN"
    "http://www.w3.org/TR/xhtml1/DTD/xhtml1-transitional.dtd">
<html xmlns="http://www.w3.org/1999/xhtml">
<head runat="server">
    <title>Calendar SelectionChanged Demo Part 2</title>
</head>

<body>
    <form id="form1" runat="server">
    <div>
        <asp:Calendar ID="Calendar1" runat="server"
            SelectionMode="DayWeekMonth"
            OnSelectionChanged="Calendar1_SelectionChanged">
        </asp:Calendar>
        <br />
        <asp:Label ID="lblCount" runat="server" />
        <br />
        <asp:Label ID="lblTodaysDate" runat="server" />
        <br />
        <asp:Label ID="lblSelected" runat="server" />
        <br />

        <table>
          <tr>
            <td>
                Select a month:
            </td>
            <td>
                <asp:DropDownList ID="ddl" runat="server"
                    AutoPostBack="true"
                    OnSelectedIndexChanged="ddl_SelectedIndexChanged">
                    <asp:ListItem Text="January" Value="1" />
                    <asp:ListItem Text="February" Value="2" />
                    <asp:ListItem Text="March" Value="3" />
                    <asp:ListItem Text="April" Value="4" />
                    <asp:ListItem Text="May" Value="5" />
                    <asp:ListItem Text="June" Value="6" />
                    <asp:ListItem Text="July" Value="7" />
                    <asp:ListItem Text="August" Value="8" />
                    <asp:ListItem Text="September" Value="9" />
                    <asp:ListItem Text="October" Value="10" />
                    <asp:ListItem Text="November" Value="11" />
                    <asp:ListItem Text="December" Value="12" />
                </asp:DropDownList>
            </td>
            <td>
                <asp:Button ID="btnTgif" runat="server"
                    Text="TGIF" onclick="btnTgif_Click" />
            </td>
```

Example 5-32. Calendar-MoreSelections.aspx in full (continued)

```
        </tr>
        <tr>
          <td colspan="2">
             </td>
        </tr>
        <tr>
          <td colspan="2">
            <b>Day Range</b></td>
        </tr>
        <tr>
          <td>
            Starting Day</td>
          <td>
            Ending Day</td>
        </tr>
        <tr>
          <td>
            <asp:TextBox ID="txtStart" runat="server"
              Width="25" MaxLength="2" />
          </td>
          <td>
            <asp:TextBox ID="txtEnd" runat="server"
              Width="25" MaxLength="2" />
          </td>
          <td>
            <asp:Button ID="btnRange" runat="server"
              Text="Apply" onclick="btnRange_Click" />
          </td>
        </tr>
      </table>
    </div>
    </form>
  </body>
</html>
```

Example 5-33 shows the code-behind file, *Calendar-MoreSelections.aspx.cs*, in full.

Example 5-33. Calendar-MoreSelections.aspx.cs

```
using System;
using System.Web.UI;

public partial class Calendar_MoreSelections : Page
{
    protected void Page_Load(object sender, EventArgs e)
    {
        if (!IsPostBack)
        {
            Calendar1.VisibleDate = Calendar1.TodaysDate;
            ddl.SelectedIndex = Calendar1.VisibleDate.Month - 1;
        }
        lblTodaysDate.Text = "Today's Date is "
            + Calendar1.TodaysDate.ToShortDateString();
    }
```

Example 5-33. Calendar-MoreSelections.aspx.cs (continued)

```
protected void Calendar1_SelectionChanged(object sender, EventArgs e)
{
    lblSelectedUpdate( );
    lblCountUpdate( );
    txtClear( );
}

private void lblSelectedUpdate( )
{
    if (Calendar1.SelectedDate != DateTime.MinValue)
    {
        lblSelected.Text = "The date selected is "
            + Calendar1.SelectedDate.ToShortDateString( );
    }
}

private void lblCountUpdate( )
{
    lblCount.Text = "Count of Days Selected:   "
        + Calendar1.SelectedDates.Count.ToString( );
}

protected void ddl_SelectedIndexChanged(object sender, EventArgs e)
{
    Calendar1.SelectedDates.Clear( );
    lblSelectedUpdate( );
    lblCountUpdate( );
    Calendar1.VisibleDate = new DateTime(Calendar1.VisibleDate.Year,
        Int32.Parse(ddl.SelectedItem.Value), 1);
    txtClear( );
}

protected void btnTgif_Click(object sender, EventArgs e)
{
    int currentMonth = Calendar1.VisibleDate.Month;
    int currentYear = Calendar1.VisibleDate.Year;
    Calendar1.SelectedDates.Clear( );
    for (int i = 1;
        i <= System.DateTime.DaysInMonth(currentYear, currentMonth);
        i++)
        {
        DateTime date = new DateTime(currentYear, currentMonth, i);
        if (date.DayOfWeek == DayOfWeek.Friday)
        {
            Calendar1.SelectedDates.Add(date);
        }
    }
    lblSelectedUpdate( );
    lblCountUpdate( );
    txtClear( );
}
```

Example 5-33. Calendar-MoreSelections.aspx.cs (continued)

```
    protected void btnRange_Click(object sender, EventArgs e)
    {
        int currentMonth = Calendar1.VisibleDate.Month;
        int currentYear = Calendar1.VisibleDate.Year;
        DateTime StartDate = new DateTime(currentYear, currentMonth,
            Int32.Parse(txtStart.Text));
        DateTime EndDate = new DateTime(currentYear, currentMonth,
            Int32.Parse(txtEnd.Text));
        Calendar1.SelectedDates.Clear();
        Calendar1.SelectedDates.SelectRange(StartDate, EndDate);
        lblSelectedUpdate();
        lblCountUpdate();
    }

    private void txtClear()
    {
        txtStart.Text = "";
        txtEnd.Text = "";
    }
}
```

The result of running *Calendar-MoreSelections* is shown in Figure 5-26 after selecting a range of days.

All of the selection controls are in a static HTML table so you can control the layout of the page.

The ListItem objects in the DropDownList contain the names of the months for the Text properties and the number of the months for the Value properties.

The Calendar1_SelectionChanged method has been modified by having the bulk of its code refactored into a separate method named lblSelectedUpdate, which updates the Text property of the lblSelected label. This method is then called from Calendar1_SelectionChanged, as well as several other places throughout the code. In addition, another helper method, txtClear, is called to clear the Starting Day and Ending Day text boxes.

The ddl_SelectedIndexChanged event handler method begins by clearing the SelectedDates collection:

```
    Calendar1.SelectedDates.Clear();
```

A call is made to the lblSelectedUpdate method to clear the Label control containing the first selected date and to the lblCountUpdate method to clear the Label control containing the count of selected dates. Then the VisibleDate property of the Calendar control is set to the first day of the newly selected month:

```
    Calendar1.VisibleDate = new DateTime(Calendar1.VisibleDate.Year,
        Int32.Parse(ddl.SelectedItem.Value), 1);
```

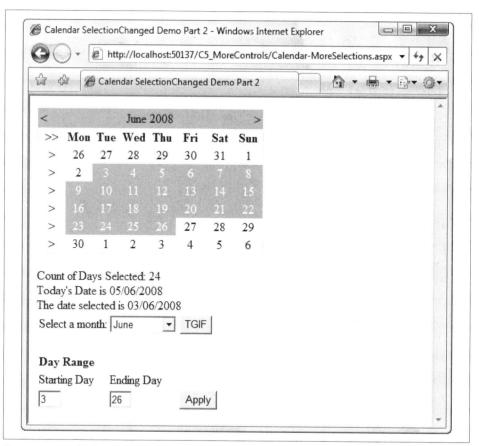

Figure 5-26. Calendar-MoreSelections.aspx in action

The VisibleDate property is of type DateTime; a new DateTime object is instantiated. The DateTime structure, like many objects in the .NET Framework, uses an overloaded constructor. An object may have more than one constructor; each must be differentiated by having different types of arguments or a different number of arguments.

In this case, you want to instantiate a DateTime object that contains only the date or the date with the time set to zero. To do so requires three integer parameters: year, month, and day. The first parameter, Calendar1.VisibleDate.Year, and the last parameter, 1, are integers. However, the month parameter comes from the Value property of the selected item in the DropDownList control. The Value property is a string, not an integer, though the characters it contains look like an integer. Therefore, it must be converted to an integer using the statement:

```
Int32.Parse(ddl.SelectedItem.Value)
```

The TGIF button is named btnTgif and has an event handler for the Click event, btnTgif_Click. This method iterates over all the days of the currently visible month and tests to see whether it is Friday. If so, it will add that date to the collection of SelectedDates.

First, the btnTgif_Click method gets the month and year of the currently visible month, using the VisibleDate property of the Calendar control, which is a DateTime object, and gets the Month and Year properties of the DateTime object:

```
int currentMonth = Calendar1.VisibleDate.Month;
int currentYear = Calendar1.VisibleDate.Year;
```

Then, it clears all the currently selected dates:

```
Calendar1.SelectedDates.Clear();
```

Now, it does the iteration. The limit part of the for loop is the number of days in the month as determined by the DaysInMonth property of the DateTime object. The month in question is specified by the currentYear and currentMonth arguments:

```
System.DateTime.DaysInMonth(currentYear, currentMonth)
```

Once inside the for loop, a DateTime variable called date is assigned to each day. Again, the DateTime object is instantiated with parameters for year, month, and day. The crucial question becomes, "Is the day of the week for this day a Friday?" If so, TGIF and add it to the collection of SelectedDates:

```
DateTime date = new DateTime(currentYear, currentMonth, i);
if (date.DayOfWeek == DayOfWeek.Friday)
{
    Calendar1.SelectedDates.Add(date);
}
```

Finally, after iterating over all the days of the month, call the lblSelectedUpdate method to update the label showing the first selected date, call the lblCountUpdate method to update the label showing the number of days selected, and call txtClear to clear the Start and End text boxes.

You will notice a Page_Load method in the code-behind file. This makes the page behave correctly the first time the TGIF button is clicked, even before the month is changed. Without this Page_Load event procedure, the page behaves correctly for the TGIF button only after the month has been changed at least once. The btnTgif_Click method uses the VisibleDate property to set the current month and year variables. If that property is not initialized during the initial page load, the values assigned to those variables will not correspond to the visible month.

In addition, the code to update the label displaying today's data, lblTodaysDate, has been moved from the Calendar1_SelectionChanged method to the Page_Load method because it makes more sense to have it there.

The controls for selecting the range are in the same static HTML table as the controls for selecting the month and all the Fridays. There are two text boxes, one named txtStart for the start day and one named txtEnd for the end day. In this example, the TextBox controls' Width and MaxLength attributes provide limited control over the user input.

The UI provided in *Calendar-MoreSelections.aspx* for selecting a range of dates is admittedly limiting because you cannot span multiple months. You could almost as easily provide three independent Calendar controls: one for the start date, one for the end date, and one for the range. Also, the day range does not apply after the month changes without reapplying the selection because the VisibleMonthChanged event is not trapped. (See "VisibleMonthChanged event," later in this chapter.)

A helper method, txtClear, is provided to clear the day range selection boxes. This method is called at appropriate points in the other methods.

The Apply button is named btnRange, with the Click event handled by the method btnRange_Click. In btnRange_Click, you set integer variables to hold the current month and year:

```
int currentMonth = Calendar1.VisibleDate.Month;
int currentYear = Calendar1.VisibleDate.Year;
DateTime StartDate = new DateTime(currentYear, currentMonth,
    Int32.Parse(txtStart.Text));
DateTime EndDate = new DateTime(currentYear, currentMonth,
    Int32.Parse(txtEnd.Text));
```

Similar to the month DropDownList described previously, the DateTime object requires the year, month, and day. You have the year and month as integers; all you need is the day. You get the day by converting the text entered in the appropriate text box to an integer.

This is not very robust code. If the user enters non-numeric data in one of the text boxes, or a value greater than the number of days in the month, an ugly error will result. If the start date is later than the end date, no error message will result, but neither will anything be selected. In a real application, you will want to use validation controls, as described in Chapter 11.

Once the method has the start and end dates as DateTime objects, it clears any currently selected dates and uses the SelectRange method of the SelectedDatesCollection class to add the range of dates to the SelectedDates collection:

```
Calendar1.SelectedDates.Clear();
Calendar1.SelectedDates.SelectRange(StartDate, EndDate);
```

The SelectRange method requires two parameters: the start date and the end date.

DayRender event

Data binding is not supported directly for the Calendar control. However, you can modify the content and formatting of individual date cells. This allows you to retrieve values from a database, process those values in some manner, and place them in specific cells.

Before the Calendar control is rendered to the browser, all of the components that comprise the control are created. As each date cell is created, it raises the DayRender event.

The DayRender event handler receives an argument of type DayRenderEventArgs. This object has two properties that can be read programmatically:

Cell
> TableCell object that represents the cell being rendered

Day
> CalendarDay object that represents the day being rendered in that cell

This next example, *Calendar-Events.aspx*, will demonstrate the DayRender event. All the weekend days will have their background color changed, and a New Year's greeting will be displayed for January 1.

Copy the previous example, *Calendar-MoreSelections.aspx*, to a new web form called *Calendar-Events.aspx*; then, change the class name in both the markup and the code-behind file to Calendar_Events. In this section, you will make the changes to handle the DayRender event. There are only three changes.

First, go into Design view, select Calendar1, click the Events icon in the Properties window (the lightning bolt), and double-click the text box next to DayRender. This will add the following attribute to the Calendar1 declaration in the content file:

```
OnDayRender="Calendar1_DayRender"
```

This will also create an empty event handler in the code-behind file. Add to this handler the code highlighted in Example 5-34.

Example 5-34. DayRender event handler in Calendar-Events.aspx.cs

```
protected void Calendar1_DayRender(object sender, DayRenderEventArgs e)
{
    // Notice that this overrides the WeekendDayStyle.
    if (!e.Day.IsOtherMonth && e.Day.IsWeekend)
    {
        e.Cell.BackColor = System.Drawing.Color.LightGreen;
    }
    if (e.Day.Date.Month == 1 && e.Day.Date.Day == 1)
    {
        e.Cell.Controls.Add(
            new LiteralControl("<br/>Happy New Year!"));
    }
}
```

You'll also need to import the System.Web.UI.WebControls namespace to use the DayRenderEventArgs class in the DayRender event handler:

```
using System.Web.UI.WebControls;
```

The first thing the Calendar1_DayRender method does is color the weekends LightGreen. Recall that a WeekendDayStyle property is set for this control which colors the weekends LavenderBlush. The DayRender method overrides the WeekendDayStyle. (The distinction may not be apparent in the printed book, but you will see the colors when you run the web page in a browser.)

The event handler method is passed two parameters:

```
protected void Calendar1_DayRender(object sender, DayRenderEventArgs e)
```

DayRenderEventArgs contains properties for the Day and the Cell. The Day is tested to see whether it is both the current month and a weekend day:

```
(!e.Day.IsOtherMonth && e.Day.IsWeekend)
```

The Day property is a member of the CalendarDay class, which has the properties shown in Table 5-24 (all of which are read-only except for IsSelectable).

Table 5-24. Properties of the CalendarDay class

Property	Type	Description
Date	DateTime	Date represented by this Day. Read-only.
DayNumberText	String	String representation of the day number of this CalendarDay object. Read-only.
IsOtherMonth	Boolean	Indicates that this CalendarDay object is in a different month than the month currently displayed by the Calendar control. Read-only.
IsSelectable	Boolean	Indicates whether the CalendarDay object can be selected. Not read-only.
IsSelected	Boolean	Indicates whether the CalendarDay object is selected.
IsToday	Boolean	Indicates whether the CalendarDay object is today's date.
IsWeekend	Boolean	Indicates whether the CalendarDay object is a weekend date.

If the date is both in the current month and a weekend day, the Cell.BackColor property is assigned a color:

```
e.Cell.BackColor=System.Drawing.Color.LightGreen;
```

Calendar1_DayRender then tests to see whether the selected date is New Year's Day. Again, the Day property of the DayRenderEventArgs object is tested; this time to see whether the Month of the Date is 1 and the Day of the Date is 1:

```
if (e.Day.Date.Month == 1 && e.Day.Date.Day == 1)
```

If so, a LiteralControl is added to the cell that adds an HTML break tag and a greeting:

```
e.Cell.Controls.Add(new LiteralControl("<br/>Happy New Year!"));
```

The thing to remember here is, like all ASP.NET server controls, what is actually sent to the browser is HTML. Thus, a calendar is rendered on the browser as an HTML table. Each selectable component of the calendar has an anchor element associated with it, along with some JavaScript that accomplishes the postback. (This is evident when you hold the cursor over any clickable element of the calendar: the status line of the browser will display the name of the JavaScript function that will be executed if the link is clicked.) Using a LiteralControl inserts the text in its argument as a control into the HTML cell as is. A look at a snippet from the source code visible on the browser confirms this:

```
<td align="center" style="width:12%;">
   <a href="javascript:__doPostBack('Calendar1','2922')"
      style="color:Black" title="01 January">1</a>
   <br/>Happy New Year!
</td>
```

When the *Calendar-Events* example is run and the month navigated to is January, you will see something like Figure 5-27.

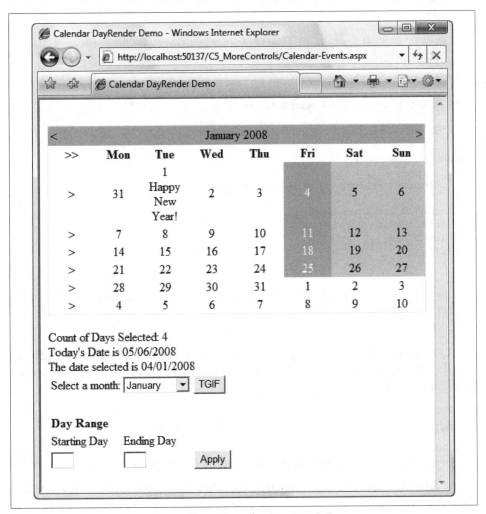

Figure 5-27. Calendar-Events.aspx adding a Literal to New Year's Day

VisibleMonthChanged event

The Calendar control also provides an event to indicate that the user has changed months. You will extend the current example, *Calendar-Events.aspx*, to handle this event.

In the same manner as you added an event handler to Calendar1 for the DayRender event, add a handler for the VisibleMonthChanged event. This will add the following attribute to the Calendar1 declaration in the content file:

```
OnVisibleMonthChanged="Calendar1_VisibleMonthChanged"
```

It will also create a default event handler code skeleton in the code-behind file, with the cursor placed ready to type. Enter into this code skeleton the code highlighted in Example 5-35.

Example 5-35. VisibleMonthChanged event handler in Calendar-Events.aspx

```
protected void Calendar1_VisibleMonthChanged
    (object sender, MonthChangedEventArgs e)
{
    if (e.NewDate.CompareTo(e.PreviousDate) == 1)
    {
        lblMonthChanged.Text = "My future's so bright...";
    }
    else
    {
        lblMonthChanged.Text = "Looking into the past";
    }
    Calendar1.SelectedDates.Clear();
    lblSelectedUpdate();
    lblCountUpdate();
    txtClear();
}
```

You will also need to add a Label control, named lblMonthChanged, to the content file just before the Calendar control:

```
<asp:Label id="lblMonthChanged" runat="server" />
```

The Calendar1_VisibleMonthChanged event handler method receives an argument of type MonthChangedEventArgs. This argument contains two properties that may be read programmatically:

NewDate
:   Represents the month currently displayed by the Calendar

PreviousDate
:   Represents the month previously displayed by the Calendar

These values are tested in the Calendar1_VisibleMonthChanged method to see which came first. Depending on the results, one of two text strings is assigned to the Text property of lblMonthChanged.

Finally, the selected dates are cleared from the calendar, the text strings below the calendar are updated, and the day range edit boxes are cleared with the following lines of code:

```
Calendar1.SelectedDates.Clear();
lblSelectedUpdate();
lblCountUpdate();
txtClear();
```

The results of running *Calendar-Events.aspx* and navigating a month are shown in Figure 5-28.

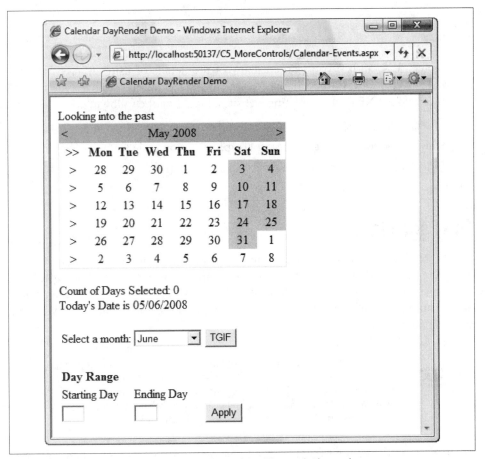

Figure 5-28. Calendar-Events.aspx with effects of VisibleMonthChanged event

CHAPTER 6

Website Fundamentals

In Chapters 3, 4, and 5, you learned many of the details of using ASP.NET server controls in web pages. In this chapter, you will learn techniques to help you use the full power of ASP.NET when creating websites, including the following:

- Understanding the Page class, posting, and cross-page posting
- Using code-behind files to segregate the presentation code from the logic
- Understanding the life cycle of a web page and controls
- Managing state in ASP.NET

The Page Class

An ASP.NET page consists of, at a minimum, a single file with an extension of *.aspx*, though typically, other files will be associated with the page, as we will describe later. In the parlance of Visual Studio 2008 (VS2008), this *.aspx* file is called the *content file*, because it contains primarily the visual content of the page, that is, HTML, text, and ASP.NET server controls.

> Do not confuse the *content file* nomenclature, as used in this context, with the use of the same term when talking about master pages, where the content file is replaceable content that is inserted onto a master page. We use the terms *markup page* and *code-behind file* to help prevent confusion. We cover master pages in Chapter 13.

Any content in the content file that is not part of a server control or server-side code is treated as normal HTML markup. It is passed from the server to the browser exactly as is, so the browser can deal with it as it would any other HTML.

The *.aspx* file can contain script blocks. These are written in a scripting (noncompiled) language, such as JavaScript or VBScript, which will execute on the client (i.e., the browser, if it supports that scripting language—JavaScript is ubiquitous; VBScript is Internet Explorer-only). It may also contain server-side code blocks, written in any .NET supported language, such as C# or Visual Basic, though these code blocks are more commonly contained in a separate code-behind file, as we will describe in the next section.

When a browser requests the *.aspx* file from a web server, ASP.NET (installed on the server) processes the page. If this is the first time the page has been requested since the web application started, the ASP.NET runtime will compile from the page a class that derives from the base System.Web.UI.Page class. The compiled class contains all the control declarations and code that make up the page, including properties, event handlers, and other methods.

 Everyone knows what an application is, more or less. Still, we more rigorously define an ASP.NET application in Chapter 18.

The class is then compiled into an *assembly*, which is what the framework runtime actually runs to render output to the client. That assembly is cached in server memory, so subsequent calls to the page do not require the compilation step, and the request can be serviced more quickly.

 You will notice this lag time the first time a page is viewed, and it can be significant for complex pages. Web Site Projects in VS2008 include the ability to precompile all the pages of a website to avoid this problem after deployment. In contrast, Web Application Projects do not. We cover deployment, as well as the difference between the two types of projects, in Chapter 20.

The name of the compiled class is derived from the name of the *.aspx* file. If you keep the default name for a VS2008 content page, *Default.aspx*, the class name will be _Default. For any other page name, the class name will be the same as the page name minus the extension, so *SomePage.aspx* will inherit from a class called SomePage.

For an *.aspx* file to be processed by the ASP.NET runtime, it must have a *page directive* as the first line in the file. We will cover directives in detail later in this chapter, but for now the important point is they provide information to the compiler, such as the language in use, the name of the code-behind file, if any, and the name of the page's class.

The class hierarchy for the Page class is shown in Figure 6-1.

Because the Page class derives from Control, as do all the ASP.NET server controls, it shares all of the members of the Control class, including properties such as Controls, EnableTheming, EnableViewState, ID, SkinID, and Visible, all of which we described in Table 3-4 in Chapter 3. It also has a number of properties of its own, the most commonly used of which are listed in Table 6-1. All except ErrorPage are read-only properties.

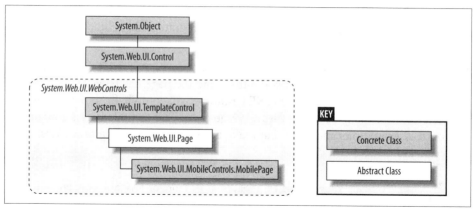

Figure 6-1. Page class hierarchy

Table 6-1. Commonly used Page class properties (read-only except where noted)

Name	Type	Description
Application	Application	Retrieves a reference to the `Application` object for the current request.
Cache	Cache	Retrieves the `Cache` object of the application.
ClientQueryString	String	Retrieves the query string portion of the URL (if any).
Controls	ControlCollection	Retrieves a reference to the collection of `Controls` on the page. Inherited from `Control`.
ErrorPage	String	Read/write. The name of the page to redirect the browser to if there is an error. See Chapter 19 for coverage of error handling.
IsCrossPagePostBack	Boolean	If `true`, this page has been called from another ASP.NET page in the site.
IsPostBack	Boolean	If `true`, this page is being loaded in response to a client post. If `false`, it is being loaded for the first time.
IsValid	Boolean	If `true`, validation succeeded for all the controls on the page.
MaintainScroll-PositionOnPostback	Boolean	If `true`, the scroll position of the page in the browser will be preserved across postbacks. The default is `false`.
Master	MasterPage	Retrieves a reference to the master page for this page. See Chapter 13 for coverage of master pages.
MasterPageFile	String	The filename of the master page, if any.
PreviousPage	Page	Retrieves a reference to the previous page.

The Code-Behind File

You can interweave content such as HTML, text, server controls, and program code in a single file, as was done with traditional ASP. This is known, cleverly, as the *single-file model*.

To see an example of the single-file model, look at *CodeSingleFile.aspx*, listed in Example 6-1.

Example 6-1. CodeSingleFile.aspx

```
<%@ Page Language="C#" %>

<!DOCTYPE html PUBLIC "-//W3C//DTD XHTML 1.0 Transitional//EN"
"http://www.w3.org/TR/xhtml1/DTD/xhtml1-transitional.dtd">

<script runat="server">
    protected void btnHello_Click(object sender, EventArgs e)
    {
        lblMessage.Text = "Hello. The time is " +
            DateTime.Now.ToLongTimeString( );
    }
</script>

<html>
<head runat="server">
    <title>Single File Demo</title>
</head>
<body>
    <form id="form1" runat="server">
    <div>
        <h1>Code-Beside</h1>
        <asp:Button ID="btnHello" runat="server"
            Text="Hello" OnClick="btnHello_Click" />
        <br />
        <asp:Label ID="lblMessage" runat="server" />
    </div>
    </form>
</body>
</html>
```

If you place this file in a folder on your machine (such as *c:\websites*), create a virtual directory in Internet Information Services (IIS) pointing to that folder (named, for example, *Websites*), and then enter in your browser the URL *http://localhost/websites/CodeSingleFile.aspx*, the page will appear, containing a button that will display a text string every time it is clicked.

 IntelliSense is available as you write code blocks, HTML, and server controls. New in VS2008, IntelliSense is also available for Cascading Style Sheets (CSS) and JavaScript.

The single file still requires a Page directive, and any compiled server code is contained within <script> tags that have the runat attribute set to "server" (highlighted in Example 6-1). For this web page, the name of the generated Page class would be CodeSingleFile.

The single-file model can produce source control nightmares and difficult-to-maintain pages. ASP.NET addresses these problems by giving developers the ability to separate the executable code from the presentation code. You write the content in a content (or "markup") file, and you write the program logic in the *code-behind* (or "code") file (with a *.cs* or *.vb* extension, depending on your language choice). The term *code-behind file* refers to the "code file behind the form."

There are other types of markup/code file types in the ASP.NET Framework besides page files. These are listed in Table 6-2.

Table 6-2. Markup/code-behind file types

File type	Extension	AJAX-enabled equivalent available?
Page	*.aspx*	Yes
User Control (Chapter 15)	*.ascx*	No
Web Service (Chapter 16)	*.asmx*	No
Master Page (Chapter 13)	*.master*	Yes
WCF Service (Chapter 16)	*.svc*	Yes

The code-behind model is the default in which VS2008 operates, automatically creating both a markup file and a code-behind file whenever you create a new page (or other item as appropriate).

To better understand the code-behind model, let's look at a simple website. In VS2008, create a new website called *C6_WebSiteFundamentals* and add a new web form to it called *CodeBehind.aspx*. Make sure the checkbox marked "Place code in separate file" is checked, as shown in Figure 6-2. This generates the code-behind file.

Drag a Button and Label control onto the page, along with any other HTML adornment you like. Name the Label control lblMessage and delete the Text property so that it initially has nothing to display.

Name the Button btnHello, set its Text property to Hello, and give it a default (Click) event handler by going to Design view and double-clicking the button. The code-behind file will open with the cursor placed for typing in the Click event handler method. Enter the highlighted text listed in Example 6-2.

Example 6-2. CodeBehind.aspx.cs in full

```
using System;
using System.Web.UI;

public partial class CodeBehind : Page
{
    protected void btnHello_Click(object sender, EventArgs e)
    {
```

Example 6-2. CodeBehind.aspx.cs in full (continued)

```
        lblMessage.Text = "Hello. The time is " +
                DateTime.Now.ToLongTimeString( );
    }
}
```

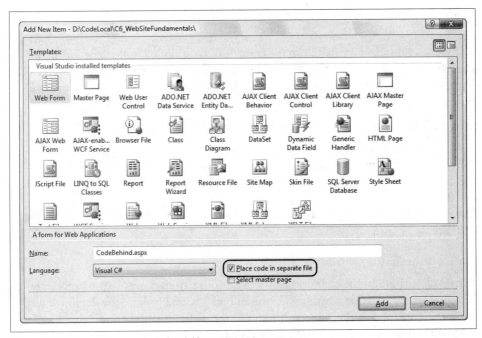

Figure 6-2. Generating a code-behind file in VS2008

The complete markup file is listed in Example 6-3 with the Button and Label controls highlighted.

Example 6-3. CodeBehind.aspx

```
<%@ Page Language="C#" AutoEventWireup="true"
    CodeFile="CodeBehind.aspx.cs" Inherits="CodeBehind" %>

<!DOCTYPE html PUBLIC "-//W3C//DTD XHTML 1.0 Transitional//EN"
    "http://www.w3.org/TR/xhtml1/DTD/xhtml1-transitional.dtd">

<html xmlns="http://www.w3.org/1999/xhtml">
<head runat="server">
    <title>Code-Behind Demo</title>
</head>
<body>
    <form id="form1" runat="server">
    <div>
      <h1>Code-Behind Demo</h1>
```

Example 6-3. CodeBehind.aspx (continued)

```
    <asp:Button ID="btnHello" runat="server"
      Text="Hello" onclick="btnHello_Click" /><br />
    <asp:Label ID="lblMessage" runat="server" />
  </div>
  </form>
</body>
</html>
```

The name of the class created from the content file is specified in the Page directive with the Inherits attribute. VS2008 defaults this to the original name of the markup file. The name of the code-behind file for this content file is specified in the CodeFile attribute.

 If you rename the content file in the Solution Explorer in VS2008, the code-behind file will automatically be renamed identically. However, the class name specified in the Page directive and in the class declaration in the code-behind file will be unchanged. If this is important to you, manually change the class name in those lines of code.

In the code-behind file, a partial class is declared that inherits from System.Web.UI.Page:

```
using System.Web.UI;

public partial class CodeBehind : Page
```

Partial classes allow the definition of a class to be split across two or more source files. In the case of code-behind files, this allows VS2008 to hide the details of initializing the controls on the page and allows you to focus on the event handlers and other methods you created in your code (*.aspx.cs*) file.

Access Modifiers

The keywords public, protected, private, and internal are access modifiers. An access modifier determines which class methods can see and use a member variable or method. Table 6-3 summarizes the access modifiers.

The default accessibility of members of a class is private. Thus, if there is no access modifier provided for a class member, it will be a private member. Regardless of this circumstance, it is always a good idea to specify the access modifier explicitly to enhance the readability of the code.

Table 6-3. Access modifiers

Access modifier	Restrictions
public	No restrictions. Members marked public are visible to any method of any class.
private	The members in class A that are marked private are accessible only to methods of class A.

Table 6-3. Access modifiers (continued)

Access modifier	Restrictions
`protected`	The members in class A that are marked `protected` are accessible to methods of class A and to methods of classes derived from class A.
`internal`	The members in class A that are marked `internal` are accessible to methods of any class in A's assembly.
`protected internal`	The members in class A that are marked `protected internal` are accessible only to methods of class A, to methods of classes derived from class A, and to any class in A's assembly. This is effectively `protected` or `internal`.

Moving to Another Page

By default, when a page is submitted to the server, it is posted back to itself. However, many times in a web application you need to direct the application flow to another page, either directly or after posting to the server. There are four different ways to do this: `HyperLink`, `Server.Transfer`, `Response.Redirect`, and cross-page posting.

HyperLink

The `HyperLink` control navigates directly to the location contained in the `NavigateUrl` property of the control without a postback to the server. We covered this control in Chapter 4.

Server.Transfer

The `Transfer` method of the `HttpServerUtility` class takes the URL of an *.aspx* or *.htm* page (but not *.asp*) as a string argument and posts back to the server. Execution of the current page is terminated and execution of the new page begins. The original and target pages must be part of the same application. The target page can access public members of the control page, as we will demonstrate shortly.

`Server.Transfer` does not verify that the current user is authorized to view the target page. If this is important for your application, you will need to use one of the other techniques described here.

After the transfer to the new page, the browser will continue to display the URL of the original page in its address box and not the current page. The browser's history does not reflect the transfer, so clicking the browser's Back button might not yield the desired results. On the other hand, that may be exactly what you do want.

An overloaded form of the method takes a Boolean argument, which if true, will indicate that the `QueryString` and `Form` collections of the original page will be preserved. The default is `false`.

This overload is particularly useful when you truly need to transfer control to another page. For example, if you were creating a multistep web-based setup wizard and you needed the order of the various steps to be conditional based on the user's selections on previous answers, you could use this Server.Transfer overload to pass complete control to the pertinent page and preserve any QueryString and Form collections from previous pages or steps in the setup wizard.

Keep in mind that view state will not be preserved from page to page even though it is stored within a hidden form variable. View state is page-scoped and invalidates when transferred to another page via Server.Transfer. You'll see more on view state later in this chapter.

Response.Redirect

The Redirect method of the HttpResponse class is the programmatic equivalent of a HyperLink. It takes a URL of an *.aspx* or *.htm* page (but not *.asp*) as a string argument and then sends a command that tells the browser to request the specified page without any further postback. (It sends an HTTP 302 response to the browser.) Consequently, it is faster than Server.Transfer. Because it is a completely new server request, it forces complete authentication and authorization.

Data from the original page is unavailable to the target page unless both pages are in the same application, in which case data can be transferred using session or application state, which we'll cover later in this chapter.

An overloaded form of this method takes a Boolean argument, which if true, indicates that the current page execution will be terminated, and the thread on which that page is being executed will be aborted and recycled.

Cross-Page Posting

A page can be submitted to the server and posted to another page. This is implemented via the PostBackUrl property of specific controls. It can transfer only to another *.aspx* page, not to an *.asp* or *.htm* page. Controls from the original page are available by using the Page.PreviousPage property. If the original page and target page are both within the same application, like all pages in an application they can share session and application state as well as public members (controls and properties) of the original page. A page can cross-post to a page outside the application, but data from the originating page is not available to the target page.

If the PreviousPage property of the target page is accessed, the original page is instantiated again and the stored view state from the original page is restored. Consequently, the performance penalty from using the PreviousPage property is directly affected by the amount of information stored in view state in the previous page. (We cover view state in more detail later in this chapter.)

Cross-page posting does not work in versions 1.0 and 1.1 of ASP.NET.

To see how these three techniques work, add a new web form called *CrossPagePostingSimple.aspx* to the *C6_WebSiteFundamentals* site created earlier in this chapter. In Design view, drag three Button controls onto the form and name them btnServerTransfer, btnRedirect, and btnCrossPage. Now double-click the first two buttons to give them default Click event handlers. btnCrossPage does not have any event handler code. However, for that button, set the PostBackUrl property to *TargetPage.aspx*. You'll create that page in a minute.

The complete code listing for the content file, *CrossPagePostSample.aspx*, is shown in Example 6-4, with the three Button declarations highlighted.

Example 6-4. CrossPagePostingSimple.aspx

```
<%@ Page Language="C#" AutoEventWireup="true"
    CodeFile="CrossPagePostingSimple.aspx.cs"
    Inherits="CrossPagePostingSimple" %>

<!DOCTYPE html PUBLIC "-//W3C//DTD XHTML 1.0 Transitional//EN"
    "http://www.w3.org/TR/xhtml1/DTD/xhtml1-transitional.dtd">
<html xmlns="http://www.w3.org/1999/xhtml">
<head runat="server">
    <title>Simple Cross Page Posting Demo</title>
</head>
<body>
    <h1>Simple Cross Page Posting Demo</h1>
    <form id="form1" runat="server">
    <div>
        <asp:Button ID="btnServerTransfer" runat="server"
          Text="Server.Transfer" OnClick="btnServerTransfer_Click" />
        <asp:Button ID="btnRedirect" runat="server"
          Text="Response.Redirect" OnClick="btnRedirect_Click" />
        <asp:Button ID="btnCrossPage" runat="server"
          Text="Cross Page Post" PostBackUrl="TargetPage.aspx" />
    </div>
    </form>
</body>
</html>
```

In the code-behind file, fill in the Button Click event handlers as highlighted in Example 6-5.

Example 6-5. CrossPagePostingSimple.aspx.cs

```
using System;
using System.Web.UI;
```

Example 6-5. CrossPagePostingSimple.aspx.cs (continued)

```
public partial class CrossPagePostingSimple : Page
{
    protected void btnServerTransfer_Click(object sender, EventArgs e)
    {
        Server.Transfer("TargetPage.aspx");
    }
    protected void btnRedirect_Click(object sender, EventArgs e)
    {
        Response.Redirect("TargetPage.aspx");
    }
}
```

Now add a new web form to the project, call it *TargetPage.aspx*, and give it a simple header for identification. For example:

```
<h1>Target Page</h1>
```

There is no code-behind for the target page at this point (other than the boilerplate created by VS2008). Now switch back to *CrossPagePostingSimple.aspx* in VS2008, right-click the editor, and choose View in Browser from the context menu. You will get something like that shown in Figure 6-3.

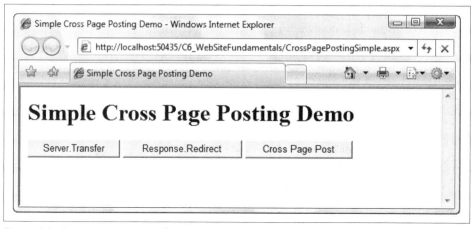

Figure 6-3. CrossPagePostingSimple.aspx in action

Clicking the Server.Transfer button will bring up the page shown in Figure 6-4.

The URL in the address bar still points to the original page, *CrossPagePostingSimple. aspx*.

Now click the browser Back button to get back to the original page and click either the Response.Redirect or the Cross Page Post button. The result will be almost the same, as shown in Figure 6-5.

Notice, however, that the URL now points to the current page, *TargetPage.aspx*. Though the end result of the Response.Redirect and the cross-page post appears the

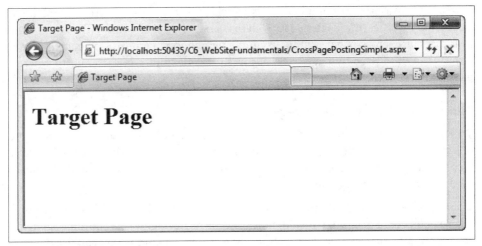

Figure 6-4. TargetPage.aspx via Server.Transfer

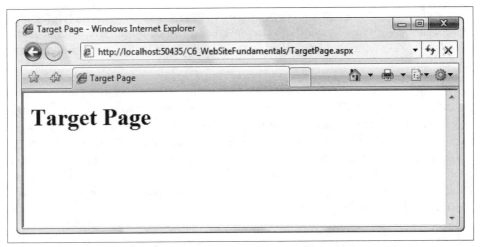

Figure 6-5. TargetPage via Response.Redirect or Cross Page Post

same, there is a fundamental difference. `Response.Redirect` tells the browser to request a new page. It may be in the same site, or it may not. `Server.Transfer`, on the other hand, tells the server to start sending the browser a new page, but without letting the browser know the page it is receiving has been changed. However, `Server.Transfer` can't send the user to an external site. Only `Response.Redirect` can do that.

The cross-page post was specified simply by setting the `PostBackUrl` property of the button; this causes the button to post to the specified page.

```
<asp:Button ID="btnCrossPage" runat="server"
    Text="Cross Page Post"
    PostBackUrl="TargetPage.aspx" />
```

PostBackUrl is a property of all controls which implement the IButtonControl interface. This includes the Button, ImageButton, and LinkButton ASP.NET server controls. Because cross-page posting is implemented on a control-by-control basis, rather than on a page-by-page basis, it gives great flexibility in directing to where a page will post back.

Retrieving data from the previous page

When you post to a different page, a typical requirement is to access controls and objects from the previous page. You could stash cross-page data in session state (described later in this chapter), but that consumes server resources and should be used cautiously with large objects.

The Page class exposes the PreviousPage property to provide a reference to the previous Page object. There are two different ways of retrieving data from this Page reference, both of which we will demonstrate shortly. The technique you can use depends on whether the Page object is strongly typed.

A strongly typed object has a very specific set of public members, with each member being of a specific type. Under these circumstances, you could retrieve a public member of a Page—say, a property called Password, of type string—with the following line of code:

```
string str = PreviousPage.Password;
```

By default, the Page object returned by the PreviousPage property is *not* strongly typed. In this case, to retrieve the contents of a control, you must use late binding— that is, wait for the class to be compiled, and then use a technique known as *reflection* to determine what controls are in the Page object's Controls collection at runtime and to find a specific control using the FindControl method of the Page class. However, late binding imposes a performance penalty and is not type-safe, so you should avoid it if possible.

 For more on reflection, have a look at *Programming C# 3.0*, Fifth Edition, by Jesse Liberty and Donald Xie (O'Reilly).

To strongly type the object representing the previous page, the content file of the target page (i.e., the page to which you are transferring) must have an additional directive, PreviousPageType, added at the top of the file. The PreviousPageType directive has two possible attributes, of which only one may be used at a time on a page:

TypeName
    A string representing the type of the previous page

VirtualPath
    A string representing the relative URL of the previous page

To see this in action, make a copy of *CrossPagePostingSimple.aspx* in the chapter website and rename it *CrossPagePostingAccessingPrevious.aspx*. In the markup file, add a DropDownList named ddlFavoriteActivity populated with a number of your favorite activities. Put it in a <p> element to space things out. Set the AutoPostback property of the DropDownList to true so you can see that when the form is posted normally, it comes back to itself. Finally, set the Inherits property for the Page directive at the top of the page to CrossPagePostingAccessingPrevious. All of these changes are highlighted in Example 6-6.

Example 6-6. CrossPagePostingAccessingPrevious.aspx

```
<%@ Page Language="C#" AutoEventWireup="true"
    CodeFile="CrossPagePostingAccessingPrevious.aspx.cs"
    Inherits="CrossPagePostingAccessingPrevious" %>

<!DOCTYPE html PUBLIC "-//W3C//DTD XHTML 1.0 Transitional//EN"
    "http://www.w3.org/TR/xhtml1/DTD/xhtml1-transitional.dtd">
<html xmlns="http://www.w3.org/1999/xhtml">
<head runat="server">
    <title>Strongly Typed Cross Page Posting Demo</title>
</head>
<body>
    <h1>Strongly Typed Cross Page Posting Demo</h1>
    <form id="form1" runat="server">
    <p>
    Select your favorite activity: 
    <asp:DropDownList ID="ddlFavoriteActivity"
        runat="server" AutoPostBack="true">
        <asp:ListItem Text="Eating" />
        <asp:ListItem Text="Sleeping" />
        <asp:ListItem Text="Programming" />
        <asp:ListItem Text="Watching TV" />
        <asp:ListItem Text="Sex" />
        <asp:ListItem Text="Skiing" />
        <asp:ListItem Text="Bicycling" />
    </asp:DropDownList>
    </p>
    <div>
        <asp:Button ID="btnServerTransfer" runat="server"
            Text="Server.Transfer" OnClick="btnServerTransfer_Click" />
        <asp:Button ID="btnRedirect" runat="server"
            Text="Response.Redirect" OnClick="btnRedirect_Click" />
        <asp:Button ID="btnCrossPage" runat="server"
            Text="Cross Page Post" PostBackUrl="TargetPage.aspx" />
    </div>
    </form>
</body>
</html>
```

Because the Page object returned by the PreviousPage property can access only public members, you must publicly expose ddlFavoriteActivity. The best way to do this is to create in the Page class a public, read-only property of type DropDownList. To do that, edit *CrossPagePostingAccessingPrevious.aspx.cs* to add the code highlighted in Example 6-7.

Example 6-7. CrossPagePostingAccessingPrevious.aspx.cs

```
using System;
using System.Web.UI;
using System.Web.UI.WebControls;

public partial class CrossPagePostingAccessingPrevious : Page
{
    public DropDownList FavoriteActivity
    {
        get { return ddlFavoriteActivity; }
    }

    protected void btnServerTransfer_Click(object sender, EventArgs e)
    {
        Server.Transfer("TargetPage.aspx");
    }
    protected void btnRedirect_Click(object sender, EventArgs e)
    {
        Response.Redirect("TargetPage.aspx");
    }
}
```

There is no inherent reason why this property must be read-only. By adding a set accessor, you could make it read/write. However, in this type of scenario, read-only is all that's needed.

Now that you have exposed a public property that returns an instance of a DropDownList, you must prepare the target page to retrieve it. Modify the markup in *TargetPage.aspx* by adding the code highlighted in Example 6-8.

Example 6-8. Revised markup in TargetPage.aspx

```
<%@ Page Language="C#" AutoEventWireup="true"
    CodeFile="TargetPage.aspx.cs" Inherits="TargetPage" %>
<%@ PreviousPageType
    VirtualPath="~/CrossPagePostingAccessingPrevious.aspx" %>

<!DOCTYPE html PUBLIC "-//W3C//DTD XHTML 1.0 Transitional//EN"
    "http://www.w3.org/TR/xhtml1/DTD/xhtml1-transitional.dtd">
<html xmlns="http://www.w3.org/1999/xhtml">
<head runat="server">
    <title>Target Page</title>
</head>

<body>
    <h1>Target Page</h1>
    <form id="form1" runat="server">
    <div>
```

Example 6-8. Revised markup in TargetPage.aspx (continued)

```
      <p>
         Your favorite activity is
         <asp:Label runat="server" ID="lblActivity" Text="Unknown" />
      </p>
   </div>
   </form>
</body>
</html>
```

You added a PreviousPageType directive, with the VirtualPath attribute set to the URL of the original page. (The ~/ preceding the filename is not required, but is put there by IntelliSense in the VS2008 editor. It resolves to the root of the website application.) You also added a Label server control to display the value retrieved from the DropDownList on the previous page.

The final step in this process is to add some code for the Page_Load event handler to the *TargetPage.aspx.cs* code-behind file, as shown in Example 6-9.

Example 6-9. TargetPage.aspx.cs in full

```
using System;
using System.Web.UI;

public partial class TargetPage : Page
{
    protected void Page_Load(object sender, EventArgs e)
    {
        if (PreviousPage != null)
        {
            lblActivity.Text =
                PreviousPage.FavoriteActivity.SelectedItem.ToString( );
        }
    }
}
```

The code in the Page_Load event handler first tests to see whether the PreviousPage property has been set. If it hasn't—for example, if you arrive here by clicking the Response.Redirect button in *CrossPagePostingSimple.aspx*—the initially declared (i.e., declared in *TargetPage.aspx*) Text property of lblActivityText will be displayed. Run *CrossPagePostingAccessingPrevious.aspx* now, select an item in the DropDownList, and then click the Server.Transfer button. You'll see the selected value in the list is now displayed in the new page, as shown in Figure 6-6.

If PreviousPage has been set, by posting the request to the server using either Server.Transfer or cross-page posting, *TargetPage.aspx* will access the DropDownList on *CrossPagePostingAccessingPrevious.aspx* using the public FavoriteActivity property you set earlier. Finally, it displays the selected item from that DropDownList in lblActivity on *TargetPage.aspx*.

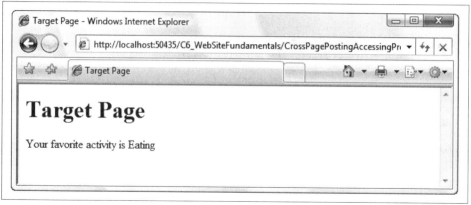

Figure 6-6. Server.Transfer makes the previous page accessible

 You could use `Page.PreviousPage` instead of just `PreviousPage` in the preceding code. However, because `Page` just returns a reference to the class representing the current page (`TargetPage`), this is necessary only for the purposes of legibility.

Return to the previous page and click the Response.Redirect button. You'll see the new page could not access the `DropDownList` through the `PreviousPage` property and so the selected value is listed as unknown, as shown in Figure 6-7.

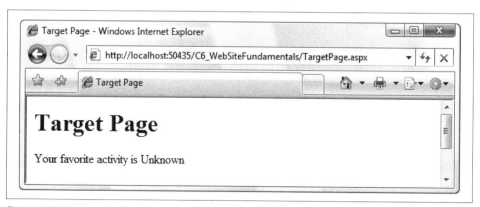

Figure 6-7. Response.Redirect loses the reference to the previous page

The implication of this entire process is that any page can be the target of a transfer by only a single other page because the previous page name is hardcoded in the `PreviousPageType` directive if you are to use strongly typed `Page` objects and the `PreviousPage` property. However, this is not the case. You can transfer or post from any page as long as all the pages have the same signature, that is, the specific list of public members and types.

If all the pages from which you need to transfer do not have the same signature, or if you cannot know at design time the name of a page to specify the types, you will have to use late-binding (or, more likely, session state). Once again, this technique incurs a small performance penalty versus the early-bound, strongly typed method while reflection does its work.

To see late binding at work, make a copy of the previous page and call it *CrossPagePostingLateBound.aspx*. The markup is unchanged aside from changing the Page's Inherits property to CrossPagePostingLateBound. In addition, in the code-behind file, the class name should be changed to CrossPagePostingLateBound, and you should delete the public property, FavoriteActivity. In *TargetPage.aspx*, delete the PreviousPageType directive. Then, in *TargetPage.aspx.cs*, replace the Page_Load method with the highlighted code from Example 6-10 and add the using statement for System.Web.UI.WebControls.

Example 6-10. TargetPage.aspx.cs adapted for late binding

```
using System;
using System.Web.UI;
using System.Web.UI.WebControls;

public partial class TargetPage : Page
{
    protected void Page_Load(object sender, EventArgs e)
    {
        if (PreviousPage != null)
        {
            DropDownList ddl =
                PreviousPage.FindControl("ddlFavoriteActivity")
                    as DropDownList;
            if (ddl != null)
            {
                lblActivity.Text =
                    ddl.SelectedItem.ToString() + " (late-bound)";
            }
        }
    }
}
```

When you remove the FavoriteActivity public property from the *CrossPagePostingAccessingPrevious.aspx.cs* file listed in Example 6-7, the Text assignment line of code in Example 6-9 fails. Instead, Page_Load in Example 6-10 uses the FindControl method of the Page class to get a reference directly to the DropDownList. The PreviousPageType directive was removed because it no longer serves any purpose.

Note as well that the PreviousPage property is still defined but only if the page was navigated to via a server post. Run the page and note that, as in the previous example, if you click the Response.Redirect button, which redirects to the target page from the browser, not from server code, lblActivity will never be populated in Page_Load, and the initial value will be used again, as shown in Figure 6-7.

How did I get here?

It is often helpful to know whether a page has been opened directly or as the result of a transfer or cross-page post. The Page class has two read-only properties of type Boolean—IsPostBack and IsCrossPagePostBack—that allow you to determine that.

The values these properties are set to are not always what you might expect at first glance. To demonstrate this, add a copy of the previous example page, *CrossPagePostingLateBound.aspx*, to the chapter's website, and rename it *CrossPagePostingPostBackProperties.aspx*. In addition to making the usual class name changes in the markup and code-behind files for this new page, add two new Label controls to the bottom of the markup page to display the values of IsPostBack and IsCrossPagePostBack as highlighted in Example 6-11.

Example 6-11. CrossPagePostingPostBackProperties.aspx

```
<%@ Page Language="C#" AutoEventWireup="true"
    CodeFile="CrossPagePostingPostBackProperties.aspx.cs"
    Inherits="CrossPagePostingPostBackProperties" %>

<!DOCTYPE html PUBLIC "-//W3C//DTD XHTML 1.0 Transitional//EN"
    "http://www.w3.org/TR/xhtml1/DTD/xhtml1-transitional.dtd">
<html xmlns="http://www.w3.org/1999/xhtml">
<head runat="server">
   <title>Cross Page Posting Properties Demo</title>
</head>
<body>
   <h1> Cross Page Posting Properties Demo </h1>
   <form id="form1" runat="server">
   <p>
   Select your favorite activity: 
   <asp:DropDownList ID="ddlFavoriteActivity"
      runat="server" AutoPostBack="true">
      <asp:ListItem Text="Eating" />
      <asp:ListItem Text="Sleeping" />
      <asp:ListItem Text="Programming" />
      <asp:ListItem Text="Watching TV" />
      <asp:ListItem Text="Sex" />
      <asp:ListItem Text="Skiing" />
      <asp:ListItem Text="Bicycling" />
   </asp:DropDownList>
   </p>
   <div>
      <asp:Button ID="btnServerTransfer" runat="server"
         Text="Server.Transfer" OnClick="btnServerTransfer_Click" />
      <asp:Button ID="btnRedirect" runat="server"
         Text="Response.Redirect" OnClick="btnRedirect_Click" />
      <asp:Button ID="btnCrossPage" runat="server"
         Text="Cross Page Post" PostBackUrl="TargetPage.aspx" />
   </div>
```

Example 6-11. CrossPagePostingPostBackProperties.aspx (continued)

```
    <p>
    IsPostBack:
    <asp:Label ID="lblIsPostBack" runat="server" Text="not defined" />
    <br />
    IsCrossPagePostBack:
    <asp:Label ID="lblIsCrossPagePostBack" runat="server" Text="not defined" />
    <br />
    PreviousPage:
    <asp:Label ID="lblPreviousPage" runat="server" Text="not defined" />
    </p>
    </form>
</body>
</html>
```

You will also need to modify the Page_Load methods in the code-behind file to populate those labels, as highlighted in Example 6-12.

Example 6-12. CrossPagePostingPostBackProperties.aspx.cs

```
using System;
using System.Web.UI;
using System.Web.UI.WebControls;

public partial class CrossPagePostingPostBackProperties : Page
{
    protected void Page_Load(object sender, EventArgs e)
    {
        lblIsPostBack.Text = IsPostBack.ToString( );
        lblIsCrossPagePostBack.Text = IsCrossPagePostBack.ToString( );
        if (Page.PreviousPage != null)
        {
            lblPreviousPage.Text = Page.PreviousPage.Title;
        }
    }

    protected void btnServerTransfer_Click(object sender, EventArgs e)
    {
        Server.Transfer("TargetPage.aspx");
    }
    protected void btnRedirect_Click(object sender, EventArgs e)
    {
        Response.Redirect("TargetPage.aspx");
    }
}
```

Finally, copy and paste the same three new Label controls highlighted in Example 6-11 into *TargetPage.aspx* under the Label that's already there. To populate them, you'll also need to add the contents of the Page_Load event handler highlighted in Example 6-12 into the Page_Load handler for *TargetPage.aspx.cs*. Example 6-13 shows the changes.

Example 6-13. The new Page_Load in TargetPage.aspx.cs

```
using System;
using System.Web.UI;
using System.Web.UI.WebControls;

public partial class TargetPage : Page
{
    protected void Page_Load(object sender, EventArgs e)
    {
        lblIsPostBack.Text = IsPostBack.ToString( );
        lblIsCrossPagePostBack.Text = IsCrossPagePostBack.ToString( );
        if (PreviousPage != null)
        {
            DropDownList ddl =
                PreviousPage.FindControl("ddlFavoriteActivity")
                    as DropDownList;
            if (ddl != null)
            {
                lblActivity.Text =
                    ddl.SelectedItem.ToString( ) + " (late-bound)";
            }
            lblPreviousPage.Text = Page.PreviousPage.Title;
        }
    }
}
```

Running *CrossPagePostingPostBackProperties.aspx* (*CP.aspx*) through the various scenarios reveals the matrix shown in Table 6-4.

Table 6-4. PostBack property values

Action	Pages	Properties	Values
CP.aspx posting to itself	*CP.aspx*	IsPostBack	true
	CP.aspx	IsCrossPagePostBack	false
	CP.aspx	PreviousPage	null
CP.aspx to *TargetPage.aspx* via Server.Transfer	*TargetPage.aspx*	IsPostBack	false
	TargetPage.aspx	IsCrossPagePostBack	false
	TargetPage.aspx	PreviousPage	Cross Page Posting Properties Demo
	CP.aspx	IsPostBack	true
	CP.aspx	IsCrossPagePostBack	false
CP.aspx to *TargetPage.aspx* via cross-page posting	*TargetPage.aspx*	IsPostBack	false
	TargetPage.aspx	IsCrossPagePostBack	false
	TargetPage.aspx	PreviousPage	Cross Page Posting Properties Demo
	CP.aspx	IsPostBack	true
	CP.aspx	IsCrossPagePostBack	true

You can see the effects of *CrossPagePostingPostBackProperties.aspx* posting back to itself by selecting a new value from the `DropDownList` because the `AutoPostBack` property is set to `true` for that control. The only difference between posting to a new page via `Server.Transfer` and cross-page posting is in the value of the original page's `IsCrossPagePostBack` property, which is `false` for the former and `true` for the latter.

State

State is the current value of all the controls and variables for the current user in the current session. The Web is inherently a *stateless* environment, which means that every time a page is posted to the server and then sent back to the browser, the page is re-created from scratch. Unless the state of all the controls is explicitly preserved before the page is posted, the state is lost and all the controls are created with default values. One of the great strengths of ASP.NET is that it automatically maintains state for server controls—both HTML and ASP.NET—so you do not need to write any code to accomplish this. This section will explore how this is done and how you can make use of the ASP.NET state management capabilities.

ASP.NET manages four types of state:

- View state (which is saved in the state bag, covered later in this chapter)
- Control state
- Application state
- Session state

Control state (described shortly in conjunction with view state) cannot be modified, accessed directly, or disabled. Table 6-5 compares the other kinds of state management.

Table 6-5. Comparison of types of state

Feature	View state	Session state	Application state
Uses server resources	No	Yes	Yes
Uses bandwidth	Yes	No	No
Times out	No	Yes	No
Security exposure	Yes	Depends on configuration	No
Optimized for nonprimitive types	No	Yes	Yes
Available for arbitrary data	Yes (if data is serializable)	Yes	Yes
Programmatically accessible	Yes	Yes	Yes
Scope	Page	Session	Application
Survives application restart	Yes	Depends on configuration	No

The following sections will examine each type of state in turn.

Session State

When you connect to an ASP.NET website, you create a session. The session imposes state on the otherwise stateless Web and allows the website to recognize that subsequent page requests are from the same browser that started the session. This allows you to maintain state across pages until you consciously end the session or the session times out. (The default timeout is 20 minutes.)

While an application is running, there will be many sessions, essentially one for each user interacting with the website.

ASP.NET provides session state with the following features:

- Works with browsers that have had cookies disabled.
- Identifies whether a request is part of an existing session.
- Stores session-scoped (user-scoped) data for use across multiple requests. The provider storing this data can be configured to persist across IIS restarts and to work in multiprocessor (web garden) and multimachine (web farm) environments, as well as in single-processor, single-server situations.
- Raises session events such as Session_Start and Session_End, which can be handled either in the *global.asax* file or in other application code.
- Automatically releases session resources if the session ends or times out.

By default, session state is stored in server memory as part of the ASP.NET process. However, as we will show shortly, you can configure it to be stored separately from the ASP.NET process, either on a separate state server or in a SQL Server database, in which case it will survive a crash or restart of the ASP.NET process.

Sessions are identified and tracked with a 120-bit SessionID that is passed from client to server and back using an HTTP cookie or a modified URL, depending on how the application is configured. The SessionID is handled automatically by the .NET Framework; there is no need to manipulate it programmatically. The SessionID consists of URL-legal ASCII characters that have two important characteristics:

- They are globally unique, so there is only a very small chance of two different sessions having the same SessionID.
- They are random, so it is difficult to guess the value of another session's SessionID after learning the value of an existing session's SessionID.

Session state is implemented using the Contents property of the HttpSessionState class. This collection is a key-value (nongeneric) dictionary containing all the session state dictionary objects that have been directly added programmatically. The dictionary objects are set and retrieved using the Session keyword, as shown in the following example, *SessionStateDemo.aspx*.

This example presents a set of radio buttons. Selecting one of the radio buttons and clicking the Submit button sets three session dictionary objects—two strings and a string array. These session dictionary objects are then used to populate a label control and a drop-down list control.

To create this example, add *SessionStateDemo.aspx* to the chapter's web page, and drag a RadioButtonList, a Button, a Label, and an invisible DropDownList control onto the page, along with some HTML to spread things out a bit. The content file is listed in Example 6-14.

Example 6-14. SessionStateDemo.aspx

```
<%@ Page Language="C#" AutoEventWireup="true"
    CodeFile="SessionStateDemo.aspx.cs"
    Inherits="SessionStateDemo" %>

<!DOCTYPE html PUBLIC "-//W3C//DTD XHTML 1.0 Transitional//EN"
   "http://www.w3.org/TR/xhtml1/DTD/xhtml1-transitional.dtd">
<html xmlns="http://www.w3.org/1999/xhtml">
<head runat="server">
    <title>Session State Demo</title>
</head>

<body>
    <form id="form1" runat="server">
    <div>
        <h1>Session State</h1>
        <h3>Select a book category</h3>
        <asp:RadioButtonList ID="rbl" runat="server"
            CellSpacing="20" RepeatColumns="3"
            RepeatDirection="Horizontal"
            OnSelectedIndexChanged="rbl_SelectedIndexChanged">
            <asp:ListItem Value="n">.NET</asp:ListItem>
            <asp:ListItem Value="d">Databases</asp:ListItem>
            <asp:ListItem Value="h">Hardware</asp:ListItem>
        </asp:RadioButtonList>
        <asp:Button ID="btn" runat="server"
            Text="Submit" OnClick="btn_Click" />
        <br />
        <br />
        <asp:Label ID="lblMessage" runat="server" />
        <br />
        <br />
        <asp:DropDownList ID="ddl" runat="server" Visible="False" />
    </div>
    </form>
</body>
</html>
```

In the code-behind file, shown in Example 6-15, are two event handlers, one for the SelectedIndexChanged event of the RadioButtonList and one for the Click event of the Button. A using System.Text statement is required at the beginning of the file to enable use of the StringBuilder.

Example 6-15. SessionStateDemo.aspx.cs

```
using System;
using System.Text;
using System.Web.UI;
using System.Web.UI.WebControls;

public partial class SessionStateDemo : Page
{
    protected void rbl_SelectedIndexChanged(object sender, EventArgs e)
    {
        if (rbl.SelectedIndex != -1)
        {
            string[] Books = new string[3];
            Session["cattext"] = rbl.SelectedItem.Text;
            Session["catcode"] = rbl.SelectedItem.Value;
            switch (rbl.SelectedItem.Value)
            {
                case "n":
                    Books[0] = "Programming C#";
                    Books[1] = "Programming ASP.NET";
                    Books[2] = "C# Essentials";
                    break;
                case "d":
                    Books[0] = "Oracle & Open Source";
                    Books[1] = "SQL in a Nutshell";
                    Books[2] = "Transact-SQL Programming";
                    break;
                case "h":
                    Books[0] = "PC Hardware in a Nutshell";
                    Books[1] = "Dictionary of PC Hardware and Data
Communications Terms";
                    Books[2] = "Linux Device Drivers";
                    break;
            }
            Session["books"] = Books;
        }
    }
    protected void btn_Click(object sender, EventArgs e)
    {
        {
            if (rbl.SelectedIndex == -1)
            {
                lblMessage.Text = "You must select a book category.";
            }
            else
            {
                StringBuilder sb = new StringBuilder();
                sb.Append("You have selected the category ");
                sb.Append((string)Session["cattext"]);
                sb.Append(" with code \"");
                sb.Append((string)Session["catcode"]);
                sb.Append("\".");
                lblMessage.Text = sb.ToString();
```

Example 6-15. SessionStateDemo.aspx.cs (continued)

```
        ddl.Visible = true;
        string[] CatBooks = (string[])Session["books"];

        // Populate the DropDownList.
        int i;
        ddl.Items.Clear();
        for (i = 0; i < CatBooks.GetLength(0); i++)
        {
            ddl.Items.Add(new ListItem(CatBooks[i]));
        }
    }
  }
 }
}
```

Look first at `rbl_SelectedIndexChanged`, the `RadioButtonList` event handler in Example 6-15. This method populates the `Session` dictionary objects whenever the user selects a radio button.

After testing to ensure something is selected, `rbl_SelectedIndexChanged` defines a string array to hold the lists of books in each category. Then it assigns the selected item `Text` and `Value` properties to two `Session` dictionary objects.

```
Session["cattext"] = rbl.SelectedItem.Text;
Session["catcode"] = rbl.SelectedItem.Value;
```

`rbl_SelectedIndexChanged` next uses a `switch` statement to fill the previously declared string array with a list of books, depending on the book category selected.

Finally, the method assigns the string array to a `Session` dictionary object:

```
Session["books"] = Books;
```

This example stores only strings and an array in the `Session` dictionary objects. However, you can store any object that inherits from `ISerializable`. These include all the primitive data types and arrays composed of primitive data types, as well as the `DataSet`, `DataTable`, `HashTable`, and `Image` objects, as well as any user-created classes that implement the interface. This allows you to store query results, for example, or a collection of items in a user's shopping cart.

The other event handler method, `btn_Click`, is called whenever the user clicks the Submit button. It tests to verify a radio button has been selected. If not, the `Label` will be filled with a warning message:

```
if (rbl.SelectedIndex == -1)
{
    lblMessage.Text = "You must select a book category.";
}
```

The `else` clause of the `if` statement is the meat of this page. It retrieves the `Session` dictionary objects and uses the `StringBuilder` class to concatenate the strings to make a single string for display in the `Label` control:

```
StringBuilder sb = new StringBuilder();
sb.Append("You have selected the category ");
sb.Append((string)Session["cattext"]);
sb.Append(" with code \"");
sb.Append((string)Session["catcode"]);
sb.Append("\".");
lblMessage.Text = sb.ToString();
```

The btn_Click method unhides the DropDownList that was created and made invisible in the content file of the page. The method then retrieves the string array from the Session dictionary object and populates the DropDownList:

```
ddl.Visible = true;
string[] CatBooks = (string[])Session["books"];

// Populate the DropDownList.
int i;
ddl.Items.Clear();
for (i = 0; i < CatBooks.GetLength(0); i++)
{
    ddl.Items.Add(new ListItem(CatBooks[i]));
}
```

As you run this example, you might wonder what advantage is gained here by using session state, rather than using the programmatically accessible control values. In this trivial example, no advantage is gained. However, in a real-life application with many different pages, session state provides an easy method for values and objects to be passed from one page to the next, with all the advantages listed at the beginning of this section.

Session state configuration

The configuration of session state is controlled on a page-by-page basis by entries in the Page directive at the top of the page. On an application-wide basis, it is controlled by the *web.config* configuration file, typically located in the \root directory of the application. (We will cover Page directives in detail later in this chapter, and configuration files in detail in Chapter 18.)

Session state is enabled by default. You can explicitly enable session state for a specific page by adding the EnableSessionState attribute to the Page directive, as in the following:

```
<%@ Page Language="C#" AutoEventWireup="true"
    CodeFile="SessionStateDemo.aspx.cs"
    Inherits="SessionStateDemo" EnableSessionState="True" %>
```

To disable session state for the page, you would use the following:

```
<%@ Page Language="C#" AutoEventWireup="true"
    CodeFile="SessionStateDemo.aspx.cs"
    Inherits="SessionStateDemo" EnableSessionState="False" %>
```

To enable session state in a read-only mode—that is, values can be read but not changed—use the ReadOnly value of EnableSessionState, as in the following:

```
<%@ Page Language="C#" AutoEventWireup="true"
    CodeFile="SessionStateDemo.aspx.cs"
    Inherits="SessionStateDemo" EnableSessionState="ReadOnly" %>
```

(All of the values for EnableSessionState are case-insensitive.) The reason for disabling session state or making it read-only is to enhance performance. If you know that you will not be using session state on a page, you can gain a small performance boost and conserve server resources at the same time by disabling session state.

By default, session state is stored in server memory as part of the ASP.NET process. However, using the mode attribute of the sessionState element in *web.config*, you can configure it to be stored separately from the ASP.NET process, either on a separate state server or in a SQL Server database, in which case it will survive a crash or restart of the ASP.NET process. In addition to unplanned outages, ASP.NET is configured to perform a preventive restart periodically of each process after a specified number of requests or after a specified length of time, improving availability and stability. (This is configurable in *machine.config* and/or *web.config*. See Chapter 18 for a complete discussion of configuration.) Session state is preserved even across these restarts.

Keep in mind that *web.config* is an XML file, and as such, it must be well formed. (We describe well-formed XML files in the sidebar "Well-Formed XHTML" in Chapter 3.) The values are case-sensitive, and the file consists of sections that include elements.

Within *web.config*, the session state configuration information is contained in the <system.web> section, which itself is contained within the <configuration> section. Thus, a typical session state configuration snippet will look something like Example 6-16.

Example 6-16. Session state code snippet from web.config

```
<?xml version="1.0" encoding="utf-8" ?>
<configuration>
<system.web>
.
.
.
   <sessionState
     mode="InProc"
     cookieless="false"
     timeout="20"
   />
```

There are several possible attributes, all optional, for the sessionState section:

allowCustomSqlDatabase

> If true, the SQL database storing session data can be a custom database. The default is false, in which case the default database is *ASPState* and an Initial Catalog cannot be specified in the connection string.

mode

> Specifies whether the session state is disabled for all the pages controlled by this copy of *web.config* and, if enabled, where the session state is stored. Table 6-6 lists the permissible values.

> Storing the InProc session state is the fastest method and is well suited to small amounts of volatile data. However, it is susceptible to crashes and is unsuitable for web farms (multiple servers) or web gardens (multiple processors on a single machine). For these cases, you should use either StateServer or SqlServer. SqlServer is the most robust for surviving crashes and restarts.

Table 6-6. Possible values for the mode attribute

Value	Description
Off	Session state is disabled.
InProc	Session state is stored in process on the local server. This is the default value.
StateServer	Session state is stored on a remote server. If this attribute is used, an entry must exist for stateConnectionString, which specifies which server to use to store the session state.
SqlServer	Session state is stored on a SQL Server. If this attribute is used, an entry must exist for sqlConnectionString, which specifies how to connect to the SQL Server. The SQL Server used can be on the local or a remote machine.
Custom	Allows you to specify a custom provider.

cookieless

> Cookies are used with session state to store the SessionID so that the server knows to which session the request is connected. The permissible values of cookieless are AutoDetect, UseCookies, UseDeviceProfile, and UseUri, with UseCookies being the default.

> AutoDetect will check to see whether the requesting client supports cookies. UseDeviceProfile will determine whether cookies are supported based on HttpBrowserCapabilities, which is a set of information sent to the server by the browser identifying itself. If either of these determines that cookies are unsupported, or if UseUri is specified, the SessionID will be persisted by adding a value to the URL, as shown in the address bar in Figure 6-8. A value of cookieless that forces the SessionID to be added to the URL will not work within the VS2008 environment if you are using File System access, but it will work outside VS2008 using a virtual directory.

cookieName

> The name of the temporary cookie that stores the SessionID. The default is ASP.NET_SessionId.

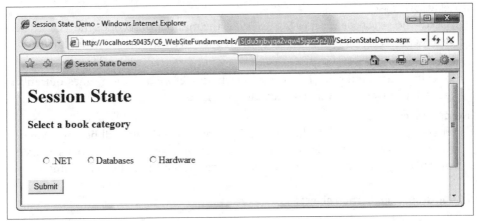

Figure 6-8. SessionStateDemo.aspx with cookieless=UseUri

customProvider

> The name of the custom session state provider you chose to create and use in place of the default ASP.NET provider.

regenerateExpiredSessionId

> For use with cookieless sessions. If true, expired SessionIDs are replaced with a new identifier. The default is false.

sqlCommandTimeout

> The number of seconds a SQL command (e.g., saving some session state information to a database) is idle before being canceled. The default value is 30.

sqlConnectionString

> Specifies a connection string to a running instance of SQL Server. It must be set if mode is set to SqlServer. This is similar to stateConnectionString in that it lends itself for use with web farms and web gardens; it will persist despite crashes and shutdowns. The session state is saved in SQL tables indexed by SessionID.

stateConnectionString

> Specifies the server and port used to save the session state. It is required if mode is set to StateServer. Use of a specific server for saving state enables easy and effective session state management in web farm or web garden scenarios. Here is an example of a stateConnectionString:
>
> ```
> stateConnectionString="tcpip=127.0.0.1:42424"
> ```
>
> In this example, a server with an IP address of 127.0.0.1 would be used. This happens to be localhost (the local machine). The port is 42424. For this to work, the server being specified must have the ASP.NET State service started (accessible via Control Panel → Administrative Tools → Services) and must have the specified port available for communications (i.e., it must not be disabled or blocked by a firewall or other security measure).

`stateNetworkTimeout`

Used when the `mode` is set to `StateServer`, the number of seconds the TCP/IP network connection can be idle before the request is canceled. The default is 10.

`timeout`

Specifies the number of minutes of inactivity before a session times out and is abandoned by the server. The default value is 20.

`useHostingIdentity`

If `true`, which is the default, the ASP.NET process identity will be impersonated by whichever custom session state provider you are using to do its work. If `false`, the provider will use the identity under which the website is running.

Session-scoped application objects

One additional way of providing information across the session is through the use of static objects, which are declared in the *global.asax* file (described in Chapter 18). Once declared with the `Scope` attribute set to `Session`, the objects are accessible by name to the session anywhere within the application code.

View State

The view state is the state of the page and all its controls. The view state is automatically maintained across posts by the ASP.NET Framework. When a page is posted to the server, the view state is read. Just before the page is sent back to the browser, the view state is built.

The view state is saved in the state bag (described in the next section) in a hidden field on the page that contains the state encoded in a string variable. Because the view state is maintained via form fields, this technique works with all browsers.

If there is no need to maintain the view state for a page, you can boost performance by disabling the view state for that page. For example, if the page does not post back to itself or if the only control on a page that might need to have its state maintained is populated from a database with every round trip to the server, there will be no need to maintain the view state for that page. To disable view state for a page, add the `EnableViewState` attribute with a value of `false` to the Page directive:

```
<%@ Page Language="C#" EnableViewState="false" %>
```

The default value for `EnableViewState` is `true`.

You can disable the view state for an entire application by setting the `EnableViewState` property to `false` in the `<pages>` section of the *web.config* configuration file (described in Chapter 18).

Maintaining or disabling the view state for specific controls is possible. You do this with the `Control.EnableViewState` property, which is a Boolean value with a default of `true`. Disabling view state for a control, just as for the page, will improve performance.

This would be appropriate, for example, in a situation where a GridView is populated from a database every time the page is loaded. In this case, the contents of the control would be overridden by the database query, so there is no point in maintaining view state for that control. If the GridView in question were named gv, the following line of code would disable its view state:

```
gv.EnableViewState = false;
```

In some situations, view state is not the best place to store data. If a large amount of data must be stored, view state is not an efficient mechanism because the data is transferred back and forth to the server with every page post. If security concerns exist about the data and the data is not being displayed on the page, including the data in view state increases the security exposure. Finally, view state is optimized only for strings, integers, Booleans, arrays, ArrayList objects, and hashtable objects. Other .NET types may be serialized and persisted in view state but will result in somewhat degraded performance and a larger view-state footprint.

In some of these instances, session state might be a better alternative; on the other hand, view state does not consume any server resources and does not time out, as session state does.

> The serialization format for view state was reformulated in ASP.NET v2, cutting the size of the hidden field that is embedded in the page by as much as 50% compared to ASP.NET v1.x.

Not timing out is perhaps more useful. In version 1.x, many controls used view state to store data required for functionality as well as data display. For example, sorting and paging of the DataGrid required that view state be enabled. If you disabled view state, you disabled that functionality. Version 2.0 separates the functional data from the display data and stores the former in a new category called *control state*. Control state cannot be disabled, so even if view state is disabled, the control will still function correctly.

State Bag

If values are not associated with any control, and you wish to preserve these values across round trips, you can store them in the page's state bag. The *state bag* is a data structure containing attribute/value pairs, stored as strings associated with objects. The valid objects are the primitive data types: integers, bytes, strings, booleans, and so on. The state bag is implemented using the StateBag class, which is a (non-type-safe) dictionary object. You add or remove items from the state bag as with any dictionary object.

> For a complete discussion of dictionary objects in C#, see *Programming C# 3.0*, Fifth Edition, by Jesse Liberty and Donald Xie (O'Reilly).

The state bag is maintained using the same hidden field as view state. Indeed, view state is actually stored within the state bag. You can set and retrieve values of things in the state bag using the ViewState keyword, as shown in the following example. This sets up a counter that is maintained as long as the page is current. Every time the Increment Counter button is clicked, the page is reloaded, causing the counter to increment.

Add a new page called *StateBagDemo.aspx* to the chapter's website, and add to it a Label control named lblCounter and a Button control named btnIncrement. The listing for the content file is shown in Example 6-17.

Example 6-17. StateBagDemo.aspx

```
<%@ Page Language="C#" AutoEventWireup="true"
    CodeFile="StateBagDemo.aspx.cs" Inherits="StateBagDemo" %>

<!DOCTYPE html PUBLIC "-//W3C//DTD XHTML 1.0 Transitional//EN"
    "http://www.w3.org/TR/xhtml1/DTD/xhtml1-transitional.dtd">
<html xmlns="http://www.w3.org/1999/xhtml">
<head runat="server">
    <title>State Bag Demo</title>
</head>
<body>
    <form id="form1" runat="server">
    <div>
        <h1>State Bag</h1>
        Counter:
        <asp:Label ID="lblCounter" runat="server" />
        <asp:Button ID="btnIncrement" runat="server" Text="Increment Counter" />
    </div>
    </form>
</body>
</html>
```

The code-behind file creates a property of type int, called Counter. The value of Counter is stored in the state bag using the ViewState property of the Page class. In the Page_Load method, the Counter property is assigned to the Label and then incremented. Because all the button is doing is submitting the form, it does not require an event handler. The complete code-behind file is shown in Example 6-18, with the Counter property highlighted.

Example 6-18. StateBagDemo.aspx.cs

```
using System;
using System.Web.UI;

public partial class StateBagDemo : Page
{
    public int Counter
    {
```

Example 6-18. StateBagDemo.aspx.cs (continued)

```
      get
      {
         if (ViewState["intCounter"] != null)
         {
            return ((int)ViewState["intCounter"]);
         }
         else
         {
            return 0;
         }
      }
      set
      {
         ViewState["intCounter"] = value;
      }
   }


   protected void Page_Load(object sender, EventArgs e)
   {
      lblCounter.Text = Counter.ToString();
      Counter++;
   }
}
```

In the get block of the Counter property, the contents of the state bag, named intCounter, are tested to see whether anything is there:

```
   if (ViewState["intCounter"] != null)
```

If the intCounter state bag is empty, 0 is returned. Otherwise, the value is retrieved and returned. The state bag returns an object that is not implicitly recognized as an integer, so it must be cast as an integer before the method returns the value.

```
   return ((int)ViewState["intCounter"]);
```

In the set block, the intCounter value is set:

```
   ViewState["intCounter"] = value;
```

In this code, value is a keyword used in the property set block to represent the implicit variable containing the value being passed in.

Then, in the Page_Load, Counter is called twice: once to retrieve the counter value to set the value of the Label control's Text property, and once to increment itself.

```
   lblCounter.Text = Counter.ToString();
   Counter++;
```

If you run the page now, you'll see that each time you click the button, the value of Counter increases. This increase is reflected on the page after each postback, as shown in Figure 6-9.

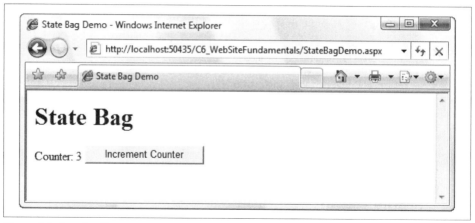

Figure 6-9. StateBagDemo.aspx in action

This demo works only because ViewState is enabled for the page and the value of Counter is stored in the StateBag. To prove this, close the page, go back to *StateBagDemo.aspx* in Source view, and add EnableViewState="False" to the Page directive at the top of the markup:

```
<%@ Page Language="C#" AutoEventWireup="true"
    EnableViewState="false"
    CodeFile="StateBagDemo.aspx.cs" Inherits="StateBagDemo" %>
```

If you save and run the page again, you'll see that the counter never increases after clicking the button, because the Counter property is not stored in view state and so its value is lost when the page is posted back to the server.

Application State

A web application consists of all the web pages, files, components, code, and images that reside in a virtual directory or its subdirectories.

The file *global.asax* contains global code for the web application. There can be only one *global.asax* file in any application. It resides in the root directory of the application. Chapter 18 discusses this file in detail. For now, we will cover only the aspects relating to application state and session state.

Among other things, the *global.asax* file contains event handlers for the Application_Start, Application_End, Application_Error, Session_Start, and Session_End events. When the application receives the first user request, the Application_Start event is fired. If the *global.asax* file is edited and the changes are saved, all current pending requests will be completed, the Application_End event will be fired, and the application will be restarted. This sequence effectively reboots the application, flushing all state information. However, the rebooting of the application is transparent to all users because it occurs only after satisfying any pending requests and before any new requests are accepted. When the next request is received, the application starts over again, raising another Application_Start event.

You can share information globally across your application via a dictionary of objects, with each object associated with a key value. This is implemented using the intrinsic Application property of the HttpApplication class. The Application property allows access to the Contents collection, whose contents have been added to the Application state directly through code.

To add a *global.asax* file to a project, click Website → Add New Item (or right-click the project root directory in the Solution Explorer and select Add New Item). From the Add New Item dialog box, select Global Application Class and accept the default name of *global.asax*. The file will be created with empty event handler methods for the application and session events mentioned earlier.

To demonstrate, add a *global.asax* file to the chapter's website. To this file, add the highlighted code in Example 6-19.

Example 6-19. An example global.asax file

```
<%@ Application Language="C#" %>
<%@ Import Namespace="System.IO" %>

<script RunAt="server">

    void Application_Start(object sender, EventArgs e)
    {
        // Code that runs on application startup
        Application["strStartMsg"] = "The application has started.";
        string[] Books =
            { "SciFi", "Fiction", "Computers", "History", "Religion" };
        Application["arBooks"] = Books;
        WriteFile("Application Starting");
    }

    void Application_End(object sender, EventArgs e)
    {
        //  Code that runs on application shutdown
        Application["strEndMsg"] = "The application is ending.";
        WriteFile("Application Ending");
    }

    void Application_Error(object sender, EventArgs e)
    {
        // Code that runs when an unhandled error occurs

    }

    void Session_Start(object sender, EventArgs e)
    {
        // Code that runs when a new session is started
```

Example 6-19. An example global.asax file (continued)

```
    }

    void Session_End(object sender, EventArgs e)
    {
        // Code that runs when a session ends.
        // Note: The Session_End event is raised only when the
        // sessionstate mode is set to InProc in the Web.config file.
        // If session mode is set to StateServer or SQLServer,
        // the event is not raised.
    }

    void WriteFile(string strText)
    {
        StreamWriter writer = new StreamWriter(@"C:\CodeLocal\test.txt", true);
        string str;
        str = DateTime.Now.ToString() + "    " + strText;
        writer.WriteLine(str);
        writer.Close( );
    }
</script>
```

A *global.asax* file is similar to a normal *.aspx* file in that a directive is on the first line followed by a script block in the language specified in the directive. In this case, the directive is not the Page directive of a normal page, but an Application directive. The example also includes an Import directive for the System.IO namespace. This works in the same way as a using statement in a code-behind file and is needed for the StreamWriter class used in the WriteFile( ) method to write a simple log to a text file hardcoded to be in the root of the C: drive.

 You'll need to assign to the ASPNET or NETWORK SERVICE users write permissions to that text file; otherwise, an ASP.NET error will occur when you start up the website.

In C#, these lines look like this:

```
<%@ Application Language="C#" %>
<%@ Import Namespace="System.IO" %>

<script runat="server">
```

You can also see that the *global.asax* file has two event handlers that actually have code to do something: one each for Application_Start and Application_End.

As mentioned previously, every time the *global.asax* file is modified, the .NET Framework detects this and automatically stops and restarts the application.

You could copy this *global.asax* file into the virtual root of any website and see it in action. However, for now, you will create a new page called *ApplicationStateDemo.aspx* in this chapter's website to demonstrate it. The markup page needs no additions other than a heading to identify it and a Label control to write to.

```
<h1>Application State Demo</h1>
<asp:Label ID="lblText" runat="server" />
```

In the Page_Load of the code-behind file, you will retrieve values from application state and write them to the page by appending them into a StringBuilder and then assigning its contents to the Label control's Text property. To do this, add the highlighted lines of code in Example 6-20 to the code-behind file.

Example 6-20. ApplicationStateDemo.aspx.cs

```
using System;
using System.Web.UI;
using System.Text;

public partial class ApplicationStateDemo : Page
{
    protected void Page_Load(object sender, EventArgs e)
    {
        StringBuilder sb = new StringBuilder();
        sb.AppendFormat("{0}<br />", (string)Application["strStartMsg"]);
        sb.AppendFormat("{0}<br />", (string)Application["strEndMsg"]);

        string[] arTest = (string[])Application["arBooks"];
        sb.AppendFormat("{0}<br />", arTest[1].ToString());

        lblText.Text = sb.ToString();
    }
}
```

The Application dictionary objects are retrieved by using the key value as an indexer into the dictionary, and then casting the object returned to the appropriate type for use in the AppendFormat method.

Run the application and you will see something like the screen shown in Figure 6-10.

At the instant the server receives and begins to process the page request, the application starts and the Application_Start event handler is called.

If you now open another browser and call some other *.aspx* file located in the same virtual directory, the application doesn't start again because it is already running. In fact, closing all your browsers and then opening a page will still not fire the Application_Start event. The application must first be ended, as described in the explanation for Example 6-21.

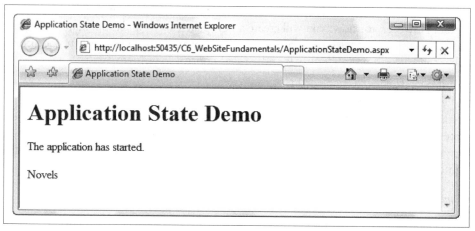

Figure 6-10. ApplicationStateDemo.aspx in action

Example 6-21. Test.txt

```
6/8/2008 3:09:59 PM   Application Starting
6/8/2008 3:10:41 PM   Application Starting
6/8/2008 3:10:57 PM   Application Ending
6/8/2008 3:11:22 PM   Application Starting
6/8/2008 3:13:32 PM   Application Ending
6/8/2008 3:13:47 PM   Application Starting
6/8/2008 4:37:18 PM   Application Ending
6/8/2008 4:53:23 PM   Application Starting
6/8/2008 4:55:51 PM   Application Ending
6/8/2008 4:55:54 PM   Application Starting
6/8/2008 5:27:13 PM   Application Ending
6/8/2008 5:35:14 PM   Application Starting
6/8/2008 5:37:05 PM   Application Ending
```

The Application property exposes a dictionary of objects linked to keys. In the
Application_Start event handler in Example 6-19, three objects are entered in the
Application dictionary: two strings and one string array. Then a call is made to
the WriteFile method, which is coded farther down in the file. WriteFile writes a
text log to the root of the C: drive. If the file does not exist, it will be created, and if it
does exist, the strings will be appended to the end of the file.

> For WriteFile to work, the process under which ASP.NET runs (in
> Windows XP, the ASPNET user; in later OSes, the NETWORK SER-
> VICE user) must have sufficient permissions to write a file to the speci-
> fied location. See the description of the FileUpload control in
> Chapter 5 for a discussion of this issue.

Finally, the `Application_End` event handler of *global.asax* puts another string object in the `Application` dictionary and makes a log entry.

ApplicationStateDemo.aspx shows how these `Application` dictionary entries are used as global variables. Though the *global.asax* file is an excellent place to initialize global `Application` objects, it is not the only place. You can set `Application` objects from anywhere in the application, including any web page or code-behind file. The benefit of using the *global.asax* file is that you can be certain the global `Application` objects will be set when the application first starts, regardless of which component of the application is accessed first. On the other hand, if the application design is such that a specific web page is always accessed first, it will be perfectly reasonable to have that web page, or its associated code-behind file, perform any initialization.

The application ends whenever *global.asax* is edited. (It also ends when IIS or the physical server is restarted or when one of the application configuration files, such as *web.config*, is edited. Chapter 18 discusses the use of these configuration files.) The results of this rebooting of the application are invisible to end-users because all pending requests are fulfilled before the application shuts down. However, they will lose state upon requesting a new page. You can see this if you force the application to end by making a minor change to *global.asax*, saving the file, and then looking at the resultant logfile, *c:\codelocal\test.txt*, in Notepad, as shown in Example 6-21.

After the application has restarted, as soon as any page in the virtual directory is requested by a browser, another line appends itself to the log, containing the words "Application Starting." However, you will never see the contents of the `strEndMsg` Application property (which was set in the `Application_End` event handler of *global.asax*, as shown in Example 6-21) displayed in your browser, because the application always ends between browser requests.

When using the application state, keep in mind the following considerations:

Concurrency and application locking

Concurrency refers to two or more pages accessing the same `Application` dictionary object simultaneously. As long as you are only reading an `Application` dictionary object, or are updating application state in the *global.asax* file, this is not a problem. However, if you are going to allow clients to modify objects held in application state, exercise great care (you'll see why in a moment). You must use the `Lock` and `Unlock` methods of the `HttpApplicationState` class to control access to the application state objects. If you fail to lock the application state objects, one client may corrupt the data used by a second client. For example, consider the following code snippet, which increments an `Application` dictionary object called `Counter`:

```
int iCtr = (int)Application["Counter"];
iCtr++;
Application["Counter"] = iCtr
```

Two clients could possibly call this code at about the same time. This code works by reading the Application["Counter"] value, adding 1 to it, and writing it back. Suppose that clients A and B read the counter when its value is 5. Client A increments and writes back 6. Client B increments and writes back 6, which is not what you want, and you've lost track of Client A's increment. If you were keeping track of inventory, that would be a serious bug. You can solve this problem by locking and unlocking the critical code:

```
Application.Lock();
// Update application state here.
Application.Unlock();
```

Now when Application A reads the counter, it locks it. When Application B comes along, it is blocked by the lock until A unlocks. Thus, the value is properly incremented but at the cost of a potential performance bottleneck.

You should always call the Unlock method as soon as possible to prevent blocking other users. If you forget to call Unlock, the lock will be automatically removed by .NET when the request completes or times out, or when an unhandled error occurs that causes the request to fail, thus minimizing prolonged locks.

Simple locks like this are fraught with danger. For example, suppose you have two resources controlled by locks: Counter and ItemsOnHand. Application A locks Counter and then tries to lock ItemsOnHand. Unfortunately, ItemsOnHand is locked, so A must wait, holding its lock on Counter. It turns out that Application B is holding the lock on ItemsOnHand waiting to get the lock on Counter. Application B must block waiting for A to let go of Counter, and A waits for B to let go of ItemsOnHand. This is called a *deadlock* or a *deadly embrace*. It is deadly to your application, which grinds to a halt.

Locks are particularly dangerous with web applications that need to scale up quickly. Use application locking with extreme caution. By extension, you should also use read/write application state with extreme caution.

Scalability

The issue of concurrency has a direct effect on scalability. Unless all the Application dictionary objects are read-only, you are liable to run into severe performance issues as the number of simultaneous requests increases, due to locks blocking other processes from proceeding.

Memory

This is a consideration for scalability also, because every Application dictionary object takes up memory. Whether you have a million short string objects or a single DataSet that takes up 50 MB, you must be cognizant of the potential memory usage of application state.

Persistence and survivability

Application state objects will not survive if the application is halted, whether intentionally because of updates to *global.asax* or a planned shutdown, or because of system crashes. If it is important to persist global application state, you must take some measures to save it, perhaps to a database or other permanent file on disk.

Expandability to web farms and web gardens

The application state is specific to a single process on a single processor. Therefore, if you are running a web farm (multiple servers) or a web garden (multiple processors in a single server), any global values in the application state will not be global across all the servers or processors, and so will not be global. As with persistence and survivability, if this is an issue, you should get and set the value(s) from a central store accessible to all the processes, such as a database or datafile.

One additional way of providing information globally across the application is through the use of static objects. These objects are declared in the *global.asax* file, described more fully in Chapter 18. Once declared with the Scope attribute set to Application, the objects are accessible by name anywhere within the application code.

Life Cycle

A user sits at her browser and types in a URL. A web page appears, with text and images and buttons and so forth. She fills in a text box and clicks a button. What is going on behind the scenes?

Every request made to the web server initiates a sequence of steps. These steps, from beginning to end, constitute the *life cycle* of the page.

When a page is requested from the server, it is loaded into server memory, processed, sent to the browser, and unloaded from memory. From one end of the life cycle to the other, the goal of the page is to render HTML to the requesting browser. At each step, methods and events are available to let you override the default behavior or add your own programmatic enhancements.

To understand the life cycle of the page and its controls, you must recognize that the Page class creates a hierarchical tree of all the controls on the page. All the components on the page, except for directives, are part of this control tree. You can see the control tree for any page by adding trace="true" to the Page directive. (We describe directives in the next section of this chapter. Chapter 19 discusses tracing in detail.)

The Page class itself is at the root of the tree. All the named controls are included in the tree, and are referenced by control ID. Static text, including whitespace, newlines, and HTML tags, is represented in the tree as LiteralControl objects. The order of controls in the tree is strictly hierarchical. Within a given level of the hierarchy, the controls are in the order in which they appear in the content file.

Web components, including the Page, go through the entire life cycle every time the page is loaded. (This involves a fair amount of performance overhead, which you can reduce somewhat by caching. We cover caching and performance in Chapter 17.) Events fire first on the page, then recursively on every object in the control tree.

The following is a detailed description of each phase of the component life cycle in a web form. There are two slightly different sequences of events in the life cycle: on the first loading of the page and on subsequent postbacks. This life cycle is shown schematically in Figure 6-11.

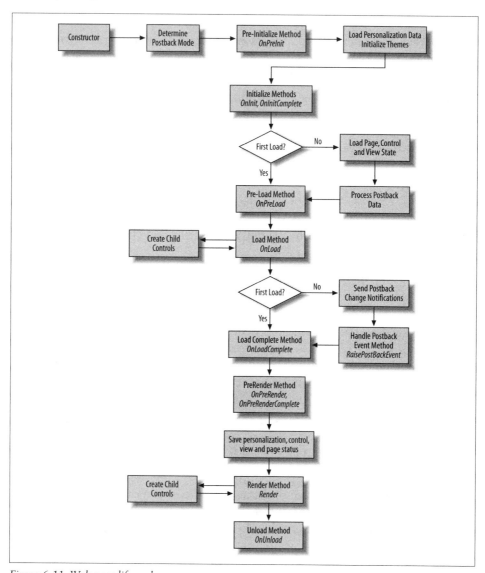

Figure 6-11. Web page life cycle

During the first page load, the life cycle is composed of the following steps:

1. The page class constructor is run. This is the first step in the life cycle for the Page or any control on the page.

2. The PostBack mode is determined. That is, is this the first load, a self-postback, or a cross-page post?

3. Preinitialization occurs, which is necessary to determine the target device before the page is initialized. PreInit is the first event in the life cycle that can be trapped and handled by overloading the OnPreInit method or creating a Page_PreInit handler.

4. Personalization and themes are loaded and initialized. (See Chapter 14 for more on these.)

5. Initialization occurs when the control tree is built. In this phase, you can initialize any values needed for the duration of the request. The initialization phase is modified by overloading the OnInit method or creating a Page_Init handler.

6. Preload occurs before postback data is loaded in the controls. You can modify this phase by overloading the OnPreLoad method or creating a Page_PreLoad handler.

7. View state information becomes available and the controls on the page are loaded into the Page's control hierarchy. You can modify the load phase by overloading the OnLoad method or creating a Page_Load handler.

8. The load process is completed, control event handlers are run, and page validation occurs. The LoadComplete event can be handled by overloading the OnLoadComplete method or creating a Page_LoadComplete handler.

9. The PreRender phase occurs, just before the output is rendered. Modifications are made via the PreRender event.

10. Personalization, control state, and view state information is saved.

11. The page and its controls are rendered as HTML. You can override the Render method or create a Page_Render handler.

12. The unload phase is the last phase of the life cycle. It gives you an opportunity to do any final cleanup and release references to any expensive resources, such as database connections. This is important for scalability. You can modify it by overriding the OnUnload method or creating a Page_Unload handler.

During postback, the life cycle is the same as during the first load, with a few changes:

1. After initialization is complete, view and control state are loaded.

2. Postback data is processed. During this phase, the data sent to the server via the Post method is processed. Any updates to the view state necessitated by the postback are performed via the LoadPostData method.

3. Preload and load are the same as on first load.

4. If any state changes between the current state and the previous state occur, change events are raised via the `RaiseChangedEvents` method. The events are raised for the controls in the order in which the controls appear in the control tree.

5. Exactly one user action caused the postback. That user action is handled now, after all the change events have been handled. The original client-side event that instigated the postback is handled in the `RaisePostBackEvent` method.

6. From here on out, it is the same as on first load.

Directives

Directives are used to pass optional settings to the ASP.NET pages and compilers. They have the following syntax:

```
<%@ directive attribute=value [attribute=value] %>
```

We will describe the many valid types of directives in detail in the following sections. Each directive can have one or more attribute/value pairs unless otherwise noted. Attribute/value pairs are separated by a space character. These pairs do *not* have any space characters surrounding the equals sign (=) between the attribute and its value.

Directives are typically located at the top of the appropriate file, though that is not a strict requirement. For example, `Application` directives are typically at the top of the *global.asax* file, and `Page` directives are typically at the top of *.aspx* files.

Application Directive

The `Application` directive is used to define application-specific attributes. It is typically the first line in the *global.asax* file, which we describe fully in Chapter 18.

Here is a sample `Application` directive:

```
<%@ Application Language="C#" %>
```

There are three possible attributes for use in the `Application` directive, and they are outlined in Table 6-7.

Table 6-7. Application directive attributes

Attribute	Description
Inherits	The name of the class from which to inherit.
Description	Text description of the application. This is ignored by the parser and compiler.
Language	Identifies the language used in any code blocks. Valid values are C#, VB, and JS, plus any other languages you install separately (such as Ruby, Python, or F#).

Assembly Directive

The Assembly directive links an assembly to the application or page at parse time. It is analogous to the /reference: command-line switch used by the C# command-line compiler.

The Assembly directive is contained in the *global.asax* file for application-wide linking, or in a page (*.aspx*) or user control (*.ascx*) file for linking to a specific page or user control. There can be multiple Assembly directives in any file. Each Assembly directive can have multiple attribute/value pairs.

Assemblies located in the *bin* subdirectory under the application's virtual root are automatically linked to the application and do not need to be included in an Assembly directive.

Two permissible attributes are listed in Table 6-8.

Table 6-8. Assembly directive attributes

Attribute	Description
Name	The name of the assembly to which to link the application or page. It does not include a filename extension. Assemblies usually have a *.dll* extension.
Src	The path to a source file to dynamically compile and link.

For example, the following Assembly directives link to the assembly or assemblies contained in the *MyAssembly.dll* file, and compile and link to a C# source code file named *SomeSource.cs*:

```
<%@ Assembly Name="MyAssembly" %>
<%@ Assembly Src="SomeSource.cs" %>
```

This directive is often used in conjunction with the Import directive, described later in this chapter.

Control Directive

The Control directive is used only with user controls and is contained in user control files (*.ascx*). There can be only one Control directive per *.ascx* file. Here is an example:

```
<%@ Control Language="C#" EnableViewState="false" %>
```

The Control directive has many possible attributes. Some of the more common attributes appear in Table 6-9.

Table 6-9. Common Control directive attributes

Attribute	Values	Description
AutoEventWireup	true, false	Enables or disables the automatic association of events to their handlers. Default is true.
ClassName	Any valid class name	The class name for the page that will be compiled dynamically. By default, it will match the control's filename.
Debug	true, false	Enables or disables compiling with debug symbols. Default is false.
Description	String	The text description of the page, ignored by the parser.
EnableViewState	true, false	Indicates whether view state is maintained across page requests. Default is true.
Explicit	true, false	If the language is VB, tells the compiler to use the Option Explicit mode. Default is false.
Inherits	Class name	The name of the code-behind file or other class from which the page inherits.
Language	VB, C#, JS, and others	The programming language used for inline code and script blocks.
Src	Filename	The relative or fully qualified name of the file containing the code-behind class.
Strict	true, false	If the language is VB, tells the compiler to use the Option Strict mode. Default is false.

Implements Directive

The Implements directive is used in page (*.aspx*) and user control (*.ascx*) files or associated code-behind files. It specifies a COM interface that the current page implements. This allows a page or user control to declare the interface's events, methods, and properties.

For example, the following Implements directive allows access to a custom IDataAccess interface contained in a custom ProgrammingASPNET namespace:

```
<%@ Implements Interface="ProgrammingASPNET.IDataAccess" %>
```

Import Directive

The Import directive imports a namespace into a page, user control, or application, making all the classes and namespaces of the imported namespace available. Imported namespaces can be part of the .NET Framework Class Library or can be custom.

If the Import directive is contained in *global.asax*, it will apply to the entire application. If it is in a page (*.aspx*) or user control (*.ascx*) file, it applies only to that page or user control.

Each Import directive can have only a single namespace attribute. If you need to import multiple namespaces, use multiple Import directives.

The following namespaces are automatically imported into all pages and user controls and do not need to be included in Import directives:

- System
- System.Collections
- System.Collections.Specialized
- System.Configuration
- System.IO
- System.Text
- System.Text.RegularExpressions
- System.Web
- System.Web.Caching
- System.Web.Security
- System.Web.SessionState
- System.Web.UI
- System.Web.UI.HtmlControls
- System.Web.UI.WebControls

The following two lines import the System.Drawing namespace from the .NET Base Class Library and a custom namespace:

```
<%@ Import namespace="System.Drawing" %>
<%@ Import namespace="ProgrammingASPNET" %>
```

Master Directive

The Master directive identifies a page file as being a master page. We cover master pages in Chapter 13.

MasterType Directive

The MasterType directive assigns a class name to the Master property of a page so that the page can be strongly typed.

OutputCache Directive

The OutputCache directive controls output caching for a page or user control. Chapter 17 discusses caching and the use of the OutputCache directive.

Page Directive

The Page directive is used to define attributes for the page parser and compiler specific to the page (*.aspx*) file. No more than one Page directive can exist for each page file. Each Page directive can have multiple attributes.

The Page directive has many possible attributes. Some of the more common attributes of the Page directive are listed in Table 6-10.

Table 6-10. Common Page directive attributes

Attribute	Values	Description
AutoEventWireup	true, false	Enables or disables Page events that are being automatically bound to methods that follow the naming convention Page_*event*; for example, Page_Load. Default is true.
Buffer	true, false	Enables or disables HTTP response buffering—whether to send the complete page once it has finished processing or to send it in chunks. Default is true.
ClassName	Any valid class name	The class name for the page that will be compiled dynamically.
ClientTarget	Any valid user-agent value or alias	Targets the user agent for which server controls should render content.
CodeFile	Filename	Indicates the name of the code-behind file.
Debug	true, false	Enables or disables compilation with debug symbols. Default is false.
Description	String	A text description of the page; ignored by the parser.
EnableSessionState	true, false, ReadOnly	Enables, disables, or makes SessionState read-only. Default is true.
EnableViewState	true, false	Enables or disables maintenance of view state across page requests. Default is true.
ErrorPage	Any valid URL	Targets the URL for redirection if an unhandled page exception occurs.
Inherits	Class name	The name of the code-behind or other class.
Language	VB, C#, JS, and others	The programming language used for inline code.
Src	Filename	The relative or fully qualified name of the file containing the code-behind class.
Trace	true, false	Enables or disables tracing. Default is false.
TraceMode	SortByTime, SortByCategory	Indicates how trace messages are to be displayed. Default is SortByTime. See Chapter 19 for more on tracing.
Transaction	NotSupported, Supported, Required, RequiresNew	Indicates whether transactions are supported on this page. Default is NotSupported.
ValidateRequest	true, false	If true (the default), all input data is validated against a hardcoded list of potentially dangerous values, to reduce the risk of cross-site scripting and SQL injection attacks.

The following code snippet is a sample Page directive:

```
<%@ Page Language="C#" AutoEventWireup="true" CodeFile="Default.aspx.cs"
    Inherits="_Default" Trace="true"%>
```

PreviousPageType Directive

The PreviousPageType directive assigns a class to a page so the page can be strongly typed and its contents accessed by a page it has called. See earlier in this chapter for more information.

Reference Directive

The Reference directive can be included in a page file (*.aspx*). It indicates another page or user control should be compiled and linked to the current page, giving you access to the controls on the linked page or user control as part of the ControlCollection object.

There are two permissible attributes: Page and Control. For either, the allowable value is a relative or fully qualified filename. For example:

```
<%@ Reference Page="AnotherPage.aspx" %>
```

Register Directive

The Register directive is used in custom server controls and user controls to associate aliases with namespaces. Chapter 15 discusses custom server controls and user controls.

CHAPTER 7

Data Source Controls and Connections

In previous chapters, you created web pages but they did not interact with real data. In this chapter, you'll look at the various sources of data with which you can fill your pages and the controls that ASP.NET provides to access them.

Then you'll look more deeply at databases, how you connect your sites to them, and how you bind the information they contain to the controls on your page. In particular, you'll look at the `SqlDataSource` control to access SQL Server and the server controls that can use it.

Sources of Data and DataSource Controls

It may be of some comfort that the various sources of data your websites can access have not changed. They are:

- Databases (e.g., SQL Server, Oracle, MySQL)
- XML documents (e.g., RSS feeds, the metabase for your Internet Information Services [IIS] web server)
- Business objects
- Flat files (e.g., IIS logfiles, CSV files, Excel files)

In addition, the various ways provided to bind data to items on a web page remain the same as well. This chapter will concentrate on the numerous data source controls available since ASP.NET 2.0.

 The name generally used to refer to the ways in which you can access and use data in ASP.NET is *ADO.NET*. The ADO.NET team at Microsoft is responsible for the contents of the `System.Data` and `System.Linq` namespaces.

A *data source control*, which is derived from the `System.Web.UI.DataSourceControl` class, provides a single object that you can define declaratively (in your web page) or programmatically (in your code-behind file). It will manage internally the connection to the data, its selection, and various options concerning its presentation (such as paging and caching) so that all you need to do is tell a UI control what data source to use and everything else is taken care of. In some cases, the controls also allow you to send changes to that data back to the source from which it came. The entire life cycle of the query to and response from the data source is encapsulated in this one control.

Many data source controls exist for accessing data from SQL Server, from ODBC or OLE DB servers, from XML files, and from business objects. They are divided into two groups: those representing sources of hierarchical data (XML and Sitemap documents) and those representing flat or table-based data (in business objects, databases, or through LINQ sources), with members of both groups binding to UI objects (such as DataList and GridView) in the same way and handling the plumbing for you. This is in marked contract to ASP.NET 1.1 development, where you had to work with the plumbing directly using the ADO.NET object model.

 In Chapter 9, you'll look at ADO.NET in some detail because as with all abstractions, a DataSource control works well up to a point, but ADO.NET has many features that a DataSource control does not include, and some UI controls just don't work with DataSource controls.

The data source controls included with .NET 3.5 for hierarchical data are:

- XMLDataSource
- SiteMapDataSource

Those for flat or table-based data include:

- ObjectDataSource
- SqlDataSource
- LinqDataSource
- AccessDataSource

You will see the SqlDataSource (and controls derived from it) used frequently in this book to access databases. We use the SiteMapDataSource in the "Navigation" section in Chapter 13, and the LinqDataSource in Chapter 10. Figure 7-1 shows how this division of controls is managed in the System.Web.UI.Control class hierarchy.

Although all of the data source controls shown in Figure 7-1 share a common parent class, the properties they inherit from it aren't actually related to their association with either a source of data or its binding to a set of UI controls. Instead, they define their own unique set of properties relevant to the type of data they access. In the case of those inheriting from the DataSourceControl class, several of these properties have similar themes, as shown in Table 7-1.

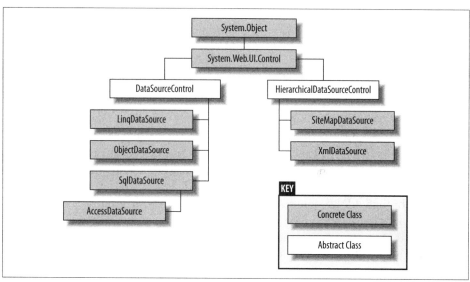

Figure 7-1. The DataSource class hierarchy

Table 7-1. DataSource properties with common themes

Theme	Properties	Description	ObjectDS	LinqDS	SqlDS
Retrieving data from a data source	SelectCommand (SQL) SelectMethod (object)	Sets a SQL command or object method that retrieves data.	Yes	No	Yes
	SelectParameters	Sets the parameters for the select command/method.	Yes	Yes	Yes
Updating a data source	UpdateCommand (SQL) UpdateMethod (object)	Sets a SQL command or object method that updates the original data store with changes made on the page.	Yes	No	Yes
	UpdateParameters	Sets the parameters for the update command/method.	Yes	Yes	Yes
Adding new data to a source	InsertCommand (SQL) InsertMethod (object)	Sets a SQL command or object method that adds new data from the page to the original data store.	Yes	No	Yes
	InsertParameters	Sets the parameters for the insert command/method.	Yes	Yes	Yes
Deleting data from a source	DeleteCommand (SQL) DeleteMethod (object)	Sets a SQL command or object method that deletes the data selected on the page from the original data store.	Yes	No	Yes
	DeleteParameters	Sets the parameters for the delete command/method.	Yes	Yes	Yes

Table 7-1. DataSource properties with common themes (continued)

Theme	Properties	Description	ObjectDS	LinqDS	SqlDS
Caching data in the DataSource control	EnableCaching	true or false. Sets whether or not retrieved data is cached by the data source object.	Yes	No	Yes
	CacheDuration	Sets the number of seconds for which the data source will cache data.	Yes	No	Yes
	CacheExpiration-Policy	Defines how the cache behaves once data in the cache has expired.	Yes	No	Yes
	CacheKeyDependency	Identifies a key for the controls that auto-expires the content of its cache if it is removed.	Yes	No	Yes

The key themes of creating, selecting, caching, changing, and finally deleting data apply to any and all data when working with web forms. Let's look at how these data source controls implement these themes across three different sources of data, starting with any business objects that you may have created for your site. Later on, you'll look at working with the data stored in XML documents and finally with any data stored in a database.

Using the ObjectDataSource Control

Most of the applications we'll look at in this book are two-tier, separating the user interface from the backend data. Many larger commercial applications, however, are *n*-tier, with at least one middle business-logic layer to separate the retrieval of data from a database from the manipulation (and validation) of that data before presentation. This separation means that business-layer logic can be more readily tested and refactored so code is not duplicated between pages when it does not need to be.

Take, for example, the Customer class in Example 7-1. It's necessarily simple for the purposes of this example and generates its own data rather than querying any external source of data, but the key idea is that it contains several methods—such as GetCustomers—returning different views of the customer data in the database as a generic DataSet container for the ObjectDataSource to then access and present onscreen.

Example 7-1. A simple business layer object class

```
using System.Data;

/// <summary>
/// An example Customer class
/// </summary>
```

Example 7-1. A simple business layer object class (continued)

```
public class Customer
{
    public int CustomerID { get; set; }
    public string Name { get; set; }
    public string City { get; set; }

    public Customer( )
    { }

    /// <summary>
    /// Gets Customers and returns them in DataSet
    /// </summary>
    public DataSet GetCustomers( )
    {
        // Add logic here for actual retrieval of data from DB

        DataSet ds = new DataSet( );

        DataTable dt = new DataTable("Customers");
        dt.Columns.Add("CustomerId", typeof(System.Int32));
        dt.Columns.Add("CustomerName", typeof(System.String));
        dt.Columns.Add("CustomerCity", typeof(System.String));

        dt.Rows.Add(new object[] {1, "Test Customer", "Glasgow"});

        ds.Tables.Add(dt);
        return ds;
    }
}
```

> Note the new C# 3.0 syntax for "automatic" properties, where:
>
> ```
> public int CustomerID { get; set; }
> ```
>
> is equivalent to:
>
> ```
> private int customerID;
> public int CutomerID
> {
>     get { return customerID;}
>     set { customerID = value; }
> }
> ```

With this class added to a website's *App_Code* directory, you can then create an ObjectDataSource to access the data returned by your GetCustomers method and bind it to a UI control on the page.

Create a new website called *C7_DataSources* and add Example 7-1 as *Customer.cs* to its *App_Code* directory. Now add a new web form to the site and call it

ObjectDataSource.aspx. In Design view, drag an `ObjectDataSource` control onto the page and select Configure Data Source from its Common Tasks panel.

 If you do not see the `ObjectDataSource` control, choose View → Visual Aids → ASP.NET Non Visual Controls from the VS2008 menu, or press Ctrl-Shift-N.

The dialog in Figure 7-2 will appear, asking you to choose a business object to bind to. Choose Customer from the drop-down list and click Next.

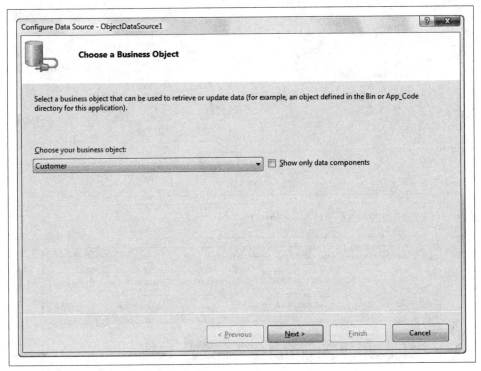

Figure 7-2. Configuring an ObjectDataSource, part 1

You're now asked to associate methods exposed by the `Customer` object with the select, update, insert, and delete operations on the database. Our simple example has only one method for selecting all data, so select GetCustomers from the drop-down list, as shown in Figure 7-3, and click Finish.

Now drag a `GridView` control onto the page, and in its Common Tasks panel, set its data source to `ObjectDataSource1`. You'll see the customer information created in the `GetCustomers` method displayed in a table, as shown in Figure 7-4.

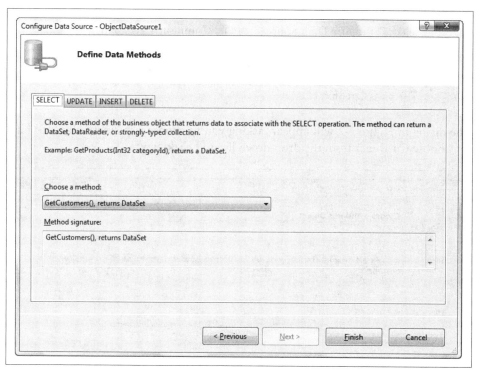

Figure 7-3. Configuring an ObjectDataSource, part 2

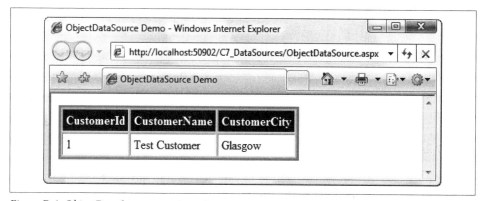

Figure 7-4. ObjectDataSource.aspx in action

 We've added some color to the GridView control to make it easier for you to see its various rows and columns in screenshots. However, the attributes to achieve that color aren't in the code samples to keep them straightforward and easy to follow. If you'd like to add some color to the GridView, open its Common Tasks panel and click Auto-Format. You can choose from a number of color schemes in the subsequent dialog. We're using "Black and Blue 2".

Behind the scenes, VS2008 has generated the following markup for the ObjectDataSource and GridView:

```
<asp:ObjectDataSource ID="ObjectDataSource1" runat="server"
    SelectMethod="GetCustomers" TypeName="Customer">
</asp:ObjectDataSource>

<asp:GridView ID="GridView1" runat="server"
    DataSourceID="ObjectDataSource1">
</asp:GridView>
```

The GridView's DataSourceID property is set to the ID of the ObjectDataSource to link the two controls. Meanwhile, the ObjectDataSource uses two properties to associate the GetCustomers method with the retrieval of data to set into the GridView. TypeName identifies the object class, and SelectMethod identifies the method within that class that the control must use to retrieve that data. If you had selected methods for another operation in the screen shown in Figure 7-3, you would see that operation's InsertMethod, UpdateMethod, and DeleteMethod properties added as appropriate.

The separation of UI layer from business logic within a website that the ObjectDataSource control offers has proven quite popular among some communities. For example, the encapsulation of several tables of information and relationships inside a middle-tier business object representing a "data entity" is a staple of the object-relational mapping (ORM) community, and the ObjectDataSource provides a direct connection from these entity classes to a website's presentation layer if required.

 In "LINQ to SQL" in Chapter 10, you'll see how Microsoft has gone another step in ASP.NET 3.5 to make the creation of data entities and hooking them into a website even easier.

Using the XmlDataSource Control

XML is pretty much everywhere these days. It's in our web services, in our AJAX calls, in our RSS feeds, and, for the standards-compliant, in every web page being created at the moment. But it's important to remember that every XML document is still a flat file that contains a uniformly structured set of hierarchical data which can be accessed with an XmlDataSource as required. And if it's not in a format you can use, the XmlDataSource lets you apply an XSLT transform to it before the data is retrieved.

Let's take an example and use an O'Reilly Atom feed for O'Reilly's new book releases (*http://feeds.feedburner.com/oreilly/newbooks*) as the source of data for a web page. Add to the chapter's website a new page called *XmlDataSource.aspx*, and drag an XmlDataSource control onto it.

 If you do not see the XmlDataSource control, choose View → Visual Aids → ASP.NET Non Visual Controls from the VS2008 menu, or press Ctrl-Shift-N.

Click Configure DataSource in the XmlDataSource's Common Tasks panel and fill it in as shown in Figure 7-5.

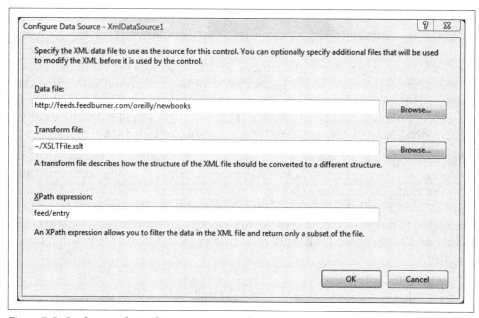

Figure 7-5. Configuring the XmlDataSource control

When binding to an XmlDataSource, an ASP.NET control automatically looks for the attributes on an XML element rather than its child elements as you might assume. For example, the Atom feed this example consumes has the following outline:

```
<feed>
   <entry>
      <title> ... </title>
      <updated>  ...  </updated>
   </entry>
   <entry>  ...  </entry>
   ...
</feed>
```

An XmlDataSource will find nothing to add to a DataGrid unless the XML it finds looks like this:

```
<feed>
   <entry title="..." updated="..."> ... </entry>
   <entry title="..." updated="..."> ... </entry>
   ...
```

```
      <entry title="..." updated="..."> ... </entry>
   </feed>
```

To this end, the XmlDataSource must use an XSLT transform to get the Atom feed in the correct form and then look at the item elements to get the needed information, which is why in Figure 7-5 it is given a transform file and an XPath document to filter out the rest of the RSS feed information.

 Extensible Stylesheet Language Transformations (XSLT) is a web standard for transforming an XML document from one format into another. XPath is also a web standard, this time for identifying an element or a set of elements within an XML document. For more information about both, have a look at *XSLT*, Second Edition, by Doug Tidwell (O'Reilly).

Create an XSLT file in the same directory as *XmlDataSource.aspx* and add the code in Example 7-2.

Example 7-2. XSLT transform code for Atom

```
<?xml version="1.0"?>
<xsl:stylesheet
   version="1.0"
   xmlns:xsl="http://www.w3.org/1999/XSL/Transform"
   xmlns:xsi="http://www.w3.org/2001/XMLSchema-instance"
   xmlns:xsd="http://www.w3.org/2001/XMLSchema"
   xmlns:atom="http://www.w3.org/2005/Atom"
   xmlns:msxsl="urn:schemas-microsoft-com:xslt">
<xsl:strip-space elements="*"/>
<xsl:output method="xml"
      omit-xml-declaration="yes"
      indent="yes"
      standalone="yes" />
<xsl:template match="/">
   <xsl:for-each select="atom:feed">
     <xsl:element name="feed">
        <xsl:for-each select="atom:entry">
          <xsl:element name="entry">
            <xsl:attribute name="title">
              <xsl:value-of select="atom:title"/>
            </xsl:attribute>
            <xsl:attribute name="updated">
              <xsl:value-of select="atom:updated"/>
            </xsl:attribute>
          </xsl:element>
        </xsl:for-each>
     </xsl:element>
   </xsl:for-each>
</xsl:template>
</xsl:stylesheet>
```

Now drag a GridView control onto the page, and in its Common Tasks panel set its data source to XmlDataSource1. Save the page and run it. You'll see the titles and dates of the new books displayed in a table, as shown in Figure 7-6.

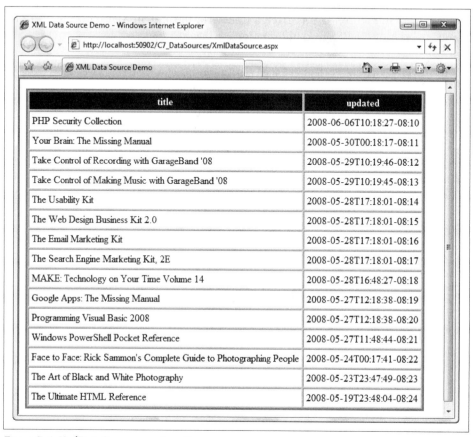

Figure 7-6. XmlDataSource.aspx in action

Behind the scenes, the markup for the XmlDataSource and GridView looks like this:

```
<asp:XmlDataSource ID="XmlDataSource1" runat="server"
    DataFile="http://feeds.feedburner.com/oreilly/newbooks"
    TransformFile="~/XSLTFile.xsl" XPath="feed/entry">
</asp:XmlDataSource>

<asp:GridView ID="GridView1" runat="server"
    DataSourceID="XmlDataSource1">
</asp:GridView>
```

As with the previous ObjectDataSource example, only the DataSourceID property needs to be set on the GridView. The onus is on the XmlDataSource to retrieve and bind the data to it. Table 7-2 lists the properties you can set on an XmlDataSource control.

Table 7-2. XmlDataSource properties

Name	Values	Description
CacheDuration	Integer	Sets the number of seconds for which the data source will cache data
CacheExpirationPolicy	Absolute, Sliding	Defines how the cache behaves once data in the cache has expired
CacheKeyDependency	String	Identifies a key for the controls that auto-expires the content of its cache if it is removed
Data	String	A string containing the XML for the XmlDataSource control to use
DataFile	String	The path to a file (relative or absolute) containing the XML for the control to use
EnableCaching	Boolean	Specifies whether or not to cache data retrieved from the XML in the control
Transform	String	A string containing the XSLT transform to be used on the target XML data before the control uses it
TransformArgumentList	XsltArgumentList	A list of arguments to be used by the transform given in the Transform or TransformFile property
TransformFile	String	The path to a file (relative or absolute) containing the XSLT transform to be used on the target XML data before the control uses it
XPath	String	An XPath expression identifying which elements in the XML should be used to provide the data for the control

Using the SqlDataSource Control

And then, of course, there are databases—relational or otherwise. Be it Microsoft's SQL Server, MySQL, Oracle, PostgreSQL, Firebird, DB/2, Access, or something else, databases are the most common way to store data for our web applications, and you'll spend the next few chapters looking at how to interact with databases successfully and efficiently.

The AdventureWorksLT Database

In this book, you'll use the sample AdventureWorksLT database running on SQL Server for all the examples. You can download it from the Releases page on *http://www.codeplex.com/MSFTDBProdSamples*. You'll need to download and run *AdventureWorksLT.msi* if you're running a 32-bit version of SQL Server or *AdventureWorksLT_x64.msi* if you're running a 64-bit version. You'll also need to make sure you're downloading the sample for the correct version of SQL Server— 2005 or 2008. Click the correct version in the Releases box on the right side of the page to make that selection.

Once you have downloaded and installed the database, you'll need to attach it to your copy of SQL Server. If you're using SQL Server Express, simply copy the *AdventureWorksLT_data.mdf* you installed to your *App_Data* directory and SQL Server Express will do the rest.

If you're using SQL Server Standard, Developer, or Enterprise, you'll need to attach it to the database engine. Open SQL Server Management Studio (SSMS) and connect to the server on which you just installed the database. Right-click the Databases node in SSMS and select Attach from the menu. In the Attach Databases dialog that appears, click Add, and select AdventureWorksLT_data.mdf, as shown in Figure 7-7. By default, this file is installed in *C:\Program Files\Microsoft SQL Server\ MSSQL.1\MSSQL\Data*. Finally, click OK.

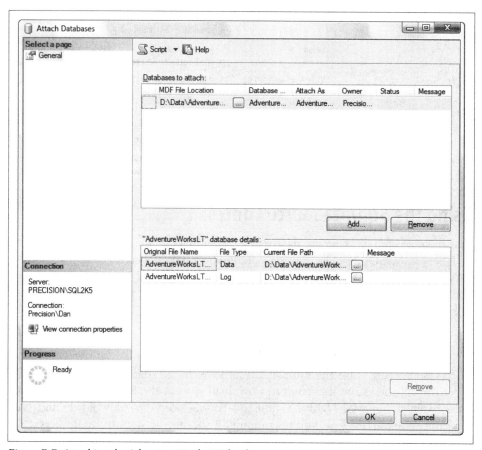

Figure 7-7. Attaching the AdventureWorksLT database

 Be aware that if you're using Windows Vista, you'll need to log on as an administrator to install the AdventureWorksLT database and then to attach the database.

Using the Server Explorer

As we mentioned in Chapter 2, the Visual Studio Server Explorer allows you to access any server to which you have network access. With respect to databases, you use the Server Explorer window (also called the Database Explorer in Visual Web Developer) to open data connections and to access and edit database information. To connect to the AdventureWorksLT database from the Server Explorer right-click the Data Connections node and select Add Connection. The dialog in Figure 7-8 appears, for which you'll need to supply the name of the database server and the database to which to connect—AdventureWorksLT. Click OK.

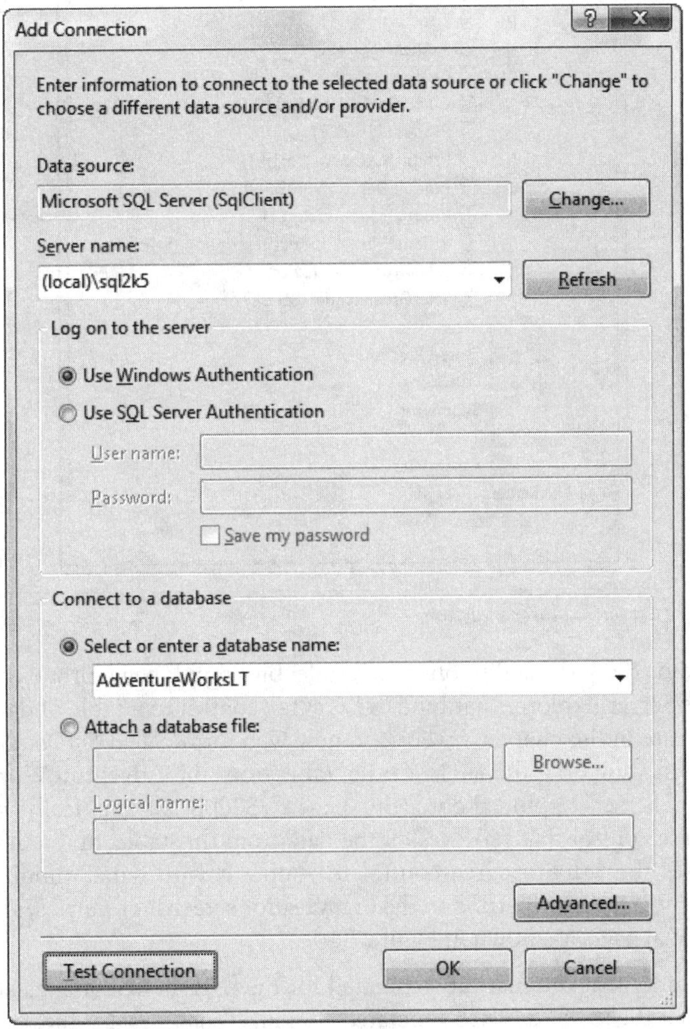

Figure 7-8. Creating a connection for the Server Explorer

The Server Explorer will now have an entry for the new connection which you can expand to view all the programmatic elements of the database. For example, Figure 7-9 shows the database in the Server Explorer, expanded to show all the tables it contains.

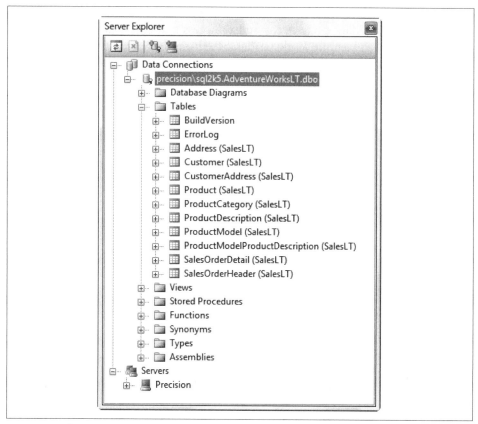

Figure 7-9. The Server Explorer in action

Visual Studio 2008 (VS2008) offers a crude but rapid page prototyping facility through the Server Explorer that binds a GridView control to a table of data. To demonstrate, create in the chapter's website a new web form called *SqlDataSource.aspx*, and in Design view drag the BuildVersion table from the AdventureWorksLT database in the Server Explorer onto the page. VS2008 automatically generates a SqlDataSource control that retrieves all the data from this table, and a GridView control that uses the SqlDataSource control to supply it with data. Running the page (after applying a little formatting to the GridView for screenshot purposes) results in a fully functional page, as shown in Figure 7-10.

If you have a look at the markup generated for the page in VS2008, as shown next, you'll see that the SqlDataSource generated contains ConnectionString, ProviderName, and SelectCommand properties. You'll look at what each of these does and how you can tweak them later in this chapter.

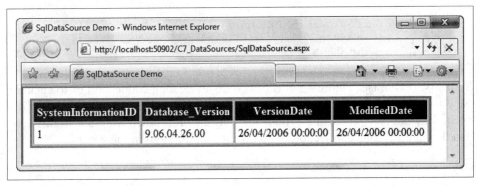

Figure 7-10. SqlDataSource.aspx in action

```
<asp:GridView ID="GridView1" runat="server"
    AutoGenerateColumns="False" DataSourceID="SqlDataSource1"
    EmptyDataText="There are no data records to display.">
    <Columns>
        <asp:BoundField DataField="SystemInformationID"
            HeaderText="SystemInformationID"
            ReadOnly="True" SortExpression="SystemInformationID"></asp:BoundField>
        <asp:BoundField DataField="Database_Version" HeaderText="Database_Version"
            SortExpression="Database_Version"></asp:BoundField>
        <asp:BoundField DataField="VersionDate" HeaderText="VersionDate"
            SortExpression="VersionDate"></asp:BoundField>
        <asp:BoundField DataField="ModifiedDate" HeaderText="ModifiedDate"
            SortExpression="ModifiedDate"></asp:BoundField>
    </Columns>
</asp:GridView>

<asp:SqlDataSource ID="SqlDataSource1" runat="server"
    ConnectionString="<%$ ConnectionStrings:AdventureWorksLTConnectionString1 %>"
    ProviderName=
        "<%$ ConnectionStrings:AdventureWorksLTConnectionString1.ProviderName %>"
    SelectCommand="SELECT [SystemInformationID], [Database Version] AS
        Database_Version, [VersionDate], [ModifiedDate] FROM [BuildVersion]">
</asp:SqlDataSource>
```

Meanwhile, VS2008 has automatically created individual columns in the GridView that map to each column in the BuildVersion table you dragged onto Design view. This represents the simplest way to bind a table of data to an ASP.NET control.

Configuring the SqlDataSource

The more conventional, flexible way to bind a table of data to an ASP.NET control is to use the Configure Data Source Wizard to set up a SqlDataSource control as you set up the ObjectDataSource and XmlDataSource controls earlier. In this next demo, you'll bind the Customer table from the AdventureWorksLT database to a GridView.

Add to the chapter's website a new web form called *SqlDataSourceWizard.aspx*. Drag a SqlDataSource control from the Toolbox onto the page and select Configure Data Source from its Common Tasks dialog.

If you do not see the SqlDataSource control, choose View → Visual Aids → ASP.NET Non Visual Controls from the VS2008 menu, or press Ctrl-Shift-N.

Your first option (see Figure 7-11) is to choose an existing connection or to click the New Connection button. You could choose to use the connection to the database created by the previous demo—you'll see it in the drop-down list—but in this case, you'll create a second connection to go through all the steps in the wizard.

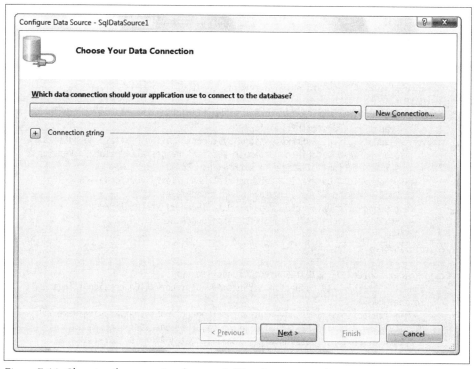

Figure 7-11. Choosing the connection for your SqlDataSource control

Click New Connection. When you create a new connection, you'll be asked to fill in the server name. Decide whether you want to use a trusted connection (Windows Authentication) or a specific username and password. You'll also be asked which database to connect to (as shown previously in Figure 7-8).

 To use a trusted connection, you will need to modify your SQL Server database through SSMS. If you're using IIS 5.x, go to the Security section and add *machineName*\ASPNET as a user. Then go to the Adventure-WorksLT database, add the ASPNET user as a user, and set its role to dbo_owner. If you're using IIS 6 or 7, perform the preceding steps but add *machinename*\NETWORK SERVICE as a user instead of *machinename*\ASPNET.

Click the Test Connection button to ensure your connection is correct. Then click OK to save the connection.

You now have the option of saving the connection string in the *web.config* file (the alternative is to save the connection string in the page as a property of the control). Generally, you'll want to save the connection string in *web.config*, as shown in Figure 7-12. Here it is more secure, as by default, *web.config* will never be sent to the browser. It can also be encrypted, but more on that later. Click Next to save the string.

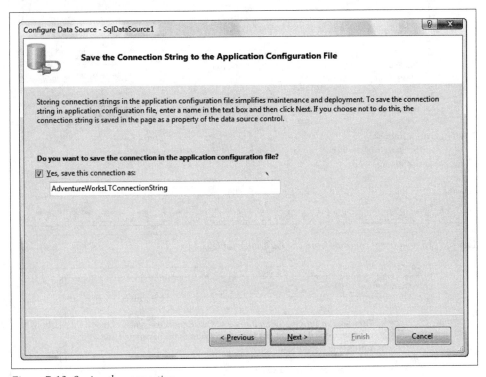

Figure 7-12. Saving the connection

The next step is to specify your query or to pick the columns you want from a specific table (see Appendix B for a crash course on relational databases and querying for data). For this example, you'll choose the CustomerID, FirstName, LastName, CompanyName, and EmailAddress columns from the Customer table, as shown in Figure 7-13.

While you are here, click the Advanced button to see that you can instruct the wizard to generate SQL statements used to update the database, which you'll look at later in this chapter. For now, however, you can leave this unchecked.

The next step in the wizard allows you to test your query. However, clicking Test Query will result in an error, as shown in Figure 7-14.

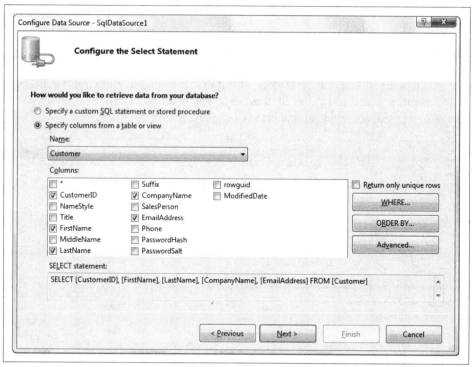

Figure 7-13. Choosing columns from the Customer table

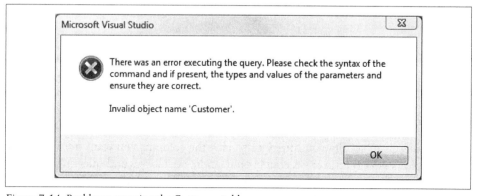

Figure 7-14. Problems querying the Customer table

So, why did this work for the BuildVersion table in the previous example but not for the Customer table? The answer lies in a feature of SQL Server 2005 called *schemas*. Like C# namespaces within an assembly, or XML namespaces within a document, the purpose of a database schema is to disambiguate the purpose of a group of tables within that database from others. It's also a way to partition database objects for security reasons. In the AdventureWorksLT database, the Customer table is part of the SalesLT schema, so all SQL statements used to access it must refer to it as `SalesLT.Customer`, something that the SqlDataSource configuration wizard doesn't do by default.

 You can spot a schema in a database by looking at its list of tables. In SSMS, all tables within a schema will be listed as *schema.tablename*. In the VS2008 Server Explorer (shown earlier in Figure 7-9), they will be listed as *tablename (schema)*.

You have two options to change the `SELECT` statement to reference the `Customer` table correctly. The first is to click Finish on the wizard, switch to Source view, and change the SQL statement in the `SqlDataSource`'s `SelectCommand` property to the following:

```
SELECT [CustomerID], [FirstName], [LastName], [CompanyName],
    [EmailAddress] FROM [SalesLT].[Customer]
```

The second option is to stay in the wizard, go back to the previous screen, and click the radio button shown in Figure 7-13, marked "Specify a custom SQL statement or stored procedure," and click Next. The wizard then allows you to write a SQL statement from scratch or to edit the one it has already generated, as shown in Figure 7-15.

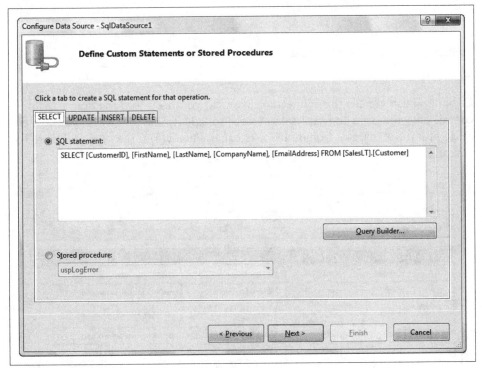

Figure 7-15. Defining a custom SQL statement for the SqlDataSource

The advantage of this option is your ability to then test that your custom `SELECT` statement works, as shown in Figure 7-16.

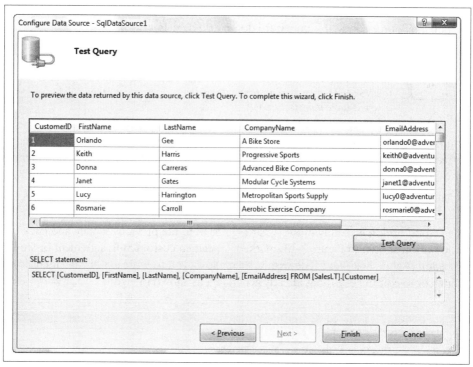

Figure 7-16. Testing the query

Clicking Finish creates the connection. Now all you need to do is drag a `GridView` control onto the page and set its `DataSource` to `SqlDataSource1` (which you just created) with the `GridView`'s Common Tasks panel. Finally, run the page and there you have it, as shown in Figure 7-17.

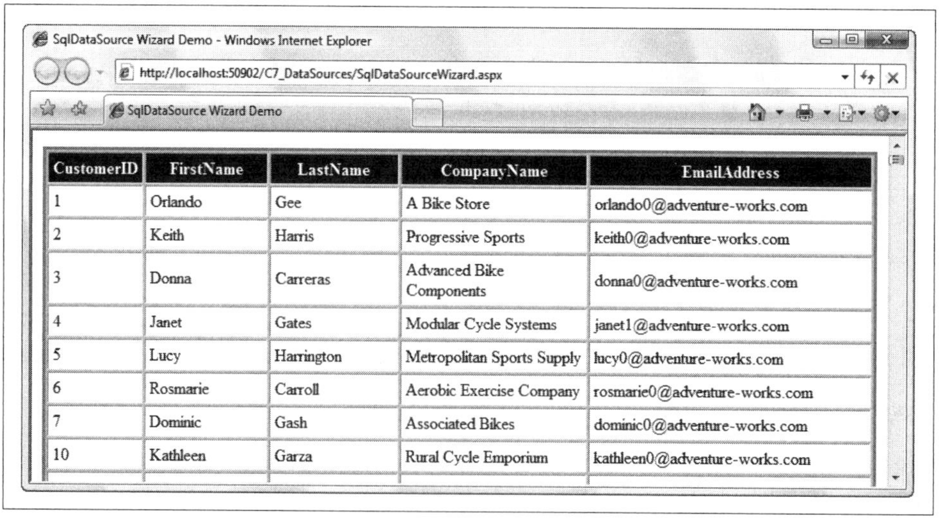

Figure 7-17. SqlDataSourceWizard.aspx in action

Example 7-3 shows the final markup for *SqlDataSourceWizard.aspx*. There is no additional code-behind to note.

Example 7-3. SqlDataSourceWizard.aspx in full

```
<%@ Page Language="C#" AutoEventWireup="true"
    CodeFile="SqlDataSourceWizard.aspx.cs"
    Inherits="SqlDataSourceWizard" %>

<!DOCTYPE html PUBLIC "-//W3C//DTD XHTML 1.0 Transitional//EN"
    "http://www.w3.org/TR/xhtml1/DTD/xhtml1-transitional.dtd">

<html xmlns="http://www.w3.org/1999/xhtml">
<head runat="server">
    <title>SqlDataSource Wizard Demo</title>
</head>

<body>
    <form id="form1" runat="server">
    <div>
        <asp:SqlDataSource ID="SqlDataSource1" runat="server"
            ConnectionString=
            "<%$ ConnectionStrings:AdventureWorksLTConnectionString %>"
            SelectCommand="SELECT [CustomerID], [FirstName], [LastName],
            [CompanyName], [EmailAddress] FROM [SalesLT].[Customer]">
        </asp:SqlDataSource>

        <asp:GridView ID="GridView1" runat="server"
            AutoGenerateColumns="False" DataKeyNames="CustomerID"
            DataSourceID="SqlDataSource1">
            <Columns>
                <asp:BoundField DataField="CustomerID"
                    HeaderText="CustomerID" InsertVisible="False"
                    ReadOnly="True" SortExpression="CustomerID">
                </asp:BoundField>
                <asp:BoundField DataField="FirstName"
                    HeaderText="FirstName" SortExpression="FirstName">
                </asp:BoundField>
                <asp:BoundField DataField="LastName"
                    HeaderText="LastName" SortExpression="LastName">
                </asp:BoundField>
                <asp:BoundField DataField="CompanyName"
                    HeaderText="CompanyName" SortExpression="CompanyName">
                </asp:BoundField>
                <asp:BoundField DataField="EmailAddress"
                    HeaderText="EmailAddress" SortExpression="EmailAddress">
                </asp:BoundField>
            </Columns>
        </asp:GridView>
    </div>
    </form>
</body>
</html>
```

Besides the mandatory ID and runat properties, VS2008 has generated two properties for the SqlDataSource control (highlighted in Example 7-3). SelectCommand contains the custom SQL SELECT statement you had to tweak to retrieve data from the database, and ConnectionString contains a reference to the connection string to the database rather than the string itself. This is one of a number of options for working with connection strings expanded upon in the next section.

In addition to those commonly themed properties already mentioned in Table 7-1, the SqlDataSource object also has the properties given in Table 7-3.

Table 7-3. Additional SqlDataSource properties

Property	Values	Description
CancelSelectOnNullParameter	Boolean	Cancels the selection of data from the database if the value of any parameter for the SelectCommand is null.
ConflictDetection	CompareAllValues, OverwriteChanges	Sets what happens if the data you want to update has already been updated before your page tries to make its changes. Default is OverwriteChanges.
ConnectionString	String	A reference to or the actual connection string to be used to connect to the database.
DataSourceMode	DataReader, DataSet	Sets which ADO.NET object the DataSource control will use to retrieve data. See Chapter 9 for the difference between the two.
FilterExpression	String	Data retrieved using the given SelectCommand will not be bound to a UI control unless it also satisfies the condition given in the FilterExpression. If not specified, all data retrieved is bound to the control.
FilterParameters	ParameterCollection	The collection of parameters associated with the FilterExpression.
ProviderName	String	The name of the .NET data provider being used by the SqlDataSource object to connect to the database.
SqlCacheDependency	String	A semicolon-delimited list of tables in the database in which a change will trigger a refresh of the cache in the DataSource control. More on this in Chapter 17.

Storing Connection Strings

In the previous example, the Configure Data Source Wizard created a connection string based on your input, saved it in *web.config*, and left a reference to it in the markup for the SqlDataSource control:

```
<asp:SqlDataSource ID="SqlDataSource1" runat="server"
    ConnectionString=
        "<%$ ConnectionStrings:AdventureWorksLTConnectionString %>"
```

```
   ...>
</asp:SqlDataSource>
```

The connection string itself is saved in the website's *web.config* file in the
<connectionStrings> element:

```
<connectionStrings>
   <add name="AdventureWorksLTConnectionString"
      connectionString="Data Source=(local)\sql2k5;
         Initial Catalog=AdventureWorksLT;Integrated Security=True"
      providerName="System.Data.SqlClient" />
</connectionStrings>
```

As you can see, the string is actually stored within a key-value pair, and the key—in
this case, AdventureWorksLTConnectionString—is then used to refer to the string itself
using this syntax:

```
"<%$ ConnectionStrings:key %>"
```

This is one of several ways to create, store, and make available a connection string to
a DataSource upon request. Other possibilities include the following:

1. Putting the connection string directly into the DataSource's ConnectionString
   property:

   ```
   <asp:SqlDataSource ID="SqlDataSource1" runat="server"
      ConnectionString=
         "Data Source=(local)\sql2k5; Initial Catalog=AdventureWorksLT;
         Integrated Security=True" ...>
   </asp:SqlDataSource>
   ```

   This isn't a good idea for two reasons: it's not very secure, and you can't reuse
   the string elsewhere unless you redeclare it, which, as proponents of Cascading
   Style Sheets (CSS) will testify, is not a good thing.

2. Extracting the connection string out of *web.config* into its own *config* file. Most
   elements in *web.config* have a configSource property that you can use to specify
   a separate file containing all the information for that element. So, instead of
   web.config containing your connection string section:

   ```
   <connectionStrings>
      <add name="AdventureWorksLTConnectionString"
         connectionString="Data Source=(local)\sql2k5;
            Initial Catalog=AdventureWorksLT;Integrated Security=True"
         providerName="System.Data.SqlClient" />
   </connectionStrings>
   ```

   you can replace it with:

   ```
   <connectionStrings configSource="~/connectionstrings.config" />
   ```

   and then create a file called *connectionstrings.config* which contains only the
   <connectionStrings> element and its contents. This has the advantage of making the connection string easier to find and to secure. Changing it also doesn't
   cause an application restart and the loss of session state. For example, you could
   put *connectionString.config* in your site's *App_Code* directory, from which IIS
   will never allow a download.

3. Using the `aspnet_setreg` utility to encrypt the data string, store it in the web server's Registry, and then leave a reference to the Registry in *web.config*.

   Although this is definitely the most secure option, you have to run `aspnet_setreg` every time you want to change the connection string. See *http://support. microsoft.com/kb/821616* for more on this technique.

4. Storing the string as a constant somewhere in your data access code and assigning it programmatically to the `DataSource` as the code-behind file is run. This has the advantage that the string is hidden in compiled code. The disadvantage is that to change the string, you have to change the code, build and redeploy it, and then restart the website. Compare this to storing it in *web.config*, where changing it there will automatically restart the web app because IIS is aware the string has been changed.

5. Using the `SqlConnectionStringBuilder` class to build up the string programmatically rather than storing it as a constant. This has the same pros and cons as storing the string as a string constant in code, but with the extra advantage that the builder class's properties present you with options they will add into the string that you might not have realized were there.

 Be aware that it's actually quite easy to decompile code and retrieve the connection string from it. Hence, options 4 and 5 are significantly less secure than the other three.

Option 5 does pose an interesting question. What information can a connection string store? Most often, the connection string to a SQL Server database looks like this if it is using Windows Security:

```
Data Source=(local)\sql2k5;
    Initial Catalog=AdventureWorksLT;Integrated Security=True"
```

Or it looks like this if it is using a SQL Server account:

```
Data Source=(local)\sql2k5;
    Initial Catalog=AdventureWorksLT;User Id=uid;Password=pwd"
```

You might be well advised to include the `Application Name` property in your connection string, which allows you to identify calls made into the database by your website, which is very handy while debugging or monitoring performance. For example:

```
Data Source=(local)\sql2k5;Initial Catalog=AdventureWorksLT;
    Integrated Security=True;Application Name=myWebSite"
```

 What else you include in your connection string will depend on how you're using your database. Perhaps you're using it as a mirror, accessing it asynchronously or connecting to it over TCP/IP rather than the default Named Pipes protocol. It will also depend on which database product you're using. Consult *http://connectionstrings.com* for a full list of possibilities.

Passing Parameters to the Select Query

Sometimes you do not want to display all the records in a table. Take, for instance, the previous example in which you simply selected all the rows in the Customer table and dumped them into a GridView; it's not easy to read, and chances are your client will want to view only portions of this full list—for example, just the customers dealt with by a particular staff member. To do this, you'll need a way to select a company and a way to pass the ID of the selected staff member to the grid to display that staff member's clients. In this example, you'll use a DropDownList.

In your website, make a copy of *SqlDataSourceWizard.aspx* and call it *SqlDataSourceParameters.aspx*. Rename SqlDataSource1 to CustomersDataSource and GridView1 to CustomerGridView.

In Design view, add a second SqlDataSource control to the page and give it the ID StaffDataSource. Use the Data Source Configuration Wizard to connect it to the AdventureWorksLT database and, by specifying a custom SQL statement in the wizard (rather than directly in the source to fix the schema problem), set its SELECT statement to:

```
SELECT DISTINCT [SalesPerson] FROM [SalesLT].[Customer]
```

The DISTINCT keyword used here ensures that staff members are included in the list only once, regardless of how many times they are actually listed in the database table. Figure 7-18 shows the wizard.

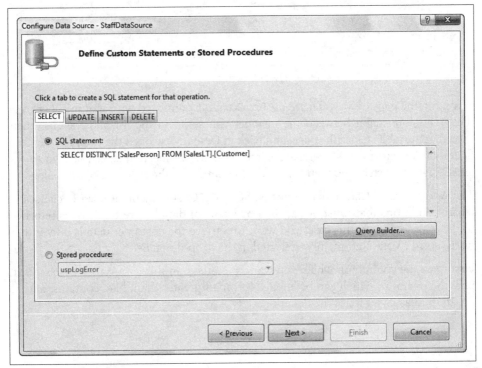

Figure 7-18. Using a SELECT DISTINCT statement

Now drag a DropDownList onto the page and click Choose a Data Source. Select StaffDataSource as the data source and SalesPerson to be both the text and the value for each item in the DropDownList, as shown in Figure 7-19. Click OK.

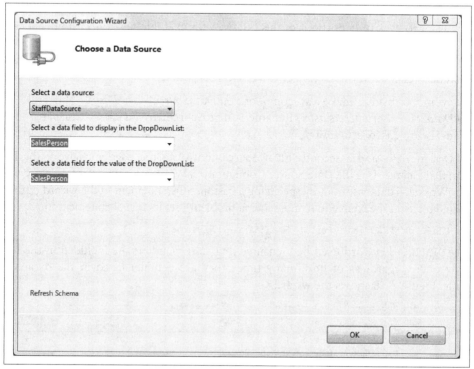

Figure 7-19. Hooking a DataSource to a DropDownList

If you run the page now, you'll see the DropDownList populated with staff members, but there's no connection between the member you select in the list and the customers shown in the table. Close the page, and back in Design view open the Data Source Configuration Wizard for CustomersDataSource. Skip the connection screen and go to the SELECT statement step, and then click the WHERE button on the right side of the dialog.

The Add WHERE Clause dialog opens. SQL SELECT statements use WHERE clauses to create conditions that must be satisfied by a row of data before that row is returned to the data source. In this case, you want to retrieve the customer details only if they were served by the staff member selected in the drop-down list.

First, pick the column on which you want to match—in this case, SalesPerson. Next, pick the operator, which can be equals, less than/greater than, like, contains, and so on. In this case, you'll use the default (=).

The third drop down (Source) lets you pick the source for the SalesPerson. You can pick None if you will be providing a source in code, or you can obtain the source from the form, a user's profile, a QueryString, or session state. In this case, you'll obtain the source of the SalesPerson from the DropDownList, so choose Control.

When you choose Control, the Parameter Properties window wakes up. You are asked to provide the ID of the Control providing the parameter, in this case DropDownList1, and (optionally) a default value. Once you've made all your choices, the screen will look like Figure 7-20.

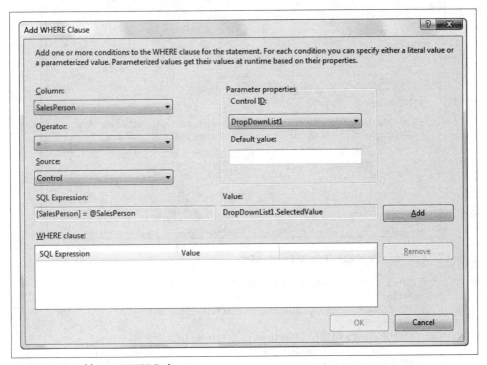

Figure 7-20. Adding a WHERE clause

Now click Add. When you do, the upper portion of the dialog returns to its initial (blank) state and the WHERE clause is added to the "WHERE clause" window.

Click OK until you are back at the Configure Select Statement dialog box. While you're at it, sort the results on the customer's LastName in ascending order by clicking the "Sort by" button, as shown in Figure 7-21.

After you finish creating this SqlDataSource control, switch to Source view and look at the declaration created by VS2008. You'll notice the wizard hasn't added the SalesLT schema to its SQL statement, so you'll need to add it, as highlighted in the following code.

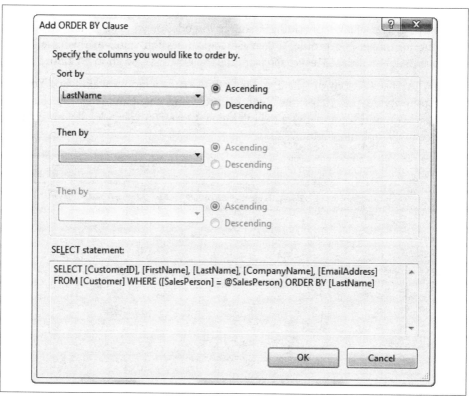

Figure 7-21. Sorting LastName in ascending order

```
<asp:SqlDataSource ID="CustomersDataSource" runat="server"
    ConnectionString=
        "<%$ ConnectionStrings:AdventureWorksLTConnectionString %>"
    SelectCommand=
        "SELECT [CustomerID], [FirstName], [LastName],
            [CompanyName], [EmailAddress]
        FROM [SalesLT].[Customer]
        WHERE ([SalesPerson] = @SalesPerson)
        ORDER BY [LastName]">
    <SelectParameters>
        <asp:ControlParameter ControlID="DropDownList1"
            Name="SalesPerson"
            PropertyName="SelectedValue" Type="String" />
    </SelectParameters>
</asp:SqlDataSource>
```

The SELECT statement now has a WHERE clause that includes a parameterized value
(@SalesPerson). In addition, within the definition of the SqlDataSource control is a
definition of SelectParameters, which includes one parameter of type asp:
ControlParameter and is a parameter that knows how to get its value from a control.
The asp:ControlParameter has one property, ControlID, that tells it which control to

check for its value, and a second property, PropertyName, that specifies which property in the DropDownList to check. A third property, Type, tells it that it is getting a value of type string, so it can properly pass that parameter to the SELECT statement.

Now run your page and try to select different names in the list. Note that the grid contents don't change because changing the selected item in a DropDownList does not automatically post the page back to the server for updates. To change this, set the AutoPostBack property for the DropDownList to true and run the page again. This time, as expected, as you select each staff member his or her clients are displayed in the grid below. Example 7-4 shows the source for *SqlDataSourceParameters.aspx* in full.

Example 7-4. SqlDataSourceParameters.aspx in full

```
<%@ Page Language="C#" AutoEventWireup="true"
    CodeFile="SqlDataSourceParameters.aspx.cs"
    Inherits="SqlDataSourceParameters" %>

<!DOCTYPE html PUBLIC "-//W3C//DTD XHTML 1.0 Transitional//EN"
    "http://www.w3.org/TR/xhtml1/DTD/xhtml1-transitional.dtd">
<html xmlns="http://www.w3.org/1999/xhtml">
<head runat="server">
    <title>Data Source Parameters Demo</title>
</head>

<body>
    <form id="form1" runat="server">
    <div>
        <asp:SqlDataSource ID="StaffDataSource" runat="server"
            ConnectionString=
            "<%$ ConnectionStrings:AdventureWorksLTConnectionString1 %>"
            SelectCommand=
            "SELECT DISTINCT [SalesPerson] FROM [SalesLT].[Customer]">
        </asp:SqlDataSource>

        <asp:DropDownList ID="DropDownList1" runat="server"
            DataSourceID="StaffDataSource" DataTextField="SalesPerson"
            DataValueField="SalesPerson" AutoPostBack="true">
        </asp:DropDownList>

        <asp:SqlDataSource ID="CustomersDataSource" runat="server"
            ConnectionString=
            "<%$ ConnectionStrings:AdventureWorksLTConnectionString %>"
            SelectCommand=
            "SELECT [CustomerID], [FirstName], [LastName],
              [CompanyName], [EmailAddress]
             FROM [SalesLT].[Customer]
             WHERE ([SalesPerson] = @SalesPerson)
             ORDER BY [LastName]">
            <SelectParameters>
                <asp:ControlParameter ControlID="DropDownList1"
                    Name="SalesPerson" PropertyName="SelectedValue"
                    Type="String" />
```

Example 7-4. SqlDataSourceParameters.aspx in full (continued)

```
            </SelectParameters>
        </asp:SqlDataSource>
    </div>

    <asp:GridView ID="CustomerGridView" runat="server"
        AutoGenerateColumns="False" DataKeyNames="CustomerID"
        DataSourceID="CustomersDataSource">
        <Columns>
            <asp:BoundField DataField="CustomerID"
                HeaderText="CustomerID" InsertVisible="False"
                ReadOnly="True" SortExpression="CustomerID" />
            <asp:BoundField DataField="FirstName"
                HeaderText="FirstName" SortExpression="FirstName" />
            <asp:BoundField DataField="LastName"
                HeaderText="LastName" SortExpression="LastName" />
            <asp:BoundField DataField="CompanyName"
                HeaderText="CompanyName" SortExpression="CompanyName" />
            <asp:BoundField DataField="EmailAddress"
                HeaderText="EmailAddress" SortExpression="EmailAddress" />
        </Columns>
    </asp:GridView>
    </form>
</body>
</html>
```

To extend the example, you could also add an AJAX `UpdatePanel` to the page so the page does not appear to post back to the server when a new staff member is chosen from the list.

Writing Data to a Database

In the *SqlDataSourceWizard.aspx* example, the `SqlDataSource` control you created has only a `SELECT` statement to extract data from the database:

```
<asp:SqlDataSource ID="SqlDataSource1" runat="server"
    ConnectionString=
        "<%$ ConnectionStrings:AdventureWorksLTConnectionString %>"
    SelectCommand=
        "SELECT [CustomerID], [FirstName], [LastName], [CompanyName],
        [EmailAddress] FROM [SalesLT].[Customer]">
</asp:SqlDataSource>
```

However, to make your work easier you can ask your data source control to create the remaining SQL `CREATE`, `UPDATE`, and `DELETE` statements using a wizard. Create a copy of *SqlDataSourceWizard.aspx* in your website and rename it *SqlReadWrite.aspx*. Open your new web form and switch to Design view.

Click the SqlDataSource's smart tag, and choose Configure Data Source. The Configure Data Source Wizard opens, displaying your current connection string. Click Next and the Configure Select Statement dialog box is displayed, as shown earlier in Figure 7-13. This time, click the Advanced button.

This opens the Advanced SQL Generation Options dialog box. Click the "Generate INSERT, UPDATE, and DELETE statements" checkbox, as shown in Figure 7-22.

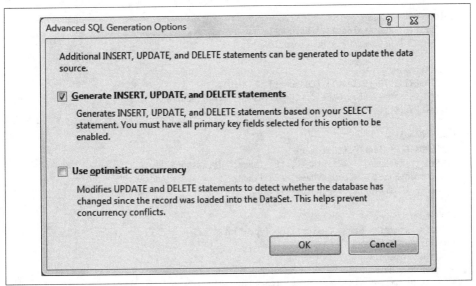

Figure 7-22. Generating SQL write statements with the Configure Data Source Wizard

Clicking this checkbox instructs the wizard to create the remaining SQL statements, and it also enables the second checkbox: "Use optimistic concurrency". Do not check this yet. Click OK, then Next, and then Finish. Your GridView is now bound to a data source control that provides all four CRUD methods.

 CRUD is shorthand for *Create*, *Retrieve*, *Update*, and *Delete*, the four basic operations you can perform on data in a database.

Open the GridView's smart tag and check Enable Editing and Enable Deleting.

Unfortunately, the wizard is no better at generating SQL write commands that use database schemas than it is at generating SQL SELECT statements, so you need to add them back in manually. Example 7-5 shows the HTML generated for the SqlDataSource control and highlights the changes you'll need to make to allow for the SalesLT schema in the AdventureWorksLT database.

Example 7-5. A newly readable/writable SqlDataSource control

```
<asp:SqlDataSource ID="SqlDataSource1" runat="server"
    ConnectionString=
        "<%$ ConnectionStrings:AdventureWorksLTConnectionString %>"
    SelectCommand=
        "SELECT [CustomerID], [FirstName], [LastName],
        [CompanyName], [EmailAddress]
        FROM [SalesLT].[Customer]"

    DeleteCommand=
        "DELETE FROM [SalesLT].[Customer]
        WHERE [CustomerID] = @CustomerID"

    InsertCommand=
        "INSERT INTO [SalesLT].[Customer]
        ([FirstName], [LastName], [CompanyName], [EmailAddress])
        VALUES (@FirstName, @LastName, @CompanyName, @EmailAddress)"

    UpdateCommand=
        "UPDATE [SalesLT].[Customer]
        SET [FirstName] = @FirstName, [LastName] = @LastName,
        [CompanyName] = @CompanyName, [EmailAddress] = @EmailAddress
        WHERE [CustomerID] = @CustomerID">

    <DeleteParameters>
        <asp:Parameter Name="CustomerID" Type="Int32" />
    </DeleteParameters>
    <UpdateParameters>
        <asp:Parameter Name="FirstName" Type="String" />
        <asp:Parameter Name="LastName" Type="String" />
        <asp:Parameter Name="CompanyName" Type="String" />
        <asp:Parameter Name="EmailAddress" Type="String" />
        <asp:Parameter Name="CustomerID" Type="Int32" />
    </UpdateParameters>
    <InsertParameters>
        <asp:Parameter Name="FirstName" Type="String" />
        <asp:Parameter Name="LastName" Type="String" />
        <asp:Parameter Name="CompanyName" Type="String" />
        <asp:Parameter Name="EmailAddress" Type="String" />
    </InsertParameters>
</asp:SqlDataSource>
```

Working through this, the SqlDataSource has seven properties. You've seen the ID, runat, ConnectionString, and SelectCommand properties before. The last three, however, are new—each representing one of the SQL write statements you just generated—and are accompanied by new child elements representing the parameters that each statement requires to work.

The DeleteCommand deletes the record in the Customer table containing the CustomerID stored in the parameter @CustomerID which is specified in the DeleteParameters element:

```
DeleteCommand=
    "DELETE FROM [SalesLT].[Customer]
    WHERE [CustomerID] = @CustomerID"

<DeleteParameters>
    <asp:Parameter Name="CustomerID" Type="Int32" />
</DeleteParameters>
```

The UpdateCommand makes changes to some, all, or none of the values in the Customer record with the CustomerID stored in the parameter @CustomerID. It contains a parameter for each field that the DataSource control retrieves in its SelectCommand (not each field the table contains), which will be filled either with the current value of the field or with a new one according to the user.

```
UpdateCommand=
    "UPDATE [SalesLT].[Customer]
    SET [FirstName] = @FirstName, [LastName] = @LastName,
    [CompanyName] = @CompanyName, [EmailAddress] = @EmailAddress
    WHERE [CustomerID] = @CustomerID">

<UpdateParameters>
    <asp:Parameter Name="FirstName" Type="String" />
    <asp:Parameter Name="LastName" Type="String" />
    <asp:Parameter Name="CompanyName" Type="String" />
    <asp:Parameter Name="EmailAddress" Type="String" />
    <asp:Parameter Name="CustomerID" Type="Int32" />
</UpdateParameters>
```

Finally, the InsertCommand adds a new Customer record to the table containing the values given by the parameters in the command. Note that CustomerID is not included because it is generated automatically by the database.

```
InsertCommand=
    "INSERT INTO [SalesLT].[Customer]
    ([FirstName], [LastName], [CompanyName], [EmailAddress])
    VALUES (@FirstName, @LastName, @CompanyName, @EmailAddress)"

<InsertParameters>
    <asp:Parameter Name="FirstName" Type="String" />
    <asp:Parameter Name="LastName" Type="String" />
    <asp:Parameter Name="CompanyName" Type="String" />
    <asp:Parameter Name="EmailAddress" Type="String" />
</InsertParameters>
```

Save and run *SqlReadWrite.aspx*. The contents of the customer database table are loaded into the GridView just as they were in the previous example, *SqlDataSourceWizard.aspx*. The difference now is the addition of the two links on the left side of each row marked Edit and Delete, as shown in Figure 7-23.

When you click the Edit link, the GridView automatically enters edit mode. You'll notice that the editable text fields change to text boxes, and the links change from Edit and Delete to Update and Cancel, as shown in Figure 7-24.

Figure 7-23. New Edit and Delete buttons for the GridView

Figure 7-24. Editing a record

Make a change to a field and click Update. When you do, the grid and the database are updated, as you can see on the page and in the `Customer` table itself using VS2008's Server Explorer window. If you click Delete against a row, the `DataSource` control will attempt to delete that `customer` from the database. Note, though, that the database may not allow that to happen if the customer has any orders logged for it.

> In this example, the parameters for the `UpdateCommand` are set transparently by the `GridView`. You'll look at how to set them explicitly in Chapter 8.

If you prefer to have buttons for Edit and Delete, rather than links, click the smart tag and then click Edit Columns. When the Fields dialog box opens, click Selected

Fields on the Command Field entry. This brings up the Command Field properties in the righthand window, where you can change the ButtonType from Link to Button by clicking ButtonType in the Appearance section of the Fields editor.

 You'll find more GridView customizations in Chapter 8.

Multiuser Updates

As things stand now, you read data from the database and move the data into your GridView through the SqlDataSource. You have now added the ability to update (or delete) that information. Of course, more than one person may be interacting with the database simultaneously (few web applications support only single-user access).

You can easily imagine that this could cause tremendous problems of data corruption. Consider, for example, two people downloading a record:

    Co-operative Web Ltd. / Birmingham / Dan Maharry

The first editor changes the city from Birmingham to London. The second editor changes the contact name from Dan Maharry to Dan Mahoney. Now, things get interesting. The first editor writes back the data record and the database has the following record:

    Co-operative Web Ltd. / London / Dan Maharry

A moment later, the second editor updates the database. Now the database has the following record:

    Co-operative Web Ltd. / Birmingham / Dan Mahoney

The values updated earlier are overwritten and lost. The technical term for this is *bad*.

To prevent this problem, you might be tempted to use any of the following strategies:

- Lock the records. When one user is working with a record, other users can read the record but they cannot update it. This is called *pessimistic record locking*, and if you have many users, the database quickly becomes fully locked and unusable.

- Update only the columns you change. This is great in theory, but it exposes you to the risk of having a database that is internally consistent but no longer reflects reality. Suppose two salespeople each check the inventory for a given book. The NumberOnHand is 1. They each change only the NumberOnHand field to 0. The database is perfectly happy, but one customer is not going to get the book because you can sell a given book only once (much to our chagrin). To prevent this, you are back to locking records, and you already read we don't like that solution.

- You could decide that before you make an update, you'll check to see whether the record has changed and make the update only to unchanged records. Unfortunately, this still does not solve the problem. If you look at the database before updating it, there is the (admittedly small) chance that someone else will update the database between the time you peek at it and the time you write your changes. Given enough transactions over enough time, collisions and corrupted data will occur.

  This is also inefficient because it requires accessing the database twice for each update (to read and then to write). In a high-volume application, the performance hit will be costly.

- Attempt the change in a way that is guaranteed to generate an error if the record has changed, and then handle these (rare) errors as they occur. This is called *optimistic concurrency*.

To implement optimistic concurrency, your WHERE clause will include the original values (stored for you automatically by the data set) so you can ensure the record will not be updated if it has been changed by another user. Thus, you do not need to "preread" the record; you can write (once) and if the record has changed, it will not be updated.

This approach has tremendous efficiency advantages. In the vast majority of cases, your update will succeed, and you will not have bothered with extra reads of the database. If your update succeeds, no lag exists between checking the data and the update, so there is no chance of someone sneaking in another write. Finally, if your update fails, you will know why and can take corrective action.

For this approach to work, your updates must fail if the data has changed in the database since the time you retrieved the data. Because the data source can tell you the original values it received from the database, you only need to pass those values back into the stored procedure as parameters and then add them to the Where clause in your Update statement. That is, you must extend your Where statement to say "where each field still has its original value."

When you update the record, the original values are checked against the values in the database. If they are different, you will not update any records until you fix the problem (which could only have been caused by someone else updating the records before you did).

To see how this is done, let's go back and turn on optimistic concurrency. Go back to Design view for *SqlReadWrite.aspx*, reopen the Data Source Configuration Wizard and click Next. Because you changed the SQL statements to use the [SalesLT]. [Customer] table, you can't click the Advanced button yet. Check the radio button to specify columns from a table or view and reselect CustomerID, FirstName, LastName, CompanyName, and EmailAddress from the Customer table. Now you can click Advanced and select both checkboxes to enable optimistic concurrency.

Now click OK, then Next, and then Finish to close the wizard. You'll need to go back into the source code now to add the schema back into the SQL statements, as shown earlier, but that requires much less effort than writing all the additional code you just generated, as highlighted in Example 7-6.

Example 7-6. SQL statements using optimistic concurrency

```
<asp:SqlDataSource ID="SqlDataSource1" runat="server"
    ConnectionString=
        "<%$ ConnectionStrings:AdventureWorksLTConnectionString %>"
    SelectCommand=
        "SELECT [CustomerID], [FirstName], [LastName],
        [CompanyName], [EmailAddress] FROM [SalesLT].[Customer]"

    DeleteCommand="DELETE FROM [SalesLT].[Customer]
        WHERE [CustomerID] = @original_CustomerID
        AND [FirstName] = @original_FirstName
        AND [LastName] = @original_LastName
        AND [CompanyName] = @original_CompanyName
        AND [EmailAddress] = @original_EmailAddress"

    InsertCommand=
        "INSERT INTO [SalesLT].[Customer]
        ([FirstName], [LastName], [CompanyName], [EmailAddress])
        VALUES (@FirstName, @LastName, @CompanyName, @EmailAddress)"

    UpdateCommand=
        "UPDATE [SalesLT].[Customer]
        SET [FirstName] = @FirstName, [LastName] = @LastName,
        [CompanyName] = @CompanyName, [EmailAddress] = @EmailAddress
        WHERE [CustomerID] = @original_CustomerID
        AND [FirstName] = @original_FirstName
        AND [LastName] = @original_LastName
        AND [CompanyName] = @original_CompanyName
        AND [EmailAddress] = @original_EmailAddress"
        ConflictDetection="CompareAllValues"
        OldValuesParameterFormatString="original_{0}">

    <DeleteParameters>
        <asp:Parameter Name="original_CustomerID" Type="Int32" />
        <asp:Parameter Name="original_FirstName" Type="String" />
        <asp:Parameter Name="original_LastName" Type="String" />
        <asp:Parameter Name="original_CompanyName" Type="String" />
        <asp:Parameter Name="original_EmailAddress" Type="String" />
    </DeleteParameters>
    <UpdateParameters>
        <asp:Parameter Name="FirstName" Type="String" />
        <asp:Parameter Name="LastName" Type="String" />
        <asp:Parameter Name="CompanyName" Type="String" />
        <asp:Parameter Name="EmailAddress" Type="String" />
        <asp:Parameter Name="original_CustomerID" Type="Int32" />
        <asp:Parameter Name="original_FirstName" Type="String" />
        <asp:Parameter Name="original_LastName" Type="String" />
```

Example 7-6. SQL statements using optimistic concurrency (continued)

```
        <asp:Parameter Name="original_CompanyName" Type="String" />
        <asp:Parameter Name="original_EmailAddress" Type="String" />
    </UpdateParameters>
    <InsertParameters>
      <asp:Parameter Name="FirstName" Type="String" />
      <asp:Parameter Name="LastName" Type="String" />
      <asp:Parameter Name="CompanyName" Type="String" />
      <asp:Parameter Name="EmailAddress" Type="String" />
    </InsertParameters>
</asp:SqlDataSource>
```

Don't panic. There are only two actual differences between Examples 7-5 and 7-6. First, the WHERE clause of the Delete and Update commands has been extended to ensure that the record being deleted or updated has not been altered in between the data being retrieved to the page and the command being executed. This is the purpose of the original_*xxx* parameters.

The wizard has also added the following attributes:

```
    ConflictDetection="CompareAllValues"
    OldValuesParameterFormatString="original_{0}">
```

The two possible values for the ConflictDetection parameter are CompareAllValues (in which case no changes will be made to the database if the original values have changed) and OverwriteChanges (in which case the new values will overwrite the old).

 OverwriteChanges blasts away anything anyone else has entered and writes your updates to the database. As you can imagine, this is used rarely and only with great caution. Most of the time, you'll use CompareAllValues.

Finally, OldValuesParameterFormatString simply indicates the naming convention used to identify the parameters representing the original values for the record being updated.

Tracking the Data Source with Events

Some programmers get nervous when a control does so much work invisibly. After all, when all goes well, it is great not to have to sweat the details, but if something does go wrong, how can you tell whether your connection failed, no records were updated, an exception was thrown, or exactly what happened? Related to that, what if you want to modify the behavior of the control in some way?

The ASP.NET controls in general, and the data controls in particular, overcome these concerns by providing numerous events that you can handle. For example, the SqlDataSource control described in this chapter has nine events you can handle that are not inherited from its parent control. There is an event you can handle when the DataSource is about to run a SELECT statement (Selecting) and one that you can handle immediately after the SELECT statement has finished executing (Selected). Indeed, there are three other pairs of events for each of the other SQL statements that a DataSource works with, as shown in Table 7-4. The ninth event, Filtering, can be used to validate or alter the values being used in WHERE clauses before they are used with a statement.

Table 7-4. SQL statements and their respective DataSource events

SQL statement	Event occurring before statement is run	Event occurring after statement has run
SELECT	Selecting	Selected
INSERT	Inserting	Inserted
UPDATE	Updating	Updated
DELETE	Deleting	Deleted
WHERE clause	Filtering	N/A

To see this at work, let's use the Selected event to reflect back to the page how many customers a staff member is associated with.

Make a copy of *SqlDataSourceParameters.aspx* on the site and call it *SqlDataSourceEvents.aspx*. In Design view, drag a Label control onto the page above the GridView, but below the DropDownList control. Give it the ID lblSelectStats and delete the Text property.

Now select the CustomerDataSource control, and in the Properties dialog click the lightning bolt icon to bring up a list of the control's events. Double-click in the space next to the Selected event and add the highlighted code to the empty handler which is generated for you in *SqlDataSourceEvents.aspx.cs*:

```
protected void CustomersDataSource_Selected(
    object sender, SqlDataSourceStatusEventArgs e)
{
    lblSelectStats.Text =
        String.Format("Number of rows selected: {0}", e.AffectedRows);
}
```

Now run the page and you'll see that the Label reflects the number of rows in the GridView each time you select a staff member, as shown in Figure 7-25.

In this example, the SqlDataSourceStatusEventArgs object provides a handle to the number of rows selected from the database through its AffectedRows property. Its three other properties provide access to the actual SELECT command sent to the database (Command), any exception thrown as a result of the command (Exception), and a value indicating to the DataSource whether the exception was handled (ExceptionHandled). This last property can come in handy if you need to ignore an Exception (by setting it to true) more directly than through a try-catch construct.

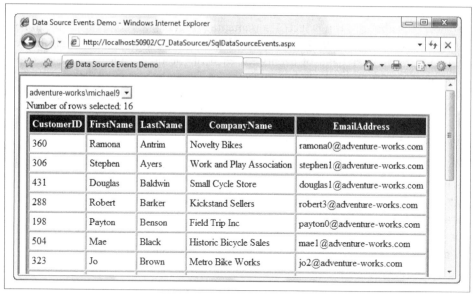

Figure 7-25. Using the Selected event in SqlDataSourceEvents.aspx

Looking back at the other DataSource objects you've seen in this chapter, the XmlDataSource supports only one event—Transforming—that occurs just before your XSLT stylesheet is applied to the XML document being used as your source of data. In comparison, the ObjectDataSource supports the same nine events as the SqlDataSource control, plus an additional three signifying that the object being used as the source of data is going to be created (ObjectCreating), has been created (ObjectCreated), and is being disposed of by .NET (ObjectDisposing).

In the next chapter, you'll look at all the various DataSource-aware controls supplied by .NET, how they work, and how to customize them to your specifications.

Using Data-Aware Controls

In Chapter 7, you looked at the go-to control for data access in ASP.NET: the DataSource control. In this chapter, you'll look at the various DataSource-aware controls available out of the box with Visual Studio and how to use them to read and write (tabular) data through a data source.

To begin, you're going to spend a few moments looking at the rest of the Visual Studio 2008 (VS2008) server control toolbox and consider:

- Which controls can be bound to a DataSource in the same way you've seen the GridView work in earlier examples

- Whether they work with tables, lists, records, or individual pieces of data

- Whether they only display data or can use a DataSource control to reflect changes back to the original source—a database in this case

- What other controls exist to which you can bind data, but do not accept DataSource objects

Technically speaking, every web form control must understand how to bind data to at least its properties (known as *inline binding*) because it inherits the DataBind method as something it must implement from its parent Control class. Thus, every ASP.NET web form control understands inline binding, and can set its properties to values from a database using the ADO.NET DataBind method that you'll look at in Chapter 9.

The question here concerns which controls know how to bind records, lists, or columns of data into their structure through DataSource controls. The technically accurate answer is the controls derived from System.Web.UI.WebControls. BaseDataBoundControl, as shown in Figure 8-1.

It's the BaseDataBoundControl class that gives a control its DataSource and DataSourceID properties, as well as the four abstract classes derived from it that handily group the ASP.NET data-aware controls by purpose.

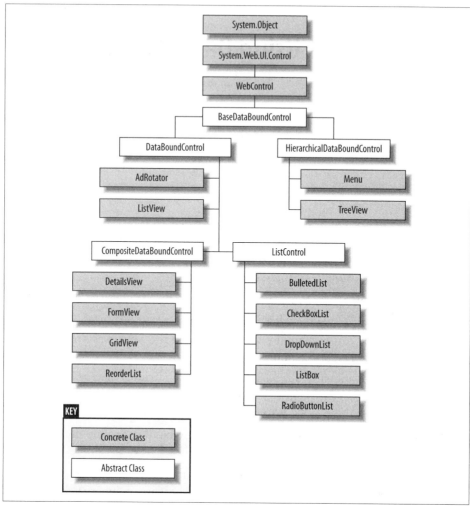

Figure 8-1. DataSource-aware controls derived from BaseDataBoundControl

Hierarchical Data Controls

Controls derived from the HierarchicalDataBoundControl, as listed in Table 8-1, display their data in hierarchical form, such as in a menu or a tree view. They might typically be bound to a SiteMapDataSource, XmlDataSource, or LinqDataSource control presenting data from a hierarchical source (such as an XML document) but they could equally use data from a database or business object to present a flat list of items as desired.

Table 8-1. Hierarchical data controls

Control name	Read/write?	Notes
Menu, TreeView	Read-only	Both the Menu and TreeView controls are used for website navigation. See Chapter 13 for more information.

Tabular Data Controls

Controls derived from the DataBoundControl class all display their data as a list or table of some form. As Figure 8-1 demonstrates, two additional abstract classes then further divide this set of controls by implementation. Controls derived from CompositeDataBoundControl present either individual records or whole tables of data. The *composite* moniker indicates that these controls contain their own collection of controls to present this data. Meanwhile, controls derived from ListControl present lists of data from which one or more items can be selected.

Tables 8-2, 8-3, and 8-4 list the controls used for presenting individual records, lists, and tables of data, respectively, that can use a DataSource control.

Table 8-2. Server controls for displaying individual records

Control name	Read/write?	Notes
DetailsView, FormView	Read, add, update, delete	DetailsView uses DataRow controls to which to bind fields in the record. FormView allows you to define a template for the record using any server controls you want.

Those list controls deriving from the ListControl class (i.e., those in Table 8-3 with the exception of the ReorderList) bind to the data source control in the same way—using the control's DataTextField property to specify the data table column name containing the text for each item in the list, and the DataValueField property to specify the column containing the value to be taken from the list if that item were selected.

Table 8-3. Server controls for lists of data

Control name	Read/write?	Notes
BulletedList	Read-only	Renders a list of data as a bulleted list on the page. None of the items in the list is selectable or can be changed.
ReorderList	Read-only	Part of the AJAX Control Toolkit. Behaves as a bulleted list with the exception that the user can reorder the items in the list by dragging and dropping them onscreen.
DropDownList, RadioButtonList	Read-only	Renders a list of data as a drop-down list or group of radio buttons, respectively. Users can select only one of the items from either of these lists.

Table 8-3. Server controls for lists of data (continued)

Control name	Read/write?	Notes
ListBox	Read-only	Renders a list of data on-screen as an HTML `<select>` list-box. By default, users can select only one of the items from this list, but you can change this so many items can be selected by changing the ListBox's SelectionMode property from Single to Multiple.
CheckBoxList	Read-only	Renders a list of data as a list of checkboxes. By default, all, some, or none of the items in the list can be selected.

Only the GridView, an update to the DataGrid control from ASP.NET v1, really presents tables of data from a source as tabular data on-screen per se. However, the AdRotator control also needs a table of data to work—it just doesn't look like it. Table 8-4 lists the controls that use tables of data, rather than columns or rows.

Table 8-4. Server controls for tables of data

Control name	Read/write?	Notes
AdRotator	Read-only	Uses a table of data to determine which advertisement should be displayed on a website. See Chapter 5 for more on this control.
GridView	Read, update, delete	Renders a table of data as an HTML `<table>`. Includes built-in support for data paging and sorting. Each column of data can be automatically generated by the control or can have a specific template created for it.
Repeater	Read-only	Completely relies on you to define a template for the display of the data within it. Therefore, it is one of the most flexible and powerful data-bound controls, but it requires more effort than most. Compare and contrast with the ListView control.
DataList	Read, update, delete	Completely template-based, like the repeater, but with the intention of laying out whole records in a grid rather than individual records as the GridView does.
ListView	Read, add, delete, update	This control is new to ASP.NET 3.5 and acts mostly as a souped-up version of the DataList control with all the control of the Repeater. Its unique selling point is that it is deliberately standards-friendly, generating no more HTML than you have specifically told it to generate. Supports paging with the help of the DataPager control.

Lists of Data

Let's start with the most straightforward controls to which to bind data—read-only selection lists. As you saw in Chapter 4, there are several different server controls we can use to create a list of items to choose from based on data you provide to them:

- CheckBoxList
- DropDownList

- RadioButtonlist
- BulletedList
- ReorderList

Indeed, you already saw how to bind data from an array to these lists in Chapter 4. Binding data from a DataSource control is just as straightforward.

 All the properties highlighted in this section on lists are available for all five list controls, not just for the DropDownList control used in the following examples.

Binding Data to a List

Open VS2008 and create a new website for this chapter, called *C8_DataAccess*. Delete *Default.aspx* and add a new web form to the site, called *SelectionList.aspx*. In Design view, drag a SqlDataSource onto the page and rename it dsCustomers. Choose Configure Data Source from its smart tag and, as you did in Chapter 7, use the wizard to set the DataSource so that it connects to the AdventureWorksLT database. However, when asked how to retrieve the data from the database, choose "Specify a custom SQL statement or stored procedure" and click Next.

Selection lists need only two values from a database—one to display and one to use as the value corresponding to the display—so use the following statement and click Next. You'll use the full name of the customer to display in the list, and the CustomerID will be the value to carry forward. The query also remembers to deal with the schema name on the table and orders all the names alphabetically so they are easy to locate in the list.

```
SELECT [CustomerID], [FirstName] + ' ' + [LastName] as FullName
FROM [SalesLT].[Customer]
ORDER BY FullName
```

Finally, test the query to make sure it works, and click Finish to close the wizard.

 This query obeys a simple rule of thumb for writing SQL SELECT statements: query only for the data you are going to use. Avoid using SELECT * FROM *some_table* if you don't need to. We've used it a couple of times in this chapter purely to keep the size of the code listings on the small side.

Now drag a BulletedList onto the page and click Choose Data Source from its smart tag. The dialog shown in Figure 8-2 will appear, asking you for the ID of the data source to use (dsCustomers), the field to display (FullName), and the field to use as a value (CustomerID).

Click OK and then press F5 to run the page.

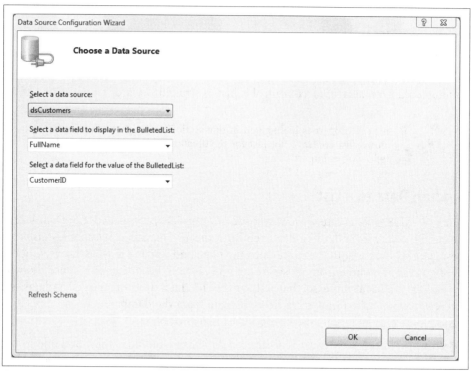

Figure 8-2. Setting the data source for a list

 If you're running this page from the download, you'll likely need to change the connection string in *web.config* to point correctly to your database.

Also, the version of *SelectionList.aspx* to this point is saved in the download for the chapter as *BulletedList.aspx*.

Enable debugging if you're asked, and then you'll see the list on the page, as shown in Figure 8-3.

Looking at the generated source code for this new page (Example 8-1), you can see that the list (abridged here for clarity) contains one customer name per list item as expected. The BulletedList control does not allow items to be selected, so the ID is not included in the list.

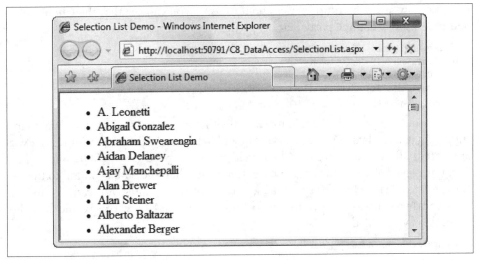

Figure 8-3. SelectionList.aspx in action

Example 8-1. The bound bulleted list (abridged)

```
<ul id="BulletedList1">
    <li>A. Leonetti</li>
    <li>Abigail Gonzalez</li>
    <li>Abraham Swearengin</li>
    ...
    <li>Yao-Qiang Cheng</li>
    <li>Yuhong Li</li>
    <li>Yuping Tian</li>
    <li>Yvonne McKay</li>
</ul>
```

Now swap out the BulletedList control for a DropDownList, choosing dsCustomers as its data source, FullName as the display field, and CustomerId as the value field again. Press F5 to view the generated source code. You'll see the CustomerId values appear, bound to an item in turn with the corresponding full name, as shown in Example 8-2.

Example 8-2. The bound drop-down list (abridged)

```
<select name="DropDownList1" id="DropDownList1">
    <option value="202">A. Leonetti</option>
    <option value="345">Abigail Gonzalez</option>
    <option value="511">Abraham Swearengin</option>
    ...
    <option value="183">Yao-Qiang Cheng</option>
    <option value="124">Yuhong Li</option>
    <option value="533">Yuping Tian</option>
    <option value="562">Yvonne McKay</option>
</select>
```

Looking now at the markup for *SelectionList.aspx*, you can see that the Choose Data Source Wizard sets three particular properties for the DropDownList:

```
<asp:DropDownList ID="DropDownList1" runat="server"
    DataSourceID="dsCustomers"
    DataTextField="FullName"
    DataValueField="CustomerID">
</asp:DropDownList>
```

As you would expect, the DataSourceID links the DropDownList with the data source supplying it with data. The DataTextField and DataValueField properties (as the wizard noted) allow you to set up which field being supplied by the SQL statement is being displayed and which is being used as a value when the data is bound to the list. If your DataTextField is, for example, a date or currency value, you can also use the list's DataTextFormatString property to format it as and how you would like. For example, if you added:

```
DataTextFormatString = "Mr. {0}"
```

to the markup for the DropDownList, the text for each list item would start with "Mr. ". For example:

```
<select name="DropDownList1" id="DropDownList1">
    <option value="202">Mr. A. Leonetti</option>
    <option value="345">Mr. Abigail Gonzalez</option>
```

These two properties work as though you had called:

```
ListItem.Text = String.Format(DataTextFormatString, DataTextField);
```

for each row of data being bound to the list. Note, however, that if you want to use multiple fields from the database to generate a text value for your list, you'll need to do one or both of the following:

- Generate the combined text value in the SQL statement as we did in this example.
- Use ADO.NET code to manipulate the text prior to binding it to the list. See Chapter 9 for more on this.

The DataTextFormatString works with only the one value that was given to it in the DataTextField.

 You can find out more about format strings at *http://msdn2.microsoft. com/en-us/library/26etazsy.aspx*.

Retrieving the Selected Value from a List

Binding data to a list is all very well, but it serves no purpose unless the value selected can be retrieved from the list. All list controls contain three properties that allow access to this very information:

SelectedIndex
>   Returns the zero-based index of the selected item in the list

SelectedValue
>   Returns the value of the selected item

SelectedItem
>   Returns the ListItem object representing the selected item

To demonstrate, you'll extend *SelectionList.aspx* to display the index, text, and value of an item in the list once it has been selected. To this end, you must do three things.

First, add a Label control to the page just beneath the DropDownList and give it an ID of lblSelection to display the selected information.

Next, set the DropDownList's AutoPostBack property to true. A page would not normally react to the selection of a new item in the list automatically, so you must force it to do so by setting this property.

Now handle the SelectedIndexChanged event of the DropDownList. Double-click the list in Design view or on the empty box for the event in the Properties dialog to generate the event handler for it, and add the following highlighted code:

```
protected void DropDownList1_SelectedIndexChanged(object sender, EventArgs e)
{
    lblSelection.Text =
        String.Format("<p>Selected Index : {0}<br />
            Selected Text : {1}<br />Selected Value : {2}</p>",
            DropDownList1.SelectedIndex.ToString(),
            DropDownList1.SelectedItem.Text,
            DropDownList1.SelectedValue);
}
```

Run the page again and select a new item in the list. The page will post back and show the required information about the selected item, as shown in Figure 8-4.

Adding Static Values to a Data-Bound List

Before we move on, one common task when adding a list to a form is to add a "select one of the following" item to the top of the list which is selected initially. If it is still selected when the form is submitted, it will be treated as though no choice has been made from the list and it will work hand in hand with validation controls (see Chapter 11), checking that a selection has been made. You can accomplish this task in two ways.

The first way is to insert the extra item into the list in the code-behind file after the data has already been bound into the list. The following lines of code will suffice:

```
DropDownList1.Items.Insert(0, new ListItem("Select a customer", ""));
DropDownList1.Items[0].Selected = true;
```

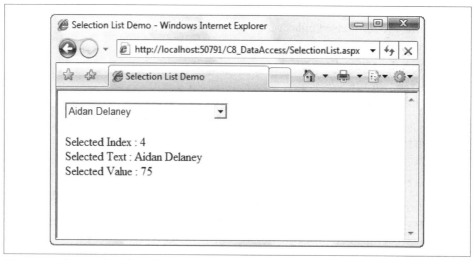

Figure 8-4. Showing the selected information in the list

This works only if you have full control over when the data is bound into the list. Simply adding these two lines into the Page_Load handler in *SelectionList.aspx.cs*, for instance, will have no effect because the data is bound after the item is inserted into the list and overwrites it.

The second way to add items to your list is to add them directly into the markup for your page. However, those items will be overwritten as well when data is bound to the list unless you also set the list control's AppendDataBoundItems property to true. For instance:

```
<asp:DropDownList ID="DropDownList1" runat="server"
    DataSourceID="dsCustomers" DataTextField="FullName"
    DataValueField="CustomerID"
    AutoPostBack="true"
    onselectedindexchanged="DropDownList1_SelectedIndexChanged"
    AppendDataBoundItems="true">
    <asp:ListItem Selected="True" Text="Select a customer" Value="" />
</asp:DropDownList>
```

This property indicates that data bound to the list from the data source should be in addition to rather than instead of the static list shown in the markup.

One Record at a Time: DetailsView

With lists in hand, let's expand your frame of data view from a couple of fields per row to an entire row. ASP.NET v2 introduced two new controls, the DetailsView and the FormView, to work with one row of information at a time. The DetailsView, which you'll look at now, applies a structure to the presentation of this information—it places it in the rows and columns of an HTML table—whereas the FormView, which you'll look at later, removes that structure and asks you to define your own.

To demonstrate the basic workings of the DetailsView, add to the *C8_DataAccess* website a new page called *DetailsView.aspx* and add a SqlDataSource to it that retrieves all the information from the Customer table. Then, add a DetailsView control to the page and use its Common Tasks panel to connect it to the data source. Example 8-3 shows the resultant markup.

Example 8-3. DetailsView.aspx initial markup

```
<%@ Page Language="C#" AutoEventWireup="true"
    CodeFile="DetailsView.aspx.cs" Inherits="DetailsView" %>

<!DOCTYPE html PUBLIC "-//W3C//DTD XHTML 1.0 Transitional//EN"
    "http://www.w3.org/TR/xhtml1/DTD/xhtml1-transitional.dtd">
<html xmlns="http://www.w3.org/1999/xhtml">
<head runat="server">
    <title>DetailsView Page</title>
</head>
<body>
    <form id="form1" runat="server">
    <div>
      <asp:SqlDataSource ID="dsCustomers" runat="server"
          ConnectionString=
            "<%$ ConnectionStrings:AWLTConnection%>"
          SelectCommand="SELECT * FROM [SalesLT].[Customer]" />
      <asp:DetailsView ID="DetailsView1"
          runat="server" DataSourceID="dsCustomers">
      </asp:DetailsView>
    </div>
    </form>
</body>
</html>
```

If you run the page, the result should look similar to Figure 8-5.

There are a number of things to note:

- Only the first row of data in the Customer table is shown. The rest of the rows are accessible if you enable paging.

- The DetailsView generates a clean HTML table markup with no visual style information. The control has properties you can use to add color using either inline styles or with CSS classes. (CSS purists might want to use the ListView for really fine-grained control.)

- The information is read-only. However, you can enable the creation, editing, and deletion of a record as required.

- The DetailsView automatically generates a row in the HTML table for each field selected in the data source. You can disable this automatic generation and manually define which fields will be displayed.

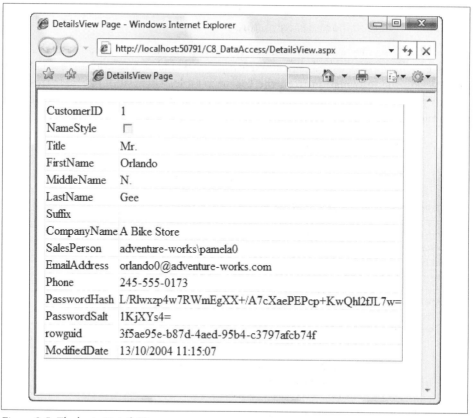

CustomerID	1
NameStyle	☐
Title	Mr.
FirstName	Orlando
MiddleName	N.
LastName	Gee
Suffix	
CompanyName	A Bike Store
SalesPerson	adventure-works\pamela0
EmailAddress	orlando0@adventure-works.com
Phone	245-555-0173
PasswordHash	L/Rlwxzp4w7RWmEgXX+/A7cXaePEPcp+KwQhl2fJL7w=
PasswordSalt	1KjXYs4=
rowguid	3f5ae95e-b87d-4aed-95b4-c3797afcb74f
ModifiedDate	13/10/2004 11:15:07

Figure 8-5. The basic DetailsView

- The `DetailsView` translates the different types of data in the table as best it can into a visual fashion. For example, `DateTime` values are returned in standard format and Booleans are rendered as checkboxes, checked or not checked depending if the value is `true` or `false`. You can tweak this when you manually define the fields being displayed.

We'll work through each of these points in turn, as well as look at how to get selected or edited data back out of this control and into something else on the page, and what events it exposes.

Paging Through Records

The `DetailsView` control may show only one record at a time, but it does keep an internal note of where that record is in the table, and by enabling paging you can easily navigate through the contents of the table. To do this, set the control's `AllowPaging` property to `true`. Now if you run the page again, you'll see that the bottom row of the table generated by the control contains links to show the different records in the table, as shown in Figure 8-6. There are more than 10 rows in the table, so an ellipsis (...) is also shown to allow access to the next 10 records after those shown.

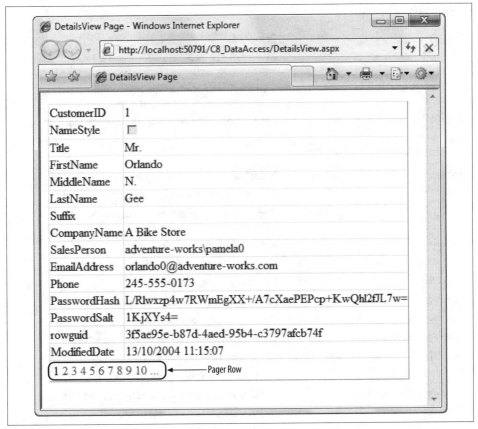

Figure 8-6. The DetailsView control with paging enabled

This looks brilliant, but you should take care. The paging functionality made available through the DataSource controls works by downloading all the data into the page and then figuring out which page is being shown, and hence which data to display. This means that if you want to display 10 rows of a table with 100 million rows in it, you'll pull all 100 million rows down from the database onto the web server first before the page decides which to show. As you can imagine, this isn't a great state of affairs and can be a huge memory and bandwidth hog if not kept in check. Solutions to this problem include writing your own paging routines as stored procedures saved on the database and calling them from your data source, or using Language Integrated Query (LINQ) to find the correct data for the page before it is returned from the database, or simply making sure your SELECT statement returns as few rows as possible for the DataSource to work with if stored procedures and LINQ are not options.

Style and color aside, several properties are related to paging for your use, as listed in Table 8-5, and a few more with the prefix PagerSettings- that control how the links in the pager row are shown. These are detailed in Table 8-6.

Table 8-5. Paging properties

Property	Default	Description
AllowPaging	false	Enables paging for the DetailsView control and makes the pager row visible.
EnablePagingCallbacks	false	If true, adds client-side code to the page that enables the change between pages without the page posting back.
PageIndex	0	Zero-based index of the record to be shown when the page is first loaded.

Table 8-6. PagerSettings properties

Property	Default	Description
Mode	Numeric	The style of buttons shown in the pager row.
Position	Bottom	The location of the pager buttons on the GridView. Can be Top, Bottom, or TopAndBottom.
Visible	true	Makes the pager controls visible.
FirstPageImageUrl	""	The URL to an image to display for the first-page button.
FirstPageText	<<	The text to use as the first-page button.
LastPageImageUrl	""	The URL to an image to display for the last-page button.
LastPageText	>>	The text to use as the last-page button.
NextPageImageUrl	""	The URL to an image to display for the next-page button.
NextPageText	&gt;	The text to use as the next-page button.
PageButtonCount	10	The number of page links to be shown at a time in the pager row.
PreviousPageImageUrl	""	The URL to an image to display for the previous-page button.
PreviousPageText	&lt;	The text to use as the previous-page button.
Visible	true	Sets whether the pager row is visible or not.

The Customer table in the example contains quite a few customers, so adding a few more page buttons and a first and last link to the pager row is probably a good idea. For example, if you alter the markup for the DetailsView control as shown in the following code, you'll get a more navigable set of records which don't cause the page to post back when you choose to view a new one:

```
<asp:DetailsView ID="DetailsView1" runat="server"
    DataSourceID="dsCustomers"
    AllowPaging="True" EnablePagingCallbacks="True" PageIndex="5">
    <PagerSettings Mode="NumericFirstLast"
        PageButtonCount="20" Position="TopAndBottom" />
</asp:DetailsView>
```

The results are shown in Figure 8-7, and you can see them in *DetailsViewPagerSettings.aspx* in the download.

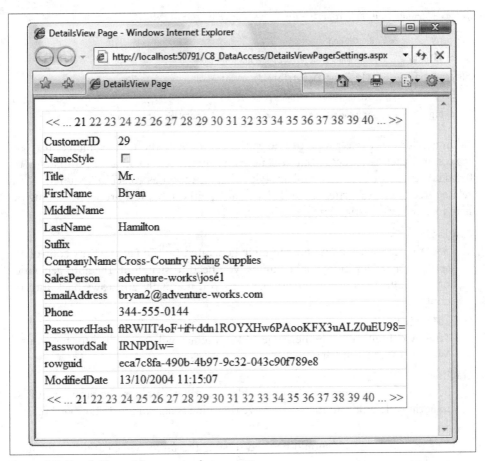

Figure 8-7. DetailsView with customized pager settings

Improving Presentation and Accessibility

The results thus far are functional, but perhaps not as informational or accessible as they might be. Fortunately, the DetailsView control also has several properties that allow you to add some explanatory text to the table generated by the control for context and to improve access to the table within it, as given in Table 8-7. By default, all of these properties are blank.

Table 8-7. Additional text properties for the DetailsView

Property	Description
AccessKey	Adds a shortcut key to the top of the table by setting the table's accesskey attribute
Caption	Sets the contents of the table's <caption> element
EmptyDataText	Sets the text displayed by the DetailsView if the DataSource it is bound to returns no data to display

Table 8-7. Additional text properties for the DetailsView (continued)

Property	Description
FooterText	Adds and sets the text of a footer row to the table
HeaderText	Adds and sets the text of a header row to the table
TabIndex	Sets the table's `tabindex` property
Tooltip	Adds and sets the text of a tool tip to the table (the table's `title` attribute)

Adding values to these properties gives the contents of the table some context and makes it easier to access, but it's not very pretty to look at. Fortunately, the DetailsView also has some familiar style-related properties to set as required. Many relate directly to properties for an HTML table, although a few are worth calling out here for further investigation:

CssClass

> Sets the CSS class name for the table generated by the DetailsView control. To set the classes for individual columns, you need to switch off the auto-generation of rows and then add the class name as you manually add rows back into the control.

EnableTheming

> True by default, sets whether styles set in themes will be applied to this control. We cover themes in Chapter 14.

GridLines

> Sets which, if any, grid lines in the table should be visible in the browser. It is set to Both by default, but it can also have the value None, Horizontal, or Vertical.

SkinID

> Sets the skin file that should be used to style the table. See Chapter 14 for more on skins.

Like the PagerSettings properties listed earlier, the DetailsView also allows you to set a common set of style properties for 10 specific row types in the table generated by the DetailsView control, seven of which are illustrated in Figure 8-8 and in *DetailsViewMultiRow.aspx* in the download.

The three not covered in Figure 8-8 are:

EditRowStyle

> The style applied to rows when the control is in edit mode

EmptyDataRowStyle

> The style applied when there is no data to show

InsertRowStyle

> The style applied to rows when the control is in insert mode

Settings these properties for a specific row type will override the same setting as applied to the DetailsView as a whole. For example, in Figure 8-8, the Font-Name

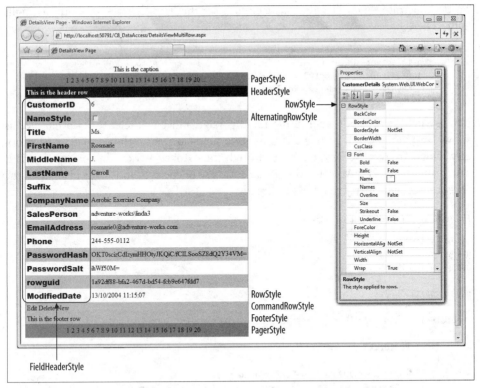

Figure 8-8. *Seven different types of row styles in a DetailsView*

property for the DetailsView is set to Arial, but is overridden in the FieldHeaderStyle area where it is set to Arial Black.

> Many color-coordinated styles are available for use in the control's Smart Tag menu by selecting Apply Format.

Retrieving Values from the Current Record

Presenting information well on-screen is one battle, but it's another battle altogether to then do something useful with it. The first skirmish in that respect is to retrieve the information currently selected on-screen. When dealing with lists earlier, you used the SelectedValue property to retrieve the value of the item selected in the list. You can still use the SelectedValue property for this purpose, but how do you know which field will be retrieved? In the list example, there was only one to choose from. In this DetailsView example, there are 15. The answer is to specify the column or columns in the control's DataKeyNames property. Typically, this property is used to identify the primary key columns in the table, which are most often used when passing parameters to SELECT statements in other data source controls or stored procedures.

To demonstrate, open *DetailsView.aspx* and set the DataKeyNames property as highlighted here:

```
<asp:DetailsView ID="CustomerDetails"
    runat="server" DataSourceID="dsCustomers"
    AllowPaging="True" EmptyDataText="No data was found"
    DataKeyNames="CustomerID, RowGuid">
</asp:DetailsView>
```

Now switch to the code-behind file for this page and edit the Page_Load handler as shown in Example 8-4. In this example, two fields are set in the DataKeyNames property which are retrieved by iterating through the DataKey.Values dictionary object. If only one field is given in the DataKeyNames property, you can also use the SelectedValue property to access it directly.

Example 8-4. DetailsView.aspx.cs in full

```
using System;
using System.Text;
using System.Web.UI;

public partial class DetailsView : Page
{
    protected void Page_Load(object sender, EventArgs e)
    {
        if (IsPostBack)
        {
            StringBuilder info = new StringBuilder();
            info.AppendFormat("You are viewing record {0} of {1}<br />",
                CustomerDetails.DataItemIndex.ToString(),
                CustomerDetails.DataItemCount.ToString());

            for (int i = 0; i < CustomerDetails.DataKeyNames.Length; i++)
            {
                info.AppendFormat("{0} : {1}<br />",
                    CustomerDetails.DataKeyNames[i],
                    CustomerDetails.DataKey.Values[i]);
            }

            info.AppendFormat("Selected Value : {0}",
                CustomerDetails.SelectedValue.ToString());

            lblInfo.Text = info.ToString();
        }
    }
}
```

Note that all of the code executes only after the page is posted back for the first time. This is because the record shown initially is not considered to be selected by the control. Building on this, Table 8-8 lists the read-only properties of the DetailsView that give you access to the various areas of the control.

Table 8-8. *Read-only, non-style-related DetailsView properties*

Property	Type	Description
BottomPagerRow	DetailsViewRow	The bottom pager row in the DetailsView.
CurrentMode	DetailsViewMode	The current mode of the DetailsView control. Value can be ReadOnly, Insert, or Edit.
DataItem	Object	Returns a reference to the current item displayed in the DetailsView.
DataItemCount	Integer	The number of items in the data source.
DataItemIndex	Integer	Zero-based index of the current item in the data source.
DataKey	DataKey	Returns the primary key of the current item.
Fields	DataControlFieldCollection	The collection of fields being used in the DetailsView.
FooterRow	DetailsViewRow	The footer row in the DetailsView.
HeaderRow	DetailsViewRow	The header row in the DetailsView.
PageCount	Integer	The number of records in the data source.
Rows	DetailsViewRowCollection	The collection of rows in the DetailsView.
SelectedValue	Object	Returns the DataKey value in the current item.
TopPagerRow	DetailsViewRow	The top pager row in the DetailsView.

Adding, Updating, and Deleting Records

Besides simply displaying data on a page, the DetailsView control also enables the creation, updating, and deletion of data. You saw in Chapter 7 how to add INSERT, UPDATE, and DELETE statements to your DataSource objects. In the DetailsView, all you need to do is set the AutoGenerateDeleteButton, AutoGenerateEditButton, and AutoGenerateInsertButton properties to true (or you can check the Enable Inserting, Editing, and Deleting buttons in the control's Smart Tag menu). This will add three links into the DetailsView's command row (shown earlier in Figure 8-8) to delete the currently displayed record, edit it, or add a new one to the database.

However, leaving ASP.NET to deal automatically with the alteration of data is not always successful. To demonstrate, make a copy of *DetailsView.aspx* in the website and rename it *DetailsViewRW.aspx*. In Design view, run the Configure Data Source Wizard again and use it to generate INSERT, UPDATE, and DELETE statements for you on the Customer table, as shown in Chapter 7. You'll need to remove any reference to the SalesLT schema in the SELECT statement, generate the new SQL statements, and then add the SalesLT schema back in again. Do not enable optimistic concurrency. Now set the three AutoGenerate*Button properties to true on the DetailsView, and set its DataKeyNames property to CustomerID so the new SQL statements can use the primary key in the table as a parameter. The final markup should look like that in Example 8-5.

Example 8-5. DetailsViewRW.aspx

```
<%@ Page Language="C#" AutoEventWireup="true"
    CodeFile="DetailsViewRW.aspx.cs" Inherits="DetailsViewRW" %>

<!DOCTYPE html PUBLIC "-//W3C//DTD XHTML 1.0 Transitional//EN"
    "http://www.w3.org/TR/xhtml1/DTD/xhtml1-transitional.dtd">
<html xmlns="http://www.w3.org/1999/xhtml">
<head runat="server">
    <title>DetailsView Read Write Demo</title>
</head>
<body>
    <form id="form1" runat="server">
    <asp:SqlDataSource ID="dsCustomers" runat="server"
        ConnectionString="<%$ ConnectionStrings:AWLTConnection %>"
        DeleteCommand=
            "DELETE FROM [SalesLT].[Customer]
                WHERE [CustomerID] = @CustomerID"
        InsertCommand=
            "INSERT INTO [SalesLT].[Customer]
            ([NameStyle], [Title], [FirstName], [MiddleName],
            [LastName], [Suffix], [CompanyName], [SalesPerson],
            [EmailAddress], [Phone], [PasswordHash], [PasswordSalt],
            [rowguid], [ModifiedDate])
            VALUES (@NameStyle, @Title, @FirstName, @MiddleName,
            @LastName, @Suffix, @CompanyName, @SalesPerson,
            @EmailAddress, @Phone, @PasswordHash, @PasswordSalt,
            @rowguid, @ModifiedDate)"
        SelectCommand= "SELECT * FROM [SalesLT].[Customer]"
        UpdateCommand=
            "UPDATE [SalesLT].[Customer]
            SET [NameStyle] = @NameStyle, [Title] = @Title,
                [FirstName] = @FirstName, [MiddleName] = @MiddleName,
                [LastName] = @LastName, [Suffix] = @Suffix,
                [CompanyName] = @CompanyName, [SalesPerson] = @SalesPerson,
                [EmailAddress] = @EmailAddress, [Phone] = @Phone,
                [PasswordHash] = @PasswordHash,
                [PasswordSalt] = @PasswordSalt,
                [rowguid] = @rowguid, [ModifiedDate] = @ModifiedDate
            WHERE [CustomerID] = @CustomerID">
        <DeleteParameters>
            <asp:Parameter Name="CustomerID" Type="Int32" />
        </DeleteParameters>
        <UpdateParameters>
            <asp:Parameter Name="NameStyle" Type="Boolean" />
            <asp:Parameter Name="Title" Type="String" />
            <asp:Parameter Name="FirstName" Type="String" />
            <asp:Parameter Name="MiddleName" Type="String" />
            <asp:Parameter Name="LastName" Type="String" />
            <asp:Parameter Name="Suffix" Type="String" />
            <asp:Parameter Name="CompanyName" Type="String" />
            <asp:Parameter Name="SalesPerson" Type="String" />
            <asp:Parameter Name="EmailAddress" Type="String" />
            <asp:Parameter Name="Phone" Type="String" />
```

Example 8-5. DetailsViewRW.aspx (continued)

```
                <asp:Parameter Name="PasswordHash" Type="String" />
                <asp:Parameter Name="PasswordSalt" Type="String" />
                <asp:Parameter Name="rowguid" Type="Object" />
                <asp:Parameter Name="ModifiedDate" Type="DateTime" />
                <asp:Parameter Name="CustomerID" Type="Int32" />
            </UpdateParameters>
            <InsertParameters>
                <asp:Parameter Name="NameStyle" Type="Boolean" />
                <asp:Parameter Name="Title" Type="String" />
                <asp:Parameter Name="FirstName" Type="String" />
                <asp:Parameter Name="MiddleName" Type="String" />
                <asp:Parameter Name="LastName" Type="String" />
                <asp:Parameter Name="Suffix" Type="String" />
                <asp:Parameter Name="CompanyName" Type="String" />
                <asp:Parameter Name="SalesPerson" Type="String" />
                <asp:Parameter Name="EmailAddress" Type="String" />
                <asp:Parameter Name="Phone" Type="String" />
                <asp:Parameter Name="PasswordHash" Type="String" />
                <asp:Parameter Name="PasswordSalt" Type="String" />
                <asp:Parameter Name="rowguid" Type="Object" />
                <asp:Parameter Name="ModifiedDate" Type="DateTime" />
            </InsertParameters>
        </asp:SqlDataSource>
        <div>
            <asp:DetailsView ID="DetailsView1" runat="server"
                AllowPaging="True" DataSourceID="dsCustomers"
                DataKeyNames="CustomerID" AutoGenerateDeleteButton="true"
                AutoGenerateEditButton="true"
                AutoGenerateInsertButton="true">
            </asp:DetailsView>
        </div>
        </form>
    </body>
</html>
```

Running the page proceeds well enough, but if you try to add or update a customer in the database, you'll quickly run into the following error:

> Server Error in '/C8_DataAccess' Application.
>
> Implicit conversion from data type sql_variant to uniqueidentifier is not allowed. Use the CONVERT function to run this query.

The issue here is that the DetailsView has identified the rowGuid field as a generic object, and it doesn't know to turn it into a value of SQL Server's uniqueidentifier type, which would be the correct thing to do. Fortunately, the database itself already provides a solution, as by default it will generate a new GUID for a new record using the TSQL newid( ) function when a new record is added to the Customer table. All you need to do, then, is remove the addition of the rowguid field from the INSERT statement along with its parameter list to get past this problem.

The same is true of the Customer table's ModifiedDate column, which contains the date and time the record was last changed. In this case, the SQL getdate( ) function is called by default when a new record is created; this adds the current date and time to that record at the moment of creation. So, remove references to the ModifiedDate column from the INSERT statement and parameters or you'll see the following error. Indeed, if you omit a value from many of the other fields, you'll see a similar error.

> Server Error in '/C8_DataAccess' Application.
>
> Cannot insert the value NULL into column 'ModifiedDate', table 'Adventure-WorksLT.SalesLT.Customer'; column does not allow nulls. INSERT fails. The statement has been terminated.

Finally, you'll be able to add a new customer to the table as long as you add a valid PasswordSalt and PasswordHash value, and so on. Likewise, there will be issues of foreign key violation if you try to delete any records you haven't added first.

Manually Setting the Contents of the Control

As you can see, there are quite a few issues to work out here if you're to use this control, or indeed any others, to alter the contents of the database. For example:

- If the database already gives a default value to a field, you could either not display that field or leave the value as read-only when adding or editing a record.
- If you're allowing a user to delete a record, you might need to delete records in other tables linked to this one.
- If you're adding a date to the database, you might want to display it as a string in read-only mode, but then offer a calendar control when adding or editing the record.
- It's a bad practice to store plain text passwords in the database for people to find, so a safer way to store them is to use a one-way hashing algorithm and store the hash in the database instead. (*One-way* also means you can't retrieve a password for the user if he forgets it.) A *salt* is a random string of characters added to the password before it is hashed so that two users with the same password end up with different hashes.

    If you're storing a password hash and salt in your database rather than the password itself, you'll want to enter the password in plain text when you add a record and have the hash and salt as read-only fields the rest of the time.

In situations such as these, the solution is to set AutoGenerateRows to false and manually set the rows that the DetailsView control will show, and how they will work in the three modes that the control can be in: read-only, edit, and insert.

You can make these changes by handcoding the HTML in Source view or by clicking the smart tag for the DetailsView and choosing either Add New Field or Edit Fields.

Doing the former brings up a simple one-page wizard for generating a row in the
`DetailsView` for one of the fields in your database or for buttons to switch between its
read-only and read/write modes. Using this wizard, as shown in Figure 8-9, ensures
that the necessary information is required for the row to function.

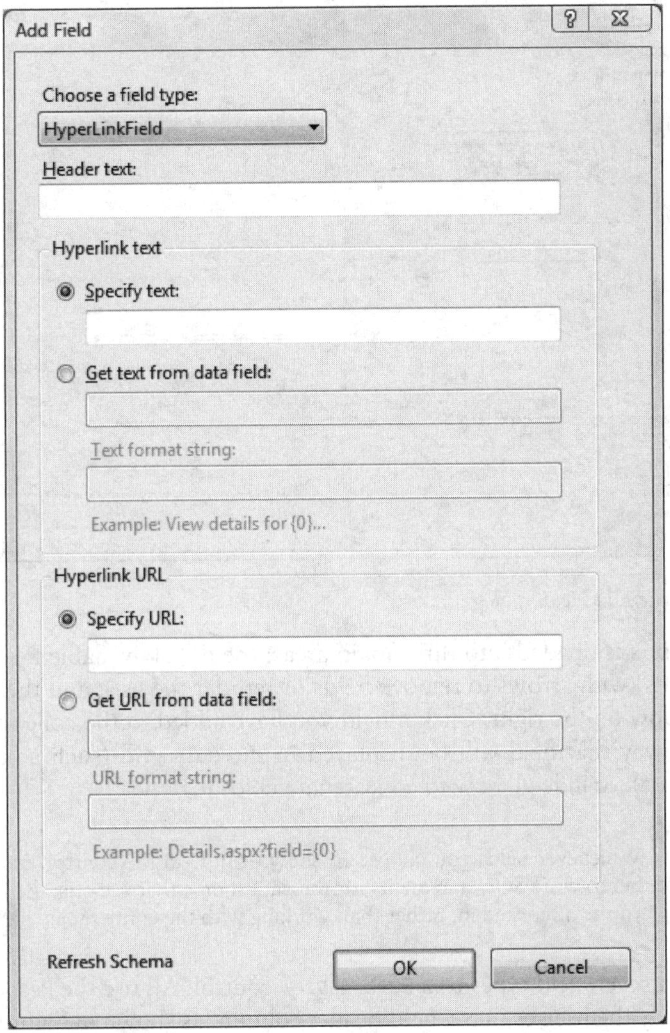

Figure 8-9. The Add New Field Wizard

The Edit Fields dialog shown in Figure 8-10, builds on the simple Add New Field
Wizard by offering the ability to add new fields, as well as edit and remove current
fields from the `DetailsView`. You also can review and set all the properties available
to each field.

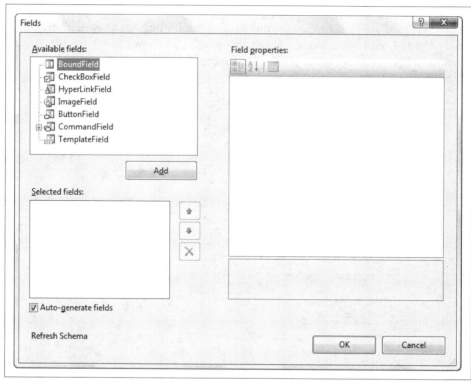

Figure 8-10. The Edit Fields dialog

The dialog box is divided into three main areas: the list of available fields, the list of selected fields (with arrows to remove fields or reorder the list), and the "Field properties" window on the right. Click a field you have added to the collection, and you can set the way that field will be displayed in the data grid (such as changing the header to Name), or indeed, how to concatenate fields together.

 Whichever fields you choose to show or hide in the control, remember to write SQL statements for the data source that use only the fields you're interested in, rather than working with the entire table.

You can add seven field types to a DetailsView control. All use the HeaderText property to identify themselves in the field header column, as shown in Figure 8-10.

BoundField

This is the standard row type used when rows are generated automatically by the DetailsView. Use the DataField property to set the name of the field to be bound to this column. Unless ReadOnly is set to true, this column type will allow a user to alter its contents and save them to the database in insert or edit mode.

`CheckBoxField`
> This works like the `BoundField`, except it should be bound only to a Boolean field in the database and will be rendered as a checkbox. Again, this field is read/write by default.

`HyperLinkField`
> This extends the `BoundField` to render (a combination of) fields as hyperlinks in the `DetailsView`. The `DataField` property is used to set the text shown on-screen and the `HyperlinkDataField` property is used to bind a field to the URL for the hyperlink. Alternatively, the text shown or the URL can be given constant values with the `Text` and `NavigateUrl` properties, respectively. A `HyperlinkField` is read-only in all three edit modes.

`ButtonField`
> This adds a row to the `DetailsView` containing a link or button for hooking up to one of the six standard commands: `Cancel`, `Edit`, `Insert`, `Delete`, `Update`, or `New`. Compare and contrast this to the `CommandField`.

`CommandField`
> This adds the predefined `CommandRow` to the `DetailsView` (see Figure 8-8, previously) containing some or none of the following pairs of commands: `Delete`, `Edit`/`Update`, `New`/`Insert`, or `Cancel`. These predefined buttons change their command types depending on the current mode of the `DetailsView`. Buttons defined in `ButtonFields` do not change their command types.

`ImageField`
> This adds a row that uses an HTML `<img>` tag to display an image stored somewhere online (not in the database). The `DataField` property binds to the name of the image stored in the database, and you can format it into a valid URL using the `DataImageUrlFormatString` property.

`TemplateField`
> This is the most flexible of all fields. It lets you define the behavior of the row in each of the control's three edit modes using its `<ItemTemplate>`, `<EditItemTemplate>`, and `<InsertItemTemplate>` subelements. It has no properties itself, except for `HeaderText`.

To demonstrate some of these different field types, you'll create a new page containing a customized `DetailsView` working against the `Customer` table. You'll work through each field in the table and reason how it should be displayed and written to through the `SqlDataSource` control that will provide the binding between it and the database. Add a new web form to the *C8_DataAccess* website and call it *DetailsViewCustomRows.aspx*. Drag a `DetailsView` control onto the page and set `AutoGenerateRows` to `false`. Also set `AllowPaging` to `true` so you can access any record in the table along with any pager settings you might want to change. Now work through each column in the table to see what to do with them (we will discuss the event handlers declared here in due course).

```
<asp:DetailsView ID="dvwCustomers" runat="server" AllowPaging="True"
   AutoGenerateRows="False" DataSourceID="dsCustomers"
   onmodechanged="dvwCustomers_ModeChanged" DataKeyNames="CustomerID"
   oniteminserting="dvwCustomers_ItemInserting">
   <PagerSettings FirstPageText="First"
      LastPageText="Last" PageButtonCount="5" />
   <EmptyDataTemplate>
      No customers found I&#8217;m afraid
   </EmptyDataTemplate>
```

The `CustomerID` field is the primary key for the `Customer` table, so it will need to be
present in the `DetailsView` for use by the `INSERT` and `UPDATE` statements if changes are
made or added. However, it is created automatically by the database when a new
record is added and should never be changed. The easiest way to do this is to create a
`BoundField` for the `CustomerID` field and set it to be read-only and not visible. The
`DataSource`'s `DataKeyNames` property should also be set to `CustomerID` as shown earlier.

```
<asp:BoundField DataField="CustomerID"
   ReadOnly="True" Visible="False" />
```

The next six fields in the table, `NameStyle`, `Title`, `FirstName`, `MiddleName`, `LastName`,
and `Suffix`, all record details of a customer's name. The aim in this demo is to have
all six of these fields available to edit if adding or changing a customer record, but
hidden in favor of one field with just the customer's full name if in read-only mode.
Therefore, you should add seven fields to the `DetailsView` control: one for the
`FullName`, which will be read-only, and six more for each database field. `BoundFields`
will also do for these seven, with the exception of the `NameStyle` field, which is a
Boolean field and therefore is more suited to a `CheckBoxField`. The `DetailsView`
appears in read-only mode by default, so each of the field's `Visible` properties is set
to `false` initially and will be toggled when the `DetailsView`'s edit mode changes.
More on that in a bit.

```
<asp:BoundField
   DataField="FullName" HeaderText="Name" ReadOnly="true" />
<asp:CheckBoxField HeaderText="Non-western name?"
   DataField="NameStyle" Visible="false" />
<asp:BoundField
   DataField="Title" HeaderText="Title" Visible="false" />
<asp:BoundField
   DataField="FirstName" HeaderText="First Name" Visible="false" />
<asp:BoundField
   DataField="MiddleName" HeaderText="Middle Name" Visible="false" />
<asp:BoundField
   DataField="LastName" HeaderText="Surname" Visible="false" />
<asp:BoundField
   DataField="Suffix" HeaderText="Suffix" Visible="false" />
```

The NameStyle field is a Boolean field that indicates whether the customer's name is Western (False) and therefore reads as 'FirstName LastName', or Eastern (True) and therefore reads as 'LastName FirstName'. As noted before, the easiest way to concatenate fields, as required for this example, is to do so in the SQL SELECT statement, which you'll see later. However, for clarity, the SELECT statement does not take account of the NameStyle field and assumes that all names are Westernized.

After the company name, which should also be rendered as a BoundField, you have the EmailAddress field. Ideally, this should present itself as a hyperlink in the form "mailto:*some.address@here.com*" in read-only mode and as an editable string in insert and edit modes. However, the standard hyperlink field won't do this, so you'll need to add a TemplateField and define this behavior yourself.

```
<asp:BoundField DataField="CompanyName" HeaderText="Company" />
<asp:TemplateField HeaderText="Email Address">
    <ItemTemplate>
        <asp:HyperLink ID="hypEmailReadOnly" runat="server"
            NavigateUrl='<%# Eval("EmailAddress", "mailto:{0}") %>'
            Text='<%# Eval("EmailAddress") %>' />
    </ItemTemplate>
    <EditItemTemplate>
        <asp:TextBox ID="txtEmailEdit" runat="server"
            Text='<%# Bind("EmailAddress") %>' />
    </EditItemTemplate>
    <InsertItemTemplate>
        <asp:TextBox ID="txtEmailInsert" runat="server"
            Text='<%# Bind("EmailAddress") %>' />
    </InsertItemTemplate>
</asp:TemplateField>
```

The four highlighted lines of code illustrate the two ways to bind a value into the property of an ASP.NET control (harking back to the days of classic ASP spaghetti code). Eval implies that data is bound only into the property and cannot be read back by the data source, so it is used in the ItemTemplate to be shown when the DetailsView is in read-only mode. Meanwhile, Bind, denotes a two-way binding so that any value entered into the TextBox will be sent back to the database when the Insert or Add button is clicked, and is used in both EditItem and InsertItem templates.

Both the Phone and SalesPerson fields can be bound into standard BoundFields. The ModifiedDate field, however, needs a bit of thought. In read-only mode, it should show only the date in some readable format rather than the default one straight from .NET (using the DataTextFormat property), and it should be updated automatically rather than have the user remember to update it herself. The database itself will add to the table the date on which a new record is added using the SQL GetDate( ) function if you do not supply one yourself, and it would seem prudent to do the same when updating a customer record. The strategy, then, is to make ModifiedDate a read-only field and to add or modify it directly in the SQL INSERT and UPDATE statements used by the DataSource, which you'll add after dealing with the rest of the table.

```
<asp:BoundField DataField="ModifiedDate"
    DataFormatString="{0:hh:mm, dd MMM yyyy}"
    HeaderText="Last Modified" ReadOnly="true" />
```

The password fields will need the most work as you'll have to add some code behind the page to generate the hash and salt to be stored in the database based on the plain text password given to the customer when she is added to the database initially.

As you did with the name fields, it makes sense to make the PasswordSalt and PasswordHash fields read-only and to hide them in other modes. For the purposes of this demonstration, you'll also add a Password field to the DetailsView which will be visible only when a new customer record is being created.

```
<asp:BoundField DataField="PasswordHash" HeaderText="Password Hash"
    ReadOnly="True" SortExpression="PasswordHash" />
<asp:BoundField DataField="PasswordSalt" HeaderText="Password Salt"
    ReadOnly="True" SortExpression="PasswordSalt" />
<asp:TemplateField HeaderText="Password" Visible="false">
    <InsertItemTemplate>
        <asp:TextBox ID="txtPasswordInsert" runat="server" />
    </InsertItemTemplate>
</asp:TemplateField>
```

Note that the TemplateField for the plain text password has only an InsertItemTemplate declared, but still has its Visible property set to false. This is because if you left Visible set to true, the row containing the Password field would still be shown—it just wouldn't contain anything, which isn't the desired effect. Also note that you're not binding the Password value to anything in the database; it's just being used as the seed for the two other values.

Finally, you'll need to add a CommandField with Edit and Insert buttons. The rowguid field is filled automatically when a row is created and should be read-only after that, so there's no need to select it at all from the database.

```
<asp:CommandField ButtonType="Button"
    ShowEditButton="True" ShowInsertButton="True" />
</Fields>
</asp:DetailsView>
```

With the DetailsView display taken care of, you need to automate a couple of things. First, there's the matter of making rows visible or invisible depending on whether the DetailsView control is in read-only mode. To achieve this, you can handle the DetailsView's ModeChanged event, which fires whenever a switch is made between read-only, insert, and edit modes. The code for this handler simply toggles the

Visible property for some of the fields in the DetailsView. Note that no custom fields have ID values, so they must be referenced in code by index number. (Just make sure you don't start swapping the rows around after you write code like this or you'll need to change the code too!)

```csharp
using System.Security.Cryptography;
using System.Text;
using System.Web.UI;
using System.Web.UI.WebControls;

public partial class DetailsViewCustomRows : Page
{
    protected void dvwCustomers_ModeChanged(object sender, EventArgs e)
    {
        bool readOnly =
            (dvwCustomers.CurrentMode == DetailsViewMode.ReadOnly);

        dvwCustomers.Fields[1].Visible = readOnly;    //FullName
        dvwCustomers.Fields[2].Visible = !readOnly;   //NameStyle
        dvwCustomers.Fields[3].Visible = !readOnly;   //Title
        dvwCustomers.Fields[4].Visible = !readOnly;   //FirstName
        dvwCustomers.Fields[5].Visible = !readOnly;   //MiddleName
        dvwCustomers.Fields[6].Visible = !readOnly;   //LastName
        dvwCustomers.Fields[7].Visible = !readOnly;   //Suffix
        dvwCustomers.Fields[12].Visible = readOnly;   //ModifiedDate
        dvwCustomers.Fields[13].Visible = readOnly;   //PasswordHash
        dvwCustomers.Fields[14].Visible = readOnly;   //PasswordSalt

        //Password field can only be viewed when adding a new record,
        //so a little different logic
        if (dvwCustomers.CurrentMode == DetailsViewMode.Insert)
        {
            dvwCustomers.Fields[15].Visible = true;
        }
        else
        {
            dvwCustomers.Fields[15].Visible = false;
        }
    }
}
```

The only other code you need to write grabs the plain text password for a customer and converts it into a hash and salt for storing in the database. This needs to occur once the Add button has been clicked, but before the actual insert, so you'll need to handle the DetailsView's ItemInserting event handler, which is raised at exactly this point.

Note that because it is embedded inside a template inside the DetailsView, you can't reference the TextBox control containing the password directly. Instead, you have to use the FindControl method first, cast the object returned into TextBox, and then carry on from there.

```csharp
// before item is inserted, password hash and salt must be generated
protected void dvwCustomers_ItemInserting(object sender,
    DetailsViewInsertEventArgs e)
```

```
{
    string password =
        ((TextBox)dvwCustomers.FindControl("txtPasswordInsert")).Text;
    string salt = GetSalt();
    string hash = GetHashFromPlainTextAndSalt(password, salt);
    e.Values["PasswordHash"] = hash;
    e.Values["PasswordSalt"] = salt;
}
```

The DetailsViewInsertEventArgs parameter in the handler has a property called Values. This is a collection of all the values about to be sent to the database. Thankfully, the items in the collection can be accessed by name (unlike the DetailsView. Fields collection). Once the salt and hash are generated, they are set to their respective values for adding to the database.

The general policy in this book is to explain how all code works in detail, but in the case of the following methods for generating the salt and hash, we have the exception that proves the rule. In overview, a salt is a random string that is appended to your password. That string is then hashed (encoded) and saved to the database. The hashing algorithm is one-way, so you can't simply decrypt the encoded string and retrieve the password. When a user logs in, the salt stored in the database for his account is appended to the password he supplies and is hashed again. If the resultant hashed string is the same as that in the database, he is logged in successfully.

```
private string GetHashFromPlainTextAndSalt(
    string password, string salt)
{
    SHA1CryptoServiceProvider hasher =
        new SHA1CryptoServiceProvider();
    byte[] clearBytes = Encoding.UTF8.GetBytes(salt + password);
    byte[] hashedBytes = hasher.ComputeHash(clearBytes);
    return Convert.ToBase64String(hashedBytes);
}

private string GetSalt()
{
    byte[] buffer = new byte[5];
    RNGCryptoServiceProvider rng = new RNGCryptoServiceProvider();
    rng.GetBytes(buffer);
    return Convert.ToBase64String(buffer);
}
}
```

That's all the code behind the page. All you have to do now is add the SqlDataSource for the DetailsView control to the page with SELECT, INSERT, and UPDATE commands that bear in mind what you saw before. Note that the SELECT command builds up the customer's FullName, because the DetailsView can't.

```
<asp:SqlDataSource ID="dsCustomers" runat="server"
    ConnectionString="<%$ ConnectionStrings:AWLTConnection %>"
    SelectCommand="SELECT    [CustomerID], [NameStyle],
        CASE WHEN [Title] IS NULL THEN ''
            ELSE [Title] + ' ' END +
```

```
        [FirstName] + ' ' +
        CASE WHEN [MiddleName] IS NULL THEN ''
            ELSE [MiddleName] + ' ' END +
        [LastName] +
        CASE WHEN [Suffix] IS NULL THEN ''
            ELSE ' ' + [Suffix] END as 'FullName',
        [Title], [FirstName], [MiddleName], [LastName], [Suffix],
        [CompanyName], [SalesPerson], [ModifiedDate], [EmailAddress],
        [Phone], [PasswordHash], [PasswordSalt]
        FROM [SalesLT].[Customer]"

        InsertCommand="INSERT INTO [SalesLT].[Customer]
([NameStyle], [Title], [FirstName], [MiddleName], [LastName], [Suffix],
[CompanyName], [SalesPerson], [EmailAddress], [Phone], [PasswordHash],
[PasswordSalt]) VALUES (@NameStyle, @Title, @FirstName, @MiddleName, @LastName,
@Suffix, @CompanyName, @SalesPerson, @EmailAddress, @Phone, @PasswordHash,
@PasswordSalt)"
        UpdateCommand="UPDATE [SalesLT].[Customer] SET [NameStyle] = @NameStyle,
[Title] = @Title, [FirstName] = @FirstName, [MiddleName] = @MiddleName, [LastName]
= @LastName, [Suffix] = @Suffix, [CompanyName] = @CompanyName, [SalesPerson] =
@SalesPerson, [EmailAddress] = @EmailAddress, [Phone] = @Phone, [ModifiedDate] =
GetDate() WHERE [CustomerID] = @CustomerID">
        <UpdateParameters>
            <asp:Parameter Name="NameStyle" Type="Boolean" />
            <asp:Parameter Name="Title" Type="String" />
            <asp:Parameter Name="FirstName" Type="String" />
            <asp:Parameter Name="MiddleName" Type="String" />
            <asp:Parameter Name="LastName" Type="String" />
            <asp:Parameter Name="Suffix" Type="String" />
            <asp:Parameter Name="CompanyName" Type="String" />
            <asp:Parameter Name="SalesPerson" Type="String" />
            <asp:Parameter Name="EmailAddress" Type="String" />
            <asp:Parameter Name="Phone" Type="String" />
            <asp:Parameter Name="CustomerID" Type="Int32" />
        </UpdateParameters>
        <InsertParameters>
            <asp:Parameter Name="NameStyle" Type="Boolean" />
            <asp:Parameter Name="Title" Type="String" />
            <asp:Parameter Name="FirstName" Type="String" />
            <asp:Parameter Name="MiddleName" Type="String" />
            <asp:Parameter Name="LastName" Type="String" />
            <asp:Parameter Name="Suffix" Type="String" />
            <asp:Parameter Name="CompanyName" Type="String" />
            <asp:Parameter Name="SalesPerson" Type="String" />
            <asp:Parameter Name="EmailAddress" Type="String" />
            <asp:Parameter Name="Phone" Type="String" />
            <asp:Parameter Name="PasswordHash" Type="String" />
            <asp:Parameter Name="PasswordSalt" Type="String" />
        </InsertParameters>
    </asp:SqlDataSource>
```

Save the page, run it, and switch among the different modes. Figures 8-11, 8-12, and 8-13 shows the DetailsView you've just created in read-only, insert, and edit modes, respectively.

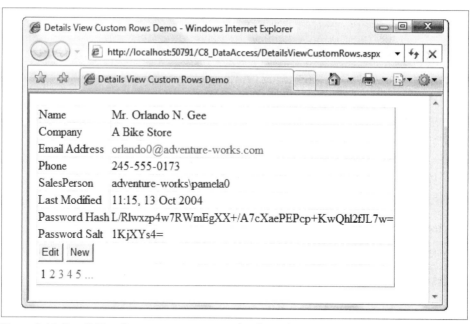

Figure 8-11. DetailsViewCustomRows.aspx in read-only mode

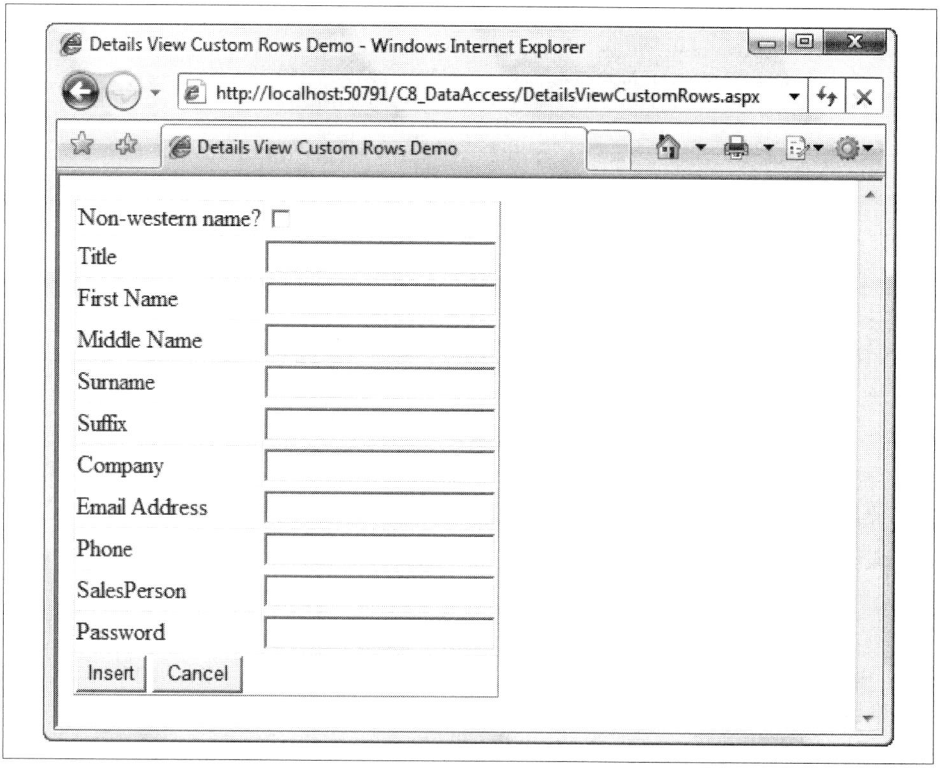

Figure 8-12. DetailsViewCustomRows.aspx in insert mode

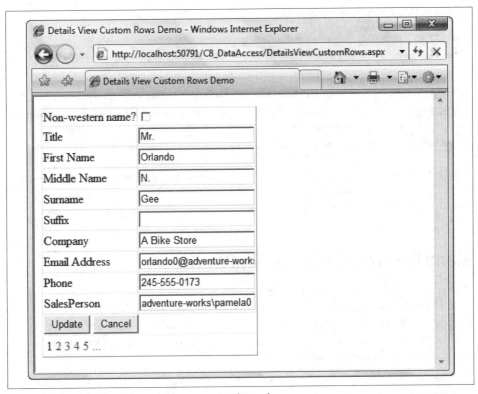

Figure 8-13. DetailsViewCustomRows.aspx in edit mode

This example demonstrates how custom fields and a touch of code can present views on data that are much easier for a user to handle and work with than the DetailsView control's own auto-generated solution. Not giving users access to fields they shouldn't edit is one way to keep your data consistent, and should you add some validation controls (shown in Chapter 11) to this page as well, you're on your way to helping your users as much as you can to keep that data consistent.

All that remains before looking at other data-bound controls is to look quickly at the events the DetailsView control exposes, two of which you used in the previous example. They are listed in Table 8-9.

Table 8-9. DetailsView events

Event name	When does it fire?
ItemCommand	When a command button is clicked
ItemCreated	When a new record (item) is created and displayed by the control
ItemDeleted	After a Delete button is clicked and the record has been deleted in the database
ItemDeleting	After a Delete button is clicked but before the record has been deleted in the database
ItemInserted	After an Insert button is clicked and the record has been added to the database

Table 8-9. DetailsView events (continued)

Event name	When does it fire?
ItemInserting	After an Insert button is clicked but before the record has been added to the database
ItemUpdated	After an Update button is clicked and the record has been changed in the database
ItemUpdating	After an Update button is clicked but before the record has been changed in the database
ModeChanged	After the DetailsView control has switched to edit mode and its CurrentMode property has been updated
ModeChanging	After the DetailsView control has switched to edit mode but before its CurrentMode property has been updated
PageIndexChanged	After a link to another page has been clicked and the control's PageIndex property has been updated
PageIndexChanging	After a link to another page has been clicked but before the control's PageIndex property has been updated

Many Records at a Time: GridView

Whereas the DetailsView control works with one record from a query at a time on-screen, the GridView control displays many, as shown in Figure 8-14. It is the go-to control for displaying tabular data on-screen and, as it is also derived from the CompositeDataBoundControl class, it shares many of its properties, events, and methods with the DetailsView control.

To demonstrate, create a new web page called *GridView.aspx* in the *C8_DataAccess* website and drag a SqlDataSource and a GridView control onto it. Set the DataSource to select all the data from the Customer table and then set the GridView to use the data source using its DataSourceID property, as shown in Example 8-6.

Example 8-6. Bare-bones markup for GridView.aspx

```
<%@ Page Language="C#" AutoEventWireup="true"
   CodeFile="GridView.aspx.cs" Inherits="GridView" %>

<!DOCTYPE html PUBLIC "-//W3C//DTD XHTML 1.0 Transitional//EN"
   "http://www.w3.org/TR/xhtml1/DTD/xhtml1-transitional.dtd">
<html xmlns="http://www.w3.org/1999/xhtml">
<head runat="server">
   <title>GridView Demo</title>
</head>

<body>
   <form id="form1" runat="server">
   <div>
      <asp:SqlDataSource ID="dsCustomers" runat="server"
         ConnectionString="<%$ ConnectionStrings:AWLTConnection %>"
         SelectCommand="SELECT * FROM [SalesLT].[Customer]" />
      <asp:GridView ID="gvwCustomers"
         runat="server" DataSourceID="dsCustomers" />
   </div>
```

Example 8-6. Bare-bones markup for GridView.aspx (continued)

```
    </form>
</body>
</html>
```

If you compare this to the bare-bones markup for the DetailsView in Example 8-3, you'll see the code is almost identical, except for the control name. The result, however, is markedly different, as (partially) shown in Figure 8-14. Instead of a simple table of 15 rows and two columns displaying the contents of the first customer record in the database, the GridView generates a much larger table of 442 rows and 15 columns displaying *all* the customer records in the table at once.

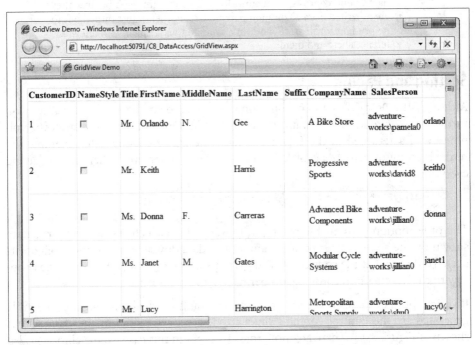

Figure 8-14. A simple noncustomized GridView control

There are a number of things to note:

- The presentation and discovery of data inside a GridView can be significantly improved over this bare-bones example using styles and paging. The GridView can also allow the user to sort the data on a field as you would in a SQL statement using the ORDER BY clause.

- The information is read-only. However, you can edit and delete records in a GridView, although you *cannot* add new records.

- The GridView automatically generates a row in the table for each record in the selected data.

- Each field retrieved from the database is grouped in a column rather than a row, as is the case with the DetailsView control. Thus, when you need to customize the presentation of the GridView, you'll set its AutoGenerateColumns property to false, rather than its AutoGenerateRows property.

- Like the DetailsView, the GridView shows different types of data it retrieves from a database in different ways. Most are shown as text formatted to your requirements, but others, such as Boolean values, are shown using a more appropriate HTML element: a CheckBox.

 Although the GridView shares many of the same properties as other data-bound controls, it's a curiosity to note that this isn't because they are inherited from a common parent class. Rather, it just turned out to be prudent for them to work in a common way, albeit with a few differences here and there.

Sorting and Paging

Although the DetailsView may show only one record at a time, the GridView will throw everything on the page, unless you rein it in. One option is to restrict the volume of data returned in the SQL statement (the preferred way)—for example, by retrieving only a certain set of fields in your SQL statement rather than selecting everything:

```
SELECT [CustomerId], [FirstName], [LastName], [EmailAddress]
FROM [SalesLT].[Customer]
```

The other option is to enable paging in the GridView (which restricts only the data shown on the screen rather than the amount of data downloaded, as mentioned earlier). To do this, set the control's AllowPaging property to true and its PageSize property to the number of records shown per page—for example, 5.

If you do both of these and run the page again, you'll see the bottom row of the table generated by the control contains links to view other records in the data set, as shown in Figure 8-15. There are more than 10 pages in this case, so the ellipsis is also shown to allow access to the next 10 pages after those currently shown.

The PagerSettings properties that control how the links are displayed in the pager row are the same as those for the DetailsView control, as listed earlier in Table 8-5.

The GridView also supports the sorting of data by any given field in the selected data. To enable this, set the GridView's AllowSorting property to true. Now when you run the page, you'll see that all the column headings are hyperlinks. Clicking any of them will sort the data by that field.

A full set of the GridView's properties related to paging and sorting is listed in Table 8-10.

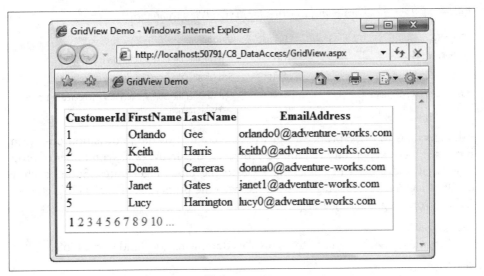

Figure 8-15. A GridView with paging enabled

Table 8-10. Paging and sorting properties for the GridView

Property	Default	Description
AllowPaging	false	Enables paging for the GridView control and makes the pager row visible
AllowSorting	false	Enables sorting for the GridView
EnableSortingAndPagingCallbacks	false	If true, adds client-side code that hides the postback between page changes and re-sorting of data
PageIndex	0	Zero-based index of the record to be shown when the page is first loaded
PageSize	10	Sets the number of records to be displayed on a single page

Improving Presentation and Accessibility

With paging (and sorting) enabled, you now have a GridView that isn't quite as over-whelming with information as the original bare-bones example. Specific data is also easier to find now, although the context of that data is now lacking. To deal with that, the GridView has a number of properties to add that context and also improve your page's accessibility. These are listed in Table 8-11.

Table 8-11. Text and accessibility properties for the GridView

Property	Default	Description
Caption	""	Sets the contents of the <table>'s caption element
EmptyDataText	""	Sets the text displayed by the DetailsView if the DataSource it is bound to returns no data to display

Property	Default	Description
ShowFooter	false	Sets whether the table's footer row is displayed
ShowHeader	false	Sets whether the table's header row is displayed
UseAccessibleHeader	true	Sets whether the table's header row is rendered in a more accessible fashion

Adding values to these properties gives some context to the information on-screen, but it's still not very pretty to look at. However, the GridView has a number of properties that add a dash of color and style to the table it generates. Some, such as CellPadding and CellSpacing, relate directly to the properties of the HTML <table>. Others worth highlighting are:

BackImageURL
> Sets the URL for an image to be displayed in the background of the table.

CaptionAlign
> Sets the horizontal or vertical alignment of the <caption> element set by the Caption property. It is set to NotSet by default, but it can have the value Top, Left, Bottom, or Right.

CssClass
> Sets the CSS class name for the table generated by the DetailsView control. To set the classes for individual columns, you need to switch off the auto-generation of rows and then add the class name as you manually add rows back into the control.

EnableTheming
> True by default, sets whether styles set in themes will be applied to this control. We cover themes in Chapter 14.

GridLines
> Sets which, if any, grid lines in the table should be visible in the browser. It is set to Both by default, but it can also have the value None, Horizontal, or Vertical.

SkinID
> Sets the skin file that should be used to style the table. See Chapter 14 for more on skins.

The GridView control also provides a common set of style properties for eight defined types of rows. Six of these row types are illustrated in Figure 8-16 along with the properties they can have set for them. You can find the code for this screenshot in the download as *GridViewMultiRow.aspx*.

The two not shown in Figure 8-16 are:

EditRowStyle
> The style applied to rows when the control is in edit mode

EmptyDataRowStyle
> The style applied when there is no data to show

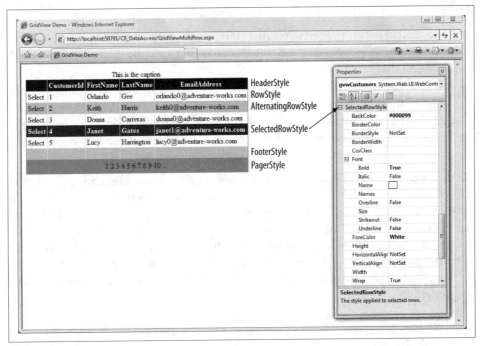

Figure 8-16. Six different types of rows in a GridView

Setting these properties for a specific row type will override the same setting applied to the GridView as a whole. For example, in Figure 8-16, the Font-Names property for the GridView is set to Times New Roman but is overridden in the HeaderStyle settings, where it is set to Arial Black.

Don't forget to experiment with the predefined styles available to you in the GridView's Smart Tag menu under Apply Format.

Retrieving Values from the Selected Record

So far in this chapter, you've seen different strategies for retrieving selected values from lists and from DetailsView controls. Retrieving selected values from a GridView is akin to the latter, albeit with a little more complexity. A DetailsView only shows one record at a time, so ASP.NET assumes that's the record from which you want to retrieve the value. A GridView, on the other hand, shows multiple records at once, so a bit more work needs to be done.

First you need to enable the selection of a row in the GridView by one of these methods:

- Checking Enable Selection in the GridView's Smart Tag menu
- Setting its AutoGenerateSelectButton property to true
- Manually adding a select button column to the GridView

There are two routes to the selected data in a GridView:

- The SelectedRow property returns the entire row currently selected as a GridViewRow object whose individual values can then be accessed through its Cells property.

- You can set the GridView's DataKeyNames property to specify the column (or columns) to be made available to you through its SelectedValue and SelectedDataKey properties. Typically, this approach is used to provide quick access to the primary key value(s) of the selected record for use in other data source controls or stored procedures as a parameter value.

To demonstrate, open *GridView.aspx* and add a Label control beneath the GridView to display some information about the row selected. Now set the AutoGenerateSelectButton and DataKeyNames properties as highlighted in the following code, and use the Properties window to generate a handler for the GridView's SelectedIndexChanged event. This event signifies a record has been selected in the GridView and thus there are some values to retrieve. You'll also need to add RowGuid to the list of fields selected from the database to match the DataKeyNames property you're setting.

```
<asp:SqlDataSource ID="dsCustomers" runat="server"
    ConnectionString="<%$ ConnectionStrings:AWLTConnection %>"
    SelectCommand="
        SELECT [CustomerId], [FirstName], [LastName],
               [EmailAddress], [RowGuid] FROM [SalesLT].[Customer]" />
<asp:GridView ID="gvwCustomers" runat="server"
    DataSourceID="dsCustomers" AllowPaging="True" PageSize="5"
    AutoGenerateSelectButton="true" DataKeyNames="CustomerID, RowGuid" />
<asp:Label runat="server" ID="lblInfo" />
```

Now switch to the code-behind page for *GridView.aspx* and edit the gvwCustomers_SelectedIndexChanged handler you just added, as shown in Example 8-7. In this example, both the SelectedRow and DataKeyNames routes are demonstrated.

Example 8-7. GridView.aspx.cs in full

```
using System;
using System.Text;
using System.Web.UI;

public partial class GridView : Page
{
    protected void gvwCustomers_SelectedIndexChanged(
        object sender, EventArgs e)
    {
        StringBuilder info = new StringBuilder();
        info.AppendFormat("You are viewing record {0} of {1} (SelectedIndex)<br />",
            gvwCustomers.SelectedIndex.ToString(),
            gvwCustomers.Rows.Count.ToString());
```

Example 8-7. GridView.aspx.cs in full (continued)

```
            info.AppendFormat("You are viewing record {0} of {1} (DataKeys)<br />",
                gvwCustomers.SelectedIndex.ToString(),
                gvwCustomers.DataKeys.Count);
            info.AppendFormat("You are viewing page {0} of {1} (PageCount)<br />",
                gvwCustomers.PageIndex.ToString(),
                gvwCustomers.PageCount.ToString());

            info.AppendFormat(
                "<p>Using SelectedRow, Email Address= {0}<br />",
                gvwCustomers.SelectedRow.Cells[4].Text);

            info.Append("Using SelectedDataKey<br />");

            for (int i = 0; i < gvwCustomers.DataKeyNames.Length; i++)
            {
                info.AppendFormat("{0} : {1}<br />",
                    gvwCustomers.DataKeyNames[i],
                    gvwCustomers.SelectedDataKey.Values[i]);
            }

            info.AppendFormat("Selected Value : {0}",
                gvwCustomers.SelectedValue.ToString());

            lblInfo.Text = info.ToString();
        }
    }
}
```

Figure 8-17 shows the results of running the page and selecting the first row. Note that the GridView's Rows.Count and DataKeys.Count properties return only a value of 5, rather than 442, which is the actual number of customers in the database table. This is because the GridView is only aware of the data given to it by a DataSource, and because it has instructed the DataSource to return only five rows (set in the PageSize property) that's all it gets and is aware of. You could multiply the PageSize by the PageCount property to get an approximate number of total records returned by the DataSource's SELECT statement, but the only way to get an accurate number would be to run a SELECT COUNT query on the database as well.

Note that changing pages after selecting a row has no effect on the row currently selected. A row does not have to be visible to be marked as selected. Also, no row is selected by default when the page initially loads.

Table 8-12 lists all the properties of the GridView control that give you access to the selected values and other areas of the control.

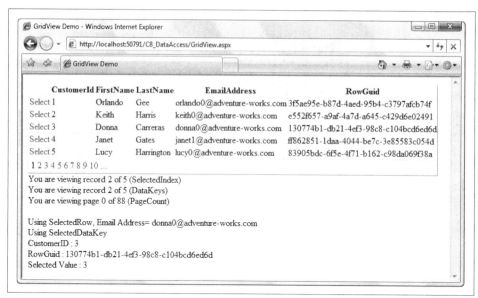

Figure 8-17. Getting selected values from the GridView

Table 8-12. Read-only, non-style-related GridView properties

Property	Type	Description
BottomPagerRow	GridViewRow	The bottom pager row in the GridView.
Columns	DataControlFieldCollection	The collection of Columns shown in the GridView.
DataKeys	DataKeyArray	The collection of DataKeys for all of the rows on the current page of the GridView.
FooterRow	GridViewRow	The footer row in the GridView.
HeaderRow	GridViewRow	The header row in the GridView.
PageCount	Integer	The number of pages required to display all the records returned by the associated DataSource's SelectCommand, given the number of records being shown per page as set in the PageSize property.
Rows	GridViewRowCollection	The collection of Rows shown in the GridView.
SelectedDataKey	DataKey	The DataKey object for the currently selected row.
SelectedRow	GridViewRow	The currently selected row in the GridView.
SelectedValue	Object	The first DataKey value in the currently selected row.
SortDirection	SortDirection	The order in which the items in the GridView are currently sorted. Possible values are Ascending and Descending.
SortExpression	String	The column on which the GridView is currently being sorted.
TopPagerRow	GridViewRow	The top pager row in the GridView.

Updating and Deleting Records

As we mentioned earlier, you can also use the GridView to update and delete data. You'll need to use a DetailsView or FormView control to add a new record to the data source, though; adding records using only a GridView is not supported. Once you've added an UPDATE and a DELETE statement to the DataSource control that binds data to the GridView, just set its AutoGenerateDeleteButton and AutoGenerateEditButton properties to true (or check the Enable Editing and Deleting boxes in its Smart Tag menu). This will add an Edit and a Delete link to each row in the table generated in a command column, as shown in Figure 8-18.

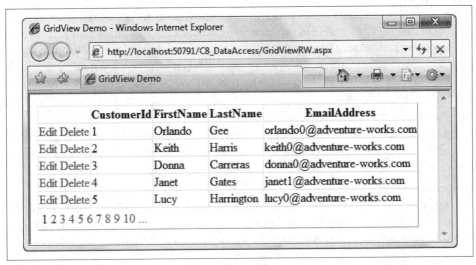

Figure 8-18. Enabling edit and delete actions on a GridView

However, as you saw in the *DetailsViewRW* example, which enabled editing and deletion on a DetailsView control, ASP.NET doesn't do a good job of figuring out which columns a user should be allowed to change, or indeed how to deal with the constraints of the database itself. To work around these problems, you can set AutoGenerateColumns to false and manually set up the columns generated by the GridView in the same way you can manually add rows to a DetailsView. The two methods for achieving this are also the same: writing them in directly in the page's markup, or using the dialogs in the Smart Tag menu. In this instance, you have a choice of Add Columns, which helps you set the minimum properties necessary to populate a column; and Edit Columns, which gives you access to all the options. With the exception of the names, the dialogs presented after clicking these two links are the same as those shown earlier in Figures 8-9 and 8-10, respectively.

You can add seven field types to the GridView's Columns collection. All use the HeaderText property to identify themselves in the header row of the table.

BoundField

> The standard column type used when columns are generated automatically by the GridView. Use the DataField property to set the name of the field to be bound to this column. Unless ReadOnly is set to true, this column type will allow a user to alter its contents and save them to the database in edit mode.

CheckBoxField

> Works like the BoundField, except it should be bound only to a Boolean field in the database and will be rendered as a checkbox. Again, this field is read/write by default.

HyperLinkField

> Extends the BoundField to render (a combination of) fields as hyperlinks in the DetailsView. The DataField property is used to set the text shown on-screen, and the HyperlinkDataField property is used to bind a field to the URL for the hyperlink. Alternatively, the text shown or the URL can be given constant values with the Text and NavigateUrl properties, respectively. A HyperlinkField is read-only in all three edit modes.

ButtonField

> Adds a column to the GridView containing a link or button for hooking up to one of the five standard commands: Cancel, Edit, Delete, Update, and Select. Compare and contrast this to the CommandField.

CommandField

> Adds a column to the GridView containing some or none of the following commands: Delete, Edit/Update, Select, and Cancel. These predefined buttons change their command types depending on the current mode of the DetailsView. Buttons defined in ButtonFields do not.

ImageField

> Adds a column that uses an HTML <img> tag to display an image stored somewhere online (not in the database). The DataField property binds to the name of the image stored in the database and can be formatted into a valid URL using the DataImageUrlFormatString property.

TemplateField

> The most flexible of all fields. The TemplateField lets you define the behavior of the column in each of read-only and edit modes using its <ItemTemplate> and <EditItemTemplate> subelements.

To demonstrate, Example 8-8 shows the code for the *DetailsViewCustomRows.aspx* example discussed earlier, adapted to work with a GridView. The code relating to the addition of a customer has been removed as the GridView doesn't support that. Aside from removing the data source's InsertCommand property and InsertParameters collection, the only change to the markup is the swap from using a DetailsView to a GridView—its Columns collection contains exactly the same fields as the previous example, with the exception of the Password field, which was used only for adding records and thus is deleted. The GridView properties not used in *GridView.aspx* are highlighted.

Example 8-8. GridViewCustomRows.aspx (abridged)

```
<%@ Page Language="C#" AutoEventWireup="true"
    CodeFile="GridViewCustomRows.aspx.cs"
    Inherits="GridViewCustomRows" %>

<!DOCTYPE html PUBLIC "-//W3C//DTD XHTML 1.0 Transitional//EN"
    "http://www.w3.org/TR/xhtml1/DTD/xhtml1-transitional.dtd">
<html xmlns="http://www.w3.org/1999/xhtml">
<head runat="server">
    <title>GridView Custom Rows Demo</title>
</head>
<body>
    <form id="form1" runat="server">
    <div>
        <asp:SqlDataSource ID="dsCustomers" runat="server"
            ConnectionString="<%$ ConnectionStrings:AWLTConnection %>"
            SelectCommand=" ... "
            UpdateCommand=" ... ">
            <UpdateParameters>
                ...
            </UpdateParameters>
        </asp:SqlDataSource>
        <asp:GridView ID="gvwCustomers" runat="server"
            AllowPaging="True"
            AutoGenerateColumns="False"
            DataSourceID="dsCustomers" DataKeyNames="CustomerID"
            onrowediting="gvwCustomers_RowEditing"
            onrowcancelingedit="gvwCustomers_RowCancelingEdit"
            onrowupdated="gvwCustomers_RowUpdated">
            <PagerSettings FirstPageText="First"
                LastPageText="Last" PageButtonCount="5" />
            <EmptyDataTemplate>
                No customers found I&#8217;m afraid
            </EmptyDataTemplate>
            <Columns>
                ...
            </Columns>
        </asp:GridView>
    </div>
    </form>
</body>
</html>
```

The GridView control has no onModeChanged event, so to toggle the display of columns required for read-only and edit modes, the three GridView events related to editing data are handled instead. RowEditing denotes the user wants to edit the selected row, and RowCancelingEdit and RowUpdated cover the two ways a user can end the editing session and return to read-only mode. Example 8-9 shows the code-behind page in full.

Example 8-9. GridViewCustomRows.aspx.cs in full

```
using System.Web.UI;
using System.Web.UI.WebControls;

public partial class GridViewCustomRows : Page
{

    protected void gvwCustomers_RowEditing(
        object sender, GridViewEditEventArgs e)
    {
        SwitchVisibleColumns(false);
    }

    protected void gvwCustomers_RowCancelingEdit(
        object sender, GridViewCancelEditEventArgs e)
    {
        SwitchVisibleColumns(true);
    }

    protected void gvwCustomers_RowUpdated(
        object sender, GridViewUpdatedEventArgs e)
    {
        SwitchVisibleColumns(true);
    }

    private void SwitchVisibleColumns(bool inReadOnlyMode)
    {
        gvwCustomers.Columns[1].Visible = inReadOnlyMode;    //FullName
        gvwCustomers.Columns[2].Visible = !inReadOnlyMode;   //NameStyle
        gvwCustomers.Columns[3].Visible = !inReadOnlyMode;   //Title
        gvwCustomers.Columns[4].Visible = !inReadOnlyMode;   //FirstName
        gvwCustomers.Columns[5].Visible = !inReadOnlyMode;   //MiddleName
        gvwCustomers.Columns[6].Visible = !inReadOnlyMode;   //LastName
        gvwCustomers.Columns[7].Visible = !inReadOnlyMode;   //Suffix
        gvwCustomers.Columns[12].Visible = inReadOnlyMode;   //ModifiedDate
        gvwCustomers.Columns[13].Visible = inReadOnlyMode;   //PasswordHash
        gvwCustomers.Columns[14].Visible = inReadOnlyMode;   //PasswordSalt
    }
}
```

Figures 8-19 and 8-20 show the GridView in read-only and edit modes, respectively.

To conclude this section, Table 8-13 lists all the events the GridView exposes.

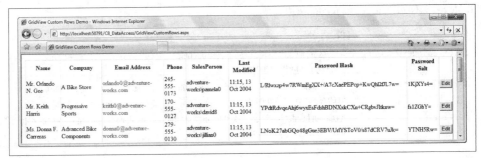

Figure 8-19. GridViewCustomRows.aspx in read-only mode

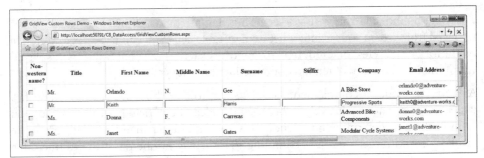

Figure 8-20. GridViewCustomRows.aspx in edit mode

Table 8-13. GridView events

Event	Occurs when...
PageIndexChanged	A link is clicked in the pager row and the page change has been made.
PageIndexChanging	A link is clicked in the pager row but before the page change has been made.
RowCancelingEdit	The Cancel button has been clicked to exit edit mode but before edit mode has actually been exited.
RowCommand	Any command button in the GridView is clicked.
RowCreated	A row is created in the GridView.
RowDataBound	Data has been bound into a row in the GridView from the data source.
RowDeleted	A row's Delete button has been clicked and the row has been deleted.
RowDeleting	A row's Delete button has been clicked but before the row has been deleted.
RowEditing	A row's Edit button has been clicked but before edit mode has been entered.
RowUpdated	A row's Update button has been clicked and the row has been updated.
RowUpdating	A row's Update button has been clicked but before the row has been updated.
SelectedIndexChanged	A row's Select button has been clicked and the GridView's SelectedIndex property has been changed.

Table 8-13. GridView events (continued)

Event	Occurs when...
SelectedIndexChanging	A row's Select button has been clicked but before the GridView's SelectedIndex property has been changed.
Sorted	A column header has been clicked to re-sort the table data on that column, and the data has been re-sorted accordingly.
Sorting	A column header has been clicked to sort the table data on that column but before the data has been re-sorted accordingly.

Templated Controls

The data-bound controls you've seen thus far all tightly bind individual values retrieved from a data source into a list item or table cell. You can use a TemplateField (within a DetailsView or GridView) to control exactly how that value is displayed within that cell, but it will remain contained within that cell.

ASP.NET provides a complementary set of controls to those we've covered so far, which use templates exclusively to broaden the idea of one field per cell. Instead, you can use them to determine how whole rows of data rather than just fields are to be displayed. And rather than just confining that display of one data row to one table cell or one list item, two of the controls go a step further and allow you to define templates for the HTML markup that will surround the data.

- The DataList control's templates define how a row of data will be shown within a list of data.
- The FormView control's templates define how a row of data is shown on its own page, akin to the DetailsView.
- The Repeater and ListView controls are "lookless." Templates for these controls let you control everything regarding how rows of data are displayed and within which structure.

Table 8-14 summarizes the differences between the four controls and the GridView for comparison.

Table 8-14. Comparing template controls and the GridView

Feature	GridView	DataList	FormView	Repeater	ListView
Table layout	Yes	Yes	Yes	No	No
Flow layout	No	Yes	No	Yes	Yes
Column layout	No	Yes	No	No	No
Style properties	Yes	Yes	Yes	No	No
Templates	Columns/ optional	Yes	Rows/optional	Yes	Yes

Table 8-14. Comparing template controls and the GridView (continued)

Feature	GridView	DataList	FormView	Repeater	ListView
Select/edit/delete	Yes	Yes	Yes	No	Yes
Insert	No	No	Yes	No	Yes
Sort	Yes	No	No	No	Yes
Paging	Yes	No	Yes	No	Yes

 The ListView is a new control for ASP.NET 3.5.

DataList Control

The toolbox provides a DataList control for creating templated lists of data. Or rather, the DataList's templates define how a row of data will be shown as an item in a list of data. Seven different templates are available for defining the appearance of a DataList control, and they are listed in Table 8-15. Of those templates, all but the ItemTemplate are optional.

Table 8-15. DataList templates

Template name	Description
AlternatingItemTemplate	Provides content and layout for every other item. If not defined, the ItemTemplate will be used for every item in the DataList.
EditItemTemplate	Provides content and layout for the item currently being edited. If not defined, the ItemTemplate will be used for the currently edited item.
FooterTemplate	Provides content and layout for the footer. If not defined, the DataList will not have a footer.
HeaderTemplate	Provides content and layout for the header. If not defined, the DataList will not have a header.
ItemTemplate	Required. Default definition for every item's content and layout.
SelectedItemTemplate	Provides content and layout for the currently selected item. If not defined, the ItemTemplate will be used.
SeparatorTemplate	Provides content and layout for the separator between items. If not defined, item separators will not be used.

To demonstrate templating at work, add to your *C8_DataAccess* website a new web form called *DataList.aspx*. Drag a SqlDataSource control onto the page and use it to select just the first 10 CustomerID values from the SalesLT.Customer table. Now drag a DataList control onto the page and set its data source to the one you just created. If you're in Design view, you'll see that the control tells you to start editing its templates, as shown in Figure 8-21.

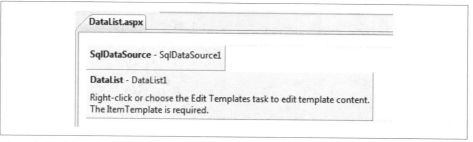

Figure 8-21. A DataList without any templates

Switch to Source view and add the four templates and styles highlighted in Example 8-10. Also, set the DataList's GridLines property to Horizontal.

> A quick way to generate a template showing all the fields in the SELECT statement is to attach the DataSource to the DataList in the latter's Smart Tag menu and then click Refresh Schema in the same menu.

Example 8-10. The basic markup for DataList.aspx

```
<%@ Page Language="C#" AutoEventWireup="true"
    CodeFile="DataList.aspx.cs" Inherits="DataList" %>

<!DOCTYPE html PUBLIC "-//W3C//DTD XHTML 1.0 Transitional//EN"
    "http://www.w3.org/TR/xhtml1/DTD/xhtml1-transitional.dtd">
<html xmlns="http://www.w3.org/1999/xhtml">
<head runat="server">
    <title>Simple DataList Demo</title>
</head>

<body>
    <form id="form1" runat="server">
    <div>
        <asp:SqlDataSource ID="dsCustomers" runat="server"
            ConnectionString="<%$ ConnectionStrings:AWLTConnection %>"
            SelectCommand="SELECT TOP 10 [CustomerID] FROM
              [SalesLT].[Customer] ORDER BY [CustomerID]" />

        <asp:DataList ID="dlCustomers" runat="server"
            GridLines="Horizontal" DataSourceID="dsCustomers">
            <HeaderTemplate>
               The DataList Header
            </HeaderTemplate>
            <FooterTemplate>
               The DataList Footer
            </FooterTemplate>
            <ItemTemplate>
               I: <%# Eval("CustomerID") %>
            </ItemTemplate>
            <AlternatingItemTemplate>
               A: <%# Eval("CustomerID") %>
            </AlternatingItemTemplate>
```

Example 8-10. The basic markup for DataList.aspx (continued)

```
            <AlternatingItemStyle HorizontalAlign="Right" />
            <ItemStyle HorizontalAlign="Left" />
        </asp:DataList>
    </div>
    </form>
</body>
</html>
```

By default, the DataList property renders each list item within a table cell, as you'll see if you run the page and look at the source code sent to the browser. If you want to render rows of data in an actual list, you'll need to use the Repeater or ListView control.

```
<table id="dlCustomers" cellspacing="0" rules="rows"
    border="1" style="border-collapse:collapse;">
    <tr><td>The DataList Header</td></tr>
    <tr><td align="left">I: 1</td></tr>
    <tr><td align="right">A: 2</td></tr>
    <tr><td align="left">I: 3</td></tr>
    <tr><td align="right">A: 4</td></tr>
    <tr><td align="left">I: 5</td></tr>
    <tr><td align="right">A: 6</td></tr>
    <tr><td align="left">I: 7</td></tr>
    <tr><td align="right">A: 10</td></tr>
    <tr><td align="left">I: 11</td></tr>
    <tr><td align="right">A: 12</td></tr>
    <tr><td>The DataList Footer</td></tr>
</table>
```

The alternative is to set the DataList's RepeatLayout property to Flow, whereupon the control renders its items inside <span> elements rather than table cells:

```
<span id="dlCustomers">
    <span>The DataList Header</span><br />
    <span align="left">I: 1</span><br />
    <span align="right">A: 2</span><br />
    <span align="left">I: 3</span><br />
    <span align="right">A: 4</span><br />
    <span align="left">I: 5</span><br />
    <span align="right">A: 6</span><br />
    <span align="left">I: 7</span><br />
    <span align="right">A: 10</span><br />
    <span align="left">I: 11</span><br />
    <span align="right">A: 12</span><br />
    <span>The DataList Footer</span>
</span>
```

You saw earlier in the chapter how you can use the Eval and Bind commands to insert field values directly into a control's property or, in this case, as raw text. To remind you, though, Eval binds the underlying data into the page. Bind does this too, but does not act as a two-way binding in templated controls.

The DataList supports neither paging nor sorting.

Presentation and accessibility

Besides RepeatLayout and GridLines, the DataList has a number of properties to alter the layout and styling of the data to which it is bound. The two properties that have the greatest effect on its layout are:

RepeatColumns
Specifies the number of columns in the table

RepeatDirection
Specifies whether the items fill the table horizontally or vertically

Figure 8-22 shows how these four properties interact, assuming that GridLines is set to Both and RepeatColumns is set to 2.

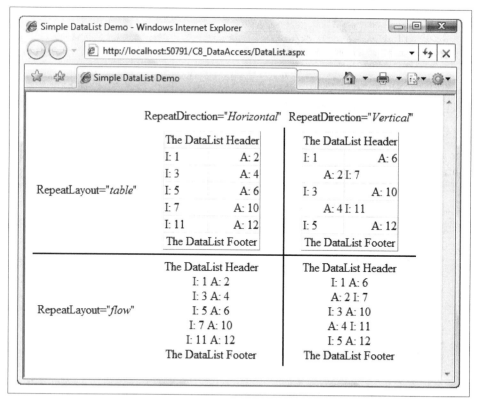

Figure 8-22. RepeatDirection and RepeatLayout

There are several other non-style properties you can use in addition to these four to improve the presentation and accessibility of the data presented by a DataList. Table 8-16 lists them.

Table 8-16. Text and accessibility properties for the DataList

Property	Default	Description
AccessKey	""	Adds a shortcut key to the top of the table by setting the table's accesskey attribute.
Caption	""	Sets the contents of the table's \<caption> element or \<span> if RepeatLayout is set to flow.
RepeatColumns	0	Specifies the number of columns to display.
RepeatDirection	Vertical	If Horizontal, items will be displayed left to right, then top to bottom. If Vertical, items will be displayed top to bottom, then left to right.
RepeatLayout	Table	If Flow, items will be displayed without a table structure; otherwise, they will be displayed with a table structure.
TabIndex	0	Sets the table's tabindex property.
Tooltip	""	Adds and sets the text of a tool tip to the table (the table's title attribute).
UseAccessibleHeader	True	Sets whether the table's header row is rendered in a more accessible fashion.

The DataList also has a number of properties that add a dash of color and style to the table it generates. Some, such as CellPadding and CellSpacing, relate directly to the properties of the HTML \<table> if RepeatLayout is set to table. Others are worth highlighting:

CaptionAlign
  Sets the horizontal or vertical alignment of the \<caption> element set by the Caption property. It is set to NotSet by default, but it can have the value Top, Left, Bottom, or Right.

CssClass
  Sets the CSS class name for either the table or the surrounding span generated by the DataList control.

EnableTheming
  True by default, sets whether styles set in themes will be applied to this control. We cover themes in Chapter 14.

GridLines
  Sets which, if any, grid lines in the table should be visible in the browser. It is set to Both by default, but it can also have the value None, Horizontal, or Vertical.

SkinID
  Sets the skin file that should be used to style the table. See Chapter 14 for more on skins.

ShowFooter

Hides or shows the `FooterTemplate`.

ShowHeader

Hides or shows the `HeaderTemplate`.

Finally, the `DataList` control also provides a common set of style properties for each template, as listed in Table 8-15. For example, the `HeaderTemplate` has a related `HeaderStyle`; the `ItemTemplate` has a related `ItemStyle`, and so on. The Apply Format option in the `DataList`'s Common Tasks menu proffers several predefined style combinations. For example, Figure 8-23 shows a more fully utilized `DataList` modeling the "Black and Blue" theme. You can find this page in the download as *DataListWithStyles.aspx*.

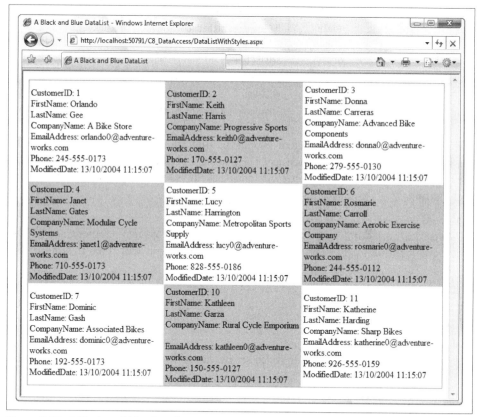

Figure 8-23. A black-and-blue DataList

 You can set all the properties mentioned in this section using the `DataList`'s Property Builder, accessible through its Smart Tag menu.

Selecting, updating, and deleting records

Unlike the DetailsView and GridView controls, enabling the selection, deletion, and editing of a record involves more than just checking the relevant "Enable action" checkbox in the DataList's Smart Tag menu. Instead, the relevant command buttons must be added into the appropriate template for the action. Then, code behind the page must be added manually (as appropriate) to the handlers for those commands that call the update and delete commands in the data source, make changes to the DataList itself, and then rebind the changed data back into the page. It sounds more complex than it is, and to prove it, you'll now reimplement the *GridViewCustomRows.aspx* example using a DataList.

Add a new page to the *C8_DataAccess* website and call it *DataListCustomRows.aspx*. Switch to Source view (if you're not already there) and copy the entire markup for the dsCustomers SqlDataSource object from *GridViewCustomRows.aspx* to this new page. It contains the necessary commands and parameter collections to enable this page.

In Design view, drag a DataList control onto the page. Select dsCustomers as its data source from its Smart Tag menu, and then click Refresh Schema on the same menu. VS2008 will auto-generate a simple ItemTemplate for you to work with.

Switch back to Source view. The DataList shows the currently selected or being-edited record using the ItemTemplate unless superseded by SelectedItemTemplate or EditItemTemplate, respectively, so copy the ItemTemplate in the DataList and paste it twice into the same control. Rename one copy as the SelectedItemTemplate and the other as the EditItemTemplate, as shown in the following code. At the very least, you'll need to add different buttons to the templates to switch back and forth between edit, selected, and read-only modes, so copying the templates at this point is a good move.

```
<asp:DataList ID="DataList1" runat="server"
    DataKeyField="CustomerID" DataSourceID="dsCustomers"
    GridLines="Vertical" RepeatColumns="3" >
    <ItemTemplate>
        ...
    </ItemTemplate>
    <EditItemTemplate>
        ...
    </EditItemTemplate>
    <SelectedItemTemplate>
        ...
    </SelectedItemTemplate>
</asp:DataList>
```

When working with the DetailsView and GridView controls, you had to write some code behind the page to toggle which fields were visible and which were not in edit or read-only mode. All this is taken care of in the markup for templated controls, of course, so you can go ahead and delete the code for the following fields from the ItemTemplate and SelectedItemTemplate:

- CustomerID
- NameStyleTitle
- FirstName
- MiddleName
- LastName
- Suffix

You can also change the Label control in the EmailAddress into a Hyperlink control as well. Now delete the following fields from the EditItemTemplate:

- CustomerID
- FullName
- ModifiedDate
- PasswordHash
- PasswordSalt

 You can find the justification for these modifications in "Manually Setting the Contents of the Control," earlier in this chapter.

Selecting a record. The ListControl provides support for selecting, editing, and deleting items in place. All three actions require you to add a Button control for that particular action to the ItemTemplate and then setting its CommandName property to Select, Edit, or Delete, respectively.

 The CommandNames here are case-sensitive.

To enable the selection of an item in the ListView, you'll add one Button control with the CommandName "Select" to the ItemTemplate and another Button control with the CommandName "Cancel" to the SelectedItemTemplate to deselect it:

```
<asp:DataList ID="DataList1" runat="server"
    DataKeyField="CustomerID" DataSourceID="dsCustomers"
    OnCancelCommand="DataList1_CancelCommand"
    OnSelectedIndexChanged="DataList1_SelectedIndexChanged">
    <ItemTemplate>
        ...
        <asp:Button runat="server"
            ID="btnSelect" Text="Select" CommandName="Select" />
    </ItemTemplate>
```

```
    <SelectedItemTemplate>
        ...
        <asp:Button runat="server"
            ID="btnCancelSelect" Text="Deselect" CommandName="Cancel" />
    </SelectedItemTemplate>
</asp:DataList>
<asp:Label ID="lblInfo" runat="server" />
```

When you run this page after adding the buttons, clicking Select will mark that record as selected and will display it using the SelectedItemTemplate and SelectedItemStyle if they have been defined. But note that the data will need to be rebound to the data source for the contents of the SelectedItemTemplate to be displayed correctly. You could achieve this by handling the DataList's ItemCommand event and seeing whether a SELECT command was initiated, or, as highlighted in the following code, by handling the control's SelectedIndexChanged event. The details and contents of the selected record will then be available using the properties listed in Table 8-17.

```
protected void DataList1_SelectedIndexChanged(
    object sender, EventArgs e)
{
    StringBuilder info = new StringBuilder();
    info.AppendFormat("You are viewing record {0} of {1} <br />",
        DataList1.SelectedIndex.ToString(),
        DataList1.Items.Count.ToString());
    info.AppendFormat("You are viewing record {0} of {1} <br />",
        DataList1.SelectedIndex.ToString(), DataList1.DataKeys.Count);

    info.Append("Using DataKey<br />");
    info.AppendFormat("{0} : {1}<br />", DataList1.DataKeyField,
        DataList1.SelectedValue.ToString());

    lblInfo.Text = info.ToString();

    DataList1.DataBind();
}
```

Table 8-17. DataList properties for retrieving selected records

Property	Type	Description
DataKeyField	String	The fields to be returned in a DataKey for the selected row. Typically used to identify primary key values.
DataKeys	DataKeyArray	The collection of DataKeys for all the records in the DataList.
SelectedIndex	Integer	The zero-based index of the selected item in the list.
SelectedItem	DataListItem	The currently selected item in the DataList.
SelectedValue	Object	The value of the first named DataKeyField in the currently selected item.

To deselect a record in the ListView, it is not enough to simply add a Cancel button to the SelectedItemTemplate and have the user click it. You must also reset the

ListItem's SelectedIndex property to -1 in its CancelCommand event handler and rebind the data back to the control again:

```
protected void DataList1_CancelCommand(
    object source, DataListCommandEventArgs e)
{
    DataList1.EditItemIndex = -1;
    DataList1.SelectedIndex = -1;
    lblInfo.Text = "";

    DataList1.DataBind();
}
```

Updating a record. To enable the editing of data, first you must add an UDPATE command to the DataSource that supplies the DataList. Then there are two changes to make to your ListItem. First, add an EditItemTemplate to your DataList. You can do this by copying the ItemTemplate and pasting it as EditItemTemplate into your markup file (unfortunately, you cannot use drag and drop to add an EditItemTemplate), and then using search and replace (within the selected EditItemTemplate) to replace Label with Textbox (replace the control and the ID). You'll also need to add two buttons: one with CommandName set to Update and one set to Cancel the update and go back to read-only mode.

```
<EditItemTemplate>
    NameStyle: <asp:CheckBox ID="NameStyleCheckBox" runat="server"
        Checked='<%# Bind("NameStyle") %>' />
    <br />
    Title: <asp:TextBox ID="TitleTextBox" runat="server"
        Text='<%# Bind("Title") %>' />
    <br />
    FirstName: <asp:TextBox ID="FirstNameTextBox" runat="server"
        Text='<%# Bind("FirstName") %>' />
    <br />
    MiddleName: <asp:TextBox ID="MiddleNameTextBox" runat="server"
        Text='<%# Bind("MiddleName") %>' />
    <br />
    LastName: <asp:TextBox ID="LastNameTextBox" runat="server"
        Text='<%# Bind("LastName") %>' />
    <br />
    Suffix: <asp:TextBox ID="SuffixTextBox" runat="server"
        Text='<%# Bind("Suffix") %>' />
    <br />
    CompanyName: <asp:TextBox ID="CompanyNameTextBox" runat="server"
        Text='<%# Bind("CompanyName") %>' />
    <br />
    SalesPerson: <asp:TextBox ID="SalesPersonTextBox" runat="server"
        Text='<%# Bind("SalesPerson") %>' />
    <br />
    EmailAddress: <asp:TextBox ID="EmailAddressTextBox" runat="server"
        Text='<%# Bind("EmailAddress") %>' />
    <br />
```

```
Phone: <asp:TextBox ID="PhoneTextBox" runat="server"
    Text='<%# Bind("Phone") %>' />
<br />
<asp:Button runat="server" ID="btnUpdate" Text="Update"
    CommandName="Update" />
<asp:Button runat="server" ID="btnCancel" Text="Cancel"
    CommandName="Cancel" />
</EditItemTemplate>
```

Second, you must provide a way to enter edit mode from your existing ItemTemplate. The easiest way is to add a button to the ItemTemplate. Set the button's CommandName attribute to Edit to cause the list to fire the EditCommand event, for which you can then create a handler:

```
<ItemTemplate>
    ...
    <asp:Button runat="server" ID="btnSelect" Text="Select"
        CommandName="Select" />
    <asp:Button runat="server" ID="btnEdit" Text="Edit"
        CommandName="Edit" />
</ItemTemplate>
```

The EditCommand event handler receives a DataListCommandEventArgs object as its second parameter. The DataListCommandEventArgs contains an Item property, representing the list item the user wants to edit. The DataListItem returned by the Item property has an ItemIndex property, which you'll assign to the EditItemIndex property of the DataList. You'll then rebind the DataList:

```
protected void DataList1_EditCommand(
    object source, DataListCommandEventArgs e)
{
    DataList1.SelectedIndex = -1;
    DataList1.EditItemIndex = e.Item.ItemIndex;
    DataBind();
}
```

As you can see, it sounds harder than it is. Once the user has changed any record details required and clicked the Update button, you'll need to handle the DataList's UpdateCommand event to retrieve the values from the controls in the EditItemTemplate and assign them to the SqlDataSource's update parameters, and then call UPDATE on the DataSource. Finally, you'll need to rebind the data to the control again.

```
protected void DataList1_UpdateCommand(
    object source, DataListCommandEventArgs e)
{
    dsCustomers.UpdateParameters["CustomerID"].DefaultValue =
        (DataList1.DataKeys[e.Item.ItemIndex]).ToString();
    dsCustomers.UpdateParameters["NameStyle"].DefaultValue =
        ((CheckBox)e.Item.FindControl("NameStyleTextBox")).Checked.ToString();
    dsCustomers.UpdateParameters["Title"].DefaultValue =
        ((TextBox)e.Item.FindControl("TitleTextBox")).Text;
    dsCustomers.UpdateParameters["FirstName"].DefaultValue =
        ((TextBox)e.Item.FindControl("FirstNameTextBox")).Text;
```

```
dsCustomers.UpdateParameters["MiddleName"].DefaultValue =
    ((TextBox)e.Item.FindControl("MiddleNameTextBox")).Text;
dsCustomers.UpdateParameters["LastName"].DefaultValue =
    ((TextBox)e.Item.FindControl("LastNameTextBox")).Text;
dsCustomers.UpdateParameters["Suffix"].DefaultValue =
    ((TextBox)e.Item.FindControl("SuffixTextBox")).Text;
dsCustomers.UpdateParameters["CompanyName"].DefaultValue =
    ((TextBox)e.Item.FindControl("CompanyNameTextBox")).Text;
dsCustomers.UpdateParameters["SalesPerson"].DefaultValue =
    ((TextBox)e.Item.FindControl("SalesPersonTextBox")).Text;
dsCustomers.UpdateParameters["EmailAddress"].DefaultValue =
    ((TextBox)e.Item.FindControl("EmailAddressTextBox")).Text;
dsCustomers.UpdateParameters["Phone"].DefaultValue =
    ((TextBox)e.Item.FindControl("PhoneTextBox")).Text;

dsCustomers.Update();

DataList1.EditItemIndex = -1;
DataBind();
}
```

Deleting a record. To allow your user to delete a record from a DataList, first you'll need to add a DeleteCommand to your DataSource control:

```
<asp:SqlDataSource ID="dsCustomers" runat="server"
    ConnectionString="<%$ ConnectionStrings:AWLTConnection %>"
    DeleteCommand="
     DELETE FROM [SalesLT].[Customer] WHERE [CustomerID] = @CustomerID"
    ...>
    <DeleteParameters>
        <asp:Parameter Name="CustomerID" Type="Int32" />
    </DeleteParameters>
    ...
</asp:SqlDataSource>
```

With this done, add a Delete button to the ItemTemplate:

```
<ItemTemplate>
    ...
    <asp:Button runat="server" ID="btnSelect"
        Text="Select" CommandName="Select" />
    <asp:Button runat="server" ID="btnEdit"
        Text="Edit" CommandName="Edit" />
    <asp:Button runat="server" ID="btnDelete"
        Text="Delete" CommandName="Delete" />
</ItemTemplate>
```

When a user clicks this button, the DataList's DeleteCommand event is fired. Its handler has five steps:

1. Get the record ID from the selected record (the one whose Delete button was clicked).

2. Get the parameter from the Parameters collection of the new data source object.

3. Set the parameter's `DefaultValue` to the record ID of the record to be deleted.

4. Call `DELETE` on the data source.

5. Rebind the `DataList`.

These steps are performed with the following code:

```
protected void DataList1_DeleteCommand(
    object source, DataListCommandEventArgs e)
{
    // (1) Get the recordID from the selected item
    string recordID = (DataList1.DataKeys[e.Item.ItemIndex]).ToString( );

    // (2) Get a reference to the customerID parameter
    Parameter param = dsCustomers.DeleteParameters["CustomerID"];

    // (3) Set the parameter's default value to the value for
    // the record to delete
    param.DefaultValue = recordID;

    // (4) Delete the record
    dsCustomers.Delete( );

    // (5) Rebind the list
    DataBind( );
}
```

Note how step 1 retrieves the `CustomerID` of the record to be deleted. You cannot use the `DataList`'s `SelectedValue` property here, even if its `DataKeyField` is set to `CustomerID`, because clicking the Edit button does not also select the item to be deleted. You still use the `DataKeys` collection to retrieve the `CustomerID`, but now you must retrieve it through the index of the item for which the Delete button was pressed, which is stored in the `DataListCommandEventArgs` parameter for the event handler.

As demonstrated in the `UpdateCommand` handler, the first three steps here can be expressed in one line of code:

```
dsCustomers.DeleteParameters["CustomerID"].DefaultValue =
    (DataList1.DataKeys[e.Item.ItemIndex]).ToString( );
```

 Don't forget that most likely your attempt to delete one of the existing records in the AdventureWorksLT database will fail because the database will not let you delete any customer records with orders attached to them.

FormView Control

The fully templated alternative to the `DetailsView` control is the `FormView`. They share almost all the same properties as listed previously in Tables 8-5 through 8-8, but rather than a `Fields` collection and a set of `Style` properties for those fields, the

FormView has the templates listed in Table 8-18 for you to define. The FormView also supports the addition of new records into a table, just as the DetailsView does.

Table 8-18. FormView templates

Template name	Description
EditItemTemplate	Provides content and layout for the item currently being edited. If not defined, the ItemTemplate will be used for the currently edited item.
EmptyDataTemplate	Provides content to be shown when there is no data to be bound into the FormView.
FooterTemplate	Provides content and layout for the footer. If not defined, the FormView will not have a footer.
HeaderTemplate	Provides content and layout for the header. If not defined, the FormView will not have a header.
InsertItemTemplate	Provides the form layout for the insertion of a new record into the database.
ItemTemplate	Required. Default definition for every item's content and layout.
PagerTemplate	Provides the layout and content for the FormView's pager row.

Indeed, the FormView supports exactly the same events as the DetailsView, so re-creating a page that replaces a DetailsView with a FormView is mostly a matter of making sure the FormView templates match the design of the DesignView and that the various IDs of the controls shown in the various templates match up.

 You can find an example of using the FormView in the code download for this chapter.

Repeater Control

The Repeater control provides a subset of the functionality of the DataList that was described earlier and, until the ListView was introduced in ASP.NET 3.5, was used to present data on a page if none of the other controls could manage it.

- On the one hand, it provides no support for selecting, editing, deleting, or adding data to a data source. It is read-only.
- On the other hand, it is "lookless." It adds no markup to the page other than the markup you specify in your templates. It is totally transparent in that respect.

The Repeater control has only five templates, listed in Table 8-19.

Table 8-19. Repeater templates

Template name	Description
AlternatingItemTemplate	Used as you would the item template; however, the alternating item is rendered for every other row in the control.
FooterTemplate	Elements to render after all items and other templates have been rendered.
HeaderTemplate	Elements to render before any other templates are rendered.

Table 8-19. Repeater templates (continued)

Template name	Description
ItemTemplate	Elements rendered once for each row in the data source.
SeparatorTemplate	Elements to render between each row in the data source.

Note there is no pager template, nor any for editing or inserting data. These five templates combine to define how data is presented on-screen only. If that involves the data being bound into text boxes for editing, that editing and subsequent update or addition to the data source must be implemented using some of the techniques shown in the previous examples or using the techniques shown in Chapter 9.

To demonstrate, add to the website a new page called *Repeater.aspx*. You'll use a Repeater to create a simple, unordered HTML list and add to it a SqlDataSource control which returns the first 10 CustomerIDs and customer names from the [SalesLT]. [Customer] table in the AdventureWorksLT database. Now add a Repeater control to the page. Note that aside from assigning a SqlDataSource to the Repeater in its Common Tasks menu, you must do everything else in source code. Switch to Source view and fill out the templates for the Repeater, as shown in Example 8-11.

Example 8-11. Repeater.aspx.cs in full

```
<%@ Page Language="C#" AutoEventWireup="true"
    CodeFile="Repeater.aspx.cs" Inherits="Repeater" %>

<!DOCTYPE html PUBLIC "-//W3C//DTD XHTML 1.0 Transitional//EN"
    "http://www.w3.org/TR/xhtml1/DTD/xhtml1-transitional.dtd">
<html xmlns="http://www.w3.org/1999/xhtml">
<head runat="server">
    <title>Repeater Demo</title>
</head>

<body>
    <form id="form1" runat="server">
    <div>
        <asp:SqlDataSource ID="SqlDataSource1" runat="server"
            ConnectionString="<%$ ConnectionStrings:AWLTConnection %>"
            SelectCommand="
                select top 10 CustomerID, FirstName, LastName
                    from [SalesLT].Customer order by CustomerID" />
        <asp:Repeater ID="Repeater1" runat="server"
            DataSourceID="SqlDataSource1">
            <HeaderTemplate>
                <ul>
            </HeaderTemplate>
            <ItemTemplate>
                <li>
                    <%# Eval("CustomerID") %>: <%# Eval("FirstName") %>
                    <%# Eval("LastName") %>
                </li>
            </ItemTemplate>
```

Example 8-11. Repeater.aspx.cs in full (continued)

```
            <FooterTemplate>
                </ul>
            </FooterTemplate>
        </asp:Repeater>
    </div>
    </form>
</body>
</html>
```

If you run this page and look at the source code for it, you'll see that there really is no additional code added, as there is, for example, in a DetailsView or a GridView:

```
<ul>
    <li>1: Orlando Gee</li>
    <li>2: Keith Harris</li>
    <li>3: Donna Carreras</li>
    <li>4: Janet Gates</li>
    <li>5: Lucy Harrington</li>
    <li>6: Rosmarie Carroll</li>
    <li>7: Dominic Gash</li>
    <li>10: Kathleen Garza</li>
    <li>11: Katherine Harding</li>
    <li>12: Johnny Caprio</li>
</ul>
```

Table 8-20 lists all the Repeater methods, properties, and events besides the templates already listed in Table 8-19.

Table 8-20. Repeater members

Name	Type	Description
DataBind	Method	Binds the contents of the Repeater to the data source
Controls	Property	The collection of child controls within the Repeater
DataMember	Property	The name of the table to use in the data source if it has more than one table
DataSource	Property	The data source being used to populate the Repeater
DataSourceID	Property	The ID of the data source being used to populate the Repeater
EnableTheming	Property	Indicates whether any themes are applied to the control
Items	Property	The collection of Items (rows of data) bound into the repeater
ItemCommand	Event	Occurs when a button is clicked in the Repeater control
ItemCreated	Event	Occurs when a new item is added to the Repeater but before data binding
ItemDataBound	Event	Occurs after an item has been data-bound but before it is rendered to the screen

ListView Control

Introduced as one of the new controls in ASP.NET 3.5, the ListView takes all the functionality of the DataList control, adds the template-only-based approach of the Repeater for presentation, and tops it off with the ability to add items to the database directly. It really is the one data-bound control that currently has it all.

As with the other templated controls, the ListView contains an ItemTemplate with which you define how the contents of a data record returned by a DataSource control are displayed on-screen. Defining this template is mandatory or the page will not build. It also has a second mandatory template—the LayoutTemplate—which defines whether any markup should surround that generated by the ItemTemplates. It's easiest to think of it as a combination of the HeaderTemplate and FooterTemplate from other controls. The LayoutTemplate also takes a cue from ASP.NET master pages and uses a Placeholder control to indicate where in the layout the ItemTemplates should be placed.

To demonstrate, add to the chapter's website a new page called *ListView.aspx* and add a SqlDataSource control to it that returns just the first 10 CustomerID values from the Customer table in the AdventureWorksLT database. Now drag a ListView control onto the page. You'll see that in Design view, VS2008 first prompts you to select a data source for the ListView and then to add a LayoutTemplate and an ItemTemplate. Switch to Source view and add the code shown in Example 8-12.

Example 8-12. The bare minimum ListView

```
<%@ Page Language="C#" AutoEventWireup="true"
   CodeFile="ListView.aspx.cs" Inherits="ListView" %>

<!DOCTYPE html PUBLIC "-//W3C//DTD XHTML 1.0 Transitional//EN"
   "http://www.w3.org/TR/xhtml1/DTD/xhtml1-transitional.dtd">

<html xmlns="http://www.w3.org/1999/xhtml">
<head runat="server">
    <title>ListView Demo</title>
</head>

<body>
    <form id="form1" runat="server">
    <div>
       <asp:SqlDataSource ID="dsCustomers" runat="server"
          ConnectionString="<%$ ConnectionStrings:AWLTConnection %>"
          SelectCommand="
             SELECT TOP 10 [CustomerID] FROM [SalesLT].[Customer]
             ORDER BY [CustomerID]">
       </asp:SqlDataSource>

       <asp:ListView ID="ListView1"
          runat="server" DataSourceID="dsCustomers">
          <LayoutTemplate>
            <table class="LayoutTemplate" border="1">
               <tr>
               <asp:PlaceHolder runat="server" ID="itemPlaceholder" />
               </tr>
            </table>
          </LayoutTemplate>
          <ItemTemplate>
            <td><%# Eval("CustomerID") %></td>
```

Example 8-12. The bare minimum ListView (continued)

```
            </ItemTemplate>
        </asp:ListView>

    </div>
    </form>
</body>
</html>
```

If you run this page and look at the source code generated, you'll see that the control produces just the markup specified in the templates, much like the Repeater control:

```
<table class="LayoutTemplate" border="1">
  <tr>
    <td>1</td>
    <td>2</td>
    <td>3</td>
    <td>4</td>
    <td>5</td>
    <td>6</td>
    <td>7</td>
    <td>10</td>
    <td>11</td>
    <td>12</td>
  </tr>
</table>
```

One problem with the Repeater control that the ListView addresses is its inability to generate tables with more than one row or column in the way you could with a DataList control (using its RepeatColumns property) or nested lists, which no ASP.NET 2.0 control can do with ease.

Toward this end, the ListView has a GroupTemplate that defines the markup to surround a group of items and a GroupItemCount property that specifies the number of items in a group. Aside from adding this template and property to the ListView definition, the only other tweak is to change the name of the placeholder so that the LayoutTemplate contains the GroupTemplate, which contains the ItemTemplate, as highlighted in the following code:

```
<asp:ListView ID="ListView1" runat="server" DataSourceID="dsCustomers"
    GroupItemCount="3">
    <LayoutTemplate>
        <table class="LayoutTemplate" border="1">
            <asp:PlaceHolder runat="server" ID="groupPlaceholder" />
        </table>
    </LayoutTemplate>

    <GroupTemplate>
        <tr class="GroupTemplate">
            <asp:PlaceHolder runat="server" ID="itemPlaceholder" />
        </tr>
    </GroupTemplate>
```

```
<ItemTemplate>
    <td><%# Eval("CustomerID") %></td>
</ItemTemplate>
</asp:ListView>
```

Running the page again, you can see the difference onscreen and in the source code straight away:

```
<table class="LayoutTemplate" border="1">
  <tr class="GroupTemplate">
    <td>1</td>
    <td>2</td>
    <td>3</td>
  </tr>
  <tr class="GroupTemplate">
    <td>4</td>
    <td>5</td>
    <td>6</td>
  </tr>
  <tr class="GroupTemplate">
    <td>7</td>
    <td>10</td>
    <td>11</td>
  </tr>
  <tr class="GroupTemplate">
    <td>12</td>
  </tr>
</table>
```

These three templates form the basis for the ListView's presentation of data on-screen and are linked together through the use of Placeholder controls which indicate how one fits into the other (much like Russian dolls). By default, GroupTemplates and ItemTemplates will be inserted into a Placeholder with the IDs groupPlaceholder and itemPlaceholder, respectively, as shown earlier. Should you wish to change the Placeholder's ID, though, you will also need to set the ListView's GroupPlaceholderID or ItemPlaceholderID property to reflect this change. For example:

```
<asp:ListView ID="ListView1" runat="server"
    DataSourceID="dsCustomers" GroupItemCount="3"
    GroupPlaceholderID="AllMyGroups" ItemPlaceholderID="AllMyItems">
    <LayoutTemplate>
        <table class="LayoutTemplate" border="1">
            <asp:PlaceHolder runat="server" ID="AllMyGroups" />
        </table>
    </LayoutTemplate>

    <GroupTemplate>
        <tr class="GroupTemplate">
            <asp:PlaceHolder runat="server" ID="AllMyItems" />
        </tr>
    </GroupTemplate>

    <ItemTemplate>
```

```
            <td><%# Eval("CustomerID") %></td>
        </ItemTemplate>
    </asp:ListView>
```

Eight additional templates are available for use, as listed in Table 8-21.

Table 8-21. Templates for the ListView control

Template name	Description
LayoutTemplate	Required. Provides the content and layout to surround all items (and groups).
GroupTemplate	Provides the content and layout to surround all the items in a group.
GroupSeparatorTemplate	Provides the content and layout for the separator between groups. If not defined, item separators will not be used.
ItemTemplate	Required. Default definition for every item's content and layout.
AlternatingItemTemplate	Provides the content and layout for every other item. If not defined, the ItemTemplate will be used for every item in the DataList.
ItemSeparatorTemplate	Provides the content and layout for the separator between items. If not defined, item separators will not be used.
EmptyDataTemplate	Provides the content to be displayed if no data is bound to the ListView.
EmptyItemTemplate	Provides the content to be displayed if there is no data to be bound into an item—for example, what to display in the 11th and 12th items of a 4 × 3 grid when only 10 items are bound to it.
EditItemTemplate	Provides the content and layout for the item currently being edited. If not defined, the ItemTemplate will be used.
InsertItemTemplate	Provides the layout for a form to add a new item to the data source. If not defined, the ItemTemplate will be used.
SelectedItemTemplate	Provides the content and layout for the currently selected item. If not defined, the ItemTemplate will be used.

Once you've defined a LayoutTemplate and ItemTemplate for a ListView, VS2008 can use them as a basis for creating several more templates if you wish. Simply switch back to Design view and open the ListView's Smart Tag menu, shown in Figure 8-24.

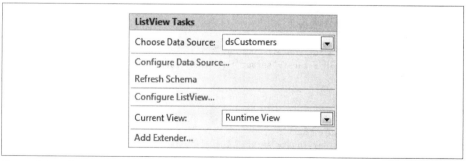

Figure 8-24. The ListView's Smart Tag menu

The Current View drop down lets you switch between editing the Item and LayoutTemplates and seeing how the control will lay out at runtime. Should you click Configure ListView you'll be able to choose among several standard layouts and styles, as shown in Figure 8-25.

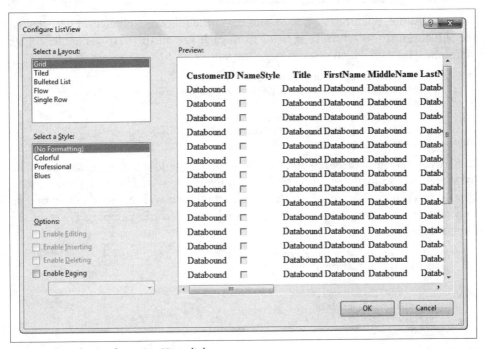

Figure 8-25. The Configure ListView dialog

You can also choose to enable paging on this dialog, as well as enable editing, inserting, and deleting data if your DataSource includes the required commands to do so.

Sorting and paging

The ListView supports the sorting and paging of data just like a GridView. However, the ListView has no predefined way to present a set of links or buttons that invoke paging or sorting, like the GridView has a pager row or links in the column headings. Instead, you must determine where these links will appear in the templates and hook them up to the required functionality.

Fortunately, this last part is quite straightforward. Where the *View controls have a pager row containing links to show various pages of data, the ListView can use the new DataPager control to provide the same functionality.

Likewise, there are two simple ways to add sorting to the ListView:

- By adding a Button control to one of the ListView's templates with the CommandName "Sort"
- By calling the Sort method on the ListView

To demonstrate, open *ListView.aspx* and make the following changes. First, change the SqlDataSource to return four fields from each row in the Customer table to give you some data with which you can page and sort:

```
<asp:SqlDataSource ID="dsCustomers" runat="server"
    ConnectionString="<%$ ConnectionStrings:AWLTConnection %>"
    SelectCommand="
        SELECT [FirstName], [LastName], [EmailAddress],
        [ModifiedDate] FROM [SalesLT].[Customer]">
</asp:SqlDataSource>
```

In between the SqlDataSource and ListView controls, add a DataPager control. The DataPager acts similarly to an AJAX Control Extender in that once it knows which control it is responsible for (set in the PagedControlID) it will restrict the flow of data into that control as pages of data. The number of records per page is set in the PageSize property.

```
<asp:DataPager ID="DataPager1" runat="server"
    PagedControlID="ListView1" PageSize="10">
    <Fields>
        <asp:NextPreviousPagerField  />
        <asp:NumericPagerField  />
    </Fields>
</asp:DataPager>
```

Finally, make a couple of changes to the ListView itself. The ItemTemplate is changed to use the data retrieved by the DataSource control and two buttons are added to the LayoutTemplate to sort the data. The first button, btnSortOnDate, needs no code behind the page with its CommandName property set to Sort and its CommandArgument property set to the field on which the data will be sorted: in this case, ModifiedDate. Clicking this button will switch the sort direction of the data between ascending and descending order.

```
<asp:ListView ID="ListView1" runat="server" DataSourceID="dsCustomers">
    <LayoutTemplate>
        <p>
            <asp:Button ID="btnSortOnDate" runat="server"
                CommandName="Sort" CommandArgument="ModifiedDate"
                Text="Sort on date" />
            <asp:Button ID="btnSortOnLastName" runat="server"
                Text="Sort by Last Name"
                OnClick="btnSortOnLastName_Click"  />
        </p>
        <div id="CustomerReport">
            <asp:PlaceHolder runat="server" ID="itemPlaceholder" />
        </div>
    </LayoutTemplate>
```

```
    <ItemTemplate>
        <p>
            <a href="<%# Eval("EmailAddress", "mailto:{0}") %>">
                <%# Eval("FirstName") %> <%# Eval("LastName") %>
            </a>
            last contacted us on
            <%# Eval("ModifiedDate", "{0:dd MMM yyyy}") %>
        </p>
    </ItemTemplate>
</asp:ListView>
```

The second new button in the `LayoutTemplate`, `btnSortOnLastName`, uses the alternative approach to enable sorting by calling the `ListView`'s `Sort` method in its `OnClick` event handler. The `ListView` exposes two properties, `SortExpression` and `SortDirection`, which let you know on which field the data in the `ListView` is currently sorted, and in which direction. By checking this, the handler makes sure to sort the data by `LastName` in ascending order first if it is sorted on a different field already, and then alternately in ascending and descending order after that.

```
protected void btnSortOnLastName_Click(object sender, EventArgs e)
{
    // Order ascending if data isn't currently ordered by LastName
    if (ListView1.SortExpression != "LastName")
    {
        ListView1.Sort("LastName", SortDirection.Ascending);
    }
    // If it is, change sortdirection
    else
    {
        ListView1.Sort("LastName",
            (ListView1.SortDirection == SortDirection.Ascending ?
                SortDirection.Descending : SortDirection.Ascending));
    }
}
```

 The ternary operator, `?:`, acts as shorthand for an `if...then...else` statement. Therefore, a ? b : c should be read as "if a then b else c."

Run the page now and you'll be able to page and sort the data presented by the `ListView`. As Figure 8-26 shows, the `DataPager` displays the links for navigating through the data as laid out in its `Fields` collection—in this example, a `NextPreviousPagerField` followed by a `NumericPagerField`. You can also use a `TemplatePagerField` within the `DataPager` field to define a custom paging UI if you'd rather not use the standard First, Back, Forward, Last, and page number links.

Figure 8-26 shows the `NextPreviousPagerField` and `NumericPagerField` controls at their default settings, the former showing Previous and Next links and the latter showing links to the first five pages individually and then one for the next five. Their properties closely match those of the `PagerSettings` class in Table 8-6, but are listed here in Tables 8-22 and 8-23, respectively, for easy reference.

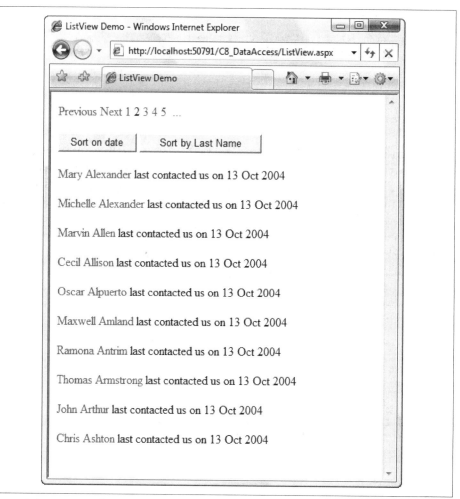

Figure 8-26. Paging and sorting with the ListView

Table 8-22. NextPreviousPagerField properties

Name	Default	Description
ButtonCssClass	" "	The CSS class for the pager buttons.
ButtonType	Link	The type of button control used as pager buttons. Possible values are Link, Image, and Button.
FirstPageImageUrl	" "	The URL to an image to display for the first-page button.
FirstPageText	First	The text to use as the first-page button.
LastPageImageUrl	" "	The URL to an image to display for the last-page button.
LastPageText	Last	The text to use as the last-page button.
NextPageImageUrl	" "	The URL to an image to display for the next-page button.

Table 8-22. NextPreviousPagerField properties (continued)

Name	Default	Description
NextPageText	Next	The text to use as the next-page button.
PreviousPageImageUrl	""	The URL to an image to display for the previous-page button.
PreviousPageText	Previous	The text to use as the previous-page button.
RenderDisbledButtonAsLabels	false	Specifies whether the text of a pager button is rendered as a Label rather than in a button if the button would be disabled.
RenderNonBreakingSpaces-BetweenControls	true	Specifies whether is added between pager buttons so they are always displayed on the same line in the page.
ShowFirstPageButton	false	Specifies whether to display the first-page button.
ShowLastPageButton	false	Specifies whether to display the last-page button.
ShowNextPageButton	true	Specifies whether to display the next-page button.
ShowPreviousPageButton	true	Specifies whether to display the previous-page button.

Table 8-23. NumericPagerField properties

Name	Default	Description
ButtonCount	5	The number of buttons to individual pages to display.
ButtonType	Link	The type of button control used as pager buttons. Possible values are Link, Image, and Button.
CurrentPageLabelCssClass	""	The CSS class to apply to the link representing the current page.
NextPageImageUrl	""	The URL to an image to display for the next-page button.
NextPageText	...	The text to use as the next-page button.
NextPreviousButtonCssClass	""	The CSS class to apply to the next and previous links.
NumericButtonCssClass	""	The CSS class to apply to the numeric page links.
PreviousPageImageUrl	""	The URL to an image to display for the previous-page button.
PreviousPageText	...	The text to use as the previous-page button.
RenderNonBreakingSpacesBetweenControls	true	Specifies whether is added between pager buttons so they are always displayed on the same line in the page.

Selecting, adding, updating, and deleting data in a ListView

The selection of a data record through a ListView control follows exactly the same steps as those we already discussed with the DataList control:

- Add a Select button to the ItemTemplate (CommandName="Select"). When the button is clicked, rebind the data to the control so the SelectedItemTemplate is populated correctly.

- Add a button that deselects the current item to the SelectedItemTemplate (CommandName="Cancel"). When the button is clicked, use the ListView's ItemCanceling event handler to reset its SelectedItemIndex to –1 and rebind the data to the control.

Indeed, it shares the same set of properties for the retrieval of data from the currently selected record as the DataList. You can find these back in Table 8-17.

Editing and deleting data through a ListView also requires the same steps as a DataList:

- Add an Edit button to the ItemTemplate (CommandName="Edit"). When the button is clicked, use the control's ItemCommand event handler to set its EditIndex to the index number of the item containing the button just clicked, and rebind the data to the control so the EditItemTemplate is populated correctly.

- Add an Update button to the EditItemTemplate (CommandName="Update"). When the button is clicked, use the control's ItemUpdating event handler to retrieve the values to update from controls in the EditItemTemplate, assign them to the UpdateParameters specified by the DataSource control, and then call Update( ) on the DataSource. Finally, reset the ListView's EditIndex property to –1 and rebind the data to the control.

- Add a Cancel button to the EditItemTemplate (CommandName="Cancel") to cancel the update and reset the control. When the button is clicked, use the ListView's ItemCommand event handler to reset its EditIndex to –1 and rebind the data to the control.

- Add a Delete button to the ItemTemplate (CommandName="Delete"). When the button is clicked, use the ListView's DeleteCommand event handler to retrieve the primary key(s) of the data item to delete—most likely from the DataKey or SelectedValue property—and assign them to the DeleteParameters specified by the DataSource control. Call Delete( ) on the DataSource and then rebind the data to the ListView.

The Configure ListView dialog in VS2008, shown in Figure 8-25, will set this up for you if you check Enable Deleting and Enable Editing. (They're disabled in the screenshot because an UpdateCommand and a DeleteCommand haven't been added to the DataSource control.) Be warned, however, that checking these options will also cause VS2008 to regenerate most of the ListView's templates based on its LayoutTemplate and ItemTemplate, overwriting any customizations you may have already made. The same is also true of the Enable Inserting checkbox, which adds an InsertItemTemplate to the ListView to allow the addition of new records to the data source.

Again, with respect to the addition of new data, using the ListView requires the same steps as adding new data using a DetailsView or FormView control:

- Make sure the InsertItemTemplate contains places to add all the data required to satisfy the rules of the database. If the field contains values auto-generated by the database (a primary key, a GUID, a modified date), don't let the user try to set them. Either set them in the INSERT statement or let the database do it by itself.

- Add an Insert button to the InsertItemTemplate (CommandName="Insert"). When the button is clicked, use the ListView's ItemInserting event handler to retrieve and generate the values to be added to the database, assign them to the DataSource's InsertParameters collection, and then call Update() on the DataSource. Finally, rebind the data source to the ListView.

- Add a Clear button to the InsertItemTemplate (CommandName="Clear"). When the button is clicked, any values entered into the template from before the click should be cleared.

 The download for this chapter contains a page called *ListViewCustomRows.aspx* that demonstrates all of these rules.

To conclude this chapter, Table 8-24 lists the events the ListView exposes.

Table 8-24. ListView events

Event	Occurs when...
ItemCanceling	The Cancel button has been clicked to exit, edit, or insert mode, but before edit mode has actually been left.
ItemCommand	Any command button in the ListView is clicked.
ItemCreated	An item is created in the ListView.
ItemDeleted	An item's Delete button has been clicked and the item has been deleted from the database.
ItemDeleting	An item's Delete button has been clicked but before the item has been deleted.
ItemEditing	An item's Edit button has been clicked but before edit mode has been entered.
ItemInserted	An item's Insert button has been clicked and the row has been added.
ItemInserting	An item's Insert button has been clicked but before the item has been added.
ItemUpdated	An item's Update button has been clicked and the item has been updated.
ItemUpdating	An item's Update button has been clicked but before the item has been updated.
LayoutCreated	The LayoutTemplate has been created in the ListView control.
PagePropertiesChanged	A paging link (presumably from the related DataPager) has been clicked and the ListView has set its new paging values.
PagePropertiesChanging	A paging link (presumably from the related DataPager) has been clicked but before the ListView has set its new paging values.
SelectedIndexChanged	An item's Select button has been clicked and the ListView's SelectedIndex property has been changed.
SelectedIndexChanging	An item's Select button has been clicked but before the item's SelectedIndex property has been changed.
Sorted	A sort operation has been requested and the data has been re-sorted accordingly.
Sorting	A sort operation has been requested and the data is being re-sorted accordingly.

CHAPTER 9

ADO.NET

For many web applications, you will use the DataSource controls and you need not know anything at all about the underlying "plumbing" that interacts with the database. However, most *serious* commercial applications will have needs that go beyond what a DataSource control can do, and you will then need to dive into the ADO.NET object model to understand how the data source works and how to accomplish more advanced tasks.

To illustrate the utility of understanding the ADO.NET object model, you'll undertake two tasks in this chapter:

- Make use of connection-based transactions.

- Create a business-tier object that mediates between the user-interface level and the database, binding the UI to an instance of ObjectDataSource.

Before you can accomplish either of these tasks, we must back up and examine the ADO.NET object model.

The ADO.NET Object Model

The goal of ADO.NET is to provide a bridge between your objects in ASP.NET and your backend data store. ADO.NET provides an object-oriented view into the database, encapsulating many of the database properties and relationships within ADO.NET objects. Further, and in many ways most important, the ADO.NET objects encapsulate and hide the details of database access; your objects can interact with ADO.NET objects without you knowing or worrying about the details of how the data is moved to and from the database.

An overview of the ADO.NET architecture is shown in Figure 9-1. We will return to the aspects of this figure throughout this chapter.

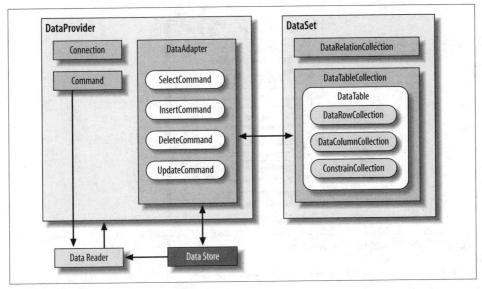

Figure 9-1. ADO.NET architecture diagram

The DataSet Class

The ADO.NET object model is rich, but at its heart it is a fairly straightforward set of classes. One of the key classes is the DataSet (shown in the upper-right corner of Figure 9-1), which is located in the System.Data namespace.

The DataSet represents a rich subset of the entire database, cached in session state or in memory, without a continuous connection to the database. Periodically, you'll reconnect the DataSet to its parent database, which is how you update the database with changes to the DataSet you've made, and update the DataSet with changes in the database made by other processes.

The DataSet doesn't just capture a few rows from a single table, but rather can represent a set of tables with all the metadata necessary to signify the relationships and constraints among the tables recorded in the original database, as shown in Figure 9-2.

The DataSet consists of DataTable objects as well as DataRelation objects. These are accessed as the Tables and Relations properties, respectively, of the DataSet object. The most important methods and properties of the DataSet class are shown in Tables 9-1 and 9-2.

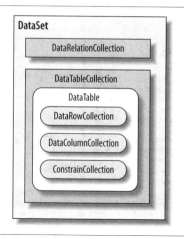

Figure 9-2. The DataSet and its children

Table 9-1. Important DataSet properties (all read-only)

Property name	Type	Description
DefaultViewManager	DataViewManager	Returns a view of the data in the DataSet that allows filtering, searching, and navigation.
HasErrors	Boolean	Returns true if there are any errors in any of the rows of any of the tables.
Relations	DataRelationCollection	Returns a collection of DataRelation objects.
Tables	DataTableCollection	Returns a collection of DataTable objects.

Table 9-2. Important DataSet methods

Method name	Return type	Description
AcceptChanges	void	Accepts all the changes made since the DataSet was loaded or since the last time AcceptChanges was called (see GetChanges).
Clear	void	Clears the DataSet of any data.
GetChanges	DataSet	Returns a copy of the DataSet containing all the changes made since it was loaded or since AcceptChanges was called.
GetXML	String	Returns the XML representation of the data in the DataSet.
GetXMLSchema	String	Returns the XSD schema for the XML representation of the data in the DataSet.
Merge	void	Merges the data in this DataSet with another DataSet. Overloaded.
ReadXML	XmlReadMode	Reads an XML schema and data into the DataSet. Overloaded.
ReadXMLSchema	void	Reads an XML schema into the DataSet.

Table 9-2. Important DataSet methods (continued)

Method name	Return type	Description
RejectChanges	void	Rolls back to the state since the last AcceptChanges (see AcceptChanges).
WriteXML	void	Writes out the XML schema and data from the DataSet. Overloaded.
WriteXMLSchema	void	Writes the structure of the DataSet as an XML schema. Overloaded.

The DataSet class contains a DataRelationCollection object, which contains DataRelation objects. Each DataRelation object represents a relationship between two tables through DataColumn objects. For example, in the AdventureWorksLT database the SalesOrderHeader table is in a relationship with the Customer table through the CustomerID column. The nature of this relationship is parent/child: for any given order represented in the SalesOrderHeader table there will be exactly one customer, but any given customer may be represented in any number of orders.

The DataTable class

The DataSet object's Tables property returns a DataTableCollection collection, which in turn contains all the DataTable objects in the data set. For example, the following line of code creates a reference to the first DataTable in the Tables collection of a DataSet object named myDataSet:

```
DataTable dataTable = myDataSet.Tables[0];
```

The DataTable has a number of public properties, including the Columns property, which returns the ColumnsCollection object, which in turn consists of DataColumn objects. Each DataColumn object represents a column in a table.

The most important properties and methods of the DataTable class are shown in Tables 9-3 and 9-4.

Table 9-3. Important DataTable properties (read-only except where stated)

Property name	Type	Description
ChildRelations	DataRelationCollection	Returns the collection of child relationships (see the Relations object).
Columns	DataColumnCollection	Returns the Columns collection.
Constraints	ConstraintCollection	Returns the Constraints collection.
DataSet	DataSet	Returns the DataSet to which this table belongs.
DefaultView	DataView	Returns a view of the table for filtering.
ParentRelations	DataRelationCollection	Returns the ParentRelations collection.
PrimaryKey	DataColumn	Read/write. An array of columns as the primary key for this table.
Rows	DataRowCollection	Returns the Rows collection.

Table 9-4. Important DataTable methods

Method name	Return type	Description
AcceptChanges	void	Commits all the changes since the last AcceptChanges.
Clear	void	Clears the table of all data.
GetChanges	DataTable	Returns a copy of the DataTable that contains all the changes since the last AcceptChanges (see AcceptChanges).
GetErrors	DataRow[]	Returns an array of rows with errors.
ImportRow	void	Copies a row into a table, including all settings and values.
LoadDataRow	DataRow	Finds and updates a specific row. Creates a new row if no matching row is found. Overloaded.
Merge	void	Merges the specified DataTable with the current DataTable. Overloaded.
NewRow	DataRow	Creates a new DataRow with the same schema as the table.
RejectChanges	void	Rolls back changes since the last AcceptChanges (see AcceptChanges).
Reset	void	Resets the table to its original state.
Select	DataRow[]	Returns an array of DataRow objects. Overloaded.

The DataTable DefaultView property returns an object of type DataView, which can be used for data binding to controls such as the GridView.

The DataRow class

The Rows property of a DataTable returns a set of rows for any given table. You use this collection to examine the results of queries against the database, iterating through the rows to examine each record in turn.

Programmers experienced with classic ADO may be confused by the absence of the RecordSet, with its moveNext and movePrevious commands. With ADO.NET, you do not iterate through the data set; instead, you access the table you need, and then you can iterate through the rows collection, typically with a foreach loop.

The most important methods and properties of the DataRow class are shown in Tables 9-5 and 9-6.

Table 9-5. Important DataRow properties

Name	Type	Description
HasErrors	Boolean	Read-only. Returns true if the row has any errors.
Item	Object	Read/write. Gets or sets the data stored in a specific column (in C#, this is the indexer).
ItemArray	Object	Read/write. Gets or sets all the values for the row using an array.
Table	DataTable	Read-only. Gets the table to which this row belongs.

Table 9-6. Important DataRow methods

Name	Return type	Description
AcceptChanges	void	Accepts all the changes since the last time AcceptChanges was called.
BeginEdit	void	Begins the edit operation.
CancelEdit	void	Cancels the edit operation.
Delete	void	Deletes the DataRow from the DataTable.
EndEdit	void	Ends the edit operation.
GetChildRows	DataRows[]	Gets the child rows for this row. Overloaded.
GetParentRow	DataRow	Gets the parent row of this row. Overloaded.
GetParentRows	DataRow[]	Gets parent rows of a DataRow. Overloaded.
RejectChanges	void	Rejects all the changes since the last time AcceptChanges was called (see AcceptChanges).

DbCommand and DbConnection

The DbConnection object represents a connection to a data source. This connection may be shared among different command objects and is used in support of transactions (explained later in this chapter).

The DbCommand object allows you to send a command (typically a SQL statement or the name of a stored procedure) to the database. Often, DbCommand objects are implicitly created when you create your data set, but you can explicitly access these objects as you'll see in a subsequent example.

The DataAdapter Object

Rather than tie the DataSet object too closely to your database architecture, ADO.NET uses a DataAdapter object to mediate between the DataSet object and the database. This decouples the data set from the database and allows a single data set to represent more than one database or other data source.

ASP.NET provides different versions of the DataAdapter object. For example, there is one for use with SQL Server and another for use with OLE DB providers such as Access. If you are connecting to a SQL Server database (or SQLExpress) you will increase the performance of your application by using SqlDataAdapter (from System.Data.SqlClient) along with SqlCommand and SqlConnection.

The DataAdapter class provides several properties, such as AcceptChangesDuringFill, AcceptChangesDuringUpdate, and ContinueUpdateOnError, to control the behavior of the object. It has a number of useful methods; the three most important are listed in Table 9-7.

Table 9-7. Important DataAdapter methods

Name	Return type	Description
Fill	Integer	Fills a DataTable by adding or updating rows in the data set. The return value is the number of rows successfully added or updated. Overloaded.
FillSchema	DataTable[]	Adds a DataTable object to the specified data set. Configures the schema (the logical design of the database) to the specified SchemaType. Returns a DataTable object containing the schema data.
Update	Integer	Updates all the modified rows in the specified table of the DataSet. Returns the number of rows successfully updated.

The DataReader Object

An alternative to the DataSet and DataAdapter combination is the DataReader object. The DataReader provides database-connected, forward-only access to records executing a SQL statement or a stored procedure. DataReaders are lightweight objects ideally suited for filling a web page with read-only data, such as populating lists, and then breaking the connection to the backend database.

The base class for all DataReaders is DbDataReader in the System.Data.Common namespace.

The classes derived from DbDataReader are DataTableReader, OdbcDataReader, OleDbDataReader, OracleDataReader, and SqlDataReader.

The DbDataReader class has properties such as FieldCount and HasRows for obtaining information about the data. Of particular interest is the Item property, which returns an object representing the value of a specified column in the row. In C#, the Item property is the indexer for the class.

The DbDataReader class has a large number of methods for extracting the data as you iterate through the reader, such as GetBytes, GetData, GetName, and GetString. Other important methods are listed in Table 9-8.

Table 9-8. Important DbDataReader methods

Name	Return type	Description
Close	void	Closes the data reader. Overridden.
NextResult	Boolean	When reading the results of a batch SQL statement, advances to the next result set (set of records). Will return true if there are more result sets. Overridden.
Read	Boolean	Advances to the next record. Will return true if there are more records.

The DataReader is a powerful object, but you don't often use many of its methods or properties. Most of the time, you use the DataReader to retrieve and iterate through the records that represent the result of your query.

Getting Started with ADO.NET

Create a new website called *C9_ADONET* and add a new web form to it called *SimpleADONetGridView.aspx*. Drag a GridView onto the page and accept all of its default values. Do not attach a data source. Switch to the code-behind file. In the code-behind page, you will create a DataSet and then assign one of the tables from that DataSet to the DataSource property of the GridView.

To get started, add to your source code a using statement for the SqlClient namespace:

```
using System.Data.SqlClient;
```

You'll need to add this using statement in all the examples in this chapter.

With that done, you will implement the Page_Load method to get the SalesLT.Customer table from the AdventureWorksLT database and bind it to your GridView. You do this in a series of steps:

1. Create a connection string and a command string.
2. Pass the strings to the constructor of the SqlDataAdapter.
3. Create an instance of a DataSet.
4. Ask the DataAdapter to fill the DataSet.
5. Extract the table from the DataSet.
6. Bind the GridView to that table.

The complete source code for this example is shown in Example 9-1.

Example 9-1. SimpleADONetGridView.aspx.cs in full

```
using System;
using System.Data;
using System.Data.SqlClient;
using System.Web.UI;
```

Example 9-1. SimpleADONetGridView.aspx.cs in full (continued)

```
public partial class SimpleADONetGridView : Page
{
    protected void Page_Load(object sender, EventArgs e)
    {
        // 1. Create the connection string and command string
        string connectionString =
          "Data Source=<your_Database>;Initial Catalog=AdventureWorksLT;" +
          "Integrated Security=True";

        string commandString = "Select [CustomerId], [FirstName],
          [LastName], [EmailAddress] from SalesLT.Customer";

        // 2. Pass the strings to the SqlDataAdapter constructor
        SqlDataAdapter dataAdapter =
           new SqlDataAdapter(commandString, connectionString);

        // 3. Create a DataSet
        DataSet dataSet = new DataSet( );

        // 4. fill the dataset object
        dataAdapter.Fill(dataSet,"Customers");

        // 5. Get the table from the dataset
        DataTable dataTable = dataSet.Tables["Customers"];

        // 6. Bind to the Gridview
        GridView1.DataSource=dataTable;
        GridView1.DataBind( );
    }
}
```

Easy as pie; the result is indistinguishable from using a DataSource control, as shown in Figure 9-3.

Note that in this example, you've explicitly identified the DataTable in the DataSet and bound the GridView to that. You could also have referenced it directly through the DataSet's Tables collection like so:

```
GridView1.DataSource = dataSet.Tables["Customers"];
```

Alternatively, you could have bound the GridView directly to the DataSet, and it would be bound by default to the first table in its Tables collection:

```
GridView1.DataSource = dataSet;
```

In this example, there's only the one DataTable in the DataSet, so this code would have had the desired effect, but it's always safer to identify the DataTable in question. You can do this by the name you've given it (Customers in this example) or by its index number in the Tables collection (0 in this example).

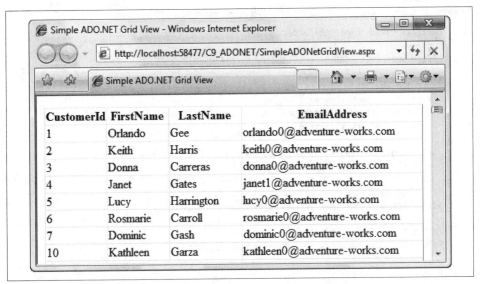

Figure 9-3. SimpleADONetGridView.aspx in action

Using a DataReader

In the previous example, the grid was filled from a table in a data set. Though data
sets are powerful, disconnected data sources, they may require more overhead than
you want. If you want to retrieve a set of records and then immediately display them,
a SqlDataReader object, introduced earlier, may be more efficient.

> A DataReader is limited compared to a DataSet. It offers only a read-
> only, forward-only iteration through a set of results directly from a
> database. The DataSet, on the other hand, stores that set of results in
> memory for easy access, editing, and updating back to the database as
> required. Indeed, the Fill method of a DataAdapter uses a DataReader
> to get the data from the database to the DataSet.

To demonstrate a DataReader, add to the website a new page called
SimpleDataReader.aspx. Drag a GridView onto the page and accept all of its default
values. Beneath it, drag a Label control. Give it an ID of lblException and clear its
Text property. Do not attach a data source. Switch to the code-behind page and
replace the default code with that in Example 9-2.

Example 9-2. SimpleDataReader.aspx.cs in full

```
using System;
using System.Data;
using System.Data.SqlClient;
using System.Web.UI;
```

Example 9-2. SimpleDataReader.aspx.cs in full (continued)

```csharp
public partial class SimpleDataReader : Page
{
    protected void Page_Load(object sender, EventArgs e)
    {
        // Create the connection string
        string connectionString =
            "Data Source=<your_database>;Initial Catalog=AdventureWorksLT;" +
            "Integrated Security=True";

        string commandString = "Select [CustomerId], [FirstName],
            [LastName], [EmailAddress] from SalesLT.Customer";

        // Create the connection object
        SqlConnection conn = new SqlConnection(connectionString);

        // Create a command object
        SqlCommand command = new SqlCommand(commandString);

        try
        {
            // open the connection
            conn.Open( );

            // attach connection to command object
            command.Connection = conn;

            // get the data reader
            SqlDataReader reader =
                command.ExecuteReader(CommandBehavior.CloseConnection);

            // bind to the data reader
            GridView1.DataSource = reader;
            GridView1.DataBind( );
        }
        catch (Exception ex)
        {
            lblException.Text = ex.Message;
        }
        finally
        {
            // make sure the connection closes
            if (conn.State != ConnectionState.Closed)
            {
                conn.Close( );
            }
        }
    }
}
```

The connection is opened in a try block and closed in the finally block. Database connections are limited resources, and it is important to ensure that they are closed. Normally, you would catch any exceptions and handle them, but you want to make sure that whatever happens, whether the page behaves as you expect or an exception occurs, the connection is explicitly closed before leaving this method.

You begin by setting the connection string and command string as you did previously. The last time you passed your connection string and a command string to the `DataAdapter` object, it implicitly created a `Connection` object and a `Command` object for you. This time you create those objects explicitly:

```
// Create the connection object
SqlConnection conn = new SqlConnection(connectionString);

// Create a command object
SqlCommand command = new SqlCommand(commandString);
```

Once your `Command` object is established, create the `DataReader`. You cannot call the `DataReader`'s constructor directly; instead, you call `ExecuteReader` on the `SqlCommand` object. The `CommandBehavior.CloseConnection` parameter given to the `ExecuteReader` method indicates that the `DataReader` will close the connection automatically once all the data returned by the query has been sent through to the page.

The call to `ExecuteReader` returns an instance of `SqlDataReader`:

```
// get the data reader
SqlDataReader reader =
    command.ExecuteReader(CommandBehavior.CloseConnection);
```

You can now bind the `GridView` to the `DataReader` you created:

```
// bind to the data reader
GridView1.DataSource = reader;
GridView1.DataBind();
```

Run the application and the `DataReader` acts as the data source, populating your grid as shown in Figure 9-4 and producing the same results as *SimpleADONetGridView.aspx*.

As mentioned earlier, unlike a `DataSet`, a `DataReader` does not store any data on the server. It is useful, then, as a lightweight alternative to the `DataSet` if all you want to do is read in data to a page, and you can remain connected to the data store while the data is being retrieved. On the other hand, you will need a `DataSet` if you need to do any of the following:

- Pass a disconnected set of data to another tier in your application or to a client application.
- Persist your results either to a file or to a `Session` object.
- Provide access to more than one table and to relationships among the tables.

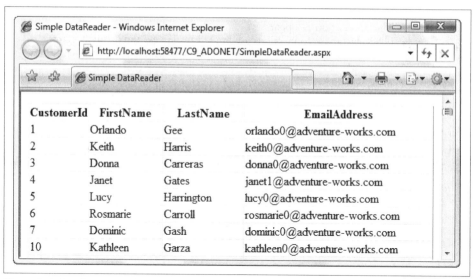

Figure 9-4. SimpleDataReader.aspx in action

- Bind the same data to multiple controls. Remember, a `DataReader` object provides forward-only access to the data; you cannot reiterate through the data for a second control.
- Jump to a particular record or go backward through a set of data.
- Update a number of records in the backend database using a batch operation.

Creating Data Relationships Within DataSets

Because the `DataSet` acts as a disconnected model of the database, it must be able to represent the tables within the database as well as the relationships among the tables.

The `DataSet` captures these relationships in a `DataRelationCollection` that you access through the read-only `Relations` property. The `DataRelationCollection` is a collection of `DataRelation` objects, each of which represents a relationship between two tables.

Each `DataRelation` object relates a pair of `DataTable` objects to each other through `DataColumn` objects. The relationship is established by matching columns in the two tables, such as matching a customer's orders to the customer by matching the `CustomerID` column in both tables (see Appendix B).

The `DataRelation` objects retrieved through the `Relations` property of the `DataSet` provide you with metadata: that is, data about the relationships among the tables in the database. You can use the metadata in a number of ways. For example, you can generate a schema for your database from the information contained in the data set, and you can get child rows and manipulate them as a unit when a relationship is defined.

In the next example, you will create `DataRelation` objects to model two relationships within the AdventureWorksLT database. The first `DataRelation` object you create will represent the relationship between the `SalesOrderHeader` table and the `SalesOrderDetail` table through the `SalesOrderID`. The second relationship you will model is between the `SalesOrderDetail` table and the `Product` table through the `ProductID`.

To begin, create a new web form named *DataRelations.aspx*. Add three `GridView` controls, one of which is in a panel. The first, `OrderGridView`, displays the orders in the database with a button to select a particular order:

```
<asp:GridView ID="OrderGridView" runat="server"
    AutoGenerateColumns="False" DataKeyNames="SalesOrderID"
    onselectedindexchanged="OrderGridView_SelectedIndexChanged">
    <Columns>
        <asp:ButtonField CommandName="Select" Text="Details" />
        <asp:BoundField DataField="SalesOrderID" HeaderText="OrderID" />
        <asp:BoundField DataField="OrderDate" HeaderText="Order Date" />
        <asp:BoundField DataField="CompanyName" HeaderText="Company" />
        <asp:BoundField DataField="Contact" HeaderText="Contact" />
        <asp:BoundField DataField="TotalDue" HeaderText="Total Due" />
    </Columns>
</asp:GridView>
```

Note that the columns are not automatically created; they will be created at your discretion. We did this by using the Edit Columns dialog in the `GridView`'s smart tag, as shown in Figure 9-5.

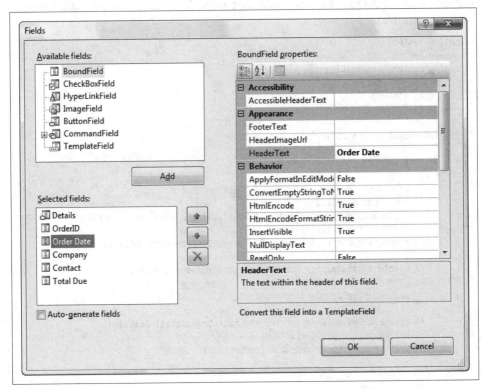

Figure 9-5. Setting the fields for OrderGridView

The second `GridView` control, `OrderDetailsGridView`, displays the details for the order you selected from the first `GridView`. It is in a `Panel`, so it can be hidden if no `Order` has been selected yet. Again, the columns are created by our design with `AutoGenerateColumns` set to False.

```
<asp:Panel ID="OrderDetailsPanel" runat="server">
   <asp:GridView ID="OrderDetailsGridView" runat="server"
      AutoGenerateColumns="False">
      <Columns>
         <asp:BoundField DataField="Name" HeaderText="Product" />
         <asp:BoundField DataField="OrderQty" HeaderText="Quantity" />
         <asp:BoundField DataField="UnitPrice"
             HeaderText="Price Per Unit" />
         <asp:BoundField DataField="LineTotal" HeaderText="Total" />
      </Columns>
   </asp:GridView>
</asp:Panel>
```

Finally, the third `GridView` control, `OrderRelationsGridView`, displays the relationships created in the DataSet:

```
<asp:GridView ID="OrderRelationsGridView" runat="server">
</asp:GridView>
```

In the code-behind file for the page, the key to the page is the `CreateDataSet` method. The job of this method is to create a `DataSet` with three tables and two relationships between the tables.

```
using System;
using System.Data;
using System.Data.SqlClient;
using System.Text;
using System.Web.UI;
using System.Web.UI.WebControls;

public partial class DataRelations : Page
{
   private DataSet CreateDataSet()
   {
      // Create connection string and Connection object
      string connectionString =
         "Data Source=<your_database>;Initial Catalog=AdventureWorksLT;" +
          "Integrated Security=True";
      SqlConnection connection = new SqlConnection(connectionString);

      // Create a DataAdapter for the SalesOrderHeader GridView
      SqlDataAdapter OrdersAdapter =
        CreateAdapterForOrders(connection);

      // Create a 2nd DataAdapter for the SalesOrderDetail GridView
      SqlDataAdapter OrderDetailsAdapter =
        CreateAdapterForOrderDetails(connection);
```

```
// Create a 3rd DataAdapter for the Product table
SqlDataAdapter ProductsAdapter =
    CreateAdapterForProducts(connection);

// Create the dataset and use the data adapter to fill it
DataSet dataSet = new DataSet();
try
{
    OrdersAdapter.Fill(dataSet);
    OrderDetailsAdapter.Fill(dataSet);
    ProductsAdapter.Fill(dataSet);
}
finally
{
    if (connection.State != ConnectionState.Closed)
    {
        connection.Close();
    }
}

// Create the relationships between the tables in the DataSet
CreateRelationsInDataSet(dataSet);
return dataSet;
}
```

First a connection to the AdventureWorksLT database is created and then
CreateAdapterForOrders is called. This creates a DataAdapter to query for some infor-
mation in the SalesOrderHeader table and maps it to a DataTable in the DataSet called
Orders.

```
private static SqlDataAdapter CreateAdapterForOrders(
                                    SqlConnection connection)
{
    //Build the SQL command
    StringBuilder s = new StringBuilder(
        "select o.SalesOrderID, o.OrderDate, o.TotalDue, ");
    s.Append("c.CompanyName, c.FirstName + ' ' + c.LastName as 'Contact'");
    s.Append(" from SalesLT.SalesOrderHeader o ");
    s.Append("inner join SalesLT.Customer c on c.CustomerID = o.CustomerID");

    SqlDataAdapter OrdersAdapter = new SqlDataAdapter();
    OrdersAdapter.SelectCommand = new SqlCommand(s.ToString(), connection);
    OrdersAdapter.TableMappings.Add("Table", "Orders");
    return OrdersAdapter;
}
```

A second DataAdapter is created to produce the OrderDetails DataTable in the DataSet.
This will contain further information for an Order selected in the OrderGridView.
Note that the SQL statement used joins the Product table to the SalesOrderDetail
table to turn a ProductID into a product name.

```
private static SqlDataAdapter CreateAdapterForOrderDetails(
    SqlConnection connection)
{
    // Build the SQL command
```

```
StringBuilder s = new StringBuilder(
    "select d.SalesOrderId, p.Name, p.ProductID, d.OrderQty, ");
s.Append("d.UnitPrice, d.LineTotal ");
s.Append("from SalesLT.SalesOrderDetail d ");
s.Append("inner join SalesLT.Product p on d.productid = p.productid");

SqlDataAdapter OrderDetailsAdapter = new SqlDataAdapter();
OrderDetailsAdapter.SelectCommand = new SqlCommand(s.ToString(), connection);
OrderDetailsAdapter.TableMappings.Add("Table", "Details");
return OrderDetailsAdapter;
}
```

Finally, a third DataAdapter is created to retrieve all the product names and IDs from the database and store them in a third DataTable called Products. This isn't bound to any GridView control, but it is required for us to map a relationship between the SalesOrderDetail and Product tables that's implied in the SQL statement for the second DataAdapter.

```
private static SqlDataAdapter CreateAdapterForProducts(
    SqlConnection connection)
{
    string cmdString = "Select ProductID, Name from SalesLT.Product";

    SqlDataAdapter ProductsAdapter = new SqlDataAdapter();
    ProductsAdapter.SelectCommand = new SqlCommand(cmdString, connection);
    ProductsAdapter.TableMappings.Add("Table", "Products");
    return ProductsAdapter;
}
```

With the three adapters created, a DataSet is created and Fill(dataSet) is called on each adapter to create and populate a DataTable within the dataSet with the names Orders, Details, and Products, respectively. These calls are all made within a try block to make sure the connection is closed as soon as the data has been retrieved. Calling Fill on a DataAdapter also opens the connection associated with the DataAdapter, so there's no need to open it explicitly in the try block.

Once the connection has been closed, CreateDataSet makes one more call to CreateRelationsInDataSet to establish the relationships among the three DataTables that are now full. DataColumn objects are used to identify the primary and foreign keys in the related tables and a DataRelation object is used to link the two columns together before being added to the DataSet object to establish the relationship.

First the relationship between the Orders and Details tables is created:

```
private static void CreateRelationsInDataSet(DataSet dataSet)
{
    // declare the DataRelation and DataColumn objects
    DataRelation dataRelation;
    DataColumn dataColumn1;
    DataColumn dataColumn2;
    // set the dataColumns to create the relationship
    // between Bug and Order Details on the OrderID key
    dataColumn1 = dataSet.Tables["Orders"].Columns["SalesOrderID"];
```

```
dataColumn2 = dataSet.Tables["Details"].Columns["SalesOrderID"];
dataRelation = new DataRelation("OrdersToDetails", dataColumn1,
                                dataColumn2);
// add the new DataRelation to the dataset
dataSet.Relations.Add(dataRelation);
```

Then the relationship between the Details and Product tables is created:

```
// reuse the DataColumns and DataRelation objects
// to create the relation between Order Details and Products
dataColumn1 = dataSet.Tables["Products"].Columns["ProductID"];
dataColumn2 = dataSet.Tables["Details"].Columns["ProductID"];
dataRelation = new DataRelation("ProductIDToName", dataColumn1,
                                dataColumn2);
dataSet.Relations.Add(dataRelation);
return;
}
```

The result of CreateDataSet is a re-creation of the SalesOrderHeader, SalesOrderDetail, and Product tables, and their relationships in the Adventure-WorksLT database. The Page_Load method in *DataRelations.aspx.cs* receives this DataSet from CreateDataSet and binds the Orders table within it to OrderGridView.

 We've given names to the DataTables in this example, although it is not necessary. DataTables are indexed in a DataSet's Tables collection by the order of their creation, so you could equally use ds.Tables[0] for the Orders table, ds.Tables[1] for the Details table, and so on.

```
protected void Page_Load(object sender, EventArgs e)
{
    if (!IsPostBack)
    {
        UpdateDetailsGrid();

        DataSet ds = CreateDataSet();
        OrderGridView.DataSource = ds.Tables["Orders"];
        OrderGridView.DataBind();
```

Next, it creates a DataView object representing a filtered view of the Details table, which is then saved to session state and bound to OrderDetailsGridView:

```
// create the dataview and bind to the details grid
DataView detailsView = new DataView(ds.Tables["Details"]);
OrderDetailsGridView.DataSource = detailsView;
Session["DetailsView"] = detailsView;
OrderDetailsGridView.DataBind();
```

Finally, it binds the DataSet's Relations collections to OrderRelationsGridView to display all the relationships in the DataSet:

```
// bind the relations grid to the relations collection
OrderRelationsGridView.DataSource = ds.Relations;
OrderRelationsGridView.DataBind();
    }
}
```

When the page is loaded initially, no order is selected in OrderGridView, so the OrderDetailsPanel's Visible property must be set to false. This is done through a call to UpdateDetailsGrid. Likewise, when an order is selected, UpdateDetailsGrid is also used to handle the SelectedIndexChanged event appropriately.

```
protected void OrderGridView_SelectedIndexChanged(object sender,
                                                  EventArgs e)
{
    UpdateDetailsGrid( );
}
```

When OrderGridView was added to *DataRelations.aspx*, its DataKeyValues property was set to OrderID. When called, the UpdateDetailsGrid method asks the OrderGridView for its DataKeys collection. This returns a collection of the fields set in DataKeyValues for the row currently selected on the GridView—or in brief, the OrderID for the order currently selected in OrderGridView.

```
private void UpdateDetailsGrid( )
{

    int index = OrderGridView.SelectedIndex;
    if (index != -1)
    {
        // get the order id from the data grid
        DataKey key = OrderGridView.DataKeys[index];
        int orderID = (int)key.Value;
```

Having cast the key's value as an integer, it then extracts the view of the Details table from session state, applies a row filter (corresponding to a WHERE clause in SQL) to get only those rows with the appropriate OrderID, and then binds the OrderDetailsGridView to the resultant view:

```
        DataView detailsView = (DataView)Session["detailsView"];
        detailsView.RowFilter = "SalesOrderID = " + orderID;
        OrderDetailsGridView.DataSource = detailsView;
        OrderDetailsGridView.DataBind( );
        OrderDetailsPanel.Visible = true;
    }
    else
    {
        OrderDetailsPanel.Visible = false;
    }
}
} // end of DataRelations.aspx.cs
```

The net result is that the details for the given order are displayed in the GridView (now visible in the Panel), as shown in Figure 9-6.

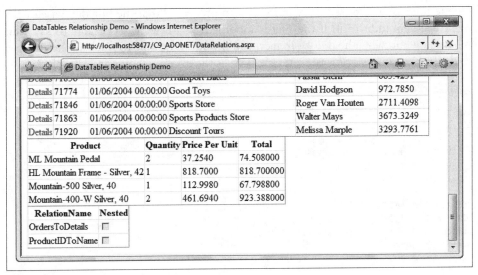

Figure 9-6. DataRelations.aspx in action

Creating Data Objects by Hand

In all of the examples so far, you have created the DataSet object and its DataTable and DataRow objects by selecting data from the database. Sometimes, however, you will want to fill a data set or a table by hand.

For example, you may want to gather data from a user and push that data into the database. It can be convenient to add records to a table manually and update the database from that table.

The DataSet is an excellent transport mechanism for data. You may even want to create a DataSet by hand only to pass it to another tier in your application where it will be used as a data source.

A Simple Database Design

Rather than use the AdventureWorksLT database for the next exercise, you will create part of a database for tracking bugs in a software development project. Think about the kinds of information you would want to capture in the database and how that information will be used. You will want to allow any user of the system to create a bug report for a product. You'll also want certain users (such as developers and Quality Assurance, or QA) to update the bug reports. Developers will want to be able to record progress in fixing a bug or to mark a bug as fixed. QA will want to check the fix and close the bug or reopen it for further investigation. The original reporter of the bug will want to find out who is working on the bug and track his progress.

One requirement imposed early in the design process is that the bug database ought to provide an audit trail. If the bug is modified, you'll want to be able to say who modified it and when he did so. In fact, you'll want to be able to track all the changes to the bug so you can generate a report such as the excerpt shown in Example 9-3.

Example 9-3. Excerpts from a bug report

```
Bug 101 - System crashes on login
101.1 - Reporter: Osborn
Date: 8/1/2008  Original bug filed
Description: When I login I crash.
Status: Open
Owner: QA

101.2 - Modified by: Smith
Date: 8/2/2008 Changed Status, Owner
Action: Confirmed bug. Set severity 2
Status: Assigned
Owner: Maharry

101.3 - Modified by Maharry
Date 8/2/2008 Changed Status
Action: I'll look into this but I don't think it is my code.
Status: Accepted
Owner: Maharry

101.4 - Modified by Maharry
Date 8/3/2008 Changed Status, Owner
Action: Fault lies in login code. Reassigned to Liberty
Status: Assigned
Owner: Liberty

101.5 - Modified by Liberty
Date: 8/3/2008 Changed Status
Action: Yup, this is mine.
Status: Accepted
Owner: Liberty

101.6 - Modified by Liberty
Date 8/4/2008 Changed Status, Owner
Action: Added test for null loginID in DoLogin( )
Status: Fixed
Owner: QA

101.7 - Modified by Smith
Date: 8/4/2008 Changed Status
Action: Tested and confirmed
Status: Closed
Owner: QA
```

To track this information, you'll need to know the date and time of each modification, who made it, and what he did. You will probably want to capture other information as well, though this may become more obvious as you build the application and use it.

One way to meet these requirements is to create two tables to represent each bug. Each record in the Bugs table will represent a single bug, but you'll need an additional table to keep track of the revisions. Call this second table BugHistory.

A bug record will have a BugID and will include the information that is constant for the bug throughout its history. A BugHistory record will have the information specific to each revision.

The bug database design described in this chapter includes three significant tables: Bugs, BugHistory, and People. Bugs and BugHistory work together to track the progress of a bug. For any given bug, a single record is created in the Bugs table, and a record is created in BugHistory each time the bug is revised in any way. The People table tracks the developers, QA, and other personnel who might be referred to in a bug report. See the design diagram in Figure 9-7.

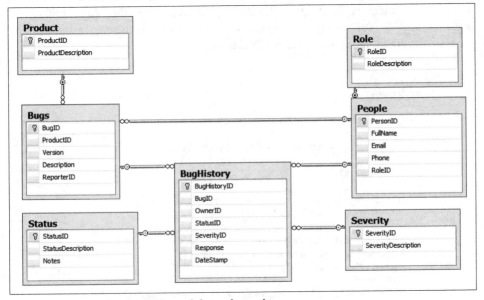

Figure 9-7. The BugTracker tables and their relationships

 This is a simplified design that meets the detailed specifications, but which focuses on the key technologies; a robust professional design would necessarily be more complex.

When a bug is first entered, a record is created in the Bugs and BugHistory tables. Each time the bug is updated, a record is added to BugHistory. During the evolution of a bug, the status, severity, and owner of a bug may change, but the initial description and reporter will not. Those items that are consistent for the entire bug are in the Bugs table; those that are updated as the bug is corrected are in the BugHistory table.

Creating a DataSet by Hand

In the next example, you'll create a DataSet and populate three tables by hand: Bugs, Product, and People. Once the tables are created, you'll set constraints on a number of columns, set default values, establish identity columns, and create keys. You'll also establish a foreign key relationship between two tables, and you'll create a data relationship tying two tables together. Don't worry; it sounds like more work than it really is.

Add to the website a new web form named *BugTrackerByHand.aspx*. Drag two GridView objects onto the form. Name the first BugsGridView and the second BugConstraintsGridView. You need make no further changes to them except for using AutoFormat to make them look reasonably nice. Switch to the code-behind page.

As we're focused for the time being on creating the database rather than the functionality of the page, Page_Load simply calls the CreateDataSet method to build the database in memory and then binds BugsGridView to the Bugs table and BugConstraintsGridView to the Constraints collection within the Bugs table to demonstrate the creation of constraints in the data set:

```
using System;
using System.Data;
using System.Web.UI;

public partial class BugTrackerByHand : Page
{
    protected void Page_Load(object sender, EventArgs e)
    {
        if (!IsPostBack)
        {
            // call the method that creates the tables and the relations
            DataSet ds = CreateDataSet();

            // set the data source for the grid to the first table
            BugsGridView.DataSource = ds.Tables["Bugs"];
            BugsGridView.DataBind();

            BugConstraintsGridView.DataSource = ds.Tables["Bugs"].Constraints;
            BugConstraintsGridView.DataBind();
        }
    }
}
```

Like the previous example, CreateDataSet is the heart of this page, creating the DataSet, creating and adding the Bugs, Product, and People tables and adding them to the DataSet, and establishing relationships among the Bugs table and the other two tables.

```
private DataSet CreateDataSet()
{
    // Create a new DataSet object for tables and relations
    DataSet dataSet = new DataSet();

    // Create the Bugs table and add it to the DataSet
    DataTable tblBugs = CreateBugsTable();
    dataSet.Tables.Add(tblBugs);
```

```
        // Create the Product table and add it to the DataSet
        DataTable tblProduct = CreateProductTable( );
        dataSet.Tables.Add(tblProduct);

        // Create the People table and add it to the DataSet
        DataTable tblPeople = CreatePeopleTable( );
        dataSet.Tables.Add(tblPeople);

        // Create the Foreign Key Constraint
        // People.PersonID = Bugs.ReporterID
        CreateForeignKeyAndDataRelation
          (dataSet, "BugToPerson", tblPeople, "PersonID",
           tblBugs, "ReporterID");

        // Create the Foreign Key Constraint
        // Product.ProductID = Bugs.ProductID
        CreateForeignKeyAndDataRelation
          (dataSet, "BugToProduct", tblProduct, "ProductID",
           tblBugs, "ProductID");

        return dataSet;
    }
```

You create a DataTable in much the same way as you do in SQL Server Management
Studio (SSMS) or SQL. First, you create the table itself, then its columns, and then its
data. If it has any relationships with other tables, they are created once the other tables
have been created. For example, the CreateBugsTable method generates a DataTable
object to be added to the DataSet.

Creating a DataTable

First you declare a DataTable object, passing in the name of the table as a parameter to
the constructor. Then columns are added to the table, and finally, data is added into it.

```
    private DataTable CreateBugsTable( )
    {
        DataTable tblBugs = new DataTable("Bugs");

        // Add columns
        AddNewPrimaryKeyColumn(tblBugs, "BugID");
        AddNewColumn(tblBugs, "System.Int32", "ProductID", false, 1);
        AddNewColumn(tblBugs, "System.String", "Version",
                    false, "0.1", 50);
        AddNewColumn(tblBugs, "System.String", "Description",
                    false, "", 8000);
        AddNewColumn(tblBugs, "System.Int32", "ReporterID", false);

        // Add some rows to the table
        AddNewBug(tblBugs, 1, "0.1", "Crashes on load", 5);
        AddNewBug(tblBugs, 1, "0.1",
                    "Does not report correct owner of bug", 5);
        AddNewBug(tblBugs, 1, "0.1",
                    "Does not show history of previous action", 6);
        AddNewBug(tblBugs, 1, "0.1", "Fails to reload properly", 5);
```

```
        AddNewBug(tblBugs, 2, "0.1", "Loses data overnight", 5);
        AddNewBug(tblBugs, 2, "0.1", "HTML is not shown properly", 6);
        return tblBugs;
    }
```

Adding DataColumns to the DataTable

To create new DataColumns within a DataTable, you call the Add( ) method on its Columns collection, as highlighted in the next code snippet. This will create the DataColumn, add it to the DataTable, and return a reference to it by which you can set more of its properties in addition to its name and type. In this example, up to three other properties are set for each DataColumn (which isn't a primary key column):

- AllowDBNull sets whether a value in that column can ever be null or not.
- DefaultValue sets the default value for that column.
- MaxLength sets the maximum length of that column if it is of type String.

Because not all columns require DefaultValue or MaxLength to be set, AddNewColumn has two overloads, setting those properties to their default values as appropriate:

```
private void AddNewColumn(
    DataTable table, string ColumnType, string ColumnName,
    bool AllowNulls, object DefaultValue, int MaxLength)
{
    DataColumn newColumn =
        table.Columns.Add(ColumnName, Type.GetType(ColumnType));
    newColumn.AllowDBNull = AllowNulls;
    newColumn.MaxLength = MaxLength;
    newColumn.DefaultValue = DefaultValue;
}

private void AddNewColumn(
    DataTable table, string ColumnType,
    string ColumnName, bool AllowNulls, object DefaultValue)
{
    AddNewColumn(table, ColumnType, ColumnName,
                AllowNulls, DefaultValue, -1);
}

private void AddNewColumn(
    DataTable table, string ColumnType, string ColumnName,
    bool AllowNulls)
{
    AddNewColumn(table, ColumnType, ColumnName,
                AllowNulls, null, -1);
}
```

Adding primary key columns

Using the AddNewColumn methods to add new columns to a DataTable is fine in general, but further properties must be set to identify a column as the primary key for the DataTable. In this sample database, all primary keys are integer identity columns and so the AddNewPrimaryKeyColumn method calls AddNewColumn and then a bit more. First it creates a reference to the new column and calls it PkColumn:

```
private void AddNewPrimaryKeyColumn(DataTable table,
                                    string ColumnName)
{
    AddNewColumn(table, "System.Int32", ColumnName, false);
    DataColumn PkColumn = table.Columns[ColumnName];
```

Because this is to be an identity column, you'll want to set its AutoIncrement property to true and its AutoIncrementSeed and AutoIncrementStep properties to set the seed and step values to 1. The AutoIncrementSeed property sets the initial value for the identity column, and the AutoIncrementStep property sets the increment for each new record. Thus, if the seed were 5 and the step were 3, the first five records would have IDs of 5, 8, 11, 14, and 17. In the case shown, where the seed and step are 1, the first four records have IDs of 1, 2, 3, and 4.

```
// Set column as auto-increment field
PkColumn.AutoIncrement = true;        // autoincrementing
PkColumn.AutoIncrementSeed = 1;       // starts at 1
PkColumn.AutoIncrementStep = 1;       // increments by 1
```

Primary keys must be unique and must not be null. The latter requisite is taken care of in the call to AddNewColumn, and the former can be done in two ways. You can either set the Unique property of the DataColumn object to true, or create a UniqueConstraint object for the column and add it to the DataTable, as done here. The only difference is the first way creates an unnamed constraint in the DataTables Constraints collection, whereas the second way creates a named one, which is easier to reference.

```
// Make sure all values are unique
string constraintName = String.Format("Unique_{0}", ColumnName);
UniqueConstraint constraint =
                new UniqueConstraint(constraintName, PkColumn);
table.Constraints.Add(constraint);
```

Finally, the DataColumn must be added to the DataTable's PrimaryKey property. Note that this property expects an array of DataColumn objects because a table's primary key could span two or more columns rather than just the one in this case.

```
// Set column as primary key for table
DataColumn[] columnArray = new DataColumn[] { PkColumn };
table.PrimaryKey = columnArray;
}
```

Adding data to the table

With all the DataColumns added to the DataTable and the identity column set, you're ready to add rows of data to the table. You do this by calling the DataTable object's NewRow( ) method, which returns an empty DataRow object with the right structure for the DataTable to which it belongs. For example, to add data to the Bugs table, CreateBugsTable makes several calls to AddNewBug, which calls NewRow and then fills in the data appropriately.

```
private void AddNewBug(
   DataTable bugTable, int product, string version,
   string description, int reporter)
{
   DataRow newRow = bugTable.NewRow();
   newRow["ProductID"] = product;
   newRow["Version"] = version;
   newRow["Description"] = description;
   newRow["ReporterID"] = reporter;
   bugTable.Rows.Add(newRow);
}
```

Adding Data a Different Way

An alternative way to add data to the table exists through the DataTable's Rows.Add()
method. This method takes an array of Objects and adds the contents to a new row in
the table, one Object per column. As such, AddNewBug could have been written like so:

```
private void AddNewBug(
    DataTable bugTable, int BugID, int product,
    string version, string description,
    int reporter)
{
    Object[] BugArray = new Object[5];
    BugArray[0] = BugID;
    BugArray[1] = product;
    BugArray[2] = version;
    BugArray[3] = description;
    BugArray[4] = reporter;
    bugTable.Rows.Add(BugArray);
}
```

Or it could have been written even more generically, so as to not need specific methods
to add a row to each other table:

```
private void AddNewRow(
    DataTable table, params Object[] values)
{
    table.Rows.Add(values);
}
```

In this case, you must manually add a value for the identity column, BugID. When you
created the row object, the identity column value was automatically created for you
with the right increment from the previous row. Because you are creating an array of
objects, you must do this by hand.

Though this technique works, it is generally not desirable. The overloaded version of
the Add() method that takes a DataRow object is type-safe. Each column must match the
definition of the column you've created. With an array of objects, just about anything
goes; in .NET, everything derives from Object, and thus, you can pass in any type of
data to an array of objects.

With the Bugs table created, `CreateDataSet` first calls `CreateProductTable`, and then `CreatePeopleTable` to add to the DataSet.

```
private DataTable CreateProductTable( )
{
    DataTable tblProduct = new DataTable("lkProduct");

    // Add columns
    AddNewPrimaryKeyColumn(tblProduct, "ProductID");
    AddNewColumn(
        tblProduct, "System.String", "ProductDescription",
        false, "", 8000);

    // Add rows to the Product table
    AddNewProduct(tblProduct, "BugX Bug Tracking");
    AddNewProduct(tblProduct, "PIM - My Personal Information Manager");
    return tblProduct;
}

private void AddNewProduct(DataTable productTable, string description)
{
    DataRow newRow = productTable.NewRow( );
    newRow["ProductDescription"] = description;
    productTable.Rows.Add(newRow);
}

private DataTable CreatePeopleTable( )
{
    DataTable tblPeople = new DataTable("People");

    // Add column
    AddNewPrimaryKeyColumn(tblPeople, "PersonID");
    AddNewColumn(tblPeople, "System.String", "FullName",
                false, "", 8000);
    AddNewColumn(tblPeople, "System.String", "Email",
                false, "", 100);
    AddNewColumn(tblPeople, "System.String", "Phone",
                false, "", 20);
    AddNewColumn(tblPeople, "System.Int32", "Role", false, 0);

    // Add new people
    AddNewPerson(tblPeople, "Dan Maharry",
                "danm@hmobius.com", "212-555-0285", 1);
    AddNewPerson(tblPeople, "Jesse Liberty",
                "jliberty@libertyassociates.com", "617-555-7301", 1);
    AddNewPerson(tblPeople, "Dan Hurwitz",
                "dhurwitz@stersol.com", "781-555-3375", 1);
    AddNewPerson(tblPeople, "John Galt",
                "jGalt@franconia.com", "617-555-9876", 1);
    AddNewPerson(tblPeople, "John Osborn",
                "jOsborn@oreilly.com", "617-555-3232", 3);
    AddNewPerson(tblPeople, "Ron Petrusha",
                "ron@oreilly.com", "707-555-0515", 2);
```

```
        AddNewPerson(tblPeople, "Tatiana Apandi",
                     "tatiana@oreilly.com", "617-555-1234", 2);
        return tblPeople;
    }

    private void AddNewPerson(
        DataTable table, string name, string email,
        string phone, int role)
    {
        DataRow newRow = table.NewRow( );
        newRow["FullName"] = name;
        newRow["email"] = email;
        newRow["Phone"] = phone;
        newRow["Role"] = role;
        table.Rows.Add(newRow);
    }
```

Creating foreign keys and data relationships

As you saw earlier in the chapter, you can encapsulate the relationship between tables in a DataRelation object. This connects a column in the parent table (typically the primary key column) with one in the child table. You can further define the relationship between the columns by applying a ForeignKeyConstraint to the Constraints collection of the child table. This allows rules to be set on what happens to rows in the child table when rows in the parent table are changed or deleted.

The DeleteRule property of a ForeignKeyConstraint object determines the action that will occur when a row is deleted from the parent table. Similarly, its UpdateRule property determines what will happen when a row is updated in the parent column. The potential values are enumerated by the Rule enumeration, as shown in Table 9-9.

Table 9-9. ForeignKeyConstraint rule options

Rule value	Description
Cascade	Delete or update related rows. This is the default action.
None	Take no action on related rows.
SetDefault	Set the values in the related rows to the value contained in the DefaultValue property.
SetNull	Set the related rows to null.

In this case, the values are set to Rule.Cascade; if a record is deleted or updated from the parent table, the associated child records will be deleted or updated as well.

```
        private void CreateForeignKeyAndDataRelation(
            DataSet dataSet, string relationName,
            DataTable parentTable, string primaryKeyColumnName,
            DataTable childTable, string foreignKeyColumnName)
        {
            // Get references to related columns
            DataColumn primaryKeyColumn =
                parentTable.Columns[primaryKeyColumnName];
```

```
        DataColumn foreignKeyColumn =
            childTable.Columns[foreignKeyColumnName];
        String foreignKeyConstraintName =
            String.Format("FK_{0}", relationName);

        // Create foreign key constraint
        ForeignKeyConstraint fk = new ForeignKeyConstraint(
            foreignKeyConstraintName, primaryKeyColumn, foreignKeyColumn);
        fk.DeleteRule = Rule.Cascade;
        fk.UpdateRule = Rule.Cascade;
        childTable.Constraints.Add(fk);

        // Add a DataRelation representing the FKConstraint to the DataSet
        DataRelation relation = new DataRelation(
            relationName, primaryKeyColumn, foreignKeyColumn);
        dataSet.Relations.Add(relation);
    }
} // end of BugTrackerByHand.aspx.cs
```

Both relationships between the Bugs table and the People table, and the Bugs table
and the Product table, are set in this fashion. When run, *BugTrackerByHand.aspx*
presents the contents of the Bugs table and the Constraints laid upon it, as shown in
Figure 9-8.

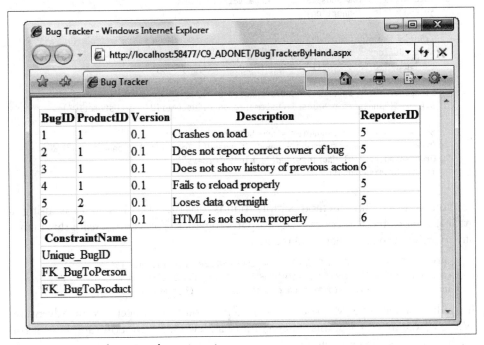

Figure 9-8. BugTrackerByHand.aspx in action

Stored Procedures

The examples in this book have thus far interacted with the database only through SQL statements. Many real-world applications interacting with SQL Server or other large databases use *stored procedures*, which are compiled by the database in advance of execution and, thus, offer better performance over SQL statements, which are compiled on the fly. They are also much more secure as the only requests made to the database are to run the stored procedures rather than the plain SQL, which could have been altered by malicious users and, for example, could result in the deletion of data.

Creating a Simple Stored Procedure

The easiest way to create a stored procedure (often referred to as a *sproc*) is to begin with a working SQL statement. To see this at work, you'll adapt *DataRelations.aspx* to fill its two main *GridView* controls using stored procedures rather than SQL statements.

When creating the DataSet to contain the information for the page, the CreateAdapterForOrders method created a SELECT statement for the first DataAdapter.

```
private static SqlDataAdapter CreateAdapterForOrders(
    SqlConnection connection)
{
    //Build the SQL command
    StringBuilder s = new StringBuilder(
        "select o.SalesOrderID, o.OrderDate, c.CompanyName, ";
    s.Append("c.FirstName + ' ' + c.LastName as 'Contact', o.TotalDue");
    s.Append(" from SalesLT.SalesOrderHeader o ");
    s.Append("inner join SalesLT.Customer c on c.CustomerID = o.CustomerID");

    SqlDataAdapter OrdersAdapter = new SqlDataAdapter();
    OrdersAdapter.SelectCommand = new SqlCommand(s.ToString(), connection);
    OrdersAdapter.TableMappings.Add("Table", "Orders");
    return OrdersAdapter;
}
```

As you can see, the method simply builds up the SELECT statement using a StringBuilder object to concatenate its parts together. You can re-create this manually to arrive at the complete statement.

```
select o.SalesOrderID, o.OrderDate, c.CompanyName, c.FirstName + ' '
+ c.LastName as 'Contact', o.TotalDue from SalesLT.SalesOrderHeader o
inner join SalesLT.Customer c on c.CustomerID = o.CustomerID
```

If you have a copy of SSMS, you should find that you can connect to your Adventure-WorksLT database, paste this statement into a New Query window, and have it run the first time, as shown in Figure 9-9.

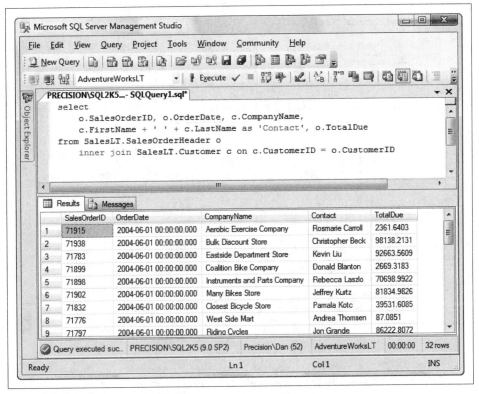

Figure 9-9. Running a query in SSMS

Or, if you're using SQL Server Express Edition and haven't downloaded Management Studio Express (from *http://www.microsoft.com/express/sql/download/default.aspx*), you can open the Server Explorer (the Database Explorer in Visual Web Developer) in Visual Studio 2008 (VS2008), right-click the data connection to your Adventure-WorksLT database there, and click New Query. Once you've closed the Add Table dialog, you'll be able to paste the query directly into the SQL window (the third one down) and click Execute for the same result, as shown in Figure 9-10.

Creating a stored procedure called spOrders which runs this SELECT statement over the AdventureWorksLT database is very straightforward. If you're using SSMS, expand the *Programmability* folder under the database entry in the Object Explorer, and right-click the *Stored Procedures* folder and select New Stored Procedure. This opens a New Query window with the skeleton of a SQL query to add a new stored procedure. To keep things simple, delete this template and paste the SELECT statement into the blank query. Preface the SELECT statement with the string "CREATE PROCEDURE dbo.spOrders AS" and then click Execute to create a new sproc named spOrders, as shown in Figure 9-11.

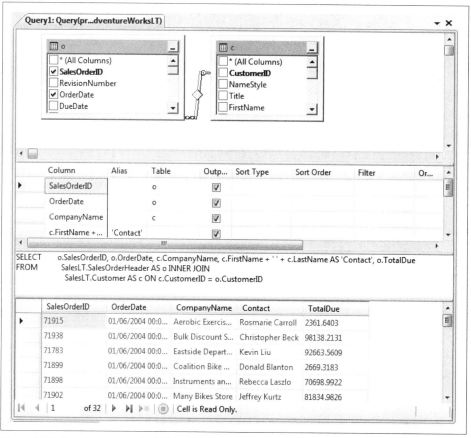

Figure 9-10. Running a query in VS2008

Alternatively, in VS2008, right-click the *Stored Procedures* folder directly under the connection to the AdventureWorksLT database listed in the Server Explorer. Select Add New Stored Procedure from the menu and, again, preface the SELECT statement with the string "CREATE PROCEDURE dbo.spOrders AS" to create the sproc, as shown in Figure 9-12. Click Save to finish creating the stored procedure.

Creating a Stored Procedure with Parameters

In *DataRelations.aspx*, you downloaded all the order details to a DataView stored in session state and then selected which details to show in the grid in the panel by using a filtered view based on the OrderID of the order selected. This time, you'll create a parameterized stored procedure to retrieve the details for the specific orderID selected. Note, however, this will not be stored in session state as the stored procedure will requery the database each time the page is posted back rather than just filter the whole SalesOrderDetail table stored in session state.

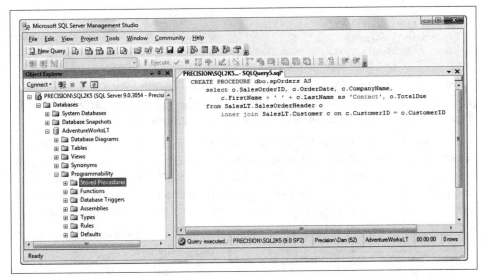

Figure 9-11. Creating a new stored procedure in SSMS

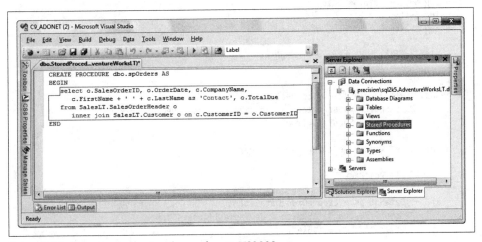

Figure 9-12. Creating a new stored procedure in VS2008

 Which approach is more efficient will depend on the volume of data, the frequency with which you want to go back to the database, how much data you can hold in memory, and so forth. Typically, you'll use the filtered view whenever possible to reduce the number of connections to the database.

Create a new stored procedure named spOrderDetails as follows:

```
CREATE PROCEDURE spOrderDetails
    @OrderID int
AS
```

```
Select d.SalesOrderId, p.Name, p.ProductID, d.OrderQty,
d.UnitPrice, d.LineTotal
from SalesLT.SalesOrderDetail d
inner join SalesLT.Product p on d.productid = p.productid
where d.SalesOrderId = @OrderID
```

Parameterized stored procedures should be read much like any C# method with parameters. In this case, the integer value passed through to spOrderDetails in the @OrderID will be used in the WHERE clause at the end of the SELECT statement.

Now to write a page that makes use of these two stored procedures. Add a copy of *DataRelations.aspx* to the *C9_ADONET* website and rename it *StoredProcedures.aspx*. In Design view, delete the third GridView (OrderRelationsGridView), and in Code view, delete all the code except for the using statements. Although the code will look similar, in this case it's easier to start fresh than to make small adjustments everywhere.

For example, in *DataRelations.aspx*, Page_Load called CreateDataSet, which created the main source of data for the page. This has changed slightly.

```
using System;
using System.Data;
using System.Data.SqlClient;
using System.Web.UI;
using System.Web.UI.WebControls;

public partial class StoredProcedures : Page
{

    private readonly string connectionString =
        "Data Source=<your_database>;Initial Catalog=AdventureWorksLT;
         Integrated Security=True";

    protected void Page_Load(object sender, EventArgs e)
    {
        if (!IsPostBack)
        {
            DataSet ds = CreateOrderDataSet();
            OrderGridView.DataSource = ds.Tables["Orders"];
            OrderGridView.DataBind();

            UpdateDetailsGrid();
        }
    }

    protected void OrderGridView_SelectedIndexChanged(
        object sender, EventArgs e)
    {
        UpdateDetailsGrid();
    }
```

To accommodate the parameterized stored procedure generating the DataSet for the page, CreateOrderDataSet—as it is now called—fills a DataSet only with the contents of the SalesOrderHeader table. The UpdateDetailsGrid method now creates a second DataSet for the OrderDetailsGridView.

```csharp
private DataSet CreateOrderDataSet()
{
    // Create a database connection
    SqlConnection connection =
        new SqlConnection(connectionString);

    // Create a DataAdapter for the SalesOrderHeader GridView
    SqlDataAdapter OrdersAdapter =
        CreateAdapterForOrders(connection);

    // Create the dataset and use the data adapter to fill it
    DataSet dataSet = new DataSet();

    try
    {
        connection.Open();
        OrdersAdapter.Fill(dataSet);
    }
    finally
    {
        if (connection.State != ConnectionState.Closed)
        {
            connection.Close();
        }
    }
    return dataSet;
}

private void UpdateDetailsGrid()
{

    int index = OrderGridView.SelectedIndex;
    if (index != -1)
    {
        // get the order id from the data grid
        DataKey key = OrderGridView.DataKeys[index];
        int orderID = (int)key.Value;

        DataSet ds = CreateOrderDetailsDataSet(orderID);

        OrderDetailsGridView.DataSource = ds;
        OrderDetailsGridView.DataBind();
        OrderDetailsPanel.Visible = true;
    }
    else
    {
        OrderDetailsPanel.Visible = false;
    }
}
```

The significant change in this page is that the SqlDataAdapters which fill the DataSets from the database now call the stored procedures you added to the database rather than the SELECT statements. To achieve this, the SqlCommand's CommandText property is set to the name of the stored procedure (spOrders or spOrderDetails) and its CommandType property is set to the enumerated constant CommandType.StoredProcedure, as highlighted in the following code:

```
private SqlDataAdapter CreateAdapterForOrders(
    SqlConnection connection)
{
    // Set the command to use the spOrders sproc
    SqlCommand cmd = new SqlCommand("spOrders", connection);
    cmd.CommandType = CommandType.StoredProcedure;

    // Set adapter to use sproc as command
    SqlDataAdapter OrdersAdapter = new SqlDataAdapter(cmd);
    OrdersAdapter.TableMappings.Add("Table", "Orders");
    return OrdersAdapter;
}
```

When it comes to calling a stored procedure with a parameter, the SqlCommand object is set to the appropriate CommandText and CommandType as before, but a SqlParameter object representing the parameter and the value being passed in must be added to the SqlCommand's Parameters collection. In CreateAdapterForOrderDetails, this is done using the collection's AddWithValue method (highlighted in the following code snippet), although you could create the SqlParameter object first and then use the collection's Add method to add it.

```
private SqlDataAdapter CreateAdapterForOrderDetails(
    SqlConnection connection, int orderId)
{
    // Set the command to use the spOrderDetails sproc and parameter
    SqlCommand cmd = new SqlCommand("spOrderDetails", connection);
    cmd.CommandType = CommandType.StoredProcedure;

    SqlParameter orderIdParameter =
        cmd.Parameters.AddWithValue("@OrderId", orderId);
    orderIdParameter.Direction = ParameterDirection.Input;
    orderIdParameter.DbType = DbType.Int32;

    // Set adapter to use sproc as command
    SqlDataAdapter OrderDetailsAdapter = new SqlDataAdapter(cmd);
    OrderDetailsAdapter.TableMappings.Add("Table", "OrderDetails");
    return OrderDetailsAdapter;
}
} // end of StoredProcedures.aspx.cs
```

The method also sets the SqlParameter's Direction property to input and its DbType property to Int32. This is optional as these are the default values, but it is a good programming practice to set them explicitly. If you need to get a value out of a stored procedure, set the Direction property to ParameterDirection.Output. You can then pick up the value after calling the stored procedure, in the same way you do with an out parameter in a C# method:

```
string retVal = command.Parameters["@MyOutputValue"].
    Value.ToString();
```

You can also set the Direction property to ParameterDirection. ReturnValue, in which case the parameter will be set to the value returned by the stored procedure using the SQL RETURN statement rather than the value the parameter is left with after the stored procedure has finished running.

Running *StoredProcedure.aspx* will demonstrate that the call to the stored procedures has the same effect as calling the query directly, with the advantage that, in larger applications, the stored procedure will be more efficient because your database will optimize its execution, and more secure because your database will be sent only commands to run the stored procedure rather than raw SQL which could instruct it to do anything.

Updating with SQL and ADO.NET

There are two aspects to writing web applications that allow users to update data. The first aspect is to provide the user with a form that facilitates data modification. The second is to provide the programmatic support for the update: how do you insert new records, or modify or delete existing records once you know what changes you want to make, if you use the ADO.NET object model directly?

Updating data in a database is simple if you update a single table, but once you update related tables, things get complicated. You can use transactions to ensure the integrity of your data, as we will show shortly.

The simplest way to update the database using ADO.NET objects directly is to generate a SQL Insert, Update, or Delete statement, and execute it using the Command object's ExecuteNonQuery method. To demonstrate this, you'll create a new web page called *UpdatingDBDirectly.aspx*. This will display the contents of the ProductCategory table in a GridView and a small form to allow you to add records from that table, as shown in Figure 9-13. You will also be able to select a row to either edit or delete from the database. An extra bit of complexity here is to ensure that any new categories have a valid parent category (by enforcing the selection through a DropDownList) and that those parent categories cannot be changed (by not including them in the GridView).

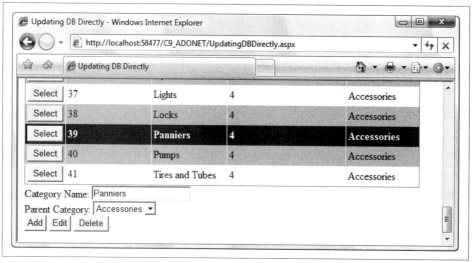

Figure 9-13. UpdatingDBDirectly.aspx in action

Once you've added a new web form to your site and called it *UpdatingDBDirectly.aspx*, drag a GridView onto the design pane to display the various categories, and add a Select button to the first column of the grid. Give the GridView an ID of CategoryGridView and use AutoFormat to give it some color.

Below the grid, add the following:

- A HiddenField control called hdnCategoryID to store the ID of the category you've selected in the GridView.

- A TextBox called txtName to display the category's name.

- A DropDownList called ddlParentCategory that contains all the possible parent categories.

- Three Button controls—btnAdd, btnEdit, and btnDelete—which will add, edit, or delete the category whose details are currently shown. Each has its OnClick event handled.

The layout for these controls is shown in Figure 9-13 and the markup for the whole page (minus any formatting properties) is in Example 9-4.

Example 9-4. UpdatingDBDirectly.aspx in full

```
<%@ Page Language="C#" AutoEventWireup="true"
    CodeFile="UpdatingDBDirectly.aspx.cs" Inherits="UpdatingDBDirectly" %>

<!DOCTYPE html PUBLIC "-//W3C//DTD XHTML 1.0 Transitional//EN"
    "http://www.w3.org/TR/xhtml1/DTD/xhtml1-transitional.dtd">
<html xmlns="http://www.w3.org/1999/xhtml">
<head runat="server">
    <title>Updating DB Directly</title>
</head>
```

Example 9-4. UpdatingDBDirectly.aspx in full (continued)

```
<body>
    <form id="form1" runat="server">
    <div>
        <asp:GridView ID="CategoryGridView" runat="server"
            DataKeyNames="ProductCategoryId"
            OnSelectedIndexChanged="CategoryGridView_SelectedIndexChanged">
            <Columns>
                <asp:CommandField ButtonType="Button" ShowSelectButton="True" />
            </Columns>
        </asp:GridView>

        <asp:HiddenField ID="hdnCategoryID" runat="server" />
        <asp:Label ID="Label1" runat="server" Text="Category Name: " />
        <asp:TextBox ID="txtName" runat="server" /><br />
        <asp:Label ID="Label2" runat="server" Text="Parent Category: " />
        <asp:DropDownList ID="ddlParentCategory" runat="server" />
        <br />
        <asp:Button ID="btnAdd" runat="server" Text="Add"
            OnClick="btnAdd_Click" />
        <asp:Button ID="btnEdit" runat="server" Text="Edit"
            OnClick="btnEdit_Click" />
        <asp:Button ID="btnDelete" runat="server" Text="Delete"
            OnClick="btnDelete_Click" />
    </div>
    </form>
</body>
</html>
```

This time, you set AutoGenerateColumns to True, but you added an additional column for the CommandField. You can do this declaratively (in the .*aspx*) or through the properties in the Design window.

Note the two ID fields for the category and its parent from the ProductCategory table are deliberately not hidden to help you keep in your head how this page fits together. Away from a demonstration, you would probably hide these columns by settings AutoGenerateColumns to false and adding two BoundColumns to the GridView, like so:

```
<asp:GridView ID="CategoryGridView" runat="server"
    DataKeyNames="ProductCategoryId"
    AutoGenerateColumns="false"
    OnSelectedIndexChanged="CategoryGridView_SelectedIndexChanged">
    <Columns>
        <asp:CommandField ButtonType="Button" ShowSelectButton="True" />
        <asp:BoundField HeaderText="Category" DataField="Category" />
        <asp:BoundField HeaderText="Parent" DataField="ParentCategory" />
    </Columns>
</asp:GridView>
```

The IDs would still be retrieved under the covers, but would just not be shown on the page.

In the code-behind file, this page has five tasks:

- Populate the GridView and DropDownList when the page is first loaded.
- Set the category details in the TextBox and DropDownList when a category is selected in the list view.
- Add a new category to the table and update the GridView to reflect the addition.
- Update the selected category in the table and update the GridView to reflect the edit.
- Delete the selected category from the table and update the GridView to reflect the deletion.

It's no surprise to find that the Page_Load event simply calls two methods (highlighted in the following code), one to populate the DropDownList and one to populate the GridView, which will also be called after each alteration to the database has finished so that it can be reflected on the page:

```csharp
using System;
using System.Data;
using System.Data.SqlClient;
using System.Text;
using System.Web.UI;
using System.Web.UI.WebControls;

public partial class UpdatingDBDirectly : Page
{
    private readonly string connectionString =
        "Data Source=<your_database>;Initial Catalog=AdventureWorksLT;" +
        "Integrated Security=True";

    protected void Page_Load(object sender, EventArgs e)
    {
        if (!IsPostBack)
        {
            PopulateCategoryList();
            PopulateGrid();
        }
    }
}
```

PopulateCategoryList takes advantage of the fact that there are only two levels of product category in the ProductCategory table: categories and subcategories. Fortunately, there are no subcategories of a subcategory. Within the table, each row has a ParentProductCategoryID field, which refers to the CategoryID of another category in the table. So, if ParentProductCategoryID is NULL it is a parent category and should be added to the DropDownList.

Also, we chose to use a DataReader here as creating the list is a one-time operation and the data being used here did not need to be persisted after its initial use:

```csharp
private void PopulateCategoryList( )
{
    // Create connection to AdventureWorksLT
    SqlConnection connection = new SqlConnection(connectionString);

    // Create SqlCommand
    StringBuilder cmdString = new StringBuilder( );
    cmdString.Append("SELECT DISTINCT ProductCategoryID, Name ");
    cmdString.Append("FROM SalesLT.ProductCategory ");
    cmdString.Append("WHERE (ParentProductCategoryID IS NULL) ");
    cmdString.Append("ORDER BY ProductCategoryID");
    SqlCommand cmd = new SqlCommand(cmdString.ToString( ), connection);

    try
    {
        connection.Open( );
        SqlDataReader dr = cmd.ExecuteReader(CommandBehavior.CloseConnection);

        while (dr.Read( ))
        {
            ddlParentCategory.Items.Add(new ListItem(
                dr["Name"].ToString( ), dr["ProductCategoryID"].ToString( )));
        }

        dr.Close( );
    }
    finally
    {
        if (connection.State != ConnectionState.Closed)
        {
            connection.Close( );
        }
    }
}
```

PopulateGrid also uses a DataReader rather than a DataGrid because the data must be refreshed from the table each time a change is made, and a DataReader is faster than a DataSet for this purpose. In addition, because AutoGenerateColumns is set to true on the GridView control, you can simply set its DataSource property to the DataReader and call DataBind( ) to get the desired results.

Also, note the SELECT statement performs between the ProductCategory table and itself to retrieve the name of each category's parent category:

```csharp
private void PopulateGrid( )
{
    // Create connection to AdventureWorksLT
    SqlConnection connection = new SqlConnection(connectionString);

    // Create SqlCommand string
    StringBuilder cmdString = new StringBuilder( );
```

```
cmdString.Append("SELECT child.ProductCategoryId, ");
cmdString.Append("child.Name AS 'Category', ");
cmdString.Append("child.ParentProductCategoryID, ");
cmdString.Append("parent.Name AS 'ParentCategory' ");
cmdString.Append("FROM SalesLT.ProductCategory AS child ");
cmdString.Append("INNER JOIN SalesLT.ProductCategory AS parent ON ");
cmdString.Append("child.ParentProductCategoryID = parent.ProductCategoryID");

SqlCommand cmd = new SqlCommand(cmdString.ToString(), connection);

try
{
    connection.Open();
    SqlDataReader dr = cmd.ExecuteReader(CommandBehavior.CloseConnection);
    CategoryGridView.DataSource = dr;
    CategoryGridView.DataBind();

    dr.Close();
}
finally
{
    if (connection.State != ConnectionState.Closed)
    {
        connection.Close();
    }
}
}
```

With the page presentable, the next task is to react to a category being selected in the GridView and to set the controls below it to the appropriate values. The code for this is set up in the GridView's SelectedIndexChanged event handler and uses the GridView's Cells collection for the selected row to discover the values to use. Note that the items in the Cells collection are accessible only by index number from left to right as they appear in the GridView, so you need to make sure you know which Cell you're referencing. For instance, in this example, the content of Cells[0] is the Select button rather than the selected category's ID:

```
protected void CategoryGridView_SelectedIndexChanged(
    object sender, EventArgs e)
{
    int selectedIndex = CategoryGridView.SelectedIndex;

    if (selectedIndex != -1)
    {
        TableCellCollection selectedValues =
            CategoryGridView.Rows[selectedIndex].Cells;

        // Have to know the order of these cells in the Grid
        hdnCategoryID.Value = selectedValues[1].Text;
        txtName.Text = selectedValues[2].Text;
        ddlParentCategory.SelectedValue = selectedValues[3].Text;
    }
}
```

Last but not least, each button has an event handler. The Add button picks up the new category name from the TextBox and its parentProductCategoryId from the DropDownList and adds a new record to the table by passing a command string to the UpdateDB method and then refreshing the GridView. The Edit and Delete buttons work in the same way, but also using the ID of the currently selected category stored in the HiddenField control.

```
protected void btnAdd_Click(object sender, EventArgs e)
{
    StringBuilder insertCommand = new StringBuilder();
    insertCommand.Append("insert into SalesLT.ProductCategory ");
    insertCommand.Append("([ParentProductCategoryID], [Name]) ");
    insertCommand.AppendFormat(
        "values ('{0}', '{1}')",
        ddlParentCategory.SelectedValue, txtName.Text);
    UpdateDB(insertCommand);
    PopulateGrid();
}

protected void btnEdit_Click(object sender, EventArgs e)
{
    StringBuilder updateCommand = new StringBuilder(
        "Update SalesLT.ProductCategory SET ");
    updateCommand.AppendFormat(
        "Name='{0}', ", txtName.Text);
    updateCommand.AppendFormat(
        "ParentProductCategoryID='{1}' ", ddlParentCategory.SelectedValue);
    updateCommand.AppendFormat(
        "where ProductCategoryID='{2}'", hdnCategoryID.Value);
    UpdateDB(updateCommand);
    PopulateGrid();
}
protected void btnDelete_Click(object sender, EventArgs e)
{
    string deleteCommand = String.Format(
        "delete from SalesLT.ProductCategory where ProductCategoryID ='{0}'",
        hdnCategoryID.Value);
    UpdateDB(deleteCommand);
    PopulateGrid();
}
```

Lastly, the UpdateDB command, which all three Click handlers call, simply takes in the command string passed to it by the handlers, creates a Command object for it, and then calls ExecuteNonQuery on it. Note that ExecuteNonQuery returns the number of rows affected by the command but that this value is not used here. You could easily build in error checking to ensure that the expected number of rows was changed as appropriate.

```
private void UpdateDB(string cmdString)
{
    SqlConnection connection = new SqlConnection(connectionString);
    SqlCommand command = new SqlCommand(cmdString, connection);
```

```
      try
      {
        connection.Open( );
        command.ExecuteNonQuery( );
      }
      finally
      {
        if (connection.State != ConnectionState.Closed)
        {
          connection.Close( );
        }
      }
    }
  } // end of UpdatingDBDirectly.aspx.cs
```

As an exercise, you might want to extend this page so that it can create subcategories of subcategories and allow the editing and addition of new top-level categories.

Updating Data with Transactions

An important feature of most industrial-strength databases is support for transactions. A *transaction* is a set of database operations that must all complete or fail together. That is, either all the operations must complete successfully (commit the transaction), or all must be undone (roll back the transaction) so that the database is left in the state it was in before the transaction began.

A good example of a transaction is transferring money at an ATM. If you transfer $50 from checking to savings, the bank will first reduce your checking account by $50 and then increase your savings account by $50. If it does the first step but not the second, you will be annoyed.

The bank system treats the entire set of reducing one account and increasing the other as a single transaction. The entire transaction occurs or none of it occurs; it is not valid for it to occur "partially."

The ACID Test

Database designers define the requirements of a transaction with the so-called "ACID" test. ACID is an acronym for *Atomic, Consistent, Isolated,* and *Durable.* Here's a brief summary of what each of these terms means:

Atomic

An atomic interaction is indivisible, that is, it cannot be partially implemented. Every transaction must be atomic. For instance, in the previous banking example, it must be impossible to decrement your checking account but fail to increment your savings account. If the transaction fails, it must return the database to the state it would have been in without the transaction.

All transactions, even failed ones, affect the database in trivial ways: resources are expended, performance is affected, and the logfile is updated. The atomic requirement only implies that, if a transaction is rolled back, all of the tables and data (other than log tables) will be in the state they would have been in had the transaction not been attempted at all.

Consistent

The database is presumed to be in a consistent state before the transaction begins, and the transaction must leave it in a consistent state when it completes. While the transaction is being processed, the database need not be in a consistent state. To continue with our example of transferring money, the database need not be consistent during the transaction. (It is okay to decrement my checking account before incrementing my savings account.) It must end in a consistent state, that is, when the transaction completes, the books must balance.

Isolated

Transactions are not processed one at a time. Typically, a database may be processing many transactions at once, switching its attention among various operations. This creates the possibility that a transaction can view and act upon data that reflects intermediate changes from another transaction that is still in progress and that therefore currently has its data in an inconsistent state. Transaction isolation is designed to prevent this problem. For a transaction to be isolated the effects of the transaction must be exactly as though the transaction were acted on alone; there can be no effects or dependencies on other database activities. For more information, see the upcoming "Data Isolation" sidebar.

Durable

Once a transaction is committed, the effect on the database is permanent.

Implementing Transactions

You can implement transactions in ASP.NET in two ways. You can allow the database to manage the transaction by using transactions within your stored procedure, or you can use connection-based transactions in ADO.NET. In the latter case, the transaction is created and enforced outside the database. This allows you to add transaction support to databases that do not otherwise provide for it or to wrap several stored procedures and other database calls inside a single transaction.

In the following example, you will build a web page called *Transactions.aspx*, shown in Figure 9-14. A GridView lists the current orders in the AdventureWorksLT database, and selecting one of the orders shows its details in a DetailsView control. Underneath these controls, a small form allows you to add a new order to the database.

Data Isolation

Creating fully isolated transactions in a multiuser environment is a nontrivial exercise. Isolation can be violated in three ways:

Lost update
> One user reads a record, a second updates the record, and the first overwrites the second's update.

Dirty read
> User 1 writes data; user 2 reads what user 1 wrote. User 1 overwrites the data or rolls back the transaction, thus leaving user 2 with old data.

Unrepeatable read
> User 1 reads data; the data is overwritten by user 2. User 1 tries to reread the data, but the data has changed.

Database experts identify four degrees of isolation:

Degree 0
> Limited only to preventing the overwriting of data by any other transaction that is of degree 1 or greater.

Degree 1
> Has no lost updates.

Degree 2
> Has no lost updates and no dirty reads but may have unrepeatable reads.

Degree 3
> Has no lost updates, no dirty reads, and no unrepeatable reads.

Clicking the Add button will update the `SalesOrderHeader` and `SalesOrderDetail` tables with the new order. To ensure that either both tables or neither table is updated these two actions will be run inside a transaction. The form allows you the choice of running the transaction either within a stored procedure on the database or within a .NET transaction object generated from the connection.

To begin, create *Transactions.aspx* as a new web form in the *C9_ADONET* website and switch to Design view. You'll need to add a `GridView` to display the orders (with an ID of `OrdersGridView`) and a `DetailsView` with an ID of `OrderDetailsView` to display the details of the selected order. This second control should be inside a `Panel` (with an ID of `OrderDetailsPanel`) so that it can be hidden when an order is not currently selected.

Create an HTML table below the panel with three rows and six columns for the form shown in Figure 9-14. In it, you should place the following:

- Two `DropDownLists`—`ddlCompany` and `ddlProduct`—which will contain the various companies and products to which the new order could relate. These go in the top row.

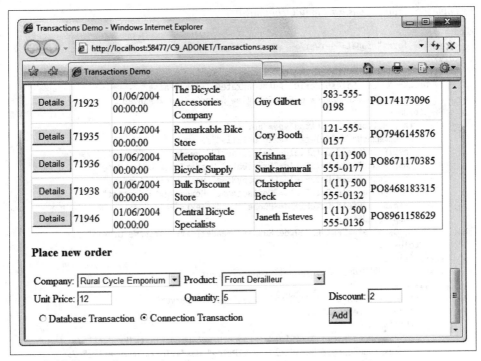

Figure 9-14. Transactions.aspx in action

- Three TextBoxes—txtUnitPrice, txtQuantity, and txtDiscount—which allow you to set the price per unit of the product being ordered, the number of units being sold, and the discount per unit on the order. These go in the middle row.

- A RadioButtonList, rbTransactionType, to allow you to set the type of transaction used when adding the order to the database.

- A Button to start the transaction (btnAdd) and a Label (lblNewOrderID) to display the SalesOrderID of the new order in the database.

Example 9-5 shows the full markup for *Transactions.aspx*. Any properties changed from their defaults or events being handled on the controls are highlighted.

Example 9-5. Transactions.aspx in full

```
<%@ Page Language="C#" AutoEventWireup="true"
   CodeFile="Transactions.aspx.cs" Inherits="Transactions" %>

<!DOCTYPE html PUBLIC "-//W3C//DTD XHTML 1.0 Transitional//EN"
   "http://www.w3.org/TR/xhtml1/DTD/xhtml1-transitional.dtd">
<html xmlns="http://www.w3.org/1999/xhtml">
<head runat="server">
   <title>Transactions Demo</title>
</head>
```

Example 9-5. Transactions.aspx in full (continued)

```
<body>
   <form id="form1" runat="server">
   <div>
      <asp:GridView ID="OrdersGridView" runat="server"
         DataKeyNames="SalesOrderID" AutoGenerateColumns="False"
         OnSelectedIndexChanged="OrdersGridView_SelectedIndexChanged">
         <Columns>
            <asp:ButtonField ButtonType="Button"
               CommandName="Select" Text="Details" />
            <asp:BoundField DataField="SalesOrderID" HeaderText="OrderID" />
            <asp:BoundField DataField="OrderDate" HeaderText="Order Date" />
            <asp:BoundField DataField="CompanyName" HeaderText="Company" />
            <asp:BoundField DataField="ContactName" HeaderText="Contact" />
            <asp:BoundField DataField="Phone" HeaderText="Phone" />
            <asp:BoundField
               DataField="PurchaseOrderNumber" HeaderText="Purchase Order#" />
         </Columns>
      </asp:GridView>
      <asp:Panel ID="OrderDetailsPanel" runat="server"
         Visible="false">
         <asp:DetailsView ID="OrderDetailsView" runat="server"
            AutoGenerateRows="False">
            <Fields>
               <asp:BoundField DataField="ProductName" HeaderText="Product" />
               <asp:BoundField DataField="UnitPrice" HeaderText="Unit Price" />
               <asp:BoundField DataField="OrderQty" HeaderText="Quantity" />
            </Fields>
         </asp:DetailsView>
      </asp:Panel>

      <h3>
         Place new order</h3>
      <table>
         <tr>
            <td>
               Company:
            </td>
            <td>
               <asp:DropDownList ID="ddlCompany" runat="server"
                  DataValueField="CustomerID" DataTextField="CompanyName" />
            </td>
            <td>
               Product:
            </td>
            <td>
               <asp:DropDownList ID="ddlProduct" runat="server"
                  DataValueField="ProductID" DataTextField="Name" />
            </td>
            <td></td><td></td>
         </tr>
         <tr>
```

Example 9-5. Transactions.aspx in full (continued)

```
            <td>
               Unit Price:
            </td>
            <td>
               <asp:TextBox ID="txtUnitPrice" runat="server" Text="0" />
            </td>
            <td>
               Quantity:
            </td>
            <td>
               <asp:TextBox ID="txtQuantity" runat="server" Text="0" />
            </td>
            <td>
               Discount:
            </td>
            <td>
               <asp:TextBox ID="txtDiscount" runat="server" Text="0" />
            </td>
         </tr>
         <tr>
            <td colspan="4">
               <asp:RadioButtonList ID="rbTransactionType" runat="server"
                  RepeatDirection="Horizontal">
                  <asp:ListItem Value="DB" Selected="true">
                     Database Transaction</asp:ListItem>
                  <asp:ListItem Value="Connection">
                     Connection Transaction</asp:ListItem>
               </asp:RadioButtonList>
            </td>
            <td>
               <asp:Button ID="btnAdd" runat="server"
                  Text="Add" OnClick="btnAdd_Click" />
            </td>
            <td>
               <asp:Label ID="lblNewOrderID" runat="server" />
            </td>
         </tr>
      </table>
   </div>
   </form>
</body>
</html>
```

With the markup done, switch to the code-behind page for this example. The Page_
Load handler does nothing more than populate the DropDownLists and OrdersGridView
with the required data when the page is initially loaded. Any refreshing of data will
be dealt with in the various event handlers this page uses.

```
using System;
using System.Data;
using System.Data.SqlClient;
using System.Text;
```

```
using System.Web.UI;
using System.Web.UI.WebControls;

public partial class Transactions : Page
{
   private readonly string connectionString =
      "Data Source=<your_database>;Initial Catalog=AdventureWorksLT;" +
      "Integrated Security=True";

   protected void Page_Load(object sender, EventArgs e)
   {
      if (!IsPostBack)
      {
         SqlConnection conn = new SqlConnection(connectionString);

         try
         {
            conn.Open( );
            BindCustomerList(conn);
            BindProductList(conn);
            BindOrdersGridView(conn);
         }
         finally
         {
            if (conn.State != ConnectionState.Closed)
            {
               conn.Close( );
            }
         }
      }
   }

}
```

One new approach used here is to use the same open connection for all queries to
the database. In previous examples, the end of each call to the database would be followed immediately by closing the connection. To this extent, the methods populating the controls with data take the open connection as a parameter but take care to
close only the DataReader and not the connection once data binding has occurred.

```
private void BindProductList(SqlConnection conn)
{
   SqlDataReader productReader = GetDataReader(conn, "Product");
   ddlProduct.DataSource = productReader;
   ddlProduct.DataBind( );
   productReader.Close( );
}

private void BindCustomerList(SqlConnection conn)
{
   SqlDataReader companyReader = GetDataReader(conn, "Customer");
   ddlCompany.DataSource = companyReader;
   ddlCompany.DataBind( );
   companyReader.Close( );
}
```

Previous examples in this chapter have used `DataViews` stored in `ViewState` to keep a disconnected copy of the `SalesOrderDetail` table available for showing an order's details on the page. In this example, you'll use a `DataReader` to return only the details for the currently selected order directly from the database (in the `GridView`'s `SelectedIndexChanged` event handler).

Using a `DataReader` is more appropriate given that new orders are being added to the database and it makes more sense to update the database as soon as the order is made, rather than store all new orders in a `DataSet` in session state and then synchronize them with the database later on. This asynchronous approach might cause an issue, for example, with stock levels being exhausted before the order was added to the database, even though they were not exhausted when the order was made. For the same reason, a `DataReader` is used to refresh the main `OrdersGridView` rather than a `DataTable`; there's no need to keep the data around if it is likely to need refreshing after a postback and a `DataReader` is faster than a `DataTable`.

```
private void BindOrdersGridView(SqlConnection conn)
{
    SqlDataReader orderReader = GetDataReader(conn, "Orders");
    OrdersGridView.DataSource = orderReader;
    OrdersGridView.DataBind();

    //Close DataReader but keep connection open
    orderReader.Close();
}

protected void OrdersGridView_SelectedIndexChanged(object sender,
                                                   EventArgs e)
{
    SqlConnection conn = new SqlConnection(connectionString);

    try
    {
        conn.Open();
        BindOrdersGridView(conn);
        SqlDataReader drDetails = GetDataReader(conn, "OrderDetails");

        if (drDetails.HasRows)
        {
            OrderDetailsPanel.Visible = true;
            OrderDetailsView.DataSource = drDetails;
            OrderDetailsView.DataBind();
        }
        else
        {
            OrderDetailsPanel.Visible = false;
        }
    }
    finally
    {
        if (conn.State != ConnectionState.Closed)
```

```
            {
                conn.Close();
            }
        }
    }
```

In this example, all the methods and event handlers that need data use a SqlDataReader object to retrieve the data from the database. Therefore, they all call into the GetDataReader method with the table they need to access and the method returns the appropriate object.

This approach has several pros and cons. On the positive side, it has the advantage of centralizing all the select queries in one place, which means it could prove easier to read and debug the page. On the negative side, the approach wouldn't work too well if you needed the SELECT queries to be parameterized. How would you pass in the various numbers of parameters as required and still keep things tidy? However, it works well in this example:

```
private SqlDataReader GetDataReader(
    SqlConnection conn, string infoRequired)
{
    StringBuilder cmdString = new StringBuilder();

    switch (infoRequired)
    {
      case "Orders":
        cmdString.Append(
          "select o.salesorderid, o.orderdate, ");
        cmdString.Append(
          "c.FirstName + ' ' + c.LastName as 'ContactName', ");
        cmdString.Append(
          "c.companyname, c.phone, o.PurchaseOrderNumber ");
        cmdString.Append(
          "from SalesLT.SalesOrderHeader o ");
        cmdString.Append(
          "inner join SalesLT.Customer c on o.CustomerId = c.CustomerId ");
        cmdString.Append("order by o.salesorderid");
        break;
      case "OrderDetails":
        int index = OrdersGridView.SelectedIndex;
        int orderId = -1;

        if (index != -1)
        {
            //get the orderId from the GridView
            DataKey key = OrdersGridView.DataKeys[index];
            orderId = (int)key.Value;
        }

        cmdString.Append(
          "select d.UnitPrice, d.OrderQty, p.Name as 'ProductName' ");
```

```
            cmdString.Append("from SalesLT.SalesOrderDetail d ");
            cmdString.Append(
                "inner join SalesLT.Product p on d.ProductId = p.ProductId ");
            cmdString.AppendFormat(
                "where d.SalesOrderId = {0}", orderId.ToString());
            break;
        case "Customer":
            cmdString.Append(
                "select CustomerID, CompanyName from SalesLT.Customer");
            break;
        case "Product":
            cmdString.Append("select ProductID, Name from SalesLT.Product");
            break;
        default:
            throw new ArgumentException(
                "GetDataReader was given an incorrect request for data");
    }

    SqlCommand cmd = new SqlCommand(cmdString.ToString(), conn);

    return cmd.ExecuteReader();
}
```

To create a new order, choose a customer and a product from the DropDownLists, fill
in the Unit Price, Quantity, and Discount text boxes, select a transaction type, and
click the Add button. The Click handler for the button parses the values from the
form into values for the database—in this case, they should all be integers—and then
reads the RadioButtonList to see which type of transaction should be called.

```
protected void btnAdd_Click(object sender, EventArgs e)
{
    int ProductId = Convert.ToInt32(ddlProduct.SelectedValue);
    int Quantity = Convert.ToInt32(txtQuantity.Text);
    int Discount = Convert.ToInt32(txtDiscount.Text);
    int PricePerUnit = Convert.ToInt32(txtUnitPrice.Text);
    int CustomerId = Convert.ToInt32(ddlCompany.SelectedValue);

    string whichTransaction =
        rbTransactionType.SelectedValue.ToString();

    if (whichTransaction == "DB")
    {
        PerformDBTransaction(
            CustomerId, ProductId, Quantity, Discount, PricePerUnit);
    }
    else
    {
        PerformConnectionTransaction(
            CustomerId, ProductId, Quantity, Discount, PricePerUnit);
    }
}
```

Using database transactions

If you choose Database Transaction, btnAdd_Click calls PerformDBTransaction, which simply passes in the values to a stored procedure called spAddOrderTransactions, and then updates the page once it has run.

```
private void PerformDBTransaction(
    int CustomerId, int ProductId, int Quantity,
    int Discount, int PricePerUnit)
{
    // Create connection and command
    SqlConnection conn = new SqlConnection(connectionString);
    SqlCommand cmd = new SqlCommand("spAddOrderTransactions", conn);
    cmd.CommandType = CommandType.StoredProcedure;

    // Add Input Parameters
    cmd.Parameters.Add(
        "@CustomerId", SqlDbType.Int).Value = CustomerId;
    cmd.Parameters.Add(
        "@ProductId", SqlDbType.Int).Value = ProductId;
    cmd.Parameters.Add(
        "@Quantity", SqlDbType.Int).Value = Quantity;
    cmd.Parameters.Add(
        "@Discount", SqlDbType.Money).Value = Discount;
    cmd.Parameters.Add(
        "@UnitPrice", SqlDbType.Money).Value = PricePerUnit;

    // Add Output Parameter
    SqlParameter salesOrderIdParam =
        cmd.Parameters.Add("@SalesOrderId", SqlDbType.Int);
    salesOrderIdParam.Direction = ParameterDirection.Output;

    // Set up new order id
    int OrderId = -1;

    try
    {
        conn.Open();

        // run transaction in DB
        cmd.ExecuteNonQuery();

        // get new order id
        OrderId = Convert.ToInt32(salesOrderIdParam.Value);

        // update gridview
        BindOrdersGridView(conn);
    }
    catch (Exception e)
    {
        Trace.Write(e.Message);
    }
    finally
```

```
    {
        if (conn.State != ConnectionState.Closed)
        {
            conn.Close( );
        }
    }

    //Reset the form
    txtDiscount.Text = string.Empty;
    txtQuantity.Text = string.Empty;
    txtUnitPrice.Text = string.Empty;
    lblNewOrderID.Text = OrderId.ToString( );
}
```

The responsibility of managing the transaction, committing it if both tables are updated, and rolling it back if anything goes wrong is entirely within the stored procedure. The only job of PerformDBTransaction is to invoke the stored procedure and pass in the appropriate parameters. The code to create this stored procedure, spAddOrderTransactions, is shown next:

```
CREATE PROCEDURE [dbo].[spAddOrderTransactions]
    @SalesOrderId integer out,
    @CustomerID int,
    @Quantity int,
    @ProductId int,
    @UnitPrice money,
    @Discount money
AS
    Begin Transaction

        -- add new Order to SalesOrderHeader table
        insert into SalesLT.SalesOrderHeader
            (DueDate, CustomerID, ShipMethod)
        values
            ( GetDate( )+5, @CustomerID, 'CARGO TRANSPORT 5')

        -- get new SalesOrderID
        select @SalesOrderID = scope_identity( )

        -- if there's a problem skip to ErrorHandler
        if @@Error <> 0 goto ErrorHandler

        -- Add order details to SalesOrderDetail table
        Insert into SalesLT.SalesOrderDetail
            (SalesOrderID, OrderQty, ProductID,
             UnitPrice, UnitPriceDiscount)
        values
            (@SalesOrderID, @Quantity, @ProductId,
             @UnitPrice, @Discount)

        -- again, if there's a problem skip to ErrorHandler
        if @@Error <> 0 goto ErrorHandler
```

```
    -- if no problems, commit transaction and exit
    commit transaction
    return

    -- else roll back the transaction and exit
    ErrorHandler:
    rollback transaction
    return
```

Using connection transactions

If you choose to add the order to the database using the connection and .NET to manage the transaction, your C# for creating and managing the transaction is a little more complex. The steps are as follows:

1. Create a SqlConnection object to your database.
2. Create a SqlCommand object for your database queries and assign it the SqlConnection object.
3. Open the connection.
4. Create a SqlTransaction object by calling BeginTransaction( ) on your open connection.
5. Assign the new SqlTransaction object to the SqlCommand's Transaction property.
6. Run any commands as required, and if all is well, call Commit( ) on the SqlTransaction.
7. If any errors occur, call Rollback( ) on the SqlTransaction.
8. Finally, close the connection.

Within this particular transaction, two commands are sent. First, the stored procedure spAddOrder (shown next) is used to add the new order to the SalesOrderHeader table and return the new ID of the order in the table. Then the details of the order are added to the SalesOrdersDetail table using the new ID as a reference to link the information across the two tables.

```
CREATE PROCEDURE [dbo].[spAddOrder]
    @SalesOrderID integer out,
    @CustomerID integer
AS
    -- add new Order to SalesOrderHeader table
    insert into SalesLT.SalesOrderHeader
        (DueDate, CustomerID, ShipMethod)
    values
        (GetDate( )+5, @CustomerID, 'CARGO TRANSPORT 5')

    -- get new SalesOrderID
    select @SalesOrderID = scope_identity( )
RETURN
```

Note how the try/catch/finally construct is used to manage the transaction. The call to roll back a transaction is in the catch block if an exception is thrown, and the call to commit is in the try block.

```
private void PerformConnectionTransaction(
    int CustomerId, int ProductId, int Quantity, int Discount, int PricePerUnit)
{
    // Get connection
    SqlConnection conn = new SqlConnection(connectionString);

    // Set up command to run sproc spAddOrder
    SqlCommand cmd = new SqlCommand("spAddOrder", conn);
    cmd.CommandType = CommandType.StoredProcedure;

    // Set up Parameters for spAddOrder
    SqlParameter customerIdParam =
        cmd.Parameters.Add("@CustomerID", SqlDbType.Int);
    customerIdParam.Value = CustomerId;
    customerIdParam.Direction = ParameterDirection.Input;

    SqlParameter salesOrderIdParam =
        cmd.Parameters.Add("@SalesOrderID", SqlDbType.Int);
    salesOrderIdParam.Direction = ParameterDirection.Output;

    // Declare transaction
    SqlTransaction transaction = null;
    int OrderID = -1;

    try
    {
        // Open connection
        // Create transaction and add to command
        conn.Open();
        transaction = conn.BeginTransaction();
        cmd.Transaction = transaction;

        // Execute the stored procedure and get
        // the ID for the new order
        cmd.ExecuteNonQuery();
        OrderID =
            Convert.ToInt32(cmd.Parameters["@SalesOrderID"].Value);

        // Now add the details for the order
        StringBuilder cmdAddDetails =
            new StringBuilder("insert into SalesLT.SalesOrderDetail ");
        cmdAddDetails.Append(
            "(SalesOrderID, OrderQty, ProductID, UnitPrice, UnitPriceDiscount) ");
        cmdAddDetails.AppendFormat("values ({0}, {1}, {2}, {3}, {4})",
            OrderID.ToString(), Quantity, ProductId, PricePerUnit, Discount);

        // Reuse the command object for this update and execute it
```

```
        cmd.CommandType = CommandType.Text;
        cmd.CommandText = cmdAddDetails.ToString();
        cmd.ExecuteNonQuery();

        // commit the transaction
        transaction.Commit();

        BindOrdersGridView(conn);
    }
    catch (Exception e)
    {
        Trace.Write(e.Message);
        transaction.Rollback();
    }
    finally
    {
        if (conn.State != ConnectionState.Closed)
        {
            conn.Close();
        }
    }

    //Reset the form
    txtDiscount.Text = string.Empty;
    txtQuantity.Text = string.Empty;
    txtUnitPrice.Text = string.Empty;
    lblNewOrderID.Text = OrderID.ToString();
    }
} // end of transactions.aspx.cs
```

Note that if you ever want to redirect the user to a new page once a transaction has committed—for example, to a page informing the user she should expect her new CDs in the mail and the money has been taken out of her account—you'll need to be careful if you use Server.Transfer rather than Response.Redirect (see Chapter 6 for complete descriptions of these calls). Server.Transfer ends the page being transferred from, which always raises a ThreadAbortException.

This is usually not an issue, but if the Server.Transfer occurs as part of a connection-based database transaction inside a try block, where the Rollback method is called in a catch block as demonstrated earlier, the transaction will never commit because the transaction Commit method will be negated by the ThreadAbortException, unless you specifically catch the ThreadAbortException, as in the following code snippet:

```
try
{
    //  Do database stuff, then commit the transaction.
    transaction.Commit();

    //  Navigate to another page assuming a successful commit.
    //  This will raise a ThreadAbortException every time.
    Server.Transfer("OrderDetails.aspx?OrderID=" + strOrderID);
}
```

```
catch (ThreadAbortException ex)
{
    //  Placeholder to catch the routine exception.
}
catch (Exception ex)
{
    //  There was a problem with the commit, so roll back.
    transaction.Rollback();
}
finally
{
    //  Always close the connection.
    connection.Close();
}
```

Binding to Business Objects

Most of the applications we've looked at in this book have been two-tier, separating the user interface from the backend data. Many larger commercial applications, however, are *n*-tier, with at least a middle business-logic layer to separate retrieval of data from the database from manipulation (and validation) of that data before presentation.

In Chapter 7, you saw how you can use the `ObjectDataSource` to reference a class that provides the data to be presented on the page. Taking this example one step further, you can create a simple Model-View-Controller (MVC) style designed site which uses a stateless class to encapsulate business logic, and a "model" class that knows how to load and store data from the database.

To illustrate implementing the *n*-tier MVC pattern, you'll create a stateless business class, `CustomerBusinessLogic`, and a "model" of the `Customer` table in the Adventure-WorksLT database, named `AWCustomer`. You'll bind an `ObjectDataSource` to the stateless business-logic class, which will use the `Model` class to get and retrieve data about customers in the database.

 This is a much simplified example of the MVC model made to fit within a few pages of a book. Fully fledged MVC site templates are available to download for almost all languages. Ruby on Rails is the most well-known example, but Microsoft is also working on its own MVC site templates for Visual Studio development. See Chapter 21 for more information on that.

To begin, add a new class called *CustomerBusinessLogic.cs* to the *App_Code* folder in the *C9_ADONET* website. This will contain both the static business logic class and the model class for the web page.

First we'll discuss the business logic class, which contains three methods. `UpdateCustomerInformation` will lock into the `Update` method for the `ObjectDataSource` (but it's stubbed out for this example), and GetCustomer returns an individual customer instance given a CustomerID.

```
using System;
using System.Collections;
using System.Data;
using System.Data.SqlClient;
using System.Text;
using System.Web.UI;
using System.Web.UI.WebControls;

/// <summary>
/// Stateless business logic that encapsulates what
/// can be done with a Customer object
/// All methods are static
/// </summary>
public static class CustomerBusinessLogic
{
    public static void UpdateCustomerInformation(
        AdvWorksCustomer customer)
    {
        bool returnValue = customer.Save();
        if (returnValue == false)
        {
            throw new ApplicationException("Unable to update customer");
        }
    }

    public static AdvWorksCustomer GetCustomer(string custID)
    {
        return new AdvWorksCustomer(custID);
    }
}
```

The only interesting method is GetAllCustomers, whose job is to return an ICollection to which the grid may bind via the ObjectDataSource control. You do this by creating an instance of SqlDataSource initialized with the connection string and a SELECT statement that gets all the CustomerIDs from the Customer table. What you get back from calling dataSource.Select (passing in no arguments) is a collection of DataRowViews.

You enumerate the collection, extracting each DataRowView, and from that you extract the CustomerID. Using that CustomerID, you instantiate an AdvWorksCustomer object which you add to your ArrayList. Once you have created an instance of the AdvWorksCustomer for every ID in the database, that collection is used as the data source for the GridView.

This process allows you to manipulate the data object (the AdvWorksCustomer) to add business logic to any or all of its properties. In this example, the AdvWorksCustomer object does nothing more than store the data for a customer from the Customer table, but you can imagine it performing operations on that data or extending the definition of a customer beyond a single table (or even beyond the data in a single database).

```
public static ICollection GetAllCustomers()
{
    ArrayList allCustomers = new ArrayList();
    String cmdAllCustomersString =
        "Select CustomerID from SalesLT.Customer";
    String connString =
        "Data Source=<your_database>;Initial " +
        "Catalog=AdventureWorksLT;Integrated Security=True";
    SqlDataSource dataSource =
        new SqlDataSource(connString, cmdAllCustomersString);

    try
    {
        // select with no arguments
        IEnumerable CustomerIDs =
            dataSource.Select(DataSourceSelectArguments.Empty);

        IEnumerator enumerator = CustomerIDs.GetEnumerator();
        while (enumerator.MoveNext())
        {
            DataRowView drv = enumerator.Current as DataRowView;
            if (drv != null)
            {
                string customerID =
                    drv["CustomerID"].ToString();
                AdvWorksCustomer cust =
                    new AdvWorksCustomer(customerID);
                allCustomers.Add(cust);
            }
        }
    }
    finally
    {
        dataSource.Dispose();
    }
    return allCustomers;
}
} // end of CustomerBusinessLogic class
```

The AdvWorksCustomer "model" class reflects the fields in the Customer table:

```
public class AdvWorksCustomer
{
    private object customerID;
    public string FirstName { get; set; }
    public string MiddleName { get; set; }
    public string LastName { get; set; }
    public string Suffix { get; set; }
    public string CompanyName { get; set; }
    public string SalesPerson { get; set; }
    public string EmailAddress { get; set; }
    public string Phone { get; set; }
    public DateTime ModifiedDate { get; set; }
    public string PasswordHash { get; set; }
    public string PasswordSalt { get; set; }
```

```
public bool Save()
{
   return true;
}
```

It also has two constructors. The first has no parameters and returns an instance with blank values:

```
public AdvWorksCustomer()
{
   customerID = DBNull.Value;
   FirstName = String.Empty;
   MiddleName = String.Empty;
   LastName = String.Empty;
   Suffix = String.Empty;
   CompanyName = String.Empty;
   SalesPerson = String.Empty;
   EmailAddress = String.Empty;
   Phone = String.Empty;
   PasswordHash = String.Empty;
   PasswordSalt = String.Empty;
   ModifiedDate = DateTime.MinValue;
}
```

The second constructor takes an integer representing the customer's ID in the database and returns an instance of the class populated with all the information for that customer:

```
public AdvWorksCustomer(string customerID)
{
   String connString =
      "Data Source=<your_database>;Initial Catalog=AdventureWorksLT;" +
      "Integrated Security=True";

   StringBuilder cmdString = new StringBuilder(
      "Select FirstName, MiddleName, LastName, Suffix, ");
   cmdString.Append("CompanyName, SalesPerson, EmailAddress, Phone, ");
   cmdString.Append("PasswordHash, PasswordSalt, ModifiedDate ");
   cmdString.Append("from SalesLT.Customer ");
   cmdString.Append("where CustomerID = @customerID");

   // Create connection and command objects
   SqlConnection conn = new SqlConnection(connString);
   SqlCommand cmd = new SqlCommand(cmdString.ToString(), conn);
   cmd.Parameters.Add("@customerID", SqlDbType.VarChar).Value = customerID;

   try
   {
      conn.Open();
      SqlDataReader dr = cmd.ExecuteReader(CommandBehavior.CloseConnection);
      if (dr != null && dr.Read())
      {
         FirstName = dr["FirstName"].ToString();
         MiddleName = dr["MiddleName"].ToString();
         LastName = dr["LastName"].ToString();
```

```
                  Suffix = dr["Suffix"].ToString( );
                  CompanyName = dr["CompanyName"].ToString( );
                  SalesPerson = dr["SalesPerson"].ToString( );
                  EmailAddress = dr["EmailAddress"].ToString( );
                  Phone = dr["Phone"].ToString( );
                  PasswordHash = dr["PasswordHash"].ToString( );
                  PasswordSalt = dr["PasswordSalt"].ToString( );
                  ModifiedDate = Convert.ToDateTime(dr["ModifiedDate"]);
               }
               else
               {
                  throw new ApplicationException(
                     "Data not found for customer ID " + customerID);
               }
               dr.Close( );
            }
            finally
            {
               if (conn.State != ConnectionState.Closed)
               {
                  conn.Close( );
               }
            }
         }
      }
   }
```

Note that after the DataReader and the connection are closed, the instance of AdvWorksCustomer is fully instantiated and can be used to bind data in the GridView through the ObjectDataSource. Indeed, now that both classes are complete, it's time to create the web form to display the customer data.

Add to *C9_ADONET* a new web form called *BusinessObjects.aspx* and add an ObjectDataSource object to the page. Use its configuration wizard to select the CustomerBusinessLogic class as your business object and GetAllCustomers( ) as its SELECT method. Then add a GridView to the page and select the ObjectDataSource control you just created as its data source. No code needs to be added to *BusinessObjects.aspx.cs*. The markup for the page is shown in Example 9-6.

Example 9-6. BusinessObjects.aspx in full

```
<%@ Page Language="C#" AutoEventWireup="true"
   CodeFile="BusinessObjects.aspx.cs" Inherits="BusinessObjects" %>

<!DOCTYPE html PUBLIC "-//W3C//DTD XHTML 1.1//EN"
   "http://www.w3.org/TR/xhtml11/DTD/xhtml11.dtd">

<html xmlns="http://www.w3.org/1999/xhtml" >
<head runat="server">
   <title>Binding To Business Objects</title>
</head>
<body>
   <form id="form1" runat="server">
   <div>
```

Example 9-6. BusinessObjects.aspx in full (continued)

```
    <asp:GridView ID="GridView1" runat="server"
        DataSourceID="ObjectDataSource1" />

    <asp:ObjectDataSource ID="ObjectDataSource1" runat="server"
        SelectMethod="GetAllCustomers"
        TypeName="CustomerBusinessLogic" />

  </div>
  </form>
</body>
</html>
```

When the application is run, the GridView is bound to the ObjectDataSource and the data is displayed appropriately, as shown in Figure 9-15.

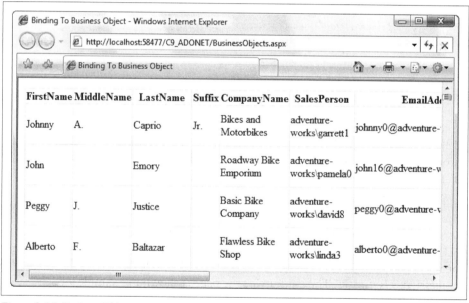

Figure 9-15. BusinessObjects.aspx in action

In the example shown, the data in the database is isomorphic with the fields in the business object, but in a real-world application, the customer business object might be larger, smaller, or more complex than the data stored in a single table in the database.

Two of the new technologies that became available in this .NET 3.5 release that address this style of binding to business objects are Language Integrated Query (LINQ) and the ASP.NET MVC website project. We'll look at the latter item in Chapter 21. We introduce LINQ in the next chapter.

CHAPTER 10

Presenting LINQ

One of the main additions to the .NET Framework for the v3.5 release is Language Integrated Query (LINQ), a new *application programming interface* (API) that is essentially a collection of namespaces and classes with a common purpose: to query data from any and all sources.

You might well wonder why Microsoft has chosen to provide yet another way to do what data source objects and ADO.NET do perfectly well already. Isn't LINQ a bit pointless? Well, no. You saw in Chapter 7 how .NET DataSource objects provide a level playing field for working with data in different sources—whether it is a business object, an XML file, or a database. You also saw in Chapter 9 how ADO.NET offers more precise control of access to databases. But let's take a step back and think about how you work with data from day to day:

- Very rarely are you in the position where all the data you need is in the same source. Some may be in a database, some in business objects, some on the end of a web service, and so on.

- The ease with which you can access data is entirely dependent on where it is stored. Accessing an in-memory object is much simpler than accessing data in an XML file or database.

- The raw data itself is not often the end product. Once collated, it needs to be sorted, altered, grouped, ordered, looped over, merged into one data pool, and so on. Take the following code snippet, for example:

```
List<Book> books = GetBooks();

//sort
books.SortByPrice(delegate(Book first, Book second))
{
    return ((double)(second.Price - first.Price));
}

// looping and aggregating
double totalIncome = 0;
```

```
books.ForEach(delegate(Book book))
{
    totalIncome += (book.Price * book.TotalSales);
}
```

- Here you have sorting, looping, and aggregation in six short lines. But this is assuming the price isn't fed in through reading some separate catalog as a spreadsheet, web service, or XML file.

So, why not have a better API for querying data? One that makes all data sources as easy to access as the rest, which provides a way to join that data from disparate data sources and then perform some standard data processing operations on it, all in one line of code. For instance, one operation that ensures all data fields are strongly typed so there's no worry about casting an Object into the right type when it's retrieved from a database. Another can be easily extensible for developers to create providers to access sources of data that aren't already supported. That's LINQ, and it looks something like this:

```
var query = from book in Books
    where book.QuarterlySales > 0
    select book => {Name, (Price * QuarterlySales) as QuarterlyIncome}
    orderby QuarterlySales;
```

LINQ uses a number of new features in C# 3.0 to present a familiar SQL-like syntax which you can use over any number of disparate data sources to query and process their contents for your use. It's a really powerful API.

In this chapter, you'll learn how it works, why it works so well, and how you can integrate it into your ASP.NET pages. In particular, you'll look at using LINQ with a SQL Server database and the support built into Visual Studio 2008 (VS2008) to make it almost trivial to enable. You'll also look at the LinqDataSource, a new DataSource control that uses LINQ expressions for its commands.

 LINQ is a big topic; big enough for its own books as well as those on the technologies which may use it, such as this one. For a more complete look at LINQ, consider *LINQ in Action* by Fabrice Marguerie et al. (Manning), and *Pro LINQ* by Joseph C. Ratz, Jr. (Apress). You might also like to look at the 500+ code samples hosted on the MSDN Code Gallery at *http://code.msdn.microsoft.com/csharpsamples*.

Deconstructing LINQ

Let's get straight into some code and see a very basic LINQ expression in action. Open VS2008 and create a new website called *C10_LINQ* for all the samples in this chapter. You'll start by creating and then running some queries over an in-memory list of books to demonstrate the basic query syntax that LINQ offers.

Click Website → Add New Item in VS2008, and then select the Class type to add to the website. Call the new class *Book.cs*, set its language to C#, and then click Add. Give it the code shown in Example 10-1.

Example 10-1. Book.cs in full

```
using System;
using System.Collections.Generic;

public class Book
{
    public string ISBN { get; set; }
    public string Title { get; set; }
    public decimal Price { get; set; }
    public DateTime ReleaseDate { get; set; }

    public static List<Book> GetBookList()
    {
        List<Book> list = new List<Book>();
        list.Add(new Book { ISBN = "0596529562",
            ReleaseDate = Convert.ToDateTime("2008-07-15"),
            Price = 30.0m, Title = "Programming ASP.NET 3.5" });
        list.Add(new Book { ISBN = "059652756X",
            ReleaseDate = Convert.ToDateTime("2008-06-15"),
            Price = 26.0m, Title = "Programming .NET 3.5" });
        list.Add(new Book { ISBN = "0596518455",
            ReleaseDate = Convert.ToDateTime("2008-07-15"),
            Price = 28.0m, Title = "Learning ASP.NET 3.5" });
        list.Add(new Book { ISBN = "0596518439",
            ReleaseDate = Convert.ToDateTime("2008-03-15"),
            Price = 25.0m, Title = "Programming Visual Basic 2008" });
        list.Add(new Book { ISBN = "0596527438",
            ReleaseDate = Convert.ToDateTime("2008-01-15"),
            Price = 31.0m, Title = "Programming C# 3.0" });

        return list;
    }
}
```

As you can see, the Book class contains four properties and one static method that returns a list of five books to any page that needs one. It also demonstrates one of the new language features in C# 3.0—object initializers—with which you can construct an instance of an object without using a constructor that has already been defined.

 You'll learn more about object initializers and other new C# 3.0 features in the next few pages.

Now add to the website a new web form called *SimpleQuery.aspx*, and add to the page a Label control called lblBooks. Switch to the code-behind page and add the code shown in Example 10-2.

Example 10-2. SimpleQuery.aspx.cs

```
using System;
using System.Collections.Generic;
using System.Linq;
using System.Web.UI;

public partial class SimpleQuery : Page
{
    protected void Page_Load(object sender, EventArgs e)
    {
        List<Book> books = Book.GetBookList();

        // Using inline binding
        var bookTitles =
            from b in books
            select b.Title;

        foreach (var title in bookTitles)
        {
            lblBooks.Text += String.Format("{0}<br />", title);
        }
    }
}
```

If you save and run this page, you'll see that the Label displays just the titles of the books from the list, as shown in Figure 10-1.

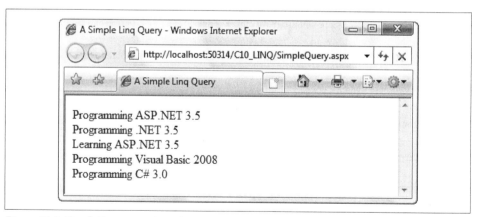

Figure 10-1. SimpleQuery.aspx in action

So, how is all this working? You can apply any LINQ query to any data-bearing class that inherits from IEnumerable<T>, such as List<Book> in the preceding example. And to make sure that queries are to be made on older .NET v1.x collections, lists, and the like, the System.Linq namespace, which contains the implementation for all the query operators (select, from, etc.), also includes the OfType<T> method, which you can apply to any class inheriting from IEnumerable to convert it into one inheriting from IEnumerable<T> (if you prefer not to cast the class) and so be LINQ-able too.

> If you're wondering what the <T> is doing suffixed to class names here, this is the way to declare *Generics*, a language feature introduced in C# 2.0. In C# 1.0, you could declare a List, but its contents were always treated as generic C# objects rather than as a Book or a Customer. The generic types, methods, and interfaces introduced in C# 2.0 allow you to replace T in their declaration with any type name and that type will be preserved throughout the generic's operation—hence, List<Book> or OfType<Customer>. For more on Generics, check out *Programming C# 3.0* by Jesse Liberty and Donald Xie (O'Reilly).

The actual LINQ query is very straightforward and can be interpreted much like a SQL statement, albeit with the clauses in a slightly different order:

```
var bookTitles =
    from b in books
    select b.Title;
```

> LINQ queries can be written on one line, but they are infinitely more readable split over several, much as you would do with SQL. Don't forget, though, that the similarity between LINQ and SQL is only in the keywords and not in the processing underneath. The order of the query reflects that.

The query iterates over the list of Books and returns a collection that implements IEnumerable<T> where T is the type of the result object. Each collection item is the title of a book as a string, so bookTitles is actually of type IEnumerable<String> (a StringCollection object), but because you can make use of the new anonymous types feature of C# 3.0, you don't need to figure this out before making the query. You can let the compiler figure it out for you. Phew!

You also can rewrite this query like so:

```
var bookTitles = books.Select(b => b.Title);
```

Though less straightforward to read, it points out a second new feature of C# 3.0 which this simple query uses. Lambda expressions, denoted by the => operator, take an object or set of objects and return (project) some of their properties to the Select method (or other query operator) for use elsewhere. We'll discuss lambda expressions in more detail later in this chapter.

Armed with the knowledge that LINQ queries return collections of some type and that you know what is in it, the final line then runs through the results of the query and puts all the book titles into the Text property of the Label control:

```
foreach (var title in bookTitles)
{
    lblBooks.Text += String.Format("{0}<br />", title);
}
```

Again, you can make use of anonymous typing in the foreach statement to make
your life simpler when working with the results of LINQ queries. The var keyword
here is still strongly typed—it's just inferred by the compiler—and is not a variant
type as the var keyword may imply for any Visual Basic users currently reading this.

So, can you set the DataSource property of one of the data controls you saw in
Chapter 8 to the result of a LINQ query? Let's find out; add to the website a new
page called *SimpleQuery2.aspx* and add a GridView control called gvwBooks to its content. Switch to the code-behind page and copy the Page_Load method and using
statements from Example 10-2 there. The only change you'll need to make is to
delete the foreach loop and replace it with the following to assign bookTitles as the
GridView's DataSource:

```
gvwBooks.DataSource = bookTitles;
gvwBooks.DataBind();
```

Run the page, and sure enough, the GridView is populated with the book titles, as
shown in Figure 10-2. But note that the column header says "Item".

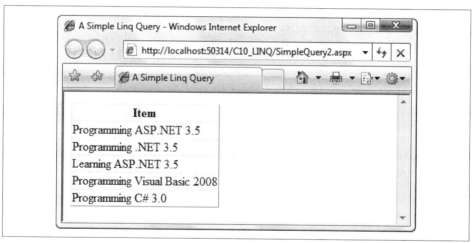

Figure 10-2. LINQ query results as a GridView data source

Look again at the LINQ expression you're using to return the book titles from the
List:

```
var bookTitles =
    from b in books
    select b.Title;
```

Unlike a SQL statement such as:

```
SELECT title from Books
```

the results in the LINQ statement are a collection of anonymous values, hence the GridView calling the column Item. It knows that there are values there, but not what the property/field name is called—because it hasn't been named. The issue isn't so much a problem with a GridView, but if you replace a GridView with a templated control such as a ListView, the problem is more apparent. So, let's do that. Delete the GridView from *SimpleQuery2.aspx* and add in a ListView, as shown in Example 10-3.

Example 10-3. SimpleQuery2.aspx with ListView

```
<%@ Page Language="C#" AutoEventWireup="true"
    CodeFile="SimpleQuery2.aspx.cs" Inherits="SimpleQuery" %>

<!DOCTYPE html PUBLIC "-//W3C//DTD XHTML 1.0 Transitional//EN"
    "http://www.w3.org/TR/xhtml1/DTD/xhtml1-transitional.dtd">

<html xmlns="http://www.w3.org/1999/xhtml">
<head runat="server">
    <title>A Simple Linq Query</title>
</head>
<body>
    <form id="form1" runat="server">
    <div>
      <asp:ListView runat="server" ID="lvwBooks">
        <LayoutTemplate>
           <ul>
               <asp:PlaceHolder runat="server" ID="itemPlaceholder" />
           </ul>
        </LayoutTemplate>
        <ItemTemplate>
           <li><%# Eval("Title") %></li>
        </ItemTemplate>
      </asp:ListView>
    </div>
    </form>
</body>
</html>
```

The main issue is what to name the field being bound to in the highlighted code. You're selecting b.Title here, so perhaps we can call it "Title". If you save and run the field, you'll see the error in Figure 10-3.

The solution is to give each value being selected a name to which you can bind. Example 10-4 shows the code to solve the problem.

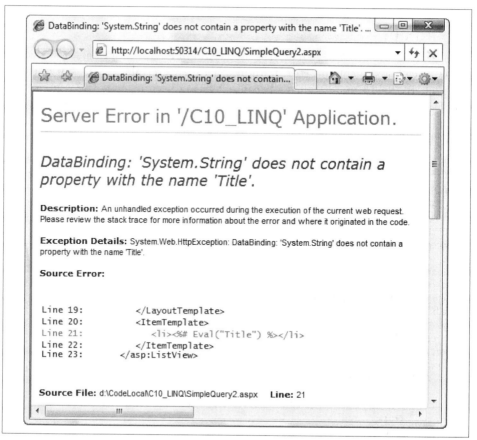

Figure 10-3. Problems binding to anonymous values selected by LINQ

Example 10-4. Adding names to selected properties

```
using System;
using System.Collections.Generic;
using System.Linq;
using System.Web.UI;

public partial class SimpleQuery : Page
{
    protected void Page_Load(object sender, EventArgs e)
    {
        List<Book> books = Book.GetBookList();

        // Using the DataSource property
        var bookTitles =
            from b in books
            select new { Title = b.Title };
```

Example 10-4. Adding names to selected properties (continued)

```
    lvwBooks.DataSource = bookTitles;
    this.DataBind( );
  }
}
```

As shown earlier in Example 10-1, you can name the properties for the resultant bookTitles collection and hence give templated controls something to bind to. Save and run this page again and the ListView binds to the query results as you would hope.

In this example, the query creates a new *anonymous type* with one property called Title for each book in the book list. It then *projects* the title of the book into the Title property of the new type.

```
    select new { Title = b.Title }
```

Because the type is anonymous, this is known as *anonymous projection*. You could also create a new named type on the fly if you prefer:

```
    select new CatalogItem {Title = b.Title}
```

In this case, the query performs a *nonanonymous projection*.

LINQ Syntax

So far, you've seen only the from and select operators in a LINQ query. In fact, there are several more, which implement all the common query clauses, as shown in Table 10-1.

Table 10-1. Common LINQ query clauses in order of execution

Keywords	Description
from	Defines the initial range (set) of data being queried
join, on	Define an additional set of data to be incorporated into the query and how it relates to the first set of data described in the from clause
let	Defines a variable for use in grouping or filtering
where	Filters the set of data by some Boolean condition
orderby, orderbydescending	Define a sort order for the results of the query
select	Defines the values to be returned from the items in the range of data (often as properties of an anonymously typed object)
group	Defines how the range of data should be grouped around a variable defined by the let clause or one of the properties in the data

We'll look at each of these in turn and then end with a quick look at the full set of query operators that LINQ implements.

The from clause

The first clause in a LINQ query is always the `from` clause:

```
from book in Books
```

This defines the main source of data in the query which must implement `IEnumerable<T>`. If the type of the Books variable in the preceding code snippet implemented only `IEnumerable`, you could use LINQ's `OfType<T>` method to convert it:

```
from book in Books.OfType<Book>()
```

Example 10-5 shows the `OfType<T>` method used in this way to convert an array of `BookStats` objects, which you'll use in a moment to demonstrate the `join` clause, into a type inheriting from `IEnumerable<BookStats>`. Add to the website's *App_Code* folder a new class file called *BookStats.cs*, and then add the code in Example 10-5.

Example 10-5. BookStats.cs: Using OfType<T>

```csharp
using System.Collections.Generic;
using System.Linq;

public class BookStats
{
   public int Sales { get; set; }
   public int Pages { get; set; }
   public int Rank { get; set; }
   public string ISBN { get; set; }

   public static IEnumerable<BookStats> GetBookStats()
   {
      BookStats[] stats = {
         new BookStats { ISBN = "0596529562", Pages=904,
                         Rank=1, Sales=109000},
         new BookStats { ISBN = "0596527438", Pages=607,
                         Rank=2, Sales=58000},
         new BookStats { ISBN = "059652756X", Pages=704,
                         Rank=3, Sales=75000},
         new BookStats { ISBN = "0596518455", Pages=552,
                         Rank=4, Sales=120000},
         new BookStats { ISBN = "0596518439", Pages=752,
                         Rank=5, Sales=37500}
      };

      return stats.OfType<BookStats>();
   }
}
```

The join clause

If you wish to incorporate any additional data sources into your query, use the `join` clause and the `on` keyword to define how they relate to the data already in the query.

For example, to join `BookStats` described in Example 10-5 with the list of books in Example 10-1, you might use the following code:

```
IEnumerable<Book> books = Book.GetBookList();
IEnumerable<BookStats> stats = BookStats.GetBookStats();

var bookTitles =
    from b in books
    join s in stats on b.ISBN equals s.ISBN
    select new { Name = b.Title, Pages = s.Pages };
```

In this case, the code joins the two sets of data based on the only information they share—the book's ISBN number. The query results returned can then span both the books and stats sets of data. In essence, this works in much the same way as a SQL `INNER JOIN` statement and, like SQL, can be used as many times as required to join all the disparate sources of data together into the one query.

 Have a look at *SimpleJoin.aspx* in the download project for this chapter to see this query at work.

The let clause

The `let` clause allows you to define a value for use in any of the subsequent parts of the query. You can use it in the same manner as you would a variable local to a method, only rather than its scope being the duration of the method's execution it is the length of one iteration over the source of data by the query.

Suppose, for example, you needed to calculate the gross profit of the books in your collection. You could use the following query to add it to the result set:

```
IEnumerable<Book> books = Book.GetBookList();
IEnumerable<BookStats> stats = BookStats.GetBookStats();

var bookTitles =
    from b in books
    join s in stats on b.ISBN equals s.ISBN
    let profit = (b.Price * s.Sales)
    select new { Name = b.Title, GrossProfit = profit };
```

If you bind these values into a `ListView` or other data-bound control, you'd see the gross profit calculated correctly for each book in turn, as shown in Figure 10-4.

Note that you can add as many let clauses as you need into your query.

 You can find this example as *SimpleLet.aspx* in the code download for this chapter.

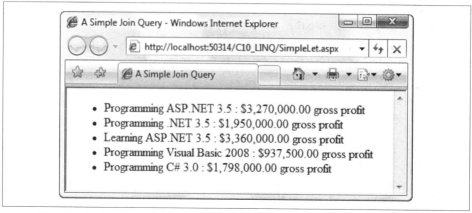

Figure 10-4. The let clause at work

The where clause

The where clause allows you to apply conditional filters to the data set you are querying. If the filter is true for the current object being iterated over in the collection, it is added to the query result set. If it is false, the current object is omitted from the results.

For example, you might want to return a list of books that have sold more than 60,000 units (oh, happy day!). The query would look like this:

```
IEnumerable<Book> books = Book.GetBookList();
IEnumerable<BookStats> stats = BookStats.GetBookStats();

var bookTitles =
    from b in books
    join s in stats on b.ISBN equals s.ISBN
    where s.Sales > 60000
    select new { Name = b.Title, Sales = s.Sales};
```

Multiple filters are allowed as well. For example, if you wanted a list of books not released yet that contain more than 700 pages, the query would have two where clauses:

```
var bookTitles =
    from b in books
    join s in stats on b.ISBN equals s.ISBN
    where b.ReleaseDate > DateTime.Now
    where s.Pages > 700
    select new {Name = b.Title, ReleaseDate = b.ReleaseDate, Pages = s.Pages};
```

As long as the where condition returns a Boolean value, you can use it within a where clause.

 We demonstrate these two queries in *SimpleWhere.aspx* and *SimpleWhere2.aspx* in the code download for this chapter.

The orderby and orderbydescending clauses

The orderby and orderbydescending clauses allow you to sort the query results in a given order based on the value of one or more of the properties in the results. For example, the following query will return all the books in the collection ordered by release date from earliest to latest, and then by the number of pages if more than one book has the same release date:

```
IEnumerable<Book> books = Book.GetBookList();
IEnumerable<BookStats> stats = BookStats.GetBookStats();

var bookTitles =
    from b in books
    join s in stats on b.ISBN equals s.ISBN
    orderby b.ReleaseDate, s.Pages
    select new {Name = b.Title, Pages = s.Pages, ReleaseDate = b.ReleaseDate};
```

Using orderbydescending rather than orderby reverses the order of the sort.

 We demonstrate this query in *SimpleOrderBy.aspx* in the code download for this chapter.

The select clause

The last part of a LINQ query must always be a select clause—either by itself or as the last part of a group clause, which you'll see in a minute. These clauses are the ones that define the information returned by the query. As you've already seen, you can use select to do the following:

- *Select* a single piece of information in an anonymous or named type.
- *Project* multiple pieces of information into an anonymous or named type.
- *Select* the entire object being queried.

Furthermore, the properties of these named or anonymous types will be given names, although they must be set explicitly to register when being data-bound to an ASP.NET server control. If they are not set explicitly, they are implicitly given the same name as the property that is being selected in the first place.

For example, this query returns a collection of instances of an anonymous type with a property named Title:

```
var bookTitles =
    from b in books
    select b.Title;
```

This query returns a collection of CategoryItem objects, each of which has two properties, one called Title and the other BookId:

```
var bookTitles =
    from b in books
    select new CategoryItem { b.Title, BookId = b.ISBN };
```

Finally, this query returns the set of objects stored in `bookTitles`. These objects will retain their names and properties if they aren't anonymous types already.

```
var bookTitles =
    from b in books
    where b.ReleaseDate > DateTime.Now
    select b;
```

You can also use the `select` clause to transform information into results that are easier to work with:

```
var bookTitles =
    from b in books
    select new { ISBN = b.ISBN, ISBN13 = "978-" + b.ISBN  };
```

```
var bookTitles =
    from b in books
    select new { ISBN = b.ISBN,
        Released = (b.ReleaseDate < DateTime.Now ? "Out now" : "Coming soon")};
```

 We demonstrate this last query in *SimpleSelect.aspx* in the code download for this chapter.

The groupby clause

The group clause defines how the results of the query should be returned as groups and the key property on which the grouping should be based. For example, if you want to get a list of books grouped by whether they have been released yet, you could use the following query:

```
var bookTitles =
    from b in books
    join s in stats on b.ISBN equals s.ISBN
    let outYet = (b.ReleaseDate < DateTime.Now ? "Out now" : "Coming Soon")
    orderby s.Rank
    group new { Title = b.Title, Price = b.Price, Pages = s.Pages }
    by outYet
        into groupedBooks
        select new
        {
            Status = groupedBooks.Key,
            Values = groupedBooks
        };
```

As you can see, grouping leads to a query that's a little more involved, but consider the results you'll be getting back. Rather than a single collection of results (IEnumerable<Results>, if you will), the query divides this single collection into several based on the value of a key value. So, the query now returns a *collection of* (a collection of results and the value of the property by which they've been grouped). In fact, IntelliSense shows you the true structure of the results if you hover your cursor over `bookTitles` in the code, as shown in Figure 10-5.

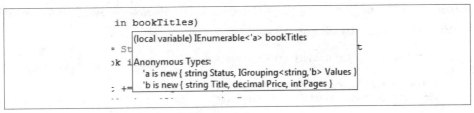

Figure 10-5. The structure of grouped data revealed

Back to the query; the group clause highlighted in the preceding code comprises two distinct parts. The first line defines the actual information that should be retrieved for each book (simply replace the group keyword with select to make sense of this line):

```
group new { Title = b.Title, Price = b.Price, Pages = s.Pages }
```

The remainder defines how the actual information is divided into groups. You've defined the local variable outYet to have two possible values, so the book information will be divided into two groups depending on which value for outYet each book has:

```
by outYet
```

Each group (referred to locally as the name given after the into keyword) will store the common value of outYet in its Key value:

```
into groupedBooks
```

To finish the query, the grouped data is collected with the value of the key by which it is grouped:

```
select new
{
    Status = groupedBooks.Key,
    Values = groupedBooks
};
```

The new structure of the query results means you can't just use them as the data source for a simple data-bound control such as a ListView now. Instead, you have to iterate over the top collection to retrieve the grouped data and the key values manually, and then iterate again over the grouped data to retrieve the information returned. To demonstrate, add to the *C10_LINQ* website a new page called *SimpleGroupBy.aspx* and add a single Label control to the page called lblBooks. Replace the contents of the code-behind page with the code in Example 10-6.

Example 10-6. Creating and using a grouped LINQ result set in SimpleGroupBy.aspx.cs

```
using System;
using System.Collections;
using System.Collections.Generic;
using System.Linq;
using System.Web.UI;
```

```
public partial class SimpleGroupBy : Page
{
    protected void Page_Load(object sender, EventArgs e)
    {
        IEnumerable<Book> books = Book.GetBookList();
        IEnumerable<BookStats> stats = BookStats.GetBookStats();

        var bookTitles =
            from b in books
            join s in stats on b.ISBN equals s.ISBN
            let outYet =
                (b.ReleaseDate < DateTime.Now ? "Out now" : "Coming Soon")
            orderby s.Rank
            group new { Title = b.Title, Price = b.Price, Pages = s.Pages }
            by outYet
                into groupedBooks
                select new
                {
                    Status = groupedBooks.Key,
                    Values = groupedBooks
                };


        foreach (var group in bookTitles)
        {
            lblBooks.Text += String.Format("<h2>{0}</h2>", group.Status);
            foreach (var book in group.Values)
            {
                lblBooks.Text += String.Format(
                    "<p>{0}, {1:c} : {2} pages</p>",
                    book.Title, book.Price, book.Pages);
            }
        }
    }
}
```

Figure 10-6 shows the page once you save and run it.

Note that although the names would seem to associate them, the purpose of the
ListView control's group template is not the same as the grouping in a LINQ query,
so don't try to map one onto the other.

Other LINQ query operators

Beyond these seven standard query clauses, LINQ implements two dozen more standard query operators you might already be familiar with in part.

> For a much more detailed look at all the operators, take the time to
> download the C# samples for VS2008 from the MSDN Code Gallery
> at *http://code.msdn.microsoft.com/csharpsamples*. These contain some
> 500 LINQ query examples showing off each operator in far more
> detail than we have room to do here.

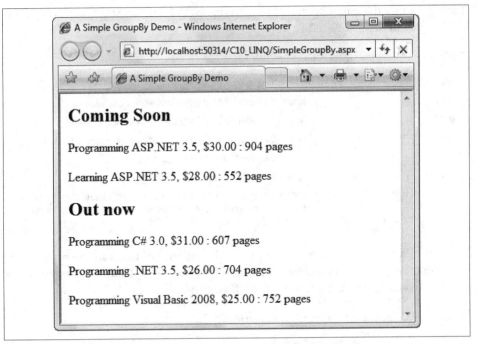

Figure 10-6. SimpleGroupBy.aspx in action

Table 10-2 lists the query operators that take two sets of data and return a combination (in some fashion) of them.

Table 10-2. Set arithmetic operators implemented in LINQ

Operator	Description
Union(set1, set2)	Used to create one set of data from two, containing only the unique elements of both
Except(set1, set2)	Used to create one set of data from two, containing only the values in set1 that are not also in set2
Intersect(set1, set2)	Used to create one set of data from two, containing only the values in set1 that are also in set2
Concat(set1, set2)	Used to create one set of data from two, with the contents of set2 following set1

Table 10-3 lists the query operators that generate a new set of data for your code to use.

Table 10-3. Set generation operators implemented in LINQ

Operator	Description
Range(seed, length)	Returns a set of all the integers between seed and (seed + length–1)
Repeat(result, number)	Returns a set containing the given number instances of result
Empty( )	Returns an empty set

Table 10-4 lists the query operators that group a set of data together, perform a function over all of them, and return a single result.

Table 10-4. Mathematical operators implemented in LINQ

Operator	Description
Count( )	Returns the number of items in the set on which it is called.
Sum( )	Returns the sum of the items (assumed to all be numeric) in the set.
Min( )	Returns the lowest value of the items (assumed to all be numeric) in the set.
Max( )	Returns the highest value of the items in the set.
Average( )	Returns the average values of a set of numbers.
Aggregate(function)	Performs the given function on the first two numbers in the set, then between that total and the third number in the set, then between the running total and the fourth number in the set, etc.

Table 10-5 lists the operators that influence the number of items in the result of the query that are actually returned to the code. For example, if 12 items satisfy a query, First( ) would return just one item from those results.

Table 10-5. Set member operators implemented in LINQ

Operator	Description
Take(int)	Specifies the number of items in the base data set to include in the result of the query.
Skip(int)	Specifies the number of items in the base data set to not include in the result of the query.
Reverse( )	Reverses the order of the items in the results.
Distinct( )	Ensures the results contain no duplicates.
First( )	Returns only the first result for the query.
FirstOrDefault( )	Returns only the first result for the query or the default value for that type if the query results collection is empty.
ElementAt(index)	Returns only the query result with the given index in the collection.
Last( )	Returns only the last result for the query.
LastOrDefault( )	Returns only the last result for the query or the default value for that type if the query results collection is empty.
ElementAtOrDefault(index)	Returns only the query result with the given index in the collection or the default value for that type if the query results collection is empty.
Single(expression)	Returns the single value in the results that satisfies the given expression or an error if no or more than one result exists.
SingleOrDefault(expression)	Returns the single value in the results that satisfies the given expression or an error if more than one result exists. If no results exist, the default value for that type is returned.

Finally, Table 10-6 lists the operators that you can include in the where clause of a query.

Table 10-6. Boolean operators implemented in LINQ

Operator	Description
Any(condition)	Returns a Boolean value indicating whether the given condition is satisfied by any of the items in the set
All(condition)	Returns a Boolean value indicating whether the given condition is satisfied by all of the items in the set
SequenceEqual(seqB)	Returns true if seqB contains exactly the same elements in the same order as the sequence on which SequenceEqual is called
Contains(value)	Returns true if the set contains the given value

Behind the Scenes of a LINQ Query: C# 3.0 at Work

Behind the scenes, a LINQ query may be using up to five of the new language features in C# 3.0 at any one time. The C# compiler uses these features to rewrite the query and its handling of the query results into the following method calls and type declarations it can actually use:

- Anonymous types and object initializers
- Implicitly typed local variables
- Extension methods
- Lambda expressions

We'll take a look at each of these in turn.

Anonymous types and object initializers

Often, you do not want to create a new class just for storing the result of a query. The .NET 3.x languages provide *anonymous types*, which allow you to declare both an anonymous class and an instance of that class using object initializers. For instance, you can initialize an anonymous book object as follows:

```
new { Title = "Programming ASP.NET 3.5",
      ReleaseDate = Convert.ToDateTime("2008-07-15"),
      Stats = bookStats };
```

This declares an anonymous class with three properties—Title, ReleaseDate, and Stats—and initializes it with a string, an instance of the DateTime class, and an instance of the BookStats class. The C# compiler can infer the property types with the types of assigned values, so here the ReleaseDate property type is the DateTime class and the Stats property type is the BookStats class. Just like a normal, named class, anonymous classes can have properties of any type.

Behind the scenes, the C# compiler generates a unique name for the new type. Because this name cannot be referenced in application code, it is considered nameless.

If you're curious, you can use an application such as Reflector (*http://www.red-gate.com/products/reflector/index.htm*) to discover exactly what these classes are called.

Implicitly typed local variables

In every example, you've seen how the results of the query are assigned to a variable of type var:

```
var bookTitles =
    from b in books
    select b.Title;
```

Because the select clause returns an instance of an anonymous type, you cannot define an explicit type IEnumerable<T>. Fortunately, C# 3.0 provides another feature, called implicitly typed local variables, which solves this problem.

You can declare an implicitly typed local variable by specifying its type as var:

```
var pages = 902;
var isbn = "0596529562";
var stats = new List<BookStats>();
var book = new {ISBN = "059652756X",
                ReleaseDate = Convert.ToDateTime("2008-06-15"),
                Price = 26.0m, Title = "Programming .NET 3.5"};
```

The C# compiler infers the type of an implicitly typed local variable from its initialized value. Therefore, you must initialize such a variable when you declare it. In the preceding code snippet, the type of pages will be set as an integer, the type of isbn as a string, and the type of stats as a strongly typed List<T> of BookStats objects. The type of the last variable, book, is an anonymous type containing four properties: ISBN, ReleaseDate, Price, and Title. Although this type has no name in your code, the C# compiler secretly assigns it one and keeps track of its instances. In fact, Visual Studio IDE IntelliSense is also aware of anonymous types, as shown in Figure 10-7.

```
var book = new
AnonymousType 'a

Anonymous Types:
  'a is new { string ISBN, DateTime ReleaseDate, decimal Price, string Title }
        Title = "Programming .NET 3.5"
};
```

Figure 10-7. IntelliSense keeping track of anonymous types

As we explained earlier, the result of any LINQ query is a variable of type IEnumerable<T>, where the argument T is the type (anonymous or named) that contains the properties named in the select or group clause. And with the query defined, the results can be iterated over with a foreach loop, as they were in Example 10-2:

```
var bookTitles =
  from b in books
  select b.Title;

foreach (var title in bookTitles)
{
    lblBooks.Text += String.Format("{0}<br />", title);
}
```

Because the result is an implicitly typed IEnumerable<T> where T is a string, the iteration variable is also implicitly typed to the same class, string. For each object in the
result list, this example simply prints its properties. The same principle applies for
the results of the grouped query in Example 10-6:

```
foreach (var group in bookTitles)
{
    lblBooks.Text += String.Format("<h2>{0}</h2>", group.Status);
    foreach (var book in group.Values)
    {
        lblBooks.Text += String.Format(
            "<p>{0}, {1:c} : {2} pages</p>",
            book.Title, book.Price, book.Pages
        );
    }
}
```

The iteration variable group in the outer loop is of type IEnumerable<T> where T is the
implicit type {string, IGrouping<string, U>}, and U is the implicit type of the iteration variable book, {string, decimal, int}.

Extension methods

Extension methods are a compiler trick—static methods that appear to extend
classes to which you cannot otherwise add a method. For example:

```
"someString".PrefixWith("asd"); // returns asdsomeString
```

instead of:

```
StringExt.PrefixWith("someString", "asd");
```

If you already know a little SQL, the query expressions we introduced in previous
sections are quite intuitive and easy to understand because LINQ is phrased in a similar way to SQL. Because C# code is ultimately executed by the .NET CLR, the C#
compiler has to translate query expressions to the format understood by the .NET
runtime. Because the CLR understands method calls that can be executed, the LINQ
query expressions written in C# are translated into a series of method calls.

For example, the following query:

```
var query =
  from book in books
  where book.Price > 25m
  select book;
```

is translated by the compiler into:

```
var query =
    books.Where(book => book.Price > 25m)
        .Select(book => book);
```

Because the select method does nothing to the book (it does not *project* the book object into a different form), it can be omitted altogether:

```
var query =
    books.Where(book => book.Price > 25m);
```

If the query returned only the price of the book, for example, the select statement would remain as follows:

```
var query =
    books.Where(book => book.Price > 25m)
        .Select(book => book.Price);
```

Indeed, all the standard LINQ operators are extension methods, and will be rewritten like this by the compiler at compile time.

Creating your own extension

Like all the features we've described here, you can write your own extension methods for your convenience in any application. If you've ever written a class called Utils, StringExt, DateExt, and so forth, chances are that the utility methods within those classes are prime candidates for being rewritten as extension methods.

Let's take an example; one possible utility method in the StringExt class is called PrefixWith( ), and as you would expect, it adds a specified prefix string to an existing one. Before it was turned into an extension method, it was called like this:

```
StringExt.PrefixWith(someString, prefixString);
```

Implemented as an extension method, it can now be called as shown in the following support, almost as though the actual System.String class contains this method:

```
someString.PrefixWith(prefixString);
```

The change from "standard" to "extension" method is pretty trivial. Example 10-7 shows the full code for the class in which PrefixWith is defined as an extension method and highlights the difference.

Example 10-7. Extensions.cs

```
using System;

public static class StringExt
{
    public static string PrefixWith(
        this string someString, string prefixString)
    {
        return prefixString + someString;
    }
}
```

In C#, an extension method must be defined as a static method in a static class, and the first parameter of an extension method, prefixed with the this keyword, is always the target type, which is the string class in this example. The preceding code therefore defines PrefixWith as an extension to the string class.

Any subsequent parameters are just normal parameters of the extension method. The method body has no special treatment compared to regular methods either. Here this function simply returns the transformed string.

To use an extension method, it must be in the same scope as the client code. If the extension method is defined in another namespace, you must add a using directive to import the namespace where the extension method is defined. You can't use fully qualified extension method names as you would with a normal method. The use of extension methods is otherwise identical to any built-in methods of the target type. In this example, you simply call it like a regular System.String method even though it is still actually a member of the StringExt class.

 It is worth mentioning, however, that extension methods are somewhat more restrictive than regular member methods—extension methods can access only public members of target types. This prevents the breach of encapsulation of the target types.

Lambda expressions

You can use lambda expressions to define inline delegate definitions. In the following expression:

```
book => book.Price > 25m
```

the left operand, book, is the input parameter. The right operand is the lambda expression that checks whether the book's Price property is greater than 25 and then projects it into a named or anonymous type that will be the result of the expression. Therefore, for a given book object, you're checking whether its price is greater than 25. This lambda expression is then passed into the Where( ) method to perform this comparison operation on each book in the book list.

Queries defined using extension methods are called *method-based queries*. Although the query and method syntaxes are different, they are semantically identical and the compiler translates them into the same IL code. You can use either of them based on your preference.

IEnumerable Good, IQueryable Better

As we've said so far, you can apply LINQ queries only to types implementing IEnumerable<T>, but it's worth noting that if the class containing your base set of data implements IQueryable<T> as well (which inherits from IEnumerable<T>), this is a far preferable situation.

Suppose you have a Collection object that maps to 1,000 records on another machine, and you make the following query:

```
for Customer c in Customers
where c.Country == "uk"
where c.Age > 35
select ......
```

If the Customers object implements only IEnumerable<Customer>, the query will pull across all 1,000 records to your local machine before doing any filtering on them, and then will work through each filter (where clause) in turn, as shown in Figure 10-8.

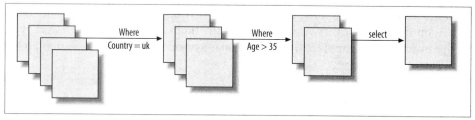

Figure 10-8. IEnumerable<T> sources of data applying filters sequentially

The query is iterated through for each clause in the LINQ query, but if the data source has changed between executions, the result will be different.

In comparison, if the Customers object implements IQueryable<Customer>, all the filtering is combined into one (in technical terms, it's combined into one expression tree), which means that the query is run only once on the remote machine *when the results are required*. The technical term for this is *deferred execution*, and it's a faster and more reliable way to provide results over (large) sources of data, as shown in Figure 10-9.

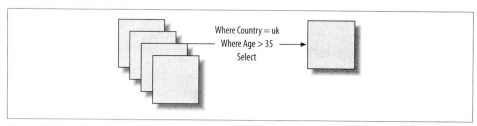

Figure 10-9. Deferred execution, whereby all filters are applied at once

Should you need to, it is also possible to force the query to execute at any time by calling ToList<T> on the query itself or on the results of the query. For example:

```
List<Book> books =
    bookList.Select(book => book.Price > 25m).ToList<Book>();
```

LINQ Providers

So, with the assistance of C# 3.0, LINQ acts as an intermediary between C# and any data store. The libraries in System.Linq implement the various query clauses and operators listed earlier in Tables 10-1 through 10-6, which in turn talk to LINQ providers, which know how to apply these queries to a specific data source, as shown in Figure 10-10.

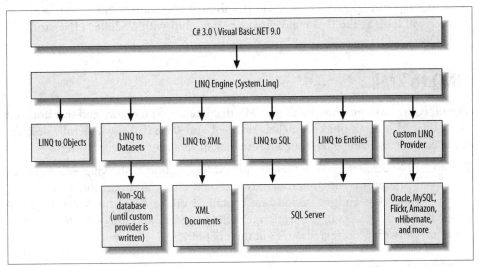

Figure 10-10. The LINQ stack and predefined providers

The .NET Framework v3.5 comes with four LINQ providers built in:

- The ability to query over arrays, lists, dictionaries, and other in-memory sources of information demonstrated so far in this chapter is known as *LINQ to Objects* and is also part of System.Linq.

- The ability to query over any XML document is known as *LINQ to XML* and is implemented in System.Xml.Linq.

- The ability to query over any SQL Server database is known as *LINQ to SQL* and is implemented in System.Data.Linq.

- The ability to query over any other type of database is currently implemented by pulling data into an in-memory DataSet object from the database and then querying the DataSet object. A set of extensions implemented in System.Data.DataSetExtensions makes this possible.

A fifth LINQ provider, known as *LINQ to Entities*, is also available as part of .NET 3.5 Service Pack 1. This is an "enterprise-level" version of LINQ to SQL.

As Figure 10-10 suggests, a number of third-party LINQ providers also provide queryable access over a wide range of other sources of data, including Oracle, MySQL, Flickr, Amazon Web Services, NHibernate, and more.

Find a list of current third-party LINQ providers at *http://oakleafblog. blogspot.com/2007/03/third-party-linq-providers.html*, although as they pretty much are all called "LINQ to *xyz*," Google is probably also your friend in discovering whether there is a provider out there for the source you want to use.

The subject of writing your own LINQ provider is well beyond the scope of this book, but there are plenty of resources out there if you want to try. The rest of this chapter will look at the two main providers that ship with VS2008: LINQ to XML and LINQ to SQL.

LINQ to XML

The LINQ to XML provider loads an XML document into memory and transforms it into a queryable set of objects (such as XElement and XAttribute) which fully describe the document and can be navigated through in an XPath or XQuery fashion.

Example 10-8 demonstrates a very simple XML document showing which books have been written by which authors. You should create and add this to the *C10_LINQ* website. The authors' details are contained in the AdventureWorksLT database which you'll access in the section on LINQ to SQL, and the book details are in the in-memory objects created earlier in this chapter.

Example 10-8. Authors.xml

```
<?xml version="1.0" encoding="utf-8" ?>
<authorlist>
    <author id="1">
        <book isbn="0596529562" />
        <book isbn="059652756X" />
    </author>
    <author id="10">
        <book isbn="059652756X" />
        <book isbn="0596527438" />
    </author>
    <author id="38">
        <book isbn="0596518439" />
    </author>
    <author id="201">
        <book isbn="0596518439" />
        <book isbn="0596527438" />
    </author>
</authorlist>
```

First, you'll create a page that displays just the author IDs. Add to the *C10_LINQ* website a new page called *SimpleXmlQuery.aspx*, and then add a Label control called lblAuthors to the page. Replace the code-behind page with the code in Example 10-9.

Example 10-9. SimpleXmlQuery.aspx

```
using System;
using System.Linq;
using System.Web.UI;
using System.Xml.Linq;

public partial class SimpleXmlQuery : Page
{
    protected void Page_Load(object sender, EventArgs e)
    {
        XElement doc = XElement.Load(Request.ApplicationPath + "\\authors.xml");

        var authorIds = from authors in doc.Elements("author")
                        select authors.Attribute("id").Value;

        foreach (var id in authorIds)
        {
            lblAuthors.Text += String.Format("<p>{0}</p>", id);
        }
    }
}
```

Should you run the page, you'll see the four author IDs—1, 10, 38, and 201—displayed as shown in Figure 10-11.

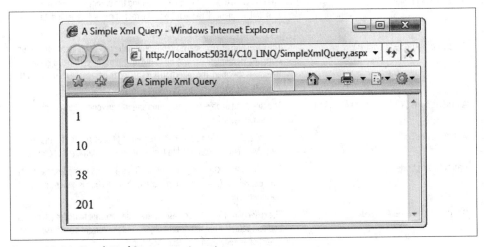

Figure 10-11. SimpleXmlQuery.aspx in action

The key code in this example is highlighted in Example 10-9. First, you use the XElement class to load the XML document into memory, and then you query the collection of all elements in the document with the name "author" for the value of each of their id attributes.

Note that XElement.Load requires a path on the filesystem for the *authors.xml* file (e.g., *C:\codelocal\authors.xml*) rather than a virtual URL (*http://localhost/authors.xml*), and so we use `Request.ApplicationPath` to convert the root directory of the website into its filesystem equivalent.

If you wish to try, you can use the query result variable `authorIds` as a `DataSource` and `DataBind( )` it to a data-bound control. It's easier to rephrase the query, however, and to give the author ID string in the results a name if you wish to bind it to a templated data-bound control:

```
var authorIds = from authors in doc.DescendantsAndSelf("author")
    select new { AuthorId = authors.Attribute("id").Value };
```

 You can find an example using this query bound to a `ListView` in *SimpleXmlQuery2.aspx* in the download for this chapter.

The `XElement` class provides a number of different methods, such as `Elements` in the preceding example, which return an `IEnumerable<T>` collection for a query over which to iterate. They are listed in Table 10-7.

Table 10-7. Collections available in an XElement object

Collection	Description
`Ancestors(name)`	The collection of `XElements` representing the parent elements of the current XML element all the way up to the root. If *name* is specified, the collection is restricted to only those elements with that name.
`AncestorsAndSelf(name)`	The collection of `XElements` representing the parent elements of the current XML element all the way up to the root, plus the current object itself. If *name* is specified, the collection is restricted to only those elements with that name.
`Annotations(T),Annotations<T>( )`	The collection of objects representing annotations on the current object of the named type `T`.
`Attributes(name)`	The collection of `XAttributes` representing the attributes for the current XML element. Restricted to those with the given *name* if specified.
`DescendantNodes( )`	The collection of `XNodes` representing all the descendant nodes (elements and text values) from the current object. The collection is generated in document order.
`DescendantNodesAndSelf( )`	The collection of `XNodes` representing all the descendant nodes (elements and text values) from the current object, and the current object itself. The collection is generated in document order.
`Descendants(name)`	The collection of `XElements` representing all the descendant XML elements from the current object. The collection is generated in document order. Restricted to those with the given *name* if specified.
`DescendantsAndSelf(name)`	The collection of `XElements` representing all the descendant XML elements from the current object, and the current object itself. The collection is generated in document order. Restricted to those with the given *name* if specified.
`Elements(name)`	The collection of `XElements` representing all the child XML elements of the current object. Restricted to those with the given *name* if specified.

Table 10-7. Collections available in an XElement object (continued)

Collection	Description
ElementsBeforeSelf(*name*), ElementsAfterSelf(*name*)	The collection of sibling XElements before or after the current one in document order. Restricted to those with the given *name* if specified.
Nodes(*name*)	The collection of XNodes representing all the child XML nodes (elements and text) of the current object. Restricted to those with the given *name* if specified.
NodesBeforeSelf(*name*), NodesAfterSelf(*name*)	The collection of sibling XNodes before or after the current one in document order. Restricted to those with the given *name* if specified.

Note how all the methods return collections of objects representing XML objects *relative to the current object*. If this doesn't make much sense to you, consider that these extension methods can be concatenated with each other. So, if you wanted to return all the ID values for the authors who had written the book with ISBN 059652756X, there are at least two ways to phrase the query.

First, it could look at each <book> element in *authors.xml* and, if it has the correct value for the isbn attribute, look at that element's parent <author> element and retrieve its ID attribute:

```
var authorIds =
    from book in doc.DescendantsAndSelf("book")
        let authorId = book.Ancestors("author").Attributes("id").Single()
        where book.Attribute("isbn").Value == "059652756X"
        select new { AuthorId = authorId.Value };
```

Or it could iterate over all the author elements and then inspect the collection of all the isbn attributes for all the author's child <book> elements. If any of them has the right value, the query keeps the value of the current <author> element's id attribute.

```
var authorIds2 =
    from author in doc.DescendantsAndSelf("author")
        where author.Elements("book").Attributes("isbn")
                .Any(attr => attr.Value == "059652756X")
        select new { AuthorId = author.Attribute("id").Value };
```

 We demonstrate both of these queries in *SimpleXmlQuery3.aspx* available in the download for this chapter.

Joining XML to a Different Type of Data

One of the big advantages in using LINQ is its ability to join different types of data seamlessly as though they were of the same data type. In this example, you'll create a page that joins the Books list created earlier in *Books.cs* with the data in *authors.xml* and groups the authorIds by the names of the books which the authors have written. Essentially, the page will invert the author-to-book relationship described in the XML file, and will use the book list to describe the book by its title rather than its ISBN.

To begin, add a new page to the *C10_LINQ* website. Call it *XmlToMemoryJoin.aspx* and add to it a single Label control called lblBooks. Now switch to the code-behind page and replace the code with that in Example 10-10.

Example 10-10. XmlToMemoryJoin.aspx.cs in full

```
using System;
using System.Collections.Generic;
using System.Linq;
using System.Web.UI;
using System.Xml.Linq;

public partial class XmlToMemoryJoin : Page
{
    protected void Page_Load(object sender, EventArgs e)
    {
        List<Book> bookList = Book.GetBookList();
        XElement doc =
            XElement.Load(Request.ApplicationPath + "\\authors.xml");

        var authorsByBooks =
            from book in doc.DescendantsAndSelf("book")
            join bookInfo in bookList on book.Attribute("isbn").Value
                equals bookInfo.ISBN
            let authorId = book.Parent.Attribute("id").Value
            orderby bookInfo.Title
            group new { AuthorId = authorId }
            by bookInfo.Title
                into groupedAuthors
                select new
                {
                    Title = groupedAuthors.Key,
                    Authors = groupedAuthors
                };

        foreach (var book in authorsByBooks)
        {
            lblBooks.Text += String.Format("<h2>{0}</h2>", book.Title);
            foreach (var author in book.Authors)
            {
                lblBooks.Text += String.Format("Author ID: {0}<br />",
                    author.AuthorId);
            }
        }
    }
}
```

Now save and run the page, and you'll see the results shown in Figure 10-12.

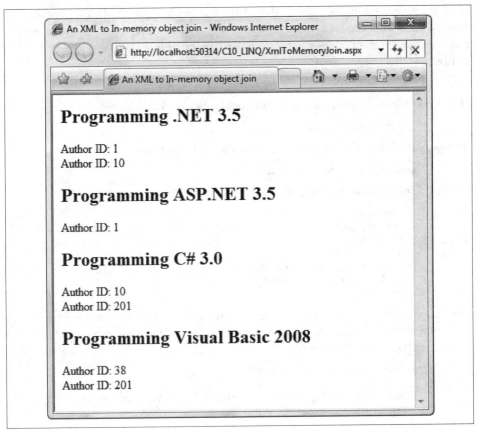

Figure 10-12. XmlToMemoryJoin.aspx in action

Let's review the contents of the Page_Load method. First the two data sources are created:

```
protected void Page_Load(object sender, EventArgs e)
{
    List<Book> bookList = Book.GetBookList();
    XElement doc =
        XElement.Load(Request.ApplicationPath + "\\authors.xml");
```

Then the query starts. The two sources are going to join by the value of the book's ISBN string, so the query iterates over the <book> elements in the XML document rather than over the <author> elements and then joins the two data sources:

```
var authorsByBooks =
    from book in doc.DescendantsAndSelf("book")
    join bookInfo in bookList on book.Attribute("isbn").Value
        equals bookInfo.ISBN
```

Now the query establishes the authorId for the book in the XML document. You already know that the <author> element is the parent of the <book> element, so you can use the XElement class's Parent method to retrieve it and the value of its id attribute with a minimum of fuss:

```
let authorId = book.Parent.Attribute("id").Value
```

Having set the grouped results to be ordered by the books' titles:

```
orderby bookInfo.Title
```

the query then does the actual grouping of the author's Ids:

```
group new { AuthorId = authorId }
```

by the title of the book to which they have contributed:

```
by bookInfo.Title
    into groupedAuthors
    select new
    {
        Title = groupedAuthors.Key,
        Authors = groupedAuthors
    };
```

And finally, having finished processing the data, the function iterates over the results to display first the book title as the key value for each group of author IDs and then the author IDs themselves:

```
foreach (var book in authorsByBooks)
{
    lblBooks.Text += String.Format("<h2>{0}</h2>", book.Title);
    foreach (var author in book.Authors)
    {
        lblBooks.Text += String.Format("Author ID: {0}<br />",
            author.AuthorId);
    }
}
```

What's important to note here is that the general shape of the query didn't change at all despite the fact that it was working with two completely different types of data.

Writing XML with LINQ

Up to now, you might well assume that LINQ is a read-only API and has no capacity to write new or transformed data back to the source from whence it came. However, although this is true of LINQ itself, it's not true of the various LINQ providers, and you can indeed use LINQ to XML to write new XML documents to the browser or back to file on disk. This functionality comes thanks to the flexibility of the new XML API used by LINQ.

The XElement has an overloaded constructor of the following form:

```
XElement xml = new XElement(string name, object childElements)
```

The key here is you can use a LINQ query to populate this childElements object and thus build up the XElement object whose ToString( ) method will render it as an XML document.

Let's look at an example. Add to the *C10_LINQ* website a new page called *XmlLinqWriter.aspx*. Switch to Source view and delete everything but the @Page directive. This page will output raw XML, so there's no need for any HTML to get in the way. Now switch to the code-behind page and replace its contents with that in Example 10-11.

Example 10-11. XmlLinqWriter.aspx.cs in full

```
using System;
using System.Collections.Generic;
using System.Linq;
using System.Web.UI;
using System.Xml.Linq;

public partial class XmlLinqWriter : Page
{
    protected void Page_Load(object sender, EventArgs e)
    {
        List<Book> bookList = Book.GetBookList();
        XElement doc =
            XElement.Load(Request.ApplicationPath + "\\authors.xml");

        XElement xml = new XElement("authors",
            from author in doc.DescendantsAndSelf("author")
            select new XElement("author",
              new XAttribute("id", author.Attribute("id").Value)
              )
          );

        Response.Write(new XDeclaration("1.0", "utf-8", "yes").ToString());
        Response.Write(xml.ToString());

    }
}
```

If you save and run the page, you'll see the XML generated by the page displayed in your browser, as shown in Figure 10-13.

Looking at the code, you'll see that the LINQ query has been embedded into the constructor for an XElement object:

```
XElement xml = new XElement("authors",
    from author in doc.DescendantsAndSelf("author")
    select new XElement("author",
      new XAttribute("id", author.Attribute("id").Value)
      )
  );
```

The outer constructor creates the root element of the new document, <authors>:

```
XElement xml = new XElement("authors", childObjects);
```

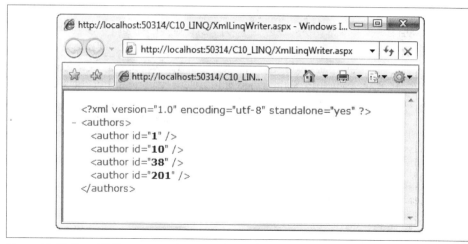

Figure 10-13. Raw XML written to the screen by XmlLinqWriter.aspx

But in this case, childObjects will be the result of the LINQ query. Stripping away the XML insertion for a minute, the actual query here is very straightforward. It iterates over the <author> elements in *authors.xml* and returns a collection of all author id values:

```
from author in doc.DescendantsAndSelf("author")
select new { author.Attribute("id").Value };
```

The only difference between this more familiar query and the preceding one is that instead of creating an instance of an anonymous type, the select clause is creating a new XElement and embedding the id values into it. Indeed, you can embed query values directly into any type as required.

Let's take a more complex query and generate another XML document. In Example 10-10, you joined *authors.xml* with an in-memory book list to return a list of authors for each book in the list. Assuming you want to generate an XML document with the following structure:

```
<books>
    <book title="...">
        <author id="..." />
        ...
    </book>
    ...
</books>
```

you can embed the LINQ query in Example 10-10 into an XElement constructor for the root element, <books>, and create the desired document. Indeed, the constructor will look like this (the actual XML-generating parts of the query are highlighted):

```
XElement xml = new XElement("books",
    from book in doc.DescendantsAndSelf("book")
```

```
join bookInfo in bookList on book.Attribute("isbn").Value
    equals bookInfo.ISBN
let authorId = book.Parent.Attribute("id").Value
orderby bookInfo.Title
group new XElement("author", new XAttribute("id", authorId))
by bookInfo.Title
    into groupedAuthors
    select new XElement("book",
        new XAttribute("title", groupedAuthors.Key),
        groupedAuthors
    )
);
```

If you add this to the code in *XmlLinqWriter.aspx.cs*, comment out the other
XElement constructor, and run the page, you'll see the final document, as shown in
Figure 10-14.

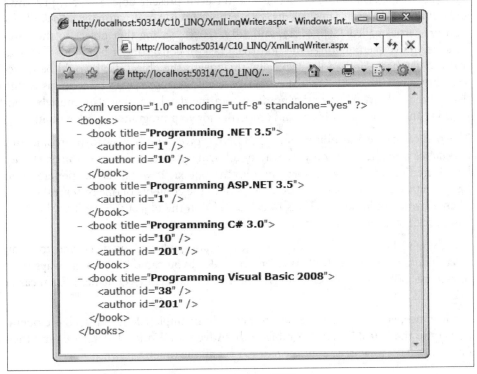

Figure 10-14. Using a grouped LINQ query to generate XML

 For many more examples of LINQ to XML queries, take the time to
download the C# samples for VS2008 from the MSDN Code Gallery
at *http://code.msdn.microsoft.com/csharpsamples*.

LINQ to SQL

Let's move on to databases, which most likely are the main data source for your website. Microsoft includes a LINQ provider for talking to SQL Server with .NET v3.5, along with a couple of other tools for use in VS2008 to make your life a bit simpler, including a `LinqDataSource` object and something called an Object Relational Designer. The point of the former is fairly obvious, but to explain the latter, here's a question:

> What can't you create, update, or delete in SQL Server?
> Answer: *objects*.

From Relations to Objects

The problem is that SQL Server doesn't present you with objects that inherit from `IQueryable` or `IEnumerable`. In fact, it doesn't even present objects at all, just rows and columns. No properties, events, or methods even. So, if you have a `Book` object with properties called `ISBN`, `Title`, and `ReleaseDate`, saving that object to the database, as you've seen, involves the nontrivial task of converting it back into raw data that the database can handle. Typically, this means the object itself would be represented by a row in a table and the properties would be represented by columns within that row. Similarly, when retrieving data from the database, that data must be converted to the appropriate objects and properties for your program to work with it.

The use of `DataSource` objects and ADO.NET gives you a way to overcome this *impedance mismatch*, but only by way of allowing you to define how things should be selected or saved to a database in a given context. It would be far preferable to have a data access tier that mapped objects onto the contents of one or several tables. Then all you would need to do is to call `Save( )` on the object to save it to the database, or `Select( )` and have it return a collection.

Well, you've been able to do this for ages, creating what is often referred to as an *object-relational mapping* (ORM) layer, and indeed you can do it in many ways right now in VS2008 with some C# and ADO.NET. Certainly, LINQ makes it even easier than it used to be.

For instance, you could use the skeleton code in Example 10-12 to map basic operations onto the `SalesLT.Customer` table in the AdventureWorksLT database (and then finally not have to worry about the SalesLT bit all the time).

Example 10-12. LINQ offers a neat syntax to map a table to a class

```
[Database(Name="AdventureWorksLT")]
public partial class AdventureWorksLT : DataContext
{
    [Table(Name="SalesLT.Customer")]
    public partial class Customer
    {
```

Example 10-12. LINQ offers a neat syntax to map a table to a class (continued)

```
    [Column(Storage="_CustomerID", DbType="Int NOT NULL IDENTITY",
            IsPrimaryKey=true, IsDbGenerated=true)]
    public int CustomerID { get; set; }

    [Column(Storage="_NameStyle", DbType="Bit NOT NULL")]
    public bool NameStyle { get; set; }

    ...
    }
}
```

Of course, it would take ages to write the full code for this table and the rest of the database, but fortunately, you do not have to. Instead, you can use the Object Relational Designer built into VS2008 to generate this ORM layer for as many of a database's tables as needed. This layer contains the following:

The classes, or entities, to represent the database

Every table will be mapped to its own class and every column within that table will be mapped to a property in that class. As a bonus, each property is strongly typed to match the type of its corresponding column in the database and warnings from the compiler if you attempted to give a column a value of the wrong type.

A DataContext class to act as a bridge between the LINQ object model and the database itself

This object will be used to send and receive data between your entities and the database.

The DataContext designer is not unique in its ability to create an ORM layer over the contents of a database. There are at least half a dozen mature ORM products on the market at the moment and several open source variants available free to download as well. Although not entirely responsible, the interest and popularity of the ActiveRecord model used by Ruby on Rails to generate data models for its Model-View-Controller (MVC) web framework certainly helped highlight and popularize the use of such products in the web space.

With that said, let's take an example and put the Object Relational Designer through its paces.

Using the Object Relational Designer

To use the Object Relational Designer to create an ORM layer for LINQ to use in your web pages, click Website → Add New Item in VS2008 and select the LINQ to SQL Classes option in the dialog that appears. You're going to create a layer over the customer information in the AdventureWorksLT database in this example, so set the name of the file to be created to *AwltCustomer.dbml*, as shown in Figure 10-15. If you're asked, agree to let the code be saved in the site's *App_Code* folder.

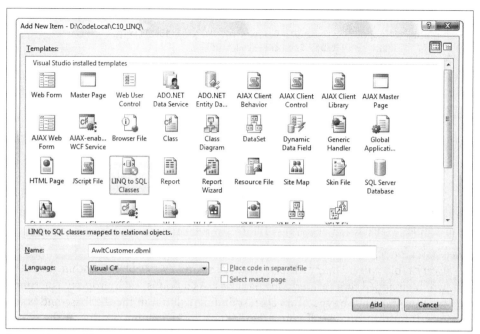

Figure 10-15. Adding a new ORM layer to your website in VS2008

After a moment of whirring, *AwltCustomer.dbml* will be added to the website's *App_ Code* folder and the designer will appear in the main VS2008 window, as shown in Figure 10-16.

At this point, the Toolbox contains controls available to use in the Object Relational Designer. You can create your own classes by dragging the Class control onto the design surface. You can add properties to that class by right-clicking the class and selecting Add → Property. You can also create relationships between classes with the Association and Inheritance controls. We will not be using these controls in this book, although they can be very useful in more advanced scenarios.

With the Object Relational Designer open, you are ready to start building your object model from the database. Open the Server Explorer and expand the connection to the AdventureWorksLT database by clicking the plus sign next to it. Then expand the list of tables by clicking the plus sign next to Tables. Now click and drag the Customer table from the Server Explorer onto the left pane of the Object Relational Designer. The screen should look something like Figure 10-17.

You'll also need to drag the Address and CustomerAddress tables onto the designer. Once you've got them arranged as you like, you'll notice that the relationships between the tables are denoted in much the same way that SQL Server Management Studio (SSMS) highlights them. As Figure 10-18 shows, an arrowed line joins the two tables with the arrowhead pointing at the table containing the foreign key field. Because the database defined relationships between these tables, those relationships

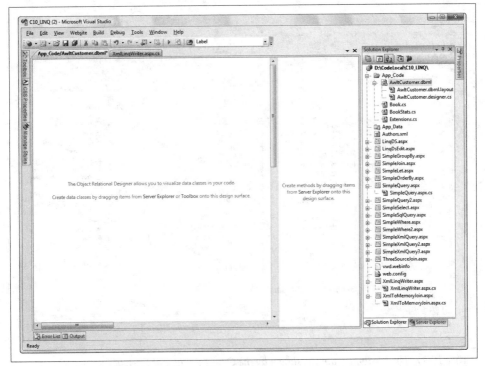

Figure 10-16. An empty Object Relational Designer

are reflected in the visual data model. More importantly, those relationships are now reflected in the underlying classes created by the tool.

And that's it. VS2008 generates the actual code for the object relational layer as you drag tables on or off the designer. If you have any stored procedures you want LINQ to use as well (e.g., for saving customers back to the database), you would drag them onto the righthand pane in the designer.

Under the hood, the Solution Explorer provides you access to the actual code just generated by the designer, as shown in Figure 10-19.

The Object Relational Designer generates three files:

- *AwltCustomer.dbml* is an XML file that describes the tables you've dragged onto the designer surface, their contents, and their relationships with one another.

- *AwltCustomer.dbml.layout* keeps track of the visual location and other design aspects of each table on the designer surface.

- *AwltCustomer.designer.cs* contains the actual Table and DataContext classes. Boilerplate code aside, this file defines three subclasses within the overall AwltCustomersDataContext class, one for each table. Within each subclass, there is a public property for each column in the table. You can see that each property has the same data type as the corresponding column in the table. In fact, it's structured in pretty much the same way as Example 10-12.

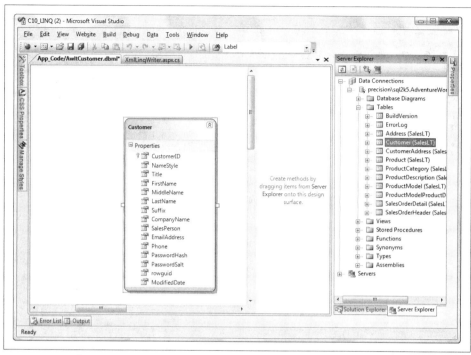

Figure 10-17. The Customer table as shown by the Object Relational Designer

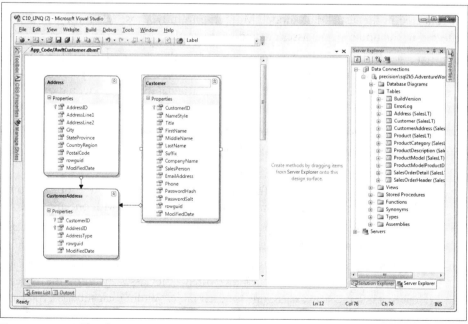

Figure 10-18. Table relationships noted visually in the Object Relational Designer

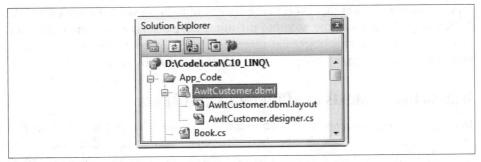

Figure 10-19. The code generated by the Object Relational Designer

With the `AwltCustomersDataContext` providing the queryable bridge between LINQ and the database, all you need to do now is create some pages that use it.

Querying DataContext Objects Manually

Once you've established the `DataContext` object, you can query it with a LINQ statement in the same way you query in-memory objects or XML documents. The only difference now is that in returning the results of the query to the page, a connection to a database is opened and then closed again. It's wise, then, to make sure you dispose of the connection implicit in the `DataContext` with a `using` statement, as shown in Example 10-13, which is the code-behind file for a page running a basic LINQ to SQL query.

Example 10-13. SimpleSqlQuery.aspx.cs in full

```
using System;
using System.Collections.Generic;
using System.Linq;
using System.Web.UI;

public partial class SimpleSqlQuery : Page
{
    protected void Page_Load(object sender, EventArgs e)
    {
        using (AwltCustomersDataContext db = new AwltCustomersDataContext())
        {
            var firstFiveCustomers =
                from customer in db.Customers.Take(5)
                select customer;


            foreach (var customer in firstFiveCustomers)
            {
                lblCustomers.Text += String.Format("<p>{0} {1}</p>",
                    customer.FirstName, customer.LastName);
            }
        }
    }
}
```

Like the XElement object that loads in the document to begin with, the instance of the DataContext object offers the way into the in-memory objects representing the database. In this instance, the object has three methods—Customers, CustomerAddresses, and Addresses, each representing the contents of its respective table.

Joining DataContexts to a Different Type of Data

In the preceding example you queried over the Customer table and retrieved the first and last names for each of the first five customers in the database. As in Example 10-10, however, where you wrote a query to join an XML document to an in-memory object, it's perfectly possible to join the contents of a SQL database through its DataContext layer to another data source. In this demonstration, we'll expand on Example 10-10 and join an in-memory object containing book information with a SQL table containing author information (OK, it's called *customers*, but hey…) through an XML document which lays out who has written which book.

Make a copy of *XmlToMemoryJoin.aspx* in the *C10_LINQ* website and rename it *ThreeSourceJoin.aspx*. The markup can stay the same, but the code-behind page needs to incorporate the DataContext. Example 10-14 shows the complete code for *ThreeSourceJoin.aspx.cs*, highlighting the new or changed lines.

Example 10-14. ThreeSourceJoin.aspx.cs in full

```
using System;
using System.Collections.Generic;
using System.Linq;
using System.Web.UI;
using System.Xml.Linq;

public partial class ThreeSourceJoin : Page
{
    protected void Page_Load(object sender, EventArgs e)
    {
        List<Book> bookList = Book.GetBookList();
        XElement doc =
            XElement.Load(Request.ApplicationPath + "\\authors.xml");

        using (AwltCustomersDataContext db = new AwltCustomersDataContext())
        {
            var authorsByBooks =
                from book in doc.DescendantsAndSelf("book")
                join bookInfo in bookList on
                    book.Attribute("isbn").Value equals bookInfo.ISBN
                join authorInfo in db.Customers on
                    book.Parent.Attribute("id").Value equals
                        authorInfo.CustomerID.ToString()
                let authorName = authorInfo.FirstName + " "
                                + authorInfo.LastName
                orderby bookInfo.Title
                group new { Name = authorName}
                by bookInfo.Title
```

Example 10-14. ThreeSourceJoin.aspx.cs in full (continued)

```
                    into groupedAuthors
                    select new
                    {
                        Title = groupedAuthors.Key,
                        Authors = groupedAuthors
                    };

                foreach (var book in authorsByBooks)
                {
                    lblBooks.Text += String.Format("<h2>{0}</h2>", book.Title);
                    foreach (var author in book.Authors)
                    {
                        lblBooks.Text += String.Format("Author: {0} <br />",
                            author.Name);
                    }
                }
            }
        }
    }
}
```

If you save and run the page, you'll see the customer names from the database and the book names from the List object are being correctly joined together through the XML document, as shown in Figure 10-20.

Note that in the join between the DataContext object and the XML document, you had to call ToString() on authorInfo.CustomerID because the DataContext correctly types it as an integer, which is how it is typed in the database. However, the Value property for the XAttribute object returns a string, and as the LINQ join clause will do no casting of its own, the call to ToString() must be made so that the join is actioned on two strings.

```
join authorInfo in db.Customers on
    book.Parent.Attribute("id").Value equals
    authorInfo.CustomerID.ToString()
```

Writing to the Database with LINQ

Adding, updating, or deleting data from a database is also possible using the DataContext object. Unlike writing out a new XML document, however, making changes to a database can involve no LINQ queries at all. Instead, the procedure for adding new data is to create a new object representing data in the table you want to add, set its properties, set it for insertion by calling InsertOnSubmit on the object representing the table to which it will be added, and then calling SubmitChanges() on the DataContext object. For example:

```
using (AwltCustomersDataContext db = new AwltCustomersDataContext())
{
    Address addr = new Address();
    addr.AddressLine1 = "1c Sharp Way";
    addr.City = "Seattle";
    addr.PostalCode = "98011";
    addr.StateProvince = "Washington";
```

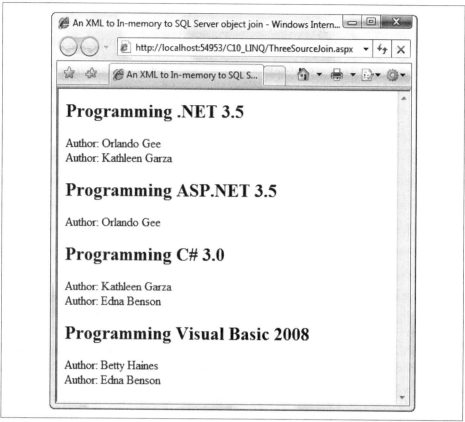

Figure 10-20. ThreeSourceJoin.aspx in action

```
addr.CountryRegion = "United States";
addr.ModifiedDate = DateTime.Today;
addr.rowguid = Guid.NewGuid( );

db.Addresses.InsertOnSubmit(addr);
db.SubmitChanges( );
}
```

Similarly, updating a row in the table involves retrieving the object that represents it, setting the object's properties with new values, and then calling SubmitChanges( ) again:

```
using (AwltCustomersDataContext db = new AwltCustomersDataContext( ))
{
    Address addr = db.Addresses.Single(
        a => (a.AddressLine1 == "1c Sharp Way" && a.City == "Seattle"));

    addr.AddressLine1 = "12b Pointy Street";
    db.SubmitChanges( );
}
```

Or, if an object has been detached from the `Context`—for example, because it has been parsed through a web service or stored as its own middle-tier business—you can call `Attach` on its respective collection in the `Context` and then `SubmitChanges( )`:

```
using (AwltCustomersDataContext db = new AwltCustomersDataContext( ))
{
    db.Addresses.Attach(updatedAddress, true);
    db.SubmitChanges( );
}
```

Note that the Boolean parameter in the call to `Attach` states whether the object has been modified since it was detached from the `Context`.

Finally, deleting a row in the table involves retrieving the object that represents it, calling `DeleteOnSubmit` on the object representing the table from which it will be deleted, and then calling `SubmitChanges( )` again:

```
using (AwltCustomersDataContext db = new AwltCustomersDataContext( ))
{
    Address addr = db.Addresses.Single(
        a => (a.AddressLine1 == "12b Pointy Street "
            && a.City == "Seattle"));

    db.Addresses.DeleteOnSubmit(addr);
    db.SubmitChanges( );
}
```

If the deletion of the row causes no issues because it does not violate a relationship between two tables, the row will be deleted.

Data Consistency

One issue for database managers is that of data consistency. To understand how this works, you must first understand the concept of *normalization*, which, among other things, implies that data is not unnecessarily duplicated in a relational database.

Thus, for example, if you have a database that tracks customers and their orders, rather than duplicate the information about each customer (the customer's name, address, phone, etc.) in each order, you would create a customer record and assign each customer a unique `CustomerID`. Each order would then contain a `CustomerID` that would identify the customer who "owns" that order.

This has many advantages, one of which is if you change the customer's phone number, you need to change it only in the customer record, not in every order record.

The data would be inconsistent, however, if the `CustomerID` in an order did not refer to any customer at all (or worse, if it referred to the wrong customer!). To avoid this, database administrators like databases that enforce consistency rules, such as you cannot delete a customer record unless you've deleted all the orders for that customer first (thus, not leaving any "orphan" orders that have no associated customer) and never reusing a `CustomerID`.

Introducing the LinqDataSource Object

Quite a lot of code is involved in retrieving, updating, adding, and deleting data from a database via LINQ, so to make things simpler, Microsoft has included a LinqDataSource object with VS2008 that encapsulates all this code into one object, which mirrors those you already saw in Chapter 7. The only difference is that instead of SQL statements defining its select, insert, delete, and update commands for a database, the LinqDataSource expects just LINQ select queries. These can be made against any LINQ provider (LINQ to XML, LINQ to Objects, LINQ to SQL, etc.), and the LinqDataSource will automatically figure out how to insert, delete, and update data to that data store if the provider you are using supports it.

To demonstrate, add to the *C10_LINQ* website a new page called *LinqDS.aspx*, and in Design view add a LinqDataSource control to the page. If you select Configure Data Source from the LinqDataSource control's Smart Tag menu, you'll bring up the Configure Data Source Wizard, which is very similar in operation to the wizard of the same name for the SqlDataSource control.

The first step in the wizard is to specify the DataContext object representing the database tables and stored procedures you want to work with, as shown in Figure 10-21.

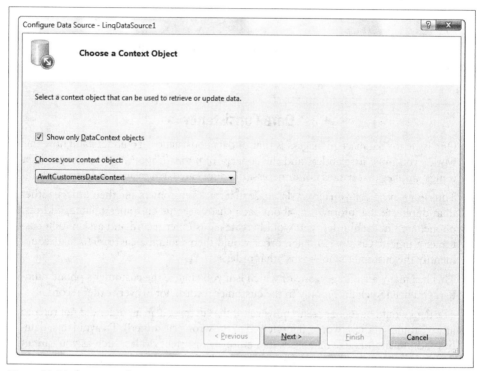

Figure 10-21. Setting up the DataContext for the LinqDataSource

All the available DataContext objects are listed in the drop down, but in this case, there is only one, the AwltCustomersDataContext you created earlier, so click Next. If you uncheck the "Show only DataContext objects" checkbox, you'll also be able to select any non-LINQ to SQL contexts to query against.

The next step asks you which fields to display from which table in the database, as shown in Figure 10-22.

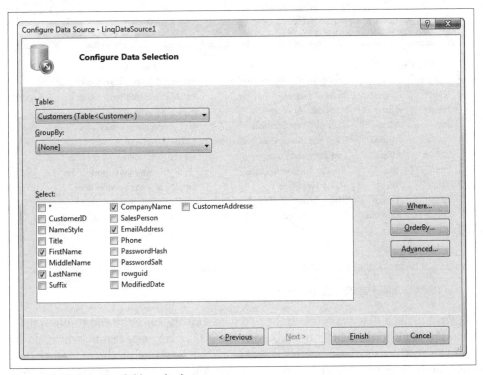

Figure 10-22. Selecting fields to display

Just as you did in Chapter 7, select the Customer table along with FirstName, LastName, CompanyName, and EmailAddress, and then click Finish to complete the wizard. Note that you also have the opportunity to group the data being returned by the LINQ query as well, although we do not cover that in this book.

Looking at the markup generated by the wizard, you'll see that only the select clause of the LINQ query that would otherwise be present is shown by the DataSource control's Select property. The rest of it is hidden from prying coders.

Next, switch back to Design view and add a GridView control to the page, using its Smart Tag menu to set LinqDataSource1 to be its data source. Immediately the GridView will redraw in Design view to show the columns you have configured the data source to return.

While the smart tag is open, check the Enable Paging and Enable Sorting check-boxes, and then run the page. You will see something identical to Figure 10-23, with paging and sorting fully implemented, except it is based on the LinqDataSource rather than the SqlDataSource.

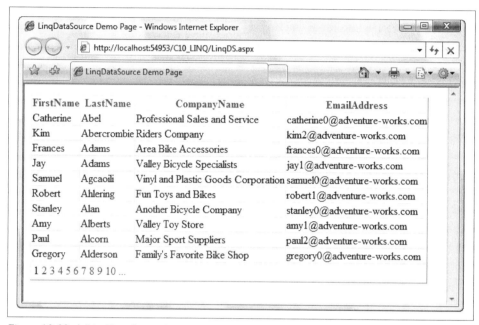

Figure 10-23. A LinqDataSource in action

So, what is the difference between the two data sources, since the end result in these examples is identical? As mentioned earlier, LINQ is a language feature which allows you to construct database queries directly in your language of choice, rather than using SQL. Back in Chapter 7, you saw the markup generated by the SqlDataSource control. It included a ConnectionString and a SelectCommand. The latter consists of this SQL statement:

```
SELECT FirstName, LastName, CompanyName, EmailAddress
FROM SalesLT.Customer
```

If you look at *LinqDS.aspx* in Source view, you will see the following markup for the LinqDataSource control:

```
<asp:LinqDataSource ID="LinqDataSource1" runat="server"
    ContextTypeName="AwltCustomersDataContext" OrderBy="LastName"
    Select="new (FirstName, LastName, CompanyName, EmailAddress)"
    TableName="Customers">
</asp:LinqDataSource>
```

Instead of a ConnectionString attribute pointing to a database, it has a ContextTypeName attribute specifying the DataContext class you created with the Object Relational Designer. It's the DataContext class that stores the connection string.

Furthermore, instead of a `SelectCommand` attribute with a SQL statement, it has a `Select` attribute with a LINQ statement for selecting properties from the table specified in the `TableName` attribute. It also has `Where`, `OrderBy`, `GroupBy`, and `OrderGroupsBy` attributes, which correspond to the respective parts of a LINQ query.

The `LinqDataSource` control can also work with the `GridView` to easily allow for editing of your data, as long as the data source is configured to return all the columns of the table and is not performing a `GroupBy` operation. (Recall from an earlier example that using `GroupBy` changes the structure of the results returned from the query into something to which you can't assign and bind a `GridView`.) The `GridView` does not have to display all the columns, but the `LinqDataSource` must select all the columns.

To demonstrate, open *AwltCustomers.dbml* in the Object Relational Designer again, delete the `Address` and `CustomerAddress` tables from the pane, and save it.

Now add another page, *LinqDsEdit.aspx*, in either Source or Design view, and drag a `LinqDataSource` control and a `GridView` control onto it from the Data section of the Toolbox. In Design view, open the smart tag of the `LinqDataSource` control and click Configure Data Source. As before, verify that `CustomersDataContext` is chosen and click Next.

By default, the only table available, `Customer`, should already be selected and the first checkbox in the first column (the one with an asterisk in it, to select all the fields) should be checked, as shown in Figure 10-24.

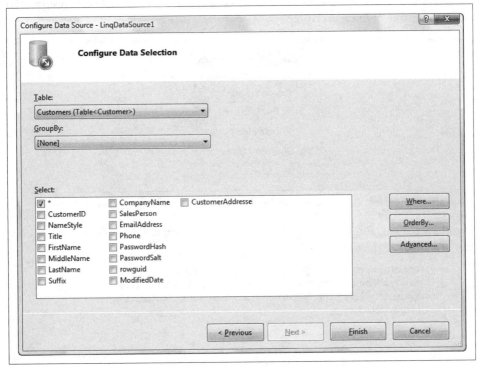

Figure 10-24. Checking the asterisk to return all the fields

If no tables or fields are visible in the dialog, cancel the dialog and click Build → Build Website to build the website. Then try again.

Click the Advanced button to get the options shown in Figure 10-25.

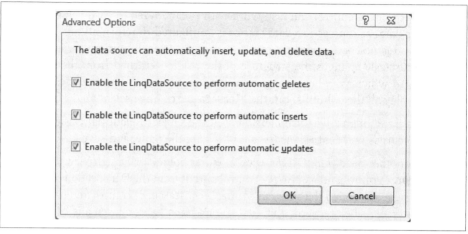

Figure 10-25. Advanced query operations

Check all three checkboxes, then click OK and then Finish. The smart tag for the control will now show checkboxes, all checked, for enabling deletes, inserts, and updates, as shown in Figure 10-26.

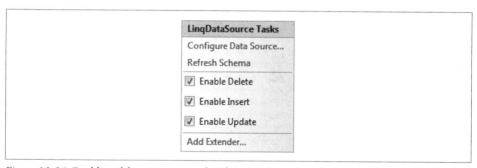

Figure 10-26. Enabling deletes, inserts, and updates on the LinqDataSource control

If you switch to Source view and look at the declaration for the LinqDataSource control, you will see the following:

```
<asp:LinqDataSource ID="LinqDataSource1" runat="server"
    ContextTypeName="AwltCustomersDataContext" EnableDelete="True"
    EnableInsert="True" EnableUpdate="True" TableName="Customers">
</asp:LinqDataSource>
```

If you compare this with the earlier markup for the LinqDataSource, you will see that not only does this have attributes to enable deletes, inserts, and updates, but it also does not have a Select attribute returning specific columns, so all the columns are returned from the database.

Now click the smart tag for the GridView. Choose the DataSource to be LinqDataSource1. Immediately the GridView will redraw with every column in the table, which is more than we want to display. If you recall from Chapter 9, there are two basic ways to remove unwanted fields from a GridView:

- The GUI way is to click Edit Columns in the smart tag, to get the Fields editor, and delete the unwanted fields by selecting them, one at a time, from the listbox in the lower-left corner of the dialog and then clicking the red X button.

- The text-based way is just to delete the undesired BoundField declarations from within the Columns element.

Remove the unwanted fields using the text-based way, removing all the BoundField declarations as required.

Now one last step: go back to the smart tag for the GridView. It will have two new checkboxes in addition to the checkboxes you saw previously: Enable Editing and Enable Deleting. Check those, as shown in Figure 10-27.

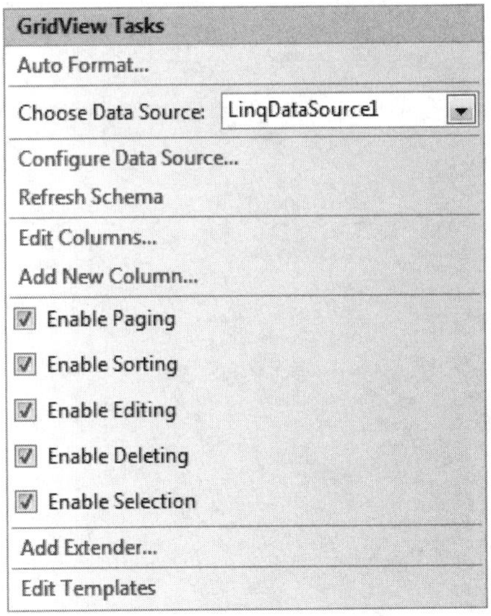

Figure 10-27. Enabling deletes, inserts, and updates on the GridView control

If you save and run the page now, you'll see that barring any problem with referential integrity, you'll be able to edit, insert, and delete from the Customer table.

For more information about the LINQ API and the LINQ providers that are installed as part of .NET 3.5 and .NET 3.5 Service Pack 1, start by checking out the LINQ Project home page at *http://msdn. microsoft.com/en-us/netframework/aa904594.aspx* and its base at *http:// msdn.microsoft.com/en-us/library/bb397926.aspx*. You also can find an extensive list of LINQ-related books at *http://blogs.msdn.com/charlie/ archive/2008/02/17/linq-books.aspx*.

CHAPTER 11

Validation

As you saw in previous chapters, many web applications involve user input. Sadly, however, users make mistakes: they skip required fields, they enter phone numbers with the wrong number of digits, and they send to your application all manner of incorrectly formatted data. Your database routines can choke on corrupted data, and orders can be lost, for example, if a credit card number is entered incorrectly or an address is omitted, so it is imperative to validate user input.

Traditionally, it takes a great deal of time and effort to write reliable validation code. Each field must be checked, and routines must be created for ensuring data integrity. If bad data is found, error messages must be displayed so that the user knows there is a problem and knows how to correct it.

In a given application, you may choose to validate that certain fields have a value, that the values fall within a given range, or that the data is formatted correctly. For example, when processing an order, you may need to ensure the user has input an address and phone number, the phone number has the right number of digits (and no letters), and that the Social Security number entered is in the appropriate form of nine digits separated with hyphens.

Some applications require more complex validation, in which one field is validated to be within a range established by two other fields. For example, in one field you might ask what date a customer wishes to arrive at your hotel, and in a second field you might ask for the departure date. When the user books dinner, you'll want to ensure the date is between the arrival and departure dates.

There is no limit to the complexity of the validation routines you may need to write. Credit cards have checksums built into their values, as do ISBN numbers. Zip and postal codes follow complex patterns, as do international phone numbers. You may need to validate passwords, membership numbers, dollar amounts, dates, runway choices, and launch codes.

In addition, you usually want all of this validation to happen on the client side, so you can avoid the delay of repeated round trips to the server while the user is tinkering with his input. In the past, this was solved by writing client-side JavaScript to validate the input, and then writing server-side script to handle input from browsers that don't support client-side programming. In addition, as a security check, you may want to do server-side validation even though you have client-side validation, because users can circumvent validation code by deliberately spoofing requests. Traditionally, this involved writing your validation code twice, once for the client and once for the server.

As you can see, validating user input can require a lot of hard work, but ASP.NET simplifies this process considerably by providing rich controls for this task. The validation controls allow you to specify how and where the error messages will be displayed: inline with the input controls, aggregated together in a summary report, or both. These controls can be used to validate input for both HTML and ASP.NET server controls.

You add validation controls to your ASP.NET document as you would add any other control. Within the declaration of the validation control, you specify which other control is being validated. You may freely combine the various validation controls, and you may even write your own custom validation controls, as you'll see later in this chapter.

With up-level browsers that support DHTML, such as Internet Explorer 4 and later, .NET validation is done on the client side, avoiding the necessity of a round trip to the server. With down-level browsers or browsers with scripting turned off, your code is unchanged, but the code sent to the client ensures validation at the server.

 Even when client-side validation is done, the values are also validated on the server side as a security measure.

Because client-side validation will prevent your server-side code from ever running if the control is invalid, sometimes you may want to force server-side validation. In that case, add a `ClientTarget` attribute to the @Page directive:

```
<% @Page Language="C#" AutoEventWireup="true"
    CodeFile="Default.aspx.cs" Inherits="Default_aspx"
    ClientTarget="downlevel"
%>
```

This directive will cause the validation to occur on the server even if your browser would have supported DHTML and client-side validation.

Sometimes you don't want any validation to occur, such as when a Cancel button is clicked. To specify this, many server controls, such as `Button`, `ImageButton`, `LinkButton`, `ListControl`, and `TextBox`, have a `CausesValidation` property, which dictates whether validation is performed on the page when the control's default event is raised.

If `CausesValidation` is set to `true`, which is the default value, the postback will not occur if any control on the page fails validation. If `CausesValidation` is set to `false`, however, no validation will occur when that button is used to post the page.

ASP.NET supports the following validation controls:

RequiredFieldValidator

> Ensures the user does not skip over your input control. A RequiredFieldValidator can be tied to a TextBox to force input into the TextBox. With selection controls, such as a DropDownList or RadioButtons, the RequiredFieldValidator ensures the user makes a selection other than the default value you specify. The RequiredFieldValidator does not examine the validity of the data, but only ensures that some data is entered or chosen.

RangeValidator

> Ensures the value entered is within a specified lower and upper boundary. You can check the range within a pair of numbers (greater than 10 and less than 100), a pair of characters (greater than D and less than K), or a pair of dates (after 1/1/09 and before 2/28/09).

CompareValidator

> Compares the user's entry against another value. It can compare against a constant you specify at design time, or against a property value of another control. It can also compare against a database value.

RegularExpressionValidator

> One of the most powerful validators, RegularExpressionValidator compares the user's entry with a regular expression you provide. You can use this validator to check for valid Social Security numbers, phone numbers, passwords, and so on.

CustomValidator

> For use if none of the previous controls meets your needs. CustomValidator checks the user's entry against whatever algorithm you provide in a custom method.

In the remainder of this chapter, we'll examine how to use each of these controls to validate data in ASP.NET applications. You'll also see how some of the extender controls that come with the ASP.NET AJAX Control Toolkit aid in guiding a user's input toward the desired entry.

The RequiredFieldValidator

The RequiredFieldValidator ensures the user provides a valid value for your control. To demonstrate, create for the chapter a new website called *C11_Validation* and then add a new web page called *RequiredFieldValidator.aspx*. You'll create a simple form nominally for reporting bugs, as shown in Figure 11-1.

Validator controls will be added to the form such that when the user clicks the Submit Bug button, the page is validated to ensure that each field has been modified. If not, the offending field is marked with an error message in red. See Figure 11-2.

To help with layout, add an HTML table to the page with five rows and three columns. (You could equally put each row of the table in a <div> or <p> tag and lay things out with CSS, but that would just complicate the code here.) In the first row,

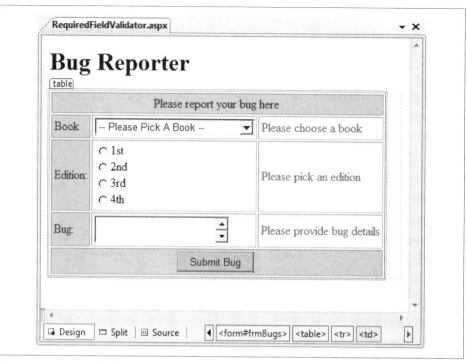

Figure 11-1. RequiredFieldValidator.aspx design

add a Label control called lblMsg. Later on, you'll use the Page_Load method to change its Text property depending on whether the page is valid or not.

```
<%@ Page Language="C#" AutoEventWireup="true"
    CodeFile="RequiredFieldValidator.aspx.cs" Inherits="RequiredFieldValidator" %>

<!DOCTYPE html PUBLIC "-//W3C//DTD XHTML 1.0 Transitional//EN"
    "http://www.w3.org/TR/xhtml1/DTD/xhtml1-transitional.dtd">
<html xmlns="http://www.w3.org/1999/xhtml">

<head>
    <title>Required Field Validator Demo</title>
</head>

<body>
    <h1>Bug Reporter</h1>
    <form runat="server" id="frmBugs">
    <table>
        <tr>
            <td colspan="3" align="center">
                <asp:Label ID="lblMsg" Text="Please report your bug here"
                runat="server" />
            </td>
        </tr>
```

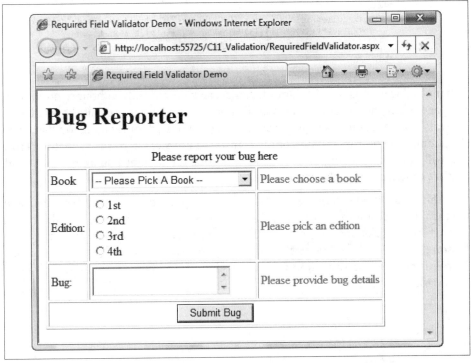

Figure 11-2. Required field validation errors reported when page is submitted

The second row contains a `DropDownList` control (`ddlBooks`) and a `RequiredFieldValidator` control (`rfvBooks`). Besides the mandatory `runat` and `ID`, its most important properties are `ControlToValidate`, which identifies the control that it should validate, and `ErrorMessage`, which contains the text the control will display if a value has not been selected in the list, or if the value selected is the same as the one given in the `InitialValue` property.

`rfvBooks` also has a `Display` property, which is set to `Static`. This tells ASP.NET to allocate room on the page for the validator regardless of whether there is a message to display. If this property is set to `Dynamic`, space will not be allocated until (and unless) an error message is displayed.

```
<tr>
    <td>Book</td>
    <td>
        <asp:DropDownList ID="ddlBooks" runat="server">
            <asp:ListItem>-- Please Pick A Book --</asp:ListItem>
            <asp:ListItem>Programming ASP.NET</asp:ListItem>
            <asp:ListItem>Learning ASP.NET With AJAX</asp:ListItem>
            <asp:ListItem>Programming C# 2008</asp:ListItem>
            <asp:ListItem>Programming Visual Basic 2008</asp:ListItem>
        </asp:DropDownList>
    </td>
</tr>
```

```
<td>
  <asp:RequiredFieldValidator ID="rfvBooks" ControlToValidate="ddlBooks"
      Display="Static" InitialValue="-- Please Pick A Book --"
      runat="server" ErrorMessage="Please choose a book" />
</td>
</tr>
```

Dynamic allocation is powerful, but it can cause your controls to bounce around on the page when the message is displayed. For example, if you set all the validation controls to Dynamic on this page, no space will be allocated for them. If you then click the Submit Bug button and one of the controls is not validated, the validators' error text will display, widening the table and relocating the Submit Bug button and Label that are centered across the whole table.

The third row in the table contains a RadioButtonList control (rblEdition) and another RequiredFieldValidator (rfvEdition) set to validate it. In this case, rfvEdition does not have its InitialValue property set. Because the control is a radio button list, the validator knows the user is required to pick one of the buttons; if any button is chosen, the validation will be satisfied. If no button is chosen, the validator's error message will be displayed.

```
<tr>
  <td>
    Edition:
  </td>
  <td>
    <asp:RadioButtonList ID="rblEdition" RepeatLayout="Flow"
      runat="server">
        <asp:ListItem>1st</asp:ListItem>
        <asp:ListItem>2nd</asp:ListItem>
        <asp:ListItem>3rd</asp:ListItem>
        <asp:ListItem>4th</asp:ListItem>
    </asp:RadioButtonList>
  </td>
  <td>
    <asp:RequiredFieldValidator ID="rfvEdition"
        ControlToValidate="rblEdition"
        Display="Static" runat="server"
        ErrorMessage="Please pick an edition" />
  </td>
</tr>
```

To complete the example, the fourth row contains a multiline TextBox (txtBug) and a third RequiredFieldValidator (rfvBug) set to monitor it. Again, a user has either added some text to the TextBox or not, so no InitialValue property needs to be set on rfvBug.

The fifth and final row in the table contains a simple Button control, which when clicked automatically causes the page to initiate validation on the browser according to the rules set out in the three validation controls you've added to the page.

```
        <tr>
          <td>Bug: </td>
          <td>
            <asp:TextBox ID="txtBug" runat="server" TextMode="MultiLine" />
          </td>
          <td>
            <asp:RequiredFieldValidator ID="rfvBug"
              ControlToValidate="txtBug" Display="Static"
              runat="server" ErrorMessage="Please provide bug details" />
          </td>
        </tr>
        <tr>
          <td colspan="3" align="center">
            <asp:Button ID="btnSubmit" Text="Submit Bug" runat="server" />
          </td>
        </tr>
      </table>
    </form>
  </body>
</html>
<!-- end of RequiredFieldValidator.aspx -->
```

If you run the page now and click the Submit Bug button without making any changes on the form, each control being validated is checked and error messages are displayed, as shown previously in Figure 11-2.

Once validation has occurred, ASP.NET then posts back to the server when any server-side validation occurs. If that validation also passes, the Page's IsValid property is set to true or false depending on whether the value in every control being monitored is valid.

To demonstrate, add to the code-behind page in *RequiredFieldValidator.aspx* a handler for the Submit Bug button's Click event, and then add the highlighted code in Example 11-1.

Example 11-1. RequiredFieldValidator.aspx.cs in full

```
using System;
using System.Web.UI;

public partial class RequiredFieldValidator : Page
{
    protected void btnSubmit_Click(object sender, EventArgs e)
    {
        if (Page.IsValid)
        {
            lblMsg.Text = "Page is valid";
        }
        else
        {
            lblMsg.Text = "Some of the fields still have no value";
        }
    }
}
```

If you run the page again, notice that when the Submit Bug button is clicked, the page is posted to the server only if all client-side validation routines return true. If you view the source for the page, you'll see the following code, which is injected into the page and enforces this behavior:

```
<script type="text/javascript">
//<![CDATA[
function WebForm_OnSubmit() {
if (typeof(ValidatorOnSubmit) == "function" &&
        ValidatorOnSubmit() == false) return false;
return true;
}
//]]>
</script>
```

 The text that AJAX Control Toolkit extender controls, such as the WatermarkExtender and MaskedEditExtender, add into a TextBox does not affect whether the RequiredFieldValidator works. The watermark or mask does not count as a value having been entered.

The Summary Control

You can decide how and where validation errors are reported. You are not required to place validator controls alongside the control they are validating, although it does help to identify which text box or list control has been filled out incorrectly. For forms of any size, though, a good strategy to help a user identify her mistakes is to summarize all the validation failures with a ValidationSummary control. This control can place a summary of the errors in a bulleted list, a simple list, or a paragraph that appears on the web page or in a pop-up message box.

To demonstrate, add to the website a new page called *ValidationSummary.aspx* and copy the contents of *RequiredFieldValidator.aspx* into it. Add a ValidationSummary control at the bottom of the page, between the closing </table> and </form> tags.

```
    ...
        <tr>
            <td colspan="3" align="center">
                <asp:Button ID="btnSubmit" Text="Submit Bug" runat="server" />
            </td>
        </tr>
    </table>
    <asp:ValidationSummary ID="ValidationSummary1" runat="server"
        DisplayMode="BulletList"
        HeaderText="The following errors were found: "
        ShowSummary="true" />
    </form>
</body>
</html>
```

Three properties are set on the ValidationSummary control besides the mandatory runat and ID:

DisplayMode

Sets the way in which those errors are shown in the summary. Possible values are BulletList (shown in Figure 11-3), List, and SingleParagraph.

HeaderText

Sets the header that will be displayed if there are any errors to report.

ShowSummary

Indicates that the errors should be shown in the body of the HTML document. It has a sister property, ShowMessageBox, which will display the errors in a pop-up message box if set to true. You can set both to true if desired.

Now save and run the page. If you click the Submit Bug button, the text in the validator controls' ErrorMessage attributes will be displayed in the summary if this control reports a validation error, as shown in Figure 11-3.

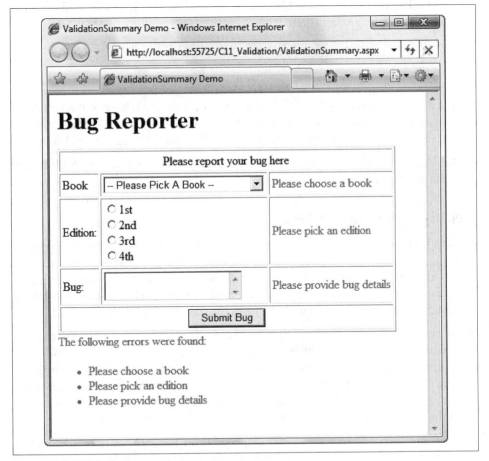

Figure 11-3. ValidationSummary.aspx

Figure 11-4 shows the ValidationSummary with ShowMessageBox set to true.

Figure 11-4. ValidationSummary as a MessageBox

You can avoid having the same error messages displayed by both the validator controls and the ValidationSummary control by setting the Text property on the validators. For example, set the Text property on the three RequiredFieldValidator controls to *:

```
<asp:RequiredFieldValidator ID="rfvBooks" ControlToValidate="ddlBooks"
    Display="Static" InitialValue="-- Please Pick A Book --"
    runat="server" ErrorMessage="Please choose a book"
    Text="*" />
```

Now run the page and click the Submit Bug button again. You'll see that the Text property overrides the ErrorMessage displayed by the validator control. Meanwhile, the ValidationSummary control continues displaying the ErrorMessage, as Figure 11-5 shows.

Figure 11-6 shows the results of ValidationSummary's DisplayMode set to List (left) and SingleParagraph (right).

Identifying the User's Errors

Filling in a form only to have the page throw it back at you and say you've completed it incorrectly isn't a great user experience. Rather than having error messages strewn all over the place, you've seen how to use the ValidationSummary control to group all the error messages in one area for review, leaving more discreet identifying marks against the form control with the incorrect value.

If you have a large form, however, first finding the control to correct and then associating which error message applies to it can be tricky. You can help users with their corrections by placing the focus on the first control that fails validation. To do so, add the SetFocusOnError property to each validation control and set it to true. When one or more controls use SetFocusOnError and if the page is invalid, the focus will be set to the first control that fails validation and has this property set to true.

You can also use a ValidatorCallout extender from the AJAX Control Toolkit to more clearly highlight the control in error, as shown in Figure 11-7.

As you can see, the ValidatorCallout control displays the contents of a validator control's ErrorMessage property in a callout box pointing at the control with an erroneous

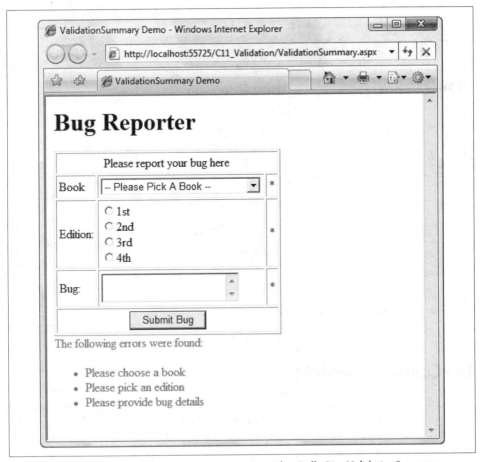

Figure 11-5. Using Text and ErrorMessage properties with a BulletList ValidationSummary

value in it. What you can't see is that the callout box appears only when the user has selected the control (set the focus on it), so this extender works well with the SetFocusOnError property. When a page is marked as invalid, focus is set on the first erroneous value by SetFocusOnError and the callout box appears.

ValidatorCallout requires only markup, using its TargetControlId property to identify the validator control it is extending and HighlightCssClass to give the callout box color.

```
<asp:RequiredFieldValidator ID="rfvBooks"
    ControlToValidate="ddlBooks" Display="Static"
    InitialValue="-- Please Pick A Book --" Text="*"
    runat="server" ErrorMessage="Please choose a book"
    SetFocusOnError="true" />
<cc1:ValidatorCalloutExtender ID="rfvBooks_ValidatorCalloutExtender"
    runat="server" Enabled="True" TargetControlID="rfvBooks"
    HighlightCssClass="validatorCalloutHighlight" />
```

You can find the code that demonstrates this in the download for this chapter as *ValidatorCallout.aspx.*

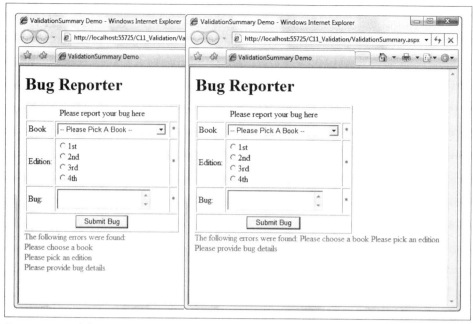

Figure 11-6. ValidationSummary as List and SingleParagraph

The Compare Validator

Although the ability to ensure the user has made some sort of entry is great, you will often want to validate that the entry content is within certain guidelines. One of the most common requirements for validation is to compare the user's input to a value constant, the value of another control, or a database value. To do this, you can use a CompareValidator control.

To demonstrate, add to the site a new web page called *CompareValidator.aspx*. Copy the <body> of *ValidationSummary.aspx* into it and then add a new row to the main <table> immediately above the row containing the Submit Bug button. This row will contain a TextBox control to specify a page number where the bug was found and two validator controls: a RequiredFieldValidator and a CompareValidator.

```
<tr>
    <td>Page Number:</td>
    <td>
        <asp:TextBox ID="txtNumPurch" runat="server" />
    </td>
    <td>
        <asp:RequiredFieldValidator runat="server" ID="rfvPageNumber"
            ControlToValidate="txtPageNumber"
            ErrorMessage="You did not enter the page number" Text="*" />

        <asp:CompareValidator runat="server" ID="cmpPageNumber"
            ControlToValidate="txtPageNumber"
```

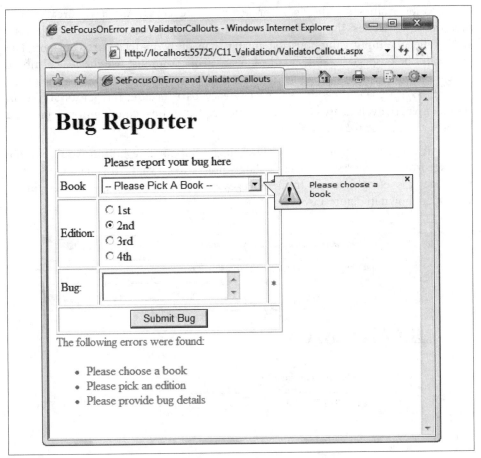

Figure 11-7. ValidatorCallout controls in action

```
                  ErrorMessage="Invalid page number" Type="Integer"
                  Operator="GreaterThan" ValueToCompare="0" Text="*" />
      </td>
   </tr>
```

Both validators are placed into the same cell in the table, and both validators validate the same control: txtPageNumber.

 You need the RequiredFieldValidator because the CompareValidator will always return true for null or empty values.

The CompareValidator's ValueToCompare attribute takes a constant, in this case zero. The Operator attribute determines how the comparison will be made (i.e., how the input value must be related to ValueToCompare).

The possible values for the `Operator` attribute are `Equal`, `NotEqual`, `GreaterThan`, `GreaterThanEqual`, `LessThan`, `LessThanEqual`, and `DataTypeCheck`. In this example case, to be valid, the input value must be greater than the `ValueToCompare` constant. The error can't be on page 0, so it's marked as an error. You must use the `Type` attribute to tell the control what type of value it is using. The `Type` attribute takes one of the `ValidationDataType` enumerated values: `Currency`, `Date`, `Double`, `Integer`, or `String`. In the example, the values are compared as integers, and thus, entering (for example) a character will cause the validation to fail.

Save and run the page. If you initially click the Submit Bug button, you'll see the message from `rfvPageNumber` appear telling you to enter a value. If you enter 0 (zero), you'll get the error message from `cmpPageNumber` instead, telling you that this is wrong, as shown in Figure 11-8.

Figure 11-8. The CompareValidator control at work

Checking the Input Type

Instead of checking that the page number is greater than zero, you might want to check that it is a number at all (rather than a letter or date). To do this, you should make the following changes to the CompareValidator:

- Remove the ValueToCompare attribute.
- Change the Operator attribute from GreaterThan to DataTypeCheck.

The Type attribute is already set to Integer, so the control will report any integer value as valid, and following those changes its code will look like this:

```
<asp:CompareValidator runat="server" ID="cmpPageNumber"
    ControlToValidate="txtPageNumber" Text="*"
    ErrorMessage="Invalid page number" Type="Integer"
    Operator="DataTypeCheck" />
```

Comparing to Another Control

You can also compare a value in one control to the value in another control rather than to a constant. A classic use of this technique might be to ask a user to enter his password twice and then validate that both entries are identical.

The common scenario is that you've asked the user to pick a new password. For security, when the password is entered, the text is disguised with asterisks or dots (depending on your browser). Because this will be the password the user will need in order to log in, you must validate that the user entered the password as intended. The usual solution is to ask the user to reenter the password, and then you validate that the same password was entered each time. The CompareValidator is perfect for this.

To demonstrate, add another two rows to the table in *CompareValidator.aspx* just above the row containing the Submit Bug button. Both rows will contain a TextBox in Password mode and a RequiredFieldValidator to make sure passwords were supplied in both boxes. The second row will also contain a CompareValidator which tries to match the contents of the second TextBox to the first.

```
<tr>
    <td>Enter your password:</td>
    <td>
        <asp:TextBox ID="txtPassword1" runat="server" TextMode="Password" />
    </td>
    <td>
        <!-- required to enter the password -->
        <asp:RequiredFieldValidator runat="server" ID="rfvPassword1"
            ControlToValidate="txtPassword1"
            ErrorMessage="Please enter your password" Text="*" />
    </td>
</tr>
<!-- Second password for comparison -->
```

```
<tr>
    <td>Re-enter your password:</td>
    <td><asp:TextBox ID="txtPassword2" runat="server" TextMode="Password" />
    </td>
    <td>
        <!-- Second password is required -->
        <asp:RequiredFieldValidator runat="server" ID="rfvPassword2"
            ControlToValidate="txtPassword2"
            ErrorMessage="Please re-enter your password" Text="*" />

        <!-- Second password must match the first -->
        <asp:CompareValidator runat="server" ID="cmpPasswords"
            ControlToValidate="txtPassword2"
            ErrorMessage="Passwords do not match"
            Type="String" Operator="Equal"
            ControlToCompare="txtPassword1" Text="*" />
        </td>
    </tr>
```

This says that the CompareValidator (whose ID is CmpPasswords) is validating the TextBox control whose ID is txtPassword2 by comparing its value with the TextBox control whose ID is txtPassword1. The Operator property is set to Equal and the Type property is set to String, so the two strings must match.

 Both text boxes need a RequiredFieldValidator because the CompareValidator will validate as matching a string against a null or empty string value.

Checking Password Strength

In this particular scenario, you may also consider adding a PasswordStrength control from the AJAX Control Toolkit to help a user create a strong password. This extender targets the TextBox control (using its TargetControlID property) where a password is being entered, and gives the user hints on how secure his new password is based on criteria set in six of its properties:

- MinimumLowerCaseCharacters
- MinimumNumericCharacters
- MinimumSymbolCharacters
- MinimumUpperCaseCharacters
- PreferredPasswordLength
- RequiresUpperAndLowerCaseCharacters

The default for all of these properties is 0 (zero), with the exception of RequiresUpperAndLowerCaseCharacters which is false by default, and PreferredPasswordLength which is 10. Once you've set the criteria for a password, as the user enters the password the extender scores the password between 0 and 100 based on how well the password fulfills those criteria. The score is also weighted with respect to how the password matches up to its length, numeric, casing, and symbol requirements based on the extender's CalculationWeightings property. By default, this is set to 50;15;15;20 for length, numbers, casing, and symbols, respectively.

The scores are then reflected on the page either as a bar chart or as text depending on whether the StrengthIndicatorType property is set to Text or BarIndicator. If it is set to Text, you must also provide the various strings to indicate the current strength of the password. You do this as a semicolon-separated list of strings in the control's TextStrengthDescriptions property in order of strength. For example:

```
TextStrengthDescriptions="Awful;Poor;OK;Strong;RockSolid!"
```

If a password is scored between 0 and 20, the extender will show "Awful" onscreen, 21–40 will receive "Poor," and so on. You must include between 2 and 10 strings in this property.

Finally, the PasswordStrength control also has a number of properties to control how it appears on-screen, as given in Table 11-1.

Table 11-1. Style-related properties for the PasswordStrength control

Property	Description
DisplayPosition	Where the score will be shown on-screen with respect to the TextBox containing it. Default is AboveRight.
PrefixText	Text to prefix the current score string.
TextCssClass	The default CSS style for the text-based score.
BarIndicatorCssClass	The default CSS style for the bar of a bar chart-based score.
BarBorderCssClass	The default CSS style for the bar border of a bar chart-based score.
StrengthStyles	A semicolon-separated list of CSS styles to override TextCssClass or BarIndicatorCssClass as the score increases. Works in the same way as TextStrengthDescriptions.

To demonstrate, add a new page to the *C11_Validation* website and call it *ComparePasswordStrength.aspx*. Copy the contents of *CompareValidator.aspx* to this new page. Find txtPassword1 on the page and add a PasswordStrength extender to the page, setting its properties as shown here:

```
<td>
    Enter your password:
</td>
<td>
    <asp:TextBox ID="txtPassword1" runat="server" TextMode="Password" />
    <cc1:PasswordStrength ID="txtPassword1_PasswordStrength"
        runat="server" Enabled="True"
        TargetControlID="txtPassword1" DisplayPosition="RightSide"
        StrengthIndicatorType="Text"
        PreferredPasswordLength="10" PrefixText="Strength:"
        TextStrengthDescriptions="Very Poor;Weak;Average;Strong;Excellent"
```

```
            StrengthStyles="VPoor;Weak;Average;Strong;Excellent"
            MinimumNumericCharacters="0" MinimumSymbolCharacters="0"
            RequiresUpperAndLowerCaseCharacters="false">
        </cc1:PasswordStrength>
    </td>
```

Note how we've deliberately matched up the CSS class names in StrengthStyles to
the scores in TextStrengthDescriptions. It's not mandatory, but it is handy when
you're trying to remember which style represents which score. Speaking of styles,
you'll also need to add to the page the CSS classes given in StrengthStyles:

```
<style media="screen" type="text/css">
    .VPoor
    {
        background-color: Gray;
        color: White;
        font-family: Arial;
        font-size: x-small;
        font-style: italic;
        padding: 2px 3px 2px 3px;
        font-weight: bold;
    }
    .Weak
    {
        background-color: Gray;
        color: Yellow;
        font-family: Arial;
        font-size: x-small;
        font-style: italic;
        padding: 2px 3px 2px 3px;
        font-weight: bold;
    }
    .Average
    {
        background-color: Gray;
        color: #FFCAAF;
        font-family: Arial;
        font-size: x-small;
        font-style: italic;
        padding: 2px 3px 2px 3px;
        font-weight: bold;
    }
    .Strong
    {
        background-color: Gray;
        color: Aqua;
        font-family: Arial;
        font-size: x-small;
        font-style: italic;
        padding: 2px 3px 2px 3px;
        font-weight: bold;
    }
```

```
    .Excellent
    {
        background-color: Gray;
        color: #93FF9E;
        font-family: Arial;
        font-size: x-small;
        font-style: italic;
        padding: 2px 3px 2px 3px;
        font-weight: bold;
    }
</style>
```

When you run the page and start typing, you'll see the score for your password appear above and to the right of the text box where you are typing, as shown in Figure 11-9. As you type, you'll see the score change until the password is more than 10 characters long.

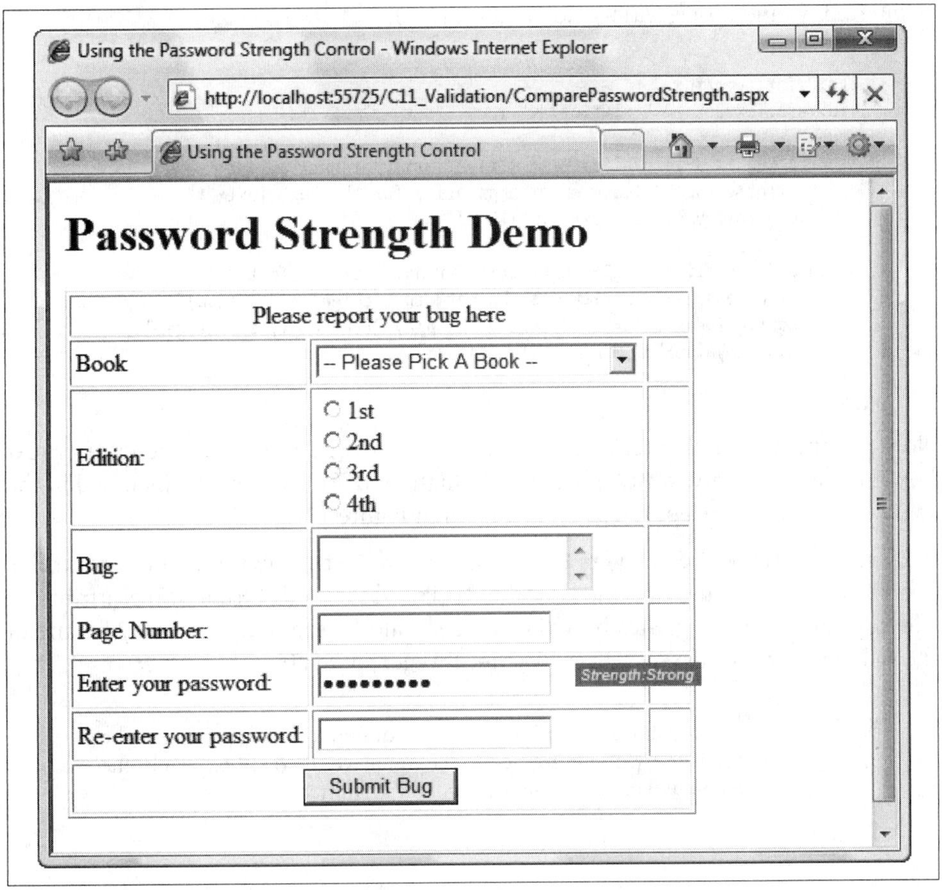

Figure 11-9. The PasswordStrength control as text

Range Checking

At times, you'll want to validate that a user's entry falls within a range. That range can be within a pair of numbers, characters, or dates. In addition, you can express the boundaries for the range by using constants or by comparing its value with values found in other controls.

To demonstrate, add a new web page to the *C11_Validation* website and name it *RangeValidator.aspx*. Copy the contents of *CompareValidator.aspx* to this new page. In this example, you'll add another row to the bug tracker form to allow the user to specify the priority of the bug. This must be a number between 1 and 7.

Add a new row to the table in *RangeValidator.aspx* between the page number TextBox and the first password TextBox. You'll need to add a TextBox control (txtPriority) and two validators to the control: a RequiredFieldValidator (rfvPriority) and a RangeValidator (rngPriority).

```
<tr>
    <td>Priority:</td>
    <td><asp:TextBox ID="txtPriority" runat="server" /></td>
    <td>
        <asp:RequiredFieldValidator ID="rfvPriority" runat="server"
            ErrorMessage="Please enter a priority for the bug" Text="*"
            ControlToValidate="txtPriority" />

        <asp:RangeValidator ID="rngPriority" runat="server" Text="*"
            ErrorMessage="Priority must be between 1 (high) and 7 (low)"
            ControlToValidate="txtPriority" Display="Static" Type="Integer"
            MaximumValue="7" MinimumValue="1" />
    </td>
</tr>
```

Now run the page and enter a value that is not between 1 and 7 in the Priority text box. The text "Priority must be between 1 (high) and 7 (low)" will be included in the ValidationSummary area of the page, as shown in Figure 11-10.

A RangeValidator will display its ErrorMessage and Text if the value in the control is not between the values specified by the MinimumValue and MaximumValue attributes. The Type attribute designates how the value should be evaluated and may be any of the following types: Currency, Date, Double, Integer, or String.

The RequiredFieldValidator is also required on this page lest the TextBox is left without any words. If you leave the text box blank, the validation will pass and the page will be submitted.

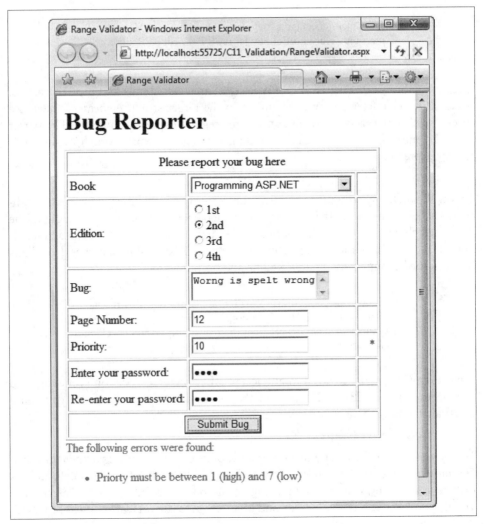

Figure 11-10. The RangeValidator in action

Regular Expressions

Often, a simple value or range check is insufficient; you must check that the form of the data entered is correct. For example, you may need to ensure that a zip code is five digits, an email address is in the form name@place.com, a credit card matches the right format, and so forth.

A regular expression validator allows you to validate that a text field matches a regular expression. Regular expressions are a language for describing and manipulating text.

For complete coverage of regular expressions, see *Mastering Regular Expressions*, Third Edition, by Jeffrey E.F. Friedl (O'Reilly).

A regular expression consists of two types of characters: literals and metacharacters. A *literal* is a character you wish to match in the target string. A *metacharacter* is a special symbol that acts as a command to the regular expression parser. (The parser is the engine responsible for understanding the regular expression.) Consider this regular expression:

```
^\d{5}$
```

This will match any string that has five numerals. The initial metacharacter, ^, indicates the beginning of the string. The second metacharacter, \d, indicates a digit. The third metacharacter, {5}, indicates five of the digits, and the final metacharacter, $, indicates the end of the string. Thus, this regular expression matches five digits between the beginning and end of the line and nothing else.

 When you use a RegularExpressionValidator control with client-side validation, the regular expressions are matched using JScript. This may differ in small details from the regular expression checking done on the server.

A more sophisticated algorithm might accept a five-digit zip code, or a nine-digit zip code in the format 12345-1234. Rather than using the \d metacharacter, you could designate the range of acceptable values:

```
[0-9]{5}|[0-9]{5}-[0-9]{4}
```

To demonstrate, make a copy of *RangeValidator.aspx* and call it *RegexValidator.aspx*. On this page, you'll add another row to the form for the user to enter her email address (so you can acknowledge the submission of the bug by email) in a TextBox control. You'll use a RequiredFieldValidator and RegularExpressionValidator control to check that the email address is valid.

Add a new row to the table in *RangeValidator.aspx* between the priority TextBox and the first password TextBox. You'll need to add a TextBox control (txtEmail) and two validators to the control: a RequiredFieldValidator (rfvEmail) and a RegularExpressionValidator (rgxEmail).

```
<tr>
    <td>Email Address:</td>
    <td><asp:TextBox ID="txtEmail" runat="server" /></td>
    <td>
        <asp:RequiredFieldValidator ID="rfvEmail" runat="server"
            ErrorMessage="Please enter an email address" Text="*"
            ControlToValidate="txtEmail" />
```

```
        <asp:RegularExpressionValidator ID="rgxEmail" runat="server"
          ErrorMessage="Please enter a valid email address" Text="*"
          ControlToValidate="txtEmail" Display="Static"
          ValidationExpression=
            "\w+([-+.']\w+)*@\w+([-.]\w+)*\.\w+([-.]\w+)*" />
    </td>
  </tr>
```

Rather than type out the regular expression shown here, Visual Studio 2008 (VS2008) stores a number of preset regular expressions that you can use for this purpose. To access them, switch your page to Design view, select the RegularExpressionValidator on the form, and then look for the ValidationExpression entry in the Properties window. When you click in the area for the entry, click the button that appears. The Regular Expression Editor window appears, from which you can choose the pattern matching common email addresses, as shown in Figure 11-11.

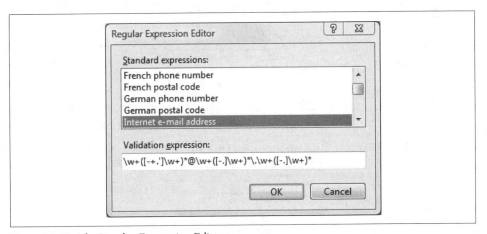

Figure 11-11. The Regular Expression Editor

Choose the regular expression you want to use and then click OK to have it set in the validator's ValidationExpression property.

If you run the page and click Select, the RequiredFieldValidator will ask you to enter an email address, and if you enter, for example, just a name rather than an email address, the RegularExpressionValidator will kick in and ask you to supply a valid email address, as shown in Figure 11-12.

 If you want to use your own regular expression in the validator, you can enter it directly into the markup, or you can choose Custom from the "Validation expression" drop-down menu. This will leave the property blank for you to alter directly. For help with creating custom regular expressions, we recommend the program RegexBuddy (*http:// www.RegExBuddy.com*).

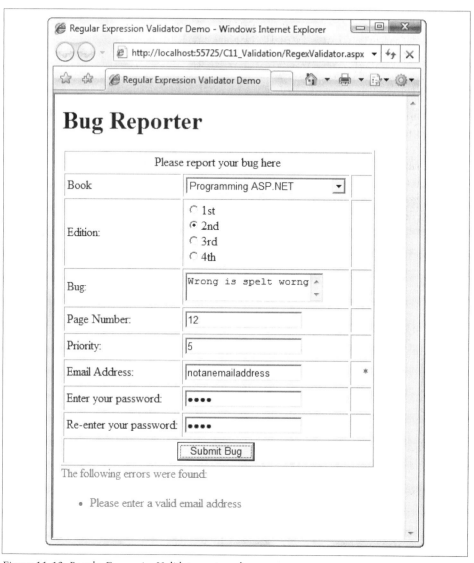

Figure 11-12. RegularExpressionValidators at work

Custom Validation

Sometimes the validation of your data is so specific to your application that you will need to write your own validation method. The CustomValidator is designed to provide all the infrastructure support you need. You point to your validation method and have it return a Boolean value: true or false. The CustomValidator control takes care of the rest.

Because validation can be done on the client or on the server, depending on the browser, the CustomValidator has attributes for specifying a server-side and a client-side method for validation. You can write the server-side method in any .NET language, such as C# or VB.NET, but you must write the client-side method in a scripting language the browser can understand, such as VBScript or JavaScript.

To demonstrate, add a copy of *RegexValidator.aspx* to the *C11_Validation* website and call it *CustomValidator.aspx*. In this example, you'll add a new row to ensure that the user enters an even number before the bug is submitted.

 In the real world, antispam measures such as CAPTCHA and Akismet randomly generate a series of characters for the user to type rather than just a number divisible by 2. You could also use this technique to perform a checksum on a credit card or ISBN or otherwise perform complex data checking. However, we're demonstrating the CustomValidator here, and not those systems.

Add a new row to the table immediately above the Submit Bug button row. You'll need to add a TextBox control (txtEvenNumber) for the user input, and two validators to make sure that it has a valid Text value. The RequiredFieldValidator (rfvEvenNumber) will check that the TextBox has a value before the CustomValidator (cvalEvenNumber) checks it. Unlike the other validator controls, the CustomValidator control actually can deal with an empty value gracefully if you set its ValidateEmptyText property to true or false. When the control is set to false, it will simply mark the value it is set to monitor as not valid if it is empty. When it is set to true, you'll need to deal with empty values yourself in your validation routines.

```
<tr>
    <td>Are you human?<br />Enter an even number</td>
    <td>
        <asp:TextBox ID="txtEvenNumber" runat="server" />
    </td>
    <td>
        <asp:RequiredFieldValidator runat="server" ID="rfvEvenNumber"
            ControlToValidate="txtEvenNumber"
            ErrorMessage="Please enter an even number" Text="*" />
        <asp:CustomValidator runat="server" ID="cvalEvenNumber"
            ControlToValidate="txtEvenNumber"
            ErrorMessage="No odd numbers please" Text="*"
            ValidateEmptyText="false"
            ClientValidationFunction="IsNumberEven"
            onservervalidate="cvalEvenNumber_ServerValidate" />
    </td>
</tr>
```

The key to making your custom validator work is in setting the client-side validator, which you identify in the control's ClientValidationFunction property. In this example, it is set to IsNumberEven, a JavaScript function added at the top of the page.

This function examines the value passed to the script by the validator, and if it is an even number, it will return true; otherwise, it will return false.

```
<script type="text/javascript" language="javascript">
   function IsNumberEven(source, args)
   {
      if (args.Value % 2 == 0)
         args.IsValid=true;
      else
         args.IsValid=false;
      return;
   }
</script>
```

To add a server-side validation routine to the CustomValidator, you'll need to add it into or call it from the control's ServerValidate event handler, which you'll find in *CustomValidator.aspx.cs*. This method does the same thing as the client-side validator, only in C# rather than in JavaScript.

Note that the value the CustomValidator is examining is passed to your routine as the Value property of the ServerValidateEventArgs event argument. It's passed as a generic object, though, so it has to be cast back to an integer before it is used.

```
using System;
using System.Web.UI;
using System.Web.UI.WebControls;

public partial class CustomValidator : Page
{
   protected void cvalEvenNumber_ServerValidate(
      object source, ServerValidateEventArgs args)
   {
      args.IsValid = false;
      int evenNumber = Int32.Parse(args.Value);
      if (evenNumber % 2 == 0)
      {
         args.IsValid = true;
      }
   }
}
```

If you run this program in an up-level browser and enter an odd number, the page will never be posted back to the server; the JavaScript handles the validation. If you enter an even number, however, the client-side script *and* the server-side script will run (to protect against spoofing from the client).

Validation Groups

We have kept the examples shown in this chapter intentionally simple. In a real application, however, you might have a page with many controls on it. In addition, the page may be divided into sections, with more than one button that can submit the page, depending on what the user is doing.

At times, it is convenient to be able to say, "When I click the first button I want to validate only these first five controls, but when I click the second button I want to validate only the last four controls." This allows you to create forms in which you expect that some of the controls will be invalid. For example, you might have a page in which you ask the user to enter her username and password (if registered) or to enter other information if creating a new account. Clearly, one or the other will be left blank.

To accomplish this, you set the ValidationGroup property on all the controls (and the button that submits the page) to the same value for each group. In the example just described, the first five controls and the first button might all have ValidationGroup set to GroupOne, yet all the other controls would have ValidationGroup set to GroupTwo. By default, all controls have their ValidationGroup property set to the empty string so they all validate at the same time until the property is set to something else.

To demonstrate, add a copy of *CompareValidator.aspx* to the website; call it *ValidationGroup.aspx*, and make two changes. First, move the two rows for password entry after the row that holds the Submit Bug button. Then, add an additional row after the passwords containing a new button (btnLogin) with the Text property set to Login.

```
<tr>
    <td colspan="3" align="center">
        <asp:Button ID="btnLogin" Text="Login" runat="server" />
    </td>
</tr>
```

Your page should look like Figure 11-13.

With that done, add a ValidationGroup property to each validation control and button on the page:

- For all the controls *above* the Submit Bug button and for the Submit Bug button itself, add the group name Bug.

- For all the controls *below* the Submit Bug button, add the group name Login (as in this example):

```
<asp:RequiredFieldValidator runat="server" ID="rfvPassword2"
    ControlToValidate="txtPassword2"
    ErrorMessage="Please re-enter your password" Text="*"
    ValidationGroup="Login" />
```

The drop-down lists have their AutoPostBack property set to true. This will cause a postback (and, thus, validation) when the drop-down value changes. Be sure to set the ValidationGroup to Bug for these controls as well.

Figure 11-13. The design for ValidationGroup.aspx

Now when you click a button, only the controls in its group are validated. Furthermore, the ValidationSummary control now displays error messages for only one ValidationGroup. If its ValidationGroup were not set at all, it would show the error messages only for those invalid controls that also were not assigned to any validation group.

Click the Submit Bug button. The password fields are not flagged as invalid even though they have a required field validator. Because the Submit Bug button was clicked, and the validators for the password controls were not in the Bug group, they were not validated at all. If you click Login, the password controls will be validated, but none of the other controls will be validated.

Forms-Based Security

Back in the primitive days of personal computing, when each user's computer stood alone and isolated, security was not such a big deal. Until computers became networked and viruses were let loose as a scourge on the Internet, security for most PCs meant screensaver passwords and a lock on the office door.

All of that has changed. Today's computers are interconnected in myriad ways, on local networks and over the Internet. The pipes of data that connect your machine to the rest of the world are tremendously beneficial, but at the same time potentially harmful, opening your machine to outsiders. Some of those outsiders are malicious or just plain unwelcome. In any case, it is the job of security to let the good stuff in and keep the bad stuff out.

As part of the .NET Framework, ASP.NET 2.0 has a robust security infrastructure. ASP.NET is designed to work with Microsoft Internet Information Services (IIS), Windows 2000 to 2008, and the NTFS filesystem. Consequently, there is tight integration with the security provided inherently in those environments. If you are on an intranet and are certain that all your clients will be using Windows and Internet Explorer, there are features you can use to make your job as software developer easier. Alternatively, you can implement your security system independent of Windows and NTFS using the new forms-based security controls.

The fundamental role of security in ASP.NET is to restrict access to portions of a website. It does this through the following methods:

Authentication
> Verifying that a client is who he says he is.

Authorization
> Determining whether the client has permission to access the resource he is requesting.

Impersonation

 ASP.NET assumes the role of the user or process gaining access, granting or limiting system access to that which is allowed to the user.

Delegation

 A more powerful form of impersonation that allows remote resources to be accessed by the web server while it is impersonating the client.

The decision to allow or deny access is based on Windows and NTFS security features in conjunction with IIS or by verifying credentials against a security database. ASP.NET makes creating a security database simple; setting up all the tables you need for authentication and authorization as well as for personalization (Chapter 14) and role-based access.

One major change to note between the release of .NET 2.0 and .NET 3.5 is that IIS 7.0 was completely rewritten for Windows Vista, and IIS 7.0 has several key security changes which may catch you off guard if you're used to IIS 5.0, 5.1, or 6.0. The main change requires a brief explanation. In versions of IIS earlier than 7.0, ASP.NET was simply a plug-in for IIS, which meant that both it and IIS made their own security check for each web request, as shown in Figure 12-1.

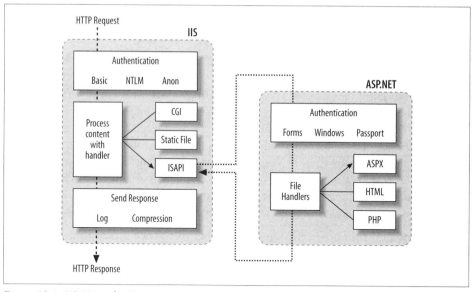

Figure 12-1. IIS 5/6 and ASP.NET as a plug-in

In IIS 7.0, although this "classic mode" is still available, ASP.NET is now a module which integrates directly into the IIS web server pipeline. In effect, this means that issues of security previously dealt with by ASP.NET are now looked after by IIS, as shown in Figure 12-2.

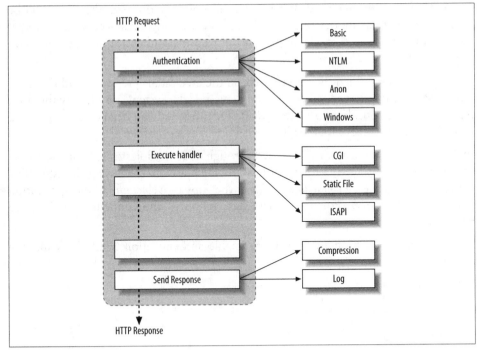

Figure 12-2. IIS 7 and ASP.NET in integrated mode

Microsoft's IIS team maintains a great site about IIS 7 at *http://www.iis.net*. In particular, check out Mike Volodarsky's article about the new integrated IIS/ASP mode at *http://www.iis.net/go/928*, and two more articles at *http://www.iis.net/go/1023* and *http://www.iis.net/go/1027* which look at more of the new security features in IIS 7 than we cover here.

Authentication

Authentication is the process of ensuring that clients are who they claim to be. Authentication is accomplished using credentials, or some form of identification. The requesting client presents the credentials to IIS and the ASP.NET application, usually in the form of a username and password.

The credentials are validated against some authority. Depending on how authentication is configured, that authority might be Windows security, or it might be a store of names, passwords, and rights maintained in a configuration file such as *web.config*, a relational database such as SQL Server (preferably), your Active Directory, or an XML file.

Authentication is not required. If no authentication is performed, the client will be an anonymous user. By default, all websites allow anonymous access. However, if you need to restrict access to any part of the website, authentication is a necessary step.

If the system cannot identify a user based on the credentials presented and if anonymous users are disallowed, access will be denied. If the system can identify the user, that user will be considered an authenticated identity and will be allowed to proceed to authorization. Sometimes the identity is known as a *principal*.

In ASP.NET, authentication is provided through code modules called *authentication providers*. Once installed, authentication providers are enabled using the ASP.NET configuration files, either *machine.config* or the copy of *web.config* in the application virtual root directory. (For a complete description of the configuration files, see Chapter 18.)

A typical entry in a configuration file to enable authentication would look like the following:

```
<configuration>
    <system.web>
        <authentication mode="Windows" />
    </system.web>
</configuration>
```

The mode attribute determines which authentication provider is used. There are four possible values for the mode attribute, as shown in Table 12-1. We will describe each authentication mode in the following sections.

Table 12-1. Values of the authentication key's mode attribute

Mode value	Description
None	No authentication will be performed by ASP.NET, although IIS 5/6 may still have some form of authentication enabled. Enables anonymous access.
Windows	Windows authentication will be used in conjunction with IIS. This is the default.
Passport	Centralized commercial authorization service offered by Microsoft to website developers, providing single logon across websites. Not supported by IIS 7, but supported by ASP.NET 2.0 in IIS 5/6. *Passport has been officially deprecated by Microsoft.*
Forms	Unauthenticated requests are redirected to an ASP.NET web page that you specify that gathers credentials from the user and submits them to the application for authentication.

Anonymous Access

Anonymous access occurs when a web application does not need to know the identity of users. In this case, credentials are not requested by IIS, and authentication is not performed. Allowing anonymous access is the default configuration for websites.

To configure IIS 7.0 to disable anonymous access, open the Windows Start menu, type **IIS** to highlight the IIS Manager, and press Enter. Alternatively, press Windows-R to open a Run dialog, type **InetMgr.exe**, and press Enter.

To run IIS, you must be logged in as an administrator.

If you want to disable anonymous access for just one website, expand the Web Site tree on the left, select the one you want to change, and double-click the Authentication icon (as shown in Figure 12-3) in the main window. If you want to make a change for all websites, select the root of the tree (marked with the computer name) and then double-click Authentication.

Figure 12-3. The main IIS 7.0 dialog

When the Authentication panel appears right-click the entry for Anonymous Authentication and select Disable, as shown in Figure 12-4.

Anonymous access is appropriate if your application has no need to know the username or password of the person or application calling the application, and if the information or service contained in the application is considered public. You can also personalize a site without requiring a login, through the use of cookies.

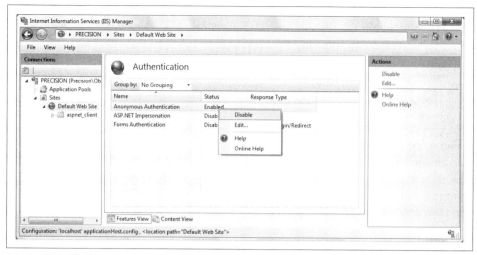

Figure 12-4. Disabling anonymous access in IIS 7.0

This would be useful when the content on the site is public, but you want to preserve user preferences or previous selections. For more information about personalization, see Chapter 14.

Of all the security configurations available to a website, anonymous access provides the best performance but is the least secure.

The IUSR account

Because all requests made to IIS must have credentials, anonymous requests are assigned to a standard Windows user account. This account defaults to the built-in IUSR account, created when IIS is installed on the machine. It has a limited set of permissions, just enough to allow access to websites on the server computer.

 In IIS 5.0, 5.1, or 6.0, the anonymous user account is called *IUSR_MachineName*. IIS 7 will create an *IUSR_MachineName* account in addition to IUSR if you install the FTP server along with the web server.

If you think you'll need to give the IUSR account further permissions to enable a certain website's functionality (e.g., writing to a directory or a file), you might want to change the anonymous user account to something else so that you can leave IUSR with the bare minimum permissions for other websites.

To change the account assigned to anonymous access in IIS 7, return to the Authentication panel shown in Figure 12-3, right-click Anonymous Authentication, and select Edit. In the resultant dialog (shown in Figure 12-5), you can either choose to go with the user account that the worker process for the site's application pool is running as, or choose to use an account with minimal privileges that you've already created by clicking the Set button and giving the appropriate details to the user request box that appears.

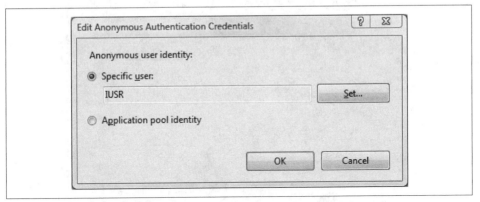

Figure 12-5. Changing the IUSR account in IIS 7

 An application pool is the application domain (the isolated process) inside which a website runs. By default, all websites run inside the same application pool, but if you believe there is a need (hacking, tendency to crash, etc.) you can create a new pool for a website. Inside that application pool, the website cannot affect any other website that is not also in that particular pool. The worker process for an application pool is set to *MachineName*\NETWORKSERVICE by default.

The IIS 5/6 Directory Security panel

For pre-Vista users, all security options are dealt with in the Directory Security tab of the Properties dialog in IIS 5.x or 6.0. To access it select Start → Control Panel → Administrative Tools → Internet Information Services to bring up the IIS Manager application.

If you want to change settings for just one website, expand the tree on the left until you find the one you want to change, right-click it, and select Properties. If you want to change settings for all websites, expand the tree until you can right-click the node marked Web Sites and then select Properties. In both cases, the resultant dialog will have a Directory Security tab, as shown in Figure 12-6.

The Directory Security tab has sections for enabling server certificates and imposing restrictions based on Internet Protocol (IP) address and domain name. (This latter section will be available only for Windows Server 2000, 2003, and 2008 and will be grayed out for Windows 2000 Professional and Windows XP Professional, as in Figure 12-6.)

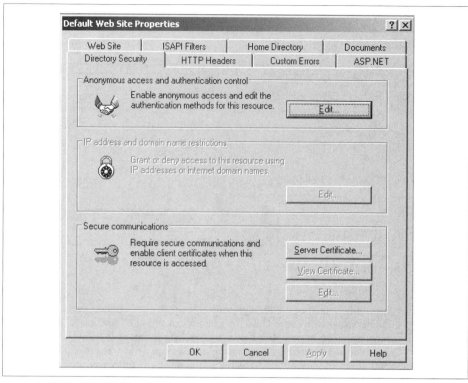

Figure 12-6. The IIS 5/6 Directory Security panel

To change between the authentication methods mentioned in this chapter, click the Edit button in the "Anonymous access and authentication control" section. You will get the dialog box shown in Figure 12-7.

From here, you can enable each type of authentication by checking or unchecking the appropriate box. You can change the anonymous access user account by clicking the Browse button and setting the account in the Select User dialog box. You also can configure Basic authentication to assume a default domain or realm using the two Select buttons. We will discuss exactly what these options mean in the relevant sections of this chapter.

Windows Authentication

Windows authentication offers the developer a way to make use of the security built into the Windows platform and the NTFS filesystem. It also takes advantage of the security built into IIS. Using Windows authentication, you can build a high level of security into an ASP.NET application with little or no code. The trade-off is that

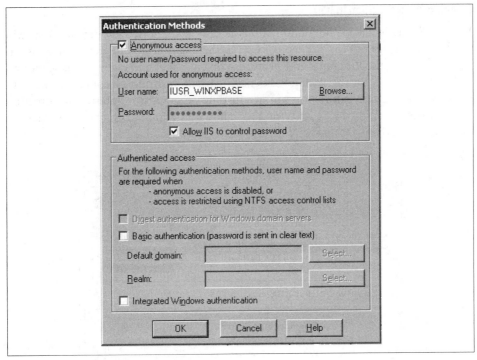

Figure 12-7. Authentication methods in IIS 5/6

Windows authentication works only if the client is using a Windows platform and has a user account on the web server or in the Windows domain to which the web server belongs.

There are five types of Windows authentication:

- Basic authentication
- Digest authentication
- Integrated Windows authentication
- IIS Client Certificate Mapping authentication
- Active Directory Client Certificate Mapping authentication

We describe them in the following sections.

If more than one type of authentication access is enabled, IIS will first attempt to use Certificate Mapping and then Integrated Windows authentication, if they are checked. If that fails, it will attempt Digest authentication if that is checked. Finally, if all else fails, it will use Basic authentication. In other words, it tries the most secure option first, and then falls back to less-secure options.

Enabling authentication in IIS 7

When IIS 7 is installed, only anonymous access is supported by default. You will need to install support for any type of user authentication should you want to use it. To do so, open the Programs and Features control panel and click "Turn Windows features on or off" in the lefthand sidebar. (An administrator account will need to approve this request before you go any further.) Expand the Internet Information Services tree down to the Security node as shown in Figure 12-8, check the method of Windows authentication required, and click OK to install it.

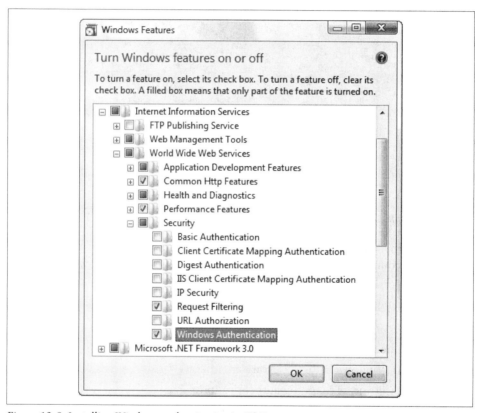

Figure 12-8. Installing Windows authentication in IIS 7

Once it is installed, you can return to the Authentication panel shown in Figure 12-4, right-click the Authentication method, and select Enable. You will also need to disable Anonymous Authentication while you're there.

 The first request that all browsers send to a web server is for anonymous access to server content. If you do not disable Anonymous Authentication (or if you have the anonymous user account's file access revoked), users can anonymously access all the content on your server, regardless of what other authentication methods are enabled on your server.

Finally, you must include the following section in the appropriate *web.config* configuration file:

```
<configuration>
  <system.web>
    <authentication mode="Windows" />
  </system.web>
</configuration>
```

Note that in Figure 12-8, the entry marked "Windows Authentication" actually means Integrated Windows authentication and is not some sort of prerequisite for Basic, Digest, or some other authentication type, which you might misconstrue to be the case. All of these installation options are independent of one another.

Basic authentication

Basic authentication is the simplest and least secure type of Windows authentication. It is an implementation of the Basic authentication scheme found in Section 11 of the HTTP 1.0 specification. In this type of authentication, the browser presents a standard Windows-supplied dialog box for the user to enter his credentials, consisting of a username and password. These credentials are compared against valid user accounts on the domain server or on the local machine. If the credentials match, the user will be authenticated and access to the requested resource will be provided.

Basic authentication is the least secure method of authentication because the username and password are sent to the server encoded as a base64 string. However, your username and password are *not* encrypted. The username and password are available to your application code in clear text. A skilled person using a network sniffer can easily intercept and extract the username and password. Therefore, Basic authentication is best suited for those applications where a high level of security is not a requirement, or where no other authentication method will work.

You can use Basic authentication in conjunction with Secure Sockets Layer (SSL) to achieve a high level of security. This encrypts the information passed over the network and prevents the password from being deciphered, though the performance hit from SSL is significant and you may end up spending a lot of money on dedicated SSL servers to regain that performance.

By default, the local domain of the web server is active and is used for Basic authentication. If you wish to authenticate against a different domain, go to the Authentication panel for your site in IIS (shown earlier in Figure 12-4), right-click Basic Authentication, and then click Edit to select a different default domain.

Basic authentication works across proxy servers and through firewalls. It is supported by essentially all browsers. Basic authentication allows for delegation of credentials from one computer to another but only for a single hop, that is, to only one other computer. If you need to access resources beyond the first hop, you will need to log on locally to each of the other computers in the call chain. This is possible because the username and password are available to your application in clear text.

Digest authentication

Digest authentication is similar to Basic authentication, except that the credentials are encrypted and a hash is sent over the network to the server. It is a fairly secure method of authentication, though not as secure as Basic authentication used with SSL, as Integrated Windows authentication, or as Certificate authentication. Like Basic authentication, Digest authentication works through firewalls and proxy servers. Digest authentication does not support delegation, that is, impersonated requests to remote machines.

Digest authentication works only with Internet Explorer 5.x and later and .NET web services. It requires that the web server is running on Windows 2000 or later and that all users have Windows accounts stored in an Active Directory store. Because of these requirements, Digest authentication is generally limited to intranet applications.

 In IIS 7.0, Digest authentication works only against Windows Server 2003- or 2008-based domain controllers. Windows 2000 domain controllers are not supported.

When the user requests a resource that requires Digest authentication, the browser presents the same credentials dialog box as with Basic authentication. The username and password are combined with a server-specified string value and are encrypted to a hash value. This hash value is sent over the network. Because the server knows the string used to create the hash, it is able to decrypt the hash and extract the username and password. These are compared with the user accounts to determine whether the user is authenticated, and if so, whether the user has permission to access the requested resource.

For a user to be able to use Digest authentication, the user account must be set to store the password using reversible encryption. To do this, go to the Management console for Active Directory Users and Computers on the domain controller. Open the domain you want to administer and double-click the username that you want to use Digest authentication. On the Account Options tab, select "Store password using reversible encryption".

Integrated Windows authentication

Integrated Windows authentication uses the current user's credentials presented at the time he logged in to Windows. A dialog box is never presented to the user to gather credentials unless the Windows logon credentials are inadequate for a requested resource.

Integrated Windows authentication comprises two different types of authentication: NT LAN Manager (NTLM) challenge/response, and Kerberos. NTLM is the protocol used in Windows NT, Windows 2000 work groups, and environments with mixed NT and 2000 domains. If the environment is a pure Windows 2000 or Windows XP Active Directory domain, NTLM is automatically disabled and the authentication protocol switches to Kerberos. In Windows Server 2008, NTLM is disabled by default.

 Kerberos is named after the three-headed, dragon-tailed dog (Cerberus) who guarded the entrance to Hades in Greek mythology.

Integrated Windows authentication works well in intranet environments, where all the users have Windows domain accounts and presumably all users are using Internet Explorer 3.01 or later. It is secure because the encrypted password is not sent over the network. Integrated Windows authentication does not work through a proxy server. NTLM does not support delegation, though Kerberos does.

Integrated Windows authentication does not require any login dialog boxes. This is more convenient for the user and is well suited to automated applications, such as those using web services.

Kerberos is faster than NTLM, though neither is as fast as Basic authentication or well-designed custom authentication methods. If you are anticipating a large number of concurrent users or are delegating security to backend servers (such as SQL Server), scalability may become an issue with Integrated Windows authentication.

Role-based security

Windows also provides *role-based security*. In this security scheme, *roles*, also known as *groups*, are defined. A role defines the range of actions and access that is permitted to users assigned to the role. Users are assigned to one or more roles, or groups. For example, if a user is a member of the Administrator role, that person will have complete access to the computer and all of its resources. If a user is a member of only the Guest group, he will have very few permissions.

You assign groups and users by going to the Control Panel, clicking Administrative Tools, and then clicking on Computer Management. You will see the MMC console shown in Figure 12-9.

All the groups shown in Figure 12-9 were installed by default or by SQL Server 2005.

Windows users log in to the operating system, providing a username and password. These constitute their credentials. At login time, those credentials are authenticated by the operating system. Once their credentials are verified, they will have certain permissions assigned, depending on which role(s) they have been assigned. As you will see, ASP.NET uses these credentials and roles if the web application makes use of Windows authentication.

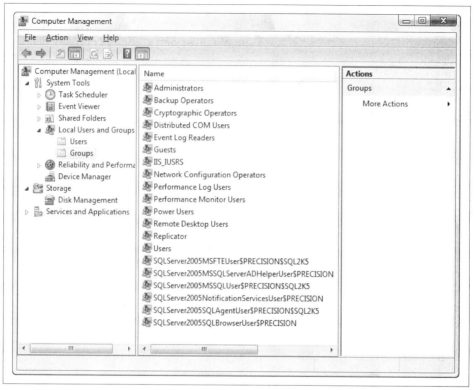

Figure 12-9. Groups in the Computer Management console

When a client requests an ASP.NET page or web service, all the requests are handled by IIS. If Windows authentication is the currently configured authentication scheme, IIS will hand off the authentication chores to Windows. The user is authenticated based on the credentials that were presented when he first logged in to his Windows system. These credentials are verified against the Windows user accounts contained on the web server or on the domain controller that handles the web server.

Client certificate mapping

Client certificate mapping is a technique whereby IIS will ask clients accessing the website for a certificate to identify themselves. Once provided, the certificate is then mapped to a user account which the client will use for the rest of the session. No dialog box will pop up as it would for Basic, Digest, or Windows authentication, because the authentication is done automatically through the certificate.

Because certificates are unique, it becomes very easy to map them across many servers, but it is also more time-consuming to set up and configure. You'll need to:

- Create an online certificate authority on your domain controller.
- Issue each user with a certificate signed by your new certificate authority, saving a copy on your server against which to match it.

- Decide whether IIS or Windows Active Directory should perform the mapping and install the correct authentication module.
- Configure SSL for your site with IIS.
- Map a certificate (or group of certificates) to a user account.

You cannot use both IIS and Active Directory to map client certificates, so you'll need to choose which you'll use and then configure your mappings accordingly. To map them for IIS, you'll need to add each mapping manually to the appropriate *web.config* file:

```
<configuration>
    <system.webServer>
        <security>
            <authentication>
                <iisClientCertificateMappingAuthentication enabled="true"
                    oneToOneCertificateMappingsEnabled="true">
                <oneToOneMappings>
                    <add username="..." password="..."
                        certificate="..." />
                </oneToOneMappings>
                </iisClientCertificateMappingAuthentication>
            </authentication>
        </security>
    </system.webServer>
</configuration>
```

The key code is in bold. Here, a set of one-to-one mappings between a certificate (given as a base64-encoded string) and a Windows username and password are laid out. You can also choose to map to a single account many certificates using a set of criteria with the following changes:

```
<configuration>
    <system.webServer>
        <security>
            <authentication>
                <iisClientCertificateMappingAuthentication enabled="true"
                    manyToOneCertificateMappingsEnabled="true">
                <manyToOneMappings>
                    <add name="mappingName" enabled="true"
                        permissionMode="Allow" username="..."
                        password="...">
                        <rules>
                            <add certificateField="Subject"
                            certificateSubField="..."
                            matchCriteria="regEx" />
                        </rules>
                    </add>
                </manyToOneMappings>
                </iisClientCertificateMappingAuthentication>
            </authentication>
        </security>
    </system.webServer>
</configuration>
```

In this case, rather than simply defining the mapping, you define a rule for IIS to match a certificate against its Subject (or Issuer) field, and a regular expression (the matchCriteria) for a specific field on the certificate. If the rule (or rules) is satisfied, the named user account is assigned to the client.

Should you prefer to use Active Directory for mapping, you'll need to set up the mapping in the Active Directory administrative tool and then enable it on the website with the following addition to *web.config*:

```
<configuration>
  <system.webServer>
    <security>
      <authentication>
        <clientCertificateMappingAuthentication enabled="true" />
      </authentication>
    </security>
  </system.webServer>
</configuration>
```

Passport Authentication

Passport is a centralized authentication service provided by Microsoft. It offers a single logon for all websites that have registered with the Passport service, accepted the license agreement, paid the requisite fee, and installed the Passport SDK.

Passport authentication is not supported by IIS 7.0 on either Windows Vista or Windows Server 2008. Indeed, it has been deprecated by Microsoft. This section is here for legacy reasons only.

You should use another digital identity system such as OpenID, Windows CardSpace, or Active Directory Federation Services (ADFS) if this is the route you want to take for your site's security. Go to *http://www.openid.org*, *http://netfx3.com*, and *http://www.microsoft.com/windowsserver2003/techinfo/overview/adfsoverview.mspx*, respectively, for more information on these systems.

When a client makes a request to a Passport-protected site, the server detects that the request does not contain a valid Passport ticket as part of the query string. The client is redirected to the Passport Logon Service along with encrypted parameters about the original request. The Passport Logon Service presents the client with a logon form, which the user fills out and posts back to the logon server using the SSL protocol. If the logon server authenticates the user, the request is redirected back to the original site, this time with the ticket authenticating the user encrypted in the query string. When the original site receives this new request, it detects the authentication ticket and authenticates the request.

Subsequent requests to the same site are authenticated using the same authentication ticket. Provisions exist for expiring the authentication ticket and for using the same ticket at other sites.

For sites that have implemented Passport and installed the Passport SDK, the `PassportAuthenticationModule` provides a wrapper around the SDK for ASP.NET applications.

Passport uses Triple-DES encryption to encrypt and decrypt the authentication key when passed as part of the query string. When a site registers with the Passport service, it is given a site-specific key that is used for this encryption and decryption.

Using delegation is impossible if you are using Passport authentication.

To use Passport authentication, you must configure ASP.NET by including the following section in the relevant *web.config* configuration file:

```
<configuration>
  <system.web>
    <authentication mode="Passport" />
  </system.web>
</configuration>
```

Forms Authentication

Integrated Windows authentication offers many advantages to the developer who is deploying to an environment where all the clients are known to have user accounts in the requisite Windows domain or Active Directory, and are known to be using a recent version of Internet Explorer. However, in many web applications, one or both of these conditions will not be true. In these cases, forms authentication allows the developer to collect credentials from the client and authenticate them.

In *forms authentication*, a login form that you create as an ASP.NET web page is presented to the user to gather credentials. This form then posts those credentials to application code that performs the authentication. The application code generally authenticates by comparing the credentials submitted with usernames and passwords contained in a data store of some sort rather than Windows domain accounts. ASP.NET can do most of the work of setting up the database to support forms authentication, as described shortly.

The credentials submitted by the login form are sent unencrypted over the network and are vulnerable to interception by a skilled and malicious user of a network sniffer. A forms authentication scheme can be made fully secure by sending the credentials and all subsequent authenticated requests using the SSL protocol.

You can find a handy guide to configuring SSL on IIS 7.0 at *http://learn.iis.net/page.aspx/144/how-to-setup-ssl-on-iis-7/*.

Once the client is authenticated, the server returns a small piece of data, called a *cookie*, back to the client. This authentication cookie is then passed from the client to the server on each subsequent request, which informs the server that this client has been authenticated. If a request is made without a valid authentication cookie, the user will be automatically redirected to the login form, where credentials are again gathered and authenticated.

Setting Up Forms-Based Authentication

For the rest of this chapter, you'll see how to set up a forms-based authentication system for a website. In particular, you'll look at how to:

- Create the database to support forms-based authentication.
- Create a website that hooks into the database.
- Create the user accounts.
- Group users into roles (groups).
- Restrict users' and groups' activities on the site.

Your initial goal will be to have four pages: a default page that displays different information to users who are logged in than to users who are not yet logged in, a login page that allows the user to log in, one that allows users to retrieve their password if they have forgotten it, and one to change it if they require. To have users log in, however, you must create a database of users. Thus, the most important part of this process is setting up the database correctly, so you'll start there.

Creating the Database

ASP.NET forms-based security is based on a set of tables that must be created in your database, typically SQL Server or SQL Server Express. Fortunately, ASP.NET provides a utility named *aspnet_regsql.exe*, located in the *%windows%\Microsoft.NET\Framework\v2.0.50727* folder on your web server, which sets up the tables for you. This utility program will create the required database and all its tables.

> You can also use the ASP.NET Web Site Administration Tool (WAT) to set up the tables for you, but it assumes you are happy with the default options of using a SQL Express database stored in your site's *App_Data* folder. If you are, just run the tool; it will create a new *aspnetdb.mdf* in the *App_Data* folder for the current website, and will make the appropriate settings in the *config* file, all automatically.

The easiest way to use this utility is to run the *aspnet_regsql.exe* utility from the command line with no arguments. A wizard will start that will walk you through the process. Click Next to start it. The first screen (shown in Figure 12-10) is to confirm that you want to add the tables to a database rather than remove them. Make sure "Configure SQL Server for application services" is checked and click Next.

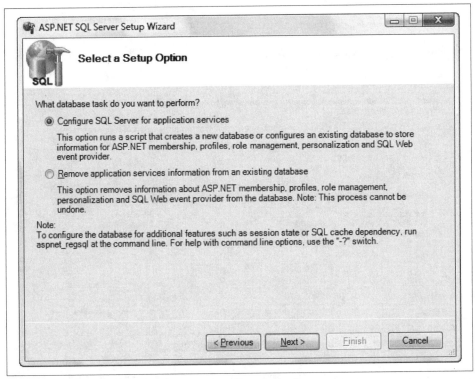

Figure 12-10. The ASP.NET SQL Server Setup Wizard, step 1

The next step asks you to identify which database on which server you want to add the tables to and how to connect to it. The default setup in ASP.NET is to use a database running in SQL Server Express, called *aspnetdb*. If you installed SQL Server Express along with Visual Studio, simply change the server name to `.\SQLEXPRESS` and leave the database name at `<default>`.

If you want to use another name for the database or some non-Express version of SQL Server, fill in the appropriate details and then click Next. In Figure 12-11, for example, the wizard will generate the tables in a database called Membership on a local instance of SQL Server.

 If the database you specify doesn't exist, the wizard will try to create it for you before adding the tables to it. If you leave the database name at *<default>*, it will create a database called *aspnetdb* if it doesn't exist already.

Click Next again to confirm your settings and create the tables. If your login doesn't have permission to make the required addition and changes or if the wizard can't reach the database server in question, you'll be told there is an issue to correct before you can try again.

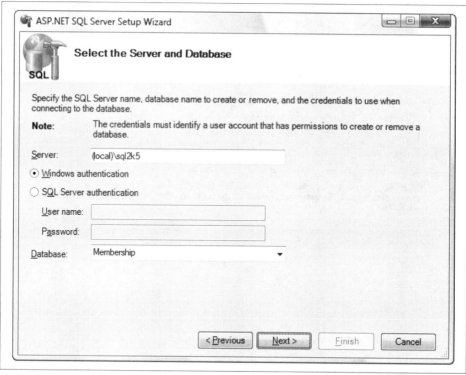

Figure 12-11. The ASP.NET SQL Server Setup Wizard, step 2: Specifying the database

You can confirm the tables' creation after the wizard has finished by opening your database in Visual Studio's Server Explorer window or SQL Server Management Studio (SSMS) and looking at the list of tables. Those created begin with "aspnet_", as shown in Figure 12-12.

If you're using SQL Express, you'll need to retrieve the newly created *aspnetdb.mdf* file and copy it to your site's *App_Data* folder. It will have been created in *C:\Program Files\Microsoft SQL Server\MSSQL.1\DATA*.

If you ever want to remove the tables from a database, just run the wizard again and check the "Remove application services information from an existing database" box shown in Figure 12-10. It will not attempt to delete the database entirely, however, so you'll need to do that separately if that is your intent.

Creating and Configuring the Website

With the database tables created, you'll need to create and configure a website that accesses them correctly. To begin, open Visual Studio 2008 (VS2008) and create a new website called *C12_Security*. If you created the tables in the default database on .\SQLEXPRESS, as shown in the previous section, you need to do only one thing, as

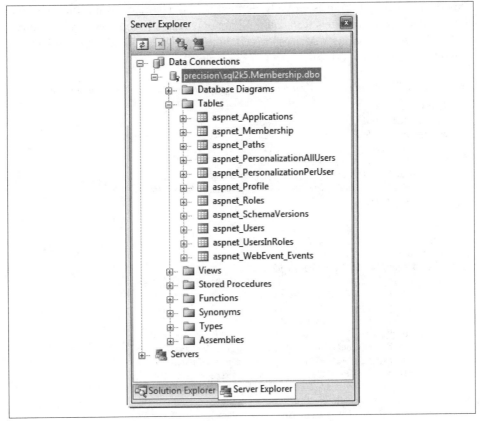

Figure 12-12. The newly generated user tables

this is the default configuration for a forms-based authenticated website. Change one line in *web.config* from this:

```
<authentication mode="Windows" />
```

to this:

```
<authentication mode="Forms" />
<membership defaultProvider="AspNetSqlMembershipProvider" />
```

You can confirm this setting is now working by opening Visual Studio's WAT at Website → ASP.NET Configuration and clicking the Security tab. If you can start adding users to your website, your site configuration is correct. If not, the WAT will report an error connecting to the database. We'll cover creating users and roles later in this chapter.

> Making sure the WAT works against the configuration given to your website isn't the only measure of whether things are working, of course, but it *is* a good rule of thumb even if you then don't go on to use the tool.

This default configuration is actually defined in .NET's main config file, *machine. config*, which your website's *web.config* file may override if you so choose. You can find it in the *%windows%\Microsoft.NET\Framework\v2.0.50727\CONFIG* folder. The relevant pieces of code are shown in Example 12-1.

Example 12-1. The default authentication database configuration in the .NET Framework

```
<configuration>
  <connectionStrings>
    <add name="LocalSqlServer"
      connectionString="data source=.\SQLEXPRESS;
        Integrated Security=SSPI;
        AttachDBFilename=|DataDirectory|aspnetdb.mdf;
        User Instance=true" providerName="System.Data.SqlClient"/>
  </connectionStrings>

  <system.web>
    <membership>
      <providers>
        <add name="AspNetSqlMembershipProvider"
          type="System.Web.Security.SqlMembershipProvider, System.Web,
              Version=2.0.0.0, Culture=neutral,
              PublicKeyToken=b03f5f7f11d50a3a"
          connectionStringName="LocalSqlServer"
          enablePasswordRetrieval="false" enablePasswordReset="true"
          requiresQuestionAndAnswer="true" applicationName="/"
          requiresUniqueEmail="false" passwordFormat="Hashed"
          maxInvalidPasswordAttempts="5" minRequiredPasswordLength="7"
          minRequiredNonalphanumericCharacters="1"
          passwordAttemptWindow="10"
          passwordStrengthRegularExpression=""/>
      </providers>
    </membership>
  </system.web>
</configuration>
```

As you can see, .NET defines a provider within the `<system.web>` element to look after users and passwords (the membership provider) that expects the database specified by the connection string called `LocalSqlServer` to contain the correct tables, and that connection string points to a SQL Server Express database called *aspnetdb*.

Therefore, the best way to override these defaults is to make changes to your website's *web.config* file such that these three items are removed and replaced to use the database containing the tables you've just created, as shown in Example 12-2. In this case, the site is now configured to use the Membership database to which we added tables in Figure 12-11.

Example 12-2. Overriding web.config with your Membership database

```
<configuration>
  <connectionStrings>
    <clear />
```

```
    <add name="MembershipDB"
      connectionString="Data Source=(local)\sql2k5;
      Initial Catalog=Membership;Integrated Security=True;
      Application Name=C12"
      providerName="System.Data.SqlClient" />
  </connectionStrings>

  <system.web>
    <membership>
      <providers>
        <remove name="AspNetSqlMembershipProvider"/>
        <add name="AspNetSqlMembershipProvider"
          connectionStringName="MembershipDB" applicationName="C12"
          type="System.Web.Security.SqlMembershipProvider, System.Web,
            Version=2.0.0.0, Culture=neutral,
            PublicKeyToken=b03f5f7f11d50a3a"/>
      </providers>
    </membership>
  </system.web>
</configuration>
```

Again, once you've made your changes to *web.config*, you can check that they work correctly by trying to open the WAT and seeing whether you can add a user to the site.

You could just rename your connection string to `LocalSqlServer` and override only that, rather than the role and membership providers as well. On the other hand, in addition to storing membership data in the database you want, rather than the one proscribed, overriding the providers also means you can redefine their properties (listed in Table 12-2). Also, by removing the `LocalSqlServer` connection string name, any other references to it in *machine.config* (or the global *web.config* in the same directory) won't be able to resolve and thus do something in the background you'd rather didn't happen.

Table 12-2. Properties for a SQL-based membership provider

Property	Default value	Description
name		Required. The ID of the provider.
type		Required. Sets the class of membership provider that this is. Two are provided by .NET out of the box: `SqlMembershipProvider` and `ActiveDirectoryMembershipProvider`.
connectionStringName		Required. The name of the connection string pointing to the user database.
applicationName	The virtual path to the root of the website	Identifies the website sending the user information if more than one is using the same database.
commandTimeout	30	Number of seconds before the command to the database times out.

Table 12-2. Properties for a SQL-based membership provider (continued)

Property	Default value	Description
description		Optional description of this provider.
enablePasswordRetrieval	false	Sets whether the provider allows the retrieval of passwords.
enablePasswordReset	true	Sets whether the provider supports password resets.
requiresQuestionAndAnswer	true	Sets whether users must answer a question before their password can be retrieved.
requiresUniqueEmail	true	Sets whether each user's email must be unique.
passwordFormat	Hashed	Sets how the passwords are stored in the database. Valid values are Clear (a bad idea), Hashed, and Encrypted.
maxInvalidPasswordAttempts	5	Number of login attempts allowed before the user account is locked out.
passwordAttemptWindow	10	Number of minutes during which the number of login attempts is tracked before a user is locked out.
minRequiredPasswordLength	1. Value must be between 0 and 128.	Number of characters a user password must contain.
minRequiredNonalphanumeric Characters	1. Value must be between 0 and 128.	Number of nonalphanumeric characters a user password must contain.
passwordStrength RegularExpression	Empty string	Sets a regular expression a user password must match to be valid.

 You may need to go through a similar procedure of overriding *web.config* if you want to use your own user database rather than the default when working with user profiles, as covered in Chapter 14, or with user roles, as covered later in this chapter.

Creating Users

With your user database now in sync with your website, you need to create some user accounts. You can do this in two ways:

- With the WAT
- By creating your own web page

We'll look briefly at both. The WAT is initially the most convenient way to do this and get some user accounts up and running for testing purposes, but once the website is deployed live, you should always have a page available to create user accounts. Your copy of VS2008 should never have access to your website's live database. (OK, *never* is a big word, but the best-case scenario is that a live web server and database should be far removed from your local development environment. If they aren't perhaps you should wonder why that is so.)

Using the Web Site Administration Tool

To add a user to the website with the WAT, follow these steps:

1. Choose Website → ASP.NET Configuration to open the WAT.

2. Click the Security tab. You'll see a section in the lower-left corner of the page indicating no users currently exist for your application (see Figure 12-13).

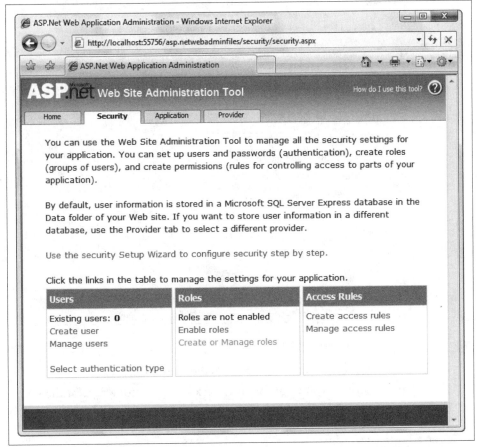

Figure 12-13. The main WAT security page: No users created

3. Click Create User.

4. Fill in the details for a new user, as shown in Figure 12-14, and click Create User. If your password doesn't satisfy the restrictions you set up with the properties in Table 12-2, you'll be alerted to retry with some password that does satisfy them. If all is well, you'll be told the user was created successfully.

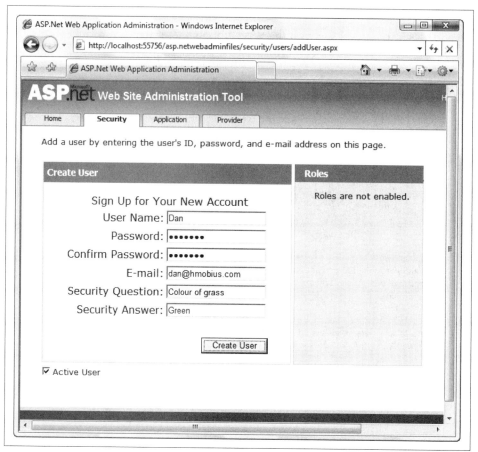

Figure 12-14. Creating a new user with WAT

5. Click Continue, and you'll be taken back to the Create User screen.

6. Add more accounts if you want, or click Back in the bottom right of the screen (you may need to scroll the window to the right) to return to the main security screen in Figure 12-13 where the number of existing user accounts will have been adjusted accordingly.

Using a Create User web page

Prior to ASP.NET 2.0, creating a page such as the one in Figure 12-14 was quite laborious, but then the CreateUserWizard control was added to the basic server control toolbox, making it all much simpler.

1. Add to the *C12_Security* website a new C# web form called *CreateAccount.aspx*.

2. Switch to Design view and drag onto the page a `CreateUserWizard` control from the Login section of the Visual Studio Toolbox.

   The `CreateUserWizard` prompts the user for a username, a password (twice), an email address, and a security question and answer, just as you saw in the WAT. All of this is configurable through properties of this control or, more commonly, through its Common Tasks panel, as shown in Figure 12-15.

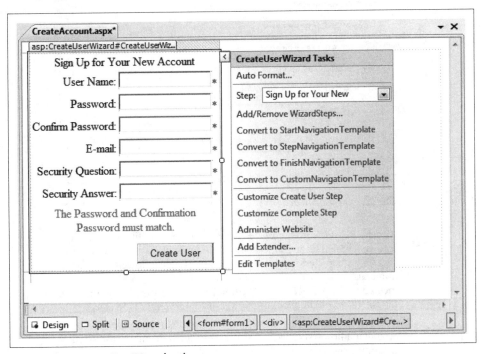

Figure 12-15. CreateUserWizard tasks

3. Click the control and scroll through the Properties window to find the `ContinueDestinationPageURL`. Click the Browse button and choose the create account page (*CreateAccount.aspx*), so you'll be brought back to the same page after the new user is confirmed.

4. Set the *CreateAccount.aspx* page as your Start page and fire up the application. You will be prompted to add a new user, as shown in Figure 12-16.

5. When you click Create User, the account is created, and you are brought to a confirmation screen. Click Continue, and you are brought back to the Create Account screen to create a second account.

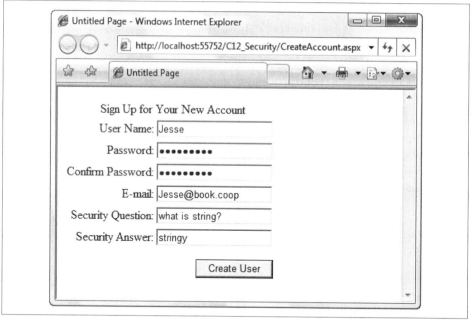

Figure 12-16. CreateAccount.aspx in action

 By default, passwords must be "strong," which is defined as having at least six characters and at least one element of at least three of the four types of characters: English uppercase, English lowercase, Arabic numerals, and special characters (such as ! and @). This is documented in the MSDN article "Strong Password Enforcement and Passfilt.dll" (*http://msdn.microsoft.com/en-us/library/ms722458.aspx*).

The CreateUserWizard control has a PasswordRegularExpression property that allows you to substitute your own regular expression to determine the characteristics of acceptable passwords.

If you add a couple of accounts, close the page, and look at the aspnet_Users table in your membership database, as shown in Figure 12-17, you'll see the accounts you've just set up.

Creating User-Aware Pages

Now that you have a few active users in your database, you need to build some pages that are "user aware." You'll create a default page that displays different information to users who are logged in as opposed to users who are not yet logged in and a login page that allows the user to log in.

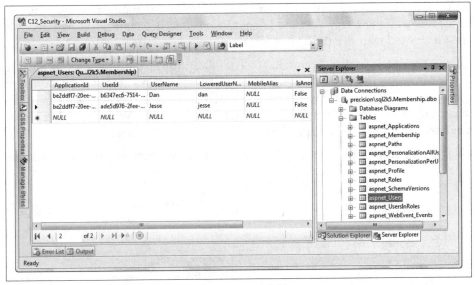

Figure 12-17. User accounts stored in the aspnet_Users table

The Welcome page

With your user database in place, you are ready to create your Welcome page that will welcome the logged-in user.

Add a new page called *Welcome.aspx* to the website. Drag onto the new page a LoginStatus control from the Login section of the Toolbox. A link marked "Login" is placed on the page. Click the smart tag and you'll see you are looking at the template for when no user is logged in, as shown in Figure 12-18.

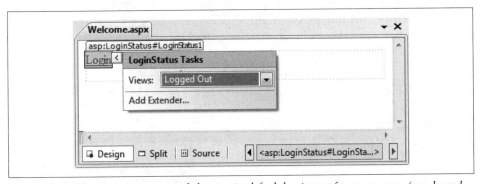

Figure 12-18. The LoginStatus control showing its default log-in text for anonymous (non-logged in) users

You can set the properties of the LoginStatus control, for example, to change the text of the link with the Login Text and Logout Text properties. You can also drop down the Views window to see the link and text for Logged In status.

Drag a LoginView control from the Toolbox, and drop it onto the page below the LoginStatus control. Here you may enter text and controls that will be displayed based on whether the user is logged in. This control has two views visible from the smart tag: Anonymous Template and Logged In Template. Which template's contents will be displayed will depend on whether the user has logged in.

Click the smart tag, confirm that the view is set to Anonymous Template, and type some text into the box, as shown in Figure 12-19.

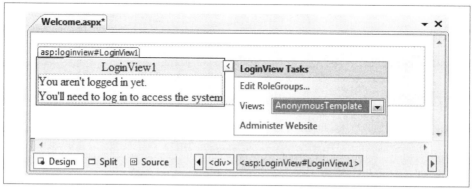

Figure 12-19. The LoginView control showing its contents for anonymous (non-logged in) users

Now set some text for users when they have logged in with the LoggedInTemplate. Open the LoginView's smart tag and choose LoggedInTemplate from the Views drop-down box. The LoginName control displays the name of the user currently logged in, so you can use that within the LoggedInTemplate to welcome the user by name. After typing some text onto the LoginView template, drag the LoginName control right onto the LoginView template, as shown in Figure 12-20.

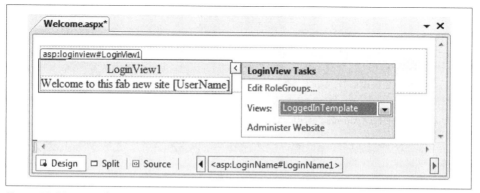

Figure 12-20. Using the LoginName control within a LoginView control

You could also add a link beneath the `LoginView` control that points to *CreateAccount.aspx* so more users can add an account for themselves to your site.

Also, reopen *CreateAccount.aspx* and change the `CreateUserWizard`'s `ContinueDestinationPageUrl` to point to *Welcome.aspx*.

The Login page

Now to create the Login page; add a new page named *Login.aspx* to the site and drag a `Login` control onto the page, as shown in Figure 12-21. That's it. Simple, eh?

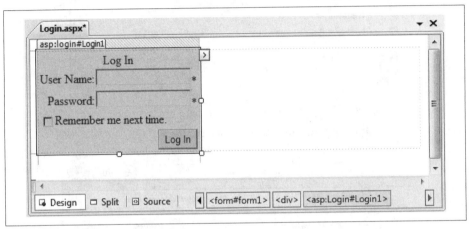

Figure 12-21. The Login control

Set the Welcome page as the start page and run the application. The Welcome page will display its "Not Logged In" message. Click the link to go to the Login page.

Enter a false name or an incorrect password. The `Login` control will let you know that your login attempt was incorrect, as shown in Figure 12-22.

Now enter a correct name and password, and you will be brought back to the Welcome page. Your status as logged in is noted, you are greeted by name, and you are offered the opportunity to log out, as shown in Figure 12-23.

You may have noticed that the `Login` link provided by the `LoginStatus` control automatically links to *Login.aspx*. This is another default that you can override in your site's *web.config* file. For example, to change the default login page for your site to *SignInHere.aspx*, make the following additions to the <authentication> section of your file:

```
<configuration>
  <system.web>
    ...
    <authentication mode="Forms">
      <forms loginUrl="SignInHere.aspx" />
    </authentication>
  </system.web>
</configuration>
```

Figure 12-22. The Login control alerting the user to a failed login

Figure 12-23. Logging in correctly takes you to the Welcome page

Similarly, if you wish to define the page to which users are redirected once they have logged in successfully, you should also add a `defaultUrl` attribute to the `<forms>` element in the site's *web.config* file:

```
<authentication mode="Forms">
  <forms loginUrl="SignInHere.aspx" defaultUrl="Welcome.aspx" />
</authentication>
```

The Password Recovery page

One problem with users is that they are prone to forgetting things, especially passwords. Fortunately, ASP.NET provides the `PasswordRecovery` control, which makes the developer's life that much easier to help the user gain access to her account once again. By default, this control will allow the user to answer the question she set when adding her user account and have a new password emailed to her. When she logs in to the site she can then change her password to something she wants. This is the default behavior because unless you changed them, your membership provider has its enablePasswordReset property set to true and enablePasswordRetrieval property set to false. The provider's passwordFormat property is also set by default to Hashed, which means the user's password is stored in an encrypted state and cannot be decrypted to send back to the user anyway; a new password must be generated, sent to the user, and then hashed and saved in the database.

If you want the PasswordRecovery control to send the user's actual password to her, you'll need to set enablePasswordReset to false, enablePasswordRetrieval to true, and passwordFormat to Clear. This is a far less secure alternative to the default, though, and it is not recommended to do this.

 The PasswordRecovery control requires the use of an email server to send users their passwords and for the details of an email account to use to be given in your site's *web.config* folder. See Chapter 18 for how to do this.

The convention for password recovery is to have a link to such a facility on the same page as the login form. Switch to or reopen *Login.aspx* in Design view, and select the Login control. Open the control's smart tag and click Convert to Template.

You can now customize the UI of the Login control. Drag a Hyperlink control beneath the log-in button that's already there, as shown in Figure 12-24, and change its Text property to some suitable text to link to the password recovery page.

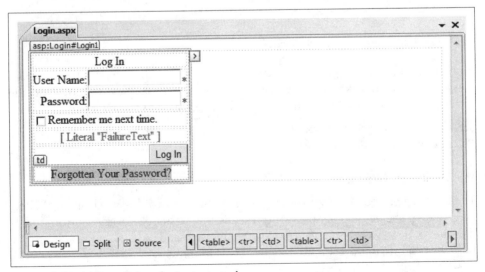

Figure 12-24. Adding a link to the Login control

Set the Hyperlink's NavigateURL property to *RecoverPW.aspx*, which you'll create next. This page will hold your PasswordRecovery control.

Your next step is to create the new *RecoverPW.aspx* page to your site. Add it as a new web form and then drag a PasswordRecovery control onto this new page. This control has three views that you can change if required:

- One to ask the user for her username (UserName)
- One to ask the user her secret question and wait for her answer (Question)
- One to confirm that her answer was correct and her password is being sent to her (Success)

Simply open the control's smart tag and choose the template you wish to view, as shown in Figure 12-25.

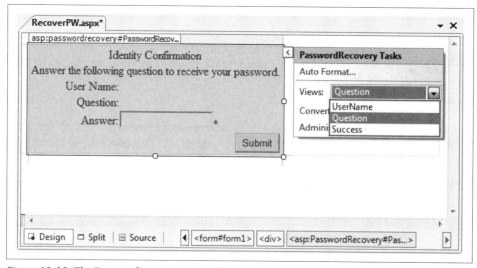

Figure 12-25. The PasswordRecovery control

You can then change the Success text or other text fields (e.g., QuestionInstructionText, QuestionLabelText) in the Properties window for the PasswordRecovery control to see how they will be rendered in the main panel.

Set the SuccessPageUrl property for the control to *Login.aspx* and then save *RecoverPW.aspx*.

The Change Password page

The final page to build allows a user to change her password—which she will likely need to do if she has had her password reset by the PasswordRecovery control. Add to the site a new web form called *ChangePW.aspx* and add a link to it in the LoggedInTemplate of the LoginView control in *Welcome.aspx*.

In Design view, drag a ChangePassword control onto *ChangePW.aspx*, as shown in Figure 12-26, and set its ContinueDestinationPageURL property to *Login.aspx*. Like the PasswordRecovery control, the ChangePassword control has two views which you can switch between using its smart tag:

- A form to make the password change
- A view to confirm the password has been changed

You may want to confirm or change the Success text as well as the other text fields (e.g., ChangePasswordTitleText, ChangePasswordFailureText), but the defaults are fine for this demonstration.

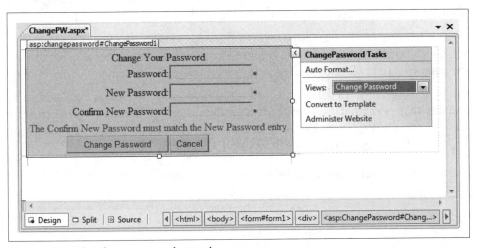

Figure 12-26. The ChangePassword control

Finally, on *Login.aspx*, make sure the DestinationPageURL property of the Login control is set to *Welcome.aspx*.

Now run the application. You should be able to log in and out, change your password, and so forth. You have added the essential aspects of form-based security without writing any code.

Restricting Access to Users

So far, you have set up user authentication for your website—that is, you now have a way to tell who a user is. The next step is to add authorization, which is the set of rules that determines which users can get access to which pages in the site.

There are three ways to restrict access to a page based on which user has just logged in. One is to put a restriction on a role (group) to which the user belongs. You'll see this later in this chapter. The other two are to:

- Check for the username in the code-behind page and allow or restrict access accordingly.
- Set the restrictions in the *web.config* file for the page.

In the code-behind page

ASP.NET associates a special HttpContext object with every web request, which you can automatically access in your code-behind page as HttpContext.Current. For quick access, a lot of its properties are also available directly rather than having to access them through HttpContext.Current. One such property is the User object which contains details about the currently logged-in user. You can check that object for the User's name and act appropriately.

To demonstrate, you'll create two more pages for the website. The first, *Restricted.aspx*, will check for the identity of the user logged in, and if the user is not allowed to view the page, the user will be redirected to the second page, *NoPrivs.aspx*.

Add a new web form to the site and call it *Restricted.aspx*. In Design view, add some content that permitted users may see and then double-click the page to create a handler for the Page_Load event. When the code-behind page for *Restricted.aspx* appears, add the highlighted code in Example 12-3 to it.

Example 12-3. Restricted.aspx.cs

```
using System;

public partial class Restricted : System.Web.UI.Page
{
    protected void Page_Load(object sender, EventArgs e)
    {
        if (User.Identity.Name == "Jane")
        {
            Response.Redirect("NoPrivs.aspx");
        }
    }
}
```

You'll need to change Jane to the name of a user you've created yourself. Now add a second web form called *NoPrivs.aspx* to the site which just contains some text indicating access is restricted.

If you run the website and log in as Jane (or whoever you chose to restrict access), when you navigate to *Restricted.aspx*, you'll be instantly redirected to *NoPrivs.aspx* without seeing any content. Log in as any other user and you'll be allowed to stay on the page and see its content.

You've now created a very simple blacklist for *Restricted.aspx*. However, it soon gets hard to maintain if you have to keep adding checks for each name. Blacklisting the users in a role (or whitelisting them, for that matter) is much easier to maintain, and you can then use the techniques seen here to cater to any exceptional cases where the role as a whole is granted access to a page, except for one or two users in the role who are denied it. You will see how to do this later in this chapter.

In web.config

The second way to restrict users from accessing a page (or a directory) is by altering the <authorization> section of your *web.config* file. In this section, you can add authorization rules that specify who may (or may not) access pages in the site. A benefit of using this approach is that you can use wildcards to indicate groups of users, rather than having to name them individually as you did in the preceding code example. (You can name them individually in the *web.config* file too, if that's practical in your application.)

For example, add the following to the <system.web> section of your *web.config* file:

```
<configuration>
  <system.web>
    ...
    <authorization>
      <deny users="?"/>
      <deny users="Jane"/>
      <allow users="*"/>
    </authorization>
    ...
  </system.web>
</configuration>
```

The three rules added here are given in order of priority. The first rule that matches the user or the role the user is in is the one used. The first two rules deny the anonymous user account (denoted as ?) and the user called Jane access to the pages in the same directory as this *web.config* file. The third rule establishes that all users (who aren't ? or Jane) can view all the pages in the directory (* is used as the wildcard for all users).

Save this to your *web.config* file and run the site. You'll start it as the anonymous user (as you aren't logged in) and will be instantly redirected to the Login page because *web.config* has denied you access to *Welcome.aspx*. The same will happen if you try to navigate to any other page in the site.

This directory-wide approach with *web.config* can be very handy if you group your admin pages in one area, but it is less useful here. Fortunately, you can target your access rules by wrapping them in a `<location>` element as shown here:

```
<configuration>
  ...
  <location path="restricted.aspx">
    <system.web>
      <authorization>
        <deny users="?"/>
        <deny users="Jane"/>
        <allow users="*"/>
      </authorization>
    </system.web>
  </location>
  ...
  <system.web>
    ...
  </system.web>
</configuration>
```

If you save and run *web.config* again, you'll be able to access all but *Restricted.aspx* as the anonymous user again.

> Note that `<location>` is a child of `<configuration>` and not of `<system.web>`.
>
> If you are using the ASP.NET Development Server to test these pages, and if you find your authorization settings don't seem to be working as you expect, try closing all the pages, stopping the server, and then running the pages again.

Enabling Roles

As noted in the preceding section, if you're going to create a blacklist or whitelist with a nontrivial number of users on it, the best solution is to assign that group of users a role and then to assign permissions or restrictions to the role. For example, the `Bloggers` role might allow users in that role access to their blogs but not to the forums for which they would also need to be in the `ForumUsers` role.

> Typically, there's a `SystemAdmin` role of some kind, which gives access to all the admin areas of a website. Some might consider the existence of users within this role to be a security risk, though it's your decision whether to include it.

To enable and integrate roles into your site's security strategy, you need to follow a few steps:

1. Create the database tables to support roles.

2. Hook the website into that database.

---

3. Create the roles.

4. Group users into roles (groups).

5. Restrict users' activities on the site by role.

Fortunately, the first of these steps is already done. Running *aspnet_regsql.exe* as you did at the beginning of the chapter creates all the tables needed to support roles. Indeed, if you look at the database created by *aspnet_regsql.exe*, you'll see the aspnet_Roles table listed, which is exactly what we need.

And if you decided to use the default *aspnetdb* database running on SQL Server Express Edition, all you'll need to do now is add the following lines to the <system.web> element of your *web.config* file to enable the role manager:

```
<configuration>
   <system.web>
   ...
      <roleManager enabled="true"
                   defaultProvider="AspNetSqlRoleProvider" />
   ...
   </system.web>
</configuration>
```

If you decided to create your membership and roles tables in a different database, you'll need to override the default RoleProvider setting in the website's *web.config* file in the same way you did for the membership provider in Example 12-2. Continuing that example, Example 12-4 demonstrates how this would look for the same database—called Membership running in a SQL Server instance called sql2k5 on the same machine as the web server.

 If you had already overridden the membership provider you'd likely already have set up a connection string to your database and wouldn't need to add it again. We included it in this example for completeness and ease of reference.

Example 12-4. Overriding the default role provider settings

```
<configuration>
  <connectionStrings>
    <clear />

    <add name="MembershipDB"
      connectionString="Data Source=(local)\sql2k5;
      Initial Catalog=Membership;Integrated Security=True;
      Application Name=C12"
      providerName="System.Data.SqlClient" />
  </connectionStrings>

  <system.web>
    <roleManager enabled="true">
      <providers>
        <remove name="AspNetSqlRoleProvider"/>
```

Example 12-4. Overriding the default role provider settings (continued)

```
        <add connectionStringName="MembershipDB"
          applicationName="C12 "
          name="AspNetSqlRoleProvider"
          type="System.Web.Security.SqlRoleProvider, System.Web,
                Version=2.0.0.0, Culture=neutral,
                PublicKeyToken=b03f5f7f11d50a3a"/>
      </providers>
    </roleManager>
  </system.web>
</configuration>
```

If all is well, you'll be able to confirm that roles are now enabled and configured correctly for your website by running the WAT from VS2008 and opening the Security tab. In the Roles section at the bottom of the page, the Roles area will now implicitly tell you that roles are enabled because the Disable Roles link is displayed. It will also state that there are no roles created so far, as shown in Figure 12-27.

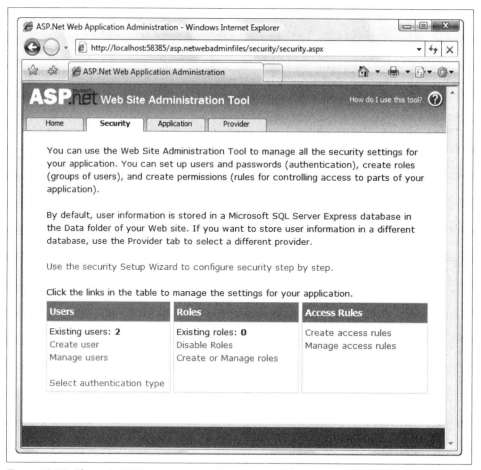

Figure 12-27. The main WAT security page: No roles created

Table 12-3 shows the various attributes you can give to the role provider if you decide to override the default.

Table 12-3. Properties for a SQL-based role provider

Property	Default value	Description
name		Required. The ID of the provider.
type		Required. Sets the class of the membership provider. Three are provided by .NET out of the box: `SqlRoleProvider`, `WindowsTokenRoleProvider`, and `AuthorizationStoreRoleProvider`.
connectionStringName		Required. The name of the connection string pointing to the user database.
applicationName	The virtual path of the website	Identifies the website sending the user information if more than one is using the same database.
commandTimeout	30	Number of seconds before the command to the database times out.
description		Optional description of this provider.

Creating Roles

With your role manager enabled, you now have two options for creating roles and assigning or removing users from those roles:

- Using the WAT
- Creating a page in your site which does the WAT's job for you

To finish the demonstration of restricting access to pages via roles, you'll create a role called Member, and add a user to it.

Using the Web Site Administration Tool

To create a role for your website, follow these steps:

1. Choose Website → ASP.NET Configuration to open the WAT.
2. Click the Security tab. You'll see a section in the lower-left corner of the page indicating no roles currently exist for your application.
3. Click Create or Manage Roles.
4. Enter the name of the role to create (Member) into the "New role name" text box, as shown in Figure 12-28, and click Add Role.

To assign a user to one or more roles, you have two choices. The first is through managing the user accounts. This approach is better suited to assigning multiple roles to a single user.

1. From the main Security page, click Manage Users.
2. Find the user to which you want to assign a role and click Edit Roles in the row for that user.
3. Check the box for each role you want to assign to the user, as Figure 12-29 shows.

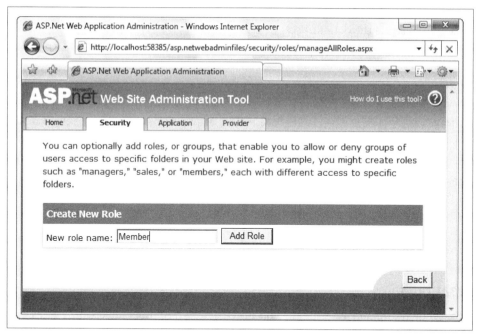

Figure 12-28. *Creating a new role with the WAT*

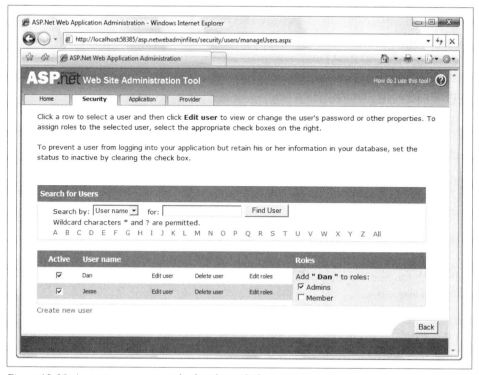

Figure 12-29. *Assigning a user to multiple roles with the WAT*

The second method is to edit the role membership. This approach is better suited to assigning a role to multiple users.

1. From the main Security page, click Create or Manage Roles.

2. Find the role to which you want to assign users from the table and click Manage in the row for that role.

3. In the next screen, you need to search for the user to add to the role. If you know the name of the user you want to add to the role, add the name to the empty text box and click Find User; otherwise, enter the wildcard character, *, and click Find User to return a list of all the users you've added to the site so far, as shown in Figure 12-30.

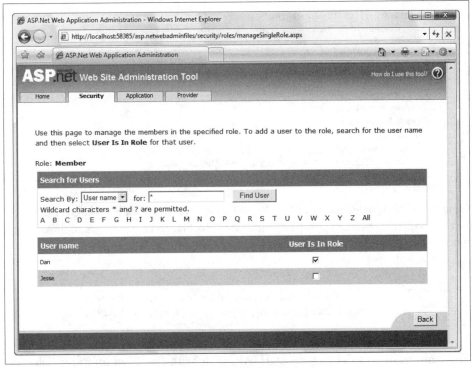

Figure 12-30. Assigning multiple users to a role with the WAT

4. Check or uncheck the box marked User Is In Role for the user you wish to add or remove from the role. The action will occur automatically.

5. When you've finished, click the Back button twice to return to the main Security page.

When you next return to the Manage Role page, a list of users already in the role will be displayed automatically.

Using a Create Roles web page

No server controls are available out of the box for managing roles in the same way there are for managing users, so creating your own equivalent to the WAT role management pages takes a bit more effort.

Start by adding a link to a new page, *ManageRoles.aspx*, from the LoginView control of the *Welcome.aspx* page. Only those logged in should be able to access this, so add the link to the LoginView's LoggedInTemplate, as shown here:

```
<asp:LoginView ID="LoginView1" runat="server">
    <LoggedInTemplate>
        Welcome to this fab new site
        <asp:LoginName ID="LoginName1" runat="server" />
        <br />
        <asp:HyperLink ID="HyperLink2" runat="server"
            NavigateUrl="~/ChangePW.aspx">
            Change your password
        </asp:HyperLink><br />
        <asp:HyperLink ID="HyperLink3" runat="server"
            NavigateUrl="~/ManageRoles.aspx">
            Manage Roles
        </asp:HyperLink>
    </LoggedInTemplate>
    <AnonymousTemplate>
        You aren&#8217;t logged in yet.<br />
        You&#8217;ll need to log in to access the system.
    </AnonymousTemplate>
</asp:LoginView>
```

Now to create *ManageRoles.aspx* itself; add a new web form called *ManageRoles.aspx* to the chapter website. It's quite complicated, so Figure 12-31 shows its layout as a guide while you follow the text. If you get lost, Example 12-5 shows the markup for the site in full.

 Of course, you can download this page and the rest of the website for this chapter from *http://www.oreilly.com/catalog/9780596529567*.

The main feature of the page is an HTML table with two rows and four columns. Above that is a Hyperlink control with an ID of linkHome which points back to *Welcome.aspx*, and a Label control with an ID of Msg and an empty Text property which will return service messages as roles are created and users are assigned.

From left to right across the columns, the top row of the main table contains:

- The word "Roles" to identify the ListBox in the next column.
- A ListBox control with an ID of RolesListBox, AutoPostBack set to True, and Rows set to 8. This shows the current roles for the website, and selecting one will post back the page and have the users in that role shown in the GridView control in the second row of the table.

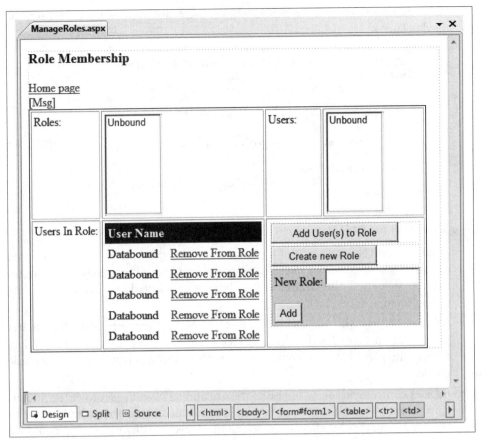

Figure 12-31. The basic layout of ManageRoles.aspx

- The word "Users" to identify the ListBox in the next column.

- A ListBox control with an ID of UsersListBox, and Rows set to 8. Also, the DataTextField property is set to Username. This control shows all the created users for the website. You will be able to select several and then click the button marked Add User(s) to Role to add them to the currently selected role.

The first two columns in the second row contain the following:

- The words "Users in Role" to identify the GridView control in the next column.

- A GridView control with an ID of UsersInRoleGrid, and CellPadding, CellSpacing, and GridLines properties set to 4, 0, and None, respectively. This control binds to an array of the usernames in the currently selected role so that it has no data source set at design time, and uses Container.DataItem.ToString( ) to indicate its UserName column will bind to the string representation of each item in that array (i.e., the usernames). Its AutoGenerateColumns property is set to false. It has two columns, a template field for the username to be shown and a button field to click and remove the user from the role. The source for these columns is as follows.

(You should also create a handler for the OnRowCommand event of the GridView to be filled in later.)

```
<asp:GridView runat="server" CellPadding="4" ID="UsersInRoleGrid"
    AutoGenerateColumns="false" GridLines="None" CellSpacing="0"
    OnRowCommand="UsersInRoleGrid_RemoveFromRole">
    <HeaderStyle BackColor="navy" ForeColor="white" />
    <Columns>
        <asp:TemplateField HeaderText="User Name">
            <ItemTemplate>
                <%# Container.DataItem.ToString() %>
            </ItemTemplate>
        </asp:TemplateField>
        <asp:ButtonField Text="Remove From Role" ButtonType="Link" />
    </Columns>
</asp:GridView>
```

The last area of the table spans two columns and contains the following:

- A Button control with an ID of btnAddUsersToRole, the Text property set to "Add user(s) to Role", and an event handler for its Click event ready for filling in later. As suggested, this handler will add the users selected in UsersListBox to the role selected in RolesListBox.

- A Button control with an ID of btnCreateRole, the Text property set to "Create New Role", and an event handler for its Click event ready for filling in later. When clicked, the panel below it, containing controls to create a new role, will be made visible.

- A Panel control with an ID of pnlCreateRole and its visibility set to false. It contains a TextBox called txtNewRole and a Button called btnNewRole with Text set to "Add" and an event handler set up for its Click event. When clicked, a new Role with the name given in the txtNewRole will be added to the website.

Example 12-5. ManageRoles.aspx in full

```
<%@ Page Language="C#" AutoEventWireup="true"
    CodeFile="ManageRoles.aspx.cs" Inherits="ManageRoles" %>

<!DOCTYPE html PUBLIC "-//W3C//DTD XHTML 1.0 Transitional//EN"
    "http://www.w3.org/TR/xhtml1/DTD/xhtml1-transitional.dtd">
<html xmlns="http://www.w3.org/1999/xhtml">
<head id="Head1" runat="server">
    <title>Manage Roles</title>
</head>

<body>
    <form id="form1" runat="server">
    <h3>Role Membership</h3>
    <asp:HyperLink ID="linkHome" runat="server"
                NavigateUrl="Welcome.aspx">
        Home page
```

Example 12-5. ManageRoles.aspx in full (continued)

```
</asp:HyperLink><br />
<asp:Label ID="Msg" ForeColor="maroon" runat="server" />
<br />

<table cellpadding="3" border="1"
        style="border: solid 1px black">
    <tr>
        <td valign="top">Roles: </td>
        <td valign="top">
            <asp:ListBox ID="RolesListBox" runat="server"
                Rows="8" AutoPostBack="True" />
        </td>
        <td valign="top">Users:</td>
        <td valign="top">
            <asp:ListBox ID="UsersListBox"
                DataTextField="Username" Rows="8"
                SelectionMode="Multiple" runat="server" />
        </td>
    </tr>
    <tr>
        <td valign="top">Users In Role:</td>
        <td valign="top">
            <asp:GridView runat="server" CellPadding="4"
                ID="UsersInRoleGrid"
                AutoGenerateColumns="false"
                GridLines="None" CellSpacing="0"
                AllowSorting="False"
                OnRowCommand="UsersInRoleGrid_RemoveFromRole">
                <HeaderStyle BackColor="navy"
                    ForeColor="white" />
                <Columns>
                    <asp:TemplateField
                        HeaderText="User Name">
                        <ItemTemplate>
                            <asp:Label runat="server"
                                ID="lblUserName"
                                Text=" <%# Container.DataItem.ToString( ) %>" />
                        </ItemTemplate>
                    </asp:TemplateField>
                    <asp:ButtonField Text="Remove From Role"
                        ButtonType="Link" />
                </Columns>
            </asp:GridView>
        </td>
        <td valign="top" visible="false" colspan="2">
            <asp:Button Text="Add User(s) to Role"
                ID="btnAddUsersToRole"
                runat="server"
                OnClick="btnAddUsersToRole_Click" /><br />
            <asp:Button Text="Create new Role"
                ID="btnCreateRole" runat="server"
                OnClick="btnCreateRole_Click" />
```

Example 12-5. ManageRoles.aspx in full (continued)

```
                <asp:Panel ID="pnlCreateRole" runat="server"
                    Visible="False" BackColor="#E0E0E0">
                     New Role: 
                    <asp:TextBox ID="txtNewRole" runat="server" />
                    <br /><br />
                     
                    <asp:Button ID="btnAddRole" runat="server"
                        Text="Add" OnClick="btnAddRole_Click" />
                    <br />
                </asp:Panel>
            </td>
        </tr>
    </table>
    </form>
</body>
</html>
```

In the code-behind page, you need to set up the four event handlers for the controls and implement the Page_Load handler. To serve this end, your class will declare three member variables:

- A string array named rolesArray
- A string array named usersInRole
- An instance of MembershipUserCollection named users

The MembershipUserCollection is defined by the framework to hold MembershipUser objects (surprise!). A MembershipUser object, in turn, is defined by the framework to represent a single user in the membership data store (in this case, the tables created by *aspnet_regsql.exe* or the WAT). This class exposes information about the user such as the user's email address, and methods such as those needed to change or reset the user's password.

```
using System;
using System.Web.Security;
using System.Web.UI;
using System.Web.UI.WebControls;

public partial class ManageRoles : Page
{
    private string[] rolesArray;
    private string[] usersInRole;
    MembershipUserCollection users;
```

Page_Load has three tasks. If it is the first time the page has loaded, it binds the names of the current roles and users to the RolesListBox and UsersListBox controls, respectively. If not, it checks to see whether a role has been selected, and if so, it populates the GridView control with the users in that role. It also clears the Msg label on each visit.

```
protected void Page_Load(object sender, EventArgs e)
{
    Msg.Text = string.Empty;
    if (!IsPostBack)
    {
        rolesArray = Roles.GetAllRoles();
        RolesListBox.DataSource = rolesArray;
        RolesListBox.DataBind();
        users = Membership.GetAllUsers();
        UsersListBox.DataSource = users;
        UsersListBox.DataBind();
    }
    if (RolesListBox.SelectedItem != null)
    {
        usersInRole = Roles.GetUsersInRole
            (RolesListBox.SelectedItem.Value);
        UsersInRoleGrid.DataSource = usersInRole;
        UsersInRoleGrid.DataBind();
    }
}
```

Next, the handler to add users to a role; first, checks are made to ensure that both users and a role to which to add them have been selected. Then it loops through the selected users in the ListBox control and adds their names to a string array. That string array is then passed to the static Roles.AddUsersToRole .NET method, which does the actual adding for us and stores it back in our usersInRole variable. This is then rebound to the GridView, which is updated on the page.

```
protected void btnAddUsersToRole_Click(object sender, EventArgs e)
{
    if (RolesListBox.SelectedItem == null)
    {
        this.Msg.Text = "Please select a role.";
        return;
    }
    if (UsersListBox.SelectedItem == null)
    {
        Msg.Text = "Please select one or more users";
        return;
    }

    int sizeOfArray =
        UsersListBox.GetSelectedIndices().Length;
    string[] newUsers = new string[sizeOfArray];

    // get the array of selected indexes from the
    //(multiselect) listbox
    int[] selectedIndices = UsersListBox.GetSelectedIndices();

    for (int i = 0; i < newUsers.Length; i++)
    {
        // Get the selectedIndex that corresponds
        // to the counter[i].
```

```
    int selectedIndex = selectedIndices[i];
    // Get the list item in the UserListBox Items
    // collection at that offset.
    ListItem myListItem = UsersListBox.Items[selectedIndex];
    // Get the string that is that list item's value property.
    string newUser = myListItem.Value;
    // Add that string to the newUsers collection of strings.
    newUsers[i] = newUser;
}

// Add users to the selected role.
Roles.AddUsersToRole(newUsers, RolesListBox.SelectedItem.Value);
usersInRole =
    Roles.GetUsersInRole(RolesListBox.SelectedItem.Value);
UsersInRoleGrid.DataSource = usersInRole;
UsersInRoleGrid.DataBind();
}
```

As noted, clicking the Create Role button simply makes the panel containing the AddRole controls visible. The Click handler for btnAddRole first makes sure a new role name has been supplied and that it isn't the same as another one that currently exists before it adds the new role to the site, and then updates the RolesListBox with the new list. When the role is added, the TextBox is cleared and the panel is made invisible again.

```
protected void btnCreateRole_Click(object sender, EventArgs e)
{
    pnlCreateRole.Visible = true;
}
protected void btnAddRole_Click(object sender, EventArgs e)
{
    if (txtNewRole.Text.Length > 0)
    {
        string newRole = txtNewRole.Text;
        if (Roles.RoleExists(newRole))
        {
            Msg.Text = "Role already exists!";
        }
        else
        {
            Roles.CreateRole(newRole);
            rolesArray = Roles.GetAllRoles();
            RolesListBox.DataSource = rolesArray;
            RolesListBox.DataBind();
        }
    }
    txtNewRole.Text = string.Empty;
    pnlCreateRole.Visible = false;
}
```

Finally, the Remove from Role link handler first must establish the name of the user to be removed, then removes it from the role and refreshes the GridView with the new list of role members:

```
protected void UsersInRoleGrid_RemoveFromRole(
    object sender, GridViewCommandEventArgs e)
{
    int index = Convert.ToInt32(e.CommandArgument);
    Label userLabel =
        (Label)UsersInRoleGrid.Rows[index].FindControl("lblUserName");

    Roles.RemoveUserFromRole(
        userLabel.Text, RolesListBox.SelectedItem.Value);
    usersInRole =
        Roles.GetUsersInRole(RolesListBox.SelectedItem.Value);
    UsersInRoleGrid.DataSource = usersInRole;
    UsersInRoleGrid.DataBind();
}
}
```

Run *ManageRoles.aspx* and add a few roles, as well as a user or two to each role. You can confirm that the users have been added to the roles successfully either by looking directly in the database or by opening the WAT and checking there.

Restricting Access to User Roles

Once you have created some roles and assigned users to them, you can set access rights to pages or directories for roles in a very similar way as you did for individual users. Again, you have two choices:

- Check whether the user is in a role in the code-behind page and allow or restrict access accordingly.
- Set the restrictions in the *web.config* file for the page (or directory).

In the code-behind page

You can take the same approach to creating a blacklist or a whitelist based on role membership as you did for user identity earlier in this chapter. Again, the User object supplied by ASP.NET with the page request can be used to test for a logged-in user's roles; this time using its User.IsInRole method.

Add to the chapter's site a new web form called *RoleRestricted.aspx*. In Design view, add some content that permitted role members may see and then double-click the page to create a handler for the Page_Load event. When the code-behind page for *RoleRestricted.aspx* appears, add the highlighted code in Example 12-6 to it.

Example 12-6. RoleRestricted.aspx.cs

```
using System;
using System.Web.UI;

public partial class RoleRestricted : Page
{
    protected void Page_Load(object sender, EventArgs e)
    {
```

Example 12-6. RoleRestricted.aspx.cs (continued)

```
        if (User.IsInRole("Member"))
        {
            Response.Redirect("NoPrivs.aspx");
        }
    }
}
```

Run your site and use *ManageRoles.aspx* to create a role called Member and add a user to it, if that role doesn't already exist. Now log on to the site as a user who is in that role and navigate to *RoleRestricted.aspx*. You'll instantly be redirected to *NoPrivs.aspx*.

In web.config

As with restriction by username, you can use *web.config* to restrict directory access to a role's members by adding rules to an <authorization> element inside the <configuration>\<system.web> element, as shown in the following code snippet, or to restrict access to the page by creating a <location> element directly under <configuration> and then adding <system.web>\<authorization> to it.

```
<configuration>
    <system.web>
    ...
        <authorization>
            <deny users="?"/>
            <deny roles="Member" />
            <allow users="*"/>
        </authorization>
        ...
    </system.web>
</configuration>
```

Or, if you are restricting access to a particular file, such as *RoleRestricted.aspx*, you would add a <location> element to your *web.config* file:

```
<configuration>
    ...
    <location path="rolerestricted.aspx">
        <system.web>
            <authorization>
                <deny users="?"/>
                <deny roles="Member"/>
                <allow users="*"/>
            </authorization>
        </system.web>
    </location>
    ...
    <system.web>
        ...
    </system.web>
</configuration>
```

CHAPTER 13

Master Pages and Navigation

Websites look better and are less confusing to users when they have a consistent look and feel as you move from page to page. ASP.NET facilitates the creation of consistency with *master pages*, which allow you to create a consistent frame in which each page will place its content.

Navigation adds to the user's ease of use by providing a site map, or by providing "bread crumbs" that tell the user how he got to the current page. By placing your navigation aids in master pages, you can provide consistent navigational cues to your users, making for an enhanced user experience.

You can also control the user's browser history so he can quickly and accurately move back or forward to different asynchronous postbacks on the same AJAX-enabled page.

Master Pages

A master page provides shared HTML, controls, and code that you can use as a template for all of the pages of a site. Unlike CSS, which helps to ensure that similar controls have similar appearances (see "Themes and Skins" in Chapter 14), master pages ensure that all the pages have common elements, such as logos, headers, footers, or navigation aids. Everything on your master page is shown on every page that uses it. For example, you might have a master page with a logo and a menu; these will show on every "child" of the master page. Each master page can have multiple content areas in which you put the content that varies on each child page.

The O'Reilly website is a good example of a site that could be implemented using a master page. With a master page, the O'Reilly logo (the tarsier) and an image (the O'Reilly header) can be shared across multiple pages, as shown in Figure 13-1.

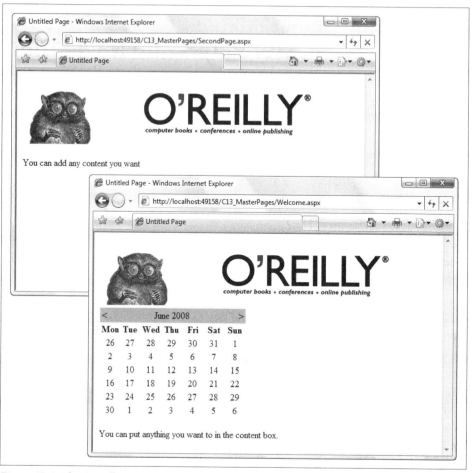

Figure 13-1. The O'Reilly site with master pages

> The O'Reilly site shown in these examples is a mockup and is not taken from the actual O'Reilly site, which you can reach at *http://www.oreilly.com*.

To use master pages, you'll take the following steps:

1. Create a new website.
2. Add a master page to the site.
3. Add content pages based on the master page.

To begin, create a new website and call it *C13_MasterPages*. After the new site opens, right-click the project and choose Add New Item. In the dialog box that opens, choose Master Page and name your master page *SiteMasterPage.master*, as shown in Figure 13-2.

All master pages *must* have the extension *.master*.

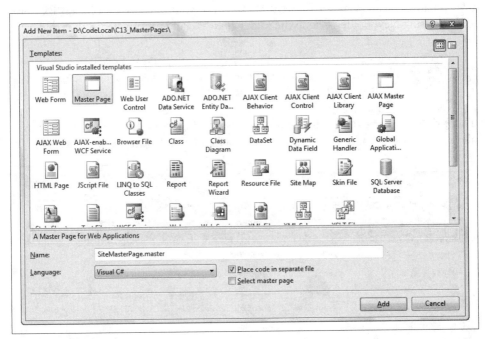

Figure 13-2. Adding the master page

Your new master page has been created with two `<asp:contentplaceholder>` controls already in place. One is in the HTML `<head>` element with an ID of head, the other is in the `<body>` called `ContentPlaceHolder1`:

```
<head runat="server">
   <title>Untitled Page</title>
   <asp:ContentPlaceHolder ID="head" runat="server">
   </asp:ContentPlaceHolder>
</head>
<body>
   <form id="form1" runat="server">
   <div>
       <asp:ContentPlaceHolder ID="ContentPlaceHolder1" runat="server">
       </asp:ContentPlaceHolder>
   </div>
   </form>
</body>
```

These placeholders will be filled by the page content that uses this master page (the content pages). Within the master page, you may add anything you like surrounding the `<asp:contentplaceholder>`. For example, if you are creating pages such as those in Figure 13-1, you might add the logos at the top of the page using a pair of image controls.

To set this up, download the images that come with the source code, or save your own images. Create a folder by right-clicking the solution in the Solution Explorer and choosing New Folder. Name the folder *Images*. Put your images in that folder.

 As usual, you can download the images used in this book, along with the source code, from *http://www.oreilly.com*. Click Books, scroll down to this book, and click Source Code.

Then, right-click the *Images* folder and choose Add Existing Item. You can highlight all your images and add them to the project, as shown in Figure 13-3.

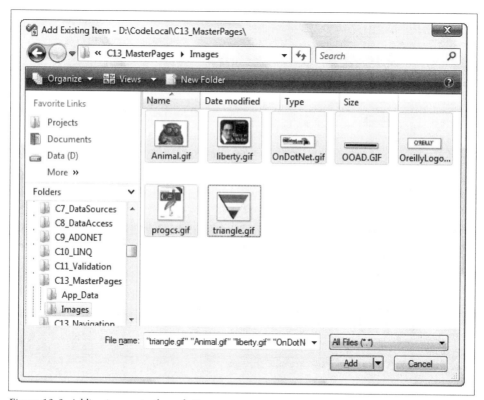

Figure 13-3. Adding images to the website

Add two image controls to the master page just above the ContentPlaceHolder1 control. You can drag these onto the page in either design or source mode. Set the ID for the first to imgAnimal, and set its ImageURL by clicking the ellipsis in the Properties window and navigating to the appropriate image, as shown in Figure 13-4.

Figure 13-4. Locating animal.gif

Name the second image control imgOreilly, and set its ImageURL to the *OreillyLogo.gif* file. Your form now has three objects, as shown in Figure 13-5:

- The first image
- The second image
- The ContentPlaceHolder object

You may add text to the master page's ContentPlaceHolder by typing directly onto it, which will act as default text (typically replaced in the pages that use this master page).

The *.master* page file that resulted in Figure 13-5 is listed in Example 13-1. The ID property of the ContentPlaceHolder control has been changed from its default value to TopPageContent in preparation for use in the example.

 Remember to save your master page before you create a content page based on it, especially if you decide to change the ID for one of the master page's ContentPlaceHolder controls.

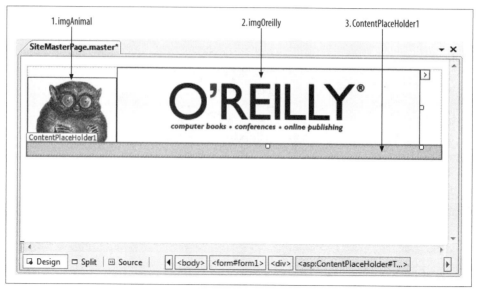

Figure 13-5. Three areas on the master page

Example 13-1. SiteMasterPage.aspx in full

```
<%@ Master Language="C#" AutoEventWireup="true"
   CodeFile="SiteMasterPage.master.cs" Inherits="SiteMasterPage" %>

<!DOCTYPE html PUBLIC "-//W3C//DTD XHTML 1.0 Transitional//EN"
   "http://www.w3.org/TR/xhtml1/DTD/xhtml1-transitional.dtd">
<html xmlns="http://www.w3.org/1999/xhtml">

<head runat="server">
   <title>Untitled Page</title>
   <asp:ContentPlaceHolder ID="head" runat="server">
   </asp:ContentPlaceHolder>
</head>

<body>
   <form id="form1" runat="server">
   <div>
      <asp:Image ID="imgAnimal" runat="server"
         ImageUrl="~/Images/Animal.gif"  />
      <asp:Image ID="imgOreilly" runat="server"
         ImageUrl="~/Images/OreillyLogo.gif" />
      <asp:ContentPlaceHolder ID="TopPageContent" runat="server">
      </asp:ContentPlaceHolder>
   </div>
   </form>
</body>
</html>
```

Adding Content Pages

The pages you'll add that will use this master page will merge all their content into the `ContentPlaceHolder` controls that are on the master page. Feel free to add any number of `ControlPlaceHolder` controls to a master page. For example, you might use one for a page's content, another for a sidebar, and another for the footer. In this example, however, you'll stick to using just one `ControlPlaceHolder` control, namely `TopPageContent`. You can use the `Head` `ContentPlaceHolder` to add further stylesheet information or meta information for specific pages beyond that added to the master page in your own web pages.

Add to the site a new web form called *Welcome.aspx*, but check "Select master page" in the Add New Item dialog, as shown in Figure 13-6.

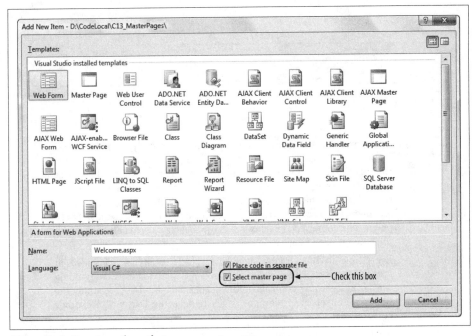

Figure 13-6. Creating a form that uses a master page

When you click the Add button, the Select a Master Page dialog will open, as shown in Figure 13-7. Choose *SiteMasterPage.master* and click OK.

Switch to Design view, and you will see *Welcome.aspx* within the master page. The outlined Content area representing the `TopPageContent` control will allow you to add any content you like, including controls, text, and so forth, but the contents of the master page will be disabled, as shown in Figure 13-8. Viewing a content page in Design view allows you to see how it will look when it is combined with the master page at runtime. For example, in Figure 13-8 we have added a `Calendar` control and some text.

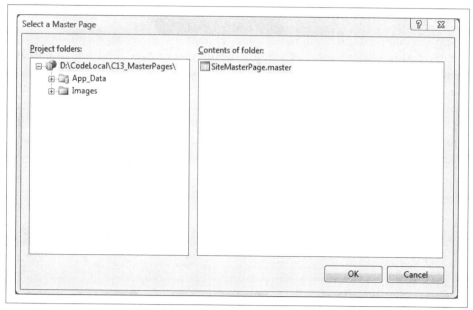

Figure 13-7. Selecting a master page for Welcome.aspx

The terminology can get a bit confusing, so let's clarify. A master page contains one or more empty ContentPlaceHolder controls. At runtime, this placeholder control is populated with markup that's defined in content pages. A content page is a normal *.aspx* file, with a Page directive but minus the <html>, <form>, <head>, and <body> tags (i.e., minus all the elements which constitute the basic containers for an HTML page). The content page is bound to the master page via an attribute in the content page's Page directive.

Everything in the content page is (in fact, must be) contained in Content controls. These Content controls are matched to corresponding ContentPlaceHolder controls on the master page by ID. At runtime, the Content controls from content pages replace the ContentPlaceHolder controls in the master page.

That's not really that confusing, is it?

When a content page is viewed in Design view, the Smart Tag menu for each control thereon has one option, Default to Master's Content. Selecting this option actually deletes the Content control from the page and leaves any text or server controls you added to the ContentPlaceHolder control on the master page visible to the user.

Add to the site a second web form called *SecondPage.aspx*. Give it the same master page as *Welcome.aspx*—*SiteMasterPage.master*—thus ensuring the look and feel of

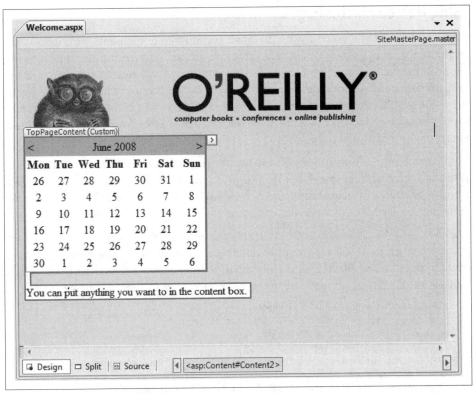

Figure 13-8. Adding content to the Content page

the two pages is identical. If you look at the source for this view, you'll see the `MasterPageFile` attribute in the @Page directive links the content page with its master, and that it has a `Content` control for each `ContentPlaceHolder` in the master:

```
<%@ Page Language="C#" AutoEventWireup="true"
    CodeFile="SecondPage.aspx.cs" Inherits="SecondPage"
    Title="Untitled Page"
    MasterPageFile="~/SiteMasterPage.master" %>

<asp:Content ID="Content1" ContentPlaceHolderID="head" Runat="Server">
</asp:Content>
<asp:Content ID="Content2" ContentPlaceHolderID="TopPageContent"
    Runat="Server">
</asp:Content>
```

Add some simple text to this page inside the `Content` controls, and then run the site in your browser. If you view both *Welcome.aspx* and *SecondPage.aspx*, you will notice a consistency of style much like the two pages shown back in Figure 13-1.

Using Nested Master Pages

It is not unusual for you to want to have certain stable elements throughout the entire application, as well as elements that are shared only within one part of your application. For example, you might have a company-wide header for your site but need to display division-wide elements as well, depending on where you are in the site. ASP.NET lets you create nested master pages. You can combine any given web page with a nested master page or with the original master, whichever makes more sense for that individual page.

To illustrate this, add to the site a new master page called *ASPNet.master*, but make sure the "Select master page" box in the Add New Item dialog is checked as it was when you created *Welcome.aspx* and *SecondPage.aspx*. Select *SiteMasterPage.master* as its master page, as shown earlier in Figure 13-7.

Click OK, and Visual Studio 2008 (VS2008) will generate the page for you. If you look at its source code, you'll see the only difference between this and a newly generated content page is the @Master directive rather than the @Page directive. It too has a MasterPageFile attribute indicating that it is a nested page to *SiteMasterPage.master*.

```
<%@ Master MasterPageFile="~/SiteMasterPage.master"
    AutoEventWireup="false" CodeFile="ASPNet.master.cs"
    Language="C#" Inherits="ASPNet" %>

<asp:Content ID="Content1" ContentPlaceHolderID="head" Runat="Server">
</asp:Content>
<asp:Content ID="Content2" ContentPlaceHolderID="TopPageContent"
    Runat="Server">
</asp:Content>
```

The intention for this nested master page is for you to add more structure to your website's pages. You do this by adding text, controls, and further ContentPlaceHolders for the content pages that will use this page as its master page within the Content controls generated for you, as shown in Figure 13-9. As with *SiteMasterPage.master*, switching to Design view will show you the current design of *ASPNet.master*, combining your work on this page and its master page.

 This combined view of topmost and nested master pages, as shown in Figure 13-9, is new to VS2008, as is the ability to add a nested master page to a site through the Add New Item dialog.

Note that the name of the ContentPlaceHolder (TopPageContent) is now shown to the right of its outline to differentiate between it in this nested page and in the original. And, as with content pages, you can easily delete the Content control on the page by choosing the Default to Master's Content option in its Smart Tag menu and display the content in the master page's ContentPlaceHolder control instead.

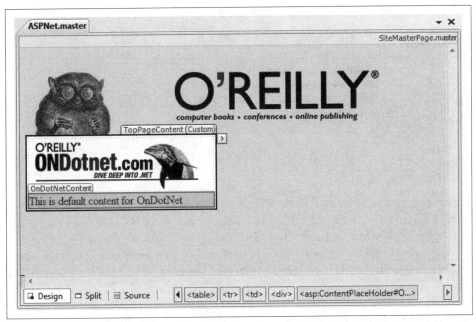

Figure 13-9. Viewing a nested master page's design

To demonstrate using a nested master page, you'll first add some content to *ASPNet.master* and then create two content pages based on it. Add an HTML table to the TopPageContent control in *ASPNet.master*. It should have one column with two rows in it, the top row containing *OnDotNet.gif* in an Image control and the bottom row another ContentPlaceHolder control with its ID set to OnDotNetContent and some default text. Example 13-2 shows the final source for *ASPNet.master* and Figure 13-9 its final design.

Example 13-2. ASPNet.master in full

```
<%@ Master Language="C#" MasterPageFile="~/SiteMasterPage.master"
    AutoEventWireup="false" CodeFile="ASPNet.master.cs"
    Inherits="ASPNet" %>

<asp:Content ID="Content1" ContentPlaceHolderID="head" runat="Server">
</asp:Content>

<asp:Content ID="Content2"
    ContentPlaceHolderID="TopPageContent" runat="Server">
    <table>
        <tr>
            <td>
                <asp:Image ID="Image1"
                    runat="server" ImageUrl="~/Images/OnDotNet.gif" />
            </td>
        </tr>
```

Example 13-2. ASPNet.master in full (continued)

```
    <tr>
      <td>
        <div>
          <asp:ContentPlaceHolder
              ID="OnDotNetContent" runat="server">
              This is default content for OnDotNet
          </asp:ContentPlaceHolder>
        </div>
      </td>
    </tr>
  </table>
</asp:Content>
```

To create a new page using *ASPNet.master* as its master, just add a new web form to the site and make sure to select *ASPNet.master* when asked. VS2008 takes care of the rest. Add *OnDotNetPage1.aspx* and *OnDotNetPage2.aspx* to the site in this way. Have a look at their source code and note that they have only one Content control. This corresponds to the one ContentPlaceHolder control in *ASPNet.master*. The ContentPlaceHolder controls in *SiteMasterPage.master* are not inherited by nested master pages. Therefore, there is no Content control in *OnDotNetPage1.aspx* or *OnDotNetPage2.aspx* for the ContentPlaceHolder with an ID of head that is on *SiteMasterPage.master*. Those pages contain Content controls only for the ContentPlaceHolder control named OnDotNetContent on the *ASPNet.master* page.

Add some sample text to both new pages and the results should have the same look and feel as Figure 13-10.

There is a theoretical limit to the number of times you can nest a master page after which VS2008 breaks—many dozen—but if you start building page designs that need that many nested masters, you should stop and reconsider your design.

Dynamically Modifying Master Page Contents from Content Pages

You may decide that in response to certain events, you'd like to reach up into the master page from a content page and change its presentation. To do this, you create a public property in your master page that content pages can access.

To see this in action, add the following property to *SiteMasterPage.master.cs*:

```
public Image AnimalImage
{
   get { return imgAnimal; }
   set { imgAnimal = value; }
}
```

In this case, imgAnimal refers to the Image control you added to *SiteMasterPage.master* at the beginning of the chapter:

```
<asp:Image ID="imgAnimal" runat="server"
    ImageUrl="~/Images/Animal.gif"  />
```

Figure 13-10. Pages based on ASPNet.master

To demonstrate how to access this property, add to the website a new page called *Welcome2.aspx*. Check the Select Master Page checkbox in the Add New Item dialog as you create it. Select *SiteMasterPage.master* as its master page in the Select a Master Page dialog box.

In Source view, add the following directive at the top of *Welcome2.aspx*:

```
<%@ MasterType TypeName="SiteMasterPage" %>
```

This directive tells ASP.NET to generate a reference to the SiteMasterPage class that provides strongly typed access to the master page. You can get a reference to this strongly typed object via the Master property of the current (i.e., content) page.

You can now write code in *Welcome2.aspx.cs* that accesses the SiteMasterPage and sets its property, as highlighted in the following code snippet:

```
protected void Page_Load(object sender, EventArgs e)
{
    Master.AnimalImage.ImageUrl = "~/images/progcs.gif";
}
```

> You may need to build the website before IntelliSense picks up the AnimalImage property.

Add some content to *Welcome2.aspx* for identification purposes. For example:

```
<asp:Content ID="Content2"
  ContentPlaceHolderID="TopPageContent" Runat="Server">
  <h1>This is Welcome 2</h1>
</asp:Content>
```

When you run the pages, you can see that *Welcome2.aspx* has had its master page modified at runtime, as shown in Figure 13-11.

Figure 13-11. Modifying the master page

The alternative to making content on the master page available by using properties is to use late binding. If you replace the Page_Load method in *Welcome2.aspx* with the following, the results will be identical (if a bit slower):

```
protected void Page_Load(object sender, EventArgs e)
{
    Control ctrl = Master.FindControl("imgAnimal");
    Image img = ctrl as Image;
    if (img != null)
    {
        img.ImageUrl = "~/images/progcs.gif";
    }
}
```

In this case, rather than using a property, you are finding the Image control at runtime and then setting its ImageUrl property. Both approaches work, but the use of properties is preferred because late binding is less efficient and harder to maintain.

Navigation

As websites become larger and more complex, developers need to incorporate navigational hints and menus to keep visitors from getting lost. ASP.NET 2.0 included controls for creating "bread crumbs" (how did I get to this page?) and site maps (how do I find that other page?). Most of the time you will want these features to be present on every page, and thus master pages are a great asset. If you change the site map or the control, you have to update only the master and all the other pages are "updated" automatically.

With Service Pack 1, ASP.NET 3.5 also includes a way to control a browser's history list. This is useful if you use AJAX features of ASP.NET so you can offer users logical navigation in an AJAX-enabled page.

Customizing Browser History

Using ASP.NET AJAX to perform asynchronous postbacks makes the UI in a page lively and makes it possible for the page to communicate with the server in the background, without full postbacks. However, AJAX introduces a navigation problem that hasn't been an issue in plain HTML pages or ASP.NET web pages. (Well, not much of an issue in ASP.NET pages, anyway.)

Consider an AJAX-enabled page that lets the user make various settings in various controls. The user selects an item in a listbox, and the page makes an asynchronous postback. He checks a checkbox, and there's another asynchronous postback. He clicks a radio button, and there's yet another asynchronous postback. Wait, no, the user decides that he didn't mean to click that radio button after all. So, he clicks the browser's back button. What happens next is probably *not* what the user intends: the page that the user is working on is unloaded completely, and the browser obligingly goes back (as requested) to the page the user was on *before* he started working on your AJAX-enabled page.

This is technically correct, but it's often not logically correct. However, in AJAX-enabled pages, the definition of "back" for purposes of the back button often means that the user wants to go back to *the preceding state of the current page*, not to the preceding page. In this example, the user wants to go back to the state before the radio button was clicked, not to the preceding page.

The problem is that the browser knows nothing about any of these asynchronous postbacks, because they don't register anything with the browser. To help solve this problem, ASP.NET 3.5 introduces *browser history*. Browser history lets you, the page developer, capture the state of a page each time something interesting happens, and store that state as a *history point* in the browser's history stack. ("Something interesting" is usually when the state of a control changes or an asynchronous postback occurs.)

History points consist of the state information appended to the URL of the current page. The result of storing state, then, is that you push URLs onto the browser's history stack—that is, URLs with state information in them.

Imagine the earlier example, but this time with browser history enabled. When the user makes a selection from the list, your code does whatever it normally does to respond to the choice, plus it adds a history point to the browser's history stack. It does the same with the checkbox and with the radio button, for a total of three history points. As before, when the user clicks the browser's back button, the browser pops the URL off the top of the history stack and loads the page. This time, though, the most recent URL is a history point—the current page's URL plus some state data.

ASP.NET raises a navigation event that notifies you that the user has clicked the back button and makes the state data available to you. You unpack the state data, and then use it to reset the controls to that state. As far as the user is concerned, the page went back in the usual way. If the user clicks the back button again, another URL with state data is popped off the stack, and you reset the page to whatever state *that* data represents. As you can deduce, all of this works just as well if the user now decides to click the forward button, which likewise raises a navigation event and gives you the state to restore.

As a bonus, browser history lets you solve a problem that even full postbacks have. If you run a page that posts back to the server six times, the browser's history list simply has six entries for that page showing only the page's title with no indication of what "stage" in the page each entry reflects, as shown in Figure 13-12.

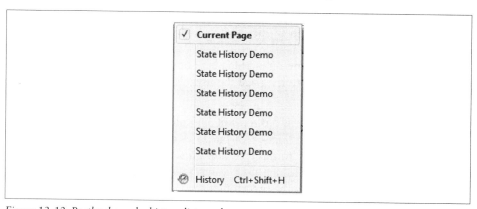

Figure 13-12. Postbacks make history lists useless

If you were looking at this list and wanted to return back to view details of a book on this page which menu item would you click?

Browser history helps you address this by letting you specify a title each time you save a history point. If you do so, it would be clear what list item to select, as shown in Figure 13-13.

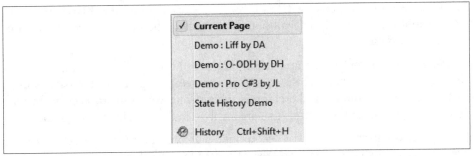

Figure 13-13. Using EnableHistory makes history lists useful again

To demonstrate how to use this new functionality, create a new website called *C13_ Navigation*. Right-click the website in the Solution Explorer and add a new AJAX-enabled page called *StateHistoryDemo.aspx*.

The browser history functionality works by letting the ScriptManager for the page manage a name-value collection. Each time the page posts back asynchronously, you can call the AddHistoryPoint method of the ScriptManager control to store the state description of the page (in this case, Step 1, Step 2, Step 3, etc.) and set the title of the page as you want it to appear in the browser history list. When a user clicks the forward or back button in the browser, the ScriptManager control raises its Navigate event, at which point you can pull the state of the page being navigated out of the page and use it as you will.

To start using browser history, add two new properties to the ScriptManager control on *StateHistoryDemo.aspx*:

```
<%@ Page Language="C#" AutoEventWireup="true"
    CodeFile="StateHistoryDemo.aspx.cs" Inherits="StateHistoryDemo" %>

<!DOCTYPE html PUBLIC "-//W3C//DTD XHTML 1.0 Transitional//EN"
    "http://www.w3.org/TR/xhtml1/DTD/xhtml1-transitional.dtd">
<html xmlns="http://www.w3.org/1999/xhtml">

<head runat="server">
    <title>State History Demo</title>
    <script type="text/javascript">
      function pageLoad( ) {
      }
    </script>
</head>

<body>
    <form id="form1" runat="server">
    <div>
      <asp:ScriptManager ID="sm" runat="server"
          EnableHistory="true" OnNavigate="RestoreHistoryPoint" />
```

The EnableHistory property switches browser history on, and the OnNavigate property identifies the method that will handle the event when a user clicks forward or back in his browser.

The ScriptManager control can update only the page history collection during an asynchronous update. The next step is to add an UpdatePanel control to the page with its ContentTemplate surrounding the controls whose state you want to keep in history. (That is, it will contain the controls that are involved in the asynchronous postbacks.)

In this case, you'll wrap the UpdatePanel around a DropDownList (ddlAuthors) containing a few authors, a RadioButtonList (rblBooks) containing a few books, and a single Button (btnSave) which will trigger the asynchronous postbacks. When each postback occurs you'll save the current state of each control and reflect it in the title of the page.

```
<asp:UpdatePanel runat="server" ID="updHistory"
                 UpdateMode="Always">
    <ContentTemplate>
        Authors :
        <asp:DropDownList ID="ddlAuthors" runat="server">
            <asp:ListItem Text="Jesse Liberty" Value="JL"
                        Selected="True" />
            <asp:ListItem Text="Dan Hurwitz" Value="DH" />
            <asp:ListItem Text="Dan Maharry" Value="DM" />
            <asp:ListItem Text="Douglas Adams" Value="DA" />
        </asp:DropDownList>
        <br />
        Books : 
        <asp:RadioButtonList ID="rblBooks" runat="server">
            <asp:ListItem Text="Professional C# 3.0"
                Value="Pro C#3" Selected="True" />
            <asp:ListItem
                Text="Object Oriented Design Heuristics"
                Value="O-ODH" />
            <asp:ListItem Text="The Meaning of Liff"
                Value="Liff" />
        </asp:RadioButtonList>
        <br />
        <asp:Button ID="btnSave" runat="server"
            OnClick="SaveHistoryPoint" Text="Save" />
    </ContentTemplate>
</asp:UpdatePanel>
    </div>
    </form>
</body>
</html>
```

The next step is to add calls to the SaveHistoryPoint method, which will be called each time the Save button is clicked. History state is stored in a NameValueCollection object, so you must include the System.Collections.Specialized namespace to use it.

```
using System;
using System.Web.UI;
using System.Web.UI.WebControls;
using System.Collections.Specialized;
```

The method itself does three things:

- It gathers the state of the controls on the page and stores them in the NameValueCollection object. In this case, the currently selected values of the lists are stored in the state.
- It generates the title to associate with the new state of the page to be sent to the browser.
- It calls AddHistoryPoint on the ScriptManager to add both state and title to the page's history stack:

```
protected void SaveHistoryPoint(object sender, EventArgs e)
{
    NameValueCollection state = new NameValueCollection( );
    state.Add("book", rblBooks.SelectedValue);
    state.Add("author", ddlAuthors.SelectedValue);

    string newTitle = String.Format("Demo : {0} by {1}",
        rblBooks.SelectedValue, ddlAuthors.SelectedValue);

    sm.AddHistoryPoint(state, newTitle);
}
```

Two further versions of AddHistoryPoint cater to the situation where just a single piece of information needs to be stored regarding the state of a page in the history stack:

AddHistoryPoint(string key, string value, string title)
: Adds a new key-value pair to the history stack to represent the new state of the page and a title to associate with that state

AddHistoryPoint(string key, string value)
: Adds a new key-value pair to the history stack to represent the new state of the page, but uses the current page title to associate with that state

Having saved the page state to your history stack, the final step is to deal with the event raised when the browser history list has been used to move forward and backward to a new page, or to a different page state. In this case, you'll need to get the appropriate page state from the history stack, and use it to reset the page to that state. All of this is done in the event handler for the ScriptManager control's Navigate event handler:

```
protected void RestoreHistoryPoint(object sender,
                                   HistoryEventArgs e)
{
    if (e.State != null)
    {
        if (String.IsNullOrEmpty(e.State["author"]))
        {
            ddlAuthors.SelectedIndex = 0;
        }
        else
        {
```

```
            ddlAuthors.SelectedIndex = ddlAuthors.Items.IndexOf(
                ddlAuthors.Items.FindByValue(e.State["author"]));
        }

        if (String.IsNullOrEmpty(e.State["book"]))
        {
            rblBooks.SelectedIndex = 0;
        }
        else
        {
            rblBooks.SelectedIndex = rblBooks.Items.IndexOf(
                rblBooks.Items.FindByValue(e.State["book"]));
        }
      }
    }
  }
} // end of StateHistoryDemo.aspx.cs
```

When the page is initially loaded, no state will be saved, so this method must deal with the case where there is no state and reset the controls to their original states. For example, the author list has Jesse Liberty selected initially, so it must be reset to that if the user returns to the initial state of the page.

```
if (String.IsNullOrEmpty(e.State["author"]))
{
    ddlAuthors.SelectedIndex = 0;
}
```

In any other case, the list must have selected the author saved to the state on the history stack. This is done by retrieving the selected value of the author list from the state e.State["author"], finding which item in the list contains that value, and then marking it as selected. The book list works in the same way.

```
else
{
    ddlAuthors.SelectedIndex = ddlAuthors.Items.IndexOf(
        ddlAuthors.Items.FindByValue(e.State["author"]));
}
```

Save and run *StateHistoryDemo.aspx*, and then save different choices of items from the two lists by clicking the Save button. If you look at the browser history list, you'll see that each page state is now more easily identifiable (as shown in Figure 13-13) and that if you select any entry in the history, the page state will be restored as it was when the Save button was clicked.

You'll also see that the state for the current page is stored as an encrypted string in the URL for the page. For example:

```
http://localhost:50278/C13_Navigation/StateHistoryDemo.aspx#&&/wEXAgU
GYXVOaG9yBQJEQQUEYm9vawUETGlnZ+wJIzrByGiR2+StzSbiDrE3Nb/h
```

It is recommended that you leave it encrypted to ward off prying eyes. However, you can create it as an unencrypted string in the URL by setting the ScriptManager's EnableSecureHistoryState to false (it is true by default):

```
<asp:ScriptManager ID="sm" runat="server"
    EnableHistory="true" OnNavigate="RestoreHistoryPoint"
    EnableSecureHistoryState="false"
/>
```

With this property set, the URL will now look like this:

```
http://localhost:50278/C13_Navigation/StateHistoryDemo.aspx#
&&book=Liff&author=DA
```

Note that although browser history works across all browsers, there are a couple of gotchas that you might need to bear in mind.

A browser's page history list is usually a fixed width, so although you can give each page state a unique name in the list it may not be fully legible to the user. *StateHistoryDemo.aspx*, for instance, could have saved the full names of the currently selected book and author in the page title, but the browser's history list would have shown only the first 20 or so characters of that title which might not have been that useful. Hence, it used abbreviated versions of author and title.

If a user initially comes to a page through a named anchor, browser history doesn't work on the page because a named anchor also uses the # character and this causes confusion. You'll have to rework your page without named anchors if you want to use browser history.

Getting Started with Site Navigation

The new browser history functionality is great for finding your way around the different states of a page, but without some way for a user to find his way around your site, it's debatable whether he will ever find the page for you to worry about, if it's a site of any size. The most common way to provide a navigation aid to a page is to add a Menu, a SiteMapPath, or a TreeView control to the site's master page. You'll see how to use all three controls in this chapter, but first you'll look at their main common factor: a data source that provides them with information on each page in the site.

The most common way to create this *site navigation data source* is to create an XML file. You can use a database, multiple XML files, and other sources, but for now let's keep things simple.

Right-click the *C13_Navigation* website in the Solution Explorer and choose Add New Item. When the Add New Item dialog box appears, choose Site Map and verify that the name provided is *Web.sitemap*, as shown in Figure 13-14.

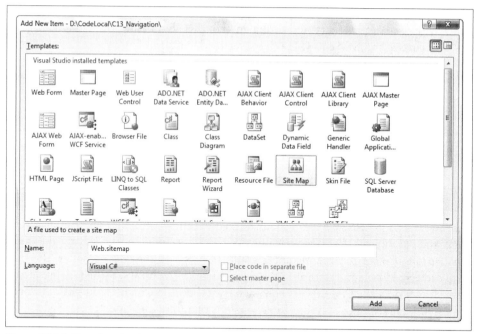

Figure 13-14. Creating the site map

When you click Add, *Web.sitemap* is added to your website, and the skeleton of a site map is provided for you, as shown in Example 13-3.

Example 13-3. A skeleton Web.sitemap file

```
<?xml version="1.0" encoding="utf-8" ?>
<siteMap xmlns="http://schemas.microsoft.com/AspNet/SiteMap-File-1.0">
    <siteMapNode url="" title=""  description="">
        <siteMapNode url="" title=""  description="" />
        <siteMapNode url="" title=""  description="" />
    </siteMapNode>
</siteMap>
```

The title attribute defines the text that is (usually) used as the link, and the description attribute is used in the tool tip.

 VS2008 provides no drag-and-drop support for creating your site map file. You can implement your own SiteMap provider to automate this process or to get the site map from another source (such as a database), but this is a very advanced topic that is beyond the scope of this book. You can find one documented attempt at *http://msdn.microsoft.com/magazine/cc163657.aspx.*

Replace the contents of *Web.sitemap* with the site map XML shown in Example 13-4.

Example 13-4. Web.sitemap for C13_Navigation

```xml
<?xml version="1.0" encoding="utf-8" ?>
<siteMap xmlns="http://schemas.microsoft.com/AspNet/SiteMap-File-1.0">
    <siteMapNode title="Welcome" description="Welcome"
        url="~/welcome.aspx">
        <siteMapNode title="Writing" description="Writing"
            url="~/Writing.aspx">
            <siteMapNode title="Books" description="Books"
                url="~/Books.aspx">
                <siteMapNode title="In Print Books"
                    description="Books in Print"
                url="~/BooksInPrint.aspx" />
                <siteMapNode title="Out Of Print Books"
                    description="Books no longer in Print"
                url="~/OutOfPrintBooks.aspx" />
            </siteMapNode>
            <siteMapNode title="Articles" description="Articles"
                url="~/Articles.aspx" />
        </siteMapNode>
        <siteMapNode title="Programming"
            description="Contract Programming"
            url="~/Programming.aspx">
            <siteMapNode title="On-Site Programming"
                description="On-site contract programming"
                url="~/OnSiteProgramming.aspx" />
            <siteMapNode title="Off-Site Programming"
                description="Off-site contract programming"
                url="~/OffSiteProgramming.aspx" />
        </siteMapNode>
        <siteMapNode title="Training"
            description="On-Site Training"
            url="~/OnSiteTraining.aspx">
            <siteMapNode title="C# Training"
                description="C# Training"
                url="~/TrainCSharp.aspx" />
            <siteMapNode title="ASP.NET Training"
                description="ASP.NET Training"
                url="~/TrainASPNET.aspx" />
            <siteMapNode title="Windows Forms Training"
                description="Windows Forms Training"
                url="~/TrainWinForms.aspx" />
        </siteMapNode>
        <siteMapNode title="Consulting"
            description="Consulting"
            url="~/Consulting.aspx">
            <siteMapNode title="Application Analysis"
                description="Analysis"
                url="~/ApplicationAnalysis.aspx" />
            <siteMapNode title="Application Design"
                description="Design"
                url="~/ApplicationDesign.aspx" />
            <siteMapNode title="Mentoring"
                description="Team Mentoring"
                url="~/Mentoring.aspx" />
```

Example 13-4. Web.sitemap for C13_Navigation (continued)

```
      </siteMapNode>
    </siteMapNode>
</siteMap>
```

The site map file has a single `<sitemap>` element that defines the namespace:

```
<siteMap xmlns="http://schemas.microsoft.com/AspNet/SiteMap-File-1.0">
```

Within the `siteMap` element is nested exactly one `<SiteMapNode>` (in this case, `Welcome`). Nested within that first `<SiteMapNode>`, however, is any number of children `<SiteMapNode>` elements.

In Example 13-4, there are four such children: `Writing`, `Programming`, `Training`, and `Consulting`. Nested within each of these `<SiteMapNode>` elements can be more nodes. For example, `Writing` has `Books` and `Articles`. You may nest the nodes to any arbitrary depth. The `Books` node has nested within it nodes for `"Books in Print"` and `"Books no longer in Print"`.

 ASP.NET is configured to protect files with the extension *.sitemap* so that they cannot be downloaded to a client (web browser). If you change providers and need to use a different extension, be sure to place your file in the protected *App_Data* folder.

Setting Up the Pages

To work with the site map file, add a new master page to *C13_Navigation*. Leave its name as *MasterPage.master*, the default that VS2008 has given to it.

 All the controls you will now add to the master page must be placed outside the `ContentPlaceHolder` tags, but inside the `<\form>` tag.

From the Toolbox, drag a `SiteMapDataSource` control from the Data tab and a `TreeView` control from the Navigation tab onto the master page. By default, the `SiteMapDataSource` control will look for and use the file named *Web.sitemap*.

In Design view, open the `TreeView`'s Smart Tag menu and set the data source to the `SiteMapDataSource` control you just created, as shown in Figure 13-15.

VS2008 will automatically update the `TreeView` to reflect the contents of the *Web. sitemap* file, as shown in Figure 13-16.

To control the layout of the master page, add an HTML table to the page with one row and two columns. Into the first column drag the `TreeView` control, and into the second add a `SiteMapPath` control. This control adds another type of navigation aid to your pages: bread crumbs. These are links, often at the top of a page, that show how the user arrived at the current page—for example, "Main Page → Books → Programming ASP.NET".

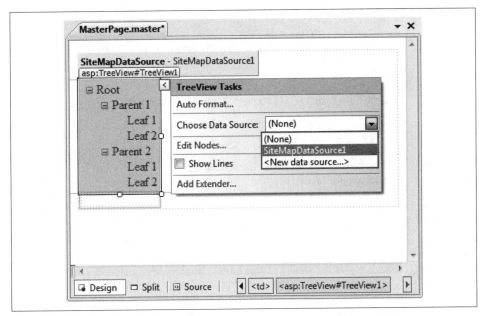

Figure 13-15. Setting the TreeView's data source

Under the SiteMapPath control, add a couple of line breaks and the ContentPlaceHolder control already on the page. The layout is shown in Design view in Figure 13-17, and in code in Example 13-5.

Note that the SiteMapPath displays Root Node → Parent Node → Current Node in VS2008 as it updates only at runtime and not at design time.

Example 13-5. MasterPage.master in full

```
<%@ Master Language="C#" AutoEventWireup="true"
   CodeFile="MasterPage.master.cs" Inherits="MasterPage" %>

<!DOCTYPE html PUBLIC "-//W3C//DTD XHTML 1.0 Transitional//EN"
   "http://www.w3.org/TR/xhtml1/DTD/xhtml1-transitional.dtd">
<html xmlns="http://www.w3.org/1999/xhtml">
<head runat="server">
   <title>Navigation Demo Site</title>
   <asp:ContentPlaceHolder ID="head" runat="server">
   </asp:ContentPlaceHolder>
</head>

<body>
   <form id="form1" runat="server">
   <div>
      <asp:SiteMapDataSource ID="SiteMapDataSource1"
                             runat="server" />
      <table>
        <tr>
          <td>
```

Example 13-5. MasterPage.master in full (continued)

```
                <asp:TreeView ID="TreeView1"
                    runat="server" DataSourceID="SiteMapDataSource1">
                </asp:TreeView>
            </td>
            <td>
                <asp:SiteMapPath ID="SiteMapPath1" runat="server">
                </asp:SiteMapPath>
                <br />
                <br />
                <asp:ContentPlaceHolder
                    ID="ContentPlaceHolder1" runat="server">
                </asp:ContentPlaceHolder>
            </td>
        </tr>
    </table>
</div>
</form>
</body>
</html>
```

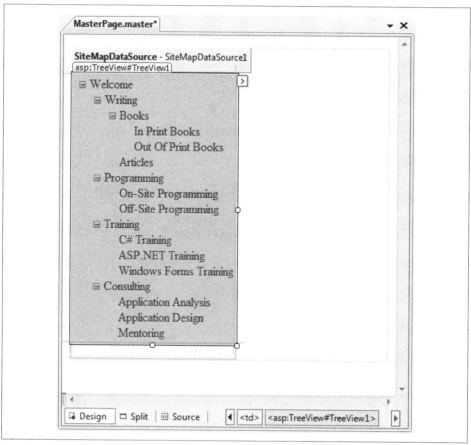

Figure 13-16. The TreeView control automatically updates to reflect its data source

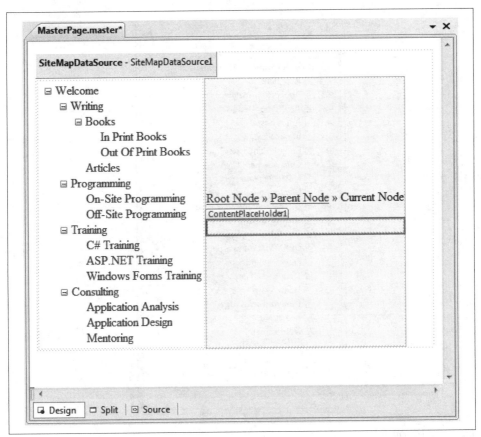

Figure 13-17. MasterPage.master layout

To test this master page, you'll need to create at least a few of the pages defined in the site map. Delete *Default.aspx* from the website and create a new page named *Welcome.aspx*. Check the "Select master page" checkbox and set the master page to *MasterPage.master*. Within the content control, add the following line of code shown in bold:

```
<asp:Content ID="Content2"
    ContentPlaceHolderID="ContentPlaceHolder1" Runat="Server">
    <h1>Welcome</h1>
</asp:Content>
```

Create each of the other pages, providing whatever stubbed out data you want as long as you can tell what page you are on. When you are done, your Solution Explorer should look more or less like Figure 13-18. Set *Welcome.aspx* as the start page.

Start the application and navigate from the Welcome page to another page, such as Mentoring, as shown in Figure 13-19.

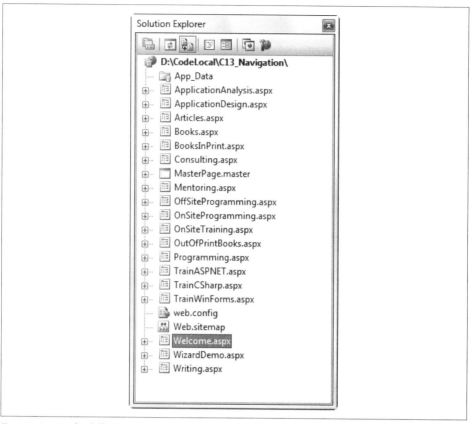

Figure 13-18. The full set of pages for C13_Navigation

There are a few things to notice about this page. The tree view was built for you by reading the XML file through the SiteMapDataSource control. You can see that each node can be collapsed (like the Training node) or expanded (like the Writing node). When you click a node (in this case, Mentoring), you are brought directly to that page. The bread crumbs, put in place by the SiteMapPath, show you how you got here and how to get back to home.

Customizing the Look and Feel

You can set a number of properties for the TreeView. To begin with, you may click the smart tag and choose Auto Format to bring up the AutoFormat dialog, which offers a series of preset formats for the tree, as shown in Figure 13-20.

In addition, you can click the TreeView control and then set its properties through the Properties window. Most of the TreeView's properties have to do with the styles used for the various nodes. Some of the most important properties are shown in Figure 13-21.

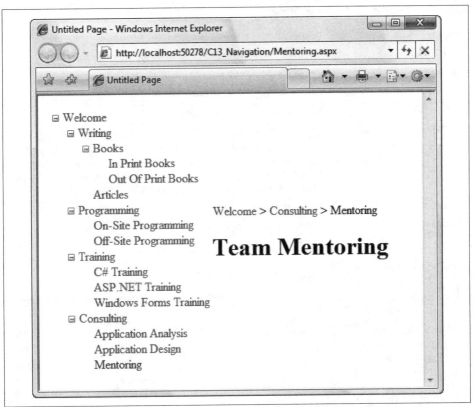

Figure 13-19. The SiteMapPath control reflects the position of Mentoring.aspx in Web.sitemap

There are a large number of other properties, many of which are listed in Table 13-1.

Table 13-1. TreeView properties

Property	Description
AutoGenerateDataBindings	If set to true, the default, lets you manually set the bindings between data and tree nodes.
CheckedNodes	Returns a collection of TreeNode objects that contains only those nodes whose checkbox was selected.
CollapseImageToolTip	The tool tip to display when the node is collapsed.
CollapseImageUrl	The URL for the image to display when the node is collapsed.
ExpandDepth	The number of levels to which the tree should be expanded when it is first displayed.
ExpandImageToolTip	The tool tip to display when the node is expanded.
ExpandImageUrl	The URL for the image to display when the node is expanded.
HoverNodeStyle	The TreeNodeStyle object to set the appearance of a node when the mouse pointer is hovering over it.
NodeIndent	The number of pixels that child nodes are indented from their parent.

Table 13-1. TreeView properties (continued)

Property	Description
NodeStyle	The TreeNodeStyle object to set the default appearance of a node.
NodeWrap	If true, the text of a node wraps if it runs out of space. Default is false.
PathSeparator	The character used to delimit the node values.
SelectedNode	Returns the selected TreeNode object.
SelectedNodeStyle	The TreeNodeStyle object to set the appearance of the selected node.
ShowCheckBoxes	A bitwise combination of TreeNodeTypes to indicate which types of nodes will display with checkboxes. In this example, none of the nodes has checkboxes; in other applications, you might open a TreeView control to display, for example, directories, and allow the user to check which directories are to be acted on (e.g., deleted).
ShowExpandCollapse	If true, the default, the expand/collapse indicators will be displayed.
ShowLines	If true, lines connecting the nodes will be displayed. Default is false.

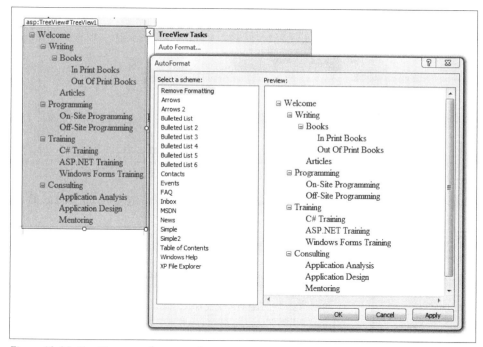

Figure 13-20. TreeView auto-format options

The TreeView has a number of public methods that allow you to poke into the control and pick out specific nodes or to programmatically change, expand, and contract nodes. The most important methods are shown in Table 13-2.

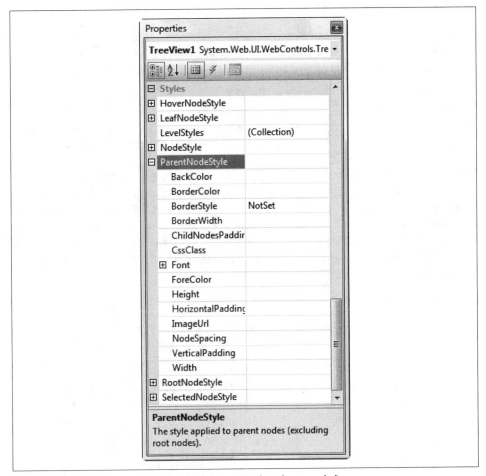

Figure 13-21. TreeView node styles (with ParentNodeStyle expanded)

Table 13-2. TreeView methods

Method	Description
CollapseAll	Collapses the entire tree
ExpandAll	Expands the entire tree
FindNode	Retrieves the designated TreeNode

Finally, a number of events that the TreeView control raises allow you to hook into the user's interaction with the TreeView and modify the results. The most important events are shown in Table 13-3.

Table 13-3. TreeView events

Event	Description
SelectedNodeChanged	Raised when a node is selected in the TreeView
TreeNodeCheckChanged	Raised when the checkbox status of a node is changed
TreeNodeCollapsed	Raised when a node is collapsed
TreeNodeExpanded	Raised when a node is expanded
TreeNodePopulate	Raised when a node whose PopulateOnDemand property is set to true is expanded in the TreeView (gives you an opportunity to fill in the subnodes for that node)

Similarly, you can modify the SiteMapPath control by using the smart tag to set auto-formatting or by setting properties on the control. Some common tasks include customizing the link *style* properties (such as RootNodeStyle-Font-Names and RootNodeStyle-BorderWidth). You can set these declaratively in the declaration of the control itself. IntelliSense will help; when you press the Space bar while you're within the declaration of the control, a list of its properties, methods, and events will pop up, as shown in Figure 13-22.

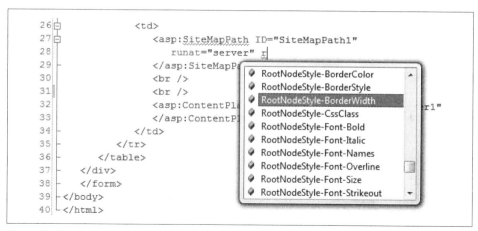

Figure 13-22. SiteMapPath properties via IntelliSense

> In addition to setting styles for the RootNode, you can set separate styles for the ParentNode, the CurrentNode, and the PathSeparator. You can use the NodeTemplate to customize the style of all the links at once.

In the preceding example, the bread crumbs separated the various pages with the greater-than symbol (>). Changing that symbol is easy with the PathSeparator property. For example:

```
<asp:SiteMapPath ID="SiteMapPath1"
    runat="server" PathSeparator=" &raquo; ">
```

results in bread crumbs, as shown in Figure 13-23.

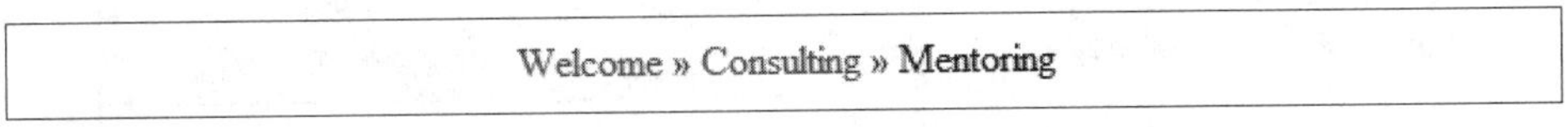

Welcome » Consulting » **Mentoring**

Figure 13-23. A different bread crumb separator

For "deep" websites, the bread crumbs may become unwieldy. You have the option to limit the number of levels shown by setting the ParentLevelDisplayed property:

```
<asp:SiteMapPath ID="SiteMapPath1" runat="server"
    ParentLevelDisplayed="3" />
```

Populating on Demand

You may decide you would like your tree view to populate on demand. That is, rather than loading all the contents of each node when the tree is first shown and displaying the full tree, you can display (for example) the first node, and as each node is clicked, it will populate the next level.

To do this, you'll make some simple changes to the master page. First, modify the TreeView not to be a self-closing element; you'll be adding content between the opening and closing tags. Add an ExpandDepth attribute to the TreeView, which you will set to 0 (or whatever level, zero-based, you want the tree to expand to when loaded).

Within the TreeView, you'll add a DataBindings element, and within that, you'll add a TreeNodeBinding control, as shown in Example 13-6.

Example 13-6. Adding tree node bindings for Populate on Demand

```
<asp:TreeView ID="TreeView1" runat="server"
    DataSourceID="SiteMapDataSource1"
    ExpandDepth="0">
    <DataBindings>
        <asp:TreeNodeBinding DataMember="SiteMapNode"
            NavigateUrlField="URL" PopulateOnDemand="true"
            TextField="Title" />
    </DataBindings>
</asp:TreeView>
```

Run the application with *Welcome.aspx* as the start page. The tree is fully closed. Expand the TreeView to choose Off-Site Programming. When you get to the page, again the tree is fully closed, as shown in Figure 13-24.

The nodes will be loaded as you click each level of the menu.

Figure 13-24. Menu fully closed

Using a Menu for Navigation

Open *MasterPage.master* in source mode and locate the TreeView control. Comment it out and replace it with a menu:

```
<%--
    <asp:TreeView ID="TreeView1" runat="server"
        DataSourceID="SiteMapDataSource1" />
--%>
<asp:Menu ID="Menu1" runat="server"
    DataSourceID="SiteMapDataSource1" />
```

Run the application. Presto! You have a menu control for navigation, as shown in Figure 13-25.

In this case, we hovered over Welcome (opening the next level) and then hovered over Programming (opening the third level). If the menus start to eat into your content, you can set their Orientation property to Horizontal (the default is Vertical) and rearrange your table to make room for them.

Enumerating the Site Map Programmatically

Sometimes you may want access to the current node and its subnodes so you can manipulate them programmatically. You can add code to a page to get that information. In the next example, you will display the name of the current node in the *Programming.aspx* page, and you will also display its subnodes. Add the code in Example 13-7 inside the Content tags in *Programming.aspx*.

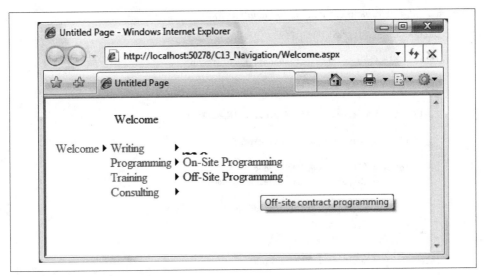

Figure 13-25. Using a menu for navigation

Example 13-7. New content for Programming.aspx

```
<table>
   <tr>
      <td>
         <b>Current Node:</b>
      </td>
      <td>
         <asp:Label ID="lblCurrentNode" runat="server" />
      </td>
   </tr>
   <tr>
      <td>
         <b>Child Nodes:</b>
      </td>
      <td>
         <asp:Label ID="lblChildNodes" runat="server" />
      </td>
   </tr>
</table>
```

You have added two labels: lblCurrentNode and lblChildNodes. Open the code-behind file for this page and modify the Page_Load method, as shown in Example 13-8.

Example 13-8. Programming.aspx.cs in full

```
using System;
using System.Web;
using System.Web.UI;
```

Example 13-8. Programming.aspx.cs in full (continued)

```
public partial class Programming : Page
{
    protected void Page_Load(object sender, EventArgs e)
    {
        try
        {
            lblCurrentNode.Text = SiteMap.CurrentNode.Title;

            if (SiteMap.CurrentNode.HasChildNodes)
            {
                foreach (SiteMapNode childNode in
                        SiteMap.CurrentNode.ChildNodes)
                {
                    lblChildNodes.Text += childNode.Title + "<br/>";
                }
            }
        }
        catch (System.NullReferenceException)
        {
            lblCurrentNode.Text =
                "The xml file is not in the site map!";
        }
        catch (Exception ex)
        {
            lblCurrentNode.Text = "Exception! " + ex.Message;
        }
    }
}
```

In this code, you are setting the text of lblCurrentNode to reflect the SiteMap's CurrentNode. The SiteMap is an in-memory representation of a site's navigational structure. The SiteMap object itself is created by the site map provider (in this case, by the SiteMapDataSource).

The CurrentNode property returns an object of type SiteMapNode, and the Text property of that SiteMapNode returns that SiteMapNode's title.

The SiteMapNode's property, HasChildNodes, returns a Boolean, true, if there are sub-nodes to the SiteMapNode. If this is the case, you can iterate through the SiteMapNodeCollection returned by the ChildNodes property.

When you view this page, the labels display the name of the current node and all its child nodes, as shown in Figure 13-26.

Filtering Based on Security

In Chapter 12, we covered the creation of login accounts and roles. In the next example, we'll use that information combined with the navigation tools we've also already covered to make aspects of the navigation aids visible and accessible to users in specific roles.

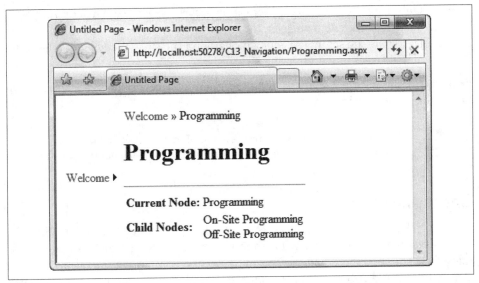

Figure 13-26. Accessing the current node's properties

To get started, copy the *C12_Security* website folder and all its contents to a new folder called *C13_SecureNavigation*, and then open that website in VS2008. To recap, in the preceding chapter, this website demonstrated the creation of user accounts and user roles and then used both code-behind files in individual pages and the *web.config* file to restrict access to pages and directories based on either the user identity or the role in which the user was grouped.

Table 13-4 lists the users and roles set up in the membership database for *C12_ Security*. You may have created others, but for the purposes of this chapter, this is what will be assumed. Feel free to follow along using the users and roles you created, or use the download.

Table 13-4. Users and roles defined for C13_SecureNavigation

User ID	Password	Role
Dan	Dan@123	Admins, Member
Jane	Jane@123	
Jesse	Jesse@123	Member

Two pages have access restricted to them: one by user ID (*Restricted.aspx*) and the other by role (*RoleRestricted.aspx*). You should also create two new folders within the site, one called *Admins* and the other called *Members*, and add a new page into each of them: *AdminsOnly.aspx* and *MembersOnly.aspx*.

The aim of the demonstration is to make sure only Admins can see the links to *AdminsOnly.aspx* in the site map and only Members and Admins can see the links to

MembersOnly.aspx. You do this by activating *security trimming* whereby ASP.NET removes links from the site map given the user logged in, its associated roles, and the access rules for the site set in *web.config* files around the site. (We will not take code-behind-enforced rules into account here.)

Before activating security trimming, you need to create access rules and a *Web.sitemap* file for the site to be trimmed.

 You'll also need to add a `TreeView` control to *Welcome.aspx* to reflect the trimming of the site map. The suggested layout is in Figure 13-26.

Creating Access Rules

Open the Web Site Administration Tool (WAT) by clicking Website → ASP.NET Configuration. Click the Security tab, and under Access Rules, click "Create access rules". Click first on the *Admins* folder. In the second column, set the rule to apply to a specific role and choose Admins from the drop down. In the third column, click the Allow radio button, as shown in Figure 13-27.

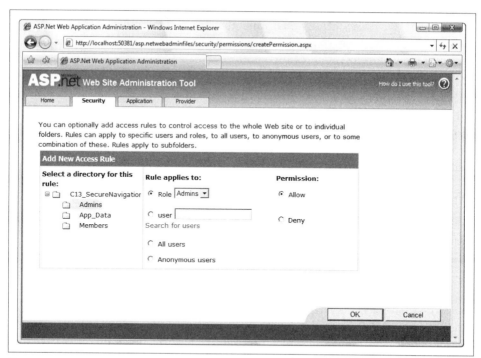

Figure 13-27. Creating an access rule for the Admins folder

Click OK and you are returned to the WAT home page. Repeat the same steps to create an access rule for the *Members* folder, granting permission only to the `Members` role.

Return to the WAT home page and click Manage Access Rules. Click the *Admins* folder and click Add New Access Rule. This time, with the *Admins* folder highlighted, click the "All users" radio button and set the permission to Deny, then click OK. Do the same for *Members*.

You've now created four rules. The *Admins* folder rules specify that users in the role of Admins are allowed access and all others are denied. The same is true for the *Members* folder: only Members have access. Click Done and then close the WAT.

 By default in Internet Information Services (IIS) 7, the order in which these rules are written does not matter; they are "combined" and then applied to the user being checked against them. However, in IIS 5, 6, and 7 running an ASP.NET application in Classic mode, the rules are checked in order of their appearance.

So, if a Deny All rule is at the top of the list and someone tries to access that page, he will be denied. On the other hand, if you set the order as Allow Authors, then Deny All, Authors will be granted access and all other roles (including users who are not identified or not in a role) will be denied access to the page.

If you refresh the folder view in the Solution Explorer, you'll see that the WAT has created two new *web.config* files in the site's subfolders containing the rules you've just set.

Creating a Permission-Driven Site Map

The goal is to limit which parts of the SiteMap are displayed to the user based on the groups (or roles) of which the user is a member. To get started, create a site map as described earlier. Right-click the website root in the Solution Explorer and select Add New Item, and then choose SiteMap. Accept the default name, *Web.sitemap*, and copy the SiteMap shown in Example 13-9.

Example 13-9. Web.sitemap

```xml
<?xml version="1.0" encoding="utf-8" ?>
<siteMap xmlns="http://schemas.microsoft.com/AspNet/SiteMap-File-1.0" >
   <siteMapNode url="~/Welcome.aspx"
      title="Welcome"  description="Home">
      <siteMapNode url="~/CreateAccount.aspx"
         title="Create Account"  description="Create Account" />
      <siteMapNode url="~/ManageRoles.aspx"
         title="Manage Roles"  description="Manage Roles" />
      <siteMapNode url="~/Admins/AdminsOnly.aspx"
         title="Admins Only" description="Admins Only" />
      <siteMapNode url="~/Members/MembersOnly.aspx"
         title="Members Only" description="Members Only" />
      <siteMapNode url="~/Login.aspx"
         title="Login" description="Login"
         securityTrimmingEnabled="true" />
   </siteMapNode>
</siteMap>
```

At this point, you have three users, two roles, a default page, a login page, and a
SiteMap. You are all set to add security trimming to your SiteMap navigation so control
over which parts of the SiteMap are displayed will be determined by which role the user
is in.

Enabling Security Trimming

You cannot set security trimming programmatically—you set it in the configuration
for the site's site map provider. By default, security trimming is turned off for an
ASP.NET site, so you'll need to override the default settings laid out in the default
web.config with your own in *web.config*. Add the highlighted code in Example 13-10
to the `<system.web>` element.

Example 13-10. Switching on security trimming

```
<configuration>
    <system.web>
    ...
        <siteMap defaultProvider="XmlSiteMapProvider">
            <providers>
                <clear />
                <add name="XmlSiteMapProvider"
                    type="System.Web.XmlSiteMapProvider"
                    siteMapFile="Web.sitemap"
                    securityTrimmingEnabled="true" />
            </providers>
        </siteMap>
    ...
    </system.web>
</configuration>
```

You've put some pages into secured folders and established which roles should have
access to those folders. When you turn security trimming on, ASP.NET checks
whether the page is available to the current user, and if it isn't available, the page will
not be displayed in any representation of the site map.

You can see this by running the site and opening *Welcome.aspx*. Without being
logged on, the links to Admins Only and Members Only are not visible, as shown in
Figure 13-28.

Now log in as Dan. Dan is a member of both the Members and Admins roles, so
both links are now visible in *Welcome.aspx*, as shown in Figure 13-29.

If you log in as Jesse, you'll see that the Members Only link becomes visible but not
the Admins Only link, reflecting Jesse's membership of the Members role but not
Admins. Finally, if you log in as Jane, neither link will be visible, reflecting that she is
not a member of either role.

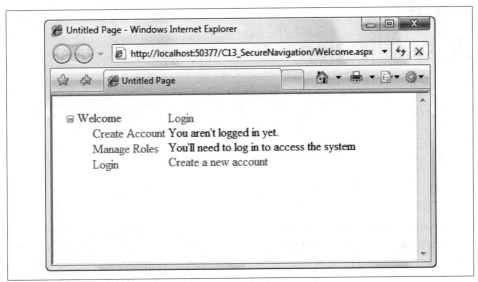

Figure 13-28. The TreeView is trimmed for anonymous users

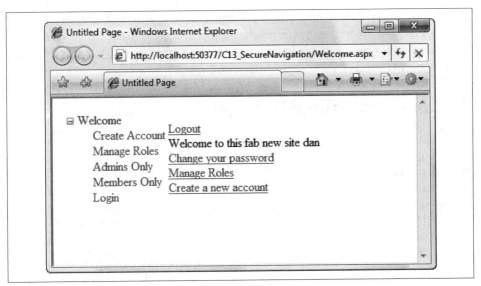

Figure 13-29. All options available to the right user

CHAPTER 14

Personalization

Most modern websites are designed for users to visit repeatedly, and therefore, they support some level of personalization: the ability to remember a user's preferences and, if appropriate, previous user choices. For example, in what color did the user prefer to see the site? In what language did he view the site? What are his name and email address?

In this chapter, you'll see how ASP.NET enables the creation of user profiles and how they are used to enable the personalization of a site. In particular, you'll see how to store different types of values in a user's profile and then how to use them to affect the design and layout of the site.

Creating Personalized Websites

The simplest form of personalization is to record information about the user and then to make that information available whenever the user logs on. This requires a kind of persistence that goes beyond session state. To create true personalization, you'll want to store the user's choices and information in a database that associates the saved information with a particular user, and persists indefinitely. Fortunately, ASP.NET provides all of the plumbing required. You do not need to design, edit, or manage the database tables; all of that is done for you.

You saw in Chapter 12 that by default, ASP.NET relies on a database to store the information for a site's users and the roles to which they belong. That same database is also used in part to support the personalization of a website in conjunction with some alterations to the site's *web.config* file. In this chapter, you'll use a copy of the site created in Chapter 12 as a basis for working with ASP.NET's profile provider.

 You can find instructions on how to generate the ASP.NET membership database for your website in "Setting Up Forms-Based Authentication" in Chapter 12.

So, then, to get started, copy the *C12_Security* website folder and all its contents to a new folder called *C14_Personalization*, and then open that website in Visual Studio 2008 (VS2008). Set *Welcome.aspx* as the start page and run the program to make sure you have a working duplicate.

 Profiles are related to specific users and not to the roles to which they are assigned. This site has three users, called Dan, Jane, and Jesse, with passwords Dan@123, Jane@123, and Jesse@123, respectively.

Configuring the Site for Profiles

Profiles must be set up in *web.config*. Unlike membership and roles, VS2008's Web Site Administration Tool (WAT) will not help you. (You can also use the ASP.NET section of Internet Information Services [IIS] 7.0 to make changes to *web.config* through dialogs if you prefer, but we'll leave that until Chapter 18 when we look at website configuration in more detail.)

If you created the tables in the default database (*ASPNETDB*) on `.\SQLEXPRESS`, as shown in Chapter 12, all you need to do in *web.config* is add the highlighted code in Example 14-1 to the `<system.web>` element.

Example 14-1. Enabling the default profile provider in web.config

```
<configuration>
    <system.web>
    ...
        <profile enabled="true">
            <properties>
                <add name="lastName" />
                <add name="firstName" />
                <add name="phoneNumber" />
                <add name="birthDate" type="System.DateTime" />
            </properties>
        </profile>
    ...
    </system.web>
</configuration>
```

This will enable the profile service and cause the Profile API to create storage for four pieces of information: `lastName`, `firstName`, `phoneNumber`, and `birthDate`. The default storage type is `string`. Notice, however, that you are storing the `birthdate` as a `DateTime` object.

 The `<properties>` element is mandatory for the `<profile>` element. It can be empty, but you have to include it.

This default configuration, like that for membership and roles, uses a provider defined in .NET's main config file, *machine.config*, which your website's *web.config* file may override if you so choose. You can find it in the *%windows%\Microsoft.NET\ Framework \v2.0.50727/CONFIG* folder. The relevant pieces of code are shown in Example 14-2.

Example 14-2. The default profile provider configuration in .NET

```
<configuration>
  <connectionStrings>
    <add name="LocalSqlServer"
      connectionString="data source=.\SQLEXPRESS;
        Integrated Security=SSPI;
        AttachDBFilename=|DataDirectory|aspnetdb.mdf;
        User Instance=true" providerName="System.Data.SqlClient"/>
  </connectionStrings>

  <system.web>
    <profile>
      <providers>
        <add name="AspNetSqlProfileProvider"
          connectionStringName="LocalSqlServer"
          applicationName="/"
          type="System.Web.Profile.SqlProfileProvider, System.Web,
            Version=2.0.0.0, Culture=neutral,
            PublicKeyToken=b03f5f7f11d50a3a"/>
      </providers>
    </profile>
  </system.web>
</configuration>
```

Because you did not specify which provider to use in Example 14-1, ASP.NET defaults to using AspNetSqlProfileProvider. If you're using a database other than the default one to store your membership and profile data, you'll need to override these defaults in your *web.config* file. Example 14-3 shows the code to override these defaults using a connection string called Membership running on an instance of SQL Server called sql2k5 on the web server.

Example 14-3. Overriding web.config with your profile database

```
<configuration>
  <connectionStrings>
    <clear />

    <add name="MembershipDB"
      connectionString="Data Source=(local)\sql2k5;
      Initial Catalog=Membership;Integrated Security=True;
      Application Name=C14"
      providerName="System.Data.SqlClient" />
  </connectionStrings>

  <system.web>
```

Example 14-3. Overriding web.config with your profile database (continued)

```
    <profile enabled="true">
      <providers>
        <remove name="AspNetSqlProfileProvider"/>
        <add name="AspNetSqlProfileProvider"
          connectionStringName="MembershipDB"
          applicationName="C14"
          type="System.Web.Profile.SqlProfileProvider, System.Web,
            Version=2.0.0.0, Culture=neutral,
            PublicKeyToken=b03f5f7f11d50a3a"/>
      </providers>
      <properties>
        <add name="lastName" />
        <add name="firstName" />
        <add name="phoneNumber" />
        <add name="birthDate" type="System.DateTime" />
      </properties>
    </profile>
  </system.web>
</configuration>
```

Alternatively, you could redefine the `LocalSqlServer` connection string or use a different name for your `ProfileProvider`. In the latter case, you'd also need to add a `defaultProvider` attribute to `<profile>`:

```
    <profile enabled="true" defaultProvider="myProfileProvider">
      <properties>
        ...
      </properties>
      <providers>
        <remove name="AspNetSqlProfileProvider"/>
        <add name="myProfileProvider" ... />
      </providers>
    </profile>
```

If you do use your own configuration, you can use the attributes listed in Table 14-1 to tweak the profile provider's properties as required.

Table 14-1. Properties for the <profile> element

Property	Default value	Description
enabled	true	Sets whether profiles are enabled.
defaultProvider	AspNetSql-ProfileProvider	Sets the name of the profile provider to be used.
inherits		Rather than specifying the properties for the profile in the config file, you can create a class inherited from `ProfileBase` which contains properties for the profile, and set `inherits` to the name of the class.
automaticSaveEnabled	true	Specifies whether the user profile is automatically saved at the end of the execution of an ASP.NET page.

Working with Profile Data

With your website configured to support the gathering of user profile data, a database to store that data ready and waiting, and the information to store in a user profile specified, all you need to do now is gather it. To keep the example simple, just add a new hyperlink to the LoggedInTemplate in *Welcome.aspx* to point to the page where it can be entered:

```
<asp:LoginView ID="LoginView1" runat="server">
    <LoggedInTemplate>
        Welcome to this fab new site
        <asp:LoginName ID="LoginName1" runat="server" />
        <br />
        <asp:HyperLink ID="HyperLink2" runat="server"
            NavigateUrl="~/ChangePW.aspx">
            Change your password</asp:HyperLink><br />
        <asp:HyperLink ID="HyperLink3" runat="server"
            NavigateUrl="~/ManageRoles.aspx">
            Manage Roles</asp:HyperLink><br />
        <asp:HyperLink ID="HyperLink4" runat="server"
            NavigateUrl="~/ProfileInfo.aspx">
            Add Profile Information</asp:HyperLink>
    </LoggedInTemplate>
    <AnonymousTemplate>
        You aren&#39;t logged in yet.<br />
        You&#39;ll need to log in to access the system
    </AnonymousTemplate>
</asp:LoginView>
```

As you can see, the link brings you to *ProfileInfo.aspx*, a page you should now add to the website. Add to the page an HTML table with two columns and five rows, and within it four TextBoxes, some descriptive text, and a Save button, as shown in Figure 14-1.

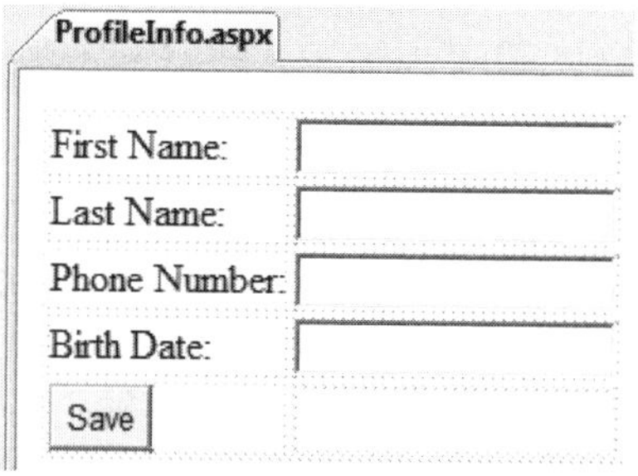

Figure 14-1. ProfileInfo.aspx in Design view

From top to bottom, the controls have the IDs txtFirstName, txtLastName, txtPhone, txtBirthDate, and btnSave. The full source for *ProfileInfo.aspx* is in Example 14-4.

Example 14-4. ProfileInfo.aspx in full

```
<%@ Page Language="C#" AutoEventWireup="true"
   CodeFile="ProfileInfo.aspx.cs" Inherits="ProfileInfo" %>

<!DOCTYPE html PUBLIC "-//W3C//DTD XHTML 1.0 Transitional//EN"
   "http://www.w3.org/TR/xhtml1/DTD/xhtml1-transitional.dtd">
<html xmlns="http://www.w3.org/1999/xhtml">
<head runat="server">
   <title>Profile Info Demo</title>
</head>

<body>
   <form id="form1" runat="server">
   <div>
      <table>
         <tr>
            <td>First Name:</td>
            <td><asp:TextBox ID="txtFirstName" runat="server" /></td>
         </tr>
         <tr>
            <td>Last Name:</td>
            <td><asp:TextBox ID="txtLastName" runat="server" /></td>
         </tr>
         <tr>
            <td>Phone Number:</td>
            <td><asp:TextBox ID="txtPhone" runat="server" /></td>
         </tr>
         <tr>
            <td>Birth Date:</td>
            <td><asp:TextBox ID="txtBirthDate" runat="server" /></td>
         </tr>
         <tr>
            <td>
               <asp:Button ID="btnSave" Text="Save" runat="server"
                  onClick="btnSave_Click" />
            </td>
            <td>
            </td>
         </tr>
      </table>
   </div>
   </form>
</body>
</html>
```

The eagle-eyed among you will note that the Click event for btnSave is handled. Double-click btnSave in Design view to generate the handler for its Click event if you haven't done so already, and add the code following this paragraph. You can also add some code to the Page_Load event to get initial values for the TextBoxes from the Profile object. By doing so, you make any profile information previously entered by a user available for editing rather than having the user enter everything from scratch again.

```
using System;
using System.Web.UI;

public partial class ProfileInfo : Page
{
    protected void Page_Load(object sender, EventArgs e)
    {
        if (!IsPostBack)
        {
            if (Profile.IsAnonymous == false)
            {
                txtLastName.Text = Profile.lastName;
                txtFirstName.Text = Profile.firstName;
                txtPhone.Text = Profile.phoneNumber;
                txtBirthDate.Text = Profile.birthDate.ToShortDateString( );
            }
        }
    }

    protected void btnSave_Click(object sender, EventArgs e)
    {
        if (Profile.IsAnonymous == false)
        {
            Profile.lastName = txtLastName.Text;
            Profile.firstName = txtFirstName.Text;
            Profile.phoneNumber = txtPhone.Text;
            DateTime birthDate = DateTime.Parse(txtBirthDate.Text);
            Profile.birthDate = birthDate;
        }
        Response.Redirect("Welcome.aspx");
    }
}
```

 If IntelliSense does not recognize the `Profile.lastName` field, leave the `if` statement empty, build the application, and try again. This will force VS2008 to reread the configuration file and generate a class that implements this field and the others listed in *web.config*. We'll discuss this class in more detail in "Inheriting Profile Properties," later in this chapter.

When you start the application, you are asked to log in. Once you're logged in, a new hyperlink appears: Add Profile Info. This was created by the hyperlink you added to the `LoggedInTemplate` (earlier). Clicking that link brings you to your new profile page.

The `Profile` object has properties that correspond to the properties you added in *web.config*. To test that the `Profile` object has stored this data, you want to add a panel to the bottom of the Welcome page just before the closing `</div>` tag:

```
<asp:Panel ID="pnlInfo" runat="server" Visible="False">
    <br />
    <table>
        <tr>
            <td>
                <asp:Label ID="lblFullName" runat="server"
                    Text="Full name unknown" /></td>
        </tr>
        <tr>
            <td>
                <asp:Label ID="lblPhone" runat="server"
                    Text="Phone number unknown" /></td>
        </tr>
        <tr>
            <td>
                <asp:Label ID="lblBirthDate" runat="server"
                    Text="Birthdate unknown" /></td>
        </tr>
    </table>
</asp:Panel>
```

The panel has a table with three rows, and each row has a Label initialized indicating the value is unknown (this is not normally needed, but it is included here to ensure the data you see was in fact retrieved from the Profile object). When the page is loaded, you check to see whether you have Profile data for this user and, if so, you assign that data to the appropriate controls.

To do so, implement Page_Load in *Welcome.aspx.cs*:

```
protected void Page_Load(object sender, EventArgs e)
{
    if (Profile.UserName != null && Profile.IsAnonymous == false)
    {
        pnlInfo.Visible = true;
        lblFullName.Text = Profile.firstName + " " + Profile.lastName;
        lblPhone.Text = Profile.phoneNumber;
        lblBirthDate.Text = Profile.birthDate.ToShortDateString();
    }
    else
    {
        pnlInfo.Visible = false;
    }
}
```

Run the application, log in, and click Add Profile Information. You will be brought to the Profile Information form, as shown in Figure 14-2.

When you click Save and return to the Welcome page, the Page_Load event fires, both parts of the if statement return true, that is, the UserName value is in the profile (and is not null), and the user is logged in and is not anonymous.

```
if (Profile.UserName != null && Profile.IsAnonymous == false)
```

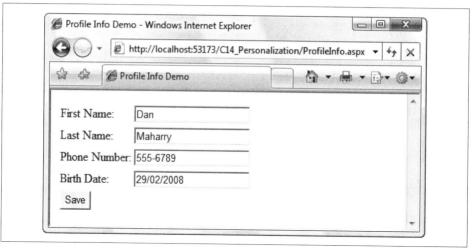

Figure 14-2. ProfileInfo.aspx in action

Your profile information is displayed, as shown in Figure 14-3.

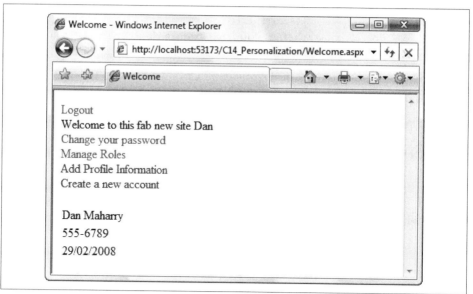

Figure 14-3. Saved profile information displayed in Welcome.aspx

Returning to the profile information page, you'll see that all the profile data is already in the text boxes ready for editing right where you left it in Figure 14-2.

The Page_Load handler in *ProfileInfo.aspx.cs* adds profile information to the TextBox controls only if the page has not posted back. This is because when the Save button is clicked and the page posts back, Page_Load runs first, overwriting any changes made on the screen before the Click handler saves the now overwritten changes back to the Profile. Try removing the check for IsPostBack from the Page_Load event and changing some profile data. You'll find that you can't do it. It's a subtle bug, but with an obvious effect.

So, how is a user's profile data stored in the database?

Exploring the Profile Tables

Open the Server Explorer window in VS2008 (or the Database Explorer if you're using Visual Web Developer) and look at the tables in your membership database. In turn, right-click on the following two tables and select Show Table Data from the menu:

- aspnet_Users (which lists all the users your security system knows about)
- aspnet_Profile (which lists the profile information for those users)

Right-click the tab for the window showing the aspnet_Users table and click New Horizontal Tab Group so you can compare both tables at the same time, as shown in Figure 14-4. The Users table shows you that each user has a unique UserID. The Profile table has a foreign key into that table (UserID) and lists the PropertyNames and PropertyValues, also in Figure 14-4.

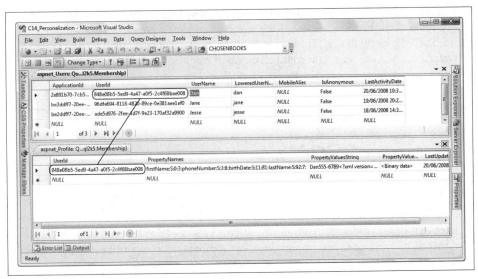

Figure 14-4. Comparing the Users and Profile tables

PropertyNames matches up with the entries you created in the <profile> section of *web.config*:

```
<profile>
   <properties>
      <add name="lastName" />
      <add name="firstName" />
      <add name="phoneNumber" />
      <add name="birthDate" type="System.DateTime"/>
   </properties>
</profile>
```

Each property is named (such as phoneNumber), and is given a type (S for string), a starting offset (phoneNumber begins at offset 3), and a length (phoneNumber's value has a length of 8). The offset and value are used to find the value within the PropertyValueString field; hence, the following value in the table:

```
firstName:S:0:3:phoneNumber:S:3:8:birthDate:S:11:81:lastName:S:92:7:
```

Note that birthDate is listed as a string that begins at offset 11 and is 81 characters long, but if you look at the propertyValuesString column, you'll find that the birth date is encoded as XML:

```
<?xml version="1.0" encoding="utf-16"?><dateTime>
2008-02-29T00:00:00</dateTime>
```

Profile Property Groups

If a user profile is going to contain many different properties, you might consider grouping them in the same way that a server control's properties are grouped in VS2008's Property dialog. To do this, add a <group> element under <properties> in *web.config*. For example, you could change *web.config* in *C14_Personalization* to read as follows:

```
<profile>
   <properties>
      <group name="PersonalInfo">
         <add name="lastName" />
         <add name="firstName" />
         <add name="phoneNumber" />
         <add name="birthDate" type="System.DateTime" />
      </group>
   </properties>
</profile>
```

Each of the four properties in the group can now be accessed as Profile.PersonalInfo.* rather than Profile.* to keep things clear—a trick that IntelliSense makes doubly useful.

Personalizing with Complex Types

Although personalizing a site for your users is terrific, you often need to store complex user-defined types (classes) or collections.

In the next exercise, you'll edit the *web.config* file to add a collection of strings called *favoriteBooks*. Doing so will allow the user to choose one or more books and have those choices stored in the user's profile.

Add a line to *web.config* for your new property:

```
<profile>
   <properties>
      <add name="lastName" />
      <add name="firstName" />
      <add name="phoneNumber" />
      <add name="birthDate" type="System.DateTime" />
      <add name="favoriteBooks"
         type="System.Collections.Specialized.StringCollection" />
   </properties>
</profile>
```

To see this collection at work, edit the page *ProfileInfo.aspx* and insert a row with a checkbox list just above the row with the Save button, as shown here:

```
... top of profileinfo.aspx
<tr>
   <td>
      Birth Date:
   </td>
   <td>
      <asp:TextBox ID="txtBirthDate" runat="server" />
   </td>
</tr>
<tr>
   <td>Books</td>
   <td>
      <asp:CheckBoxList ID="cblFavoriteBooks" runat="server">
         <asp:ListItem>Programming C# 3.5</asp:ListItem>
         <asp:ListItem>Programming ASP.NET</asp:ListItem>
         <asp:ListItem>Programming .NET Apps</asp:ListItem>
         <asp:ListItem>Programming Silverlight</asp:ListItem>
         <asp:ListItem>Object Oriented Design Heuristics
            </asp:ListItem>
         <asp:ListItem>Design Patterns</asp:ListItem>
      </asp:CheckBoxList>
   </td>
</tr>
```

```
      <tr>
         <td>
            <asp:Button ID="btnSave" Text="Save" runat="server"
                        OnClick="btnSave_Click" />
         </td>
         <td>
         </td>
      </tr>
      ... bottom of ProfileInfo.aspx
```

You'll also need to modify both the Page_Load and btnSave_Click handlers in
ProfileInfo.aspx.cs to add the selected books to the profile and show them preselected in
the list. The changes are shown in Example 14-5.

Example 14-5. ProfileInfo.aspx.cs modified to add a StringCollection value

```
using System;
using System.Web.UI;
using System.Web.UI.WebControls;
using System.Collections.Specialized;

public partial class ProfileInfo : Page
{
   protected void Page_Load(object sender, EventArgs e)
   {
      if (!IsPostBack)
      {
         if (Profile.IsAnonymous == false)
         {
            txtLastName.Text = Profile.lastName;
            txtFirstName.Text = Profile.firstName;
            txtPhone.Text = Profile.phoneNumber;
            txtBirthDate.Text = Profile.birthDate.ToShortDateString( );

            if (Profile.favoriteBooks != null)
            {
               foreach (ListItem li in cblFavoriteBooks.Items)
               {
                  foreach (string profileString
                           in Profile.favoriteBooks)
                  {
                     if (li.Text == profileString)
                     {
                        li.Selected = true;
                     }
                  }
               }
            }
         }
      }
   }
}
```

Example 14-5. ProfileInfo.aspx.cs modified to add a StringCollection value (continued)

```
protected void btnSave_Click(object sender, EventArgs e)
{
    if (Profile.IsAnonymous == false)
    {
        Profile.lastName = txtLastName.Text;
        Profile.firstName = txtFirstName.Text;
        Profile.phoneNumber = txtPhone.Text;
        DateTime birthDate = DateTime.Parse(txtBirthDate.Text);
        Profile.birthDate = birthDate;
        Profile.favoriteBooks = new StringCollection( );
        foreach (ListItem li in cblFavoriteBooks.Items)
        {
            if (li.Selected)
            {
                Profile.favoriteBooks.Add(li.Value.ToString( ));
            }
        }
    }
    Response.Redirect("Welcome.aspx");
}
```

 Each time you save the books, you create an instance of the string collection and then iterate through the checked listboxes, looking for the selected items. Each selected item is added to the StringCollection within the profile (the favoriteBooks property).

To confirm that this data has been stored, add a listbox (lbBooks) into the table displaying profile data in *Welcome.aspx*:

```
<tr>
    <td>
        <asp:ListBox ID="lbBooks" runat="server" />
    </td>
</tr>
```

Then update the Page_Load handler in *Welcome.aspx.cs* to reflect the chosen books in the profile:

```
protected void Page_Load(object sender, EventArgs e)
{
    if (Profile.UserName != null && Profile.IsAnonymous == false)
    {
        pnlInfo.Visible = true;
        lblFullName.Text = Profile.firstName + " " + Profile.lastName;
        lblPhone.Text = Profile.phoneNumber;
        lblBirthDate.Text = Profile.birthDate.ToShortDateString( );

        lbBooks.Items.Clear( );
        if (Profile.favoriteBooks != null)
```

```
        {
            foreach (string bookName in Profile.favoriteBooks)
            {
                lbBooks.Items.Add(bookName);
            }
        }
    }
    else
    {
        pnlInfo.Visible = false;
    }
}
```

Save all the changes and run the site. Once you've logged on, click Add Profile Information and you'll now be able to add books to your user's profile, as shown in Figure 14-5.

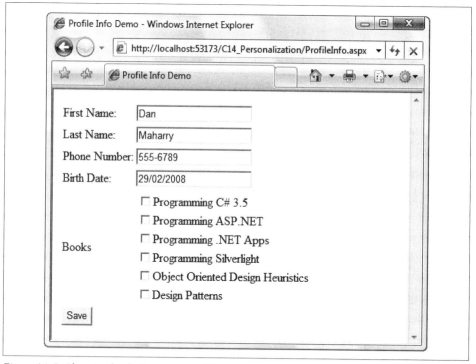

Figure 14-5. Choosing books for a user profile

Once you've chosen a couple, click Save and your choices will be reflected on the Welcome page through your profile, as shown in Figure 14-6.

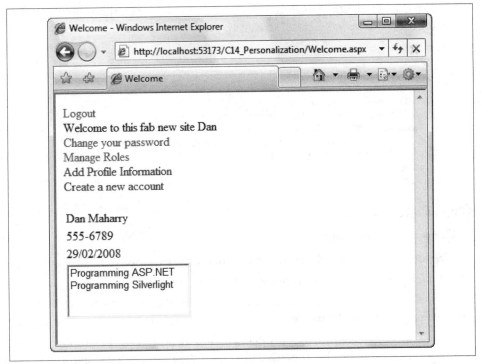

Figure 14-6. Showing the books saved to your profile

Anonymous Personalization

It is common to allow your users to personalize your site before identifying themselves. A classic example of this is Amazon.com, which lets you add books to your shopping cart *before* you log in (you need to log in only when you are ready to purchase what is in your cart).

ASP.NET supports the ability to link anonymous personalized data with a specific user's personalized data, once that user logs in (you don't want to lose what's in your cart when you do log in).

To demonstrate, you'll enable anonymous personalization in the *C14_ Personalization* website and allow browsers to select their favorite books before copying them to their profile when they log in.

A little more configuration

To enable anonymous personalization, you must update your *web.config* file, adding the following in the `<system.web>` section:

```
<anonymousIdentification enabled="true" />
```

You'll also need to identify which profile elements can be set by the anonymous user by adding the attribute-value pair `allowAnonymous="true"` to them:

```
<profile>
   <properties>
      <add name="lastName" />
      <add name="firstName" />
      <add name="phoneNumber" />
      <add name="birthDate" type="System.DateTime" />
      <add name="favoriteBooks"
           type="System.Collections.Specialized.StringCollection"
           allowAnonymous="true" />
   </properties>
</profile>
```

A little more code

You'll need to make changes to:

- *Welcome.aspx* to show the chosen books of the anonymous user
- *ProfileInfo.aspx* to allow the choice of books for the anonymous user
- *Global.asax* to migrate the choice of books from the anonymous profile into a user's profile when the user logs in

Redesign your *Welcome.aspx* page so the hyperlink that links to the profile information page and the `lbBooks` list is between the `LoginView` and the `Panel` control so that you can see the hyperlink and the list even if you are not logged in. While you are at it, rename Add Profile Info to Edit Profile Info, because you will be using this link to add, and edit, the profile info.

```
...
</asp:LoginView>
<asp:HyperLink ID="HyperLink1" runat="server"
   NavigateUrl="~/CreateAccount.aspx">
   Create a new account
</asp:HyperLink>
<br />
<asp:HyperLink ID="HyperLink4"
   runat="server" NavigateUrl="~/ProfileInfo.aspx">
   Edit Profile Information</asp:HyperLink>
<br />
<asp:ListBox ID="lbBooks" runat="server" />
<br />
<asp:HyperLink ID="HyperLink1" runat="server"
   NavigateUrl="~/CreateAccount.aspx">
   Create a new account</asp:HyperLink>
<asp:Panel ID="pnlInfo" runat="server" Visible="False">
...
```

You'll also need to change the `Page_Load` handler in *Welcome.aspx.cs* to display the list of books for the anonymous user:

```
protected void Page_Load(object sender, EventArgs e)
{
    if (Profile.UserName != null && Profile.IsAnonymous == false)
    {
        pnlInfo.Visible = true;
        lblFullName.Text = Profile.firstName + " " + Profile.lastName;
        lblPhone.Text = Profile.phoneNumber;
        lblBirthDate.Text = Profile.birthDate.ToShortDateString( );

        lbBooks.Items.Clear( );
    }
    else
    {
        pnlInfo.Visible = false;
    }

    if (Profile.favoriteBooks != null)
    {
        foreach (string bookName in Profile.favoriteBooks)
        {
            lbBooks.Items.Add(bookName);
        }
    }
}
```

Now to the profile information page; *ProfileInfo.aspx* currently assumes that a user has logged in, so all five pieces of information are available to edit. However, only favoriteBooks is set to be stored for an anonymous user, so you'll wrap the rest of the controls in a Panel control, as shown in Example 14-6, and use the Page_Load handler to hide it if the user isn't logged in.

Example 14-6. Modifying ProfileInfo.aspx for anonymous profile data

```
<%@ Page Language="C#" AutoEventWireup="true"
   CodeFile="ProfileInfo.aspx.cs" Inherits="ProfileInfo" %>

<!DOCTYPE html PUBLIC "-//W3C//DTD XHTML 1.0 Transitional//EN"
   "http://www.w3.org/TR/xhtml1/DTD/xhtml1-transitional.dtd">
<html xmlns="http://www.w3.org/1999/xhtml">
<head runat="server">
   <title>Profile Info Demo</title>
</head>

<body>
   <form id="form1" runat="server">
   <div>
     <asp:Panel ID="pnlNonAnonymousInfo" runat="server">
     <table>
       <tr>
          <td>First Name:</td>
          <td><asp:TextBox ID="txtFirstName" runat="server" />
          </td>
       </tr>
```

```
            <tr>
                <td>Last Name:</td>
                <td><asp:TextBox ID="txtLastName" runat="server" /></td>
            </tr>
            <tr>
                <td>Phone Number:</td>
                <td><asp:TextBox ID="txtPhone" runat="server" /></td>
            </tr>
            <tr>
                <td>Birth Date:</td>
                <td><asp:TextBox ID="txtBirthDate" runat="server" />
                </td>
            </tr>
        </table>
    </asp:Panel>
    <table>
        <tr>
            <td>Books</td>
            <td>
                <asp:CheckBoxList ID="cblFavoriteBooks"
                    runat="server" >
                    <asp:ListItem>Programming C# 3.5</asp:ListItem>
                    <asp:ListItem>Programming ASP.NET</asp:ListItem>
                    <asp:ListItem>Programming .NET Apps</asp:ListItem>
                    <asp:ListItem>Programming Silverlight</asp:ListItem>
                    <asp:ListItem>
                        Object Oriented Design Heuristics</asp:ListItem>
                    <asp:ListItem>Design Patterns</asp:ListItem>
                </asp:CheckBoxList>
            </td>
        </tr>
        <tr>
            <td>
                <asp:Button ID="btnSave" Text="Save" runat="server"
                    OnClick="btnSave_Click" />
            </td>
        </tr>
    </table>
    </div>
    </form>
</body>
</html>
```

When an anonymous user chooses books, that user will automatically be assigned a Globally Unique Identifier (GUID), and an entry will be made in the database. However, only those properties marked with allowAnonymous will be stored, so you must modify the btnSave_Click event handler in *ProfileInfo.aspx.cs* as well as Page_Load. In both cases, the alterations are mostly to ensure that the favoriteBooks property is saved and shown whether the user is anonymous or not, as shown in Example 14-7.

Example 14-7. Modifying ProfileInfo.aspx.cs to work with the anonymous user profile

```csharp
using System;
using System.Web.UI;
using System.Web.UI.WebControls;
using System.Collections.Specialized;

public partial class ProfileInfo : Page
{
    protected void Page_Load(object sender, EventArgs e)
    {
        if (!IsPostBack)
        {
            if (Profile.IsAnonymous == true)
            {
                pnlNonAnonymousInfo.Visible = false;
            }
            else
            {
                txtLastName.Text = Profile.lastName;
                txtFirstName.Text = Profile.firstName;
                txtPhone.Text = Profile.phoneNumber;
                txtBirthDate.Text = Profile.birthDate.ToShortDateString();
            }

            if (Profile.favoriteBooks != null)
            {
                foreach (string bookName in Profile.favoriteBooks)
                {
                    cblFavoriteBooks.Items.FindByText(bookName).Selected
                        = true;
                }
            }
        }
    }

    protected void btnSave_Click(object sender, EventArgs e)
    {
        if (Profile.IsAnonymous == false)
        {
            Profile.lastName = txtLastName.Text;
            Profile.firstName = txtFirstName.Text;
            Profile.phoneNumber = txtPhone.Text;
            DateTime birthDate = DateTime.Parse(txtBirthDate.Text);
            Profile.birthDate = birthDate;
        }

        Profile.favoriteBooks = new StringCollection();
        foreach (ListItem li in cblFavoriteBooks.Items)
        {
            if (li.Selected)
            {
                Profile.favoriteBooks.Add(li.Value.ToString());
            }
```

Example 14-7. Modifying ProfileInfo.aspx.cs to work with the anonymous user profile (continued)

```
        }
        Response.Redirect("Welcome.aspx");
    }
}
```

Run the application. Do *not* log in; click the Profile Info link. Select a few books and click Save. When you return to the Welcome page, you will still not be logged in, but your selected books will be displayed, as shown in Figure 14-7.

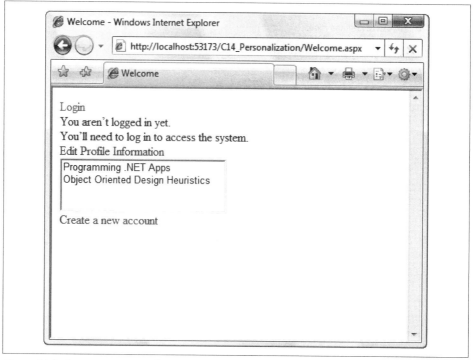

Figure 14-7. Anonymous user information

Stop the application and reopen the database. Open the `aspnet_Users` table and the `aspnet_Profile` tables. You'll see that an ID has been created for the anonymous user (and the `UserName` has been set to the GUID generated). In addition, the chosen books list has been stored in the corresponding record, as shown in Figure 14-8.

The GUID is also stored in a cookie on the user's machine so if the user leaves before logging in, his profile will be retained in the database for his return as long as he returns to the site without clearing all his cookies from the browser or before that particular cookie expires. By default, this cookie is named *.ASPXANONYMOUS*, but you can change this in your *web.config* file by adding to the `anonymousIdentification` element:

```
<anonymousIdentification enabled="true"
    cookieName=".C14_AnonymousCookieName"/>
```

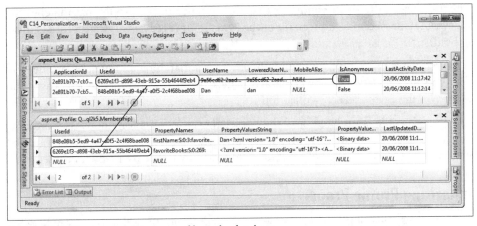

Figure 14-8. The anonymous user profile in the database

When the user returns to the site, the GUID in the cookie is sent on each request to the server so that the server can retrieve that user's anonymous profile. If the user logs in, you must migrate the profile data accumulated for the anonymous user to the appropriate authenticated user's record (so, for example, the user's favorite books are not lost). You do this by writing a handler for the global MigrateAnonymous event that is fired when a user logs in. This handler must be named Profile_MigrateAnonymous (case-sensitive) and is created within the script tags in *Global.asax*:

```
void Profile_MigrateAnonymous(object sender,
                              ProfileMigrateEventArgs e)
{
    ProfileCommon anonymousProfile = Profile.GetProfile(e.AnonymousID);

    if (anonymousProfile != null
                    && anonymousProfile.favoriteBooks != null)
    {
        // add anonymous user choices to named user profile
        foreach (string s in anonymousProfile. favoriteBooks)
        {
            Profile.favoriteBooks.Remove(s);  // Remove duplicates
            Profile.favoriteBooks.Add(s);
        }

        // Clear anonymous profile
        anonymousProfile.favoriteBooks.Clear( );
    }
}
```

 If your project does not have a *Global.asax* file, right-click the project and choose Add New Item. One of your choices will be Global Application Class, and it will default to the name *Global.asax*. Click Add.

The first step in the event handler is to get a reference to the profile that matches the AnonymousID passed in as a property of the ProfileMigrateEventArgs structure (shown in bold).

If the reference is not null, you will know there is a matching anonymous profile, and that you may pick up whatever data you need from that profile. In this case, you copy over the favoriteBooks collection.

The user's profile is updated, and the books chosen as an anonymous user are now part of that user's profile. To finish, the anonymous user profile is then cleared of chosen books as they have been migrated successfully to the user's own profile.

Inheriting Profile Properties

So, how does a list of profile properties in *web.config* get turned into a strongly typed set of properties? When you press F5, the ASP.NET compiler parses the <profile> element in *web.config* and auto-generates a class derived from System.Web.Profile. ProfileBase, which it saves in the Temporary ASP.NET Files directory. Each profile property has a corresponding C# property generated for it that looks like this:

```
public virtual string lastName {
  get {
    return ((string)(this.GetPropertyValue("lastName")));
  }
  set {
    this.SetPropertyValue("lastName", value);
  }
}
```

To see this for yourself, you can either seek out the generated file in *C:\Users\ <YourUserName>\AppData\Local\Temp\Temporary ASP.NET Files\c14_personalization* or set a breakpoint on any code-behind line involving a profile property and step into it (more on debugging in Chapter 19).

This is all well and good, but it would be nicer if you could influence how the values are stored in the properties. Indeed, you can by creating your own C# class inheriting from the ProfileBase class and tying that into your website's profile provider. For instance, Example 14-8 shows how to implement the five properties in the profile used in this chapter as a CustomProfile class. You'll need to save it in your website's *App_Code* directory.

Example 14-8. CustomProfile.cs

```
using System;
using System.Collections.Specialized;
using System.Web.Profile;

/// <summary>
/// Summary description for CustomProfile
/// </summary>
```

Example 14-8. CustomProfile.cs (continued)

```csharp
public class CustomProfile : ProfileBase
{
   public string lastName
   {
      get { return base["LastName"] as string; }
      set { base["LastName"] = value; }
   }

   public string firstName
   {
      get { return base["FirstName"] as string; }
      set { base["FirstName"] = value; }
   }

   public string phoneNumber
   {
      get { return base["PhoneNumber"] as string; }
      set { base["PhoneNumber"] = value; }
   }

   public DateTime birthDate
   {
      get { return (DateTime)(base["BirthDate"]); }
      set { base["BirthDate"] = value; }
   }

   [SettingsAllowAnonymous(true)]
   public StringCollection favoriteBooks
   {
      get { return base["FavoriteBooks"] as StringCollection; }
      set { base["FavoriteBooks"] = value; }
   }
}
```

To get your website to use this class rather than the class generated by the ASP.NET class, replace the <profile> element and its contents in *web.config* with this:

```
<profile inherits="CustomProfile" />
```

You'll now be able to run the website again using your own class as the backbone of the profile. This is useful if you want to add extra logic to the Profile properties. For example, you could make sure all first and last names have their first letter capitalized before saving them, or that a birth date is given a sensible value rather than 10,000 BC.

Note that if you've created your custom profile class outside the *App_Code* folder, you'll need to add its fully qualified name to the inherits property:

```
<profile inherits="Full.Namespace.CustomProfile" />
```

Saving Profile Properties

Whether you are working with the profile capabilities provided by ASP.NET, or a custom profile class such as the one in Example 14-8, the page a user is visiting will save all the profile values to the data store specified by the Profile provider at the end of its execution unless you tell it otherwise. For example, if most of the pages in your site don't use any profile information, you might consider the extra trips to the database as each page closes to be a waste of resources and prefer to save it to the database only when there's a chance of it having been changed.

If you do wish to save profile values manually, you'll need to set the automaticSaveEnabled property of the <profile> element in *web.config* to false:

```
<profile enabled="true"
    automaticSaveEnabled="false">
```

Once you've done this, you'll need to make sure to call Profile.Save( ) whenever you need to update profile properties. For example, in *ProfileInfo.aspx.cs*, you would add the call to the btnSave_Click method just before the redirect back to the Welcome page:

```
...
    foreach (ListItem li in cblFavoriteBooks.Items)
    {
        if (li.Selected)
        {
            Profile.favoriteBooks.Add(li.Value.ToString( ));
        }
    }
    Profile.Save( );
    Response.Redirect("Welcome.aspx");
}
```

Themes and Skins

Many users like to personalize their favorite websites by setting the look and feel of the site's controls to meet their own personal aesthetic preferences. ASP.NET 3.5 provides support for *themes* that enable you to offer that level of personalization to your users.

A theme is a collection of skins. A skin describes how a control should look. A skin can define stylesheet attributes, images, colors, and so forth.

Having multiple themes allows your users to choose how they want your site to look by switching from one set of skins to another at the touch of a button. Combined with personalization, your site can remember the look and feel your user prefers.

There are two types of themes:

- *Stylesheet themes* define styles that may be overridden by the page or control. These are, essentially, equivalent to CSS stylesheets.
- *Customization themes* define styles that cannot be overridden.

You set a stylesheet theme by adding the StyleSheetTheme attribute to the Page directive, and similarly, you set a customization theme by setting the Theme attribute in the Page directive.

 You can set the default theme for the entire website in *web.config* by adding the pages element to the system.web element within the configuration element, as follows:

```
<configuration>
    <system.web>
        <pages theme="Psychedelic" />
    </system.web>
</configuration>
```

Settings in the page will override those in *web.config*.

In any given page, the properties for the controls are set in this order:

1. Properties are applied first from a stylesheet theme.
2. Properties are then overridden based on properties set in the control.
3. Properties are then overridden based on a customization theme.

The customization theme is guaranteed to have the final word in determining the look and feel of the control.

Skins come in two flavors: default skins and explicitly named skins. Thus, you might create a Labels skin file with this declaration:

```
<asp:Label runat="server"
    ForeColor="Blue" Font-Size="Large"
    Font-Bold="True" Font-Italic="True" />
```

Or, more preferably and in line with web standards:

```
<asp:Label runat="server" CssClass="BlueLabel" />
```

This is a default skin for all Label controls. It looks like the definition of an asp:Label server control, but it is housed in a skin file and is used to define the look and feel of all Label objects.

In addition, however, you might decide that some labels must be red. To accomplish this, you create a second skin, but you assign this skin a SkinID property:

```
<asp:Label runat="server"
    SkinID="RedLabel"
/>
```

Any Label that does not have a SkinID attribute will receive the default skin; any Label that sets SkinID="RedLabel" will receive your named skin.

The steps to providing a personalized website are as follows:

1. Create the test site.
2. Organize your themes and skins.
3. Enable themes and skins for your site.
4. Specify themes declaratively if you wish.

Creating the Test Site

To demonstrate the use of themes and skins, you'll need some controls whose look and feel you can set. Open *Welcome.aspx* and add the following controls to the page, using the code shown in Example 14-9 (add this new code after the panel but before the closing <div>).

Example 14-9. Extra controls for Welcome.aspx to demonstrate skins

```
<table>
   <tr>
      <td>
         <asp:Label ID="lblListBox" runat="server" Text="ListBox" />
      </td>
      <td>
         <asp:ListBox ID="lbItems" runat="server">
            <asp:ListItem>First Item</asp:ListItem>
            <asp:ListItem>Second Item</asp:ListItem>
            <asp:ListItem>Third Item</asp:ListItem>
            <asp:ListItem>Fourth Item</asp:ListItem>
         </asp:ListBox>
      </td>
      <td>
         <asp:Label ID="lblRadioButtonList" runat="server"
            Text="Radio Button List" />
      </td>
      <td>
         <asp:RadioButtonList ID="RadioButtonList1" runat="server">
            <asp:ListItem>Radio Button 1</asp:ListItem>
            <asp:ListItem>Radio Button 2</asp:ListItem>
            <asp:ListItem>Radio Button 3</asp:ListItem>
            <asp:ListItem>Radio Button 4</asp:ListItem>
            <asp:ListItem>Radio Button 5</asp:ListItem>
            <asp:ListItem>Radio Button 6</asp:ListItem>
         </asp:RadioButtonList>
         <br />
      </td>
   </tr>
   <tr>
      <td>
         <asp:Label ID="lblCalendar" runat="server" Text="Calendar" />
      </td>
```

```
      <td>
         <asp:Calendar ID="Calendar1" runat="server" />
      </td>
      <td>
         <asp:Label ID="lblTextBox" runat="server" Text="TextBox" />
      </td>
      <td>
         <asp:TextBox ID="TextBox1" runat="server" />
      </td>
   </tr>
</table>
```

You will use skins to change the look and feel of these controls, and you will organize sets of skins into themes.

Organizing Site Themes and Skins

Themes are stored in your project in a folder named *App_Themes*. To create this folder, go to the Solution Explorer, right-click the project folder, and choose Add ASP.NET Folder → Theme. The folder *App_Themes* will be created automatically, with a theme folder under it. Name the new folder *DarkBlue*. Create a second theme folder by right-clicking the *App_Themes* folder and choosing Add ASP.NET Folder → Theme. Name it *Psychedelic*.

Right-click the *DarkBlue* theme folder and choose Add New Item. From the Templates list, choose Skin File and name it *Button.skin* (to hold all the button skins for your *DarkBlue* theme), as shown in Figure 14-9.

Each skin file is a text file that contains a definition for the control type but with no ID. For example, your *Button.skin* file might look like this (for the *DarkBlue* theme):

```
<asp:Button Runat="server"
    ForeColor="Blue" Font-Size="Large"
    Font-Bold="True" Font-Italic="True" />
```

Create skin files for each of the following types in both themes:

- *Button.skin*
- *Calendar.skin*
- *Label.skin*
- *ListBox.skin*
- *RadioButton.skin*
- *Text.skin*

At this point, your solution should look more or less like Figure 14-10.

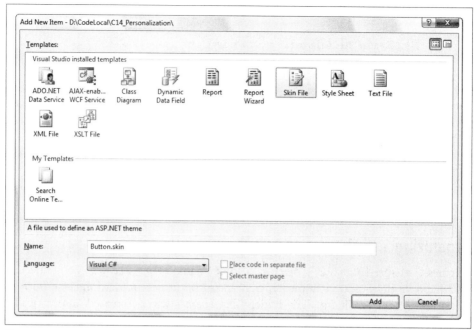

Figure 14-9. Creating the skin file

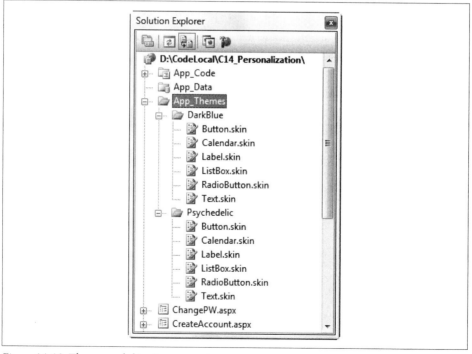

Figure 14-10. Themes and skins in your project

Enabling Themes and Skins

To let your users choose the theme they like and have it stored in their profile, you need to add a single line to the <properties> element in the <profile> element of *web.config*:

```
<add name="theme" />
```

Save and rebuild your application to make sure the class implementing the profile is set properly.

Specifying Themes for Your Page

You can set the themes on your page declaratively or programmatically. To set a theme declaratively, add the Theme attribute to the Page directive. For example:

```
<%@ Page Language="C#" AutoEventWireup="true"
    CodeFile="Welcome.aspx.cs" Inherits="Welcome"
    Theme="DarkBlue"%>
```

This will set the theme for *Welcome.aspx* to the *DarkBlue* theme you've created.

You can set the theme programmatically by hardcoding it, or (even better) by setting it from the user's profile.

Setting Stylesheet Themes

You set stylesheet themes by overriding the StyleSheetTheme property for the page. IntelliSense will help you with this. Open *Welcome.aspx.cs*, and scroll to the bottom of the class. Type the words **public override** and all the members you can override are shown. Start typing **sty** and IntelliSense will scroll to the property you want, StyleSheetTheme, as shown in Figure 14-11.

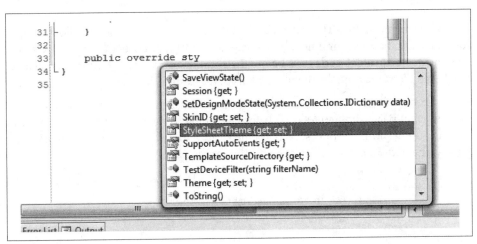

Figure 14-11. Overriding the stylesheet theme

Once IntelliSense finds the method you want, press the Tab key to accept that property. Fill in the accessors as follows:

```
public override string StyleSheetTheme
{
  get
  {
    if ((!Profile.IsAnonymous) && Profile.Theme != null)
    {
      return Profile.Theme;
    }
    else
    {
      return "DarkBlue";
    }
  }
  set
  {
    Profile.Theme = value;
  }
}
```

Setting Customization Themes

If you are going to set a customization theme programmatically, you must do so from the PreInit event handler for the page because the theme must be set before the controls are created.

```
protected void Page_PreInit(object sender, EventArgs e)
{
  if (!Profile.IsAnonymous)
  {
    Page.Theme = Profile.Theme;
  }
}
```

Setting the theme in PreInit creates a bit of a difficulty when you want to allow the user to change the theme at runtime. If you create a control that posts the page back with a new theme, the PreInit code runs before the event handler for the button that changes the theme, so by the time the theme is changed, the buttons have already been drawn.

To overcome this you must either refresh the page or, as in this example, set the theme on a different page (*ProfileInfo.aspx*) before returning to the page (*Welcome.aspx*) with the call to Page_PreInit that sets its theme. Add two buttons to the *ProfileInfo.aspx* page at the bottom of the table at the bottom of the page:

```
<tr>
    <td>
        <asp:Button ID="ThemeBlue" Text="DarkBlue"
          Runat="server" OnClick="Set_Theme" />
    </td>
```

```
<td>
    <asp:Button ID="ThemePsych" Text="Psychedelic"
        Runat="server" OnClick="Set_Theme" />
</td>
</tr>
```

The two buttons share a single Click event handler. An easy way to have VS2008 set up that event handler for you is to switch to Design view and click one of the buttons. Click the lightning bolt in the Properties window to go to the events, and double-click the Set_Theme event handler. You are ready to implement the event handler. You'll cast the sender to Button and check its text, setting the theme appropriately:

```
protected void Set_Theme(object sender, EventArgs e)
{
    Button btn = (Button)sender;
    if (btn.Text == "Psychedelic")
    {
        Profile.Theme = "Psychedelic";
    }
    else
    {
        Profile.Theme = "DarkBlue";
    }
}
```

When the user is not logged on, the page's default theme will be used. Once the user sets a theme in the profile, that theme will be used. Create skins for your two themes and run the application to see the effect of applying the themes.

Alternatively, you can use the skins included with the copy of this chapter's website in the code download for this book.

Using Named Skins

You can override the theme for particular controls by using named skins. For example, you can set the lblRadioButtonList label in *Welcome.aspx* to be red even in the *DarkBlue* theme, by using a named skin. To accomplish this, create two Label skins in the *Label.skin* file within the *DarkBlue* folder:

```
<asp:Label Runat="server"
    ForeColor="Blue" Font-Size="Large"
    Font-Bold="True" Font-Italic="True" />

<asp:Label Runat="server"
    SkinID="Red"
    ForeColor="Red" Font-Size="Large"
    Font-Bold="True" Font-Italic="True" />
```

The first skin is the default, and the second is a named skin because it has a SkinID property set to Red. Open the source for *Welcome.aspx*, find the label you want to make red, and add the attribute SkinID="Red", as shown in the following code snippet:

```
<asp:Label ID="lblRadioButtonList" Runat="server"
    Text="Radio Button List"
    SkinID="Red"/>
```

When you log in and set your theme to *DarkBlue*, you'll find that the label for the RadioButtonList is Red (honest!), as shown in Figure 14-12.

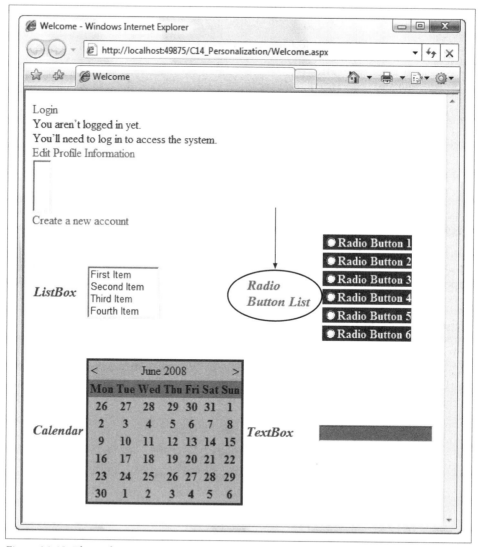

Figure 14-12. The RadioButtonList's label is red (honest)

Web Parts

Web parts allow your users to reconfigure sections of your site to meet their own needs and preferences. Many information providers allow users to pick which content they want displayed and in which column to display it. Web parts allow you to provide that functionality with drag and drop "parts" of your page.

Web Parts Architecture

Web parts are created and managed on top of personalization using a structural component, called the WebPartManager control, to manage the interaction of web parts and UI controls to create user-managed interfaces.

Every web part page has a WebPartManager control. This invisible control tracks all the individual web part controls and manages the web part zones (described shortly). It also tracks the different display modes of the page, and whether personalization of your web part page applies to a particular user or to all users.

You'll need to make sure the WebPartManager is placed at the top of the page. ASP.NET will throw an error if you run this page and the WebPartManager is declared lower in the source than any of the web parts that it is managing: between the form and div tags at the top of the page should be fine. For example:

```
<body>
    <form id="form1" runat="server">
        <asp:WebPartManager ID="WebPartManager1" runat="server" />
        <div>
            ... rest of page ...
```

The WebPartManager uses another ASP.NET provider, this time the AspNetSqlPersonalizationProvider, to store the current location of the contents in the web parts in your database. Like the providers for users, roles, and profiles, this one also has a default configuration defined, although this time, you'll find it in the global *web.config* file rather than in *machine.config* in *%windows%\Microsoft.NET\Framework\v2.0.50727/CONFIG*. The relevant pieces of code are shown in Example 14-10.

Example 14-10. The default personalization provider configuration

```
<configuration>
  <connectionStrings>
    <add name="LocalSqlServer"
      connectionString="data source=.\SQLEXPRESS;
        Integrated Security=SSPI;
        AttachDBFilename=|DataDirectory|aspnetdb.mdf;
        User Instance=true" providerName="System.Data.SqlClient"/>
  </connectionStrings>

  ...
```

Example 14-10. The default personalization provider configuration (continued)

```
  <system.web>
    <webParts>
      <personalization>
        <providers>
          <add connectionStringName="LocalSqlServer"
            name="AspNetSqlPersonalizationProvider"
            type="System.Web.UI.WebControls.WebParts.
                    SqlPersonalizationProvider,
                  System.Web, Version=2.0.0.0, Culture=neutral,
                  PublicKeyToken=b03f5f7f11d50a3a"/>
        </providers>
      </personalization>
    </webParts>
  </system.web>
</configuration>
```

Because you did not specify which provider to use in your site's *web.config* file, ASP.NET uses the defaults. If you're using something other than the default SQL Express-based database to store your membership and profile data, you'll need to override these defaults in your site's *web.config* file. Example 14-11 shows the code to override these defaults using a connection string called `MembershipDB`.

Example 14-11. Overriding web.config with your personalization database

```
<configuration>
  ...
  <webParts>
    <personalization defaultProvider="LocalPersonalizationProvider">
      <providers>
        <clear />
        <add name="LocalPersonalizationProvider"
          connectionStringName="MembershipDB" applicationName="C14"
            type="System.Web.UI.WebControls.WebParts.
                    SqlPersonalizationProvider,
                  System.Web, Version=2.0.0.0, Culture=neutral,
                  PublicKeyToken=b03f5f7f11d50a3a"/>
      </providers>
    </personalization>
  </webParts>
  ...
</configuration>
```

Or, as noted before, simply define your own connection string called `LocalSqlServer` and this will have the same effect:

```
<connectionStrings>
  <clear/>
  <add name="LocalSqlServer"
    connectionString="<your_connection_string>"
    providerName="System.Data.SqlClient"/>
</connectionStrings>
```

With your changes to *web.config* in place, you can start building a page that uses web parts.

Creating Zones

A page that uses web parts is divided into *zones*: areas of the page that can contain content and controls that derive from the Part class (Part controls). They can contain consistent UI elements (header and footer styles, border styles, etc.) known as the *chrome* of the control.

To see a simple example of web parts at work, follow these steps:

1. Create a new page called *WebParts.aspx*.

2. Open the WebParts section of your Toolbox and drag a WebPartManager onto your page. The job of the WebPartManager is to track and coordinate all the web part controls on the page. It will not be visible when the page is running.

3. Add a new table, made up of two rows and three columns. Rearrange the columns so that they are not of even size.

4. Drag a WebPartZone into each of the six table cells. Each WebPartZone will have a default name (such as WebPartZone6) and a default heading. You can modify either or both of these properties in the Properties window, as shown in Figure 14-13.

5. Set the HeaderText property for WebPartZone1 to News.

Adding Controls to Zones

Drag a Label control into WebPartZone1. The Label is wrapped in a GenericWebPart control, and its title is set to Untitled, as shown in Figure 14-14.

Switch to Source view and change the Title property of the label to "Today's News" and the text to the following:

```
<br/>
Penguin Classics releases new translation of "In Search of Lost Time".
```

 Title is not normally a property of the Label control and will not show up in the Properties window or IntelliSense. However, when you add it to a WebPartZone, it is wrapped, at runtime, in a GenericWebPart control that does recognize this property.

Switch back to Design view and drag a ListBox control into the top-right WebPartZone control. Set the header text for the WebPartZone to "Our Sponsors". Click the ListBox and then its smart tag and Edit Items to open the ListItems Collection Editor. Add a few items to the listbox. Back in Source view set the ListBox's Title property to "Our Sponsors". (This control, like the Label control, does not inherently have a Title property, so IntelliSense will complain; as the earlier note explains, all will be well.)

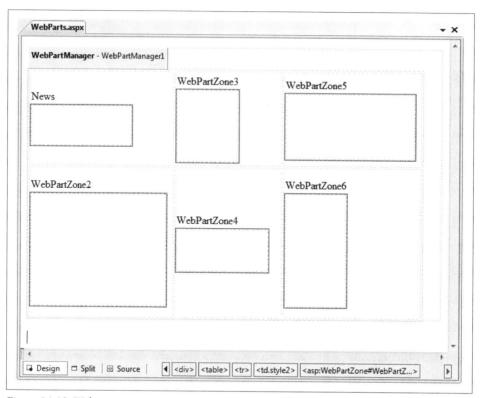

Figure 14-13. Web part zones

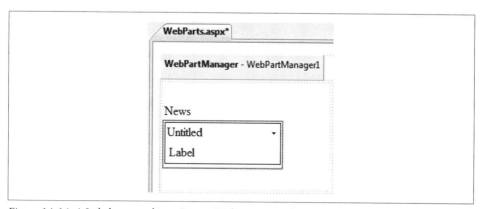

Figure 14-14. A Label wrapped in a GenericWebPart control

Finally, add a hyperlink to *Welcome.aspx* pointing to *WebParts.aspx* so that you can access the page. Now run the site and log in. Click the link to the web part page which you added to *Welcome.aspx*. You should see two web parts, complete with Minimize and Close commands, as shown in Figure 14-15.

If you don't log in, the web parts will not have the Minimize and Close commands.

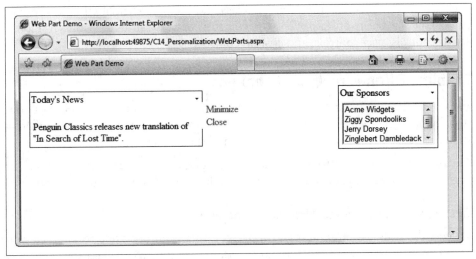

Figure 14-15. Two web parts visible in their zones

Minimizing and Restoring

Click the Minimize tag and a menu appears allowing you to minimize or close the web part, as just shown in Figure 14-15.

If you choose Minimize, the web part will be minimized to its title, and the minimize tag will offer a choice of Restore or Close, as shown in Figure 14-16.

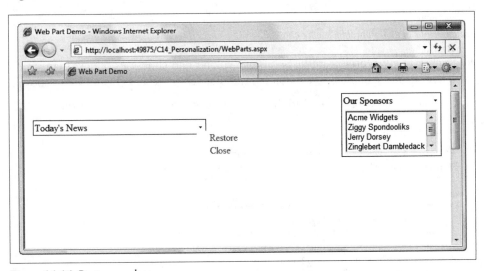

Figure 14-16. Restore or close

Exit the application. Restart, sign back in, and navigate to these pages. Aha! The minimized zone remains minimized. The individual's personalized web parts are automatically persisted through the personalization database.

Web part controls derive from the Part class and are the essential UI of a web part page. You can create custom web part controls, or you can use existing ASP.NET server controls, user controls, and custom controls.

Enabling Editing and Layout Changes

Web parts provide users with the ability to change the layout of the web part controls by dragging them from zone to zone. You may also allow your users to modify the appearance of the controls, their layout, and their behavior.

The built-in web part control set provides basic editing of any web part control on the page. You can create custom editor controls that let users do more extensive editing.

Creating a user control to enable changing page layout

To edit the contents of zones or to move controls from one zone to another, you need to be able to enter Design and Edit mode. To do this, you will create a new user control called DisplayModeMenu.ascx (see Chapter 15 for information on creating user controls), which will allow the user to change modes among Browse, Design, and Edit, as shown in Figure 14-17.

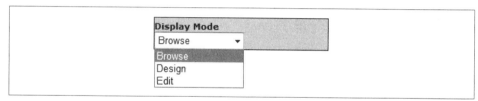

Figure 14-17. The DisplayMode user control

Right-click the web project in the Solution Explorer and choose Add New Item. Select Web User Control; name the new user control DisplayModeMenu, as Figure 14-18 shows.

Add the code in Example 14-12 to the content file of your new user control.

Example 14-12. DisplayMode.aspx in full

```
<%@ Control Language="C#" AutoEventWireup="true"
   CodeFile="DisplayModeMenu.ascx.cs" Inherits="DisplayModeMenu" %>

<div>
   <asp:Panel ID="Panel1" runat="server" BorderWidth="1"
      Width="230" BackColor="lightgray"
      Font-Names="Verdana, Arial, Sans Serif">
      <asp:Label ID="Label1" runat="server" Text="Display Mode"
         Font-Bold="true" Font-Size="8" Width="120" />
      <asp:DropDownList ID="ddlDisplayMode" runat="server"
         AutoPostBack="true" EnableViewState="false" Width="120"
         OnSelectedIndexChanged="ddlDisplayMode_SelectedIndexChanged" />
   </asp:Panel>
</div>
```

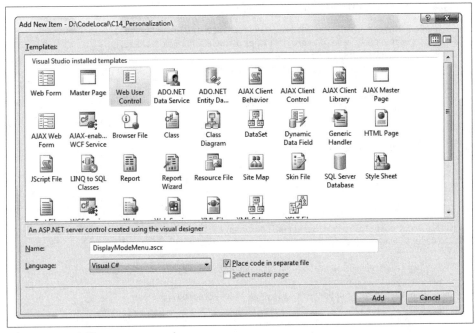

Figure 14-18. Adding a user control

This code creates a panel, and within that panel it adds a single drop-down list (ddlDisplayMode). It sets the event handler for when the Selected item changes in the drop-down list. To support this page, open the code-behind file (*DisplayModeMenu.ascx.cs*) and add the code shown in Example 14-13.

Example 14-13. DisplayModeMenu.aspx.cs

```csharp
using System;
using System.Web.UI;
using System.Web.UI.WebControls;
using System.Web.UI.WebControls.WebParts;

public partial class DisplayModeMenu : UserControl
{

    // will reference the current WebPartManager control.
    WebPartManager webPartManager;

    public void Page_Init(object sender, EventArgs e)
    {
        Page.InitComplete += new EventHandler(InitComplete);
    }

    // when the page is fully initialized
    public void InitComplete(object sender, EventArgs e)
    {
```

Example 14-13. DisplayModeMenu.aspx.cs (continued)

```
        webPartManager = WebPartManager.GetCurrentWebPartManager(Page);
        String browseModeName = WebPartManager.BrowseDisplayMode.Name;
        foreach (WebPartDisplayMode mode in
                webPartManager.SupportedDisplayModes)
        {
            String modeName = mode.Name;
            if (mode.IsEnabled(webPartManager))
            {
                ListItem listItem = new ListItem(modeName, modeName);
                ddlDisplayMode.Items.Add(listItem);
            }
        }
    }

    // Change the page to the selected display mode.
    public void ddlDisplayMode_SelectedIndexChanged
        (object sender, EventArgs e)
    {
        String selectedMode = ddlDisplayMode.SelectedValue;
        WebPartDisplayMode mode =
            webPartManager.SupportedDisplayModes[selectedMode];
        if (mode != null)
        {
            webPartManager.DisplayMode = mode;
        }
    }

    // Set the selected item equal to the current display mode.
    public void Page_PreRender(object sender, EventArgs e)
    {
        ListItemCollection items = ddlDisplayMode.Items;
        int selectedIndex =
            items.IndexOf(items.FindByText(
                            webPartManager.DisplayMode.Name));
        ddlDisplayMode.SelectedIndex = selectedIndex;
    }
}
```

Now open *WebParts.aspx*, and in Design mode make a space between the WebPartManager and the table of zones. Drag the *DisplayModeMenu.ascx* file from the Solution Explorer into that space. Change to Source view. VS2008 has done two things for you. First, it has registered the new control:

```
<%@ Register src="DisplayModeMenu.ascx"
    tagname="DisplayModeMenu" tagprefix="uc1" %>
```

Second, it has placed the control into the form:

```
<form id="form1" runat="server">
    <asp:WebPartManager ID="WebPartManager1" runat="server" />
    <uc1:DisplayModeMenu ID="DisplayModeMenu1" runat="server" />
    <div>
        ...
```

Before testing this, drag an `EditorZone` control onto the page underneath the table (currently unoccupied) and drag an `AppearanceEditorPart` and a `LayoutEditorPart` onto the `EditorZone`: you'll need to drop it onto the TextBox-like area above the OK, Cancel, and Apply zones, as shown in Figure 14-19.

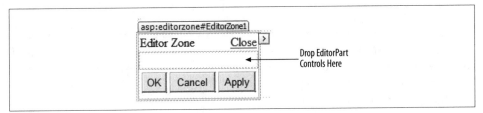

Figure 14-19. An empty EditorZone control

To make the `EditorZone` stand out, click its smart tag and choose AutoFormat and then Professional. Your `EditorZone` control should now look more or less like Figure 14-20.

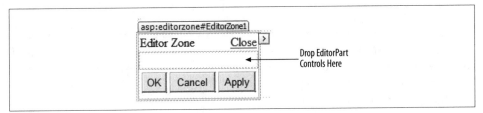

Figure 14-20. A formatted EditorZone control

WebPartZones may not be nested inside a WebPart.

Moving a part

Run the application. When you log in and go to the web part page, you are in Browse mode. Use the Display mode drop down to switch to Design mode and all the zones (except the editing zone) appear. You can click any web part (e.g., Our Sponsors) and drag it to any zone. Pressing the Alt key while dragging will animate this dragging, as shown in Figure 14-21.

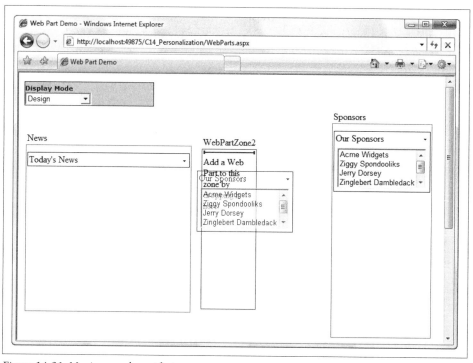

Figure 14-21. Moving a web part between zones

Next, change the drop down to Edit mode. Nothing much happens, but click the drop-down tag on one of the web part controls. A menu appears that now includes Edit, as shown in Figure 14-22.

Click Edit and the `EditorZone` appears, allowing you to edit the current web part, as shown in Figure 14-23.

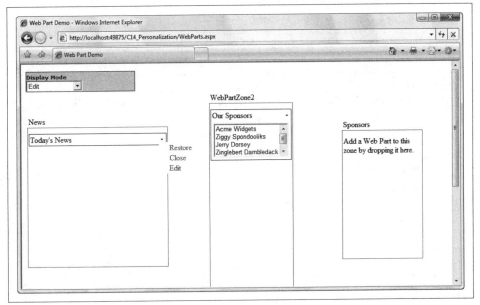

Figure 14-22. A new edit option in web part Edit mode

The Appearance Editor lets you change the title and look of the web part, and the Layout lets you change, among other things, in which zone the WebPart will appear.

Adding Parts from a Catalog

You may want to provide a catalog of web parts from which your users can add to the various zones. To do so, open *WebParts.aspx* in Source view, and delete the bottom-left WebPartZone control. The table cell that contained it should now be empty. Switch to Design view and drag a CatalogZone control into the newly empty cell. Click the zone, and in the Properties window set the HeaderText property to CatalogZone if it isn't already. Drag a DeclarativeCatalogPart control into the zone, as shown in Figure 14-24.

Click the smart tag on the DeclarativeCatalogPart and select Edit Templates. From the Standard tab of the Toolbox drag on a Calendar and a FileUpload control into the WebPartsTemplate, as shown in Figure 14-25. This is the only template for the DeclarativeCatalogPart.

Before you run your program, switch to Source view and find the CatalogZone you added. Within the <WebPartsTemplate> element, add a Title attribute to both the Calendar and the FileUpload controls, as shown in Example 14-14. (Again, Intelli-Sense will not like this attribute, but be strong and do it anyway.)

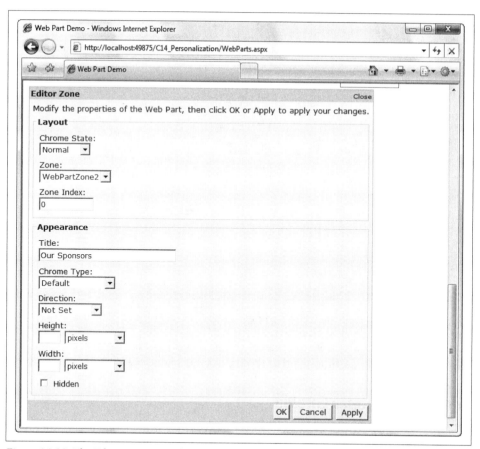

Figure 14-23. The EditorZone control in action

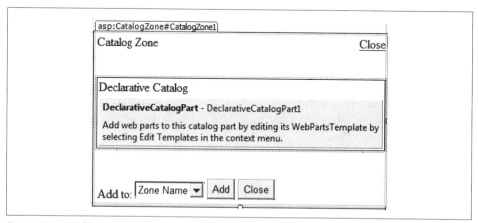

Figure 14-24. Adding a DeclarativeCatalogPart control

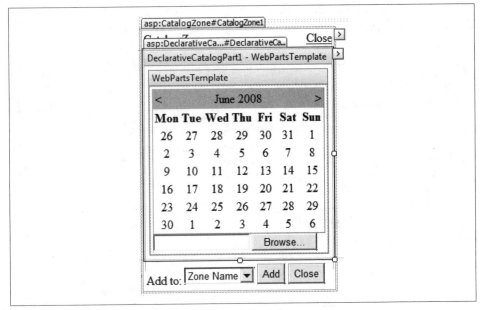

Figure 14-25. Dragging controls into the WebPartsTemplate

Example 14-14. Adding titles in the CatalogZone

```
<asp:CatalogZone ID="CatalogZone1" runat="server">
 <ZoneTemplate>
    <asp:DeclarativeCatalogPart
       ID="DeclarativeCatalogPart1" runat="server">
       <WebPartsTemplate>
          <asp:Calendar ID="Calendar1" runat="server"
             Title="Calendar" />
          <asp:FileUpload ID="FileUpload1" runat="server"
             Title="Upload Files" />
       </WebPartsTemplate>
    </asp:DeclarativeCatalogPart>
 </ZoneTemplate>
</asp:CatalogZone>
```

Save and run the application. Log in and switch to *WebParts.aspx*. You'll see that the Catalog mode has been added automatically to the Display Mode drop-down menu, as shown in Figure 14-26.

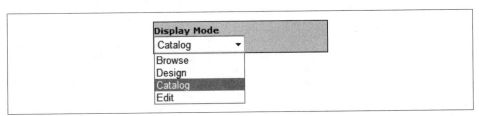

Figure 14-26. Catalog mode now available in the menu

When you select Catalog, the catalog zone will be exposed. You may select one of the controls and decide which zone to place it in, as shown in Figure 14-27.

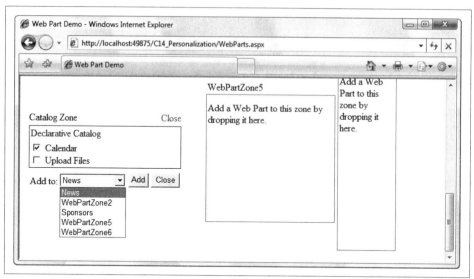

Figure 14-27. Adding a control from the catalog

Once you've picked your control and the zone to which to add it, click Add and the control instantly appears in the designated zone.

Web parts are the building blocks (along with personalization, themes, and skins) for the next generation of web applications, in which the user (rather than the designer) decides how the site appears and which information is given prominence.

CHAPTER 15

Custom and User Controls

This chapter looks at controls which you, the developer, will create for your websites. They can be divided into two main categories: *custom controls* and *user controls*.

User controls are segments of ASP.NET pages that can be reused from within other pages. This is similar to "include files" familiar to ASP developers. However, user controls are far more powerful. User controls support properties and events and, thus, provide reusable functionality as well as reusable HTML.

Custom controls are compiled controls that act, from the client's perspective, much like ASP.NET controls. You can create custom controls in one of three ways:

- By deriving a new custom control from an existing control (e.g., deriving your own specialized text box from asp:TextBox). This is known as a *derived custom control*.

- By composing a new custom control out of two or more existing controls. This is known as a *composite custom control*.

- By deriving from the base control class, thus creating a new custom control from scratch. This is known as a *full custom control*.

All three of these methods, and the three control types that correspond to them, are variations on the same theme.

 Strictly speaking, user controls are a subset of custom controls, with the emphasis on ease of creation as you'll see in the next section.

User Controls

User controls allow you to save a part of an existing ASP.NET page and reuse it in many other ASP.NET pages. A user control is almost identical to a normal *.aspx* page, with the following differences:

- User controls have an *.ascx* extension rather than an *.aspx* extension.
- User controls may not have <html>, <body>, or <form> tags.
- User controls have a Control directive rather than a Page directive.

The simplest user control is one that displays only HTML. A classic example of a simple user control is an HTML page that displays a copyright notice.

 User controls were originally called *pagelets*, which we think is more descriptive; alas, Microsoft has elected to call them user controls and so shall we. When you see the term *user control*, think this: *a bit of a content page that can be reused in other content pages.*

Visual Studio 2008 (VS2008) provides support for creating user controls. To see this at work, create a new website named *C15_UserControls*. Right-click the *website* folder in the Solution Explorer and choose Add New Item to bring up the Add New Item dialog box. Select Web User Control and give it the name *Copyright.ascx*.

This choice opens the new file in Source view. Initially, the file contains only a Control directive:

```
<%@ Control Language="C#" AutoEventWireup="true"
    CodeFile="Copyright.ascx.cs" Inherits="Copyright" %>
```

This directive, similar to the Page directive described in Chapter 6, sets the language, the name of the code-behind file, the class, and so on.

Copy the following code into the new *.ascx* file below the Control directive:

```
<table>
    <tr>
        <td align="center">
            Copyright &copy;2008 O'Reilly Inc.
        </td>
    </tr>
    <tr>
        <td align="center">
            Support at http://www.ora.com and http://www.hmobius.com
        </td>
    </tr>
</table>
```

You can now add this user control to any number of pages. You'll begin by returning to *Default.aspx* and adding a couple of server controls to the page. Drag a Label control onto the page and set its Text property to "Hello". Drag a Button control onto the page and set its Text property to Change. Double-click the button in Design view to go to its default event handler and enter the following line of code:

```
Label1.Text = "Changed!";
```

Default.aspx now has a label and a button, but we want to add the copyright. You can reuse the copyright user control by adding two lines to *Default.aspx*: the Register directive for the user control and an instance of the user control itself.

Switch to Source view and, at the top of the *Default.aspx* file, add the following Register directive immediately after the Page directive:

```
<%@ Register src="Copyright.ascx"
    tagname="Copyright" tagprefix="OReilly" %>
```

The Register directive establishes your tagprefix (OReilly) and the tagname of your user control (Copyright) so that the control can be uniquely defined on the page. Compare this to the Label control, where its tagprefix is asp and its tagname is Label.

You can add an instance of your user control like any other control. The complete source for the content file for *Default.aspx* is shown in Example 15-1, which highlights the Register directive and user control.

Example 15-1. Default.aspx in full

```
<%@ Page Language="C#" AutoEventWireup="true"
    CodeFile="Default.aspx.cs" Inherits="_Default" %>

<%@ Register src="Copyright.ascx"
    tagname="Copyright" tagprefix="OReilly" %>

<!DOCTYPE html PUBLIC "-//W3C//DTD XHTML 1.0 Transitional//EN"
    "http://www.w3.org/TR/xhtml1/DTD/xhtml1-transitional.dtd">

<html xmlns="http://www.w3.org/1999/xhtml">
<head runat="server">
    <title>User Controls Demo</title>
</head>

<body>
    <form id="form1" runat="server">
    <div>
        <asp:Label ID="Label1" runat="server" Text="Hello" />
        <asp:Button ID="Button1" runat="server"
            Text="Change" onclick="Button1_Click" />
    </div>
    <OReilly:Copyright ID="Copyright1" runat="server" />
    </form>
</body>
</html>
```

Run the program and the copyright user control is displayed as though you had put its HTML into the content file, as shown in Figure 15-1.

You can reuse the user control in any *.aspx* page. If you update the copyright, you will make that update in only the one *.ascx* file, and it will be displayed appropriately in all the pages that use that control.

If you do use the control on many pages, rather than adding in the Register directive to each page before you can use it, you can "preregister" the control in the site's *web.config* file. You must add an entry for each control to the <pages>\<controls> section of the file, as shown in Example 15-2.

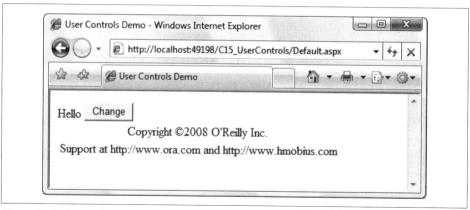

Figure 15-1. Copyright user control

Example 15-2. Registering a user control in web.config

```
<configuration>
    <system.web>
        ...

        <pages>
            <controls>
                <add src="~/UserControls/Copyright.ascx"
                    tagName="Copyright" tagPrefix="OReilly"/>
            </controls>
        </pages>

        ...
    </system.web>
</configuration>
```

A couple of gotchas, though: first, note that the uppercase letters in this declaration are slightly different between the declaration in *web.config* and that on the page. The site will not compile correctly if you get them around the wrong way in the wrong file. Second, if you are going to register your user controls or server controls centrally in *web.config*, you'll need to put them in a folder separate from any page or other control that uses them.

 For the rest of this chapter, we'll continue to register all user and custom controls in the page that uses them rather than in *web.config*.

User Controls with Code

User controls can have events and other code associated with them to make for more sophisticated reusable code. Suppose, for example, that you'd like to reuse the customer data list you developed in Chapter 8 in *DataListCustomRows.aspx*.

To convert this *.aspx* page and the code behind the page into a reusable user control, you will need to do the following:

1. Add a new web user control called *CustomerDataList.ascx* to the *C15_UserControls* website.

2. Open *DataListCustomRows.aspx* from the *C8_DataAccess* website, copy from it the SqlDataSource control, the DataList control, and the <div> element surrounding it, and paste them all into the new *CustomerDataList.ascx*.

3. Open *DataListCustomRows.aspx.cs* and copy the five event handlers from that page to the code-behind page for the new user control, *CustomerDataList.ascx.cs*. You'll also need to remove the references to lblInfo in the CancelCommand and SelectIndexChanged events and add System.Text to the list of namespaces being used. Finally, you can also delete the empty handler for the Page_Load event in this new page if you wish.

4. Copy and paste the <connectionStrings> element from *web.config* in the *C8_DataAccess* website into the *web.config* for *C15_UserControls*. For reference, it should read something like this (the name may vary):

```
<connectionStrings>
    <add name="AWLTConnection"
     connectionString="Data Source=machineName;
        Initial Catalog=AdventureWorksLT;Integrated Security=True"
     providerName="System.Data.SqlClient"/>
</connectionStrings>
```

Your control is now ready to save and use. You can add it to *Default.aspx* in the *C15_UserControls* website in two steps. First, register it by adding a Register directive and then place an instance of the control under the Button control, as highlighted in Example 15-3.

Example 15-3. Default.aspx with new CustomerDataList user control

```
<%@ Page Language="C#" AutoEventWireup="true"
    CodeFile="Default.aspx.cs" Inherits="_Default" %>

<%@ Register src="Copyright.ascx"
    tagname="Copyright" tagprefix="OReilly" %>
<%@ Register src="CustomerDataList.ascx"
    tagname="CustomerDL" tagprefix="OReilly" %>

<!DOCTYPE html PUBLIC "-//W3C//DTD XHTML 1.0 Transitional//EN"
    "http://www.w3.org/TR/xhtml1/DTD/xhtml1-transitional.dtd">

<html xmlns="http://www.w3.org/1999/xhtml">
<head runat="server">
    <title>User Controls Demo</title>
</head>
<body>
    <form id="form1" runat="server">
    <div>
        <asp:Label ID="Label1" runat="server" Text="Hello"></asp:Label>
```

Example 15-3. Default.aspx with new CustomerDataList user control (continued)

```
        <asp:Button ID="Button1" runat="server"
          Text="Change" onclick="Button1_Click" />
        <OReilly:CustomerDL ID="CustomerDL1" runat="server" />
    </div>
    <OReilly:Copyright ID="Copyright1" runat="server" />
    </form>
</body>
</html>
```

When you save and run *Default.aspx*, it comes up with the complete and populated DataList in place as you would expect, as shown in Figure 15-2.

Clicking the Edit button puts the record into edit mode as it did before you turned your page into a reusable data control, as shown in Figure 15-3.

The @Control Directive

There can be only one @Control directive for each user control. The ASP.NET page parser and compiler use this directive to set attributes for your user control, as listed in Table 15-1.

Table 15-1. @Control attributes

Attribute	Type	Description
AutoEventWireup	Boolean	Sets whether the control's events must be fired manually (false) or whether they are hooked up automatically (true). Default is true.
ClassName	String	The class name for the control.
CodeFile	String	The name of the code-behind file for the control. (Also called CodeBehind for backward compatibility.)
CodeFileBaseClass	String	The path to the base class for the control. Most likely, this contains new member definitions for the control shared among several different controls for consistency. CodeFile must also be declared.
CompilationMode	String	Sets whether a control should be compiled at runtime. Possible values are Always (the default), Never, and Auto. The last option will not compile the control if it doesn't need to.
CompilerOptions	String	A set of compiler command-line switches used to compile the control.
Debug	Boolean	Sets whether to compile with debug symbols. Default is true.
Description	String	A text description of the control for IntelliSense. Ignored by the compiler.
EnableTheming	Boolean	Sets whether themes can be applied to the control. Default is true.
EnableViewState	Boolean	Sets whether the current state of the control is saved in ViewState when the page is posted back to the server. Default is true.
Explicit	Boolean	Sets whether the control should be compiled using VB.NET Option Explicit mode. Default is true.
Inherits	String	Sets a code-behind class derived from UserControl for the control to inherit.
Language	String	The .NET-supported language used for inline rendering and server-side script blocks.
Src	String	The name of the source (markup) file for the control.

Table 15-1. @Control attributes (continued)

Attribute	Type	Description
Strict	Boolean	Sets whether the control should be compiled using VB.NET Option Strict mode. Default is `false`.
WarningLevel	Integer	Sets the level at which compiler warnings are treated as errors preventing your control from compiling successfully. Valid values are between 0 (zero) and 4.

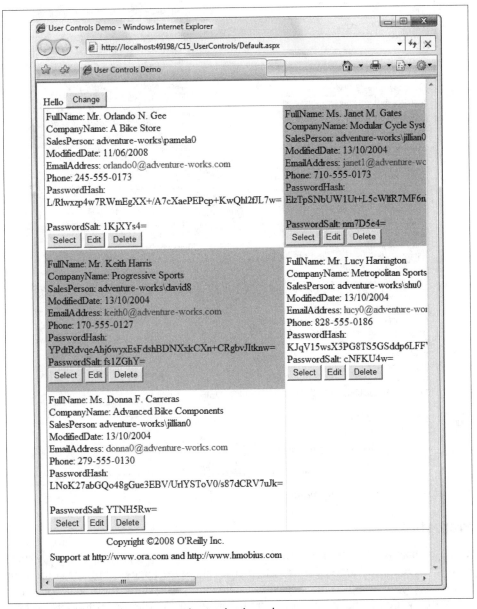

Figure 15-2. The DataList user control in read-only mode

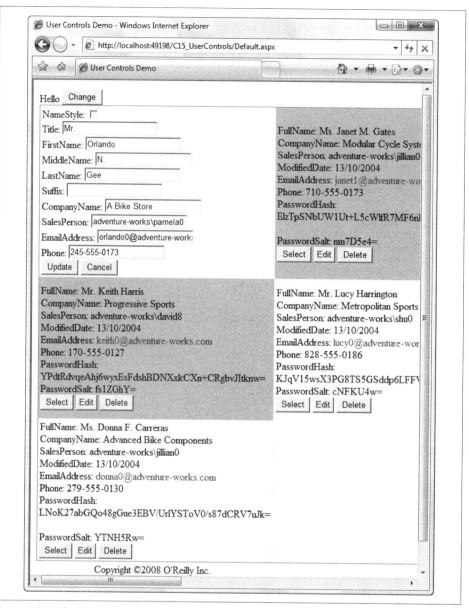

Figure 15-3. The DataList user control in edit mode

Properties

You can make your user control much more useful by giving it properties like the standard set of ASP.NET server controls. Properties allow the page hosting the control (in this case, *Default.aspx*) to interact with it, allowing you to alter their behavior either declaratively (in the page's markup) or programmatically (in the code behind the page).

You can, for example, give your CustomerDataList control properties for the number of columns to render and whether to add data into the table to produce either row by row (horizontally) or column by column (vertically). You do this in four steps:

1. Add properties to the control. You must decide whether you will provide read/write, read-only, or write-only properties. For this example, you'll provide read/write properties.

2. Provide an underlying value for the properties. You can do this by computing the property, retrieving it from a database, or, as you'll do here, storing the underlying value in a private member variable. You must decide whether you'll provide a default value for your properties.

3. Integrate the underlying values into the body of the code; you'll do that, in this case, by setting these values in the PreRender event of the control.

4. Set the properties from the page hosting the control declaratively (as an attribute) or programmatically. In this case, you'll set them programmatically in response to user input.

Creating a property

There is nothing special about creating a property for a user control; you create it as you would any property for a class. To demonstrate, add the following code to the CustomerDataList class in *CustomerDataList.ascx.cs*:

```
public int NumOfColumns
{
    get { return numOfColumns; }
    set { numOfColumns = value; }
}

public RepeatDirection direction
{
    get { return direction; }
    set { direction = value; }
}
```

Providing an underlying value for the property

You can compute the value of a property or look up the value in a database. In this example, you'll create member variables to hold the underlying value. Add these two lines of code to *CustomerDataList.ascx.cs*:

```
private int numOfColumns = 3;
private RepeatDirection direction = RepeatDirection.Horizontal;
```

 As you saw in Chapter 8, RepeatDirection has two possible values, Horizontal and Vertical. IntelliSense will assist you in choosing one or the other.

Integrating the property into your code

Having declared the properties, you must modify the code so that these values are used when creating the control. You can't do this in the Page_Load of the user control code-behind file because the event handler for setting the properties runs after Page_Load. You want to use the new property values before you render the control, so put the following code in the code-behind file to handle the PreRender event:

```
protected void Page_PreRender(object sender, EventArgs e)
{
    DataList1.RepeatColumns = NumOfColumns;
    DataList1.RepeatDirection = direction;
}
```

Setting the property from the client

If you save the changes to the CustomerDataList control now and open *Default.aspx*, you'll see no change. The default values set for the two properties are the same as those originally set in the DataList. To see the new properties at work, add a new value to the properties in *Default.aspx*. For example:

```
<OReilly:CustomerDL ID="CustomerDL1" runat="server"
    NumOfColumns="4" direction="Vertical" />
```

Run the page again and you'll see that the DataList's nine customer records are laid out across four columns from top to bottom, left to right.

To demonstrate the use of these properties programmatically, add to the website a new page called *UserControlProperties.aspx*. Add a DropDownList (ddlColumns) for the number of columns in which to lay out the DataList, and another (ddlDirection) for the user to specify the direction of layout. Finally, add a Button (btnSubmit) to the page to set those values in a postback and then add the CustomerDataList control itself. You'll also need to add the @Register directive at the top of the page for the CustomerDataList control.

Example 15-4 shows the complete markup for this page.

Example 15-4. UserControlProperties.aspx in full

```
<%@ Page Language="C#" AutoEventWireup="true"
    CodeFile="UserControlProperties.aspx.cs"
    Inherits="UserControlProperties" %>
<%@ Register src="CustomerDataList.ascx"
    tagname="CustomerDL" tagprefix="OReilly" %>

<!DOCTYPE html PUBLIC "-//W3C//DTD XHTML 1.0 Transitional//EN"
    "http://www.w3.org/TR/xhtml1/DTD/xhtml1-transitional.dtd">

<html xmlns="http://www.w3.org/1999/xhtml">
<head runat="server">
    <title>User Control Properties</title>
</head>
```

Example 15-4. UserControlProperties.aspx in full (continued)

```
<body>
    <form id="form1" runat="server">
    <div>
      <p>
        Number of columns:
        <asp:DropDownList ID="ddlColumns" runat="server">
           <asp:ListItem Text="1" Value="1" />
           <asp:ListItem Text="2" Value="2" />
           <asp:ListItem Text="3" Value="3" />
           <asp:ListItem Text="9" Value="9" />
        </asp:DropDownList>
        <br />
        Layout direction :
        <asp:DropDownList ID="ddlDirection" runat="server">
           <asp:ListItem Text="Horizontal" Value="Horizontal" />
           <asp:ListItem Text="Vertical" Value="Vertical" />
        </asp:DropDownList>
        <br />
        <asp:Button ID="btnSubmit" runat="server" Text="Submit"
          OnClick="btnSubmit_Click" />
      </p>
      <OReilly:CustomerDL ID="CustomerDL1" runat="server" />
    </div>
    </form>
</body>
</html>
```

As highlighted in Example 15-4, the Click event for the Button is handled by a method called btnSubmit_Click in the code-behind page for *UserControlProperties.aspx*. This handler checks the selected values of the two DropDownList controls and sets them into their respective properties on the user control. Example 15-5 shows the full code-behind file for this page.

Example 15-5. UserControlProperties.aspx.cs in full

```
using System;
using System.Web.UI;
using System.Web.UI.WebControls;

public partial class UserControlProperties : Page
{
    protected void btnSubmit_Click(object sender, EventArgs e)
    {
        CustomerDL1.HowManyColumns =
                Convert.ToInt32(ddlColumns.SelectedValue);

        switch (ddlDirection.SelectedValue)
        {
            case "Horizontal":
                CustomerDL1.Direction = RepeatDirection.Horizontal;
                break;
```

Example 15-5. UserControlProperties.aspx.cs in full (continued)

```
            case "Vertical":
                CustomerDL1.Direction = RepeatDirection.Vertical;
                break;
        }
    }
}
```

When you run the application, the control is displayed on the page using the default values for its properties. If you choose new values and then click Submit, the new values will be placed into the control's properties and will be used when the control is rendered, as shown in Figure 15-4.

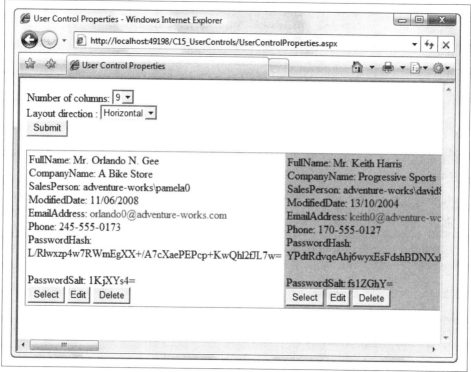

Figure 15-4. UserControlProperties.aspx in action

Handling Events

Event handling with user controls can be a bit confusing. Within a user control (e.g., CustomerDataList), you may have other controls (e.g., buttons). If those internal controls fire events, you'll need to handle them within the user control. The page the user control is placed in will never see those events.

With that said, a user control can raise its own events. You may raise an event in response to events raised by internal controls, user actions or system activity, or for any reason you choose.

Your user control can publish any event it chooses, and the page hosting the control may respond to those events if it chooses. Here are the steps:

1. The user control defines a delegate for the event.
2. The user control defines the event.
3. The user control defines a method that raises the event if anyone has registered to receive the event.
4. The user control calls that method from the place in the code where the event should be raised.
5. If the user control needs to pass along additional information for an event, the user control will define a class that derives from EventArgs, add a parameter of that class to the delegate definition, and create an instance of that EventArgs-derived class when raising the event.
6. The consuming class registers for the event, indicating which method should be called if the event is raised.
7. The consuming class's event handler handles the event in whatever way is appropriate.

To demonstrate how all of this is accomplished, you'll add two events to the CustomerDataList control and then handle them in a web page. The first event, EditRecord, will be raised when a record is being edited, and will pass along the name of the company in ChangedRecordEventArgs (derived from EventArgs). The second event, FinishedEditRecord, will be raised when the user either saves the update or cancels the update.

Start by creating a new web form in your website and call it *UserControlEvents.aspx*. Copy and replace all but the @Page directive from *Default.aspx* into this new page, and similarly, copy over the event handlers from *Default.aspx.cs* to *UserControlEvents.aspx. cs*. You'll add handlers for the user control's events here once you've created them.

You declare new events for the user control as you would for any class. In this case, you'll declare two delegates and two events for the CustomerDataList in the code-behind file for the user control. Open *CustomerDataList.ascx.cs* and add the following code just below the two properties:

```
public delegate void EditRecordHandler(
    object sender, ChangedRecordEventArgs e);
public event EditRecordHandler EditRecord;

public delegate void FinishedEditRecordHandler(
    object sender, EventArgs e);
public event FinishedEditRecordHandler FinishedEditRecord;
```

The first delegate has, as its second argument, a ChangedRecordEventArgs object. This is a class defined within the definition of the CustomerDataList class, specifically to pass along the company name that is being edited:

```
public partial class CustomerDataList : UserControl
{
    public class ChangedRecordEventArgs : EventArgs
    {
        private string companyName;

        public string CompanyName
        {
            get { return companyName; }
        }

        public ChangedRecordEventArgs(string companyName)
        {
            this.companyName = companyName;
        }
    }
    ... rest of CustomerDataList class ...
}
```

The company name is set in the constructor, and there is a read-only property for the event handler to read the name of the company being edited.

In addition to declaring the two events, you must declare methods in the CustomerDataList class that fire the events if anyone has registered to receive them:

```
protected virtual void OnEditRecord(ChangedRecordEventArgs e)
{
    if (EditRecord != null)
    {
        EditRecord(this, e);
    }
}

protected virtual void OnFinishedEditRecord(EventArgs e)
{
    if (FinishedEditRecord != null)
    {
        FinishedEditRecord(this, e);
    }
}
```

Finally, you must add calls to these methods to the places in your code at which point you want the events to be raised. The first place is when the user clicks the Edit button. An event handler exists for the EditCommand event of the DataList control. Add the highlighted lines from the following snippet to add these calls:

```
protected void DataList1_EditCommand(
    object source, DataListCommandEventArgs e)
{
```

```
DataList1.SelectedIndex = -1;
DataList1.EditItemIndex = e.Item.ItemIndex;
DataBind();

// Now raise OnEditRecord event
Label lbl = (Label)e.Item.FindControl("CompanyNameLabel");
string companyName = lbl.Text;
ChangedRecordEventArgs cre =
            new ChangedRecordEventArgs(companyName);
OnEditRecord(cre);
}
```

The first three lines are unchanged. The next two lines extract the company name from the CompanyNameLabel within the selected DataList item. The next line creates an instance of your new ChangedRecordEventArgs class, and the final line calls the method that will raise the event.

You'll want to modify the preexisting UpdateCommand and CancelCommand event handlers to raise the OnFinishedEditRecord. Add the highlighted line from the following snippet to both of those event handlers:

```
protected void DataList1_UpdateCommand(
    object source, DataListCommandEventArgs e)
{
    ...
    dsCustomers.Update();

    DataList1.EditItemIndex = -1;
    DataList1.DataBind();

    OnFinishedEditRecord(new EventArgs());
}

protected void DataList1_CancelCommand(
    object source, DataListCommandEventArgs e)
{
    DataList1.EditItemIndex = -1;
    DataList1.SelectedIndex = -1;
    DataList1.DataBind();

    OnFinishedEditRecord(new EventArgs());
}
```

There is no data to pass in, so instead, pass in a new instance of the placeholder class EventArgs to follow the convention that every event has an EventArgs argument.

Now to handle these two events; *UserControlEvents.aspx* must be registered to receive these events. You can do this either declaratively in the markup:

```
<OReilly:CustomerDL ID="CustomerDL1" runat="server"
    HowManyColumns="4" WhichDirection="Vertical"
    OnEditRecord="CustomerDL1_EditRecord"
    OnFinishedEditRecord="CustomerDL1_FinishedEditRecord" />
```

or programmatically in the Page_Load method:

```
protected void Page_Load(object sender, EventArgs e)
{
   CustomerDL1.EditRecord +=
      new CustomerDataList.EditRecordHandler(CustomerDL1_EditRecord);
   CustomerDL1.FinishedEditRecord +=
      new CustomerDataList.FinishedEditRecordHandler(
         CustomerDL1_FinishedEditRecord);
}
```

The first line registers that you want to receive the EditRecord event and indicates that the method to call is CustomerDL1_EditRecord. The second line registers that you want to receive the FinishedEditRecord event and indicates that the method to call is CustomerDL1_FinishedEditRecord.

Both methods add or remove text to a Label control with an ID of lblDisplayCompany, which you should add to the top of the page between the Change button and the CustomerDataList control, as highlighted in the following code:

```
<div>
   <p>
      <asp:Label ID="Label1" runat="server" Text="Hello"></asp:Label>
      <asp:Button ID="Button1"
         runat="server" Text="Change" OnClick="Button1_Click" />
   </p>
   <p>
      <asp:Label ID="lblDisplayCompany" runat="server" />
   </p>
      <OReilly:CustomerDL ID="CustomerDL1" runat="server" />
</div>
```

Now all you need to do is write the event handlers themselves. As with all the event handlers you've seen so far, these are added to the code-behind file for the page in *UserControlEvents.aspx.cs*, as highlighted in Example 15-6.

Example 15-6. UserControlEvents.aspx.cs in full

```
using System;
using System.Web.UI;

public partial class UserControlEvents : Page
{
   protected void Page_Load(object sender, EventArgs e)
   {
      CustomerDL1.EditRecord +=
         new CustomerDataList.EditRecordHandler(CustomerDL1_EditRecord);
      CustomerDL1.FinishedEditRecord +=
         new CustomerDataList.FinishedEditRecordHandler(
            CustomerDL1_FinishedEditRecord);
   }

   protected void Button1_Click(object sender, EventArgs e)
```

Example 15-6. UserControlEvents.aspx.cs in full (continued)

```
    {
        Label1.Text = "Changed!";
    }

    protected void CustomerDL1_EditRecord(
        object sender, CustomerDataList.ChangedRecordEventArgs e)
    {
        lblDisplayCompany.Text = "Editing " + e.CompanyName;
    }

    protected void CustomerDL1_FinishedEditRecord(object sender,
                                                  EventArgs e)
    {
        lblDisplayCompany.Text = String.Empty;
    }
}
```

The result is when you are editing a record, the name of the record you are editing is displayed by *Default.aspx*, as shown in Figure 15-5.

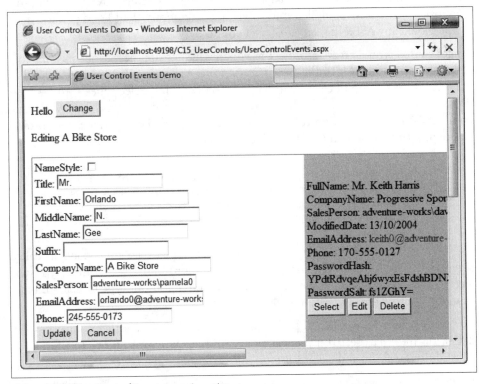

Figure 15-5. UserControlEvents.aspx in action

You can find the final code for this example in this chapter's download at *http://www.oreilly.com*.

Custom Controls

In addition to creating user controls, which are essentially reusable portions of web pages, you can create your own compiled custom controls. As noted earlier, there are three ways to create custom controls: derive a control from an existing control, create a control that combines existing controls, or create a new control from scratch.

 Custom controls are also often called "custom server controls" or even just "server controls." However, to keep the distinction between the ASP.NET server controls that are a part of .NET and the controls created in this chapter, we'll keep referring to them as "custom controls."

Composite controls are most similar to user controls. The key difference being that composite controls are compiled into a dynamic link library (DLL) and you use them as you would any ASP.NET server or user control.

To get started, you'll create a project in which you'll create the various custom controls for this chapter. Open the *C15_UserControls* website in VS2008 and right-click the solution at the top of the tree in the Solution Explorer. Select File → Add → New Project. In the New Project dialog box, select Visual C# Projects, then Web, and then ASP.NET Server Control from the project templates. Name the project *CustomControls*, as shown in Figure 15-6, and click OK.

 In VS2005, this project type was called Web Control Library and was found in the Windows category. Fortunately, this has been amended in VS2008, although the actual project template file is still called *WebControlLibrary.zip*.

VS2008 adds a new project and creates a complete custom control called `ServerControl1`. If you build the project (or solution) and try to run it, you will receive a message informing you that a project with an output type of Class Library cannot be started directly, as shown in Figure 15-7.

To use this control, you'll need to place it in a web page (or another control) as you did with the `CustomerDataList` example. Add a new web form to the *C15_UserControls* website and call it *CustomControl1.aspx*.

In the previous user control examples, you saw that to register the control on the page you must add an @`Register` directive to the top of the page (or its equivalent to *web.config*) and reference the *.ascx* file containing the control. A custom control, on

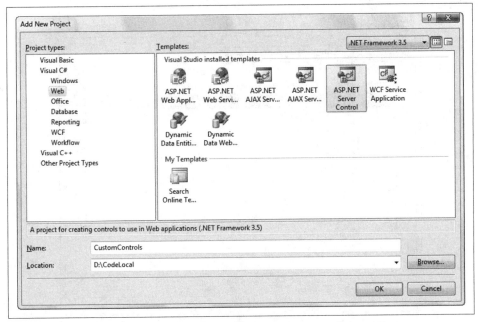

Figure 15-6. Creating an ASP.NET server control project

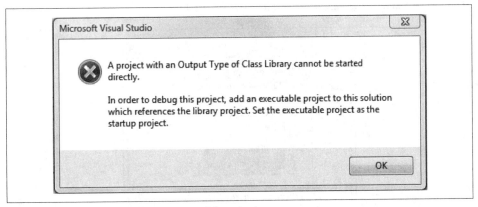

Figure 15-7. You can't run a server control directly

the other hand, is compiled into a DLL file, which must be added as a reference to the website before it can be registered on a page. Therefore, to add a reference to the *CustomControls* project, and by extension to the DLL file it generates, right-click the *C15_UserControls* website *project* entry (not the solution) and click Add Reference. When the dialog appears, switch to the Projects tab, as shown in Figure 15-8, select CustomControls, and then click OK.

The Solution Explorer will reflect the new reference, as shown in Figure 15-9. The website project will now have a *bin* folder in it containing *CustomControls.dll*.

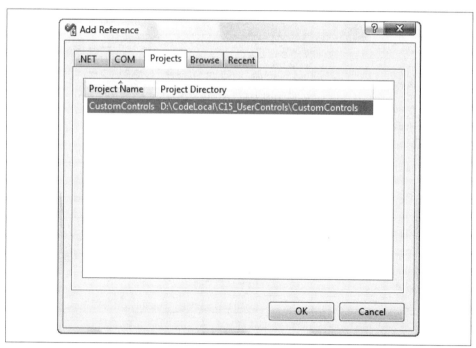

Figure 15-8. Adding a reference to the custom control project

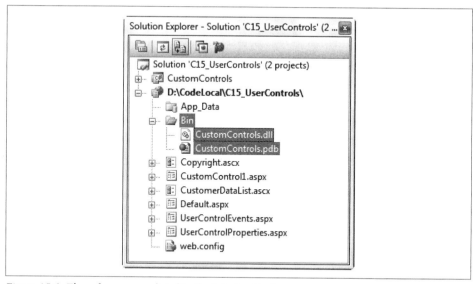

Figure 15-9. The reference now listed in the Solution Explorer

Now you are ready to add the custom control to *CustomControl1.aspx*. First, add the
Register directive just beneath the @Page directive. Rather than providing a TagName

and Src, however, you provide a Namespace and Assembly, which uniquely identify the control and the DLL that the page must use.

```
<%@ Register Assembly="CustomControls"
    Namespace="CustomControls" TagPrefix="OReilly" %>
```

Second, add the control to the page. The two attributes you must set are the Runat attribute, which is needed for all server-side controls, and the Text attribute, which dictates how the control is displayed at runtime. The complete content file, listed in Example 15-7, highlights these additions.

Example 15-7. CustomControl1.aspx in full

```
<%@ Page Language="C#" AutoEventWireup="true"
    CodeFile="CustomControl1.aspx.cs" Inherits="CustomControl1" %>
<%@ Register Assembly="CustomControls"
    Namespace="CustomControls" TagPrefix="OReilly" %>

<!DOCTYPE html PUBLIC "-//W3C//DTD XHTML 1.0 Transitional//EN"
    "http://www.w3.org/TR/xhtml1/DTD/xhtml1-transitional.dtd">

<html xmlns="http://www.w3.org/1999/xhtml">
<head runat="server">
    <title>ASP.NET Custom Server Control Demo</title>
</head>
<body>
    <form id="form1" runat="server">
    <div>
      <OReilly:ServerControl1 runat="server"
        Text="Hello Custom Control!" />
    </div>
    </form>
</body>
</html>
```

When you save and view this page, the control's Text property is displayed onscreen, as shown in Figure 15-10. Yes, the sample control supplied with the project is the server control equivalent of a Hello World application.

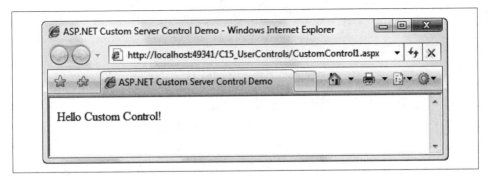

Figure 15-10. CustomControl1.aspx in action

If you look at the code in *ServerControl1.cs*, despite its simplicity, all the basics of creating a custom control are there to see. First, a few using statements; a few more than this are actually generated by default, but they aren't included here as they aren't necessary.

```
using System;
using System.ComponentModel;
using System.Web.UI;
using System.Web.UI.WebControls;
```

Next the namespace and class declarations; the namespace will be used in the @Register directive, and the class name is the name of the control to be used in pages consuming the control.

```
namespace CustomControls
{
    [DefaultProperty("Text")]
    [ToolboxData("<{0}:ServerControl1 runat=server></{0}:ServerControl1>")]
    public class ServerControl1 : WebControl
    {
```

Finally, the definition of the Text property, whose getter and setter methods save its contents to ViewState so they can persist between postbacks, and a single method, RenderContents, which overrides the method of the same name in its parent WebControl class, and simply writes the contents of the Text property to the page.

```
        [Bindable(true)]
        [Category("Appearance")]
        [DefaultValue("")]
        [Localizable(true)]
        public string Text
        {
            get
            {
                String s = (String)ViewState["Text"];
                return ((s == null) ? "[" + this.ID + "]" : s);
            }

            set
            {
                ViewState["Text"] = value;
            }
        }

        protected override void RenderContents(HtmlTextWriter output)
        {
            output.Write(Text);
        }
    }
}
```

Note the attributes adorning the class and property declarations in the preceding code. These aren't necessary for the runtime behavior of a custom control, but they are useful if you continue to use the custom control within VS2008. In fact, their sole purpose is to help VS2008 assist you in using them correctly. For example:

- The `DefaultProperty` attribute identifies the property of the control to be assigned any literal text left between its markup tags. In this example, the `Text` property will be assigned any values between the control's `<ServerControl1>` and `</ServerControl1>` tags.

- Assuming you add this custom control to the Toolbox pane in VS2008, the `ToolboxData` attribute defines what markup will be added to a page when you drag it from the Toolbox onto the page in Design or Source view. The {0} leaves space for the `TagPrefix` set in the `@Register` directive on the page for this control.

Table 15-2 lists the most commonly used attributes for custom controls and what they do. You can find a full list of attributes at *http://msdn2.microsoft.com/en-us/library/ms178658(VS.80).aspx*.

Table 15-2. Common custom control attributes

Name	Description
Bindable	Specifies whether VS2008 will display this control in the Data Bindings dialog box.
Browsable	Specifies whether the property can be displayed in the VS2008 Design pane.
Category	Specifies in which category this property will be displayed when the Properties dialog is sorted by category.
DefaultProperty	The default property of the class.
DefaultValue	The default value.
Description	The text you provide to be displayed in the Description box in the Properties panel.
ToolboxData	Used to provide the tag when the object is dragged from the Toolbox.

Properties

Custom controls can expose properties just as with any other class. You access these properties programmatically (in the code-behind file), or declaratively by setting attributes of the custom control as you did in *CustomControl1.aspx*:

```
<OReilly:ServerControl1 runat="server"
    Text="Hello Custom Control!" />
```

The Text property of the control is accessed through the Text attribute in the custom control declaration on the web page.

In the case of the Text property and the Text attribute, the mapping between the attribute and the underlying property is straightforward because both are strings.

However, ASP.NET will provide intelligent conversion of other types. For example, if the underlying type is an integer or a long, the attribute will be converted to the appropriate value type. If the value is an enumeration, ASP.NET will match the string value against the evaluation name and set the correct enumeration value. If the value is a Boolean, ASP.NET will match the string value against the Boolean value, that is, it will match the string "True" to the Boolean value true.

The Render Method

The key (and only) method of the custom control is RenderContents. This method is declared in the base class and must be overridden in your derived class if you wish to take control of rendering to the page. The RenderContents method uses the HtmlTextWriter object passed in as a parameter. In the case of the boilerplate custom control code provided by VS2008, this is used to write the string held in the Text property.

The HtmlTextWriter class derives from TextWriter and provides rich formatting capabilities. HtmlTextWriter will ensure that the elements produced are well formed, and it will manage the attributes, including style attributes, such as the following:

```
output.AddStyleAttribute("color", "fuchsia");
```

This style attribute needs to be attached to a tag. To do this, rewrite the RenderContents method in *ServerControl1.cs* like so:

```
protected override void RenderContents(HtmlTextWriter output)
{
    output.AddStyleAttribute("color", "fuchsia");
    output.RenderBeginTag("p");
    output.Write(Text);
    output.RenderEndTag( );
}
```

The style attribute is attached to an opening <p> tag, the text is written, and the RenderEndTag method renders the end tag for the most recent begin tag:

```
<div>
    <span><p style="color:fuchsia;">Hello Custom Control!</p></span>
</div>
```

Updating the Control

Each time you modify the control in the custom control library, you must get the rebuilt DLL into the *bin* directory of your website. You can do this in a few different ways.

If you're building the control as part of the same solution as the website that uses it (as is the case in this chapter), click Build → Build Solution (F6) and VS2008 will automatically add a new copy of the DLL into the *bin* directory.

If the server control project is not in the same solution as the website, you have two options:

- Delete the DLL file from the *bin* directory and then re-add the reference to it manually.
- Configure the server control project to build its DLL directly into the website's *bin* directory. To do this, click any file in the CustomControls project in the Solution Explorer. Now click Project → CustomControls Properties in VS2008, and then switch to the Build tab and set the "Output path" to the path for your website, as shown in Figure 15-11. Now each time you make a change in the custom controls, rebuild the project and the DLL will be placed in the correct directory for your web application.

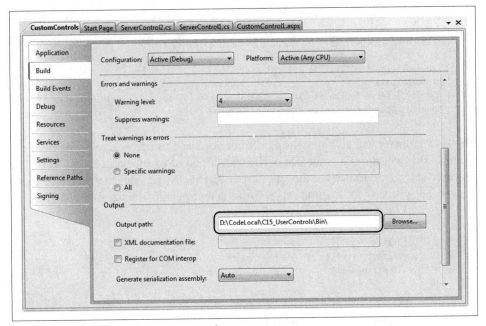

Figure 15-11. Setting a project's output path

Maintaining State

One of the issues you'll want to address when creating your own custom controls is how much of your control's settings will survive a postback to the server by being saved in ViewState or in control state. If you recall from Chapter 6, ViewState can be disabled, but control state cannot. However, saving values in control state should be left only for those values that are integral to a control's core functionality.

Maintaining view state

In the next example, you'll add a button to the custom control to increase the size of the text. The current size of the text will also be saved in view state along with the text being rendered on-screen. In the example after that, you'll see how to store the size of the text in control state instead of view state.

To start, create a copy of *ServerControl1.cs* in your CustomControls project and rename it to *ServerControlViewState.cs*. You'll also need to find the three references to ServerControl1 and replace them with ServerControlViewState. Fortunately, they are all in the class definition. The using statements required stay the same as well.

```csharp
using System;
using System.ComponentModel;
using System.Web.UI;
using System.Web.UI.WebControls;

namespace CustomControls
{
    [DefaultProperty("Text")]
    [ToolboxData(
        "<{0}:ServerControlViewState runat=server></{0}:ServerControlViewState>")]
    public class ServerControlViewState : WebControl
    {
```

The Text property will also stay the same, but you need to add a Size property to the control. This will store the font size of the text displayed by the control, in pixels. The property get method retrieves the value from ViewState and converts the value to an integer. The property set method stashes a string representing the size into ViewState.

```csharp
        [Bindable(true)]
        [Category("Appearance")]
        [DefaultValue("")]
        [Localizable(true)]
        public string Text
        {
            get
            {
                String s = (String)ViewState["Text"];
                return ((s == null) ? "[" + this.ID + "]" : s);
            }

            set
            {
                ViewState["Text"] = value;
            }
        }

        public int Size
        {
            get { return Convert.ToInt32(ViewState["Size"]); }
            set { ViewState["Size"] = value; }
        }
```

To ensure that a valid value for Size is in ViewState to begin with, add a constructor to initialize the value to 9:

```
public ServerControlViewState( )
{
    ViewState["Size"] = 9;
}
```

Finally, add a new line to the RenderContents method. This adds a font-size property into the <p> tag's style attribute set to the value of the Size property as it stands.

```
protected override void RenderContents(HtmlTextWriter output)
{
    output.AddStyleAttribute("color", "fuchsia");
    output.AddStyleAttribute("font-size",
        String.Format("{0}pt", Size.ToString( )));
    output.RenderBeginTag("p");
    output.Write(Text);
    output.RenderEndTag( );
}
}
} // ServerControlViewState.cs
```

Now when you run a page that uses ServerControlViewState, you'll see that it generates the following HTML:

```
<span id="sizeControl">
    <p style="color:fuchsia;font-size:9pt;">Text</p>
</span>
```

To demonstrate, add to the *C15_UserControls* website a new web page called *ViewStateControl.aspx*, and drag a Button control onto it. When clicked, this will post back the page, increase the Size property on ServerControlViewState, and then render the page again, effectively growing the size of the text being displayed. Set the Button's ID to btnSize and its Text to "Increase Size".

In Design view, double-click the button to create the skeleton of an event handler for the Click event in the code-behind file. Add one line of code to the handler, as shown here:

```
protected void btnSize_Click(object sender, EventArgs e)
{
    sizeControl.Size += 2;
}
```

Back in *ViewStateControl.aspx*, you'll need to add the @Register directive for the custom control to the top of the page along with the actual control beneath the button, as shown in Example 15-8.

Example 15-8. ViewStateControl.aspx in full

```
<%@ Page Language="C#" AutoEventWireup="true"
    CodeFile="ViewStateControl.aspx.cs" Inherits="ViewStateControl" %>
```

Example 15-8. ViewStateControl.aspx in full (continued)

```
<%@ Register Assembly="CustomControls"
    Namespace="CustomControls" TagPrefix="OReilly" %>
<!DOCTYPE html PUBLIC "-//W3C//DTD XHTML 1.0 Transitional//EN"
    "http://www.w3.org/TR/xhtml1/DTD/xhtml1-transitional.dtd">

<html xmlns="http://www.w3.org/1999/xhtml">
<head runat="server">
    <title>View State Custom Server Control Demo</title>
</head>
<body>
    <form id="form1" runat="server">
    <div>
        <asp:Button ID="btnSize" runat="server"
            OnClick="btnSize_Click" Text="Increase Size" />
        <OReilly:ServerControlViewState ID="sizeControl"
            runat="server" Text="Eat me, drink me, grow me" />
    </div>
    </form>
</body>
</html>
```

The @Register directive is identical to that used in *CustomControl1.aspx* even though you are using a second control. Because they are both in the same control library, you only need to register the library and not each individual control.

Save and run the page. The text on the screen is initially drawn in a 9-point font. Each time the button is clicked, the state variable Size is incremented. When the page is drawn, the state variable is retrieved and is used to set the size of the text.

Maintaining control state

The problem with view state is that it can be turned off, and that might render your control nonfunctional. Take, for example, the PageSize property of the GridView server control. If that property was not persisted across postbacks, the GridView wouldn't know how many records to show on a page and would throw an error. For this purpose, although view state can be disabled, control state cannot.

One of the design decisions you may need to make when creating your custom controls is which of the control's properties should be stored in view state and which in control state. To demonstrate, open *ViewStateControl.aspx* and disable view state on the control you created in the preceding example:

```
<OReilly:ServerControlViewState ID="sizeControl"
    runat="server" Text="Text"
    EnableViewState="false"/>
```

Run the page and click the button two or more times. You'll notice that on the second and subsequent clicks, the text does not increase in size any further. This is because view state has been disabled and the page is working in the following way:

1. When the page loads, the font size is set to 9 point in the control's constructor.

2. When the button is clicked the first time, btnSize_Click gets the control's Size property and adds 2 to it. The text is rendered in an 11-point font, but because view state is disabled for the control, the control's new Size property is not saved to view state.

3. When the button is clicked the second time, btnSize_Click tries to get the control's current Size property, but because view state is disabled for the control, it gets its initial value of 9 and adds to it again. Thus, the text is rendered in an 11-point font, the new value is not saved in view state again, and so the cycle continues.

As you can see, disabling view state can have an immediate effect on controls; even controls as simple as these, built for the purposes of demonstration. It's also safe to say that although it's inconvenient that the Size property isn't persisted across postbacks, it's not critical to its use on pages, so it's not a good candidate for being stored in control state rather than view state in this scenario. Likewise, it's debatable whether the control's Text property is a candidate for saving in control state. If view state is turned off, the control continues to display the text it was initially set to display, so there's no malfunction.

For the purposes of demonstration, however, let us assume that the control's Size property was central enough to its operation that it has to be stored in control state. Create a copy of *ServerControlViewState.cs* and rename it *ServerControlControlState.cs*. You'll need to find and replace all the instances of ServerControlViewState in the file with ServerControlControlState to start.

With the housekeeping out of the way, the first task is to create a structure that can store the fontSize and can itself be saved in control state. The structure must be able to be serialized so it can be saved within the page's source code.

```
using System;
using System.ComponentModel;
using System.Web.UI;
using System.Web.UI.WebControls;

namespace CustomControls
{
    [DefaultProperty("Text")]
    [ToolboxData("<{0}:ServerControlControlState runat=server>
                  </{0}:ServerControlControlState>")]
    public class ServerControlControlState : WebControl
    {
        [Serializable()]
        private struct ControlStateProperties
        {
            public int fontSize;
        }

        private ControlStateProperties controlState =
            new ControlStateProperties();
```

The Text property will remain stored in view state, so it remains as it was in *ServerControlViewState.cs*. The Size property, on the other hand, must now be linked to the fontSize property in the ControlStateProperties structure that is to be saved into control state. Likewise, the control's constructor must now set the fontSize property to 9 rather than its equivalent view state property.

```csharp
public string Text
{
    get
    {
        String s = (String)ViewState["Text"];
        return ((s == null) ? "[" + this.ID + "]" : s);
    }

    set
    {
        ViewState["Text"] = value;
    }
}

public int Size
{
    get
    {
        return controlState.fontSize;
    }
    set
    {
        controlState.fontSize = value;
        SaveControlState();
    }
}

public ServerControlControlState()
{
    controlState.fontSize = 9;
}
```

Note the call to SaveControlState in the setter for the Size property. This ensures the new value for Size is saved to control state as soon as it is set. You'll need to override both SaveControlState and LoadControlState. Both are defined in the WebControl class from which ServerControlControlState inherits, but are not set to work with the ControlStateProperties structure. Fortunately, neither method needs much work.

```csharp
protected override object SaveControlState()
{
    return controlState;
}

protected override void LoadControlState(object savedState)
{
```

```
    controlState = new ControlStateProperties();
    controlState = (ControlStateProperties)savedState;
}
```

The last addition to make is to handle the control's Init event and tell the page that it must maintain control state for this control. This is done by overriding WebControl's OnInit method:

```
protected override void OnInit(EventArgs e)
{
    Page.RegisterRequiresControlState(this);
    base.OnInit(e);
}
```

There are no changes to how the control should render on the screen, so the RenderContents method should remain untouched.

```
protected override void RenderContents(HtmlTextWriter output)
{
    output.AddStyleAttribute("color", "fuchsia");
    output.AddStyleAttribute("font-size",
        String.Format("{0}pt", Size.ToString()));
    output.RenderBeginTag("p");
    output.Write(Text);
    output.RenderEndTag();
}
}
} // end of ServerControlControlState.cs
```

To test this new control-state-enabled control, create a copy of *ViewStateControl.aspx* in the *C15_UserControls* website, and rename it *ControlStateControl.aspx*. Replace the ServerControlViewState control in *ViewStateControl.aspx* with this new one, leaving all the properties as they were, especially EnableViewState set to false.

```
<OReilly:ServerControlControlState
    ID="sizeControl" EnableViewState="false"
    runat="server" Text="Eat me, drink me, grow me"
/>
```

Now run the page and click the button a few times. You'll see that the font size of the text continues to increase even though view state is disabled for the control.

Derived Controls

Sometimes it is not necessary to create your own control from scratch. For instance, you may want to extend the behavior of an existing control type. You can derive from an existing control as you might derive from any class. Imagine, for example, that you would like a button to maintain a count of the number of times it has been clicked. Such a button might be useful in any number of applications; unfortunately, the ASP.NET Button control does not provide this functionality.

To overcome this limitation of the Button class, you'll derive a new custom control from System.Web.UI.WebControls.Button. Add a new ASP.NET server control to your *CustomControls* project, called *CountedButton.cs*. You'll find the option by clicking Project → Add New Item → Web, as shown in Figure 15-12.

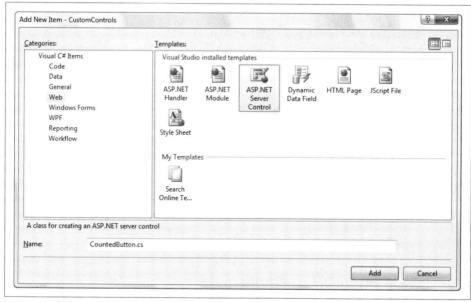

Figure 15-12. Adding a new ASP.NET server control

Delete everything in the file and replace it with the following code. You begin by deriving your new class from the existing Button type:

```
using System;
using System.ComponentModel;
using System.Web.UI;
using System.Web.UI.WebControls;

namespace CustomControls
{
    [DefaultProperty("Text")]
    [ToolboxData("<{0}:CountedButton runat=server></{0}:CountedButton>")]
    public class CountedButton : Button
    {
```

The work of this class is to maintain its state: how many times the button has been clicked. You provide a public property, Count, which is backed not by a private member variable, but rather by a value stored in ViewState. This is necessary because the Button will post the page; otherwise, the state would be lost.

```
public int Count
{
    get { return Convert.ToInt32(ViewState["Count"]); }
    set { ViewState["Count"] = value; }
}
```

To retrieve the value "Count" from ViewState, you use the string Count as an offset into the ViewState collection. What is returned is an object that you cast to an int.

To ensure that the property will return a valid value, you initialize the Count property in the constructor, where you set the initial text for the button:

```
public CountedButton( )
{
    Text = "Click me";
    ViewState["Count"] = 0;
}
```

Because CountedButton derives from Button, it is easy to override the behavior of a Click event. In this case, when the user clicks the button, you will increment the Count value held in ViewState, and update the text on the button to reflect the new count. You will then call the base class's OnClick method to carry on with the normal processing of the Click event.

```
protected override void OnClick(EventArgs e)
{
    Count = Count + 1;
    Text = Count.ToString( ) + " clicks";
    base.OnClick(e);
}
}
} // End of CountedButton.cs
```

Now add to the *C15_UserControls* website a new web form called *CustomButton.aspx*; add to it the @Register directive for the CustomControls assembly you've used before and an instance of the CountedButton control, as shown in Example 15-9.

Example 15-9. CustomButton.aspx in full

```
<%@ Page Language="C#" AutoEventWireup="true"
    CodeFile="CustomButton.aspx.cs" Inherits="CustomButton" %>
<%@ Register Assembly="CustomControls"
    Namespace="CustomControls" TagPrefix="OReilly" %>
<!DOCTYPE html PUBLIC "-//W3C//DTD XHTML 1.0 Transitional//EN"
    "http://www.w3.org/TR/xhtml1/DTD/xhtml1-transitional.dtd">

<html xmlns="http://www.w3.org/1999/xhtml">
<head runat="server">
    <title>CountedButton Custom Server Control Demo</title>
</head>
```

Example 15-9. CustomButton.aspx in full (continued)

```
<body>
    <form id="form1" runat="server">
    <div>
      <OReilly:CountedButton ID="CountedButton1" runat="server" />
    </div>
    </form>
</body>
</html>
```

When you build and run the page, the button reflects the current count of clicks, as shown in Figure 15-13.

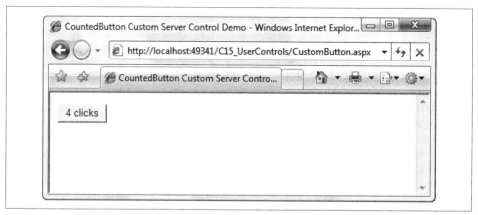

Figure 15-13. CountedButton.aspx in action

Composite Controls

The third way to create a custom control is to combine two or more existing controls. In the next example, you will act as a contract programmer and we will act as the client. We'd like you to build a more complex control we can use to keep track of the number of inquiries we receive regarding our books.

As your potential client, we may ask you to write a control that lets us put in one or more books; each time we click on a book, the control will keep track of the number of clicks for that book, as shown in Figure 15-14.

To start, add to *C15_UserControls* a new web form called *BookCounter.aspx*. The complete listing for the content file is shown in Example 15-10.

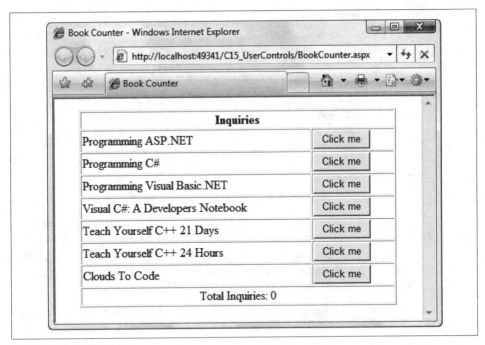

Figure 15-14. Book counter

Example 15-10. BookCounter.aspx

```
<%@ Page Language="C#" AutoEventWireup="true"
    CodeFile="BookCounter.aspx.cs" Inherits="BookCounter" %>
<%@ Register TagPrefix="OReilly"
    Namespace="CustomControls" Assembly="CustomControls" %>
<!DOCTYPE html PUBLIC "-//W3C//DTD XHTML 1.0 Transitional//EN"
    "http://www.w3.org/TR/xhtml1/DTD/xhtml1-transitional.dtd">

<html xmlns="http://www.w3.org/1999/xhtml">
<head runat="server">
    <title>Book Counter</title>
</head>
<body>
    <form id="form1" runat="server">
    <div>
        <div>
            <OReilly:BookInquiryList ID="bookInquiry1" Runat="Server">
                <OReilly:BookCounter ID="Bookcounter1"
                    Runat="server" BookName="Programming ASP.NET" />
                <OReilly:BookCounter ID="Bookcounter2"
                    Runat="server" BookName="Programming C#" />
                <OReilly:BookCounter ID="Bookcounter3"
                    Runat="server" BookName="Programming Visual Basic.NET" />
```

Example 15-10. BookCounter.aspx (continued)

```
        <OReilly:BookCounter ID="Bookcounter4"
          Runat="server" BookName="Visual C#: A Developers Notebook" />
        <OReilly:BookCounter ID="Bookcounter5"
          Runat="server" BookName="Teach Yourself C++ 21 Days" />
        <OReilly:BookCounter ID="Bookcounter6"
          Runat="server" BookName="Teach Yourself C++ 24 Hours" />
        <OReilly:BookCounter ID="Bookcounter7"
          Runat="server" BookName="Clouds To Code" />
      </OReilly:BookInquiryList>
    </div>
  </form>
</body>
</html>
```

The key point to note in this code is that the BookInquiryList component contains a number of BookCounter elements. There is one BookCounter element for each book we want to track in the control. The control is quite flexible. We can track one, seven (as shown here), or any arbitrary number of books. Each BookCounter element has a BookName attribute used to display the name of the book being tracked.

You can see in Figure 15-14 that each book is tracked using a CountedButton custom control, but you do not see a declaration of the CountedButton in the *.aspx* file. The CountedButton control is encapsulated entirely within the BookCounter custom control.

The complete architecture, therefore, is as follows:

1. The BookInquiryList composite control derives from WebControl and implements INamingContainer (described shortly).

2. The BookInquiryList control has a Controls property it inherits from the Control class (through WebControl) that returns a collection of child controls.

3. Within this Controls collection is an arbitrary number of BookCounter controls.

4. BookCounter is a composite control that derives from WebControl and implements INamingContainer.

5. Each instance of BookContainer has two properties, BookName and Count:

   BookName

   > Backed by ViewState and initialized through the BookName in the *.aspx* file

   Count

   > Delegates to a private CountedButton object, which is instantiated in BookContainer.CreateChildControls( )

The BookInquiryList object has two purposes: it acts as a container for the BookCounter objects, and it is responsible for rendering itself and ensuring that its contained BookCounter objects render themselves on demand.

The best way to see how all this operates is to work your way through the code from the inside out. The most contained object is the CountedButton.

Modifying the CountedButton Derived Control

CountedButton needs minor modification. To keep the code clear, create a new custom control named CountedButton2 and have it derive from Button, as shown in Example 15-11.

Example 15-11. CountedButton2.cs

```
using System;
using System.ComponentModel;
using System.Web.UI;
using System.Web.UI.WebControls;

namespace CustomControls
{
   [DefaultProperty("Text")]
   [ToolboxData("<{0}:CountedButton2 runat=server>
      </{0}:CountedButton2>")]
   public class CountedButton2 : Button
   {
      private string displayString;

      // default constructor
      public CountedButton2()
      {
         displayString = "clicks";
         InitValues();
      }

      // overloaded, takes string to display (e.g., 5 books)
      public CountedButton2(string text)
      {
         displayString = text;
         InitValues();
      }

      // called by constructors
      private void InitValues()
      {
         if (ViewState["Count"] == null)
         {
            Count = 0;
         }
         Text = "Click me";
      }

      // count as property maintained in view state
      public int Count
      {
         get
         {
            return (int)ViewState["Count"];
         }
```

Example 15-11. CountedButton2.cs (continued)

```
      set
      {
          ViewState["Count"] = value;
      }
   }

   // override the OnClick to increment the count,
   // update the button text and then invoke the base method
   protected override void OnClick(EventArgs e)
   {
      Count = Count + 1;
      Text = Count.ToString() + " " + displayString;
      base.OnClick(e);
   }
  }
}
```

Because you want the button to be able to display the string "5 Inquiries" rather than "5 clicks", you must change the line within the OnClick method that sets the button's text:

```
Text = Count.ToString() + " " + displayString;
```

Rather than hardwiring the string, you'll use a private member variable, displayString, to store a value passed in to the constructor:

```
private string displayString;
```

You must set this string in the constructor. To protect client code that uses the default constructor (with no parameters), you'll overload the constructor, adding a version that takes a string:

```
public CountedButton2(string text)
{
   displayString = text;
   InitValues();
}
```

You can now modify the default constructor to set the displayString member variable to a reasonable default value:

```
public CountedButton2()
{
   displayString = "clicks";
   InitValues();
}
```

The code that is common to both constructors has been factored out to the private helper method, InitValues, which ensures the Count property is initialized to zero and sets the initial text for the button:

```
private void InitValues()
{
   if (ViewState["Count"] == null)
```

```
        {
            Count = 0;
        }
        Text = "Click me";
    }
```

With these changes, the CountedButton is ready to be used in the first composite control, BookCounter.

Creating the BookCounter Composite Control

The BookCounter composite control is responsible for keeping track of and displaying the number of inquiries regarding an individual book. Create in CustomControls a new server control named BookCounter, and modify it as shown in Example 15-12.

Example 15-12. BookCounter.cs in full

```
using System.ComponentModel;
using System.Web.UI;
using System.Web.UI.WebControls;

namespace CustomControls
{
    [ToolboxData("<{0}:BookCounter runat=server></{0}:BookCounter>")]
    public class BookCounter : WebControl, INamingContainer
    {
        // intialize the counted button member
        CountedButton2 btn = new CountedButton2("inquiries");

        public string BookName
        {
            get { return (string)ViewState["BookName"]; }
            set { ViewState["BookName"] = value; }
        }

        public int Count
        {
            get { return btn.Count; }
            set { btn.Count = value; }
        }

        public void Reset()
        {
            btn.Count = 0;
        }

        protected override void CreateChildControls()
        {
            Controls.Add(btn);
        }
    }
}
```

INamingContainer

The BookCounter class implements the INamingContainer interface. This is a "marker" interface that has no methods. This interface identifies a container control that creates a new ID namespace, guaranteeing that all child controls have IDs that are unique to the page.

Containing CountedButton2

The BookCounter class contains an instance of CountedButton2:

```
CountedButton2 btn = new CountedButton2("inquiries");
```

The btn member is instantiated in the CreateChildControls method inherited from System.Control:

```
protected override void CreateChildControls()
{
    Controls.Add(btn);
}
```

CreateChildControls is called in preparation for rendering, and offers the BookCounter class the opportunity to add the btn object as a contained control.

The complete control life cycle is presented in Chapter 6. That same life cycle applies to custom controls as it does to ASP.NET web controls.

There is no need for BookCounter to override the Render method; the only thing it must render is the CountedButton, which can render itself. The default behavior of Render is to render all the child controls, so you need not do anything special to make this work.

BookCounter has two properties: BookName and Count. BookName is a string to be displayed in the control and is managed through ViewState:

```
public string BookName
{
    get { return (string)ViewState["BookName"]; }
    set { ViewState["BookName"] = value; }
}
```

Count is the count of inquires regarding this particular book; responsibility for keeping track of this value is delegated to the CountedButton2:

```
public int Count
{
    get { return btn.Count; }
    set { btn.Count = value; }
}
```

There is no need to place the value in ViewState because the button is responsible for its own data.

Creating the BookInquiryList Composite Control

Each BookCounter object is contained within the Controls collection of the BookInquiryList. Create another control in the CustomControls project, named BookInquiryList, and modify it as shown in Example 15-13. BookInquiryList has no properties or state. Its only method is Render.

Example 15-13. BookInquiryList.cs in full

```csharp
using System;
using System.Web.UI;
using System.Web.UI.WebControls;
using System.Collections;

namespace CustomControls
{
    [ToolboxData(
        "<{0}:BookInquiryList runat=server></{0}:BookInquiryList>")]
    [ControlBuilderAttribute(typeof(BookCounterBuilder)),
        ParseChildren(false)]
    public class BookInquiryList : WebControl, INamingContainer
    {
        protected override void Render(HtmlTextWriter output)
        {
            int totalInquiries = 0;
            BookCounter current;

            // Write the header
            output.Write("<Table border='1' width='90%' cellpadding='1'"
                + "cellspacing='1' align = 'center' >");
            output.Write("<tr><td colspan = '2' align='center'>");
            output.Write("<b> Inquiries </b></td></tr>");

            // if you have no contained controls, write the default msg.
            if (Controls.Count == 0)
            {
                output.Write("<tr><td colspan='2' align='center'>");
                output.Write("<b> No books listed </b></td></tr>");
            }
            // otherwise render each of the contained controls
            else
            {
                // iterate over the controls collection and
                // display the book name for each
                // then tell each contained control to render itself
                for (int i = 0; i < Controls.Count; i++)
                {
                    current = (BookCounter)Controls[i];
                    totalInquiries += current.Count;
                    output.Write("<tr><td align='left'>" +
                        current.BookName + "</td>");
                    output.RenderBeginTag("td");
                    current.RenderControl(output);
```

Example 15-13. BookInquiryList.cs in full (continued)

```
            output.RenderEndTag( );  // end td
            output.Write("</tr>");
          }
          output.Write("<tr><td colspan='2' align='center'> " +
            " Total Inquiries: " +
            totalInquiries + "</td></tr>");
        }
        output.Write("</table>");
      }
    }

    internal class BookCounterBuilder : ControlBuilder
    {
      public override Type GetChildControlType(
        string tagName, IDictionary attributes)
      {
        if (tagName == "BookCounter")
          return typeof(BookCounter);
        else
          return null;
      }

      public override void AppendLiteralString(string s)
      { }
    }
}
```

ControlBuilder and ParseChildren attributes

The BookCounter class must be associated with BookInquiryClass so that ASP.NET can translate the elements in the *.aspx* page into the appropriate code. This is done by adding the ControlBuilderAttribute attribute to the BookInquiryList class declaration:

```
[ToolboxData(
   "<{0}:BookInquiryList runat=server></{0}:BookInquiryList>")]
[ControlBuilderAttribute(typeof(BookCounterBuilder)),
   ParseChildren(false)]
public class BookInquiryList : WebControl, INamingContainer
{
```

The first argument to the ControlBuilderAttribute attribute is a Type object that you obtain by passing in BookCounterBuilder, a class you will define to return the type of the BookCounter class given a tag named BookCounter. BookCounterBuilder is defined in the following code, added to *BookInquiryList.cs* inside the CustomControls namespace:

```
internal class BookCounterBuilder : ControlBuilder
{
  public override Type GetChildControlType(
    string tagName, System.Collections.IDictionary attributes)
  {
    if (tagName == "BookCounter")
      return typeof(BookCounter);
    else
```

```
        return null;
    }

    public override void AppendLiteralString(string s)
    { }
}
```

ASP.NET will use this BookCounterBuilder class, which derives from ControlBuilder, to determine the type of the object indicated by the BookCounter tag. Through this association, each BookCounter object will be instantiated and added to the Controls collection of the BookInquiryClass.

The BookCounterBuilder's method, GetChildControlType, uses the classic (nongeneric) IDictionary interface.

The second argument of the ControlBuilderAttribute attribute, ParseChildren, must be set to false to tell ASP.NET you have handled the children attributes and no further parsing is required. A value of false indicates that the nested child attributes are not properties of the outer object, but rather are child controls.

Render method

The only method of the BookInquiryList class is the override of Render. The purpose of Render is to draw the table shown earlier in Figure 15-14, using the data managed by each BookCounter child control. The BookInquiryList class provides a count of the total number of inquiries, as shown in Figure 15-15.

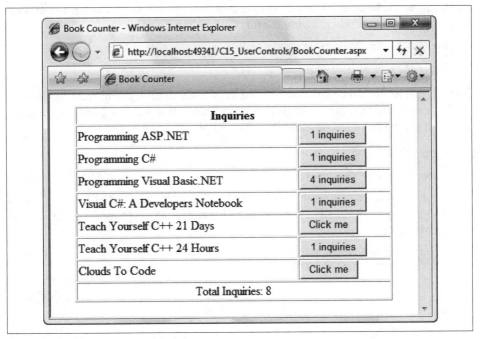

Figure 15-15. Total inquiries displayed

The code tallies inquiries by initializing an integer variable, totalInquiries, to 0 and then iterating over each control in turn, asking the control for its Count property:

```
totalInquiries += current.Count;
```

The Count property of the control delegates to the CountedButton's Count property.

Rendering the output

That same loop in the overridden Render method of the BookInquiryList class renders each child control by iterating over each control, building up the output HTML:

```
for (int i = 0; i < Controls.Count; i++)
{
    current = Controls[i] as BookCounter;

    if (current != null)
    {
        totalInquiries += current.Count;
        output.Write("<tr><td align='left'>" +
        current.BookName + "</td>");
        output.RenderBeginTag("td");
        current.RenderControl(output);
        output.RenderEndTag();  // end td
        output.Write("</tr>");
    }
}
```

The local BookCounter object, current, is assigned to each object in the Controls collection in succession. Each object is cast to a BookCounter object using the as keyword, so if the object is not a BookCounter, current is set to null.

```
for (int i = 0; i < Controls.Count; i++)
{
    current = Controls[i] as BookCounter;
```

If current is not a BookCounter object and thus is set to null, the current iteration of the loop ends and current is assigned another object. If it is a BookCounter object, the code can get the Count, as described previously:

```
if (current != null)
{
totalInquiries += current.Count;
```

Then you proceed to render the object. The HTMLTextWriter is used first to create a row and to display the name of the book, using the BookName property of the current BookCounter object:

```
output.Write("<tr><td align='left'>" +
    current.BookName + "</td>");
```

You then render a td tag, and within that tag you tell the BookCounter object to render itself. Finally, you render an ending td tag using RenderEndTag and an ending row tag using the Write method of the HTMLTextWriter:

```
output.RenderBeginTag("td");
current.RenderControl(output);
output.RenderEndTag( );  // end td
output.Write("</tr>");
```

You tell the contained control to render itself:

```
current.RenderControl(output);
```

When you do this, the Render method of BookCounter is called. Because you have not overridden this method, the Render method of the base class is called, which tells each contained object to render itself. The only contained object is CountedButton2. Because you have not overridden Render in CountedButton2, the base Render method in Button is called, and the button is rendered.

Assignment of Responsibilities

This example of a composite control is interesting because the various responsibilities are spread among the participating objects. The BookInquiryList object assumes all responsibility for laying out the control, creating the table, and deciding what will be rendered where. However, it delegates responsibility for rendering the Button object to the individual contained controls.

Similarly, the BookInquiryList is responsible for the total number of inquiries—because that information transcends what any individual BookCounter object might know. However, the responsibility for the count held by each BookCounter is delegated to the BookCounter itself. As far as the BookInquiryList is concerned, it gets that information directly from the BookCounter's Count property. It turns out, however, that BookCounter delegates that responsibility to the CountedButton2.

Rendering the summary

Once all of the child controls have been rendered, the BookInquiryList creates a new row to display the total inquiries:

```
output.Write("<tr><td colspan='2' align='center'> " +
  " Total Inquiries: " +
  totalInquiries + "</td></tr>");
```

CHAPTER 16

Web Services

The information you publish in web pages is meant to be seen and read, and the forms on those pages are meant to be filled in by hand. When designing your web pages, you use design elements such as layout, fonts, and color that make your website visually appealing to people. However, the information and services your website provides may also be useful to other website applications.

A *web service* is web-based functionality that you access using the protocols of the Web, but it is designed to be easy to use by programs. Unlike web pages, web services are not meant to be accessed in a browser or look good to people.

For example, most search engines are capable of limiting their searches to a single site. If you could call a search engine's functionality like a function, you could easily add search functionality to your own site. However, if there is no standard way to access this behavior, you will need to write this functionality yourself, or you will need to try to access the pages with code that acts like a browser or with screen scraping. Since the pages are meant for people to read and not for programs to use, you cannot be guaranteed that data in a page will be easy to parse, or even that it will remain the same.

The goal of web services is to create web-based applications that interact with other applications with no user interface. If you're a web page developer, having such web services can make your data or site functionality available to other sites in mashups, and can increase the visibility of your site. Inside an enterprise, different groups can make their applications integrate via web services to keep them loosely coupled. For example, an accounting system can expose transaction recording functionality to the e-commerce system. Then, either could be upgraded or changed as long as the service interface remained the same. Your applications can communicate with each other, exchanging data in standard formats.

There are two broad aspects to web service development: creating the web service and consuming the web service. This chapter will show how easy it is to do both of those using the tools built into Visual Studio 2008 (VS2008).

Introducing Web Services

Web services are *loosely coupled*, which means they are entirely independent of the operating system or programming language used on either the server side or the client side. Unlike previous technologies for distributed computing (such as Java's RMI or .NET Remoting), web services do not require that both ends of the connection be programmed in the same language. For example, the server code might be written in Visual Basic on Windows Vista while the client is written in C++ running on a Unix machine.

However, if you are implementing both the client and the server, web services may not be the best solution. You will get better performance by using .NET Remoting, a tightly coupled, proprietary format that sends binary data over the wire.

> For more information on .NET Remoting, see *Advanced .NET Remoting*, Second Edition, by Ingo Rammer and Mario Szpuszta (Apress).

As mentioned in Chapter 1, Microsoft introduced the Windows Communication Foundation (WCF) as part of .NET 3.0. This completely redefines how services are created and lets you write code for a service which you can deploy as either a web service or a .NET Remoting service by changing its associated *.config* file rather than its code.

> For more information on WCF, see *Learning WCF* by Michele Leroux Bustamante (O'Reilly), and *Programming WCF Services* by Juval Löwy (O'Reilly).

In this chapter, we'll look at implementing web services, the preferred choice when you need to make the service available to as many platforms as possible. This is often the case when calling and consuming services over the Internet using HTTP, since firewalls and proxies will already be set up for web browsing; web services can be accessed in the same fashion as websites are by a browser. The only difference is that rather than the web browser requesting a new page from a server, it is the web page making a request to the web service for information that it will then use to complete its own display on the user's screen.

All that is necessary to create a web service is that both the server and the client support the industry-standard web protocol, HTTP, and can read and write messages according to whichever web service architecture they are using. Often, the term *web service* refers to a service using Simple Object Access Protocol (SOAP), because that was one of the first architectures to gain wide popularity. However, there are many ways to talk to a service over the Web (another option is to combine REST and JSON, which we'll see later in this chapter). We will use the word *SOAP* when referring to a SOAP web service and the term *web service* when referring to any service architecture that uses HTTP.

Understanding Web Service Protocols and Standards

Web services are built using a number of industry-standard protocols. Although covering these in detail is beyond the scope of this book, the following overview will help you understand the architecture of web services.

A *protocol* is a set of rules that describe the transmission and receipt of data between two or more computing devices. For example, Transmission Control Protocol/Internet Protocol (TCP/IP) governs the low-level transport of packets of data on the Internet.

HTTP

Hypertext Transfer Protocol (HTTP) is used to enable servers and browsers on the Web to communicate. It is primarily used to establish connections between servers and browsers and to transmit data, such as HTML pages or images, to the client browser.

The client sends an HTTP request to the server, which then processes the request. The server typically returns HTML pages to be rendered by the client browser. HTTP requests start with a *verb*. The typical verbs used by browsers are GET and POST (web servers also support PUT for creating new resources, DELETE for deleting them, HEAD for getting the metadata for a resource, and others). In a typical HTML form page, GET is used to access the HTML that shows the form and POST is used to process it (for more information visit *http://www.w3.org/Protocols/rfc2616/rfc2616-sec9.html*).

Since the verbs could technically be used interchangeably, there are guidelines for when to use GET and when to use POST. You should use a GET request to read data; the user should safely be able to refresh a page that was accessed by GET. When your request is changing data, use POST. The browser will warn the user if he tries to refresh the page. These guidelines are not always followed on web pages, but web service standards are written to expect closer adherence to these guidelines.

HTTP-GET

In GET requests, the name/value pairs are appended directly to the URL. The data is encoded (which guarantees that only legal ASCII characters are passed over the wire) and then appended to the URL, separated from the URL by a question mark.

For example, consider the following URL:

```
http://localhost/StockTicker/Service.asmx/GetName?StockSymbol=msft
```

The question mark indicates that this is an HTTP-GET request, the name of the variable passed to the GetName method is StockSymbol, and the value is msft.

GET requests are suitable when all the data that needs to be passed can be handled by name/value pairs, there are few fields to pass, and the length of the fields is relatively short. GET requests are also suitable when security is not an issue. This last point arises because the URL is sent over the wire and is included in server logs as plain text. As such, they can be easily captured by a network sniffer or an unscrupulous person.

The .NET Framework provides a class, `HttpGetClientProtocol` (shown in Figure 16-1), for using the HTTP-GET protocol in your clients.

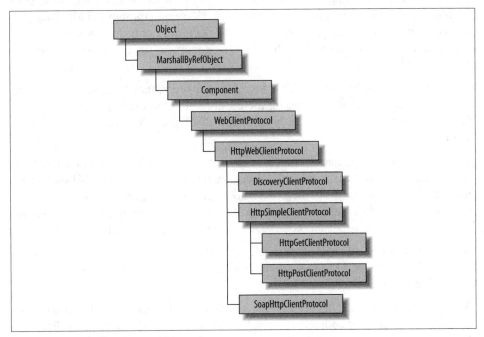

Figure 16-1. WebClientProtocol hierarchy

HTTP-POST

In POST requests, the name/value pairs are also encoded, but instead of being appended to the URL, they are sent as part of the request message.

POST requests are suitable for large numbers of fields or when lengthy parameters need to be passed. If security is an issue, a POST request is safer than a GET request since the HTTP request can be encrypted.

The .NET Framework provides a class, `HttpPostClientProtocol` (see Figure 16-1), for using the HTTP-POST protocol in your clients.

XML

Extensible Markup Language (XML) is an open standard ratified by the World Wide Web Consortium (W3C) as a means of describing data. (For more information, visit *http://www.w3.org/XML/*.) The latest version of the XML protocol is version 1.1, recommended by the W3C in February 2004 and updated in August 2006. However, the version of XML currently in widespread use, including in VS2008, is version 1.0.

XML is similar to HTML. In fact, both XML and HTML are derived from Standard Generalized Markup Language (SGML). Like HTML documents, XML documents are plain-text documents containing elements. However, though HTML uses predefined elements that specify how the HTML document will display in a browser, only XML allows elements to be defined by the document developer so that virtually any data can be conveyed.

XML documents are human-readable text files. However, they typically are meant to be read only by the developers doing the programming and debugging. Most often, XML documents are "read" by programs, and .NET provides extensive support for creating and reading XML.

XML documents are generally much larger than binary files containing the same data, but binary files must use proprietary encoding; the point of XML is to be a platform-neutral and language-neutral standard. In any case, file size, per se, is rarely an issue since the difference in transmission time over the Internet is usually negligible at today's speeds, especially when data compression is taken into account.

An XML *schema* is a file used to define the elements and how they relate to one another within a given XML document or set of documents. In the schema, both the element names and the content types are specified.

One significant difference between HTML and XML is that most HTML readers (web browsers) are tolerant of coding errors; XML readers are not. XML must be *well formed*. (For a complete discussion of well-formed XML markup, see the XHTML sidebar in Chapter 3.) For example, though browsers generally do not care whether elements are uppercase or lowercase, in XML they must be lowercase or an error will be generated.

SOAP

Simple Object Access Protocol (SOAP) is an XML grammar that's tailored for exchanging web service data. In a .NET web service, you'll usually send SOAP messages over HTTP. SOAP is a simple, lightweight protocol for the exchange of information over the Internet. Like XML, the SOAP standard is promulgated by the W3C.

A SOAP message consists of the message content, plus one or more header blocks, all wrapped within the so-called SOAP envelope. The SoapEnvelope class derives from the System.Xml.XmlDocument class, so all the functionality provided by the .NET Framework for dealing with XML applies to SOAP.

SOAP uses XML syntax to format its content. It is, by design, as simple as possible and provides a minimum of functionality. Therefore, it is modular and flexible. Since SOAP messages consist of XML, which is plain text, they can easily pass through firewalls, unlike many proprietary, binary formats. At the time of this writing, the latest SOAP version is 1.2 (recommended by the W3C in June 2003). SOAP was originally developed by Compaq, HP, IBM, Lotus, Microsoft, and others.

SOAP is not limited to name/value pairs as HTTP-GET and HTTP-POST are. Instead, SOAP can be used to send more complex objects, including data sets, classes, and other objects.

One drawback to using SOAP to pass requests back and forth to web services is that SOAP messages tend to be verbose because of the nature of XML. Therefore, if bandwidth or transmission performance is an issue, you may be better off using HTTP-GET or HTTP-POST.

The .NET Framework provides a class, `SoapHttpClientProtocol` (see Figure 16-1), for using SOAP in your clients.

Using SOAP Web Services

SOAP allows two programs to exchange XML documents over HTTP. Using this simple mechanism, it is possible to create a Remote Procedure Call (RPC) model, which many web services do. In that style of SOAP, the documents describe operations to call and the parameters they take. The response document describes the return value of the RPC. SOAP services are usually accompanied by Web Services Description Language (WSDL) documents that describe the calls available in a service and descriptions of the types they use. In the web service world, WSDL documents play the same role that reflection does in .NET. It makes it possible for generic tools to operate with web services without knowing their details beforehand.

The SOAP web service infrastructure has several defining characteristics:

- Both the web service server and the client application are connected to the Internet.
- The data format with which the two ends of the connection communicate conforms to the same open standard. SOAP messages usually consist of self-describing, text-based XML documents.
- The systems at the two ends of the connection are loosely coupled. In other words, web services do not care what operating system, object model, or programming language is used on either end of the connection as long as both the web service and the consuming application are able to send and receive messages that conform to the proper protocol standard.

The logic behind the web service process is shown schematically in Figure 16-2.

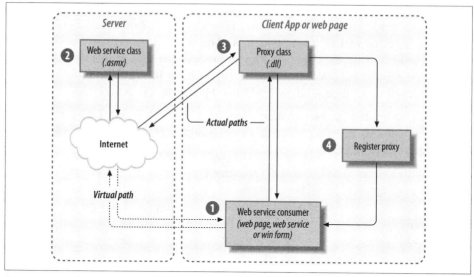

Figure 16-2. What goes on behind a web service

In Figure 16-2, at position 1, a web service consumer (a program that uses a particular web service, sometimes called the *consuming program*) makes a call to the web service (position 2). The consumer thinks it is talking directly to the web service over the Internet. This is an illusion.

The actual call is being made to a proxy class (position 3), which is local to the consumer. The proxy handles all the complex infrastructure of sending the request over the Internet to the server machine, as well as getting results back and presenting them to the consumer.

All of this is made possible because the proxy was previously registered with the consuming application (position 4). This is done by the developer of the consuming application. If the service has a WSDL description, tools can create the proxy for us.

In addition to creating and consuming the web service, there are other aspects to consider:

Protocol

> The web service must communicate with the client, and vice versa, in a manner that both sides will understand.

Directories

> Web services will be developed by thousands, or tens of thousands, of companies. Directories will be created to list these services and make them available to developers. For directories to be useful, however, there must be conventions for discovery and description:

Discovery

Potential clients will need to locate, or *discover*, documents that describe the web service. Thus, the service will often provide discovery documents, that is, XML files that contain information allowing potential clients to find other files that describe the web service.

Description

Once a web service has been identified, through discovery or other means, it must make a document available that describes the protocols it supports (typically SOAP) and the programmatic interface to its usage. The WSDL describes all of the exposed methods and properties, including each method's parameters and return type.

Security

Most servers connected to the Internet are set up to be conscious of security, with firewalls and other means of blocking all traffic except that which is deemed safe. Web services must live within these security constraints. Web services must not be portals for malicious people or software to enter your network.

It is often necessary to restrict access to specific clients. For example, suppose you are developing a stock ticker for a brokerage firm. You might want to restrict access to the web service to paying clients, excluding anyone who has not paid a usage fee.

State

Like web pages, web services use HTTP, which is a stateless protocol. And as with web pages, the .NET Framework will provide tools to preserve state if the application requires this.

Creating a Proxy

Before a client application can use a web service, a *proxy* must be created. A proxy is a stand-in for the actual code you want to call. It is responsible for *marshaling* the call across the machine boundaries. Requests to the web service on the server must conform to the proper protocol and format, usually SOAP and/or HTTP. You could write all the code to serialize and send the proper data to the web service yourself, but that would be a lot of work. The proxy does it all for you.

The proxy is registered with the client application. Then the client application makes method calls *as though it were calling a local object*. The proxy does all the work of taking your calls, wrapping them in the proper format, and sending them as a SOAP request to the server. When the server returns the SOAP package to the client, the proxy decodes everything and presents it to the client application as though it were returning from a method on a local object. This process is shown schematically in Figure 16-3.

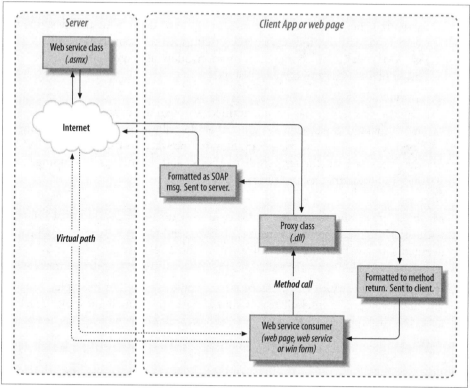

Figure 16-3. Web service proxy operation

To make this work, a developer must create the proxy and register it with the client application under development. This registration consists of a list of the exposed web methods and their signatures. The owner of the web service can add new web methods or update existing ones without changing their signature, and the existing proxy will not break.

Creating a Consumer

The consumer of a web service can be a desktop application, a web page, or another web service. All that is required is that the consumer be able to send and receive SOAP or HTTP packages.

The proxy class is compiled into an assembly, which must be registered with the consuming application. In the next chapter, you will see several ways to do this, ranging from a fully automated technique using VS2008 to a series of manual steps, either using VS2008 or not.

The consuming application is called the *client*, and the proxy is located on the client's machine. Once the proxy is created and registered with the client, all the client needs to do to use your web service is make a method call against that proxy object as though it were a call against a local object.

Developing an ASP.NET SOAP Web Service

Before WCF and VS2008, the process of developing a web service was nearly identical to that for developing a web page. That approach remains an option, even though it has been superseded by newer WCF facilitated techniques. Here is a list of features that ASP.NET web pages and legacy ASP.NET web services share:

- All the source files that make up both web pages and services are text files. They can be created and edited in any text editor, and class files can be compiled using a command-line tool from a command prompt.

- Both web pages and web services can use either the *code-behind* or the inline coding model. Code-behind is generally considered a technique intended to separate visual content from programmatic content in web pages. As such, its use in web services is less imperative since a web service does not have any visual content. (For a full discussion of the code-behind technique, see Chapter 6.)

- Both web pages and web services make full use of the CLR and the .NET Framework.

Whereas a web page is defined by its *.aspx* file, a web service is defined by its *.asmx* file.

Think of a web service as a class in which some (but not necessarily all) of the methods are exposed to clients over the Internet.

You can easily test an *.asmx* file by entering its URL into any browser, as in this example:

```
http://localhost/websites/StockTickerInLine.asmx
```

The result is shown in Figure 16-4. This test shows a list of usable links to each web method exposed by the web service. It also displays useful information and links pertaining to its deployment, including code samples in C#, Visual Basic, and C++.

Creating a web service this way is still possible in VS2008, and for some deployments it may still be necessary. For new web services, it is recommended that you use WCF for creating web services, but here is a quick overview of how to create ASP.NET-style web services in Visual Studio.

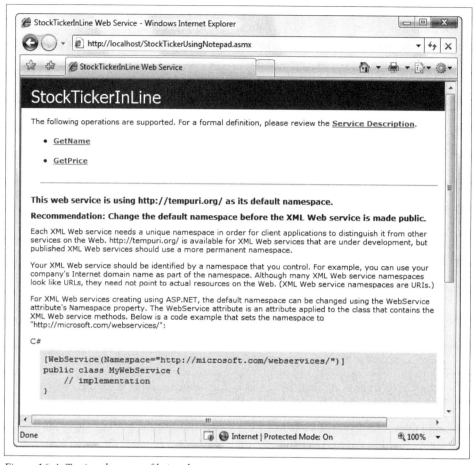

Figure 16-4. Testing the .asmx file in a browser

Creating a Web Service

Though a web service has no user interface and no visual component, the architecture and files used to create a web service are similar to those used to create a web page, which we described in detail in previous chapters. Some of these similarities include the following:

- Access to the full implementation of the .NET Framework and CLR, including the object-oriented architecture, all the base class libraries, and features such as caching, state, and data access
- Nearly identical file and code structures
- All source code files in plain text, which can be created in any text editor

- Full support of Visual Studio, with all its productivity features, including Intelli-Sense, code completion, and integrated debugging
- Configurable on a global or application-wide basis using plain-text configuration files and the Web Site Administration Tool (WAT) in Visual Studio

With that said, web pages and web services are conceptually very different. A web page entails an interface designed for interaction with a person sitting at a web browser. A web service, on the other hand, consists only of methods, some of which are available for remote calls by client applications.

A web service can be coded inline, in a single file with an extension of *.asmx*. Alternatively, the application logic of the web service can be segregated into a code-behind file, which is the default behavior of VS2008. We will show one inline example here, to aid in your understanding of how web services work, but for all the other examples we will use code-behind files from within VS2008.

Code-Behind in Web Services

The rationale for code-behind is that it provides a clean separation between the presentation and programmatic portions of an application. Though this is extremely useful in the development of web pages, it is irrelevant to web services. However, since code-behind is the default coding technique for Visual Studio (which offers so many productivity enhancements) it becomes the de facto preferred technique.

In addition, code-behind will confer a performance advantage over inline code the first time the web service app is run, *if* the web service class is manually compiled and placed in the *bin* directory under the virtual root, because the *.asmx* file is compiled into a class every time it is run. You won't see this advantage, by default, when using ASP.NET 2.0 or later, which places the class source code in the *App_Code* directory and compiles on first use under all circumstances.

You can manually compile the class file and place it in the *bin* directory. We will cover manual compilation and deployment issues in Chapter 20.

Whether you're using an inline or code-behind architecture, the *.asmx* file is the target URL you enter into the browser for testing, or is referenced by the utilities that create the proxy DLL.

As a first step in understanding how web services work, you will create a simple web service twice, the first called *StockTickerInLine*, using any favorite text editor. As the name implies, this example will use the inline coding model. This is the only web service example in this book using that coding model and the only example made outside VS2008. Then you will create essentially the same example, called *StockTickerSimple*, in VS2008.

The StockTicker services will emulate an online source for stock price information. Clients can query about the name and price of a stock given a ticker symbol (e.g., MSFT for Microsoft). In our examples, we'll hardcode the stock prices and store them in a two-dimensional array. When requests come in to the service, we'll respond with the values in this array. The example demonstrates how to define and implement a service. If this web service were an actual production program, the data returned would be fetched from a live database. For a complete discussion of accessing a database, see Chapters 7 through 10. This example web service will expose two web methods:

GetName

> Expects a stock symbol as an argument and returns a string containing the name of the stock

GetPrice

> Expects a stock symbol as an argument and returns a number containing the current price of the stock

Inline with a text editor

To create this web service without the benefit of VS2008 open Notepad or your favorite editor that is capable of creating a flat text file (e.g., not Microsoft Word unless you want to jump through hoops). Enter into the file the code in Example 16-1.

Example 16-1. StockTickerUsingNotepad.asmx

```
<%@ WebService Language="C#" Class="ProgAspNet.StockTickerUsingNotepad" %>

using System;
using System.Web.Services;

namespace ProgAspNet
{
    public class StockTickerUsingNotepad : WebService
    {
        // Construct and fill an array of stock symbols and prices.
        // Note: the stock prices are as of 7/30/08.
        string[,] stocks =
        {
            {"MSFT","Microsoft","26.23"},
            {"DELL","Dell Inc","24.00"},
            {"HPQ","Hewlett-Packard","45.06"},
            {"GOOG","Google","482.70"},
            {"YHOO","Yahoo!","20.03"},
            {"GE","General Electric","28.97"},
            {"IBM","International Business Machines","128.86"},
            {"GM","General Motors","11.40"},
            {"F","Ford Motor Company","4.84"}
        };
```

Example 16-1. StockTickerUsingNotepad.asmx (continued)

```
[WebMethod]
public double GetPrice(string StockSymbol)
// Given a stock symbol, return the price.
{
    // Iterate through the array, looking for the symbol.
    for (int i = 0; i < stocks.GetLength(0); i++)
    {
        // Do a case-insensitive string compare.
        if (String.Compare(StockSymbol, stocks[i,0], true) == 0)
            return Convert.ToDouble(stocks[i,2]);
    }
    return 0;
}


[WebMethod]
public string GetName(string StockSymbol)
// Given a stock symbol, return the name.
{
    // Iterate through the array, looking for the symbol.
    for (int i = 0; i < stocks.GetLength(0); i++)
    {
        // Do a case-insensitive string compare.
        if (String.Compare(StockSymbol, stocks[i,0], true) == 0)
            return stocks[i,1];
    }
    return "Symbol not found.";
}
    }
}
```

To see your service "in action," you'll need to access the page in a browser, so you can save your code as *StockTickerUsingNotepad.asmx* in either a virtual directory you've set up already (see Chapter 4 for how to do this) or the default home directory for Internet Information Services (IIS) (*C:\inetpub\wwwroot*). Vista users, however, should note that you'll need to be an administrator to perform the latter option directly. If you're not, you'll need to save the file in your *Documents* folder first and then move it. The text editor will simply refuse to save the file directly, but moving the file will give you the opportunity to supply an administrative password to complete the move.

Now you can open a browser and point it at *http://localhost/StockTickerUsingNotepad.asmx*. IIS will realize you're requesting a web service directly and will generate a page through which you can access it, such as the one shown back in Figure 16-4.

This *.asmx* file contains the entire web service inline. It defines a namespace called ProgAspNet and creates a class called StockTickerUsingNotepad. The class instantiates and fills an array to contain the stock data and then creates the two WebMethods that comprise the public aspects of the web service.

If you're familiar with web page code, you may notice in Example 16-1 that the code for a web service is almost identical to that in a code-behind page for an equivalent web page. There are some differences, however, which are highlighted in the code example.

The first difference is in the use of a WebService directive at the top of the file rather than a Page directive. As with Page directives (covered in detail in Chapter 6), the WebService directive provides the compiler with necessary information. In this example, it specifies the language in use and the name of the web service class.

The next difference is that the web service class inherits from System.Web.Services.WebService, rather than the Page class. Though this is not a strict requirement, it generally makes your life as a developer much easier. We will cover this issue in detail later in this chapter.

The final difference is that any method that is to be made available as part of the web service, called *web methods*, is decorated with the WebMethod attribute.

Creating an ASP.NET Web Service with VS2008

VS2008 offers the programmer several advantages over a plain-text editor in addition to automating the creation of code-behind. Among them are color-coding of the source code, integrated debugging, IntelliSense, integrated compilation, and full integration with the development environment. Chapter 2 covers VS2008 in detail.

To create a web service equivalent to the previous example in VS2008, select File → New → Web Site and then select ASP.NET Web Service, as shown in Figure 16-5. Leave the Location selection as File System, name it *C16_WebServices*, and click OK.

As with a normal website, VS2008 will create several files and directories, though the specifics are different for web services. In particular, though, it creates a web service file called *Service.asmx* and places its code-behind file, *Service.cs*, in the *App_Code* directory.

 If you had added a new web service to a Web Deployment Project rather than to a Web Site Project, as you've done (implicitly) here, the code-behind file would be kept in the same directory as the *.asmx* file.

We discuss further differences between Web Site and Web Application Projects in Chapter 20.

Before you add the code to the service, let's give it a more meaningful name. In the Solution Explorer, rename *Service.asmx* and *Service.cs* to *StockTickerSimple.asmx* and *StockTickerSimple.cs*, respectively, by right-clicking each file and choosing Rename; now double-click *StockTickerSimple.asmx* to open it. You'll see that it consists of a single WebService directive identifying its code-behind file. You'll need to change it slightly to reflect the renamed code-behind file, as highlighted in Example 16-2. And, for consistency, you'll change the name of the class, too.

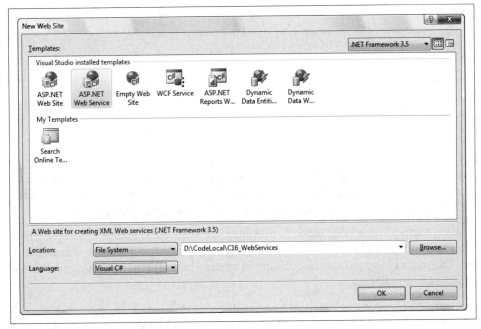

Figure 16-5. Creating a new web service project

Example 16-2. StockTickerSimple.asmx

```
<%@ WebService Language="C#"
    CodeBehind="~/App_Code/StockTickerSimple.cs"
    Class="StockTickerSimple" %>
```

Now double-click *StockTickerSimple.cs* to open that as well. You'll see that the code generated in it by default is your basic Hello World type of program with a few attributes decorating both the class declaration and the HelloWorld method it contains, as shown in Example 16-3.

Example 16-3. The default web service code-behind file

```
using System;
using System.Collections.Generic;
using System.Linq;
using System.Web;
using System.Web.Services;

[WebService(Namespace = "http://tempuri.org/")]
[WebServiceBinding(ConformsTo = WsiProfiles.BasicProfile1_1)]
// To allow this Web Service to be called from script,
// using ASP.NET AJAX, uncomment the following line.
// [System.Web.Script.Services.ScriptService]
public class Service : System.Web.Services.WebService
{
    public Service () {
```

Example 16-3. The default web service code-behind file (continued)

```
        //Uncomment the following line if using designed components
        //InitializeComponent( );
    }

    [WebMethod]
    public string HelloWorld( ) {
        return "Hello World";
    }

}
```

The code-behind file contains a class, named after the web service file, which derives from the System.Web.Services.WebService class. This class has two attributes, WebService and WebServiceBinding, both of which we will describe shortly.

Within the Service class, there is a boilerplate method called HelloWorld, which returns a string. This method is decorated with the WebMethod attribute, which identifies this method as available to consuming applications. We will cover the WebMethod attribute in detail shortly.

To complete the simple web service example, you'll need to rename the class StockTickerSimple to match the WebService declaration you changed earlier and then replace the code within the class with the code highlighted in Example 16-4. This is the same code used in *StockTickerUsingNotepad.asmx*. Finally, you'll need to reference the System namespace with a using statement so that .NET can work with strings.

Example 16-4. StockTickerSimple.cs

```
using System;
using System.Web.Services;

[WebService(Namespace = "http://tempuri.org/")]
[WebServiceBinding(ConformsTo = WsiProfiles.BasicProfile1_1)]
// To allow this Web Service to be called from script,
// using ASP.NET AJAX, uncomment the following line.
// [System.Web.Script.Services.ScriptService]
public class StockTickerSimple : WebService
{
    // Construct and fill an array of stock symbols and prices.
    // Note: the stock prices are as of 7/30/08.
    string[,] stocks =
      {
          {"MSFT","Microsoft","26.23"},
          {"DELL","Dell Inc","24.00"},
          {"HPQ","Hewlett-Packard","45.06"},
          {"GOOG","Google","482.70"},
          {"YHOO","Yahoo!","20.03"},
          {"GE","General Electric","28.97"},
          {"IBM","International Business Machines","128.86"},
```

Example 16-4. StockTickerSimple.cs (continued)

```
          {"GM","General Motors","11.40"},
          {"F","Ford Motor Company","4.84"}
      };

  [WebMethod]
  public double GetPrice(string StockSymbol)
      //  Given a stock symbol, return the price.
  {
      //  Iterate through the array, looking for the symbol.
      for (int i = 0; i < stocks.GetLength(0); i++) {
          //  Do a case-insensitive string compare.
          if (String.Compare(StockSymbol, stocks[i, 0], true) == 0)
              return Convert.ToDouble(stocks[i, 2]);
      }
      return 0;
  }

  [WebMethod]
  public string GetName(string StockSymbol)
      //  Given a stock symbol, return the name.
  {
      //  Iterate through the array, looking for the symbol.
      for (int i = 0; i < stocks.GetLength(0); i++) {
          //  Do a case-insensitive string compare.
          if (String.Compare(StockSymbol, stocks[i, 0], true) == 0)
              return stocks[i, 1];
      }
      return "Symbol not found.";
  }
}
```

Running the web service app will again produce a standard web service test page, as shown in Figure 16-4. In the following sections, you will learn about the WebService directive and the various attributes used in Examples 16-2 and 16-4.

The WebService Directive

You can see the first difference between a web service and a web page in the web service file listed in Example 16-2. A normal *.aspx* file will have a Page directive as its first line, but a web service has a WebService directive as reproduced here:

```
<%@ WebService Language="C#"
    CodeBehind="~/App_Code/StockTickerSimple.cs" Class="StockTickerSimple" %>
```

The WebService directive is required of all web services. Like all directives, it has the following syntax.

```
<%@ DirectiveName attribute="value" [attribute="value"...]%>
```

You can have multiple attribute/value pairs. The order of the attribute/value pairs does not matter.

Language

The WebService directive's Language attribute specifies the language used in the web service. Legal values include C#, VB, and JS for C#, VB.NET, and JScript .NET, respectively. The value is not case-sensitive. The Language attribute is not required. If it is missing, the compiler will deduce the language in use from the extension of the class file.

Class

The WebService directive's Class attribute specifies the name of the class implementing the web service. The Class attribute is required. The class specified can reside either in a separate code-behind file, or inline in a script block in the *.asmx* file.

CodeBehind

The WebService directive's CodeBehind attribute will specify the name and location of the source code file that implements the WebService class if the class is not contained inline with the (*.asmx*) web service file.

Debug

If true, the WebService directive's Debug attribute specifies that the web service will be compiled with debugging enabled. The default is false.

When you develop within VS2008, this attribute is typically omitted and the debug status is controlled by an entry in the *web.config* configuration file.

Deriving from the WebService Class

In the *StockTickerSimple* web service, with the class file listed in Example 16-4, the Service class inherits from the WebService class. Deriving from the WebService class is optional, but it offers several advantages. The principle one being you gain access to several common ASP.NET objects:

Application *and* Session

These objects allow the application to take advantage of state management. For a complete discussion of state management, see Chapter 6.

User

This object is useful for authenticating the caller of a web service. For a complete discussion of security, see Chapter 12.

Context

This object provides access to all HTTP-specific information about the caller's request contained in the HttpContext class.

The main reason you may not want to inherit from WebService is to overcome the limitation imposed by the .NET Framework that a class can inherit from only one other class. Multiple inheritance is not supported. It would be very inconvenient to be restricted to inheriting from WebService if you needed to inherit from another class.

Calling the Web Service

You've already seen that ASP.NET will create a page to view in your browser if you navigate to a web service directly, but nine times out of 10 this won't be how a web service is accessed. Instead, a user will browse to a page that calls the web service behind the scenes for information. In this section, you'll create a simple web page that *consumes* the *StockTickerSimple* web service you just created. As you'll see, VS2008 does all the heavy lifting for you.

With *C16_WebServices* still open in VS2008, click File → Add → New Web Site and create a new website called *C16_WebServiceClients*. Click OK, and you'll see it appear in the Solution Explorer above *C16_WebServices*, as shown in Figure 16-6.

Figure 16-6. Two projects in the Solution Explorer

Now delete *Default.aspx* and add a new web form called *StockTickerClient.aspx*. This page will consume your web service. To demonstrate, add a Label control called lblMessage and two Button controls, btnPost and btnWebService, to the page, as highlighted in Example 16-5. The Click event handler for btnWebService will call the web service and display the stock price for Microsoft in lblMessage. Clicking btnPost will cause the page to post back and the Page_Load handler will show the current time in lblMessage.

Example 16-5. StockTickerClient.aspx

```
<%@ Page Language="C#" AutoEventWireup="true"
    CodeFile="StockTickerClient.aspx.cs" Inherits="StockTickerClient" %>

<!DOCTYPE html PUBLIC "-//W3C//DTD XHTML 1.0 Transitional//EN"
    "http://www.w3.org/TR/xhtml1/DTD/xhtml1-transitional.dtd">
```

Example 16-5. StockTickerClient.aspx (continued)

```
<html xmlns="http://www.w3.org/1999/xhtml">
<head runat="server">
    <title>Stock Ticker Client</title>
</head>
<body>
    <h1>Stock Ticker Simple Client</h1>
    <form id="form1" runat="server">
    <div>
      <p>
        <asp:Label ID="lblMessage" runat="server" />
      </p>
      <p>
        <asp:Button ID="btnPost" runat="server" Text="Post"  />
        <asp:Button ID="btnWebService" runat="server" Text="Web Service"
          onclick="btnWebService_Click" />
      </p>
    </div>
    </form>
</body>
</html>
```

Before you can call the web service in btnWebService_Click, you must first add a web reference to it in VS2008. This will transparently create a proxy class that knows how to call the web service and receive responses from it. It will be the proxy class you actually call in btnWebService_Click. Figures 16-2 and 16-3 illustrate this calling by proxy.

VS2008 can add a web reference to a web service that is:

- In the same solution as the consuming page
- Being served from a virtual directory on your development machine
- Available over the Internet in a location known to a web service (UDDI) directory

To add the web reference, right-click the project entry for the *C16_WebServiceClients* website (it's the one highlighted in Figure 16-6) and click Add Web Reference. You'll get the Add Web Reference dialog shown in Figure 16-7.

In this example, the service is in the same solution, so click the hyperlink marked "Web services in this solution". VS2008 searches for all web services in the solution and returns a list of them, as shown in Figure 16-8.

If you had picked "Web services on the local machine", VS2008 would have searched through all the websites and virtual directories being served by IIS on your local machine and returned a list of the web services they contained.

 For developers using Vista, a list of web services on the local machine is shown only if you are running VS2008 as an administrator and you have installed the "IIS Metabase and IIS 6 configuration compatibility" feature for IIS.

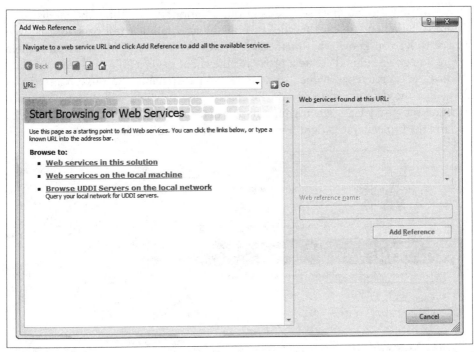

Figure 16-7. The Add Web Reference dialog box

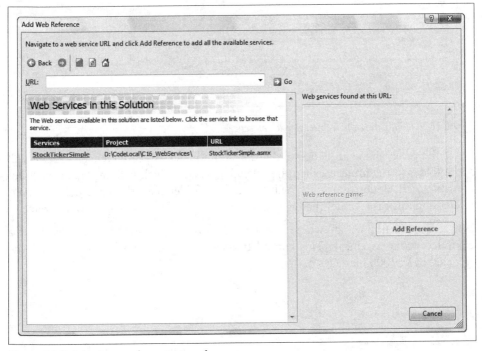

Figure 16-8. Selecting a web service to reference

Only the *StockTickerSimple* service is in our solution, so it's the only one listed in Figure 16-8. When you click it, you'll see the by-now-familiar test page for that web service to let you know what methods it makes available and for you to test them before you go ahead and create a proxy for the client page. You'll also see a text box marked "Web reference name" that allows you to rename the proxy class if you don't like the default, and the Add Reference button which will direct VS2008 to generate the proxy class when you're happy that the service is the one you want to use and the proxy name is right. Figure 16-9 shows the full dialog.

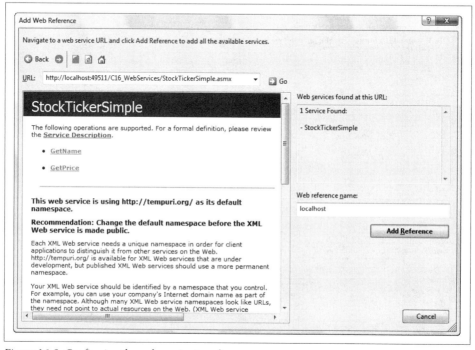

Figure 16-9. Confirming the web service to reference

Leave the proxy name at its default, *localhost*, and click Add Reference. VS2008 will add a folder to the project, called *App_WebReferences*, which will display in the Solution Explorer. Under that folder will be another folder named after the web server, *localhost* in this case. Under that will be files that are used to *describe* the web service.

What you will not see anywhere is either the source code for the proxy class or a compiled proxy assembly. This compiled assembly is there somewhere behind the scenes, but VS2008 manages it.

The reference is made available to the web page at runtime via an entry added to the *web.config* file in *C16_WebServiceClients*. Note that the *xxxx* will be the port number from which the development web server (not IIS) is set to run the web service.

```
<appSettings>
    <add key="localhost.StockTickerSimple"
        value="http://localhost:xxxx/C16_WebServices/StockTickerSimple.asmx"/>
</appSettings>
```

Once the web reference has been added, add the highlighted code in Example 16-6 to *StockTickerClient.aspx.cs* to access the web service when btnWebService is clicked and to display the time when btnPost is clicked (see Example 16-6).

Example 16-6. StockTickerClient.aspx.cs in full

```
using System;
using System.Web.UI;
using localhost;

public partial class StockTickerClient : Page
{
    protected void Page_Load(object sender, EventArgs e)
    {
        if (!IsPostBack)
        {
            lblMessage.Text = "First loaded at " + DateTime.Now.ToLongTimeString( );
        }
        else
        {
            lblMessage.Text = "Postback at " + DateTime.Now.ToLongTimeString( );
        }
    }

    protected void btnWebService_Click(object sender, EventArgs e)
    {
        StockTickerSimple proxy = new StockTickerSimple( );
        lblMessage.Text = String.Format("Current MSFT Price: {0}",
                                proxy.GetPrice("MSFT").ToString( ));
    }
}
```

Run the page and click the Web Service button. The page will access the *StockTickerSimple* web service in the background and return Microsoft's stock price, as shown in Figure 16-10.

As you can see, once the web reference is added to the website, the web service is referenced by creating an instance of the proxy class and then calling one of the service's methods as you would a method on any other class.

Figure 16-10. StockTickerClient.aspx in action

Developing a WCF Web Service

In contrast to ASP.NET web services which were introduced in .NET v1.0 and built into VS2002 at launch, the Windows Communication Foundation (WCF) was introduced in .NET 3.0, a release not tied to any particular release of Visual Studio. Coming after the launch of VS2005, VS2008 is the first release of Visual Studio with built-in support for WCF: project templates and wizards to match those we just demonstrated for ASP.NET web services. Of course, the files generated and the wizards used aren't exactly the same, as the goals of WCF are different from those of ASP.NET services. Unlike building web services in ASP.NET, web services built with WCF can be used in non-web contexts. You can share most of the code you write to implement the same service deployed as a .NET Remoting service, or as a local object, and even if you keep it as a web service, you can choose among several web service standards, not just SOAP.

Creating a WCF Service

WCF is designed around the concept of contracts, which are .NET classes and interfaces that describe your service to would-be users. WCF uses interfaces to define a service because they are completely decoupled from any implementation details. In C#, an interface has just the declarations for methods but no implementations, and any class that implements the interface must provide a definition for each method. Since any client to the service will know only about the interface, this ensures that clients do not tie any of their code to a specific implementation of the service, and will therefore be able to be changed to use other implementations easily.

For more information on interfaces, see *Programming C# 3.0* by Jesse Liberty and Donald Xie (O'Reilly).

A *service contract* is an interface that contains the methods your service exposes. In WCF, each method is defined as an *operation contract*, which defines the name, parameters, and return value. For example, here is a simple service contract with operations:

```
[ServiceContract]
public interface IStockTickerService
{
    [OperationContract]
    int GetStockTickerCount( );

    [OperationContract]
    string GetTickerSymbol(int index);
}
```

As you can see, nothing in this code has anything to do with the Web. You could imagine classes that implement this service could be implemented with a simple class and not use any kind of service.

WCF uses the .NET attributes ServiceContract and OperationContract to mark the parts of the interface that define the service. ServiceContract is used on the interface, and OperationContract is used for each method that is part of the service.

Since the operations in this service use simple .NET types such as int and string, WCF has a built-in mechanism for passing them to the service. If you need to use custom classes, you need to define them as a WCF *data contract*. Example 16-7 shows the same service with a new operation that uses a custom class called StockInfo.

Example 16-7. The IStockTickerServiceWcf interface

```
[ServiceContract]
public interface IStockTickerServiceWcf
{
    [OperationContract]
    int GetStockTickerCount( );

    [OperationContract]
    string GetTickerSymbol(int index);

    [OperationContract]
    StockInfo GetStockInfo(string ticker);
}
```

For GetStockInfo to work, WCF needs more information about what a StockInfo object has in it. Example 16-8 demonstrates how you define the StockInfo class and use the DataContract and DataMember .NET attributes from WCF to indicate which properties should be included (serialized) in responses from the web service.

Example 16-8. Defining the StockInfo DataContract

```
[DataContract]
public class StockInfo
{
    [DataMember]
    public string Ticker { get; set; }
    [DataMember]
    public string Name { get; set; }
    [DataMember]
    public double Price { get; set; }
}
```

Again, this class is not tied to web services in any way. You could use this class in a number of contexts. To continue with this service, you would need to implement IStockTickerServiceWcf. Example 16-9 shows a simple implementation.

Example 16-9. Implementing IStockTickerServiceWcf

```
using System;

public class StockTickerServiceWcf : IStockTickerServiceWcf
{
    string[,] stocks =
      {
          {"MSFT","Microsoft","26.23"},
          {"DELL","Dell Inc","24.00"},
          {"HPQ","Hewlett-Packard","45.06"},
          {"GOOG","Google","482.70"},
          {"YHOO","Yahoo!","20.03"},
          {"GE","General Electric","28.97"},
          {"IBM","International Business Machines","128.86"},
          {"GM","General Motors","11.40"},
          {"F","Ford Motor Company","4.84"}
      };

    public int GetStockTickerCount() {
        return stocks.GetLength(0);
    }

    public string GetTickerSymbol(int index) {
        return stocks[index, 0];
    }

    public StockInfo GetStockInfo(string ticker) {
        StockInfo info = new StockInfo();
        for (int i = 0; i < stocks.GetLength(0); ++i) {
            if (stocks[i, 0] != ticker) continue;
            info.Ticker = stocks[i, 0];
            info.Name = stocks[i, 1];
            info.Price = Double.Parse(stocks[i, 2]);
            return info;
        }
        return null;
```

Example 16-9. Implementing IStockTickerServiceWcf (continued)

```
    }
}
```

With these three classes—IStockTickerServiceWcf, StockTickerServiceWcf, and StockInfo—you have defined everything you need for WCF to generate the web service.

To demonstrate these classes in action and create a WCF service, right-click the project node for your *C16_WebServices* in the Solution Explorer and click Add New Item. Select WCF Service from the Add New Item dialog, as shown in Figure 16-11, name it *StockTickerServiceWcf.svc*, and click Add.

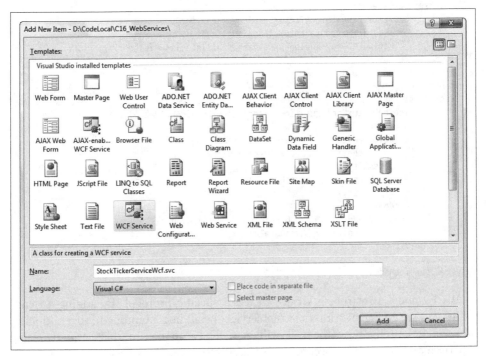

Figure 16-11. Adding a WCF service to your project

VS2008 will create three new files for you:

StockTickerServiceWcf.svc
> This is just a placeholder for the entry point to your service, much as the *.asmx* file is for a SOAP service. It also contains only one line of code—a ServiceHost directive identifying the class that implements it in its Service attribute and the file that contains the class in its CodeBehind attribute.

App_Code\IStockTickerServiceWcf.cs
> This is the file that contains the ServiceContract and any DataContracts for the service. Copy the code in Examples 16-7 and 16-8 into this file, replacing all but the using statements.

App_Code\StockTickerServiceWcf.cs
   This is the file that implements the ServiceContract. Replace all the code in this
   file with that in Example 16-9.

Open *web.config* and scroll to the bottom to see how the service is configured. The
endpoint element highlighted in Example 16-10 is what makes your service a SOAP
service, by setting the binding to wsHttpBinding.

Example 16-10. The default WCF configuration for a SOAP service

```
<system.serviceModel>
    <behaviors>
        <serviceBehaviors>
            <behavior name="StockTickerServiceWcfBehavior">
                <serviceMetadata httpGetEnabled="true" />
                <serviceDebug includeExceptionDetailInFaults="false" />
            </behavior>
        </serviceBehaviors>
    </behaviors>
    <services>
        <service behaviorConfiguration="StockTickerServiceWcfBehavior"
            name="StockTickerServiceWcf">
            <endpoint address="" binding="wsHttpBinding"
                    contract="IStockTickerServiceWcf">
                <identity>
                    <dns value="localhost" />
                </identity>
            </endpoint>
            <endpoint address="mex" binding="mexHttpBinding"
                    contract="IMetadataExchange" />
        </service>
    </services>
</system.serviceModel>
```

In WCF, *bindings* instruct a service to use a specific protocol. By adding an endpoint, you are giving an address to our service. By adding a binding to that endpoint,
you are describing how the call will actually be made. In this case, by using
wsHttpBinding, the service becomes a SOAP web service.

Note that WCF also added another endpoint, called "mex," with the binding set to
mexHttpBinding. This binding is put here to enable discovery of your service and
automatic proxy generation.

Since WCF is for implementing any kind of remote service, not just web services, it
provides other bindings that are not related to the Web.

 For more on configuration options in WCF, see *Learning WCF* by
Michele Leroux Bustamente (O'Reilly), and *Programming WCF Services* by Juval Löwy (O'Reilly).

To see the service running, right-click *StockTickerServiceWcf.svc* and choose View in Browser. You will get a page with instructions on how to create a client, as shown in Figure 16-12.

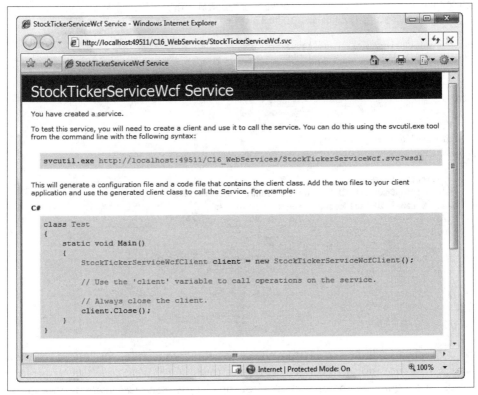

Figure 16-12. Viewing a WCF service directly in a browser

In the next section, you'll see how to follow these instructions and use WCF to create a web page that consumes this web service.

Consuming a WCF Service

To demonstrate how to consume a WCF service, add a new web form to the *C16_WebServiceClients* website and call it *StockTickerWcfClient.aspx*. Add to the page a DropDownList called ddlStocks, a Label called lblMessage, and a Button called btnGetPrice, as shown in Example 16-11. When the page loads, it will call the web service for a list of all the stocks it knows about to populate ddlStocks. When you select a stock in the list and click the Button, the web service will be called again for the stock information to be shown in the Label.

Example 16-11. StockTickerWcfClient.aspx

```
<%@ Page Language="C#" AutoEventWireup="true"
    CodeFile="StockTickerWcfClient.aspx.cs" Inherits="StockTickerWcfClient" %>

<!DOCTYPE html PUBLIC "-//W3C//DTD XHTML 1.0 Transitional//EN"
    "http://www.w3.org/TR/xhtml1/DTD/xhtml1-transitional.dtd">

<html xmlns="http://www.w3.org/1999/xhtml">
<head runat="server">
  <title>WCF Stock Ticker Service Client</title>
</head>
<body>
  <h1>
    WCF Stock Ticker Service Client</h1>
  <form id="form1" runat="server">
  <div>
    <p>
      Select a Stock :
      <asp:DropDownList ID="ddlStocks" runat="server" />
      <asp:Label ID="lblMessage" runat="server" />
    </p>
    <p>
      <asp:Button ID="btnGetPrice" runat="server"
          OnClick="btnGetPrice_Click" Text="Get Stock Price" />
    </p>
  </div>
  </form>
</body>
</html>
```

Before you can call the service from the code behind your page, you'll need to add a *service reference* (not a web reference) for it to the *C16_WebServiceClients* project. To do this, right-click the project node for the *C16_WebServiceClients* website in the Solution Explorer and then you click Add Service Reference. The Add Service Reference dialog appears, allowing you to choose to which WCF service you want to create a reference. Because the service you want to add a reference to is local to your solution, you can click the Discover button and select it from the list of services in the solution, as shown in Figure 16-13. You can also view the ServiceContract it uses by expanding its entry, also shown in Figure 16-13.

If the service you wanted to reference was not part of your solution, you would need to copy the WSDL URL for the service into the address box and click Go. You can find the WSDL URL by viewing the service's endpoint in a browser, as shown back in Figure 16-12. It is the URL highlighted at the top of the page next to *svcutil.exe*. Typically, it is the service's endpoint address suffixed with ?wsdl.

When you've identified and selected the service to reference, you can change the namespace for the proxy class that VS2008 will generate for you once you click OK.

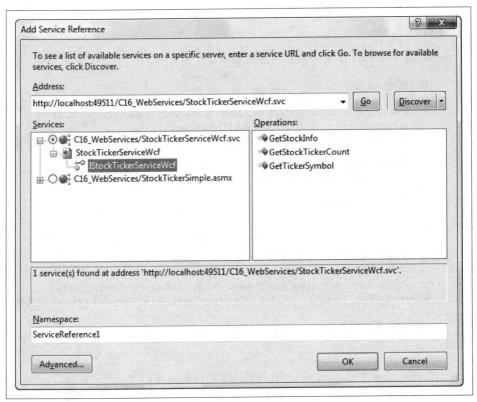

Figure 16-13. Adding a service reference to a WCF service

Note that VS2008 will always name the proxy class by appending the word "Client" to the name of the service—in this case, StockTickerServiceWcfClient—so don't change it to that. Indeed, leave it as the default ServiceReference1 and click OK. As occurred with the ASP.NET web service, VS2008 now generates a folder under *App_ WebReferences* containing all the discovery files for the WCF service, but the code for the proxy class itself remains hidden.

With the reference and proxy class created, you can add the code to access the service to the code-behind page, *StockTickerWcfClient.aspx.cs*, as highlighted in Example 16-12.

Example 16-12. StockTickerWcfClient.aspx.cs in full

```
using System;
using System.Web.UI;
using System.Web.UI.WebControls;
using ServiceReference1;
```

Example 16-12. StockTickerWcfClient.aspx.cs in full (continued)

```
public partial class StockTickerWcfClient : Page
{
    protected void Page_Load(object sender, EventArgs e)
    {
        if (!IsPostBack)
        {
            StockTickerServiceWcfClient svcClient = new StockTickerServiceWcfClient();
            int stockCount = svcClient.GetStockTickerCount();
            for (int i = 0; i < stockCount; ++i)
            {
                ddlStocks.Items.Add(
                    new ListItem(svcClient.GetTickerSymbol(i)));
            }
            svcClient.Close();
        }
    }

    protected void btnGetPrice_Click(object sender, EventArgs e)
    {
        StockTickerServiceWcfClient svcClient = new StockTickerServiceWcfClient();
        lblMessage.Text = svcClient.GetStockInfo(ddlStocks.SelectedValue).Price.ToString(
);
        svcClient.Close();
    }
}
```

Save all your work and then view *StockTickerWcfClient.aspx* in a browser. You'll see the DropDownList does indeed get populated through the web service. Select a stock and click the button. The stock price will be returned to you, as shown in Figure 16-14.

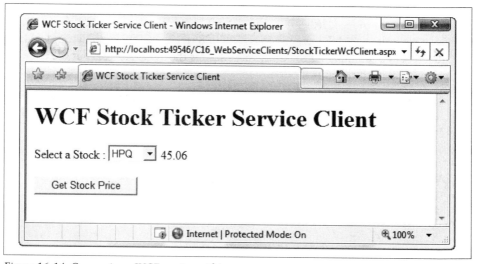

Figure 16-14. Consuming a WCF service within a page

Visual Studio generated `StockTickerServiceWcfClient` when you added the service reference to the project. It implements the `IStockTickerServiceWcf` interface by turning each method call into a web request to the web service that actually implements the functionality.

In *web.config*, including the service reference adds a `<client>` section defining the endpoint for the service to the `<system.serviceModel>` element:

```
<system.serviceModel>
  <client>
    <endpoint
address="http://localhost:xxxx/C16_WebServices/StockTickerServiceWcf.svc"
        binding="wsHttpBinding"
bindingConfiguration="WSHttpBinding_IStockTickerServiceWcf"
        contract="ServiceReference1.IStockTickerServiceWcf"
        name="WSHttpBinding_IStockTickerServiceWcf">
      <identity>
        <dns value="localhost"/>
      </identity>
    </endpoint>
  </client>
```

The endpoint node's address attribute is configured to the URL that was used to create the reference, and can be changed later. Note that the highlighted ***xxxx*** will be the port number from which the development web server (not IIS) is set to run the web service. The bindingConfiguration is set to `WSHttpBinding_IStockTickerServiceWcf`, which refers to a binding element that is also in *web.config*. VS2008 gives the endpoint this same name, and although there is no conflict, it might be better for you to change the name attribute of the endpoint to something that is more memorable, such as `StockTickerEndpoint`, so that there is no confusion. The code generated in `StockTickerServiceWcfClient` will find the endpoint configuration by its contract attribute, not its name, but since you could want to use a name in your own code, it's better to make it clear. The dns element in the identity element will need to be updated when the service is deployed into production. The identity is used to help a client verify that the service is being served from the server for which it was written and can help to detect fraudulent web services.

Once you create an object of `StockTickerServiceWcfClient`, you can call the operations in it just like any other object. In `Page_Load`, the service is used to get the list of ticker symbols to populate the drop-down list. First, `GetStockTickerCount` is called to get the count of ticker symbols, and then in the loop, `GetTickerSymbol` is called for each stock in the list to get the symbol to put in the list.

In `btnGetPrice_Click`, you again create a `StockTickerServiceClient` object and call `GetStockInfo` to return the information for the chosen symbol in the `DropDownList`. Then the `Price` property of the `StockInfo` object returned by the service is displayed in the `Label` on the page.

Using WCF to Call a Public Service

Not only can you call services you create, but you can also call services created and hosted by others. Since SOAP is an open standard, it is often used to implement services on the public Internet. The Microsoft Live Search web API uses SOAP and WSDL to implement the Microsoft search service. The WSDL URL you'll need to create a reference to this service is *http://soap.search.msn.com/webservices.asmx?wsdl*. To demonstrate, you'll create a new web page that uses the Live Search Web Service to search for pages on the Internet given a keyword.

 To follow this demonstration, you'll need to generate a developer key to call the MS Live API. This is so Microsoft can monitor who is using the web services and can set a limit on how much any one developer uses it over a period of time. To generate the key, follow these steps:

1. Go to *http://search.msn.com/developer*.
2. Click the "Create and Manage your application IDs" link.
3. Log in with your Windows Live ID.
4. Click "Get a new App ID" and follow the instructions.
5. At the end of the process, Microsoft will assign you a unique string to use in your search requests. Copy that to somewhere local for easy reference.

If you are using a new App ID, it may take a few minutes before it is activated.

Add to *C16_WebServiceClients* a new web form called *LiveClient.aspx*, and add to it a TextBox called txtSearchFor, a Button named btnSearch, and a Label named lblResults, as shown in Example 16-13.

Example 16-13. LiveSearch.aspx

```
<%@ Page Language="C#" AutoEventWireup="true"
    CodeFile="LiveClient.aspx.cs" Inherits="LiveClient" %>

<!DOCTYPE html PUBLIC "-//W3C//DTD XHTML 1.0 Transitional//EN"
    "http://www.w3.org/TR/xhtml1/DTD/xhtml1-transitional.dtd">

<html xmlns="http://www.w3.org/1999/xhtml">
<head runat="server">
  <title>MS Live Search Service Client</title>
</head>
<body>
  <h1>MS Live Search Service Client</h1>
  <form id="form1" runat="server">
  <div>
    <p>
      <asp:TextBox ID="txtSearchFor" runat="server"></asp:TextBox>
      <asp:Button ID="btnSearch" runat="server" Text="Search" OnClick="btnSearch_Click" />
    </p>
```

Example 16-13. LiveSearch.aspx (continued)

```
    <p>
       <asp:Label runat="server" ID="lblResults" />
    </p>
  </div>
  </form>
</body>
</html>
```

To add a reference to the Live Search Web Service, right-click the *C16_WebServiceClients* project item in the Solution Explorer, and click Add Service Reference. When the Add Service Reference dialog appears, type *http://soap.search.msn.com/webservices. asmx?wsdl* into the Address box and click Go. VS2008 will retrieve a description of the web service at that address and show it in the dialog, as shown in Figure 16-15.

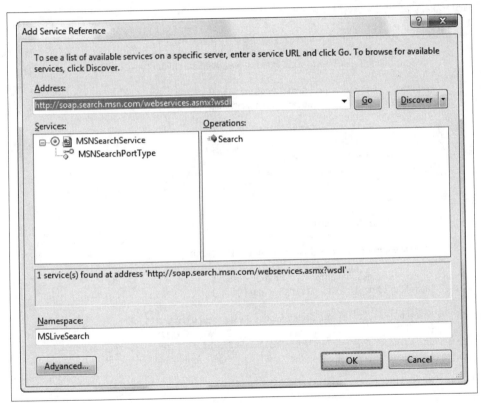

Figure 16-15. Adding a service reference to MS Live Search

Change the namespace for this service from ServiceReference2 to MSLiveSearch and then click OK. Once again, VS2008 will create all the DataContract, ServiceContract, and proxy classes and will configure an endpoint and binding for us in our *web.config* file. To consume the service in *LiveClient.aspx*, you'll need to add code to the handler for btnSearch_Click which will call the service, sending it the contents of the txtSearch, and retrieving search results for that text for display in the Label, as shown in Example 16-14.

 You must change the line in Example 16-14 where req.AppID is assigned to use your key rather than *xxxx*.

Example 16-14. LiveSearch.aspx.cs

```
using System;
using System.Text;
using System.Web.UI;
using MSLiveSearch;

public partial class LiveClient : Page
{
    protected void btnSearch_Click(object sender, EventArgs e)
    {
        MSNSearchPortTypeClient srchClient = new MSNSearchPortTypeClient( );

        SearchRequest req = new SearchRequest( );
        req.AppID = "xxxx"; // update with your App ID
        req.Query = txtSearchFor.Text;

        SourceRequest[] srcReq = new SourceRequest[1];
        srcReq[0] = new SourceRequest( );
        srcReq[0].Source = SourceType.Web;
        srcReq[0].ResultFields = ResultFieldMask.Url | ResultFieldMask.Title;

        req.Requests = srcReq;
        req.CultureInfo = "en-US";

        SearchResponse srchResponse = srchClient.Search(req);

        // create links based on the search results
        StringBuilder sb = new StringBuilder( );

        foreach (Result res in srchResponse.Responses[0].Results)
        {
            sb.AppendFormat("<a href='{0}'>{1}</a><br />", res.Url, res.Title);
        }

        lblResults.Text = sb.ToString( );
    }
}
```

Save your code and view *LiveClient.aspx* in your browser. Search for some text as you would in your favorite search engine and click the button. You'll get the top results back for that text, as shown in Figure 16-16.

Figure 16-16. Accessing MS Live Search as a web service

In this code, MSNSearchPortTypeClient is an automatically generated proxy class. SearchRequest, SourceRequest, Result, and many other classes are DataContract classes and were also automatically generated. If you look in your *web.config* file, you'll see that another client endpoint and binding have been defined and configured in the <system.serviceModel> section to point to the service. The WSDL from *http://soap.search.msn.com/webservices.asmx?wsdl* has all of the information that WCF needs to create the classes and this configuration section. The endpoint node ties together the address, the type of service, and the contract that it provides.

Creating and Consuming AJAX-Enabled Web Services

AJAX (Asynchronized JavaScript and XML) is a popular way to enhance web pages to make them more interactive for the user. In an AJAX style, instead of submitting an entire page to the server and generating a new page, you make connections to servers with JavaScript and then use the results to change the existing page. Originally, this was done with XML, but the data can be in any format and still be considered AJAX. In VS2008, there is direct support for AJAX in ASP.NET, and combined with WCF you can call web services directly from the browser in JavaScript.

When you're building a service for use in ASP.NET AJAX, VS2008 can perform most of these steps for you. Let's build an AJAX page using this built-in support.

In the preceding example, you created a page to search for text using Microsoft's MS Live Search service. In this demonstration, you'll repeat the exercise but you'll use AJAX to view the results without page refreshes. In contrast to the preceding example, rather than calling the Live Search service directly from the page, you must first create an AJAX-enabled WCF service of your own that will call Live Search on behalf of your page's. The page itself must also be AJAX-enabled.

To create the new service, right-click the *C16_WebServiceClients* project in the Solution Explorer and click Add New Item. From the Add New Item dialog, select "AJAX-enabled WCF Service" and call it *LiveSearchWithAjax.svc*, as shown in Figure 16-17. Click Add to generate the required files.

Do not add the new service to the *C16_WebServices* project. It's important that when you call server resources (in this case, a web service) from JavaScript that you always call back to the same site that served the page with the JavaScript code, since the browser will consider it to be a cross-domain scripting security issue otherwise. Having both the service and the consuming page on the same site will mean we don't have any cross-domain scripting issues and it should work fine in any browser.

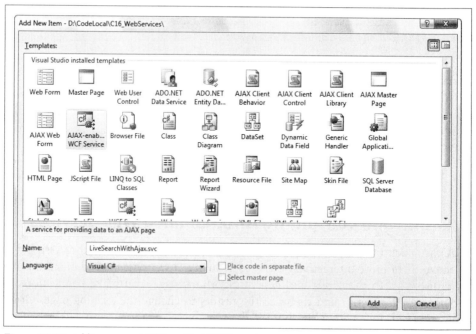

Figure 16-17. Adding a new AJAX-enabled WCF service

Now you can incorporate the code that called the Live Search service in Example 16-14 into the code for the new AJAX-enabled web service. Open *LiveSearchWithAjax.cs* and replace the contents with the code in Example 16-15, remembering to replace ***xxxx*** with your own application key.

Example 16-15. LiveSearchWithAjax.cs

```
using System;
using System.Collections.Generic;
using System.Runtime.Serialization;
using System.ServiceModel;
using System.ServiceModel.Activation;
using MSLiveSearch;

[ServiceContract(Namespace = "")]
[AspNetCompatibilityRequirements(RequirementsMode = AspNetCompatibilityRequirementsMode.
Allowed)]
public class LiveSearchWithAjax
{
    [OperationContract]
    public List<LinkInfo> Search(String query) {
        MSNSearchPortTypeClient srchClient = new MSNSearchPortTypeClient();

        SearchRequest req = new SearchRequest();
        req.AppID = "xxxx"; // replace with your App ID
        req.Query = query;

        SourceRequest[] srcReq = new SourceRequest[1];
        srcReq[0] = new SourceRequest();
        srcReq[0].Source = SourceType.Web;
        srcReq[0].ResultFields = ResultFieldMask.Url | ResultFieldMask.Title;

        req.Requests = srcReq;
        req.CultureInfo = "en-US";

        SearchResponse srchResponse = srchClient.Search(req);

        // create links based on the search results
        List<LinkInfo> li = new List<LinkInfo>();
        foreach (Result res in srchResponse.Responses[0].Results) {
            LinkInfo link = new LinkInfo();
            link.url = res.Url;
            link.title = res.Title;
            li.Add(link);
        }
        return li;
    }
}

[DataContract]
public class LinkInfo
```

Example 16-15. LiveSearchWithAjax.cs (continued)

```
{
    [DataMember]
    public string url { get; set; }
    [DataMember]
    public string title { get; set; }
}
```

The new service makes available a single method called Search which takes in some text with which to query Live Search and returns a list of LinkInfo objects defined in the DataContract at the end of Example 16-15. Each LinkInfo contains two strings: one for the title of the result page and one for its URL.

With the web service created, you'll need to create a page to consume it. Add to the *C16_WebServiceClients* website a new AJAX-enabled web form called *LiveAjaxClient.aspx*. Following the client-side approach, you'll use standard HTML elements to re-create the layout of *LiveClient.aspx* and client-side JavaScript to enable its calls to the web service. Add the highlighted code in Example 16-16 to *LiveAjaxClient.aspx* to achieve this. There is no code to add to *LiveAjaxClient.aspx.cs*.

Example 16-16. LiveAjaxClient.aspx

```
<%@ Page Language="C#" AutoEventWireup="true"
    CodeFile="LiveAjaxClient.aspx.cs" Inherits="LiveAjaxClient" %>

<!DOCTYPE html PUBLIC "-//W3C//DTD XHTML 1.0 Transitional//EN"
    "http://www.w3.org/TR/xhtml1/DTD/xhtml1-transitional.dtd">

<html xmlns="http://www.w3.org/1999/xhtml">
<head runat="server">
  <title>Ajax-Enabled Live Search Client</title>
  <script type="text/javascript">
    function Search(query)
    {
        LiveSearchWithAjax.Search(query, OnSearchSucceeds);
    }

    function OnSearchSucceeds(results)
    {
        var html = "";
        for (var i = 0; i < results.length; ++i)
        {
            html += '<a href="'+results[i].url+'">'+results[i].title + "</a><br/>";
        }
        document.getElementById('pnlResults').innerHTML = html;
    }
  </script>
</head>
```

Example 16-16. LiveAjaxClient.aspx (continued)

```
<body>
  <h1>Ajax-Enabled Live Search Client</h1>
  <form id="form1" runat="server">
  <div>
    <asp:ScriptManager ID="ScriptManager1" runat="server">
      <Services>
        <asp:ServiceReference Path="~/LiveSearchWithAjax.svc" />
      </Services>
    </asp:ScriptManager>
    <input type="text" id="tbSearchFor" />
    <input type="button" id="btnSearch" value="Search"
      onclick="Search(document.getElementById('tbSearchFor').value);" />
    <div id="pnlResults" />
  </div>
  </form>
</body>
</html>
```

Save and run *LiveAjaxClient.aspx*. Once again, you'll be able to search the Web for any term you add to the page, as shown in Figure 16-18.

Figure 16-18. LiveAjaxClient.aspx in action

This page puts a simple search form on the page and sets the onclick event of the button to call a JavaScript function called Search( ). As in the previous example, you have an automatically generated proxy object (LiveSearchWithAjax) which was created by the <ServiceReference> tag inside the ScriptManager tag:

```
<asp:ScriptManager ID="ScriptManager1" runat="server">
    <Services>
        <asp:ServiceReference Path="~/LiveSearchWithAjax.svc" />
    </Services>
</asp:ScriptManager>
```

The ScriptManager tag uses the service information it contains to request that the service send JavaScript code to create a proxy that can be used to make the web service call from the browser. The class will match the name of the service class, LiveSearchWithAjax.

In the Search( ) function, Search( ) is called on the LiveSearchWithAjax object passing in the query and a function to call when the function succeeds (OnSearchSucceeds). Because this call is asynchronous, you can't process the results here; you must wait for the call to finish. If it's successful, it will call OnSearchSucceeds( ) for you and will pass in the results.

```
function Search(query)
{
    LiveSearchWithAjax.Search(query, OnSearchSucceeds);
}
```

In OnSearchSucceeds, you can use the return value that is passed in as the results argument. Since LiveSearchWithAjax.Search( ) on the server side returned a List<LinkInfo> object, WCF automatically generates a JavaScript array with objects that match the LinkInfo DataContract you defined. You can simply access results[i].title and results[i].url to build up the links to the search results:

```
function OnSearchSucceeds(results)
{
    var html = "";
    for (var i = 0; i < results.length; ++i)
    {
        html += '<a href="'+results[i].url+'">'+results[i].title + "</a><br/>";
    }
    document.getElementById('pnlResults').innerHTML = html;
}
```

It is worth reiterating here that because both the web service and the HTML are hosted by the same server, we don't have any cross-domain scripting issues and it should work fine in any browser. It's important when you call server resources from JavaScript that you always call back to the same server that served the page with the JavaScript code, since the browser will consider it to be a security issue otherwise. In our case, since we want to ultimately call a service on a third-party server (MS Live), we make that call from the server where we have control.

Introducing REST and JSON

SOAP is just one standard for implementing web services, but it is not the only one. Another popular style of implementation is to use REST to define a service's location and make calls to the service, and JSON to define the data. REST is a simple style of calling web services that is closely tied to the verbs (e.g., GET and POST) provided by HTTP, and JSON is a simple alternative to XML that is based on how data is defined in JavaScript. One important advantage of SOAP is that it is strictly defined, and when it is coupled with WSDL, it is easier to write tools that automatically generate proxies. REST and JSON are very simple protocols which are easy to code against in any language without the need for tools, and parsing of JSON is built into JavaScript. JSON also often uses less bandwidth than XML.

REST

REST stands for Representational State Transfer, and it is a style of service rather than an exact specification. REST services consist of a number of uniquely identifiable "resources," and there are only four operations one can perform with a resource: read it, modify it, delete it, or create a new one.

When REST services are exposed over HTTP (as is typically the case), URIs are used to refer to server-side resources, and operations on those resources are represented as the HTTP verbs GET, POST, DELETE, and PUT.

A simple example is a book database. A URI to a book could be:

http://bookdatabase.oreilly.com/books/ISBN/<isbn_id>

where *isbn_id* is the unique identifier for the book. The URI is used to uniquely identify the book, which is the resource in this case.

A GET request is what happens when you type a URL into a browser. In REST, GET is used for getting server-side resources, and should never change their state. Since GET is read-only, it is safe to make the same request over and over (refreshing in a browser or having a proxy retry a request), and there are defined caching behaviors. In the book example, if you issue a GET on the URI for a book, you should get data describing the book.

If you need to change the state of an existing server-side resource, use POST. In a browser, POST is what happens on most forms that update the site's data. One of the main differences between POST and GET is that since POST changes the resource, you cannot arbitrarily retry it. You have probably seen this in your browser if you have ever refreshed a page that was the result of submitting a form—the browser will warn you that refreshing will actually repeat the action (such as placing an order). This can have unforeseen consequences if the site doesn't guard against it. The same is true for web services built around POST.

PUT and DELETE are not commonly used on most websites, which usually use POST to add and delete resources. If the preceding book example had a web user interface, you would expect that the delete and add functionality would be implemented by forms that use POST.

REST services use PUT and DELETE. The advantage of PUT and DELETE over POST for these operations is that they can be safely retried. A PUT or DELETE of the same resource done twice in a row is usually safe because the HTTP standard defines these operations as *idempotent*, which means that repeated identical requests should have the same result as a single request (for more information, visit *http://www.w3.org/Protocols/rfc2616/rfc2616-sec9.html*). Also, by using PUT and DELETE you are declaring your intent more specifically. GET, POST, PUT, and DELETE are analogous to the SQL commands SELECT, UPDATE, INSERT, and DELETE, which are separate commands for a lot of the same reasons.

REST doesn't specify how to form resource URIs, query strings, POST data, or what the result formats from any of these operations will be. Any REST-based (or RESTful) service will need to be documented to provide this information.

JSON

JSON, or JavaScript Object Notation, is the subset of JavaScript that is used to define values such as integers, Booleans, and arrays. Because of this, and because JavaScript provides functions to parse itself, JSON is very easy to use in JavaScript. The format is simple enough to parse in any language, and parsers for many other languages are available on *http://json.org*.

JSON is used in a lot of places where you might use XML. Its main benefits are that it is much lighter in weight (both to humans and on bandwidth), and it is easy and fast to parse in JavaScript. Let's look at an example.

Here's some simple XML to represent a collection of books:

```
<books>
    <book title="Frankenstein" author="Mary Shelley" />
    <book title="1984" author="George Orwell" />
    <book title="The Sun Also Rises" author="Ernest Hemingway" />
    <book title="Pride and Prejudice" author="Jane Austen" />
</books>
```

In JSON, it might look like this:

```
{ "books": [
    { "title": "Frankenstein", "author": "Mary Shelley" },
    { "title": "1984", "author": "George Orwell" },
    { "title": "The Sun Also Rises", "author": "Ernest Hemingway" },
    { "title": "Pride and Prejudice", "author": "Jane Austen" }
  ]}
```

The basic structure is to use curly braces to enclose an object. An object has keys and values separated by colons and delimited with commas. Strings are enclosed in double quotation marks, and the keys of an object are always a string. The values of an object can be any JSON-supported type, including strings, other objects, numbers, Booleans (true or false), a special null value, and arrays. JSON arrays are enclosed in square brackets and are a comma-separated list of any JSON type (including objects and arrays).

Table 16-1 demonstrates some other simple types defined in JSON.

Table 16-1. .NET types and their JSON-equivalent definitions

JSON	Description
`"hello world"`	The string `"hello world"`
`123`	The number 123
`123.45`	The number 123.45

`{ "name" : "Bob" }`	An object with one property, name, which is set to `"Bob"`. In JavaScript, you could use it like this:
	`    obj.name`
	or like this:
	`    obj["name"]`

`{`
`  "name": "Bob",`
`  "age" : 40`
`}`
	An object as in the preceding table entry, but with a second property, age, set to 40. In JavaScript, the age is a number and can be used as such:
	`    var ageInOneYear = obj.age + 1;`

`[ 1, 2, 3, 4 ]`	An array of the numbers from 1 to 4
`[ 1, "hello" ]`	A heterogeneous array with the number 1 and the string `"hello"`

`{`
`  "name": "Bob",`
`  "age":  40,`
`  "kids": ["Sally","John"]`
`}`
	Another object with name `"Bob"`, age 40, and a property called `kids` set to the array with `"Sally"` as the first element and `"John"` as the second. Access it like this:
	`    var firstKid = obj.kids[0];`

Arrays can nest other arrays and objects, and objects can nest other objects and arrays.

> You can find the full specification for JSON at *http://json.org*, which also has open source JSON parsers for almost every common programming language, and an alternative parser for JavaScript which can be used for JSON strings on which it is unsafe to call eval( ).

If the earlier book list were stored in a JavaScript variable named jsonString, you could parse it like this:

```
var bookList = eval('(' + jsonString + ')');
```

Then you could use it like this:

```
for (var i = 0; i < bookList.books.length; ++i)
{
    document.write(bookList.books[i].title +
        " was written by " + bookList.books[i].author + "<br/>");
}
```

The JavaScript function, eval( ), runs any JavaScript string you pass to it, not just JSON (which is a subset of JavaScript). This means that if you did not create the string yourself, it isn't safe to use eval( ), because the string might contain malicious JavaScript code. If your JSON string is made up of user-supplied data, use the JavaScript JSON parser from *http://json.org*. Either method will result in a full JavaScript object that is easy to use in the rest of your code.

Also, although JSON is a popular choice for REST-based web services, the two are not linked together. REST can return any resource type (HTML, XML, PDF, JPEG, plain text, etc.), and JSON can be used outside RESTful services.

Consuming a RESTful Web Service

Google provides standard ways to conduct searches programmatically. The server-side search API from Google is based on REST over HTTP and the response format is JSON. Like the MS Live Search example, this example uses a public web service to implement a search over a single website, but because the service is not self-describing, we won't be able to use a wizard and will have to write the code to call the service and parse its results manually.

 Complete documentation for Google's search web service is available online at *http://code.google.com/apis/ajaxsearch/documentation/#fonje*.

To demonstrate, you'll create another simple search form, but this time you'll write the code to query and parse the results from the service yourself. To begin, create a new web form called *GoogleClient.aspx* in your *C16_WebServiceClients* website and add a TextBox, Button, and Label to your page to enable the search and viewing of the results, as shown in Example 16-17.

Example 16-17. GoogleSearch.aspx

```
<%@ Page Language="C#" AutoEventWireup="true"
    CodeFile="GoogleClient.aspx.cs" Inherits="GoogleClient" %>

<!DOCTYPE html PUBLIC "-//W3C//DTD XHTML 1.0 Transitional//EN"
    "http://www.w3.org/TR/xhtml1/DTD/xhtml1-transitional.dtd">
<html xmlns="http://www.w3.org/1999/xhtml">
```

Example 16-17. GoogleSearch.aspx (continued)

```
<head runat="server">
  <title>Google Search Client</title>
</head>
<body>
  <h1>
    Google Search Client</h1>
  <form id="form1" runat="server">
  <div>
    <p>
      <asp:TextBox ID="txtSearchFor" runat="server"></asp:TextBox>
      <asp:Button ID="btnSearch" runat="server"
                  Text="Search" OnClick="btnSearch_Click" />
    </p>
    <p>
      <asp:Label runat="server" ID="lblResults" />
    </p>
  </div>
  </form>
</body>
</html>
```

Initially, at least, the code to call the Google search service is minimal and runs completely in the Button's Click event handler. Open *GoogleClient.aspx.cs* and replace its contents with the code in Example 16-18.

Example 16-18. The event handler for the Button's Click event

```
using System;
using System.Net;
using System.Web.UI;

public partial class GoogleClient : Page
{
    protected void btnSearch_Click(object sender, EventArgs e)
    {
        WebClient wc = new WebClient( );
        String url = String.Format(
            "http://ajax.googleapis.com/ajax/services/search/web?v=1.0&q={0}",
                Server.UrlEncode(txtSearchFor.Text));

        String json = wc.DownloadString(url);
        lblResults.Text = json;
    }
}
```

If you save and run *GoogleClient.aspx* now, the page will indeed query Google for the text you've specified, but the results are returned in raw JSON and are not particularly legible, as shown in Figure 16-19.

Figure 16-19. GoogleClient.aspx mark 1: it works, but the results need to be parsed

The code itself is straightforward. The documentation for the service states that this URL, *http://ajax.googleapis.com/ajax/services/search/web?v=1.0&q=<search_term>*, should be used to access the service where *search_term* should be replaced by your query. The `DownloadString` method of the `WebClient` class makes an HTTP connection to the URL and makes a GET request. Google's web service responds with the search results in JSON format and that's sent directly to the `Label`.

To make a useful page, you'll have to parse the result. Fortunately, WCF introduced the `DataContractJsonSerializer` class (in the `System.Runtime.Serialization.Json` namespace) to aid in parsing JSON in .NET 3.5.

To use the serializer, you must create classes that correspond to your JSON format. The `DataContractJsonSerializer` uses reflection on a type that you provide to match the parts of the JSON string to its member variables. The Google JSON is a little complex to start with, so let's look at an example for the book list JSON we had earlier:

```
{ "books": [
    { "title": "Frankenstein", "author": "Mary Shelley" },
    { "title": "1984", "author": "George Orwell" },
    { "title": "The Sun Also Rises", "author": "Ernest Hemingway" },
    { "title": "Pride and Prejudice", "author": "Jane Austen" }
    ]}
```

Serialization

Serialization is a process whereby an in-memory object is transformed into a stream of bytes that can be used to store the object's state (in a file or database) or send the object's state over a network. Reformatting the bytes back into an object is called *deserialization*. The exact format of the bytes is implemented by the serializer/deserializer, and in .NET, you can find standard ones in the System.Runtime.Serialization namespace.

.NET serializers store the bytes into Stream objects from the System.IO namespace. A *stream* is simply a place where you can store bytes and read them. If you want to store the bytes in a file, use a FileStream; to keep the bytes in memory, use a MemoryStream.

You need to create a class for each object type, with a public member variable for each key. The classes should have a DataContract attribute, and the members should have a DataMember attribute. Use a .NET array type for JSON arrays.

The names of these members should correspond to the key names in JSON. Here are the classes into which this JSON string would parse:

```
[DataContract]
public class Book
{
    [DataMember]
    public string title;
    [DataMember]
    public string author;
}

[DataContract]
public class Booklist
{
    [DataMember]
    public Book[] books;
}
```

You need the following using statements for the classes you're using here:

```
using System.Runtime.Serialization;
using System.Runtime.Serialization.Json;
using System.IO;
using System.Text;
```

To parse it, use this code:

```
public Booklist ParseBooksJson(string json)
{
    using (MemoryStream ms = new MemoryStream(Encoding.ASCII.GetBytes(json)))
    {
        DataContractJsonSerializer jsonSerializer =
            new DataContractJsonSerializer(typeof(Booklist));
        return jsonSerializer.ReadObject(ms) as Booklist;
    }
}
```

The json argument contains the JSON string that represents the book list:

```
{ "books": [
    { "title": "Frankenstein", "author": "Mary Shelley" },
    { "title": "1984", "author": "George Orwell" },
    { "title": "The Sun Also Rises", "author": "Ernest Hemingway" },
    { "title": "Pride and Prejudice", "author": "Jane Austen" }
]}
```

The ReadObject method in DataContractJsonSerializer takes a stream containing that string and tries to parse it into a class you specify (in this case, Booklist). Serializers read from streams so you can point them to files, databases, network connections, or anywhere you get bytes. A MemoryStream is an easy way to take an array of bytes you already have in memory and present it as a stream to a serializer.

ReadObject parses the string by matching the keys in the JSON with the members of the class by name. The "books" key at the beginning of the JSON string corresponds to the books field in the Booklist class. Since the books field is an array, the parser expects the value of the JSON "books" key will be an array (which it is). It tries to parse each array element as a Book class, which means matching the title and author keys in the JSON with the title and author fields in the Book class.

Now that you've seen how to translate JSON into a set of classes that will let .NET parse it, you can create the classes to parse the Google Search API. The format of the JSON string returned by the Google API is described here:

http://code.google.com/apis/ajaxsearch/documentation/#fonje

The resultant JSON is more complex than the book example, but if you go through the same process as before, you will end up with the classes that DataContractJsonSerializer can use to parse the data automatically.

The JSON example given in the documentation is:

```
{"responseData": {
 "results": [
  {
   "GsearchResultClass": "GwebSearch",
   "unescapedUrl": "http://en.wikipedia.org/wiki/Paris_Hilton",
   "url": "http://en.wikipedia.org/wiki/Paris_Hilton",
   "visibleUrl": "en.wikipedia.org",
   "cacheUrl": "http://www.google.com/search?q\u003dcache:TwrPfhd22hYJ:en.wikipedia.
org",
   "title": "\u003cb\u003eParis Hilton\u003c/b\u003e - Wikipedia, the free
encyclopedia",
   "titleNoFormatting": "Paris Hilton - Wikipedia, the free encyclopedia",
   "content": "\[1\] In 2006, she released her debut album..."
  },
  {
   "GsearchResultClass": "GwebSearch",
   "unescapedUrl": "http://www.imdb.com/name/nm0385296/",
   "url": "http://www.imdb.com/name/nm0385296/",
```

```
    "visibleUrl": "www.imdb.com",
    "cacheUrl": "http://www.google.com/search?q\u003dcache:1i34KkqnsooJ:www.imdb.com",
    "title": "\u003cb\u003eParis Hilton\u003c/b\u003e",
    "titleNoFormatting": "Paris Hilton",
    "content": "Self: Zoolander. Socialite \u003cb\u003eParis Hilton\u003c/b\u003e..."
    },
    ...
  ],
  "cursor": {
    "pages": [
    { "start": "0", "label": 1 },
    { "start": "4", "label": 2 },
    { "start": "8", "label": 3 },
    { "start": "12","label": 4 }
    ],
    "estimatedResultCount": "59600000",
    "currentPageIndex": 0,
    "moreResultsUrl": "http://www.google.com/search?oe\u003dutf8\u0026ie\u003dutf8..."
  }
}
, "responseDetails": null, "responseStatus": 200}
```

The returned object has three properties—responseData, responseDetails, and
responseStatus—so we can define a class to hold this object as follows:

```
[DataContract]
public class GoogleSearchResponse
{
    [DataMember]
    public GoogleResponseData responseData;
    [DataMember]
    public string responseDetails;
    [DataMember]
    public int responseStatus;
}
```

Since responseData is itself an object, you will need to create GoogleResponseData to
hold its members. It has one property called results which is an array of search
results, and another called cursor which has a pages array with search results page
information—it can be used to find out how many pages of search results there are
(the length of the array), the index of the first search result on the page, and more
information about the page of results. Here is the definition of the
GoogleResponseData class:

```
[DataContract]
public class GoogleResponseData
{
    [DataMember]
    public GoogleResult[] results;
    [DataMember]
    public GoogleCursor cursor;
}
```

GoogleResult is a simple class of string members that define the search result. You simply name each member for each key in the JSON:

```
[DataContract]
public class GoogleResult
{
    [DataMember]
    public string GsearchResultClass;
    [DataMember]
    public string unescapedUrl;
    [DataMember]
    public string url;
    [DataMember]
    public string visibleUrl;
    [DataMember]
    public string cacheUrl;
    [DataMember]
    public string title;
    [DataMember]
    public string titleNoFormatting;
    [DataMember]
    public string content;
}
```

GoogleCursor and GooglePage are similarly defined.

Putting this all to practice, Example 16-19 presents the complete code for the revised *GoogleClient.aspx.cs* with the changes to btnSearch_Click highlighted for your reference.

Example 16-19. GoogleClient.aspx.cs revised

```
using System;
using System.IO;
using System.Net;
using System.Runtime.Serialization;
using System.Runtime.Serialization.Json;
using System.Text;
using System.Web.UI;

[DataContract]
public class GoogleResult
{
    [DataMember]
    public string GsearchResultClass;
    [DataMember]
    public string unescapedUrl;
    [DataMember]
    public string url;
    [DataMember]
    public string visibleUrl;
    [DataMember]
    public string cacheUrl;
```

Example 16-19. GoogleClient.aspx.cs revised (continued)

```csharp
    [DataMember]
    public string title;
    [DataMember]
    public string titleNoFormatting;
    [DataMember]
    public string content;
}

[DataContract]
public class GooglePage
{
    [DataMember]
    public string start;
    [DataMember]
    public int label;
}

[DataContract]
public class GoogleCursor
{
    [DataMember]
    public GooglePage[] pages;
    [DataMember]
    public string estimatedResultCount;
    [DataMember]
    public int currentPageIndex;
    [DataMember]
    public string moreResultsUrl;
}

[DataContract]
public class GoogleResponseData
{
    [DataMember]
    public GoogleResult[] results;
    [DataMember]
    public GoogleCursor cursor;
}

[DataContract]
public class GoogleSearchResponse
{
    [DataMember]
    public GoogleResponseData responseData;
    [DataMember]
    public string responseDetails;
    [DataMember]
    public int responseStatus;
}

public partial class GoogleClient : Page
{
    protected void btnSearch_Click(object sender, EventArgs e)
```

Example 16-19. GoogleClient.aspx.cs revised (continued)

```
    {
        WebClient wc = new WebClient( );

        // Google requires that you provide an accurate referer
        wc.Headers.Add(HttpRequestHeader.Referer, Request.Url.ToString( ));

        // make the request
        String url = String.Format(
            "http://ajax.googleapis.com/ajax/services/search/web?v=1.0&q={0}",
                Server.UrlEncode(txtSearchFor.Text));
        String json = wc.DownloadString(url);

        // Parse the JSON with DataContractJsonSerializer
        GoogleSearchResponse srchResponse = null;
        using (MemoryStream ms = new MemoryStream(Encoding.ASCII.GetBytes(json)))
        {
            DataContractJsonSerializer jsonSerializer =
                new DataContractJsonSerializer(typeof(GoogleSearchResponse));
            srchResponse = jsonSerializer.ReadObject(ms) as GoogleSearchResponse;
        }

        // create links based on the search results
        StringBuilder sb = new StringBuilder( );
        foreach (GoogleResult res in srchResponse.responseData.results)
        {
            sb.AppendFormat("<a href='{0}'>{1}</a><br />",
                res.unescapedUrl, res.title);
        }
        lblResults.Text = sb.ToString( );
    }
}
```

Now if you save and run the page, you'll see the search results displayed in a much more legible way, as shown in Figure 16-20.

You used the WebClient class to make an HTTP connection, and formed the URL to the Google search web service. Since the documentation for the Google web service asked that you send a referrer page with the request, you have added the line:

```
wc.Headers.Add(HttpRequestHeader.Referer, Request.Url.ToString( ));
```

which tells Google the URL of the page that is making the request.

After calling DownloadString, which makes the HTTP GET request to the web service, you use the DataContractJsonSerializer to parse the JSON string that the web service returns.

Just as in the books example, you need to take the JSON string and convert to a stream. To do that, you use the MemoryStream (which takes bytes in memory and allows access to them as a stream). Then we create a DataContractJsonSerializer with the type of the GoogleSearchResponse class so it knows how to parse the JSON string. Again, the parser will match the keys in the JSON with the fields in the class.

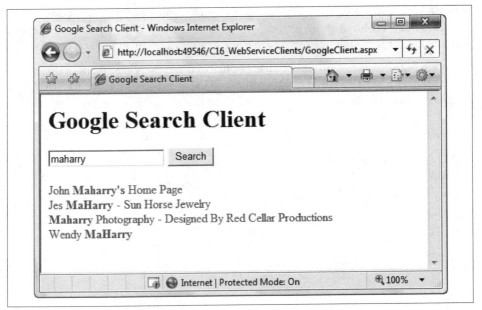

Figure 16-20. GoogleClient.aspx working correctly

Once you have a `GoogleSearchResponse` class, we can loop through the results (available in the `responseData.results` field). The URL of the search result is in the `unescapedUrl` field of the `res` object and the text describing the link is in the `title` field. To put links on our page, we construct `HyperLink` objects with the URL and title and add them to the panel on the page.

Learning More About Web Services

In this chapter, you saw how to use web services to make the information on your website easy to use in other programs. Since web services have become more widely used, there are many public web services that you can use in your projects, even if you don't choose to create any yourself. Adding a site search based on Microsoft Live or Google is almost as simple as calling a method in a local object when using a proxy.

Many topics that are important to implementing web services, such as state, security, and transactions, are beyond the scope of this chapter, but many other resources are available to learn about them.

Before VS2008 and WCF, the support for web services was built into ASP.NET and closely followed the model for creating web pages. For more details about ASP.NET-based web services, see *Programming .NET Web Services* by Alex Ferrara and Matthew MacDonald (O'Reilly), or *Programming .NET XML Web Services* by Damien Foggon et al. (Microsoft Press).

Starting with .NET 3.0, the recommended way to implement web services in .NET is with WCF. To learn more about WCF, see *Learning WCF* by Michele Leroux Bustamente (O'Reilly), and *Programming WCF Services* by Juval Löwy (O'Reilly).

Although SOAP was the prototype that popularized web services, many web services are based on REST. To learn more about how to use REST in .NET, see *RESTful .NET* by Jon Flanders (O'Reilly).

CHAPTER 17

Caching and Performance

There are several ways to achieve higher performance and better scalability in ASP.NET. One way is through the use of caching. *Caching* is a technique whereby frequently requested data is stored in memory so that the next time the same information is requested, it can be fetched from memory rather than generated by the application.

This can result in a significant performance boost, especially for dynamically generated content (such as ASP.NET web pages and components) and in cases where the data underlying the response is expensive to gather (such as database queries).

Most web browsers cache pages they receive, so if the same page is requested again, it does not have to be sent over the Internet, but rather is retrieved directly from the local hard drive. Most operating systems also employ caching of some sort to store frequently requested data in memory, rather than requiring additional hard-drive reads. The only caching this chapter is concerned with is server-side caching performed by the .NET Framework.

In some respects, caching is similar to the storage of *state objects*. (See Chapter 6 for a complete discussion of state in ASP.NET.) In both cases, data is saved for use across multiple requests, and in the case of application state, across multiple sessions. However, don't be misled by this apparent similarity. With state objects, the developer explicitly saves a particular piece of data in a particular place, intending to retrieve that piece of data at a later time in the session or in other sessions. The data stored in state objects will last as long as the session or application and will not be lost until the developer specifies that it is to be removed or replaced. In short, the developer can count on the data in a state object being available.

In contrast, cached data is nondeterministic. You cannot assume that any piece of data you are looking for will be in the cache. As we will show later in this chapter, whenever your program attempts to retrieve data from the cache, it must test to see whether the data is there and make provisions to retrieve the data elsewhere if it is not in the cache. The data may be missing because its lifetime expired, because the application freed memory for other purposes, or because the cache was never populated.

Types of Caching

There are several different types of caching in ASP.NET. Some are automatic and require no intervention on the developer's part, whereas others require explicit coding.

In all types of caching, data or objects are placed in the *cache*, an area of memory managed by the server. Subsequent requests for that information are retrieved from the cache rather than the underlying source. If the cached item has *expired*, either because the underlying data has changed, the time limit has run out, or some dependency has changed, the cache will be invalidated and the next request will retrieve fresh content from the underlying source rather than the cache. Your code can then refresh the cache. There are many ways to add items to the cache and expire items already in the cache, depending on the type of cache. We cover the types of cache in the next few sections, and the many ways of populating and expiring the cache in subsequent sections.

Class Caching

A web page or web service (*.aspx*, *.asmx*, or *.svc* file) is compiled into a page class in an assembly the first time the page or service is run. This causes some delay, but that compiled assembly is then cached on the server and is called directly every subsequent time the page (or service) is referenced. This is done automatically; no user or developer interaction is required for this to happen.

The CLR watches for source code changes. If the source code changes, the CLR will know to recompile the assembly the next time the page or service is called.

Configuration Caching

Application-wide configuration information is contained in the configuration files. Chapter 18 discusses the specifics of configuration in detail. For now, the relevant point is that when the application is started (the first time a page or service is called from the application's virtual root directory), all the configuration information must be loaded. This can take some time, especially if the configuration files are extensive. Configuration caching, which occurs automatically, allows the application to store the configuration information in memory, thus saving time when the information is subsequently needed.

Data Caching

Caching data from a database is one of the most effective ways to improve the performance and scalability of a web application, because database hits are a relatively expensive operation, especially when compared to retrieving the data from server memory. The DataSource controls are specifically designed to enable easy and effective caching of data. We will cover data caching shortly.

Output Caching

Output caching is the caching of pages or portions of pages that are sent to the client. This is one of the most significant performance-enhancing techniques available to the website developer. Because the page does not have to be re-created from scratch each time a request for it is made, the website throughput, for example, measured in requests fulfilled per second, can be significantly increased.

We will discuss output caching later in this chapter.

Object Caching

Object caching is the caching of objects on the page, such as data-bound controls. Object caching stores the cached data in server memory. We will cover object caching in detail later in this chapter.

Data Caching

Data caching is (surprise!) the caching of data from a data source. As long as the cache is not expired, a request for data will be fulfilled from the cache rather than the original data source. If the cache is expired for whatever reason, fresh data will be obtained by the data source and the cache will be refreshed. The cache can expire for many reasons, as you will see. These can include timeouts, changed data, or changes to other objects.

There are two kinds of data caching; both are very useful:

- DataSourceControl caching
- SQL cache dependency

DataSourceControl Caching

As we showed in Chapters 7 through 10, DataSource controls represent data in a data source, such as a database or an XML file. Of those that derive from the abstract DataSourceControl class (see Figure 7-1 in Chapter 7), the ObjectDataSource, the SqlDataSource, and its derived types have a number of read/write properties for implementing caching, as listed in Table 17-1.

Table 17-1. Data source control properties for caching

Property	Type	Description
CacheDuration	Integer	Length of time, in seconds, that data is cached before the cache is invalidated. Default value is Infinite.
CacheExpirationPolicy	DataSourceCacheExpiry	Default is Absolute. The other possible value is Sliding, in which case the countdown to cache expiration is reset every time the cache is accessed.

Table 17-1. Data source control properties for caching (continued)

Property	Type	Description
CacheKeyDependency	String	Creates a dependency between cache entries and a key. When the key expires, so does the cache.
EnableCaching	Boolean	If `true`, caching will be enabled for the control. Default is `false`.

To demonstrate, create a new website called *C17_Caching* and add a new web form to it called *DataSourceCaching.aspx*. Add to it a SqlDataSource control (dsCustomers) that SELECTs the FirstName, LastName, CompanyName, EmailAddress, and Phone fields from the Customer table. Also add a GridView control (gvwCustomers) that uses dsCustomers as its data source.

To differentiate between when the page has been rendered from the server and when it has been retrieved from cache, add a Label control (lblTime) to the top of the page and the following line of code to the Page_Load handler in the code-behind file to populate the label with the current time:

```
protected void Page_Load(object sender, EventArgs e)
{
    lblTime.Text = String.Format("Page posted at {0}",
        DateTime.Now.ToLongTimeString());
}
```

When you run this website, you will get something like that shown in Figure 17-1.

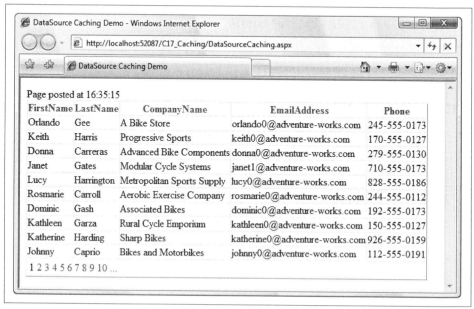

Figure 17-1. DataSourceCaching.aspx—no caching yet

At this point, the web page has no caching enabled. You can see this by refreshing the browser window and seeing the displayed timestamp update. You can change the data in the underlying database (use SQL Server Enterprise Manager, Query Analyzer, or the Server Explorer in Visual Studio 2008 [VS2008]) and see the new values appear as soon as you refresh the page.

Now implement data caching in the SqlDataSource by setting its EnableCaching and CacheDuration attributes to true and 60, respectively, as shown highlighted in Example 17-1.

Example 17-1. DataSourceCaching.aspx with caching enabled

```
<%@ Page Language="C#" AutoEventWireup="true"
CodeFile="DataSourceCaching.aspx.cs" Inherits="DataSourceCaching" %>

<!DOCTYPE html PUBLIC "-//W3C//DTD XHTML 1.0 Transitional//EN"
    "http://www.w3.org/TR/xhtml1/DTD/xhtml1-transitional.dtd">
<html xmlns="http://www.w3.org/1999/xhtml">
<head runat="server">
    <title>DataSource Caching Demo</title>
</head>
<body>
    <form id="form1" runat="server">
    <div>
        <asp:Label ID="lblTime" runat="server" />
        <asp:SqlDataSource ID="dsCustomers" runat="server"
            ConnectionString="<%$ ConnectionStrings:AWLTConnectionString
            %>"
            SelectCommand="SELECT [FirstName], [LastName],
            [CompanyName], [EmailAddress], [Phone]
            FROM [SalesLT].[Customer]"
            EnableCaching="true" CacheDuration="60" />
        <asp:GridView ID="gvwCustomers" runat="server"
            AllowPaging="True" AllowSorting="True"
            DataSourceID="dsCustomers" />
    </div>
    </form>
</body>
</html>
```

Setting EnableCaching to true implements caching, and setting the CacheDuration to 60 means the cache will expire every minute. You can verify this by changing some data in the Customer table and refreshing the web page in the browser. Though the timestamp displayed on the page will update every time, the data will not refresh until the 60 seconds have passed.

The CacheDuration is subject to the value of the CacheExpirationPolicy property, which we cover in detail in "Time dependency," later in this chapter. In short, the default value for CacheExpirationPolicy is Absolute, which causes the cache to expire at the end of the CacheDuration setting regardless of whether data access has occurred during that time.

SQL Cache Dependency

SQL cache dependency is the caching of data from a SQL Server database, specifically, SQL Server 7.0 or later, and expiring the cache whenever data in the database changes. It is not supported for other databases, such as Access and Oracle. Two different mechanisms are used to support SQL cache dependency. *Polling-based invalidation* is used for SQL Server 7.0 and 2000. *Notification-based invalidation* is used for SQL Server 2005 and 2008. We will describe both mechanisms in the following sections.

Polling-based cache invalidation

SQL cache dependency in SQL Server 7.0 and 2000 works by inserting into the database a special table, five stored procedures (all with names beginning with AspNet_SqlCache), and a trigger for each table being watched (*tableName*_AspNet_SqlCacheNotification_Trigger) to monitor whether any data has changed. One or more tables in the database can be watched. When data is modified in a table under watch, the special table for keeping track, called AspNet_SqlCacheTablesForChangeNotification, is updated. Periodically, the ASP.NET application polls the database to see whether any changes have occurred. If they have, the data cache is invalidated and fresh data is retrieved from the database.

The actual implementation of SQL cache dependency is a three-part process. In the first part, the SQL Server database is prepared to support data caching or SQL cache dependency. In the second step, the cache is set up in the *web.config* file for the application. We will cover both of those steps shortly. Finally, the data cache is actually used, typically in the context of an output cache. We will cover output caching later in this chapter.

Preparing the database. To prepare SQL Server to support SQL cache dependency, you must first run the SQL Server administrative command-line tool, *aspnet_regsql.exe*, which you first saw in Chapter 12.

You can see all the options available to this tool by running the following command from the command prompt:

```
aspnet_regsql -?
```

There is a wizard mode to this utility, which you can enter by running the command from the command line without any options, but the wizard mode does not handle setting up the database for SQL cache dependency, so you must do it all from the command line. This is easy if you have either a working connection string to the database or are using Windows integrated security on the database.

The command-line switches relevant to SQL cache dependency are listed in Table 17-2. Note that this utility serves many functions, including configuration of SQL Server Express, session state options, and other ASP.NET application services.

Table 17-2. The aspnet_regsql command-line switches relevant to SQL cache dependency

Switch	Description
-?	Displays help.
-S *servername*	SQL Server instance with which to work.
-U *loginID*	Username with which to authenticate. Requires the -P option.
-P *password*	Password with which to authenticate. Requires the -U option.
-E	Authenticates with current Windows credentials.
-C *connString*	Connection string to use instead of username, password, and server name.
-d *database*	Database name for SQL Server 7.0 and 2000. The database can optionally be specified as part of the connection string.
-ed	Enables a database for SQL cache dependency.
-dd	Disables a database for SQL cache dependency.
-et	Enables a table for SQL cache dependency. Requires the -t option.
-dt	Disables a table for SQL cache dependency. Requires the -t option.
-t *tablename*	Name of the table to enable or disable.
-lt	Lists all tables enabled for SQL cache dependency.

First, you must prepare the database by creating the table AspNet_SqlCacheTablesForChangeNotification for keeping track of changes, and then by creating the stored procedures. If you are using Windows integrated security, enter the following command:

```
aspnet_regsql -E -d Northwind -ed
```

The first argument, -E, specifies to use Windows authentication; -d specifies the database, and -ed instructs to enable data caching.

If you are using a connection string, you do not specify the database because that is in the connection string, as in the following example:

```
aspnet_regsql -C "Data Source=MyServer;Initial Catalog=AdventureWorksLT;
    Persist Security Info=True;User ID=userId;Password=secret" -ed
```

Alternatively, you could use the -S, -U, and -P options to provide the credentials individually.

Adding a table for SQL cache dependency depends on your security method. If you are using Windows integrated security, use the following line:

```
aspnet_regsql -E -d AdventureWorksLT -t Customer -et
```

or, with a connection string:

```
aspnet_regsql -C "Data Source=MyServer;
    Initial Catalog= AdventureWorksLT;
    Persist Security Info=True;
    User ID=userId;Password=secret" -t Customer -et
```

This adds a trigger called `Customer_AspNet_SqlCacheNotification_Trigger` to the Customer table, which calls the stored procedure `AspNet_SqlCacheUpdateChangeIdStoredProcedure` every time there is a change to the data in the Customer table.

To list all the enabled tables, use the following command:

```
aspnet_regsql -C "Data Source=MyServer;
    Initial Catalog=AdventureWorksLT;
    Persist Security Info=True;User ID=userId;Password=secret" -lt
```

An alternative to using the preceding command to list all the tables being monitored is to query the table `AspNet_SqlCacheTablesForChangeNotification` directly.

The database is now ready to support SQL cache dependency.

You also can accomplish all of the preceding functionality in code, using the `SqlCacheDependencyAdmin` class. This class has five methods for setting up and administering a SQL Server database for SQL cache dependency:

- `DisableNotifications`
- `DisableTableForNotifications`
- `EnableNotifications`
- `EnableTableForNotifications`
- `GetTablesEnabledForNotifications`

Usage of these `SqlCacheDependencyAdmin` classes is beyond the scope of this book.

Editing web.config. The second step in implementing SQL cache dependency is to edit the *web.config* file for the website. Open *web.config* for *C17_Caching* and add a new `<caching>` element to the `<system.web>` section, as highlighted in Example 17-2.

Example 17-2. The web.config file with SqlCacheDependency enabled (abridged)

```
<?xml version="1.0"?>
<configuration>
  ...
  <connectionStrings>
    <add name="AWLTConnectionString"
        connectionString="Data Source=<your_server>;
          Initial Catalog=AdventureWorksLT;Integrated Security=True"
        providerName="System.Data.SqlClient"/>
  </connectionStrings>
  <system.web>
    <caching>
      <sqlCacheDependency enabled="true">
        <databases>
          <clear />
          <add name="AdventureWorksLT"
            connectionStringName="AWLTConnectionString"
            pollTime="1000" />
```

```
        </databases>
      </sqlCacheDependency>
    </caching>
    ...
  </system.web>
  ...
</configuration>
```

The `<sqlCacheDependency>` element has two possible attributes:

- `enabled` can be `true` or `false`.
- `pollTime` is the number of milliseconds between polls that SQL Server waits to determine whether the data has changed. If the latter is omitted from this element, the value in the `<add>` sections for individual databases will apply.

Within the `<sqlCacheDependency>` element are one or more `<databases>` sections. These contain `<add>`, `<clear>`, or `<remove>` sections. To add a database, as in Example 17-2, you provide the `name`, `connectionString`, and `pollTime` properties as attributes. To remove a database, you need only provide the `name` attribute. `<clear />` takes no attributes.

With the SQL cache dependency configured in *web.config*, you are ready to cache the data and have the cache expire when the data changes.

Notification-based cache invalidation

SQL cache dependency in SQL Server 2005 and 2008 works by using the query change notification mechanism built into the database. It requires much less setup than polling-based cache invalidation used in earlier versions of SQL Server. There is no need to configure the database with *aspnet_regsql.exe*, and there is no need to add any `<sqlCacheDependency>` element to *web.config*.

To enable notification-based cache invalidation for a page, add a `SqlDependency` attribute to the `OutputCache` directive, described shortly, with a value of `CommandNotification`:

```
<%@ OutputCache Duration="999999"
    SqlDependency="CommandNotification"
    VaryByParam="none" %>
```

To enable notification-based cache invalidation for a `DataSource` control, add a `SqlCacheDependency` attribute to the control declaration, again with a value of `CommandNotification`:

```
<asp:SqlDataSource ID="SqlDataSource1" runat="server"
    SqlCacheDependency="CommandNotification"
    EnableCaching="true"
    CacheDuration="Infinite">
    ...
</asp:SqlDataSource>
```

In both cases ASP.NET and ADO.NET will work together to create a cache dependency that detects change notifications sent from SQL Server and that invalidates the cache when the data is changed.

Output Caching

Output caching is the caching of pages or portions of pages that are output to the client. This does not happen automatically. The developer must enable output caching using either the OutputCache directive or the HttpCachePolicy class. We will describe both methods.

You can apply output caching to an entire page or to a portion of a page. To cache only a portion of a page, you apply the caching to a user control contained within the page. We will describe this later in this chapter.

The OutputCache Directive

The OutputCache directive, like all page directives, is placed at the top of the page file. (For a complete description of page directives, see Chapter 6.) A typical example of an OutputCache directive looks something like the following:

```
<%@ OutputCache Duration="60" VaryByParam="*" %>
```

The full syntax is:

```
<%@ OutputCache
    Duration="number of seconds"
    VaryByParam="parameter list"
    CacheProfile=""
    DiskCacheable=""
    Location="Any | Client | Downstream | Server | None"
    NoStore=""
    SqlDependency="database:table"
    VaryByControl="control list"
    VaryByCustom="custom output"
    VaryByHeader="header list" %>
```

Only the first two parameters, Duration and VaryByParam, are required, though the VaryByParam attribute will not be required for user controls if there is a VaryByControl attribute.

The VaryBy... parameters allow different versions of the cached page to be stored with each version satisfying the combination of conditions being varied.

We describe the various parameters in the following sections.

Duration

The Duration parameter specifies the number of seconds that the page or user control is cached. Items placed in the output cache are valid only for this specified time period.

When the time limit is reached, the cache is said to be expired. The next request for the cached page or user control after the cache is expired causes the page or user control to be regenerated, and the cache is refilled with the fresh copy.

To demonstrate, add a new web page to the *C17_Caching* website and call it *OutputCaching.aspx*. Add a single `Label` control (`lblTime`) to the page and the same code to `Page_Load` as in *DataSourceCaching.aspx* which displays the current time in the `Label`.

```
protected void Page_Load(object sender, EventArgs e)
{
    lblTime.Text = String.Format("Page posted at {0}",
        DateTime.Now.ToLongTimeString( ));
}
```

Finally, add an @OutputCache directive to the top of the markup file, as highlighted in Example 17-3.

Example 17-3. OutputCaching.aspx in full

```
<%@ Page Language="C#" AutoEventWireup="true"
    CodeFile="OutputCaching.aspx.cs" Inherits="OutputCaching" %>

<%@ OutputCache Duration="10" VaryByParam="*" %>

<!DOCTYPE html PUBLIC "-//W3C//DTD XHTML 1.0 Transitional//EN"
    "http://www.w3.org/TR/xhtml1/DTD/xhtml1-transitional.dtd">

<html xmlns="http://www.w3.org/1999/xhtml">
<head runat="server">
    <title>Output Caching Demo</title>
</head>
<body>
    <form id="form1" runat="server">
    <div>
      <asp:Label ID="lblTime" runat="server" />
    </div>
    </form>
</body>
</html>
```

This OutputCache directive is all that is necessary to implement output caching. It specifies a Duration of 10 seconds. (We will explain the other parameter, VaryByParam, in the next section.) This means that if the same page is requested from the server within 10 seconds of the original request, the subsequent request will be served out of the cache rather than be regenerated by ASP.NET.

This is easy to verify. Run the page and note the time. Quickly refresh the page in the browser. If you refresh within 10 seconds of originally running the page, the displayed time will not have changed. You can refresh the page as many times as you wish, but the displayed time will not change until 10 seconds have passed.

VaryByParam

The `VaryByParam` parameter allows you to cache different versions of the page depending on which parameters are submitted to the server when the page is requested. These parameters are contained in a semicolon-separated list of strings.

In the case of a `GET` request, the strings in the parameter list represent query string values contained in the URL. In the case of a `POST` request, the strings represent variables sent as part of the form.

There are two special values for the `VaryByParam` parameter:

> Don't vary by parameter, that is, save only a single version of the page in the cache and return that version, no matter what query string values or form variables are passed in as part of the request.

*

> Save a separate version of the page in cache for each unique combination of query string values or form variables. The order of the query string values or form variables has no effect on the caching. However, the parameter values are case-sensitive: `state=ma` differs from `state=MA`.

To see the effects of the `VaryByParam` parameter, modify the previous example, *OutputCaching.aspx*. Add two Labels (`lblUserName` and `lblState`) for displaying parameters passed in as a query string as part of the URL in a `GET` request. Also, change the `Duration` parameter for the `@OutputCache` page directive to 60 seconds to give you more time to explore the effects, as shown in Example 17-4.

Example 17-4. OutputCaching.aspx modified to use VaryByParam

```
<%@ Page Language="C#" AutoEventWireup="true"
   CodeFile="OutputCaching.aspx.cs" Inherits="OutputCaching" %>
<%@ OutputCache Duration="60" VaryByParam="*" %>
<!DOCTYPE html PUBLIC "-//W3C//DTD XHTML 1.0 Transitional//EN"
   "http://www.w3.org/TR/xhtml1/DTD/xhtml1-transitional.dtd">

<html xmlns="http://www.w3.org/1999/xhtml">
<head runat="server">
   <title>Output Caching Demo</title>
</head>
<body>
   <form id="form1" runat="server">
   <div>
     <asp:Label ID="lblTime" runat="server" /><br />
     <asp:Label ID="lblUserName" runat="server" /><br />
     <asp:Label ID="lblState" runat="server" />
   </div>
   </form>
</body>
</html>
```

You'll also need to add a bit more code to the Page_Load handler in the code-behind page to reflect the values in the query string in the Labels you've just added, as highlighted in Example 17-5.

Example 17-5. OutputCaching.aspx.cs modified to demonstrate VaryByParam

```
using System;
using System.Web.UI;

public partial class OutputCaching : Page
{
    protected void Page_Load(object sender, EventArgs e)
    {
        lblTime.Text = String.Format("Page posted at {0}",
            DateTime.Now.ToLongTimeString());
        lblUserName.Text = String.Format("UserName : {0}",
            Request.QueryString["UserName"]);
        lblState.Text = String.Format("State : {0}",
            Request.QueryString["State"]);
    }
}
```

To test this version of *OutputCaching.aspx*, save and run the page. Then add a query string to the URL in the browser as follows:

```
http://localhost/C17_Caching/OutputCaching.aspx?username=Dan&state=UK
```

This will give the result shown in Figure 17-2.

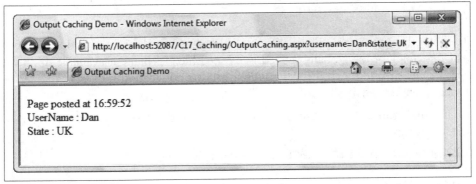

Figure 17-2. OutputCaching.aspx in action with VaryByParam

Now enter the same URL but with different parameters—say, username=Jesse and state=NY, as in:

```
http://localhost/c17_Caching/OutputCaching/default.aspx?username=Jesse&state=NY
```

This will give a different time in the resultant page. Now go back and enter the original URL with username=Dan and state=UK. You will see the original time shown in Figure 17-2, assuming 60 seconds have not passed since you first entered the URL.

Suppose the preceding example was part of an application where the username was needed for login purposes and the state was used to query a database to return information about publicly traded firms in that state. In that case, it would make no sense to cache based on the username, but it would make a lot of sense to cache based on the state parameter.

To accomplish this, set VaryByParam equal to the parameter(s) by which you wish to cache. So, for example, to cache only by state, use the following OutputCache directive:

```
<%@ OutputCache Duration="60" VaryByParam="state" %>
```

If you need to cache by the unique combination of two parameters—say, state and city—use a directive similar to this:

```
<%@ OutputCache Duration="60" VaryByParam="state;city" %>
```

CacheProfile

If you find yourself using the same OutputCache directives on many pages, you can use CacheProfiles to reuse the same attributes. To do this, add an <outputCacheProfiles> section to a configuration file. The <add> element specifies the name of the profile, as well as all the directive attributes, as in the following code snippet:

```
<outputCacheProfiles>
    <add name="StateCityCacheProfile"
        enabled="true"
        duration="60"
        varyByParam="state;city" />
</outputCacheProfiles>
```

To make this CacheProfile available to all the pages on the server, add it to either *machine.config* or the globally scoped *web.config* file. To make it available to only a specific website, add it to the *web.config* file in the application root (see Chapter 18 for more on *.config* files).

To use this profile, use the CacheProfile attribute of the OutputCache directive, as in the following:

```
<%@ OutputCache CacheProfile="StateCityCacheProfile" %>
```

DiskCacheable

ASP.NET will remove items from cache if the amount of memory available falls below a certain threshold, in a practice known as *scavenging*. We describe this later in this chapter. By default, ASP.NET also saves the output cache to disk. That way, the data can be retrieved from disk rather than regenerated from scratch even if memory is short. In addition, this enables cached data to survive an application restart.

To disable disk caching, set the DiskCacheable attribute to false, as in the following:

```
<%@ OutputCache Duration="60" VaryByParam="*" DiskCacheable="false" %>
```

Location

The Location parameter specifies the machine where the cached data is stored. The permissible values for this parameter are contained in the OutputCacheLocation enumeration written out in Table 17-3.

Table 17-3. OutputCacheLocation values

Value	Description
Client	The cache is located on the same machine as the client browser. This is useful if the page requires authentication.
Downstream	The cache is located on a server downstream from the web server. This might be a proxy server.
Server	The cache is located on the web server processing the request.
None	Output caching is disabled.
Any	The output cache can be located either on the client, on a downstream server, or on the web server. This is the default value.

The Location parameter is not supported when output caching user controls.

SqlDependency

The SqlDependency attribute of the OutputCache directive allows you to expire the output cache when the underlying data changes. To implement this requires setting up the database and editing *web.config*, as described in "SQL Cache Dependency," earlier in this chapter.

To demonstrate, add a copy of *DataSourceCaching.aspx* to the *C17_Caching* website and rename it *SqlDependencyCaching.aspx*. Remove the EnableCaching and CacheDuration attributes from the SqlDataSource declaration. Add the following OutputCache directive to the top of the content file:

```
<%@ OutputCache SqlDependency="AdventureWorksLT:Customer"
    Duration="600" VaryByParam="none" %>
```

The value supplied to the SqlDependency attribute is a concatenation of the database name that was previously set up for SQL cache dependency, specified in the *web.config* file listed in Example 17-2, and the table that was also previously set up for SQL cache dependency, in this case the Customer table. The database name and table name are separated by a colon.

In this example, the OutputCache duration is set for 10 minutes and VaryByParam is disabled (none).

When you run the page, you can refresh the page all you want and the displayed timestamp will not be updated for 10 minutes. However, go into the database, change a value in the Customer table, and refresh the page, and the timestamp will be updated immediately.

You can see that the page will expire whenever the specified duration is exceeded or the data changes, whichever occurs first.

VaryByControl

The VaryByControl parameter is used when caching user controls, which we will describe shortly, in "Fragment Caching: Caching Part of a Page." This parameter is not supported in OutputCache directives in web pages (.*aspx* files).

The values for this parameter consist of a semicolon-separated list of strings. Each string represents a fully qualified property name on a user control.

VaryByCustom

The VaryByCustom parameter allows the cache to be varied by browser if the value of the parameter is set to browser. In this case, the cache is varied by browser name and major version. In other words, there will be separate cached versions of the page for Internet Explorer 4, 5, 6, 7, and 8, Firefox, Safari, or any other browser type or version used to access the page.

VaryByHeader

The VaryByHeader parameter allows the cache to vary by HTTP header. The value of the parameter consists of a semicolon-separated list of HTTP headers. This parameter is not supported in OutputCache directives in user controls.

Fragment Caching: Caching Part of a Page

All the examples shown so far have cached the entire page. Sometimes all you want to cache is part of the page. To do this, wrap that portion of the page you want to cache in a user control and cache the user control. This is known as *fragment caching*. (For a complete discussion of user controls, see Chapter 15.)

For example, suppose you develop a stock portfolio analysis page, where the top portion of the page displays the contents of the user's stock portfolio and the bottom portion contains a data grid showing historical data about one specific stock. There would be little benefit in caching the top portion of the page because it will differ for every user. However, it is likely that in a heavily used website, many people will be requesting historical information about the same stock, so there would be a benefit to caching the bottom portion of the page. This is especially true because generating the historical data requires a relatively expensive database query. In this case, you can wrap the data grid in a user control and cache just that.

To demonstrate fragment caching, add to the *C17_Caching* website a new web form called *FragmentCaching.aspx* and a new user control called *SimpleUserControl.ascx*, which will be cached in the page. This control will do no more than display the current time, as with previous examples, so add a Label control to show the time and an @OutputCache directive with a Duration of 10 seconds, as shown here:

```
<%@ Control Language="C#" AutoEventWireup="true"
    CodeFile="SimpleUserControl.ascx.cs" Inherits="SimpleUserControl" %>
<%@ OutputCache Duration="10" VaryByParam="*" %>

<hr />
<asp:Label ID="lblTime" runat="server" />
<hr />
```

Its code-behind file likewise does nothing more than set the Label's Text property appropriately:

```
using System;
using System.Web.UI;

public partial class SimpleUserControl : UserControl
{
    protected void Page_Load(object sender, EventArgs e)
    {
        lblTime.Text = String.Format("Control Time is {0}",
            DateTime.Now.ToLongTimeString( ));
    }
}
```

Once the user control is ready, you can add some content to *FragmentCaching.aspx*, as shown in Example 17-6. Again, another Label is set to the current time on the page: with the control being cached, these should go out of sync upon refreshing the page. Note that the web page that uses the user control does not have any caching implemented; there is no OutputCache directive.

Example 17-6. FragmentCaching.aspx in full

```
<%@ Page Language="C#" AutoEventWireup="true"
    CodeFile="FragmentCaching.aspx.cs" Inherits="FragmentCaching" %>
<%@ Register Src="~/SimpleUserControl.ascx"
    TagPrefix="OReilly" TagName="CachedControl" %>
<!DOCTYPE html PUBLIC "-//W3C//DTD XHTML 1.0 Transitional//EN"
    "http://www.w3.org/TR/xhtml1/DTD/xhtml1-transitional.dtd">

<html xmlns="http://www.w3.org/1999/xhtml">
<head runat="server">
    <title>Fragment Caching Demo</title>
</head>
<body>
    <form id="form1" runat="server">
    <div>
      <asp:Label ID="lblPageTime" runat="server" />
      <br />
      <OReilly:CachedControl ID="CachedControl1" runat="server" />
    </div>
    </form>
</body>
</html>
```

Again, the code behind the page just sets the text for the Label in the Page_Load handler:

```
using System;
using System.Web.UI;

public partial class FragmentCaching : Page
{
    protected void Page_Load(object sender, EventArgs e)
    {
        lblPageTime.Text = String.Format("Page time is {0}",
            DateTime.Now.ToLongTimeString());
    }
}
```

When you run *FragmentCaching.aspx*, you will initially see something like
Figure 17-3, with the time displayed for both the user control and the containing
page being identical.

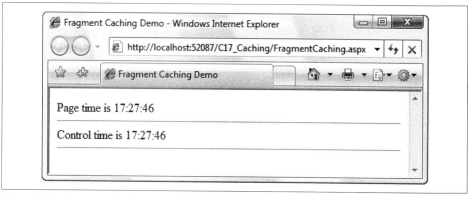

Figure 17-3. FragmentCaching.aspx initially

However, if you refresh the view, you will notice that the time the page was loaded
will be the current time and the time the user control was loaded is static until the
10-second cache duration has expired.

When caching user controls, keep in mind the caveat that you cannot programmatically
manipulate the user control being cached. This is because a user control in cache is generated dynamically only the first time it is requested. After that, the object is unavailable
for the code to interact with. If you need to manipulate the contents of the user control
programmatically, the code to do so must be contained within the user control.

To demonstrate this, open *SimpleUserControl.ascx* and add to it a Label control
(lblUserName) to display a user's name. For now, this label is hardcoded to "Dan".

```
<hr />
<asp:Label ID="lblTime" runat="server" /><br />
<asp:Label ID="lblUserName" runat="server" Text="Dan" />
<hr />
```

Also add a public property, called UserName, with a Get and a Set method to the code-
behind file of the user control, *SimpleUserControl.ascx.cs*:

```
public partial class SimpleUserControl : UserControl
{
    public string UserName
    {
        get { return lblUserName.Text; }
        set { lblUserName.Text = value; }
    }

    protected void Page_Load(object sender, EventArgs e)
    {
        lblTime.Text = String.Format("Control time is {0}",
            DateTime.Now.ToLongTimeString());
    }
}
```

Now to create a page to host this new control; add to the *C17_Caching* website a new page called *FragmentCachingWithProperty.aspx* and copy over the contents of *FragmentCaching.aspx*. Add to the markup page a Label (lblUserName) to display the value of the user control property, UserName, and a button (btnChange) to change the value of the property.

```
<head runat="server">
    <title>Fragment Caching Demo</title>
</head>
<body>
    <form id="form1" runat="server">
    <div>
      <asp:Label ID="lblPageTime" runat="server" /><br />
      <OReilly:CachedControl ID="CachedControl1" runat="server" />
        <br />
      <asp:Label ID="lblUserName" runat="server" /><br />
      <asp:Button ID="btnChange" runat="server" Text="Change Name"
          onclick="btnChange_Click" />
    </div>
    </form>
</body>
```

The code-behind file adds a line in the Page_Load method to populate that label, as well as a Click event handler for the button:

```
public partial class FragmentCachingWithProperty : Page
{
    protected void Page_Load(object sender, EventArgs e)
    {
        lblPageTime.Text = String.Format("Page time is {0}",
            DateTime.Now.ToLongTimeString());
        lblUserName.Text = CachedControl1.UserName;
    }

    protected void btnChange_Click(object sender, EventArgs e)
    {
        CachedControl1.UserName = "Janey";
    }
}
```

 Remember that this example demonstrates the error that occurs when attempting to manipulate a cached user control programmatically.

The *FragmentCachingWithProperty* example works fine when the page is first called, giving the result shown in Figure 17-4.

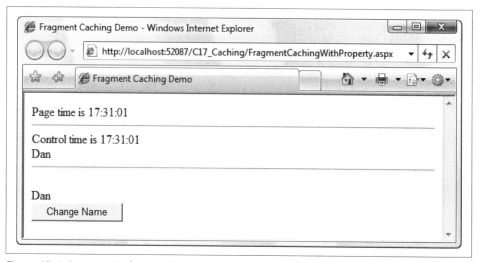

Figure 17-4. FragmentCachingWithProperty.aspx in action

It will even work as expected if you click the button to change the name to Jane. This is because the button causes the form to be posted to the server, so everything is regenerated and the request for the user control is not being satisfied from the cache. However, as soon as you refresh the page in the browser, either by clicking the browser Refresh icon or clicking the Change Name button a third time, ASP.NET attempts to satisfy the request for the user control from the cache, and a server error occurs.

The only way around this is to move all the code that accesses the user control property into the user control itself. To see this, copy *FragmentCachingWithProperty.aspx* to a new web form, called *FragmentCachingWithPropertyCorrect.aspx*. Remove the lblUserName control from the page and then move the Button control into *SimpleUserControl.ascx*.

```
<%@ Control Language="C#" AutoEventWireup="true"
    CodeFile="SimpleUserControl.ascx.cs" Inherits="SimpleUserControl" %>
<%@ OutputCache Duration="10" VaryByParam="*" %>

<hr />
<asp:Label ID="lblTime" runat="server" /><br />
<asp:Label ID="lblUserName" runat="server" Text="Dan" /><br />
```

```
<asp:Button ID="btnChange" runat="server" Text="Change Name"
    onclick="btnChange_Click" />
<hr />
```

You should also move the Button's onClick event handler into the control's code-behind page:

```
using System;
using System.Web.UI;

public partial class SimpleUserControl : UserControl
{
    public string UserName
    {
        get { return lblUserName.Text; }
        set { lblUserName.Text = value; }
    }

    protected void Page_Load(object sender, EventArgs e)
    {
        lblTime.Text = String.Format("Control time is {0}",
            DateTime.Now.ToLongTimeString());
    }

    protected void btnChange_Click(object sender, EventArgs e)
    {
        lblUserName.Text = "Jane";
    }
}
```

If you run the page now, you'll see that no errors occur when the page is refreshed.

Though this restriction on programmatically modifying user controls that are in the cache might seem significant, as a practical matter it should not be. The entire point of putting user controls in the cache is that they will not change while cached. If that is not the case, they will probably not be a good candidate for caching.

Object Caching

All the examples in the preceding section have cached pages, or parts of pages wrapped in user controls. But ASP.NET allows you much more caching flexibility. You can use object caching to place any object in the cache. The object can be of any type: a data type, a web control, a class, a DataSet, and so on.

The object cache is stored in server memory, a limited resource, and the careful developer will conserve that resource. With that said, it is an easy way to buy significant performance benefits when used wisely, especially because ASP.NET will evict older items if memory becomes scarce.

Suppose you are developing a retail shopping catalog web application. Many of the page requests contain queries against the same database to return a relatively static price list and description data. Instead of your control querying the database each time the data is requested, the data set is cached, so subsequent requests for the data will be satisfied from the high-speed cache rather than forcing a relatively slow and expensive regeneration of the data. You might want to set the cache to expire every minute, every hour, or every day, depending on the needs of the application and the frequency with which the data is likely to change.

Object caching is implemented by the Cache class. One instance of this class is created automatically per application when the application starts. The class remains valid for the life of the application. The Cache class uses syntax very similar to that of session and application state. Objects are stored in Cache as key/value pairs in a dictionary object. The object being stored is the value, and the key is a descriptive string.

To demonstrate, you'll create a new web form displaying a GridView containing data from the AdventureWorksLT database. Data will be selected from the database into a DataSet and then will store the DataSet in cache for subsequent requests.

Add to the *C17_Caching* website a new web form called *ObjectCaching.aspx* and drag into it a Label control (lblMessage), a GridView control (gvwCustomers), and two Button controls (btnClear and btnPost). Double-click btnClear in Design view to create a placeholder for its onClick event handler in the code-behind page. Note that no @OutputCache directive is needed for this example because it does not use output caching.

```
<%@ Page Language="C#" AutoEventWireup="true"
    CodeFile="ObjectCaching.aspx.cs" Inherits="ObjectCaching" %>

<!DOCTYPE html PUBLIC "-//W3C//DTD XHTML 1.0 Transitional//EN"
    "http://www.w3.org/TR/xhtml1/DTD/xhtml1-transitional.dtd">

<html xmlns="http://www.w3.org/1999/xhtml">
<head runat="server">
    <title>Object Caching Demo</title>
</head>
<body>
    <form id="form1" runat="server">
    <div>
       <asp:Label ID="lblMessage" runat="server" /><br />
       <asp:GridView ID="gvwCustomers" runat="server" /><br />
       <asp:Button ID="btnClear" runat="server" Text="Clear Cache"
          onclick="btnClear_Click" />
       <asp:Button ID="btnPost" runat="server" Text="Post" />
    </div>
    </form>
</body>
</html>
```

It would simplify matters greatly if you could just use a SqlDataSource control, set the EnableCache property of that control, and then set the DataSource property of the GridView to point to the SqlDataSource. However, there are certain circumstances in which you must "manually" create the data source and bind the source to the control.

We cover this in detail in Chapter 9, but two of these circumstances are when you need to implement connection-based transactions or you are building an *n*-tier data architecture and your data is being retrieved from a business object.

In *ObjectCaching.aspx.cs*, Page_Load calls a method named CreateGridView every time the page is loaded:

```
using System;
using System.Configuration;
using System.Data;
using System.Data.SqlClient;
using System.Web.UI;

public partial class ObjectCaching : Page
{
    protected void Page_Load(object sender, EventArgs e)
    {
        CreateGridView();
    }
```

CreateGridView itself is quite straightforward; its purpose is to provide and bind a DataSet to the GridView control, gvwCustomers. First it looks in the cache to see whether the DataSet has been cached there as an object with the key GridViewDataSet. If it has, it uses this cached version. If it hasn't, it pulls the required data from the database using the GetDataSet method, stores it in the cache with the GridViewDataSet key, and then binds it to the GridView. Finally, it uses lblMessage to state whether it has used a cached DataSet.

```
    private void CreateGridView()
    {
        DataSet dsGrid;
        dsGrid = (DataSet)Cache["GridViewDataSet"];
        if (dsGrid == null)
        {
            dsGrid = GetDataSet();
            Cache["GridViewDataSet"] = dsGrid;
            lblMessage.Text = "Data from database.";
        }
        else
        {
            lblMessage.Text = "Data from cache.";
        }

        gvwCustomers.DataSource = dsGrid.Tables[0];
        gvwCustomers.DataBind();
    }
```

As with the Session and Application objects seen in Chapter 6, whatever is retrieved from the Cache object must be explicitly cast, or converted, to the correct data type—in this case, DataSet. For this purpose, C# uses an explicit cast:

```
dsGrid = (DataSet)Cache["GridViewDataSet"];
```

You can use the Cache, Session, and View syntax even from within *Global.asax* files (see Chapter 18 for a complete discussion of the *Global.asax* file). However, in that case, you must qualify the keyword with the current context:

```
dsGrid = (DataSet)HttpContext.Current.Cache["GridViewDataSet"];
```

The GetDataSet method is also straightforward, using the techniques demonstrated in Chapter 9 to return a DataSet containing a single DataTable containing the IDs, names, and email addresses of the first 10 customers in the Customer table.

```
private DataSet GetDataSet()
{
   // connect to the Northwind database
   string connectionString = ConfigurationManager.
      ConnectionStrings["AWLTConnectionString"].ConnectionString;

   // get records from the Customer table
   string commandString =
      "SELECT TOP 10 CustomerID, FirstName, LastName, " +
      "EmailAddress FROM SalesLT.Customer";

   // create the data set command object and the DataSet
   SqlDataAdapter dataAdapter =
      new SqlDataAdapter(commandString, connectionString);

   DataSet dsData = new DataSet();

   // fill the data set object
   dataAdapter.Fill(dsData, "Customers");

   return dsData;
}
```

Finally, the OnClick event handler for the btnClear button removes the customer DataSet from the cache and then calls CreateGridView to force the page to re-create the DataSet from the database:

```
protected void btnClear_Click(object sender, EventArgs e)
{
   Cache.Remove("GridViewDataSet");
   CreateGridView();
}
}
```

The result of running *ObjectCaching.aspx* is shown in Figure 17-5.

The first time the web page is run, the Label just above the GridView control will indicate that the data is coming directly from the database. Every subsequent time the form is requested by pressing F5 or clicking the Post button, the Label will change to "Data from cache." Even opening a new browser instance on a different machine will cause the data to come from the cache unless the application on the server is restarted. That is because the cache is available to the entire application just as the Application object is.

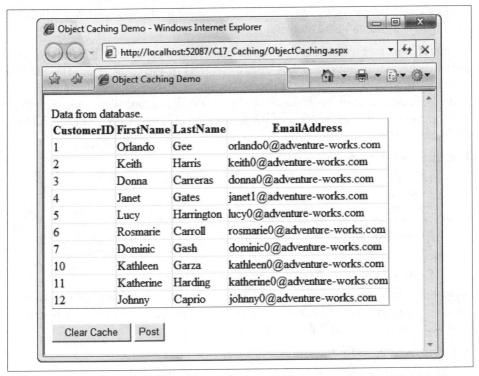

Figure 17-5. ObjectCaching.aspx in action

When you click the Clear button, however, the form is forced to empty the cache thanks to a call to the Cache.Remove method. This method removes the cache record specified by the key named as the parameter to the method.

```
Cache.Remove("GridViewDataSet");
```

As an exercise in observing different behavior, comment out the line that calls CreateGridView in the btnClear_Click method and observe the different behavior when you repost the page after clicking the Clear Cache button. When the line calling the CreateGridView method is not commented out, the next time a browser is opened after the Clear Cache button is clicked, the data will still come from the cache. But if the line is commented out, the next browser instance will get the data directly from the database.

Cache Class Functionality

The previous example, *ObjectCaching.aspx*, demonstrates how to add values to, retrieve values from, and delete values in the Object cache using a dictionary syntax of key/value pairs. The Cache class exposes much more functionality than this, including the ability to set dependencies, manage expirations, and control how memory used by cached objects can be recovered for more critical operations. We will cover all of these features in detail in upcoming sections.

This additional functionality is exposed through a different syntax for adding objects to the cache that uses the Add and Insert methods of the Cache class. The Add and Insert methods are very similar in effect. The only difference is that the Add method requires parameters for controlling all the exposed functionality, and the Insert method allows you to make some of the parameters optional, using default values for those parameters.

The syntax for the Add method is:

```
Cache.Add(
    KeyName,
    KeyValue,
    Dependencies,
    AbsoluteExpiration,
    SlidingExpiration,
    Priority,
    CacheItemRemovedCallback);
```

KeyName is a string with the name of the key in the Cache dictionary, and KeyValue is the object, of any type, to be inserted into the cache. We will discuss the remaining parameters in the sections following this one.

The syntax examples for the overloaded Insert methods are:

- To insert a key/value pair with default values for all the other parameters:

    ```
    Cache.Insert(KeyName, KeyValue);
    ```

- To insert a key/value pair with dependencies and with default values for the other parameters:

    ```
    Cache.Insert(KeyName, KeyValue, Dependencies);
    ```

- To insert a key/value pair with dependencies and expiration policies and with default values for the other parameters:

    ```
    Cache.Insert(KeyName, KeyValue, Dependencies, AbsoluteExpiration,
    SlidingExpiration);
    ```

- To insert a key/value pair with dependencies, expiration policies, and priority policy, and a delegate to notify the application when the inserted item is removed from the cache:

    ```
    Cache.Insert(KeyName, KeyValue, Dependencies, AbsoluteExpiration,
    SlidingExpiration, Priority, CacheItemRemovedCallback);
    ```

To see this call in action, replace a single line from *ObjectCaching.aspx*. Find the line in the CreateGridView method that looks like this:

```
Cache["GridViewDataSet"] = dsGrid;
```

Replace it with the following:

```
Cache.Insert("GridViewDataSet", dsGrid);
```

On running the modified page in a browser, you will see no difference from the prior version. By using the Insert method rather than the Add method, you are required to provide only the key and value, just as with the dictionary syntax.

Dependencies

One useful feature exposed by the Cache class is dependencies. A *dependency* is a relationship between a cached item and a point in time or an external object. If the designated point in time is reached or if the external object changes, the cached item will expire and will be removed from the cache.

The external object controlling the dependency can be a file, a directory, an array of files or directories, another item stored in the cache (represented by its key), or an array of items stored in the cache. The designated point in time can be either an absolute time or a relative time. In the following sections, we'll examine each of these dependencies and how you can use them to control the contents of the cache programmatically.

One of the more useful dependencies is data dependency, where the cache is expired if the data in the underlying SQL Server database changes. This feature is not part of object caching but is available to DataSourceControls and output caching. We covered data dependencies earlier in this chapter.

File change dependency

With a file change dependency, a cached item will expire and be removed from the cache if a specified file changes. This feature is typically used when a cached data set is derived from an XML file. You do not want the application to get the DataSet from the cache if the underlying XML file has changed.

To generate an XML file containing the first five records from the Customer table of the AdventureWorksLT database (an excerpt of which is listed in Example 17-7), perform the following steps if you're using SQL Server 2000:

1. Select Start → Programs → Microsoft SQL Server → Configure SQL XML Support in IIS.
2. Set a virtual directory called *AWLT*. Be sure to check the checkbox on the Settings tab, which enables sql=URL queries.
3. Open the following URL in a browser:

    http://localhost/AWLT?sql=select+top+5*+from+SalesLT.Customer +for+xml+auto&root=ROOT

If you're using SQL Server 2005:

1. Open SQL Server 2005 Management Studio (SSMS).
2. Connect to your AdventureWorksLT database.

3. Select File → New → Query with Current Connection (Ctrl-N).

4. Run the following query:

```
select top 5 * from saleslt.customer for xml auto, root('root')
```

Once you've opened the URL or run the query, you'll need to add a new XML file called *Customers.xml* to the *C17_Caching* website and then copy the XML you've generated into it beneath the XML prologue line, highlighted in Example 17-7. Note that you should change the prologue to read utf-16 rather than utf-8. This 16-bit character set allows the higher-order characters common to many non-English languages.

Example 17-7. Excerpt from Customers.xml

```
<?xml version="1.0" encoding="utf-16" ?>
<root>
  <saleslt.customer CustomerID="1" NameStyle="0" Title="Mr."
    FirstName="Orlando" MiddleName="B." LastName="Gee"
    CompanyName="A Bike Store" ... />
  <saleslt.customer CustomerID="2" NameStyle="0" Title="Mr."
    FirstName="Keith" MiddleName="h" LastName="Harris"
    CompanyName="Progressive Sports" ... />
  <saleslt.customer CustomerID="3" NameStyle="0" Title="Ms."
    FirstName="Donna" MiddleName="F." LastName="Carreras"
    CompanyName="Advanced Bike Components" ... />
  <saleslt.customer CustomerID="4" NameStyle="0" Title="Ms."
    FirstName="Janet" MiddleName="M." LastName="Gates"
    CompanyName="Modular Cycle Systems" ... />
  <saleslt.customer CustomerID="5" NameStyle="0" Title="Mr."
    FirstName="Lucy" LastName="Harrington"
    CompanyName="Metropolitan Sports Supply" ... />
</root>
```

The next example will use this XML file as a data source. You can then edit the XML file to demonstrate a file change dependency. To demonstrate, add a copy of the previous example, *ObjectCaching.aspx*, to the *C17_Caching* website and rename it *ObjectCachingFileDependency.aspx*.

The contents of the markup file remain the same, but the code-behind page needs a few tweaks. You will modify the GetDataSet method to populate the data set from the XML file rather than from the AdventureWorksLT database, and you will modify the CreateGridView method to implement a Cache object with a file change dependency.

You start by adding a couple of new using statements at the top of the file for Caching and Xml and removing those for database access:

```
using System;
using System.Data;
using System.Web.UI;
using System.Web.Caching;
using System.Xml;
```

```
public partial class ObjectCachingFileDependency : Page
{
    protected void Page_Load(object sender, EventArgs e)
    {
        CreateGridView();
    }
```

The goal of the GetDataSet method is still to return a data set. However, the source of the data for the data set is now the XML file called *Customers.xml*. Because ASP.NET stores data sets internally as XML, moving back and forth between XML and data sets is easy. The XML object equivalent to a data set is the XmlDataDocument. An XmlDataDocument object named doc is instantiated. This XmlDataDocument object is filled using the ReadXml method. The MapPath method maps a virtual path of a file on the server to a physical path.

The DataSet object is obtained from the DataSet property of the XmlDataDocument object, and then is returned to the calling method:

```
private DataSet GetDataSet()
{
    DataSet dsData = new DataSet();
    XmlDataDocument doc = new XmlDataDocument();
    doc.DataSet.ReadXml(Server.MapPath("Customers.xml"));
    dsData = doc.DataSet;
    return dsData;
}
```

In the CreateGridView method, only three lines have changed from the original ObjectCaching example. A CacheDependency object is defined against the source XML file. Again, MapPath is used to map the virtual path to a physical path.

The dictionary syntax used in the original ObjectCaching example to add the item to the cache is changed to use the Insert method of the Cache class. Using the Insert method allows you to specify a dependency in addition to the key name and value.

The text string assigned to the label has been updated to reflect that the data is now coming from an XML file rather than a database:

```
private void CreateGridView()
{
    DataSet dsGrid;
    dsGrid = (DataSet)Cache["GridViewDataSet"];
    if (dsGrid == null)
    {
        dsGrid = GetDataSet();
        CacheDependency fileDepends =
            new CacheDependency(Server.MapPath("Customers.xml"));
        Cache.Insert("GridViewDataSet", dsGrid, fileDepends);
        lblMessage.Text = "Data from XML file.";
    }
    else
    {
        lblMessage.Text = "Data from cache.";
    }
```

```
    gvwCustomers.DataSource = dsGrid.Tables[0];
    gvwCustomers.DataBind( );
}
```

The OnClick event handler for btnClear remains the same:

```
protected void btnClear_Click(object sender, EventArgs e)
{
    Cache.Remove("GridViewDataSet");
    CreateGridView( );
}
} // end of ObjectCachingFileDependency.aspx.cs
```

When you run this page, you will get something similar to Figure 17-6.

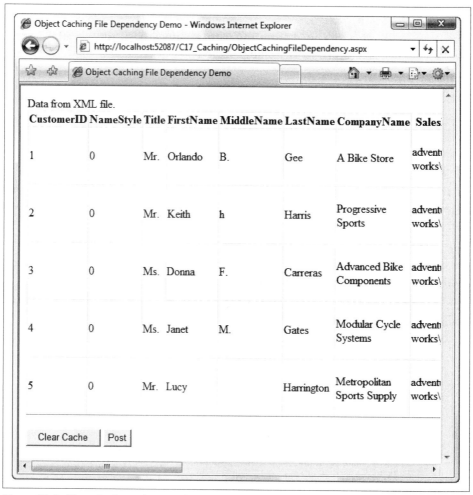

Figure 17-6. ObjectCachingFileDependency.aspx in action

If you repost the page by highlighting the URL and pressing Enter, the label at the top of the page will indicate that the data is coming from the cache.

Now open the *Customers.xml* file in a text editor and make a change to one of the values in one of the records. Remember to save the XML file. When you repost the page in the browser, instead of the data still coming from the cache, it will once again be coming from the XML file.

As soon as the XML source file was changed, the cached data set was expired and removed from the cache. The next time the page requested the data set from the server, it had to retrieve it fresh from the XML file.

If you want the cache dependency to monitor an array of files or directories, the syntax for the CacheDependency constructor in *ObjectCachingFileDependency.aspx.cs* can take an array of file paths or directories rather than a single filename. So, for example, the single line of code that defines the CacheDependency object would be preceded by code defining a string array with one or more files or paths, and the CacheDependency constructor itself would take the array as a parameter. It would look like this:

```
string[] fileDependsArray =
    {Server.MapPath("Customers.xml"), Server.MapPath("Employees.xml")};
CacheDependency fileDepends = new CacheDependency(fileDependsArray);
```

Cached item dependency

A cached item can be dependent on other items in the cache. If a cached item is dependent on one or more other cached items, it will be expired and removed from the cache if any of those cached items upon which it depends changes. These changes include either removal from the cache or a change in value.

To make a cached item dependent on other cached items, the keys of all of the controlling items are put into an array of strings. This array is passed to the CacheDependency constructor, along with an array of file paths. (If you do not want to define a dependency on any files or paths, the array of file paths can be null.)

To demonstrate, create a copy of the previous example in the *C17_Caching* website, rename it *ObjectCachingItemDependency.aspx*, and add two more Button controls to the page, as highlighted in the following code. The first button (btnInit) initializes several other cached items. The second button (btnChange) changes the value of the cached text string in one of the controlling cached items. As with the previous examples, a label near the top of the page indicates whether the data was retrieved directly from an XML file or from cache. The Clear Cache and Post buttons are unchanged.

```
<div>
    <asp:Label ID="lblMessage" runat="server" /><br />
    <asp:GridView ID="gvwCustomers" runat="server" /><br />
    <asp:Button ID="btnClear" runat="server" Text="Clear Cache"
        onclick="btnClear_Click" />
```

```
<asp:Button ID="btnPost" runat="server" Text="Post" /><br />
<asp:Button ID="btnInit" runat="server" Text="Initialize Keys"
    OnClick="btnInit_Click" />
<asp:Button ID="btnChange" runat="server" Text="Change Key 0"
    OnClick="btnChange_Click" />
</div>
```

The only changes to the code-behind file, shown in the following code, are a slight modification to CreateGridView and the new Click event handlers for the two new buttons:

```
private void CreateGridView( )
{
    DataSet dsGrid;
    dsGrid = (DataSet)Cache["GridViewDataSet"];
    if (dsGrid == null)
    {
        dsGrid = GetDataSet( );
        string[] fileDependsArray = { Server.MapPath("Customers.xml") };
        string[] cacheDependsArray = { "Depend0", "Depend1", "Depend2" };
        CacheDependency cacheDepends = new CacheDependency
                (fileDependsArray, cacheDependsArray);
        Cache.Insert("GridViewDataSet", dsGrid, cacheDepends);
        lblMessage.Text = "Data from XML file.";
    }
    else
    {
        lblMessage.Text = "Data from cache.";
    }

    gvwCustomers.DataSource = dsGrid.Tables[0];
    gvwCustomers.DataBind( );
}
```

In the btnInit_Click event handler, the controlling cache items are created. The values of the cached items are unimportant for this example, except as something to change when the Change Key 0 button is clicked, which is done in the event handler for that button, btnChange_Click:

```
protected void btnInit_Click(object sender, EventArgs e)
{
    Cache["Depend0"] = "This is the first dependency.";
    Cache["Depend1"] = "This is the 2nd dependency.";
    Cache["Depend2"] = "This is the 3rd dependency.";
}

protected void btnChange_Click(object sender, EventArgs e)
{
    Cache["Depend0"] = "This is a changed first dependency.";
}
```

The real action here occurs in the CreateGridView method. Two string arrays are defined, one to hold the file to depend upon and one to hold the keys of the other cached items to depend upon.

The file dependency is exactly as described in the preceding section. If you do not wish to implement any file or directory dependency here, use null:

```
CacheDependency cacheDepends = new CacheDependency(null, cacheDependsArray);
```

Running the `ObjectCachingItemDependency` example brings up the page shown in Figure 17-7.

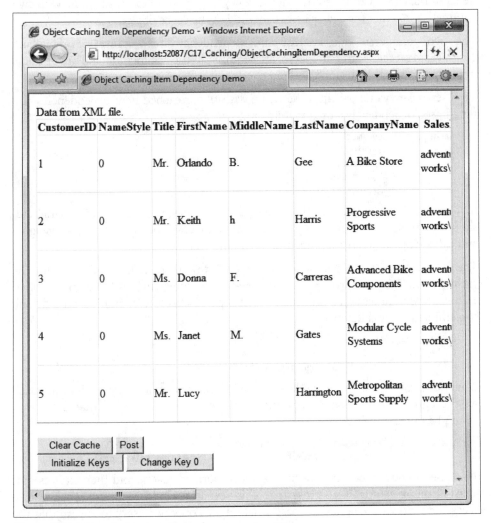

Figure 17-7. ObjectCachingItemDependency.aspx in action

Initially, the label above the data grid will show that the data is from the XML file. After you click the Initialize Keys button, clicking the Post button or reentering the URL will cause the data to come from the cache. Clicking any of the other buttons or changing the contents of *Customers.xml* will cause the cached data set to expire and the data to be retrieved fresh from the XML file the next time the page is posted.

Note that this example does not explicitly demonstrate what would happen if one of the controlling cached items was removed from the cache; this would also cause the dependent cached item to expire.

Time dependency

Items in the cache can be given a dependency based on time. This is done with two parameters in either the Add or Insert method of the Cache object.

The two parameters that control time dependency are AbsoluteExpiration and SlidingExpiration. Both parameters are required in the Add method and are optional in the Insert method through method overloading.

To insert a key/value pair into the cache with file or cached item dependencies and time-based dependencies, use the following syntax:

```
Cache.Insert(KeyName,
             KeyValue,
             Dependencies,
             AbsoluteExpiration,
             SlidingExpiration);
```

If you don't want any file or cached item dependencies, the Dependencies parameter should be null. If this syntax is used, default values will be used for the scavenging and callback parameters (described in upcoming sections).

The AbsoluteExpiration parameter is of type DateTime. It defines a lifetime for the cached item. The time provided can be an absolute time, such as March 31, 2008 at 1:23:45 P.M. The code to implement that type of absolute expiration would look something like the following:

```
DateTime expDate = new DateTime(2008,3,31,13,23,45);
Cache.Insert("GridViewDataSet", dsGrid, null, expDate,
             Cache.NoSlidingExpiration);
```

Obviously, this is not very flexible. Of greater utility is an absolute expiration based on the current time—say, 30 minutes from now. The syntax for that expiration would be the following:

```
Cache.Insert("GridViewDataSet", dsGrid, null,
             DateTime.Now.AddMinutes(30), Cache.NoSlidingExpiration);
```

This line of code inserts the specified data set into the cache and then expires that item 30 minutes after it was inserted. This scenario would be useful when you're accessing a slowly changing database where it was only necessary to ensure that the data presented was no more than 30 minutes old.

Suppose that the data was volatile or needed to be very current. Perhaps the data presented must never be more than 10 seconds old. The following line of code implements that scenario:

```
Cache.Insert("DataGridDataSet", dsGrid, null,
             DateTime.Now.AddSeconds(10), Cache.NoSlidingExpiration);
```

If your web page is receiving hundreds of hits per minute, implementing a 10-second cache would provide a huge performance boost by reducing the number of database queries by a factor of 20 or more. Even a one-second cache can provide a significant performance enhancement to heavily trafficked web servers.

The other time-based parameter is SlidingExpiration, of type TimeSpan. This parameter specifies a time interval between when an item is last accessed and when it expires. If the sliding expiration is set for 30 seconds, for example, the cached item will expire if the cache is not accessed within 30 seconds. If it is accessed within that time period, the clock will be reset, so to speak, and the cached item will persist for at least another 30 seconds. If the cache were accessed every 29 seconds, for example, it would never expire. You might use this for data that does not change often but is not used often either. To implement this scenario, use the following line of code:

```
Cache.Insert("DataGridDataSet", dsGrid, null,
            Cache.NoAbsoluteExpiration, TimeSpan.FromSeconds(30));
```

Cache.NoAbsoluteExpiration is used for the AbsoluteExpiration parameter. Alternatively, you could use DateTime.MaxValue. This constant is the largest possible value of DateTime, corresponding to 11:59:59 P.M., 12/31/9999. (That's a millennium problem we can live with.) This indicates to ASP.NET that absolute expiration should not be used. If you attempt to use both types of expiration policies at once (absolute and sliding), an error will occur.

Scavenging

ASP.NET can scavenge memory by removing seldom-used or low-priority items from the cache if server memory falls below a given threshold. Doing so frees up memory to handle a higher volume of page requests.

Scavenging is influenced by the Priority parameter of the Add and Insert methods of the Cache class. This parameter is required of the Add method and is optional for the Insert method.

The Priority parameter indicates the value of the cached item relative to the other items stored in the cache. This parameter is used by the cache when it evicts objects to free up system memory when the web server runs low on memory. Cached items with a lower priority are evicted before items with a higher priority.

The legal values of the Priority parameter are contained in the CacheItemPriority enumeration, as shown in Table 17-4 in descending order of priority.

Table 17-4. The CacheItemPriority enum

Value	Description
NotRemovable	Items with this priority level will not be evicted.
High	Items with this priority level are the least likely to be evicted.
AboveNormal	Items with this priority level are less likely to be evicted than items assigned Normal priority.

Table 17-4. The CacheItemPriority enum (continued)

Value	Description
Default	This is equivalent to Normal.
Normal	The default value.
BelowNormal	Items with this priority level are more likely to be evicted than items assigned Normal priority.
Low	Items with this priority level are the most likely to be evicted.

To implement scavenging, use the following line of code:

```
Cache.Insert("DataGridDataSet", dsGrid, null,
            Cache.NoAbsoluteExpiration,
            Cache.NoSlidingExpiration,
            CacheItemPriority.High,
            null);
```

The final parameter in the preceding line of code pertains to callback support, which we will cover in the next section.

Because the Insert method calls use all seven parameters, you could use the Add method with the same parameters.

Callback Support

A CacheItemRemovedCallback event is raised when an item is removed from the cache for any reason. You may want to implement an event handler for this event, perhaps to reinsert the item into the cache or to log the event to evaluate whether your server needs more memory. The Add and Insert methods take a parameter that specifies the event handler (callback) method.

The next example demonstrates using the CacheItemRemovedCallback event. This example will behave identically to the previous example, shown in Figure 17-7, except that it will make an entry in a logfile, *test.txt*, every time the cache is expired.

 You'll need to make sure the user account you're running the page as has permissions to create files in the directory in which you want to hold *test.txt*; otherwise, the page will fail.

Add a copy of *ObjectCachingItemDependency.aspx* to the *C17_Caching* website and call it *ObjectCachingCallback.aspx*. There are no changes to make to the markup for the page, but several to make in the code behind the page, as follows.

You start by adding System.IO to the list of namespaces to use in this file. You'll need it to write the logfile to disk.

```
using System;
using System.Data;
using System.IO;
using System.Web.Caching;
```

```
using System.Web.UI;
using System.Xml;

public partial class ObjectCachingCallback : Page
{
```

The callback method is encapsulated within a *delegate*, which is a reference type that encapsulates a method with a specific signature and return type. The callback method is of the same type and must have the same signature as the CacheItemRemovedCallback delegate. The callback method is declared as a private member of the Page class with the following line of code:

```
public static CacheItemRemovedCallback onRemove = null;

protected void Page_Load(object sender, EventArgs e)
{
    CreateGridView( );
}
```

The callback delegate is then instantiated in CreateGridView by passing a reference to the method RemovedCallback, which will actually do the work when a cache item is removed. You'll also see that the call to Insert an item in the Cache in CreateGridView now includes onRemove (in addition to the three parameters for time and priority dependencies). This is the callback.

```
private void CreateGridView( )
{
    DataSet dsGrid;
    dsGrid = (DataSet)Cache["GridViewDataSet"];

    onRemove = new CacheItemRemovedCallback(this.RemovedCallback);

    if (dsGrid == null)
    {
        dsGrid = GetDataSet( );
        string[] fileDependsArray =
            { Server.MapPath("Customers.xml") };
        string[] cacheDependsArray =
            { "Depend0", "Depend1", "Depend2" };
        CacheDependency cacheDepends = new CacheDependency
            (fileDependsArray, cacheDependsArray);

        Cache.Insert("GridViewDataSet", dsGrid, cacheDepends,
            DateTime.Now.AddSeconds(10), Cache.NoSlidingExpiration,
            CacheItemPriority.Default,
            onRemove);

        lblMessage.Text = "Data from XML file.";
    }
    else
    {
        lblMessage.Text = "Data from cache.";
    }
```

```
gvwCustomers.DataSource = dsGrid.Tables[0];
gvwCustomers.DataBind();
}
```

The signature for the RemovedCallback method itself consists of the three required parameters:

- A string containing the key of the cached item
- An object that is the cached item
- A member of the CacheItemRemovedReason enumeration

This last parameter, CacheItemRemovedReason, provides the reason that the cached item was removed from the cache. It can have one of the values shown in Table 17-5.

Table 17-5. The CacheItemRemovedReason enumeration

Value	Description
DependencyChanged	A file or item key dependency has changed.
Expired	The cached item has expired.
Removed	The cached item has been explicitly removed by the Remove method or replaced by another item with the same key.
Underused	The cached item was removed to free up system memory.

```
public void RemovedCallback(
    string cacheKey, Object cacheObject,
    CacheItemRemovedReason reasonToRemove)
{
    WriteFile("Cache removed for following reason: " +
        reasonToRemove.ToString());
}
```

In this example, the only thing the RemovedCallback method does is call WriteFile to make a log entry. It does this by instantiating a StreamWriter on the logfile. The second parameter for the StreamWriter class, the Boolean, specifies to append to the file if it exists and to create the file if it doesn't exist. If false, it would have overwritten the file if it existed. For this to work as written, the account used by the ASP.NET process must have sufficient rights to create files in the root directory. The WriteLine method is then used to write the string to be logged to the logfile.

```
private void WriteFile(string strText)
{
    StreamWriter writer = new StreamWriter("~\test.txt", true);
    writer.WriteLine(String.Format("{0} {1}",
        DateTime.Now.ToString(), strText));
    writer.Close();
}
```

To give the ASP.NET process account the right to create files in the root directory of your website, right-click the directory in Windows Explorer and click Properties from the menu. Choose the Security tab and click Edit to add an entry for the account (ASPNET on IIS 5 and earlier, NETWORK SERVICE on IIS 6 or later) to the dialog. With the account selected, check the Modify and Write checkboxes and then click OK twice to close the dialog and save the permissions for the account on the directory.

The rest of the code in this file, GetDataSet() and the OnClick event handlers, remains the same:

```
private DataSet GetDataSet()
{
    DataSet dsData = new DataSet();
    XmlDataDocument doc = new XmlDataDocument();
    doc.DataSet.ReadXml(Server.MapPath("Customers.xml"));
    dsData = doc.DataSet;
    return dsData;
}
protected void btnClear_Click(object sender, EventArgs e)
{
    Cache.Remove("GridViewDataSet");
    CreateGridView();
}

protected void btnInit_Click(object sender, EventArgs e)
{
    // Initialize caches to depend on.
    Cache["Depend0"] = "This is the first dependency.";
    Cache["Depend1"] = "This is the 2nd dependency.";
    Cache["Depend2"] = "This is the 3rd dependency.";
}

protected void btnChange_Click(object sender, EventArgs e)
{
    Cache["Depend0"] = "This is a changed first dependency.";
}
} // end of ObjectCachingCallback.aspx.cs
```

The HttpCachePolicy Class

Just as the OutputCache directive provides a high-level API for implementing caching, a low-level API is available through the HttpCachePolicy class. This class is contained within the System.Web namespace. It uses HTTP headers to control the caching. The HttpCachePolicy class mirrors the functionality provided by the page directive. It also provides additional low-level control, comparable to the type of control provided for object caching.

To use the `HttpCachePolicy` class to control output caching, do not include an `OutputCache` directive in the page file. Instead, use the `Response.Cache` syntax, as shown in the next example, *OutputCacheLowLevel.aspx*. Create this example by adding a copy of *OutputCaching.aspx* to the *C17_Caching* website and renaming it *OutputCacheLowLevel.aspx*.

The content file of *OutputCacheLowLevel.aspx* is functionally unchanged from the previous example, except for removing the `OutputCache` directive from the top of the file. If you leave the `OutputCache` directive in, it will override the calls using `Response.Cache`.

The code-behind file has two additional lines added to the `Page_Load` method, highlighted in Example 17-8.

Example 17-8. OutputCacheLowLevel.aspx.cs in full

```
using System;
using System.Web;
using System.Web.UI;

public partial class OutputCachingLowLevel : Page
{
    protected void Page_Load(object sender, EventArgs e)
    {
        Response.Cache.SetExpires(DateTime.Now.AddSeconds(10));
        Response.Cache.SetCacheability(HttpCacheability.Public);

        lblTime.Text = String.Format("Page posted at {0}",
            DateTime.Now.ToLongTimeString());
        lblUserName.Text = String.Format("UserName : {0}",
            Request.QueryString["UserName"]);
        lblState.Text = String.Format("State : {0}",
            Request.QueryString["State"]);
    }
}
```

The first highlighted line in Example 17-8 sets the cache duration to 10 seconds. It is equivalent to a `Duration` parameter in an `OutputCache` directive.

The second line corresponds to the `Location` parameter in the `OutputCache` directive.

For reference, Table 17-6 compares the possible `Location` parameter values for an `OutputCache` directive with their equivalent values in a call to `Response.Cache.SetCacheability`. These are all members of the `HttpCacheability` enumeration.

Table 17-6. Location values versus the HttpCacheability enumeration

Location	SetCacheability value	SetCacheability description
Client	Private	The response is cacheable on the client. This is useful if the page requires authentication. This is the default.
Downstream	Public	Uses the `SetNoServerCaching` method to disallow caching on the web server.

Location	SetCacheability value	SetCacheability description
Server	Server	The response is cached on the web server.
None	NoCache	Disables caching.
Any	Public	The response is cacheable by clients and shared (proxy) caches.

Many other `HttpCachePolicy` methods and properties are available. Some of the more common ones include the following:

SetMaxAge

> Another method, in addition to `SetExpires`, to set an expiration. Accepts a `TimeSpan` value. The following line of code would set the expiration time to 45 seconds:

```
Response.Cache.SetMaxAge(new TimeSpan(0,0,45))
```

SetNoServerCaching

> Disables all further server caching. For example:

```
Response.Cache.SetNoServerCaching()
```

SetSlidingExpiration

> A method to enable sliding expiration. Takes a Boolean parameter. If true, it will enable sliding expiration. Sliding expiration forces the clock to restart, so to speak, every time the cache is accessed. So, if `SetMaxAge` (described earlier in this list) is set to 30 seconds, every time the cache is accessed the 30-second clock will be reset to zero. As long as the cache is accessed at least every 30 seconds, it will never expire. The following statement, for example, enables sliding expiration of the cache:

```
Response.Cache.SetSlidingExpiration(true)
```

VaryByParams

> The equivalent of the `VaryByParam` parameter in the `OutputCache` directive (note the slight difference in spelling). It forces a separate cache for each unique combination of parameters passed to the server in the page request.

> To duplicate the `VaryByParam` parameter in the following `OutputCache` directive:

```
<%@ OutputCache Duration="60" VaryByParam="state;city" %>
```

> you would use the following lines of code:

```
Response.Cache.VaryByParams.Item("state")=true
Response.Cache.VaryByParams.Item("city")=true
```

Performance

Performance is often an important issue in computer applications, especially in web applications receiving a large number of requests. One obvious way to improve performance is to buy faster hardware with more memory. But you can also tune your code to enhance performance in many ways, some of them significant. We'll begin by examining some of the areas specific to ASP.NET that offer the greatest performance improvements and then examine some of the general .NET topics related to improving performance.

 Several Microsofties involved with writing the .NET Framework used the word *performant* to mean that something is delivering higher performance. We can't find it in any dictionary, but it seems like a good word.

ASP.NET-Specific Issues

Correctly using the following features of ASP.NET offers the greatest performance improvements when an ASP.NET application is running.

Session state

Session state is a wonderful thing, but not all applications or pages require it. ASP.NET must execute more code and makes more network requests to process, alter, and maintain session state for every page request and postback that a user makes. So, if your website contains any pages that do not need to use session state, disable it. You can disable session state for a page by setting the EnableSessionState attribute in the Page directive to false, as in this example:

```
<%@ Page Language="C#" EnableSessionState="false"%>
```

If a page will not be creating or modifying session variables but still needs to access them, set the session state to read-only:

```
<%@ Page Language="C#" EnableSessionState="ReadOnly"%>
```

By default, web services do not have session state enabled. They have access to session state only if the EnableSession property of the WebMethod attribute is set to true:

```
[WebMethod(EnableSession=true)]
```

You can disable session state for an entire application by editing the sessionState section of the application's *web.config* file:

```
<sessionState mode="off" />
```

Session state can be stored in one of three ways:

- In-process
- Out-of-process, as a Windows service
- Out-of-process, in a SQL Server database

Each has advantages and disadvantages. Storing session state in-process is by far the most performant. The out-of-process stores are necessary in web farm or web garden scenarios (see "Web gardening and web farming," later in this chapter) or if the data must not be lost if a server or process is stopped and restarted.

For a complete discussion of session state, see Chapter 6.

View state

Automatic view state management is another great feature of ASP.NET server controls that enables the controls to show property values correctly after a round trip with no work on the part of the developer. However, there is a performance penalty. This information is passed back and forth via a hidden field, which consumes bandwidth and takes time to process. To see the amount of data used in view state, enable tracing (see Chapter 19) and look at the ViewState column of the Control Tree table displayed as part of the trace output.

By default, view state is enabled for all server controls. To disable view state for a server control, set the EnableViewState attribute to false, as in the following example:

```
<asp:TextBox id="txtBookName" runat="server"
   text="Enter book name." toolTip="Enter book name here."
   EnableViewState="false" />
```

You can disable view state for an entire page by setting the EnableViewState attribute of the Page directive to false, as in this example:

```
<%@ Page Language="C#" EnableViewState="false" %>
```

Caching

Use output and data caching whenever possible. This is especially valuable for database queries that return relatively static data or have a limited range of query parameters. Effective use of caching can have a profound effect on the performance of a website.

Server controls

Server controls—those bundled with .NET and those user and custom controls you build yourself—are convenient and offer many advantages. In VS2008, they are practically the default type of control. However, they have a certain amount of overhead and are sometimes not the optimal type of control to use.

In general, if you do not need to manipulate a control programmatically, do not use a server control. Use a classic HTML control instead. For example, if you're placing a simple label on a page, there will be no need to use a server control unless you need to read or change the value of the label's Text property.

If you need to substitute values into HTML sent to the client browser, you can achieve the desired result (without using a server control) by using data binding or a simple rendering. For instance, the following example shows three ways of displaying a hyperlink in a browser:

```
<script language="C#" runat="server">
   string strLink = "www.anysite.com";

   void Page_Load(Object sender, EventArgs e)
   {
      //..retrieve data for strLink here
      //  Call the DataBind method for the page.
      DataBind();
   }
</script>

<%--the server control is not necessary....--%>
<a href='<%# strLink %>' runat="server">The Name of the Link</a>
<br /><br />

<%-- use DataBinding to substitute literals instead....--%>
<a href='<%# strLink %>' > The Name of the Link</a>
<br /><br />

<%-- or a simple rendering expression....--%>
<a href='<%= strLink %>' > The Name of the Link</a>
```

Web gardening and web farming

The practice of adding multiple processors to a computer, by using either multicore processors or many physical CPU chips, is called *web gardening*. The .NET Framework takes advantage of this by distributing work to several processes, one per CPU.

For truly high-traffic sites, multiple web server machines can work together to serve the same application. This is referred to as a *web farm*.

At the least, locating the web server on one machine and the database server on another will buy a large degree of stability and scalability. Or you can go one step further and start doubling up machines for a single purpose and create machine clusters.

Round trips

Round trips to the server are expensive. In low-bandwidth situations they are slow for the client, and in high-volume applications they bog down the server and inhibit scaling. You should design your applications to minimize round trips.

The only truly essential round trips to the server are those that read or write data. Most validation and data manipulations can occur on the client browser. ASP.NET server controls do this automatically for validation with up-level browsers (Internet Explorer 4 and later and any other browser that supports ECMAScript).

When developing custom server controls, having the controls render client-side code for up-level browsers will reduce the number of round trips.

Another way to minimize round trips is to use the IsPostBack property in the Page_Load method. Often, you will want the page to perform some process the first time the page loads, but not on subsequent postbacks. For example, the following code shows how to make code execution conditional on the IsPostBack property:

```
void Page_Load(Object sender, EventArgs e) {
   if (! IsPostBack)
   {
       // Do the expensive operations only the
       // first time the page is loaded.
   }
}
```

For a complete discussion of the IsPostBack property, see Chapter 3.

General .NET Issues

Many of the performance enhancements that affect an ASP.NET application are general ones that apply to any .NET application. This section lists some of the major .NET-related areas to consider when developing your ASP.NET applications.

String concatenation

Strings are immutable in the .NET Framework. This means that methods and operators that appear to change the string are actually returning a modified copy of the string. This has huge performance implications. If you're doing a lot of string manipulation, using the StringBuilder class is much faster.

Consider the code shown in Example 17-9. It measures the time to create a string from 10,000 substrings in two different ways. The first time a simple string concatenation is used, and the second time the StringBuilder class is used. If you want to see the resultant string, uncomment the two commented lines in the code.

Example 17-9. String concatenation benchmark in C#, StringConcat-cs.aspx

```
<%@ Page Language="C#" AutoEventWireup="true"
   CodeFile="String-Concat.aspx.cs" Inherits="String_Concat" %>

<script runat="server">
   void Page_Load(Object Source, EventArgs E)
   {
       int intLimit = 10000;
       DateTime startTime;
       DateTime endTime;
       TimeSpan elapsedTime;
       string strSub;
       string strWhole = "";

       // Do string concat first
       startTime = DateTime.Now;
       for (int i=0; i < intLimit; i++)
       {
```

```
            strSub = i.ToString( );
            strWhole = strWhole + " " + strSub;
        }
        endTime = DateTime.Now;

        elapsedTime = endTime - startTime;
        lblConcat.Text = elapsedTime.ToString( );
        //lblConcatString.Text = strWhole;

        //  Do stringBuilder next
        startTime = DateTime.Now;
        StringBuilder sb = new StringBuilder( );
        for (int i=0; i < intLimit; i++)
        {
            strSub = i.ToString( );
            sb.Append(" ");
            sb.Append(strSub);
        }
        endTime = DateTime.Now;
        elapsedTime = endTime - startTime;
        lblBuild.Text = elapsedTime.ToString( );
        //lblBuildString.Text = sb.ToString( );
    }
</server>

<!DOCTYPE html PUBLIC "-//W3C//DTD XHTML 1.0 Transitional//EN"
    "http://www.w3.org/TR/xhtml1/DTD/xhtml1-transitional.dtd">
<html>
<head>
    <title>String Concatenation Benchmark</title>
</head>
<body>
    <form id="Form1" runat="server">
    <h1>String Concatenation Benchmark</h1>
    <h2>Concatenation:</h2>
    <asp:Label ID="lblConcat" runat="server" />
    <br />
    <asp:Label ID="lblConcatString" runat="server" />
    <h2>StringBuilder:</h2>
    <asp:Label ID="lblBuild" runat="server" />
    <br />
    <asp:Label ID="lblBuildString" runat="server" />
    </form>
</body>
</html>
```

When this page is run, you should see something like Figure 17-8. The difference between the two techniques is dramatic: the StringBuilder's Append method is some 150 times faster than string concatenation.

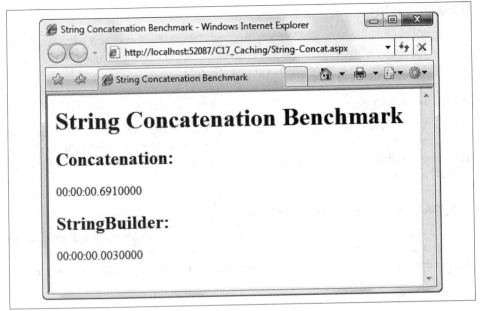

Figure 17-8. String concatenation benchmark results

Minimizing exceptions

You can use try...catch blocks to control program flow (see Chapter 19). However, this coding technique is a serious impediment to performance. You will do much better if you first test whether some condition will cause a failure; if so, code around it.

For example, rather than dividing two integers inside a try...catch block and catching any Divide By Zero exceptions thrown, first test whether the divisor is zero; if it is, do not do the operation. Similarly, it is as expensive to throw exceptions of your own creation, though there are times when it cannot be avoided.

Using early binding

.NET languages allow both early and late binding. Early binding occurs when all objects are declared and the object type is known at compile time. Late binding occurs when the object type is not determined until runtime, at which point the CLR determines the type of object it is working with.

Early binding is much faster than late binding, though the latter can be very convenient. Late binding is implemented with reflection, the details of which are beyond the scope of this book.

Disabling debug mode

When you deploy your application, remember to disable debug mode. For a complete discussion of deployment issues, refer to Chapter 20.

Database Issues

Almost all applications involve some form of database access, and accessing data from a database is necessarily an expensive operation. You can make data access more efficient, however, by focusing on several areas.

Using a DataReader class

There are two main ways to get data from a database: from a DataReader object or from a DataSet object. The DataReader classes (SqlDataReader, OleDbDataReader, and OracleDataReader) are a much faster way of accessing data if all you need is a forward-only data stream.

Using SQL or Oracle classes rather than OleDB classes

Some database engines have managed classes specifically designed for interacting with that database. It is much better to use the database-specific classes rather than the generic OleDB classes. So, for example, it is faster to use a SqlDataReader rather than an OleDbDataReader.

Benchmarking and Profiling

Benchmarking is the process of conducting reproducible performance tests to see how fast an application is running. It may involve coding the same task two different ways and seeing which one runs faster. The web page shown previously in Example 17-9, which tested the relative speed of string concatenation techniques, is an example of a simple benchmarking program. Obviously, benchmarking programs will often be more complex than that example. You should design them to emulate your environment as closely as possible.

Profiling is the gathering of performance information about an application. There are several ways to profile an application. Two that are part of the .NET Framework are the following:

- Windows XP and Windows Vista System Performance Monitor
- The .NET performance counters API

You can use the Performance Monitor to watch a huge variety of system parameters, both .NET-specific and otherwise, in real time. You can open the Performance Monitor by opening a Command Prompt and typing in **perfmon**. When the Performance Monitor opens, click the Add icon on the Toolbar to select and add any number of performance counters. The available counters cover the processor, memory, hard disk, SQL Server, .NET, and ASP.NET.

The performance counter's API includes several classes. You can use the PerformanceCounter component in the System.Diagnostics namespace for reading existing performance counters and for creating and writing to custom counters.

 Benchmarking is a vast subject and this section only scratches the surface. Many articles and books have been written on the topic. To see what support is available within the .NET Framework, search for *Monitoring Performance* in the documentation index or search for "monitoring performance site:microsoft.com" in your favorite search engine.

CHAPTER 18

Application Logic and Configuration

ASP.NET provides easy access to application-wide program logic through the *Global.asax* file. This text file allows you to create event handlers for many events exposed by the application as a whole and by individual sessions. You can also include variables and methods that will apply globally to the entire application.

You can configure web applications using the XML configuration files *machine.config* and *web.config*, which provide a flexible and hierarchical configuration scheme. Configuration settings can apply to every application on the web server, to specific applications, or to specific subdirectories within an application. New to Windows Vista and Windows Server 2008 as a complement to ASP.NET 3.5 is the ability to configure Internet Information Services (IIS) 7.0 through *web.config* and use it to change *web.config*, in addition to the Web Site Administration Tool (WAT) in Visual Studio 2008 (VS2008). If you're using Windows XP, you also can use IIS 5.1 and its ASP.NET Configuration Settings dialog box as an alternative to hand-editing application-specific configuration files.

Because all of the configuration and control for ASP.NET applications is done with text files, either XML or some other variant of plain text, you can maintain and update a web application remotely. You don't need to be physically present at a web server to reconfigure the application through IIS (though access to these files is tightly controlled so that your users cannot modify them).

Introducing IIS 7.0

This chapter assumes that you are using IIS 7.0, the version that is included with the Windows Vista operating system. This version of IIS was rewritten from the ground up for many and varied reasons and looks quite a bit different from IIS v5.x and v6.0, as you will see. Suffice it to say for now that IIS 7.0 continues to support websites written in classic ASP, ASP.NET v1 through v3.5, and beyond.

You can determine which version of IIS is serving a page by enabling tracing on that page (see Chapter 19 for more on tracing) and looking for the value of SERVER_SOFTWARE under Server Variables. Alternatively, add a Label control to the form and set its Text property as follows:

```
lblVersion.Text = Request.ServerVariables["SERVER_SOFTWARE"];
```

If the page is being served from VS2008 rather than IIS, the value of SERVER_SOFTWARE will be blank.

You can access IIS 7.0 on your machine in a number of different ways:

- From Windows Explorer, right-click My Computer and select Manage. You can find IIS under Services and Applications.
- Click Start → Settings → Control Panel → Administrative Tools → Internet Information Services (IIS) Manager.
- Click Start → Run, enter **%SystemRoot%\system32\inetsrv\InetMgr.exe** in the dialog, and click OK.

 You must be an administrator to run IIS 7.0 at any time.

IIS 7.0 will appear as shown in Figure 18-1.

It has three distinct windows, from left to right:

- The Connections window allows you to select the websites you will configure in the other two windows.
- The main window presents two views on the currently selected site in the Connections window. The Features View, shown in Figure 18-1, presents you with various configuration options for the currently selected site, some of which will be reflected in *web.config* and some not. The Contents View, shown in Figure 18-2, displays the files and folders contained in the currently selected site or folder within it.
- The Actions window is context-sensitive to the folder or site selected in the Connections window and also to whether the Features View or Contents View is being shown in the main window. It presents you with a list of all the common tasks to perform, such as starting and stopping a site, adding a virtual directory to the site, editing permissions, and more.

If you've used IIS v5.x or v6.0 before, you'll be familiar with the Contents View as it is more akin to those previous iterations of IIS.

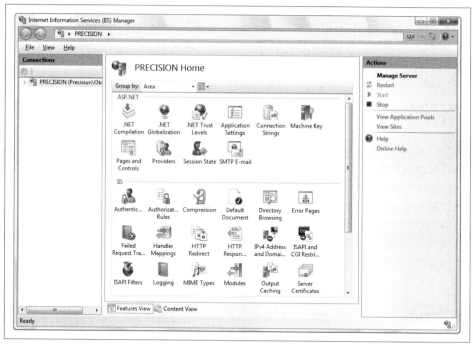

Figure 18-1. IIS 7.0 at first glance: The Features View

Figure 18-2. IIS 7.0: The Contents View

The Default Website

When IIS is installed on a machine, it creates *C:\inetpub\wwwroot* and a few files within it to provide a default page for the default website. You can see this by directing your browser to *http://localhost*.

If your web server is accessible over the Internet through a domain name, a remote user at a browser who entered that domain name as a URL (say, for example, as *http://www.SomeDomainName.com*) would see the same thing.

You will not see anything in the browser (other than help pages put up by IIS) unless one of the following conditions is true:

- A suitably named file (*default.htm*, *default.asp*, *Default.aspx*, or *iisstart.htm*) containing a valid web page exists in the physical directory.
- Directory Browsing is enabled by selecting the Default Web Site, double-clicking Directory Browsing from the Features View, and clicking Enable in the Actions View.

 Be aware that enabling Directory Browsing can present a serious gap in security. It is generally not something to do on a production site unless you have a very good reason and suitable security precautions are in place, such as stringent permissions.

Compare the contents of the default website in Figure 18-2 with the actual contents of *c:\inetpub\wwwroot* shown in Figure 18-3. You can see that all the files and directories in the physical directory are also in the default website in Figure 18-2. These physical directories, such as *aspnet_client*, are normal directories with standard Explorer-style directory icons.

In addition to normal directories, *virtual directories* are denoted by a folder with a shortcut icon overlaid on it. Web applications, which we will cover after virtual directories, are denoted by a globe icon overlaid with pages. Both icons are shown in Figure 18-4.

Virtual Directories

When you work with web applications, you will frequently need to create, configure, or examine the properties of a virtual directory. Virtual directories in IIS are central to web applications. A virtual directory is any directory on the server, or accessible to the server, that has been made available by IIS to requests from the Web. Virtual directories are isomorphic with applications, that is, each virtual directory is a separate application, and each IIS-served application must have a single virtual root directory.

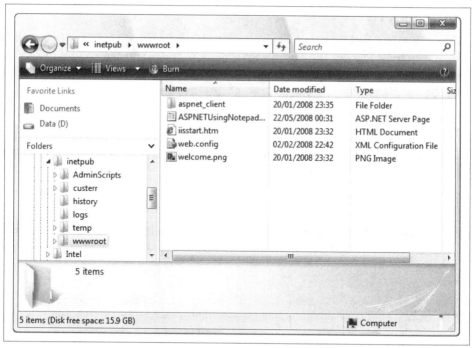

Figure 18-3. C:\inetpub\wwwroot

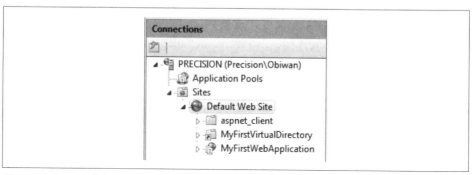

Figure 18-4. Virtual directory and web application icons

Virtual directories are accessible to requests from browsers coming in over the Internet. The URL is the domain name, followed by the virtual directory and the web page (or service) file. For example, if an application with a starting web page called *MyPage.aspx* was using a virtual directory called *MyVirtualDirectory*, and the domain name of the hosting web server was *http://www.somedomainname.com*, the URL to access that application would be *http://www.SomeDomainName.com/MyVirtualDirectory/MyPage.aspx*.

If the virtual directory is added to the Default Web Site added when IIS is installed, the URL to access *MyPage.aspx* would be *http://localhost/MyVirtualDirectory/ MyPage.aspx*.

Creating the virtual directory

When a new web application is created in VS2008 and the Location is set to HTTP, an IIS virtual directory for the app is created automatically. If the Location is set to either File System (the default) or FTP, IIS does not come into play and no virtual directory is created. In these latter two cases, VS2008 provides its own built-in, lightweight web server to serve the pages during development only.

 For a discussion of the Location setting, see Chapter 2.

If you wish to deploy the application or look at the application in a browser without running the website from Visual Studio, you will have to create the virtual directory manually using IIS.

To create a virtual directory in IIS 7.0 once it is open, follow these steps:

1. Expand the tree in the Connections pane on the lefthand side of the window. You'll be able to drill down through the machine into the *Sites* folder to the website to which you want to add the virtual directory. In Figure 18-5, we're using the Default Web Site to demonstrate.

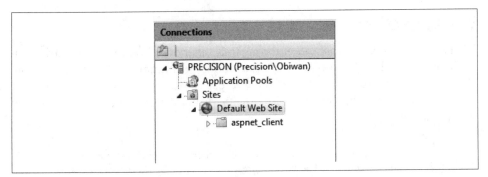

Figure 18-5. Selecting the Default Web Site in the Connections pane

2. Switch to the Contents View. The main window will show the contents of the physical directory that corresponds to the Default Web Site which is *C:\inetpub\ wwwroot*, unless you've changed it.

3. Select Add Virtual Directory from the Actions pane. Specify the name of the virtual directory and the physical folder it will point to and click OK. A new folder with a shortcut icon will appear in the Contents View, denoting your new virtual directory.

Virtual directory security and zones

When you create a virtual directory, it is mapped to a physical directory. To then access the virtual directory, you can enter one of the following URLs from a browser, depending on whether you are on a local machine or are accessing the application over a local intranet or the Internet:

- *http://localhost/VDir* (local)
- *http://SomeComputerName/VDir* (intranet)
- *http://www.SomeDomainName.com/VDir* (Internet)

Internet Explorer can determine whether a URL is pointing to an intranet or an Internet address by the presence of periods in the first node. If there are any periods, it is an Internet address. For example, both of the following URLs are Internet addresses:

- *http://www.SomeDomainName.com/Websites*
- *http://123.456.789.123/Websites*

This determination is important for imposing the proper security settings. Localhost, intranet, and Internet sites all map into one of the security zones for which Internet Explorer and other browsers maintain different security settings. Although you cannot foresee how a user may individually set her security settings for each zone, it is useful to understand the differences between them in their defaults.

You can find the Internet Explorer settings by choosing Tools → Internet Options → Security, selecting one of the four preset zones, and then selecting "Custom level" to see the various settings.

Web Applications

We have used the term *application* throughout this book. You probably know intuitively what a web application is. Here is a working definition for a web application: "A web application consists of all of the web pages, files, code, objects, executables, images, and other resources located in an IIS virtual directory or a subdirectory of that virtual directory."

 Web application directories can be either physical directories or virtual directories. The virtual directories created by developers are also application directories by default. To convert a virtual directory into a web application directory, right-click it in the Connections pane and select Convert to Application.

A web application will start the first time any of its pages is requested from the web server. It will run until any of a number of events causes it to shut down. These events include the following:

- Editing *Global.asax* or a configuration file
- Restarting IIS
- Restarting the machine
- Updating any of the assemblies in the application
- Encountering an unhandled exception or fault

If a page is requested and the application is not running, the application will automatically restart.

Unlike traditional desktop applications, web applications allow a user to request a specific entry point. Instead of clicking an icon, a user enters a URL in a browser. The flow and security of web applications should be designed accordingly.

For example, a virtual directory may contain three web pages: *Default.aspx*, *Login.aspx*, and *Bugs.aspx*. If you enter the URL *http://localhost* in a browser, you will go to *Default.aspx*, which may send you to *Login.aspx*.

On the other hand, users may enter *http://localhost/login.aspx* to go directly to the login page.

Once logged in, they can go to *Bugs.aspx*. If a user tries to go directly to *Bugs.aspx* without logging in, your code should redirect her to *Login.aspx* to log in first.

Classic ASP, PHP, and ASP.NET applications can coexist side by side on the same server and also in the same application directory. However, configuration, application, and session objects cannot be shared between them. They are totally distinct and independent.

Application Pools and Domains

Each ASP.NET web application runs in its own *application domain*, which the runtime server creates. The application domain allows the web application to run in memory that is isolated from other applications. If one application crashes or otherwise compromises its own stability, it limits the effect on other domains. This improves security and stability.

Because each application is independent from any other application, this means each application has its own independent configuration and control structures.

Each application domain is part of an *application pool*, also created and governed within IIS. Each application pool is created by the runtime server and is isolated from every other application pool. Thus, if one application crashes or otherwise compromises the stability of its application pool, it will affect only the sites in the same pool. Hence, it is a good practice to create an application pool for each site or domain. This greatly enhances security and stability.

To create a new application pool in IIS 7.0, find and select the Application Pools entry in the Connections view. It should be directly under the name of the machine you want to create it on, as shown in Figure 18-6.

Figure 18-6. IIS 7.0 Application Pools page

Click Add Application Pool in the Actions pane. A dialog will appear, as shown in Figure 18-7, where you can give it a name, select whether the pool should be based on .NET 2.0 or no managed code, and select which type of pipeline mode it should use.

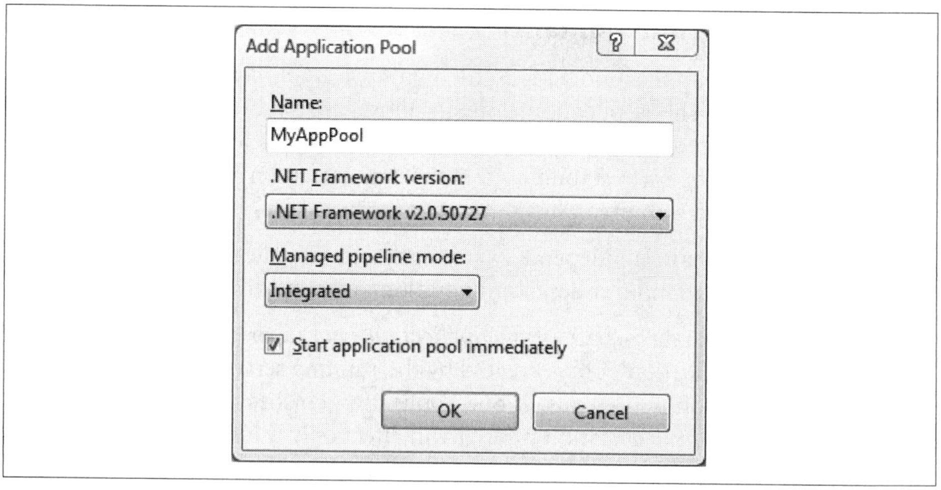

Figure 18-7. The Add Application Pool dialog

Please consult the beginning of Chapter 12 for the distinction between classic mode, as illustrated in Figure 12-1, and integrated mode, as illustrated in Figure 12-2.

Application-Wide Logic

All code contained in the Page class is scoped to the page. In other words, it is visible only to other code within that Page class. This is true for variables and members such as methods, properties, and events. For most code, this is the appropriate behavior. However, often it is either convenient or necessary to have code scoped more globally. For example, you may have a common method used in several pages. Though you can replicate the code on all the pages, it is far better to have a single source. Another example would be an application where a variable—a TrackingID, for example—is needed by every page as the user moves from page to page.

It is possible to scope your code application-wide (rather than per page). There are several ways of doing this:

- Using the HttpApplication object
- Using the *Global.asax* file
- Using HTTP handlers and modules

The HttpApplication Object

Just as a web page instantiates the Page class, when an application runs it instantiates an object from the HttpApplication class. This object has methods, properties, and events available to all the objects within the application. It provides several objects that allow you to interact with the HTTP request:

- The Application object for using application state
- The Request object for getting access to the incoming request
- The Response object for sending an HttpResponse back to the client
- The Session object for access to session state

ASP.NET maintains a pool of HttpApplication instances during the lifetime of each application. Every time a page is requested from the server, an HttpApplication instance is assigned to it. This instance manages the request from start to finish. Once the request is completed, that instance is freed up for reuse.

You can also program against the HttpApplication object by using a file called *Global.asax*, described next.

The Global.asax File

The *Global.asax* file is a text file that provides code which the application may run independently of any pages that are currently being requested, and in some cases code which is available to any page at any time. Such code can include event handlers for application and session events, methods, and static variables. This file is sometimes called an *application file*.

Any code contained in the *Global.asax* file becomes part of the application in which it is located. There can be only one *Global.asax* file per application, located in the root directory of the application. However, this file is optional. If there is no *Global.asax* file, the application will run using default behavior for all the events exposed by the HttpApplication class if no HTTP handlers and modules are attached to the application.

 Classic ASP had a file with similar format and structure, called *global.asa*. In fact, if you copy all the code from a working copy of *global.asa* into *Global.asax*, the application should run fine.

When the application runs, the contents of *Global.asax* are compiled into a class that derives from the HttpApplication class. Thus, all the methods, classes, and objects of the HttpApplication class are available to your application.

ASP.NET monitors *Global.asax* for changes. If it detects a change in the file, a new copy of the application will be started automatically, creating a new application domain. Any requests that the old application domain is currently handling are allowed to complete, but any new requests are handled by the new application domain. When the last request on the old application domain is finished, that application domain is removed. This effectively reboots the web application without any users being aware of the fact.

To prevent application users from seeing the code underlying the application, ASP.NET is configured by default to prevent users from seeing the contents of *Global.asax*. If someone enters "http://localhost/progaspnet/Global.asax" in a browser, she will receive a 403 (forbidden) error message or an error message similar to the following:

```
This type of page is not served.
```

 Web.config files, described shortly, have behaviors similar to *Global.asax*. If these files are changed, the application will be "invisibly rebooted" in the same way mentioned earlier. It is also not possible to view *web.config* files in a browser.

The *Global.asax* file looks and is structured similarly to a page file (*.aspx*). It can have one or more sections, which we will describe in detail shortly:

- Directives
- Script blocks
- Object declarations

Just like web pages and custom controls, the *Global.asax* file can use the code behind the page. However, unlike the situation with web pages and web services, the default behavior of VS2008 is not to use the code-behind technique with *Global.asax*.

Versions of Visual Studio prior to 2005 by default did use the code-behind model with *Global.asax*. The code-behind model is still supported, though not used by default.

To use the code-behind technique with *Global.asax*, the Application directive at the top of the file (which is analogous to the Page directive in a page file and will be described fully in the next section) has an Inherits property that points to the code-behind class created in *Global.asax.cs*.

There is also a CodeBehind attribute, which you can use to point to a code-behind file. However, if this points to a file located anywhere other than the *App_Code* folder, the class file will have to be compiled manually.

You can add a *Global.asax* file to a web application by right-clicking the website in the Solution Explorer, or clicking the Website menu and selecting Add New Item, then selecting Global Application Class, as shown in Figure 18-8. Leave the default name of *Global.asax* and click Add.

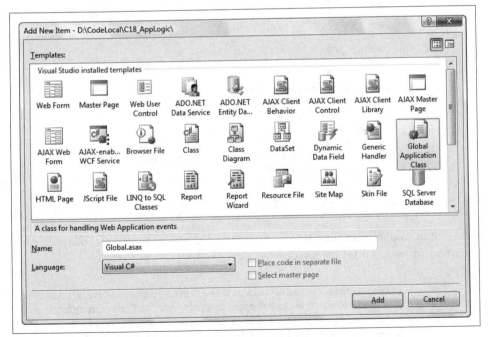

Figure 18-8. Adding Global.asax to a website

Create a new website called *C18_AppLogic* with VS2008 and add a *Global.asax* file to it. VS2008 will create the file listed in Example 18-1. This boilerplate has empty declarations for five events: `Application_Start` and `_End`, `Session_Start` and `_End`, and `Application_Error`.

Example 18-1. The default Global.asax file

```
<%@ Application Language="C#" %>

<script runat="server">

    void Application_Start(object sender, EventArgs e)
    {
        // Code that runs on application startup
    }

    void Application_End(object sender, EventArgs e)
    {
        //  Code that runs on application shutdown
    }

    void Application_Error(object sender, EventArgs e)
    {
        // Code that runs when an unhandled error occurs
    }

    void Session_Start(object sender, EventArgs e)
    {
        // Code that runs when a new session is started
    }

    void Session_End(object sender, EventArgs e)
    {
        // Code that runs when a session ends.
        // Note: The Session_End event is raised only when
        // the sessionstate mode is set to InProc in the
        // Web.config file. If session mode is set to StateServer
        // or SQLServer, the event is not raised.
    }

</script>
```

The sample *Global.asax* file listed in Example 18-2 sets some values in Application state and writes an entry to a logfile every time the application starts.

 In this example, the logfile in located in *C:* because everyone has a *C:* directory. However, to use this example, the ASP.NET account must have permission to write to that directory *C:*, and giving permissions like this is not recommended in a production system. If the site is hacked, the hacker could get access to your entire *C:* drive. It's better if you relocate the logfile to another directory before you run this example and give the ASP.NET account write access to that. Vista users, for example, can use *C:\Users\Public* for this demo as all users have access to it.

Example 18-2. A sample Global.asax

```
<%@ Application  Language="C#"%>
<script runat="server">

   protected void Application_Start(Object sender, EventArgs e)
   {
      Application["strConnectionString"] =
                "SERVER=MyServer;DATABASE=MyDB;UID=myID;PWD=secret;";

      string[] Books = {"SciFi","Novels", "Computers",
                "History", "Religion"};
      Application["arBooks"] = Books;

      WriteFile("Application Starting");
   }

   protected void Application_End(Object sender, EventArgs e)
   {
      WriteFile("Application Ending");
   }

   void WriteFile(string strText)
   {
      using (System.IO.StreamWriter writer =
                new System.IO.StreamWriter(@"C:\test.txt",true))
      {
         string str;
         str = DateTime.Now.ToString() + "   " + strText;
         writer.WriteLine(str);
         writer.Close();
      }
   }
}
</script>
```

Directives

As with web page and web service files, the *Global.asax* file may begin with any number of directives. These specify settings the application compilers are to use when they process the ASP.NET files. As with Page directives, Application directives use a dictionary structure that accepts one or more attribute/value pairs. There are three supported directives: Application, Import, and Assembly.

Application. The Application directive specifies application-specific attributes used by the compiler. For example:

```
<%@ Application Language="C#"
    Inherits="WebServiceConsumer.Global"
    Description="A sample application" %>
```

- The Language attribute is usually set to C# or Visual Basic, but can be set to any third-party language that supports the .NET platform. The default is C#.

The language specified here applies only to the language used in the *Global.asax* file and not to any of the other code files in the application. It is perfectly legal to use C# in the *Global.asax* file and VB.NET in the *.aspx* file, or vice versa, for example.

- The Inherits attribute specifies the name of a class from which to inherit, typically a class in a code-behind file.

- The Description attribute accepts a text description of the application for your own reference, which the parser and compiler then ignore.

- You can use the CodeBehind attribute (not shown in the preceding code snippet) to identify the code-behind file for *Global.asax*, but its use is optional, as mentioned earlier.

Import. The Import directive takes a single attribute, a namespace. The specified namespace is explicitly imported into the application, making all of its classes and interfaces available. The imported namespace can be part of the .NET Framework or a custom namespace. For example:

```
<%@ Import Namespace="System.Data" %>
```

There can be only one Namespace attribute. If you need to import multiple namespaces, use multiple Import directives.

ASP.NET automatically imports the following namespaces into all web applications (specified in the global *web.config* file for the server) and so do not need an Import directive:

- System
- System.Collections
- System.Collections.Specialized
- System.Configuration
- System.IO
- System.Text
- System.Text.RegularExpressions
- System.Web
- System.Web.Caching
- System.Web.Security
- System.Web.SessionState
- System.Web.Profile
- System.Web.UI
- System.Web.UI.HtmlControls
- System.Web.UI.WebControls
- System.Web.UI.WebControls.WebParts

Assembly. The `Assembly` directive links an assembly to the current application during compilation. This makes all the assembly's classes and interfaces available to the application.

 Assemblies are, typically, *.dll* or *.exe* files, and we describe them in detail in Chapter 20.

Using the `Assembly` directive enables both early and late binding because the assembly can be referenced at compile time, then loaded into the application domain at runtime.

Assemblies that are physically located in the application assembly cache (i.e., the *bin* directory and code files located in the *App_Code* directory) are automatically linked to the application. Therefore, any assemblies located in the *bin* directory, or any assemblies compiled from code contained in the *App_Code* directory, need not be linked with an `Assembly` directive.

There are two possible attributes for the `Assembly` directive: `Name` and `Src`. `Name` is a string with the name of the assembly to link to the application. It should not include a path. `Src` is the path (relative only) to a source file that will be dynamically compiled and linked.

Each `Assembly` directive can have only one attribute. If you need to link to multiple assemblies use multiple `Assembly` directives.

`Assembly` directives will look something like this:

```
<%@ Assembly Name="SomeAssembly" %>
<%@ Assembly Src="sources/SomeSourceFile.cs" %>
```

Script blocks

The typical *Global.asax* file contains the bulk of its code in a script block contained between script tags:

```
<script runat="server">
    .
    .
    .
</script>
```

If you are using the code-behind technique, the code contained within the code-behind class in the code-behind file is equivalent to putting the code in a script block, although code in the code-behind file itself is not enclosed in script tags.

The code contained within the script block can consist of event handlers or methods, as we will demonstrate in the following section.

Events

Just as web pages and the controls they contain expose events, the application and the sessions running within the application also expose events. These events can be handled by event handlers contained in the *Global.asax* file, as well as in page-specific files. For example, the Application_Start event is fired when the application starts, and the Application_End event is fired when the application ends. Some of the application events fire every time a page is requested, whereas others, such as Application_Error, fire under only certain conditions.

The sample *Global.asax* file shown in Example 18-2 demonstrates event handlers for the Application_Start and Application_End events. The Application_Start event in Example 18-2 sets two Application properties: a string called strConnectionString and an array of strings called arBooks. The event handler then calls the helper method, WriteFile, which is also contained within the *Global.asax* file. This helper method writes a line containing the string argument to a logfile. WriteFile is reproduced here from Example 18-2:

```
void WriteFile(string strText)
{
    using(System.IO.StreamWriter writer =
        new System.IO.StreamWriter(@"C:\test.txt",true))
    {
        string str;
        str = DateTime.Now.ToString() + "   " + strText;
        writer.WriteLine(str);
        writer.Close();
    }
}
```

The WriteFile method is a simple logging method. It opens a StreamWriter object on a text file, hardcoded to be *c:\test.txt*. It adds a line to the file containing a timestamp and whatever text string is passed in to the method. The Boolean parameter, true, in the StreamWriter method call specifies that if the file already exists, the line will be appended to the file. If the file does not exist, it will be created.

The Application_End event handler makes another call to WriteFile to make a log entry that the application has ended.

To see the results of these two event handlers, make some meaningless edit to *Global.asax* and save the file. This will force the application to end. Then request any URL in the virtual directory. For this example, use one of the web pages from a previous chapter—it doesn't really matter which one—or a web page of your own creation. Example 18-3 shows an excerpt from the resultant logfile.

Example 18-3. Excerpt from test.txt

```
28/06/2008 13:21:53  Application Starting
28/06/2008 13:23:44  Application Ending
28/06/2008 13:23:52  Application Starting
```

Just as there are Start and End events for the Application, there are Start and End events for each session: Session_Start and Session_End. This allows you to have code that will run every time each session within the application starts and ends.

By putting an event handler in *Global.asax* for every possible application event, as shown in Example 18-4 with all the method names highlighted for readability, it is easy to see the cycle of application events as the page request is received, processed, and rendered.

Example 18-4. Global.asax event demonstration

```
<%@ Application  Language="C#" %>

<script RunAt="server">

    protected void Application_Start(Object sender, EventArgs e)
    {
        WriteFile("Application Starting");
    }

    protected void Application_End(Object sender, EventArgs e)
    {
        WriteFile("Application Ending");
    }

    protected void Session_Start(Object sender, EventArgs e)
    {
        Response.Write("Session_Start" + "<br/>");
    }

    protected void Session_End(Object sender, EventArgs e)
    {
        Response.Write("Session_End" + "<br/>");
    }

    protected void Application_Disposed(Object sender, EventArgs e)
    {
        Response.Write("Application_Disposed" + "<br/>");
    }

    protected void Application_Error(Object sender, EventArgs e)
    {
        string strError;
        strError = Server.GetLastError().ToString();

        if (Context!= null)
        {
            Context.ClearError();

            Response.Write("Application_Error" + "<br/>");
            Response.Write("<b>Error Msg: </b>" + strError + "<br/>" +
                    "<b>End Error Msg</b><br/>");
        }
```

Example 18-4. Global.asax event demonstration (continued)

```
    }

    protected void Application_BeginRequest(Object sender, EventArgs e)
    {
        Response.Write("Application_BeginRequest" + "<br/>");
    }

    protected void Application_EndRequest(Object sender, EventArgs e)
    {
        Response.Write("Application_EndRequest" + "<br/>");
    }

    protected void Application_AcquireRequestState(
        Object sender, EventArgs e)
    {
        Response.Write("Application_AcquireRequestState" + "<br/>");
    }

    protected void Application_AuthenticateRequest(
        Object sender, EventArgs e)
    {
        Response.Write("Application_AuthenticateRequest" + "<br/>");
    }

    protected void Application_AuthorizeRequest(
        Object sender, EventArgs e)
    {
        Response.Write("Application_AuthorizeRequest" + "<br/>");
    }

    protected void Application_PostRequestHandlerExecute(
        Object sender, EventArgs e)
    {
        Response.Write("Application_PostRequestHandlerExecute"
                    + "<br/>");
    }

    protected void Application_PreRequestHandlerExecute(
        Object sender, EventArgs e)
    {
        Response.Write("Application_PreRequestHandlerExecute"
                    + "<br/>");
    }

    protected void Application_PreSendRequestContent(
        Object sender, EventArgs e)
    {
        Response.Write("Application_PreSendRequestContent" + "<br/>");
    }

    protected void Application_PreSendRequestHeaders(
        Object sender, EventArgs e)
```

Example 18-4. Global.asax event demonstration (continued)

```
    {
        Response.Write("Application_PreSendRequestHeaders" + "<br/>");
    }

    protected void Application_ReleaseRequestState(
        Object sender, EventArgs e)
    {
        Response.Write("Application_ReleaseRequestState" + "<br/>");
    }

    protected void Application_ResolveRequestCache(
        Object sender, EventArgs e)
    {
        Response.Write("Application_ResolveRequestCache" + "<br/>");
    }

    protected void Application_UpdateRequestCache(
        Object sender, EventArgs e)
    {
        Response.Write("Application_UpdateRequestCache" + "<br/>");
    }

    void WriteFile(string strText)
    {
        System.IO.StreamWriter writer =
            new System.IO.StreamWriter(@"C:\test.txt",true);
        string str;
        str = DateTime.Now.ToString() + "   " + strText;
        writer.WriteLine(str);
        writer.Close();
    }
</script>
```

The following are all the events fired with every page request, in the order in which they are fired:

Application_BeginRequest

Raised for every request handled by ASP.NET. Code in this event handler is executed before the web page or service processes the request.

Application_AuthenticateRequest

Raised prior to authentication of the request. (As we covered in Chapter 12, authentication is the process whereby a user is verified as being who she says she is.) Code in this event handler allows custom security routines to be implemented.

Application_AuthorizeRequest

Raised prior to authorization of the request. (Authorization is the process of determining whether the requesting user has permission to access a resource, as discussed in Chapter 12.) Code in this event handler allows custom security routines to be implemented.

`Application_ResolveRequestCache`

Raised before ASP.NET determines whether the output should be generated fresh or filled from cache. Code in this event handler is executed in either case.

`Application_AcquireRequestState`

Raised prior to acquiring the session state.

`Application_PreRequestHandlerExecute`

Raised just prior to the request being passed to the handler that is servicing the request. After the event is raised, the page is processed by the HTTP handler processing the request.

`Application_PostRequestHandlerExecute`

Raised when the HTTP handler is finished with the page request. At this point, the Response object now has the data to send back to the client.

`Application_ReleaseRequestState`

Raised when the session state is released and updated.

`Application_UpdateRequestCache`

Raised when the output cache is updated, if the output is to be cached.

`Application_EndRequest`

Raised when the request is finished.

`Application_PreSendRequestHeaders`

Raised prior to sending the HTTP headers to the client. If response buffering is enabled, meaning that none of the data will be sent until all the data is ready (the default condition), this event will always follow `Application_EndRequest`. If response buffering is disabled, this event will be raised whenever the data is sent back to the client. Response buffering is controlled by an attribute to a `Page` directive or, in the case of web services, a `WebMethod` attribute.

`Application_PreSendRequestContent`

Raised prior to sending the HTTP content to the client. As with `Application_PreSendRequestHeaders`, the order in which the event is raised depends on whether response buffering is enabled.

The following are the application events that fire under only certain conditions:

`Application_Start`

Raised whenever the application is started. An application is started the first time any page is requested from an application virtual directory and the application is not already running.

`Application_End`

Raised whenever an application ends. An application ends whenever one of the configuration files (*Global.asax*, *Global.asax.cs*, *Global.asax.vb*, or *web.config*) or an assembly is modified, or the server is crashed or restarted. Cleanup code, such as closing database connections, is normally executed in this event handler.

Session_Start

> Raised for every session that starts. This is a good place to put code that is session-specific.

Session_End

> Raised for every session that ends. This provides an opportunity to save any data stored in session state.

Application_Disposed

> Raised when the CLR removes the application from memory.

Application_Error

> Raised whenever an unhandled error occurs anywhere in the application. This provides an excellent opportunity to implement generic application-wide error handling.

> You should handle specific error conditions where necessary in your code, using try...catch blocks. You should trap errors at the page level using the ErrorPage attribute of the Page directive. Any errors handled in these ways will not trigger the Application_Error event.

To test this new version of *Global.asax*, create a page called *GlobalEvents.aspx* in the *C18_AppLogic* website and give it the code shown in Example 18-5.

Example 18-5. GlobalEvents.aspx

```
<%@ Page Language="C#" AutoEventWireup="true"
    CodeFile="GlobalEvents.aspx.cs" Inherits="GlobalEvents" %>

<!DOCTYPE html PUBLIC "-//W3C//DTD XHTML 1.0 Transitional//EN"
    "http://www.w3.org/TR/xhtml1/DTD/xhtml1-transitional.dtd">

<html xmlns="http://www.w3.org/1999/xhtml">
<head runat="server">
    <title>Global Events Demo</title>
</head>
<body>
    <form id="form1" runat="server">
    <div>
        <h1>Global Events</h1>
        <asp:Button ID="btnPost" runat="server" Text="Post" />
        <asp:Button ID="btnEndSession" runat="server"
            Text="End Session" OnClick="btnEndSession_Click" />
        <asp:Button ID="btnError" runat="server"
            Text="Generate Error" OnClick="btnError_Click" />
    </div>
    </form>
</body>
</html>
```

You'll also need to add handlers for the Click event on two of the buttons to the code-behind page, *GlobalEvents.aspx.cs*, as shown in Example 18-6.

Example 18-6. GlobalEvents.aspx.cs

```csharp
using System;
using System.Web.UI;

public partial class GlobalEvents : Page
{
    protected void btnEndSession_Click(object sender, EventArgs e)
    {
        Session.Abandon();
    }

    protected void btnError_Click(object sender, EventArgs e)
    {
        int a = 5;
        int b = 0;
        int c;
        c = a / b;
    }
}
```

When this web page is run, you will get the screen shown in Figure 18-9.

Figure 18-9. GlobalEvents.aspx in action

In Figure 18-9, you see that a series of application events have fired. About midway through the sequence of events, the *.aspx* file itself is finally rendered, followed by another series of application events.

The first time the page is displayed the Session_Start event is fired, but on subsequent displays the Session_Start event may not be fired. This is because the request is part of the same session. Clicking the End Session button causes the Session.Abandon method to be called, which ends the current session. The next time the page is submitted to the server, the Session_Start event will fire.

The Post button simply provides a way to repost the page.

Most of the Application event handlers in Example 18-4 use the Response.Write method to indicate that the event has been called. However, the Application_Start and Application_End methods call the WriteFile method instead. If you try using Response.Write in these event handlers, they will not display on the web page because the session in which the page is to be rendered is not running. However, by examining the logfile, *c:\test.txt*, you will see entries that indicate when the application starts and ends.

The sample *Global.asax* file shown in Example 18-4 demonstrates one way of using the Application_Error event. That code is reproduced here for reference:

```
protected void Application_Error(Object sender, EventArgs e)
{
    string strError;
    strError = Server.GetLastError( ).ToString( );

    if (Context!= null)
    {
        Context.ClearError( );

        Response.Write("Application_Error" + "<br/>");
        Response.Write("<b>Error Msg: </b>" + strError + "<br/>" +
                "<b>End Error Msg</b><br/>");
    }
}
```

This event handler uses the HttpServerUtility object's GetLastError method to report the last error that occurred. That error is converted to a string and assigned to a string variable:

```
strError = Server.GetLastError( ).ToString( );
```

Next the HttpContext object's ClearError method is called to clear all the errors for the current HTTP request:

```
Context.ClearError( );
```

If the errors are not cleared, the error will still display on the client browser and the subsequent Response.Write statements will remain invisible.

Finally, the `Response.Write` statements display a message and the current error to the client browser.

An alternative technique for reporting an error to the user would display a custom error-handling page. To do this, replace the `Response.Write` lines in the `Application_Error` event handler with the following line of code:

```
Response.Redirect(
    "CustomErrorPage.aspx?Msg=" + Server.UrlEncode(strError));
```

This line of code uses the `HttpServerUtility` object's `UrlEncode` method to pass the error message as a query string parameter to the custom error page coded in *CustomErrorPage.aspx*. *CustomErrorPage.aspx* would have a `Label` control, called `lblMessage`, and the following code in its `Page_Load` method:

```
void Page_Load(Object Source, EventArgs E)
{
    lblMessage.Text = Request.QueryString["Msg"];
}
```

The Generate Error button on *GlobalEvents.aspx.cs* intentionally causes an error to see error handling in action. The `Click` event handler for that button contains the following code, which will raise a Divide by Zero exception:

```
protected void btnError_Click(object sender, EventArgs e)
{
    int a = 5;
    int b = 0;
    int c;
    c = a / b;
}
```

Server-side includes

You can include external source code files in the application using server-side includes much as you could in classic ASP. The code contained within an include file is added to *Global.asax* before it is compiled. The language used in the include file must match the language used in the *Global.asax* file, though that may be different from the language(s) used within the application.

The following syntax is used for a server-side include:

```
<!--#Include PathType="fileName" -->
```

In this syntax, `PathType` can have one of two values, as shown in Table 18-1.

Table 18-1. PathType attributes

Path type	Description
File	The `fileName` is a string containing a relative path from the directory containing the *Global.asax* file.
Virtual	The `fileName` is a string containing a full virtual path from a virtual directory in your website.

Add the following line as the second line in the sample *Global.asax* file listed in Example 18-4:

```
<!--#Include File="IncludeFile.cs" -->
```

Create a new text file, called *IncludeFile.cs*, and store it in the same directory that contains *Global.asax*. This file requires a pair of script tags as with the *Global.asax* file.

Move a copy of the WriteFile method from *Global.asax* to the include file. Finally, comment out (or delete) the WriteFile method from *Global.asax*. The include file should look like Example 18-7.

Example 18-7. IncludeFile.cs in full

```
<script runat="server">
   void WriteFile(string strText)
   {
      using (System.IO.StreamWriter writer =
         new System.IO.StreamWriter(@"c:\test.txt", true))
      string str;
      str = DateTime.Now.ToString() + "   " + strText;
      writer.WriteLine(str);
      writer.Close();
   }
</script>
```

If you run any of your web pages, there should be no difference in behavior because all you did was move the code for a method from one file to another.

Just as ASP.NET watches for changes in *Global.asax* and restarts the application if any occur it also watches for changes in any include files. If an include file changes, the application will restart for that as well.

Include files are useful for including the same standard code into multiple applications. This common code could include such things as methods for accessing databases, writing log entries, handling errors, logging in users, or any number of infrastructure-type pieces that are part of every application.

Object declarations

An additional way to include code in the *Global.asax* file is as declarative object tags. These static objects are declared as either Application or Session objects. They are then available for the duration of the application or each session.

Here is a code snippet showing how an object might be declared in the *Global.asax* file. This snippet would be located outside the script block in the file.

```
<object id="strDSN" class="System.String"
   scope="Application" runat="server"/>
```

The object in this snippet can be referred to in the application by the value of the id attribute, which in this example is strDSN.

The class attribute specifies the type of this object. In this case, it is a string object. The class attribute implies that the object is derived from a .NET assembly. Alternatively, you can use a progid or classid instead of the class attribute to instantiate a COM object rather than a .NET object. Each object declaration can have only one class, progid, or classid.

In this snippet, the scope attribute specifies that this will be an Application object. The other legal value for this attribute is Session.

Objects declared in this way are not created upon declaration. They are created the first time they are referenced in the application. To reference in your code the static object shown in the preceding code snippet, refer to the following:

```
Application["strDSN"];
```

Storing application or session information elsewhere is also possible, such as in the *web.config* file, which we will describe shortly.

Global Members

We noted previously that the code contained in the *Global.asax* file is compiled into a class derived from HttpApplication and becomes part of the application. You can also create a separate class file that will contain globally available code, such as public member variables and methods. These global members can be either static or instance.

Static methods and member variables are those that do not require that the class containing the method or variable be instantiated. You define static member variables in C# using the static keyword. Instance members require an instance of the class to be invoked. Any member not declared as static is an instance member. We will demonstrate both static and instance members in this chapter.

The trick to getting access to this global class is to place the class file in the *App_Code* directory under the application root. Placed there, it will automatically be compiled every time the application is run. (Alternatively, the class can be manually compiled and the resultant assembly can be located in the *bin* directory.) The class can then be referred to throughout the application, making available global static and instance members.

 Version 1.x of ASP.NET provided a ClassName attribute of the Application directive, which allowed you to directly specify the name of the global class. That attribute is no longer supported as of version 2.0. Though it will not cause a compiler error, it will be ignored.

To see this in action, right-click the website root folder for *C18_AppLogic* in the Solution Explorer, or click the Website menu item and select Add ASP.NET Folder → App_Code Folder. Then right-click the new *App_Code* folder in the Solution Explorer and select Add New Item. From the Add New Item dialog click Class. Change the name to *GlobalMembers.cs*.

 The name used for this file and for the name of the class within the file is not important as long as it is consistent throughout the application.

This class file will open in the editor with the class declared and an empty default constructor. Add the highlighted lines of code listed in Example 18-8.

Example 18-8. GlobalMembers.cs in full

```
using System;
using System.IO;

public class GlobalMembers
{
    public static int successRate = 50;

    public GlobalMembers()
    {
    }

    protected void Application_Start(Object sender, EventArgs e)
    {
        WriteFile("Application Starting");
    }

    protected void Application_End(Object sender, EventArgs e)
    {
        WriteFile("Application Ending");
    }

    public void WriteFile(string strText)
    {
        using (StreamWriter writer =
            new StreamWriter(@"C:\test.txt", true))
        {
            string str;
            str = DateTime.Now.ToString() + " " + strText;
            writer.WriteLine(str);
            writer.Close();
        }
    }

    public static void StaticWriteFile(string strText)
    {
```

Example 18-8. GlobalMembers.cs in full (continued)

```
    using (StreamWriter writer =
        new StreamWriter(@"C:\test.txt", true))
    {
        string str;
        str = DateTime.Now.ToString() + " " + strText;
        writer.WriteLine(str);
        writer.Close();
    }
  }
}
```

The first highlighted line of code in Example 18-8 implements a global static variable, called successRate. You can access this variable from anywhere in the application simply by prepending the class name. So, for example, if your web page has a Label control named lblGlobalStatic, you could set its Text property with the following line of code:

```
    lblGlobalStatic.Text = GlobalMembers.successRate.ToString();
```

The ToString method must be called to convert the variable to a string so that it can be assigned to the Text property of the label.

The next two highlighted methods are event handlers for the Application_Start and Application_End events, exactly the same as in the previous example, *GlobalEvents.aspx*. These event handlers call the method WriteFile, listed farther down in the class file. The public accessibility modifier has been added to the WriteFile method declaration, changing it from the default accessibility of private. This makes the method available to the entire application.

WriteFile is not static. That is, it requires an instance of the class to be invoked. The following two lines of code in a web page code-behind file get a reference to an instance of the class, and then invoke WriteFile:

```
    GlobalMembers g = new GlobalMembers();
    g.WriteFile("Instance method - Now in Page_Load of web page.");
```

Example 18-7 also demonstrates a static version of WriteFile, called StaticWriteFile. It is made static by the use of the static keyword. You can invoke it directly without first instantiating the class, similar to the static variable:

```
    GlobalMembers.StaticWriteFile(
        "Static method - Now in Page_Load of web page.");
```

In this example, there is no real reason to use the static instead of the instance methods, because the method content itself is identical. In the general case, however, instance methods are required when the method needs to refer to the specific instance of the class. Suppose the global method is working with a DataSet or some other object specific to this invocation of the page; then an instance global method would be called for. Otherwise, you can use a static global method.

HTTP Handlers and Modules

Two further options for working with your code at the application level are the use of HTTP modules and handlers:

- HTTP modules allow you to process and make changes to both the requests coming into the server for a file and the responses to those requests as they leave the server.

- HTTP handlers allow you to handle the requests for files with a specific file extension.

To put that into context, take a look at Figure 18-10. As a request comes into the web server (say, for an *.aspx* file), it is passed to any number of HTTP modules for preprocessing. These modules may be either built into IIS (e.g., user authentication, authorization, and caching modules) or built specifically for and attached to a web application (e.g., a URL rewriter). Once all preprocessor modules have dealt with the request, the web server identifies the correct handler for the request (by file extension) and the handler prepares the initial response for the client—an image perhaps, or some HTML. As the response is then pushed back through the pipeline and out to the client, any post-processing modules (e.g., logging, compression, and caching modules) then work with and may alter it before sending it out to the client.

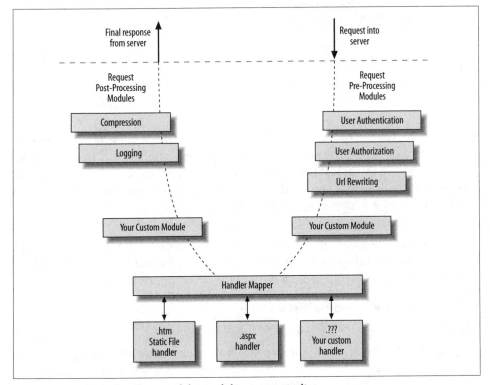

Figure 18-10. HTTP handlers, modules, and the request pipeline

In the next example, you'll write a simple HttpModule that logs the page being requested to the same *test.txt* file you've been using throughout this chapter. To implement a new HttpModule, you only need to create a class that inherits and implements the IHttpModule interface.

Add a new class file to the *App_Code* directory in *C18_AppLogic*. Call it *TextLoggerModule.cs*. Delete the contents and replace them with the code in Example 18-9.

Example 18-9. TextLoggerModule.cs

```
using System;
using System.Web;

public class TextLoggerModule : IHttpModule
{
    public void Init(HttpApplication context)
    {
        context.PreRequestHandlerExecute += new
            EventHandler(context_PreRequestHandlerExecute);
    }

    void context_PreRequestHandlerExecute(object sender, EventArgs e)
    {
        GlobalMembers.StaticWriteFile(
            HttpContext.Current.Request.RawUrl);
    }

    public void Dispose()
    {
        throw new NotImplementedException();
    }
}
```

And that's it. The IHttpModule interface requires you to implement two methods, Init and Dispose. The Init method is the way you can add any functionality to the module. The HttpApplication parameter gives you access to the current HttpApplication context if you need to use it, and you can hook up any of the events listed in Table 18-2 to define at what point during the request pipeline the processing by the module takes place.

In this example, you handle the PreRequestHandlerExecute event for the logging to take place just before each request is sent to the appropriate handler for processing. In the event handler, the URL requested is written to the file, acting as rudimentary logging.

Table 18-2. Events that an HttpModule can handle

Event	Occurs
AcquireRequestState	When the session state for the current request is about to be loaded.
AuthenticateRequest	When ASP.NET is about to authenticate the identity of the user making the request.

Table 18-2. Events that an HttpModule can handle (continued)

Event	Occurs
AuthorizeRequest	When ASP.NET is about to authorize the user for the files that she is trying to access.
BeginRequest	When ASP.NET receives a new request.
Disposed	When ASP.NET has completed the processing of a request.
EndRequest	When the final response is about to be sent to the user.
Error	When an unhandled exception occurs during a request.
PostRequestHandlerExecute	When an HTTP handler has finished executing the request and prepared an initial response.
PreRequestHandlerExecute	Just before an HTTP handler begins processing the current request. The handler begins processing immediately after this event occurs if it is not handled.
PreSendRequestContent	Just before ASP.NET sends the content of its response to the request back to the user.
PreSendRequestHeaders	Just before ASP.NET sends the HTTP headers for its response to the request back to the user.

To register the module with a website running in classic mode (i.e., any website running under IIS 5.1, 6.0, or 7.0 in classic mode), you'll need to add an entry for it in the <system.web>\<httpModules> section:

```
<configuration>
...
    <system.web>
    ...
        <httpModules>
            ...
            <add name="TextLoggerModule" type="TextLoggerModule,
                                             app_Code" />
        </httpModules>
    ...
    </system.web>
...
</configuration>
```

If you're running the site under IIS 7.0 and want to run the module using integrated mode rather than classic mode (see Figures 12-1 and 12-2 in Chapter 12 for the difference between the two), you'll need to add the entry for the module to the <system.webServer>\<modules> section instead:

```
<configuration>
...
    <system.webServer>
    ...
        <modules>
            ...
            <add name="TextLoggerModule" type="TextLoggerModule,
                                             App_Code"/>
        </modules>
    ...
```

```
        </system.webServer>
    ...
    </configuration>
```

Run the website now and browse to *GlobalEvents.aspx*. Manually change the URL in the browser to try to get to some of the other files in the site, or even ones that don't exist. When you look at *test.txt*, you'll see that all the files you've tried to access have been logged:

```
28/06/2008 17:30:33  Application Starting
28/06/2008 17:30:33  /C18_AppLogic/GlobalEvents.aspx
28/06/2008 17:30:38  /C18_AppLogic/GlobalEvents1234.aspx
28/06/2008 17:30:42  /C18_AppLogic/default.html
28/06/2008 17:31:04  Application Ending
```

In contrast to HTTP modules, which can occur at many different points during a request's journey through the ASP.NET pipeline, HTTP handlers work on a request at only one point (see Figure 18-10) and are mapped to specific file extensions. They are the code that takes a request and prepares an initial response for further processing by any post-processing HTTP modules.

Writing HTTP handlers for a given file extension is very similar to writing an HTTP module. At a minimum, it requires only a class to implement the IHttpHandler interface, and this interface only requires you to create a property, IsReusable, and a method, ProcessRequest.

To demonstrate, you'll create a handler for the *.log* file extension. Its purpose is to log and highlight requests for any file ending in *.log* in the *test.txt* file. To start, add a new class file, called *TextLogHandler.cs*, to the *App_Code* directory in your *C18_AppLogic* website. Delete the contents and replace them with the code in Example 18-10.

Example 18-10. TextLogHandler.cs

```
using System.Web;

public class TextLogHandler : IHttpHandler
{
    public bool IsReusable
    {
        get { return false; }
    }

    public void ProcessRequest(HttpContext context)
    {
        GlobalMembers.StaticWriteFile(
            ".log handler running for " + context.Request.RawUrl);
        context.Response.ContentType = "text/html";
        context.Response.Write(
            "Logged request for " + context.Request.RawUrl + "<br />");
    }
}
```

The IsReusable property is used to state whether another request coming into the server can use the same instance of the handler. This is set to false. The ProcessRequest method, meanwhile, logs the request for the file, and then sets the response type for the request to HTML and acknowledges the request for the file in the response.

To register the handler with a website running in classic mode (i.e., any website running under IIS 5.1, 6.0, or 7.0 in classic mode), you'll need to add an entry for it in the <system.web>\<httpHandlers> section:

```
<configuration>
...
    <system.web>
    ...
        <httpHandlers>
            ...
            <add verb="*" path="*.log" type="TextLogHandler, App_Code"/>
        </httpHandlers>
    ...
    </system.web>
...
</configuration>
```

If you're running the site under IIS 7.0 and want to run the handler using integrated mode rather than classic mode (see Figures 12-1 and 12-2 in Chapter 12 for the difference between the two), you'll need to add the entry for the module to the <system.webServer>\<handlers> section instead:

```
<configuration>
...
    <system.webServer>
    ...
        <handlers>
            ...
            <add name="TextLogHandler" verb="*" path="*.log"
                type="TextLogHandler, App_Code" />
        </handlers>
    ...
    </system.webServer>
...
</configuration>
```

Run the website now and try to browse to *logthis.log*. The file doesn't exist; but ASP.NET will pass the request to the handler and will log the request in *test.txt*:

```
28/06/2008 23:10:38  Application Starting
28/06/2008 23:10:42 /C18_AppLogic/logthis.log
28/06/2008 23:10:42 .log handler running for /C18_AppLogic/logthis.log
```

Now three different files are logging to this logfile:

- *Global.asax* adds to the log when the application begins.

- The HttpModule *TextLoggerModule.cs* then logs the file request because it logs any file request.

- The HttpHandler *TextLogHandler.cs* then also logs the file because it is a request specifically for a file with a *.log* file extension.

In this simple demonstration, the handler is used to deal with any type of request for any *.log* file when it is added to *web.config*:

```
<add verb="*" path="*.log" type="TextLogHandler, App_Code"/>
```

You can add more specific values to the verb and path attributes to narrow down the focus of the handler's remit. For example, the TextLogHandler might only be supposed to log requests for the retrieval of files, so it applies only to the GET and POST HTTP verbs rather than to HEAD, PUT, and DELETE as well. If this was the case, you could tweak its declaration in *web.config* like so:

```
<add verb="GET,POST" path="*.log" type="TextLogHandler, App_Code"/>
```

Similarly, if you wanted only to log requests for certain *.log* files, you could replace the path attribute with a comma-separated list of the files in question.

For much more on creating HTTP handlers and modules, try *Professional IIS 7 and ASP.NET Integrated Programming* by Shahram Khosravi (Wrox).

Configuring the Application

ASP.NET is configured with XML files. The base server-wide configuration file is called *machine.config*, described in the next section. This is supplemented by an optional server-wide *web.config* file located in the same directory as *machine.config*, and a number of application-specific configuration files, all called *web.config*, located in the application root directory and subdirectories.

VS2008 goes one step further, offering a different default *web.config* for ASP.NET 2.0 and ASP.NET 3.5 websites. The main differences between them are the inclusion of Language Integrated Query (LINQ) and AJAX in the 3.5 variant along with the assumption that the site will use the new IIS 7.0 integrated security pipeline. The 2.0 variant is the same as that generated by VS2005.

You can edit the XML files that control the configuration with any standard text editor. It is not necessary to use the IIS control panel, as was the case with classic ASP. Although you can edit the configuration files in any text editor, VS2008 and IIS provide UIs for editing the most common configurations.

Because the configuration is accomplished with XML files and because files are text, it is easy to administer your configuration remotely. Anyone with suitable security clearance can create or edit files from a development machine and then copy them into place via FTP or remote network access. There is no need for the developer to be physically present at the server machine hosting the application to perform configuration chores.

The configuration system is hierarchical. Each application inherits a baseline configuration from *machine.config*, located on the server. An optional *web.config* file, located in the same folder as *machine.config*, layers on top of that baseline configuration. The application-specific *web.config* files then apply successive configuration attributes and parameters as the application directory tree structure is traversed. We will explain this in detail in the next section. A corollary of the hierarchical nature of the system is that each application can have its own independent configuration. All applications do not need to share a server-wide configuration.

The configuration system is extensible. The baseline system provides configurability to a large number of standard program areas. In addition, you can add custom parameters, attributes, and section handlers as required by your application. We will explain this in detail later in this chapter.

You can modify the configuration of a running application without needing to manually stop and restart either the application or the server. Instead, the application will restart itself and the changes will automatically and immediately apply themselves to any new client requests. Any clients online at the time the changes are made will be unaware that changes are being made, other than perhaps experiencing a slight delay for the first request made after the change is put in place.

The configuration settings for each unique URL are computed at application runtime, using all the hierarchical configuration files. These configuration settings are then cached so that requests to each URL can retrieve the configuration settings in a performant manner. ASP.NET automatically detects whether any configuration files anywhere in the hierarchy are modified and recomputes and recaches the configuration settings accordingly.

Configuration files are hidden from browser access. If a browser directly requests a configuration file in a URL, an HTTP access error 403 (forbidden) will be returned. This is the same behavior you would see if you tried to request the *Global.asax* file directly from a browser.

Hierarchical Configuration

The configuration system is hierarchical. The file at the top of the hierarchy is called *machine.config*. You'll find this in *C:\Windows\Microsoft.NET\Framework\<version>\ CONFIG*, where *version* will be replaced with the version of the .NET runtime installed on your machine. VS2008 and ASP.NET currently use the .NET 2.0 runtime to function, so the version folder in question is currently v2.0.50727.

All the other configuration files are called *web.config*, of which there might be several:

- A machine-scoped *web.config* can be located in the same directory as *machine.config*.

- A *web.config* applicable to the whole of a *website* will be found in its root directory as defined in IIS.

- Any configuration instructions specific to a folder or virtual directory within a website will be found in a *web.config* file in that folder or virtual directory.

These files are optional: if there are none in an application virtual directory or its subdirectories, the configuration settings contained in *machine.config* or the machine-scoped *web.config* will apply to your application without any modifications.

Each directory and subdirectory contained in the application can have, at most, a single *web.config* file. The configuration settings contained in a specific instance of *web.config* apply to the directory in which it is contained and to all its child directories. If a specific instance of *web.config* contains a setting that is in conflict with a setting higher up in the configuration hierarchy (i.e., in a parent directory or *machine.config*), the lower-level setting will override and apply to its own directory and all child subdirectories below it (unless, of course, any of those child subdirectories have their own copies of *web.config*, which will further override the settings).

For example, consider the directory structure shown in Figure 18-11. The virtual root of the website is called MyWebSite, corresponding to the physical directory *c:\inetpub\wwwroot\MyWebSite*. Underneath the virtual root are two subdirectories, each with additional subdirectories. The URL for this website would be *http://mywebsite.com* (assuming that the domain name *http://mywebsite.com* was registered to the Internet Protocol [IP] address assigned to the server and the startup page was named *Default.aspx* or one of the other default document names specified in IIS, as we will describe shortly).

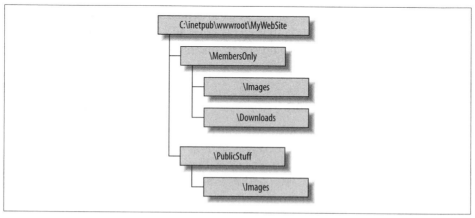

Figure 18-11. A website is a hierarchical structure

Given this directory structure, the following is true of the site's configuration settings:

- If there were no *web.config* files in any of these directories, the entire configuration would come directly from the globally scoped *web.config*. If that file was not present, it would come from *machine.config*.

- If there is a *web.config* in the directory *MyWebSite*, any settings it contains will apply to the entire application (but only to that application), including all the subdirectories beneath it.

- If there were another version of *web.config* in the *MembersOnly* directory, its configuration settings would apply to the *MembersOnly* directory and its subdirectories, but not to *PublicStuff*.

- If any of the settings in the *web.config* in *MembersOnly* conflicted with those in *machine.config* or the *web.config* in *MyWebSite*, the settings in *MembersOnly* would be in effect.

It is important to note that the hierarchical nature of the configuration files is based on application virtual directories. Refer again to Figure 18-11. The only virtual directory defined so far for that application is *MyWebSite*. However, suppose another virtual directory, *MyPublicWebSite*, were defined, corresponding to *C:\inetpub\wwwroot\MyWebSite\PublicStuff*. The URL for this application might be *http://mypublicwebsite.com*. This application would inherit the configuration settings from *machine.config* but not from *C:\inetpub\wwwroot\MyWebSite\web.config*.

Though *C:\inetpub\wwwroot\MyWebSite* is the physical parent directory of *C:\inetpub\wwwroot\MyWebSite\PublicStuff*, it is not the virtual parent. In fact, *C:\inetpub\wwwroot\MyWebSite\PublicStuff* is a virtual root and does not have a virtual parent. Configuration settings inherit from virtual parents and *not* from physical parents.

Format

Most of the content of the application-specific configuration files, *web.config*, can be handled by the configuration tools, covered in the next two sections. However, it is often useful to be able to look at and edit a *web.config* file directly, and the tools provided by VS2008 do not modify *machine.config* at all (although IIS 7.0 will edit the machine-scoped *web.config*). Therefore, it is worth examining the format requirements of these files.

The configuration files, *machine.config* and *web.config*, are XML files. As such, they must be well-formed. (For a description of well-formed XML, see the sidebar "Well-Formed XHTML" in Chapter 3.) Specifically, these files consist of a nested hierarchy of XML tags. All opening tags must have the corresponding closing tag or be self-closing (with a trailing / character just inside the closing angle bracket). The tags must not overlap, though tags may be nested. All tags may have attributes. All of these elements are case-sensitive.

You can find the complete schema for *machine.config* and *web.config* installed in *C:\Program Files\Microsoft Visual Studio 9.0\Xml\Schemas\ DotNetConfig.xsd* and complete, unexpurgated docs explaining all the minutiae at *http://msdn2.microsoft.com/en-us/library/zeshe0eb.aspx.*

Typically, tag and attribute names consist of one or more words run together. Tag and attribute names are camel-cased. Attribute values are usually Pascal-cased.

Camel-casing means that all the characters are lowercase, including the first character, except for the first character of each run-on word after the first word. Examples of camel-casing are appSettings, configSections, section, and sessionState.

Pascal-casing is the same as camel-casing, except that the first character of the name is also uppercase. Examples of Pascal-casing are SortByTime, InProc, and StateServer.

There are a couple of exceptions to these naming conventions:

- true and false are always lowercase.
- Literal strings do not adhere to either camel- or Pascal-casing. A database connection string may be specified as:

      SERVER=MyServer;DATABASE=MyDB;UID=sa;PWD=secret;

  If the value is the name of another tag in a configuration file, it will be camel-cased.

The first line in the configuration file declares the file to be an XML file, with attributes specifying the version of the XML specification to which the file adheres and the character encoding used. Here is a typical XML declaration line:

    <?xml version="1.0" encoding="UTF-8" ?>

The character encoding specified here is UTF-8, which is a superset of ASCII. You can omit the character encoding parameter if, and only if, the XML document is written in either UTF-8 or UTF-32. Therefore, if the XML file is written in pure ASCII, you can omit the encoding parameter, though self-documentation is enhanced if the attribute is included.

The next line in the configuration file is the opening <configuration> tag:

    <configuration>

The entire contents of the configuration file, except the initial XML declaration, is contained between the opening <configuration> tag and the closing </configuration> tag, which comprise the <configuration> element.

You can include comments in the file using the standard XML (and HTML) format:

    <!-- Your comments here -->

Within the <configuration> element are two broad categories of entries. They are, in the order in which they appear in the configuration files:

- Configuration section handler declarations
- Configuration sections

Configuration section handler declarations

The configuration section handler declarations are contained between an opening <configSections> tag and a closing </configSections> tag. Each configuration handler declaration specifies the name of a configuration section, contained elsewhere in the file, which provides specific configuration data. Each declaration also contains the name of the .NET class that will process the configuration data in that section.

This terminology can be confusing. The first part of the file is enclosed in <configSections> tags, but contains only a list of the configuration sections and their handlers and not the configuration sections themselves. And, as you will see shortly, the configuration sections are contained within tags, but there is no grouping tag to contain all the separate configuration sections, analogous to <configSections>.

The *machine.config* file contains, in the default installation, many configuration section handler declarations that cover the areas subject to configuration by default. These include sections for the compilation of the website, authentication rules for it, and email settings. The default *web.config* file generated by VS2008 for an ASP.NET 3.5 website then adds another set of sections relating to the use of ASP.NET AJAX in your website.

Because this is an extensible system, you can also create your own. A typical entry containing a handler declaration (in this case for the section concerning database connection strings) is shown in Example 18-11. In the actual *machine.config* file, the contents of Example 18-11 are on a single line. It is wrapped here for readability.

Example 18-11. Typical configuration section handler declaration

```
<section name="compilation"
    type="System.Web.Configuration.CompilationSection,
        System.Web,
        Version=2.0.0.0, Culture=neutral,
        PublicKeyToken=b03f5f7f11d50a3a"/>
```

Despite appearances to the contrary, the <section> tag has only two attributes: name and type. In Example 18-11, the name is compilation. This implies that somewhere else in the configuration file is a configuration section called compilation that will contain the actual configuration settings. These settings are name/value pairs to be used by the application(s). We will describe them in detail shortly.

The type attribute has a lengthy parameter enclosed in quotation marks. This parameter contains the following:

- The class that will handle the named configuration section
- The assembly file (*.dll*) that contains that class
- Version and culture information to coordinate with the assembly file
- A public-key token used to verify that the *.dll* being called is secure

Each handler need be declared only once: in the base-level *machine.config* file or in a *web.config* file farther down the configuration hierarchy. The configuration section it refers to can then be specified as often as desired in other configuration files.

Example 18-12 presents an abridged version of *machine.config* to demonstrate how these configSections map into the rest of a *.config* file.

Example 18-12. How configSections map to sibling elements in machine.config

```
<?xml version="1.0" encoding="UTF-8"?>
<configuration>
  <configSections>
    <section name="appSettings"
             type="System.Configuration.AppSettingsSection,.../>
    <section name="connectionStrings"
             type="System.Configuration.ConnectionStringsSection,.../>
    <section name="mscorlib"
             type="System.Configuration.IgnoreSection,.../>

    <sectionGroup name="system.net"
                  type="System.Net.Configuration.NetSectionGroup,...>
      <section name="authenticationModules"
       type="System.Net.Configuration.AuthenticationModulesSection,.../>
      <section name="connectionManagement"
        type="System.Net.Configuration.ConnectionManagementSection,.../>
      <section name="defaultProxy"
         type="System.Net.Configuration.DefaultProxySection,.../>
      <sectionGroup name="mailSettings"
         type="System.Net.Configuration.MailSettingsSectionGroup,...>
        <section name="smtp"
                 type="System.Net.Configuration.SmtpSection,.../>
      </sectionGroup>
      <section name="requestCaching"
          type="System.Net.Configuration.RequestCachingSection,.../>
      <section name="settings"
          type="System.Net.Configuration.SettingsSection,.../>
      <section name="webRequestModules"
          type="System.Net.Configuration.WebRequestModulesSection,.../>
    </sectionGroup>

    <sectionGroup name="system.web"
          type="System.Web.Configuration.SystemWebSectionGroup,...>
```

```
        <section name="compilation"
              type="System.Web.Configuration.CompilationSection,.../>
        <section name="customErrors"
                type="System.Web.Configuration.CustomErrorsSection,.../>
        <sectionGroup name="caching"
        type="System.Web.Configuration.SystemWebCachingSectionGroup,...>
          <section name="cache"
                  type="System.Web.Configuration.CacheSection,.../>
          <section name="outputCache"
                  type="System.Web.Configuration.OutputCacheSection,.../>
        </sectionGroup>
      </sectionGroup>
    </configSections>

    <runtime />

    <connectionStrings>
      <add name="LocalSqlServer"
        connectionString="data source=.\SQLEXPRESS;Integrated
                        Security=SSPI;
                        AttachDBFilename=|DataDirectory|aspnetdb.mdf;
                        User Instance=true"
        providerName="System.Data.SqlClient" />
    </connectionStrings>

    <system.web>
      <processModel autoConfig="true" />
      <httpHandlers />
      <membership>
        <providers>
          <add name="AspNetSqlMembershipProvider"
                type="System.Web.Security.SqlMembershipProvider,.../>
        </providers>
      </membership>
      <profile>
        <providers>
          <add name="AspNetSqlProfileProvider"
                connectionStringName="LocalSqlServer"
                applicationName="/"
                type="System.Web.Profile.SqlProfileProvider,.../>
        </providers>
      </profile>
      <roleManager>
        <providers>
          <add name="AspNetSqlRoleProvider"
                connectionStringName="LocalSqlServer"
                applicationName="/"
                type="System.Web.Security.SqlRoleProvider,.../>
        </providers>
      </roleManager>
    </system.web>
</configuration>
```

We included in Example 18-12 only a small subset of the entries in *machine.config*. We edited the type attribute of each entry to remove all but the class, and we broke lines to enhance the readability.

In Example 18-12, you can see that many of the handler declarations are contained within <sectionGroup> tags. The name attribute of these tags corresponds to the namespace that contains the handlers. This groups together all the configuration sections that are handled out of the same namespace.

Configuration sections

The configuration sections contain the actual configuration data. Each is contained within tags corresponding to the name of the section specified in the configuration section handler declaration. Alternatively, a single self-closing tag can be used. For example, the following two configuration sections are equivalent:

```
<globalization requestEncoding="utf-8" responseEncoding="utf-8" />
```

and:

```
<globalization
    requestEncoding="utf-8"
    responseEncoding="utf-8">
</globalization>
```

Configuration sections contain name/value pairs that hold the configuration data. They may also contain subsections.

Machine.config contains one configuration section for each handler declaration. If the handler declaration was contained within a <sectionGroup> tag, its corresponding configuration section would be contained within a tag containing the name of the <sectionGroup>. You can see this in Example 18-12 for *system.web*.

The two configuration tools described in the next several sections provide an easy-to-use UI for editing and maintaining the configuration files. You can also edit any of them using any text editor, including Notepad.

The sections that follow provide a description of each configuration section contained in the default *machine.config*. There are other configuration sections, including *system.diagnostics*, *system.runtime.remoting*, and *system.windows.forms*, but they are beyond the scope of this book.

Web.config v2.0 and v3.5

Before we start looking at the various alterations you can make to *web.config*, let's take time to look at the default contents of the file when VS2008 first creates a website so that you understand the baseline your alterations will change. As mentioned earlier, VS2008 changes the default contents of *web.config* depending on whether the website targets ASP.NET 3.5.

If the site targets either ASP.NET 2.0 or ASP.NET 3.0, *web.config* is quite minimal, as shown in Example 18-13.

Example 18-13. Web.config for .NET 2.0 (with comments omitted)

```
<?xml version="1.0"?>
<configuration>
    <appSettings/>
    <connectionStrings/>
    <system.web>
      <compilation debug="false">
      </compilation>
      <authentication mode="Windows"/>
    </system.web>
    <system.codedom>
    </system.codedom>
    <system.webServer>
    </system.webServer>
</configuration>
```

Aside from leaving placeholders for some of the common configuration sections, all the file does is switch debug mode off (something VS2008 will ask to switch back on as soon as you try to run the website by pressing F5) and set the website to use Windows security to authenticate users. (See Chapter 12 for more on types of security.)

 VS2005 users may not recognize the <system.webServer> element here. This is new for use with IIS 7.0 only and can safely be ignored if the site is not being run on IIS 7.0. We'll discuss this in more detail in a minute.

In contrast, the default *web.config* file for ASP.NET 3.5 is much larger, but for all its changes it really does only four things over and above *web.config* for .NET 2.0.

First, it defines some new configuration sections which you'll use to customize how your ASP.NET AJAX Extensions work:

```
<?xml version="1.0"?>
<configuration>
    <configSections>
      <sectionGroup name="system.web.extensions" ...>
        <sectionGroup name="scripting" ...>
          <section name="scriptResourceHandler" .../>
          <sectionGroup name="webServices" ...>
            <section name="jsonSerialization" .../>
            <section name="profileService" .../>
            <section name="authenticationService" .../>
            <section name="roleService" .../>
          </sectionGroup>
        </sectionGroup>
      </sectionGroup>
    </configSections>

    <appSettings/>
    <connectionStrings/>
```

Then it tells the .NET compiler to use the v3.5 framework to compile the website:

```
<system.codedom>
  <compilers>
    <compiler language="c#;cs;csharp" extension=".cs" ...>
      <providerOption name="CompilerVersion" value="v3.5"/>
      <providerOption name="WarnAsError" value="false"/>
    </compiler>
    <compiler language="vb;vbs;visualbasic;vbscript"
              extension=".vb" ...>
      <providerOption name="CompilerVersion" value="v3.5"/>
      <providerOption name="OptionInfer" value="true"/>
      <providerOption name="WarnAsError" value="false"/>
    </compiler>
  </compilers>
</system.codedom>

<runtime>
  <assemblyBinding xmlns="urn:schemas-microsoft-com:asm.v1">
    <dependentAssembly>
      <assemblyIdentity name="System.Web.Extensions" .../>
      <bindingRedirect oldVersion="1.0.0.0-1.1.0.0"
                       newVersion="3.5.0.0"/>
    </dependentAssembly>
    <dependentAssembly>
      <assemblyIdentity name="System.Web.Extensions.Design" .../>
      <bindingRedirect oldVersion="1.0.0.0-1.1.0.0"
                       newVersion="3.5.0.0"/>
    </dependentAssembly>
  </assemblyBinding>
</runtime>
```

Next, it adds the assemblies for LINQ and the ASP.NET AJAX Extensions into the site for your convenience, and sets up the ASP.NET AJAX Extension server controls (UpdatePanel, etc.) to use the <asp:...> tag prefix:

```
<system.web>
  <compilation debug="false">
    <assemblies>
      <add assembly="System.Core, .../>
      <add assembly="System.Web.Extensions, .../>
      <add assembly="System.Xml.Linq, .../>
      <add assembly="System.Data.DataSetExtensions, .../>
    </assemblies>
  </compilation>

  <authentication mode="Windows"/>

  <pages>
    <controls>
      <add tagPrefix="asp" namespace="System.Web.UI"
        assembly="System.Web.Extensions, .../>
```

```
      <add tagPrefix="asp" namespace="System.Web.UI.WebControls"
         assembly="System.Web.Extensions, .../>
    </controls>
  </pages>
```

Finally, it lets the website know how to handle requests for *.asmx*, *ScriptResource.axd*, and *_AppService.axd* files, which are all related to the ASP.NET AJAX Extensions library in the System.Web.Extensions assembly, albeit a little counterintuitively. First it adds in the handling instructions in the <httpHandlers> element for users of IIS v5 and v6. Then, in anticipation of the website being hosted on IIS 7.0, it uses the <system.webServer> element to replace those handling instructions with new ones that use IIS 7.0's integrated pipeline rather than the classic version which mimics that of v5 and v6.

```
    <httpHandlers>
      <remove verb="*" path="*.asmx"/>
      <add verb="*" path="*.asmx" validate="false"
         type="System.Web.Script.Services.ScriptHandlerFactory,
            System.Web.Extensions, .../>
      <add verb="*" path="*_AppService.axd" validate="false"
         type="System.Web.Script.Services.ScriptHandlerFactory,
            System.Web.Extensions, .../>
      <add verb="GET,HEAD" path="ScriptResource.axd"
         validate="false"
         type="System.Web.Handlers.ScriptResourceHandler,
            System.Web.Extensions, .../>
    </httpHandlers>

    <httpModules>
      <add name="ScriptModule"
         type="System.Web.Handlers.ScriptModule,
            System.Web.Extensions, .../>
    </httpModules>
  </system.web>

  <system.webServer>
    <validation validateIntegratedModeConfiguration="false"/>
    <modules>
      <remove name="ScriptModule"/>
      <add name="ScriptModule" preCondition="managedHandler"
         type="System.Web.Handlers.ScriptModule,
            System.Web.Extensions, .../>
    </modules>
    <handlers>
      <remove name="WebServiceHandlerFactory-Integrated"/>
      <remove name="ScriptHandlerFactory"/>
      <remove name="ScriptHandlerFactoryAppServices"/>
      <remove name="ScriptResource"/>
      <add name="ScriptHandlerFactory" verb="*" path="*.asmx"
         preCondition="integratedMode"
         type="System.Web.Script.Services.ScriptHandlerFactory,
            System.Web.Extensions, .../>
```

```
            <add name="ScriptHandlerFactoryAppServices" verb="*"
                path="*_AppService.axd" preCondition="integratedMode"
                type="System.Web.Script.Services.ScriptHandlerFactory,
                    System.Web.Extensions, .../>
            <add name="ScriptResource" verb="GET,HEAD"
                path="ScriptResource.axd"
                preCondition="integratedMode"
                type="System.Web.Handlers.ScriptResourceHandler,
                    System.Web.Extensions, .../>
        </handlers>
    </system.webServer>
</configuration>
```

If you're using .NET 3.5 but not with IIS 7.0, you can safely delete the `<system.webServer>` section of *web.config* to avoid any confusion. Only IIS 7.0 interprets `<system.webServer>`, however, so if you do decide to leave it in, it will be safely ignored.

With the default settings covered, now we will look at some of the common ways to alter *web.config* and thus the behavior of the website.

Modifying web.config with IIS 7.0

As you saw earlier in this chapter, you can use the Features View of IIS 7.0's main central window to change *web.config* for a website or indeed within the machine-wide *web.config*. Which you change is decided by the selected item in its Connections pane on the left of the window, as shown before in Figure 18-5.

If you select the machine name, you'll alter the machine-wide *web.config*. If you select a website, you'll change the *web.config* file for the whole of that website. If you select a subfolder within a website, be it a normal, virtual, or web application, you'll alter the *web.config* file for that subfolder, creating it automatically if it doesn't already exist.

Once you've selected the item to configure, you can use the Features View to select the particular aspect of the site or folder to configure. Figure 18-2 shows these features grouped by area. You can also choose to view them grouped by category, as shown in Figure 18-12, and this is how we'll review them here.

IIS 7.0 is installed with only a limited number of features by default. This is to reduce the potential number of ways for hackers to attack a website installed on it. If you cannot see a feature we describe in your copy of IIS, you may need to install it if you want to use it. The option to do this is at Start → Settings → Control Panel → Programs and Features → Turn Windows Features On or Off.

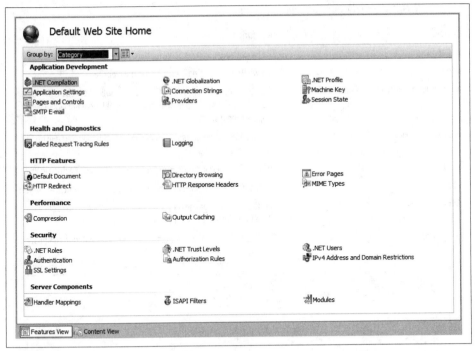

Figure 18-12. IIS 7.0 features grouped by category

Application Development

All the options in this category support the actual development of the web application, allowing you to set up database connections, mail servers, compiler options, and the like toward this goal.

.NET Compilation

All the options in the .NET Compilation dialog (shown in Figure 18-13) reflect attributes of the <compilation> element in *web.config*, as listed in Table 18-3, with the exception of Assemblies, which is actually a child element of <compilation>.

Table 18-3. The <compilation> attributes

Attribute	Description
batch	If true, will cause all the uncompiled files in a website to be precompiled. This increases the execution delay when the app is started but eliminates any compilation delay after that. Default is false.
maxBatchGeneratedSize	Specifies the maximum size (in kilobytes) of generated files per batched compilation.
maxBatchSize	Specifies the maximum number of pages per batched compilation.

Table 18-3. The <compilation> attributes (continued)

Attribute	Description
batchTimeout	The timeout period, in seconds, for batch compilation.
debug	Sets whether debugging is enabled on the website.
numRecompilesBefore AppRestart	Sets the number of times ASP.NET can recompile the website on the fly (e.g., after a change is made to a content page) before the whole website or application restarts.
urlLinePragmas	If true, ASP.NET *line pragmas* (instructions to the compiler) will use URLs rather than physical paths.
explicit	Switches Option Explicit on in your pages and web service if written in VB.NET.
strict	Switches Option Strict on in your pages and web service if written in VB.NET.
defaultLanguage	Sets the default language for your code in the website. Choices in IIS are c# and vb, but you can set any .NET-aware language here.
tempDirectory	Specifies a directory to use for temporary file storage during compilation.

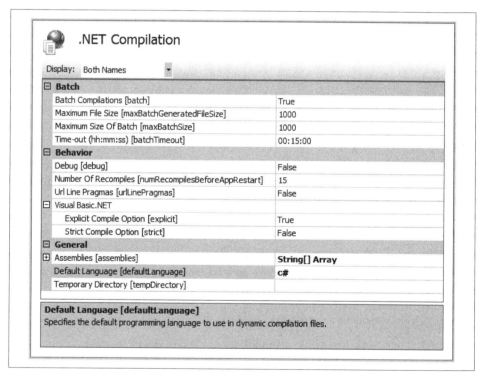

Figure 18-13. NET Compilation options

The .NET Compilation dialog also allows you to specify a list of assemblies to be imported into the compiled website for use in code-behind files. For example, the default *web.config* for ASP.NET 3.5 sites uses this to add the assemblies for LINQ and the AJAX extensions to your site and is reflected in the <assemblies> child element of <compilation>. In addition to <assemblies>, Table 18-4 lists the three other child elements for <compilation>. They are not editable through the .NET Compilation dialog.

Table 18-4. The <compilation> child elements

Child element	Description
<compiler>	Used to specify compilers and what language extension maps with what compiler. It also specifies the class containing the code provider and version information.
<assemblies>	Specifies which assembly files are to be included when the project is compiled.
<codeSubDirectories>	Specifies subdirectories containing files to be compiled at runtime. The default value is App_Code, though this value is not contained in any configuration file. Multiple directories can be specified. The order in which they are listed dictates the order in which the code is compiled.
<buildProviders>	Specifies build providers used to compile custom resource files.

.NET Globalization

The .NET Globalization panel shown in Figure 18-14 gives you control over the attributes of the <system.web>/<globalization> element, listed in Table 18-5.

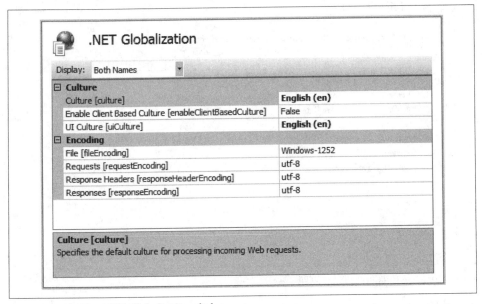

Figure 18-14. The .NET Globalization dialog

Table 18-5. The <globalization> attributes

Attribute	Description
culture	Specifies the default culture for incoming requests
enableClientBasedCulture	Specifies whether culture and uiCulture should be set by the browser in its AcceptLanguages request header
uiCulture	Specifies the default culture for locale-dependent resource searches
fileEncoding	Specifies the default encoding for parsing *.aspx*, *.asmx*, and *.asax* files
requestEncoding	Specifies the encoding assumed for incoming requests
responseHeaderEncoding	Specifies the encoding of a response's header
responseEncoding	Specifies the encoding of a response's content

Note that if any of the last three *Encoding properties (i.e., not including fileEncoding) are not specified in any configuration file, their value will default to the computer's Regional Options locale setting.

.NET Profile

The .NET Profile dialog provides a graphical UI, shown in Figure 18-15, for defining the contents of a user profile, as discussed in Chapter 14.

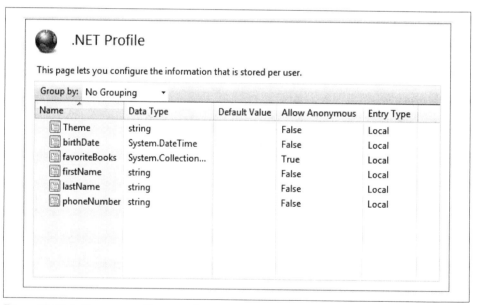

Figure 18-15. Setting user profile properties

To add a property to the site's user profile, click Add Property or Add Property to Group in the Actions pane. You'll see the dialog in Figure 18-16 where you can set the property's name, type, serialization options, default value, and whether it is part of the anonymous user profile as well.

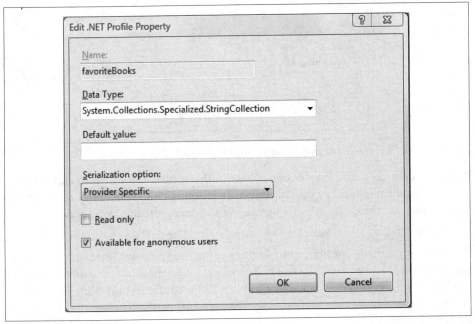

Figure 18-16. Adding a profile property

 Please read Chapter 14 for more on user profiles and personalization.

Application Settings

The Application Settings grid allows you to store application-wide name/value pairs for read-only access. For example, you might want to store a book name in a property called appTitle. Click Add in the Actions pane and you'll get the dialog in Figure 18-17 to fill in.

Once you fill in the name and value of the setting and click OK, this setting is saved within *web.config* files as a child of <configuration>/<appSettings>:

```
<configuration>
    <appSettings>
        <add key="appISBN" value="0-596-00487-7" />
        <add key="appTitle" value="Programming ASP.NET" />
    </appSettings>
</configuration>
```

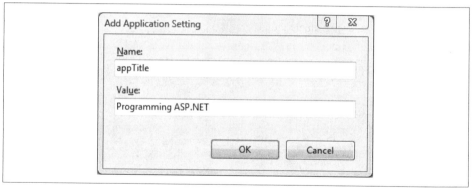

Figure 18-17. Adding an application setting to the site

Now you can access those values anywhere in the application to which this configuration is applicable (i.e., its current directory and any child directories in which the value is not overridden by another *web.config* file) using the following code:

```
string siteName = ConfigurationManager.AppSettings["appTitle"];
```

An application reads configuration settings using the static `AppSettings` property of the `ConfigurationManager` class. This class provides methods and properties for reading configuration settings in an application's configuration files. It is part of the `System.Configuration` namespace, which is automatically imported into every ASP.NET application.

The `AppSettings` property of the `ConfigurationManager` class is of type `NameValueCollection`. It takes a key as a parameter and returns the value associated with that key.

Connection Strings

The Connection Strings dialog (see Figure 18-18) shows you which database connection strings are currently available to the website. This means those you have explicitly defined for the website you're working on and those it has inherited from machine-wide *.config* files.

By default, then, this dialog will always show the following `LocalSqlServer` connection string inherited from *machine.config* until you remove it explicitly:

```
<connectionStrings>
  <add name="LocalSqlServer"
      connectionString=
        "data source=.\SQLEXPRESS;Integrated Security=SSPI;
         AttachDBFilename=|DataDirectory|aspnetdb.mdf;User Instance=true"
      providerName="System.Data.SqlClient" />
</connectionStrings>
```

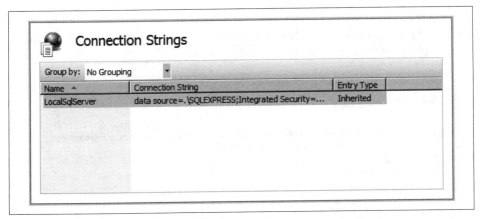

Figure 18-18. The Connection Strings dialog

Use the Actions pane to add, edit, or remove connection strings for the website. The Add dialog, shown in Figure 18-19, assumes that the connection is for a SQL Server database (not a SQL Express database, though) and will build a connection string for you as you enter database and login details. Connections to non-SQL Server databases will need you to specify a custom string and enter it in full instead.

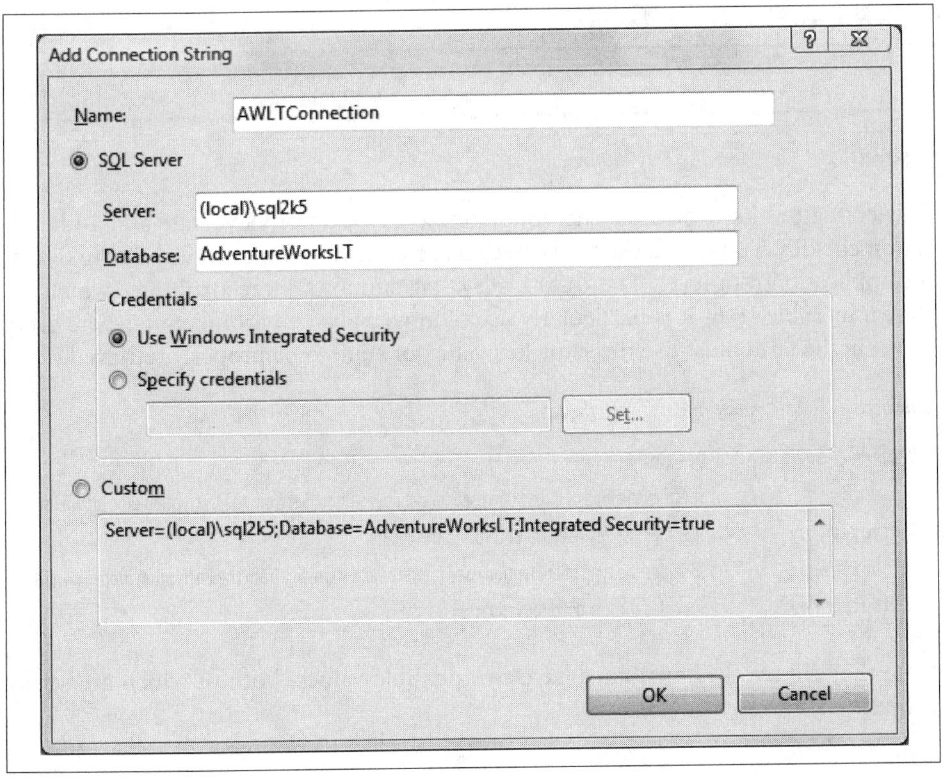

Add Connection String

Name: AWLTConnection

◉ SQL Server

  Server: (local)\sql2k5

  Database: AdventureWorksLT

  Credentials
  ◉ Use Windows Integrated Security
  ○ Specify credentials

  [   ] Set...

○ Custom

  Server=(local)\sql2k5;Database=AdventureWorksLT;Integrated Security=true

  OK   Cancel

Figure 18-19. The Add Connection String dialog

Machine Key

The Machine Key dialog (shown in Figure 18-20) allows you to set attribute values on the <system.Web>\<machineKey> element.

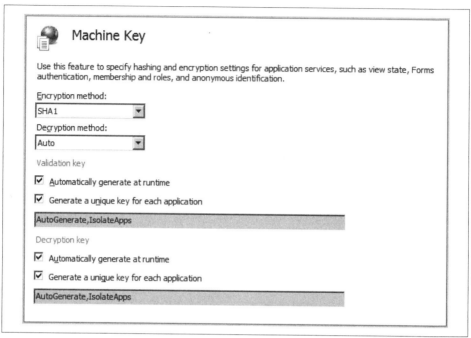

Figure 18-20. The Machine Key dialog

This configures keys used for encryption and decryption of view state and authentication cookies. You can declare this section at the server level or in *web.config* files at the application root level. The <machineKey> tag supports three attributes, which are shown in Table 18-6. It is particularly useful in web farm environments, where every server in the farm must use the same key value for state to be properly retrieved.

Table 18-6. The <machineKey> attributes

Attribute	Description
decryption	Specifies the type of encryption used for data decryption. Set from the Decryption drop-down list.
decryptionKey	Specifies the key used for decrypting the cookie.
validation	Specifies the type of encryption used for data validation. Set from the Encryption drop-down list.
validationKey	Specifies the key used for validation.

Note that the two key attributes have two possible values, both of which are set by default:

`AutoGenerate`

Specifies that ASP.NET will generate a random key at runtime.

`Key_string`

Click Generate Keys in the Actions pane to manually set keys in the *.config* file. This will allow operation across a web farm and will be between 40 and 128 hexadecimal characters long (between 20 and 64 bytes).

Pages and Controls

On initial appearance, the Pages and Controls dialog, shown in Figure 18-21, allows you to set the values for some of the attributes for the `<system.Web>/<pages>` element in *.config* files. These are all related in some way to how pages within a site function—for example, the default theme, master page, or base class for a page.

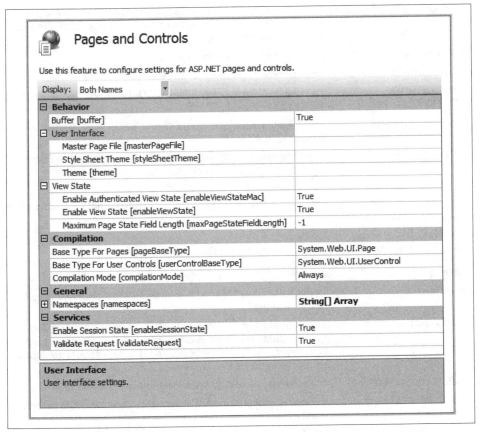

Figure 18-21. The Pages and Controls dialog

The attributes you can set in the dialog are listed in Table 18-7.

Table 18-7. The <pages> attributes

Attribute	Description
buffer	If true, response buffering will be used.
masterPageFile	Sets the default master page for pages in the site. See Chapter 13 for more on master pages.
styleSheetTheme	Sets the default stylesheet theme for pages in the site. See Chapter 13 for more on stylesheet themes.
theme	Sets the default theme for pages in the site. See Chapter 13 for more on themes.
enableViewStateMac	If true, an encrypted version of the view state, called the message authentication code, is included on postback to verify that the view state has not been tampered with. Default is false.
enableViewState	Specifies whether the view state is used for the page. Valid values are true (the default) and false.
maxPageStateFieldLength	Specifies the maximum length of the view state hidden field, in bytes. If this value is exceeded, the field will be broken into chunks and sent separately. Default value is -1, which indicates no maximum size.
pageBaseType	Specifies the base type for all pages in the site.
userControlBaseType	Specifies the base type for all controls in the site.
compilationMode	Valid values are Always (the default), Auto (ASP.NET will compile only if necessary), and Never.
enableSessionState	Specifies whether session state is used for the page. Valid values are true (the default), false, and ReadOnly.
validateRequest	If true (the default), ASP.NET will examine all browser input for potentially dangerous data. If found, an HttpRequestValidationException will be raised.

In addition to these, the Pages element has six other attributes that you can alter manually. These are listed in Table 18-8.

Table 18-8. The <pages> attributes not settable in the Pages and Controls dialog

Attribute	Description
asyncTimeout	The length of time to wait for an asynchronous handler to finish processing on the page. Default is 45 seconds.
autoEventWireup	If true (the default), the .NET Framework will call page events (Page_Init and Page_Load) automatically with no code necessary to explicitly add an event handler to an event delegate. If autoEventWireup is false, you will have to explicitly add event handler methods to the event delegates.
enableEventValidation	If true, the page will validate postback and callback events. Default is true.
maintainScrollPosition OnPostBack	If true, the position of the page will be maintained between postbacks to the server. Default is false.
pageParserFilterType	Sets a filter class derived from PageParserFilter that the ASP.NET parser should use to determine whether an item is allowed in the page at parse time.
smartNavigation	*This feature is deprecated in ASP.NET v2.0 and later.* Enables smart navigation for Internet Explorer 5.5 and later.

The <pages> element also provides two child elements, <namespaces> and <controls>, which you also can edit through the Pages and Controls dialog. The <namespaces> child element specifies namespaces referenced by default by the page. Namespaces added via the <namespaces> child element need not be explicitly referenced at compile time but are still accessible to the code. Those added in the default global *web.config* file are immediately listed under the namespaces, as shown in Figure 18-22.

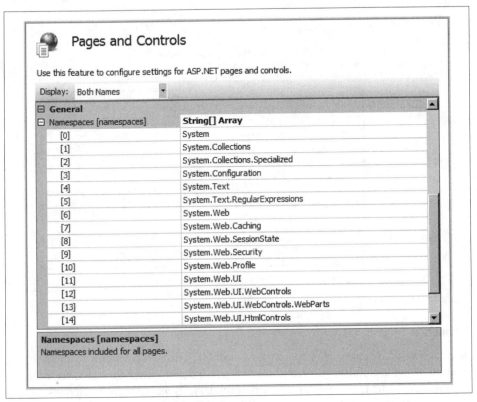

Figure 18-22. Namespaces imported by default

The <controls> child element associates tagPrefixes with a namespace and assembly. For example, the default *web.config* file for ASP.NET 3.5 websites associates the <asp:...> tag with System.Web.Extensions and System.Web.UI.WebControls for the new AJAX, ListView, and DataPager controls with this code:

```
<controls>
    <add tagPrefix="asp" namespace="System.Web.UI"
        assembly="System.Web.Extensions, Version=3.5.0.0,
        Culture=neutral, PublicKeyToken=31BF3856AD364E35" />
    <add tagPrefix="asp" namespace="System.Web.UI.WebControls"
        assembly="System.Web.Extensions, Version=3.5.0.0,
        Culture=neutral, PublicKeyToken=31BF3856AD364E35" />
</controls>
```

This is reflected in the IIS Controls dialog, shown in Figure 18-23, which you can access by clicking Register Controls in the Actions pane while the Pages and Controls dialog is open. Use the Actions pane again to add, edit, and remove <controls> from *web.config*. Also shown in Figure 18-23 is the add/edit dialog for controls.

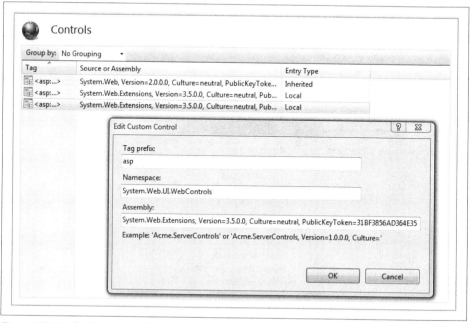

Figure 18-23. The Controls dialog

Providers

In Chapters 12, 13, and 14, you saw how ASP.NET uses "providers" to maintain an account of the users, user roles, and user profiles your site uses to enable security and personalization features. You also saw that by default, *machine.config* defines a set of providers for each of these features based on a SQL Express database created using the *aspnet_regsql.exe* utility.

If you would prefer to set up these providers to use a different database or a different nondatabase mechanism, you will need to add details of those new providers to *web.config*. You can use the Providers dialog, shown in Figure 18-24, to make this simpler.

Session State

The Session State dialog, shown in Figure 18-25, allows you to set all the attributes for the <sessionState> element in *web.config*. These relate to how session state is stored for the duration of a user's session and how cookies are handled.

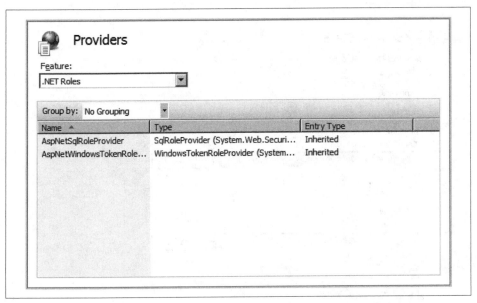

Figure 18-24. The Providers dialog

The dialog is divided into two parts. The top part sets values for the mode attribute. From top to bottom, these values are:

Not enabled
: Disables session state.

In process (default)
: Session state is stored inside the worker process for ASP.NET.

Custom
: Session state is stored inside a custom provider which you have built.

State Server
: Session state is stored by the out-of-process aspnet_state.exe Windows service. With this option you can set how to connect to the service and how long (in seconds) to wait for the service to respond before timing out.

SQL Server
: Session state is stored inside a SQL Server database prepared with the *InstallSqlState.sql* script. Again, you can set the connection string to the database and connection timeout values for this option. Finally, you can check the "Enable custom database" box to use your own database configuration to store session state.

In the bottom part of the dialog you can set up how the site should deal with browsers and devices that do not support cookies (to store session information). The Mode drop-down list offers four values for the <sessionState> element's cookieless attribute.

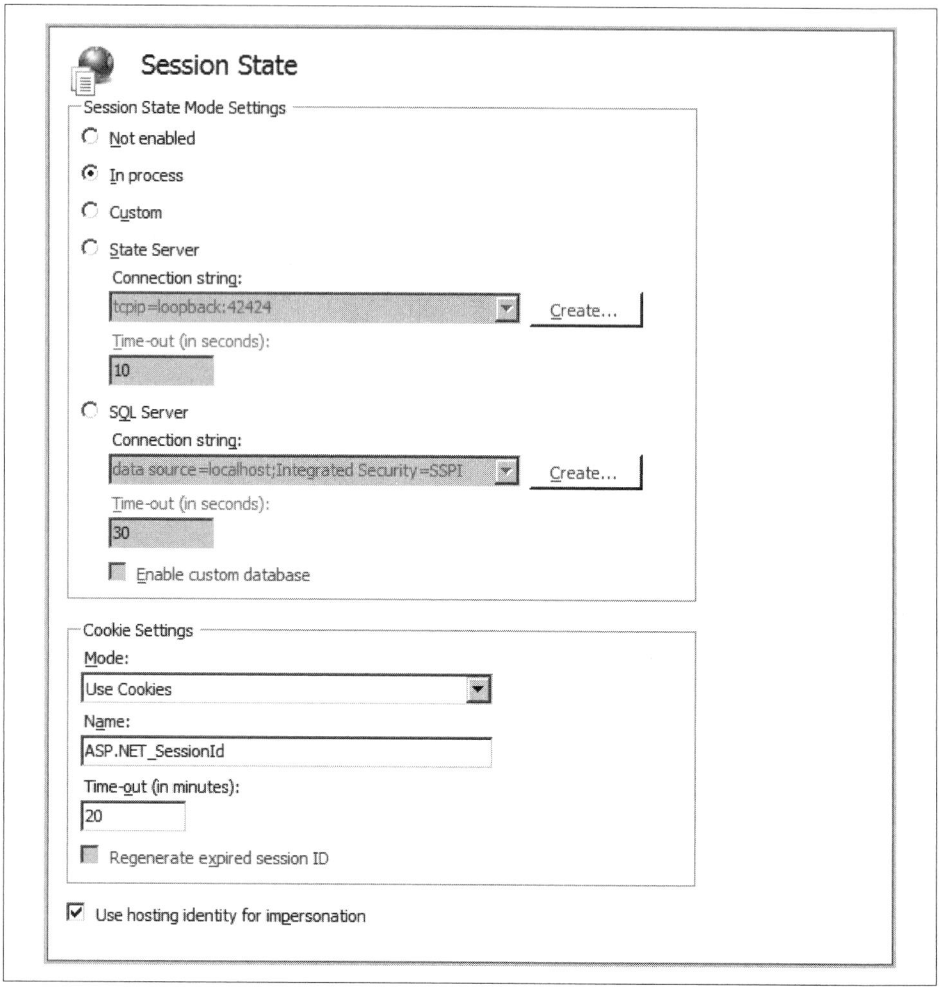

Figure 18-25. The Session State dialog

AutoDetect

Assumes cookies are enabled, but tries to detect whether this is the case and switches to cookieless if not.

Use Cookies

Requires cookies to be used at all times.

Use Device Profile

Checks the device profile to see whether cookies are supported, and uses them if so. If not, ASP.NET switches to cookieless mode where session information is stored in the URI of the page.

Use URI

Stores session information in the page URI at all times. Effectively, the site is always in cookieless mode.

If cookies are being used, you can also set the name of the cookie to be used for session state by the site and how long it should exist before it expires. In addition, you can state whether ASP.NET should regenerate session IDs once they have expired. This is a good idea to prevent replay attacks by ne'er-do-wells. Finally, you can tell IIS to impersonate the NETWORK SERVICE account when the website wants to make any remote connections.

SMTP E-mail

As its name suggests, the SMTP E-mail dialog, shown in Figure 18-26, helps you set up the default settings for the site to send emails as necessary.

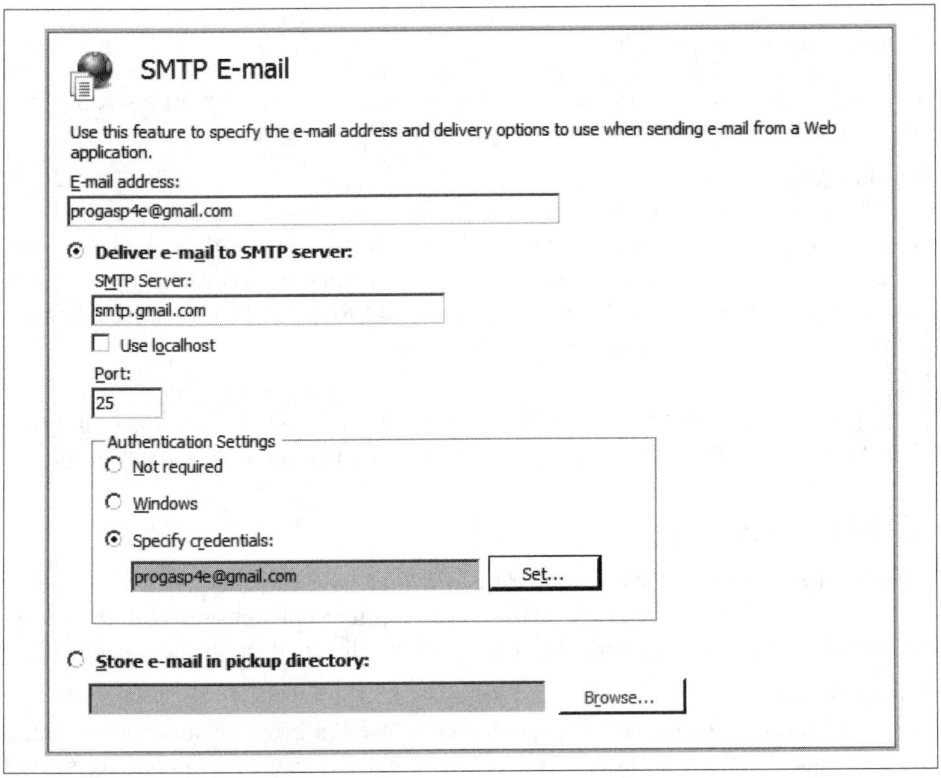

Figure 18-26. The SMTP E-mail dialog

Using this dialog adds an entry under the <system.net>/<mailSettings> element. For example, the settings in Figure 18-26 translate into the following:

```
<configuration>
    <system.net>
        <mailSettings>
            <smtp from="progasp4e@gmail.com">
                <network defaultCredentials="false"
                    host="smtp.gmail.com" password="password"
                    userName="progasp4e@gmail.com" />
```

```
            </smtp>
        </mailSettings>
    </system.net>
</configuration>
```

Many of you will have noticed that Vista does not come with a built-in SMTP server as previous versions did. Although several open source SMTP servers are available for you to use for testing on your development boxes before deploying to a staging server, another option is to check the radio button marked "Store e-mail in pickup directory". When this is checked, rather than trying to find an SMTP server to send the email, ASP.NET will save the email in a nominated directory for inspection and sending later on—very handy indeed for testing.

Health and Diagnostics

Both dialogs grouped under health and diagnostics are website-agnostic settings that do not have counterparts in an ASP.NET *.config* file:

Failed Request Tracing Rules
> This dialog allows you to set up how IIS traces and logs request errors and time-outs and the information contained within that log entry. First, however, you must enable this feature for the website by selecting the website in the Connections pane and then clicking Configure Failed Request Tracing in the Actions pane. You can enable it in the resultant dialog.

Logging
> You can set this only at the website or machine-wide level. This dialog, as in previous versions of IIS, allows you to configure how IIS logs requests to the website.

HTTP Features

Although these features look slightly different, they have direct equivalents in previous versions of IIS and set up basic HTTP responses for your website. With the exception of HTTP Response Headers, they do not have a direct effect on a *web.config* file.

Default Document
> Let's you set a list of default page names to use if a browser does not request a page specifically (e.g., *http://www.google.com*). The pages in the list are sought after from top to bottom.

 If *app_offline.htm* exists in the root directory of your website, that will override this list.

Directory Browsing
> Allows you to enable or disable directory browsing for your website or a directory therein.

Error Pages

Allows you to set default pages in IIS for dealing with HTTP errors. This is a separate feature from the ASP.NET custom errors settings you'll see in "Custom Error Pages" in Chapter 19, and caters to websites which don't support custom error pages themselves.

HTTP Redirect

Sets an automatic redirect (with either HTTP code 301 Permanent, 302 Found, or 307 Temporary) from the requested page or directory to a nominated URL.

HTTP Response Headers

Sets up any HTTP headers that you want to add to all the pages being served from the current website or directory. Once added in the dialog, these are reflected in the site's *web.config* within the <system.webServer>\<httpProtocol>\ <customHeaders> element.

The forthcoming Internet Explorer 8 is using HTTP headers to identify whether a website should be rendered using its new standards-compatible rendering engine. If so, add a new header either to the page directly or to the site overall through IIS using this dialog with the settings shown in Figure 18-27.

After adding this header in IIS, the following is added to your *web.config* file:

```
<system.webServer>
    <httpProtocol>
        <customHeaders>
            <add name="X-UA-Compatible" value="IE=8" />
        </customHeaders>
    </httpProtocol>
</system.webServer>
```

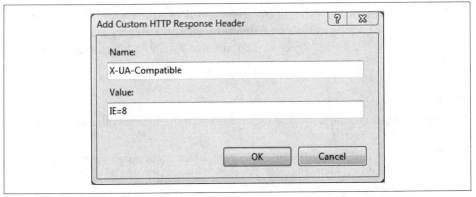

Figure 18-27. Setting up the standards mode HTTP header in Internet Explorer 8

MIME Types

Sets up the MIME types for any static files (movies, pictures, etc.) being served by IIS.

Performance

In Chapter 17, you looked at caching and performance within the context of an ASP.NET website—for example, the caching of a control's output based on some dependency. IIS also provides ways to cache and compress its responses to a request, hence providing a performance gain. Changes to the settings in these dialogs do not affect *web.config*.

> For more information on IIS performance features, have a look at *http://learn.iis.net/page.aspx/93/optimizing-performance/*.

Compression
> Lets you set whether content is compressed depending on whether it is static or dynamically generated.

Output Caching
> Lets you set up caching for files with a given extension (*.htm*, *.aspx*, etc.). Caching can take place inside either the ASP.NET worker process (user mode) or the *http.sys* kernel-mode driver. The latter is a more performant cache, but it does have some limitations. For instance, it does not support page caching based on query string values, and it does not support features that must run in user mode, such as Basic or Windows authentication. The page will be served but not cached.

Security

With the exception of the .NET Trust Levels and IPv4 Address and Domain Restrictions dialogs, the options available to use in the security category map directly to the security issues covered in Chapter 12 and are also available for editing through the WAT.

.NET Roles

The .NET Roles dialog allows you to add user roles to the site's membership databases.

> For this dialog to work and be relevant, an appropriate membership database, user, and role provider must be set up (as shown in Chapter 12) and forms authentication must be enabled.

.NET Trust Levels

The .NET Trust Levels dialog allows you to set one of five trust levels to be applied to the code in the website, as shown in Table 18-9.

Table 18-9. Code access security trust levels

Level	Description
Full	The website has access to any resources subject to Windows security.
High	The website cannot call unmanaged code, call serviced components, write to the event log, access message queues, or access ODBC, OleDB, or Oracle data sources.
Medium	Applies high trust restrictions and prevents access to files outside the website directory, the Registry, and web services.
Low	Applies medium trust restrictions and prevents the creation or modification of files and calling the Assert method.
Minimal	The website can only execute itself.

This translates into setting the level attribute for the `<system.web>\<trust>` element. For example:

```
<configuration>
  <system.web>
    <trust level="medium" />
  </system.web>
</configuration>
```

The `<trust>` element has two attributes in addition to level which you must set manually in *web.config*. They are listed in Table 18-10.

Table 18-10. The <trust> attributes

Attribute	Description
level	Sets the website's trust level.
originUrl	Sets a URL for use in setting permissions in medium trust to call a web service.
processRequestInApplicationTrust	If false, page requests may run under full trust even if the level attribute is set otherwise. The default is true, which enforces the trust level on all page requests.

.NET Users

The .NET Users dialog allows you to add user accounts to the site's membership databases.

 For this dialog to work and be relevant, an appropriate membership database, user, and role provider must be set up (as shown in Chapter 12) and forms authentication must be enabled.

This dialog presents a two-step wizard for adding users to the membership database similar to that of the WAT (see Chapter 12). The first screen, shown on the left of Figure 18-28, sets up the user account details, and the second, shown on the right, allows you to assign the new account to any roles already established.

Figure 18-28. The IIS 7.0 Add .NET User Wizard

Authentication

The Authentication dialog, shown in Figure 18-29, allows you to establish which methods of authentication will be used to authenticate users and which user account the website will impersonate if not the account of the currently logged on user.

 IIS 7.0 does not install all of the options shown in Figure 18-29 by default.

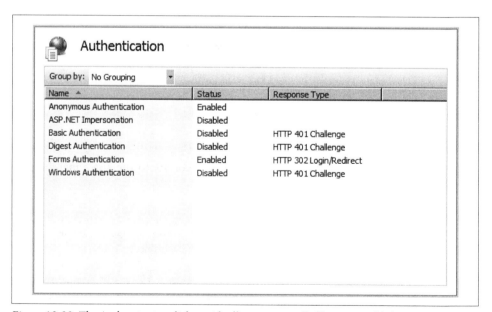

Figure 18-29. The Authentication dialog with all options installed but not enabled

To enable any of the various forms of authentication, select it in the main window and choose Enable from the Actions window. You can then edit the settings for that particular type of authentication by clicking Edit, also in the Actions window. Note that forms and Windows authentication are mutually exclusive and cannot be enabled at the same time. You can find a description of each type of security in Chapter 12.

Enabling either forms or Windows authentication alters the `<system.web>/` `<authentication>` element, changing its mode attribute from the default of none to either Forms or Windows, respectively. This attribute can also take the value Passport, but this method of authentication has been deprecated and is included for legacy reasons only.

The `<authentication>` element also has two possible subelements. They are `<forms>` and `<passport>`. Here is a typical `<authentication>` element with a `<forms>` subelement, as populated by editing the settings for forms authentication:

```
<authentication mode="Forms">
    <forms cookieless="UseCookies" protection="Encryption"
        requireSSL="true" timeout="60" />
</authentication>
```

To edit these settings, select Forms Authentication in the Authentication dialog and click Edit in the Actions panel. You'll see the dialog shown in Figure 18-30.

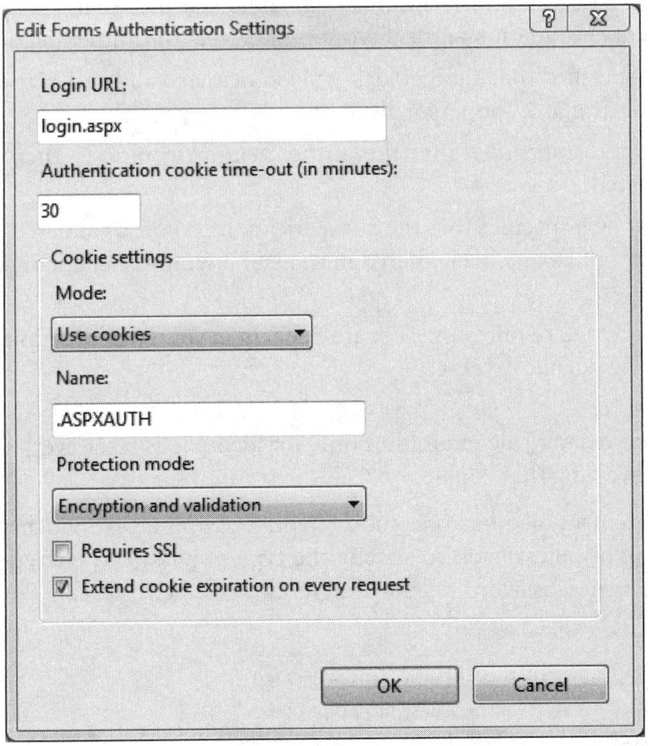

Figure 18-30. Forms authentication settings

The seven options in the dialog match to seven attributes for the <forms> element. From top to bottom, these are:

loginUrl

The web form to which to redirect unauthenticated users should they try to access restricted pages.

timeout

The period (in minutes) after which a user's authentication cookie expires and she must log in again.

cookieless

Defines how the browser will store a user's authentication information in the situation where cookies are not enabled on the browser. It uses the same values as the cookieless attribute for the <sessionState> element.

Name

Specifies the name of the HTTP cookie used for authentication. The default name is .ASPXAUTH.

protection

Sets how the authentication cookie is to be protected by ASP.NET. It has four legal values:

- All, the default and recommended value, specifies that the application use both data validation and encryption to protect the authentication cookie.

- None specifies that the cookies will be neither validated nor encrypted but will be available for personalization.

- Encryption specifies that the authentication cookie is encrypted but not validated.

- Validation specifies that the authentication cookie is validated (i.e., it is verified as not having been altered in transit between the client and the server).

requireSSL

If true, the page requires that Secure Sockets Layer (SSL) be implemented to be viewed. The default is false.

slidingExpiration

If true, the default, the expiration time for a cookie is reset every time a request is made involving that cookie.

The <forms> element also has one subelement, <credentials>, which you must create manually. This allows you to specify the type of password encryption used and also to define name/password pairs within its child element, <user>. For example:

```
<authentication mode="Forms">
    <forms>
        <credentials passwordFormat="SHA1">
            <user name="dan" password="password"/>
        </credentials>
    </forms>
</authentication>
```

The `<credentials>` element's `passwordFormat` attribute has three legal values, shown in Table 18-11.

Table 18-11. Values for the <credentials> tag's passwordFormat attribute

Value	Description
Clear	Passwords are not encrypted.
MD5	Passwords are encrypted using the MD5 hash algorithm.
SHA1	Passwords are encrypted using the SHA-1 hash algorithm.

The `<credentials>` element enables you to specify user/password pairs using the `<user>` subelement. The `<user>` subelement has two attributes: `name` and `password`. Their values are the username and password, respectively.

Impersonation. Listed in the Authentication dialog, the entry for ASP.NET Impersonation controls the identity of the application at runtime and is reflected in *web.config* by the `<system.web>\<identity>` element. Should you enable impersonation and edit the settings, you'll see the dialog shown in Figure 18-31.

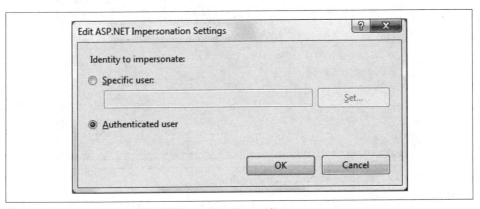

Figure 18-31. Configuring ASP.NET impersonation settings

The default option, "Authenticated user," tells ASP.NET to impersonate the user currently logged in. It translates to the following in *web.config*:

```
<identity impersonate="true" />
```

If you want ASP.NET to impersonate a specific account, check "Specific user" and then click Set to set the username and password of that account. Or, in *web.config*:

```
<identity impersonate="true" password="pwd" userName="uid" />
```

Authorization rules

Authorization is how ASP.NET security controls access to URL resources. The Authorization page allows you to configure this access by either allowing or denying access based on any combination of user, role, and HTTP verb. This information is saved in an ⟨authorization⟩ element in *web.config*, as demonstrated in Chapter 13.

If you prefer not to write these manually, click either Add Allow Rule or Add Deny Rule from the Actions pane in IIS. You'll get the same dialog shown in Figure 18-32.

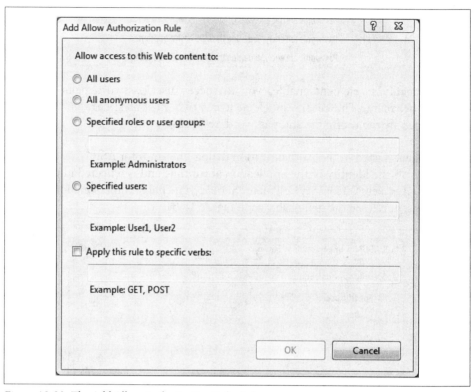

Figure 18-32. The Add Allow Authorization Rule dialog

The ⟨authorization⟩ element supports two subelements, ⟨allow⟩ and ⟨deny⟩, which correspond to whether you choose to add an allow rule or a deny rule in the first place.

Both subelements have the same set of three attributes, controlling the verb, the user, and the roles. Each of these attributes, listed in Table 18-12 and accessible in the Edit Rule dialog, are used to define access rules that are iterated at runtime.

Table 18-12. Attributes of the ⟨allow⟩ and ⟨deny⟩ subtags

Attribute	Description
users	Comma-separated list of users either allowed or denied access. A question mark (?) allows anonymous users. An asterisk (*) allows all users.
roles	Comma-separated list of roles that are allowed or denied access.
verbs	Comma-separated list of HTTP verbs that are allowed or denied access. Registered verbs are GET, HEAD, POST, and DEBUG.

Note that if you are using the new IIS 7.0 integrated pipeline to parse these access rules, all the rules that apply to a page or directory are "added" together first before access is granted or denied. In classic mode (the only way IIS 5 or 6 works) the rules are evaluated in the order found and the first rule that explicitly allows or denies access is taken.

IPv4 Address and Domain Restrictions

The IPv4 Address and Domain Restrictions dialog allows you to create rules for IIS to grant or deny access to a user based on the request's incoming IPv4 address. Rules can be based on individual addresses and subranges.

SSL Settings

The SSL Settings dialog makes available various settings relating to the website working under SSL using an *https://* URL moniker. Note that this dialog becomes available only after you have added a binding for the website to HTTPS.

Server Components

The three dialogs in this category are used to map incoming requests to the server to the ISAPI filters and handlers that know what to do with those files and the HTTP modules that know how to process those requests having been called by the handler or filter. You saw how to create HTTP handlers and modules earlier in this chapter.

There is a fairly extensive mapping in the default machine-level *web.config* file, which maps standard file types to a specific class. For example, Figure 18-33 shows the handler dialog documenting just some of the handlers set up by default by this file.

Web Site Administration Tool

The Web Site Administration Tool (WAT), shown in Figure 18-34, is another tool that eases common configuration chores. As with IIS 7.0, this tool edits the *web.config* file. However, unlike IIS 7.0, the WAT only edits the *web.config* file in the current application. You can access it inside VS2008 by choosing Website → ASP.NET Configuration.

As you saw in Chapter 12, some of the configuration data is stored in a SQL Server database file.

 When VS2008 is first installed on a machine, the Security tab will be available, but will report a problem accessing the data store. You must first configure the SQL Server database file, which is used to store much of the security configuration information. Do this by going to the Provider tab in this tool, clicking either of the links, and then clicking the Test link for the provider you wish to initialize. Or, follow the instructions in Chapter 12 to roll your own membership database.

Three tabs are available in the WAT: Security, Application, and Provider.

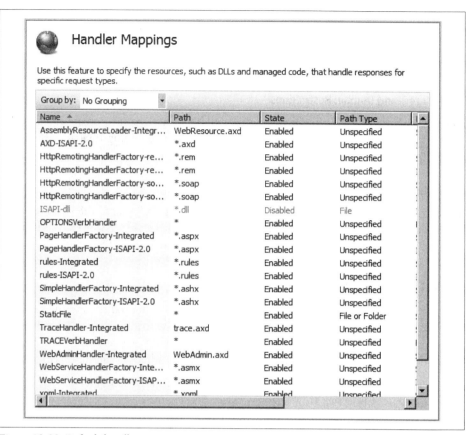

Figure 18-33. Default handler mappings

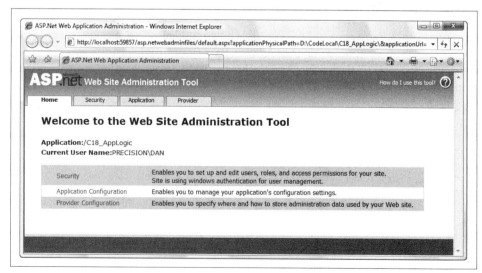

Figure 18-34. The WAT

Security

The Security page offers you a way to configure user accounts, role groups, and access rules for those users and roles, much in the same way the .NET Roles, .NET Users, and Authorization dialogs in IIS 7.0 do. We cover its use in Chapters 12 and 14, so we won't duplicate that here.

Application

The Application tab of the WAT brings up a page that looks like that shown in Figure 18-35.

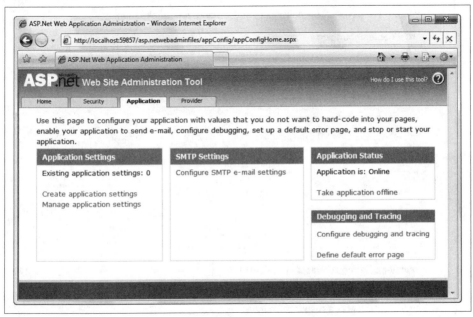

Figure 18-35. The WAT Application page

The Application Settings column has two links for creating and managing application settings, analogous to the Application Settings dialog in IIS 7.0.

The "Configure SMTP e-mail settings" link allows you to configure the SMTP mail server on the web server, much like the SMTP E-mail dialog in IIS 7.0.

The link under Application Status allows you to toggle the online status of the application. Taking the application offline hides the website from browser requests by adding the following child element to <system.web>:

```
<httpRuntime enable="false" />
```

The "Configure debugging and tracing" link brings up the page shown in Figure 18-36, which allows you to set various debugging and tracing parameters.

All except the top checkbox add and configure the `<system.web>\<trace>` element in *web.config*.

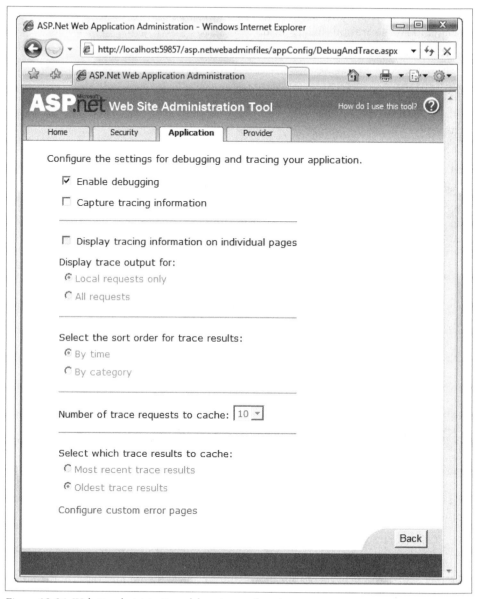

Figure 18-36. Website administration, debugging, and tracing

The `<trace>` element configures the ASP.NET trace service. Chapter 19 describes tracing fully. The `<trace>` element supports the attributes shown in Table 18-13.

Table 18-13. The <trace> attributes

Attribute	Description
enabled	Enables (true) or disables (false) tracing. Default is false.
requestLimit	The number of trace requests to store on the server.
pageOutput	true specifies that trace output is appended to each page. false (the default) specifies that trace output is accessible only through the trace utility.
traceMode	Specifies the sort order of the trace display. SortByTime, the default value, specifies that trace information is sorted in the order processed. SortByCategory specifies that trace information is displayed alphabetically by user-defined category.
localOnly	If true (the default), will specify that the trace viewer is available only on the host web server. false specifies that the trace viewer is available remotely.

The typical <trace> element might look something like the following:

```
<trace
    enabled="false"
    localOnly="true"
    pageOutput="false"
    requestLimit="10"
    traceMode="SortByTime"
/>
```

The "Configure custom error pages" page allows you to specify a default error page that you've created instead of the standard ASP.NET error pages supplied by IIS. By doing so, you add the <system.web>/<customErrors> element to *web.config*:

```
<customErrors defaultRedirect="~/myDefaultErrorPage.aspx" />
```

Beyond this dialog, you can add more to the customErrors element manually to set up a custom error page for each type of HTTP request error, just as you can set up IIS in a more general way to do the same. For example:

```
<customErrors mode="On" defaultRedirect="~/myDefaultErrorPage.aspx">
    <error statusCode="404" redirect="err404.htm" />
    <error statusCode="407" redirect="err407.htm" />
</customErrors>
```

When custom errors are enabled, if an error occurs, the web page specified in defaultRedirect is presented to the client rather than the standard ASP.NET error page. The mode attribute specifies how custom errors are enabled. There are three possible values for this mode:

On
: Custom errors are enabled for all users.

Off
: Custom errors are disabled for all users.

RemoteOnly
: Custom errors are shown only to remote clients, not to local clients. This setting allows developers to see the full error message provided by ASP.NET, while showing end-users the error page you wish them to see.

You can add multiple <error> tags to present specific error pages for specific errors.

In the preceding example, error 404 will result in the page *err404.htm* being presented to the client, error 407 will result in *err407.htm*, and all other errors will result in *StdError.htm* being presented. In any case, the developer working on the local machine will see none of these custom error pages, but rather will see the standard error page put up by ASP.NET.

Provider

A significantly limited version of the IIS 7.0 Providers dialog, the Provider tab allows you to select which of the already defined membership providers should be used to manage users and roles for the website.

In addition to all the configuration settings described so far in this chapter, many other configuration sections are available in the configuration files. To use these settings, you must manually edit the relevant file, either *machine.config* or the appropriate *web.config*, as described in "Hierarchical Configuration," earlier in this chapter.

These configuration sections are described in the online guide to the ASP.NET settings files at *http://msdn2.microsoft.com/en-us/library/zeshe0eb.aspx*.

Custom Configuration Sections

In addition to all the predefined configuration sections, you can also add your own custom configuration sections. You might wish to add two different types of custom configuration sections:

- Sections that provide access to a collection of name/value pairs, similar to appSettings
- Sections that return any type of object

We will demonstrate both here.

Name/Value Pairs

Earlier in this chapter, you saw how to add an <appSettings> element to store strings containing an ISBN number and a title. Suppose you wanted to store connection strings for multiple databases—say, one called Test (for testing purposes) and one called Content (to hold the production content). Using a custom configuration section for each database is one way to handle this situation, the code for which is shown in Example 18-14.

Example 18-14. Custom sections in web.config

```
<configSections>
    <section name="altDB"
             type="System.Configuration.DictionarySectionHandler,
                   System, Version=2.0.0.0, Culture=neutral,
                   PublicKeyToken=b77a5c561934e089" />
</configSections>

<altDB>
    <add key="Test"
       value="SERVER=(local)\sql2k5;DATABASE=Test;UID=sa;PWD=secret;" />
    <add key="Content"
       value="SERVER=(local)\sql2k5;DATABASE=Content;UID=sa;PWD=secret;" />
</altDB>
```

There are three steps to adding a custom configuration section that returns a name/ value pair:

1. Determine which specific configuration file to which to add the custom section. This will determine the scope, or visibility, of the custom section, as described earlier in this chapter in "Hierarchical Configuration."

2. Adding the section to *machine.config* or the machine-level *web.config* will make it available to every application on that machine. Adding it to a *web.config* file in the Default Web Site, *C:\inetpub\wwwroot*, will make it available to every website under the default website. Adding it to a *web.config* file in the application root will make the section visible to that entire application but to no other applications. Adding it to a *web.config* file in an application subdirectory will make it visible only to that subdirectory and its child subdirectories.

3. Declare the section handler by adding a line to the <configSections> section of the designated configuration file. This tells ASP.NET to expect a configuration section with the specified name and which class and assembly file to use to process the section.

4. Add the highlighted lines between the <configSections> tags in Example 18-14 to the designated configuration file. If the file you are editing does not have a pair of <configSections> tags, you will need to add those as well. The <configSections> element should be the first child of the root <configuration> element.

5. Add the custom section itself to the configuration file. This consists of the high-lighted lines in Example 18-14 between the <altDB> tags. This custom configuration section contains two entries, one named Test and the other named Content, each with its own value attribute.

The type in the <section> element specifies the DictionarySectionHandler class in the *System.dll* assembly file. For further documentation, check the SDK documentation, search on "Custom Elements," and choose "Custom Element for NameValueSection-Handler."

To read the contents of this custom configuration section, you again use a method from the ConfigurationManager class, this time the GetSection method. The code for doing this is highlighted in Example 18-15, which assumes that the content page has two labels named lblTest and lblContent. Notice the using statement referencing the System.Collections namespace at the top of the code-behind file. This is necessary to allow use of the Hashtable object without having to code a fully qualified name.

Example 18-15. Reading custom configuration values

```
using System;
using System.Collections;
using System.Configuration;

protected void Page_Load(object sender, EventArgs e)
{
    if (!IsPostBack)
    {
        string strTest;
        strTest = ((Hashtable)ConfigurationManager.
                        GetSection("altDB"))["Test"].ToString( );
        lblTest.Text = strTest;

        lblContent.Text = ((Hashtable)ConfigurationManager.
                        GetSection("altDB"))["Content"].ToString( );
    }
}
```

The code in Example 18-15 shows two equivalent ways of displaying the contents of the key value. One way is to assign the value to a string and then assign the string to the Text property of a Label. The other way is to assign the value directly to the Text property. Though the latter technique is more concise, the former is often easier to debug.

The GetSection method takes a configuration section name as a parameter and returns an object of type Hashtable. The desired value in the collection is retrieved by using the key as an offset into the collection, using the get property syntax. In C#, the property is retrieved using square brackets.

The C# code first casts or converts the value returned by GetSection to type Hashtable because C# does not support late binding. In addition, the value returned is of type object, so it must be converted to a string using the static ToString method.

Objects

appSettings and custom configuration sections are very useful. However, they suffer from the same limitation of being able to return only a name/value pair. Sometimes it would be useful to return an object.

For example, suppose you have a standard query into a database. You could store the query string in an appSettings tag and then open a database connection after retrieving the string. However, it would be more convenient to store the query string in *web.config* and then have the configuration system return a DataSet directly.

To do this, you must add a <section> tag and a configuration section to the designated configuration file as with the custom section returning name/value pairs, described in the previous section.

Edit the *web.config* file used in the previous example and shown in Example 18-15, adding the lines of code highlighted in Example 18-16.

Example 18-16. Custom sections returning objects in web.config

```
<?xml version="1.0" encoding="utf-8" ?>
<configuration>
    <configSections>
        <section name="altDB"
            type="System.Configuration.NameValueSectionHandler, System" />
        <sectionGroup name="system.web">
            <section name="DataSetSectionHandler"
                        type="DataSetSectionHandler,SectionHandlers" />
            </section>
        </sectionGroup>
    </configSections>

    <altDB>
        <add key="Test"
            value=
                "SERVER=(local)\sql2k5;DATABASE=Test;UID=sa;PWD=secret;" />
        <add key="Content"
            value=
                "SERVER=(local)\sql2k5;DATABASE=Content;UID=sa;PWD=secret;"
        />
    </altDB>

    <system.web>
        ...
        <!-- Custom config section returning an object -->
        <DataSetSectionHandler
            str="Select CompanyName,ContactName,City
                from SalesLT.Customers"  />
        ...
    </system.web>
</configuration>
```

In the <sectionGroup> child element within the <configSections> element, a handler declaration is created for the DataSetSectionHandler within the system.web group. This specifies that elsewhere within the file, there will be a custom configuration section called DataSetSectionHandler within the system.web element. Furthermore, it specifies that the class that will handle the configuration section is called DataSetSectionHandler, and the class will be found in an assembly file called *SectionHandlers.dll* located in the *bin* directory.

Farther down in the file, within the <system.web> section, there is a section called DataSetSectionHandler. It has a single attribute, str. This is a string containing the SQL statement you wish to pass to the database.

Next you must create the DataSetSectionHandler class and place it in a file called *SectionHandler.cs*. To do this in VS2008, right-click the application root in the Solution Explorer. Select Add New Item. Select a new Class and name the file *SectionHandlers.cs*. Delete its contents and add the code from Example 18-17.

Example 18-17. SectionHandler.cs

```
using System;
using System.Configuration;
using System.Data;
using System.Data.SqlClient;
using System.Xml;

public class DataSetSectionHandler : IConfigurationSectionHandler
{
   public Object Create(Object parent, Object configContext,
                        XmlNode section)
   {
      string strSql = section.Attributes.Item(0).Value;
      string connString =
         "server=(local)\\sql2k5;Integrated Security=true;" +
         "database=AdventureWorksLT";

      // create the data set command object and the DataSet
      SqlDataAdapter da = new SqlDataAdapter(strSql, connectionString);
      DataSet dsData = new DataSet();

      // fill the data set object
      da.Fill(dsData, "Customers");
      return dsData;      }
}
```

The name of the class has been changed to DataSetSectionHandler to match the class name used in the *web.config* listed in Example 18-16. This class inherits from IConfigurationSectionHandler.

 Set the connection string to match your specific database. You might need to set a specific username and password to access it.

We cover the database aspects of the code in this example thoroughly in Chapters 8 and 9.

For a class to be used as a configuration section handler, it must be derived from the IConfigurationSectionHandler interface. In C#, this is indicated by a colon between the class or method name and the class or interface being inherited.

 A full discussion of object-oriented concepts such as inheritance, base classes, and interfaces is beyond the scope of this book. For now, you should just know that an interface acts as a contract that the implementing class must fulfill. The interface may, for example, dictate the signature of methods that the implementing class must implement, or it may dictate which properties the class must provide.

The IConfigurationSectionHandler interface has only one method, Create. Therefore, the implementing class must implement the Create method with the specified signature. The three parameters are dictated by the interface. The first two parameters are rarely used and we will not discuss them further here. The third parameter is the XML data from the configuration file.

The XML node is parsed, and the value of the first item in the Attributes collection is assigned to a string variable in this line:

```
string strSql = section.Attributes.Item(0).Value
```

Once the SQL string is in hand, the connection string is hardcoded, a SqlDataAdapter object is instantiated and executed, and the DataSet is filled and then returned.

Before this class can be used, it must be compiled and placed in the application assembly cache located in the *bin* directory under the application root.

 The assembly referenced in the type attribute of the <section> tag must be precompiled and available to the application. You cannot just put the source code for the class into the *App_Code* directory and have it automatically compiled at runtime, as is the normal practice, because the name of the assembly is required at compile time and not just its contents.

Open a command prompt by clicking Start → Microsoft Visual Studio 2008 → Visual Studio Tools → Visual Studio 2008 Command Prompt. Use the cd command to make the application root the current directory. This assumes that the application root directory already has a child directory called *bin*. If not, you'll have to make one. Then enter the following command line (all on one line):

```
csc /t:library /out:bin\SectionHandlers.dll
    /r:system.dll,System.data.dll,System.xml.dll SectionHandlers.cs
```

The target type of output is set to be library, that is, a dynamic link library (DLL). The name of the output file to be placed in the *bin* directory will be *SectionHandlers.dll*. Three DLL files are referenced. The input source file is *SectionHandler.cs*. When the source file is compiled, you will have the output DLL in the *bin* directory, where the classes it contains will automatically be available to the application.

A typical way to utilize this custom configuration section would be to have a GridView on a page which data-binds to the data set returned by this section. Assuming the GridView control was named gv the code listed in Example 18-18 would retrieve the data set and bind the control.

Example 18-18. Code for retrieving custom configuration object

```
protected void Page_Load(object sender, EventArgs e)
{
   if (!IsPostBack)
   {
      CreateGrid( );
   }
}

private void CreateGrid( )
{
   DataSet dsGrid = new DataSet( );
   dsGrid = (DataSet)ConfigurationManager.
                     GetSection("system.web/DataSetSectionHandler");
   gv.DataSource = dsGrid.Tables[0];
   gv.DataBind( );
}
```

The interesting work in Example 18-18 is done in the CreateGrid method. Rather than supplying connection information and a SQL query string, a call is made to the GetSection method of the ConfigurationManager class, which returns a DataSet object directly. Then the DataSet object is set as the DataSource of the GridView control, and the control is data-bound. The parameter of the GetSection method is a string containing the name of the section containing the configuration settings. The syntax with the section name (*system.web*) is separated from the subsection name (DataSetSectionHandler) by a slash.

CHAPTER 19

Tracing, Debugging, and Error Handling

Every computer programmer has run into bugs. It comes with the territory. Many bugs are found during the coding process. Others pop up only when an end-user performs a specific and unusual sequence of steps or the program receives unexpected data. It is highly desirable to find bugs early in the development process, and it is very important to avoid having end-users find your bugs for you. Countless studies have shown that the earlier you find a bug, the easier and less expensive it is to fix.

In the event that your program does run into a problem, you will want to recover quickly and invisibly, or, at worst, fail gracefully. ASP.NET provides tools and features to help you reach these goals:

Tracing
> You can trace program execution at either the page or the application level. ASP.NET provides an extensible trace log with program life cycle information.

Symbolic debugging
> You can step through your program, set breakpoints, examine and modify variables and expressions, and step into and out of classes, even those written in other languages.

Error handling
> You can handle standard or custom errors at the application or page level. You can also show different error pages for different errors.

To get started exploring the ASP.NET debugging tools, you'll create a simple website to which you will add tracing code. You will then introduce bugs into the program and use the debugger to find and fix the bugs.

Creating the Sample Application

To begin, open Visual Studio 2008 (VS2008) and create a new website called *C19_Debugging*. Drag a Label control onto *Default.aspx* and give it an ID of lblHeader. Beneath it, add a DropDownList called ddlBooks, another Label called lblBooks to reflect the selected item in the DropDownList, and finally a Hyperlink control called hypBookLink. Change hypBookLink's Text property to "Link To" and its NavigateUrl property to *TestLink.aspx*. No page with this name exists. This is an intentional error to demonstrate error handling later in this chapter.

To make the connection between ddlBooks and lblBooks, change ddlBooks' AutoPostBack property to true and double-click it in Design view to create an event handler for its SelectedIndexChanged handler. Example 19-1 shows the complete markup for *Default.aspx* with additional code for the header label included.

Example 19-1. Default.aspx in full

```
<%@ Page Language="C#" AutoEventWireup="true"
   CodeFile="Default.aspx.cs" Inherits="_Default" %>

<!DOCTYPE html PUBLIC "-//W3C//DTD XHTML 1.0 Transitional//EN"
   "http://www.w3.org/TR/xhtml1/DTD/xhtml1-transitional.dtd">

<html xmlns="http://www.w3.org/1999/xhtml">
<head runat="server">
   <title>Tracing, Debugging & Error Handling</title>
</head>

<body>
   <form id="form1" runat="server">
   <div>
      <asp:Label ID="lblHeader" runat="server"
         Font-Bold="True" Font-Names="Arial Black"
         Text="Tracing, Debugging and Error Handling" />
      <br />
      <asp:DropDownList ID="ddlBooks"
         runat="server" AutoPostBack="True"
         OnSelectedIndexChanged="ddlBooks_SelectedIndexChanged" />
      <br />
      <asp:Label ID="lblBooks" runat="server"></asp:Label>
      <br />
      <asp:HyperLink ID="hypBookLink"
         runat="server" NavigateUrl="TestLink.aspx">
         Link To
      </asp:HyperLink>
   </div>
   </form>
</body>
</html>
```

The code-behind file for the page (shown in Example 19-2) is also very straightforward. Page_Load builds an array of books for the DropDownList to display and, as mentioned, the DropDownList's SelectedIndexChanged handler updates the Label beneath it with the name and ISBN of the book currently selected.

Example 19-2. Default.aspx.cs in full

```csharp
using System;
using System.Web.UI;
using System.Web.UI.WebControls;

public partial class _Default : Page
{
    protected void Page_Load(object sender, EventArgs e)
    {
        // Initialize list of books for DropDownList
        if (!IsPostBack)
        {
            string[,] bookList = {
                {"9780596513979", "Learning ASP.NET 2.0 with AJAX"},
                {"9780596510503", "Building a Web 2.0 Portal
                                   with ASP.NET 3.5"},
                {"9780596514822", "Head First C#"},
                {"9780596514242", "Programming ASP.NET AJAX"},
                {"059652756X", "Programming .NET 3.5"},
                {"9780596526993", "Programming WCF Services"}
            };

            // Now populate the list
            for (int i = 0; i < bookList.GetLength(0); i++)
            {
                ddlBooks.Items.Add(
                    new ListItem(bookList[i, 1], bookList[i, 0]));
            }
        }
    }

    protected void ddlBooks_SelectedIndexChanged(
            object sender, EventArgs e)
    {
        // Check to verify an item has been selected
        if (ddlBooks.SelectedIndex != -1)
        {
            lblBooks.Text = String.Format("{0}, ISBN : {1}",
                ddlBooks.SelectedItem.Text, ddlBooks.SelectedValue);
        }
    }
}
```

Although this chapter uses *Default.aspx* to demonstrate tracing, debugging, and error handling, the demonstration website contains two pages, *AtChapterStart.aspx* and *AtChapterEnd.aspx*, which contain the code for *Default.aspx* as given at this point in the chapter and at the end of the chapter, respectively.

Run the web page, clicking OK to enable debugging in *web.config*, and select one of the items from the list. You should see something similar to Figure 19-1.

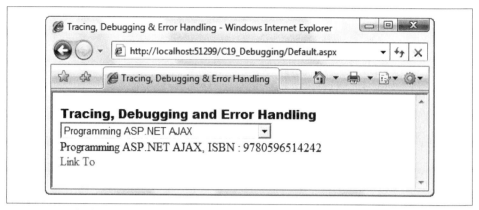

Figure 19-1. The debugging test page in action

You will use this application through the rest of this chapter to demonstrate various techniques for analyzing and debugging code in ASP.NET and for handling errors in your application.

Tracing

Tracing is an easy way to determine what is going on in your program. Back in the days of classic ASP, the only way to trace what was happening in your code was to insert `Response.Write` statements in strategic places. This allowed you to see that you had reached a known point in the code and, perhaps, to display the value of some variables. The big problem with this hand-tracing technique, aside from the amount of work involved, was that you had to laboriously remove or comment out all those statements before the program went into production.

ASP.NET provides better ways of gathering the trace information. You can add tracing at the application level or at the page level. With application-level tracing every page is traced, and with page-level tracing you choose the pages to which to add tracing.

Page-Level Tracing

To add page-level tracing, modify the `Page` directive at the top of your *.aspx* page, by adding a `Trace` attribute and setting its value to `true`. For example, to enable tracing on *Default.aspx*, the Page directive should read as follows:

```
<%@ Page Language="C#" AutoEventWireup="true"
    CodeFile="Default.aspx.cs" Inherits="_Default"
    Trace="true" %>
```

Now when you save and view *Default.aspx*, there will be tables at the bottom that contain a wealth of information about your web application, as shown in Figure 19-2.

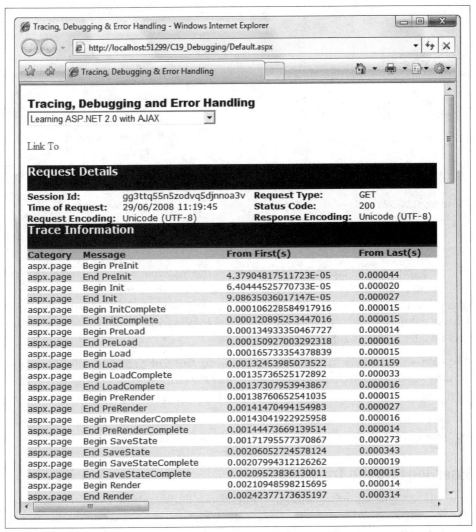

Figure 19-2. Some trace information for Default.aspx

The top section, labeled Request Details, shows basic information, including the Session ID, the Time of Request, the Request Type, and the HTTP Status Code sent from the server for the page request (see Table 19-1). Every time the page is posted to the server, this information is updated. If you change the selection (remember that AutoPostBack is set to true), you will see that the Time of Request is updated, but the Session ID remains constant.

Table 19-1. HTTP status codes

Category	Number	Description
Informational (100–199)	100	Continue
	101	Switching protocols
Successful (200–299)	200	OK
	204	No content
Redirection (300–399)	301	Moved permanently
	305	Use proxy
	307	Temporary redirect
Client Errors (400–499)	400	Bad request
	402	Payment required
	404	Not found
	408	Request timeout
	417	Expectation failed
Server Errors (500–599)	500	Internal server error
	503	Service unavailable
	505	HTTP version not supported

The next section, labeled Trace Information, is the *trace log*, which provides life cycle information. This includes elapsed times, in seconds, since the page was initialized [the From First(s) column] and since the previous event in the life cycle [the From Last(s) column]. You can add custom trace information to the trace log, as we explain later in this chapter.

The next section in the trace, under the heading Control Tree, lists all the controls on the page in a hierarchical manner, including the name of the control, its type, and its size in bytes, both on the page and in the ViewState state bag.

This is followed by Session and Application State summaries, and itemizations of the Cookies and Headers collections. Finally, there is a list of all the server variables.

Inserting into the Trace Log

You can add custom information to the trace output by writing to the Trace object. This object, encapsulated in the TraceContext class, exposes two methods for putting your own statements into the trace log: Write and Warn. The only difference between the two methods is that Warn writes to the log in red. The Warn and Write methods are overloaded to take a single argument, two arguments, or two strings and an exception object, as the following cases illustrate:

Trace.Warn("Warning Message")

Inserts a record into the trace log with the message passed in as a string

```
Trace.Warn("Category","Warning Message")
```
Inserts a record into the trace log with the category and message you pass in

```
Trace.Warn("Category","Warning Message", exception)
```
Inserts a record into the trace log with a category, warning message, and exception

To see this in action, add the highlighted lines of code into the top of the Page_Load function in *Default.aspx*:

```
protected void Page_Load(object sender, EventArgs e)
{
    Trace.Write("In Page_Load");

    // Initialize list of books for DropDownList
    if (!IsPostBack)
    {
        Trace.Write("Page_Load", "Not Postback");
        string[,] bookList = {
            {"9780596513979", "Learning ASP.NET 2.0 with AJAX"},
...
```

Similarly, add the following lines of code into the SelectedIndexChanged handler:

```
protected void ddlBooks_SelectedIndexChanged(
                object sender, EventArgs e)
{
    // Force an exception
    try
    {
        int a = 0;
        int b = 5 / a;
    }
    catch (Exception ex)
    {
        Trace.Warn("UserAction", "Calling b=5/a", ex);
    }

    // Check to verify an item has been selected
    if (ddlBooks.SelectedIndex != -1)
    {
        lblBooks.Text = String.Format("{0}, ISBN : {1}",
            ddlBooks.SelectedItem.Text, ddlBooks.SelectedValue);
    }
}
```

The first message is added in the Page_Load method to signal that you've entered that method:

```
Trace.Write("In Page_Load");
```

The second message is added if the page is not a postback:

```
if (! IsPostBack)
{
    Trace.Write("Page_Load", "Not Postback.");
```

This second message is categorized as Page_Load; using a category can help you organize the trace output. The effect of these two Write statements is shown in Figure 19-3.

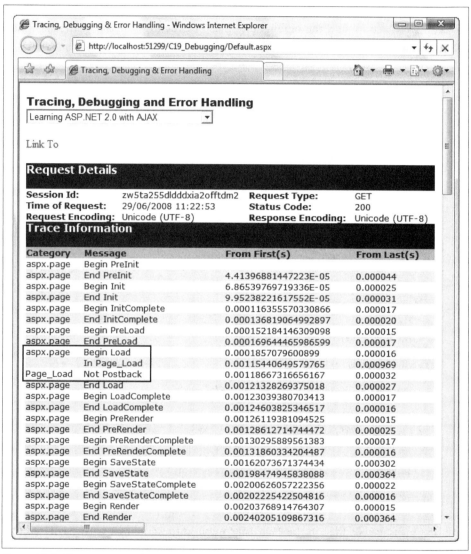

Figure 19-3. Trace.Write results

The third message is added to demonstrate the process of inserting an exception into the error log. The ddlBooks_SelectedIndexChanged event handler now contains code to force an exception by dividing by zero. The code catches that exception and logs the exception with a Trace statement, as shown in Figure 19-4.

Figure 19-4. Trace.Warn results

Because this Trace statement was written calling the Warn method rather than the Write method, the trace output appears in red on-screen (though not in your copy of this book). Notice that the string you passed in, Calling b=5/a, is displayed, followed by an error message extracted automatically from the exception object.

Implementing Trace statements is easy, and when it is time to put your page into production, all these statements can remain in place. The only modification you need to make is to change the Trace attribute in the Page directive from true to false.

Application-Level Tracing

Application-level tracing applies to all the pages in a given website. It is configured through the *web.config* file, which we described in Chapter 18.

The *web.config* file is typically located in the root directory of the website. If there is a *web.config* file in a subdirectory of the application root, that copy will apply only to the pages in that subdirectory and in the subdirectories under it. If tracing is enabled application-wide from the root directory, tracing will be applied across the application uniformly. The exception is when a specific page has a contradictory page directive, which supersedes the application directive.

Web.config is an XML file that consists of sections delimited by tags. The trace configuration information is contained in the `<trace>` section within the `<system.web>` section, which is contained within the `<configuration>` section.

 Web.config, like all XML documents, must consist of well-formed XML. We discuss the elements of a well-formed XML file in the sidebar "Well-Formed XHTML" in Chapter 3. Note that XML is case-sensitive.

A typical trace configuration snippet will look something like Example 19-3.

Example 19-3. Enabling tracing application-wide in web.config

```
<?xml version="1.0"?>
<configuration xmlns="http://schemas.microsoft.com/
.NetConfiguration/v2.0" >

  <system.web>
.
.
.

    <trace
        enabled="true"
        requestLimit="10"
        pageOutput="false"
        traceMode="SortByTime"
        localOnly="true"
    />
```

You can enable application-level tracing by editing *web.config* manually and by using the Web Site Administration Tool (WAT) in VS2008. The option here is under Application Settings → Debugging and Tracing.

There are seven possible properties in the `<trace>` section. These properties appear in Table 19-2. Several of these properties affect the trace viewer, which we will describe in the following section.

Table 19-2. The <trace> attributes and their uses

Property	Values	Description
enabled	true, false	Enables or disables application-level tracing. Default is false. If enabled, all pages in the application will display trace information unless a specific page has Trace=false in the Page directive.
localOnly	true, false	Indicates whether the trace viewer is available only on the host web server. Default is true.
mostRecent	true, false	If true, will discard older requests when the value of the RequestLimit property is exceeded. If false, the default, the trace service will be disabled when the RequestLimit is reached.
pageOutput	true, false	Dictates whether trace information is displayed both on the application pages and in the trace viewer. Default is false. Pages with tracing enabled are not affected by this setting.
requestLimit	Integer	Number of trace requests that will be stored on the server and visible in the trace viewer. Default is 10.
traceMode	SortByTime, SortByCategory	Dictates whether the trace log is sorted by time or category. Default is TraceMode.SortByTime.
writeToDiagnosticsTrace	true, false	If true, messages from the trace log are forwarded to the Trace class. Default is false.

Trace Viewer

If application-level tracing is enabled, you can view the trace log directly from your browser for any application, even across multiple page requests. The trace facility provides a trace viewer, called *trace.axd*. Aim your browser toward *trace.axd* as though it were a page in the application, with the following URL, for example:

> *http://localhost/C19_Debugging/trace.axd*

You will see a summary of all the entries in the trace log, as shown in Figure 19-5.

Debugging

Tracing provides you with a snapshot of the steps your code has taken after the code has run. At times, however, you'd like to monitor your code while it is running. What you want is more of a CAT scan than an autopsy. The code equivalent of a CAT scan is a *symbolic debugger*.

When you run your code in the debugger, you can watch your code work, step by step. As you walk through the code, you can see the variables change values, and you can watch as objects are created and destroyed.

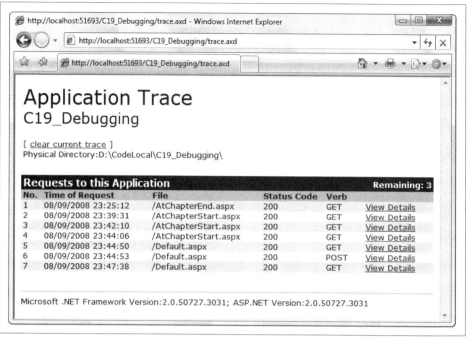

Figure 19-5. The ASP.NET trace viewer

This section will provide a brief introduction to the most important parts of the debugger that accompanies the VS2008 integrated development environment (IDE). For complete coverage of how to use the debugger, we urge you to spend time with the documentation and to experiment freely. The debugger is one of the most powerful tools at your disposal for learning ASP.NET.

There are some fantastic debugging blogs out there with some large, deep examples of exactly how far you can go into the rabbit hole of debugging. Check out these two for starters:

- Tess Ferrandez at *http://blogs.msdn.com/tess/*
- Mike Stall at *http://blogs.msdn.com/jmstall/*

You can configure an application to either enable or disable debugging. As with tracing, you do this in *web.config*. Often, you'll enable debugging when the site is first run in VS2008, and it displays a prompt asking whether the website should be enabled for debugging, as shown in Figure 19-6.

Whether you choose to enable debugging at that point by clicking OK, or to enable it later by modifying *web.config*, the end result is the same: the <compilation> element inside <system.web> will have its debug attribute set to true, as shown in Example 19-4.

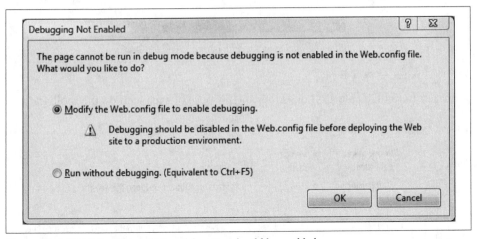

Figure 19-6. VS2008 asking whether debugging should be enabled

Example 19-4. Debugging enabled in web.config

```
<?xml version="1.0"?>
<configuration>
    ...
    <system.web>
        <compilation debug="true">
            <assemblies>
                ...
            </assemblies>
        </compilation>
        ...
    </system.web>
    ...
</configuration>
```

Don't forget, though, to set debug back to false before you deploy your website to a live server. This will remove all the debugging information out of your compiled site and help it run faster. Of course, it will run even faster if there are no bugs in it to start with, so let's look at the tools VS2008 provides to help debug our sites.

The Debug Toolbar

The Debug toolbar, shown in Figure 19-7, is your constant companion in VS2008, and it contains all the basic commands to inch your way through your code until you find your bug. It automatically becomes visible once you run your website in the VS2008 debugger by pressing F5, but you can also beckon it forward through the View → Toolbars menu option or by right-clicking the Toolbar area of VS2008 and selecting Debug from there.

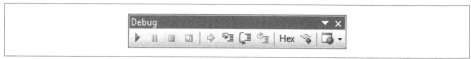

Figure 19-7. The Debug toolbar

From left to right, Table 19-3 describes the purpose of each icon on the toolbar.

Table 19-3. Debug toolbar icons

Icon	Debug menu equivalent	Keyboard shortcut	Purpose
	Start Debugging	F5	Starts or continues executing the website.
	Break All	Ctrl-Alt-Break	Pauses program execution at the currently executing line.
	Stop Debugging	Shift-F5	Stops debugging.
	Restart	Ctrl-Shift-F5	Stops the current debugging sessions and restarts them from scratch.
			Highlights the next statement to be executed in the program.
	Step Into	F11	Moves to the next line of code to be executed. If this is inside a method being called, focus is moved to that method.
	Step Over	F10	Moves to the next line of code to be executed in the current block of code. Will not step into any methods being called on the current line.
	Step Out	Shift-F11	Moves to the next line of code to be executed after the one that made the call into the current block of code.
Hex			Hexadecimal display toggle.
			Shows the various threads being executed in the source (for multithreaded apps).
	Windows submenu	Various	The main icon toggles the Breakpoints window. The drop-down icon shows the menu of all other debug windows that can be shown. More on those later in the chapter.

Breakpoints

Breakpoints are at the heart of debugging. A breakpoint is an instruction to .NET to run to a specific line in your code, and then stop and wait for you to examine the current state of the application. As the execution is paused, you can do the following:

- Examine and modify values of variables and expressions.
- Single-step through the code.
- Move into and out of methods and functions, even stepping into classes written in other CLR-compliant languages.
- Perform any number of other debugging and analysis tasks.

Setting a breakpoint

You can set a breakpoint in any window editing a .NET-compliant language, such as C# and VB.NET, by single-clicking the gray vertical bar along the left margin of the window. A red dot will appear in the left margin and the line of code will be highlighted, as shown in Figure 19-8.

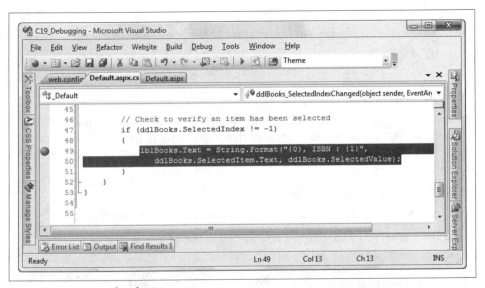

Figure 19-8. Setting a breakpoint

Breakpoints window

You can see all the breakpoints currently set by looking at the Breakpoints window. To display the Breakpoints window, perform any one of the following actions:

- Press Ctrl-Alt-B.
- Select Breakpoints from the Debug → Windows menu command.
- Click the rightmost icon of the Debug toolbar and select Breakpoints.

The Breakpoints window is shown in Figure 19-9.

You can toggle a breakpoint between Enabled and Disabled by clicking the corresponding checkbox in the Breakpoints window.

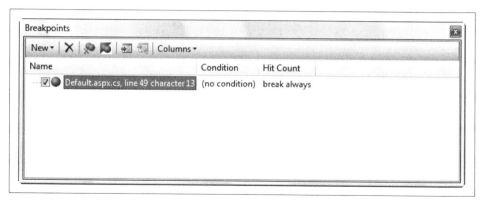

Figure 19-9. The Breakpoints window

 The Breakpoints window is not available in Visual Web Developer.

Breakpoint properties

Sometimes you don't want a breakpoint to stop execution every time the line is reached. VS2008 offers several properties that you can set to modify the behavior of a breakpoint. You can set these properties via the Property menu, arrived at in one of the following ways:

- Right-click the breakpoint glyph in the left margin.
- Open the Breakpoints window and right-click the desired breakpoint.

In the latter case, you will see the menu shown in Figure 19-10.

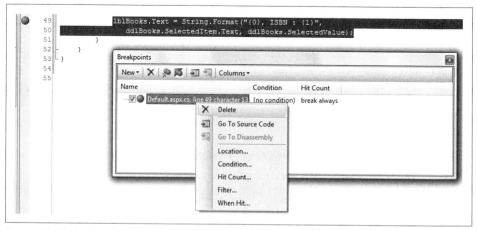

Figure 19-10. Breakpoint Properties menu

In both menus, the first option allows you to delete the selected breakpoint. If you right-clicked a breakpoint in the Code window, the second option allows you to disable it. If you right-clicked it in the Breakpoints window, the second and third options focus on and highlight the source code and disassembly code linked to the breakpoint, respectively.

After that, the menu options are the same.

Location. The Location menu item brings up the dialog box shown in Figure 19-11, which is fairly self-explanatory.

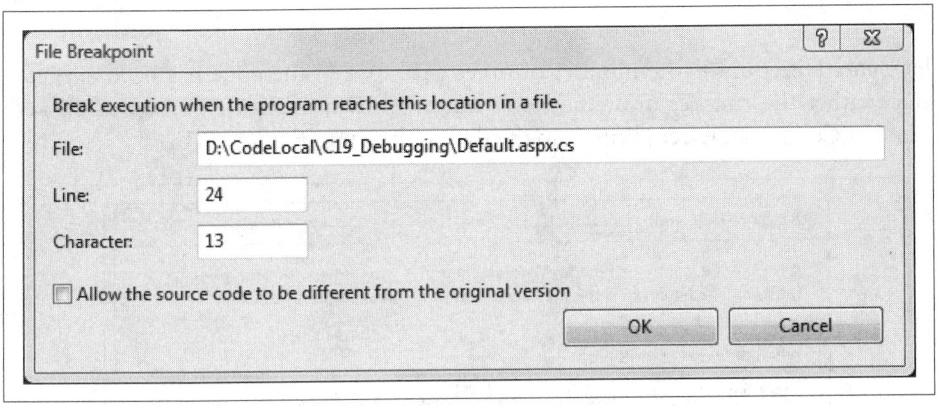

Figure 19-11. File Breakpoint dialog box

Condition. The Condition menu item brings up the dialog shown in Figure 19-12.

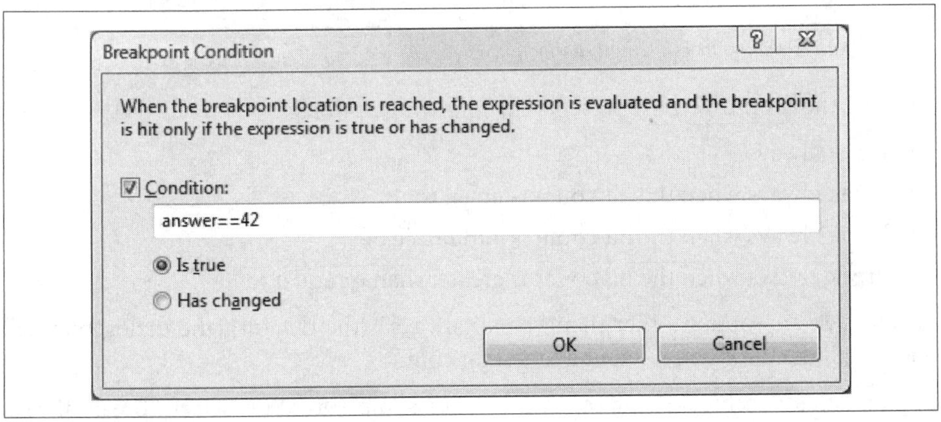

Figure 19-12. Breakpoint Condition dialog box

You can enter any valid expression in the edit field. This expression is evaluated when program execution reaches the breakpoint. Depending on which radio button is selected and how the condition expression evaluates, the program execution will either pause or move on. The two radio buttons are labeled:

Is true

If the condition entered evaluates to a Boolean true, the program will pause.

Has changed

If the condition entered has changed, the program will pause. On the first pass through the piece of code being debugged, the breakpoint will never pause execution because there is nothing to compare against. On the second and subsequent passes, the expression will have been initialized and the comparison will take place.

Hit count. Hit count is the number of times that spot in the code has been executed since either the run began or the Reset button shown in Figure 19-13 was clicked. The Hit Count menu item brings up the dialog shown in Figure 19-13.

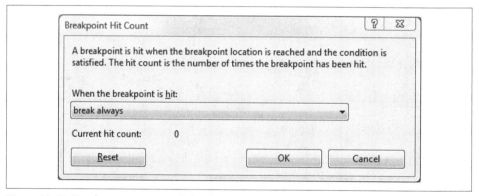

Figure 19-13. Breakpoint Hit Count dialog box

Clicking the drop-down list presents the following options:

- Break always
- Break always when the hit count is equal to
- Break always when the hit count is a multiple of
- Break always when the hit count is greater than or equal to

If you click any option other than "break always" (the default), the dialog box will add an edit field for you to enter a target hit count.

Suppose this is a breakpoint set in a loop of some sort. You select "break always when the hit count is a multiple of" and enter **5** in the edit field. The program will pause execution every fifth time it runs.

When a hit count is set, the red breakpoint icon in the left margin of the window has a plus sign in the middle of it.

Filter. Setting a breakpoint filter allows you to specify machines, processes, or threads, or any combination thereof, for which a breakpoint will be in effect. The Filter menu item brings up the dialog box shown in Figure 19-14.

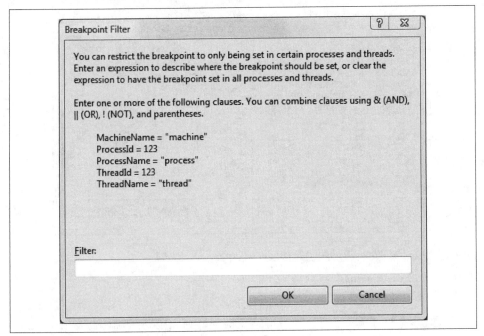

Figure 19-14. Breakpoint Filter dialog box

When Hit. The When Hit menu item brings up the dialog box shown in Figure 19-15. By default, the "Print a message" checkbox is unchecked. When this box is checked, the red circular breakpoint icon in the left margin of the window changes to a diamond shape.

You can also elect to run one of a large selection of predefined macros, such as FindCase, SaveView, and SaveBackup.

By default, the "Continue execution" checkbox is checked.

Breakpoint icons

Each breakpoint symbol, or glyph, conveys a different type of breakpoint. These glyphs appear in Table 19-4.

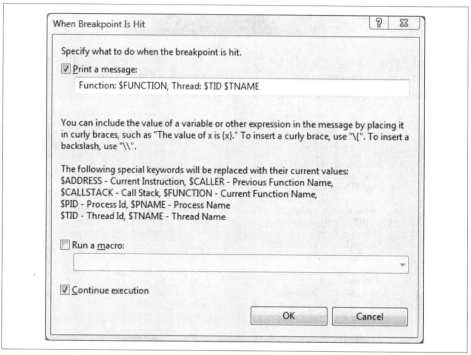

Figure 19-15. The When Breakpoint Is Hit dialog box

Table 19-4. Breakpoint icons

Icon	Type	Description
	Enabled	A normal, active breakpoint. If breakpoint conditions or hit count settings are met, execution will pause at this line.
	Disabled	Execution will not pause at this line until the breakpoint is re-enabled.
	With Condition	Execution will not pause at this line until a condition has been passed.
	Error	The location or condition of the breakpoint is not valid.
	Warning	The code at this line is not yet loaded, so a breakpoint can't be set. If the code is subsequently loaded, the breakpoint will become enabled.

Stepping Through Code

One of the most powerful techniques for debugging an application is to single-step through the code, giving you the opportunity to see the execution flow and to examine the value of variables, properties, objects, and so on. To see this in action, go to the code-behind file in the example. Place a breakpoint on the call to the Add method of the `DropDownList` control's `Items` collection, the line in the `Page_Load` method where the items are added to the `DropDownList`. Set the Hit Count to be a multiple of five (break always when the hit count is a multiple of five). Then press F5 to open *Default.aspx*.

The breakpoint will be hit, and the program will stop execution at the line of code containing the breakpoint, which will turn yellow. The breakpoint glyph in the left margin will have a yellow arrow on top of it. The VS2008 screen should look like Figure 19-16.

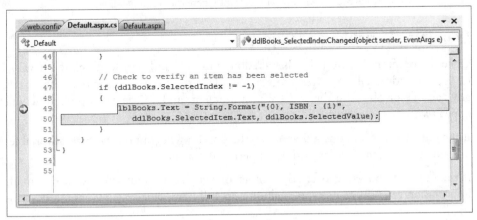

Figure 19-16. Code is highlighted when a breakpoint is hit

You can now move forward one statement or line at a time, stepping into any of the methods or functions as you go, by using one of the following techniques:

- Select the Debug → Step Into menu command.
- Click the Step Into icon (see Table 19-3 for a picture of the icon).
- Press F11.

You can step through the code without going through called functions or methods. That is, you can step over the calls rather than into the calls, using one of the following techniques:

- Select the Debug → Step Over menu item.
- Click the Step Over icon (see Table 19-3 for a picture of the icon).
- Press F10.

Finally, if you are debugging in a called method or function, you can step out of that method or function call, using one of the following techniques:

- Select the Debug → Step Out menu command.
- Click the Step Out icon (see Table 19-3 for a picture of the icon).
- Press Shift-F11.

The process of stepping through code is not limited to server-side code. You can also step through JavaScript as well (which is very handy for figuring out why your AJAX scripts aren't working as planned). To enable this, open Internet Explorer and select Tools → Options from the menu. Switch to the Advanced tab and under the group of options marked Browsing, uncheck the two boxes labeled "Disable Script Debugging (Internet Explorer)" and "Disable Script Debugging (Other)". Now when a JavaScript error occurs, you'll be given the option to break into the program flow of the page and open a Visual Studio window at the point where the script is failing.

Examining Variables and Objects

Once the program is stopped, it is incredibly intuitive and easy to examine the value of objects and variables currently in scope. Place the mouse cursor over the top of any variable or object in the code, wait a moment, and a little pop-up window will appear with its current value.

If the cursor is hovering over a variable, the pop up will contain the type of variable, its value (if relevant), and any other properties it may have.

If the cursor is hovering over some other object, the pop-up window will contain information relevant to its type, including its full namespace, syntax, and a descriptive line of help.

Debug Windows

The debug windows are optimized to show program information in a specific way. The following sections will describe each of the windows.

You can access all of the windows in one of three ways: with a shortcut key combination, from the Debug → Windows menu command, or from the Windows icon of the Debug toolbar. Table 19-5 summarizes all the windows, along with the shortcut keys for accessing each window.

Table 19-5. Accessing the debug windows

Window name	Shortcut keys	Description
Immediate	Ctrl-Alt-I	View any variable or expression.
Autos	Ctrl-Alt-V, A	View all variables in the current and previous statements.
Locals	Ctrl-Alt-V, L	View all variables in the current context.
Watch	Ctrl-Alt-W, followed by either 1, 2, 3, or 4	View up to four different sets of variables of your choosing.
Call Stack	Ctrl-Alt-C	View all methods on the call stack.
Threads	Ctrl-Alt-H	View and control threads.

Table 19-5. Accessing the debug windows (continued)

Window name	Shortcut keys	Description
Modules	Ctrl-Alt-U	View all modules in use.
Disassembly	Ctrl-Alt-D	View the current program in assembly code.
Registers	Ctrl-Alt-G	View microprocessor registers.
Memory	Ctrl-Alt-M, followed by *n*, where *n* is either 1, 2, 3, or 4	View the contents of up to four different memory addresses.

 Some of these debugging windows are not available in Visual Web Developer.

Immediate window

The Immediate window allows you to type almost any variable, property, or expression and immediately see its value.

You can enter expressions for immediate execution in the Immediate window. For instance, if the breakpoint is on the line shown in Figure 19-16, you will see the value of the string lblBooks.Text by entering either of the following lines in the Immediate window and pressing Enter:

```
?lblBooks
lblBooks
?lblBooks.Text
lblBooks.Text
```

Figure 19-17 demonstrates using ?lblBooks. When given the ID of an object, the Immediate window lists its base type, public properties, and the current values of those properties. When the given property of an object is named, the Immediate window shows the current value of that property. Figure 19-17 also shows the process of assigning a new value to lblBooks.Text. If you change the value of a variable in the Immediate window and then continue to run the program, the new value will now be in effect.

You can clear the contents of the Immediate window by right-clicking anywhere in the window and selecting Clear All. Close the window by clicking the X in the upper-right corner. If you close the window and subsequently bring it back up in the same session, it will still have all the previous contents.

Autos window

The Autos window shows all the variables used in the current statement and the previous statement displayed in a hierarchical table. For example, Figure 19-18 shows the Autos window at the point when the breakpoint on *Default.aspx* is hit.

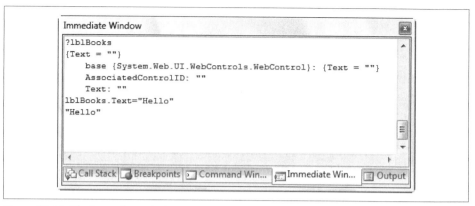

Figure 19-17. The Immediate window

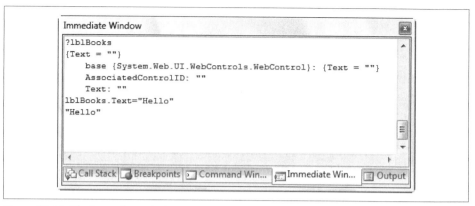

Figure 19-18. The Autos window

There are columns for the name of the object, its value, and its type. A plus sign next to an object indicates that it has child objects that are not displayed, and a minus sign indicates that its child objects are visible. Clicking a plus symbol expands the tree and shows any children, whereas clicking a minus symbol contracts the tree and displays only the parent. Values that change in the current step display in red.

You can select and edit the value of any variable. The value will display as red in the Autos window. Any changes to values take effect immediately.

Locals window

The Locals window, shown in Figure 19-19, is the same as the Autos window, except that it shows variables local to the current context. The current context is the method or function containing the current execution location.

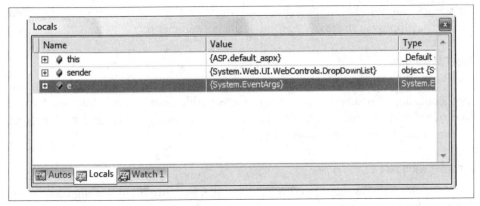

Figure 19-19. The Locals window

Watch window

The Watch window is the same as the Autos window, except that it shows only variables, properties, or expressions you enter into the Name field in the window or drag from another window. The advantage of using a Watch window is that it allows you to watch objects from several different source windows simultaneously. This overcomes the inability to add object types other than the specified type to any of the other debug windows.

In addition to typing in the name of the object you want to watch, you can also drag and drop variables, properties, or expressions from a code window. Select the object in the code you want to put in the Watch window and then drag it to the Name field in the open Watch window.

You can also drag and drop objects from any of the following windows into the Watch window:

- Locals
- Autos
- This
- Disassembly

To drag something from one of these windows to the Watch window, both the source window and the Watch window must be open. Highlight a line in the source window and drag it down over the Watch tab. The Watch window will come to the foreground. Continue dragging the object to an empty line in the Watch window.

Call Stack window

The Call Stack window displays the names of the methods on the call stack and their parameter types and values. You can control which information is displayed in the

Call Stack window by right-clicking anywhere in the window and toggling field names that appear in the lower portion of the pop-up menu.

Threads window

The Threads window allows you to examine and control threads in the program you are debugging. Threads are sequences of executable instructions. Programs can be single-threaded or multithreaded. The whole topic of threading and multiprocess programming is beyond the scope of this book.

Modules window

The Modules window allows you to examine the *.exe* and *.dll* files being used by the program being debugged. For example, as the breakpoint is hit in *Default.aspx*, Figure 19-20 shows the current state of the Modules window.

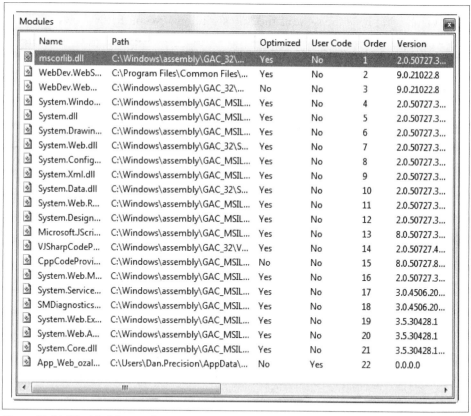

Figure 19-20. The Modules window

By default, the modules are shown in the order in which they were loaded. You can re-sort the table by clicking any of the column headers.

Disassembly window

The Disassembly window, as shown in Figure 19-21, shows the current program in assembly code. If you are debugging managed code, such as that which comes from VB.NET, C#, or Managed C++, this will correspond to Microsoft Intermediate Language (MSIL) code.

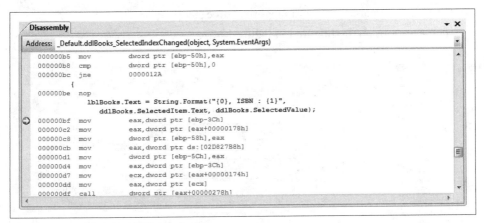

Figure 19-21. The Disassembly window

Unlike the previous windows discussed in this chapter, the Disassembly window displays as a tabbed item as part of the main work surface. You can set breakpoints anywhere in the window, just as you can for any other source code window.

Registers window

The Registers window allows you to examine the contents of the microprocessor's registers. Values that have changed recently are displayed in red.

You can select which pieces of information to view by right-clicking anywhere in the Registers window and clicking the information you would like displayed.

Memory windows

Four Memory windows are available for viewing memory dumps of large buffers, strings, and other data that will not display well in any other window. These four memory windows are for watching four different memory addresses.

Debugging ASP.NET Source Code

The actual process of debugging an application, be it web- or desktop-based, remains the same as it has in all the previous versions of Visual Studio. With VS2008, however, Microsoft has added the ability to step through the source code for the .NET Framework, providing one more avenue to explore while attempting to discover why your pages are malfunctioning.

There are three steps to enable this:

1. Open VS2008 and choose Tools → Options from the menu. In the dialog that appears, find the Debugging → General section. If it isn't apparent, check Show All Settings in the bottom-left corner first. In this section, do the following:

   • Uncheck "Enable Just My Code (Managed only)".
   • Check "Enable .NET Framework source stepping".

   These options are highlighted in Figure 19-22.

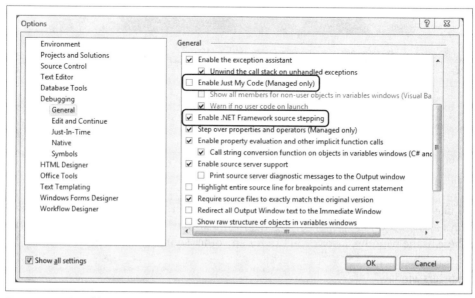

Figure 19-22. Enabling .NET source code browsing: Step 1

2. Visual Studio will prompt you for a place to download the symbols for the .NET source code, so switch to the Debugging → Symbols section.

   • Choose a local directory your account has read/write access to, where the .NET source code symbols will be downloaded to.

   Figure 19-23 shows the dialog with these options set.

3. Finally, click OK to accept the changes. A dialog will appear letting you know that the .NET symbols are being downloaded.

To demonstrate this new facility, set a breakpoint on *Default.aspx* and run the page. When the breakpoint is reached, open the Call Stack window in VS2008 (Ctrl-Alt-C).

You can now view the source code by either stepping into it from your own code or double-clicking one of the blacked-in frames on the call stack. If a frame is grayed out, right-click it and choose Load Symbols From → Microsoft Symbol Servers from

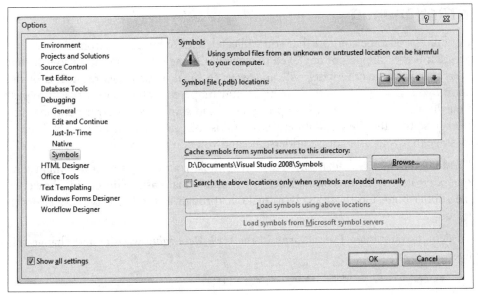

Figure 19-23. Enabling .NET source code browsing: Step 2

the menu that appears. This will load the symbols for the assembly named in the frame, and all frames in the call stack referencing that assembly will be blacked in and line numbers added.

 One caveat: at the time of this writing, some of the source code for the framework was not available, although it was planned to be. The assemblies currently available are:

- *Mscorlib.DLL*
- *System.DLL*
- *System.Data.DLL*
- *System.Drawing.DLL*
- *System.Web.DLL*
- *System.Web.Extensions.DLL*
- *System.Windows.Forms.DLL*
- *System.XML.DLL*
- WPF (*UIAutomation*.dll, System.Windows.DLL, System.Printing.DLL, System.Speech.DLL, WindowsBase.DLL, WindowsFormsIntegration. DLL, Presentation*.DLL*, and others)
- *Microsoft.VisualBasic.DLL*

Trying to load the symbols for any other assembly will result in an Open File dialog asking for the debugging symbols (*.pdb*) file related to the assembly, because it isn't available in the location you specified earlier.

Error Handling

It should be of some comfort that you will catch a lot of bugs and errors in your code before it is ever shipped or deployed to a client. On the other hand, it's also true that users, innocent or otherwise, will find ways to break your pages regardless of the efforts you make to validate their input and (imperceptibly) control their progression through your site. And it's up to you to add some level of error handling into the site so that the site does not crash or, if possible, return some cryptic .NET error message that your users don't understand and you don't get to see.

Fortunately, VS2008 will simply refuse to compile your code at all if it contains any syntax errors—violations of the rules of C# and Visual Basic. Those aside, however, the subtler bugs and those likely to make it through to the live server are errors in logic.

To demonstrate, open *Default.aspx* in the *C19_Debugging* website and change this line:

```
for (int i = 0; i < bookList.GetLength(0); i++)
```

to this:

```
for (int i = 0; i < bookList.GetLength(0) + 2; i++)
```

When this code runs, it will try to add more items to the book array than the array has space allotted for, thus causing a runtime error. This is not a subtle bug, but it serves to demonstrate how the system reacts to runtime errors. If you run the page, the error is detected straight away and a generic error page (a yellow screen of death) appears with full details of the error, as shown in Figure 19-24.

This error page is actually fairly useful to the developer or technical support person who will be trying to track down and fix any bugs. It tells you the error type, the line in the code that is the approximate error location, and a stack trace to help in tracking down how that line of code was reached.

This is great for the developer, but not something you want your users to see. Fortunately, you can control who gets to see what by setting the mode attribute of the CustomErrors element in the configuration file.

Custom Error Pages

To intercept an error in a page before it has a chance to send the generic error page to the client, you can make changes on an application-wide basis by adding error-handling settings in *web.config*, the site's configuration file. Indeed, a newly generated *web.config* file has its <customErrors> section, wherein error handling is configured and commented out, so none is configured at all.

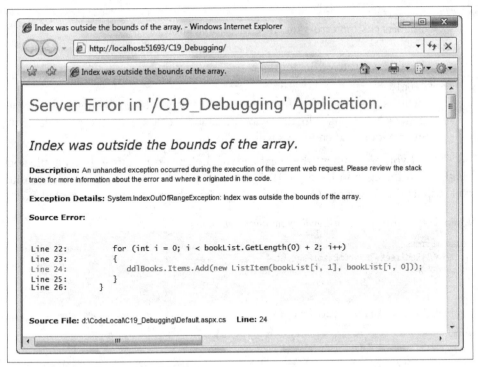

Figure 19-24. A yellow screen of death

```
<configuration>
   <system.web>
      <!--
      <customErrors mode="RemoteOnly"
         defaultRedirect="GenericErrorPage.htm">
         <error statusCode="403" redirect="NoAccess.htm" />
         <error statusCode="404" redirect="FileNotFound.htm" />
      </customErrors>
      -->
   </system.web>
</configuration>
```

There are two possible attributes for the <customErrors> section:

- defaultRedirect is a text string that contains the URL of the page to display in the case of any error not otherwise handled. Or rather, the URL for your own generic yellow screen of death. The example in *web.config* is *GenericErrorPage.htm*, which would be contained in the same application virtual root directory. If the custom error page to be displayed is not in the application virtual root, you need to include either a relative or a fully qualified URL in the defaultRedirect attribute.

- mode is an attribute that enables or disables custom error pages for the application. It can have three possible values:

On

Enables custom errors for the entire application.

Off

Disables custom errors for the entire application.

RemoteOnly

Enables custom errors for only remote clients. Local clients will see the generic error page. In this way, developers can see all the possible error information, but end-users will see the custom error page.

So, then, if you uncomment the <customErrors> element in your *web.config* file and change it to the code in Example 19-5, any unhandled errors in the sample website will redirect the browser to *CustomErrorPage.htm*, which is listed in Example 19-6.

Example 19-5. A simple error-handling tweak to web.config

```
<customErrors
    defaultRedirect="CustomErrorPage.htm"
    mode="On"
/>
```

Example 19-6. CustomErrorPage.htm

```
<html>
    <body>
        <h1>Sorry - you've got an error.</h1>
    </body>
</html>
```

If you now try to open *Default.aspx*, you'll see *CustomErrorPage.htm* in your browser, as shown in Figure 19-25, rather than the screen you saw in Figure 19-24.

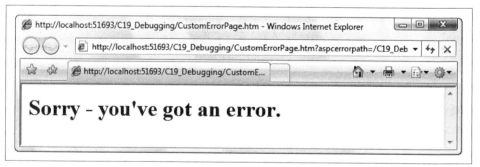

Figure 19-25. Your own custom error page

You'll want to put more information on your custom error page, such as instructions or contact information for the user, but you get the idea. Showing dynamic information about the error on the custom error page is also possible.

You can even use a different custom error page for different errors. To do this, you need to include one or more <error> subtags in the <customErrors> section of *web.config*. You might, for example, modify *web.config* to look like the following:

```
<customErrors
    defaultRedirect="CustomErrorPage.htm"
    mode="On" >

    <error statusCode="400" redirect="CustomErrorPage400.htm"/>
    <error statusCode="404" redirect="CustomErrorPage404.htm"/>
    <error statusCode="500" redirect="CustomErrorPage500.htm"/>

</customErrors>
```

If you make three copies of *CustomErrorPage.htm* and rename them to the names highlighted in the preceding code, you'll see that the 500 error page is displayed when you run *Default.aspx* again. This is because the faulty for loop generates a server error which translates into a code 500 server error according to the HTTP protocol, and so the 500 page is sent to the browser.

Fix the for loop so that *Default.aspx* loads correctly, and run the page again. Now click the link at the bottom of the page and, sure enough, the server returns a 404 "Page Not Found" error, or rather the custom error page you've just created for any 404 errors that occur (see Figure 19-26).

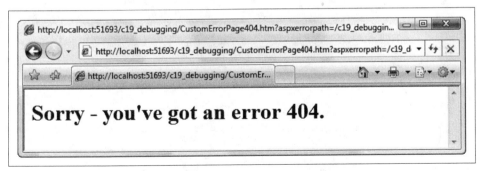

Figure 19-26. Your custom 404 error page

Be aware that you can display custom error pages only for errors generated on *your* server. So, for example, if the hyperlink had been set to a nonexistent page—say, *http://TestPage.comx* (note the intentional misspelling of the extension)—you will not see your custom error page for error 404. Instead, you'll see the error page for which the remote server or your browser is configured.

In addition to displaying a custom error page, you can add code to the Application_ OnError event handler in the *Global.asax* file to be executed every time an error occurs. We discuss application and session events, as well as the *Global.asax* file, in detail in Chapter 18. Here would be a good place to put functionality such as logging an error message, shutting down connections, cleaning up resources, and so on.

You can also override the application-level error pages for any specific page by modifying the Page directive. (Chapter 6 fully discusses Page directives.) For example, you could modify the Page directive in *Default.aspx* so that it appears as follows:

```
<%@ Page Language="C#" AutoEventWireup="true"
    CodeFile="Default.aspx.cs"
    Inherits="_Default" Trace="true"
    ErrorPage="PageSpecificErrorPage.htm" %>
```

If there is an error on this page, the *PageSpecificErrorPage.htm* page will be displayed. If there is an application-level custom error page defined in *web.config*, it will be overridden by the Page directive.

CHAPTER 20

Deployment

Perhaps one of the most useful features in Visual Studio that goes mostly unheralded is the ease with which you can deploy ASP.NET websites. Indeed, with two types of Visual Studio projects for a website—a *Web Site Project* and a *Web Application Project*—there are now even more options than before with respect to deployment. ASP.NET derives all of this deployment bliss by virtue of being part of the .NET Framework and being implemented on Visual Studio. This means that:

- If you use Web Site Projects, source code files need only be located in a specific directory (*App_Code*) to be automatically compiled and available.

- Precompiled *.dll* files only have to be located in a specific directory (*bin*) to be visible to an application.

- You don't need to register objects, either in the Registry or elsewhere, for an application to use the contents of a *.dll*. Installation does not require any registering of components with *regsrvr32* or any other utility, though globally available components may be placed in the Global Assembly Cache.

- Websites can be deployed with installer files (*.msi*) or by using XCOPY or a Web Deployment Project. You can also use Visual Studio 2008 (VS2008) to deploy your website with a single click of the Publish button.

- Websites can be updated without stopping the web server or the application.

- There are no versioning issues with conflicting *.dll* files.

- Web Application Projects can be integrated into automated builds and given pre- and post-compilation tasks.

Understand that with all the different deployment scenarios, the fundamental requirement is that you are deploying your site to a web server (or to servers in the case of a web farm) which is running Internet Information Services (IIS), as described in Chapter 18. Even if you developed the application in VS2008 using a filesystem location on a machine without IIS installed, you must deploy to a virtual directory on a server running IIS if you want your site to be visible to other users.

A warning for Vista Standard users: at the time of this writing, building Web Setup and Web Deployment projects required Visual Studio to be running with administrative privileges to succeed. Likewise, using XCOPY to deploy files to folders that are not owned by your account will also see the User Account Control (UAC) dialog pop up to get admin permission for your actions.

Assemblies

An *assembly* is the .NET unit of versioning and deploying code modules. An assembly consists of Portable Executable (PE) files. PE files can be either dynamic link library (*.dll*) files or *.exe* files. These PE files are in the same basic format as normal Windows PE files but with a slight difference; they use the PE header, but the contents are in Microsoft Intermediate Language (MSIL) rather than machine binaries.

Assemblies contain versioning information. An assembly is the minimum unit for a single version of a piece of code. Multiple versions of the same code can run side by side in different applications, with no conflicts, by packaging the different versions into separate assemblies and specifying in the configuration files which version is current.

Assemblies are *self-describing* because they contain *metadata* that fully describes the assembly and the classes, methods, and types the assemblies contain. One of the files in the assembly contains a *manifest* as part of the metadata, which details exactly what is in the assembly. This includes identification information (e.g., name, version), a list of the types and resources in the assembly, a map to connect public types with the implementing code, and a list of other assemblies referenced by this assembly.

Sites created in both Web Site Projects and Web Application Projects consist of all the files and resources in their virtual root directory and its subdirectories. One standard subdirectory is the *bin* directory. Any assemblies placed in this directory are considered *private assemblies* and are automatically made available to the application.

Another standard subdirectory within Web Site Projects only is *App_Code*. Any source code placed in this folder is automatically compiled at runtime, and the resultant private assembly is copied to the *Temporary ASP.NET Files* directory on the server and made available to the site.

Any classes generated and compiled automatically by ASP.NET before the site is up and running (such as the profile class mentioned in Chapter 14) are also saved to the *Temporary ASP.NET Files* directory (henceforth referred to as *TempAspFiles*). Whether in the site's *bin* directory or the server's *TempAspFiles* directory, the physical location of the assembly files for the site is unimportant because the CLR handles all aspects of managing these assemblies. It just works.

If an assembly file is placed in either location, all the classes contained in that assembly are automatically available to the application. No developer or user action is required for this to occur. Any class, method, or type defined in these folders or the Global Assembly Cache (described later in this chapter) is available to the rest of the application, subject to the access modifiers in Table 20-1.

Table 20-1. VB.NET and C# access modifiers

C#	VB.NET
public	Public
protected	Protected
private	Private
internal	Friend
internal protected	Protected Friend

 ASP.NET is configured to prohibit web access to the *bin* and *App_ Code* subdirectories. This prevents web users from examining or tampering with your source code or assemblies. Likewise, the *TempAspFiles* directory is not available through any website.

When the CLR loads an assembly from its disk file (a DLL) into memory, the file is not locked. This allows a new version of the file to be copied in at any time. When that happens, any web requests using the old version at that moment will run to completion on the old version. New requests will use the new version, even if the new requests come in while an old request is still running. Eventually, all requests that were using the old version will finish, and the old version of the assembly will be "unloaded"—the CLR will reclaim its memory.

The CLR constantly monitors the *bin* and *TempAspFiles* folders and the Global Assembly Cache to see whether any new assemblies have been added, or any of the existing assemblies have changed. If a new or updated source code file in *App_Code* is detected, and there is a new web request for something in that file, it will be recompiled and the resultant assembly file (a DLL) will be copied to *TempAspFiles*. If a new or updated assembly file is detected, the classes it contains are automatically available to the application. In either case, all pending requests to the old version of the assembly are allowed to complete, but all new requests are handled by the new version. When the last request to the old version is finished, the copy of that version in memory is allowed to expire and the transition is complete.

There are two broad categories of deployment: *local* and *global*:

- With local deployment, the entire application is self-contained within a virtual directory. All of the content and assemblies (described shortly) that make up the application are contained within the virtual directory and are available to this single application.
- With global deployment, assemblies are made available to every application running on the server.

Within the category of local deployment, several scenarios are available for the preparation of website files for deployment:

Automatic runtime compilation of all content and code
> This provides the most convenience and flexibility but the least security and slowest performance on first load. It is the default model used by Web Site Projects.

Manual precompilation of assemblies
> Assemblies are compiled and then placed in the *bin* or *TempAspFiles* folder. This is the compilation model for Web Application Projects and provides better performance the first time the assembly is called than automatic runtime compilation.

Full precompilation of all content and code
> This provides the best performance and security at the expense of convenience and flexibility.

Precompilation of all code only
> The content files are not precompiled, and they remain available for update after deployment. This provides nearly the performance of full precompilation, but it retains the ability to modify the content files after deployment, without a full redeploy.

Once the files are ready, four different techniques are available for their actual deployment: XCOPY, Web Deployment Project, Microsoft Installer, and the Publish Website option in VS2008. Your choice of which method to use will be driven by the requirements of your situation. We will describe all of these, with the pros and cons of each, later in this chapter.

Microsoft Intermediate Language (MSIL)

When a .NET application is compiled from C# or another .NET language into an executable file, that file does not contain machine code (the managed C++ compiler can produce assemblies containing native machine code, but this is the exception). Instead, the compiler output is in a language known as Microsoft Intermediate Language (MSIL), or IL for short. When the program is run, the .NET Framework calls a Just-In-Time (JIT) compiler to compile the IL code into machine code, which is then executed.

In theory, a program can be written in any .NET-compliant language to produce the same IL code. Though this is not always precisely true in practice (managed C++ is the exception), it is fair to say that for all practical purposes, all the .NET languages are equivalent.

The use of IL offers several advantages. First, it allows the JIT compiler to optimize the output for the platform. As of this writing, the .NET platform is supported on Windows environments running on Intel Pentium-compatible processors, and as an open source platform named Mono (*http://go-mono.org*) on some flavors of Linux. It is not a stretch to imagine the framework being ported to other operating environments, such as other flavors of Linux or Unix, the Mac OS, or other hardware platforms. Even more likely is that as new generations of processor chips become available, Microsoft could release new JIT compilers that detect the specific target processor and optimize the output accordingly. The Silverlight 2.0 platform, meanwhile, is a browser-based cross-platform subset of the .NET Framework for those who can't wait for it to be ported completely.

The second major advantage of an IL architecture is that it enables the framework to be language-neutral. To a large degree, language choice is no longer dictated by the capabilities of one language over another, but rather by the preferences of the developer or the team. You can even mix languages in a single application. A class written in C# can be derived from a VB.NET class, and an exception thrown in a C# method can be caught in a VB.NET method.

A third advantage is that the CLR analyzes the code to determine compliance with requirements such as type safety. Things like buffer overflows and unsafe casts are caught at compile time, greatly reducing maintenance headaches and security risks.

ILDASM

You can examine the contents of a compiled .NET EXE or DLL using Intermediate Language Disassembler (ILDASM), a tool provided as part of the Windows SDK for Windows Server 2008 and .NET Framework 3.5. ILDASM parses the contents of the file, displaying its contents in human-readable format. It shows the IL code, as well as namespaces, classes, methods, and interfaces.

 For details on IL programming, we recommend *Expert .NET 2.0 IL Assembler* by Serge Lidin (APress).

To access ILDASM, click Start → Programs → Microsoft Windows SDK v6.1 → Tools → IL Disassembler.

Or, you can click Start → Programs → Microsoft Visual Studio 2008 → Visual Studio Tools → Visual Studio Command Prompt. When the command prompt appears, enter **ildasm** to open the program.

Once the program is open, click File → Open to open the file you wish to look at, or drag the file from Windows Explorer onto the ILDASM window.

Alternatively, at the command prompt enter:

```
ildasm <full path>\<appname.exe>
```

where the full path (optional if the *.exe* or *.dll* is in the current directory) and name of the *.exe* or *.dll* will be given as an argument. In either case, you will get something similar to that shown in Figure 20-1. You can click the plus sign next to each node in the tree to expand that node and so drill down through the file.

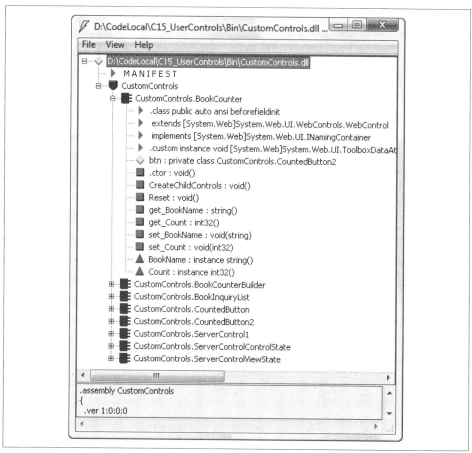

Figure 20-1. ILDASM in action

In Figure 20-1, the file being examined is *CustomControls.dll*, the assembly containing the custom controls created in Chapter 15. You can see that it has a manifest (which we will describe shortly) and it contains a class called CustomControls. BookCounter which contains several properties, fields, and methods.

The icons used in ILDASM are listed in Table 20-2. Because this is a monochrome book, the colors in which the icons are displayed are mentioned.

Table 20-2. ILDASM icons

Icon	Represents	Description
	Namespace	Blue icon with red top edge
	Class	Blue icon

Table 20-2. ILDASM icons (continued)

Icon	Represents	Description
	Interface	Blue icon with yellow letter I
	Value class	Brown icon
	Enum	Brown icon with purple letter E
	Method	Pink icon
	Static method	Pink icon with yellow letter S
	Field	Aqua icon
	Static field	Aqua icon with dark blue letter S
	Event	Green icon
	Property	Red icon
	Manifest or class info item	Red icon

Manifests

Assemblies in .NET are self-describing: they contain *metadata*, which describes the files contained in the assembly and how they relate to each other (e.g., references to types), version and security information relevant to the assembly, and dependencies on other assemblies. This metadata is contained in the assembly manifest. Each assembly must have exactly one assembly manifest.

Looking back at Figure 20-1, you can see that a manifest is in the file. Double-clicking the manifest in ILDASM will bring up a window that displays the contents of the manifest, as shown in Figure 20-2.

Looking at the manifest displayed in Figure 20-2, you can see that three external assemblies are referenced: System.Web, mscorlib, and System. All are part of the .NET Framework. This assembly itself is referred to with the following section:

```
.assembly CustomControls
```

All of these assemblies have version attributes, and the framework assemblies also have public key token attributes. We will discuss both of these attributes shortly.

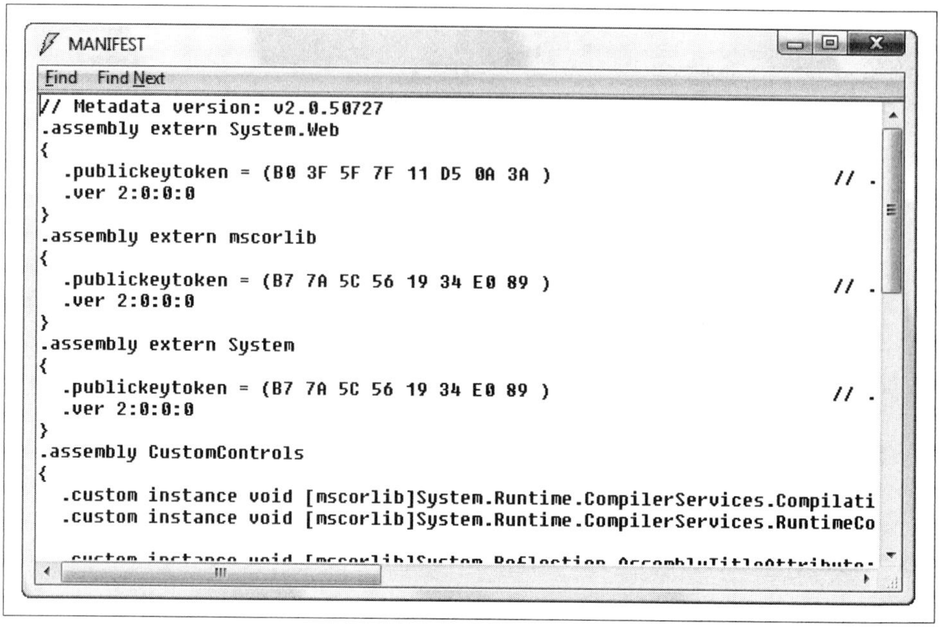

```
// Metadata version: v2.0.50727
.assembly extern System.Web
{
  .publickeytoken = (B0 3F 5F 7F 11 D5 0A 3A )              // .
  .ver 2:0:0:0
}
.assembly extern mscorlib
{
  .publickeytoken = (B7 7A 5C 56 19 34 E0 89 )              // .
  .ver 2:0:0:0
}
.assembly extern System
{
  .publickeytoken = (B7 7A 5C 56 19 34 E0 89 )              // .
  .ver 2:0:0:0
}
.assembly CustomControls
{
  .custom instance void [mscorlib]System.Runtime.CompilerServices.Compilati
  .custom instance void [mscorlib]System.Runtime.CompilerServices.RuntimeCo
  .custom instance void [mscorlib]System.Reflection.AssemblyTitleAttribute:
```

Figure 20-2. An assembly manifest

Versioning

Every assembly can have a four-part version number assigned to it, of the following form:

<major version>.<minor version>.<build number>.<revision number>

Each part of the version can have any meaning you wish to assign. There is no enforced meaning to the first number as opposed to the second, for example. The generally recommended meanings are that the major version represents a distinctly new release that may not be backward-compatible with previous versions, the minor version represents a significant feature enhancement that probably is backward-compatible, the build number represents a bug fix or patch level, and the revision number represents a specific compilation. Of course, your marketing department may have other ideas, and you are free to assign any versioning meaning you wish to the parts of the version number.

Though there is no enforced meaning to the four parts of the version number, the fact that they are ordered from most significant to least significant is used in the assembly binding process if you specify a range of versions to redirect.

Looking back at the manifest shown in Figure 20-2, every assembly has a version associated with it. For example, in that figure System.Web has the following version attribute:

```
.ver 2:0:0:0
```

This corresponds to a major version of 2, a minor version of 0, a build number of 0, and a revision number of 0.

Version numbers are part of the identity of an assembly. The CLR considers two assemblies that differ only in version number to be two distinctly different assemblies. This allows for multiple versions of the same assembly to reside side by side in the same application, not to mention on the same machine.

 Though it is possible to have side-by-side versions of the same assembly in the same application, this is rarely a good idea as a practical matter. You must go out of your way to make this work, and it can be a maintenance headache.

As you will see shortly, the CLR differentiates between two different types of assemblies: *private* (those assemblies located in the application assembly cache, described earlier) and *shared*. The CLR ignores the version number of private assemblies. Adding a version number to a private assembly is a form of self-documentation, for the benefit of people examining the source code or the manifest. However, if an assembly is shared, which we will explain in detail shortly, the CLR will be cognizant of the version and can use it to allow or disallow the assembly to load, depending on which version is called for.

In Web Site Projects, you assign versions to an assembly with assembly attributes, either at the top of your main source file or at the top of a separate source file compiled into the assembly.

Any source file that is going to include attributes must make reference to the System. Reflection namespace (unless you type in fully qualified attribute names). In C#, include the following using statement:

```
using System.Reflection;
```

The attribute, or attributes, must be at the top of the source file, after the using statements but before any class definitions. In C#, it looks something like this:

```
[assembly: AssemblyVersion("1.1.*")]
```

Version syntax in manifests uses colons to separate the numbers, and attributes in source code use periods.

The argument provided to the attribute is a string. Though the four parts of the version number have the meanings described earlier (major, minor, build, and revision), you can use any values you want. To the extent that the CLR checks the version number, it does not enforce any meaning other than to compare whether the total version number is equal to, greater than, or less than a specified value or falls within a specified range.

With that said, the framework does impose some rules, and it also provides some shortcuts for automatically generating meaningful version numbers:

- If you specify the version, you must specify at least the major revision number. That is, specifying "1" will result in version 1.0.0.0.

- You can specify all four parts of the version. If you specify fewer than four parts, the remaining parts will default to zero. For example, specifying "1.2" will result in version 1.2.0.0.

- You can specify the major and minor numbers plus an asterisk for the build. The build will then be equal to the number of days since January 1, 2000 and the revision will be equal to the number of seconds since midnight local time, divided by 2 and truncated to the nearest integer. For example, specifying "1.2.*" will result in version 1.2.1963.28933 if the file was compiled May 17, 2005 at 4:04:27 P.M.

- You can specify the major, minor, and build numbers plus an asterisk for the revision. The revision will then be equal to the number of seconds since midnight local time, divided by 2 and truncated to the nearest integer. For example, "1.2.3.*" will result in version 1.2.3.28933 if the file was compiled at 4:04:27 P.M.

In Web Application Projects, you use a file called *AssemblyInfo.cs* (or *AssemblyInfo.vb*) which is automatically added to the project when it is created. You can also use the project's Properties page to set assembly properties by clicking the Assembly Information button on the Application tab. Figure 20-3 shows the resultant dialog. The changes made there will also be saved in *AssemblyInfo.cs*.

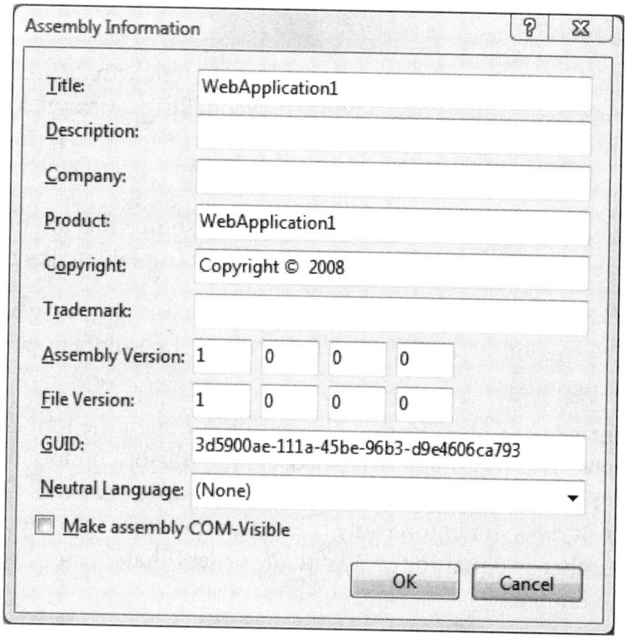

Figure 20-3. The Web Application Project Assembly Information dialog

Private Versus Shared Assemblies

Broadly speaking, there are two types of assemblies: private and shared.

- A *private* assembly is one that is used by only a single application.
- A *shared* assembly is one that can be used by more than one application.

A private assembly is located in one of two locations. If you are using full runtime compilation, where source files are located in the *App_Code* directory, the assemblies compiled from that source code and the content files will be located in a system folder somewhere on the machine, managed by the CLR. In addition, any assembly files located in the *bin* directory will be private assemblies.

Any public member (such as a method, field, or property) contained in a private assembly will be available to any application in that directory by virtue of its presence in the directory. There is no need to register the assembly with the Registry, for example, as is the case with COM.

Private assemblies make no provision for versioning. The CLR does not check the version of private assemblies, and it cannot make load decisions based on version number. From this, it follows that it is not possible to have multiple versions of the same assembly in the same directory. However, it also follows that different directories can each have their own copy of a given assembly regardless of their respective versions. Be careful with this: it is easy to find yourself with inexplicable results when more than one version of an assembly is in use at the same time.

COM allows only a single copy of a given DLL on a machine, to be used by all the applications requiring that DLL. (Support for side-by-side COM DLLs has been added to Windows XP, but this is a relatively new feature.) Back in the days when hard-disk space was a precious commodity, single copies of each DLL was a laudable, if imperfectly implemented, goal. Now, with large hard drives, it makes more sense to allow multiple copies of DLLs, one for each application that needs it. The benefits of this approach are the elimination of DLL Hell, and simplified installation and management. We will discuss the deployment ramifications of private assemblies in "Local Deployment," later in this chapter.

> *DLL Hell* is the following phenomenon: the user installs a new program (A) and suddenly a different program (B) stops working. As far as the user is concerned, A has nothing to do with B, but unbeknownst to the user, A and B share a DLL. Unfortunately, they require different versions of that same DLL. This problem goes away with .NET; each application can have its own private version of the DLL, or the application can specify which version of the DLL it requires.

In contrast, a shared assembly is one that can be made available to multiple applications on the machine. Typically, shared assemblies are located in a special area of the drive called the *Global Assembly Cache* (GAC). We'll cover the GAC in more detail shortly.

Technically, you don't need to put shared assemblies in the GAC because you can specify an alternative location with a <CodeBase> element in a configuration file.

There are often reasons for creating a shared assembly other than to share an assembly between applications. For example, to take advantage of Code Access Security (CAS), an assembly must have a strong name (described shortly), which effectively makes it shared.

Shared assemblies also eliminate DLL Hell because the version of the assembly is part of its identity. An application will use the version of the assembly it was originally compiled with, or the version specified by the version policy contained in a controlling configuration file.

Of course, nothing prevents a developer from releasing a new assembly with the same version numbers as a previous release. In this circumstance, you will have replaced DLL Hell with Assembly Hell.

Shared assemblies in the GAC offer some benefits over shared assemblies not in the GAC, and shared assemblies in general offer several benefits over private assemblies, though they are more of a bother to prepare, install, and administer. These benefits include the following:

Performance

- The CLR looks for an assembly first in the GAC and then in the application assembly cache.

- Assemblies stored in the GAC do not need to have their public key signature verified every time they are loaded, but shared assemblies not in the GAC do. However, private assemblies never have their signatures verified because they do not have a strong name (described shortly).

- The files in a shared assembly in the GAC are verified to be present and neither tampered with nor corrupted when the assembly is installed in the GAC. For shared assemblies not in the GAC, this verification step is performed every time the assembly is loaded.

Versioning

- An application, or different applications, can use different versions of the same assembly. This feature is known as side-by-side execution. Private assemblies in different application directories can be different versions.

- An application will use the same version of an assembly that it was originally compiled with unless overridden by a binding policy specified in a configuration policy.

- Applications can be redirected to use a different version of an assembly (allowing for easy updating).

Robustness

- Files cannot be deleted except by an administrator.
- All the files in a shared assembly are verified to be present and neither tampered with nor corrupted.
- The shared assembly, whether in the GAC or another location, is signed with a public key to ensure that it has not been tampered with.

Strong Names

For an assembly to be shared, it must have a strong name. A strong name uniquely identifies a particular assembly. It is composed of a concatenation of the following:

- The text name of the assembly (without any file extension)
- The version
- The culture
- A public key token

A strong name with all four parts is *fully qualified*, whereas one with fewer than all four components is *partially qualified*. If the culture is omitted, it can be specified as neutral. If the public key token is omitted, it can be specified as null.

A typical fully qualified name might look something like this:

```
myAssembly,Version=1.0.0.1,Culture=en-US,PublicKeyToken=9e9ddef18d355781
```

The public key identifies the developer or organization responsible for the assembly. Functionally, it replaces the role of Globally Unique Identifiers (GUIDs) in COM, guaranteeing the uniqueness of the name. It is the public half of a public key encryption scheme. The token listed as part of the strong name is a hash of the public key.

A public key encryption scheme, also called *asymmetric encryption*, relies on two numbers: a public key and a private key. They are mathematically related in such a way that if one key is used to encrypt a message, that message can be decrypted only by the other key, and vice versa. Furthermore, it is computationally infeasible, though possible, to determine one key given only the other. (Given enough time with a supercomputer, any encryption scheme can be broken.)

Many algorithms are available for calculating hashes. The only two directly supported by the .NET Framework at this time are the MD5 and SHA-1 algorithms. The algorithm used for an assembly is indicated in the manifest by the keywords .hash algorithm, followed by 0x00008003 for MD5 or 0x00008004 for SHA-1.

The general principle is this: you generate a pair of keys, one of which you designate as private and one as public. You keep your private key very safe and very secret.

A hash code is generated for the assembly using the specified encryption algorithm, commonly SHA-1. That hash code is then encrypted using RSA encryption and the private key. The encrypted hash code is embedded in the assembly manifest along with the public key. (The spaces where the encrypted hash code and the public key will go in the manifest are set to zeros before the encryption and are taken into account by the encryption program.)

The CLR decrypts the hash code included in the manifest using the public key. The CLR also uses the algorithm indicated in the manifest, again typically SHA-1, to hash the assembly. The decrypted hash code is compared to the just-generated hash code. If they match, the CLR can be sure the assembly has not been altered since it was signed.

Creating a strong name

Two steps are required to generate a strong name for an assembly.

The first step is to create the public/private pair of keys. The .NET Framework provides a command-line tool for this purpose, *sn.exe*. Generate a pair of keys by executing sn with the -k option and the name of the file to hold the keys:

```
sn -k KeyPair.snk
```

 The options passed to *sn.exe* are case-sensitive.

Save this file and guard it carefully if you are going to use the keys to provide proof of origin. Make a copy and put it in a secure place, such as a safe deposit box. (If you are using the keys for testing purposes or as a guaranteed unique identifier, there is no need for this level of security.) This file contains the private key which you should use for all the assemblies created by your organization.

In a large organization where it is not feasible for all the developers to have access to the private key, you can use a procedure known as *delayed signing*. We will explain this in the next section.

The second step is to compile the source code, including the key file, into an assembly. We will cover the specifics of doing so shortly, in "Local Deployment." For now, note the name and location of the key file for use in that process.

Delayed signing

As we mentioned, the private key must be a closely guarded item. However, this presents a quandary: access to the private key is necessary to create a strong name for an assembly. Creating a strong name is necessary to develop and test a shared assembly. Yet it may be imprudent to provide the firm's private key to all the developers working on the project who legitimately need to create strong names.

To get around this quandary, you can use *delayed signing*, sometimes called *partial signing*. In this scenario, you create the strong-named assembly using only the public key, which is safe to disseminate to anybody who wants it. You do all your development and testing. Then when you are ready to do the final build, you sign it properly with both the private and public keys.

The first step in delayed signing is to extract the public key from the key file, which contains both the private and public keys. This is done from the command line using the sn tool again, passing it the -p option, the name of the key file, and the name of a file to hold the public key. In the following command, only the public key is contained in *PublicKey.snk*:

```
sn -p KeyPair.snk PublicKey.snk
```

During the publish process, described shortly, you can check the Delay Signing checkbox and include the key file with only the public key.

Local Deployment

Strictly speaking, all you need to do to deploy most .NET applications, including ASP.NET, is to copy the new files to the proper directories on the proper machine, overwriting any previous versions of files if they exist. This is referred to as *XCOPY deployment*.

XCOPY deployment is so simple as to cause experienced developers to ask, "Is that all there is to it?" It provides all the deployment benefits of .NET except for the ability to deploy assemblies globally (i.e., to use application code modules for multiple applications) and to precompile the application. To implement globally available code modules, you will use global deployment, described later in this section. We will cover precompilation scenarios of local deployment shortly.

 XCOPY is a command-prompt command that originated in the DOS days and has been enhanced for use in modern networks. It is used to copy files and directories from one location to another. The basic syntax is:

```
XCOPY source destination switches
```

Both source and destination can be either filenames or directories. There is full support for wildcards. A multitude of switches are available that control such things as resetting (or not) the archive bit, copying (or not) any empty subdirectories, controlling the screen display during copying, and copying (or not) security information about the files. For a full list of the switches available, go to a command prompt and enter:

```
XCOPY /?
```

All command-prompt commands (known colloquially as DOS commands, though DOS is no more) are case-insensitive, unless otherwise noted.

You can, of course, copy the files in any manner you wish, including dragging and dropping in Windows Explorer or FTP over the Internet. It is called XCOPY deployment to convey the essential fact that all that is required for deployment is to copy the application virtual root and all its subdirectories.

The CLR automatically handles any changes to application files seamlessly and invisibly to the user. If the *Global.asax* or *web.config* file changes, the application will be automatically restarted. If a page, web service, or custom or user control file changes, the next request to come in to the application will get the new version. If an assembly file changes, the CLR will handle the transition from the old version to the new one for any pending requests. It doesn't get much easier than this.

Because all the files necessary to the application are contained within the application virtual root and its child directories, this implies that if two different applications on a server use a *.dll* of the same name, they will be two independent copies of the file. They may be identical copies, but they don't have to be. It is possible to have two or more different versions of a *.dll* on the same machine, each in its own application directory structure, with no conflict between applications. This relegates DLL Hell to something that old programmers will tell war stories about, like 64 KB boundaries or running out of conventional memory in DOS.

Within the category of local deployment, several scenarios are available, as discussed in the next several sections. You can use .NET's full compilation of all content and code at runtime, you can compile the assemblies manually, and you can completely precompile all the content and code, or just the code.

Full Runtime Compilation

Compiling all the content and code at runtime is the easiest and most convenient way to compile applications, because no work is required on the part of the developer other than to place any source code files requiring compilation in the *App_Code* directory under the application root.

This is how Web Site Projects operate in VS2008. When you right-click a site's root directory in the Solution Explorer, you will see a menu item for adding a folder. One of the choices is *App_Code*. Further, if you attempt to add a class file to a web application, you will be prompted to place it in the *App_Code* directory. You can decline and place it wherever you wish, but VS2008 tries to guide you to this approach.

If a source file is located outside the *App_Code* directory, you will have to take active steps to compile the file and make the resultant assembly available to the app, using one of three scenarios described here.

Full runtime compilation is independent of VS2008. Even if you create all the application files in Notepad, as long as the source files are in the *App_Code* directory under the application virtual root, they will be compiled by the CLR at runtime.

The big advantage to this technique is convenience and automatic synchronicity between content and code files. If you have to remember to do a complete recompile before deploying, it is possible for deployment errors to slip in.

There are two downsides to this compilation scenario:

Performance

A page or class is not compiled until it is first called. The lag time on first call is noticeable, sometimes significant, but it occurs only the first time a page or class is called. There is no performance penalty after the first hit because the compiled assemblies are cached on the server and are immediately available on subsequent calls.

Security

Deploying an app in this manner means the source code and content files are all present on the server as plain text files. Though ASP.NET and IIS are configured to prohibit access to these files, there is always the possibility that a hacker might penetrate security and gain access to the server's filesystem (or that a disgruntled or unscrupulous employee will steal or corrupt the code). In a hosting scenario, where your website is hosted by a commercial hosting service, your source files will be available for any prying eyes with sufficient access rights.

Manual Compilation of Assemblies

In Web Application Projects, any class files in the project, or indeed any class library projects included in the solution and referenced by the web application, will be compiled, added to the site's *bin* folder, and automatically made available to the application. The key is that they must be manually compiled first either in Visual Studio or by using the command-line compiler, as described shortly. If you choose to use Visual Studio, once they are compiled, you can right-click the project's root folder in the Solution Explorer and click Publish to quickly copy the site to the desired location. The Publish Web dialog shown in Figure 20-4 allows you to copy the site locally or to enter an FTP or HTTP URL to deploy to a remote server.

Aside from the inconvenience of manual compilation (which you can automate with batch files, a make system, or MSBuild), this approach provides good performance and security (at least for the compiled source code files; the content files are still present in plain text). In some cases, such as when using custom configuration sections (covered in Chapter 19), having a manually compiled assembly is a requirement.

To compile a class file manually, go to Start → All Programs → Microsoft Visual Studio 2008 → Visual Studio Tools → Visual Studio 2008 Command Prompt, to open a command prompt window.

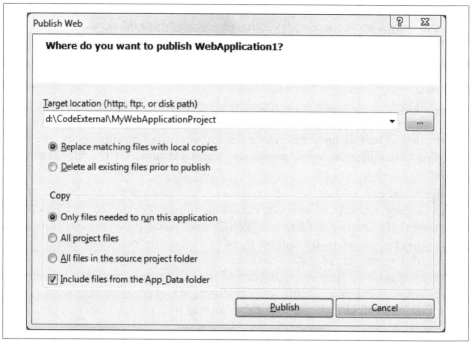

Figure 20-4. The Web Application Project Publish Web dialog

Change the current directory of the command window to be the directory containing the source file. The command to do this looks something like this:

```
cd \websites\MyWebApp
```

The generic syntax for the C# compiler is:

```
csc [parameters] inputFile.ext
```

For example, the following command (the command is wrapped here for readability; in reality, it would be on a single line) will output an assembly file called *MyClasses.dll* in the *bin* directory, using *\websites\MyWebApp\MyClasses.cs* as the input source code file:

```
csc /out:bin\MyClasses.dll /t:library
    /r:system.dll,system.web.dll,MyClasses.cs
```

The command-line compiler has a large number of parameters available to it, three of which are used here. To see the complete list of parameters available, enter the following command at the command prompt:

```
csc /?
```

Table 20-3 lists the parameters used in the preceding command lines.

Table 20-3. C# compiler parameters

Parameter	Short form	Description
/out:*<filename>*		Output filename. If not specified, the output filename will be derived from the first source file.
/target:*<type>*	/t:*<type>*	Specifies the type of file to build. Possible values are library, exe, winexe, and module.
/reference:*<file list>*	/r:*<file list>*	References the specified assembly files. If more than one file exists, include either multiple reference parameters or separate filenames with commas within a single reference parameter. Do not include any spaces between filenames.

Full Precompilation

If you're using a Web Site Project rather than a Web Application Project and you do not want to subject the website users to any compilation delay the first time a page or class is hit, you can precompile the entire site, including the content files. This allows you to deploy only compiled assembly files, which will have no delay the first time they are called and will keep them resistant to prying eyes. No plain text source code files will be deployed.

> For greater security, you can obfuscate the compiled assemblies to make them more difficult to decompile and reverse-engineer. An obfuscator, called the Dotfuscator Community Edition, is included with VS2008 under the Tools menu. It is an option in the VS2008 installer, though, so if you can't see it, check to see whether it is installed.

You can accomplish this full precompile from the command line using the *aspnet_compiler.exe* utility. However, the easier way to do it in VS2008 is by right-clicking the Web Site Project in the Solution Explorer and choosing Publish Web Site. This integrates in the MSBuild build engine.

After clicking that command, you will get the dialog box shown in Figure 20-5. The default target location, if you're using a File System location, will be a folder called *PrecompiledWeb* under the VS2008 project file location. You can enter an FTP or HTTP URL to deploy to a remote server.

For a full precompile with maximum security, that is, including the content files, uncheck the checkbox labeled "Allow this precompiled site to be updatable."

To use strong names with a key file, as described previously, check the checkbox labeled "Enable strong naming on precompiled assemblies" and enter or browse to the key file location. There is a checkbox to implement Delay signing as described earlier. The Key container controls allow you to use RSA Key Containers (a topic beyond the scope of this book) rather than a key file.

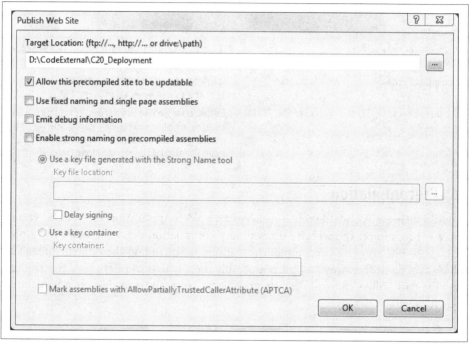

Figure 20-5. The Web Site Project: Publish Web Site dialog box

The result of this precompile will be a directory structure, suitable for XCOPY deployment to a production server, in the location specified in the dialog box. In that directory structure will be a *bin* directory containing all the compiled *.dll*s, plus compiled versions of the content files. The content files will not be present, although stub files named identically to the original content files will be there. These stub files provide a target for browser requests but are used only to redirect the request to the compiled version in the *bin* directory.

If you want to make any changes to any file, you must do so in VS2008 and recompile.

Precompilation of Code Only

Even though the full recompile is often what you need, sometimes you want the flexibility to make minor modifications to the content files after they have been deployed, without the hassle of a full recompile and redeploy. In this case, check the checkbox in Figure 20-5 labeled "Allow this precompiled site to be updatable."

The result will be the same as with a full precompile, except that the content files will be the original version rather than stub versions. These content files can be edited after deployment, and those changes will take effect with any subsequent requests, transparently to any users of the site.

Global Deployment

In the preceding section, we stated that most applications are deployed by copying files to the proper directory. The exception occurs when you wish to use the same assembly in more than one application. In this case, you use *global deployment*.

There are many scenarios in which you might want to have a common assembly file accessible to multiple applications. A firm might have two different websites on a server, both providing access to the same database. One website is free of charge and open to the public, but is of limited functionality; the other is fully functional, requiring a paid subscription. Because both sites access the same database, they will have common database query routines. They may also have common login routines. Using the same assembly to contain those common routines will enhance maintainability. Another scenario might be a web-hosting firm that has many websites running on a server. It may want to offer some functionality to all of its client websites. Encapsulating this functionality in a globally available assembly would make this easy to offer and maintain.

Another consideration is versioning. When assemblies are local to an application, each application can have its own version of common assemblies. The .NET Framework allows for global assemblies to have multiple versions. Each application making use of the global assembly can either specify the version it wants to use or take the latest version. By specifying the version, an application will not break if a newer version of the assembly introduces signature changes or bugs.

To provide global availability of an assembly, it must be installed to the GAC. The GAC is a machine-wide location for code to be shared among multiple applications on that machine. Typically, it is physically located at *C:\windows\assembly*.

To make an assembly file suitable for inclusion in the GAC, it must have assembly information compiled into it. You can do this using Assembly attributes. These Assembly attributes either can be included in the same source code file as the class or classes being compiled into the assembly, or can be in a separate source code file that is compiled into the assembly along with the class source code file(s). The format of the Assembly attributes looks like this:

```
[Assembly:attributeName(attributeValue)]
```

attributeName is the name of the Assembly attribute, and *attributeValue* is the string value assigned to the attribute. So, for example, if you're assigning the AssemblyVersionAttribute, it would look like the following:

```
[Assembly: AssemblyVersionAttribute ("1.0.3.101")]
```

Table 20-4 lists the available Assembly attributes with a brief description.

Table 20-4. Assembly attributes

Attribute	Description
AssemblyAlgorithmIdAttribute	Sets the hash algorithm for the files in the assembly.
AssemblyCompanyAttribute	A string containing the company name.
AssemblyConfigurationAttribute	A string configuration, such as Retail or Debug. Not used by the CLR.
AssemblyCopyrightAttribute	A string containing copyright information.
AssemblyCultureAttribute	A field indicating the culture supported by the assembly.
AssemblyDefaultAliasAttribute	A string containing the default alias for the assembly. It can contain a friendly name.
AssemblyDelaySignAttribute	A Boolean indicating delayed application of the digital signature.
AssemblyDescriptionAttribute	A string containing a short description of the assembly.
AssemblyFileVersionAttribute	A string containing the Win32 file version number. Defaults to the assembly version.
AssemblyFlagsAttribute	A flag indicating the kind of side-by-side execution allowed.
AssemblyInformationalVersionAttribute	A string containing version information not used by the CLR.
AssemblyKeyFileAttribute	A string containing the name of the file with either a public key signature if using delayed signing, or both public and private keys. The filename is relative to the output file path and not to the source file path.
AssemblyKeyNameAttribute	A string containing the key container.
AssemblyName	A string containing an assembly's unique name.
AssemblyNameProxy	A string containing a version of the assembly's unique name that can be used to access it remotely.
AssemblyProductAttribute	A string containing product information.
AssemblyTitleAttribute	A string containing the friendly name for the assembly.
AssemblyTrademarkAttribute	A string containing trademark information.
AssemblyVersionAttribute	A numeric version representation, in the form *major.minor. build.revision*.

If you are using Assembly attributes in a source file, you must reference the System. Reflection namespace with the using keyword in C#. If you're using AssemblyAlgorithmIdAttribute, you must also include System.Configuration. Assemblies.

For an assembly to be included in the GAC, it must have a strong name.

Once all of this is in place, you can drag the assembly file into *C:\windows\assembly* using Windows Explorer to add the assembly to the GAC, or you can use *GacUtil.exe*. The syntax is:

```
gacutil /i pathToDLL\myDLL.DLL
```

where *pathToDLL* is the path to the directory containing the assembly file, and *myDLL.DLL* is the name of the assembly file.

The *GacUtil.exe* utility has several command-line switches. For a complete list, enter the following at a command prompt:

```
gacutil /?
```

Some of the more commonly used switches are described in Table 20-5.

Table 20-5. Some common GacUtil.exe switches

Switch	Description
/i	Installs an assembly to the GAC.
/u	Uninstalls an assembly from the GAC. If the name of the assembly to be uninstalled has no qualifying information, such as version, all assemblies of that name will be uninstalled.
/l	Lists all the assemblies installed in the GAC.

To use a global assembly in applications, it must be registered in the *machine.config* file or the machine-level *web.config* file. To add the preceding assembly to the configuration file, add the following line to the `<configuration><system.web><compilation>` `<assemblies>` section:

```
<add assembly="myDLL, Version=1.0.3.101, Culture=neutral,
    PublicKeyToken=nnnnnnnn"/ >
```

where *nnnnnnnn* is obtained from *GacUtil* by running:

```
gacutil /l
```

from the command line, finding `myDLL` in the listing, and copying the public key token into place.

Windows Installer

XCOPY deployment works well for many websites. However, it falls short in some situations. For example, XCOPY does not automate the installation of assemblies into the GAC, nor does it make Registry edits. Further, if you need to install to multiple servers, such as a web farm, or if you have a precisely scripted and repeatable installation process, XCOPY may get tedious and error-prone. For all of these scenarios, you need an installation tool with more robust capabilities. Several third-party installation tools are available, such as InstallShield, InstallAnywhere, and Wise.

Windows has its own installation technology, known as Windows Installer, which has been included with all of the Windows operating systems starting with Windows 2000.

Windows Installer provides installation, removal, and management of applications. It also supports features such as automatic repair of existing installations, transactional operations (a set of operations performed by the installer can be undone if installation does not complete successfully), installation on demand (application features are not installed until the first time a user tries to use that feature), and installation in locked-down environments if an administrator approves an installation package by means of Group Policy.

The Windows Installer is based on a database. Each application to be installed has a file associated with it, with an extension of *.msi*, which contains the data for that application, including rules for controlling the installation.

You can open an *.msi* file in several ways. Double-clicking the file will open the Windows Installer for that application. If the application is not currently installed on the machine, you will be presented with a series of dialog boxes for installing the application. Depending on how the installation package was customized (described shortly), these dialogs will allow the user to select a target destination, offer installation for the current user or all users, present software license information, and so on.

If the application is already installed on the machine, you will be presented with a dialog box offering the choice to repair or remove the installation.

If you right-click an *.msi* file in Windows Explorer, the context menu will include three relevant menu items: Install, Repair, and Uninstall. These options perform the same operations you might access by double-clicking the file.

 You can execute the Windows Installer from a command prompt. To install an application, use the following command:

```
msiexec /i MyApp.msi
```

To uninstall the app, use the following command:

```
msiexec /x MyApp.msi
```

To repair an installation, use this line:

```
msiexec /f MyApp.msi
```

Interestingly, *msiexec.exe* is one of the few command-line tools provided by Microsoft that does not display a list of parameters when executed with the */?* switch. However, executing the command with no command-line switches will bring up a dialog box with a list of all the command-line switches.

Probably the easiest way to run the Installer is to execute *setup.exe*, the Installer Bootstrapper, which VS2008 creates in a process that we will describe shortly. Do so by double-clicking the file in Windows Explorer.

The Windows Installer automatically logs installations and removals in the Application Log of the Event Viewer found in Control Panel → Administrative Tools. Each entry in the log will have the MsiInstaller as the value for Source.

The Windows Installer is integrated into VS2008. You create installation packages for your application by adding one or more setup projects to the web application. By having more than one setup project as part of an application, you can easily deploy the same application with different configurations.

VS2008 uses MSBuild, the Microsoft build engine, to perform the builds that get packaged into the *.msi* files. You can create powerful and flexible MSBuild projects. MSBuild is also available outside VS2008, from the command line, with the *MSBuild.exe* utility. Going into all the detail of MSBuild is beyond the scope of this book.

To demonstrate using VS2008 to build deployment packages, you will first create a three-page Web Site Project called *C20_Deployment*, with the pages named *Default.aspx*, *FirstPage.aspx*, and *SecondPage.aspx*. Each page will consist of two buttons to navigate to the other two pages. In addition, you will create a class file, *Class1.cs*, in the *App_Code* directory, which will have a single static public method called GetTime that returns a string representing the current time.

All three content files along with their associated code-behind files and the class file are listed in Examples 20-1 through 20-7. (You might want to download these code examples from *http://www.oreilly.com*, because the code itself is not the focus of this section, but rather how to deploy the code.)

Example 20-1. C20_Deployment\Default.aspx

```
<%@ Page Language="C#" AutoEventWireup="true"
    CodeFile="Default.aspx.cs" Inherits="_Default" %>

<!DOCTYPE html PUBLIC "-//W3C//DTD XHTML 1.0 Transitional//EN"
    "http://www.w3.org/TR/xhtml1/DTD/xhtml1-transitional.dtd">
<html xmlns="http://www.w3.org/1999/xhtml">
<head runat="server">
    <title>Deployment Example</title>
</head>
<body>
    <form id="form1" runat="server">
    <div>
        <h1>Deployment Example</h1>
        <h2>Home Page</h2>
        <asp:Label ID="lblTime" runat="server" />
        <br />
        <asp:Button ID="btn1stPage" runat="server"
            Text="Go To First Page" OnClick="btn1stPage_Click" />
        <asp:Button ID="btn2ndPage" runat="server"
            Text="Go To Second Page" OnClick="btn2ndPage_Click" />
    </div>
    </form>
</body>
</html>
```

Example 20-2. C20_Deployment\Default.aspx.cs

```
using System;
using System.Web.UI;

public partial class _Default : Page
{
    protected void Page_Load(object sender, EventArgs e)
```

Example 20-2. C20_Deployment\Default.aspx.cs (continued)

```
   {
      lblTime.Text = Class1.GetTime( );
   }

   protected void btn1stPage_Click(object sender, EventArgs e)
   {
      Response.Redirect("FirstPage.aspx");
   }

   protected void btn2ndPage_Click(object sender, EventArgs e)
   {
      Response.Redirect("SecondPage.aspx");
   }
}
```

Example 20-3. C20_Deployment\FirstPage.aspx

```
<%@ Page Language="C#" AutoEventWireup="true"
   CodeFile="FirstPage.aspx.cs" Inherits="FirstPage" %>

<!DOCTYPE html PUBLIC "-//W3C//DTD XHTML 1.0 Transitional//EN"
   "http://www.w3.org/TR/xhtml1/DTD/xhtml1-transitional.dtd">
<html xmlns="http://www.w3.org/1999/xhtml">
<head runat="server">
   <title>Deployment Example</title>
</head>
<body>
   <form id="form1" runat="server">
   <div>
      <h1>Deployment Example</h1>
      <h2>First Page</h2>
      <asp:Button ID="btnHomePage" runat="server"
         Text="Go To Home Page" OnClick="btnHomePage_Click" />
      <asp:Button ID="btn2ndPage" runat="server"
         Text="Go To Second Page" OnClick="btn2ndPage_Click" />
   </div>
   </form>
</body>
</html>
```

Example 20-4. C20_Deployment\FirstPage.aspx.cs

```
using System;
using System.Web.UI;

public partial class FirstPage : Page
{
   protected void btnHomePage_Click(object sender, EventArgs e)
   {
      Response.Redirect("Default.aspx");
   }
```

Example 20-4. C20_Deployment\FirstPage.aspx.cs (continued)

```
    protected void btn2ndPage_Click(object sender, EventArgs e)
    {
        Response.Redirect("SecondPage.aspx");
    }

}
```

Example 20-5. C20_Deployment\SecondPage.aspx

```
<%@ Page Language="C#" AutoEventWireup="true"
    CodeFile="SecondPage.aspx.cs" Inherits="SecondPage" %>

<!DOCTYPE html PUBLIC "-//W3C//DTD XHTML 1.0 Transitional//EN"
    "http://www.w3.org/TR/xhtml1/DTD/xhtml1-transitional.dtd">
<html xmlns="http://www.w3.org/1999/xhtml">
<head runat="server">
    <title>Deployment Example</title>
</head>
<body>
    <form id="form1" runat="server">
    <div>
        <h1>Deployment Example</h1>
        <h2>Second Page</h2>
        <asp:Button ID="btnHomePage" runat="server"
            Text="Go To Home Page" OnClick="btnHomePage_Click" />
        <asp:Button ID="btn1stPage" runat="server"
            Text="Go To First Page" OnClick="btn1stPage_Click" />
    </div>
    </form>
</body>
</html>
```

Example 20-6. C20_Deployment\SecondPage.aspx.cs

```
using System;
using System.Web.UI;

public partial class SecondPage : Page
{
    protected void btnHomePage_Click(object sender, EventArgs e)
    {
        Response.Redirect("default.aspx");
    }

    protected void btn1stPage_Click(object sender, EventArgs e)
    {
        Response.Redirect("FirstPage.aspx");
    }

}
```

Example 20-7. C20_Deployment\App_Code\Class1.cs

```
using System;

public class Class1
{
    public static string GetTime()
    {
        return DateTime.Now.ToLongTimeString();
    }
}
```

Build Configurations

By default, websites created in VS2008 are configured not to enable debugging. As soon as you press F5, however, you will be prompted to run them in debug mode so that if any unhandled errors occur, the user will automatically be brought into the debugger. The price for being in debug mode is reduced performance.

You can configure a website to disable debugging. In this mode, all breakpoints will be ignored and any unhandled errors will result in an error page being displayed to the user. The nondebug (release) mode is more performant than the debug mode and is typically used when a web application is deployed.

You can select debug or nondebug mode with an entry in the <compilation> element in *web.config*. (We covered configuration in Chapter 18.) You can configure this by manually editing *web.config* or by running the Web Site Administration Tool (WAT).

To edit the file manually, set the debug attribute of the <compilation> tag to true or false, as in the following code snippet:

```
<compilation debug="true" />
```

To use the WAT, click the Website → ASP.NET Configuration menu item. When the tool opens, click the Application tab, then the "Configure debugging and tracing" link. On that page, check or uncheck the "Enable debugging" checkbox. Doing so will automatically make the correct entry in *web.config*.

> Visual Studio provides two default build configurations for Web Application Projects: Debug and Release. A Release build produces different, smaller binaries than a Debug build. You can run either with Debug=true in *web.config*. A Release-mode application can still have breakpoints on method exits and possibly other places, but not on individual lines of code.
>
> Web Site Projects have only one build configuration by default: Debug.

Adding a Setup Project with the Setup Wizard

You are now ready to add a project to the website that will take advantage of the Setup Wizard to walk you through the steps of creating an installation package. This installation package will install a version of the application with the debug mode set to the value currently indicated in *web.config*, as described in the preceding section. For this example, verify that debug mode is set to true.

With the website root directory highlighted in the Solution Explorer click the File → Add → New Project menu item. From the tree view on the left, select Setup and Deployment under Other Project Types. From the list on the right, select Setup Wizard. Name the project Setup-Debug and leave the default location. The dialog box will look something like that shown in Figure 20-6.

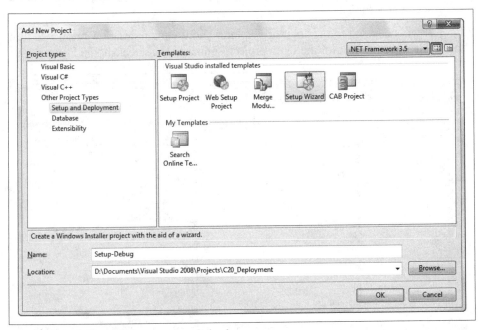

Figure 20-6. The Setup Wizard project dialog box

By using the default location, you ensure that the setup project will be located in its own folder under the root location for all your project files (set using Tools → Options). You might want to consider changing the location of this setup project to be in a subdirectory of the project it is setting up.

The wizard will take you through five screens:

- The first is a splash screen.
- The second screen asks you to choose a Project Type. Select "Create a setup for a web application."
- The third screen asks you to select the outputs from all the projects in the solution. Check the only checkbox available, next to "Content Files from C:\ <*directory*>\C20_Deployment." (Your directory structure may be different from those shown here.) Click the Next button.
- The fourth screen allows you to include other files, such as READMEs, of which there are none.
- The fifth and final screen displays a summary of all the settings for this setup project. Click Finish.

A project will be added to the Solution Explorer and the main design window will now show a File System editor for the setup project, similar to the screenshot in Figure 20-7.

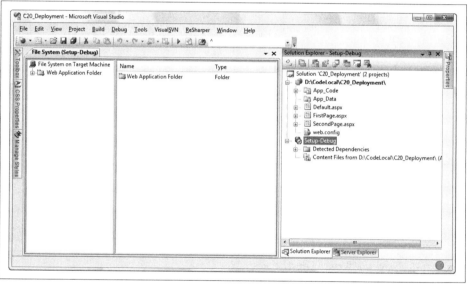

Figure 20-7. The Setup Project, open in VS2008

Build the setup project by right-clicking the project name in the Solution Explorer and selecting the Build menu item.

Build will build the application, taking all dependencies into account but not building any components that are up-to-date. In a large solution where current development work is being done on only one or two projects, it makes for a faster build process.

The Rebuild menu item first deletes all intermediary files and previous build outputs and then builds the entire app from scratch. It may take longer, but it is smart to do a rebuild before testing the final build.

You can open the Output window to view a log of the build process by clicking View →
Other Windows → Output. At the end of the build process, it should say:

```
Build: 2 succeeded or up-to-date, 0 failed, 0 skipped
```

The number 2 refers to the two projects in this application, that is, the Web Site
Project and the setup project.

Two files are created by this build process, which actually need to be deployed:
setup.exe and *Setup-Debug.msi*. Copying these files to the deployment target (the
server) and double-clicking the setup file will cause the contents of the *.msi* file to be
installed on the local machine.

The output files from the build process will be located in the *Setup-Debug* directory
created for the Setup-Debug project. This will contain a *.vdproj* file which contains
information VS2008 uses to properly handle the project, and two other subdirectories: *Debug* and *Release*. These folder names correspond to the two possible build
configurations for the setup project. The deployment output files, *setup.exe* and
Setup-Debug.msi, will be contained in the folder called *Debug*, because that is the
name of the current active build configuration. When you switch the current build
configuration to Release (using Build → Configuration Manager), the files will be
saved in the *Release* folder.

Adding a Setup Project Manually

You can create a setup project manually without using the Setup Wizard. This gets
you to the same place as using the wizard, trading convenience for greater control.

To begin, repeat the process of clicking the File → Add → New Project menu item.
This time select the Web Setup Project template, and name the project Setup-
Release, as this time you'll create a nondebug (release) version.

Edit *web.config* for the *C20_Deployment* website to set the debug attribute of the
<compilation> tag to false, or open the WAT, go to the Application page, click
"Configure debugging and tracing," and uncheck "Enable debugging".

You must manually add the output files to the setup project this time, so right-click
the setup project in the Solution Explorer and select Add → Project Output. Select
Content Files from the list at the top of the dialog box, as shown in Figure 20-8.

You can select multiple outputs using standard Windows techniques with the Ctrl or
Shift key.

As soon as the output is added, any dependencies are detected and the class library is
automatically included in the build.

The new project with that name will display in the Solution Explorer with the primary outputs, similar to that shown in Figure 20-9.

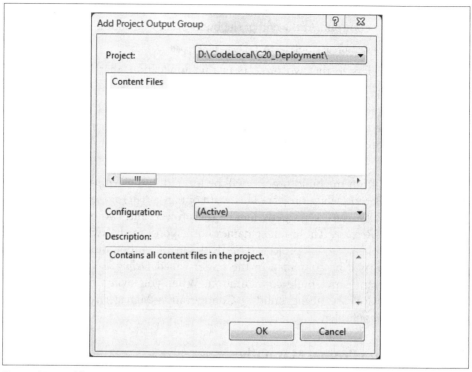

Figure 20-8. Adding project output manually

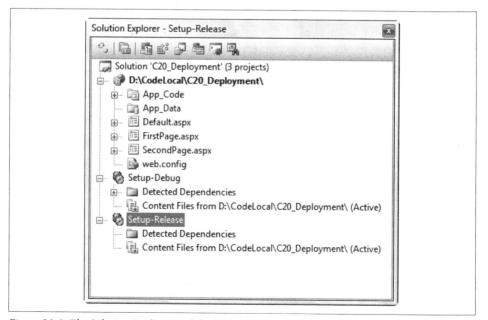

Figure 20-9. The Solution Explorer and the Web Setup projects

Further Customizations

Whether the setup project came from the wizard or not, a number of customizations are available to you. Specifically, right-clicking a setup project in the Solution Explorer and selecting View or clicking the View → Editor menu item will bring up six different editor choices, as shown in Figure 20-10.

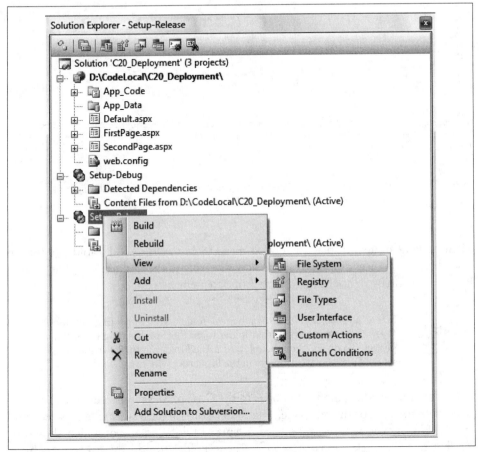

Figure 20-10. Further setup project customizations in the Solution Explorer

Clicking any of these editors will display that editor for that project in the main pane. (When you first add a setup project, the File System editor is what you're looking at.)

File System editor

The File System editor, shown in Figure 20-11, lets you control where files are added to the end-user's machine. The items in the leftmost pane are named folders on the target machine, such as the *Web Application* folder, the directory where the application is installed. Clicking any of the named folders displays its contents in the right pane.

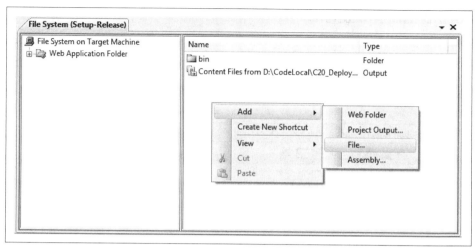

Figure 20-11. The File System editor

Web Setup Projects present only one named folder on the left side of this editor: the *Web Application* folder.

Right-clicking an item displays a context menu. Select Add to add a folder, a file, an assembly, or a project output. You can add shortcuts to the desktop or to the Start → Programs menu by right-clicking the appropriate item.

Before adding any files to a named folder, you must first set the AlwaysCreate property of that folder to true before building the setup project. To do so, click the relevant named folder in the left pane, and set the AlwaysCreate property in the Properties window.

Use this editor to add shared assemblies to the GAC on the target machine. To do so right-click the root of the left pane, File System on Target Machine, and select Add Special Folder. You will see a plethora of special folders, many of which should be familiar to you. Click Global Assembly Cache Folder to add this to the left pane. Right-click it and select Add → Assembly to add an assembly to the GAC. For an assembly to be added to the GAC, it must first have a strong name.

Registry editor

The Registry editor allows your setup program to make entries in the Registry of the target machine. The screenshot in Figure 20-12 shows a new key called TestValue inserted in *HKEY_LOCAL_MACHINE\Software\<Manufacturer>*, where *<Manufacturer>* will be replaced with the value of the Manufacturer property of the setup project. (It defaults to the organization entered when VS2008 was installed.)

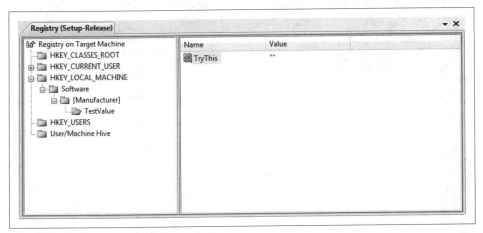

Figure 20-12. The Setup Project Registry editor

You can add new keys to the Registry by right-clicking a node in the left pane and selecting New → Key. If you want to add a value to a key, right-click that key and select New. Then select one of the following:

- String Value
- Environment String Value
- Binary Value
- DWORD Value

You can name the new value in the right pane or in the Properties window. The value is set in the Properties window.

File Types editor

The File Types editor allows you to associate file extensions with the application. If an associated file type has been double-clicked in Windows Explorer, the application will open with that filename passed in as an argument.

To add a file type to the project right-click File Types on Target Machine and select Add File Type. A default document type will appear with the &Open command below it. In the Properties window, change the name to something meaningful—say, *MyApp Data File*—and enter the extension in the Extensions property—say, *abc*—as shown in Figure 20-13.

Now if a file on the target machine with an extension of .*abc*—say, *SomeData.abc*—is double-clicked in Windows Explorer, the application will open with that file.

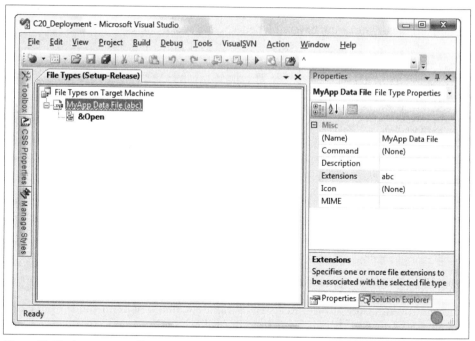

Figure 20-13. Associating a file extension with your project

User Interface editor

The User Interface editor allows you to customize the dialog boxes that are displayed during the installation process. The process is divided into two categories: Install and Administrative Install. The first is for normal installation by users on their local machine, and the latter is for installation to a network for use by members of a workgroup.

Each category is further divided into three phases: Start, Progress, and End. The default configuration looks like that shown in Figure 20-14.

Right-clicking any item in the window and selecting the Add Dialog menu item brings up a selection of standard dialog boxes which can be added and further customized, such as dialogs with radio buttons, checkboxes, or text boxes, a customer information screen, a splash screen, a license agreement, and so on.

Again, because this example is based on a Web Setup Project, the middle node under Start is Installation Address. If you had based the project on a Setup Project, those nodes would be Installation Folder.

Any dialog box added in this way will have properties for text files or bitmaps to display, executables to run, and so on.

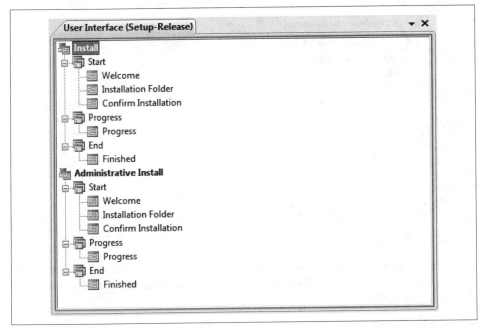

Figure 20-14. The User Interface editor

Custom Actions editor

The Custom Actions editor displays the four phases of the installation process: Install, Commit, Rollback, and Uninstall. You can assign an executable or script file to execute at the conclusion of any of these phases.

Launch Conditions editor

The Launch Conditions editor allows you to create conditional installs. For example, you can specify that a certain version of Windows be installed, a certain file is present, or a certain Registry entry has the correct value.

By default, Web Setup Projects verify that IIS has been installed with a version greater than or equal to 4, as shown in Figure 20-15.

Deploying the Website

To deploy the website created by building a setup project, copy the two output files, *setup.exe* and *setup.msi*, to the target machine and double-click *setup.exe* in Windows Explorer. The installation program will run, opening the Setup Wizard. If you're running Vista, you'll get a UAC dialog asking for administrative permission to run the install.

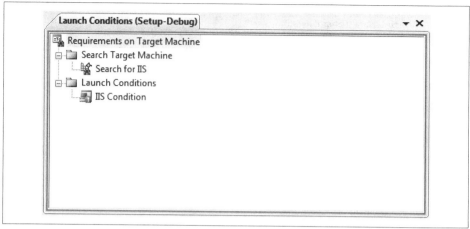

Figure 20-15. Setting up a conditional install

Clicking the Next button will bring up a dialog box showing all the websites available on that machine in the Site drop-down. You can enter the name of the virtual directory you wish to use.

Clicking the Disk Cost button will bring up a dialog box detailing the drive space required and available on the local machine.

After looking at the drive space, click the Next button on the Setup Wizard dialog box to go to a confirmation page.

Click Next one more time to start the installation.

Assuming that the installation succeeds, you will see the new virtual directory created in IIS. You can then run the website by opening a browser and navigating to the new URL, with a web address similar to the following:

```
http://localhost/setup-debug/default.aspx
```

Web Deployment Projects

One of several out-of-band releases for VS2005 and VS2008 has been the Web Deployment Project, an additional project type to add to your solution, which will automatically compile and deploy your Web Site Project for you according to the settings you've set for it. It also works with Web Application Projects, but is targeted at Web Site Projects to give them a build script to automate. Web Application Projects already have a build script—their *.csproj* project file—of which the Web Deployment Project will work independently. Web Site Projects do not have a *.csproj* file.

It fits in rather neatly between XCOPY deployment and using a Web Setup Project, automating the deployment of your website, but performing when you build the website in VS2008 rather than when a user runs an installer. This makes the Web Deployment Project excellent for deploying the latest build of a website to a staging server for testing, either manually or through some sort of automated integration server such as Cruise Control or Team System.

The VS2008 Web Deployment Project was released to the Web in January 2008; it is available for download from *http://www.microsoft. com/downloads/details.aspx?familyId=0AA30AE8-C73B-4BDD-BB1B-FE697256C459*.

Download hotfixes for it at *https://connect.microsoft.com/VisualStudio/ Downloads/DownloadDetails.aspx?DownloadID=10826*.

Once you've installed the Web Deployment Project (admin rights required, Vista users!), right-click a Web Site Project in the Solution Explorer and select Add Web Deployment Project from the context menu to add one to your current solution. A dialog will appear asking you to name the project and where to save it, as shown in Figure 20-16.

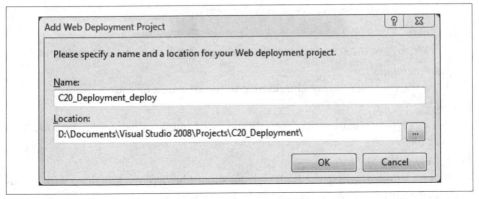

Figure 20-16. Adding a Web Deployment Project to your solution

The deployment project actually maps to a single MSBuild file which you can read and alter by right-clicking the new entry in the Solution Explorer and selecting Open Project File.

If you're not entirely convinced that editing an MSBuild file directly is a good idea, you'll be relieved to know that just double-clicking the deployment project file in the Solution Explorer will bring up a dialog which is much simpler to deal with, as shown in Figure 20-17.

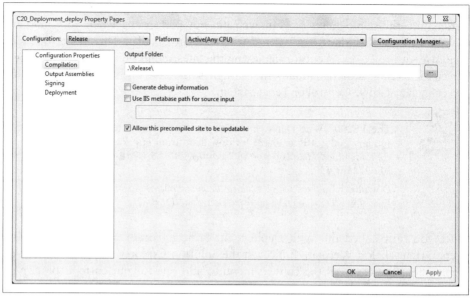

Figure 20-17. The Web Deployment Project edit dialog

The dialog has four screens to deal with different options:

Compilation
Where to save the compiled website and how much of it should be compiled

Output Assemblies
How the compiler output should map to the structure of your website

Signing
Whether the website assemblies should be strongly named and signed with an .*snk* file

Deployment
Once compiled, where the built website should be deployed to along with a couple of additional tasks

We'll look at each of these in turn.

Unless you have a good reason to deploy your site each time you create a Debug build of your site, you'll want to disable the deployment project for Debug builds. To do this, open the Configuration Manager in VS2008, select Debug in the Active Solution Configuration drop-down list, and then uncheck the checkbox for the deployment project in the Build column, as shown in Figure 20-18.

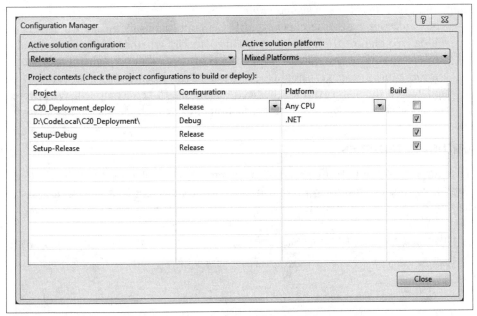

Project	Configuration	Platform	Build
C20_Deployment_deploy	Release	Any CPU	☐
D:\CodeLocal\C20_Deployment\	Debug	.NET	☑
Setup-Debug	Release		☑
Setup-Release	Release		☑

Figure 20-18. Disabling the deployment project for Debug builds

Compilation

The Compilation tab, shown in Figure 20-17, lets you specify four things related to the actual compilation of the website:

Output Folder
: This indicates where to save the compiled files.

Generate debug information
: This indicates whether debug symbols should be included in the compiled assemblies. By default, this is on for Debug builds and off for Release builds. This will also switch debugging on or off in *web.config*.

Use IIS metabase path for source input
: If you're working with a website hosted by IIS rather than on the filesystem, you can choose to specify the website for compilation to the deployment project by its virtual directory name in the IIS metabase, rather than leaving it to Visual Studio. This more precise approach deals with the problem that Visual Studio will compile the website in the virtual directory and any other websites in subdirectories by default, which will cause a crash. By using the metabase's directory name, however, you ensure that this inclusion of other websites will not occur.

Allow this precompiled site to be updatable

The same option as the checkbox of the same name in the Publish Website dialog (see Figure 20-5), this allows you to specify whether all pages, code, and content should be compiled into a (group of) assemblies or whether the *.aspx* and *.ascx* markup pages should be left out of the assembly so that they can be updated on the server without the need for the site to be recompiled. We covered this choice in more depth in "Precompilation of Code Only," earlier in this chapter.

Output Assemblies

The purpose of the Output Assemblies screen, shown in Figure 20-19, is to determine how the structure of your website should be reflected, if at all, by the assemblies into which it is compiled.

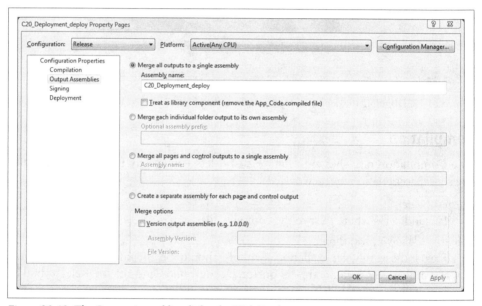

Figure 20-19. The Output Assemblies dialog for Web Deployment Projects

The options are to compile the entire contents of the website given the settings in the Compilation dialog into (from top to bottom):

- A single assembly
- One assembly per folder in the website
- One assembly for all the pages and controls in the website and another for the special folders, such as *App_Code* and *App_WebReferences*
- One assembly for each page and control in the website and also one each for the special folders, such as *App_Code* and *App_WebReferences*

The final option on this page is to add a version number to your assemblies.

The Web Deployment Project will take this number from *assemblyinfo.cs* if you are using a Web Application Project or have added one to your *App_Code* folder, or you can generate one automatically in MSBuild if required.

Signing

The Signing dialog, shown in Figure 20-20, allows you to give your website assemblies a strong name for sharing among applications, as described earlier in "Strong Names."

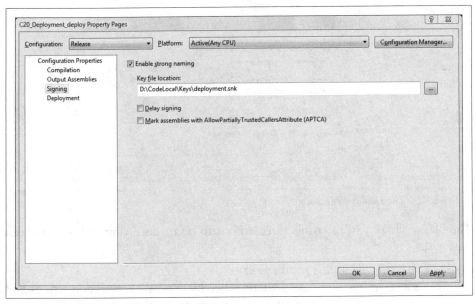

Figure 20-20. The Signing dialog for Web Deployment Projects

You have the option to enable strong naming and to sign it during the build with a key file which you specify, or to delay signing it for later.

The other option here is to mark the website assemblies with the `AllowPartiallyTrustedCallers` attribute, which means that when placed in the GAC, this assembly can be called by any (possibly malevolent) code. This attribute overrides the default in which this is not the case. A discussion of why you would want to enable this is beyond the scope of this book (yet is easily discoverable on Google or Live Search), but leaving this option unchecked is fairly wise.

Deployment

The Deployment screen, shown in Figure 20-21, allows you to customize your website post-deployment.

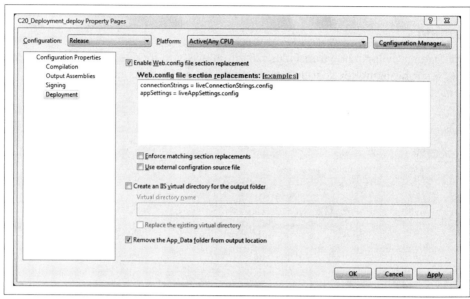

Figure 20-21. The Deployment dialog

The dialog allows you to enable three actions to occur once your website has been deployed:

Enable Web.config file section replacement

This addresses the common scenario whereby database connection strings and other website settings are most likely to differ in a live environment from those on your development box. Rather than having to remember to go in and edit your *web.config* file and put in the right settings once the site is deployed, you can use the Web Deployment Project to replace named sections of your *web.config* file. Simply add into the box a semicolon-separated list of sections to replace along with the name of the XML file containing the settings to replace them with and you're on your way.

By default, these settings will be copied into *web.config*, but checking the "Use external configuration source file" box will instead set the configSource attribute for that setting to use the replacement file directly. (See Chapter 18 for more on configSource.) Checking the "Enforce matching section replacements" box will force the deployment project to make sure that the settings replacing those currently in *web.config* have the same number of elements as those being replaced or else an error will occur.

Create an IIS virtual directory for the output folder

If checked, the deployment project will create a new virtual directory with the specified name pointing to the directory containing the new website assemblies, if one does not exist. If one does exist, it will be deleted and re-created if the "Replace the existing virtual directory" box is checked.

Remove the App_Data folder from output location

This removes the *App_Data* folder from the compiled version of the website. This might come in handy if, for example, you're using SQL Server Express for development and SQL Server Standard on a staging or live server.

Because a Web Deployment Project is just another MSBuild file, your website's deployment can be customized beyond the options that these four dialogs offer. However, it also means working directly with MSBuild, which is beyond the scope of this book. If you'd like to look into this more, visit *http://msdn2.microsoft.com/en-us/library/ aa479568.aspx* for more on the specifics of the MSBuild file behind the Web Deployment Project, and *http://msdn2.microsoft.com/en-us/ library/ms171452.aspx* for Microsoft's guide to the MSBuild syntax.

CHAPTER 21

Epilogue: From Now to vNext

So, that's the core of ASP.NET within the .NET Framework version 3.5 as supported by Visual Studio 2008 (VS2008). You may believe that in these 1,000+ pages we've covered a little more than the core, or you might think we haven't covered it all. Either way, this book contains a lot of information, and if you dig into any one of the topics covered in a single chapter you're sure to find that there's a lot more to the subject than you thought. That's one of the beauties of ASP.NET. It's relatively easy to start learning it and there's always more to discover. Indeed, the folks over in Redmond Campus, Building 42, are always busy developing even more for us beleaguered web developers, promising richer UI experiences, more powerful data access, and clever integration with other technologies in the .NET Framework.

That's where this epilogue comes in, with a short overview of what's known to be in the cooking pot so far for the VS2008/.NET 3.5 web developer.

 Disclaimer: This was the perceived plan for the next iteration of ASP.NET and surrounding technologies in mid-2008. Microsoft is not bound to this and may well change how some or all of this fits together.

(Some of) The Winnowing Process

But first, a note on how our benefactors on the ASP.NET team are starting to make their ideas and plans more transparent, rather than operating in a black box, as they did with earlier releases. The ASP.NET community site at *http://www.asp.net* has always been a central source of information and answers for ASP.NET development. Its Downloads page, as shown in Figure 21-1, is now also one possible portal into the future.

The Sandbox projects in the General Downloads area are independent projects from members of the ASP.NET team. They can comprise interesting prototypes such as Blinq, useful code libraries such as the RSS Toolkit or the Anti-Cross Site Scripting Library, or plug-ins for Visual Studio. Some of them evolve into ASP.NET or Visual Studio features going forward.

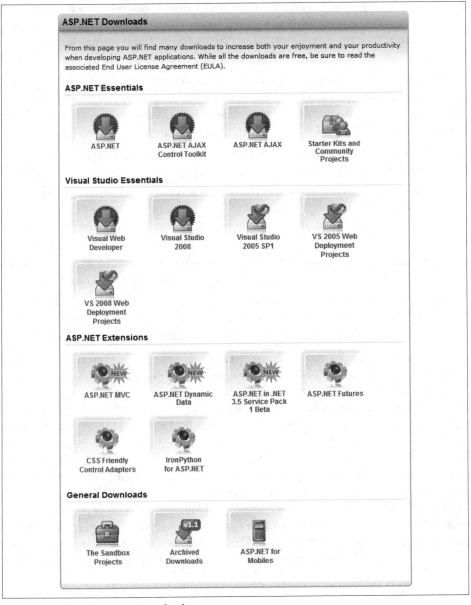

Figure 21-1. The ASP.NET Downloads page

Likewise the ASP.NET Futures download shown in the fourth row in Figure 21-1; this is the place to find a set of alpha technologies the ASP.NET team has put together for initial reaction from the development community in the ASP.NET Futures forum at *http://forums.asp.net/1127.aspx*. New Community Technology Preview (CTP) builds of the Futures package appear from time to time. They may include new or completely rewritten libraries, or they may be missing libraries.

For example, the Model-View-Controller (MVC) framework mentioned later in this chapter was originally part of the ASP.NET Futures download, but it is now its own separate entity. The first service pack for .NET 3.5 also contains three features originally in the Futures download.

From the time the projects are announced (e.g., through Scott Guthrie's blog at *http:// weblogs.asp.net/scottgu* or the ASP.NET team's collective blog at *http://weblogs.asp.net/ aspnet-team*), the feedback from the community sent via the forums on Asp.net, newsgroups, or an individual's blog helps to determine what happens to these libraries:

- Lots of positive feedback will likely push the library into a CTP and full effort to be released as an interim extension to ASP.NET.

- If the library receives a positive, albeit not incredibly enthusiastic, reception, it may remain in the Futures package for a while until it fits into another interim project or is rewritten into something that gets more positive feedback from the community.

- Less than enthusiastic feedback may see it pushed onto Codeplex.com for the community to work on directly and out of the Futures package altogether.

Of course, a lot more is going on behind the scenes than just these libraries, but it's good to know that we humble developers can have a small influence on the future of ASP.NET v4 and Visual Studio 10 (codenamed "Hawaii" at the time of this writing).

The ADO.NET team follows a similar process, albeit at a higher level. Although there may never be an ADO.NET Futures download per se, the ADO.NET team blog (*http://blogs.msdn.com/adonet/*) is a good place to learn about any new sample drops at the team's various CodePlex projects when they happen together with the development of and on top of any interim extensions to the Data Programmability platform between Visual Studio releases, such as the Entity Framework which we mentioned in Chapter 10 and will touch on again in a minute. CTP drops of so-called "incubator projects" from the ADO.NET team are also announced on this blog and are subject to the same feedback influence as the ASP.NET Futures releases. Witness the announcement of the "Astoria" and "Jasper" projects at the beginning of May 2007. Allowing the community to guide them partially, Astoria is now being geared up as a full release known as ADO.NET Data Services, for release in .NET 3.5 Service Pack 1, and Jasper remains on the back burner, its future uncertain. We'll look at both in a minute.

On the Stove

So, what's cooking for the period between Orcas and Hawaii? All Visual Studio .NET releases have been named after islands in Puget Sound, so the choice of *Hawaii* may indicate that the team will stretch itself further in the next few years. Alternatively, it may simply indicate that they all wish Building 42 could be located on a beach in Maui.

Richer Community Experiences

Wherever they may be, we, as part of a community of several million .NET developers, will continue to be spread out around the world, joined through the Internet at community sites such as *http://www.asp.net* and *http://www.aspinsiders.com*. Microsoft can't spread itself so thin as to answer every question on every forum (there are many MVPs and excellent programmers out there to help out besides those in Redmond), but it has committed itself to improving and giving responses to 99% of all the questions on *http://forums.microsoft.com* and *http://forums.asp.net*.

Its intention, presumably, is to make its own sites the number one resource for getting your questions answered. The enabling of community contributions to the MSDN Library website through the Community Content and Click to Rate and Give Feedback buttons (shown in Figure 21-2), added to the top of all its content pages, is also a precursor of things to come. Microsoft wants MSDN to be a community platform for developers to contribute to as well as to find information.

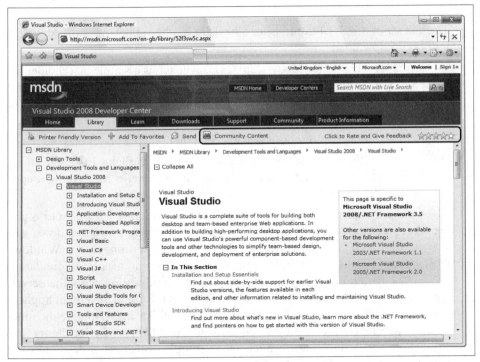

Figure 21-2. MSDN's community contribution buttons

A standalone Wiki will also be added to MSDN for developers to add to the already generated documentation, along with a translation Wiki where documentation can be translated to other languages. In the meantime, the ASP.NET team has already made a Wiki available for web developers at *http://wiki.asp.net*.

And if you have finished writing your own code for the day, there are also a handful of .NET-specific community sites you can visit and collaborate with other people. They are:

CodePlex (http://www.codeplex.com)
For open source projects. Anyone can upload his own projects to this site, as well as contribute to other people's projects.

Code Gallery (http://code.msdn.microsoft.com)
For code samples and white papers.

Rich Media Experiences with Silverlight

One topic you may feel was surprisingly absent from this book is Silverlight. Its initial branding as Microsoft's Flash killer is justified, especially in the realm of media streaming. However, there are quite a lot of reasons why Silverlight is growing beyond this initial judgment and into a justification for a lot of books this size, if not larger:

- The first set of ASP.NET controls for Silverlight has been brewing in the ASP.NET Futures for download:
  - `<asp:Silverlight>` (formerly `<asp:Xaml>`) will act as a simple placeholder for a Silverlight application on a web page, but with the added ability to check a user's web browser for the correct version of the Silverlight plug-in and ask the user to download it if required.
  - `<asp:MediaPlayer>` presents a skinable Silverlight media player on your page.
- Using Microsoft's AJAX JavaScript library within Silverlight 1.0 applications enables asynchronous updates and all the AJAXified benefits for Silverlight apps that we already have for our ASP.NET websites.
- Silverlight 2.0 is just around the corner. Beta 2 was recently released and is giving some indication of the power it will provide. Packing a stripped-down version of the .NET runtime that includes a fair proportion of the Windows Presentation Foundation (WPF) and Windows Communication Foundation (WCF) for better presentation and backend communication with the server, respectively, it will come with close to 100 controls for use in Silverlight applications when it's finally released. Version 2 will consolidate and reinforce the functionality developers are already using through the AJAX JavaScript library and will enable the embedding of much more complex business code within the Silverlight plug-in. Here perhaps is one future endpoint of Microsoft's Software as a Service (SaaS) initiative. It certainly seems to tie in with the Oslo view of the future, as covered later. Not so much .NET My Services as .NET My Applications.

- Popfly, the no-code-required mashup creator, is re-creating the bridge between power users and programmers that was destroyed about the time that 16-bit computers decided not to include BASIC at the command prompt. This could be incredibly important in creating a new generation of bedroom coders, and it's a Silverlight application. Add to it the Popfly Explorer plug-in, which seamlessly gives access to those mashups to Visual Studio Express users (14 million downloads and counting, so far), and that's a fantastic door for many new programmers.

If you're interested in learning more about Silverlight development, go straight to *http://silverlight.net/GetStarted/* and start watching the tutorials there. They will be updated with each new release and are an excellent place to start.

Rich Data Experiences

VS2008 could easily be described as a collection of point releases rather than something completely new (that'll be Visual Studio 10); the UI tweaks, AJAX integration, and support for Language Integrated Query (LINQ) are reactions to new creations elsewhere, rather the proactive work of the Visual Studio team per se. OK, that's a bit of an oversimplification, but it's on about the right level. SQL Server 2008 could also be considered a point release for the major work that was SQL Server 2005. Of most interest to us nominally is the SQL IntelliSense in the Query window and the next version of SQL Server Compact Edition, which will replace SQL CE 2005 as the default database engine for mobile devices. There are the ever-present (claimed) improvements in performance and security as well, but worth noting here is that the Entity Framework/LINQ to Entities mentioned in Chapter 10 is not a SQL Server 2008 feature. It is part of .NET 3.5 Service Pack 1.

SQL Server 2008 has no specific support for the Entity Framework. However, the Entity Framework will be able to take advantage of some of the new features in SQL Server 2008 (such as geo data types) that other databases probably don't have.

 There was no firm home for information regarding the Entity Framework and LINQ to Entities on the MSDN site at the time of this writing. However, an overview of them both as a beta product was available at *http://msdn.microsoft.com/en-us/library/bb386964.aspx*. When they are released as part of Service Pack 1, the LINQ home page at *http://msdn.microsoft.com/en-us/netframework/aa904594.aspx* will be a good place to start for more information.

Also in the works as this book went to press is *Programming Entity Framework*, written by Julia Lerman for O'Reilly, which should be worth a read.

It's great that Microsoft is finally offering an object-relational mapping (ORM) facility for its databases. Not just because it means that the already available libraries, such as NHibernate, EntityBroker, and Genome, will now be pushed to even greater heights while the Entity Framework matures, but also because it looks like Microsoft is going to use the Entity Framework as a platform for some genuinely interesting and useful projects of its own. On the developer front, the aforementioned Astoria and Jasper incubator projects look to be good examples of this, and SQL Reporting looks to be getting an overhaul using this technology as well.

Astoria, or rather, ADO.NET Data Services, is built on top of the Entity Framework and WCF to present a data entity model—that is, the contents of your database as a set of objects—as a set of REST-based web services. The beauty of Microsoft's approach to Astoria is that, for a change, nothing new is being created to enable these web services. As you saw in Chapter 16, REST web services use HTTP verbs—GET, PUT, POST, DELETE, and so forth—to retrieve data and return it as applicable. Astoria uses the Entity Framework to generate and maintain the service responses and cross-links to other information. It uses the WCF to create the services to begin with.

ADO.NET Data Services is being released as part of .NET 3.5 Service Pack 1. You can find up-to-date tutorials and information about it at *http://astoria.mslivelabs.com*.

Jasper, or Dynamic ADO.NET, as it might be known, is another Entity Framework-based project currently on the back burner in favor of development on Astoria. Briefly described as Ruby on Rails via the Entity Framework, Jasper generates a web-based MVC-style read/write view over a generated entity model of your database for reading and writing. Nothing much has been seen of it since its first CTP release in May 2007, but it will be interesting to see whether it has been redesigned as a scaffold generator over an entity model for the ASP.NET MVC framework when the next CTP appears.

At the time of this writing, you could find Jasper on the MSDN Data Access Incubation Projects home page, at *http://msdn.microsoft.com/ en-us/data/bb419139.aspx*.

An Alternative Web Framework

Perhaps the most interesting beta download currently in circulation is the ASP.NET MVC framework. You'll still produce a website at the end of it, but the way in which pages are requested and produced is substantially different from the web forms model we've all used up to now.

This is not going to replace web forms. It's here as an alternative. There's no need to panic that Microsoft is ditching support for all the websites you've labored over for the past five years.

The three parts of MVC are pretty straightforward to understand:

- The *Model* represents your data; in this case, it's the model over your database. It could be generated using LINQ to SQL, the Entity Framework, Rails, Subsonic; the choice is yours. All it does is make your data available—perhaps read-only, perhaps read/write.

- The *View* represents the presentation of the data in the model on the page. And that's all. It has no business logic in it; it's just a dumb terminal slaved to the model by the controller.

- The *Controller* contains the logic in the website, parsing the request from the browser, performing any required logic, and plugging in the required data from the model into the required view.

Diagrammatically, this looks like Figure 21-3.

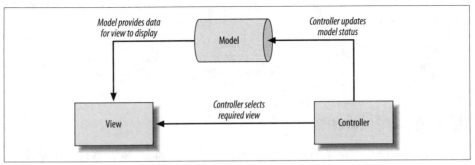

Figure 21-3. Model, View, and Controller

Programmatically, this means a shift in thinking and a possible gain in developing. With the data access, business, and presentation layers of your website becoming completely separate, the ability to unit-test a site's business logic becomes that much easier.

The most well-known MVC framework of recent years is Ruby on Rails, wherein Rails is pointed at a database providing the data model for the site, and generates a *scaffold* for the developer's use in building the site. The scaffold provides an ORM layer over the data model with which the controller classes can populate views or push updates back down to the model as required. Indeed, as Ruby is a dynamic language and Rails actually generates a new set of language calls, maybe that's one type of scaffold Microsoft will offer over the top of its dynamic language runtime once it's formally released. Indeed, one of the known goals of IronRuby is to have Rails work on it. It also looks like Visual Basic 10 (VBx) will either become a dynamic language or have a dynamic variant to it in parallel with IronPython and IronRuby, which are already in the works, so maybe a Visual Basic on Rails MVC flavor will appear at some point.

For now, though, if you're not happy to work from scratch on the ASP.NET MVC framework, Microsoft has already stated that its intention is to keep the framework itself "scaffold-agnostic" (for want of a better term). Microsoft also expressed its intent to assist any scaffold code project to generate code that is friendly to its MVC offering. The Castle Project team (*http://www.castleproject.org*) had already inquired about this for their ActiveRecord library as this book went to press.

Because of how MVC works, a new set of ASP.NET controls will be made available which tie into the separation of presentation and business logic more closely. The current web form controls amalgamate the two, and available demos of the MVC framework use only HTML in the view code, so who knows what will happen on this front. Perhaps the standards-compliant web form controls hinted at by the CSS Adaptors download, ListView in .NET 3.5, and AJAX standards compliance tweaks in the Futures download will come in a second flavor for MVC. Perhaps a new set of controls is being built from scratch that more accurately maps to common usage patterns in an MVC framework.

 You can find the current download of the MVC framework, along with many tutorials and a forum, at *http://www.asp.net/MVC/*.

On the Far Horizon

At the time of this writing, very few specifics had been made known regarding .NET v4 and the other technologies that make up the Oslo platform. We know that its focus is on Service-Oriented Architecture (SOA) and the creation of business software as a service. Indeed, Microsoft's Patterns and Practices team has already started down that road, producing a first guidance document for creating a platform for SOA applications using BizTalk 2006.

In his general session at TechEd Europe 2007, Pat Helland pointed out that the way in which the hardware we use is created, assigned a cost, and treated has changed, and will continue to change, over at least the next five years. Moore's Law may still hold true until 2020, but the ever-shrinking transistor is giving rise not to the creation of CPUs with ever-higher frequencies, but rather to multicore CPUs. Today, dual- and quad-core CPUs crop up in home hardware, and anything up to 32-core chips is available in high-end server farms. These chips, memory, storage, and bandwidth have all become so cheap to manufacture that cost-benefit analysis of some scenarios shows that low- to no-maintenance disposable data centers may be the way forward rather than the traditional, carefully maintained center that may be feasible for only absolutely critical data. The point is that changes in the way we use hardware will affect how we write our software to make full use of it.

Creating software that's available as a disconnected software service is one possibility, and Microsoft's Volta technology preview at *http://labs.live.com/volta/* would seem to indicate one way to develop this type of software that the company is investigating. Microsoft's Project Velocity (*http://msdn.microsoft.com/en-us/data/cc655792.aspx*) might also indicate a way that is it investigating increasing the speed of software being run over the wire as a service. To quote, "Velocity fuses memory across multiple computers to give a single unified cache view to applications."

The few press releases regarding Oslo would indicate that .NET 4.0 will most likely contain an evolution of WCF and support for some sort of explicit modeling language (read: domain-specific language) known as "D," although that may remain in the Visual Studio SDK where that support lives at the moment.

On a small scale at least, we can consider the following ideas to be in sync with this sort of thinking:

- Using RESTful web services to facilitate interaction with the remote application (sounds like the old dumb terminal arrangement, doesn't it?) in the same way that Google's online Office suite works.

- Streaming applications through a Silverlight container into a browser. We know Silverlight will contain a reduced version of the .NET runtime from 2.0 onward. The questions are what exactly will be in this subset as time goes on and .NET evolves, and what will the offline experience be for a Silverlight user?

- With the parallel Moonlight project to run Silverlight applications on Linux (or rather, on the Mono .NET Framework for Linux), is Silverlight the first foray into full-blown, multiplatform .NET for Microsoft, or will this ambition stay restricted to browsers?

The really burning question, though, is how this slow shift to SOA and SaaS will affect us as ASP.NET developers. How will .NET 4 or Visual Studio 10 help and hinder us in our development? And the only answer to that is to wait and see. The first hints at what they are aiming at in Oslo indicate a lot of work ahead once you get past the buzzwords. (You might even want to look at *http://blog.jemm.net/2008/05/24/the-future-of-net-visual-studio-and-more/* for one person's thoughts on this based on his inspection of current development job openings at Microsoft.)

One thing is for sure, though: we won't be waiting until the official release of .NET 4 and Visual Studio 10 to know what Oslo will contain. The transparency in development and documentation that the MSDN, ASP.NET, and ADO.NET teams are beginning to work with should ensure that we'll understand the contents of the new code stacks before they are officially RTM'd. Long may that continue.

Installing the AJAX Control Toolkit

This book sometimes makes use of the AJAX Control Toolkit, an open source set of some three dozen AJAX-enabled server controls developed by the Microsoft ASP.NET team and the public and available on the CodePlex website (*http://www.codeplex.com*). It builds on and uses the AJAX server controls that are now part of ASP.NET 3.5, but it is by no means a mandatory download for developing ASP.NET websites.

This appendix explains how to install the Toolkit and integrate the controls into Visual Studio 2008 (VS2008).

Downloading the Code

First, download the latest release of the Toolkit from *http://www.codeplex.com/ AjaxControlToolkit/Release/ProjectReleases.aspx*. In this example, that's release 20229. The Toolkit is under continuous development as an open source project, but the method of installation is the same. Don't worry if the release number is greater than 20229. It's to be expected. (Of course, if it's lower, it may be time to ask questions.)

The page for release 20229 has four options, as shown in Figure A-1.

This release has four possible downloads, two for running in VS2005 and .NET v3.0 and two for VS2008 and .NET 3.5. You'll want the latter for this book, so download *AjaxControlToolkit-Framework3.5.zip*. This file includes the source code for the controls, which may come in handy when debugging pages that contain them.

When you do select the file, you'll be ask to agree to the terms of the license under which the code is made available, as shown in Figure A-2. You can find the full terms at *http://www.microsoft.com/resources/sharedsource/licensingbasics/publiclicense.mspx*.

Once the ZIP file has downloaded, extract all the files to a convenient folder. Figure A-3 shows the top-level contents of the download.

Figure A-1. The Toolkit Releases page on CodePlex

Building the Code and Looking Around

Open *AjaxControlToolkit.sln* in VS2008. You may get a warning that you have extracted the code into an unsafe location. Click OK to carry on. A second security warning appears. Choose to Load the Project Normally and click OK. Repeat these choices when the dialog appears again for another project in the solution.

The solution contains the four projects shown in Figure A-4. From top to bottom, they are:

- The code for the server controls themselves
- A website for demonstrating each control

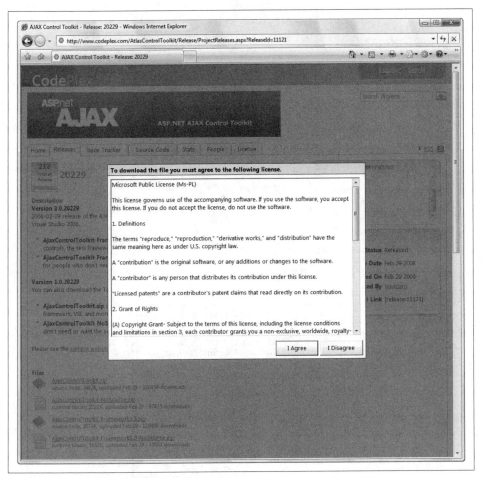

Figure A-2. Agreeing to the Microsoft Public License

- A website containing a full set of tests for each control
- A template project for use with VS2008

Select Build → Build Solution to build all four projects in the solution, and then press F5 to open the demonstration website using VS2008's built-in web server. The home page is shown in Figure A-5.

 You'll need to install the Visual J# Redistributable (Second Edition) package to build the TemplateVSI project, or else the build will fail, saying it is missing *vjslib.dll*. You can download and install it from *http://msdn2.microsoft.com/en-us/vjsharp/bb188598.aspx*. You'll need the x86 download for 32-bit Windows and the x64 download for 64-bit Windows.

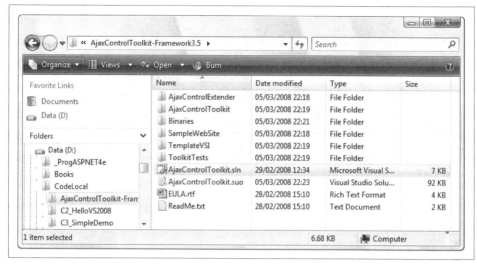

Figure A-3. The contents of the Toolkit

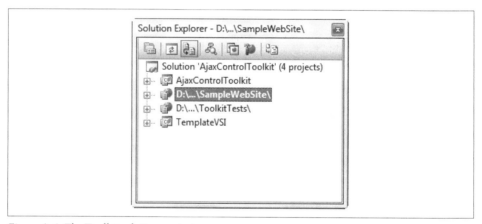

Figure A-4. The Toolkit solution projects

 You may also want to put the compiled code for the Toolkit in a place that's easier to locate. You'll find a copy of it in the *bin* or *bin/debug* folder of the Toolkit, sample website, and test website to move elsewhere. The file is called *AjaxControlToolkit.dll*.

Integrating the Toolkit with VS2008

When you've finished looking at the website, close both the website and VS2008. Open Windows Explorer and browse to the folder to which you extracted the Toolkit files. Open the *TemplateVSI\bin* directory and double-click the

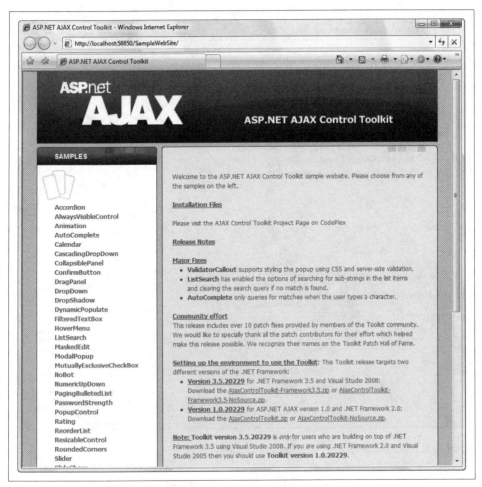

Figure A-5. The Toolkit sample website

AjaxControlExtender.vsi file therein. Figure A-6 shows the dialog that pops up, asking you which templates to install. If you haven't installed both C# and Visual Basic support with VS2008, deselect the appropriate templates and then click OK. You'll get another warning dialog saying the content you are trying to install has not been signed. Click Yes to continue installing and then Finish to exit the wizard.

Finally, you can add the Toolkit controls to the VS2008 toolbar. Open VS2008, and then make the Toolbox window visible (View → Toolbox) if it isn't already. Without a project open, it will just be showing the General tab, but that's OK.

Right-click the Toolbox window in the space under the General tab; then select Add Tab from the context menu that appears. Give the new tab the name "AJAX Control Toolkit" and press Enter. Figure A-7 shows the Toolbox as it now looks.

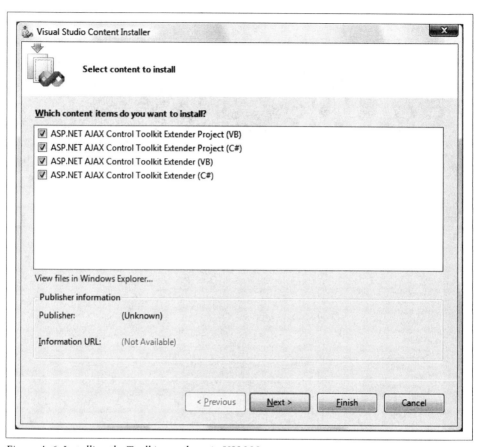

Figure A-6. Installing the Toolkit templates in VS2008

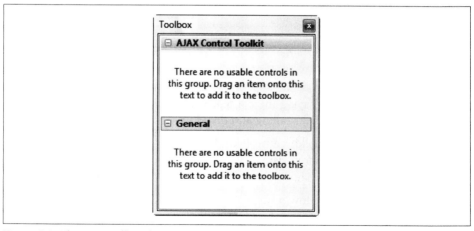

Figure A-7. The new Toolkit tab

To add the controls to the new tab, right-click the tab and select Choose Items from the context menu. After about 30 seconds, the Choose Toolbox Items dialog (see Figure A-8) appears, open at the .NET Framework Components tab. Click Browse and then locate a copy of the *AjaxControlToolkit.dll* file you built previously. Select it and click OK.

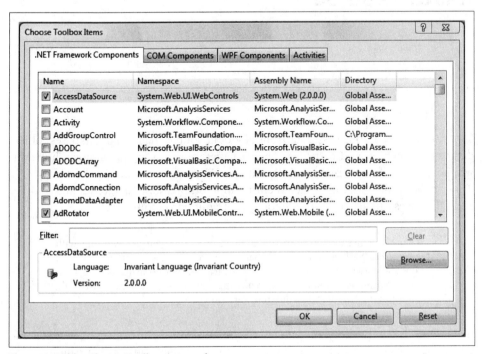

Figure A-8. The Choose Toolbox Items tab

The controls in the dynamic link library (DLL) will be added to and highlighted in the Choose Toolbox Items dialog. Click OK.

 Although they aren't visible initially, the Toolkit controls have now been added to the Toolbox. To confirm this, open an AJAX-enabled web page in VS2008 and look at the Toolbox again.

Note that if you've added the Toolkit controls to VS2008 and then decide to install VS2008 Service Pack 1, you'll see that the service pack installer resets the Toolbox to its default settings. You'll need to add the Toolkit controls to the Toolbox again.

Relational Database Technology: A Crash Course

You can use .NET to access data from any data source: relational databases, object databases, flat files, and text files. The vast majority of web applications, however, will access data from a relational database such as SQL Server, Oracle, or MySQL. Though we could certainly write an entire book on relational databases and another on SQL, the essentials of these technologies are not hard to understand.

 All of the examples in this appendix assume you are working with either SQL Server or SQL Server Express. Users of other relational databases will find that the lessons learned here transfer well to their environment, but be careful with applications such as Oracle, MySQL, and Access that use a different variation of SQL.

A *database* is a repository of data. A *relational database* organizes your data into tables that are connected to one another by the data they contain. For example, one table might contain a customer's information and a second table might contain information about orders, and each order is owned by an individual customer.

Similarly, you might have one table of cars and a second table of car parts. Each part can be in one or more cars, and each car is made up of many parts. Or you might have a table for bugs and a table for developers. Each bug is owned by one developer, and each developer has a list of bugs he owns.

Tables, Records, and Columns

The principal division of a database is into *tables*. Every table in a relational database is organized into rows, where each row represents a single record. The rows are organized into columns. All the rows in a table have the same column structure. For example, a Customer table might have columns for the customer ID (the unique ID of the customer placing the order), the name of the customer, the email address of the customer, and so forth.

It is common to make an analogy between tables and classes and between rows and objects. The Customer table, for example, tells you a great number of things about a customer, just as a Customer class does. Each row in the Customer table describes a particular customer, much as an instance of the Customer would do.

This analogy is compelling, but limited. Tables, like classes, typically describe one logical entity and all of what you know about that entity. The mapping isn't reflexive, though—classes can contain properties that actually map across several different tables. This is similar to the notion of relationships between tables to ensure that consistent data in a database is not reflected back as relationships between classes.

One of the challenges facing an object-oriented programmer is overcoming these and other design differences between the object model on the one hand and the database model on the other. Typically, the interface between the backend relational database and the objects in the application is managed by creating a database interface layer of objects that negotiate between the creation of objects and the storage of information in the database tables, all created by hand. The past few years, however, have seen a number of products known as *object-relational mappers*, which can scan the structure of a database and, with a little help from the developer, produce a set of classes which represent the entities and relationships and make that transition between your code and your database that much easier. Language Integrated Query (LINQ), covered in Chapter 10, actually includes two object-relational mappers:

- LINQ to SQL looks after the simpler case where your classes generally have a one-to-one relationship with tables in the database.
- LINQ to Entities (available with VS2008 Service Pack 1) deals with the more enterprise-level case where your classes generally map to information in more than one table in your database.

This distinction is not a hard and fast rule by any means, but it does make the general distinction between the two that Microsoft is using.

Several other mappers are also available, including:

- NHibernate (*http://www.nhibernate.org*)
- SubSonic (*http://www.codeplex.com/subsonic*)

Table Design

To understand the issues in table design, consider a database for recording orders (such as the AdventureWorksLT database used in this book). You need to know who placed each order, and it would be useful to know the email address, phone number, and other identifying information about each person as well.

You can imagine a form in which you display details about a given order, and in that detail page you offer the email address and phone number of the customer so the salesperson working on the order can contact that customer in case of a delay or stock issue.

You could store the identifying information with each order in an Orders table (named SalesOrderHeader in the database, for reasons we'll mention in a minute), but that would be inefficient. If John Doe placed 50 orders, you'd rather not repeat John Doe's email address and phone number in 50 records. It's also a data maintenance nightmare. If John Doe changes his email address and phone number, you'd have to make the change in 50 places.

Instead, the customer details are kept in a second table, called Customer, in which each row represents a single customer. In the Customer table, there will be a column for the CustomerID. Each customer will have a unique ID, and that field will be marked as the *primary key* for the Customer table. A primary key is the column or combination of columns that uniquely identifies a record in a given table.

The Orders table will use the PersonID column as a *foreign key*. A foreign key is a column (or combination of columns) that is a primary (or otherwise unique) key from a different table. The Orders table uses the CustomerID, which is the primary key in Customer, to identify which person placed the order. If you need to determine the email address for that person, you can use the CustomerID to look up the Customer record in the Customer table and that will give you all the detailed information about that person.

By "factoring out" the details of the person's address into a Customer table, you reduce the redundant information in each Order record. This process of taking out redundant information from your tables is called *normalization*.

The same process explains why an order is actually stored in two tables—SalesOrderDetail and SalesOrderHeader—rather than one. An order can be split into individual requests for products and so the SalesOrderHeader table stores the details of the order as a whole—when it is due, when it was shipped, how much it cost in total, and so on—whereas rows in the SalesOrderDetail table contain details for each separate product in the order.

Normalization

Normalization makes your use of the database more efficient, and it reduces the likelihood of data corruption. If you kept the customer's email address in the Customer table and in the SalesOrderHeader table, you would run the risk that a change in one table might not be reflected in the other. Thus, if you changed the person's email address in the Customer table, that change might not be reflected in every row in the SalesOrderHeader table (or it would be a lot of work to make sure that it was reflected). By keeping only the CustomerID in SalesOrderHeader, you are free to change the email address or other personal information in Customer, and the change will automatically be reflected for each order.

Just as Visual Basic and C# programmers want the compiler to catch bugs at compile time rather than at runtime, database programmers want the database to help them avoid data corruption. A compiler helps avoid bugs by enforcing the rules of the language. For example, in C# you can't use a variable you've not defined. SQL Server and other modern relational databases help you avoid bugs by enforcing constraints that you create. For example, the Customer table marks the CustomerID field as a primary key. This creates a primary key constraint in the database, which ensures that each CustomerID is unique. If you were to enter a person named Dan Maharry with a PersonID of 123, and then you were to try to add Jesse Liberty with a PersonID of 123, the database would reject the second record because of the primary key constraint. You would need to give one of these people a different, and unique, CustomerID.

Declarative Referential Integrity

Relational databases use *Declarative Referential Integrity* (DRI) to establish constraints on the relationships among the various tables. For example, you might declare a constraint on the SalesOrderHeader table that dictates that no order may have a CustomerID unless that CustomerID represents a valid record in the Customer table. This helps you avoid two types of mistakes. First, you cannot enter a record with an invalid CustomerID. Second, you cannot delete a Customer record if that CustomerID is used in any order. The integrity of your data and the relationships among records is thus protected.

SQL

The language of choice for querying and manipulating databases is *Structured Query Language*, often referred to as SQL. SQL is often pronounced "sequel." SQL is a declarative language, as opposed to a procedural language, and it can take awhile to get used to working with a declarative language if you are used to languages such as Visual Basic and C#.

Most programmers tend to think in terms of a sequence of steps: "Find me all the orders, then get the customer's ID, then use that ID to look up that customer's records in Customer, then get me the email address." In a declarative language, such as SQL, you declare the entire query and the query engine returns a set of results. You are not thinking about a set of steps; rather, you are thinking about designing and "shaping" a set of data. Your goal is to make a single declaration that will return the right records. You do that by creating temporary "wide" tables that include all the fields you need and then filtering for only those records you want: "Widen the SalesOrderHeader table with the Customer table, joining the two on the CustomerID, then filter for only those that meet my criteria."

The heart of SQL is the query. A query is a statement that returns a set of records from the database. Typically, queries are in this form:

```
Select column,column,column from table where column = value
```

For example, you might like to see information about the customers served by Janet. To do so you would write:

```
Select FirstName, LastName, CompanyName from Customer where SalesPerson = 'Janet'
```

Joining Tables

SQL is capable of much more powerful queries (see the upcoming "SQL Select Statement" sidebar for the full syntax as provided by Microsoft).

For example, suppose you'd like to know about all the orders by all the customers served by Janet after January 1, 1997. You might create this query:

```
Select c.FirstName, c.LastName, c.CompanyName, o.OrderDate, o.TotalDue
    from Customers c
inner join SalesOrderHeader o on o.customerID = c.customerID
where c.SalesPerson = 'Janet' and o.OrderDate > '1/1/97'
```

At first glance, you appear to be selecting orderDate from the Customer table, but that is not possible because the Customer table does not have an orderDate. You must take care to identify the table that each field comes from by prefixing each field with an "alias" defined in the query. The key phrase is:

```
inner join SalesOrderHeader o on o.customerID = c.customerID
```

It is as though the join phrase creates a temporary table that is the width of the Customer table and the SalesOrderHeader table joined together. The on keyword dictates how the tables are joined. In this case, the tables are joined on the CustomerID column in Customer and in SalesOrderHeader.

Each record in Customer (represented by the alias c) is joined to the appropriate record in Orders (represented by the alias o) when the CustomerID fields match in both records.

When you join two tables you can say "get every record that exists in one table but not necessarily the other" (this is called an *outer join*), or you can say, as we've done here, "get only those records that exist in both tables" (called an *inner join*).

 Inner joins are the default, so writing join is the same as writing inner join.

The inner join shown in the preceding code snippet says: get only the records in Orders that match the records in Customer by having the same value in the CustomerID field (on o.customerID = c.customerID).

SQL Select Statement

This is the complete syntax for the SELECT statement as used in SQL Server:

```
SELECT statement ::=
    < query_expression >
    [ ORDER BY { order_by_expression | column_position [ ASC | DESC ] }
        [ ,...n]    ]
    [ COMPUTE
        { { AVG | COUNT | MAX | MIN | SUM } (expression)} [ ,...n]
        [ BY expression[ ,...n]]
    ]
    [ FOR { BROWSE | XML { RAW | AUTO | EXPLICIT }
            [ , XMLDATA ]
            [ , ELEMENTS ]
            [ , BINARY base64 ]
        }
    ]
    [ OPTION ( < query_hint > [ ,...n ]) ]
< query expression > ::=
    { < query specification > | ( < query expression > ) }
    [ UNION [ ALL ] < query specification | ( < query expression > ) [...n] ]
< query specification > ::=
    SELECT [ ALL | DISTINCT ]
        [ { TOP integer| TOP integer PERCENT } [ WITH TIES ] ]
        < select_list >
    [ INTO new_table ]
    [ FROM { < table_source > } [ ,...n ] ]
    [ WHERE < search_condition > ]
    [ GROUP BY [ ALL ] group_by_expression[ ,...n ]
        [ WITH { CUBE | ROLLUP } ]
    ]
    [ HAVING < search_condition > ]
```

The where clause further constrains the search to those records where the SalesPerson field in Customer is an exact match for the string Janet and where the OrderDate in the Orders table is greater than January 1, 1997:

```
where c.SalesPerson = 'Janet' and o.orderDate > '1/1/97'
```

But because Orders is the only table with an orderDate column, there is no ambiguity if we use just the column name:

```
where c.SalesPerson = 'Janet' and orderDate > '1/1/97'
```

It's often easier to read, though, if all columns are given a prefix rather than you having to figure out which table each column is part of. SQL is able to translate the string "1/1/97" into a DateTime representing January 1, 1997.

Using SQL to Manipulate the Database

You can use SQL to search for and retrieve data and to create, update, and delete tables and generally manage and manipulate the content and the structure of the database. For example, you can update the FirstName of a specific company:

```
Update Customer set FirstName = 'Jesse' where CustomerId = '124'
```

You can add a new row to the Customer table:

```
INSERT INTO [Customer]
  ([FirstName], [LastName], [SalesPerson])
VALUES
  ('Dan', 'Maharry', 'Janet')
```

And you can delete a row from the table as well:

```
DELETE from Customer where FirstName='Dan' and LastName='Maharry'
```

Further Reference

In this book, the database server of choice is Microsoft's SQL Server 2005, but as we mentioned earlier, it is not the only kid on the block and there are a number of different free versions of the major databases to tide you over while you learn. They all have a lot of good documentation installed with them as well, making them well worth a read.

- SQL Server 2005 Express Edition (*http://www.microsoft.com/express/sql/*)
- Oracle 10g Express Edition (*http://www.oracle.com/technology/software/products/ database/xe/htdocs/102xewinsoft.html*)
- MySQL Community Server (*http://dev.mysql.com/downloads/mysql/5.0.html#win32*)

Likewise, there are many good books and websites to teach you a lot more about database design and SQL queries than you'll ever need (probably). For example:

- *http://www.sqljunkies.com*
- *http://www.sqlservercentral.com*
- *Head First SQL* by Lynn Beighley (O'Reilly), a cracking beginner's guide to SQL
- *SQL Visual Quickstart Guide* by Chris Fehily (Peachpit), a slimmer alternative to *Head First SQL*
- *SQL Queries for Mere Mortals* by John L. Viescas and Michael J. Hernandez (Addison-Wesley), the book to look at once you've got the basics of SQL in your head
- *Professional SQL Server 2005 Programming* by Rob Vieira (Wrox), the book to take you outside of just writing SQL and into thinking about SQL Server as a whole programming platform
- *Expert Oracle Database Architecture: 9i and 10g Programming Techniques* by Thomas Kyte (Apress), the equivalent to Vieira's book for Oracle users

Keyboard Shortcuts

The following tables list the default keyboard shortcuts in Visual Studio 2008 (VS2008) using the *Web Development default settings*. They do vary if you choose to use the Visual C# Development settings or one of the other preset settings instead.

> Sara Ford's blog provides a lot more detail than we provide here. Find it at *http://blogs.msdn.com/saraford/*.

To reset your settings to match those listed in this appendix and elsewhere in the book, choose Tools → Import and Export Settings and select "Reset all settings". Click Next twice, and then you'll be able to choose Web Development settings from a list of predefined options. Clicking Finish will complete the reset.

General Actions

Shortcut	Menu equivalent	Action
Ctrl-N	File → New File	Creates a new file for the project.
Ctrl-Shift-N	File → New Project	Creates a new project.
Shift-Alt-N	File → New Web Site	Creates a new website.
Ctrl-O	File → Open File	Opens a file.
Ctrl-Shift-O	File → Open Project	Opens a project.
Shift-Alt-O	File → Open Web Site	Opens a website.
Ctrl-P	File → Print	Prints the current file.
Ctrl-Shift-S	File → Save All	Saves all currently altered files.
Ctrl-S	File → Save	Saves alterations to the current file.
Ctrl-Shift-W	File → View in Browser	Opens the current HTML or ASPX file in a browser window.
Shift-Alt-A	Project → Add Existing Item	Adds an existing item to the current project.
Ctrl-Shift-A	Project → Add New Item	Adds a new item to the current project.

Shortcut	Menu equivalent	Action
Shift-F4	Project → *projectName* Properties	Views the Properties pages for the current project.
Ctrl-F4	File → Close	Closes the current file (tab).
Ctrl-Shift-B	Build → Build Solution	Builds the open solution.
Shift-Alt-D	Data → Show Data Sources	Shows the Data Sources window.
Shift-Alt-Enter	View → Full Screen	Switches VS2008 to full-screen mode.
Ctrl-/		Focuses the cursor on the command-line area in the Standard toolbar.
Alt-comma key		Visual Basic only. Changes the IntelliSense filter from Common to All.
Alt-period key		Visual Basic only. Changes the IntelliSense filter from All to Common.
Ctrl-E, Ctrl-W		Toggles word wrap in the main editor window.
Ctrl-K, Ctrl-I	Edit → IntelliSense → Quick Info	Displays a tool tip about the current symbol the cursor is on.
Ctrl-R, Ctrl-W	Edit → Advanced → View Whitespace	Displays characters on-screen representing the whitespace in the code.

Text Generation and Refactoring

Shortcut	Menu equivalent	Action
Ctrl-Shift-Space bar		Shows the IntelliSense window for the current markup tag.
Ctrl-Space bar		Shows the IntelliSense window for the current class member.
Ctrl-J	Edit → IntelliSense → List Members	Opens an IntelliSense window displaying the classes and class members you can currently use.
Ctrl-Shift-J		Updates JScript IntelliSense.
Ctrl-K, Ctrl-M	Edit → IntelliSense → Generate Method Stub	Creates a method stub for the symbol currently under the cursor (if it doesn't exist already).
Ctrl-K, Ctrl-S	Edit → IntelliSense → Surround With	Opens an IntelliSense window listing the code constructs with which you can surround the selected lines of code.
Ctrl-K, Ctrl-X	Edit → IntelliSense → Insert Snippet	Inserts a code snippet at the current cursor location.
Ctrl-Shift-Ins		Allows you to override base class methods in a derived class.
Ctrl-R, Ctrl-E	Refactor → Encapsulate Field	Encapsulates the member field into a property.
Ctrl-R, Ctrl-I	Refactor → Extract Interface	Extracts the interface definition from the current class.
Ctrl-R, Ctrl-M	Refactor → Extract Method	Extracts the selected lines of code into a separate method and replaces them with a call to that method.
Ctrl-R, Ctrl-P	Refactor → Promote Local Variable to Parameter	Encapsulates the local field declaration into a property.
Ctrl-R, Ctrl-V	Refactor → Remove Parameters	Removes the selected parameter from the constructor, indexer, method, or delegate.

Shortcut	Menu equivalent	Action
Ctrl-R, Ctrl-R	Refactor → Rename	Renames the current symbol and all instances of it throughout the solution.
Ctrl-R, Ctrl-O	Refactor → Reorder Parameters	Reorders the parameters of a constructor, indexer, method, or delegate and the calls to them appropriately.
Ctrl-Enter		Adds a blank line above the cursor.
Ctrl-Shift-Enter		Adds a blank line below the cursor.
Ctrl-K, Ctrl-D	Edit → Format Document	Formats the whole document according to the given formatting rules.
Ctrl-K, Ctrl-F	Edit → Format Selection	Formats the selected lines of text according to the given formatting rules.

Text Navigation

Shortcut	Menu equivalent	Action
Ctrl-Left Arrow		Moves the cursor left to the nearest start of some text.
Ctrl-Right Arrow		Moves the cursor right to the nearest end of some text.
Ctrl-End		Moves the cursor to the end of the document.
End		Moves the cursor to the end of the current line.
Ctrl-Home		Moves the cursor to the start of the document.
Home		Moves the cursor to the start of the current line.
PgDn		Moves the cursor to the last shown line of the file directly in line with its previous location.
PgUp		Moves the cursor to the first shown line of the file directly in line with its previous location.
Ctrl-G	Edit → Go To	Opens the Go to Line dialog.
Ctrl-Shift-G		Opens the file whose name is under the cursor or is currently selected.
F12		Moves the cursor to the definition of the method that the cursor is currently over.
Ctrl-K, Ctrl-K	Edit → Bookmarks → Toggle Bookmark	Adds/removes a bookmark to the current line of text.
Ctrl-K, Ctrl-L	Edit → Bookmarks → Clear Bookmarks	Removes all bookmarks in your project.
Ctrl-K, Ctrl-W	View → Bookmark Window	Opens the Bookmark window.
Ctrl-K, Ctrl-N	Edit → Bookmarks → Next Bookmark	Move the cursor to the next bookmark in the project.
Ctrl-Shift-K, Ctrl-Shift-N	Edit → Bookmarks → Next Bookmark in Folder	Move the cursor to the next bookmark in the folder.
Ctrl-K, Ctrl-P	Edit → Bookmarks → Previous Bookmark	Move the cursor to the previous bookmark in the project.
Ctrl-Shift-K, Ctrl-Shift-P	Edit → Bookmarks → Previous Bookmark in Folder	Move the cursor to the previous bookmark in the folder.

Shortcut	Menu equivalent	Action
Ctrl-Shift-1		Navigates to the next definition, declaration, or reference of an item within a Search Results window.
Ctrl-Shift-2		Navigates to the previous definition, declaration, or reference of an item within a Search Results window.
Ctrl-Shift-7		Navigates to the next item called in the current file.
Ctrl-Shift-8		Navigates to the previous item called in the current file.
Ctrl-hyphen key		Navigates to the previously browsed line of code.
Ctrl-Shift-hyphen key		Navigates to the next browsed line of code.
Ctrl-Shift-F12		Navigates to the next line of code containing an error.
Ctrl-]		Moves the cursor to the matching brace for the one the cursor is currently next to.
Ctrl-K, Ctrl-H	Edit → Bookmarks → Add/Remove Task List Shortcut	Creates a shortcut in the task list to the comment line the cursor is currently on.
Ctrl-M, Ctrl-H	Edit → Outlining → Hide Selection	Visual Basic only. Hides the selected text.
Ctrl-M, Ctrl-L	Edit → Outlining → Toggle All Outlining	Collapses/expands all blocks of code in the current file to their outlines.
Ctrl-M, Ctrl-M	Edit → Outlining → Toggle Outlining Expansion	Collapses/expands the block of code the cursor is currently on.
Ctrl-M, Ctrl-O	Edit → Outlining → Collapse to Definitions	Collapses all code in the current file to class, interface, and namespace definitions.
Ctrl-M, Ctrl-P	Edit → Outlining → Stop Outlining	Removes all outlining information from the current file.
Ctrl-M, Ctrl-T	Edit → Outlining → Collapse Tag	Hides the selected markup tag and replaces it with an ellipsis.
Ctrl-M, Ctrl-U	Edit → Outlining → Stop Hiding Current	Makes visible the code segment the cursor is currently over.

Text Editing and Selection

Shortcut	Menu equivalent	Action
Ctrl-C	Edit → Copy	Copies selected text to the clipboard.
Ctrl-Ins		Copies the line the cursor is currently on to the clipboard.
Ctrl-X	Edit → Cut	Cuts selected text to the clipboard.
Ctrl-L or Shift-Delete key		Cuts the line the cursor is currently on to the clipboard.
Ctrl-V or Shift-Ins	Edit → Paste	Pastes the current top text in the clipboard to the current cursor position in source code.
Ctrl-Shift-Ins		Cycles through the contents on the clipboard ring, replacing and pasting each item to the current cursor position in the source code.
Delete key	Edit → Delete	Deletes the currently selected code.
Ctrl-Shift-L		Deletes the line the cursor is currently on.

Shortcut	Menu equivalent	Action
Ctrl-Y or Ctrl-Shift-Z	Edit → Redo	Redoes the previous action.
Ctrl-A	Edit → Select All	Selects all text or controls in the main window.
Ctrl-Shift-]		Selects the block of code delimited by the brace that the cursor is currently next to.
Ctrl-Z or Alt-Back-space	Edit → Undo	Undoes the previous action.
Ctrl-period key or Shift-Alt-F10		Shows the Smart Tag menu if it's available for the current cursor position.
Ctrl-=		Selects the text between the cursor's current and previous locations.
Backspace		Deletes the character to the left of the cursor.
Ctrl-Backspace		Deletes all characters to the left of the cursor in the current word.
Ctrl-Shift-Alt-C		Copies the parameter list for a method from the IntelliSense window that appears as you write a call to it.
Ctrl-Shift-Alt-P		Pastes the parameter list for a method from the IntelliSense window generated against it directly into a call to it in the code.
Ctrl-Delete key		Deletes all characters to the right of the cursor in the current word.
Shift-Alt-Down Arrow		Adds the entire line below the cursor to the selected text.
Ctrl-Shift-End		Moves the cursor to the end of the document, selecting all the content between there and its original position.
Shift-End		Moves the cursor to the end of the current line, selecting all the content between there and its original position.
Shift-Alt-End		Moves the cursor to the end of the current line, selecting all the content between there and its original position and adding it to the already selected text.
Ctrl-Shift-Home		Moves the cursor to the start of the document, selecting all the content between there and its original position.
Shift-Home		Moves the cursor to the start of the current line, selecting all the content between there and its original position.
Shift-Alt-Home		Moves the cursor to the start of the current line, selecting all the content between there and its original position and adding it to the already selected text.
Ins		Starts overtype mode.
Ctrl-K, Ctrl-\	Edit → Advanced → Delete Horizontal White Space	Deletes the area of whitespace on the line the cursor is currently in.
Ctrl-K, Ctrl-A		Moves the cursor to the other end of the selected text.
Ctrl-K, Ctrl-C	Edit → Advanced → Comment Selection	Comments out the selected lines of text.
Ctrl-K, Ctrl-U	Edit → Advanced → Uncomment Selection	Uncomments the selected lines of text.

Shortcut	Menu equivalent	Action
Ctrl-Shift-Alt-Left Arrow		Selects the text in a block where the current and previous cursor positions are opposite corners of that block. The cursor moves one word at a time.
Ctrl-Shift-Left Arrow		Selects all the text in the current word to the left of the cursor.
Shift-Alt-Left Arrow		Selects the text in a block where the current and previous cursor positions are opposite corners of that block. The cursor moves one character at a time.
Shift-PgDn		Moves the cursor to the last shown line of the file directly in line with its previous location, selecting everything in between.
Shift-PgUp		Moves the cursor to the first shown line of the file directly in line with its previous location, selecting everything in between.
Ctrl-Shift-Alt-Right Arrow		Selects the text in a block where the current and previous cursor positions are opposite corners of that block. The cursor moves one word at a time.
Ctrl-Shift-Right Arrow		Selects all the text in the current word to the right of the cursor.
Shift-Alt-Right Arrow		Selects the text in a block where the current and previous cursor positions are opposite corners of that block. The cursor moves one character at a time.
Ctrl-Shift-T		Swaps the word the cursor is on with the next one in the code.
Ctrl-T		Swaps the character to the left of the cursor with the one to the right of it.
Shift-Alt-T		Swaps the line of text the cursor is on with the one below it.
Ctrl-Shift-U	Edit → Advanced → Make Uppercase	Makes all the selected letters uppercase.
Ctrl-U	Edit → Advanced → Make Lowercase	Makes all the selected letters lowercase.
Ctrl-W		Selects the word under the cursor.

Main Window Shortcut Keys

Shortcut	Menu equivalent	Action
F7		Opens the corresponding code-behind file (if applicable).
Shift-F7		Switches between markup and Design view for the page.
Esc key		Switches focus to the main code edit/designer window.
Ctrl-F2		Switches focus to the class selection combo in the main editor window.
Ctrl-F6		Switches the active file in the main editor window to the next tab.
Ctrl-Shift-F6		Switches the active file in the main editor window to the previous tab.

Shortcut	Menu equivalent	Action
F6		If viewing a file in a split window, moves focus to the next split.
Shift-F6		If viewing a file in a split window, moves focus to the previous split.
Ctrl-Tab or Ctrl-Shift-Tab		Opens the Select Active Window dialog with focus on files.
Ctrl-Shift-Y	View → Synchronize Views	Synchronizes the contents of Source and Design views for the web page as seen in Split view.
Ctrl-PgDn, Ctrl-PgUp		Toggles between Design, Split, and Source views for web pages.

Design View Shortcut Keys

The following shortcut keys apply only when a page or form is shown in Design view in the main edit window (there are no menu equivalents).

Shortcut	Action
Ctrl-B	Turns HTML text bold (uses `<b>` tags).
Ctrl-L	Turns HTML text into a hyperlink (uses `<a>` tags).
Ctrl-Shift-L	Turns HTML text into a bookmark (uses `<a>` tags).
Ctrl-I	Makes HTML text italic (uses `<i>` tags).
Ctrl-U	Underlines selected HTML text.
Tab	Moves focus to the next control on the page (based on TabIndex values).
Shift-Tab	Moves focus to the previous control on the page (based on TabIndex values).
Down Arrow	Moves the selected control down one pixel.
Left Arrow	Moves the selected control left one pixel.
Right Arrow	Moves the selected control right one pixel.
Up Arrow	Moves the selected control up one pixel.
Ctrl-Down Arrow	Moves the selected control down eight pixels.
Ctrl-Left Arrow	Moves the selected control left eight pixels.
Ctrl-Right Arrow	Moves the selected control right eight pixels.
Ctrl-Up Arrow	Moves the selected control up eight pixels.
Shift-Down Arrow	Increases the height of the selected control by one pixel.
Shift-Left Arrow	Decreases the width of the selected control by one pixel.
Shift-Right Arrow	Increases the width of the selected control by one pixel.
Shift-Up Arrow	Decreases the height of the selected control by one pixel.
Ctrl-Shift-Down Arrow	Increases the height of the selected control by eight pixels.
Ctrl-Shift-Left Arrow	Decreases the width of the selected control by eight pixels.
Ctrl-Shift-Right Arrow	Increases the width of the selected control by eight pixels.
Ctrl-Shift-Up Arrow	Decreases the height of the selected control by eight pixels.

Class Diagram Shortcut Keys

The following shortcut keys apply only when a class diagram is shown in the main edit window (there are no menu equivalents).

Shortcut	Action
Plus sign key (on a numeric keypad)	Shows the class member list for selected classes in the window.
Hyphen key (on a numeric keypad)	Hides the class member list for selected classes in the window.
Delete key (on a numeric keypad)	Deletes the selected class from the diagram.
Enter	Displays code for the selected class in the main edit window.
Shift-Alt-L	Selects the interface lollipop (if it exists) for the selected class.
Shift-Alt-B	Expands/collapses the base type list for the selected object.

SQL Editor Shortcut Keys

The following shortcut keys become active when the SQL Editor is active in the main edit window.

Shortcut	Menu equivalent	Action
Ctrl-R	Query Designer → Execute SQL	Runs the current SQL query.
Ctrl-1	Query Designer → Pane → Diagram	Toggles the Diagram window in the SQL Editor.
Ctrl-2	Query Designer → Pane → Criteria	Toggles the Criteria window in the SQL Editor.
Ctrl-3	Query Designer → Pane → SQL	Toggles the SQL Text window in the SQL Editor.
Ctrl-4	Query Designer → Pane → Results	Toggles the Results window in the SQL Editor.
Ctrl-T		Cancels the currently executing SQL query.

Tool Window Shortcut Keys

Shortcut	Menu equivalent	Action
F2		Renames the currently selected item.
Ctrl-K, Ctrl-B	Tools → Code Snippets Manager	Opens the Code Snippets Manager.
Ctrl-K, Ctrl-W	View → Bookmark Window	Opens the Bookmark window.
Ctrl-Shift-C	View → Class View	Opens the Class View window.
Ctrl-K, Ctrl-V		Focuses the cursor on the search combo in the Class View window.
Ctrl-\, Ctrl-D	View → Code Definition Window	Opens the Code Definition window.
Ctrl-Alt-A	View → Other Windows → Command Window	Opens the Command window.
Ctrl-Alt-T	View → Document Outline	Opens the Document Outline window.
Ctrl-\, Ctrl-E	View → Error List	Opens the Error List window.
Ctrl-Alt-F12	View → Find Results → Find Symbol Results	Opens the Find Symbol Results window.

Shortcut	Menu equivalent	Action
Ctrl-Alt-J	View → Object Browser	Opens the Object Browser window.
Ctrl-K, Ctrl-R		Focuses the cursor on the search combo in the Object Browser window.
Ctrl-Alt-O	View → Output	Opens the Output window.
F4 or Alt-Enter	View → Properties Window	Opens the Properties window.
Ctrl-Shift-E	View → Other Windows → Resource View	Opens the Resource View window.
Ctrl-Alt-S	View → Server Explorer	Opens the Server Explorer window.
Ctrl-Alt-L	View → Solution Explorer	Opens the Solution Explorer window.
Ctrl-\, Ctrl-T	View → Task List	Opens the Task List window.
Ctrl-Alt-X	View → Toolbox	Opens the Toolbox window.
Ctrl-Alt-R	View → Other Windows → Web Browser	Opens a web browser window (inside Visual Studio).
Shift-Esc key		Closes the Current Active Tool window.
Alt-F6		Moves focus among the tool windows to the next one.
Shift-Alt-F6		Moves focus among the tool windows to the previous one.
Alt-F7, Shift-Alt-F7		Opens the Select Active window dialog with focus on tool windows.

Find-and-Replace Shortcut Keys

Shortcut	Menu equivalent	Action
Ctrl-F	Edit → Find and Replace → Quick Find	Opens the Quick Find window.
Shift-F12		Finds all references to the symbol the cursor is currently on and returns them in a results window.
Ctrl-Shift-F	Edit → Find and Replace → Find in Files	Opens the Find in Files window.
F3		Highlights the next instance of the text being searched for.
Ctrl-F3		Highlights the next instance of the text being searched for within the currently selected text.
Shift-F3		Highlights the previous instance of the text being searched for.
Ctrl-Shift-F3		Highlights the previous instance of the text being searched for within the currently selected text.
Alt-F12	Edit → Find and Replace → Find Symbol	Opens the Find Symbol window.
Shift-Alt-F12		Finds all instances of the symbol the cursor is currently on and returns them in a results window.
Alt-F3, S		Stops the current search.
Ctrl-D		Focuses the cursor on the Find drop-down list in the Standard dialog.
F8		Moves the cursor to the next location in a Find Results window.
Shift-F8		Moves the cursor to the previous location in a Find Results window.

Shortcut	Menu equivalent	Action
Ctrl-H	Edit → Find and Replace → Quick Replace	Opens the Quick Replace window.
Ctrl-Shift-H	Edit → Find and Replace → Replace in Files	Opens the Replace in Files window.
Ctrl-Alt-F12	View → Find Results → Find Symbol Results	Opens the Find Symbol Results window.
Ctrl-I	Edit → Advanced → Incremental Search	Starts an incremental search looking down the page.
Ctrl-Shift-I		Starts an incremental search looking up the page.

Macro Shortcut Keys

Shortcut	Menu equivalent	Action
Alt-F8	Tools → Macros → Macro Explorer	Opens the Macro Explorer window.
Alt-F11	Tools → Macros → Macros IDE	Open the macro editing IDE.
Ctrl-Shift-R	Tools → Macros → Record Temporary-Macro	Records a temporary macro.
Ctrl-Shift-P	Tools → Macros → Run Temporary-Macro	Runs the just recorded temporary macro.

Debugging Shortcut Keys

This table lists shortcuts that are globally available while writing code.

Shortcut	Menu equivalent	Action
Ctrl-B	Debug → New Breakpoint → Break at Function	Opens the dialog to create a breakpoint at the named function.
Ctrl-Alt-B	Debug → Windows → Breakpoints	Shows the Breakpoints window.
Ctrl-Shift-F9	Debug → Delete All Breakpoints	Deletes all set breakpoints in your solution.
Ctrl-F9		Disables/re-enables the selected breakpoint.
Ctrl-Alt-E	Debug → Exceptions	Shows the dialog to set which exceptions in code will cause Visual Studio to break into the code.
Ctrl-Alt-I	Debug → Windows → Immediate	Shows the Immediate window.
Ctrl-Alt-P	Tools → Attach to Process	Opens the Attach to Process dialog box.
F5	Debug → Start Debugging	Starts the project in the debugger.
Ctrl-F5	Debug → Start Without Debugging	Starts the project without the debugger.
F9	Debug → Toggle Breakpoint	Adds/removes a breakpoint to the current line of code.
Ctrl-F11	Debug → Toggle Disassembly	Shows/hides the disassembly for the current file which has been broken into (break mode only).

The following table lists shortcuts (and menu options) that become available in addition to those in the preceding table when you are debugging code.

Shortcut	Menu equivalent	Action
Ctrl-Alt-V, A	Debug → Windows → Autos	Shows the Autos window.
Ctrl-Alt-C	Debug → Windows → Call Stack	Shows the Call Stack window.
Ctrl-Alt-D	Debug → Windows → Disassembly	Shows the Disassemble window (while debugging).
Ctrl-Alt-V, L	Debug → Windows → Locals	Shows the Locals window.
Ctrl-5		Focuses the cursor on the Process drop-down list in the Debug Location toolbar.
Ctrl-6		Focuses the cursor on the Thread drop-down list in the Debug Location toolbar.
Ctrl-7		Focuses the cursor on the Stack Frame drop-down list in the Debug Location toolbar.
Ctrl-8		Flags the thread currently displayed in the Debug Location toolbar.
Ctrl-9		Shows only flagged threads in the Debug Location toolbar.
Ctrl-Alt-M, 1	Debug → Windows → Watch → Memory 1	Shows the Memory 1 window.
Ctrl-Alt-M, 2	Debug → Windows → Watch → Memory 2	Shows the Memory 2 window.
Ctrl-Alt-M, 3	Debug → Windows → Watch → Memory 3	Shows the Memory 3 window.
Ctrl-Alt-M, 4	Debug → Windows → Watch → Memory 4	Shows the Memory 4 window.
Ctrl-Alt-U	Debug → Windows → Modules	Shows the Modules window.
Ctrl-Alt-Z	Debug → Windows → Processes	Shows the Processes window.
Shift-F9		Shows the QuickWatch dialog.
Ctrl-Alt-G	Debug → Windows → Registers	Shows the Registers window.
Ctrl-Shift-F5	Debug → Restart	Restarts the project within the debugger.
Ctrl-F10		Runs the project to the current cursor position.
Ctrl-Shift-F10		Sets the next statement in the same function to be executed in the debugger.
Alt-Num *		Highlights the next statement to be executed in the debugger.
F11	Debug → Step Into	Steps the debugger into the next block of code.
Ctrl-Alt-F11		Steps the debugger into the next block of code in the selected process in the Processes window.
Shift-F11	Debug → Step Out	Steps the debugger out of the current block of code and onto the next statement or block.
Ctrl-Shift-Alt-F11		Steps the debugger out of the current block of code and onto the next statement or block in the selected process in the Processes window.

Shortcut	Menu equivalent	Action
F10	Debug → Step Over	Steps the debugger onto the next statement or block of code at the same level of scope.
Ctrl-Alt-F10		Steps the debugger onto the next statement or block of code at the same level of scope in the selected process in the Processes window.
Shift-F5	Debug → Stop Debugging	Stops the debugger.
Ctrl-Alt-H	Debug → Windows → Threads	Shows the Threads window.
Alt-F9, A		Shows the Disassembly window for the currently selected breakpoint in the Breakpoint window.
Alt-F9, D		Deletes the currently selected breakpoint in the Breakpoint window.
Alt-F9, S		Shows the source code for the currently selected breakpoint in the Breakpoint window.
Ctrl-Alt-W, 1	Debug → Windows → Watch → Watch 1	Shows the Watch 1 window.
Ctrl-Alt-W, 2	Debug → Windows → Watch → Watch 2	Shows the Watch 2 window.
Ctrl-Alt-W, 3	Debug → Windows → Watch → Watch 3	Shows the Watch 3 window.
Ctrl-Alt-W, 4	Debug → Windows → Watch → Watch 4	Shows the Watch 4 window.

Index

We'd like to hear your suggestions for improving our indexes. Send email to *index@oreilly.com*.

E

About the Authors

Jesse Liberty is a senior program manager at Microsoft in the Silverlight Development division. His business card reads "Silverlight Geek," and he is responsible for fostering a Silverlight Developer community, primarily through Silverlight.net.

Jesse is the author or coauthor of numerous books, including O'Reilly's *Programming Silverlight 2*, *Programming .NET 3.5*, and the perennial bestseller *Programming C#*. Jesse has two decades of experience as a developer, author, and consultant, and has been a distinguished software engineer at AT&T, a software architect for PBS/Learning Link, and a vice president at Citibank. He provides full support for his writing, and access to his blogs, at *http://www.JesseLiberty.com*.

Dan Hurwitz is the president of Sterling Solutions, Inc., where for nearly two decades he has been providing contract programming and database development to a wide variety of clients. He is a coauthor, with Jesse Liberty, of O'Reilly's *Learning ASP.NET 3.5*.

Dan Maharry is a senior developer for Co-operative Web, a software development workers co-op based in the UK. He specializes in working with new technologies and has been working with .NET since its first beta. This is his twelfth book on web development for the Microsoft platform. It is his first book for O'Reilly following successful contributions to the Wrox Beginning ASP.NET and Apress Beginning ASP.NET Databases series. He lives with his lovely wife, Jane, and a rose bush that is trying to engulf his house.

Colophon

The animal on the cover of *Programming ASP.NET 3.5*, Fourth Edition, is a guitarfish, a part of the family *Rhinobatiformes* and a close relative of the rays. As their name implies, guitarfish have a unique body shape, with a flattened head and trunk and a hindbody resembling that of a shark. Their wide pectoral fins are fused to their head, giving it a distinctive spadelike shape. Many adult guitarfish grow to a length of up to 6 feet, although the giant guitarfish (*Rhynchobatus djiddensis*) can grow to 10 feet long, weighing as much as 500 pounds. Guitarfish are typically gray or brown on their dorsal side and white or cream-colored underneath. They are ovoviviparous, meaning their eggs hatch inside the female's body.

There are approximately 45 guitarfish species inhabiting tropical, subtropical, and temperate waters all over the world. They feed on bottom-dwelling creatures such as scallops and shrimp; an opening just behind their eyes called the *spiracle* allows them to breathe while scavenging for food on the ocean floor.

Well-known guitarfish species include the bowmouth and the shovelnose. The bowmouth guitarfish is also known as the shark-ray, thanks to large dorsal fins that give it a sharklike appearance. It has a ridge of spikes above its eyes and along its back and shoulders, a trait that makes it unpopular among the shrimp fisherman whose bycatch it often comprises; the bowmouth's spikes make it difficult to handle and can damage the commercial catch. The shovelnose, easily identified by its pointy snout, is a not-uncommon sight among snorkelers in southern California. Although the shovelnose is generally skittish and not considered aggressive toward humans, there is one documented case of a scuba diver in La Jolla Cove being bitten by a male shovelnose interrupted in his pursuit of a female guitarfish.

The cover image is from the Dover Pictorial Archive. The cover font is Adobe ITC Garamond. The text font is Linotype Birka; the heading font is Adobe Myriad Condensed; and the code font is LucasFont's TheSansMonoCondensed.